masculine or femini		
military		
music		
noun		
nautical		
pejorative		
personal		
photography		
physics		
plural		
politics		
possessive	*poss*	possessivo
past participle	*pp*	participio passato
prefix	*pref*	prefisso
preposition	*prep*	preposizione
present tense	*pres*	presente
pronoun	*pron*	pronome
psychology	*Psych*	psicologia
past tense	*pt*	tempo passato
someone	*qcno*	qualcuno
something	*qcsa*	qualcosa
rail	*Rail*	ferrovia
reflexive	*refl*	riflessivo
religion	*Relig*	religione
relative pronoun	*rel pron*	pronome relativo
somebody	*sb*	qualcuno
school	*Sch*	scuola
singular	*sg*	singolare
something	*sth*	qualcosa
technical	*Tech*	tecnico
telephone	*Teleph*	telefono
theatrical	*Theat*	teatrale
television	*TV*	televisione
typography	*Typ*	tipografia
university	*Univ*	università
auxiliary verb	*v aux*	verbo ausiliare
intransitive verb	*vi*	verbo intransitivo
reflexive verb	*vr*	verbo riflessivo
transitive verb	*vt*	verbo transitivo
transitive and intransitive verb	*vt/i*	verbo transitivo e intransitivo
vulgar	*vulg*	volgare
familiar	🆃	familiare
slang	⊠	gergo
cultural equivalent	≈	equivalenza culturale

Oxford
Italian
Minidictionary

THIRD EDITION

Italian–English
English–Italian

Italiano–Inglese
Inglese–Italiano

OXFORD
UNIVERSITY PRESS

OXFORD
UNIVERSITY PRESS

Great Clarendon Street, Oxford OX2 6DP

Oxford University Press is a department of the University of Oxford.
It furthers the University's objective of excellence in research, scholarship,
and education by publishing worldwide in

Oxford New York

Auckland Cape Town Dar es Salaam Hong Kong Karachi Kuala Lumpur
Madrid Melbourne Mexico City Nairobi New Delhi Shanghai Taipei
Toronto

With offices in

Argentina Austria Brazil Chile Czech Republic France Greece
Guatemala Hungary Italy Japan South Korea Poland Portugal
Singapore Switzerland Thailand Turkey Ukraine Vietnam

Oxford is a registered trade mark of Oxford University Press
in the UK and in certain other countries

© Oxford University Press 1986, 1997, 1999, 2005

First published 1986
Second edition published 1997
This edition published 2005

British Library Cataloguing in Publication Data

Data available

Library of Congress Cataloging in Publication Data

Data available

ISBN 0-19-861042-4
ISBN 978-0-19-861042-7

10 9 8 7 6 5 4 3 2 1

Typeset by Interactive Sciences Ltd, Gloucester
Printed and bound in Italy
by Legoprint S.p.A.

Contents/Indice

Third Edition/Terza edizione
Editors/Redazione
Nicholas Rollin, Francesca Logi

Second Edition/Seconda edizione
Editors/Redazione
Debora Mazza, Donatella Boi, Sonia
Tinagli-Baxter, Peter Terrell, Jane
Goldie, Francesca Logi, Carla Zipoli

First Edition/Prima edizione
Editor/Redazione
Joyce Andrews

Phrasefinder/Trovafrasi
Colin MacIntosh, Francesca Logi
Loredana Riu, Neil and Roswitha
Morris

Proprietary terms

This dictionary includes some words which are or are asserted to be, proprietary names or trademarks. Their inclusion does not imply that they have acquired for legal purposes a non-proprietary or general significance, nor is any other judgement implied concerning their legal status. In cases where the editor has some evidence that a word is used as proprietary name or trade mark this is indicated by the symbol (®), but no judgement concerning the legal status of such words is made or implied thereby.

Marchi registrati

Questo dizionario include alcune parole che sono o vengono considerate marchi registrati. La loro presenza non implica che abbiano acquisitito legalmente un significato generale, né si suggerisce alcun altro giudizio riguardo il loro stato giuridico. Qualora il redattore abbia trovato testimonianza dell'uso di una parola come marchio registrato, quest'ultima è stata contrassegnata dal simbolo ®, ma nessun giudizio riguardo lo stato giuridico di tale parola viene espresso o suggerito in tal modo.

Preface/Prefazione

This new edition of the *Oxford Italian Minidictionary* has been updated to reflect the changes in English and Italian since the last edition in 1999. Colloquial words and phrases figure largely, as do neologisms. Notable additions include terms from the spheres of computing, business and communications, that have become common in modern life. Cultural notes on important aspects of life in the Italian- and English-speaking worlds are included for the first time. The *Phrasefinder* section has been expanded to provide more useful expressions needed for everyday communication. The section is arranged thematically and covers eight key topics, *going places, keeping in touch, food and drink, places to stay, shopping and money, good timing* and *conversion charts.*

Questa nuova edizione del *Minidizionario Oxford* è stata aggiornata per riflettere i cambiamenti avvenuti nell'inglese e nell'italiano dopo la scorsa edizione del 1999. Oltre all'aggiornamento di parole ed espressioni colloquiali contiene numerosi neologismi. Tra le voci aggiunte si segnalano in particolare termini del settore informatico, commerciale e delle comunicazioni divenuti ricorrenti nella lingua di tutti i giorni. Per la prima volta sono state inserite note culturali su importanti aspetti della vita nei paesi di lingua italiana e di lingua inglese. La sezione *Trovafrasi* è stata infine ampliata per dare maggiore spazio alle espressioni necessarie alla comunicazione quotidiana. Tale sezione è presentata per tema e copre otto aree chiave: *in viaggio, comunicazioni, mangiare e bere, dove alloggiare, spese e soldi, l'ora giusta* e *tabelle di conversione.*

Introduzione

Allo scopo di fornire il maggior numero possibile di informazioni riguardo all'inglese e all'italiano, questo dizionario ricorre ad alcune convenzioni per sfruttare al meglio lo spazio disponibile.

All'interno della voce un trattino ondulato ~ è utilizzato al posto del lemma.

Qualora il lemma contenga una barra verticale |, il trattino ondulato sostituisce solo la parte del lemma che precede la barra. Ad es.: **dark|en** *vt* oscurare; **~ness** *n* buio *m* (la seconda parola in neretto va letta **darkness**).

Vengono forniti indicatori per indirizzare l'utente verso la traduzione del senso voluto di una parola. I tipi di indicatori sono:

- etichette semantiche, indicanti lo specifico settore d'uso di una parola o di un senso (commercio, informatica, fotografia ecc.);

- indicatori di significato, ad es.: **redazione** *f* (ufficio) editorial office; (di testi) editing;

- soggetti tipici di verbi, ad es.: **trovarsi** *vr* (luogo:) be;

- complementi oggetti tipici di verbi, collocati dopo la traduzione del verbo stesso, ad es.: **superare** *vt* overtake (veicolo); pass (esame);

- sostantivi che ricorrono tipicamete con certi aggettivi, ad es.: **solare** *adj* (energia, raggi) solar; (crema) sun.

Il pallino nero indica che la stessa parola viene tradotta come una diversa parte del discorso, ad es.: **calcolatore** *adj* ... ● *m* ...

La pronuncia inglese è trascritta usando l'Alfabetico Fonetico Internazionale (vedi pag. viii).

L'accento tonico nelle parole italiane è indicato dal segno ' collocato davanti alla sillaba accentata.

Le parentesi quadre racchiudono parti di espressioni che possono essere omesse senza alterazioni di significato.

Introduction

In order to give the maximum information about English and Italian in the space available, this new dictionary uses certain space-saving conventions.

A swung dash ~ is used to replace the headword within the entry.

Where the headword contains a vertical bar | the swung dash replaces only the part of the headword that comes before the |. For example: **efficien|te** *adj* efficient. **~za** *f* efficiency (the second bold word reads efficienza).

Indicators are provided to guide the user to the best translation for a specific sense of a word. Types of indicator are:

- field labels, which indicate a general area of usage (commercial, computing, photography etc);

- sense indicators, eg: **bore** *n* (of gun) calibro *m*; (person) seccatore, -trice *mf*;

- typical subjects of verbs, eg: **bond** *vt* (glue:) attaccare;

- typical objects of verbs, placed after the translation of the verb, eg: **boost** *vt* stimolare (sales); sollevare (morale);

- nouns that typically go together with certain adjectives eg: **rich** *adj* ricco; (food) pesante;

A bullet point means that a headword has changed its part of speech within an entry, eg: **partition** *n* ... • *vt* ...

English pronunciation is given for the Italian user in the International Phonetic Alphabet (see p viii).

Italian stress is shown by a ' placed in front of the stressed syllable in a word.

Square brackets are used around parts of an expression which can be omitted without altering its sense.

Pronuncia inglese

Simboli fonetici

Vocali e dittonghi

iː	see	ɔː	saw	eɪ	page	ɔɪ	join
ɪ	sit	ʊ	put	əʊ	home	ɪə	near
e	ten	uː	too	aɪ	five	eə	hair
æ	hat	ʌ	cup	aɪə	fire	ʊə	poor
ɑː	arm	ɜː	fur	aʊ	now		
ɒ	got	ə	ago	aʊə	flour		

Consonantl

p	pen	tʃ	chin	s	so	n	no
b	bad	dʒ	June	z	zoo	ŋ	sing
t	tea	f	fall	ʃ	she	l	leg
d	dip	v	voice	ʒ	measure	r	red
k	cat	θ	thin	h	how	j	yes
g	got	ð	then	m	man	w	wet

Note: ' precede la sillaba accentata.

Pronunciation of Italian

Vowels

a   is broad like *a* in *father*: **casa**

e   has two sounds: closed like *ey* in *they*: **sera**; open like e in *egg*: **sette**

i   Is like *ee* in *feet*: **venire**.

o   1. closed like *o* in *show*: **croma**. 2. open like *o* in *dog*: **bocca**.

u   is like *oo* in *moon*: **luna**

When two or more vowels come together each vowel is pronounced separately: **buono**, **baia**.

Consonants

b, d, f, l, m, n, p, t, v are pronounced as in English. When these are double, they are pronounced as separate sounds: **bello**.

c   before **a**, **o** or **u** and before consonants is like *k* in *king*: **cane**. Before **e** or **i** it is like *ch* in *church*: **cena**.

ch   is also like *k* in *king*: **chiesa**

g   before **a**, **o** or **u** is hard like *g* in *got*: **gufo**. Before **e** or **i** it is like *j* in *jelly*: **gentile**.

gh   is like *g* in *gun*: **ghiaccio**.

gl   when followed by **a, e, o** and **u** is like *gl* in *glass*: **gloria**.

gli   is like *lli* in *million*: **figlio**.

gn   is like *ni* in *onion*: **bagno**.

h   is silent.

ng   is like *ng* in *finger*: **ringraziare**.

r   is pronounced distinctly.

s   between two vowels is like *s* in *rose*: **riso**. at the beginning of a word it is like *s* in *soap*: **sapone**.

sc   before *e* or *i* is like *sh* in *shell*: **scienza**.

z   sounds like *ts* within a word: **fazione**; like *dz* at the beginning: **zoo**.

Stress is shown by the sign ' printed before the stressed syllable.

Aa

a (ad before vowel) prep to; (stato in luogo, tempo, età) at; (con mese, città) in; (mezzo, modo) by; **dire qcsa a qcno** tell sb sth; **alle tre** at three o'clock: **a vent'anni** at the age of twenty; **a Natale** at Christmas; **a dicembre** in December; **ero al cinema** I was at the cinema; **vivo a Londra** I live in London; **a due a due** two by two; **a piedi** on o by foot; **maglia a maniche lunghe** long-sleeved sweater; **casa a tre piani** house with three floors; **giocare a tennis** play tennis; **50 km all'ora** 50 km an hour; **4 euro al chilo** 4 euros a kilo; **al mattino/alla sera** in the morning/evening; **a venti chilometri/due ore da qui** twenty kilometres/two hours away

a'bate m abbot

abbacchi'ato adj downhearted

ab'bacchio m (young) lamb

abbagli'ante adj dazzling ● m headlight, high beam

abbagli'are vt dazzle. **ab'baglio** m blunder; **prendere un ~** make a blunder

abbai'are vi bark

abba'ino m dormer window

abbando'na|re vt abandon; leave (luogo); give up (piani ecc). **~rsi** vr let oneself go; **~rsi a** give oneself up to (ricordi ecc). **~to** adj abandoned. **abban'dono** m abandoning; fig abandon; (stato) neglect

abbassa'mento m (di temperatura, prezzi ecc) drop

abbas'sar|e vt lower; turn down

abbas'sa'mento see opposite

ab'basso adv below ● int down with

abba'stanza adv enough; (alquanto) quite

ab'batter|e vt demolish; shoot down (aereo); put down (animale); topple (regime), (fig: demoralizzare) dishearten. **~si** vr (cadere) fall; fig be discouraged

abbatti'mento m (morale) despondency

abbat'tuto adj despondent

abba'zia f abbey

abbel'lir|e vt embellish. **~si** vr adorn oneself

abbeve'ra|re vt water. **~'toio** m drinking trough

abbi'ente adj well-to-do

abbiglia'mento m clothes pl; (industria) clothing industry

abbigli'ar|si vr dress. **~si** vr dress up

abbina'mento m combining

abbi'nare vt combine; match (colori)

abbindo'lare vt cheat

abbocca'mento m interview; (conversazione) talk

abboc'care vi bite; (tubi) join; fig swallow the bait

abboc'cato adj (vino) fairly sweet

abbof'farsi vr stuff oneself

abbona'mento m subscription; (ferroviario ecc) season-ticket; **fare l'~** take out a subscription

abbo'na|re vt make a subscriber. **~rsi** vr subscribe (**a** to); take out a season-ticket (**a** for) (teatro, stadio).

~to, -a *mf* subscriber

abbon'dan|te *adj* abundant; (quantità) copious; (nevicata) heavy; (vestiario) roomy. ~**te di** abounding in. ~**te'mente** *adv* (mangiare) copiously. ~**za** *f* abundance

abbon'dare *vi* abound

abbor'da|bile *adj* (persona) approachable; (prezzo) reasonable. ~**ggio** *m* (Mil) boarding. ~**re** *vt* board (nave); approach (persona); (T: attaccar bottone a) chat up; tackle (compito ecc)

abbotto'na|re *vt* button up. ~**'tura** *f* [row of] buttons. ~**to** *adj fig* tight-lipped

abboz'zare *vt* sketch [out]; ~ **un sorriso** give a hint of a smile. ab'**bozzo** *m* sketch

abbracci'are *vt* embrace; take up (professione); *fig* include. ab'**braccio** *m* hug

abbrevi'a|re *vt* shorten; (ridurre) curtail; abbreviate (parola). ~**zi'one** *f* abbreviation

abbron'zante *m* sun-tan lotion

abbron'za|re *vt* bronze; tan (pelle). ~**rsi** *vr* get a tan. ~**to** *adj* tanned. ~**'tura** *f* [sun-]tan

abbrusto'lire *vt* toast; roast (caffè ecc)

abbruti'mento *m* brutalization. abbru'tire *vt* brutalize. abbru'tirsi *vr* become brutalized

abbuf'fa|rsi *vr* (T) stuff oneself. ~**ta** *f* blowout

abbuo'nare *vt* reduce

abbu'ono *m* allowance; *Sport* handicap

abdi'ca|re *vi* abdicate. ~**zi'one** *f* abdication

aber'rante *adj* aberrant

a'bete *m* fir

abi'etto *adj* despicable

'abil|e *adj* able; (idoneo) fit; (astuto) clever. ~**ità** *f inv* ability; (idoneità) fit-

ness; (astuzia) cleverness. ~**'mente** *adv* ably; (con astuzia) cleverly

abili'ta|re *vt* qualify. ~**to** *adj* qualified. ~**zi'one** *f* qualification; (titolo) diploma

abis'sale *adj* abysmal. a'**bisso** *m* abyss

abi'tabile *adj* inhabitable

abi'tacolo *m* (Auto) passenger compartment

abi'tante *mf* inhabitant

abi'ta|re *vi* live. ~**to** *adj* inhabited ● *m* built-up area. ~**zi'one** *f* house

'abito *m* (da donna) dress; (da uomo) suit. ~ **da cerimonia/da sera** formal/evening dress

abitu'al|e *adj* usual. ~**'mente** *adv* usually

abitu'ar|e *vt* accustom. ~**si a** *vr* get used to

abitudi'nario, -a *adj* of fixed habits ● *mf* person of fixed habits

abi'tudine *f* habit; **d'**~ usually; **per** ~ out of habit; **avere l'**~ **di fare qcsa** be in the habit of doing sth

abnegazi'one *f* self-sacrifice

ab'norme *adj* abnormal

abo'li|re *vt* abolish; repeal (legge). ~**zi'one** *f* abolition; repeal

abomi'nevole *adj* abominable

abor'rire *vt* abhor

abor'ti|re *vi* miscarry; (volontariamente) have an abortion; *fig* fail. ~**vo** *adj* abortive. a'**borto** *m* miscarriage; (volontario) abortion. ~**sta** *adj* pro-choice

abrasi'|one *f* abrasion. abra'sivo *adj* & *m* abrasive

abro'ga|re *vt* repeal. ~**zi'one** *f* repeal

'abside *f* apse

abu'lia *f* apathy. a'**bulico** *adj* apathetic

abu's|are *vi* ~ **di** abuse; overindulge in (alcol); (approfittare di) take advantage of; (*violentare*) rape. **~ivo** *adj* illegal

a'buso *m* abuse. **~ di confidenza** breach of confidence

a.C. *abbr* (avanti Cristo) BC

'acca *f* | ▯ | **non ho capito un'~** I understood damn all

acca'demi|a *f* academy. **A~a di Belle Arti** Academy of Fine Arts. **~co, -a** *adj* academic ● *mf* academician

acca'd|ere *vi* happen; **accada quel che accada** come what may. **~uto** *m* event

accalappi'are *vt* catch; *fig* allure

accal'carsi *vr* crowd

accal'da|rsi *vr* get overheated; *fig* get excited. **~to** *adj* overheated

accalo'rarsi *vr* get excited

accampa'mento *m* camp. **accam'pare** *vt* *fig* put forth. **accam'parsi** *vr* camp

accani'mento *m* tenacity; (*odio*) rage

acca'ni|rsi *vr* persist; (*inferire*) rage. **~to** *adj* persistent; (*odio*) fierce; *fig* inveterate

ac'canto *adv* near; **~ a** *prep* next to

accanto'nare *vt* set aside; (*Mil*) billet

accaparra'mento *m* hoarding; (*Comm*) cornering

accapar'ra|re *vt* hoard. **~rsi** *vr* grab, corner (*mercato*). **~tore, ~trice** *mf* hoarder

accapigli'arsi *vr* scuffle; (*litigare*) squabble

accappa'toio *m* bathrobe; (*per spiaggia*) beachrobe

accappo'nare *vt* **fare ~ la pelle a** q*cno* make sb's flesh creep

accarez'zare *vt* caress; *fig* cherish

accartocci'ar|e *vt* scrunch up. **~si** *vr* curl up

acca'sarsi *vr* get married

accasci'arsi *vr* flop down; *fig*

lose heart

accata'stare *vt* pile up

accatti'vante *adj* beguiling

accatti'varsi *vr* **~ le simpatie/la stima/l'affetto di q**c**no** win sb's sympathy/respect/affection

accat'tonaggio *m* begging. **accat'tone, -a** *mf* beggar

accaval'lar|e *vt* cross (*gambe*). **~si** *vr* pile up; *fig* overlap

acce'cante *adj* (*luce*) blinding

acce'care *vt* blind ● *vi* go blind

ac'cedere *vi* **~ a** enter; (*acconsentire*) comply with

accele'ra|re *vi* accelerate ● *vt* accelerate. **~to** *adj* rapid. **~tore** *m* accelerator. **~zi'one** *f* acceleration

ac'cender|e *vt* light; turn on (*luce*, *TV* ecc); *fig* inflame; **ha da ~e?** have you got a light?. **~si** *vr* catch fire; (*illuminarsi*) light up; (*TV* ecc) turn on; *fig* become inflamed

accendi'gas *m inv* gas lighter; (*su cucina*) automatic ignition

accen'dino *m* lighter

accendi'sigari *m* cigar-lighter

accen'nare *vt* indicate; hum (*melodia*) ● *vi* **~ a** beckon to; *fig* hint at; (*far l'atto di*) make as if to; **accenna a piovere** it looks like rain. **ac'cenno** *m* gesture; (*con il capo*) nod; *fig* hint

accensi'one *f* lighting; (*di motore*) ignition

accen'ta|re *vt* accent; (*con accento tonico*) stress. **~zi'one** *f* accentuation. **ac'cento** *m* accent; (*tonico*) stress

accentra'mento *m* centralizing

accen'trare *vt* centralize

accentu'a|re *vt* accentuate. **~rsi** *vr* become more noticeable. **~to** *adj* marked

accerchia'mento *m* surrounding

accerchi'are *vt* surround

accerta'mento *m* check

accer'tare *vt* ascertain; (*controllare*) check; assess (*reddito*)

ac'ceso adj lighted; (radio, TV ecc) on; (colore) bright

acces'sibile adj accessible; (persona) approachable; (spesa) reasonable

ac'cesso m access; (Med: di rabbia) fit; **vietato l'~** no entry

acces'sorio adj accessory; (secondario) of secondary importance ● m accessory; **accessori** pl (rifiniture) fittings

ac'cetta f hatchet

accet'tabile adj acceptable

accet'tare vt accept; (aderire a) agree to

accettazi'one f acceptance; (luogo) reception. **~ [bagagli]** check-in. **[banco] ~** check-in [desk]

ac'cetto adj agreeable; **essere bene ~** be very welcome

accezi'one f meaning

acchiap'pare vt catch

ac'chito m **di primo ~** at first

acciac'ca|re vt crush; fig prostrate. **~to, -a** adj essere **~to** ache all over. **acci'acco** m infirmity; **acciacchi** pl aches and pains

acciaie'ria f steelworks

acci'aio m steel; **~ inossidabile** stainless steel

acciden'ta|le adj accidental. **~l'mente** adv accidentally. **~to** adj (terreno) uneven

acci'dente m accident; (Med) stroke; **non capisce un ~ 🔳** he doesn't understand a damn thing. **acci'denti!** int damn!

accigli'a|rsi vr frown. **~to** adj frowning

ac'cingersi vr **~ a** be about to

acci'picchia int good Lord!

acciuf'fare vt catch

acci'uga f anchovy

accla'ma|re vt applaud; (eleggere) acclaim. **~zi'one** f applause

acclima'ta|re vt acclimatize. **~si** vr get acclimatized

ac'clu|dere vt enclose. **~so** adj enclosed

accoc'colarsi vr squat

accogli'en|te adj welcoming; (confortevole) cosy. **~za** f welcome

ac'cogliere vt receive; (con piacere) welcome; (contenere) hold

accol'larsi vr take on (responsabilità, debiti, doveri). **accol'lato** adj high-necked

accoltel'lare vt knife

accomia'tar|e vt dismiss. **~si** vr take one's leave (**da** of)

accomo'dante adj accommodating

accomo'dar|e vt (riparare) mend; (disporre) arrange. **~si** vr make oneself at home; **si accomodi!** come in!; (si sieda) take a seat!

accompagna'mento m accompaniment; (seguito) retinue

accompa'gna|re vt accompany; **~re qcno a casa** see sb home; **~re qcno alla porta** show sb out. **~'tore, ~'trice** mf companion; (di comitiva) escort; (Mus) accompanist

accomu'nare vt pool

acconci'a|re vt arrange. **~'tura** f hair-style; (ornamento) head-dress

accondiscen'den|te adj too obliging. **~za** f excessive desire to please

accondi'scendere vi **~ a** condescend; comply with (desiderio); (acconsentire) consent to

acconsen'tire vi consent

acconten'tar|e vt satisfy. **~si** vr be content (**di** with)

ac'conto m deposit; **in ~** on account; **lasciare un ~** leave a deposit

accop'pare vt 🔳 bump off

accoppia'mento m coupling; (di animali) mating

accoppi'a|re vt couple; mate (animali). **~rsi** vr pair off; mate. **~ta** f (scommessa) bet on two horses for first and second place

acco'rato adj sorrowful

accorci'ar|e vt shorten. **~si** vr get shorter

accor'dar|e vt concede; match (colori ecc); (Mus) tune. **~si** vr agree

ac'cordo m agreement; (Mus) chord; (armonia) harmony; andare d'**~** get on well; d'**~**! agreed!; essere d'**~** agree; prendere accordi con qcno make arrangements with sb

ac'corgersi vr **~ di** notice; (capire) realize

accorgi'mento m shrewdness, (ospediente) device

ac'correre vi hasten

accor'tezza f (previdenza) forethought

ac'corto adj shrewd; mal **~** incautious

accosta'mento m combination

acco'star|e vt draw close to; approach (persona), set ajar (porta ecc). **~si** vr **~si a** come near to

accovacci'ar|si vr crouch

accoz'zaglia f jumble; (di persone) mob

accoz'zare vt **~ colori** mix colours that clash

accredita'mento m credit; **~ tramite bancogiro** Bank Giro Credit

accredi'tare vt confirm (notizia); (Comm) credit

ac'crescere vt increase. **~ersi** vr grow larger. **~i'tivo** adj augmentative

accucci'arsi vr (cane:) lie down; (persona:) crouch

accu'dire vi **~ a** attend to

accumu'lar|e vt accumulate. **~rsi** vr accumulate. **~tore** m accumulator; (Auto) battery. **~zi'one** f accumulation.

accura'tezza f care

accu'rato adj careful

ac'cusa f accusation; (Jur) charge; essere in stato di **~** have been charged; la Pubblica A**~** the public prosecutor

accu'sa|re vt accuse; (Jur) charge; complain of (dolore); **~ re ricevuta** di acknowledge receipt of. **~to, -a** mf accused. **~tore** m prosecutor

a'cerbo adj sharp; (non maturo) unripe

a'cero m maple

a'cerrimo adj implacable

a'ceto m vinegar

ace'tone m nail-polish remover

A.C.I. abbr (Automobile Club d'Italia) Italian Automobile Association

acidità f acidity. **~ di stomaco** acid stomach

'acido adj acid; (persona) sour ● m acid

a'cidulo adj slightly sour

'acino m berry; (chicco) grape

'acne f acne

'acqua f water; fare **~** leak; **~ in bocca!** fig mum's the word!. **~ corrente** running water. **~ dolce** fresh water. **~ minerale** mineral water. **~ minerale gassata** fizzy mineral water. **~ naturale** still mineral water. **~ potabile** drinking water. **~ salata** salt water. **~ tonica** tonic water

acqua'forte f etching

ac'quaio m sink

acquama'rina adj aquamarine

acqua'rello m = ACQUERELLO

ac'quario m aquarium; (Astr) Aquarius

acqua'santa f holy water

acqua'scooter m inv water-scooter

ac'quatico adj aquatic

acquat'tarsi vr crouch

acqua'vite f brandy

acquaz'zone m downpour

acque'dotto m aqueduct

'acqueo adj vapore **~**

water vapour

acque'rello m water-colour

acqui'rente mf purchaser

acqui'si|re vt acquire. ~**to** adj acquired. ~**zi'one** f attainment

acqui'st|are vt purchase; (ottenere) acquire. **ac'quisto** m purchase; **uscire per** ~**i** go shopping; **fare** ~**i** shop

acqui'trino m marsh

acquo'lina f **far venire l'**~ **in bocca a qcno** make sb's mouth water

ac'quoso adj watery

'acre adj acrid; (al gusto) sour; fig harsh

a'crilico m acrylic

a'croba|ta mf acrobat. ~**'zia** f acrobatics pl

a'cronimo m acronym

acu'ir|e vt sharpen. ~**si** vr become more intense

a'culeo m sting; (Bot) prickle

acumi'nato adj pointed

a'custic|a f acoustics pl. ~**o** adj acoustic

acu'tezza f acuteness

acutiz'zarsi vr become worse

a'cuto adj sharp; (suono) shrill; (freddo, odore) intense; (Gram, Math, Med) acute ● m (Mus) high note

ad prep = **A** (davanti a vocale)

adagi'ar|e vt lay down. ~**si** vr lie down

a'dagio adv slowly ● m (Mus) adagio; (proverbio) adage

adattabilità f adaptability

adatta'mento m adaptation; **avere spirito di** ~ be adaptable

adat'ta|re vt adapt; (aggiustare) fit. ~**rsi** vr adapt. ~**'tore** m adaptor. **a'datto** adj suitable (**a** for); (giusto) right

addebita'mento m debit. ~ **diretto** direct debit

addebi'tare vt debit; ascribe (colpa)

ad'debito m charge

addensa'mento m thickening; (di persone) gathering

adden'sar|e vt thicken. ~**si** vr thicken; (affollarsi) gather

adden'tare vt bite

adden'trarsi vr penetrate

ad'dentro adv deeply; **essere** ~ **in** be in on

addestra'mento m training

adde'strar|e vt train. ~**si** vr train

ad'detto, -a adj assigned ● mf employee; (diplomatico) attaché. ~ **stampa** press officer

addiaccio m **dormire all'**~ sleep in the open

addi'etro adv (indietro) back; (nel passato) before

ad'dio m & int goodbye. ~ **al celibato** stag party

addirit'tura adv (perfino) even; (assolutamente) absolutely; ~**!** really!

ad'dirsi vr ~ **a** suit

addi'tare vt point at; (in mezzo a un gruppo) point out; fig point to

addi'tivo adj & m additive

addizio'nal|e adj additional. ~**'mente** adv additionally

addizio'nare vt add [up]. **addizi'one** f addition

addob'bare vt decorate. **ad'dobbo** m decoration

addol'cir|e vt sweeten; tone down (colore); fig soften. ~**si** vr fig mellow

addolo'ra|re vt grieve. ~**rsi** vr be upset (**per** by). ~**to** adj distressed

ad'dom|e m abdomen. ~**i'nale** adj abdominal; **[muscoli] addominali** pl abdominals

addomesti'ca|re vt tame. ~**tore** m tamer

addormen'ta|re vt put to sleep. ~**rsi** vr go to sleep. ~**to** adj asleep; fig slow

addos'sar|e vt ~e a (appoggiare) lean against; (attribuire) lay on. ~si vr (ammassarsi) crowd; shoulder (responsabilità ecc)

ad'dosso adv on; ~ a prep on; (molto vicino) right next to; **mettere gli occhi** ~ a qcno/qcosa hanker after sb/sth; **non mettermi le mani** ~**!** keep your hands off me!; **stare** ~ **a** qcno fig be on sb's back

ad'durre vt produce (prova, documento); give (pretesto, esempio)

adegua'mento m adjustment

adegu'a|re vt adjust. ~**rsi** vr conform. ~**to** adj adequate; (conforme) consistent

a'dempi|ere vt fulfil. ~**'mento** m fulfilment

ade'noidi fpl adenoids

ade'ren|te adj adhesive; (vestito) tight ● mf follower. ~**za** f adhesion. ~**ze** pl connections

ade'rire vi ~ **a** adhere to, support (petizione); agree to (richiesta)

adesca'mento m (Jur) soliciting

ade'scare vt bait; fig entice

adesi'one f adhesion; fig agreement

ade'sivo adj adhesive ● m sticker; (Auto) bumper sticker

a'desso adv now; (poco fa) just now; (tra poco) any moment now; **da** ~ **in poi** from now on; **per** ~ for the moment

adia'cente adj adjacent; ~ **a** next to

adi'bire vt ~ **a** put to use as

'adipe m adipose tissue

adi'ra|rsi vr get irate. ~**to** adj irate

a'dire vt resort to; ~ **le vie legali** take legal proceedings

'adito m **dare** ~ **a** give rise to

adocchi'are vt eye; (con desiderio) covet

adole'scen|te adj & mf adolescent. ~**za** f adolescence. ~**zi'ale** adj adolescent

adom'brar|e vt darken; fig veil. ~**si** vr (offendersi) take offence

adope'rar|e vt use. ~**si** vr take trouble

ado'rabile adj adorable

ado'ra|re vt adore. ~**zi'one** f adoration

ador'nare vt adorn

adot't|are vt adopt. ~**ivo** adj adoptive. **adozi'one** f adoption

adrena'lina f adrenalin

adri'atico adj Adriatic ● m **l'A**~, the Adriatic

adu'la|re vt flatter. ~**tore**, ~**trice** mf flatterer. ~**zi'one** f flattery

adulte'ra|re vt adulterate. ~**to** adj adulterated

adul'terio m adultery. **a'dultero**, **-a** adj adulterous ● m adulterer ● f adulteress

a'dulto, **-a** adj & mf adult; (maturo) mature

adu'nanza f assembly

adu'na|re vt gather. ~**ta** f (Mil) parade

a'dunco adj hooked

ae'rare vt air (stanza)

a'ereo adj aerial; (dell'aviazione) air attrib ● m aeroplane, plane

ae'robica f aerobics. ~**o** adj aerobic

aerodi'namic|a f aerodynamics sg. ~**o** adj aerodynamic

aero'nautic|a f aeronautics sg; (Mil) Air Force. ~**o** adj aeronautical

aero'plano m aeroplane

aero'porto m airport

aero'scalo m cargo and servicing area

aero'sol m inv aerosol

'afa f sultriness

af'fabil|e adj affable. ~**ità** f affability

affaccen'da|rsi vr busy oneself (a

with). ∼to *adj* busy

affacci'arsi *vr* show oneself; ∼ **alla finestra** appear at the window

affa'ma|re *vt* starve [out]. ∼**to** *adj* starving

affan'na|re *vt* leave breathless. ∼**rsi** *vr* busy oneself; (*agitarsi*) get worked up. ∼**to** *adj* breathless; **dal respiro** ∼ **to** wheezy. **af'fanno** *m* breathlessness; *fig* worry

af'fare *m* matter; (*Comm*) deal; (*occasione*) bargain; **affari** *pl* business; **non sono affari tuoi** it's none of your business. **affa'rista** *mf* wheeler-dealer

affasci'nante *adj* fascinating; (*persona, sorriso*) bewitching

affasci'nare *vt* bewitch; *fig* charm

affatica'mento *m* fatigue

affati'car|e *vt* tire; (*sfinire*) exhaust. ∼**si** *vr* tire oneself out; (*affannarsi*) strive

af'fatto *adv* completely; **non...** ∼ not... at all; **niente** ∼**!** not at all!

affer'ma|re *vt* affirm; (*sostenere*) assert. ∼**rsi** *vr* establish oneself

affermativa'mente *adv* in the affirmative

afferma'tivo *adj* affirmative

affermazi'one *f* assertion; (*successo*) achievement

affer'rar|e *vt* seize; catch (*oggetto*); (*capire*) grasp; ∼**e al volo** *fig* be quick on the uptake. ∼**si** *vr* ∼**si a** grasp at

affet'ta|re *vt* slice; (*ostentare*) affect. ∼**to** *adj* sliced; (*maniere*) affected ● *m* cold meat.

affet'tivo *adj* affective; **rapporto** ∼ emotional tie

af'fetto¹ *m* affection

af'fetto² *adj* ∼ **da** suffering from

affettuosità *f inv* (*gesto*) affectionate gesture

affettu'oso *adj* affectionate

affezio'na|rsi *vr* ∼**rsi a** grow fond of. ∼**to** *adj* devoted (**a** to)

affian'car|e *vt* put side by side; (*Mil*) flank; *fig* support. ∼**si** *vr* come side by side; *fig* stand together; ∼**si a qcno** *fig* help sb out

affiata'mento *m* harmony

affia'ta|rsi *vr* get on well together. ∼**to** *adj* close-knit; **una coppia** ∼**ta** a very close couple

affibbi'are *vt* ∼ **qcsa a qcno** saddle sb with sth; ∼ **un pugno a qcno** let fly at sb

affi'dabil|e *adj* dependable. ∼**ità** *f* dependability

affida'mento *m* (*Jur: dei minori*) custody; **fare** ∼ **su qcno** rely on sb; **non dare** ∼ not inspire confidence

affi'dar|e *vt* entrust. ∼**si** *vr* ∼**si a** rely on

affievo'lirsi *vr* grow weak

af'figgere *vt* affix

affi'lare *vt* sharpen

affili'ar|e *vt* affiliate. ∼**si** *vr* become affiliated

affi'nare *vt* sharpen; (*perfezionare*) refine

affinché *conj* so that, in order that

af'fin|e *adj* similar. ∼**ità** *f* affinity

affiora'mento *m* emergence; (*Naut*) surfacing

affio'rare *vi* emerge; *fig* come to light

af'fisso *m* bill; (*Gram*) affix

affitta'camere *m inv* landlord ● *f inv* landlady

affit'tare *vt* rent; **'af'fittasi'** 'for rent'

af'fitt|o *m* rent; **contratto d'**∼**o** lease; **dare in** ∼**o** let; **prendere in** ∼**o** rent. ∼**u'ario, -a** *mf* (*Jur*) lessee

af'fligger|e *vt* torment. ∼**si** *vr* distress oneself

af'fli|tto *adj* distressed. ∼**zi'one** *f* distress; *fig* affliction

afflosci'arsi *vr* become floppy; (*accasciarsi*) flop down; (*morale:*) decline

afflu'en|te *adj* & *m* tributary. ∼**za** *f*

flow; (di gente) crowd

afflu'ire vi flow; fig pour in

af'flusso m influx

affo'ga|re vt/i drown; (Culin) poach; ~**re** in fig be swamped with. ~**to** adj (persona) drowned; (uova) poached. ~**to al caffè** m ice cream with hot espresso poured over it

affol'la|re vt, ~**rsi** vr crowd. ~**to** adj crowded

affonda'mento m sinking

affon'dare vt/i sink

affossa'mento m pothole

affran'ca|re vt redeem (bene); stamp (lettera); free (schiavo). ~**rsi** vr free oneself. ~**trice** f franking machine. ~**tura** f stamping; (di spedizione) postage

af'franto adj prostrated; (esausto) worn out

af'fresco m fresco

affret'ta|re vt speed up. ~**rsi** vr hurry. ~**ta'mente** adv hastily. ~**to** adj hurry

affron'ta|re vt face; confront (nemico); meet (spese). ~**si** vr clash

af'fronto m affront, insult; **fare un ~ a qcno** insult sb

affumi'ca|re vt fill with smoke; (Culin) smoke. ~**to** adj (prosciutto, formaggio) smoked

affuso'la|re vt taper [off]. ~**to** adj tapering

afo'risma m aphorism

a'foso adj sultry

'Africa f Africa. **afri'cano, -a** agg & mf African

afrodi'siaco adj & m aphrodisiac

a'genda f pocket-diary

a'gente m agent; **agenti** pl **atmosferici** atmospheric agents. ~ **di cambio** stockbroker. ~ **di polizia** police officer

agen'zia f agency; (filiale) branch office; (di banca) branch. ~ **di viaggi** travel agency. ~ **immobiliare** estate agency

agevo'la|re vt facilitate. ~**zi'one** f facilitation

a'gevole adj easy; (strada) smooth. ~**mente** adv easily

agganci'ar|e vt hook up; (Rail) couple. ~**si** vr (vestito:) hook up

ag'geggio m gadget

agget'tivo m adjective

agghiacci'ante adj terrifying

agghiacci'ar|e vt fig ~ **qcno** make sb's blood run cold. ~**si** vr freeze

agghin'da|re vt ① dress up. ~**rsi** vr ① doll oneself up. ~**to** adj dressed up

aggiorna'mento m up-date

aggior'na|re vt (rinviare) postpone; (mettere a giorno) bring up to date. ~**rsi** vr get up to date. ~**to** adj up-to-date; (versione) updated

aggi'rare vt surround; (fig: ingannare) trick. ~**si** vr hang about; ~**si su** (discorso ecc:) be about; (somma:) be around

aggiudi'car|e vt award; (all'asta) knock down. ~**si** vr win

aggi'un|gere vt add. ~**ta** f addition. ~**tivo** adj supplementary. ~**to** adj added ● adj & m (assistente) assistant

aggiu'sta|re vt mend; (sistemare) settle; (①: mettere a posto) fix. ~**si** vr adapt; (mettersi in ordine) tidy oneself up; (decidere) sort things out; (tempo:) clear up

agglomera'mento m conglomeration

agglome'rato m built-up area

aggrap'par|e vt grasp. ~**si** vr ~**si a** cling to

aggra'vante (Jur) f aggravation
● adj aggravating

aggra'var|e vt (peggiorare) make worse; increase (pena); (appesantire)

a

weigh down. ~si vr worsen

aggrazi'ato adj graceful

aggre'dire vt attack

aggre'ga|re vt add; (associare a un gruppo ecc) admit. ~rsi a vr ~rsi a join. ~to a associated ● m aggregate; (di case) block

aggressi'one f aggression; (atto) attack

aggres's|ivo adj aggressive. ~ività f aggressiveness. ~ore m aggressor

aggrin'zare, aggrin'zire vt wrinkle

aggrot'tare vt ~ le ciglia/la fronte frown

aggrovigli'a|re vt tangle. ~rsi vr get entangled; fig get complicated. ~to adj entangled; fig confused

agguan'tare vt catch

aggu'ato m ambush; (tranello) trap; **stare in ~** lie in wait

agguer'rito adj fierce

agia'tezza f comfort

agi'ato adj (persona) well off; (vita) comfortable

a'gibil|e adj (palazzo) fit for human habitation. ~ità f fitness for human habitation

'agil|e adj agile. ~ità f agility

'agio m ease; **mettersi a proprio ~** make oneself at home

a'gire vi act; (comportarsi) behave; (funzionare) work; **~ su** affect

agi'ta|re vt shake; wave (mano); (fig: turbare) trouble. ~rsi vr toss about; (essere inquieto) be restless; (mare:) get rough. ~to adj restless; (mare) rough. ~'tore, ~'trice mf (persona) agitator. ~zi'one f agitation; **mettere in ~zione** qcno make sb worried

'agli = A + GLI

'aglio m garlic

a'gnello m lamb

agno'lotti mpl ravioli sg

a'gnostico, -a adj & mf agnostic

'ago m needle

ago'ni|a f agony. ~z'zare vi be on one's deathbed

ago'nistic|a f competition. ~o adj competitive

agopun'tura f acupuncture

a'gosto m August

a'grari|a f agriculture. ~o adj agricultural ● m landowner

a'gricol|o adj agricultural. ~'tore m farmer. ~'tura** f agriculture

agri'foglio m holly

agritu'rismo m farm holidays, agro-tourism

>
>
> **Agriturismo** In the 1980s many farmers began to supplement their falling incomes by offering tourists an authentic experience of the Italian countryside. Agriturismo is now a very popular form of tourism in Italy. Guests can learn traditional skills and crafts, such as cooking and wine-making, all of which helps to preserve a threatened way of life.

'agro adj sour

agroalimen'tare adj food attrib

agro'dolce adj bitter-sweet; (Culin) sweet-and-sour; **in ~** sweet and sour

agrono'mia f agronomy

a'grume m citrus fruit; (pianta) citrus tree

aguz'zare vt sharpen; **~ le orecchie** prick up one's ears; **~ la vista** look hard

aguz'zino m slave-driver; (carceriere) jailer

ahimè int alas

'ai = A + I

'aia f threshing-floor

'Aia f L'~ The Hague

Aids *mf* Aids

ai'rone *m* heron

ai'tante *adj* sturdy

aiu'ola *f* flower-bed

aiu'tante *mf* assistant ● *m* (*Mil*) adjutant ● ~ **di campo** aide decamp

aiu'tare *vt* help

ai'uto *m* help, aid; (*assistente*) assistant

aiz'zare *vt* incite; ~ **contro** set on

al = **a+il**

'ala *f* wing; **fare** ~ make way

ala'bastro *m* alabaster

'alacre *adj* brisk

a'lano *m* Great Dane

'alba *f* dawn

Alba'nia *f* Albania. **a~ese** *adj & mf* Albanian

albeggi'are *vi* dawn

albe'rato *adj* wooded; (*viale*) tree-lined. ~**'tura** *f* (*Naut*) masts *pl*. **albe-'rello** *m* sapling

al'bergo *m* hotel. ~**o diurno** hotel where rooms are rented during the daytime. ~**a'tore**, ~**a'trice** *mf* hotel-keeper. ~**hi'ero** *adj* hotel attrib

'albero *m* tree; (*Naut*) mast; (*Mech*) shaft. ~ **genealogico** family tree. ~ **maestro** (*Naut*) mainmast. ~ **di Natale** Christmas tree

albi'cocca *f* apricot. ~**o** *m* apricot-tree

al'bino, **-a** *mf* albino

'albo *m* register; (*libro ecc*) album; (*per avvisi*) notice board

'album *m* album. ~ **da disegno** sketch-book

al'bume *m* albumen

'alce *m* elk

'alcol *m* alcohol; (*Med*) spirit; (*liquori forti*) spirits *pl*; (*Mech*) spirits *pl*. **al'colici** *mpl* alcoholic drinks. **al'colico** *adj* alcoholic. **alco'lismo** *m* alcoholism. ~**iz'zato**, **-a** *adj & mf* alcoholic

alco'test® *m inv* Breathalyser®

al'cova *f* alcove

al'cun, **al'cuno** *adj & pron* any; **non ha** ~ **amico** he hasn't any/no friends. **alcuni** *pl* some, a few; ~**i suoi amici** some of his friends

alea'torio *adj* unpredictable

a'letta *f* (*Mech*) fin

alfa'betico *adj* alphabetical

alfabetizzazi'one *f* ~ **della popolazione** teaching people to read and write

alfa'beto *m* alphabet

alfi'ere *m* (*negli scacchi*) bishop

al'fine *adv* eventually, in the end

'alga *f* seaweed

'algebra *f* algebra

Alge'ria *f* Algeria. **a~no**, **-a** *agg & mf* Algerian

ali'ante *m* glider

'alibi *m inv* alibi

alie'na|re *vt* alienate. ~**rsi** *vr* become estranged; ~**rsi le simpatie di qcno** lose sb's good will. ~**to**, **-a** *adj* alienated ● *mf* lunatic

a'lieno, **-a** *mf* alien ● *adj* è ~ **da invidia** envy is foreign to him

alimen'ta|re *vt* feed; *fig* foment ● *adj* food attrib; (*abitudine*) dietary ● *m* ~**ri** *pl* food-stuffs. ~**'tore** *m* power unit. ~**zi'one** *f* feeding

> **Alimentari** Alimentari are food shops offering a range of products, from groceries, fruit, and vegetables to prepared foods like cheeses, cured hams, and salamis. Some even bake their own bread. An *alimentari* will also usually prepare *panini* (filled rolls) using their own ingredients. Small villages which have no other shops usually have an *alimentari*.
>
>

ali'mento *m* food; **alimenti** *pl* food; (*Jur*) alimony

a'liquota *f* share; (*di imposta*) rate

ali'scafo m hydrofoil

'alito m breath

'alla = A + LA

allaccia'mento m connection

allacci'are vt fasten (cintura); lace up (scarpe); do up (vestito); (collegare) connect; form (amicizia). **~si** vr do up, fasten

allaga'mento m flooding

alla'gar|e vt flood. **~si** vr become flooded

allampa'nato adj lanky

allarga'mento m (di strada, ricerche) widening

allar'gar|e vt widen; open (braccia, gambe); let out (vestito ecc); fig extend. **~si** vr widen

allar'mante adj alarming

allar'ma|re vt alarm. **~to** adj panicky

al'larme m alarm; **dare l'~** raise the alarm; **falso ~** fig false alarm. **~ aereo** air raid warning

allar'mis|mo m alarmism. **~ta** mf alarmist

allatta'mento m (di animale) suckling; (di neonato) feeding

allat'tare vt suckle (animale); feed (neonato)

'alle = A + LE

alle'a|nza f alliance. **~to, -a** adj allied ● mf ally

alle'ar|e vt unite. **~si** vr form an alliance

alle'gare¹ vt (Jur) allege

alle'gare² vt (accludere) enclose; set on edge (denti). **~to** adj enclosed ● m enclosure; **in ~to** attached. **~zi'one** f (Jur) allegation

allegge'rir|e vt lighten; fig alleviate. **~si** vr become lighter; (vestirsi leggero) put on lighter clothes

allego'ria f allegory. **alle'gorico** adj allegorical

allegra'mente adv breezily

alle'gria f gaiety

al'legro adj cheerful; (colore) bright; (brillo) tipsy ● m (Mus) allegro

alle'luia int hallelujah!

allena'mento m training

alle'na|re vt, **~rsi** vr train. **~'tore**, **~'trice** mf trainer, coach

allen'tar|e vt loosen; fig relax. **~si** vr become loose; (Mech) work loose

aller'gia f allergy. **al'lergico** adj allergic

all'erta f stare **~** be alert

allesti'mento m preparation. **~ scenico** (Theat) set

alle'stire vt prepare; stage (spettacolo); (Naut) fit out

allet'tante adj alluring

allet'tare vt entice

alleva'mento m breeding; (processo) bringing up; (luogo) farm; (per piante) nursery; **pollo di ~** battery chicken

alle'vare vt bring up (bambini); breed (animali); grow (piante)

allevi'are vt alleviate; fig lighten

alli'bito adj astounded

allibra'tore m bookmaker

allie'tar|e vt gladden. **~si** vr rejoice

alli'evo, -a mf pupil ● m (Mil) cadet

alliga'tore m alligator

alline'a'mento m alignment

alline'ar|e vt line up; (Typ) align; Fin adjust. **~si** vr fall into line

'allo = A + LO

al'locco m Zool tawny owl

al'lodola f [sky]lark

alloggi'are vt put up; (casa:) provide accommodation for; (Mil) billet ● vi stay; (Mil) be billeted. **al'loggio** m apartment; (Mil) billet

allontana'mento m removal

allonta'nar|e vt move away; (licenziare) dismiss; avert (pericolo). **~si** vr go away

al'lora adv then; (a quel tempo) at that time; (in tal caso) in that case;

d'~ in poi from then on; e ~? what now?; (e con ciò?) so what?; fino ~ until then

al'loro m laurel; (Culin) bay

'alluce m big toe

alluci'na|nte adj ① incredible; sostanza ~cínte hallucinogen. ~to, -a mf ① space cadet. ~zi'one f hallucination

alluci'nogeno adj (sostanza) hallucinatory

al'ludere vi ~ a allude to

allu'minio m aluminium

allun'gar|e vt lengthen; stretch [out] (gamba); extend (tavolo); (diluire) dilute; ~e il collo crane one's neck. ~e le mani su qcno touch sb up. ~e il passo quicken one's step. ~si vr grow longer; (crescere) grow taller; (sdraiarsi) lie down

allusi'one f allusion

allu'sivo adj allusive

alluvio'nale adj alluvial

alluvi'one f flood

al'meno adv at least; [se] ~ venisse il sole! if only the sun would come out!

a'logeno m halogen ● adj lampada alogena halogen lamp

a'lone m halo

'Alpi fpl le ~ the Alps

alpi'nis|mo m mountaineering. ~ta mf mountaineer

al'pino adj Alpine ● m (Mil) gli alpini the Alpine troops

al'quanto adj a certain amount of ● adv rather

alt int stop

alta'lena f swing; (tavola in bilico) see-saw

altale'nare vi fig vacillate

alta'mente adv highly

al'tare m altar

alta'rino m scoprire gli altarini di qcno reveal sb's guilty secrets

alte'ra|re vt alter; adulterate (vino);

(falsificare) falsify. ~rsi vr be altered; (cibo): go bad; (merci:) deteriorate; (arrabbiarsi) get angry. ~to adj (vino) adulterated. ~zi'one f alteration; (di vino) adulteration

al'terco m alteration

alter'nanza f alternation

alter'na|re vt, ~rsi vr alternate. ~tiva f alternative. ~tivo adj alternate. ~to adj alternating. ~tore m (Electr) alternator

al'terno adj alternate; a giorni ~i every other day

al'tero adj haughty

al'tezza f height; (profondità) depth; (suono) pitch; (di tessuto) width; (titolo) Highness; essere all'~ di be on a level with; fig be up to

altezzosa'mente adv haughtily. ~ità f haughtiness

altez'zoso adj haughty

al'ticcio adj tipsy, merry

altipi'ano m plateau

alti'tudine f altitude

'alto adj high; (di statura) tall; (profondo) deep; (suono) high-pitched; (tessuto) wide; (Geog) northern; a notte alta in the middle of the night; avere degli alti e bassi have some ups and downs; ad alta fedeltà high-fidelity; a voce alta, ad alta voce in a loud voice; (leggere) aloud; essere in ~ mare be on the high seas. alta finanza f high finance. alta moda f high fashion. alta tensione f high voltage ● adv high; in ~ at the top; (guardare) up; manì in ~! hands up!

alto'forno m blast-furnace

altolà int halt there!

altolo'cato adj highly placed

altopar'lante m loudspeaker

altopi'ano m plateau

altret'tanto adj & pron as much; (pl) as many ● adv likewise; buona fortuna! – grazie, ~ good luck! – thank you, the same to you

altri'menti *adv* otherwise

'altro *adj* other; un ~, un'altra another; l'altr'anno last year; domani l'~ the day after tomorrow; l'ho visto l'~ giorno I saw him the other day ●*pron* other [one]; un ~, un'altra another [one]; ne vuoi dell'~? would you like some more?; l'un l'~ one another; nessun ~ nobody else; gli altri (la gente) other people ●*m* something else; non fa ~ che lavorare he does nothing but work; desidera ~? (in negozio) anything else?; più che ~, sono stanco I'm tired more than anything; se non ~ at least; senz'~ certainly; tra l'~ what's more; ~ che! and how!

altroi'eri *m* l'~ the day before yesterday

al'tronde *adv* d'~ on the other hand

al'trove *adv* elsewhere

al'trui *adj* other people's ●*m* other people's belongings *pl*

al'tura *f* high ground; (Naut) deep sea

a'lunno, -a *mf* pupil

alve'are *m* hive

al'za|re *vt* lift; (costruire) build; (Naut) hoist; ~re le spalle shrug one's shoulders. ~rsi *vr* rise; (in piedi) stand up; (da letto) get up; ~rsi in piedi get to one's feet. ~ta *f* lifting; (aumento) rise; (da letto) getting up; (Archit) elevation. ~to *adj* up

a'mabile *adj* lovable; (vino) sweet

a'maca *f* hammock

amalga'mar|e *vt*, ~si *vr* amalgamate

a'mante *adj* ~ di fond of ●*m* lover ●*f* mistress, lover

a'ma|re *vt* love; like (musica, ecc). ~to, -a *adj* loved ●*mf* beloved

ama'rena *f* sour black cherry

ama'retto *m* macaroon

ama'rezza *f* bitterness;

(dolore) sorrow

a'maro *adj* bitter ●*m* bitterness; (liquore) bitters *pl*

ama'rognolo *adj* rather bitter

ama'tore, -'trice *mf* lover

ambasci'a|ta *f* embassy; (messaggio) message. ~tore, ~'trice *m* ambassador ●*f* ambassadress

ambe'due *adj & pron* both

ambien'ta|le *adj* environmental. ~lista *adj & mf* environmentalist

ambien'tar|e *vt* acclimatize; set (personaggio, film ecc). ~si *vr* get acclimatized

ambi'ente *m* environment; (stanza) room; *fig* milieu

ambiguità *f inv* ambiguity; (di persona) shadiness

am'biguo *adj* ambiguous; (persona) shady

ambiva'len|te *adj* ambivalent. ~za *f* ambivalence

ambizi'o|ne *f* ambition. ~so *adj* ambitious

ambu'lante *adj* wandering; venditore ~ hawker

ambu'lanza *f* ambulance

ambula'torio *m* (di medico) surgery; (di ospedale) out-patients'

a'meba *f* amoeba

a'meno *adj* pleasant

A'merica *f* America. ~ del Sud South America. ameri'cano, -a *agg & mf* American

ami'anto *m* asbestos

ami'chevole *adj* friendly

ami'cizia *f* friendship; fare ~ con qcno make friends with sb; amicizie *pl* (amici) friends

a'mico, -a *mf* friend; ~ del cuore bosom friend

'amido *m* starch

ammac'ca|re *vt* dent; bruise

(frutto). **~rsi** vr (metallo:) get dented; (frutto:) bruise. **~to** adj dented; (frutto) bruised. **~'tura** f dent; (livido) bruise

ammae'stra|re vt (istruire) teach; train (animale). **~to** adj trained

ammai'nare vt lower (bandiera); furl (vele)

amma'la|rsi vr fall ill. **~to, -a** adj ill • mf sick person; (paziente) patient

ammali'are vt bewitch

am'manco m deficit

ammanet'tare vt handcuff

ammani'cato adj essere ~ have connections

amma'raggio m splashdown

amma'rare vi put down on the sea; (nave spaziale:) splash down

ammas'sar|e vt amass. **~si** vr crowd together. **am'masso** m mass; (mucchio) pile

ammat'tire vi go mad

ammaz'zar|e vt kill. **~si** vr (suicidarsi) kill oneself; (rimanere ucciso) be killed

am'menda f amends pl; (multa) fine; fare ~ di qcsa make amends for sth

am'messo pp di ammettere • conj ~ che supposing that

am'mettere vt admit; (riconoscere) acknowledge; (supporre) suppose

ammic'care vi wink

ammini'stra|re vt administer; (gestire) run. **~'tivo** adj administrative. **~tore, ~trice** mf administrator; (di azienda) manager; (di società) director. **~tore delegato** managing director. **~zi'one** f administration; **fatti di ordinaria ~zione** fig routine matters

ammi'ragli|o m admiral. **~'ato** m admiralty

ammi'ra|re vt admire. **~to** adj restare/essere **~to** be full of admiration. **~tore, ~trice** mf admirer. **~zi'one** f admiration. **ammi'revole**

adj admirable

ammis'sibile *adj* admissible

ammissi'one f admission; (approvazione) acknowledgement

ammobilia|re vt furnish. **~to** adj furnished

am'modo adj proper • adv properly

am'mollo m in ~ soaking

ammo'niaca f ammonia

ammoni'mento m warning; (di rimprovero) admonishment

ammoni|re vt warn; (rimproverare) admonish. **~'tore** adj admonishing. **~zi'one** f Sport warning

ammon'tare vi ~ a amount to • m amount

ammonticchi'are vt heap up

ammorbi'dente m (per panni) softener

ammorbi'dir|e vt, **~si** vr soften

ammorta'mento m (Comm) amortization

ammor'tare vt pay off (spesa); (Comm) amortize (debito)

ammortiz'za|re vt (Comm) = **AMMORTARE**; (Mech) damp. **~'tore** m shock-absorber

ammosci'ar|e vt make flabby. **~si** vi get flabby

ammucchi'a|re vt, **~rsi** vr pile up. **~ta** f (🔲: orgia) orgy

ammuf'fi|re vi go mouldy. **~to** adj mouldy

ammuti'mento m mutiny

ammuti'narsi vr mutiny

ammuto'lire vi be struck dumb

amni'stia f amnesty

'amo m hook; fig bait

a'more m love; fare l'~ make love; per l'amor di Dio/del cielo! for heaven's sake!; andare d'~ e d'accordo get on like a house on fire; **amor proprio** self-respect; è un ~ (persona) he/she's a darling; **per ~ di** for the sake of; **amori** pl love affairs. **~ggi'are** vi flirt.

a

amo'revole adj loving

a'morfo adj shapeless; (fig) grey

amo'roso adj loving; (sguardo ecc) amorous; (lettera, relazione) love

ampi'ezza f (di esperienza) breadth; (di stanza) spaciousness; (di gonna) fullness; (importanza) scale

'ampio adj ample; (esperienza) wide; (stanza) spacious; (vestito) loose; (gonna) full; (pantaloni) baggy

am'plesso m embrace

amplia'mento m (di casa, porto) enlargement; (di strada) widening

ampli'are vt broaden (conoscenze)

amplifi'ca|re vt amplify; (fig magnify. ∼'tore m amplifier. ∼zi'one f amplification

am'polla f cruet

ampu'ta|re vt amputate. ∼zi'one f amputation

amu'leto m amulet

anab'bagli'ante adj (Auto) dipped ● mpl anabbaglianti dipped headlights

anacro'nis|mo m anachronism. ∼tico adj anachronistic

a'nagrafe f (ufficio) register office; (registro) register of births, marriages and deaths

ana'grafico adj dati mpl ana-grafici personal data

ana'gramma m anagram

anal'colico adj non-alcoholic ● m soft drink, non-alcoholic drink

analfa'be|ta adj & mf illiterate. ∼tismo m illiteracy

anal'gesico adj painkiller

a'nalisi f inv analysis; (Med) test. ∼ grammaticale/del periodo/logica parsing. ∼ del sangue blood test

ana'li|sta mf analyst. ∼tico adj analytical. ∼z'zare vt analyse; (Med) test

anal'lergico adj hypoallergenic

analo'gia f analogy. **a'nalogo** adj analogous

'ananas m inv pineapple

anar'chi|a f anarchy. **a'narchico, -a** adj anarchic ● mf anarchist. ∼smo m anarchism

A.N.A.S. f abbr (Azienda Nazionale Autonoma delle Strade) national road maintenance authority

anato'mia f anatomy. **ana'tomico** adj anatomical; (sedia) contoured

'anatra f duck

ana'troccolo m duckling

'anca f hip; (di animale) flank

ance'strale adj ancestral

'anche conj also, too; (persino) even; ∼ se even if

anchilo'sato adj fig stiff

an'cora[1] adv still, yet; (di nuovo) again; (di più) some more; ∼ una volta once more

'anco|ra[2] f anchor; gettare l'∼a drop anchor; ∼'raggio m anchorage. ∼'rare vt anchor

anda'mento m (del mercato, degli affari) trend

an'dante adj (corrente) current; (di poco valore) cheap ● m (Mus) andante

an'da|re vi go; (funzionare) work; ∼ via (partire) leave; (macchia): come out; ∼ [bene] (confarsi) suit; (taglia:) fit; **ti va bene alle tre?** does three o'clock suit you?; **non mi va di mangiare** I don't feel like eating; ∼ **di fretta** be in a hurry; ∼ **fiero di** be proud of; ∼ **di moda** be in fashion; **va per i 20 anni** he's nearly 20; **ma va' [là]!** come on!; **come va?** how are things?; ∼ **a male** go off; ∼ **a fuoco** go up in flames; **va spedito [entro] stamattina** it must be sent this morning; **ne va del mio lavoro** my job is at stake; **come è andata a finire?** how did it turn out?; **cosa vai dicendo?** what are you talking about?. ∼**rsene** go away; (morire) pass away ● m going; **a lungo** ∼**re** eventually '**andito** m passage

an'**drone** m entrance

a'**neddoto** m anecdote

ane'**lare** vt ~ a a long for. a'**nelito** m longing

a'**nello** m ring; (di catena) link

ane'**mia** f anaemia. a'**nemico** adj anaemic

a'**nemone** m anemone

aneste'**si|a** f anaesthesia; (sostanza) anaesthetic. ~'**sta** mf anaesthetist. ane'**stetico** adj & m anaesthetic

an'**fibi** mpl (stivali) army boots

an'**fibio** m (animale) amphibian ● adj amphibious

anfite'**atro** m amphitheatre

'**anfora** f amphora

an'**fratto** m ravine

an'**gelico** adj angelic

'**angelo** m angel. ~ custode guardian angel

angli'**c|ano** adj Anglican. ~'**smo** m Anglicism

angli'**cano** adj Anglican. ~'**smo** m Anglicism

an'**glofilo, -a** adj & mf Anglophile

an'**glofono, -a** adj & mf English speaker

anglo'**sassone** adj & mf Anglo-Saxon

ango'**la|re** adj angular. ~zi'**one** f angle shot

'**angolo** m corner; (Math) angle. ~ [di] cottura kitchenette

ango'**loso** adj angular

an'**gosci|a** f anguish. ~'**are** vt torment. ~'**ato** adj agonized. ~'**oso** adj (disperato) anguished; (che dà angoscia) distressing

angu'**illa** f eel

an'**guria** f water-melon

an'**gusti|a** f (ansia) anxiety; (penuria) poverty. ~'**are** vt distress. ~'**arsi** vr be very worried (**per** about)

an'**gusto** adj narrow

'**anice** m anise; (Culin) aniseed; (liquore) anisette

ani'**dride** f ~ **carbonica** carbon dioxide

'**anima** f soul; **non c'era** ~ **viva** there was not a soul about; **all'~-!** good grief!; **un'**~ **in pena** a soul in torment. ~ **gemella** soul mate

ani'**ma|le** adj m animal; ~**li domestici** pl pets. ~'**lesco** adj animal

ani'**ma|re** vt give life to; (ravvivare) enliven; (incoraggiare) encourage. ~**rsi** vr come to life; (accalorarsi) become animated. ~**to** adj animate; (discussione) animated; (paese) lively. ~'**tore**, ~'**trice** mf leading spirit; Cinema animator. ~**zi'one** f animation

'**animo** m (mente) mind; (indole) disposition; (cuore) heart; **perdersi d'**~ lose heart; **farsi** ~ take heart. ~**sità** f animosity

ani'**moso** adj brave; (ostile) hostile

'**anitra** f = **ANATRA**

annac'**qua|re** vt water down. ~**to** adj watered down

annaf'**fia|re** vt water. ~'**toio** m watering-can

an'**nali** mpl annals

anna'**spare** vi flounder

an'**nata** f year; (importo annuale) annual amount; (di vino) vintage

annebbia'**mento** m fog build-up; fig clouding

annebbi'**ar|e** vt cloud (vista, mente). ~**si** vr become foggy; (vista, mente) grow dim

annega'**mento** m drowning

anne'**ga|re** vt/i drown

anne'**rir|e** vt/i blacken. ~**si** vr become black

annessi'**one** f (di nazione) annexation

an'**nesso** pp di annettere ● adj attached; (stato) annexed

an'**nettere** vt add; (accludere) enclose; annex (stato)

annichi'**lire** vt annihilate

anni'**darsi** vr nest

annienta'**mento** m annihilation

annien'tar|e vt annihilate. **~si** vr abase oneself

anniver'sario adj & m anniversary. **~ di matrimonio** wedding anniversary

'anno m year; **Buon A~!** Happy New Year!; **quanti anni ha?** how old are you?; **Tommaso ha dieci anni** Thomas is ten [years old]. **~ bisestile** leap year

anno'dar|e vt knot; do up (cintura); fig form. **~si** vr become knotted

annoi'a|re vt bore; (recare fastidio) annoy. **~rsi** vr get bored; (condizione) be bored. **~to** adj bored

anno'ta|re vt note down; annotate (testo). **~zi'one** f note

annove'rare vt number

annu'a|le adj annual, yearly. **~rio** m year-book

annu'ire vi nod; (acconsentire) agree

annulla'mento m annulment; (di appuntamento) cancellation

annul'lar|e vt annul; cancel (appuntamento); (togliere efficacia a) undo; disallow (gol); (distruggere) destroy. **~si** vr cancel each other out

annunci'a|re vt announce; (preannunciare) foretell. **~tore**, **~trice** mf announcer. **A~zi'one** f Annunciation

an'nuncio m announcement; (pubblicitario) advertisement; (notizia) news. **annunci** pl **economici** classified advertisements

'annuo adj annual, yearly

annu'sare vt sniff

annuvo'lar|e vt cloud. **~si** vr cloud over

'ano m anus

a'nomalo adj anomalous

anoni'mato m **mantenere l'~** remain anonymous

a'nonimo, -a adj anonymous ● mf (pittore, scrittore) anonymous painter/writer

ano'ressico, -a mf anorexic

anor'mal|e adj abnormal ● mf deviant. **~ità** f inv abnormality

'ansa f handle; (di fiume) bend

an'sare vi pant

'ansia, ansietà f anxiety; **stare/essere in ~ per** be anxious about

ansi'oso adj anxious

antago'nis|mo m antagonism. **~ta** mf antagonist

an'tartico adj & m Antarctic

antece'dente adj preceding ● m precedent

ante'fatto m prior event

ante'guerra adj pre-war ● m pre-war period

ante'nato, -a m ancestor

an'tenna f (Radio, TV) aerial; (di animale) antenna; (Naut) yard. **~ parabolica** satellite dish

ante'porre vt put before

ante'prima f preview; **vedere qcsa in ~** have a sneak preview of sth

anteri'ore adj front attrib; (nel tempo) previous

antia'ereo adj anti-aircraft attrib

antial'lergico adj hypoallergenic

antia'tomico adj **rifugio ~** fallout shelter

antibi'otico adj & m antibiotic

anti'caglia f (oggetto) piece of old junk

antica'mente adv long ago

anti'camera f ante-room; **far ~** be kept waiting

antichità f inv antiquity; (oggetto) antique

antici'clone m anticyclone

antici'pa|re vt advance; (Comm) pay in advance; (prevedere) anticipate; (prevenire) forestall ● vi be early. **~ta'mente** adv in advance. **~zi'one** f anticipation; (notizia) advance news

an'ticipo m advance; (caparra) deposit; **in ~** early; (nel lavoro) ahead of schedule

an'tico adj ancient; (mobile ecc) antique; (vecchio) old, **all'antica** old-fashioned ● mpl **gli antichi** the ancients

anticoncezio'nale adj & m contraceptive

anticonfor'mis|mo m unconventionality. **~ta** mf nonconformist. **~tico** adj unconventional

anticonge'lante adj & m antifreeze

anticostituzio'nale adj unconstitutional

anti'crimine adj inv (squadra) crime attrib

antidemo'cratico adj undemocratic

antidolo'rifico m painkiller

an'tidoto m antidote

anti'droga adj inv (campagna) anti-drugs; (squadra) drug attrib

antie'stetico adj ugly

antifa'scismo m anti fascism

antifa'scista adj & mf anti-fascist

anti'furto m anti-theft device; (allarme) alarm ● adj inv (sistema) anti-theft

anti'gelo m antifreeze; (parabrezza) defroster

antigi'enico adj unhygienic

An'tille fpl **le ~** the West Indies

an'tilope f antelope

antin'cendio adj inv **allarme ~** fire alarm; **porta ~** fire door

anti'nebbia m inv (Auto) [faro] **~** foglamp

antinfiamma'torio adj & m anti-inflammatory

antinucle'are adj anti-nuclear

antio'rario adj anti-clockwise

anti'pasto m hors d'oeuvre

an'tipodi mpl antipodes; **essere agli ~** fig be poles apart

antiquari'ato m antique trade

anti'quario, -a m antique dealer

anti'quato adj antiquated

anti'ruggine m inv rust-inhibitor

anti'rughe adj inv anti-wrinkle attrib

anti scippo adj inv theft-proof

anti'settico adj & m antiseptic

antisoci'ale adj anti-social

antista'minico m antihistamine

anti'stante a prep in front of

anti'tarlo m woodworm treatment

antiterro'ristico adj antiterrorist attrib

an'titesi f inv antithesis

'antivirus m inv virus checker

antolo'gia f anthology

'antro m cavern

antropolo'gia f anthropology. **antro'pologo, -a** mf anthropologist

anu'lare m ring finger

'anzi conj in fact; (o meglio) or better still; (al contrario) on the contrary

anziani'tà f old age; (di servizio) seniority

anzi'ano, -a adj elderly; (di grado) senior ● mf elderly person

anziché conj rather than

anzi'tempo adv prematurely

anzi'tutto adv first of all

a'orta f aorta

apar'titico adj unaligned

apa'tia f apathy. **a'patico** adj apathetic

'ape f bee; **nido di api** honeycomb

aperi'tivo m aperitif

aperta'mente adv openly

a'perto adj open; **all'aria aperta** in the open air; **all'~** open-air

aper'tura f opening; (inizio) beginning; (ampiezza) spread; (di arco) span; (Pol) overtures pl; (Phot) aperture; **~ mentale** openness

'apice m apex

apicol'tura f beekeeping

ap'nea f immersione in ~ free diving

a'polide adj stateless ● mf stateless person

a'postolo m apostle

apostro'fare vt (mettere un apostrofo a) write with an apostrophe; reprimand (persona)

a'postrofo m apostrophe

appaga'mento m fulfilment

appa'ga|re vt satisfy. ~rsi vr ~rsi di be satisfied with

appai'are vt pair; mate (animali)

appallotto'lare vt roll into a ball

appalta'tore m contractor

ap'palto m contract; dare in ~ to contract

appan'naggio m (in denaro) annuity; fig prerogative

appan'nar|e vt mist (vetro); dim (vista). ~si vr mist over; (vista:) grow dim

appa'rato m apparatus; (pompa) display

apparecchi'a|re vt prepare ● vi lay the table. ~'tura f (impianti) equipment

appa'recchio m apparatus; (congegno) device; (radio, tv ecc) set; (aeroplano) aircraft. ~ acustico hearing aid

appa'ren|te adj apparent. ~te'mente adv apparently. ~za f appearance; in ~za apparently

appa'ri|re vi appear; (sembrare) look. ~'scente adj striking; pej gaudy. ~zi'one f apparition

apparta'mento m apartment

appar'ta|rsi vr withdraw. ~to adj secluded

apparte'nenza f membership

apparte'nere vi belong

appassio'nante adj (storia, argomento) exciting

appassio'na|re vt excite; (commuovere) move. ~rsi vr ~rsi a become excited by. ~to adj passionate; ~to di (entusiasta) fond of

appas'sir|e vi wither. ~si vr fade

appel'larsi vr ~ a appeal to

ap'pello m appeal; (chiamata per nome) rollcall; (esami) exam session; fare l'~ call the roll

ap'pena adv just; (a fatica) hardly ● conj [non] ~ as soon as

ap'pendere vt hang [up]

appen'dice f appendix. **appendi'cite** f appendicitis

Appen'nini mpl gli ~ the Apennines

appesan'tir|e vt weigh down. ~si vr become heavy

ap'peso pp di appendere adj hanging; (impiccato) hanged

appe'ti|to m appetite; aver ~to be hungry; buon ~to! enjoy your meal!. ~'toso adj appetizing; fig tempting

appezza'mento m plot of land

appia'nar|e vt level; fig smooth over. ~si vr improve

appiat'tir|e vt flatten. ~si vr flatten oneself

appic'care vt ~ il fuoco a set fire to

appicci'car|e vt stick; ~e a (fig: appioppare) palm off on ● vi be sticky. ~si vr stick; (cose:) stick together; ~si a qcno stick to sb like glue

appicci'caticcio adj sticky; fig clingy

appicci'coso adj sticky; fig clingy

appie'dato adj sono ~ I don't have the car; sono rimasto ~ I was stranded

appi'eno adv fully

appigli'arsi vr ~ a get hold of; fig stick to. **ap'piglio** m fingerhold; (per piedi) foothold; fig pretext

appiop'pare vt ~ a palm off on; (🔒: dare) give

appiso'larsi vr doze off

applau'dire vt/i applaud. **ap-'plauso** m applause

appli'cabile adj applicable

appli'care vt apply; enforce (legge ecc). **~rsi** vr apply oneself; **~ tore** m applicator. **~zi'one** f application; (di legge) enforcement

appoggi'are vt lean (a against); (mettere) put; (sostenere) back. **~si** a lean against; fig rely on. **ap-'poggio** m support

appollai'arsi vr fig perch

ap'porre vt affix

appor'tare vt bring; (causare) cause. **ap'porto** m contribution

apposita'mente adv especially

ap'posito adj proper

ap'posta adv on purpose; (espressamente) specially

appo'stare vt post (soldati). **~si** vr lie in wait

ap'prendere vt understand; (imparare) learn. **~i'mento** m learning

appren'dista mf apprentice. **~stato** m apprenticeship

apprensi'one f apprehension; **essere in ~ per** be anxious about. **appren'sivo** adj apprehensive

ap'presso adv & prep (vicino) near; (dietro) behind; **come ~** as follows

appre'stare vt prepare. **~si** vr get ready

apprez'za|bile adj appreciable. **~'mento** m appreciation; (giudizio) opinion

apprez'zare vt approach. **~to** adj appreciated

ap'proccio m approach

appro'dare vi land; **~ a** fig come to; **non ~ a nulla** come to nothing. **ap'prodo** m landing; (luogo) landing-stage

approfit'ta|re vi take advantage

(di of), profit (di by). **~'tore**, **~'trice** mf chancer

approfondi'mento m deepening; di ~ fig: (esame) further

approfon'di|re vt deepen. **~rsi** vr (divario) widen. **~to** adj (studio, ricerca) in depth

appropri'arsi vr (essere adatto a) suit; **~rsi di** take possession of. **~to** adj appropriate. **~zi'one** f (Jur) appropriation. **~zione indebita** (Jur) embezzlement

approssi'ma|re vt **~re per eccesso/difetto** round up/down. **~rsi** vr draw near. **~tiva'mente** adv approximately. **~'tivo** adj approximate. **~zi'one** f approximation

appro'va|re vt approve of; approve (legge). **~zi'one** f approval

approvvigiona'mento m supplying; **approvvigionamenti** pl provisions

approvvigio'nar|e vt supply. **~ si** vr stock up

appunta'mento m appointment; **fissare un ~** make an appointment; **darsi ~** decide to meet

appun'ta|re vt (annotare) take notes; (fissare) fix; (con spillo) pin; (appuntire) sharpen. **~si** vr **~si su** (teoria:) be based on

appun'ti|re vt sharpen. **~to** adj (mento) pointed

ap'punto[1] m note; (piccola critica) niggle

ap'punto[2] adv exactly; **per l'~!** exactly!; **stavo ~ dicendo...** I was just saying...

appu'rare vt verify

a'pribile adj that can be opened

apribot'tiglie m inv bottle-opener

a'prile m April; **il primo d'~** April Fools' Day

a'prir|e vt open; turn on (acqua ecc); (con chiave) unlock; open up (ferita ecc). **~si** vr (spaccarsi) split; (confidarsi) confide (con in)

apri'scatole *f inv* tin-opener

aqua'planing *m* andare in ∼ aquaplane

'aquil∣a *f* eagle; non è un'∼a! he is no genius!. ∼'lino *adj* aquiline

aqui'lone *m* (*giocattolo*) kite

ara'besco *m* arabesque; *hum* scribble

A'rabia Sau'dita *f* l'∼ Saudi Arabia

'arabo, -a *adj* Arab; (*lingua*) Arabic ● *mf* Arab ● *m* (*lingua*) Arabic

a'rachide *f* peanut

ara'gosta *f* lobster

a'ranci∣a *f* orange. ∼'ata *f* orangeade. ∼o *m* orange-tree; (*colore*) orange. ∼'one *adj* & *m* orange

a'ra∣re *vt* plough. ∼tro *m* plough

ara'tura *f* ploughing

a'razzo *m* tapestry

arbi'tra∣re *vt* arbitrate in; *Sport* referee. ∼'ietà *f* arbitrariness. ∼io *adj* arbitrary

ar'bitrio *m* will; è un ∼ it's very high-handed

'arbitro *m* arbiter; *Sport* referee; (*nel baseball*) umpire

ar'busto *m* shrub

'arca *f* ark; (*cassa*) chest

arca'ico *adj* archaic. ∼'ismo *m* archaism

arc'angelo *m* archangel

ar'cata *f* arch; (*serie di archi*) arcade

arche∣olo'gia *f* archaeology. ∼o'logico *adj* archaeological. ∼'ologo, -a *m* archaeologist

ar'chetto *m* (*Mus*) bow

architet'tare *vt* & *fig* devise; **cosa state architettando?** *fig* what are you plotting?

archi'tet∣to *m* architect. ∼'tonico *adj* architectural. ∼'tura *f* architecture

archivi'are *vt* file; (*Jur*) close

ar'chivio *m* archives *pl*; (*Comput*) file

archi'vista *mf* filing clerk

ar'cigno *adj* grim

arci'pelago *m* archipelago

arci'vescovo *m* archbishop

'arco *m* (*Math*) arc; (*Mus, arma*) bow; **nell'∼ di una giornata/due mesi** in the space of a day/two months

arcoba'leno *m* rainbow

arcu'a∣re *vt* bend. ∼rsi *vr* bend. ∼to *adj* bent, curved

ar'dente *adj* burning; *fig* ardent. ∼'mente *adv* ardently

'ardere *vt/i* burn

ar'desia *f* slate

ar'di∣re *vi* dare. ∼to *adj* daring; (*coraggioso*) bold; (*sfacciato*) impudent

ar'dore *m* (*calore*) heat; *fig* ardour

'arduo *adj* arduous; (*ripido*) steep

'area *f* area. ∼ **di rigore** (*nel calcio*) penalty area. ∼ **di servizio** service area

a'rena *f* arena

are'narsi *vr* run aground; *fig*: (*trattative*) reach deadlock; **mi sono arenato** I'm stuck

'argano *m* winch

argen'tato *adj* silver-plated

argente'ria *f* silver[ware]

ar'gento *m* silver

ar'gil∣la *f* clay. ∼'loso *adj* (*terreno*) clayey

argi'nare *vt* embank; *fig* hold in check, contain

'argine *m* embankment; (*diga*) dike

argomen'tare *vi* argue

argo'mento *m* argument; (*motivo*) reason; (*soggetto*) subject

argu'ire *vt* deduce

ar'gu∣to *adj* witty. ∼zia *f* wit; (*battuta*) witticism

'aria *f* air; (*aspetto*) appearance; (*Mus*) tune; **andare all'∼** *fig* come to nothing; **avere l'∼...** look...; **corrente d'∼** draught; **mandare all'** qcsa *fig* ruin sth

aridità *f* aridity, dryness

'arido *adj* arid

arieggi'a|re *vt* air. **∼to** *adj* airy

ari'ete *m* ram. **A∼** (*Astr*) Aries

arl'etta *f* (*brezza*) breeze

a'ringa *f* herring

ari'oso *adj* (*locale*) light and airy

aristo'cra|tico, -a *adj* aristocratic ● *mf* aristocrat. **∼'zia** *f* aristocracy

arit'metica *f* arithmetic

arlec'chino *m* Harlequin; *fig* buffoon

'arma *f* weapon; **armi** *pl* arms; (*forze armate*) [armed] forces; **chiamare alle armi** call up; **sotto le armi** in the army; **alle armi** *fig* inexperienced. **∼ da fuoco** firearm. **armi** *mpl* **di distruzione di massa** weapons of mass destruction.

armadi'etto *m* locker, cupboard

ar'madio *m* cupboard; (*quartanha*) wardrobe

armamen'tario *m* tools *pl*; *fig* paraphernalia

arma'mento *m* armament; (*Naut*) fitting out

ar'ma|re *vt* arm; (*equipaggiare*) fit out, (*Archi*) reinforce. **∼rsi** *vr* arm oneself (**di** with). **∼ta** *f* army; (*flotta*) fleet. **∼'tore** *m* shipowner. **∼'tura** *f* framework; (*impalcatura*) scaffolding; (*di guerriero*) armour

armeggi'are *vi* *fig* manoeuvre

armi'stizio *m* armistice

armo'ni|a *f* harmony. **ar'monica** *f* **∼ [a bocca]** mouth organ. **ar'monico** *adj* harmonic. **∼'oso** *adj* harmonious

armoniz'zar|e *vt* harmonize ● *vi* match. **∼si** *vr* (*colori*) match

ar'nese *m* tool; (*oggetto*) thing; (*congegno*) gadget; **male in ∼** in bad condition

'arnia *f* beehive

a'roma *m* aroma; **aromi** *pl* herbs.

∼tera'pia *f* aromatherapy

aro'matico *adj* aromatic

aromatiz'zare *vt* flavour

'arpa *f* harp

ar'peggio *m* arpeggio

ar'pia *f* harpy

arpi'one *m* hook; (*pesca*) harpoon

arrabat'tarsi *vr* do all one can

arrabbi'a|rsi *vr* get angry. **∼to** *adj* angry. **∼'tura** *f* rage; **prenderси una ∼tura** fly into a rage

arraf'fare *vt* grab

arrampi'ca|rsi *vr* climb [up]. **∼ta** *f* climb. **∼'tore, ∼'trice** *mf* climber. **∼'tore sociale** social climber

arran'care *vi* limp, hobble

arrangia'mento *m* arrangement

arrangi'ar|e *vt* arrange. **∼si** *vr* manage; **∼si alla meglio** get by; **arrangiati!** get on with it!

arra'parsi *vr* 🔲 get randy

arre'care *vt* bring; (*causare*) cause

arreda'mento *m* interior decoration; (*l'arredare*) furnishing; (*mobili* ecc) furnishings *pl*

arre'da|re *vt* furnish. **∼'tore, ∼'trice** *mf* interior designer. **ar'redo** *m* furnishings *pl*

ar'rendersi *vr* surrender

arren'devo|le *adj* (*persona*) yielding. **∼'lezza** *f* softness

arre'star|e *vt* arrest; (*fermare*) stop. **∼si** *vr* halt. **ar'resto** *m* stop; (*Med, Jur*) arrest; **la dichiaro in [stato d'] arresto** you are under arrest; **mandato di arresto** warrant. **arresti** *pl* **domiciliari** (*Jur*) house arrest

arre'tra|re *vt/i* withdraw; pull back (*giocatore*). **∼to** *adj* (*paese* ecc) backward; (*Mil*: *posizione*) rear; **numero ∼to** (*di rivista*) back number; **del lavoro** *m* ∼to a backlog of work ● *m* (*di stipendio*) back pay

arre'trati *mpl* arrears

arricchi'mento *m* enrichment

arric'chi|re *vt* enrich. **∼rsi** *vr* get

rich. ~to, -a mf nouveau riche

arricci'are vt curl; ~ **il naso** turn up one's nose

ar'ringa f harangue; (Jur) closing address

arrischi'a|rsi vr dare. ~to adj risky; (imprudente) rash

arri'va|re vi arrive; ~re a (raggiungere) reach; (ridursi) be reduced to. ~to, -a adj successful; **ben** ~**to!** welcome! ● mf successful person

arrive'derci int goodbye; ~ **a domani** see you tomorrow

arri'vis|mo m social climbing; (nel lavoro) careerism. ~ta mf social climber; (nel lavoro) careerist

ar'rivo m arrival; Sport finish

arro'gan|te adj arrogant. ~za f arrogance

arro'garsi vr ~ **il diritto di fare qcsa** take it upon oneself to do sth

arrossa'mento m reddening

arros'sar|e vt make red (occhi). ~si vr go red

arros'sire vi blush, go red

arro'stire vt roast; toast (pane); (ai ferri) grill. ar'rosto adj & m roast

arroto'lare vt roll up

arroton'dar|e vt round; (Math ecc) round off. ~si vr become round; (persona) get plump

arrovel'larsi vr ~ **il cervello** rack one's brains

arroven'ta|re vt make red-hot. ~rsi vr become red-hot. ~to adj red-hot

arruf'fa|re vt ruffle; fig confuse. ~to adj (capelli) ruffled

arruffianarsi vr ~ **qcno** fig butter sb up

arrug'gini|re vt rust. ~rsi vr go rusty; fig (fisicamente) stiffen up; (conoscenze): go rusty. ~to adj rusty

arruola'mento m enlistment

arruo'lar|e vt/i, ~si vr enlist

arse'nale m arsenal; (cantiere)

[naval] dockyard

ar'senico m arsenic

'arso pp di ardere ● adj burnt; (arido) dry. ar'sura f burning heat; (sete) parching thirst

'arte f art; (abilità) craftsmanship; **le belle arti** the fine arts. **arti figurative** figurative arts

arte'fa|re vt adulterate (vino); disguise (voce). ~tto adj fake; (vino) adulterated

ar'tefice mf craftsman; craftswoman; fig author

ar'teria f artery. ~ **[stradale]** arterial road

arterioscle'rosi f arteriosclerosis

'artico adj & m Arctic

artico'la|re adj articular ● vt articulate; (suddividere) divide. ~rsi vr fig ~rsi in consist of. ~to adj (Auto) articulated; fig well-constructed. ~zi'one f (Anat) articulation

ar'ticolo m article. ~ **di fondo** leader

artifici'ale adj artificial

arti'fici|o m artifice; (affettazione) affectation. ~'oso adj artful; (affettato) affected

artigia'nal|e adj made by hand; hum amateurish. ~'mente adv with craftsmanship; hum amateurishly

artigi|a'nato m craftsmanship; (ceto) craftsmen pl. ~'ano, -a m craftsman ● f craftswoman

artigli'ere m artilleryman. ~e'ria f artillery

ar'tiglio m claw; fig clutch

ar'tist|a mf artist. ~ica'mente adv artistically. ~ico adj artistic

'arto m limb

ar'trite f arthritis

ar'trosi f rheumatism

arzigo'golato adj bizarre

ar'zillo adj sprightly

a'scella f armpit

ascen'den|te adj ascending ● m

(antenato) ancestor; (influenza) ascendancy; (Astr) ascendant

ascensi'one f ascent; **l'A~** the Ascension

ascen'sore m lift, elevator Am

a'scesa f ascent; (al trono) accession, (al potere) rise

a'scesso m abscess

a'sceta mf ascetic

'ascia f axe

asciugabianche'ria m inv (stenditoio) clothes horse

asciugaca'pelli m inv hair dryer

asciuga'mano m towel

asciu'gar|e vt dry. **~si** v dry oneself; (diventare asciutto) dry up

asci'utto adj dry; (magro) wiry, (risposta) curt; **essere all'~** fig be hard up

ascol'ta|re vt listen to ● vi listen. **~tore**, **~trice** mf listener

a'scolto m listening; **dare ~** a listen to; **mettersi in ~** Radio tune in

asfal'tare vt asphalt

a'sfalto m asphalt

asfis'sia f asphyxia. **~ante** adj oppressive; fig (persona) annoying **~'are** vt asphyxiate; fig annoy

'Asia f Asia. **asi'atico**, **-a** agg & mf Asian

a'silo m shelter; (d'infanzia) nursery school. **~ nido** day nursery. **~ politico** political asylum

asim'metrico adj asymmetrical

'asino m donkey; (fig: persona stupida) ass

'asma f asthma. **a'smatico** adj asthmatic

asoci'ale adj asocial

'asola f buttonhole

a'sparagi mpl asparagus sg

a'sparago m asparagus spear

asperità f inv harshness; (di terreno) roughness

aspet'ta|re vt wait for; (prevedere) expect; **~re un bambino** be expecting [a baby]; **fare ~re qcno** keep sb waiting ● vi wait. **~rsi** vr expect. **~tiva** f expectation

a'spetto[1] m appearance; (di problema) aspect; **di bell'~** good looking

a'spetto[2] m **sala f d'~** waiting room

aspi'rante adj aspiring, (pompa) suction attrib ● mf (a un posto) applicant, (al trono) aspirant; **gli aspiranti al titolo** the contenders for the title

aspira'polvere m inv vacuum cleaner

aspi'ra|re vt inhale; (Mech) suck in ● vi **~re a** aspire to. **~tore** m extractor fan. **~zi'one** f inhalation; (Mech) suction; (ambizione) ambition

aspi'rina f aspirin

aspor'tare vt take away

aspra'mente adv (duramente) severely

a'sprezza f (al gusto) sourness; (di clima) severity; (di suono) harshness; (di odore) pungency

'aspro adj (al gusto) sour; (clima) severe, (suono, parole) harsh; (odore) pungent; (litigio) bitter

assag'gi|are vt taste. **~gini** mpl (Culin) samples. **as'saggio** m tasting; (piccola quantità) taste

as'sai adv very; (moltissimo) very much; (abbastanza) enough

assa'li|re vt attack. **~tore**, **~trice** mf assailant

as'salto m attack; **prendere d'~** storm (città); fig mob (persona): hold up (banca)

assapo'rare vt savour

assassi'nare vt murder, assassinate

assas'sin|io m murder, assassination. **~o**, **-a** adj murderous ● m murderer ● f murderess

'asse f board ● m (Techn) axle; (Math) axis. **~ da stiro** ironing board

a assecon'dare vt satisfy; (favorire) support

assedi'are vt besiege. as'sedio m siege

assegna'mento m allotment; fare ~ su rely on

asse'gna|re vt allot; award (premio). ~'tario mf recipient. ~zi'one f (di alloggio, borsa di studio) allocation; (di premio) award

as'segno m allowance; (bancario) cheque; contro ~ cash on delivery. ~ circolare bank draft. assegni pl familiari family allowance. ~ non trasferibile non-transferable cheque.

assem'blea f assembly; (adunanza) gathering

assembra'mento m gathering

assen'nato adj sensible

as'senso m assent

assen'tarsi vr go away; (da stanza) leave the room

as'sen|te adj absent; (distratto) absent-minded ● mf absentee. ~te'ismo m absenteeism. ~te'ista mf frequent absentee. ~za f absence; (mancanza) lack

asse'r|ire vt assert. ~'tivo adj assertive. ~zi'one f assertion

assesso'rato m department

asses'sore m councillor

assesta'mento m settlement

asse'star|e vt arrange; ~e un colpo deal a blow. ~si vr settle oneself

asse'tato adj parched

as'setto m order; (Aeron, Naut) trim

assicu'ra|re vt assure; (Comm) insure; register (posta); (fissare) secure; (accertare) ensure. ~rsi vr (con contratto) insure oneself; (legarsi) fasten oneself; ~rsi che make sure that. ~'tivo adj insurance attrib. ~'tore, ~'trice mf insurance agent ● adj insurance attrib. ~zi'one f assurance; (contratto) insurance

assidera'mento m exposure. as'side'rato adj (Med) suffering from exposure; ⊤ frozen

assidu|a'mente adv assiduously. ~ità f assiduity

as'siduo adj assiduous; (cliente) regular

assil'lante adj (persona, pensiero) nagging

assil'lare vt pester

as'sillo m worry

assimi'la|re vt assimilate. ~zi'one f assimilation

as'sise fpl assizes; Corte d'A~ Court of Assize[s]

assi'sten|te mf assistant. ~te sociale social worker. ~te di volo flight attendant. ~za f assistance; (presenza) presence. ~za sociale social work

assistenzi'a|le adj welfare attrib. ~'lismo m welfare

as'sistere vt assist; (curare) nurse ● vi ~ a (essere presente) be present at; watch (spettacolo ecc)

'asso m ace; piantare in ~ leave in the lurch

associ'a|re vt join; (collegare) associate. ~rsi vr join forces; (Comm) enter into partnership. ~rsi a join. ~zi'one f association

assogget'tar|e vt subject. ~si vr submit

asso'lato adj sunny

assol'dare vt recruit

as'solo m (Mus) solo

as'solto pp di assolvere

assoluta'mente adv absolutely

assolu'tismo m absolutism

asso'lu|to adj absolute. ~zi'one f acquittal; (Relig) absolution

as'solvere vt perform (compito); (Jur) acquit; (Relig) absolution

assomigli'ar|e vi ~e a resemble. ~si vr resemble each other

assom'marsi vr combine; ~ a qcsa add to sth

asso'nanza f assonance

asson'nato adj drowsy

asso'pirsi vr doze off

assor'bente adj & m absorbent. igienico sanitary towel

assor'bire vt absorb

assor'da|re vt deafen. ~nte adj deafening

assorti'mento m assortment

assor'ti|re vt match (colori). ~to adj assorted; (colori, persone) matched

as'sorto adj engrossed

assottigli'ar|e vt make thin; (aguzzare) sharpen; (ridurre) reduce. ~si vr grow thin; (finanze:) be whittled away

assue'fa|re vt accustom. ~rsi vr ~rsi a get used to. ~tto adj (a caffè, aspirina) immune to the effects; (a droga) addicted. ~zi'one f (a caffè, aspirina) immunity to the effects; (a droga) addiction

as'sumere vt assume; take on (impiegato); ~ informazioni make inquiries

as'sunto pp di assumere ● m task. assunzi'one f (di impiegato) employment

assurdità f inv absurdity; ~ pl nonsense

as'surdo adj absurd

'asta f pole; (Mech) bar; (Comm) auction; a mezz'~ at half-mast

a'stemio adj abstemious

aste'n|ersi vr abstain (da from). ~si'one f abstention

aste'nuto, -a mf abstainer

aste'risco m asterisk

astig'ma|tico adj astigmatic. ~'tismo m astigmatism

'asti|o m rancour; avere ~o contro qcno bear sb a grudge. ~'oso adj resentful

a'stratto adj abstract

astrin'gente adj & m astringent

'astro m star

astrolo'gia f astrology. a'strologo, -a mf astrologer

astro'nauta mf astronaut

astro'nave f spaceship

astro|no'mia f astronomy. ~o'nomico adj astronomical. a'stronomo m astronomer

astrusità f abstruseness

a'stuccio m case

a'stu|to adj shrewd; (furbo) cunning. ~zia f shrewdness; (azione) trick

ate'ismo m atheism

A'tene f Athens

'ateo, -a adj & mf atheist

a'tipico adj atypical

at'lant|e m atlas. ~ico adj Atlantic; l' [Oceano] A~ico the Atlantic [Ocean]

at'let|a mf athlete. ~ica f athletics sg. ~ica leggera track and field events. ~ica pesante weight-lifting, boxing, wrestling, etc. ~ico adj athletic

atmo'sfer|a f atmosphere. ~ico adj atmospheric

a'tomic|a f atom bomb. ~o adj atomic

'atomo m atom

'atrio m entrance hall

a'troc|e adj atrocious; (terribile) dreadful. ~ità f inv atrocity

atrofiz'zarsi vr atrophy

attaccabot'toni mf inv [crashing] bore

attacca'brighe mf inv troublemaker

attacca'mento m attachment

attacca'panni m inv [coat-]hanger; (a muro) clothes hook

attac'car|e vt attach; (legare) tie; (appendere) hang; (cucire) sew on; (contagiare) pass on; (assalire) attack; (iniziare) start ● vi stick; (diffondersi) catch

a on. ~**si** vr cling; (affezionarsi) become attached; (litigare) quarrel

attacca'ticcio adj sticky

at'tacco m attack; (punto d'unione) junction

attar'darsi vr stay late; (indugiare) linger

attec'chire vi take; (moda ecc:) catch on

atteggia'mento m attitude

atteggi'ar|e vt assume. ~**si** vr **si** a pose as

attem'pato adj elderly

at'tender|e vt wait for ● vi ~**e a** attend to. ~**si** vr expect

atten'dibil|e adj reliable. ~**ità** f reliability

atte'nersi vr ~ **a** stick to

attenta'mente adv attentively

atten'ta|re vi ~**re a** make an attempt on. ~**to** m act of violence; (contro politico ecc) assassination attempt. ~**tore**, ~**trice** mf (a scopo politico) terrorist

at'tento adj attentive; (accurato) careful; ~**!** look out!; **stare** ~ pay attention

attenu'ante f extenuating circumstance

attenu'a|re vt attenuate; (minimizzare) minimize; subdue (colori ecc); calm (dolore); soften (colpo). ~**rsi** vr diminish. ~**zi'one** f lessening

attenzi'one f attention; ~**!** watch out!

atter'ra|ggio m landing. ~**re** vt knock down ● vi land

atter'rir|e vt terrorize. ~**si** vr be terrified

at'tes|a f waiting; (aspettativa) expectation; **in** ~**a di** waiting for. ~**o** pp di **attendere**

atte'sta|re vt state; (certificare) certify. ~**to** m certificate. ~**zi'one** f certificate; (dichiarazione) declaration

'attico m attic

at'tiguo adj adjacent

attil'lato adj (vestito) close-fitting

'attimo m moment

atti'nente adj ~ **a** pertaining to

at'tingere vt draw; fig obtain

atti'rare vt attract

atti'tudine f (disposizione) aptitude; (atteggiamento) attitude

atti'v|are vt activate. ~**ismo** m activism. ~**ista** mf activist. **attività** f inv activity; (Comm) assets pl. ~**o** adj active; (Comm) productive ● m assets pl

attiz'za|re vt poke; fig stir up. ~**'toio** m poker

'atto m act; (azione) action; (Comm, Jur) deed; (certificato) certificate; **atti** pl (di società ecc) proceedings; **mettere in** ~ put into effect

at'tonito adj astonished

attorcigli'ar|e vt twist. ~**si** vr get twisted

at'tore m actor

attorni'ar|e vt surround. ~**si** vr ~**si di** surround oneself with

at'torno adv around, about ● prep ~ **a** around, about

attrac'care vt/i dock

attra'ente adj attractive

at'tra|rre vt attract. ~**rsi** vr be attracted to each other. ~**t'tiva** f charm

attraversa'mento m crossing. ~ **pedonale** crossing, crosswalk Am

attraver'sare vt cross; (passare) go through

attra'verso prep through; (obliquamente) across

attrazi'on|e f attraction. ~**i** pl turistiche tourist attractions

attrez'za|re vt equip; (Naut) rig. ~**rsi** vr kit oneself out; ~**tura** f equipment; (Naut) rigging

at'trezzo m tool; **attrezzi** pl equipment; Sport appliances pl; (Theat) props pl

attribu'ir|e vt attribute. ~**si** vr

ascribe to oneself; ~**si il merito di** claim credit for

attri'bu|to m attribute. ~**zi'one** f attribution

at'trice f actress

at'trito m friction

attu'abile adj feasible

attu'al|e adj present; (di attualità) topical; (effettivo) actual. ~**ità** f topicality; (avvenimento) news; **programma di** ~**ità** current affairs programme. ~**iz'zare** vt update. ~**'mente** adv at present

attu'a|re vt carry out. ~**rsi** vr be realized. ~**zi'one** f carrying out

attu'tire vt deaden, to il colpo soften the blow

au'dac|e adj audacious;. ~**ia** f boldness; (insolenza) audacity

'audience f inv (telespettatori) audience

'audio m audio

audiovi'sivo adj audiovisual

audi'torio m auditorium

audizi'one f audition; (Jur) hearing

'auge m height; **essere in** ~ be popular

augu'rar|e vt wish. ~**si** vr hope. **au'gurio** m wish; (presagio) omen; **auguri!** all the best!; (a Natale) Happy Christmas!; **tanti auguri** best wishes

'aula f classroom; (università) lecture-hall; (sala) hall. ~ **magna** (in università) great hall. ~ **del tribunale** courtroom

aumen'tare vt/i increase. **au'mento** m increase; (di stipendio) [pay] rise

au'reola f halo

au'rora f dawn

auscul'tare vt (Med) auscultate

ausili'are adj & mf auxiliary

auspi'cabile adj è ~ **che...** it is to be hoped that...

auspi'care vt hope for

au'spicio m omen; **auspici** (pl: pro-tezione) auspices

auste'rità f austerity

au'stero adj austere.

Au'strali|a f Australia. **a~'ano, -a** adj & mf Australian

'Austria f Austria. **au'striaco, -a** adj & mf Austrian

autar'chi|a f autarchy. **au'tarchico** adj autarchic

autenti'c|are vt authenticate. ~**ità** f authenticity

au'tentico adj authentic; (vero) true

au'tista m driver

'auto+ pref self +; auto-

autoabbron'zante m self-tan ● adj self-tanning

autoambu'lanza f ambulance

autoartico'lato m articulated lorry

autobio|gra'fia f autobiography. ~**'grafico** adj autobiographical

auto'botte f tanker

'autobus m inv bus

auto'carro m lorry

autocommiserazi'one f self-pity

auto'critica f self-criticism

autodi'fesa f self-defence

auto'gol m inv own goal

au'tografo adj & m autograph

autolesio'nis|mo m fig self-destruction. ~**tico** adj self-destructive

auto'linea f bus line

au'toma m robot

automatica'mente adv automatically

auto'matico adj automatic ● m (bottone) press-stud; (fucile) automatic

automatiz'za|re vt automate. ~**zi'one** f automation

auto'mezzo m motor vehicle

auto'mobi|le f [motor] car. ∼'lismo m motoring. ∼'lista mf motorist. ∼'listico adj (industria) automobile attrib

autonoma'mente adv autonomously

auto'no|mia f autonomy; (Auto) range; (di laptop, cellulare) battery life. **au'tonomo** adj autonomous

auto'psia f autopsy

auto'radio f inv car radio; (veicolo) radio car

au'tore, -'trice mf author; (di pinti) painter; (di furto ecc) perpetrator; **quadro d'**∼ genuine master

auto'revo|le adj authoritative; (che ha influenza) influential. ∼'lezza f authority

autori'messa f garage

autori|tà f inv authority. ∼'tario adj autocratic. ∼ta'rismo m authoritarianism

autori'tratto m self-portrait

autoriz'za|re vt authorize. ∼zi'one f authorization

auto'scontro m inv bumper car

autoscu'ola f driving school

auto'stop m hitch-hiking; **fare l'**∼ hitch-hike. ∼'pista f hitch-hiker

auto'strada f motorway

autostra'dale adj motorway attrib

autosuffici'en|te adj self-sufficient. ∼za f self-sufficiency

autotrasporta'|tore, ∼'trice mf haulier, carrier

auto'treno m articulated lorry

autove'icolo m motor vehicle

Auto'velox® m inv speed camera

autovet'tura f motor vehicle

autun'nale adj autumn[al]

au'tunno m autumn

aval'lare vt endorse

a'vallo m endorsement

avam'braccio m forearm

avangu'ardia f vanguard; fig

avant-garde; **essere all'**∼ be in the forefront; (Techn) be at the leading edge

a'vanti adv (in avanti) forward; (davanti) in front; (prima) before; (entrate) come in!; (suvvia) come on!; (su semaforo) cross now; **va'** ∼! go ahead!; **andare** ∼ (precedere) go ahead; (orologio): be fast; ∼ **e indietro** backwards and forwards ● adj before ● prep ∼ **a** before; (in presenza di) in the presence of

avanti'eri adv the day before yesterday

avanza'mento m progress; (promozione) promotion

avan'za|re vi advance; (progredire) progress; (essere d'avanzo) be left [over] ● vt advance; (superare) surpass; (promuovere) promote. ∼**rsi** vr advance; (avvicinarsi) approach. ∼**ta** f advance. ∼**to** adj advanced; (nella notte) late; **in età** ∼**ta** elderly. **a'vanzo** m remainder; (Comm) surplus; **avanzi** pl (rovine) remains; (di cibo) left-overs

ava'ri|a f (di motore) engine failure. ∼'ato adj (di frutta, verdura) rotten; (carne) tainted

ava'rizia f avarice. **a'varo, -a** adj stingy ● mf miser

a'vena f oats pl

a'vere

Si può usare **have** o **have got** per parlare di ciò che si possiede. *have got* non si usa nell'inglese americano

● vt have; (ottenere) get; (indossare) wear; (provare) feel; **ho fame/freddo** be hungry/cold; **ho mal di denti** I've got toothache; **cos'ha a che fare con lui?** what has it got to do with him?; ~ **da fare** be busy; **che hai?** what's the matter with you?; **nei hai per molto?** will you be long?; **quanti ne abbiamo oggi?** what date is it today?; **avercela con qcno** have it in for sb

● v aux have; **non l'ho visto** I haven't seen him; **lo hai visto?** have you seen him?; **l'ho visto ieri** I saw him yesterday

● m averi pl wealth sg

avia'tore m flyer, aviator. ~**zi'one** f aviation; (Mil) Air Force

avidità f avidness. '**avido** adj avid

avio'getto m jet

'**avo, -a** mf ancestor

avo'cado m inv avocado

a'**vorio** m ivory

Avv. abbr avvocato

avva'lersi vr avail oneself (**di** of)

avval'lamento m depression

avvalo'rare vt bear out (tesi); endorse (documento); (accrescere) enhance

avvam'pare vi flare up; (arrossire) blush

avvantaggi'are vt favour. ~**si** vr ~**si di** benefit from; (approfittare) take advantage of

avve'dersi vr (accorgersi) notice; (capire) realize. ~**uto** adj shrewd

avvele'namento m poisoning

avvele'nare vt poison. ~**rsi** vr poison oneself. ~**to** adj poisoned

avve'nente adj attractive

avveni'mento m event

avve'nire[1] vi happen; (aver luogo) take place

avve'nire[2] m future. ~'**ristico** adj futuristic

avven'tarsi vr fling oneself. ~**to** adj (decisione) rash

av'vento m advent; (Relig) Advent

avven'tore m regular customer

avven'tura f adventure; (amorosa) affair; **d'~** (film) adventure attrib. ~'**rarsi** vr venture. ~**ri'ero, -a** m adventurer ● f adventur-ess. ~'**roso** adj adventurous

avve'ra|bile adj (previsione) that may come true. ~**rsi** vr come true

av'verbio m adverb

avver'sar|e vt oppose. ~**io, -a** adj opposing ● mf opponent

avversi'l'one f aversion. ~**tà** f inv adversity

av'verso adj (sfavorevole) adverse; (contrario) averse

avver'tenza f (cura) care; (avvertimento) warning; (avviso) notice; (premessa) foreword; **avvertenze** pl (istruzioni) instructions

avverti'mento m warning

avver'tire vt warn; (informare) inform; (sentire) feel

avvez'zar|e vt accustom. ~**si** vr accustom oneself. **av'vezzo** adj avvezzo **a** used to

avvia'mento m starting; (Comm) goodwill

avvi'a|re vt start. ~**rsi** vr set out. ~**to** adj under way; **bene** ~**to** thriving

avvicenda'mento m (in agricoltura) rotation; (nel lavoro) replacement

avvicen'darsi vr alternate

avvici'namento m approach

avvici'nar|e vt bring near; approach (persona). ~**si** vr approach; ~**si a** approach

avvi'lente adj demoralizing; (umiliante) humiliating

avvili'mento m despondency; (degradazione) degradation

avvi'li|re vt dishearten; (degradare) degrade. ~**rsi** vr lose heart; (degradarsi) degrade oneself. ~**to** adj disheartened; (degradato) degraded

avvilup'par|e vt envelop. ~**si** vr

wrap oneself up; *(aggrovigliarsi)* get entangled

avvinaz'zato *adj* drunk

avvin'cente *adj (libro ecc)* enthralling. **av'vincere** *vt* enthral

avvinghi'ar|e *vt* clutch. **~si** *vr* cling

av'vio *m* start-up; **dare l'~ a qcsa** get sth under way; **prendere l'~** get under way

avvi'sare *vt* inform; *(mettere in guardia)* warn

av'viso *m* notice; *(annuncio)* announcement; *(avvertimento)* warning; *(pubblicitario)* advertisement; **a mio ~** in my opinion. **~ di garanzia** *(Jur)* notification that one is to be the subject of a legal enquiry

avvi'stare *vt* catch sight of

avvi'tare *vt* screw in; screw down *(coperchio)*

avviz'zire *vi* wither

avvo'ca|to *m* lawyer; *fig* advocate. **~tura** *f* legal profession

av'volgere *vt* wrap [up]. **~si** *vr* wrap oneself up

avvol'gibile *m* roller blind

avvol'toio *m* vulture

aza'lea *f* azalea

azi'en|da *f* business. **~ agricola** farm. **~ di soggiorno** tourist bureau. **~'dale** *adj (politica)* corporate; *(giornale)* in-house

azio'namento *m* operation

azio'nare *vt* operate

azio'nario *adj* share *attrib*

azi'one *f* action; *Fin* share; **d'~** *(romanzo, film)* action[-packed]. **azio'nista** *mf* shareholder

a'zoto *m* nitrogen

azzan'nare *vt* seize with its teeth; sink its teeth into *(gamba)*

azzar'd|are *vt* risk. **~arsi** *vr* dare. **~ato** *adj (rischioso)* risky; *(precipitoso)* rash. **az'zardo** *m* hazard; **gioco d'azzardo** game of chance

azzec'care *vt* hit; *(indovinare)* guess

azzuf'farsi *vr* come to blows

az'zur|ro *adj & m* blue; **il principe ~** Prince Charming. **~'rognolo** *adj* bluish

Bb

bab'beo *adj* foolish ● *m* idiot

'babbo *m* 🔢 dad, daddy. **B~** Natale Father Christmas

bab'buccia *f* slipper

babbu'ino *m* baboon

ba'bordo *m (Naut)* port side

baby'sitter *mf inv* baby-sitter; **fare la ~** babysit

ba'cato *adj* wormeaten

'bacca *f* berry

baccalà *m inv* dried salted cod

bac'cano *m* din

bac'cello *m* pod

bac'chetta *f* rod; *(magica)* wand; *(di direttore d'orchestra)* baton; *(di tamburo)* drumstick

ba'checa *f* showcase; *(in ufficio)* notice board. **~ elettronica** *(Comput)* bulletin board

bacia'mano *m* kiss on the hand; **fare il ~ a qcno** kiss sb's hand

baci'ar|e *vt* kiss. **~si** *vr* kiss [each other]

ba'cillo *m* bacillus

baci'nella *f* basin

ba'cino *m* basin; *(Anat)* pelvis; *(di porto)* dock; *(di minerali)* field

'bacio *m* kiss

'baco *m* worm. **~ da seta** silkworm

ba'cucco *adj* **un vecchio ~** a senile old man

'bada *f* **tenere qcno a ~** keep sb at bay

ba'dante mf carer

ba'dare vi take care (a of); (fare attenzione) look out; **bada ai fatti tuoi!** mind your own business!

ba'dia f abbey

ba'dile m shovel

'badminton m badminton

'baffi mpl moustache sg; (di animale) whiskers; **mi fa un baffo** I don't give a damn; **ridere sotto i ~** laugh up one's sleeve

baf'futo adj moustached

ba'gagli mpl baggage. **~aio** m (Rail) baggage car; (Auto) boot

ba'gaglio m baggage; **un ~ a** piece of baggage. **~ a mano** hand baggage

baggia'nata f non dire baggianate don't talk nonsense

bagli'ore m glare; (improvviso) flash; (fig: di speranza) glimmer

ba'gnante mf bather

ba'gna|re vt wet; (inzuppare) soak; (immergere) dip; (innaffiare) water; (mare:) wash; (fiume:) flow through. **~rsi** vr get wet; (al mare ecc) bathe

ba'gnato adj wet

ba'gnino, -a mf life guard

'bagno m bath; (stanza) bathroom; (gabinetto) toilet; (in casa) toilet; (al mare) bathe; **bagni** pl (stabilimento) lido; **fare il ~** have a bath; (nel mare ecc) [have a] swim; **andare in ~** go to the toilet; **mettere a ~** soak. **~ turco** Turkish bath

bagnoma'ria m bain marie

bagnoschi'uma m inv bub ble bath

'baia f bay

baio'netta f bayonet

'baita f mountain chalet

bala'ustra, balaus'trata f balustrade

balbet'tare vt/i stammer; (bambino) babble. **~io** m stammering; babble

bal'buzie f stutter. **~ente** adj stuttering ●mf stutterer

Bal'can|i mpl Balkans. **b~ico** adj Balkan

balco'nata f (Theat) balcony

balcon'cino m reggiseno a ~ underwired bra

bal'cone m balcony

baldac'chino m canopy; **letto a ~** four-poster bed

bal'danza f boldness. **~zoso** adj bold

bal'doria f revelry; **far ~** have a riotous time

ba'lena f whale

bale'nare vi lighten; fig flash; **mi è balenata un'idea** I've just had an idea

bale'niera f whaler

ba'leno m in un ~ in a flash

ba'lera f dance hall

ba'lia f in ~ di at the mercy of

'balla f bale; (fam: frottola) tall story

bal'labile adj good for dancing to

bal'la|re vi dance. **~ta** f ballad

balla'toio m (nelle scale) landing

balle'rino, -a mf dancer; (classico) ballet dancer; **ballerina** (classica) ballet dancer, ballerina

bal'letto m ballet

'ballo m dance; (il ballare) dancing; **sala da ~** ballroom; **essere in ~** (lavoro, vita:) be at stake; (persona:) be committed; **tirare qcno in ~** involve sb

ballonzo'lare vi skip about

ballot'taggio m second count (of votes)

balne'a|re adj bathing attrib. **stagione ~** swimming season. **stazione ~** seaside resort, **~zi'one** f è vietata la **~zione** no swimming

ba'lordo adj foolish; (stordito) stunned; **tempo ~** nasty weather

'balsamo m balsam; (per capelli) conditioner; (lenimento) remedy

baltico | barattolo

'baltico adj Baltic. **il** [mar] **B~** the Baltic [Sea]

balu'ardo m bulwark

'balza f crag; (di abito) flounce

bal'zano adj (idea) weird

bal'zare vi bounce; (saltare) jump; **~ in piedi** leap to one's feet. **'balzo** m bounce; (salto) jump; **prendere la palla al balzo** seize an opportunity

bam'bagia f cotton wool

bambi'nata f childish thing to do/say

bam'bi|no, -a mf child; (appena nato) baby; **avere un ~no** have a baby. **~'none, -a** mf pej big or overgrown child

bam'boccio m chubby child; (sciocco) simpleton; (fantoccio) rag doll

'bambo|la f doll. **~'lotto** m male doll

bambù m bamboo

ba'nal|e adj banal; **~ità** f inv banality; **~iz'zare** vt trivialize

ba'nan|a f banana. **~o** m banana-tree

'banca f bank. **~ [di] dati** databank

banca'rella f stall

ban'cario, -a adj banking attrib; **trasferimento ~** bank transfer • mf bank employee

banca'rotta f bankruptcy; **fare ~** go bankrupt

banchet'tare vi banquet. **ban-'chetto** m banquet

banchi'ere m banker

ban'china f (Naut) quay; (in stazione) platform; (di strada) path; **~ non transitabile** soft verge

ban'chisa f floe

'banco m (di scuola) desk; (di negozio) counter; (di officina) bench; (di gioco, banca) bank; (di mercato) stall; (degli imputati) dock; **sotto ~** under the counter; **medicinale da ~** over the counter medicines. **~ di nebbia** information desk. **~ di nebbia** fog bank

'bancomat® m inv cashpoint, ATM; (carta) bank card

ban'cone m counter; (in bar) bar

banco'nota f banknote, bill Am; **banco'note** pl paper currency

'banda f band; (di delinquenti) gang. **~ d'atterraggio** landing strip. **~ larga** broad band. **~ rumorosa** rumble strip

banderu'ola f weathercock; (Naut) pennant

bandi'e|ra f flag. **~'rina** f (nel calcio) corner flag. **~'rine** f bunting sg

ban'di|re vt banish; (pubblicare) publish; fig dispense with (formalità, complimenti). **~to** m bandit. **~'tore** m (di aste) auctioneer

'bando m proclamation; **~ di concorso** job advertisement (published in an official gazette for a job for which a competitive examination has to be taken)

bar m inv bar

> **Bar** In Italy a bar is first and foremost a place where coffee is drunk, although alcoholic and soft drinks are also served. Italians tend to drink their coffee standing up at the bar, and there is usually an additional charge for sitting at a table. ⓘ

'bara f coffin

ba'rac|ca f hut; (catapecchia) hovel; **mandare avanti la ~ca** keep the ship afloat. **~'cato** m person living in a makeshift shelter. **~'chino** m (di gelati, giornali) kiosk; Radio CB radio. **~'cone** m (roulotte) circus caravan; (in luna park) booth. **~'copoli** f inv shanty town

bara'onda f chaos

ba'rare vi cheat

'baratro m chasm

barat'tare vt barter. **ba'ratto** m barter

ba'rattolo m jar; (di latta) tin

'barba f beard; (🔧: *noia*) bore; **farsi la ~** shave; **è una ~** (*noia*) it's boring

barbabi'etola f beetroot. **~ da zucchero** sugar-beet

bar'barico adj barbaric **har'barie** f barbarity, **'barbaro** adj barbarous ● m barbarian

'barbecue m inv barbecue

barbi'ere m barber; (*negozio*) barber's

barbi'turico m barbiturate

bar'bone m (*vagabondo*) vagrant; (*cane*) poodle

bar'boso adj 🔧 boring

barbu'gliare vi mumble

bar'buto adj bearded

'barca f boat. **~ a motore** motorboat. **~ da pesca** fishing boat. **~ a remi** rowing boat. **~ di salvataggio** lifeboat. **~ a vela** sailing boat. **~'iolo** m boatman

barcame'narsi vr manage

barcol'lare vi stagger

bar'cone m barge; (*di ponte*) pontoon

bar'dare vt harness. **~si** vr hum dress up

ba'rella f stretcher. **~li'ere** m stretcher-bearer

'Barents: il mare di ~ the Barents Sea

bari'centro m centre of gravity

ba'rile m barrel. **~'lotto** m fig tub of lard

ba'rista m barman ● f barmaid

ba'ritono m baritone

bar'lume m glimmer; **un ~ di speranza** a glimmer of hope

'barman m inv barman

'baro m cardsharper

ba'rocco adj & m baroque

ba'rometro m barometer

ba'rone m baron; **i baroni** fig the

top brass. **baro'nessa** f baroness

'barra f bar; (*lineetta*) oblique; (*Naut*) tiller. **~ spazio** (*Comput*) space bar. **~ strumenti** (*Comput*) tool bar

bar'rare vt block off (strada)

barri'care v barricade. **~ta** f barricade

barri'era f barrier; (*stradale*) roadblock; (*Geol*) reef. **~ razziale** colour bar

bar'rire vi trumpet. **~to** m trumpeting

barzel'letta f joke; **~ sporca o spinta** dirty joke

basa'mento m base

ba'sare vt base. **~si** vr **~si su** be based on; **mi baso su ciò che ho visto** I'm going on [the basis of] what I saw

'basco, -a mf & adj Basque ● m (*copricapo*) beret

'base f basis, (*fondamento*) foundation; (*Mil*) base; (*Pol*) rank and file; **a ~ di containing**; **in ~ a** on the basis of. **~ dati** database

'baseball m baseball

ba'setta f sideburn

ba'silare adj basic

ba'silica f basilica

ba'silico m basil

ba'sista m grass roots politician; (*di un crimine*) mastermind

'basket m basketball

bas'sezza f lowness; (*di statura*) shortness; (*viltà*) vileness

bas'sista m bassist

'basso adj low; (*di statura*) short; (*acqua*) shallow; (*televisione*) quiet; (*vile*) despicable; **parlare a bassa voce** speak in a low voice; **la bassa Italia** southern Italy ● m lower part; (*Mus*) bass. **guardare in ~** look down

basso'fondo m (*pl* bassifondi) shallows *pl*; **bassifondi** *pl* (*quartieri* *poveri*) slums

bassorili'evo m bas-relief

bas'sotto m dachshund

ba'stardo, -a adj bastard; (*di animale*) mongrel ● mf bastard; (*animale*) mongrel

ba'stare vi be enough; (*durare*) last; **basta!** that's enough!; **basta che** (*purché*) provided that; **basta così** that's enough; **basta così?** is that enough?; (*in negozio*) anything else?; **basta andare alla posta** you only have to go to the post office

Basti'an con'trario m contrary old so-and-so

basti'one m bastion

basto'nare vt beat

baston'cino m ski pole. ~ **di pesce** fish finger, fish stick Am

ba'stone m stick; (*da golf*) club; (*da passeggio*) walking stick

ba'tosta f blow

bat'tagli|a f battle; (*lotta*) fight. ~'**are** vi battle; fig fight

bat'taglio m (*di campana*) clapper; (*di porta*) knocker

battagli'one m battalion

bat'tello m boat; (*motonave*) steamer

bat'tente m (*di porta*) wing; (*di finestra*) shutter; (*battaglio*) knocker

'batter|e vt beat; (*percorrere*) scour; thresh (*grano*); break (*record*) ● vi (*bussare, urtare*) knock; (*cuore*) beat; (*ali ecc*) flap; *Tennis* serve; ~**e a macchina** type; ~**e le palpebre** blink; ~**e le mani** clap [one's hands]; ~**e le ore** strike the hours. ~**si** vr fight

bat'teri mpl bacteria

batte'ria f battery; (*Mus*) drums pl

bat'terio m bacterium. ~'**logico** adj bacteriological

batte'rista mf drummer

bat'tesimo m baptism

battez'zare vt baptize

battiba'leno m **in un** ~ in a flash

batti'becco m squabble

batticu'ore m palpitation; **mi venne il** ~ I was scared

bat'tigia f water's edge

batti'mano m applause

batti'panni m inv carpetbeater

batti'stero m baptistery

batti'strada m inv outrider; (*di pneumatico*) tread; *Sport* pacesetter

battitap'peto m inv carpet sweeper

'battito m [heart]beat; (*alle tempie*) throbbing; (*di orologio*) ticking; (*della pioggia*) beating

bat'tuta f beat; (*colpo*) knock; (*spiritosaggine*) wisecrack; (*osservazione*) remark; (*Mus*) bar; *Tennis* service; (*Theat*) cue; (*dattilografia*) stroke

ba'tuffolo m flock

ba'ule m trunk

'bava f dribble; (*di cane ecc*) slobber; **aver la** ~ **alla bocca** foam at the mouth

bava'glino m bib

ba'vaglio m gag

'bavero m collar

ba'zar m inv bazaar

baz'zecola f trifle

bazzi'care vt/i haunt

be'arsi vr delight (**di** in)

beati'tudine f bliss. **be'ato** adj blissful; (*Relig*) blessed; **beato te!** lucky you!

beauty-'case m inv toilet bag

bebè m inv baby

bec'caccia f woodcock

bec'ca|re vt peck; fig catch. ~**rsi** vr (*litigare*) quarrel. ~**ta** f peck

beccheggi'are vi pitch

bec'chino m grave-digger

'bec|co m beak; (*di caffettiera ecc*) spout. ~'**cuccio** m spout

be'fana f Epiphany; (*donna brutta*) old witch

Befana La Befana, whose name is derived from Epifania (Epiphany), is an old woman who is said to visit children on 6 January, bringing presents and sweets. Befana is also the name for the Epiphany holiday and usually signals the end of the Christmas celebrations and the return to school.

'**beffa** f hoax; **farsi beffe di qcno** mock sb. **bef'fardo** adj derisory; (persona) mocking

bef'far|e vt mock. **~si** vr **~si di** make fun of

'**bega** f quarrel; **è una bella ~** it's really annoying

'**beige** adj & m beige

be'la|re vi bleat. **~to** m bleating

'**belga** adj & mf Belgian

'**Belgio** m Belgium

'**bella** f (in carte, Sport) decider

bel'lezza f beauty; **che ~!** how lovely!; **chiudere/finire in ~** end on a high note

'**belli|co** adj war attrib. **~'coso** adj warlike. **~ge'rante** adj & mf belligerent

'**bello** adj nice, (di aspetto) beautiful; (uomo) handsome; (moralmente) good; **cosa fai di ~ stasera?** what are you up to tonight?; **oggi fa ~** it's a nice day; **una bella cifra** a lot; **un bel piatto di pasta** a big plate of pasta; **nel bel mezzo** right in the middle; **un bel niente** absolutely nothing; **bell'e fatto** over and done with; **bell'amico!** [a] fine friend he is/you are!; **questa è bella!** that's a good one!; **scamparla bella** have a narrow escape ● **n** (di bellezza) beauty; (innamorato) sweetheart; **sul più ~** at the crucial moment, **il ~ è che...** the funny thing is that...

'**belva** f wild beast

be'molle m (Mus) flat

ben ▷**BENE**

ben'ché conj though, although

'**benda** f bandage, (per occhi) blindfold. **ben'dare** vt bandage; blindfold (occhi)

'**bene** adv well; **ben ~** thoroughly; **~! good!; star ~** (di salute) be well; (vestito, stile:) suit; (finanziariamente) be well off; **non sta ~** (non è educato) it's not nice; **sta/va ~!** all right!; **ti sta ~!** [it] serves you right!; **ti auguro ogni ~** I wish you well; **di ~ in meglio** better and better; **fare ~** (aver ragione:) do the right thing; **fare ~ a** (cibo:) be good for, **una persona per ~** a good person; **per ~** (fare) properly, **è ben difficile** it's very difficult; **come tu ben sai** as you well know; **lo credo ~!** I can well believe it! ● **m** good; **per il tuo ~** for your own good. **beni** mpl (averi) property sg; **un ~ di famiglia** a family heirloom

bene'detto adj blessed

bene'di|re vt bless. **~'one** f blessing

benedu'cato adj well-mannered

benefat'to|re, -'trice m benefactor ● f benefactress

bene'ficare vt help

benefi'cenza f charity

benefici'ar|e vi **~e di** profit by. **~io, -a** adj & mf beneficiary. **bene'ficio** m benefit. **be'nefico** adj beneficial; (di beneficenza) charitable

bene'placito m approval

be'nessere m well-being

bene'stante adj well-off ● mf well-off person

bene'stare m consent

be'nevolo adj benevolent

ben'fatto adj well-made

'**beni** mpl property sg; Fin assets; **~ di consumo** consumer goods

benia'mino m favourite

be'nigno adj kindly; (Med) benign

beninfor'mato adj well-informed

benintenzio'nato, -a adj well-meaning ● mf well-meaning person

benin'teso adv of course

benpen'sante adj selfrighteous

benser'vito m dare il ~ a qcno fire sb

bensì conj but rather

benve'nuto adj & m welcome

ben'visto adj essere ~ go down well (da with)

benvo'lere vt farsi ~ da qcno win sb's affection; **prendere qcno in** ~ take a liking to sb; **essere benvoluto da tutti** to be well-liked by everyone

ben'zina f petrol, gas Am; **far** ~ get petrol. ~ **verde** unleaded petrol. **benzi'naio, -a** mf petrol station attendant

berga'motto m bergamot

ber'lina f (Auto) saloon

Ber'lino m Berlin

ber'muda mpl (pantaloni) Bermuda shorts

ber'noccolo m bump; (disposizione) flair

ber'retto m beret, cap

bersagli'are vt fig bombard. **ber'saglio** m target

be'stemmi|a f swear-word; (maledizione) oath; (sproposito) blasphemy. ~'are vi swear

'besti|a f animal; (persona brutale) beast; (persona sciocca) fool; **andare in** ~a 🔲 blow one's top. ~'ale adj bestial; (espressione, violenza) brutal; 🔲: (freddo, fame) terrible. ~alità f inv bestiality; fig nonsense. ~'ame m livestock

'bettola f fig dive

be'tulla f birch

be'vanda f drink

bevi'tore, -'trice mf drinker

be'vut|a f drink. ~o pp di **bere**

bi'ada f fodder

bianche'ria f linen. ~ **intima** underwear

bi'anco adj white; (foglio, pagina ecc) blank ● m white; **mangiare in** ~ not eat rich food; **in** ~ **e nero** (film, fotografia) black and white; **passare una notte in** ~ have a sleepless night

bian'core m whiteness

bianco'spino m hawthorn

biasci'care vt (mangiare) eat noisily; (parlare) mumble

biasi'mare vt blame. **bi'asimo** m blame

'Bibbia f Bible

bibe'ron m inv [baby's] bottle

'bibita f [soft] drink

'biblico adj biblical

bibliogra'fia f bibliography

biblio'te|ca f library; (mobile) bookcase. ~'cario, -a mf librarian

bicarbo'nato m bicarbonate

bicchi'ere m glass

bicchie'rino m 🔲 tipple

bici'cletta f bicycle; **andare in** ~ ride a bicycle

bico'lore adj two-coloured

bidè m inv bidet

bi'dello, -a mf janitor

bido'nata f 🔲 swindle

bi'done m bin; (🔲: truffa) swindle; **fare un** ~ a qcno 🔲 stand sb up

bien'nale adj biennial

bi'ennio m two-year period

bi'etola f beet

bifo'cale adj bifocal

bi'folco, -a mf fig boor

bifor'c|arsi vr fork. ~azi'one f fork. ~uto adj forked

biga'mia f bigamy. **'bigamo, -a** adj bigamous ● mf bigamist

bighello'nare vi loaf around. bighel'lone m loafer

bigiotte'ria f costume jewellery; (negozio) jeweller's

bigliet'taio m booking clerk; (aui treni) ticket-collector. ~e'ria f ticket-office; (Theat) box-office

bigl'et|to m ticket; (lettera breve) note; (cartoncino) card; (di banca) bank-note. ~to da visita business card. ~'tone m (Ⅱ: soldi) big one

bignè m inv cream puff

bigo'dino m roller

bi'kini m inv bikini

bi'lancia f scales pl; (Comm) balance. B~ (Astr) Libra. ~'are vt balance; fig weigh. ~o m budget; (Comm) balance sheet; fare il ~o balance the books; fig take stock

'bil|e f bile; fig rage

bili'ardo m billiards sg

'bilico m equilibrium; in ~ in the balance

bi'lingue adj bilingual

bili'one m billion

bilo'cale adj two-room

'bimbo, -a m/f child

bimen'sile adj fortnightly

bime'strale adj bimonthly

bi'nario m track; (piattaforma) platform

bi'nocolo m binoculars pl

bio'chimica f biochemistry

biodegra'dabile adj bio-degradable

bio'etica f bioethics

bio'fisica f biophysics

biogra'fia f biography. bio'grafico adj biographical. bi'ografo, -a m/f biographer

biolo'gia f biology. bio'logico adj biological; (alimento, agricoltura) organic. bi'ologo, -a m/f biologist

bi'ond|a f blonde. ~o adj blond ●m fair colour; (uomo) fair-haired man

bio'sfera f biosphere

bi'ossido m ~ di carbonio carbon dioxide

bioterro'rismo m bioterrorism

biparti'tismo m two-party system

'birba f, bir'bante m rascal, rogue. bir'bone adj wicked

biri'chino, -a adj naughty ●m/f little devil

bi'rillo m skittle

'birr|a f beer; a tutta ~a fig flat out. ~a chiara lager. ~a scura brown ale. ~e'ria f beer-house; (fabbrica) brewery

bis m inv encore

bi'saccia f haversack

bi'sbetic|a f shrew. ~o adj bad-tempered

bisbigli'are vt/i whisper. bi'sbiglio m whisper

'bisca f gambling-house

'biscia f snake

bi'scotto m biscuit

bisessu'ale adj & mf bisexual

bise'stile adj anno ~ leap year

bisettima'nale adj fortnightly

bi'slacco adj peculiar

bis'nonno, -a m/f great-grandfather; great-grandmother

biso'gn|are vi ~a agire subito we must act at once; ~a farlo it is necessary to do it; non ~a venire you don't have to come. ~o m need; (povertà) poverty; aver ~o di need. ~oso adj needy; (povero) poor; ~oso di in need of

bi'sonte m bison

bi'stecca f steak

bisticci'are vi quarrel. bi'sticcio m quarrel; (gioco di parole) pun

bistrat'tare vt mistreat

bi'torzolo m lump

'bitter m inv (bitter) aperitif

bi'vacco m bivouac

'bivio m crossroads; (di strada) fork

bizan'tino adj Byzantine

'bizza f tantrum; **fare le bizze** (bambini:) play up

biz'zarro adj bizarre

biz'zeffe adv a ~ galore

blan'dire vt soothe; (allettare) flatter. **'blando** adj mild

bla'sone m coat of arms

'blatta f cockroach

blin'da|re vt armour-plate. ~to adj armoured

blitz m inv blitz

bloc'car|e vt block; (isolare) cut off; (Mil) blockade; (Comm) freeze. ~si vi (Mech) jam

blocca'sterzo m steering lock

'blocco m block; (Mil) blockade; (dei fitti) restriction; (di carta) pad; (unione) coalition; **in ~** (Comm) in bulk. ~ **stradale** road-block

bloc-'notes m inv writing pad

blog'gista mf blogger

blu adj & m blue

blue-'jeans mpl jeans

bluff m inv (carte, fig) bluff

'blusa f blouse

'boa m boa [constrictor]; (sciarpa) [feather] boa ● f (Naut) buoy

bo'ato m rumbling

bo'bina f spool; (di film) reel; (Electr) coil

'bocca f mouth; **a ~ aperta** fig dumbfounded; **in ~ al lupo!** 🔲 break a leg!; **fare la respirazione a ~ a qcno** give sb mouth to mouth resuscitation or the kiss of life

boc'caccia f grimace; **far boccacce** make faces

boc'caglio m nozzle

boc'cale m jug; (da birra) tankard

bocca'porto m (Naut) hatch

boc'cata f (di fumo) puff; **prendere una ● d'aria** get a breath of

fresh air

boc'cetta f small bottle

bocchegg'iare vi gasp

boc'chino m cigarette holder; (Mus, di pipa) mouthpiece

'bocc|ia f (palla) bowl; ~e pl (gioco) bowls sg

bocci'a|re vt (agli esami) fail; (respingere) reject; (alle bocce) hit; **essere** ~to fail; (ripetere) repeat a year. ~**tura** f failure

bocci'olo m bud

boccon'cino m morsel

boc'cone m mouthful; (piccolo pasto) snack

boc'coni adv face downwards

'boia m executioner

boi'ata f 🔲 rubbish

boicot'tare vt boycott

bo'lero m bolero

'bolgia f (caos) bedlam

'bolide m meteor; **passare come un ~** shoot past [like a rocket]

Bo'livi|a f Bolivia. **b~'ano, -a** agg & mf Bolivian

'bolla f bubble; (pustola) blister

bol'la|re vt stamp; fig brand. ~to adj fig branded; **carta** ~ta paper with stamp showing payment of duty

bol'lente adj boiling [hot]

bol'let|ta f bill; **essere in ~ta** be hard up. ~**tino** m bulletin; (Comm) list

bol'lino m coupon

bol'li|re vt/i boil. ~to m boiled meat. ~**tore** m boiler; (per l'acqua) kettle. ~**tura** f boiling

'bollo m stamp

bol'lore m boil; (caldo) intense heat; fig ardour

'bomba f bomb; **a prova di ~** bomb-proof

bombarda'mento m shelling; (con aerei) bombing; fig bombardment. **~ aereo** air raid

bombar'd|are vt shell; (con aerei) bomb; fig bombard. **~i'ere** m bomber

bom'betta f bowler [hat]

'bombola f cylinder. **~ di gas** gas cylinder

bombo'lone m doughnut

bomboni'era f wedding keep-sake

bo'naccia f (Naut) calm

bonacci'one, -a mf goodnatured person ● adj good-natured

bo'nario adj kindly

bo'nifica f land reclamation. **bonifi-'care** vt reclaim

bo'nifico m (Comm) discount (bonifico) [credit] transfer

bontà f goodness; (gentilezza) kindness

'bora f bora (cold north east wind in the upper Adriatic)

'borchia f stud. **~'ato** adj studded

bor'd|are vt border. **~'tura** f border

bor'deaux adj inv maroon

bor'dello m brothel; fig bedlam; (disordine) mess

'bordo m border; (estremità) edge; **a ~** (Aeron, Naut) on board

bor'gata f hamlet

bor'ghese adj bourgeois, (abito) civilian, **in ~** in civilian dress; (poliziotto) in plain clothes

borghe'sia f middle classes pl

'borgo m village

'bori|a f conceit. **~'oso** adj conceited

bor'lotto m [fagiolo] **~** borlotto bean

boro'talco m talcum powder

bor'raccia f flask

'bors|a f bag; (borsetta) handbag; (valori) Stock Exchange, **~ dell'acqua calda** hot-water bottle. **~a frigo** cool-box. **~a della spesa** shopping bag. **~a di studio** scholarship. **~ai'olo** m pickpocket. **~el'lino** m

purse. **bor'sista** mf Fin speculator; (Sch) scholarship holder

bor'se|llo m purse; (borsetto) man's handbag. **~tta** f handbag. **~tto** m man's handbag

bo'scaglia f woodlands pl

boscai'olo m woodman; (guardaboschi) forester

'bosco m wood. **bo'scoso** adj wooded

'Bosnia f Bosnia

'bossolo m cartridge case

bo'tanic|a f botany. **~o** adj botanical ● m botanist

'botta f blow; (rumore) bang; **fare a botte** come to blows. **~ e risposta** fig thrust and counter-thrust

'botte f barrel

bot'te|ga f shop; (di artigiano) workshop. **~gaio, -a** mf shopkeeper. **~ghino** m Theat boxoffice; (del lotto) lottery-shop

bot'tiglia f bottle; **in ~** bottled. **~e'ria** f wine shop

bot'tino m loot; (Mil) booty

'botto m bang; **di ~** all of a sudden

bot'tone m button; (Bot) bud

bo'vino adj bovine; **bovini** m cattle

box m inv (per cavalli) loosebox; (recinto per bambini) play-pen

'boxe f boxing

'bozza f draft; (Typ) proof; (bernoccolo) bump. **boz'zetto** m sketch

'bozzolo m cocoon

brac'care vt hunt

brac'cetto m **a ~** arm in arm

bracci'a|le m bracelet; (fascia) armband. **~letto** m bracelet; (di orologio) watch-strap

bracci'ante m day labourer

bracci'ata f (nel nuoto) stroke

'bracci|o m (pl f braccia) arm; (di fiume, di braccio) arm. **~'olo** m (di sedia) arm[rest]; (da nuoto) armband

'bracco m hound

bracconi'ere *m* poacher

'brac|e *f* embers *pl*; **alla** ~**e** char-grilled. ~**i'ere** *m* brazier. ~**i'ola** *f* chop

'brado *adj* **allo stato** ~ in the wild

'brama *f* longing. **bra'mare** *vt* long for. **bramo'sia** *f* yearning

'branca *f* branch

'branchia *f* gill

'branco *m* (*di cani*) pack; (*pej: di persone*) gang

branco'lare *vi* grope

'branda *f* camp-bed

bran'dello *m* scrap; **a brandelli** in tatters

bran'dire *vt* brandish

'brano *m* piece; (*di libro*) passage

Bra'sil|e *m* Brazil. **b**~**i'ano, -a** *agg &* *mf* Brazilian

bra'vata *f* bragging

'bravo *adj* good; (*abile*) clever; (*coraggioso*) brave; ~**!** well done!. **bra'vura** *f* skill

'breccia *f* breach; **sulla** ~ *fig* very successful, at the top

bre'saola *f* dried, salted beef sliced thinly and eaten cold

bre'tella *f* shoulder-strap; **bretelle** *pl* (*di calzoni*) braces

'breve *adj* brief; **in** ~ briefly; **tra** ~ shortly

brevet'tare *vt* patent. **bre'vetto** *m* patent; (*attestato*) licence

brevità *f* shortness

'brezza *f* breeze

'bricco *m* jug

bric'cone *m* blackguard; *hum* rascal

'briciol|a *f* crumb; *fig* grain. ~**o** *m* fragment

'briga *f* (*fastidio*) trouble; (*lite*) quarrel; **attaccar** ~ pick a quarrel; **prendersi la** ~ **di fare qcsa** go to the trouble of doing sth

brigadi'ere *m* (*dei carabinieri*) sergeant

bri'gante *m* bandit; *hum* rogue

bri'gare *vi* intrigue

bri'gata *f* brigade; (*gruppo*) group

briga'tista *mf* (*Pol*) member of the Red Brigades

'briglia *f* rein; **a** ~ **sciolta** at break-neck speed

bril'lante *adj* brilliant; (*scintillante*) sparkling ●*m* diamond

bril'lare *vi* shine; (*metallo:*) glitter; (*scintillare*) sparkle

'brillo *adj* tipsy

'brina *f* hoar-frost

brin'dare *vi* toast; ~ **a qcno** drink a toast to sb

'brindisi *m inv* toast

bri'tannico *adj* British

'brivido *m* shiver; (*di paura ecc*) shudder; (*di emozione*) thrill

brizzo'lato *adj* greying

'brocca *f* jug

broc'cato *m* brocade

'broccoli *mpl* broccoli *sg*

'brodo *m* broth; (*per cucinare*) stock. ~ **ristretto** consommé

'broglio *m* ~ **elettorale** gerrymandering

bron'chite *f* bronchitis

'broncio *m* sulk; **fare il** ~ sulk

bronto'l|are *vi* grumble; (*tuono ecc:*) rumble. ~**io** *m* grumbling; (*di tuono*) rumbling. ~**one, -a** *mf* grumbler

'bronzo *m* bronze

bros'sura *f* **edizione in** ~ paperback

bru'care *vt* (*pecora:*) graze

bruciacchi'are *vt* scorch

brucia'pelo *adv* **a** ~ point-blank

bruci'a|re *vt* burn; (*scottare*) scald; (*incendiare*) set fire to ●*vi* burn; (*scottare*) scald. ~**rsi** *vr* burn oneself. ~**to** *adj* burnt; *fig* burnt-out. ~**tore** *m* burner. ~**tura** *f* burn. **bruci'ore** *m* burning sensation

'bruco m grub

'brufolo m spot

brughi'era f heath

bruli'care vi swarm

'brullo adj bare

'bruma f mist

'bruno adj brown; (occhi, capelli) dark

brusca'mente adv (di colpo) suddenly

bru'schetta f toasted bread rubbed with garlic and sprinkled with olive oil

'brusco adj sharp; (persona) brusque, (improvviso) sudden

bru'sìo m buzzing

bru'tale adj brutal. **~ità** f inv brutality. **~iz'zare** vt brutalize. **'bruto** adj & m brute

brut'tezza f ugliness

'brut|to adj ugly; (tempo, tipo, situazione, affare) nasty; (cattivo) bad, **~ta copia** rough copy; **~to tiro** dirty trick. **~'tura** f ugly thing

'buca f hole; (avvallamento) hollow. **~ delle lettere** (a casa) letter-box

'buca'neve m inv snowdrop

bu'car|e vt make a hole in; (pungere) prick; punch (biglietti) ● vi have a puncture. **~si** vr prick oneself; (con droga) shoot up

bu'cato m washing

'buccia f peel, skin

bucherel'lare vt riddle

'buco m hole

bu'dello m (pl f **budella**) bowel

bu'dino m pudding

'bue m (pl **buoi**) ox; **carne di ~** beef

'bufalo m buffalo

bu'fera f storm; (di neve) blizzard

buf'fetto m cuff

'buffo adj funny; (Theat) comic ● m funny thing. **~'nata** f (scherzo) joke. **buf'fone** m buffoon; **fare il buffone** play the fool

bu'gia f lie; **~a pietosa** white lle. **~'ardo, -a** adj lying ● mf liar

bugi'gattolo m cubby-hole

'buio adj dark ● m darkness; **al ~** in the dark; **~ pesto** pitch dark

'bulbo m bulb; (dell'occhio) eyeball

Bulga'ria f Bulgaria. **'bulgaro, -a** adj & mf Bulgarian

'bullo m bully

bul'lone m bolt

'hunker m inv bunker

buona'fede f good faith

buona'notte int good night

buona'sera int good evening

buon'giorno int good morning; (di pomeriggio) good afternoon

buon'grado: di ~ adv willingly

buon'gu'staio, -a mf gourmet. **buon'gusto** m good taste

bu'ono adj good; (momento) right; **dar ~** (convalidare) accept; **alla buona** easy-going; (cena) informal; **buona notte/sera** good night/evening; **buon compleanno/Natale!** happy birthday/merry Christmas!; **buon senso** common sense; **di buon'ora** early; **una buona volta** once and for all; **buona parte di** the best part of; **tre ore buone** three good hours ● m good; (in film) goody; (tagliando) voucher; (titolo) bond; **con le buone** gently; **~ sconto** money-off coupon ● mf buono, **-a a nulla** dead loss

buontem'pone, -a mf happy-go-lucky person

buonu'more m good temper

buonu'scita f retirement bonus; (di dirigente) golden handshake

burat'tino m puppet

'burbero adj surly; (nei modi) rough

burocra|te m bureaucrat. **buro-'cratico** adj bureaucratic. **~'zia** f bureaucracy

bur'ra|sca f storm. **~'scoso** adj stormy

'burro m butter

bur'rone m ravine

bu'scar|e vt, ~si vr catch

bus'sare vt knock

'bussola f compass; **perdere la ~** lose one's bearings

'busta f envelope; (astuccio) case. ~ **paga** pay packet. ~'**rella** f bribe. **bu'stina** f (di tè) tea bag; (per medicine) sachet

'busto m bust; (indumento) girdle

but'tar|e vt throw; ~**e giù** (demolire) knock down; (inghiottire) gulp down; scribble down (scritto); ⧉ put on (pasta); ~**e via** throw away. ~**si** vr throw oneself; (saltare) jump

butte'rato adj pock-marked

Cc

caba'ret m inv cabaret

ca'bina f (Aeron, Naut) cabin; (balneare) beach hut. ~ **elettorale** polling booth. ~ **di pilotaggio** cockpit. ~ **telefonica** telephone box. **cabi'nato** m cabin cruiser

ca'cao m cocoa

'cacca f ⧉ pooh

'caccia f hunt; (con fucile) shooting; (inseguimento) chase; (selvaggina) game ● m inv (Aeron) fighter; (Naut) destroyer

cacciabombardi'ere m fighter-bomber

cacciagi'one f game

cacci'a|re vt hunt; (mandar via) chase away; (scacciare) drive out; (ficcare) shove ● vi go hunting. ~**rsi** vr (nascondersi) hide; (andare a finire) get to; ~**rsi nei guai** get into trouble; **alla** ~**tora** adj (Culin) chasseur. ~**tore**, ~**trice** mf hunter. ~**tore di frodo**

poacher

caccia'vite m inv screwdriver

ca'chet m inv (Med) capsule; (colorante) colour rinse; (stile) cachet

'cachi m inv (albero, frutta) persimmon

'cacio m (formaggio) cheese

'cactus m inv cactus

ca'da|vere m corpse. ~'**verico** adj fig deathly pale

ca'dente adj falling; (casa) crumbling

ca'denza f cadence; (ritmo) rhythm; (Mus) cadenza

ca'dere vi fall; (capelli ecc) fall out; (capitombolare) tumble; (vestito ecc) hang; **far** ~ (di mano) drop; ~ **dal sonno** feel very sleepy; **lasciar** ~ drop; ~ **dalle nuvole** fig be taken aback

ca'detto m cadet

ca'duta f fall; (di capelli) loss; fig downfall

caffè m inv coffee; (locale) café. ~ **corretto** espresso coffee with a dash of liqueur. ~ **lungo** weak black coffee. ~ **macchiato** coffee with a dash of milk. ~ **ristretto** strong espresso coffee. ~ **solubile** instant coffee. **caffe'ina** f caffeine. **caffe l'latte** m inv white coffee.

> **Caffè** If you ask for a caffè *i* in an Italian bar you will be served an espresso, a small amount of very strong coffee in a small cup. A macchiato is the same, but with the addition of a little frothy milk. Cappuccino is drunk in the morning or afternoon, never at the end of a meal. A corretto has a dash of spirits in it.

caffetti'era f coffee-pot

cafo'naggine f boorishness

cafo'nata f boorishness

ca'fone, -a mf boor

ca'gare vi 🔲 crap

cagio'nare vt cause

cagio'nevole adj delicate

cagli'are vi, ∼si vr curdle

'cagna f bitch

ca'gnara f 🔲 din

ca'gnesco adj guardare qcno in ∼ scowl at sb

'cala f creek

cala'brone m hornet

cala'maio m inkpot

cala'mari mpl squid sg

cala'mita f magnet

calamità f inv calamity

ca'lar|e vi come down; (vento:) drop; (diminuire) fall; (tramontare) set ● vt (abbassare) lower; (nei lavori a maglia) decrease ● m (di luna) waning. ∼si vr lower oneself

'caica f throng

cal'cagno m heel

cal'care[1] m limestone

cal'care[2] vt tread; (premere) press [down]; ∼ la mano fig exaggerate; ∼ le orme di qcno fig follow in sb's footsteps

'calce[1] f lime

'calce[2] m in ∼ at the foot of the page

calce'struzzo m concrete

cal'cetto m Sport five-a-side [football]

calci'are vt kick. ∼'tore m footballer

cal'cina f mortar

calci'naccio m (pezzo di intonaco) flake of plaster

'calcio[1] m (Sport) football; (di arma da fuoco) butt; **dare un ∼ a** kick. ∼ **d'angolo** corner [kick]

'calcio[2] m (chimica) calcium

'calco m tracing; (arte) cast

calco'lar|e vt calculate; (considerare) consider. ∼'tore m calculating ● m calculator; (macchina elettronica) computer

'calcolo m calculation; (Med) stone

cal'daia f boiler

caldar'rosta f roast chestnut

caldeggi'are vt support

'caldo adj warm; (molto caldo) hot ● m heat; **avere ∼** be warm/hot; **fa ∼** it is warm/hot

calen'dario m calendar

ca'libro m calibre; (strumento) callipers pl; **di grosso ∼** (persona) top attrib

'calice m goblet; (Relig) chalice

ca'ligine f fog; (industriale) smog

'call centre m call centre

calligra'fia f handwriting; (cinese) calligraphy

cal'lista mf chiropodist. **'callo** m corn; **fare il callo a** become hardened to. **cal'loso** adj callous

'calma f calm. **cal'mante** adj calming ● m sedative, **cal'mare** vt calm [down]; (lenire) soothe. **cal'marsi** vr calm down; (vento:) drop; (dolore:) die down. **'calmo** adj calm

'calo m (Comm) fall; (di volume) shrinkage; (di peso) loss

ca'lore m heat; (moderato) warmth; **in ∼** (animale) on heat. **calo'roso** adj warm

calo'ria f calorie

ca'lorico adj calorific

calo'rifero m radiator

calorosa'mente adv (cordialmente) warmly

calpe'stare vt trample [down]; fig trample on (diritti, sentimenti); **vietato ∼ l'erba** keep off the grass

calpe'stio m (passi) footsteps

ca'lunni|a f slander. ∼'are vt slander. ∼'oso adj slanderous

ca'lura f heat

cal'vario m Calvary; fig trial

cal'vizie f baldness. **'calvo** adj bald

'calz|a f (da donna) stocking; (da uomo)

sock. ~a'maglia f tights pl; (per danza) leotard

cal'zante adj fig fitting

cal'za|re vt (indossare) wear; (mettersi) put on ● vi fit

calza'scarpe m inv shoehorn

calza'tura f footwear

calzaturi'ficio m shoe factory

cal'zetta f è una mezza ~ fig he's no use

calzet'tone m knee-length woollen sock. cal'zino m sock

calzo'l|aio m shoemaker. ~e'ria f (negozio) shoe shop

calzon'cini mpl shorts. ~ da bagno swimming trunks

cal'zone m folded pizza with tomato and mozzarella or ricotta

cal'zoni mpl trousers, pants Am

camale'onte m chameleon

cambi'ale f bill of exchange

cambia'mento m change

cambi'ar|e vt/i change; move (casa); (fare cambio di) exchange; ~e rotta (Naut) alter course. ~si vi vr change. 'cambio m change; (Comm, scambio) exchange; (Mech) gear; dare il ~ a qcno relieve sb; in ~ di in exchange for

'camera f room; (mobili) [bedroom] suite; (Phot) camera; C~ (Comm, Pol) Chamber. ~ ardente funeral parlour. ~ d'aria inner tube. C~ di Commercio Chamber of Commerce. C~ dei Deputati (Pol) ≈House of Commons. ~ doppia double room. ~ da letto bedroom. ~ matrimoniale double room. ~ oscura darkroom. ~ singola single room

came'rata¹ f (dormitorio) dormitory; (Mil) barrack room

came'ra|ta² mf (amico) mate; (Pol) comrade. ~'tismo m comradeship

cameri'era f maid; (di ristorante) waitress; (in albergo) chamber-maid; (di bordo) stewardess

cameri'ere m manservant; (di ristorante) waiter; (di bordo) steward

came'rino m dressing-room

'camice m overall. cami'cetta f blouse. ca'micia f shirt; uovo in ~ poached egg. camicia da notte nightdress

cami'netto m fireplace

ca'mino m chimney; (focolare) fireplace

'camion m inv truck, lorry Br

camion'cino m van

camio'netta f jeep

camio'nista m truck driver

cam'mello m camel; (tessuto) camel-hair ● adj inv (colore) camel

cam'meo m cameo

cammi'na|re vi walk; (auto, orologio:) go. ~ta f walk; fare una ~ta go for a walk. cam'mino m way; essere in ~ be on the way; mettersi in ~ set out

camo'milla f camomile; (bevanda) camomile tea

ca'morra f local mafia

ca'moscio m chamois; (pelle) suede

cam'pagna f country; (paesaggio) countryside; (Comm, Mil) campaign; in ~ in the country. ~ elettorale election campaign. ~ pubblicitaria marketing campaign. campa'gnolo, -a adj rustic ● m countryman ● f countrywoman

cam'pale adj field attrib; giornata ~ fig strenuous day

cam'pa|na f bell; (di vetro) belljar. ~'nella f (di tenda) curtain ring. ~'nello m door-bell; (cicalino) buzzer

campa'nile m belfry

campani'lismo m parochialism

campani'lista mf person with a parochial outlook

cam'panula f (Bot) campanula

cam'pare vi live; (a stento) get by

cam'pato adj ~ in aria unfounded

campeggi'a|re vi camp; (spiccare)

stand out. **~'tore**, **~'trice** mf camper. **cam'peglio** m camping; (terreno) campsite

cam'pestre adj rural

'camping m inv campsite

campio'nari|o m [set of] samples ● adj samples; **fiera ~a** trade fair

campio'nato m championship

campiona'tura f (di merce) range of samples

campi'on|e m champion; (Comm) sample; (esemplare) specimen. **~'essa** f ladies' champion

'campo m field; (accampamento) camp. **~ da calcio** football pitch. **~ di concentramento** concentration camp. **~ da golf** golf course. **~ da tennis** tennis court. **~ profughi** refugee camp

campo'santo m cemetery

camuf'far|e vt disguise. **~si** vr disguise oneself

'Cana|da m Canada, **~'dese** agg & mf Canadian

ca'naglia f scoundrel; (plebaglia) rabble

ca'nal|e m channel; (artificiale) canal. **~iz'zare** vt channel (acque). **~izza-zi'one** f channelling, (rete) pipes pl

'canapa f hemp

cana'rino m canary

cancel'la|re vt cross out; (con la gomma) rub out; (annullare) cancel; (Comput) delete. **~'tura** f erasure. **~zi'one** f cancellation; (Comput) deletion

cancelle'ria f chancellery; (articoli per scrivere) stationery

cancelli'ere m chancellor; (di tribunale) clerk

can'cello m gate

cance'ro|geno m carcinogen ● adj carcinogenic, **~'so** adj cancerous

can'crena f gangrene

'cancro m cancer. **C~** (Astr) Cancer

candeg'gi|na f bleach. **~'are** vt

bleach. **can'deggio** m bleaching

can'de|la f candle; (Auto) spark plug. **~li'ere** m candlestick

candi'dar|si vr stand as a candidate. **~to**, **-a** mf candidate. **~'tura** f (Pol) candidacy; (per lavoro) application

'candido adj snow-white; (sincero) candid; (puro) pure

can'dito adj candied

can'dore m whiteness; fig innocence

'cane m dog; (di arma a fuoco) cock; **un tempo da cani** foul weather. **~ da caccia** hunting dog

ca'nestro m basket

cangi'ante adj iridescent; **seta ~** shot silk

can'guro m kangaroo

ca'nile m kennel; (di allevamento) kennels pl. **~ municipale** dog pound

ca'nino adj & m canine

'canna f reed; (da zucchero) cane; (di fucile) barrel; (bastone) stick; (di bicicletta) crossbar; (asta) rod; (🔧: hascisc) joint; **povero in ~** destitute. **~ da pesca** fishingrod

can'nella f cinnamon

can'neto m bed of reeds

canni'ba|le m cannibal. **~'lismo** m cannibalism

cannocchi'ale m telescope

canno'nata f cannon shot; **è una ~** fig it's brilliant

can'non|e m cannon, fig ace. **~'cino** m (dolce) cream horn

can'nuccia f [drinking] straw; (di pipa) stem

ca'noa f canoe

ca'none m canon; (affitto) rent; **equo ~** fair rents act

ca'noni|co m canon. **~z'zare** vt canonize. **~zzazi'one** f canonization

ca'noro adj melodious

ca'notta f (estiva) vest top

canot'taggio m canoeing; (voga) rowing

canotti'era f singlet

canotti'ere m oarsman

ca'notto m [rubber] dinghy

cano'vaccio m (trama) plot; (straccio) duster

can'tante mf singer

can't|are vt/i sing. **~au'tore, ~au'trice** mf singer-songwriter. **~ic-chi'are** vt sing softly; (a bocca chiusa) hum

canti'ere m yard; (Naut) shipyard; (di edificio) construction site. **~ navale** naval dockyard

canti'lena f singsong; (ninna-nanna) lullaby

can'tina f cellar; (osteria) wine shop

'canto¹ m singing; (canzone) song; (Relig) chant; (poesia) poem

'canto² m (angolo) corner; (lato) side; **dal ~ mio** for my part; **d'altro ~** on the other hand

canto'nata f **prendere una ~** fig be sadly mistaken

can'tone m canton; (angolo) corner

can'tuccio m nook

canzo'na|re vt tease. **~'torio** adj teasing. **~'tura** f teasing

can'zo|ne f song. **~'netta** f 🔲 pop song. **~ni'ere** m songbook

---

Canzone Italians are very proud of their tradition of popular song and it is celebrated at the Festival of Sanremo (Festival della Canzone Italiana). The festival has been held since 1951 and is watched by millions on Italian TV every year. The festival includes a competition for the best new song and the winner is guaranteed chart success.

'caos m chaos. **ca'otico** adj chaotic

C.A.P. m abbr (Codice di Avviamento Postale) post code, zip code Am

ca'pac|e adj able; (esperto) skilled; (stadio, contenitore) big; **~ e di** (disposto a) capable of. **~ità** f inv ability; (attitudine) skill; (capienza) capacity

capaci'tarsi vr **~ di** (rendersi conto) understand; (accorgersi) realize

ca'panna f hut

capan'nello m **fare ~ intorno a** qcno/qcsa gather round sb/sth

capan'none m shed; (Aeron) hangar

ca'parbio adj obstinate

ca'parra f deposit

capa'tina f short visit; **fare una ~ in città/da qcno** pop into town/in on sb

ca'pel|lo m hair; **~li** pl (capigliatura) hair sg. **~'lone** m hippie. **~'luto** adj hairy

capez'zale m bolster; fig bedside

ca'pezzolo m nipple

capi'en|te adj capacious. **~za** f capacity

capiglia'tura f hair

ca'pire vt understand; **~ male** misunderstand; **si capisce!** naturally!; **sì, ho capito** yes, I see

capi'ta|le adj (Jur) capital; (principale) main ● f (città) capital ● m (Comm) capital. **~'lismo** m capitalism. **~'lista** mf capitalist. **~'listico** adj capitalist

capitane'ria f **~ di porto** port authorities pl

capi'tano m captain

capi'tare vi (giungere per caso) come; (accadere) happen

capi'tello m (Archit) capital

capito'la|re vi capitulate. **~zi'one** f capitulation

ca'pitolo m chapter

capi'tombolo m headlong fall; **fare un ~** tumble down

'capo m head; (chi comanda) boss 🔲; (di vestiario) item; (Geog) cape; (in tribù) chief; (parte estrema) top; **a ~** new paragraph; **da ~** over again; **in ~ a**

un mese within a month; **giramento di** ~ dizziness; **mal di** ~ headache; ~ **d'abbigliamento** item of clothing. ~ **d'accusa** (Jur) charge ~ **di bestiame** head of cattle

capo'banda m (Mus) bandmaster; (di delinquenti) ringleader

ca'poccia f (🔲: testa) nut

capocci'one, -a mf 🔲 brainbox

capo'danno m New Year's Day

capofa'miglia m head of the family

capo'fitto m a ~ headlong

capo'giro m giddiness

capola'voro m masterpiece

capo'linea m terminus

capo'lino m fare ~ peep in

capolu'ogo m main town

capo'rale m lance-corporal

capo'squadra mf Sport team captain

capo'stipite mf (di famiglia) progenitor

capo'tavola mf head of the table

capo'treno m guard

capouf'ficio m head clerk

capo'verso m first line

capo'vol|gere vt overturn; fig reverse. ~**gersi** vr overturn; (barca:) capsize; fig be reversed. ~**to** pp di capovolgere ● adj upside-down

'cappa f cloak; (di camino) cowl; (di cucina) hood

cap'pel|la f chapel. ~'lano m chaplain

cap'pello m hat. ~ **a cilindro** top hat

'cappero m caper

'cappio m noose

cap'pone m capon

cap'potto m [over]coat

cappuc'cino m (frate) Capuchin; (bevanda) white coffee

cap'puccio m hood; (di penna stilografica) cap

'capra f goat. **ca'pretto** m kid

ca'priccio m whim; (bizzarria) freak; **fare i capricci** have tantrums. **~'cioso** adj capricious; (bambino) naughty

Capri'corno m (Astr) Capricorn

capri'ola f somersault

capri'olo m roe-deer

'capro m [billy-]goat. ~ **espiatorio** scapegoat.

ca'prone m [billy] goat

'capsula f capsule; (di proiettile) cap; (di dente) crown

cap'tare vt (Radio, TV) pick up; catch (attenzione)

cara'bina f carbine

carabini'ere m carabiniere; **carabinieri** pl Italian police

ca'raffa f carafe

Ca'raibi mpl (zona) Caribbean sg; (isole) Caribbean Islands; **il mar dei** ~ the Caribbean [Sea]

cara'mella f sweet

cara'mello m caramel

ca'rato m carat

ca'ratte|re m character; (caratteristica) characteristic; (Typ) type; **di buon** ~**re** good-natured. ~'ristico, **-a** adj characteristic; (pittoresco) quaint ● f characteristic. ~**riz'zare** vt characterize

carbon'cino m charcoal

car'bone m coal

carbu'rante m fuel

carbura'tore m carburettor

car'cassa f carcass; fig old wreck

carce'ra|rio adj prison attrib. **~to, -a** mf prisoner. **~zi'one** f imprisonment. **~zione preventiva** preventive detention

'carcer|e m prison; (punizione) imprisonment. **~i'ere, -a** mf gaoler

carci'ofo m artichoke

cardi'nale adj & m cardinal

'cardine m hinge

cardio|chi'rurgo m heart surgeon. **~lo'gia** f cardiology. **cardi'ologo** m heart specialist. **~'tonico** m heart stimulant

'cardo m thistle

ca'rena f (Naut) bottom

ca'ren|te adj **~te di** lacking in. **~za** f lack; (scarsità) scarcity

ca're'stia f famine; (mancanza) dearth

ca'rezza f caress

cari'a|rsi vi decay. **~to** adj decayed

'carica f office; (Electr, Mil) charge; fig drive. **cari'care** vt load; (Electr, Mil) charge; wind up (orologio). **~'tore** m (per proiettile) magazine

carica'tu|ra f caricature. **~'rale** adj grotesque. **~'rista** mf caricaturist

'carico adj loaded (di with); (colore) strong; (orologio) wound [up]; (batteria) charged ● m load; (di nave) cargo; (il caricare) loading; **a ~ di** (Comm) to be charged to; (persona) dependent on

'carie f [tooth] decay

ca'rino adj pretty; (piacevole) agreeable

ca'risma m charisma

carit|à f charity; **per ~à!** (come rifiuto) God forbid!. **~a'tevole** adj charitable

carnagi'one f complexion

car'naio m fig shambles

car'nale adj carnal; **cugino ~** first cousin

'carne f flesh; (alimento) meat; **~ di manzo/maiale/vitello** beef/pork/veal

car'nefi|ce m executioner. **~'cina** f slaughter

carne'va|le m carnival. **~'lesco** adj carnival

car'noso adj fleshy

'caro, -a adj dear; **cari saluti** kind regards ● m darling, dear; **i miei cari** my nearest and dearest

ca'rogna f carcass; fig bastard

caro'sello m merry-go-round

ca'rota f carrot

caro'vana f caravan; (di veicoli) convoy

caro'vita m high cost of living

'carpa f carp

carpenti'ere m carpenter

car'pire vt seize; (con difficoltà) extort

car'poni adv on all fours

car'rabile adj suitable for vehicles; **passo ~** ▷**CARRAIO**

car'raio adj **passo ~** entrance to driveway, garage etc where parking is forbidden

carreggi'ata f roadway; **doppia ~** dual carriageway, divided highway Am

carrel'lata f (TV) pan

car'rello m trolley; (di macchina da scrivere) carriage; (Aeron) undercarriage; (Cinema, TV) dolly. **~ d'atterraggio** (Aeron) landing gear

car'retto m cart

carri'e|ra f career; **di gran ~ra** at full speed; **fare ~ra** get on. **~'rismo** m careerism

carri'ola f wheelbarrow

'carro m cart. **~ armato** tank. **~ attrezzi** breakdown vehicle. **~ funebre** hearse. **~ merci** truck

car'rozza f carriage; (Rail) car. **~ cuccette** sleeping car. **~ ristorante** restaurant car

carroz'zella f (per bambini) pram;

(*per disabili*) wheelchair

carrozze'ria f bodywork; (*officina*) bodyshop

carroz'zina f pram; (*pieghevole*) push-chair, stroller Am

carroz'zone m (*di circo*) caravan

'carta f papers (*di gioco*) card; (*statuto*) charter; (Goog) map. ~ **d'argento** ≈ senior citizens' railcard. ~ **assorbente** blotting-paper. ~ **di credito** credit card. ~ **geografica** map. ~ **d'identità** identity card. ~ **igienica** toilet-paper. ~ **di imbarco** boarding card or pass. ~ **da lettere** writing-paper. ~ **da parati** wallpaper. ~ **stagnola** silver paper; (Culin) aluminium foil. ~ **straccia** waste paper. ~ **stradale** road map. ~ **velina** tissue-paper. ~ **verde** (Auto) green card. ~ **vetrata** sandpaper

cartacar'bone f carbon paper

car'taccia f waste paper

carta'modello m pattern

cartamo'neta f paper money

carta'pesta f papier mâché

carta'straccia f waste paper

cartave'trare vt sand [down]

car'tel|la f briefcase; (*di cartone*) folder; (*di scolaro*) satchel. ~**la clinica** medical record. ~**'lina** f folder

cartel'lino m (*etichetta*) label; (*del prezzi*) price-tag; (*di presenza*) time-card; **timbrare il** ~ clock in; (*all'uscita*) clock out

car'tel|lo m sign; (*pubblicitario*) poster; (*stradale*) road sign; (*di protesta*) placard; (Comm) cartel. ~**lone** m poster; (Theat) bill

carti'era f paper-mill

car'tina f map

car'toccio m paper bag; **al** ~ (Culin) baked in foil

carto'l|aio, -a mf stationer. ~**le'ria** f stationer's. ~**libre'ria** f stationer's and book shop

carto'lina f postcard. ~ **postale** postcard

carto'mante mf fortune-teller

carton'cino m (*materiale*) card

car'tone m cardboard; (*arte*) cartoon. ~ **animato** [animated] cartoon

car'tuccia f cartridge

'casa f house; (*abitazione propria*) home; (*ditta*) firm; **amico di** ~ family friend; **andare a** ~ go home; **essere di** ~ be like one of the family; **fatto in** ~ home-made; **padrone di** ~ (*pensione occ*) landlord; (*proprietario*) house owner. ~ **di cura** nursing home. ~ **popolare** council house. ~ **dello studente** hall of residence

ca'sacca f military coat; (*giacca*) jacket

ca'saccio adv a ~ at random

casa'ling|a f housewife. ~**o** adj domestic; (*fatto in casa*) home-made; (*amante della casa*) home-loving; (*semplice*) homely

ca'scante adj falling, (*floscio*) flabby

ca'sca|re vi fall [down]. ~**ta** f (*di acqua*) waterfall

ca'schetto m [capelli a] ~ bob

ca'scina f farm building

'casco m crash-helmet; (*asciugacapelli*) [hair-]drier; ~ **di banane** bunch of bananas

caseggi'ato m apartment block

casei'ficio m dairy

ca'sella f pigeon-hole. ~ **postale** post office box; (Comput) mailbox

casel'lante mf (*per treni*) signalman

casel'lario m ~ **giudiziario** record of convictions; **avere il** ~ **giudizia rio vergine** have no criminal record

ca'sello m [autostra'dale] m [motorway] toll booth

case'reccio adj home-made

ca'serma f barracks pl; (*dei carabinieri*) [police] station

casi'nista mf [🔲] muddler. **ca'sino** m [🔲] (*bordello*) brothel; (*fig: confusione*) racket; (*disordine*) mess; **un casino di** loads of

casinò *m inv* casino

ca'sistica *f* (*classificazione*) case records *pl*

'**caso** *m* chance; (*Gram, Med*), (*fatto, circostanza*) case; **a** ~ at random; ~ **mai** if need be; **far a** ~ a pay attention to; **non far** ~ a take no account of; **per** ~ by chance. ~ **[giudiziario]** [legal] case

caso'lare *m* farmhouse

'**caspita** *int* good gracious!

'**cassa** *f* till; cash; (*luogo di pagamento*) cash desk; (*mobile*) chest; (*istituto bancario*) bank. ~ **automatica prelievi** cash dispenser, ATM. ~ **da morto** coffin. ~ **toracica** ribcage

cassa'forte *f* safe

cassa'panca *f* linen chest

casseru'ola *f* saucepan

cas'setta *f* (*per registratore*) cassette. ~ **delle lettere** letterbox. ~ **di sicurezza** strong-box

cas'set|to *m* drawer. ~'**tone** *m* chest of drawers

cassi'ere, -a *mf* cashier; (*di supermercato*) checkout assistant; (*di banca*) teller

'**casta** *f* caste

ca'stagn|a *f* chestnut. **casta'gneto** *m* chestnut grove. ~o *m* chestnut[-tree]

ca'stano *adj* chestnut

ca'stello *m* castle; (*impalcatura*) scaffold

casti'gare *vt* punish

casti'gato *adj* (*casto*) chaste

ca'stigo *m* punishment

casti'tà *f* chastity. '**casto** *adj* chaste

ca'storo *m* beaver

ca'strare *vt* castrate

casu'al|e *adj* chance *attrib.* ~'**mente** *adv* by chance

ca'supola *f* little house

cata'clisma *m fig* upheaval

cata'comba *f* catacomb

cata'fascio *m* **andare a** ~ go to rack and ruin

cata'litico *adj* **marmitta catalitica** (*Auto*) catalytic converter

cataliz'za|re *vt* heighten. ~'**tore** *m* (*Auto*) catalytic converter

catalo'gare *vt* catalogue. **cata'logo** *m* catalogue

catama'rano *m* (*da diporto*) catamaran

cata'pecchia *f* hovel; 🔧 dump

catapul'tar|e *vt* eject. ~**si** *vr* (*precipitarsi*) dive

catarifran'gente *m* reflector

ca'tarro *m* catarrh

ca'tasta *f* pile

ca'tasto *m* land register

ca'tastrofe *f* catastrophe. **cata'strofico** *adj* catastrophic

cate'chismo *m* catechism

catego'ria *f* category. ~'**gorico** *adj* categorical

ca'tena *f* chain. ~ **montuosa** mountain range. **catene** *pl* **da neve** tyre-chains. **cate'naccio** *m* bolt

cate'|nella *f* (*collana*) chain. ~'**nina** *f* chain

cate'ratta *f* cataract

ca'terva *f* **una** ~ **di** heaps of

cati'nell|a *f* basin; **piovere a** ~**e** bucket down

ca'tino *m* basin

ca'trame *m* tar

cat'tedra *f* (*tavolo di insegnante*) desk; (*di università*) chair

catte'drale *f* cathedral

catti'veria *f* wickedness; (*azione*) wicked action

cattivi'tà *f* captivity

cat'tivo *adj* bad; (*bambino*)

naughty

cattoli'cesimo m Catholicism

cat'tolico, -a adj & mf [Roman] Catholic

cat'tu|ra f capture. **~'rare** vt capture

caucciù m rubber

'causa f cause; (*Jur*) lawsuit; **far ~ a qcno** sue sb. **cau'sare** vt cause

'caustico adj caustic

cauta'mente adv cautiously

cau'tela f caution

caute'lar|e vt protect. **~si** vr take precautions

cauteriz'z|are vt cauterize. **~ra ziu'ne** f cauterization

'cauto adj cautious

cauzi'one f security; (*per libertà provvisoria*) ball

'cava f quarry; *fig* mine

caval'ca|re vt ride; (*stare a cavalcioni*) sit astride. **~ta** f ride; (*corteo*) cavalcade. **~'via** m flyover

cavalci'oni: a ~ adv astride

cavali'ere m rider; (*titolo*) knight; (*accompagnatore*) escort; (*al ballo*) partner

cavalle'resco adj chivalrous. **~'ria** f chivalry; (*Mil*) cavalry. **~'rizzo, -a** m horseman **•f** horsewoman

caval'letta f grasshopper

caval'letto m trestle; (*di macchina fotografica*) tripod; (*di pittore*) easel

caval'lina f (*ginnastica*) horse

ca'vallo m horse; (*misura di potenza*) horsepower; (*scacchi*) knight; (*dei pantaloni*) crotch; **a ~** on horseback; **andare a ~** go horse-riding. **~ a dondolo** rocking-horse

caval'lone m (*ondata*) roller

caval'luccio ma'rino m sea horse

ca'var|e vt take out; (*di dosso*) take

off; **~sela** get away with it; **se la cava bene** he's doing all right

cava'tappi m inv corkscrew

ca'ver|na f cave. **~'noso** adj (*voce*) deep

'cavia f guinea-pig

cavi'ale m caviar

ca'viglia f ankle

cavil'lare vi quibble. **ca'villo** m quibble

cavità f inv cavity

'cavo adj hollow **•m** cavity; (*di metallo*) cable; (*Naut*) rope

cavo'lata f fam rubbish

cavo'letto m **~ di Bruxelles** Brussels sprout

cavolfi'ore m cauliflower

'cavolo m cabbage; **~!** fam sugar!

caz'zo int vulg fuck!

caz'zott|o m punch; **prendere qcno a ~i** beat sb up

cazzu'ola f trowel

c/c abbr (*conto corrente*) c/a

CD-Rom m inv CD-Rom

ce pers pron (*a noi*) (to) us **•** adv there; **~ ne sono molti** there are many

'cece m chick-pea

recità f blindness

ceco, -a adj & mf Czech; **la Repubblica Ceca** the Czech Republic

'cedere vi (*arrendersi*) surrender; (*concedere*) yield; (*sprofondare*) subside **•** vt give up; make over (*proprietà ecc*). **ce'devole** adj (*terreno ecc*) soft, *fig* yielding. **cedi'mento** m (*di terreno*) subsidence

'cedola f coupon

'cedro m (*albero*) cedar; (*frutto*) citron

'ceffo m (*muso*) snout; (*pej: persona*) mug

cef'fone m slap

ce'lar|e vt conceal. **~si** vr hide

cele'bra|re vt celebrate. **~zi'one** f

celebration

'celebr|e *adj* famous. ~ità *f inv* celebrity

'celere *adj* swift

ce'leste *adj* (*divino*) heavenly ● *agg & m* (*colore*) sky-blue

celi'bato *m* celibacy

'celibe *adj* single ● *m* bachelor

'cella *f* cell

'cellofan *m inv* cellophane; (*Culin*) cling film

'cellula *f* cell. ~ fotoelettrica electronic eye

cellu'lare *m* (*telefono*) cellular phone ● *adj* [furgone] ~ police van. [telefono] ~ *m* cellular phone

cellu'lite *f* cellulite

cellu'loide *adj* celluloid

cellu'losa *f* cellulose

'Celt|i *mpl* Celts. ~ico *adj* Celtic

cemen'tare *vt* cement. ce'mento *m* cement. cemento armato reinforced concrete

'cena *f* dinner; (*leggera*) supper

Cena *Cena* is the evening meal, traditionally a lighter meal than *pranzo*, although it too may start with a *primo* (often small pasta shapes in broth). A *cena* can also be a dinner party or a dinner at a restaurant, two of the principal ways in which Italians socialize.

---

ce'nacolo *m* circle

ce'nare *vi* have dinner

'cenci|o *m* rag; (*per spolverare*) duster. ~'oso *adj* in rags

'cenere *f* ash; (*di carbone ecc*) cinders

ce'netta *f* (*cena semplice*) informal dinner

'cenno *m* sign; (*col capo*) nod; (*con la mano*) wave; (*allusione*) hint; (*breve resoconto*) mention

ce'none *m* il ~ di Capodanno/Natale *special* New Year's Eve/Christmas Eve dinner

censi'mento *m* census

cen's|ore *m* censor. ~ura *f* censorship. ~u'rare *vt* censor

'cent *m inv* cent

centelli'nare *vt* sip

cente'n|ario, -a *adj & mf* centenarian ● *m* centenary. ~'nale *adj* centennial

cen'tesimo *adj* hundredth ● *m* (*di moneta*) cent; **non avere un** ~ be penniless

cen'ti|grado *adj* centigrade. ~metro *m* centimetre

centi'naio *m* hundred

'cento *adj & m* one or a hundred; **per** ~ per cent

centome'trista *mf* Sport one hundred metres runner

cento'mila *m* one or a hundred thousand

cen'trale *adj* central ● *f* (*di società ecc*) head office. ~ atomica atomic power station. ~ elettrica power station. ~ nucleare nuclear power station. ~ telefonica [telephone] exchange

centra'li|na *f* (*Teleph*) switchboard. ~'nista *mf* operator

centra'lino *m* (*Teleph*) exchange; (*di albergo ecc*) switchboard

centra'li|smo *m* centralism. ~z'zare *vt* centralize

cen'trare *vt* ~ qcsa hit sth in the centre; (*fissare nel centro*) centre; *fig* hit on the head (*idea*)

cen'trifu|ga *f* spin-drier. centrifuga [asciugaverdure] shaker. ~'gare *vt* centrifuge; (*lavatrice:*) spin

'centro *m* centre. ~ [città] city centre. ~ commerciale mall. ~ di accoglienza reception centre. ~ sociale community centre

Centro storico The layout and much of the fabric of most Italian town and city centres derive from medieval or even Roman times, with the result that the *centro storico* is a place of narrow streets. Some (like Lucca) are surrounded by city walls. This makes life difficult for the motorist, and cars have been banned from many city centres.

'**ceppo** m (di albero) stump; (da ardere) log; (fig: gruppo) stock

'**cera** f wax; (aspetto) look, ~ **per il pavimento** floor-polish

ce'**ramica** f (arte) ceramics; (materia) pottery; (oggetto) pot

ce'**rato** adj (tela) waxed

cerbi'**atto** m fawn

'**cerca** f andare in ~ **di** look for

cercaper'**sone** m inv beeper

cer'**care** vt look for ● vi ~ **di** try to

'**cerchia** f circle. ~'**are** vt circle (parola). ~'**ato** adj (occhi) black-ringed. ~'**etto** m (per capelli) hairband

'**cerchio** m circle; (giocattolo) hoop. ~'**one** m alloy wheel

cere'**ale** m cereal

cere'**brale** adj cerebral

'**cereo** adj waxen

ce'**retta** f depilatory wax

ceri'**monia** f ceremony. ~'**ale** m ceremonial. ~'**oso** adj ceremonious

ce'**rino** m [wax] match

cerni'**era** f hinge; (di borsa) clasp. ~ **lampo** zip[-fastener], zipper Am

'**cernita** f selection

'**cero** m candle

ce'**rone** m grease-paint

ce'**rotto** m [sticking] plaster

certa'**mente** adv certainly

cer'**tezza** f certainty

certifi'**care** vt certify. ~**to** m certificate

'**certo** adj certain; (notizia) definite; (indeterminativo) some; **sono** ~ **di riuscire** I am certain to succeed; **certi giorni** some days; **un** ~ **signor Giardini** a Mr Giardini; **una certa Anna** somebody called Anna; **certa gente** pej some people; **ho certi dolori!** I'm in such pain!. **certi** pron pl some; (alcune persone) some people ● adv of course; **sapere per** ~ know for certain; **di** ~ surely; ~ **che sì!** of course! ~ **che** ... of course!

cer'**vello** m brain.

'**cervo** m deer

ce'sareo adj (Med) Caesarean

cesel'**lare** vt chisel. ~**to** adj chiselled. ce'**sello** m chisel

ce'**soie** fpl shears

ce'**spuglio** m bush. ~'**oso** adj (terreno) bushy

ces'**sare** vi stop, cease ● vt stop. ~**te il fuoco** ceasefire

cessi'**one** f handover

'**cesso** m ☒ (gabinetto) bog, john Am; (fig: locale, luogo) dump

'**cesta** f [large] basket. ce'**stino** m (di lavatrice) drum

cesti'**nare** vt throw away. ce'**stino** m [small] basket; (per la carta straccia) waste-paper basket. '**cesto** m basket

'**ceto** m [social] class

'**cetra** f lyre

cetrio'**lino** m gherkin. cetri'**olo** m cucumber

cfr abbr (confronta) cf.

chat'**tare** vi (Comput) chat

che

● pron rel (persona: soggetto) who; (persona: oggetto) that, who, whom fml; (cosa, animale) that, which; **questa è la casa** ~ **ho comprato** this is the house [that] I've bought; **il** ~ **mi sorprende** which surprises me; **dal**

~ **deduco che...** from which I gather that...; **avere di ~ vi-vere** have enough to live on; **grazie! – non c'è di ~!** thank you! – don't mention it!; **il giorno ~ ti ho visto** ⬚ the day I saw you

● adj inter which, what; (esclamativo: con aggettivo) how; (esclamativo: con nome) what a; ~ **macchina prendiamo, la tua o la mia?** which car are we taking, yours or mine?; ~ **bello!** how nice!; ~ **idea!** what an ideal; ~ **bella giornata!** what a lovely day!

● pron inter what; **a ~ pensi?** what are you thinking about?

● conj that; (con comparazioni) than; **credo ~ abbia ragione** I think [that] he is right; **era così commosso ~ non riusciva a parlare** he was so moved [that] he couldn't speak; **aspetto ~ tele-foni** I'm waiting for him to phone; **è da un po' ~ non lo vedo** it's been a while since I saw him; **mi piace più Roma ~ Milano** I like Rome better than Milan; ~ **ti piaccia o not;** ~ **io sappia** as far as I know

checché indef pron whatever
chemiotera'pia f chemotherapy
chero'sene m paraffin
cheti'chella: alla ~ adv silently
'cheto adj quiet

chi

● rel pron whoever; (coloro che) people who; **ho trovato ~ ti può aiutare** I found somebody who can help you; **c'è ~ dice che...** some people say that...; **senti ~ parla!** listen to who's talking!

● inter pron (soggetto) who; (oggetto,

con preposizione) who, whom fml; (possessivo) di ~ whose; ~ **sei?** who are you?; ~ **hai incon-trato?** who did you meet?; **di ~ sono questi libri?** whose books are these?; **con ~ parli?** who are you talking to?; **a ~ lo dici!** tell me about it!

chi'acchie|ra f chat; (pettegolezzo) gossip. ~'**rare** vi chat; (far pettego-lezzi) gossip. ~'**rato** adj **essere ~rato** (persona): be the subject of gossip; ~**re** pl chitchat; **far quattro ~re** have a chat. ~'**rone, -a** adj talkative ● mf chatterer

chia'ma|re vt call; (far venire) send for; **come ti chiami?** what's your name?; **mi chiamo Roberto** my name is Robert; ~**re alle armi** call up. ~**rsi** vr be called. ~**ta** f call; (Mil) call-up

chi'appa f ⬚ cheek

chiara'mente adv clearly

chia'rezza f clarity; (limpidezza) clearness

chiarifi'ca|re vt clarify. ~'**tore** adj clarificatory. ~**zi'one** f clarification

chiari'mento m clarification

chia'rir|e vt make clear; (spiegare) clear up. ~**si** vr become clear

chi'aro adj (luminoso) bright; (colore) light. **chia'rore** m glimmer

chiaroveg'gente adj clear-sighted ● mf clairvoyant

chi'as|so m din. ~'**soso** adj rowdy

chi'av|e f key; **chiudere a ~** lock. ~**e inglese** spanner. ~**i'stello** m latch

chiaz|za f stain. ~'**zare** vt stain

chic adj inv chic

chicches'sia pron anybody

'chicco m grain; (di caffè) bean; (d'uva) grape

chi'eder|e vt ask; (per avere) ask for; (esigere) demand. ~**si** vr wonder

chi'esa f church

chi'esto pp di **chiedere**

'chiglia f keel

'chilo m kilo

chilo'grammo m kilogram[me]

chilome'traggio m (Auto) mileage

chilo'metrico adj in kilometres

chi'lometro m kilometre

chi'mera f fig illusion

'chimic|a f chemistry. **~o, -a** adj chemical ● mf chemist

'china f (declivio) slope. **inchiostro di ~** Indian ink

chi'nar|e vt lower. **~si** vr stoop

chincaglie'rie fpl knick-knacks

chinesitera'pia f physiotherapy

chi'nino m quinine

'chino adj bent

chi'notto m sparkling soft drink

chi'occia f sitting hen

chi'occiola f snail; (Comput) at sign; **scala a ~** spiral staircase

chi'odo m nail; (idea fissa) obsession. **~ di garofano** clove

chi'oma f head of hair; (fogliame) foliage

chi'osco m kiosk

chi'ostro m cloister

chiro'man|te mf palmist. **~'zia** f palmistry

chirur'gia f surgery. **chi'rurgico** adj surgical, **chi'rurgo** m surgeon

chissà adv who knows; **~ quando arriverà** I wonder when he will arrive

chi'tar|ra f guitar. **~'rista** mf guitarist

chi'uder|e vt close; (con la chiave) lock; turn off (luce, acqua); (per sempre) close down (negozio ecc); (recingere) enclose ● vi shut, close. **~si** vr shut; (tempo:) cloud over; (ferita:) heal up.

chi'unque pron anyone, anybody ● rel pron whoever

chi'usa f enclosure; (di canale) lock;

(conclusione) close

chi'us|o pp di **chiudere** ● adj shut; (tempo) overcast; (persona) reserved. **~'sura** f closing; (sistema) lock; (allacciatura) fastener. **~sura lampo** zip, zipper Am

---

ci

● pron (personale) us; (riflessivo) ourselves; (reciproco) each other; (a ciò, di ciò ecc) about it; **non ci disturbare** don't disturb us; **aspettateci** wait for us; **ci ha detto tutto** he told us everything; **ce lo manderanno** they'll send it to us; **ci consideriamo...** we consider ourselves...; **ci laviamo le mani** we wash our hands; **ci odiamo** we hate each other; **non ci penso mai** I never think about it; **pensaci!** think about it!

● adv (qui) here; (lì) there; (moto per luogo) through it; **ci siamo** we are here; **ci siete?** are you there?; **ci siamo passati tutti** we all went through it; **c'è** there is; **ce ne sono molti** there are many; **ci vuole pazienza** it takes patience; **non ci vedo/sento** I can't see/hear

---

cia'bat|ta f slipper. **~'tare** vi shuffle

ciabat'tino m cobbler

ci'alda f wafer

cial'trone m scoundrel

ciam'bella f (Culin) ring-shaped cake; (salvagente) lifebelt; (gonfiabile) rubber ring

cianci'are vi gossip

cia'notico adj (colorito) puce

ci'ao int [1] (all'arrivo) hello!, hi!; (alla partenza) bye-bye!

ciar'la|re vi chat. **~'tano** m charlatan

cias'cuno adj each ● pron everyone,

everybody; (*distributivo*) each [one]; **per** ~ each

ci'bar|e *vt* feed. ~**ie** *fpl* provisions ~ **si** *vr* eat; ~**si di** live on

ciber'netico *adj* cybernetic

'cibo *m* food

ci'cala *f* cicada

cica'lino *m* buzzer

cica'tri|ce *f* scar. ~**z'zante** *m* ointment

cicatriz'zarsi *vr* heal [up]. **cicatriz-zazi'one** *f* healing

'cicca *f* cigarette end; (: *sigaretta*) fag; (: *gomma*) [chewing] gum

cic'chetto *m* (*bicchierino*) nip; (*rim-provero*) telling-off

'ciccia *f* fat, flab

cice'rone *m* guide

cicla'mino *m* cyclamen

ci'clis|mo *m* cycling. ~**ta** *mf* cyclist

'ciclo *m* cycle; (*di malattia*) course

ciclomo'tore *m* moped

ci'clone *m* cyclone

ci'cogna *f* stork

ci'coria *f* chicory

ci'eco, -a *adj* blind ● *m* blind man ● *f* blind woman

ci'elo *m* sky; (*Relig*) heaven; **santo** ~! good heavens!

'cifra *f* figure; (*somma*) sum; (*mono-gramma*) monogram; (*codice*) code

ci'fra|re *vt* embroider with a mono-gram; (*codificare*) code. ~**to** *adj* monogrammed; coded

'ciglio *m* (*bordo*) edge; (*pl f* **ciglia**: *delle palpebre*) eyelash

'cigno *m* swan

cigo'l|are *vi* squeak. ~**io** *m* squeak

'Cile *m* Chile

ci'lecca *f* far ~ miss

ci'leno, -a *adj* & *mf* Chilean

cili'egi|a *f* cherry. ~**o** *m* cherry [tree]

cilin'drata *f* cubic capacity; **mac-china di alta** ~ highpowered car

ci'lindro *m* cylinder; (*cappello*) top hat

'cima *f* top; (*fig: persona*) genius; **da** ~ **a fondo** from top to bottom

ci'melio *m* relic

cimen'tar|e *vt* put to the test. ~**si** *vr* (*provare*) try one's hand

'cimice *f* bug; (*puntina*) drawing pin, thumbtack *Am*

cimini'era *f* chimney; (*Naut*) funnel

cimi'tero *m* cemetery

ci'murro *m* distemper

'Cina *f* China

cin cin! *int* cheers!

cincischi'are *vi* fiddle

'cine *m* cinema

cine'asta *mf* film maker

'cinema *m inv* cinema. **cine'presa** *f* cine-camera

ci'nese *adj* & *mf* Chinese

cine'teca *f* film collection

'cingere *vt* (*circondare*) surround

'cinghia *f* strap; (*cintura*) belt

cinghi'ale *m* wild boar; **pelle di** ~ pigskin

cinguet't|are *vi* twitter. ~**io** *m* twittering

'cinico *adj* cynical

ci'niglia *f* (*tessuto*) chenille

ci'nismo *m* cynicism

ci'nofilo *adj* dog-loving

cin'quanta *adj* & *m* fifty, **cinquan-'tenne** *adj* & *mf* fifty-year-old. **cin-quan'tesimo** *adj* fiftieth. **cinquan-'tina** *f* una cinquantina di about fifty

'cinque *adj* & *m* five

cinquecen'tesco *adj* sixteenth-century

cinque'cento *adj* five hundred ● *m* **il C**~ the sixteenth century

cinque'mila *adj* & *m* five thousand

'cinta *f* (*di pantaloni*) belt; **muro di** ~ [boundary] wall. **cin'tare** *vt* enclose

'cintola *f* (*di pantaloni*) belt

cin'tura f belt. ~ **di salvataggio** lifebelt. ~ **di sicurezza** (Aeron), (Auto) seat-belt

cintu'rino m ~ **dell'orologio** watch-strap

ciò pron this; that; ~ **che** what; ~ **nondimeno** nevertheless

ci'occa f lock

ciocco'la|ta f chocolate; (bevanda) [hot] chocolate. ~**tino** m chocolate. ~**to** m chocolate. ~**to al latte/ fondente** milk/plain chocolate

cioè adv that is

ciondo'lare vi dangle. **ci'ondolo** m pendant

cionono'stante adv nonetheless

ci'otola f bowl

ci'ottolo m pebble

ci'polla f onion; (bulbo) bulb

ci'presso m cypress

'cipria f [face] powder

'Cipro m Cyprus. **cipri'ota** adj & mf Cypriot

'circa adv & prep about

'circo m circus

circo'la|re adj circular ● f circular; (di metropolitana) circle line ● vi circulate. ~**torio** m (Med) circulatory. ~**zi'one** f circulation; (traffico) traffic

'circolo m circle; (società) club

circon'ci|dere vt circumcise. ~**si'one** f circumcision

circon'dar|e vt surround. ~**io** m (amministrativo) administrative district. ~**si di** vr surround oneself with

circonfe'renza f circumference. ~ **dei fianchi** hip measurement

circonvallazi'one f ring road

circo'scritto adj limited

circoscrizi'one f area. ~ **eletto-rale** constituency

circo'spetto adj wary

circospezi'one f con ~ warily

circo'stante adj surrounding

circo'stanza f circumstance; (occa-*

sione) occasion

circu'ire vt (ingannare) trick

cir'cuito m circuit

ci·cumnavi'ga|re vt circumnavigate. ~**zi'one** f circumnavigation

ci'sterna f cistern; (serbatoio) tank

'cisti f inv cyst

ci'ta|re vt quote; (come esempio) cite; (Jur) summons. ~**zi'one** f quotation; (Jur) summons sy

citofo'nare vt buzz. **ci'tofono** m entry phone; (in ufficio, su aereo ecc) intercom

ci'trullo, -a mf [!] dimwit

città f inv town; (grande) city

citta'della f citadel

citta|di'nanza f citizenship; (popo-lazione) citizens pl. ~**'dino, -a** mf citizen; (abitante di città) city dweller

ciucci'are vt [!] suck. **ci'uccio** m [!] dummy

ci'uffo m tuft

ci'urma f (Naut) crew

ci'vet|ta f owl; (fig: donna) flirt; [auto] ~**ta** unmarked police car. ~**'tare** vi flirt. ~**te'ria** f coquettishness

'civico adj civic

ci'vil|e adj civil. ~**iz'zare** vt civilize. ~**iz'zato** adj (paese) civilized. ~**izza-zi'one** f civilization. ~**'mente** adv civilly

civiltà f inv civilization; (cortesia) civility

'clacson m inv (car) horn

clacso'nare vi hoot; honk

cla'mo|re m clamour; **fare** ~**re** cause a sensation. ~**rosa'mente** adv (sbagliare) sensationally. ~**roso** adj noisy; (sbaglio) sensational

clan m inv clan; fig clique

clandestinità f secrecy

clande'stino adj secret; **movi-mento** ~ underground movement; **passeggero** ~ stowaway

clari'netto m clarinet

'**classe** f class. ~ **turistica** tourist class

classi'cis|mo m classicism. ~**ta** mf classicist

'**classico** adj classical; (tipico) classic ● m classic

clas'sifi|ca f classification; Sport results pl. ~'**care** vt classify. ~'**carsi** vr be placed. ~**ca'tore** m (cartella) folder. ~**cazi'one** f classification

clas'sista mf class-conscious person

'**clausola** f clause

claustro'fo|bia f claustrophobia. ~'**fobico** adj claustrophobic

clau'sura f (Relig) enclosed order

clavi'cembalo m harpsichord

cla'vicola f collar-bone

cle'men|te adj merciful; (tempo) mild. ~**za** f mercy

cleri'cale adj clerical. '**clero** m clergy

clic m (Comput) click; **fare** ~ **su** click on; **fare doppio** ~ **su** double-click on

clic'care vi click (**su** on)

cli'en|te mf client; (di negozio) customer. ~**tela** f customers pl

'**clima** m climate. **cli'matico** adj climatic; **stazione climatica** health resort

'**clinica** f clinic. **clinico** adj clinical ● m clinician

clo'na|re vt clone. ~**zione** f cloning

'**cloro** m chlorine

clou adj inv **i momenti** ~ the highlights

coabi'ta|re vi live together. ~**zi'one** f cohabitation

coagu'la|re vt, ~**rsi** vr coagulate. ~**zi'one** f coagulation

coaliz|i'one f coalition. ~'**zarsi** vr unite

co'atto adj (Jur) compulsory

'**cobra** m inv cobra

coca'ina f cocaine. **cocai'nomane**

mf cocaine addict

cocci'nella f ladybird

'**coccio** m earthenware; (frammento) fragment

cocciu'taggine f stubbornness. ~'**uto** adj stubborn

'**cocco** m coconut palm; 🔲 love; **noce di** ~ coconut

cocco'drillo m crocodile

cocco'lare vt cuddle

co'cente adj (sole) burning

'**cocktail** m inv (ricevimento) cocktail party

co'comero m watermelon

co'cuzzolo m top; (di testa, cappello) crown

'**coda** f tail; (di abito) train; (fila) queue; **fare la** ~ queue [up], stand in line Am. ~ **di cavallo** (acconciatura) ponytail.

co'dardo, -a adj cowardly ● mf coward

'**codice** m code. ~ **di avviamento postale** postcode, zip code Am. ~ **a barre** bar-code. ~ **fiscale** tax code. ~ **della strada** highway code.

codifi'care vt codify

coe'ren|te adj consistent. ~**za** f consistency

coesi'one f cohesion

coe'taneo, -a adj & mf contemporary

cofa'netto m casket. '**cofano** m chest; (Auto) bonnet, hood Am

'**cogliere** vt pick; (sorprendere) catch; (afferrare) seize; (colpire) hit

co'gnato, -a m brother-in-law; sister-in-law

cogni'zione f knowledge

co'gnome m surname

'**coi** = CON + I

coinci'denza f coincidence; (di treno ecc) connection

coin'cidere vi coincide

coinqui'lino m flatmate

coin'volgere vt involve. **~gi'mento** m involvement. **~to** adj involved

'coito m coitus

col = **con** + **il**

colà adv there

cola'brodo m inv strainer; **ridotto a un ~brodo** [I] full of holes. **~'pasta** m inv colander

co'lare vt strain; (versare lentamente) drip • vi (gocciolare) drip; (perdere) leak; **~re a picco** (Naut) sink. **~ta** f (di metallo) casting; (di lava) flow

colazi'one f (del mattino) breakfast; (di mezzogiorno) lunch; **prima ~** breakfast; **far ~** have breakfast/lunch. **~ al sacco** packed lunch

co'lei pron f the one

co'lera m cholera

coleste'rolo m cholesterol

colf f abbr (collaboratrice familiare) home help

'colica f colic

co'lino m (tea) strainer

'colla f glue; (di farina) paste. **~ di pesce** gelatine

collabo'rare vi collaborate. **~'tore, ~'trice** mf collaborator. **~zi'one** f collaboration

col'lana f necklace; (serie) series

col'lant m inv tights pl

col'lare m collar

col'lasso m collapse

collau'dare vt test. **col'laudo** m test

'colle m hill

col'lega mf colleague

collega'mento m connection; (Mil) liaison; Radio link; **~ iperte'stuale** hypertext link. **colle'gare** vt connect. **~si** vr link up

collegi'ale mf boarder • adj (responsabilità, decisione) collective

col'legio m (convitto) boarding-school. **~ elettorale** constituency

'collera f anger; **andare in ~** get

angry. **col'lerico** adj irascible

col'letta f collection

collet'tività f inv community. **~'tivo** adj collective; (interesse) general; **biglietto ~'tivo** group ticket

col'letto m collar

collezio'nare vt collect. **~'one** f collection. **~o'nista** mf collector

colli'mare vi coincide

col'lina f hill. **~'noso** adj (terreno) hilly

col'lirio m eyewash

collisi'one f collision

'collo m neck; (pacco) package; **a ~ alto** high necked. **~ del piede** instep

colloca'mento m placing; (impiego) employment

collo'care vt place. **~rsi** vr take one's place. **~zi'one** f placing

colloqui'ale adj (termine) colloquial. **col'loquio** m conversation; (udienza ecc) interview; (esame) oral [exam]

collusi'one f collusion

colluttazi'one f scuffle

col'mare vt fill [to the brim]; bridge (divario); **~ qeno di gentilezze** overwhelm sb with kindness. **'colmo** adj full • m top; fig height; **al colmo della disperazione** in the depths of despair; **questo è il colmo!** (con indignazione) this is the last straw!; (con stupore) I don't believe it!

co'lomba f dove. **~o** m pigeon

co'lonia f colony; **~a [estiva]** (per bambini) holiday camp. **~'ale** adj colonial

co'lonia² f **[acqua di] ~** [eau de] Cologne

co'lonico adj (terreno, casa) farm

coloniz'zare vt colonize. **~'tore, ~'trice** mf colonizer

co'lonna f column. **~ sonora** sound-track. **~ vertebrale** spine.

∼'**nato** m colonnade

colon'nello m colonel

co'lono m tenant farmer

colo'rante m colouring

colo'rare vt colour; colour in (disegno)

co'lore m colour; **a colori** in colour; **di** ∼ coloured. **colo'rito** adj coloured; (viso) rosy; (racconto) colourful ● m complexion

co'loro pron pl the ones

colos'sale adj colossal. **co'losso** m colossus

'**colpa** f fault; (biasimo) blame; (colpevolezza) guilt; (peccato) sin; **dare la** ∼ a blame; **essere in** ∼ be at fault; **per** ∼ **di** because of. **col'pevole** adj guilty ● mf culprit

col'pire vt hit, strike

'**colpo** m blow; (di arma da fuoco) shot; (urto) knock; (emozione) shock; (Med, Sport) stroke; (furto) raid; **di** ∼ suddenly; **far** ∼ make a strong impression; **far venire un** ∼ **a qcno** fig give sb a fright; **perdere colpi** (motore:) keep missing; **a** ∼ **d'occhio** at a glance; **a** ∼ **sicuro** for certain. ∼ **d'aria** chill. ∼ **di sole** sunstroke; **colpi di sole** (su capelli) highlights. ∼ **di stato** coup [d'état]. ∼ **di telefono** ring; **dare un** ∼ **di telefono a qn** give sb a ring. ∼ **di testa** [sudden] impulse. ∼ **di vento** gust of wind

col'poso adj omicidio ∼ manslaughter

coltel'lata f stab. **col'tello** m knife

colti'va|re vt cultivate. ∼'**tore**, ∼'**trice** mf farmer. ∼**zi'one** f farming; (di piante) growing

'**colto** pp di **cogliere** ● adj cultured

'**coltre** f blanket

col'tura f cultivation

co'lui pron inv m the one

'**coma** m coma; **in** ∼ in a coma

comanda'mento m commandment

coman'dante m commander; (Aeron, Naut) captain

coman'dare vt command; (Mech) control ● vi be in charge. **co'mando** m command; (di macchina) control

co'mare f (madrina) godmother

combaci'are vi fit together; (testimonianze:) concur

combat'tente adj fighting ● m combatant. **ex** ∼ ex-serviceman

com'bat|tere vt/i fight. ∼ti-'**mento** m fight; (Mil) battle; **fuori** ∼**timento** (pugilato) knocked out. ∼'**tuto** adj (gara) hard fought

combi'na|re vt/i arrange; (mettere insieme) combine; (:⃞: fare) do; **cosa stai** ∼**ndo?** what are you doing? ∼**rsi** vr combine; (mettersi d'accordo) come to an agreement. ∼**zi'one** f combination; (caso) coincidence; **per** ∼**zione** by chance

com'briccola f gang

combu'sti|bile adj combustible ● m fuel. ∼'**one** f combustion

com'butta f gang; **in** ∼ in league

<table>
<tr><td>

'**come**

● adv like; (in qualità di) as; (interrogativo, esclamativo) how; **questo vestito è il tuo** this dress is like yours; ∼ **stai?** how are you?; ∼ **va?** how are things?; ∼ **mai?** how come?; ∼**?** what?; **non sa** ∼ **fare** he doesn't know what to do; ∼ **sta bene!** how well he looks!; ∼ **no!** that will be right!; ∼ **tu sai** as you know; **fa** ∼ **vuoi** do as you like; ∼ **se** as if

● conj (non appena) as soon as
</td></tr>
</table>

co'meta f comet

'**comico, -a** adj comic ● m funny side ● mf (attore) comedian ● f (a torte in faccia) slapstick sketch

co'mignolo m chimney-pot

cominci'are vt/i begin, start; **a ~ da oggi** from today.

comi'tato m committee

comi'tiva f party, group

co'mizio m meeting

com'manda m mil commando

com'medi|a f comedy; (opera teatrale) play; fig sham. **~a musicale** musical. **~ante** mf comedian; fig pej phoney. **~'ografo**, **-a** mf playwright

commemo'ra|re vt commemorate. **~zi'one** f commemoration

commen'sale mf fellow diner

commen't|are vt comment on; (annotare) annotate. **~ario** m commentary. **~a'tore**, **~a'trice** mf commentator. **~mento** m comment

commerci'ale adj commercial; (relazioni, trattative) trade; (attività) business. **centro ~e** shopping centre. **~lista** mf business consultant; (contabile) accountant. **~liz'zare** vt market. **~lizzazi'one** f marketing

commerci'ante mf trader; (negoziante) shopkeeper. **~ all'ingrosso** wholesaler

commerci'are vi **~ in** deal in

com'mercio m commerce; (internazionale) trade; (affari) business; **in ~** (prodotto) on sale. **~ all'ingrosso** wholesale trade. **~ al minuto** retail trade

com'messo, **-a** pp di commettere • mf shop assistant. **~ viaggiatore** commercial traveller • f (ordine) order

commes'tibile adj edible. **commestibili** mpl groceries

com'mettere vt commit; make (sbaglio)

commi'ato m leave; **prendere ~ da** take leave of

commise'rar|e vt commiserate with. **~si** vr feel sorry for oneself

commissari'ato m (di polizia) police station

commis's|ario m [police] superin-

tendent; (membro di commissione) commissioner; Sport steward; (Comm) commission agent. **~ario d'esame** examiner. **~i'one** f (incarico) errand; (comitato ecc) commission; (Comm: di merce) order; **~ioni** pl (acquisti) **fare ~ioni** go shopping. **~ione d'esame** board of examiners. **C~ione Europea** European Commission

commit'tente mf purchaser

com'mo|sso pp di commuovere • adj moved. **~'vente** adj moving

commozi'one f emotion. **~ cerebrale** concussion

commu'over|e vt touch, move. **~si** vr be touched

commu'tare vt change; (Jur) commute

comò m inv chest of drawers

comoda'mente adv comfortably

como'dino m bedside table

comodità f inv comfort; (convenienza) convenience

'comodo adj comfortable; (conveniente) convenient; (spazioso) roomy; (facile) easy; **stia ~!** don't get up!; **far ~** be useful • m comfort; **fare il proprio ~** do as one pleases

compae'sano, **-a** mf fellow countryman

com'pagine f (squadra) team

compa'gnia f company; (gruppo) party; **tenere ~ a qcno** keep sb company; **essere di ~** be sociable. **~ aerea** airline

com'pagno, **-a** mf companion; (Comm, Sport, in coppia) partner; (Pol) comrade. **~ di scuola** schoolmate

compa'rabile adj comparable

compa'ra|re vt compare. **~'tivo** adj & m comparative. **~zi'one** f comparison

com'pare m (padrino) godfather; (testimone di matrimonio) witness

compa'rire vi appear; (spiccare) stand out; **~ in giudizio** appear in court

com'parso, -a pp di comparire ●f appearance; *Cinema* extra

compartecipazi'one f sharing; *(quota)* share

comparti'mento m compartment; *(amministrativo)* department

compas'sato adj calm and collected

compassi'o|ne f compassion; **aver ~ne per** feel pity for; **far ~ne** arouse pity. **~'nevole** adj compassionate

com'passo m [pair of] compasses pl

compa'tibil|e adj *(conciliabile)* compatible; *(scusabile)* excusable. **~ità** f compatibility. **~'mente** adv **~mente con i miei impegni** if my commitments allow

compa'tire vt pity; *(scusare)* make allowances for

compat'tezza f *(di materia)* compactness. **com'patto** adj compact; *(denso)* dense; *(solido)* solid; *fig* united

compene'trare vt pervade

compen'sar|e vt compensate; *(supplire)* make up for. **~si** vr balance each other out

compen'sato m *(legno)* plywood

compensazi'one f compensation

com'penso m compensation; *(retribuzione)* remuneration; **in ~** *(in cambio)* in return; *(d'altra parte)* on the other hand; *(invece)* instead

'comper|a f purchase; **far ~e** do some shopping

compe'rare vt buy

compe'ten|te adj competent. **~za** f competence; *(responsabilità)* responsibility

com'petere vi compete; **~ a** *(compito)* be the responsibility of

competi|tività f competitiveness. **~'tivo** adj *(prezzo, carattere)* competitive. **~'tore, ~'trice** mf competitor. **~zi'one** f competition

compia'cen|te adj obliging. **~za** f obligingness

compia'cer|e vt/i please. **~ersi** *(congratularsi)* congratulate. **~ersi di** *(degnarsi)* condescend. **~i'mento** m satisfaction; *pej* smugness. **~i'uto** adj satisfied; *(aria, sorriso)* smug

compi'an|gere vt pity; *(per lutto ecc)* sympathize with. **~to** adj lamented ●m grief

'compier|e vt *(concludere)* complete; commit *(delitto)*; **~e gli anni** have one's birthday. **~si** vr end; *(avverarsi)* come true

compi'la|re vt compile; fill in *(modulo)*. **~zi'one** f compilation

compi'mento m **portare a ~ qcsa** conclude sth

com'pire vt = COMPIERE

compi'tare vt spell

com'pito¹ adj polite

'compito² m task; *(Sch)* homework

compi'ut|o adj **avere 30 anni ~i** be over 30

comple'anno m birthday

complemen'tare adj complementary; *(secondario)* subsidiary

comple'mento m complement; *(Mil)* draft. **~ oggetto** direct object

comples|sità f complexity. **~siva'mente** adv on the whole. **~'sivo** adj comprehensive; *(totale)* total. **com'plesso** adj complex; *(difficile)* complicated ●m complex; *(di cantanti ecc)* group; *(di costruzione, fattori)* combination; **in ~so** on the whole

completa'mente adv completely

comple'tare vt complete

com'pleto adj complete; *(pieno)* full [up]; **essere al ~** (teatro): be sold out; **la famiglia al ~** the whole family ●m *(vestito)* suit; *(insieme di cose)* set

compli'ca|re vt complicate. **~rsi** vr become complicated. **~to** adj complicated. **~zi'one** f complication; **salvo ~zioni** all being well '**complic|e** *mf* accomplice ● *adj* (sguardo) knowing. ~**ità** *f* complicity

complimen'tar|e *vt* compliment. ~**si** *vr* ~**si con** congratulate.

compli'menti *mpl* (ossequi) regards; (congratulazioni) congratulations; **far ~** stand on ceremony

compli'mento *m* compliment

complot'tare *vi* plot

compo'nente *adj & m* component ● *m* member

compo'nibile *adj* (cucina) fitted; (mobili) modular

componi'mento *m* composition; (letterario) work

com'por|re *vt* compose; (ordinare) put in order; (Typ) set. ~**si** *vr* ~**si di** be made up of

comporta'mento *m* behaviour

compor'tar|e *vt* involve; (consentire) allow. ~**si** *vr* behave

composi'|tore, -'trice *mf* composer; (Typ) compositor. ~**zi'one** *f* composition

com'posta *f* stewed fruit; (concime) compost

compo'stezza *f* composure

com'posto *pp di* **comporre** ● *adj* composed; (costituito) comprising; **stai ~!** sit properly! ● *m* (Chem) compound

com'pra|re *vt* buy. ~**tore**, ~**trice** *mf* buyer

compra'vendita *f* buying and selling

compren|dere *vt* understand; (includere) comprise. ~**'sibile** *adj* understandable. ~**sibil'mente** *adv* understandably. ~**si'one** *f* understanding. ~**'sivo** *adj* understanding; (che include) inclusive. **com'preso** *pp di* **comprendere** ● *adj* included; **tutto compreso** all-in

com'pressa *f* compress; (pastiglia) tablet

compressi'one *f* compression. **com'presso** *pp di* **comprimere** ● *adj* compressed

com'primere *vt* press; (reprimere) repress

compro'me|sso *pp di* **compromettere** ● *m* compromise. ~**l'tente** *adj* compromising. ~**ttere** *vt* compromise

comproprietà *f* multiple ownership

compro'vare *vt* prove

compu'tare *vt* calculate

com'puter *m inv* computer. ~**iz'zare** *vt* computerize. ~**iz'zato** *adj* computerized

computiste'ria *f* book-keeping. '**computo** *m* calculation

comu'nale *adj* municipal

co'mune *adj* common; (condiviso) mutual; (ordinario) ordinary ● *m* borough; (amministrativo) commune; **fuori del ~** extraordinary. ~**'mente** *adv* commonly

comuni'ca|re *vt* communicate; pass on (malattia); (Relig) administer (communion (to). ~**rsi** *vr* receive Communion. ~**'tiva** *f* communicativeness. ~**'tivo** *adj* communicative. ~**to** *m* communiqué. ~**to stampa** press release. ~**zi'one** *f* communication; (Teleph) [phone] call; **avere la ~zione** get through; **dare la ~zione a qcno** put sb through

comuni'one *f* communion; (Relig) [Holy] Communion

comu'nis|mo *m* communism. ~**ta** *adj & mf* communist

comunità *f inv* community. **C~ [Economica] Europea** European [Economic] Community

co'munque *conj* however ● *adv* anyhow

con *prep* with; (mezzo) by; ~ **facilità** easily; ~ **mia grande gioia** to my great delight; **è gentile ~ tutti** he is kind to everyone; **col treno** by train; **~ questo tempo** in this weather

co'nato m ~ **di vomito** retching

'conca f basin; (valle) dell

concate'na|re vt link together. **~zi'one** f connection

'concavo adj concave

con'ceder|e vt grant; award (premio); (ammettere) admit. **~si** vr allow oneself (pausa)

concentra'mento m concentration

concen'tra|re vt, **~rsi** vr concentrate. **~to** adj concentrated ● m **~to di pomodoro** tomato pureé. **~zi'one** f concentration

concepi'mento m conception

conce'pire vt conceive (bambino); (capire) understand; (figurarsi) conceive of; devise (piano ecc)

con'cernere vt concern

concer'tar|e vt (Mus) harmonize; (organizzare) arrange. **~si** vr agree

concer'tista mf concert performer. **con'certo** m concert; (composizione) concerto

concessio'nario m agent

concessi'one f concession

con'cesso pp di **concedere**

con'cetto m concept; (opinione) opinion

concezi'one f conception; (idea) concept

con'chiglia f [sea] shell

'concia f tanning; (di tabacco) curing

conci'a|re vt tan; cure (tabacco); **~re qcno per le feste** give sb a good hiding. **~rsi** vr (sporcarsi) get dirty; (vestirsi male) dress badly. **~to** adj (pelle, cuoio) tanned

concili'abile adj compatible

concili'a|re vt reconcile; settle (contravvenzione); (favorire) induce. **~rsi** vr go together; (mettersi d'accordo) become reconciled. **~zi'one** f

reconciliation; (Jur) settlement

con'cilio m (Relig) council; (riunione) assembly

conci'mare vt feed (pianta). **con'cime** m fertilizer; (chimico) fertilizer

concisi'one f conciseness. **con'ciso** adj concise

conci'tato adj excited

concitta'dino, -a mf fellow citizen

con'clu|dere vt conclude; (finire con successo) achieve. **~dersi** vr come to an end. **~si'one** f conclusion; **in ~sione** (insomma) in short. **~'sivo** adj conclusive. **~so** pp di **concludere**

concomi'tanza f (di circostanze, fatti) combination

concor'da|nza f agreement. **~re** vt agree; (Gram) make agree. **~to** m agreement; (Comm, Jur) arrangement

con'corde adj in agreement; (unanime) unanimous

concor'ren|te adj concurrent; (rivale) competing ● mf (Comm), Sport competitor; (candidato) candidate. **~za** f competition. **~zi'ale** adj competitive

con'cor|rere vi (contribuire) concur; (andare insieme) go together; (competere) compete. **~so** pp di **concorrere** ● m competition; **fuori ~so** not in the official competition. **~so di bellezza** beauty contest

concreta'mente adv specifically

concre|'tare vt (concludere) achieve. **~tiz'zare** vt put into concrete form (idea, progetto)

con'creto adj concrete; **in ~** in concrete terms

concussi'one f extortion

con'danna f sentence; **pronunziare una ~** pass a sentence. **condan'nare** vt condemn; (Jur) sentence. **condan'nato, -a** mf convict

conden'sa|re vt, **~rsi** vr condense. **~zi'one** f condensation

condi'mento m seasoning, (salsa) dressing. **con'dire** vt flavour; dress (insalata)

condiscen'den|te adj indulgent; pej condescending. **~za** f indulgence; pej condescension

condi'videre vt share

condizio'na|le adj & m conditional ● f (Jur) suspended sentence

condizio'na|re vt condition. **~to** adj conditional. **~tore** m air conditioner

condizi'one f condition; a ~ che on condition that

condogli'anze fpl condolences; fare le ~ a offer condolences to

condominI'ale adj (spese) common. **condo'minio** m joint ownership; (edificio) condominium

condo'nare vt remit. **con'dono** m remission

con'dotta f conduct, (circonscrizione di medico) district; (di gara ecc) management; (tubazione) piping

con'dotto pp di condurre ● adj medico ~ district doctor ● m pipe; (Anat) duct

condu'cente m driver

con'dulrre vt lead; drive (veicoli); (accompagnare) take; conduct (gas, elettricità ecc); (gestire) run. **~rsi** vr behave. **~t'tore, ~t'trice** mf (TV) presenter; (di veicolo) driver ● m (Electr) conductor. **~t'tura** f duct

confabu'lare vi have a confab

confa'cente adj suitable. **con'farsi** vr confarsi a suit

confederazi'one f confederation

confe'renz|a f (discorso) lecture; (congresso) conference. **~a stampa** news conference. **~i'ere, -a** mf lecturer

confe'rire vt (donare) give ● vi confer

con'ferma f confirmation. **confer'mare** vt confirm

confes's|are vt, **~arsi** vr confess. **~io'nale** adj & m confessional. **~i'one** f confession. **~ore** m confessor

con'fetto m sugared almond

confet'tura f jam

confezio'na|re vt manufacture; make (abiti); package (merci). **~to** adj (vestiti) off-the-peg; (gelato) wrapped

confezi'one f manufacture; (di abiti) tailoring; (di pacchi) packaging; **confezioni** pl clothes. **~ regalo** gift pack

confic'care vt thrust. **~si** vr run into

confi'd|are vi ~are in trust ● vt confide. **~arsi** vr ~arsi con confide in. **~ente** adj confident ● mf confidant

confi'denz|a f confidence; (familiarità) familiarity; **prendersi delle ~e** take liberties. **~i'ale** adj confidential; (rapporto, tono) familiar

configu'ra|re vt (Comput) configure. **~zi'one** f configuration

confi'nante adj neighbouring

confi'na|re vi (relegare) confine ● vi ~re con border on. **~rsi** vr with-draw. **~to** adj confined

con'fin|e m border; (tra terreni) boundary. **~o** m political exile

con'fisc|a f (di proprietà) forfeiture. **~are** vt confiscate

con'flitt|o m conflict. **~u'ale** adj adversarial

conflu'enza f confluence; (di strade) junction

conflu'ire vi (fiumi:) flow together; (strade:) meet

con'fonder|e vt confuse; (turbare) confound; (imbarazzare) embarrass. **~si** vr (mescolarsi) mingle; (turbarsi) become confused; (sbagliarsi) be mistaken

confor'ma|re vt adapt. **~rsi** vr conform. **~zi'one** f conformity (a with); (del terreno) composition

con'forme adj according. ~'**mente** adv accordingly

confor'mi|smo m conformity. ~**sta** mf conformist. ~**tà** f (a norma) conformity

confor'tante adj comforting

confor't|are vt comfort. ~**evole** adj (comodo) comfortable. **con'forto** m comfort

confron'tare vt compare

con'fronto m comparison; **in** ~ **a** by comparison with; **nei tuoi confronti** towards you; **senza** ~ far and away

confusi|o'nario adj (persona) muddle-headed. ~'**one** f confusion; (baccano) racket; (disordine) mess; (imbarazzo) embarrassment. **con'fuso** pp di **confondere** ● adj confused; (indistinto) indistinct; (imbarazzato) embarrassed

conge'dar|e vt dismiss; (Mil) discharge. ~**si** vr take one's leave

con'gedo m leave; **essere in** ~ be on leave. ~ **malattia** sick leave. ~ **maternità** maternity leave

conge'gnare vt devise; (mettere insieme) assemble. **con'gegno** m device

congela'mento m freezing; (Med) frost-bite

conge'la|re vt freeze. ~**to** adj (cibo) deep-frozen. ~'**tore** m freezer

congeni'ale adj congenial

con'genito adj congenital

congestio'na|re vt congest. ~**to** adj (traffico) congested. **conge'stione** f congestion

conget'tura f conjecture

congi'unger|e vt join; combine (sforzi). ~**si** vr join

congiunti'vite f conjunctivitis

congiun'tivo m subjunctive

congi'unto pp di **congiungere** ● adj joined ● m relative

congiun'tu|ra f joint; (circostanza)

juncture; (situazione) situation. ~'**rale** adj economic

congiunzi'one f conjunction

congi'u|ra f conspiracy. ~'**rare** vi conspire

conglome'rato m conglomerate; fig conglomeration; (da costruzione) concrete

congratu'lar|si vr ~**si con qcno per** congratulate sb on. ~**zi'oni** fpl congratulations

con'grega f band

congre'ga|re vt, ~**rsi** vr congregate. ~**zi'one** f congregation

con'gresso m congress

'congruo adj proper; (giusto) fair

conguagli'are vt balance. **con-gu'aglio** m balance

coni'are vt coin

'conico adj conical

co'nifera f conifer

co'niglio m rabbit

coniu'gale adj marital; (vita) married

coniu'ga|re vt conjugate. ~**rsi** vr get married. ~**zi'one** f conjugation

'coniuge mf spouse

connessi'one f connection. **con-'nesso** pp di **connettere**

con'netter|e vt connect ● vi think rationally. ~**rsi** vr go online

conni'vente adj conniving

conno'ta|re vt connote. ~**to** m distinguishing feature; ~**ti** pl description

con'nubio m fig union

'cono m cone

cono'scen|te mf acquaintance. ~**za** f knowledge; (persona) acquaintance; (sensi) consciousness; **perdere** ~**za** lose consciousness; **riprendere** ~**za** regain consciousness

co'nosc|ere vt know; (essere a conoscenza di) be acquainted with; (fare la conoscenza di) meet. ~**i'tore**, ~**i'trice** mf connoisseur. ~**i'uto** pp di **cono-**

scere ● *adj* well known

con'quist|a *f* conquest. conqui-
'stare *vt* conquer; *fig* win

consa'cra|re *vt* consecrate; ordain
(*sacerdote*); (*dedicare*) dedicate. ∼rsi
vr devote oneself

consangu'ineo, -a *mf*
bloodrelation

consa'pevo|le *adj* conscious.
∼'lezza *f* consciousness. ∼l'mente
adv consciously

'conscio *adj* conscious

consecu'tivo *adj* consecutive; (*seguente*) next

con'segna *f* delivery; (*merce*) consignment; (*custodia*) care; (*di prigioniero*)
handover; (*Mil: ordine*) orders *pl*; (*Mil:
punizione*) confinement; **pagamento
alla ∼** cash on delivery

conse'gnare *vt* deliver; (*affidare*)
give in charge; (*Mil*) confine to
barracks

consegu'en|te *adj* consequent,
∼za *f* consequence, **di ∼za** (*perciò*)
consequently

consegui'mento *m* achievement

consegu'ire *vt* achieve ● *vi* follow

con'senso *m* consent

consensu'ale *adj* consensus-based

consen'tire *vi* consent ● *vt* allow

con'serva *f* preserve; (*di frutta*) jam;
(*di agrumi*) marmalade. ∼ **di pomodoro** tomato sauce

conser'var|e *vt* preserve; (*mante-
nere*) keep. ∼si *vr* keep; ∼si in salute keep well

conserva'tore, -'trice *mf* (*Pol*)
conservative

conserva'torio *m* conservatory

conservazi'one *f* preservation; a
lunga ∼ long-life

conside'ra|re *vt* consider; (*stimare*)
regard. ∼to *adj* (*stimato*) esteemed.
∼zi'one *f* consideration; (*osservazione,
riflessione*) remark

conside'revole *adj* considerable

consigli'abile *adj* advisable

consigli'are *vt* advise; (*raccomandare*) recommend. ∼'arsi ∼ arsi
con qcno ask sb's advice. ∼'ere, -a
mf adviser; (*membro di consiglio*) councillor

con'siglio *m* advice; (*ente*) council.
∼ d'amministrazione board of directors. C∼ dei Ministri Cabinet

consi'sten|te *adj* substantial;
(*spesso*) thick; (*fig: argomento*) valid

con'sistere *vi* ∼ in consist of

consoci'ata *f* associate company

conso'lar|e¹ *vt* console; (*rallegrare*)
cheer. ∼si *vr* console oneself

conso'lare² *adj* consular. ∼to *m*
consulate

consolazi'one *f* consolation;
(*gioia*) joy

'console *m* consul

consoli'dar|e *vt*, ∼si *vr* con-
solidate

conso'nante *f* consonant

'consono *adj* consistent

con'sorte *mf* consort

con'sorzio *m* consortium

con'stare *vi* ∼ di consist of; (*risultare*) appear, **a quanto mi consta** as
far as I know; **mi consta che** it ap-
pears that

consta'ta|re *vt* ascertain. ∼zi'one *f*
of observation

consu'eto *adj* & *m* usual. ∼tudi-
'nario *adj* (*diritto*) common; (*persona*) set in one's ways. ∼'tudine *f*
habit; (*usanza*) custom

consu'len|te *mf* consultant. ∼za *f*
consultancy

consul'tar|e *vt* consult. ∼rsi con
consult with. ∼zi'one *f* consultation

consul'tivo *adj* consultative

∼'orio *m* clinic

consu'ma|re *vt* (*usare*) consume;
wear out (*abito, scarpe*); consummate (*matrimonio*); commit (*delitto*). ∼rsi *vr* consume; (*abito,*

scarpe:) wear out; (*struggersi*) pine

consu'mato adj (politico) seasoned; (scarpe, tappeto) worn

consuma'tore, -'trice mf consumer. **∼zi'one** f (bibita) drink; (*spuntino*) snack

consu'mismo m consumerism. **∼ta** mf consumerist

con'sumo m consumption; (*di abito, scarpe*) wear; (*uso*) use; **generi di ∼** consumer goods or items. **∼ [di carburante]** [fuel] consumption

consun'tivo m [bilancio] **∼** final statement

conta'balle mf 🔢 storyteller

con'tabil|e adj book-keeping ● mf accountant. **∼ità** f accounting; **tenere la ∼ità** keep the accounts

contachilo'metri m inv mileometer, odometer Am

conta'dino, -a mf farm-worker; (*medievale*) peasant

contagi'are vt infect. **con'tagio** m infection. **∼'oso** adj infectious

conta'gocce m inv dropper

contami'na|re vt contaminate. **∼zi'one** f contamination

con'tante m cash; **pagare in contanti** pay cash

con'tare vt/i count; (tenere conto di) take into account; (proporsi) intend

conta'scatti m inv (Teleph) time-unit counter

conta'tore m meter

contat'tare vt contact. **con'tatto** m contact

'conte m count

conteggi'are vt put on the bill ● vi calculate. **con'teggio** m calculation. **conteggio alla rovescia** countdown

con'te|gno m behaviour; (*atteggiamento*) attitude. **∼'gnoso** adj dignified

contem'pla|re vt contemplate; (*fissare*) gaze at. **∼zi'one** f contemplation

con'tempo m **nel ∼** in the meantime

contempo|ranea'mente adv at once. **∼raneo, -a** adj & mf contemporary

conten'dente mf competitor. **con'tendere** vi compete; (*litigare*) quarrel ● vt contend

conte'n|ere vt contain; (*reprimere*) repress. **∼ersi** vr contain oneself. **∼i'tore** m container

conten'tarsi vr **∼ di** be content with

conten'tezza f joy

conten'tino m placebo

con'tento adj glad; (*soddisfatto*) contented

conte'nuto m contents pl; (*soggetto*) content

contenzi'oso m legal department

con'tes|a f disagreement; Sport contest. **∼o** pp di **contendere** ● adj contested

con'tessa f countess

conte'sta|re vt contest; (Jur) notify. **∼tario** adj anti-establishment. **∼tore, -'trice** mf protester. **∼zi'one** f (disputa) dispute

con'testo m context

con'tiguo adj adjacent

continen'tale adj continental. **conti'nente** m continent

conti'nenza f continence

contin'gen|te m contingent; (quota) quota. **∼za** f contingency

continua'mente adv (senza interruzione) continuously; (frequentemente) continually

continu'are vt/i continue; (riprendere) resume. **∼a'tivo** adj permanent. **∼azi'one** f continuation. **∼ità** f continuity

con'tinu|o adj continuous; (molto frequente) continual. **corrente ∼a** direct current; **di ∼o** continually

'conto m calculation; (Comm) account; (di ristorante ecc) bill; (stima) consideration; **a conti fatti** all things considered; **far ~ di** (supporre) suppose; (proporsi) intend; **far ~ su** rely on; **in fin dei conti** when all is said and done; **per ~ di** on behalf of; **per ~ mio** (a mio parere) in my opinion; (da solo) on my own; **starsene per ~ proprio** be on one's own; **rendersi ~ di qcsa** realize sth; **sul ~ di qcno** (voci, informazioni) about sb; **tener ~ di qcsa** take sth into account; **tenere da ~ qcsa** look after sth. **~ corrente** current account, checking account Am. **~ alla rovescia** countdown

con'torcere vt twist. **~si** vr twist about

contor'nare vt surround

con'torno m contour; (Culin) vegetables pl

contorsi'one f contortion. **con'torto** pp di **contorcere** ● adj twisted

contrabban'dare vt smuggle. **contrabbandi'ere, -a** mf smuggler. **contrab'bando** m contraband

contrab'basso m double bass

contraccambi'are vt return. **contrac'cambio** m return

contracce'tivo m contraceptive. **~zi'one** f contraception

contrac'colpo m rebound; (di arma da fuoco) recoil; fig repercussion

con'trada f (rione) district

contrad'detto pp di **contraddire**

contrad'dire vt contradict. **~t'torio** adj contradictory. **~zi'one** f contradiction

contraddistin'guere vt differentiate. **~to** adj distinct

contra'ente mf contracting party

contra'ereo adj anti-aircraft

contraf'fare vt disguise; (imitare) imitate; (falsificare) forge. **~tto** adj forged. **~zi'one** f disguising; (imitazione) imitation; (falsificazione) forgery

con'tralto m countertenor ● f

contralto

contrap'peso m counterbalance

contrap'por|re vt counter; (confrontare) compare. **~si** vr contrast; **~si a** be opposed to

contraria'mente adv contrary (a to)

contrari'are vt oppose; (infastidire) annoy. **~arsi** vr get annoyed. **~età** f inv adversity; (ostacolo) set-back

con'trario adj contrary; (direzione) opposite; (sfavorevole) unfavourable ● m contrary; **al ~** on the contrary

con'trarre vt contract

contras'se|gnare vt mark. **~segno** m mark; [in] **~segno** (spedizione) cash on delivery

contra'stare vt oppose; (contestare) contest ● vi clash. **con'trasto** m contrast; (litigio) dispute

contrattac'care vt counterattack. **contrat'tacco** m counter-attack

contrat'ta|re vt/i negotiate; (mercanteggiare) bargain. **~zi'one** f (salariale) bargaining

contrat'tempo m hitch

con'tratt|o pp di **contrarre** ● m contract. **~o a termine** fixed term contract. **~u'ale** adj contractual

contravve'ni|re vi contravene. **~zi'one** f contravention; (multa) fine

contrazi'one f contraction; (di prezzi) reduction

contribu'ente mf contributor; (del fisco) taxpayer

contribu'ire vi contribute. **contri'buto** m contribution

'contro prep against; **~ di me** against me ● m i pro e i **~** the pros and cons

contro'battere vt counter

controbilanci'are vt counterbalance

controcor'rente adj nonconformist ● adv upriver; fig upstream

controffen'siva f counteroffensive

controfi'gura f stand-in

controindicazi'one f (Med) contraindication

control'la|re vt control; (verificare) check; (collaudare) test. **~rsi** vr have self-control. **~to** adj controlled

con'trol|lo m control; (verifica) check; (Med) check-up. **~lo delle nascite** birth control. **~lore** m controller; (sui treni ecc) [ticket] inspector. **~lore di volo** air-traffic controller

contro'mano adv in the wrong direction

contromi'sura f countermeasure

contropi'ede m prendere in **~** catch off guard

controprodu'cente adj self-defeating

con'trordin|e m counter order; salvo **~i** unless I/you hear to the contrary

contro'senso m contradiction in terms

controspio'naggio m counter-espionage

contro'vento adv against the wind

contro'vers|ia f controversy; (Jur) dispute. **~o** adj controversial

contro'voglia adv unwillingly

contu'macia f default; in **~** in one's absence

contun'dente adj (corpo, arma) blunt

contur'ba|nte adj perturbing

contusi'one f bruise

convale'scen|te adj convalescent

con'vali|da f validation. **~'dare** vt confirm; validate (atto, biglietto)

con'vegno m meeting; (congresso) congress

conve'nevol|e adj suitable; **~i** pl pleasantries

conveni'en|te adj convenient; (prezzo) attractive; (vantaggioso) ad-

vantageous. **~za** f convenience; (interesse) advantage; (di prezzo) attractiveness

conve'nire vi (riunirsi) gather; (concordare) agree; (ammettere) admit; (essere opportuno) be convenient ● vt agree on; **ci conviene andare** it is better to go; **non mi conviene stancarmi** I'd better not tire myself out

con'vento m (di suore) convent; (di frati) monastery

conve'nuto adj fixed

convenzio'nale adj conventional. **~'one** f convention

conver'gen|te adj converging. **~za** f fig confluence

con'vergere vi converge

conver'sa|re vi converse. **~zi'one** f conversation

conversi'one f conversion

con'verso pp di convergere

conver'tibile f (Auto) convertible

conver'ti|re vt convert. **~rsi** vr be converted. **~to, -a** mf convert

con'vesso adj convex

convin'cente adj convincing

con'vin|cere vt convince. **~to** adj convinced. **~zi'one** f conviction

con'vitto m boarding school

convi'ven|te m common-law husband ● f common-law wife. **~za** f cohabitation. **con'vivere** vi live together

convivi'ale adj convivial

convo'ca|re vt convene. **~zi'one** f convening

convogli'are vt convey; convoy (navi) **con'voglio** m convoy; (ferroviario) train

convulsi'one f convulsion. **con'vulso** adj convulsive; (febbrile) feverish

coope'ra|re vi co-operate. **~'tiva** f co-operative. **~zi'one** f co-operation

coordina'mento m co-ordination

coordi'na|re vt co-ordinate. **∼ta** f (Math) coordinate. **∼te bancarie** bank (account) details. **∼zi'one** f co-ordination

co'perchio m lid; (copertura) cover

co'perta f blanket; (copertura) cover; (Naut) deck

coper'tina f cover; (di libro) dust-jacket

co'perto pp di **coprire** ● adj covered; (cielo) overcast ● m (a tavola) place; (prezzo del coperto) cover charge; **al ∼** under cover

coper'tone m tarpaulin; (gomma) tyre

coper'tura f covering; (Comm, Fin) cover

'copia f copy; **bella/brutta ∼** fair/rough copy; **carbon copy. ∼ su carta** hardcopy. **copi'are** vt copy

copi'one m script

copi'oso adj plentiful

'coppa f (calice) goblet; (per gelato ecc) dish; Sport cup. **∼ [di] gelato** ice-cream (served in a dish)

cop'petta f bowl; (di gelato) small tub

'coppia f couple; (in carte) pair

co'prente adj (pittura, vernice) covering

copri'capo m headgear

coprifu'oco m curfew

copri'letto m bedspread

copripiu'mino m duvet cover

co'prir|e vt cover; drown (suono); hold (carica). **∼si** vr (vestirsi) cover up; fig cover oneself; (cielo) become overcast

coque f **alla ∼** (uovo) soft-boiled

co'raggi|o m courage; (sfacciataggine) nerve; **∼o!** come on. **∼'oso** adj courageous

co'rale adj choral

co'rallo m coral

Co'rano m Koran

co'raz|za f armour; (di animali) shell. **∼'zata** f battleship. **∼'zato** adj (nave) armour-clad

curbelle'ria f nonsense; (sproposito) blunder

'corda f cord, (Mus, spago) string; (fune) rope; (cavo) cable; **essere giù di ∼** be depressed; **dare ∼ a qcno** encourage sb. **corde vocali** vocal cords

cordi'al|e adj cordial ● m (bevanda) cordial; **∼i saluti** best wishes. **∼ità** f cordiality

'cordless m inv cordless phone

cor'doglio m grief, (lutto) mourning

cor'done m cord; (schieramento) cordon

core|ogra'fia f choreography. **∼'ografo, -a** mf choreographer

cori'andoli mpl confetti sg

cori'andolo m (spezia) coriander

cori'car|e vt put to bed. **∼si** vr go to bed

co'rista mf choir member

'corna ▶ CORNU

cor'nacchia f crow

corna'musa f bagpipes pl

cor'nett|a f (Mus) cornet; (del telefono) receiver. **∼o** m (brioche) croissant

cor'nice f frame. **∼ci'one** m cornice

'corno m (pl f **corna**) horn; **fare le corna a qcno** be unfaithful to sb; **fare le corna** (per scongiuro) touch wood. **cor'nuto** adj horned ● m (①) manto tradito) cuckold; (insulto) bastard

'coro m chorus; (Relig) choir

co'rolla f corolla

co'rona f crown; (di fiori) wreath; (rosario) rosary. **∼'mento** m (di impresa) crowning. **coro'nare** vt crown; (sogno) fulfil

cor'petto m bodice

'corpo m body; (Mil, diplomatico) corps inv; **∼ a ∼** man to man; **andare**

di ~ move one's bowels. ~ **di ballo** corps de ballet. ~ **insegnante** teaching staff. ~ **del reato** incriminating item

corpo'rale *adj* corporal

corporati'vismo *m* corporatism

corpora'tura *f* build

corporazi'one *f* corporation

cor'poreo *adj* bodily

cor'poso *adj* full-bodied

corpu'lento *adj* stout

cor'puscolo *m* corpuscle

corre'dare *vt* equip

corre'dino *m* (*per neonato*) layette

cor'redo *m* (*nuziale*) trousseau

cor'reggere *vt* correct; lace (*bevanda*)

corre'lare *vt* correlate

cor'rente *adj* running; (*in vigore*) current; (*frequente*) everyday; (*inglese ecc*) fluent ● *f* current; (*d'aria*) draught; **essere al ~** be up to date. ~'**mente** *adv* (*parlare*) fluently

'**correre** *vi* run; (*affrettarsi*) hurry; *Sport* race; (*notizie:*) circulate; ~ **dietro a** run after ● *vt* run; ~ **un pericolo** run a risk; **lascia ~!** I don't bother!

corre'tta'mente *adv* correctly. **cor'retto** *pp di* **correggere** ● *adj* correct; (*caffè*) with a drop of alcohol. ~**zi'one** *f* correction

cor'rida *f* bullfight

corri'doio *m* corridor; (*Aeron*) aisle

corri'dore , -'**trice** *mf* racer; (*a piedi*) runner

corri'era *f* coach, bus

corri'ere *m* courier; (*posta*) mail; (*spedizioniere*) carrier

corri'mano *m* bannister

corrispet'tivo *m* amount due

corrispon'den|te *adj* corresponding ● *mf* correspondent. ~**za** *f* correspondence; **scuola/corsi per** ~ correspondence course; **vendite per** ~**za** mail-order [shopping]. **corri-**

'**spondere** *vi* correspond; (*stanza:*) communicate; **corrispondere a** (*con-traccambiare*) return

corri'sposto *adj* (*amore*) reciprocated

corrobo'rare *vt* strengthen; *fig* corroborate

cor'roder|e *vt*, ~**si** *vr* corrode

cor'rompere *vt* corrupt; (*con denaro*) bribe

corrosi'one *f* corrosion. **corro'sivo** *adj* corrosive

cor'roso *pp di* **corrodere**

cor'rotto *pp di* **corrompere** ● *adj* corrupt

corrucci'a|rsi *vr* be vexed. ~**to** *adj* upset

corru'gare *vt* wrinkle; ~ **la fronte** knit one's brows

corruzi'one *f* corruption; (*con denaro*) bribery

'**corsa** *f* running; (*rapida*) dash; *Sport* race; (*di treno ecc*) journey; **di** ~ at a run; **fare una** ~ run

cor'sia *f* gangway; (*di ospedale*) ward; (*Auto*) lane; (*di supermercato*) aisle

cor'sivo *m* italics *pl*

'**corso** *pp di* **correre** ● *m* course; (*strada*) main street; (*Comm*) circulation; **lavori in** ~ work in progress; **nel** ~ **di** during. ~ **d'acqua** watercourse

'**corte** *f* [court]yard; (*Jur*, *regale*) court; **fare la** ~ **a** qcno court sb. ~ **d'appello** court of appeal

cor'teccia *f* bark

corteggia'mento *m* courtship

corteggia're *vt* court. ~'**tore** *m* admirer

cor'teo *m* procession

cor'te|se *adj* courteous. ~'**sia** *f* courtesy; **per** ~**sia** please

cortigi'ano , -**a** *mf* courtier ● *f* courtesan

cor'tile *m* courtyard

cor'tina *f* curtain; (*schermo*) screen

'**corto** adj short; **essere a ∼ di** be short of. **∼ circuito** m short [circuit]

cortome'traggio m Cinema short

cor'vino adj jet black

'**corvo** m raven

'**cosa** f thing; (faccenda) matter; Jur, rel what; [che] ∼ what; **nessuna ∼** nothing; **ogni ∼** everything; **per prima ∼** first of all; **tante cose** so many things; (augurio) **all the best**

'**cosca** f clan

'**coscia** f thigh; (Culin) leg

cosci'en|te adj conscious. **∼za** f conscience; (consapevolezza) consciousness

co'scritto m conscript. **∼zi'one** f conscription

co'sì adv so; (in questo modo) like this, like that; (perciò) therefore; **le cose stanno ∼** that's how things stand; **fermo ∼!** hold it; **proprio ∼!** exactly!; **basta ∼!** that will do!; **ah, è ∼?** it's like that, is it?; **∼ ∼** so-so; **e ∼ via** and so on; **per ∼ dire** so to speak; **più di ∼** any more; **una ∼ cara ragazza!** such a nice girl!; **è stato ∼ generoso da aiutarti** he was kind enough to help you ● conj (allora) so ● adj inv (tale) like that; **una ragazza ∼** a girl like that

cosicché conj and so

cosid'detto adj so-called

co'smesi f cosmetics

co'smetico adj & m cosmetic

'**cosmico** adj cosmic

'**cosmo** m cosmos

cosmopo'lita adj cosmopolitan

co'spargere vt sprinkle; (disseminare) scatter

co'spetto m **al ∼ di** in the presence of

co'spicuo adj conspicuous; (somma ecc) considerable

cospi'ra|re vi conspire. **∼tore**, **∼trice** mf conspirator. **∼zi'one** f conspiracy

'**costa** f coast; (Anat) rib

costà adv there

co'stan|te adj & f constant. **∼za** f constancy

co'stare vi cost; **quanto costa?** how much is it?

co'stata f chop

costeggi'are vt (per mare) coast; (per terra) skirt

co'stei pron pron ▷COSTUI

costellazi'one f constellation

coster'na|to adj dismayed. **∼zi'one** f consternation

costi'era f stretch of coast. **∼o** adj coastal

costi'pa|to adj constipated. **∼zi'one** f constipation; (raffreddore) bad cold

costitu'ir|e vt constitute; (formare) form; (nominare) appoint. **∼si** vr (Jur) give oneself up

costituzio'nale adj constitutional. **costituzi'one** f constitution; (fondazione) setting up

'**costo** m cost; **ad ogni ∼** at all costs; **a nessun ∼** on no account

'**costola** f rib; (di libro) spine

costo'letta f cutlet

co'storo pron ▷COSTUI

co'stoso adj costly

co'stretto pp di **costringere**

co'stri|ngere vt compel; (stringere) constrict. **∼ttivo** adj coercive

costru'ire vt build. **∼ttivo** adj constructive. **∼zi'one** f construction

co'stui, **co'stei**, pl **co'storo** pron (soggetto) he, she, pl they; (complemento) him, her, pl them

co'stume m (usanza) custom; (condotta) morals pl; (indumento) costume. **∼ da bagno** swim-suit; (da uomo) swimming trunks

co'tenna f pigskin; (della pancetta) rind

coto'letta f cutlet

co'tone m cotton. ~ **idrofilo** cotton wool, absorbent cotton Am

'cottimo m **lavorare a ~ do** piece-work

'cotto pp di **cuocere** ● adj done; (🅸: infatuato) in love; (🅸: sbronzo) drunk; **ben ~** (carne) well done

'cotton fi'oc® m inv cotton bud

cot'tura f cooking

co'vare vt hatch; sicken for (malattia); harbour (odio) ● vi smoulder

'covo m den

co'vone m sheaf

'cozza f mussel

coz'zare vi ~ **contro** bump into. **'cozzo** m fig clash

C.P. abbr (Casella Postale) PO Box

'crampo m cramp

'cranio m skull

cra'tere m crater

cra'vatta f tie; (a farfalla) bow-tie

cre'anza f politeness; **mala ~ bad** manners

cre'a|re vt create; (causare) cause. **~tività** f creativity. **~'tivo** adj creative. **~to** m creation. **~tore, ~trice** mf creator. **~zi'one** f creation

crea'tura f creature; (bambino) baby; **povera ~!** poor thing!

cre'den|te mf believer. **~za** f belief; (Comm) credit; (mobile) sideboard. **~zi'ali** fpl credentials

'crede|re vt believe; (pensare) think ● vi **~ in** believe in; **credo di sì** I think so; **non ti credo** I don't believe you. **~si** vr think oneself to be. **cre'dibile** adj credible. **credibilità** f credibility

'credi|to m credit; (stima) esteem; **comprare a ~to** buy on credit. **~'tore, ~'trice** m creditor

credulità f credulity

'credu|lo adj credulous. **~'lone, -a** mf simpleton

'crema f cream; (di uova e latte) custard. ~ **idratante** moisturizer. ~ **pasticcera** egg custard. ~ **solare** suntan lotion

cre'ma|re vt cremate. **~'torio** m crematorium. **~zi'one** f cremation

'crème cara'mel f crème caramel

creme'ria f dairy (also selling ice cream and cakes)

'crepa f crack

cre'paccio m cleft; (di ghiacciaio) crevasse

crepacu'ore m heart-break

crepa'pelle: a ~ adv fit to burst; **ridere a ~** split one's sides with laughter

cre'pare vi crack; (🅸: morire) kick the bucket; ~ **dal ridere** laugh fit to burst

crepa'tura f crevice

crêpe f inv pancake

crepi'tare vi crackle

cre'puscolo m twilight

cre'scendo m crescendo

'cresc|ere vi grow; (aumentare) increase ● vt (allevare) bring up; (aumentare) increase. **~ita** f growth; (aumento) increase. **~i'uto** pp di crescere

'cresi|ma f confirmation. **~'mare** vt confirm

'crespo adj frizzy ● m crêpe

'cresta f crest; (cima) peak

'creta f clay

'Creta f Crete

cre'tino, -a adj stupid ● mf idiot

cric m car jack

cri'ceto m hamster

crimi'nal|e adj & mf criminal. **~ità** f crime. **'crimine** m crime

crimi'noso adj criminal

crin|e m horsehair. **~i'era** f mane

'cripta f crypt

crisan'temo m chrysanthemum

'crisi f inv crisis; (Med) fit

cristal'lino m crystalline

cristalliz'zar|e vt, **~si** vr crystallize; *fig*: (parola, espressione:) become part of the language

cri'stallo *m* crystal

Cristia'nesimo *m* Christianity

cristi'ano, -a *adj & mf* Christian

'Cristo *m* Christ; un povero c ● ● poor beggar

cri'terio *m* criterion; (*buon senso*) [common] sense

'criti|ca *f* criticism; (*recensione*) review. **criti'care** *vt* criticize. **~co** *adj* critical ● *m* critic. **~cone, -a** *mf* faultfinder

crivel'lare *vt* riddle (**di** with)

cri'vello *m* sieve

Cro'azia *f* Croatia

croc'cante *adj* crisp ● *m type of crunchy nut biscuit*

cro'chetta *f* croquette

'croce *f* cross; **a occhio e ~** roughly. **C~ Rossa** Red Cross

croce'via *m inv* crossroads *sg*

croci'ata *f* crusade

cro'cicchio *m* crossroads *sg*

croci'era *f* cruise. (*Archit*) crossing

croci'fi|ggere *vt* crucify. **~ssi'one** *f* crucifixion. **~sso** *pp di* **crocifiggere** ● *adj* crucified ● *m* crucifix

crogio'larsi *vr* bask

crogi[u]'olo *m* crucible; *fig* melting pot

crol'lare *vi* collapse; (*prezzi*:) slump. **'crollo** *m* collapse; (*dei prezzi*) slump

cro'mato *adj* chromium-plated. **'cromo** *m* chrome. **cromo'soma** *m* chromosome

'cronaca *f* chronicle; (*di giornale*) news; (*Radio, TV*) commentary; **fatto di ~** news item. **~ nera** crime news

'cronico *adj* chronic

cro'nista *mf* reporter

crono'logico *adj* chronological

crono'metrare *vt* time

cro'nometro *m* chronometer

'crosta *f* crust; (*di formaggio*) rind; (*di ferita*) scab; (*quadro*) daub

cro'staceo *m* shellfish

cro'stata *f* tart

cro'stino *m* croûton

cruccia'arsi *vr* worry. **'cruccio** *m* worry

cruci'ale *adj* crucial

cruci'verba *m inv* crossword [puzzle]

cru'del|e *adj* cruel. **~tà** *f inv* cruelty

'crudo *adj* raw; (*rigido*) harsh

cru'ento *adj* bloody

cru'miro *m* blackleg, scab

'crusca *f* bran

cru'scotto *m* dashboard

'Cuba *f* Cuba

cu'betto *m* **~ di ghiaccio** ice cube

'cubico *adj* cubic

cubi'tal|e *adj* **a caratteri ~i** in enormous letters

'cubo *m* cube

cuc'cagna *f* abundance; (*baldoria*) merry-making. **paese della ~** land of plenty

cuc'cetta *f* (*su un treno*) couchette; (*Naut*) berth

cucchia'ino *m* teaspoon

cucchi'a|io *m* spoon; **al ~io** (*dolce*) creamy. **~iata** *f* spoonful

'cuccia *f* dog's bed; **fa la ~!** lie down!

cucci'olata *f* litter

'cucciolo *m* puppy

cu'cin|a *f* kitchen; (*il cucinare*) cooking; (*cibo*) food; (*apparecchio*) cooker; **far da ~** cook; **libro di ~** cook[ery] book. **~ a gas** gas cooker

cuci'n|are *vt* cook. **~ino** *m* kitchenette

cu'ci|re *vt* sew; **macchina per ~re** sewing-machine. **~to** *m* sewing. **~tura** *f* seam

cucù *m inv* cuckoo

'cuculo *m* cuckoo

'cuffia f bonnet; (da bagno) bathing-cap; (ricevitore) headphones pl

cu'gino, -a mf cousin

cui pron rel (persona: con prep) who, whom fml; (cose, animali: con prep) which; (tra articolo e nome) whose; **la persona con ~ ho parlato** the person [who] I spoke to; **la ditta per ~ lavoro** the company I work for, the company for which I work; **l'amico il ~ libro è stato pubblicato** the friend whose book was published; **in ~** (dove) where; (quando) that; **per ~** (perciò) so; **la città in ~ vivo** the city I live in, the city where I live; **il giorno in ~ l'ho visto** the day [that] I saw him

culi'nari|a f cookery. **~o** adj culinary

'culla f cradle. **cul'lare** vt rock

culmi'na|nte adj culminating. **~re** vi culminate. **'culmine** m peak

'culto m cult; (Relig) religion; (adorazione) worship

cul'tu|ra f culture. **~ra generale** general knowledge. **~'rale** adj cultural

cultu'ris|mo m body-building

cumula'tivo adj cumulative; **biglietto ~** group ticket

'cumulo m pile; (mucchio) heap; (nuvola) cumulus

'cuneo m wedge

cu'netta f gutter

cu'ocere vt/i cook; fire (ceramica)

cu'oco, -a mf cook

cu'oio m leather. **~ capelluto** scalp

cu'ore m heart; **cuori** pl (carte) hearts; **nel profondo del ~** in one's heart of hearts; **di [buon] ~** (persona) kind-hearted; **nel ~ della notte** in the middle of the night; **stare a ~ a qcno** be very important to sb

cupi'digia f greed

'cupo adj gloomy; (suono) deep

'cupola f dome

'cura f care; (amministrazione) management; (Med) treatment; **a ~ di** edited by; **in ~** under treatment. **~ dimagrante** diet. **cu'rante** adj **medico curante** GP, doctor

cu'rar|e vt take care of; (Med) treat; (guarire) cure; edit (testo). **~si** vr take care of oneself; (Med) follow a treatment; **~si di** (badare a) mind

cu'rato m parish priest

cura'tore, -'trice mf trustee; (di testo) editor

'curia f curia

curio's|are vi be curious; (mettere il naso) pry (in into); (nei negozi) look around. **~ità** f inv curiosity. **curi'oso** adj curious; (strano) odd

cur'sore m (Comput) cursor

'curva f curve; (stradale) bend. **~ a gomito** U-bend. **cur'vare** vt/i curve; (strada:) bend. **cur'varsi** vr bend. **'curvo** adj curved; (piegato) bent

cusci'netto m pad; (Mech) bearing

cu'scino m cushion; (guanciale) pillow. **~ d'aria** air cushion

'cuspide f spire

cu'stod|e m caretaker. **~e giudiziario** official receiver. **~ia** f care; (Jur) custody; (astuccio) case. **custo'dire** vt keep; (badare) look after

cu'taneo adj skin attrib

'cute f skin

Dd

da prep from; (con verbo passivo) by; (moto a luogo) to; (moto per luogo) through; (stato in luogo) at; (continuativo) for; (causale) with; (in qualità di)

d

as; (con caratteristica) with; (come) like; (temporale) since, for

da si traduce con **for** quando si tratta di un periodo di tempo e con **since** quando si riferisce al momento in cui qualcosa è cominciato. Nota che in inglese si usa il passato prossimo invece del presente: **aspetto da mesi** I've been waiting for months; **aspetto da lunedì** I've been waiting since Monday

••• **da Roma a Milano** from Rome to Milan; **staccare un quadro dalla parete** take a picture off the wall; **i bambini dal 5 ai 10 anni** children between 5 and 10; **vedere qcsa da vicino/lontano** see sth from up close/from a distance; **scritto da** written by; **andare dal panettiere** go to the baker's, **passo da te più tardi** I'll come over to your place later; **passiamo da qui** let's go this way; **un appuntamento dal dentista** an appointment at the dentist's; **il treno passa da Venezia** the train goes through Venice; **dall'anno scorso** since last year; **vivo qui da due anni** I've been living here for two years; **da domani** from tomorrow; **piangere dal dolore** cry with pain; **ho molto da fare** I have a lot to do; **occhiali da sole** sunglasses; **qualcosa da mangiare** something to eat; **un uomo dai capelli scuri** a man with dark hair; **è un oggetto da poco** it's not worth much; **l'ho fatto da solo** I did it by myself; **si è fatto da sé** he is a self-made man; **non è da lui** it's not like him

dac'capo adv again; (dall'inizio) from the beginning

dacché conj since

'dado m dice; (Culin) stock cube; (Techn) nut

daf'fare m work

'dagli = DA + GLI. **'dai** = DA + I

'dai int come on!

'daino m deer; (pelle) buckskin

dal = DA + IL. **'dalla** = DA + LA. **'dalle** = DA + LE. **'dallo** = DA + LO

'dalia f dahlia

dal'tonico adj colour-blind

'dama f lady, (nei balli) partner; (gioco) draughts sg

dami'gella f (di sposa) bridesmaid

damigi'ana f demijohn

dam'meno adv non essere ~ (di qcno) be no less good (than sb)

da'naro m = DENARO

dana'roso adj (fam: ricco) loaded

da'nese adj Danish ● m/f Dane ● m (lingua) Danish

Dani'marca f Denmark

dan'na|re vt damn; far ~re qcno drive sb mad. ~to adj damned. ~zi'one f damnation

danneggia'mento m damage ● ~are vt damage; (nuocere) harm

'danno m damage; (a persona) harm. **dan'noso** adj harmful

'danza f dance; (il danzare) dancing. **dan'zare** vi dance

dapper'tutto adv everywhere

dap'poco adj worthless

dap'prima adv at first

'dardo m dart

'dar|e vt give; take (esame); have (festa); ~ **qcsa a qcno** give sb sth; ~ **da mangiare a qcno** give sb something to eat; ~ **il benvenuto a qcno** welcome sb; ~ **la buonanotte a qcno** say good night to sb; ~ **del tu/del lei a qcno** address sb as "tu"/"lei"; ~ **del cretino a qcno** call sb an idiot; ~ **qcsa per scontato** take sth for granted; **cosa danno alla TV stasera?** what's on TV tonight? ● vi ~ **nell'occhio** be conspicuous; ~ **alla testa** go to one's head; ~ **su** (finestra, casa:) look on to; ~ **sui** o **ai nervi a qcno** get on sb's nerves ● m (Comm) debit. ~**si** vr (scambiarsi) give each other; ~**si da fare** get down to it; **si è dato tanto da fare!** he went to so much trouble; ~**si** a (cominciare) take up; ~**si al bere** take to drink; ~**si per** (malato) pretend to be; ~**si per vinto** give up; **può** ~**si** maybe

'**darsena** f dock

'**data** f date. ~ **di emissione** date of issue. ~ **di nascita** date of birth. ~ **di scadenza** cut-off date

da'ta|re vt date; **a** ~**re da** as from. ~**to** adj dated

'**dato** adj given; (dedito) addicted; ~ **che** given that; ~ **di fatto** well-established fact; **dati** pl data. **da'tore** m giver. **datore, da'trice** m/f **di lavoro** employer

'**dattero** m date

dattilogra'f|are vt type. ~**ia** f typing. **datti'lografo, -a** mf typist

dat'torno adv **togliersi** ~ clear off

da'vanti adv before; (dirimpetto) opposite; (di fronte) in front ● adj inv front ● m front; ~ **a** prep in front of

da'vanzo adv more than enough

dav'vero adv really; **per** ~ in earnest; **dici** ~? honestly?

'**dazio** m duty; (ufficio) customs pl

d.C. abbr (dopo Cristo) AD

'**dea** f goddess

debel'lare vt defeat

debili'ta|nte adj weakening. ~**re** vt weaken. ~**rsi** vr become weaker

debita'mente adv duly

'**debi|to** adj due; **a tempo** ~**to** in due course ● m debt. ~**tore, ~'trice** m/f debtor

'**debo|le** adj weak; (luce) dim; (suono) faint ● m weak point; (prefe-

renza) weakness. ~'**lezza** f weakness

debor'dare vi overflow

debosci'ato adj debauched

debut'ta|nte m (attore) actor making his début ● f actress making her début. ~**re** vi make one's début. **de'butto** m début

deca'den|te adj decadent. ~'**tismo** m decadence. ~**za** f decline. (Jur) loss. **deca'dere** vi lapse.

decadi'mento m (delle arti) decline

decaffei'nato adj decaffeinated ● m decaffeinated coffee

decan'tare vt (lodare) praise

decapi'ta|re vt decapitate; behead (condannato). ~**zi'one** f decapitation; beheading

decappot'tabile adj convertible

de'ce|dere vi (morire) die. ~'**duto** adj deceased

dece'lerare vt decelerate

decen'nale adj ten-yearly. **de'cennio** m decade

de'cen|te adj decent. ~**te'mente** adv decently. ~**za** f decency

decentra'mento m decentralization

de'cesso m death; **atto di** ~ death certificate

de'cider|e vt decide; settle (questione). ~**si** vr make up one's mind

deci'frare vt decipher; (documenti cifrati) decode

deci'male adj decimal

deci'mare vt decimate

'**decimo** adj tenth

de'cina f (Math) ten; **una** ~ **di** (circa dieci) about ten

decisa'mente adv definitely

decisio'nale adj decision-making

decisi'o|ne f decision. ~'**sivo** adj decisive. **de'ciso** pp di **decidere** ● adj decided

decla'ma|re vt/i declaim. ~'**torio** adj (stile) declamatory

declas'sare vt downgrade

decli'na|re vt decline; ~**re ogni responsabilità** disclaim all responsibility • vi go down; (tramontare) set. ~**zi'one** f declension. **do'clino** m decline; **in declino** on the decline

decodificazi'one f decoding

dacol'lare vi take off

décolle'té m inv décolleté

de'collo m take-off

decolo'rante vt bleach. ~**re** vt bleach

decolorazi'one f bleaching

decom'po|rre vt, ~**rsi** vr decompose. ~. **sizi'one** f decomposition

deconcen'trarsi vr become distracted

deconge'lare vt defrost

decongestio'nare vt relieve congestion in

deco'ra|re vt decorate. ~**tivo** adj decorative. ~**to** adj (ornato) decorated. ~**'tore, ~'trice** mf decorator. ~**zi'one** f decoration

da'coro m decorum

decorosa'mente adv decorously. **decoroso** adj dignified

decor'renza f ~ **dal...** starting from...

de'correre vi pass; **a ~ da** with effect from. **de'corso** pp di **decorrere** • m passing; (Med) course

de'crepito adj decrepit

decre'scente adj decreasing. **de'crescere** vi decrease; (prezzi:) go down; (acque:) subside

decre'tare vt decree. **de'creto** m decree. **decreto legge** dooroo which has the force of law

'dedalo m maze

'dedica f dedication

dedi'car|e vt dedicate. ~**si** vr dedicate oneself

'dedi|to adj **~ a** given to; (assorto) engrossed in; (addicted to (vizi). ~**zi'one** f dedication

de'dotto pp di **dedurre**

dedu'cibile adj (tassa) allowable

de'du|rre vt deduce; (sottrarre) deduct. ~**t'tivo** adj deductive. ~**zi'one** f deduction

defal'care vt deduct

defe'rire vt (Jur) remit

defezi|o'nare vi (abbandonare) defect. ~**'one** f defection

defici'en|te adj (mancante) deficient; (Med) mentally deficient • mf mental defective ~**za** f deficiency; (lacuna) gap; (Med) mental deficiency

'deficit m inv deficit. ~**'tario** adj (bilancio) deficit attnò

defi'larsi vr (scomparire) slip away

défilé m inv fashion show

defi'ni|re vt define; (risolvere) settle. ~**tiva'mente** adv for good. ~**tivo** adj definitive. ~**to** adj definite. ~**zi'one** f definition; (soluzione) settlement

deflazi'one f deflation

deflet'tore m (Auto) quarterlight

deflu'ire vi (liquidi:) flow away; (persone:) stream out

de'flusso m (di marea) ebb

defor'mar|e vt deform (arto); fig distort. ~**si** vr lose its shape. **de'form|e** adj deformed. ~**ità** f deformity

defor'ma|to adj warped. ~**zi'one** f (di fatti) distortion

defrau'dare vt defraud

de'funto, -a adj & mf deceased

degene'ra|re vi degenerate. ~**to** adj degenerate. ~**zi'one** f degeneration. **de'genere** adj degenerate

de'gen|te mf patient. ~**za** f confinement

'degli = DI + GLI

deglu'tire vt swallow

de'gnare vi **~ qcno di uno sguardo** deign to look at sb

'degno adj worthy; (meritevole) deserving

degrada'mento m degradation

degra'da|re vt degrade. ∼**rsi** vr lower oneself; (città) fall into disrepair. ∼**zi'one** f degradation

de'grado m damage; ∼ **ambientale** m environmental damage

degu'sta|re vt taste. ∼**zi'one** f tasting

'dei = DI + I. **del** = DI + IL

dela'tore, -'trice mf [police] informer. ∼**zi'one** f informing

'delega f proxy

dele'ga|re vt delegate. ∼**to** m delegate. ∼**zi'one** f delegation

dele'terio adj harmful

del'fino m dolphin; (stile di nuoto) butterfly [stroke]

de'libera f bylaw

delibe'ra|re vt/i deliberate; ∼ **su/in** rule on/in. ∼**to** adj deliberate

delicata'mente adv delicately

delica'tezza f delicacy; (fragilità) frailty; (tatto) tact

deli'cato adj delicate

delimi'tare vt delimit

deline'a|re vt outline. ∼**rsi** vr be outlined; fig take shape. ∼**to** adj defined

delin'quen|te mf delinquent. ∼**za** f delinquency

deli'rante adj (Med) delirious; (assurdo) insane

deli'rare vi be delirious. **de'lirio** m delirium; fig frenzy

de'litt|o m crime. ∼**u'oso** adj criminal

de'lizi|a f delight. ∼**'are** vt delight. ∼**'oso** adj delightful; (cibo) delicious

'della = DI + LA. **delle** = DI + LE. **'dello** = DI + LO

delocaliz'zare vt relocate

'delta m inv delta

delta'plano m hang-glider; **fare** ∼ go hang-gliding

delucidazi'one f clarification

delu'dente adj disappointing

de'lu|dere vt disappoint. ∼**si'one** f disappointment. **de'luso** adj disappointed

demar'ca|re vt demarcate. ∼**zi'one** f demarcation

de'men|te adj demented. ∼**za** f dementia. ∼**zi'ale** adj (assurdo) zany

demilitariz'za|re vt demilitarize. ∼**zi'one** f demilitarization

demistificazi'one f debunking

demo'cra|tico adj democratic. ∼**'zia** f democracy

democristi'ano, -a adj & mf Christian Democrat

demogra'fia f demography. **demo'grafico** adj demographic

demo'li|re vt demolish. ∼**zi'one** f demolition

'demone m demon. **de'monio** m demon

demoraliz'zar|e vt demoralize. ∼**si** vr become demoralized

de'mordere vi give up

demoti'vato adj demotivated

de'nari mpl (nelle carte) diamonds

de'naro m money

deni'gra|re vt denigrate. ∼**'torio** adj denigratory

denomi'na|re vt name. ∼**'tore** m denominator. ∼**zi'one** f denomination; ∼**zione di origine controllata** guarantee of a wine's quality

deno'tare vt denote

densità f inv density. **'denso** adj dense

den'ta|le adj dental. ∼**rio** adj dental. ∼**ta** f bite. ∼**'tura** f teeth pl

'dente m tooth; (di forchetta) prong; **al** ∼ (Culin) slightly firm. ∼ **del giudizio** wisdom tooth. ∼ **di latte** milk tooth. **denti'era** f false teeth pl

denti'fricio m toothpaste

den'tista mf dentist

'dentro adv in, inside; (in casa) indoors; **da** ∼ from within; **qui** ∼ in here ● prep in, inside; (di tempo) within, by • m inside

denu'dar|e vt bare. **~si** vr strip

de'nunci|a, de'nunzia f denunciation; (alla polizia) report; (dei redditi) [income] tax return. **~'are** vt denounce; (accusare) report

denutrizi'one f malnutrition

deodo'rante adj & m deodorant

dépendance f inv outbuilding

depe'ri|bile adj perishable. **~'mento** m wasting away; (di merci) deterioration. **~re** vi waste away

depi'la|re vt depilate. **~rsi** vr shave (gambe); pluck (sopracciglia). **~'torio** m depilatory

deplo'rabile adj deplorable

deplo'r|are vt deplore; (dolersi di) grieve over. **~evole** adj deplorable

de'porre vt put down; lay (uova); (togliere da una carica) depose; (testimoniare) testify

depor'ta|re vt deport. **~to, -a** mf deportee. **~zi'one** f deportation

deposi'tar|e vt deposit; (lasciare in custodia) leave; (in magazzino) store. **~io, -a** mf (di segreto) repository. **~si** vr settle

de'posito m deposit; (luogo) warehouse; (Mil) depot. **~ to bagagli** left-luggage office. **~zi'one** f deposition; (da una carica) removal

depra'va|re vt deprave. **~to** adj depraved

depre'ca|bile adj appalling. **~re** vt deprecate

depre'dare vt plunder

depressi'one f depression. de'presso pp di deprimere • adj depressed

deprez'zar|e vt depreciate. **~si** vr depreciate

depri'mente adj depressing

de'primer|e vt depress. **~si** vr become depressed

depu'ra|re vt purify. **~'tore** m purifier

depu'ta|re vt delegate. **~to, -a** mf Member of Parliament, MP

deragli'a|mento m derailment

deragli'are vi go off the lines; far **~** derail

'derby m inv Sport local Derby

deregolamentazi'one f deregulation

dere'litto adj derelict

dere'tano m backside, bottom

de'ri|dere vt deride. **~si'one** f derision. **~'sorio** adj derisory

deri'va|re vi **~re da** (provenire) derive from • vt derive; (sviare) divert. **~si'ana** f derivation; (di fiume) di version

dermato'lo'gia f dermatology. derma'tologo, -a mf dermatologist

'deroga f dispensation. dero'gare vi derogare a depart from

der'ra|ta f merchandise. **~e alimentari** foodstuffs

deru'bare vt rob

descrit'tivo adj descriptive. de'scritto pp di descrivere

des'cri|vere vt describe. **~'vibile** adj describable. **~zi'one** f description

de'serto adj uninhabited • m desert

deside'rabile adj desirable

deside'rare vt (volere) want, (intensamente) long for; desidera? can I help you?; lasciare a **~** leave a lot to be desired

desi'de|rio m wish; (brama) desire; (intenso) longing. **~'roso** adj desirous; (bramoso) longing

desi'gnare vt designate; (fissare) fix

de'sistere vi **~** da desist from

'desktop 'publishing m desktop publishing

deso'la|re vt distress. **~to** adj desolate; (spiacente) sorry. **~zi'one** f desolation

'despota m despot

de'star|e vt waken; fig awaken. **~si**

vr waken; *fig* awaken

desti'na|re *vt* destine; (*nominare*) appoint; (*assegnare*) assign; (*indirizzare*) address. ~'**tario** *m* addressee. ~**zi'one** *f* destination; *fig* purpose

de'stino *m* destiny; (*fato*) fate

destitu'|ire *vt* dismiss. ~**zi'one** *f* dismissal

'**desto** *adj* liter awake

'**destra** *f* (*parte*) right; (*mano*) right hand; **prendere a** ~ turn right

destreggi'ar|e *vi*, ~**si** *vr* manoeuvre

de'strezza *f* dexterity, skill

'**destro** *adj* right; (*abile*) skilful

detei'nato *adj* tannin-free

dete'n|ere *vt* hold; (*polizia:*) detain. ~**uto, -a** *mf* prisoner. ~**zi'one** *f* detention

deter'gente *adj* cleaning; (latte, crema) cleansing ● *m* detergent; (*per la pelle*) cleanser

deteriora'mento *m* deterioration

deterio'rar|e *vt* deteriorate. ~**si** *vr* deteriorate

determi'nante *adj* decisive

determi'na|re *vt* determine. ~**rsi** *vr* ~**rsi a** resolve to. ~'**tezza** *f* determination. ~'**tivo** *adj* (*Gram*) definite. ~**to** *adj* (*risoluto*) determined; (*particolare*) specific. ~**zi'one** *f* determination; (*decisione*) decision

deter'rente *adj* & *m* deterrent

deter'sivo *m* detergent; ~ **per i piatti** washing-up liquid

dete'stare *vt* detest, hate

deto'nare *vi* detonate

de'tra|rre *vt* deduct (da from). ~**zi'one** *f* deduction

detri'mento *m* detriment; **a** ~ **di** to the detriment of

de'trito *m* debris

'**detta** *f* **a** ~ **di** according to

dettagli'ante *mf* retailer

dettagli'a|re *vt* detail. ~**ta'mente** *adv* in detail

det'taglio *m* detail; **al** ~ (*Comm*) retail

det'ta|re *vt* dictate. ~**to** *m*, ~'**tura** *f* dictation

'**detto** *adj* said; (*chiamato*) called; (*soprannominato*) nicknamed; ~ **fatto** no sooner said than done ● *m* saying

detur'pare *vt* disfigure

deva'sta|re *vt* devastate. ~**to** *adj* devastated

devi'a|re *vi* deviate ● *vt* divert. ~**zi'one** *f* deviation; (*stradale*) diversion

devitaliz'zare *vt* deaden (dente)

devo'lu|to *pp di* **devolvere** ● *adj* devolved. ~**zi'one** *f* devolution

de'volvere *vt* devolve

de'vo|to *adj* devout; (*affezionato*) devoted. ~**zi'one** *f* devotion

di *prep* of; (*partitivo*) some; (*scritto da*) by; (*parlare, pensare ecc*) about; (*con causa, mezzo*) with; (*con provenienza*) from; (*in comparazioni*) than; (*con infinito*) to; **la casa di mio padre/dei miei genitori** my father's house/my parents' house; **compra del pane** buy some bread; **hai del pane?** do you have any bread?; **un film di guerra** a war film; **piangere di dolore** cry with pain; **coperto di neve** covered with snow; **sono di Genova** I'm from Genoa; **uscire di casa** leave one's house; **più alto di te** taller than you; **è ora di partire** it's time to go; **crede di aver ragione** he thinks he's right; **dire di sì** says yes; **di domenica** on Sundays; **di sera** in the evening; **una pausa di un'ora** an hour's break; **un corso di due mesi** a two-month course

dia'bet|e *m* diabetes. ~**ico, -a** *adj* & *mf* diabetic

dia'bolico adj diabolical

dia'dema m diadem; (di donna) tiara

di'afano adj diaphanous

dia'framma m diaphragm; (divisione) screen

di'agnos|i f inv diagnosis. **~ti'care** vt diagnose

diago'nale adj & f diagonal

dia'gramma m diagram

dia'letto m dialect

Dialetto As Italy was not unified until 1861, standard Italian was slow to become widely used except by the cultural elite. As a result dialects are used by many Italians, with 60% using their dialect regularly. Ranging from Neapolitan and Sicilian to Milanese and Venetian, they vary considerably from each other. Tuscan dialects are the closest to standard Italian.

di'alogo m dialogue

dia'mante m diamond

di'ametro m diameter

di'amine int che **~...** what on earth...

diapo'sitiva f slide

di'ario m diary

diar'rea f diarrhoea

di'avolo m devil

di'batt|ere vt debate. **~ersi** vr struggle. **~ito** m debate; (meno formale) discussion

dica'stero m office

di'cembre m December

dice'ria f rumour

dichia'ra|re vt state; (ufficialmente) declare. **~rsi** vr si dichiara innocente he says he's innocent. **~zi'one** f statement; (documento, di guerra) declaration

dician'nove adj & m nineteen

dicias'sette adj & m seventeen

dici'otto adj & m eighteen

dici'tura f wording

didasca'lia f (di film) subtitle; (di illustrazione) caption

di'dattico adj didactic; (televisione) educational

di'dentro adv inside

didi'etro adv behind ● m hum hindquarters pl

di'eci adj & m ten

die'cina = DECINA

'diesel adj & f inv diesel

di'esis m inv sharp

di'eta f diet; essere a **~** be on a diet. **die'tetico** adj diet. **die'tista** mf dietician. **die'tologo, -a** mf dietician

di'etro adv behind ● prep behind; (dopo) after ● adj back; (di zampe) hind ● m back; le stanze di **~** the back rooms

dietro'front m inv about-turn; fig U-turn

di'fatti adv in fact

di'fen|dere vt defend. **~dersi** vr defend oneself. **~'siva** f stare sulla **~siva** be on the defensive. **~'sivo** adj defensive. **~'sore** m defender; avvocato **~sore** defence counsel

di'fes|a f defence; prendere le **~e** di qcno come to sb's defence. **~o** pp di difendere

difet'tare vi be defective; **~are di** lack. **~'ivo** adj defective

di'fet|to m defect; (morale) fault, flaw; (mancanza) lack; (in tessuto, abito) flaw; essere in **~to** be at fault; far **~to** be lacking. **~'toso** adj defective; (abito) flawed

diffa'ma|re vt (con parole) slander; (per iscritto) libel. **~'torio** adj slanderous; (per iscritto) libellous. **~zi'one** f slander; (scritta) libel

diffe'ren|te adj different. **~za** f difference; a **~za di** unlike; non fare **~za** make no distinction (fra between). **~zi'ale** adj & m differential

differenzi'ar|e vt differentiate. **~si** vr **~si da** differ from

diffe'ri|re vt postpone ● vi be different. **~ta f** in **~ta** (TV) prerecorded

dif'ficil|e adj difficult; (duro) hard; (improbabile) unlikely ● m difficulty. **~'mente** adv with difficulty

difficoltà f inv difficulty

dif'fida f warning

diffi'd|are vi **~are di** distrust ● vt warn. **~ente** adj mistrustful. **~enza f** mistrust

dif'fonder|e vt spread; diffuse (calore, luce ecc). **~si** vr spread. **diffusi'one f** diffusion; (di giornale) circulation

dif'fu|so pp di **diffondere** ● adj common; (malattia) widespread; (luce) diffuse

difi'lato adv straight; (subito) straightaway

'diga f dam; (argine) dike

dige'ribile adj digestible

dige'ri|re vt digest; [⊞] stomach. **~sti'one f** digestion. **~'stivo** adj digestive ● m digestive; (dopo cena) liqueur

digi'tale adj digital; (delle dita) finger attrib ● f (fiore) foxglove

digitaliz'zare vt digitize

digi'tare vt key in

digiu'nare vi fast

digi'uno adj essere **~** have an empty stomach ● m fast; **a ~** (bere ecc) on an empty stomach

digni|tà f dignity. **~'tario** m dignitary. **~'toso** adj dignified

digressi'one f digression

digri'gnare vi **~ i denti** grind one's teeth

dila'gare vi flood; fig spread

dilani'are vt tear to pieces

dilapi'dare vt squander

dila'ta|re vt, **~rsi** vr dilate; (metallo, gas:) expand

dilazio'nabile adj postponable

dilazio'nare vt delay. **~'one** f delay

dilegu'ar|e vt disperse. **~si** vr disappear

di'lemma m dilemma

dilet'tante mf amateur

dilet'tare vt delight

di'letto, -a adj beloved ● m delight ● mf (persona) beloved

dili'gen|te adj diligent; (lavoro) accurate. **~za f** diligence

dilu'ire vt dilute

dilun'gar|e vt prolong. **~si** vr **~si su** dwell on (argomento)

diluvi'are vi pour [down]. **di'luvio** m downpour; fig flood

dima'gr|ante adj slimming. **~i'mento** m weight loss. **~ire** vi slim

dime'nar|e vt wave; wag (coda). **~si** vr be agitated

dimensi'one f dimension; (misura) size

dimenti'canza f forgetfulness; (svista) oversight

dimenti'car|e vt, **~si** vr **~ [di]** forget. **dimentico** adj **dimentico di** (che non ricorda) forgetful of

di'messo pp di **dimettere** ● adj humble; (trasandato) shabby; (voce) low

dimesti'chezza f familiarity

di'metter|e vt dismiss; (da ospedale ecc) discharge. **~si** vr resign

dimez'zare vt halve

diminu'ire vt/i diminish; (in maglia) decrease. **~'tivo** adj & m diminutive. **~zi'one f** decrease; (riduzione) reduction

dimissi'oni fpl resignation sg; **dare le ~** resign

di'mo|ra f residence. **~'rare** vi reside

dimo'strante mf demonstrator

dimo'stra|re vt demonstrate; (pro-

varo) prove; (*mostrare*) show. **~rsi** *vr* prove [to be]. **~tivo** *adj* demonstrative. **~zi'one** *f* demonstration; (*Math*) proof

di'namico, -a *adj* dynamic. **dina'mismo** *m* dynamism

dinami'tardo *adj* attentato **~**: bomb attack

dina'mite *f* dynamite

'dinamo *f inv* dynamo

di'nanzi *adv* in front ● *prep* **~ a** in front of

dina'stia *f* dynasty

dini'ego *m* denial

dinocco'lato *adj* lanky

dino'sauro *m* dinosaur

din'torni *mpl* outskirts, **nei ~i di** in the vicinity of. **~o** *adv* around

'dio *m* (*pl* **'dei**) god; **D~** God

di'ocesi *f inv* diocese

dipa'nare *vt* wind into a ball; *fig* unravel

diparti'mento *m* department

dipen'den|te *adj* depending ● *mf* employee. **~za** *f* dependence; (*edificio*) annexe

di'pendere *vi* **~ da** depend on; (*provenire*) derive from; **dipende** it depends

di'pinger|e *vt* paint; (*descrivere*) describe. **~si** *vr* (*truccarsi*) make up. **di'pinto** *pp di* **dipingere** ● *adj* painted ● *m* painting

di'plo|ma *m* diploma. **~'marsi** *vr* graduate

diplo'matico *adj* diplomatic ● *m* diplomat; (*pasticcino*) millefeuille (*with alcohol*)

diplo'mato *mf* person with school-leaving qualification ● *adj* qualified

diploma'zia *f* diplomacy

di'porto *m* imbarcazione da **~** pleasure craft

dira'dar|e *vt* thin out; make less frequent (*visite*). **~si** *vr* thin out; (*nebbia:*) clear

dira'ma|re *vt* issue ● *vi*, **~rsi** *vr* branch out; (*diffondersi*) spread. **~zi'one** *f* (*di strada*) fork

'dire *vt* say; (*raccontare, riferire*) tell; **~ quello che si pensa** speak one's mind; **voler ~** mean; **volevo ben ~!** I wondered!; **~ di sì/no** say yes/no; **si dice che...** rumour has it that...; **come si dice "casa" in inglese?** what's the English for "casa"?; **che ne dici di...?** how about...?; **non c'è che ~** there's no disputing that; **e ~ che,...** to think that,...; **a dir poco/tanto** at least; **most** ● *vi* **~ bene/male** di speak highly/ill of; **dica pure** how can I help you?; **dici sul serio?** are you serious?

diretta'mente *adv* directly

diret'tissima / per ~ (*Jur*) omitting normal procedure

diret'tissimo *m* fast train

diret'tiva *f* directive

di'retto *pp di* **dirigere** ● *adj* direct. **~ a** (*inteso*) meant for. **essere ~ a** be heading for. **in diretta** (*trasmissione*) live ● *m* (*treno*) through train

diret'tore, -'trice *mf* manager/manageress; (*di scuola*) headmaster, headmistress. **~tore d'orchestra** conductor

direzi'one *f* direction; (*di società*) management; (*Sch*) headmaster's/headmistress's office (*primary school*)

diri'gen|te *adj* ruling ● *mf* executive; (*Pol*) leader. **~za** *f* management. **~zi'ale** *adj* managerial

di'riger|e *vt* direct; conduct (*orchestra*); run (*impresa*). **~si** *vr* verso head for

dirim'petto *adv* opposite ● *prep* **~ a** facing

di'ritto[1], dritto *adj* straight; (*destro*) right ● *adv* straight; **andare ~** go straight on ● *m* right side; (*Tennis*) forehand

di'ritt|o[2] *m* right; (*Jur*) law. **~i** *pl*

...o | discordare

88

royalties

...ra *f* straight line; *fig* hon-

~ d'arrivo *Sport* home straight

...oc'cato *adj* tumbledown

...rom'pente *adj fig* explosive

dirot'ta|re *vt* reroute (treno, aereo); (*illegalmente*) hijack; divert (traffico) ● *vi* alter course. **~'tore, ~'trice** *mf* hijacker

di'rotto *m* (pioggia) pouring; (pianto) uncontrollable; **piovere a ~** rain heavily

di'rupo *m* precipice

dis'abile *mf* disabled person

disabi'tato *adj* uninhabited

disabitu'arsi *vr* **~ a** get out of the habit of

disac'cordo *m* disagreement

disadat'tato, -a *adj* maladjusted ● *m* misfit

disa'dorno *adj* unadorned

disa'gevole *adj* (scomodo) uncomfortable

disagi'ato *adj* poor; (vita) hard

di'sagio *m* discomfort; (difficoltà) inconvenience; (imbarazzo) embarrassment; **sentirsi a ~** feel uncomfortable; **disagi** *pl* (*privazioni*) hardships

disappro'va|re *vt* disapprove of. **~zi'one** *f* disapproval

disap'punto *m* disappointment

disar'mante *adj fig* disarming

disar'mare *vt/i* disarm. **di'sarmo** *m* disarmament

disa'strato, -a *adj* devastated

di'sastro *m* disaster; (☐: grande confusione) mess; (☐: persona) disaster area. **disa'stroso** *adj* disastrous

disat'ten|to *adj* inattentive. **~zi'one** *f* inattention; (svista) oversight

disatti'vare *vt* de-activate

disa'vanzo *m* deficit

disavven'tura *f* misadventure

dis'brigo *m* dispatch

dis'capito *m* **a ~ di** to the detriment of

dis'carica *f* scrap-yard

discen'den|te *adj* descending ● *m* descendant. **~za** *f* descent; (discendenti) descendants *pl*

di'scendere *vt/i* descend; (dal treno) get off; (da cavallo) dismount; (sbarcare) land. **~ da** (trarre origine da) be a descendant of

di'scepolo, -a *mf* disciple

di'scernere *vt* discern

di'sce|sa *f* descent; (pendio) slope; **~a in picchiata** (di aereo) nosedive; **essere in ~a** (strada:) go downhill. **~a libera** (in sci) downhill race. **di-sce'sista** *mf* (sciatore) downhill skier. **~o** *pp di* **discendere**

dis'chetto *m* (Comput) diskette

dischi'uder|e *vt* open; (svelare) disclose. **~si** *vr* open up

disci'oglier|e *vt*, **~si** *vr* dissolve; (fondersi) melt. **disci'olto** *pp di* **disciogliere**

disci'pli|na *f* discipline. **~'nare** *adj* disciplinary. **~'nato** *adj* disciplined

'disco *m* disc; (Comput) disk; *Sport* discus; (Mus) record; **ernia del ~** slipped disc. **~ fisso** (Comput) hard disk. **~ volante** flying saucer

discogra'fia *f* (insieme di incisioni) discography. **disco'grafico** *adj* (industria) recording; **casa discografica** recording company

'discolo *mf* rascal ● *adj* unruly

discol'par|e *vt* clear. **~si** *vr* clear oneself

disconnet'tersi *vr* go offline

disco'noscere *vt* disown (figlio)

discontinuità *f* (nel lavoro) irregularity. **discon'tinuo** *adj* intermittent; (rendimento) uneven

discor'dan|te *adj* discordant. **~za** *f* mismatch

discor'dare *vi* (opinioni:) conflict. **dis'corde** *adj* clashing. **dis'cordia** *f* discord; (*dissenso*) dissension

dis'cor|rere vi talk (di about). **~'sivo** adj colloquial. **dis'corso** pp di **discorrere ● m** speech; (*conversazione*) talk

dis'costo adj distant **●** adv far away; **stare ~** stand apart

disco'te|ca f disco; (*raccolta*) record library

discre'pan|te adj contradictory. **~za** f discrepancy

dis'cre|to adj discreet; (*moderato*) moderate; (*abbastanza buono*) fairly good. **~zi'one** f discretion; (*giudizio*) judgement; **a ~zi'one di** at the discretion of

discrimi'nante adj extenuating

discrimi'na|re vt discriminate. **~'torio** adj (*atteggiamento*) discriminatory. **~zi'one** f discrimination

discussi'one f discussion; (*alterco*) argument. **dis'cusso** pp di **discutere ● adj** controversial

dis'cutere vt discuss; (*formale*) debate; (*litigare*) argue; **~ sul prezzo** bargain. **discu'tibile** adj debatable; (*gusto*) questionable

disde'gnare vt disdain. **dis'degno** m disdain

dis'det|ta f retraction; (*sfortuna*) bad luck; (*Comm*) cancellation. **~o** pp di **disdire**

disdi'cevole adj unbecoming

dis'dire vt retract; (*annullare*) cancel

disedu'ca'tivo adj boorish

dise'gna|re vt draw; (*progettare*) design. **~tore**, **~trice** mf designer. **di'segno** m drawing; (*progetto*, *linea*) design

diser'bante m herbicide **●** adj herbicidal

disere'da|re vt disinherit **●** mf i **~ti** the dispossessed

diser'tare vt/i desert; **~tare la scuola** stay away from school. **~'tore** m deserter. **~zi'one** f desertion

disfaci'mento m decay

dis'fa|re vt undo; strip (*letto*); (*smantellare*) take down; (*annientare*) defeat; **~re le valigie** unpack [one's bags]. **~rsi** vi fall to pieces; (*sciogliersi*) melt; **● ~rci di** (*liberarsi di*) get rid of; **~rsi in lacrime** dissolve into tears. **~tta** f defeat. **~tto** adj fig worn out

disfat'tis|mo m defeatism. **~ta** adj & mf defeatist

disfunzi'one f disorder

dis'gelo m thaw

dis'grazi|a f misfortune; (*incidente*) accident; (*sfavore*) disgrace. **~ata'mente** adv unfortunately. **~'ato, -a** adj unfortunate **●** mf wretch

disgre'gar|e vt break up. **~si** vr disintegrate

disgu'ido m **~ postale** mistake in delivery

disgu'st|are vt disgust. **~arsi** vr **~arsi di** be disgusted by **dis'gusto** m disgust. **~oso** adj disgusting

disidra'ta|re vt dehydrate. **~to** adj dehydrated

disil'lude|re vt disenchant. **~si'one** f disenchantment. **~so** adj disillusioned

disimbal'lare vt unpack

disimpa'rare vt forget

disimpe'gnar|e vt release; (*compiere*) fulfil; redeem (*oggetto dato in pegno*). **~si** vr disengage oneself; (*cavarsela*) manage. **disim'pegno** m (*locale*) vestibule

disincan'tato adj (*disilluso*) disillusioned

disinfe'sta|re vt disinfest. **~zi'one** f disinfestation

disinfet'tante vt & m disinfectant

disinfet't'are vt disinfect. **~zi'one** f disinfection

disinfor'mato adj uninformed

disini'bito adj uninhibited

disinne'scare vt defuse (*mina*). **di-**

sin'nesco m (di bomba) bomb disposal

disinse'rire vt disconnect

disinte'gra|re vt, ~rsi vr disintegrate. ~zi'one f disintegration

disinteres'sarsi vr ~ di take no interest in. disinte'resse m indifference; (oggettività) disinterestedness

disintossi'ca|re vt detoxify. ~rsi vr come off drugs. ~zi'one f giving up alcohol/drugs

disin'volto adj natural. disinvol-'tura f confidence

disles'sia f dyslexia

disli'vello m difference in height; fig inequality

dislo'care vt (Mil) post

dismi'sura f excess; a ~ excessively

disobbedi'ente adj disobedient

disobbe'dire vt disobey

disoccu'pa|to, -a adj unemployed ● mf unemployed person. ~zi'o-ne f unemployment

disonestà f dishonesty. diso'nesto adj dishonest

disono'rare vt dishonour. diso-'nore m dishonour

di'sopra adv above ● adj upper ● m top

disordi'na|re vt disarrange. ~ta-'mente adv untidily. ~to adj untidy; (sregolato) immoderate. di'sordine m disorder

disorganiz'za|re vt disorganize. ~to adj disorganized. ~zi'one f disorganization

disorienta'mento m disorientation

disorien'ta|re vt disorientate. ~rsi vr lose one's bearings. ~to adj fig bewildered

di'sotto adv below ● adj lower ● m bottom

dis'paccio m dispatch

dispa'rato adj disparate

'dispari adj odd. ~tà f inv disparity

dis'parte adv in ~ apart; stare in ~ stand aside

dis'pendi|o m (spreco) waste. ~'oso adj expensive

dis'pen|sa f pantry; (distribuzione) distribution; (mobile) cupboard; (Jur) exemption; (Relig) dispensation; (pubblicazione periodica) number. ~'sare vt distribute; (esentare) exonerate

dispe'ra|re vi despair (di of). ~rsi vr despair. ~ta'mente (piangere) desperately. ~to adj desperate. ~zi'one f despair

dis'per|dere vt, ~dersi vr disperse. ~si'one f dispersion; (di truppe) dispersal. ~'sivo adj disorganized. ~so pp di disperdere ● adj scattered; (smarrito) lost ● m missing soldier

dis'pet|to m spite; a ~ di in spite of. ~'toso adj spiteful

dispia'c|ere m upset; (rammarico) regret; (dolore) sorrow; (preoccupazione) worry ● vi mi dispiace I'm sorry; non mi dispiace I don't dislike it; se non ti dispiace if you don't mind. ~i'uto adj upset; (dolente) sorry

dispo'nibil|e adj available; (gentile) helpful. ~ità f availability; (gentilezza) helpfulness

dis'por|re vt arrange ● vi dispose; (stabilire) order; ~re di have at one's disposal. ~si vr line up

disposi'tivo m device

disposizi'one f disposition; (ordine) order; (libera disponibilità) disposal. di-s'posto pp di disporre ● adj ready; (incline) disposed; essere ben disposto verso be favourably disposed towards

dis'potico adj despotic

dispregia'tivo adj disparaging

disprez'zare vt despise. dis'prezzo m contempt

'disputa f dispute

dispu'tar|e vi dispute; (gareggiare)

compete. **~si** vr **~si qcsa** contend for sth

dissacra'torio adj debunking

dissangua'mento m loss of blood

dissangu'a|re vt, **~rsi** vr bleed. **~rsi** vi fig become impoverished. **~to** adj bloodless; fig impoverished

dissa'pore m disagreement

dissec'car|e vt, **~si** vr dry up

dissemi'nare vt disseminate; (notizie) spread

dis'senso m dissent; (disaccordo) disagreement

dissente'ria f dysentery

dissen'tire vi disagree (da with)

dissertazi'one f dissertation

disser'vizio m poor service

disse'sta|re vt upset; (Comm) damage. **~to** adj (strada) uneven. **dis'sesto** m ruin

disse'tante adj thirst-quenching

disse'ta|re vt **~re qeno** quench sb's thirst

dissi'dente adj & mf dissident

dis'sidio m disagreement

dis'simile adj unlike, dissimilar

dissimu'lare vt conceal; (fingere) dissimulate

dissi'pa|re vt dissipate; (sperperare) squander. **~rsi** vr (nebbia) clear; (dubbio) disappear. **~to** adj dissipated. **~zi'one** f squandering

dissoci'ar|e vt, **~si** vr dissociate

disso'dare vt till

dis'solto pp di **dissolvere**

disso'luto adj dissolute

dis'solver|e vt, **~si** vr dissolve; (disperdere) dispel

disso'nanza f dissonance

dissua'|dere vt dissuade. **~si'one** f dissuasion. **~sivo** adj dissuasive

distac'car|e vt detach; Sport leave behind. **~si** vr be detached. **di'stacco** m detachment; (separazione)

separation; Sport lead

di'stan|te adj far away; fig: (person) detached ● adv far away **~za** f distance. **~zi'are** vt space out; Sport outdistance

di'stare vi be distant; **quanto dista?** how far is it?

di'sten|dere vt stretch out (parte del corpo); (spiegare) spread; (deporre) lay. **~dersi** vr stretch; (sdraiarsi) lie down; (rilassarsi) relax. **~si'one** f stretching; (rilassamento) relaxation; (Pol) détente. **~sivo** adj relaxing

di'steso, -a pp di **distendere** ● f expanse

distil'l|are vt/i distil. **~azi'one** f distillation. **~e'ria** f distillery

di'stinguer|e vt distinguish. **~si** vr distinguish oneself. **distin'guibile** adj distinguishable

di'stinta f (Comm) list. **~ di pagamento** receipt. **~ di versamento** paying in slip

distinta'mente adv individually; (chiaramente) clearly

distin'tivo adj distinctive ● m badge

di'stin|to, -a pp di **distinguere** ● adj distinct; (signorile) distinguished; **~ti saluti** Yours faithfully. **~zi'one** f distinction

di'stogliere vt **~ da** remove from; (dissuadere) dissuade from. **di'stolto** pp di **distogliere**

di'storcere vt twist

distorsi'one f (Med) sprain; (alterazione) distortion

di'stra|rre vt distract; (divertire) amuse. **~rsi** vr get distracted; (svagarsi) amuse oneself; **non ti distrarre!** pay attention!. **~tta'mente** adv absently. **~tto** pp di **distrarre** ● adj absent-minded; (disattento) inattentive. **~zi'one** f absentmindedness; (errore) inattention; (svago) amusement di'stretto m district

distribu'ire vt distribute; (disporre) arrange; deal (carte). ~tore m distributor; (di benzina) petrol pump; (automatico) slot-machine. ~zi|one f distribution

distri'car|e vt disentangle; ~si fig get out of it

di'strug|gere vt destroy. ~t'tivo adj destructive; (critica) negative. ~tto pp di distruggere. ~zi|one f destruction

distur'bar|e vt disturb; (sconvolgere) upset. ~si vr trouble oneself. di'sturbo m bother; (indisposizione) trouble; (Med) problem; (Radio, TV) interference; disturbi pl (Radio, TV) static. disturbi di stomaco stomach trouble

disubbidi'en|te adj disobedient. ~za f disobedience

disubbi'dire vi ~ a disobey

disugua|gli'anza f disparity. ~ale adj unequal; (irregolare) irregular

di'suso m cadere in ~ fall into disuse

di'tale m thimble

di'tata f poke; (impronta) finger-mark

'dito m (pl f dita) finger; (di vino) finger. ~ del piede toe

'ditta f firm

dit'tafono m dictaphone

ditta'tor|e m dictator. ~i'ale adj dictatorial. ditta'tura f dictatorship

dit'tongo m diphthong

di'urno adj daytime; spettacolo ~ matinée

'diva f diva

diva'ga|re vi digress. ~zi|one f digression

divam'pare vi burst into flames; fig spread like wildfire

di'vano m sofa. ~ letto sofa bed

divari'care vt open

di'vario m discrepancy; un ~ di

opinioni a difference of opinion

dive'n|ire vi = DIVENTARE. ~uto pp di divenire

diven'tare vi become; (lentamente) grow; (rapidamente) turn

di'verbio m squabble

diver'gen|te adj divergent. ~za f divergence; ~za di opinioni difference of opinion. di'vergere vi diverge

diversa'mente adv otherwise; (in modo diverso) differently

diversifi'ca|re vt diversify. ~rsi vr differ. ~zi|one f diversification

diver|si'one f diversion. ~sità f inv difference. ~sivo m diversion. di'verso adj different; diversi pl (parecchi) several ● pron several [people]

diver'tente adj amusing. diverti'mento m amusement

diver'tir|e vt amuse. ~si vr enjoy oneself

divi'dendo m dividend

di'vider|e vt divide; (condividere) share. ~si vr (separarsi) separate

di'vieto m prohibition; ~ di sosta no parking

divinco'larsi vr wriggle

divinità f inv divinity. di'vino adj divine

di'visa f uniform; (Comm) currency

divisi'one f division

di'vismo m worship; (atteggiamento) superstar mentality

di'vi|so pp di dividere. ~sore m divisor. ~sorio adj dividing

'divo, -a mf star

divo'rar|e vt devour. ~si vr ~si da be consumed with

divorzi'a|re vi divorce. ~to, -a mf divorcee. di'vorzio m divorce

divul'ga|re vt divulge; (rendere popolare) popularize. ~rsi vr spread. ~tivo adj popular. ~zi|one f popularization

dizio'nario m dictionary

dizi'one f diction

do m (Mus) C

> **DOC** Italian wines which are grown in certain specified areas and which conform to certain regulations may be styled DOC (Denominazione di Origine Controllata). The classification DOCG (Denominazione di Origine Controllata e Garantita) is awarded to DOC wines of particular quality. Wines must conform to the DOC criteria for at least five years before they can be classified as DOCG.

'**doccia** f shower; (grondaia) gutter; **fare la ~** have a shower

do'cen|te adj teaching • mf teacher; (Univ) lecturer. **~za** f (Univ) lecturer's qualification

'**docile** adj docile

documen'tar|e vt document. • **si** vr gather information (su about)

documen'tario adj & m documentary

documen'ta|to adj well-documented; (persona) well-informed. **~zi'one** f documentation

docu'mento m document

dodi'cesimo adj & m twelfth. '**dodici** adj & m twelve

do'gan|a f customs pl; (dazio) duty. **doga'nale** adj customs. **~l'ere** m customs officer

'**doglie** fpl labour pains

'**dogma** m dogma. **dog'matico** adj dogmatic. **~'tismo** m dogmatism

'**dolce** adj sweet; (clima) mild; (voce, consonante) soft; (acqua) fresh • m (portata) dessert; (torta) cake; **non mangio dolci** I don't eat sweet things. **~'mente** adv sweetly. **dol'cezza** f sweetness; (di clima) mildness

dolce'vita adj inv (maglione) rollneck

dolci'ario adj confectionery

dolci'astro adj sweetish

dolcifi'cante m sweetener • adj sweetening

dolci'umi mpl sweets

do'lente adj painful; (spiacente) sorry

do'le|re vi ache, hurt; (dispiacere) regret. **~rsi** vr regret; (protestare) complain; **~rsi di** be sorry for

'**dollaro** m dollar

'**dolo** m (Jur) malice; (truffa) fraud

Dolo'miti fpl le **~** the Dolomites

do'lore m pain; (morale) sorrow. **do'loroso** adj painful

do'loso adj malicious

do'manda f question; (richiesta) request; (scritta) application; (Comm) demand; **fare una ~ (a qcno)** ask (sb) a question. **~ di impiego** job application

doman'dar|e vt ask; (esigere) demand; **~e qcsa a qcno** ask sb for sth. **~si** vr wonder

do'mani adv tomorrow; **~ sera** tomorrow evening • m il **~** the future; **a ~** see you tomorrow

do'ma|re vt tame; fig control (emozioni). **~'tore** m tamer

domat'tina adv tomorrow morning

do'meni|ca f Sunday. **~'cale** adj Sunday attrib

do'mestico, -a adj domestic • m servant • f maid

domicili'are adj arresti domiciliari (Jur) house arrest

domicili'arsi vr settle

domi'cilio m domicile; (abitazione) home; **recapitiamo a ~** we do home deliveries

domi'na|re vt dominate; (controllare) control • vi rule over; (prevalere) be dominant. **~rsi** vr control oneself. **~'tore, ~'trice** mf ruler; **~zi'one** f domination

do'minio m control; (Pol) dominion; (ambito) field; **di ~ pubblico** common knowledge

don m inv (ecclesiastico) Father

do'na|re vt give; donate (sangue, organo); ●vi ~**re a** (giovare esteticamente) suit. ~**tore, ~'trice** mf donor. ~**zi'one** f donation

dondo'l|are vt swing; (cullare) rock ●vi sway. ~**arsi** vr swing. ~**io** m rocking. **dondolo** m swing; **cavallo/sedia a dondolo** rocking-horse/chair

dongio'vanni m inv Romeo

'donna f woman. ~ **di servizio** domestic help

don'naccia f pej whore

'dono m gift

'dopo prep after; (a partire da) since ●adv afterwards; (più tardi) later; (in seguito) later on; ~ **di me** after me

dopo'barba m inv aftershave

dopo'cena m inv evening

dopodi'ché adv after which

dopodo'mani adv the day after tomorrow

dopogu'erra m inv post-war period

dopo'pranzo m inv afternoon

dopo'sci adj & nm inv après-ski

doposcu'ola m inv after-school activities pl

dopo-'shampoo m inv conditioner ●adj inv conditioning

dopo'sole m inv aftersun cream ●adj inv aftersun

dopo'tutto adv after all

doppi'aggio m dubbing

doppia'mente adv doubly

doppi'a|re vt double; Sport lap; Cinema dub. ~**'tore, ~'trice** mf dubber

'doppio adj & adv double. ~ **clic** m (Comput) double click. ~ **fallo** m Tennis double fault. ~ **gioco** m (attrezzatura) double-dealing. ~ **mento** m double chin. ~ **senso** m double entendre. **doppi**

vetri mpl double glazing ●m double; Tennis doubles pl. ~ **misto** Tennis mixed doubles

doppi'one m duplicate

doppio'petto adj double-breasted

dop'pista mf doubles player

do'ra|re vt gild; (Culin). brown. ~**to** adj gilt; (color oro) golden. ~**'tura** f gilding

dormicchi'are vi doze

dormigli'one, -a mf sleepyhead; fig lazy-bones

dor'mi|re vi sleep; (essere addormentato) be asleep; fig be asleep. ~**ta** f good sleep. ~**'tina** f nap. ~**'torio** m dormitory

dormi'veglia m essere in ~ be half asleep

dor'sale adj dorsal ●f (di monte) ridge

'dorso m back; (di libro) spine; (di monte) crest; (nel nuoto) backstroke

do'saggio m dosage

do'sare vt dose; fig measure; ~ **le parole** weigh one's words

dosa'tore m measuring jug

'dose f dose; **in buona ~** fig in good measure. ~ **eccessiva** overdose

dossi'er m inv file

'dosso m (dorso) back; **levarsi di ~ gli abiti** take off one's clothes

do'ta|re vt endow; (di accessori) equip. ~**to** adj (persona) gifted; (fornito) equipped. ~**zi'one** f (attrezzatura) equipment; **in ~zione** at one's disposal

'dote f dowry; (qualità) gift

'dotto adj learned ●m scholar; (Anat) duct

dotto'rato m doctorate. **dot'tore, ~'ressa** mf doctor

dot'trina f doctrine

'dove adv where; **di ~ sei?** where do you come from; **fin ~?** how far?;

per ~? which way?

do'vere *vi* (*obbligo*) have to, must; **devo andare** I have to go, I must go; **devo venire anch'io?** do I have to come too?; **avresti dovuto dirmelo** you should have told me, you ought to have told me; **devo sedermi un attimo** I must sit down for a minute, I need to sit down for a minute; **dev'essere successo qualcosa** something must have happened; **come si deve** properly ● *vt* (*essere debitore di, derivare*) owe; **essere dovuto** a be due to ● *m* duty; **per ~** out of duty. **dove'roso** *adj* only right and proper

do'vunque *adv* (*dappertutto*) everywhere; (*in qualsiasi luogo*) anywhere ● *conj* wherever

do'vuto *adj* due; (*debito*) proper

doz'zina *f* dozen. **~nale** *adj* cheap

dra'gare *vt* dredge

'drago *m* dragon

dramma *m* drama. **dram'matico** *adj* dramatic. **~atiz'zare** *vt* dramatize. **~a'turgo** *m* playwright. **dram'mone** *m* (*film*) tear-jerker

drappeggi'are *vt* drape. **drap'peggio** *m* drapery

drap'pello *m* (*Mil*) squad. (*gruppo*) band

'drastico *adj* drastic

dre'nare *vt* drain

drib'blare *vt* (*in calcio*) dribble

'dritta *f* (*mano destra*) right hand; (*Naut*) starboard; (*informazione*) pointer, tip; **a ~ e a manca** left, right and centre

'dritto *adj* = DIRITTO ● *mf* 🅳 crafty so-and-so

driz'zare *vt* straighten; (*rizzare*) prick up. **~si** *vr* straighten [up]; (*alzarsi*) raise

'dro|ga *f* drug. **~'gare** *vt* drug. **~'garsi** *vr* take drugs. **~'gato, -a** *mf* drug addict

drogh|e'ria *f* grocery. **~i'ere, -a** *mf* grocer

'dubbio *adj* doubtful; (*ambiguo*) dubious ● *m* doubt; (*sospetto*) suspicion; **mettere in ~** doubt; **essere fuori ~o** be beyond doubt; **essere in ~o** be doubtful. **~'oso** *adj* doubtful

dubi'tare *vi* doubt; **~re di** doubt; (*diffidare*) mistrust; **dubito che venga** I doubt whether he'll come. **~'tivo** *adj* ambiguous

'duca, du'chessa *mf* duke; duchess

'due *adj* & *m* two

due'cento *adj* & *m* two hundred

du'ello *m* duel

due'mila *adj* & *m* two thousand

due'pezzi *m inv* (*bikini*) bikini

du'etto *m* duo; (*Mus*) duet

'duna *f* dune

'dunque *conj* therefore; (*allora*) well [then]

'duo *m inv* duo; (*Mus*) duet

du'omo *m* cathedral

dupli'care *vt* duplicate. **~to** *m* duplicate. **'duplice** *adj* double; **in duplice** in duplicate

dura'mente *adv* (*lavorare*) hard; (*rimproverare*) harshly

du'rante *prep* during

du'r|are *vi* last; (*cibo*) keep; (*resistere*) hold out. **~ata** *f* duration. **~a'turo, ~evole** *adj* lasting, enduring

du'rezza *f* hardness; (*di carne*) toughness; (*di voce, padre*) harshness

'duro, -a *adj* hard; (*persona, carne*) tough; (*voce*) harsh; (*pane*) stale ● *mf* tough person

du'rone *m* hardened skin

'duttile *adj* (*materiale*) ductile; (*carattere*) malleable

DVD *m inv* DVD

Ee

e, ed *conj* and

'**ebano** *m* ebony

eb'bene *conj* well [then]

eb'brezza *f* inebriation; (*euforia*) elation; **guida in stato di ~** drink-driving. '**ebbro** *adj* inebriated; (*di gioia*) ecstatic

'**ebete** *adj* stupid

ebollizi'one *f* boiling

e'braico *adj* Hebrew ● *m* (*lingua*) Hebrew. **e'breo, -a** *adj* Jewish ● *mf* Jew

eca'tombe *f* **fare un'~** wreak havoc

ecc *abbr* (*eccetera*) etc

ecce'den|te *adj* (*peso, bagaglio*) excess. **~za** *f* excess; (*d'avanzo*) surplus; **avere qcsa in ~za** have an excess of sth; **bagagli in ~za** excess baggage. **~za di cassa** surplus. **ec'cedere** *vt* exceed ● *vi* go too far; **eccedere nel bere** drink too much

eccel'len|te *adj* excellent. **~za** *f* excellence; (*titolo*) Excellency; **per ~za** par excellence. **ec'cellere** *vi* excel (**in** at)

ec'centrico, -a *adj* & *mf* eccentric

eccessiva'mente *adv* excessively. **ecces'sivo** *adj* excessive

ec'cesso *m* excess; **andare agli eccessi** go to extremes; **all'~** to excess. **~ di velocità** speeding

ec'cetera *adv* et cetera

ec'cetto *prep* except; **~ che** (*a meno che*) unless. **eccettu'are** *vt* except

eccezio'nal|e *adj* exceptional. **~'mente** *adv* exceptionally; (*contrariamente alla regola*) as an exception

eccezi'one *f* exception; (*Jur*) objection; **a ~ di** with the exception of

eccita'mento *m* excitement. **ecci-** '**tante** *adj* exciting; (*sostanza*) stimulant ● *m* stimulant

ecci'ta|re *vt* excite. **~rsi** *vr* get excited. **~to** *adj* excited

eccitazi'one *f* excitement

ecclesi'astico *adj* ecclesiastical ● *m* priest

'**ecco** *adv* (*qui*) here; (*là*) there; **~!** exactly!; **~ fatto** there we are; **~ la tua borsa** here is your bag; **~ [li] mio figlio** there is my son; **~mi** here I am; **~ tutto** that is all

ec'come *adv* & *int* and how!

echeggi'are *vi* echo

e'clissi *f inv* eclipse

'**eco** *f* (*pl m* **echi**) echo

ecogra'fia *f* scan

ecolo'gia *f* ecology. **eco'logico** *adj* ecological; (*prodotto*) environmentally friendly

e commerci'ale *f* ampersand

econo'mia *f* economy; (*scienza*) economics; **fare ~ia** economize (**di** on). **eco'nomico** *adj* economic; (*a buon prezzo*) cheap. **~ista** *mf* economist. **~iz'zare** *vt/i* economize; save (*tempo, denaro*). **e'conomo, -a** *adj* thrifty ● *mf* (*di collegio*) bursar

é'cru *adj inv* raw

ec'zema *m* eczema

ed *conj vedi* **e**

'**edera** *f* ivy

e'dicola *f* [newspaper] kiosk

edifi'cabile *adj* (*area, terreno*) classified as suitable for development

edifi'cante *adj* edifying

edifi'care *vt* build

edi'ficio *m* building; *fig* structure

e'dile *adj* building *attrib*

edi'lizi|a *f* building trade. **~o** *adj* building *attrib*

edi|'tore, -'trice *adj* publishing ● *mf* publisher; (*curatore*) editor. **~to'ria** *f* publishing. **~tori'ale** *adj* publishing ● *m* editorial

edizi'one *f* edition; (*di manifestazione*)

educare | elevare

performance. **~ ridotta** abridg[e]ment. **~ della sera** (di telegiornale) evening news

edu'ca|re vt educate; (allevare) bring up. **~'tivo** adj educational. **~to** adj polite. **~'tore**, **~'trice** mf educator, **~zi'one** f education; (di bambini) upbringing; (buono maniero) [good] manners pl. **~zione fisica** physical education

e'felide f freckle

effemi'nato adj effeminate

efferve'scente adj effervescent; (frizzante) fizzy; (aspirina) soluble

effettiva'mente adv è troppo tardi – ~ it's too late – so it is

effet'tivo adj actual; (offiooo) effective; (personale) permanent; (Mil) regular ●m sum total

ef'fett|o m effect. (impressione) impression; **in ~i** in fact; **~i personali** personal belongings. **~u'are** vt carry out (controllo, sondaggio), **~u'arsi** v take place.

effi'cace adj effective. **~ia** f effectiveness

effici'en|te adj efficient. **~za** f efficiency

ef'fimero adj ephemeral

effusi'one f effusion

E'geo m **l'~** the Aegean [Sea]

E'gitto m Egypt. **egizi'ano**, **-a** agg & mf Egyptian

'egli pers pron he; **~ stesso** he himself

ego'centrico, **-a** adj egocentric

ego'is|mo m selfishness. **~ta** adj selfish ●mf selfish person. **~tico** adj selfish

e'gregio adj distinguished; **E~ Signore** Dear Sir

eiaculazi'one f ejaculation

elabo'ra|re vt elaborate; process (dati). **~to** adj elaborate. **~zi'one** f elaboration; (di dati) processing. **~zione [di] testi** word processing

elar'gire vt lavish

elastici|tà f elasticity. **~z'zato** adj (stoffa) elasticated. **e'lastico** adj elastic; (tessuto) stretch; (orario, mente) flexible; (persona) easygoing ●m elastic; (fascia) rubber band

ele'fante m elephant

ele'gan|te adj elegant. **~za** f elegance

e'leggere vt elect. **eleg'gibile** adj eligible

elemen'tare adj elementary; **scuola ~** primary school

ele'mento m element; **elementi** pl (fatti) data; (rudimenti) elements

ele'mosina f charity; **chiedere l'~** beg. **elemosi'nare** vt/i beg

elen'care vt list

e'lenco m list. **~ abbonati** telephone directory. **~ telefonico** telephone directory

elet'tivo adj (carica) elective. **e'letto**, **-a** pp di **eleggere** ●adj chosen ●mf elected member

eletto'rale adj electoral. **~to** m electorate

elet'tore, **-'trice** mf voter

elet'trauto m inv garage for electrical repairs

elettri'cista m electrician

elettri|cità f electricity. **e'lettrico** adj electric. **~z'zante** (notizia, gara) electrifying. **~z'zare** vt fig electrify. **~z'zato** adj fig electrified

elettrocardio'gramma m electrocardiogram

e'lettrodo m electrode

elettrodo'mestico m [electrical] household appliance

elet'trone m electron

elet'tronico, **-a** adj electronic ●f electronics

ele'va|re vt raise; (promuovere) promote; (erigere) erect; (fig: migliorare) better; **~ al quadrato/cubo** square/cube. **~rsi** vr rise; (edificio:) stand.

~to adj high. ~zi'one f elevation

elezi'one f election

'elica f (Aeron, Naut) propeller; (del ventilatore) blade

eli'cottero m helicopter

elimi'na|re vt eliminate. ~'toria f Sport preliminary heat. ~zi'one f elimination

é'li|te f inv élite. ~'tista adj élitist

'ella pers pron she

el'metto m helmet

elogi'are vt praise

elo'quen|te adj eloquent; fig telltale. ~za f eloquence

e'lu|dere vt elude; evade (sorveglianza). ~'sivo adj elusive

el'vetico adj Swiss

emaci'ato adj emaciated

'e-mail f e-mail; indirizzo ~ e-mail address. ~ spazzatura junk e-mail

ema'na|re vt give off; pass (legge) ● vi emanate

emanci'pa|re vt emancipate. ~rsi vr become emancipated. ~to adj emancipated. ~zi'one f emancipation

emargi'na|to m marginalized person. ~zi'one f marginalization

em'bargo m embargo

em'ble|ma m emblem. ~'matico adj emblematic

embrio'nale adj embryonic. em-bri'one m embryo

emen'da|mento m amendment. ~'dare vt amend

emer'gen|te adj emergent. ~za f emergency; in caso di ~za in an emergency

e'mergere vi emerge; (sottomarino:) surface; (distinguersi) stand out

e'merso pp di emergere

e'messo pp di emettere

e'mettere vt emit; give out (luce, suono); let out (grido); (mettere in circolazione) issue

emi'crania f migraine

emi'gra|re vi emigrate. ~to, -a mf immigrant. ~zi'one f emigration

emi'nen|te adj eminent. ~za f eminence

e'miro m emir

emis'fero m hemisphere

emis'sario m emissary

emissi'one f emission; (di denaro) issue; (trasmissione) broadcast

emit'tente adj issuing; (trasmittente) broadcasting ● f transmitter

emorra'gia f haemorrhage

emor'roidi fpl piles

emotivi'tà f emotional make-up. emo'tivo adj emotional

emozio'na|nte adj exciting; (commovente) moving. ~re vt excite; (commuovere) move. ~rsi vr become excited; (commuoversi) be moved. ~to adj excited; (commosso) moved. emozi'one f emotion; (agitazione) excitement

'empio adj impious; (spietato) pitiless; (malvagio) wicked

em'pirico adj empirical

em'porio m emporium; (negozio) general store

emu'la|re vt emulate. ~zi'one f emulation

emulsi'one f emulsion

en'ciclica f encyclical

enciclope'dia f encyclopaedia

encomi'are vt commend. en'co-mio m commendation

en'demico adj endemic

endo've|na f intravenous injection. ~'noso adj intravenous; per via ~nosa intravenously

ener'getico adj (risorse, crisi) energy attrib; (alimento) energy-giving

ener'gia f energy. e'nergico adj energetic; (efficace) strong

'enfasi f emphasis

en'fati|co adj emphatic. ~z'zare vt emphasize

e'nigma m enigma. enig'matico adj enigmatic. enig'mistica f puzzles pl

E.N.I.T. m abbr (Ente Nazionale Italiano per il Turismo) Italian State Tourist Office

en'nesimo adj (Math) nth; ⊡ umpteenth

e'norm|e adj enormous. ~e'mente adv massively. ~ità f inv enormity; (assurdità) absurdity

eno'teca f wine-tasting shop

'ente m board; (società) company, (filosofia) being

entità f inv entity; (gravità) seriousness; (dimensione) extent

entou'rage m inv entourage

en'trambi adj & pron both

en'tra|re vi go in, enter; ~re in go into; (stare in, trovar posto in) fit into; (arruolarsi) join; ~rci (avere a che fare) have to do with; tu che c'entri? what has it got to do with you? ~ta f entrance, ~te pl (Comm) takings, (reddito) income pl

'entro prep (tempo) within

entro'terra m inv hinterland

entusias'mante adj fascinating

entusias'mar|e vt arouse enthusiasm in. ~si be enthusiastic (per about)

entusi'as|mo m enthusiasm. ~ta adj enthusiastic ● mf enthusiast. ~tico adj enthusiastic

enume'ra|re vt enumerate. ~zi'one f enumeration

enunci'a|re vt enunciate. ~zi'one f enunciation

epa'tite f hepatitis

'epico adj epic

epide'mia f epidemic

epi'dermide f epidermis

Epifa'nia f Epiphany

epi'gramma m epigram

epiles'sia f epilepsy. epi'lettico, -a adj & mf epileptic

e'pilogo m epilogue

epi'sodi|co adj episodic; caso ~co one-off case. ~o m episode

'epoca f age; (periodo) period; a quell'~ in those days; auto d'~ vintage car

ep'pure conj [and] yet

epu'rare vt purge

equa'tore m equator. equatori'ale adj equatorial

equazi'one f equation

e'questre adj equestrian; circo ~ circus

equili'bra|re vt balance. ~to adj well-balanced. equi'librio m balance; (buon senso) common sense; (di bilancia) equilibrium

equili'brismo m fare ~ do a balancing act

e'quino adj horse attrib

equi'nozio m equinox

equipaggia'mento m equipment

equipaggi'are vt equip; (di persone) man

equi'paggio m crew; (Aeron) cabin crew

equipa'rare vt make equal

é'quipe f inv team

equità f equity

equitazi'one f riding

equiva'len|te adj & m equivalent. ~za f equivalence

equiva'lere vi ~ a be equivalent to

equivo'care vi misunderstand

e'quivoco adj equivocal; (sospetto) suspicious ● m misunderstanding

'equo adj fair, just

'era f era

'erba f grass; (aromatica, medicinale) herb. ~ cipollina chives pl. er'baccia f weed. er'baceo adj herbaceous

erbi'cida m weed-killer

erbo'rist|a *mf* herbalist. **∼e'ria** *f* herbalist's shop

er'boso *adj* grassy

er'culeo *adj* (*forza*) herculean

e'red|e *mf* heir; heiress. **∼ità** *f inv* inheritance; (*Biol*) heredity. **∼i'tare** *vt* inherit. **∼itarietà** *f* heredity. **∼i'tario** *adj* hereditary

ere'sia *f* heresy. **e'retico, -a** *adj* heretical ● *mf* heretic

e're|tto *pp di* **erigere** ● *adj* erect. **∼zi'one** *f* erection; (*costruzione*) building

er'gastolo *m* life sentence; (*luogo*) prison

'erica *f* heather

e'rigere *vt* erect; (*fig: fondare*) found

eri'tema *m* (*cutaneo*) inflammation; (*solare*) sunburn

er'metico *adj* hermetic; (*a tenuta d'aria*) airtight

'ernia *f* hernia

e'rodere *vi* erode

e'ro|e *m* hero. **∼ico** *adj* heroic. **∼ismo** *m* heroism

ero'ga|re *vt* distribute; (*fornire*) supply. **∼zi'one** *f* supply

ero'ina *f* heroine; (*droga*) heroin

erosi'one *f* erosion

e'rotico *adj* erotic

er'rante *adj* wandering. **er'rare** *vi* wander; (*sbagliare*) be mistaken

er'rato *adj* (*sbagliato*) mistaken

erronea'mente *adv* mistakenly

er'rore *m* error; (*di stampa*) misprint; **essere in ∼** be wrong

'erta *f* **stare all'∼** be on the alert

eru'di|rsi *vr* get educated. **∼to** *adj* learned

erut'tare *vt* (*vulcano:*) erupt ● *vi* (*ruttare*) belch. **eruzi'one** *f* eruption; (*Med*) rash

esage'ra|re *vt* exaggerate ● *vi* exaggerate; (*nel comportamento*) go over

the top; **∼re nel mangiare** eat too much. **∼ta'mente** *adv* excessively. **∼to** *adj* exaggerated; (*prezzo*) exorbitant ● *m* è un **∼to** he exaggerates. **∼zi'one** *f* exaggeration; è costato un'**∼zione** it cost the earth

esa'lare *vt/i* exhale

esal'ta|re *vt* exalt; (*entusiasmare*) elate. **∼to** *adj* (*fanatico*) fanatical ● *m* fanatic. **∼zi'one** *f* exaltation; (*in discorso*) fervour

e'same *m* examination, exam; **dare un ∼** take an exam; **prendere in ∼** examine. **∼ del sangue** blood test. **esami** *pl* **di maturità** ≈ A-levels

esami'na|re *vt* examine. **∼tore, ∼'trice** *mf* examiner

e'sangue *adj* bloodless

e'sanime *adj* lifeless

esaspe'rante *adj* exasperating

esaspe'ra|re *vt* exasperate. **∼rsi** *vr* get exasperated. **∼zi'one** *f* exasperation

esat|ta'mente *adv* exactly. **∼'tezza** *f* exactness; (*precisione*) precision; (*di risultato*) accuracy

e'satto *pp di* **esigere** ● *adj* exact; (*risposta, risultato*) correct; (*orologio*) right; **hai l'ora esatta?** do you have the right time?; **sono le due esatte** it's two o'clock exactly

esat'tore *m* collector

esau'dire *vt* grant; fulfil (*speranze*)

esauri'ente *adj* exhaustive

esau'ri|re *vt* exhaust. **∼rsi** *vr* exhaust oneself; (*merci ecc:*) run out. **∼to** *adj* exhausted; (*merci*) sold out; (*libro*) out of print; **fare il tutto ∼to** (*spettacolo:*) play to a full house

'esca *f* bait

escande'scenz|a *f* outburst; **dare in ∼e** lose one's temper

escla'ma|re *vi* exclaim. **∼'tivo** *adj* exclamatory. **∼zi'one** *f* exclamation

es'clu|dere *vt* exclude (*possibilità*,

ipotesi). **∼si'one** f exclusion. **∼'siva** f exclusive right; **in ∼siva** exclusive. **∼siva'mente** adv exclusively. **∼'sivo** adj exclusive. **∼so** pp di **escludere** ● adj **non è ∼so che ci sia** it's not out of the question that he'll be there

escogi'tare vt contrive

escursi'one f excursion; (scorreria) raid; (di temperatura) range

ese'cra|bile adj abominable. **∼re** vt abhor

esecu'tivo adj & m executive. **∼'tore, ∼'trice** mf executor: (Mus) performer. **∼zi'one** f execution; (Mus) performance

esegu'ire vt carry out; (Jur) execute; (Mus) perform

e'sempio m example; **ad o per ∼** for example; **dare l'∼ a qcno** set sb an example; **fare un ∼** give an example

esem'plare m esemplare; (di libro) copy

esen'tar|e vt exempt. **∼si** vr free oneself. **e'sente** adj exempt. **esente da imposta** duty-free. **esente da IVA** VAT-exempt

esen'tasse adj duty free

e'sequie fpl funeral rites

eser'cente mf shopkeeper

eserci'ta|re vt exercise; (addestrare) train; (fare uso di) exert; (professione) practise. **∼rsi** vr practise. **∼zi'one** f exercise; (Mil) drill

e'sercito m army

eser'cizio m exercise; (pratica) practice; (Comm) financial year; (azienda) business; **essere fuori ∼** be out of practice

esi'bi|re vt show off; produce (documenti). **∼rsi** vr (Theat) perform; fig show off. **∼zi'one** f (Theat) performance; (di documenti) production

esibizio'nis|mo m showing off

esi'gen|te adj exacting; (pignolo) fastidious. **∼za** f demand; (bisogno) need. **e'sigere** vt demand; (riscuotere) collect

e'siguo adj meagre

esila'rante adj exhilarating

'esile adj slender; (voce) thin

esili'ar|e vt exile. **∼rsi** vr go into exile. **∼to, -a** adj exiled ● mf exile. **e'silio** m exile

e'simer|e vt release. **∼si** vr **∼si da** get out of

esi'sten|te adj existing. **∼za** f existence.

e'sistere vi exist

esi'tante adj hesitating; (voce) faltering

esi'ta|re vi hesitate. **∼zi'one** f hesitation

'esito m result; **avere buon ∼** be a success

'esodo m exodus

e'sofago m oesophagus

esone'rare vt exempt. **e'sonero** m exemption

esorbi'tante adj exorbitant

esorciz'zare vt exorcize

esor'di|ente mf person making his/her début. **∼o** m début; (di opening; (di attore) début. **esor'dire** vi début

esor'tare vt (pregare) beg; (incitare) urge

e'sotico adj exotic

espa'drillas fpl espadrilles

es'pan|dere vt expand. **∼dersi** vr expand; (diffondersi) extend. **∼si'one** f expansion. **∼'sivo** adj expansive; (persona) friendly

espatri'are vi leave one's country. **es'patrio** m expatriation

espedi'ente m expedient; **vivere di ∼i** live by one's wits

es'pellere vt expel

esperi'enza f experience; **parlare per ∼enza** speak from experience. **∼'mento** m experiment

es'perto, -a adj & mf expert

espia|re vt atone for. **~'torio** adj expiatory

espi'rare vt/i breathe out

espli'care vt carry on

esplicita'mente adv explicitly. **es'plicito** adj explicit

es'plodere vi explode ● vt fire

esplo'ra|re vt explore. **~tore**, **~'trice** mf explorer; **giovane ~tore** boy scout. **~zi'one** f exploration

esplosi'one f explosion. **~'sivo** adj & m explosive

es'por|re vt expose; display (merci); (spiegare) expound; exhibit (quadri ecc). **~si** vr (compromettersi) compromise oneself; (al sole) expose oneself

espor'ta|re vt export. **~tore**, **~'trice** mf exporter. **~zi'one** f export

esposizi'one f (mostra) exhibition; (in vetrina) display; (spiegazione ecc) exposition; (posizione, fotografia) exposure. **es'posto** pp di **esporre** ● adj exposed; **esposto a** (rivolto a) facing ● m (Jur) statement

espressa'mente adv expressly; **non l'ha detto ~** he didn't put it in so many words

espressi'one f expression. **~'sivo** adj expressive

es'presso pp di **esprimere** ● adj express ● m (lettera) express letter; (treno) express train; (caffè) espresso; **per ~** (spedire) [by] express [post]

es'primer|e vt express. **~si** vr express oneself

espropri'a|re vt dispossess. **~zi'one** f (Jur) expropriation. **es'proprio** m expropriation

espulsi'one f expulsion. **es'pulso** pp di **espellere**

es'senza f essence. **~i'ale** adj essential ● m important thing. **~ial'mente** adj essentially

'essere

● vi be; **c'è** there is; **ci sono** there are; **che ora è? – sono le dieci** what time is it? – it's ten o'clock; **chi è? – sono io** who is it? – it's me; **ci sono!** (ho capito) I've got it!; **ci siamo!** (siamo arrivati) here we are at last!; **siamo in due** there are two of us; **questa camicia è da lavare** this shirt is to be washed; **non è da te** it's not like you; **~ di** (provenire da) be from; **~ per** (favorevole) be in favour of; **se fossi in te,...** if I were you,...; **sarà!** if you say so!; **come sarebbe a dire?** what are you getting at?

● v aux have; (in passivi) be; **siamo arrivati** we have arrived; **ci sono stato ieri** I was there yesterday; **sono nato a Torino** I was born in Turin; **è riconosciuto come...** he is recognized as...; **è stato detto che** it has been said that

● m being. **~ umano** human being. **~ vivente** living creature

essic'cato adj dried

'esso, -a pers pron he, she; (cosa, animale) it

est m east

'estasi f ecstasy; **andare in ~ per** go into raptures over

e'state f summer

e'sten|dere vt extend. **~dersi** vr spread; (allungarsi) stretch. **~si'one** f extension; (ampiezza) expanse; (Mus) range. **~'sivo** adj extensive

estenu'ante adj exhausting

estenu'a|re vt wear out; deplete (risorse, casse). **~rsi** vr wear oneself out

esteri'or|e adj & m exterior. **~'mente** adv externally; (di persone) outwardly

esterna'mente adv on the outside

ester'nare vt express, show

e'sterno adj external; **per uso ~** for external use only ● m (allievo) day-boy; (Archit) exterior; (in film) location shot

'estero adj foreign ● m foreign countries pl; **all'~** abroad

esterre'fatto adj horrified

e'steso pp di **estendere** ● adj extensive; (diffuso) widespread; **per ~** (scrivere) in full

e'steti|ca f aesthetics sg. **~a'mente** adv aesthetically. **~o**, -a adj aesthetic; (chirurgia, chirurgo) plastic. **este'tista** f beautician

'estimo m estimate

estin'guere vt extinguish. **~guersi** vr die out. **~to**, -a pp di **estinguere** ● mf deceased. **~'tore** m [fire] extinguisher. **~zi'one** f extinction; (di incendio) putting out

estir'pare vt extract; (dente) fig eradicate (crimine, malattia). **~zi'one** f eradication; (di dente) extraction

e'stivo adj summer

e'stor|cere vt extort. **~si'one** f extortion. **~to** pp di **estorcere**

estradizi'one f extradition

e'straneo, -a adj extraneous; (straniero) foreign ● mf stranger

estrani'ar|e vt estrange. **~si** vr become estranged

e'stra|rre vt extract; (sorteggiare) draw. **~tto** pp di **estrarre** ● m extract; (brano) excerpt; (documento) abstract. **~tto conto** statement [of account], bank statement. **~zi'one** f extraction; (sorte) draw

estrema'mente adv extremely

estre'mis|mo m extremism. **~ta** mf extremist

estremità f inv extremity; (di una corda) end ● fpl (Anat) extremities

e'stremo adj extreme; (ultimo) last; **misure estreme** drastic measures; **l'E~ Oriente** the Far East ● m (limite) extreme. **estremi** pl (di documento) main points; (di reato) essential elements; **essere agli estremi** be at the end of one's tether

'estro m (disposizione artistica) talent; (ispirazione) inspiration; (capriccio) whim. **e'stroso** adj talented; (capriccioso) unpredictable

estro'mettere vt expel

estro'verso adj extroverted ● m extrovert

estu'ario m estuary

esube'ran|te adj exuberant. **~za** f exuberance

'esule mf exile

esul'tante adj exultant

esul'tare vi rejoice

esu'mare vt exhume

età f inv age; **raggiungere la maggiore ~** come of age; **un uomo di mezz'~** a middle-aged man

'etere m ether. **e'tereo** adj ethereal

eterna'mente adv eternally

eternità f eternity; **è un'~ che non la vedo** I haven't seen her for ages

e'terno adj eternal; (questione; problema) age-old; **in ~** fig for ever

eterosessu'ale mf heterosexual

'etica f ethics

eti'chetta[1] f label; price-tag

eti'chetta[2] f etiquette

etichet'tare vt label

'etico adj ethical

eti'lometro m Breathalyzer®

Eti'opia f Ethiopia

'etnico adj ethnic

e'trusco adj adj Etruscan

'ettaro m hectare

'etto, etto'grammo m hundred grams, ≈ quarter pound

eucari'stia f Eucharist

eufe'mismo m euphemism
eufo'ria f elation; (Med) euphoria. **eu'forico** adj elated; (Med) euphoric
'euro m inv Fin euro
Euro'city m international Intercity
eurodepu'tato m Euro MP, MEP
Eu'ropa f Europe. **euro'peo, -a** agg & mf European
eutana'sia f euthanasia
evacu'a|re vt evacuate. **~zi'one** f evacuation
e'vadere vt evade; (sbrigare) deal with ● vi ~ **da** escape from
evane'scente adj vanishing
evan'gel|ico adj evangelical. **evan'gelista** m evangelist
evapo'ra|re vi evaporate. **~zi'one** f evaporation
evasi'one f escape; (fiscale) evasion; fig escapism. **eva'sivo** adj evasive
e'vaso pp di evadere ● m fugitive
eva'sore m ~ **fiscale** tax evader
eveni'enza f eventuality
e'vento m event
eventu'al|e adj possible. **~ità** f inv eventuality
evi'den|te adj evident; **è ~te che** it is obvious that. **~te'mente** adv evidently. **~za** f evidence; **mettere in ~za** emphasize; **mettersi in ~za** make oneself conspicuous
evidenzi'a|re vt highlight. **~'tore** m (penna) highlighter
evi'tare vt avoid; (risparmiare) spare
evo'care vt evoke
evo'lu|to pp di evolvere ● adj evolved; (progredito) progressive; (civiltà, nazione) advanced; **una donna evoluta** a modern woman. **~zi'one** f evolution; (di ginnasta, aereo) circle
e'volver|e vt develop. **~si** vr evolve
ev'viva int hurray; **~ il Papa!** long live the Pope!; **gridare ~** cheer
ex+ pref ex+, former

'extra adj inv extra; (qualità) first-class ● m inv extra
extracomuni'tario adj non-EU
extrater'restre mf extra-terrestrial

Extravergine Olive oil which is obtained from the first pressing of the olives is called extravergine (extra virgin). It has a distinctive peppery flavour and is often a cloudy greenish colour. A less refined grade, suitable for cooking, is obtained by using chemical methods. This is called simply olio d'oliva. **_i_**

Ff

fa¹ m inv (Mus) F
fa² adv ago; **due mesi ~** two months ago
fabbi'sogno m requirements pl
'fabbrica f factory
fabbri'cabile adj (area, terreno) that can be built on
fabbri'cante m manufacturer
fabbri'ca|re vt build; (produrre) manufacture; (fig: inventare) fabricate. **~to** m building. **~zi'one** f manufacturing; (costruzione) building
'fabbro m blacksmith
fac'cend|a f matter; **~e** pl (lavori domestici) housework sg. **~i'ere** m wheeler-dealer
fac'chino m porter
'facci|a f face; (di foglio) side; **~a a ~a** face to face; **~a tosta** cheek; **voltar ~a** change sides; **di ~a** (palazzo) opposite; **alla ~a di** (🔒: a dispetto di) in spite of. **~'ata** f façade; (di foglio) side; (fig: esteriorità) outward

appearance

fa'ceto *adj* facetious; **tra il serio e il** ~ half joking

fa'chiro *m* fakir

'facil|e *adj* easy; (*affabile*) easygoing; **essere** ~**e alla critiche** be quick to criticize; **essere** ~**e** easy to do a lot; ~**e a farsi** easy to do; **è** ~**e che piova** it's likely to rain. ~**ità** *f* ease; (*disposizione*) aptitude; **avere** ~**ità di parola** express oneself well

facili'ta|re *vt* facilitate. ~**zi'one** *f* facility; ~**zioni** *pl* special terms

facil'mente *adv* (*con facilità*) easily; (*probabilmente*) probably

faci'lone *adj* slapdash. ~**'ria** *f* slapdash attitude

facino'roso *adj* violent

facoltà *f inv* faculty; (*potere*) power. **facolta'tivo** *adj* optional; **fermata facoltativa** request stop

facol'toso *adj* wealthy

'faggio *m* beech

fagi'ano *m* pheasant

faglo'lino *m* French bean

fagi'olo *m* bean; **a** ~ (*arrivare, capitare*) at the right time

fagoci'tare *vt* gobble up (*società*)

fa'gotto *m* bundle; (*Mus*) bassoon

'faida *f* feud

fai da te *m* do-it-yourself, DIY

fal'cata *f* stride

'falce *f* scythe. **fal'cetto** *m* sickle. ~**i'are** *vt* cut; *fig* mow down. ~**ia'trice** *f* [lawn-]mower

'falco *m* hawk

fal'cone *m* falcon

'falda *f* stratum; (*di neve*) flake; (*di cappello*) brim; (*pendio*) slope

fale'gname *m* carpenter. ~**'ria** *f* carpentry

'falla *f* leak

fal'lace *adj* deceptive

fallimen'tare *adj* disastrous; (*Jur*) bankruptcy. **falli'mento** *m Fin* bankruptcy, *fig* failure

fal'li|re *vi Fin* go bankrupt; *fig* fail ● *vt* miss (colpo). ~**to, -a** *adj* unsuccessful; *Fin* bankrupt ● *mf* failure; *Fin* bankrupt

'fallo *m* fault; (*errore*) mistake; *Sport* foul; (*imperfezione*) flaw; **senza** ~ without fail

falò *m inv* bonfire

fal'sar|e *vt* alter; (*falsificare*) falsify. ~**io, -a** *mf* forger; (*di documenti*) counterfeiter

falsifi'ca|re *vt* fake; (*contraffare*) forge. ~**zi'one** *f* (*di documenti*) falsification

falsità *f* falseness

'falso *adj* false; (*sbagliato*) wrong; (*opera d'arte ecc*) fake; (*gioielli, oro*) imitation ● *m* forgery; **giurare il** ~ commit perjury

'fama *f* fame; (*reputazione*) reputation

'fame *f* hunger; **aver** ~ be hungry; **fare la** ~ barely scrape a living. **fa'melico** *adj* ravenous

famige'rato *adj* infamous

fa'miglia *f* family

famili'ar|e *adj* family *attrib*; (*ben noto*) familiar; (*senza cerimonie*) informal ● *mf* relative, relation. ~**ità** *f* familiarity; (*informalità*) informality. ~**iz'zarsi** *vr* familiarize oneself

fa'moso *adj* famous

fa'nale *m* lamp; (*Auto*) light. **fanali** *pl* **posteriori** (*Auto*) rear lights

fa'natico, -a *adj* fanatical; **essere** ~ **di calcio** be a football fanatic ● *mf* fanatic. **fana'tismo** *m* fanaticism

fanci'ul|la *f* young girl. ~**'lezza** *f* childhood. ~**lo** *m* young boy

fan'donia *f* lie; **fandonie!** nonsense!

fan'fara *f* fanfare; (*complesso*) brass band

fanfaro'nata *f* brag. **fanfa'rone, -a** *mf* braggart

fan'ghiglia *f* mud. **'fango** *m* mud.

fan'goso adj muddy

fannul'lone, -a mf idler

fantasci'enza f science fiction

fanta'si|a f fantasy; (immaginazione) imagination; (capriccio) fancy; (di tessuto) pattern. ∼'oso adj (stilista, ragazzo) imaginative; (resoconto) improbable

fan'tasma m ghost

fantasti'c|are vi day-dream. ∼he'ria f day-dream. fan'tastico adj fantastic; (racconto) fantasy

'fante m infantryman; (nelle carte) jack. ∼'ria f infantry

fan'tino m jockey

fan'toccio m puppet

fanto'matico adj phantom attrib

fara'butto m trickster

fara'ona f (uccello) guinea-fowl

far'ci|re vt stuff; fill (torta). ∼to adj stuffed; (dolce) filled

far'dello m bundle; fig burden

'fare
● vt do; make (dolce, letto ecc); (recitare la parte di) play; (trascorrere) spend; ∼ una pausa/un sogno have a break/a dream; ∼ colpo su impress; ∼ paura a frighten; ∼ piacere a please; farla finita put an end to it; ∼ l'insegnante be a teacher; ∼ lo scemo play the idiot; ∼ una settimana al mare spend a week at the seaside; 3 più 3 fa 6 3 and 3 makes 6; quanto fa? – fanno 10 000 euro how much is it? – it's 10,000 euros; far ∼ qcsa a qcno get sb to do sth; (costringere) make sb do sth; ∼ vedere show; fammi parlare let me speak; niente a che ∼ con nothing to do with; non c'è niente da ∼ (per problema) there is nothing we/you/etc. can do; fa caldo/buio it's

warm/dark; non fa niente it doesn't matter; strada facendo on the way; farcela (riuscire) manage

● vi fai in modo di venire try and come; ∼ da act as; ∼ per make as if to; ∼ presto be quick; non fa per me it's not for me

● m way; sul far del giorno at daybreak.

● farsi vr (diventare) get; farsi avanti come forward; farsi i fatti propri mind one's own business; farsi la barba shave; farsi il ragazzo 🅸 find a boyfriend; farsi male hurt oneself; farsi strada (aver successo) make one's way in the world

fa'retto m spot[light]

far'falla f butterfly

farfal'lino m (cravatta) bow tie

farfugli'are vt mutter

fa'rina f flour. fari'nacei mpl starchy food sg

fa'ringe f pharynx

fari'noso adj (neve) powdery; (mela) soft; (patata) floury

farma|'ceutico adj pharmaceutical. ∼'cia f pharmacy; (negozio) chemist's [shop]. ∼cia di turno duty chemist. ∼'cista mf chemist.

'farmaco m drug

> **Farmacia** A farmacia in Italy sells medicines and health-related products, whereas a profumeria sells not only perfume, but also beauty and personal hygiene products. For film and developing services it is necessary to go to a shop specializing in photographic equipment. ⓘ

'faro m (Auto) headlight; (Aeron) beacon; (costruzione) lighthouse

'farsa f farce

'fasci|a f band; (zona) area; (ufficiale)

sash; (*benda*) bandage. **~'are** vt bandage; cling to (*fianchi*). **~a'tura** f dressing; (*azione*) bandaging

fa'scicolo m file, (*di rivista*) issue, (*libretto*) booklet

'fascino m fascination

'fascio m bundle, (*di fiori*) bunch

fa'scis|mo m fascism. **~ta** mf fascist

'fase f phase

fa'stidio m nuisance; (*scomodo*) inconvenience; **dar ~ a** qcno bother sb; **~i** pl (*preoccupazioni*) worries; (*disturbi*) troubles. **~'oso** adj tiresome

'fasto m pomp. **fa'stoso** adj sumptuous

fa'sullo adj bogus

'fata f fairy

fa'tale adj fatal; (*inevitabile*) fated

fata'l|ismo m fatalism. **~ista** mf fatalist. **~ità** f inv fate; (*caso sfortunato*) misfortune. **~'mente** adv inevitably

fa'tica f effort, (*lavoro faticoso*) hard work; (*stanchezza*) fatigue; **a ~** with great difficulty; **è ~ sprecata** it's a waste of time; **fare ~ a fare** qcsa find it difficult to do sth; **fare ~ a finire** qcsa struggle to finish sth. **fa-ti'caccia** f pain

fati'care vi toil; **~re a** (*stentare*) find it difficult to. **~ta** f effort; (*sfacchinata*) grind. **fati'coso** adj tiring; (*difficile*) difficult

'fato m fate

fat'taccio m hum foul deed

fat'tezze fpl features

fat'tibile adj feasible

'fatto pp di **fare** ● adj done, made; **~ a mano** hand-made ● m fact; (*azione*) action; (*avvenimento*) event; **bada ai fatti tuoi!** mind your own business; **di ~** in fact; **in ~ di** as regards

fat'to|re m (*Math, causa*) factor; (*di fattoria*) farm manager. **~'ria** f farm; (*casa*) farmhouse

fatto'rino m messenger [boy]

fattucchi'era f witch

fat'tura f (*stile*) cut; (*lavorazione*) workmanship; (*Comm*) invoice

fattu'ra|re vt invoice; (*adulterare*) adulterate. **~to** m turnover, sales pl. **~zi'one** f invoicing, billing

'fatuo adj fatuous

fau'tore m supporter

'fava f broad bean

fa'vella f speech

'favilla f spark

'favo|la f fable; (*fiaba*) story; (*oggetto di pettegolezzi*) laughing stock; (*meraviglia*) dream. **~'loso** adj fabulous

fa'vore m favour; **essere a ~ di** be in favour of; **per ~** please; **di ~** (*condizioni, trattamento*) preferential. **~ggia'mento** m (*Jur*) aiding and abetting. **favo'revole** adj favourable. **~vol'mente** adv favourably

favo'ri|re vt favour; (*promuovere*) promote; **vuol ~re?** (*a cena, pranzo*) will you have some?; (*vibara*) will you come in?. **~to, -a** adj & mf favourite

fax m inv fax. **fa'xare** vt fax

fazi'one f faction

faziosità f bias. **fazi'oso** m sectarian

fazzolet'tino m **~ [di carta]** [paper] tissue

fazzo'letto m handkerchief; (*da testa*) headscarf

feb'braio m February

'febbre f fever; **avere la ~** have o run a temperature. **~ da fieno** hay fever. **feb'brile** adj feverish

'feccia f dregs pl

'fecola f potato flour

fecon'da|re vt fertilize. **~'tore** m fertilizer. **~zi'one** f fertilization. **~zione artificiale** artificial insemination. **fe'condo** adj fertile

'fede f faith; (*fiducia*) trust; (*anello*) wedding-ring; **in buona/mala ~** in good/bad faith; **prestar** ∼ **a** believe; **tener** ∼ **alla parola** keep one's word. **fe'dele** *adj* faithful ●*mf* believer; (*seguace*) follower. **fe'l'mente** *adv* faithfully. ∼**ltà** *f* faithfulness

'federa *f* pillowcase

fede'ra|le *adj* federal. ∼**'lismo** *m* federalism. ∼**zi'one** *f* federation

fe'dina *f* **avere la** ∼ **penale sporca/pulita** have a/no criminal record

'fegato *m* liver; *fig* guts *pl*

'felce *f* fern

fe'lic|e *adj* happy; (*fortunato*) lucky. ∼**ità** *f* happiness

felici'ta|rsi *vr* ∼**rsi con** congratulate. ∼**zi'oni** *fpl* congratulations

'felpa *f* (*indumento*) sweatshirt

fel'pato *adj* brushed; (*passo*) stealthy

'feltro *m* felt; (*cappello*) felt hat

femmin|a *f* female. **femmi'nile** *adj* feminine; (*abbigliamento*) women's; (*sesso*) female ●*m* feminine. ∼**ilità** *f* femininity. **femmi'nismo** *m* feminism

'femore *m* femur

'fend|ere *vt* split. ∼**i'tura** *f* split; (*in roccia*) crack

feni'cottero *m* flamingo

fenome'nale *adj* phenomenal. **fe'nomeno** *m* phenomenon

'feretro *m* coffin

feri'ale *adj* weekday; **giorno** ∼ weekday

'ferie *fpl* holidays; (*di università, tribunale ecc*) vacation *sg*; **andare in** ∼ go on holiday

feri'mento *m* wounding

fe'ri|re *vt* wound; (*in incidente*) injure; *fig* hurt. ∼**rsi** *vr* injure oneself. ∼**ta** *f* wound. ∼**to** *adj* wounded ●*m* wounded person; (*Mil*) casualty

'ferma *f* (*Mil*) period of service

ferma'capelli *m inv* hairslide

ferma'carte *m inv* paperweight

fermacra'vatta *m inv* tiepin

fer'maglio *m* clasp; (*spilla*) brooch; (*per capelli*) hair slide

ferma'mente *adv* firmly

fer'ma|re *vt* stop; (*fissare*) fix; (*Jur*) detain ●*vi* stop. ∼**rsi** *vr* stop. ∼**ta** *f* stop. ∼**ta dell'autobus** bus-stop. ∼**ta a richiesta** request stop

fermen'ta|re *vi* ferment. ∼**zi'one** *f* fermentation. **fer'mento** *m* ferment; (*lievito*) yeast

fer'mezza *f* firmness

'fermo *adj* still; (*veicolo*) stationary; (*stabile*) steady; (*orologio*) not working ●*m* (*Jur*) detention; (*Mech*) catch; **in stato di** ∼ in custody

fe'roc|e *adj* ferocious; (*bestia*) wild; (*dolore*) unbearable. ∼**e'mente** *adv* fiercely. ∼**ia** *f* ferocity

fer'raglia *f* scrap iron

ferra'gosto *m* 15 August (*bank holiday in Italy*); (*periodo*) August holidays *pl*

ferra'menta *fpl* ironmongery *sg*; **negozio di** ∼ ironmonger's

fer'ra|re *vt* shoe (*cavallo*). ∼**to** *adj* ∼**to in** (*preparato in*) well up in

'ferreo *adj* iron

'ferro *m* iron; (*attrezzo*) tool; (*di chirurgo*) instrument; **bistecca ai ferri** grilled steak; **di** ∼ (*memoria*) excellent; (*alibi*) cast-iron; **salute di** ∼ iron constitution. ∼ **battuto** wrought iron. ∼ **da calza** knitting needle. ∼ **di cavallo** horseshoe. ∼ **da stiro** iron

ferro'vecchio *m* scrap merchant

ferro'vi|a *f* railway. ∼**'ario** *adj* railway. ∼**'ere** *m* railwayman

'fertil|e *adj* fertile. ∼**ità** *f* fertility. ∼**iz'zante** *m* fertilizer

fer'vente *adj* blazing; *fig* fervent

'fervere *vi* (*preparativi:*) be well under way

'fervid|o *adj* fervent; ∼**i auguri** best wishes

fer'vore *m* fervour

fesse'ria f nonsense

'fesso pp di fendere ● adj cracked; (🄵: sciocco) foolish ● m 🄵 (idiota) fool; far ~ qcno con sb

fes'sura f crack; (per gettone ecc) slot

'festa f feast; (giorno festivo) holiday; (compleanno) birthday; (ricevimento) party; fig joy; fare ~ a qcno welcome sb; essere in ~ be on holiday; far ~ celebrate. **~i'olo** adj festive

festeggia'mento m celebration; (manifestazione) festivity

festeggi'are vt celebrate; (accogliere festosamente) give a hearty welcome to

fe'stino m party

festività fpl festivities. **fe'stivo** adj holiday; (lieto) festive. **festivi** mpl public holidays

fe'stoso adj merry

fe'tente adj evil smelling; fig revolting ● mf 🄵 bastard

fe'ticcio m fetish

'feto m foetus

'fetta f slice; **a fette** sliced. **~ biscottata** slices of crispy toast-like bread

fet'tuccia f tape, (con nome) name tape

feu'dale adj feudal. **'feudo** m feud

FFSS abbr (Ferrovie dello Stato) Italian state railways

fi'aba f fairy-tale. **fia'besco** adj fairy-tale

fi'acca f weariness; (indolenza) laziness; **battere la ~a** be sluggish. **fiac'care** vt weaken. **~o** adj weak, (indolente) slack; (stanco) weary; (partita) dull

fi'accola f torch. **~'lata** f torchlight procession

fi'ala f phial

fi'amma f flame; (Naut) pennant; in **fiamme** aflame. **andare in fiamme** go up in flames. **~ ossidrica** blowtorch

fiam'mante adj flaming, nuovo **~nte** brand new. **~ta** f blaze

fiammeggi'are vi blaze

fiam'mifero m match

fiam'mingo, -a adj Flemish ● mf Fleming ● m (lingua) Flemish

fiancheggi'are vt border; fig support

fi'anco m side; (di persona) hip; (di animale) flank; (Mil) wing; **al mio ~** by my side; **~ a** (lavorare) side by side

fi'asco m flask; fig fiasco; **fare ~** be a fiasco

fia'tare vi breathe; (parlare) breathe a word

fi'ato m breath; (vigore) stamina; **strumenti a ~** wind instruments; **senza ~** breathlessly; **tutto d'un ~** (bere, leggere) all in one go

'fibbia f buckle

'fibra f fibre; **fibre** pl (alimentari) roughage. **~ ottica** optical fibre

ficca'naso mf nosey parker

fic'care vt thrust; drive (chiodo ecc); (🄵: mettere) shove. **~si** vr thrust oneself; (nascondersi) hide; **~si nei guai** get oneself into trouble

fiche f inv (gettone) chip

'fico m (albero) fig-tree; (frutto) fig. **~ d'India** prickly pear

'fico, -a 🄵 mf cool sort ● adj cool

fidanza'mento m engagement

fidan'zarsi vr get engaged. **~to, -a** mf (ufficiale) fiancé; fiancée

fi'darsi vr **~rsi di** trust. **~to** adj trustworthy

'fido m devoted follower; (Comm) credit

fi'ducia f confidence; **degno di ~a** trustworthy; **persona di ~a** a reliable person; **di ~a** (fornitore) usual. **~'oso** adj trusting

fi'ele m bile; fig bitterness

fie'nile m barn. **fi'eno** m hay

fi'era f fair

fie'rezza f (dignità) pride. **fi'ero** adj proud

fi'evole adj faint; (luce) dim

'fifa f [1] jitters; **aver** ~ have the jitters

'figli|a f daughter; ~**a unica** only child. ~**astra** f stepdaughter. ~**'astro** m stepson. ~**o** m son; (generico) child. ~**o unico** only child

Figlio di papà With the rapid rise in living standards which took place in Italy after 1945, more children grow up in affluent families than was previously the case, and *figli unici* (only children) are often the norm. Children, both young and grown-up, are often given considerable financial help by their parents, and are sometimes termed *figli di papà*, implying that they are also spoilt.

figli'occi|a f goddaughter. ~**o** m godson

figli'ol|a f girl. ~**lanza** f offspring. ~**lo** m boy

'figo, -a ▷ FICO, -A

fi'gura f figure; (aspetto esteriore) shape; (illustrazione) illustration; **far bella/brutta** ~ make a good/bad impression; **mi hai fatto fare una brutta** ~ you made me look a fool; **che** ~**!** how embarrassing!. **figu'rac-cia** f bad impression

figu'rare vt represent; (simboleggiare) symbolize; (immaginare) imagine ● vi (far figura) cut a dash; (in lista) appear. ~**rsi** vr (immaginarsi) imagine; ~**ti!** imagine that!; **posso? – [ma] ~ti!** may I? – of course!. ~**'tivo** adj figurative

figu'rina f ≈ cigarette card

figu|ri'nista mf dress designer. ~**rino** m fashion sketch. ~**rone** m **fare un ~rone** make an excellent impression

'fila f line; (di soldati ecc) file; (di oggetti) row; (coda) queue; **di** ~ in succession; **fare la** ~ queue [up], stand in line Am

fi'lare vt spin; (Naut) pay out ● vi (andarsene) run away; (liquido): trickle; **fila!** [1] scram!; ~ **con** ([1]: amoreggiare) go out with

filar'monica f (orchestra) orchestra

fila'strocca f rigmarole; (per bambini) nursery rhyme

fi'la|to adj spun; (ininterrotto) running; (continuato) uninterrupted; **di** ~**to** (subito) immediately ● m yarn

fil di 'ferro m wire

fi'letto m (bordo) border; (di vite) thread; (Culin) fillet

fili'ale adj filial ● f (Comm) branch

fili'grana f filigree; (su carta) watermark

film m inv film. ~ **giallo** thriller. ~ **a lungo metraggio** feature film

fil'ma|re vt film. ~**to** m short film. **fil'mino** m cine film

'filo m thread; (tessile) yarn; (metallico) wire; (di lama) edge; (venatura) grain; (di perle) string; (d'erba) blade; (di luce) ray; **con un** ~ **di voce** in a whisper; **fare il** ~ **a** qcno fancy sb; **perdere il** ~ lose the thread. ~ **spinato** barbed wire

'filobus m inv trolleybus

filodiffusi'one f rediffusion

fi'lone m vein; (di pane) long loaf

filoso'fia f philosophy. **fi'losofo, -a** mf philosopher

fil'trare vt filter. **'filtro** m filter

'filza f string

fin ▷ FINE, FINO¹

fi'nal|e adj final ● m end ● f Sport final. **fina'lista** mf finalist. ~**ità** f inv finality; (scopo) aim. ~**mente** adv at last; (in ultimo) finally

fi'nan|za f finance; ~**i'ario** adj financial. ~**i'ere** m financier; (guardia di finanza) customs officer. ~**ia'mento**

m funding

finanzi'a|re *vt* fund, finance. ~**'tore**, ~**'trice** *mf* backer

finché *conj* until, (*per tutto il tempo che*) as long as

'fine *adj* fine; (*sottile*) thin; (*udito, vista*) keen; (*raffinato*) refined ● *f* end; **alla** ~ in the end; **alla fin** ~ after all; **in fin dei conti** when all's said and done; **senza** ~ endless ● *m* aim. ~ **settimana** weekend

fi'nestra *f* window. **fine'strella** *f* **di aiuto** (*Comput*) help box. **fine'strino** *m* (*Auto, Rail*) window

fi'nezza *f* fineness, (*sottigliezza*) thinness; (*raffinatezza*) refinement

'finger|e *vt* pretend; feign (*affetto ecc*). ~**si** *vr* pretend to be

fini'menti *mpl* finishing touches; (*per cavallo*) harness *sg*

fini'mondo *m* end of the world; *fig* pandemonium

fi'ni|re *vt/i* finish, end; (*smettere*) stop; (*diventare, andare a finire*) end up; ~**scila!** stop it! ~**to** *adj* finished; (*abile*) accomplished. ~**'tura** *f* finish

finlan'dese *adj* Finnish ● *mf* Finn ● *m* (*lingua*) Finnish

Fin'landia *f* Finland

'fino¹ *prep* ~ **a** till, until; (*spazio*) as far as; ~ **all'ultimo** to the last; **fin da** (*tempo*) since; (*spazio*) from; **fin qui** as far as here; **fin troppo** too much; ~ **a che punto** how far

'fino² *adj* fine; (*acuto*) subtle; (*puro*) pure

fi'nocchio *m* fennel; (🔒: *omosessuale*) poof

fi'nora *adv* so far, up till now

'finta *f* sham; *Sport* feint; **far ~ di** pretend to; **far ~ di niente** act as if nothing had happened; **per ~** (*per scherzo*) for a laugh

'fint|o, -a *pp di* **fingere** ● *adj* false; (*artificiale*) artificial; **fare il** ~**o tonto** act dumb

finzi'one *f* pretence

fi'occo *m* bow; (*di neve*) flake; (*nappa*) tassel; **coi fiocchi** *fig* excellent. ~ **di neve** snowflake

fi'ocina *f* harpoon

fi'oco *adj* weak; (*luce*) dim

fi'onda *f* catapult

flo'raio, -a *mf* florist

fiorda'liso *m* cornflower

fi'ordo *m* fiord

fi'ore *m* flower; (*parte scelta*) cream; **fiori** *pl* (*nelle carte*) clubs, **a fior d'acqua** on the surface of the water; **fior di** (*abbondanza*) a lot of: **ha i nervi a fior di pelle** his nerves are on edge; **a fiori** flowery

fioren'tino *adj* Florentine

fio'retto *m* (*scherma*) foil; (*Relig*) act of mortification

fio'rire *vi* flower; (*albero:*) blossom; *fig* flourish

fio'rista *mf* florist

fiori'tura *f* (*di albero*) blossoming

fi'otto *m* scorrere a fiotti pour out; **piove a fiotti** the rain is pouring down

Fi'renze *f* Florence

'firma *f* signature; (*nome*) name

fir'ma|re *vt* sign. ~**'tario, -a** *mf* signatory ● **~to** *adj* (*abito, borsa*) **di** signer *attrib*

fisar'monica *f* accordion

fi'scale *adj* fiscal

fischi'are *vi* whistle ● *vt* whistle; (*in segno di disapprovazione*) boo

fischiet'tare *vt* whistle. ~**io** *m* whistling

fischi'etto *m* whistle. **'fischio** *m* whistle

'fisco *m* treasury; (*tasse*) taxation; **il** ~ the taxman

'fisica *f* physics

'fisico, -a *adj* physical ● *mf* physicist ● *m* physique

'fisima *f* whim

fisio'lo'gia f physiology. ~'logico adj physiological

fisiono'mia f features, face; (di paesaggio) appearance

fisiotera'pi|a f physiotherapy. ~sta mf physiotherapist

fis'sa|re vt fix, fasten; (guardare fissamente) stare at; arrange (appuntamento, ora). ~rsi vr (stabilirsi) settle; (fissare lo sguardo) stare; ~rsi su (ostinarsi) set one's mind on; ~rsi di fare qcsa become obsessed with doing sth. ~to m obsessive. ~zi'one f fixation; (ossessione) obsession

'fisso adj fixed; **un lavoro ~** a regular job; **senza fissa dimora** of no fixed abode

fit'tizio adj fictitious

fitto¹ adj thick; **~ di** full of ● m depth

fitto² m (affitto) rent; **dare a ~** let; **prendere a ~** rent; (noleggiare) hire

fiu'mana f swollen river; fig stream

fi'ume m river; fig stream

fiu'tare vt smell. **fi'uto** m [sense of] smell; fig nose

'flaccido adj flabby

fla'cone m bottle

fla'gello m scourge

fla'grante adj flagrant; **in ~** in the act

fla'nella f flannel

'flash m inv Journ newsflash

'flauto m flute

'flebile adj feeble

'flemma f calm; (Med) phlegm

fles'sibil|e adj flexible. ~ità f flexibility

flessi'one f (del busto in avanti) forward bend

'flesso pp di flettere

flessu'oso adj supple

'flettere vt bend

flir'tare vi flirt

F.lli abbr (fratelli) Bros

'floppy disk m inv floppy disk

'florido adj flourishing

'floscio adj limp; (flaccido) flabby

'flotta f fleet. **flot'tiglia** f flotilla

flu'ente adj fluent

flu'ido m fluid

flu'ire vi flow

fluore'scente adj fluorescent

fluo'oro m fluorine

'flusso m flow; (Med) flux; (del mare) flood[-tide]; **~ e riflusso** ebb and flow

fluttu'ante adj fluctuating

fluttu'a|re vi (prezzi, moneta:) fluctuate. ~zi'one f fluctuation

fluvi'ale adj river

fo'bia f phobia

'foca f seal

fo'caccia f (pane) flat bread; (dolce) ≈ raisin bread

fo'cale adj (distanza, punto) focal. **focaliz'zare** vt get into focus (fotografia); focus (attenzione); define (problema)

'foce f mouth

foco'laio m (Med) focus; fig centre

foco'lare m hearth; (caminetto) fireplace; (Techn) furnace

fo'coso adj fiery

'foder|a f lining; (di libro) dust-jacket; (di poltrona ecc) loose cover. **fode'rare** vt line; cover (libro). ~o m sheath

'foga f impetuosity

'foggi|a f fashion; (maniera) manner; (forma) shape. ~'are vt mould

'foglia f leaf; (di metallo) foil

fogli'etto m (pezzetto di carta) piece of paper

'foglio m sheet; (pagina) leaf. **~ elettronico** (Comput) spreadsheet. **~ rosa** (Auto) provisional licence

'fogna f sewer. ~'tura f sewerage

fo'lata f gust

fol'clo|re m folklore. ~'ristico adj

folk; (bizzarro) weird

folgo'ra|re vi (splendere) shine ● vt (con un fulmine) strike. **~zi'one** f (da fulmine, elettrica) electrocution; (idea) brainwave

'folgore f thunderbolt

'folla f crowd

'folle adj mad; **in ~** (Auto) in neutral

folle'mente adv madly

fol'lia f madness; **alla ~** (amare) to distraction

'folto adj thick

fomen'tare vt stir up

fond'ale m (Theat) backcloth

fonda'men|ta fpl foundations. **~ tale** adj fundamental. **~to** m (di principio, teoria) foundation

fon'da|re vt establish; base (ragionamento, accusa). **~to** adj (ragionamento) well-founded. **~zi'one** f establishment; **~zioni** pl (di edificio) foundations

fon'delli mpl **prendere qcno per i ~** 🔲 pull sb's leg

fon'dente adj (cioccolato) dark

'fonder|e vt/i melt; (colori) blend. **~si** vr melt; (Comm) merge

'fondi mpl (danaro) funds; (di caffè) grounds

'fondo adj deep; **è notte fonda** it's the middle of the night ● m bottom; (fine) end; (sfondo) background; (indole) nature; (somma di denaro) fund; (feccia) dregs pl; **andare a ~** (nave:) sink; **da cima a ~** from beginning to end; **in ~** after all; **in ~ in ~** deep down; **fino in ~** right to the end; (capire) thoroughly. **~ d'investimento** investment trust

fondo'tinta m foundation cream

fon'duta f ≈ fondue

fo'netic|a f phonetics. **~o** adj phonetic

fon'tana f fountain

'fonte f spring; fig source ● m font

fo'raggio m forage

fo'rar|e vt pierce; punch (biglietto) ● vi puncture. **~si** vr (gomma, pallone:) go soft

'forbici fpl scissors

forbi'cine fpl (per le unghie) nail scissors

'forca f fork; (patibolo) gallows pl

for'cella f fork; (per capelli) hairpin

for'chet|ta f fork. **~'tata** f (quantità) forkful

for'cina f hairpin

'forcipe m forceps pl

for'cone m pitchfork

fo'resta f forest. **fore'stale** adj forest attrib

foresti'ero, -a adj foreign ● mf foreigner

for'fait m inv fixed price; **dare ~** (abbandonare) give up

'forfora f dandruff

'forgi|a f forge. **~'are** vt forge

'forma f form; (sagoma) shape; (Culin) mould; (da calzolaio) last; **essere in ~** be in good form; **a ~ di** in the shape of; **forme** pl (del corpo) figure sg; (convenzioni) appearances

for'maggino m processed cheese. **for'maggio** m cheese

for'male adj formal. **~ità** f inv formality. **~iz'zarsi** vr stand on ceremony. **~'mente** adv formally

for'ma|re vt form. **~rsi** vr form; (svilupparsi) develop. **~to** m size; (di libro) format; **~to tessera** (fotografia) passportsize

format'tare vt format

formazi'one f formation; Sport line-up. **~ professionale** vocational training

formico'l|are vi (braccio ecc:) tingle; **avere di** be swarming with; **mi ~a la mano** I have pins and needles in my hand. **~io** m swarming; (di braccio ecc) pins and needles pl

formi'dabile adj (tremendo) formidable; (eccezionale) tremendous

for'mina f mould

for'moso adj shapely

'formula f formula. **formu'lare** vt formulate; (esprimere) express

for'nace f furnace; (per laterizi) kiln

for'naio m baker; (negozio) bakery

for'nello m stove; (di pipa) bowl

for'ni|re vt supply (**di** with). **~'tore** m supplier. **~'tura** f supply

'forno m oven; (panetteria) bakery; **al ~** roast. **~ a microonde** microwave [oven]

'foro m hole; (romano) forum; (tribunale) [law] court

'forse adv perhaps, maybe; **essere in ~** be in doubt

forsen'nato, -a adj mad ● mf madman; madwoman

'forte adj strong; (colore) bright; (suono) loud; (resistente) tough; (spesa) considerable; (dolore) severe; (pioggia) heavy; (a tennis, calcio) good; (fig: simpatico) great; (taglia) large ● adv strongly; (parlare) loudly; (velocemente) fast; (piovere) heavily ● m (fortezza) fort; (specialità) strong point

for'tezza f fortress; (forza morale) fortitude

fortifi'care vt fortify

for'tino m (Mil) blockhouse

for'tuito adj fortuitous; **incontro ~** chance encounter

for'tuna f fortune; (successo) success; (buona sorte) luck. **atterraggio di ~** forced landing; **aver ~** be lucky; **buona ~!** good luck!; **di ~** makeshift; **per ~** luckily. **fortu'nato** adj lucky, fortunate; (impresa) successful. **~ta'mente** adv fortunately

fo'runcolo m pimple; (grosso) boil

'forza f strength; (potenza) power; (fisica) force; **di ~** by force; **a ~ di** by dint of; **con ~** hard; **~!** come on!; **~ di volontà** will-power; **~ maggiore** circumstances beyond one's control; **la ~ pubblica** the police; **per ~** against one's will; (naturalmente) of course; **farsi ~** bear up; **mare ~ 8** force 8 gale; **bella ~!** [!] big deal!. **le forze armate** the armed forces

for'za|re vt force; (scassare) break open; (sforzare) strain. **~to** adj forced; (sorriso) strained ● m convict

forzi'ere m coffer

for'zuto adj strong

fo'schia f haze

'fosco adj dark

fo'sfato m phosphate

'fosforo m phosphorus

'fossa f pit; (tomba) grave. **~ biologica** cesspool. **fos'sato** m (di fortificazione) moat

fos'setta f dimple

'fossile m fossil

'fosso m ditch; (Mil) trench

'foto f inv [!] photo; **fare delle ~** take some photos

foto'camera f camera

foto'cellula f photocell

fotocomposizi'one f filmsetting, photocomposition

foto'copi|a f photocopy. **~'are** vt photocopy. **~a'trice** f photocopier

foto'finish m inv photo finish

fotogra|'fare vt photograph. **~'fia** f (arte) photography; (immagine) photograph; **fare ~fie** take photographs. **foto'grafico** adj photographic; **macchina fotografica** camera. **fo'tografo, -a** mf photographer

foto'gramma m frame

fotomo'dello, -a mf [photographer's] model

fotoro'manzo m photo story

fou'lard m inv scarf

fra prep (in mezzo a due) between; (in un insieme) among; (tempo, distanza) in; **detto ~ noi** between you and me; **~ sé e sé** to oneself; **~ l'altro** what's more; **~ breve** soon; **~ quindici giorni** in two weeks' time;

~ **tutti, siamo in venti** there are twenty of us altogether

fracas'sar|e vt smash. ~**si** vr shatter

fra'casso m din; (di cose che cadono) crash

'tradicio adj (bagnato) soaked; (guasto) rotten; **ubriaco** ~ blind drunk

'fragil|e adj fragile; fig frail. ~**ità** f fragility; fig frailty

'fragola f strawberry

fra'go|re m uproar; (di cose rotte) clatter; (di tuono) rumble. ~**roso** adj uproarious; (tuono) rumbling; (suono) clanging

fra'gran|te adj fragrant. ~**za** f fragrance

frain'te|ndere vt misunderstand. ~**ndersi** vr be at cross-purposes. ~**so** pp di **fraintendere**

frammen'tario adj fragmentary

'frana f landslide. **fra'nare** vi slide down

franca'mente adv frankly

fran'cese adj French ● mf Frenchman; Frenchwoman ● m (lingua) French

fran'chezza f frankness

'Francia f France

'franco' adj frank; (Comm) free; **farla franca** get away with sth

'franco' m (moneta) franc

franco'bollo m stamp

fran'gente m (onda) breaker; (scoglio) reef; (fig: momento difficile) crisis; **in quel** ~ given the situation

'frangia f fringe

fra'noso adj subject to landslides

fran'toio m olive-press

frantu'mar|e vt, ~**si** vr shatter. **fran'tumi** mpl splinters; **andare in frantumi** be smashed to pieces

frappé m inv milkshake

frap'por|re vt interpose. ~**si** vr intervene

fra'sario m vocabulary; (libro)

phrase book

'frase f sentence; (espressione) phrase. ~ **fatta** cliché

'frassino m ash[-tree]

frastagli'a|re vt make jagged. ~**to** adj jagged

frastor'na|re vt daze. ~**to** adj dazed

frastu'ono m racket

'frate m friar; (monaco) monk

fratel'lanza f brotherhood. ~**stro** m half-brother

fra'telli mpl (fratello e sorella) brother and sister. ~**o** m brother

fraterniz'zare vi fraternize. **fra-'terno** adj brotherly

frat'taglie fpl (di pollo ecc) giblets

frat'tanto adv in the meantime

frat'tempo m nel ~ meanwhile, in the meantime

frat'tura f fracture. ~**'rare** vt, ~**'rarsi** vr break

'fraudo lento adj fraudulent

frazi'one f fraction; (borgata) hamlet

'freccia f arrow; (Auto) indicator. ~**'ata** f (osservazione pungente) cutting remark

fredda'mente adv coldly

fred'dare vt cool; (fig: con sguardo, battuta) cut down; (uccidere) kill

fred'dezza f coldness

'freddo adj & m cold; **aver** ~ be cold; **fa** ~ it's cold

freddo'loso adj sensitive to cold

fred'dura f pun

fre'ga|re vt rub; (🅸: truffare) cheat; (🅸: rubare) swipe. ~**rsene** 🅸 not give a damn; **chi se ne frega!** what the heck!. ~**si** vr rub (occhi). ~**ta** f rub. ~**'tura** f (🅸 (truffa) swindle; (delusione) letdown

'fregio m (Archit) frieze; (ornamento) decoration

'frem|ere vi quiver. ~**ito** m quiver

fre'na|re vt brake; fig restrain; hold back (lacrime) ● vi brake. ~**rsi** vr check oneself. ~**ta** f fare una ~**ta brusca** brake sharply

frene'sia f frenzy; (desiderio smodato) craze. **fre'netico** adj frenzied

'freno m brake; fig check; **togliere il** ~ release the brake; **usare il** ~ apply the brake; **tenere a** ~ restrain. ~ **a mano** handbrake

frequen'tare vt frequent; attend (scuola ecc); mix with (persone)

fre'quen|te adj frequent; **di** ~**te** frequently. ~**za** f frequency; (assiduità) attendance

fre'schezza f freshness; (di temperatura) coolness

'fresco adj fresh; (temperatura) cool; **stai** ~! you're for it! ● m coolness; **far** ~ be cool; **mettere/tenere in** ~ put/keep in a cool place

'fretta f hurry, haste; **aver** ~ be in a hurry; **far** ~ **a qcno** hurry sb; **in** ~ **e furia** in a great hurry. **frettolosa'mente** adv hurriedly. **fretto'loso** adj (persona) in a hurry; (lavoro) rushed, hurried

fri'abile adj crumbly

'friggere vt fry; **vai a farti** ~! get lost! ● vi sizzle

friggi'trice f chip pan

frigidità f frigidity. **'frigido** adj frigid

fri'gnare vi whine

'frigo m inv fridge

frigo'bar m inv minibar

frigo'rifero adj refrigerating ● m refrigerator

frit'tata f omelette

frit'tella f fritter; (🅣: macchia d'unto) grease stain

'fritto pp di **friggere** ● adj fried; **essere** ~ be done for ● m fried food. ~ **misto** mixed fried fish/vegetables. **frit'tura** f fried dish

frivo'lezza f frivolity. **'frivolo** adj frivolous

frizio'nare vt rub. **frizi'one** f friction; (Mech) clutch; (di pelle) rub

friz'zante adj fizzy; (vino) sparkling; (aria) bracing

'frizzo m gibe

fro'dare vt defraud

'frode f fraud. ~ **fiscale** tax evasion

'frollo adj tender; (selvaggina) high; (persona) spineless; **pasta frolla** short[crust] pastry

'fronda f [leafy] branch; fig rebellion. **fron'doso** adj leafy

fron'tale adj frontal; (scontro) head-on

'fronte f forehead; (di edificio) front; **di** ~ opposite; **di** ~ **a** opposite, facing; (a paragone) compared with; **far** ~ **a** face ● m (Mil, Pol) front. ~**ggiare** vt face

fronti'era f frontier, border

fron'tone m pediment

'fronzolo m frill

'frotta f swarm; (di animali) flock

'frottola f fib; **frottole** pl nonsense sg

fru'gale adj frugal

fru'gare vi rummage ● vt search

frul'la|re vt (Culin) whisk ● vi (ali:) whirr. ~**to** m ~**to di frutta** fruit drink with milk and crushed ice. ~**tore** m [electric] mixer. **frul'lino** m whisk

fru'mento m wheat

frusci'are vi rustle

fru'scio m rustle; (radio, giradischi) background noise; (di acque) murmur

'frusta f whip; (frullino) whisk

fru'sta|re vt whip. ~**ta** f lash. **fru'stino** m riding crop

fru'stra|re vt frustrate. ~**to** adj frustrated. ~**zi'one** f frustration

'frutt|a f fruit; (portata) dessert. **frut'tare** vi bear fruit ● vt yield. **frut'teto**

_m_ orchard. **~i'vendolo, -a** _mf_ greengrocer. **~o** _m_ fruit; _Fin_ yield; **~i di bosco** fruits of the forest. **~i di mare** seafood _sg_. **~u'oso** _adj_ profitable

f.to _abbr_ (firmato) signed

fu _adj_ (defunto) late; **il ~ signor Rossi** the late Mr Rossi

fuci'la|re _vt_ shoot. **~ta** _f_ shot

fu'cile _m_ rifle

fu'cina _f_ forge

fuga _f_ escape; (perdita) leak; (Mus) fugue; **darsi alla ~** escape

fu'gare _adj_ fleeting

fug'gevole _adj_ short-lived

fuggi'asco, -a _mf_ fugitive

fuggi'fuggi _m_ stampede

fuggi'gi|re _vi_ flee; (innamorati:) elope; _fig_ fly. **~tivo, -a** _mf_ fugitive

'fulcro _m_ fulcrum

ful'gore _m_ splendour

fu'liggine _f_ soot

fulmi'nar|e _vt_ strike by lightning; (con sguardo) look daggers at; (con scarica elettrica) electrocute. **~si** _vr_ burn out. **'fulmine** _m_ lightning. **ful'mineo** _adj_ rapid

'fulvo _adj_ tawny

fumai'olo _m_ funnel; (di casa) chimney

fu'ma|re _vt/i_ smoke; (in ebollizione) steam. **~tore, ~trice** _mf_ smoker; **non fumatori** non-smoker, nonsmoking

fu'metto _m_ comic strip; **fumetti** _pl_ comics

'fumo _m_ smoke; (vapore) steam; _fig_ hot air; **andare in ~** vanish. **fu-'moso** _adj_ smoky; (discorso) vague

fu'nambolo, -a _mf_ tightrope walker

'fune _f_ rope; (cavo) cable

'funebre _adj_ funeral; (cupo) gloomy

fune'rale _m_ funeral

fu'nesto _adj_ sad

'fungere _vi_ **~ da** act as

i funghi Wild mushrooms are an Italian passion, and the most prized is the porcino (cep), which can be bought fresh or dried. However, many Italians are also avid mushroompickers and are expert at differentiating edible mushrooms (funghi commestibili) from poisonous ones. Local authorities often have a department controlling the picking and selling of mushrooms

'fungo _m_ mushroom; (Bot) fungus

funico'lare _f_ funicular [railway]

funi'via _f_ cableway

funzio'nal|e _adj_ functional. **~ità** _f_ functionality

funziona'mento _m_ functioning

funzio'nare _vi_ work, function; **~ da** (fungere da) act as

funzio'nario _m_ official

funzi'one _f_ function; (carica) office; (Relig) service; **entrare in ~** take up office

fu'oco _m_ fire; (fisica, fotografia) focus; **far ~** fire; **dar ~ a** set fire to; **prendere ~** catch fire. **fuochi** _pl_ **d'artificio** fireworks

fuor'ché _prep_ except

fu'ori _adv_ out; (all'esterno) outside; (all'aperto) outdoors; **andare di ~** (traboccare) spill over; **essere ~ di sé** be beside oneself, **essere in ~** (sporgere) stick out; **far ~** 🄵 do in; **~ luogo** (inopportuno) out of place; **~ mano** out of the way; **~ moda** old-fashioned; **~ pasto** between meals; **~ pericolo** out of danger; **~ questione** out of the question; **~ uso** out of use ● **m** outside

fuori'bordo _m_ speedboat (with outboard motor)

fuori'classe *mf inv* champion

fuorigi'oco *m & adv* offside

fuori'legge *mf* outlaw

fuori'serie *adj* custom-made ● *f* (*Auto*) custom-built model

fuori'strada *m* off-road vehicle

fuorvi'are *vt* lead astray ● *vi* go astray

furbe'ria *f* cunning. **fur'bizia** *f* cunning

'furbo *adj* cunning; (*intelligente*) clever; (*astuto*) shrewd; **bravo ~!** nice one!; **fare il ~** to try to be clever

fu'rente *adj* furious

fur'fante *m* scoundrel

furgon'cino *m* delivery van. **fur-'gone** *m* van

'furia *f* fury; (*fretta*) haste; **a ~a di** by dint of. **~'bondo**, **~'oso** *adj* furious

fu'rore *m* fury; (*veemenza*) frenzy; **far ~** be all the rage. **~ggi'are** *vi* be a great success

furtiva'mente *adv* covertly. **fur-'tivo** *adj* furtive

'furto *m* theft; (*con scasso*) burglary; **commettere un ~** steal. **~ d'iden-tità** identity theft

'fusa *fpl* **fare le ~** purr

fu'scello *m* (*di legno*) twig; (*di paglia*) straw; **sei un ~** you're as light as a feather

fu'seaux *mpl* leggings

fu'sibile *m* fuse

fusi'one *f* fusion; (*Comm*) merger

'fuso *pp di* **fondere** ● *adj* melted ● *m* spindle. **~ orario** time zone

fusoli'era *f* fuselage

fu'stagno *m* corduroy

fu'stino *m* (*di detersivo*) box

'fusto *m* stem; (*tronco*) trunk; (*reci-piente di metallo*) drum; (*di legno*) barrel

'futile *adj* futile

fu'turo *adj & m* future

Gg

gab'bar|e *vt* cheat. **~si** *vr* **~si di** make fun of

'gabbia *f* cage; (*da imballaggio*) crate. **~ degli imputati** dock. **~ toracica** rib cage

gabbi'ano *m* [sea]gull

gabi'netto *m* consulting room; (*Pol*) cabinet; (*bagno*) lavatory; (*labora-torio*) laboratory

'gaffe *f inv* blunder

gagli'ardo *adj* vigorous

gai'ezza *f* gaiety. **'gaio** *adj* cheerful

'gala *f* gala

ga'lante *adj* gallant. **~'ria** *f* gal-lantry. **galantu'omo** *m* (*pl* **galantuo-mini**) gentleman

ga'lassia *f* galaxy

gala'teo *m* [good] manners *pl*; (*trat-tato*) book of etiquette

gale'otto *m* (*rematore*) galley-slave; (*condannato*) convict

ga'lera *f* (*nave*) galley; Ⓣ prison

'galla *f* (*Bot*) gall; **a ~** *adv* afloat; **ve-nire a ~** surface

galleggi'are *vi* float

galle'ria *f* tunnel; (*d'arte*) gallery; (*Theat*) gallery; (*arcata*) arcade. **~ d'arte** art gallery

'Galles *m* Wales. **gal'lese** *adj* welsh ● *m* Welshman; (*lingua*) Welsh ● *f* Welshwoman

gal'letto *m* cockerel; **fare il ~** show off

gal'lina *f* hen

gal'lismo *m* machismo

'gallo *m* cock

gal'lone *m* stripe; (*misura*) gallon

galop'pare *vi* gallop. **ga'loppo** *m* gallop; **al galoppo** at a gallop

'gamba *f* leg; (*di lettera*) stem; **a**

quattro gambe on all fours; **essere in ~** (*essere forte*) be strong; (*capace*) be smart

gamba'letto m pop sock

gambe'retto m shrimp. **'gambero** m prawn; (*di fiume*) crayfish

'gambo m stem; (*di pianta*) stalk

gamma f (Mus) scale; fig range

ga'nascia f jaw; **ganasce** pl **del freno** brake shoes

'gancio m hook

'ganghero m **uscire dai gangheri** fig get into a temper

'gara f competition; (*di velocità*) race; **fare a ~** compete

ga'rage m inv garage

ga'ran|te mf guarantee; (*rendersi garante*) vouch for; (*assicurare*) assure. **~'zia** f guarantee; **in ~zia** under guarantee

gar'ba|re vi like; **non mi garba I don't like it. **~to** adj courteous

'garbo m courtesy; (*grazia*) grace; **con ~** graciously

gareggi'are vi compete

garga'nella f **a ~** from the bottle

garga'rismo m gargle; **fare i gargarismi** gargle

ga'rofano m carnation

garza f gauze

gar'zone m boy. **~ di stalla** stable-boy

gas m inv gas; **dare ~** (Auto) accelerate; **a tutto ~** flat out. **~ lacrimogeno** tear gas. **~ pl di scarico** exhaust fumes

gas'dotto m natural gas pipeline

ga'solio m diesel oil

ga'solio m gasometer

gas'sare vt aerate; (*uccidere col gas*) gas. **~ato** adj gassy. **~oso**, **-a** adj gassy; (*bevanda*) fizzy ● f lemonade

'gastrico adj gastric. **ga'strite** f gastritis

gastro|no'mia f gastronomy. **~'nomico** adj gastronomic. **ga'stro‐**

nomo, **-a** mf gourmet

'gatta f **una ~ da pelare** a headache

gatta'buia f hum clink

gat'tino, **-a** mf kitten

'gatto, **-a** mf cat. **~ delle nevi** snowmobile

gat'toni adv on all fours

gay adj inv gay

'gazza f magpie

gaz'zarra f racket

gaz'zella f gazelle; (Auto) police car

gaz'zetta f gazette

gaz'zosa f clear lemonade

'geco m gecko

ge'la|re vt/i freeze. **~ta** f frost

gela't|aio, **-a** mf ice-cream seller; (*negozio*) ice-cream shop. **~e'ria** f ice-cream parlour. **~i'era** f ice-cream maker

gela'ti|na f gelatine; (*dolce*) jelly. **~na di frutta** fruit jelly.

ge'lato adj frozen ● m ice cream

'gelido adj freezing

'gelo m (*freddo intenso*) freezing cold; (*brina*) frost; fig chill

ge'lone m chilblain

gelosa'mente adv jealously

gelo'sia f jealousy. **ge'loso** adj jealous

'gelso m mulberry[-tree]

gelso'mino m jasmine

gemel'laggio m twinning

ge'mello, **-a** adj & mf twin; (*di polsino*) cuff-link; **Gemelli** pl (Astr) Gemini sg

'gem|ere vi groan; (*tubare*) coo. **~ito** m groan

'gemma f gem; (Bot) bud

'gene m gene

genea'logia f genealogy

gene'rale[1] adj general; **spese ~i** overheads

gene'rale[2] m (Mil) general

generalità f (*qualità*) generality, general nature; ~ pl (dati personali) particulars

generaliz'za|re vt generalize. ~zi'one f generalization. general'mente adv generally

gene'ra|re vt give birth to; (causare) breed; (Techn) generate. ~'tore m (Techn) generator. ~zi'one f generation

'**genere** m kind; (Biol) genus; (Gram) gender; (letterario, artistico) genre; (prodotto) product; **il ~ umano** mankind; **in ~** generally. **generi** pl **alimentari** provisions

ge'nerico adj generic; **medico generico** general practitioner

'**genero** m son-in-law

generosità f generosity. **gene'roso** adj generous

'**genesi** f inv genesis

ge'netico, -a adj genetic ●f genetics

gen'giva f gum

geni'ale adj ingenious; (congeniale) congenial

'**genio** m genius; **andare a ~** be to one's taste. **~ civile** civil engineering. **~ [militare]** Engineers

geni'tale adj genital. **genitali** mpl genitals

geni'tore m parent

gen'naio m January

'**Genova** f Genoa

gen'taglia f rabble

'**gente** f people pl

gen'til|e adj kind; **G~e Signore** (in lettere) Dear Sir. **genti'lezza** f kindness; **per gentilezza** (per favore) please. **~'mente** adv kindly. **~u'omo** (pl **~u'omini**) m gentleman

genu'ino adj genuine; (cibo, prodotto) natural

geogra'fia f geography. **geo'grafico** adj geographical. **ge'ografo, -a** mf geographer

geolo'gia f geology. **geo'logico** adj geological. **ge'ologo, -a** mf geologist

ge'ometra mf surveyor

geome'tria f geometry

ge'ranio m geranium

gerar'chia f hierarchy

ge'rente m manager ●f manageress

'**gergo** m slang; (di professione ecc) jargon

geria'tria f geriatrics sg

Ger'mania f Germany

'**germe** m germ; (fig: principio) seed

germogli'are vi sprout. **ger'moglio** m sprout

gero'glifico m hieroglyph

'**gesso** m chalk; (Med, scultura) plaster

gestazi'one f gestation

gestico'lare vi gesticulate

gesti'one f management

ge'stir|e vt manage. **~si** vr budget one's time and money

'**gesto** m gesture; (azione pl f **gesta**) deed

ge'store m manager

Gesù m Jesus. **~ bambino** baby Jesus

gesu'ita m Jesuit

get'ta|re vt throw; (scagliare) fling; (emettere) spout; (Techn), fig cast; **~re via** throw away. **~rsi** vr throw oneself; **~rsi in** (fiume:) flow into. **~ta** f throw

'**getto** m throw; (di liquidi, gas) jet; **a ~ continuo** in a continuous stream; **di ~** straight off

getto'nato adj popular. **get'tone** m token; (per giochi) counter

'**ghetto** m ghetto

ghiacci'aio m glacier

ghiacci'a|re vt/i freeze. **~to** adj frozen; (freddissimo) ice-cold

ghi'accio m ice; (Auto) black ice. **~'olo** m icicle; (gelato) ice lolly

ghi'aia f gravel

ghi'anda f acorn

ghi'andola f gland

ghigliot'tina f guillotine

ghi'gnare vi sneer

ghi ot|to adj greedy; (appetitoso) appetizing. ~'tone, -a mf glutton. ~tone'ria f (qualità) gluttony; (cibo) tasty morsel

ghir'landa f (corona) wreath; (di fiori) garland

'ghiro m dormouse; **dormire come un** ~ sleep like a log

'ghisa f cast iron

già adv already; (un tempo) formerly; ~**!** indeed!; ~ **da ieri** since yesterday

gi'acca f jacket. ~ **a vento** windcheater

giacché conj since

giac'cone m jacket

gia'cere vi lie

giaci'mento m deposit. ~ **di petrolio** oil deposit

gia'cinto m hyacinth

gi'ada f jade

giaggi'olo m iris

giagu'aro m jaguar

gial'lastro adj yellowish

gi'allo adj & m yellow; **[libro]** ~ thriller

Giap'pone m Japan. **giappo'nese** adj & mf Japanese

giardi'n|aggio m gardening. ~i'ere, -a mf gardener ●f (Auto) estate car; (sottaceti) pickles pl

giar'dino m garden. ~ **d'infanzia** kindergarten. ~ **pensile** roofgarden. ~ **zoologico** zoo

giarretti'era f garter

giavel'lotto m javelin

gi'gan|te adj gigantic ● m giant. ~'tesco adj gigantic

gigantogra'fia f blow-up

'giglio m lily

gilè m inv waistcoat

gin m inv gin

gineco|lo'gia f gynaecology. ~'lo'gico** adj gynaecological. **gine'cologo, -a** mf gynaecologist

gi'nepro m juniper

gingil'larsi vr fiddle; (perder tempo) potter. **gin'gillo** m plaything; (ninnolo) knick-knack

gin'nasio m ≈ grammar school

gin'nast|a mf gymnast. ~ica f gymnastics; (esercizi) exercises pl

ginocchi'ata f prendere una ~ bang one's knee

gi'nocchio m (pl m ginocchi o f ginocchia) knee; **in** ~**o** on one's knees; **mettersi in** ~**o** kneel down; (per supplicare) go down on one's knees. ~'oni adv kneeling

gio'ca|re vt/i play; (giocherellare) toy; (d'azzardo) gamble; (puntare) stake; (ingannare) trick. ~rsi la carriera throw one's career away. ~'tore, ~'trice mf player, (d'azzardo) gambler

glo'cattolo m toy

giocherel|l'are vi toy; (nervosamente) fiddle. ~one adj skittish

gi'oco m game; (Techn) play; (d'azzardo) gambling; (scherzo) joke; (insieme di pezzi ecc) set; **fare il doppio** ~ **con** qcno double-cross sb

giocoli'ere m juggler

gio'coso adj playful

gi'oia f joy; (gioiello) jewel; (appellativo) sweetie

gioiel|le'ria f jeweller's [shop]. ~i'ere, -a mf jeweller; (negozio) jeweller's. **gioi'ello** m jewel; **gioielli** pl jewellery

gioi'oso adj joyous

gio'ire vi ~ **per** rejoice at

Gior'dania f Jordan

giorna'laio, -a mf newsagent

gior'nale m [news]paper; (diario) journal. ~ **di bordo** logbook. ~ **radio** news bulletin

giornali'ero adj daily ●m (per sciare) day pass

giorna'lino m comic

giorna'lis|mo m journalism. ∼ta mf journalist

giornal'mente adv daily

gior'nata f day; in ∼ today

gi'orno m day; al ∼ per day; al ∼ d'oggi nowadays; di ∼ by day; un ∼ sì, un ∼ no every other day

gi'ostra f merry-go-round

giova'mento m trarre ∼ da derive benefit from

gi'ova|ne adj young; (giovanile) youthful ●m young man ●f young woman. ∼nile adj youthful. ∼'notto m young man

gio'var|e vi ∼e a be useful to; (far bene a) be good for. ∼si vr ∼si di avail oneself of

giovedì m inv Thursday. ∼ grasso last Thursday before Lent

gioventù f youth; (i giovani) young people pl

giovi'ale adj jovial

giovi'nezza f youth

gira'dischi m inv record-player

gi'raffa f giraffe; Cinema boom

gi'randola f (fuoco d'artificio) Catherine wheel; (giocattolo) windmill; (banderuola) weathercock

gi'ra|re vt turn; (andare intorno, visitare) go round; (Comm) endorse; Cinema shoot ●vi turn; (aerei, uccelli) circle; (andare in giro) wander; ∼re al largo steer clear. ∼rsi vr turn [round]; mi gira la testa I'm dizzy

girar'rosto m spit

gira'sole m sunflower

gi'rata f turn; (Comm) endorsement; (in macchina ecc) turn; fare una ∼ (a piedi) go for a walk; (in macchina) go for a ride

gira'volta f spin; fig U-turn

gi'rello m (per bambini) babywalker; (Culin) topside

gi'revole adj revolving

gi'rino m tadpole

'giro m turn; (circolo) circle; (percorso) round; (viaggio) tour; (passeggiata) short walk; (in macchina) drive; (in bicicletta) ride; (circolazione di denaro) circulation; nel ∼ di un mese within a month; senza giri di parole without beating about the bush; a ∼ di posta by return mail. ∼ d'affari (Comm) turnover. giri pl al minuto rpm. ∼ turistico sightseeing tour. ∼ vita waist measurement

giro'collo m choker; a ∼ crewneck

gi'rone m round

gironzo'lare vi wander about

girova'gare vi wander about. gi'rovago m wanderer

'gita f trip; andare in ∼ go on a trip. ∼ scolastica school trip. gi'tante mf tripper

giù adv down; (sotto) below; (dabbasso) downstairs; a testa in ∼ (a capofitto) headlong; essere ∼ be down; (di salute) be run down; ∼ di corda down; ∼ di lì, su per ∼ more or less; non andare ∼ a qcno stick in sb's craw

gi'ub|ba f jacket; (Mil) tunic. ∼'botto m bomber jacket

giudi'care vt judge; (ritenere) consider

gi'udice m judge. ∼ conciliatore justice of the peace. ∼ di gara umpire. ∼ di linea linesman

giu'dizi|o m judg[e]ment; (opinione) opinion; (senno) wisdom; (processo) trial; (sentenza) sentence; mettere ∼o become wise. ∼oso adj sensible

gi'ugno m June

giu'menta f mare

gi'ungere vi arrive; ∼ a (riuscire) succeed in ●vt (unire) join

gi'ungla f jungle

gi'unta f addition; (Mil) junta; per ∼ in addition. ∼ comunale district council

gl'unto pp di **giungere** ● m (Mech) joint

giun'tura f joint

giuo'care, giu'oco = GIO-CARE, GIOCO

giura'mento m oath; prestare ~ take the oath

giu'ra|re vt/i swear. ~to, -a adj sworn ● mf juror

giu'ria f jury

giu'ridico adj legal

giurisdizi'one f jurisdiction

giurispru'denza f jurisprudence

giu'rista mf jurist

giustifi'ca|re vt justify. ~zi'one f justification

giu'stizia f justice. ~'are vt execute. ~'ere m executioner

gl'usto adj just, fair; (adatto) right; (esatto) exact ● m (uomo retto) just man; (cosa giusta) right ● adv exactly; ~ ora just now

glace'ale adj glacial

gla'diolo m gladiolus

'glassa f (Culin) icing

gli def art mpl (before vowel and s + consonant, gn, ps, z) the; ● il ● pron (a lui) [to] him; (a esso) [to] it; (a loro) [to] them

glice'rina f glycerine

'glicine m wisteria

gli'e|llo, -a pron [to] him/her/them; (forma di cortesia) [to] you; ~ chiedo I'll ask him/her/them/you; gliel'ho prestato I've lent it to him/her/them/you. ~ne (di ciò) [of] it; ~ne ho dato un po' I gave him/her/them/you some

glo'bal|e adj global; fig overall. ~iz-za'zione f globalization. ~'mente adv globally

'globo m globe. ~ **oculare** eyeball. ~ **terrestre** globe

'globulo m globule; (Med) corpuscle. ~ **bianco** white corpuscle. ~ **rosso** red corpuscle

'glori|a f glory. ~'arsi vr ~arsi di be proud of. ~'oso adj glorious

glos'sario m glossary

glu'cosio m glucose

'gluteo m buttock

'gnorri m fare lo ~ play dumb

'gobb|a f hump. ~o, -a adj hunch-backed ● mf hunchback

'gocci|a f drop; (di sudore) bead; è stata l'ultima ~a it was the last straw. ~o'lare vi drip. ~o'lio m dripping

godi'mento m enjoyment

goffa'mente adv awkwardly. **'goffo** adj awkward

'gola f throat; (ingordigia) gluttony; (Geog) gorge; (di camino) flue; avere mal di ~ have a sore throat; far ~ a qcno tempt sb

golf m inv jersey; Sport golf

'golfo m gulf

golosità f inv greediness; (cibo) tasty morsel. **go'loso** adj greedy

'golpe m inv coup

gomi'tata f nudge

go'mito m elbow; alzare il ~ raise one's elbow

go'mitolo m ball

'gomma f rubber; (colla, da masticare) gum; (pneumatico) tyre. ~ **da masti-care** chewing gum

gommapi'uma f foam rubber

gom'mista m tyre specialist

gom'mone m [rubber] dinghy

'gondol|a f gondola. ~i'ere m gon-dolier

gonfa'lone m banner

gonfi'abile adj inflatable

gonfi'ar|e vi swell ● vt blow up; pump up (pneumatico); (esagerare) exaggerate. ~si vr swell; (acque): rise. **'gonfio** adj swollen; (pneuma-tico) inflated. **gonfi'ore** m swelling

gongo'la|nte adj overjoyed. **~re** vi be overjoyed

'gonna f skirt. **~ pantalone** culottes pl

goo'glare vt/i google

gorgogli'are vi gurgle

go'rilla m inv gorilla; (guardia del corpo) bodyguard

'gotico adj & m Gothic

gover'nante f housekeeper

gover'na|re vt govern; (dominare) rule; (dirigere) manage; (curare) look after. **~tore** m governor

go'verno m government; (dominio) rule; **al ~** in power

gps m gps

gracchi'are vi caw; fig: (persona:) screech

graci'dare vi croak

'gracile adj delicate

gra'dasso m braggart

grada'ta'mente adv gradually

gradazi'one f gradation. **~ alcoolica** alcohol[ic] content

gra'devol|e adj agreeable.

gradi'mento m liking; **indice di ~** (Radio, TV) popularity rating; **non è di mio ~** it's not to my liking

gradi'nata f flight of steps; (di stadio) stand; (di teatro) tiers pl

gra'dino m step

gra'di|re vt like; (desiderare) wish. **~to** adj pleasant; (bene accetto) welcome

'grado m degree; (rango) rank; **di buon ~** willingly; **essere in ~ di fare qcsa** be in a position to do sth; (essere capace a) to be able to do sth

gradu'ale adj gradual

gradu'a|re vt graduate. **~to** adj graded; (provvisto di scala graduata) graduated ● m (Mil) non-commissioned officer. **~toria** f list. **~zi'one** f graduation

'graffa f clip

graf'fetta f staple

graffi'a|re vt scratch. **~'tura** f scratch

'graffio m scratch

gra'fia f [hand]writing; (ortografia) spelling

'grafic|a f graphics; **~a pubblicitaria** commercial art. **~a'mente** adv graphically. **~o** adj graphic ● m graph; (persona) graphic designer

gra'migna f weed

gram'matica f grammar

'grammo m gram[me]

gran adj ▷GRANDE

'grana f grain; (formaggio) parmesan; (🔴: seccatura) trouble; (🔴: soldi) readies pl

gra'naio m barn

gra'nat|a f (Mil) grenade; (frutto) pomegranate. **~i'ere** m (Mil) grenadier

Gran Bre'tagna f Great Britain

'granchio m crab; (errore) blunder; **prendere un ~** make a blunder

grandango'lare m wide-angle lens

'grande (a volte **gran**) adj (ampio) large; (grosso) big; (alto) tall; (largo) wide; (fig: senso morale) great; (grandioso) grand; (adulto) grown-up; **ho una gran fame** I'm very hungry; **fa un gran caldo** it is very hot; **in ~** on a large scale; **in gran parte** to a great extent; **un gran ballo** a great ball ● mf (persona adulta) grown-up; (persona eminente) great man/woman. **~ggi'are** vi **~ggiare su** tower over; (darsi arie) show off

gran'dezza f greatness; (ampiezza) largeness; (larghezza) width, breadth; (dimensione) size; (fasto) grandeur; (prodigalità) lavishness; **a ~ naturale** life-size

grandi'nare vi hail; **grandina** it's hailing. **'grandine** f hail

grandiosità f grandeur. **grandi'oso** adj grand

gran'duca m grand duke

gra'nello m grain; (di frutta) pip

gra'nita f crushed ice drink

gra'nito m granite

'grano m grain; (frumento) wheat

gran'turco m maize

'granulo m granule

'grappa f grappa; (morsa) cramp

'grappolo m bunch. **~ d'uva** bunch of grapes

gras'setto m bold [type]

gras'sezza f fatness

'grasso adj fat; (cibo) fatty; (unto) greasy; (terreno) rich; (gmssolano) coarse ● m fat; (sostanza) grease. **~'soccio** adj plump

'grata f grating **gra'tella**, **gra'ticola** f (Culin) grill

gra'tifica f bonus. **~zi'one** f satisfaction

grati'na|re vt cook au gratin. **~to** adj au gratin

grati'tudine f gratitude. **'grato** adj grateful; (gradito) pleasant

gratta'capo m trouble

grattacl'elo m skyscraper

gratta e 'vinci m inv scratch card

grat'tar|e vt scratch; (raschiare) scrape; (grattugiare) grate; (sl. rubare) pinch ● vi grate. **~si** vr scratch oneself

grat'tugi|a f grater. **~'are** vt grate

gratuita'mente adv free [of charge]. **gra'tuito** adj free [of charge]; (ingiustificato) gratuitous

gra'vare vt burden ● vi **~ su** weigh on

'grave adj (pesante) heavy; (serio) serious; (difficile) hard; (voce, suono) low; (fonetica) grave; **essere ~** (ammalato) be seriously ill. **~'mente** adv seriously

gravi'danza f pregnancy. **'gravido** adj pregnant

gravità f seriousness; (Phys) gravity

gra'voso adj onerous

'grazia f grace; (favore) favour; (Jur)

pardon; **entrare nelle ~e di qcno** get into sb's good books. **~'are** vt pardon

'grazie int thank you!, thanks!; **~ mille!** many thanks!

grazi'oso adj charming; (carino) pretty

'Grec|ia f Greece. **g~o, -a** agg & mf Greek

'gregge m flock

'greggio adj raw ● m crude oil

grembi'ale, **grembi'ule** m apron

'grembo m lap; (utero) womb; fig bosom

gre'mi|re vt pack. **~rsi** vr become crowded (**di** with). **~to** adj packed

'gretto adj stingy; (di vedute ristrette) narrow-minded

'grezzo adj = **GREGGIO**

gri'dare vi shout; (di dolore) scream; (animale:) cry ● vt shout

'grido m (pl m **gridi** o f **grida**) shout; (di animale) cry; **l'ultimo ~** the latest fashion

'grigio adj & m grey

'griglia f grill; **alla ~** grilled

gril'letto m trigger

'grillo m cricket; (fig: capriccio) whim

grinfia f fig clutch

'grin|ta f grit. **~'toso** adj determined

'grinza f wrinkle; (di stoffa) crease

grip'pare vi (Mech) seize

gris'sino m bread-stick

'gronda f eaves pl

gron'daia f gutter

gron'dare vi pour; (essere bagnato fradicio) be dripping

'groppa f back

'groppo m knot

gros'sezza f size; (spessore) thickness

gros'sista mf wholesaler

'grosso adj big, large; (spesso) thick;

(*grossolano*) coarse; (*grave*) serious ● *m* big part; (*massa*) bulk; **farla grossa** do a stupid thing

grosso|lanità *f inv* (*qualità*) coarseness; (*di errore*) grossness; (*azione, parola*) coarse thing. **~'lano** *adj* coarse; (*errore*) gross

grosso'modo *adv* roughly

'grotta *f* cave, grotto

grovi'era *f* Gruyère

gro'viglio *m* tangle; *fig* muddle

gru *f inv* (*uccello, edilizia*) crane

'gruccia *f* (*stampella*) crutch; (*per vestito*) hanger

gru'gni|re *vi* grunt. **~to** *m* grunt

'grugno *m* snout

grullo *adj* silly

'grumo *m* clot; (*di farina ecc*) lump. **gru'moso** *adj* lumpy

'gruppo *m* group; (*comitiva*) party. **~ sanguigno** blood group

gruvi'era *f* Gruyère

'gruzzolo *m* nest-egg

guada'gnare *vt* earn; gain (*tempo, forza ecc*). **gua'dagno** *m* gain; (*profitto*) profit; (*entrate*) earnings *pl*

gu'ado *m* ford; **passare a ~** ford

gua'ina *f* sheath; (*busto*) girdle

gu'aio *m* trouble; **che ~!** that's just brilliant!; **essere nei guai** be in a fix; **guai a te se lo tocchi!** don't you dare touch it!

gu'anci|a *f* cheek. **~'ale** *m* pillow

gu'anto *m* glove; **guantoni** *pl* [**da boxe**] boxing gloves

guarda'coste *m inv* coastguard

guarda'linee *m inv* Sport linesman

guar'dar|e *vt* look at; (*osservare*) watch; (*badare a*) look after; (*dare su*) look out on ● *vi* look; (*essere orientato verso*) face. **~si** *vr* look at oneself; (*astenersi*) refrain from

guarda'rob|a *m inv* wardrobe; (*di locale pubblico*) cloakroom. **~i'ere, -a**

mf cloakroom attendant

gu'ardia *f* guard; (*poliziotto*) policeman; (*vigilanza*) watch; **essere di ~** be on guard; (*medico:*) be on duty; **fare la ~ a** keep guard over; **mettere in ~** qcno warn sb. **~ carceraria** prison warder. **~ del corpo** bodyguard. **~ di finanza** ≈ Fraud Squad. **~ forestale** forest ranger. **~ medica** duty doctor

guardi'ano, -a *mf* caretaker. **~ notturno** night watchman

guar'dingo *adj* cautious

guardi'ola *f* gatekeeper's lodge

guarigi'one *f* recovery

gua'rire *vt* cure ● *vi* recover; (*ferita:*) heal [up]

guarnigi'one *f* garrison

guar'ni|re *vt* trim; (*Culin*) garnish. **~zi'one** *f* trimming; (*Culin*) garnish; (*Mech*) gasket

gua'star|e *vt* spoil (*rovinare*) ruin; break (*meccanismo*). **~si** *vr* spoil; (*andare a male*) go bad; (*tempo:*) change for the worse; (*meccanismo:*) break down. **gu'asto** *adj* broken; (*ascensore, telefono*) out of order; (*auto*) broken down; (*cibo, dente*) bad ● *m* breakdown; (*danno*) damage

guazza'buglio *m* muddle

guaz'zare *vi* wallow

gu'ercio *adj* cross-eyed

gu'err|a *f* war; (*tecnica bellica*) warfare. **~ mondiale** world war. **~eggi'are** *vi* wage war. **guer'resco** *adj* (*di guerra*) war; (*bellicoso*) warlike. **~i'ero** *m* warrior

guer'rigli|a *f* guerrilla warfare. **~'ero, -a** *mf* guerrilla

'gufo *m* owl

'guglia *f* spire

gu'id|a *f* guide; (*direzione*) guidance; (*comando*) leadership; (*Auto*) driving; (*tappeto*) runner; **~a a destra/sinistra** right-/left-hand drive. **~a telefonica** telephone directory. **~a**

turistica tourist guide. **gui'dare** vt guide; (Auto) drive; steer (nave).
~**a'tore**, ~**a'trice** mf driver

guin'zaglio m leash

guiz'zare vi dart; (luce:) flash. **gu'izzo** m dart, (di luce) flash

'guscio m shell

gu'stare vt taste ● vi like. **'gusto** m taste; (piacere) liking; **mangiare di gusto** eat well; **prenderci gusto** develop a taste for. **gu'stoso** adj tasty; fig delightful

guttu'rale adj guttural

Hh

habitué mf inv regular

ham'burger m inv hamburger

'handicap m inv handicap

handicap'pare vt handicap. ~**to**, **-a** mf disabled person ● adj disabled

'hascisc m hashish

henné m henna

hi-fi m inv hi-fi

'hippy adj hippy

hockey m hockey. ~ **su ghiaccio** ice hockey. ~ **su prato** hockey

hollywoodi'ano adj Hollywood

ho'tel m inv hotel

Ii

i def art mpl the; ▷**IL**

iber'nare vi hibernate. ~**zi'one** f hibernation

i'bisco m hibiscus

'ibrido adj & m hybrid

'iceberg m inv iceberg

i'cona f icon

Id'dio m God

i'dea f idea; (opinione) opinion; (ideale) ideal; (indizio) inkling; (piccola quantità) hint, (intenzione) intention; **cambiare** ~ change one's mind; **neanche per** ~**!** not on your life!; **chiarirsi le idee** get one's ideas straight. ~ **fissa** obsession

ide'ale adj & m ideal. ~**lista** mf idealist. ~**liz'zare** vt Idealize

ide'are vt conceive. ~**tore**, ~**trice** mf originator

'idem adv the same

i'dentico adj identical

identifi'cabile adj identifiable

identifi'care vt identify. ~**zi'one** f identification

identità f inv identity

ideolo'gia f ideology. **ideo'logico** adj ideological

idi'oma m idiom, **idio'matico** adj idiomatic

idi'ota adj idiotic ● mf idiot. **idio'zia** f (cosa stupida) idiocy

idola'trare vt worship

idoleggi'are vt idolize. **'idolo** m idol

idoneità f suitability, (Mil) fitness, **esame di** ~ qualifying examination. **i'doneo** adj **idoneo a** suitable for; (Mil) fit for

i'drante m hydrant

idra'tante adj (crema, gel) moisturizing. ~**zi'one** f moisturizing

i'draulico adj hydraulic ● m plumber

'idrico adj water attrib

idrocar'buro m hydrocarbon

idroe'lettrico adj hydroelectric

i'drofilo adj ▷**COTONE**

i'drogeno m hydrogen

i'ella f [☎] bad luck; **portare** ~ be bad luck. **iel'lato** adj [☎] jinxed, plagued by bad luck

i'ena f hyena

i'eri adv yesterday; ∼ l'altro, l'altro ∼ the day before yesterday; ∼ pomeriggio yesterday afternoon; **il giornale di** ∼ yesterday's paper

ietta|'tore, -'trice mf jinx. ∼ **tura** f (sfortuna) bad luck

igi'en|e f hygiene. ∼**ico** adj hygienic. **igie'nista** mf hygienist

i'gnaro adj unaware

i'gnobile adj base; (non onorevole) dishonourable

igno'ran|te adj ignorant ● mf ignoramus. ∼**za** f ignorance

igno'rare vt (non sapere) be unaware of; (trascurare) ignore

i'gnoto adj unknown

il
def art m the

> L'articolo determinativo in inglese non si usa quando si parla in generale: **Il latte fa bene** milk is good for you
>
> ∙∙∙▶ **il signor Magnetti** Mr Magnetti; **il dottor Piazza** Dr Piazza; **ha il naso storto** he has a bent nose; **mettiti il cappello** put your hat on; **il lunedì** on Mondays; **il 1986** 1986; **5 euro il chilo** 5 euros a kilo

'ilar|e adj merry. ∼**ità** f hilarity

illazi'one f inference

illecita'mente adv illicitly. **il'lecito** adj illicit

ille'gal|e adj illegal. ∼**ità** f illegality. ∼**'mente** adv illegally

illeg'gibile adj illegible; (libro) unreadable

illegittimità f illegitimacy. **ille'gittimo** adj illegitimate

il'leso adj unhurt

illette'rato, -a adj & mf illiterate

illimi'tato adj unlimited

illivi'dire vt bruise ● vi (per rabbia)

become livid

il'logico adj illogical

il'luder|e vt deceive. ∼**si** vr deceive oneself

illumi'na|re vt light [up]; fig enlighten; ∼**re a giorno** floodlight. ∼**rsi** vr light up. ∼**zi'one** f lighting; fig enlightenment

illumi'nismo m Enlightenment

illusi'one f illusion; **farsi illusioni** delude oneself

il'luso, -a pp di **illudere** ● adj deluded ● mf day-dreamer.

illu'stra|re vt illustrate. ∼**'tivo** adj illustrative. ∼**'tore, ∼'trice** mf illustrator. ∼**zi'one** f illustration

il'lustre adj distinguished

imbacuc'ca|re vt, ∼**rsi** vr wrap up. ∼**to** adj wrapped up

imbal'la|ggio m packing. ∼**re** vt pack; (Auto) race

imbalsa'ma|re vt embalm; stuff (animale). ∼**to** adj embalmed; (animale) stuffed

imbambo'lato adj vacant

imbaraz'zante adj embarrassing

imbaraz'za|re vt embarrass; (ostacolare) encumber. ∼**to** adj embarrassed

imba'razzo m embarrassment; (ostacolo) hindrance; **trarre qcno d'**∼ help sb out of a difficulty. ∼ **di stomaco** indigestion

imbarca'dero m landing-stage

imbar'ca|re vt embark; (**⚠**: rimorchiare) score. ∼**rsi** vr embark. ∼**zi'one** f boat. ∼**zione di salvataggio** lifeboat. **im'barco** m embarkation; (banchina) landing-stage

imba'sti|re vt tack; fig sketch. ∼**tura** f tacking, basting

im'battersi vr ∼ in run into

imbat't|ibile adj unbeatable. ∼**uto** adj unbeaten

imbavagli'are vt gag

imbe'cille adj stupid ● mf imbecile

imbel'lire vt embellish

imbestia'lire vi, **~rsi** vr fly into a rage. **~to** adj enraged

im'bever|e vt imbue (di with). **~si** vr absorb

imbe'vibile adj undrinkable. **~to** adj **~to di** (acqua) soaked in; (nozioni) imbued with

imbian'c|are vt whiten ● vi turn white. **~hino** m house painter

imbizzar'rir|e vi, **~rsi** vr become restless; (arrabbiarsi) get angry

imboc'ca|re vt feed; (entrare) enter; fig prompt. **~tura** f opening; (ingresso) entrance; (Mus di strumento) mouthpiece. **im'bocco** m entrance

imbo'scar|e vt hide. **~si** vr (Mil) shirk military service

imbo'scata f ambush

imbottigli'a|re vt bottle. **~rsi** vr get snarled up in a traffic jam. **~to** adj (vino, acqua) bottled

imbot'ti|re vt stuff, pad (giacca); (Culin) fill. **~rsi** vr **~rsi di** (fig: di pasticche) stuff oneself with. **~ta** f quilt. **~to** adj (spalle) padded; (cuscino) stuffed; (panino) filled. **~'tura** f stuffing; (di giacca) padding; (Culin) filling

imbra'nato adj clumsy

imbrat'tar|e vt mark. **~si** vr dirty oneself

imbroc'car|e vt hit; **~la giusta** hit the nail on the head

imbrogli'|are vt muddle; (raggirare) cheat. **im'broglio** m tangle; (pasticcio) mess; (inganno) trick. **~one, -a** mf cheat

imbronci'a|re vi, **~rsi** vr sulk. **~to** adj sulky

imbru'nire vi get dark; **all'~** at dusk

imbrut'tire vt make ugly ● vi become ugly

imbu'care vt post, mail; (nel biliardo) pot

imbur'rare vt butter

im'buto m funnel

imi'ta|re vt imitate. **~'tore, ~'trice** mf imitator. **~zi'one** f imitation

immaco'lato adj immaculate

immagazzi'nare vt store

immagi'na|re vt imagine; (supporre) suppose; **s'immagini!** imagine that!. **~rio** adj imaginary. **~zi'one** f imagination. **im'magine** f image; (rappresentazione, idea) picture

imman'cabile adj unfailing. **~'mente** adv without fail

im'mane adj huge; (simile) terrible

imma'nente adj immanent

immangi'abile adj inedible

immatrico'la|re vt register. **~rsi** vr (studente:) matriculate. **~zi'one** f registration; (di studente) matriculation

immaturità f immaturity. **imma'turo** adj unripe; (persona) immature, (prematuro) premature

immedesi'ma|rsi vr **~rsi in** identify oneself with. **~zi'one** f identification

immedia'ta|mente adv immediately. **~'tezza** f immediacy. **imme-di'ato** adj immediate

immemo'rabile adj immemorial

immensa|'mente adv enormously. **~ità** f immensity. **im-'menso** adj immense

immensu'rabile adj immeasurable

im'merger|e vt immerse. **~si** vr plunge; (sommergibile:) dive; **~si in** immerse oneself in

immersi'one f immersion; (di sommergibile) dive. **im'merso** pp di **immergere**

immi'gra|nte adj & mf immigrant. **~re** vi immigrate. **~to, -a** mf immigrant. **~zi'one** f immigration

immi'nen|te adj imminent. **~za** f imminence

immischi'ar|e vt involve. **~si** vr ~si in meddle in

immis'sario m tributary

immissi'one f insertion

im'mobile adj motionless

im'mobili mpl real estate. **~'are** società **~are** building society, savings and loan Am

immobili|tà f immobility. **~z'zare** vt immobilize; (Comm) tie up

immo'lare vt sacrifice

immondez'zaio m rubbish bin. **immon'dizia** f filth; (spazzatura) rubbish. **im'mondo** adj filthy

immo'ral|e adj immoral. **~ità** f immorality

immorta'lare vt immortalize. **immor'tale** adj immortal

immoti'vato adj (gesto) unjustified

im'mun|e adj exempt; (Med) immune. **~ità** f immunity. **~iz'zare** vt immunize. **~izzazi'one** f immunization

immunodefici'enza f immunodeficiency

immuso'ni|rsi vr sulk. **~to** adj sulky

immuta'bile adj unchangeable. **~to** adj unchanging

impacchet'tare vt wrap up

impacci'a|re vt hamper; (disturbare) inconvenience; (imbarazzare) embarrass. **~to** adj embarrassed; (goffo) awkward. **im'paccio** m embarrassment; (ostacolo) hindrance; (situazione difficile) awkward situation

im'pacco m compress

impadro'nirsi vr ~ di take possession of; (fig: imparare) master

impa'gabile adj priceless

impagina|re vt paginate. **~zi'one** f pagination

impagli'are vt stuff (animale)

impa'lato adj fig stiff

impalca'tura f scaffolding; fig

structure

impalli'dire vi turn pale; (fig: perdere d'importanza) pale into insignificance

impa'nare vt roll in breadcrumbs

impanta'narsi vr get bogged down

impape'rarsi, impappi'narsi vr falter, stammer

impa'rare vt learn

impareggi'abile adj incomparable

imparen'ta|rsi vr ~ con become related to. **~to** adj related

'impari adj unequal; (dispari) odd

impar'tire vt impart

imparzi'al|e adj impartial. **~ità** f impartiality

impas'sibile adj impassive

impa'sta|re vt (Culin) knead; blend (colori). **im'pasto** m (Culin) dough; (miscuglio) mixture

im'patto m impact

impau'rir|e vt frighten. **~si** vr become frightened

im'pavido adj fearless

impazi'en|te adj impatient; **~te** di fare qcsa eager to do sth. **~'tirsi** vr lose patience. **~za** f impatience

impaz'zata f all **~** full speed

impaz'zire vi go mad; (maionese:) separate; **far ~** qcno drive sb mad; **~ per** be crazy about; **da ~** (mal di testa) blinding

impec'cabile adj impeccable

impedi'mento m hindrance; (ostacolo) obstacle

impe'dire vt ~ di prevent from; (impacciare) hinder; (ostruire) obstruct; **~ a qcno di fare qcsa** prevent sb [from] doing sth

impe'gna|re vt (dare in pegno) pawn; (vincolare) bind; (prenotare) reserve; (assorbire) take up. **~rsi** vr apply oneself; **~rsi a fare qcsa** commit oneself to doing sth. **~'tiva**

f referral. **~'tivo** adj binding; (lavoro) demanding. **~ato** adj engaged; (Pol) committed, **im'pegno** m engagement; (Comm) commitment; (zelo) care

impel'lente adj pressing

impen'na|rsi vr (cavallo) rear; fig bristle. **~ta** f sharp rise; (di cavallo) rearing; (di moto) wheelie

impen'sabile adj unthinkable. **~to** adj unexpected

impensie'rir|e vt, **~si** vr worry

impe'ra|nte adj prevailing. **~re** vi reign; (tendenza:) prevail

impera'tivo adj e m imperative

impera'tore, -'trice m emperor ● f empress

impercet'tibile adj imperceptible

imperdo'nabile adj unforgivable

imper'fe|tto adj & m imperfect. **~zi'one** f imperfection

imperi'a|le adj imperial. **~lismo** m imperialism

imperi'oso adj imperious; (impellente) urgent

impe'rizia f lack of skill

imperme'abile adj waterproof ● m raincoat

imperni'ar|e vt pivot; (fondare) base. **~si** vr **~si su** to be based on

im'pero m empire; (potere) rule

imperscru'tabile adj inscrutable

imperso'nale adj impersonal

imperso'nare vt personify; (interpretare) act [the part of]

imper'territo adj undaunted

imperti'nen|te adj impertinent. **~za** f impertinence

imperver'sare vi rage

im'pervio adj inaccessible

'impet|o m impetus; (impulso) impulse; (slancio) transport. **~u'oso** adj impetuous; (vento) blustering

impet'tito adj stiff

impian'tare vt install; set up

(azienda)

impi'anto m plant; (sistema) system; (operazione) installation. **~ radio** (Auto) car stereo system

impia'strare vt plaster; (sporcare) dirty. **impi'astro** m poultice; (persona noiosa) bore; (pasticcione) cack-handed person

impic'car|e vt hang. **~si** vr hang oneself

impicci'arsi vr meddle. **im'piccio** m hindrance; (seccatura) bother. **~'one, -a** mf nosey parker

impie'ga|re vt employ; (usare) use; spend (tempo, denaro); Fin invest: **l'autobus ha ~to un'ora** it took the bus an hour. **~rsi** vr get [oneself] a job

impiega'tizio adj clerical

impie'gato, -a mf employee. **~ di banca** bank clerk. **impi'ego** m employment; (posto) job; Fin investment

impieto'sir|e vt move to pity. **~si** vr be moved to pity

impie'trito adj petrified

impigli'ar|e vt entangle. **~si** vr get entangled

impi'grir|e vt make lazy. **~si** vr get lazy

impli'ca|re vt implicate; (sottintendere) imply. **~rsi** vr become involved. **~zi'one** f implication

implicita'mente adv implicitly. **im'plicito** adj implicit

implo'ra|re vt implore. **~zi'one** f entreaty

impolve'ra|re vt cover with dust. **~rsi** vr get covered with dust. **~to** adj dusty

impon'derabile adj imponderable; (causa, evento) unpredictable

impo'nen|te adj imposing. **~za** f impressiveness

impo'nibile adj taxable ● m taxable income

impopo'lar|e adj unpopular. ~**ità** f unpopularity

im'por|re vt impose; (ordinare) order. ~**si** vr assert oneself; (aver successo) be successful; ~**si di** (prefiggersi di) set oneself the task of

impor'tan|te adj important ● m important thing. ~**za** f importance

impor'ta|re vt import; (comportare) cause ● vi matter; (essere necessario) be necessary. **non** ~**l** it doesn't matter!; **non me ne** ~ **niente!** I couldn't care less!. ~**tore**, ~**trice** mf importer. ~**zi'one** f importation; (merce importata) import

im'porto m amount

importu'nare vt pester. **impor-'tuno** adj troublesome; (inopportuno) untimely

imposizi'one f imposition; (imposta) tax

imposses'sarsi vr ~ **di** seize

impos'sibil|e adj impossible ● m **fare l'~e** do absolutely all one can. ~**ità** f impossibility

im'posta¹ f tax; ~ **sul reddito** income tax; ~ **sul valore aggiunto** value added tax

im'posta² f (di finestra) shutter

impo'sta|re vt (progettare) plan; (basare) base; (Mus) pitch; (imbucare) post, mail; (domanda, problema). ~**zi'one** f planning; (di voce) pitching

im'posto pp di **imporre**

impo'store, **-a** mf impostor

impo'ten|te adj powerless; (Med) impotent. ~**za** f powerlessness; (Med) impotence

impove'rir|e vt impoverish. ~**si** vr become poor

imprati'cabile adj impracticable; (strada) impassable

imprati'chir|e vt train. ~**si** vr ~**si in** o **a** get practice in

impre'care vi curse

impreci's|abile adj indeterminable. ~**ato** adj indeterminate. ~**i'one** f inaccuracy. **impre'ciso** adj inaccurate

impre'gnar|e vt impregnate; (imbevere) soak; fig imbue. ~**si** vr become impregnated with

imprendi'tor|e, **-'trice** mf entrepreneur. ~**i'ale** adj entrepreneurial

imprepa'rato adj unprepared

im'presa f undertaking; (gesta) exploit; (azienda) firm

impre'sario m impresario; (appaltatore) contractor

imprescin'dibile adj inescapable

impressio'na|bile adj impressionable. ~**nte** adj impressive; (spaventoso) frightening

impressio|o'nare vt impress; (spaventare) frighten; expose (foto). ~**o'narsi** vr be affected; (spaventarsi) be frightened. ~**one** f impression; (sensazione) sensation; (impronta) mark; **far** ~**one a qcno** upset sb

impressio'nis|mo m impressionism. ~**ta** mf impressionist

im'presso pp di **imprimere** ● adj printed

impre'stare vt lend

impreve'dibile adj unforeseeable; (persona) unpredictable

imprevi'dente adj improvident

impre'visto adj unforeseen ● m unforeseen event

imprigio'na|mento m imprisonment. ~**'nare** vt imprison

im'primere vt impress; (stampare) print; (comunicare) impart

impro'babil|e adj unlikely, improbable. ~**ità** f improbability

improdut'tivo adj unproductive

im'pronta f impression; fig mark. ~ **digitale** fingerprint. ~ **del piede** footprint

impro'perio m insult; **improperi**

pl abuse *sg*

im'proprio *adj* improper

improvvi'sa|re *vt/i* improvise. **~rsi** *vr* turn oneself into a. **~ta** *f* surprise. **~zi'one** *f* improvisation

improv'viso *adj* sudden; **all' ~** un expectedly

impru'den|te *adj* imprudent. **~za** *f* imprudence

impu'gna|re *vt* grasp; (*Jur*) contest. **~'tura** *f* grip; (*manico*) handle

impulsività *f* impulsiveness. im'pulsivo *adj* impulsive

im'pulso *m* impulse; agire d'~ act on impulse

impune'mente *adv* with impunity. impu'nito *adj* unpunished

impun'tura *f* stitching

impurità *f inv* impurity. im'puro *adj* impure

impu'tabile *adj* attributable (a to)

impu'ta|re *vt* attribute; (*accusare*) charge. **~to, -a** *mf* accused. **~zi'one** *f* charge

imputri'dire *vi* rot

in *prep* in; (*moto a luogo*) to; (*su*) on; (*entro*) within; (*mezzi*) by; (*con materiale*) made of; **essere in casa/ufficio** be at home/at the office; **in mano/tasca** in one's hand/pocket; **andare in Francia/campagna** go to France/the country; **salire in treno** get on the train; **versa la birra nel bicchiere** pour the beer into the glass; **in alto** up there; **in giornata** within the day; **nel 1997** in 1997; **una borsa in pelle** a bag made of leather, a leather bag; **in macchina** (*viaggiare, venire*) by car; **in contanti** [in] cash; **in vacanza** on holiday; **se fossi in te** if I were you; **siamo in sette** there are seven of us

inabbor'dabile *adj* unapproachable

i'nabile *adj* incapable; (*fisicamente*) unfit. **~ità** *f* incapacity

inabi'tabile *adj* uninhabitable

inacces'sibile *adj* inaccessible; (*persona*) unapproachable

inaccet'tabi|le *adj* unacceptable. **~ità** *f* unacceptability

inacer'bi|re *vt* embitter; exacerbate (*rapporto*). **~si** *vr* grow bitter

inaci'dir|e *vt* turn sour. **~si** *vr* go sour; (*persona*) become bitter

ina'datto *adj* unsuitable

inadegu'ato *adj* inadequate

inadempi'ente *mf* defaulter. **~'mento** *m* nonfulfilment

inaffer'rabile *adj* elusive

inala|re *vt* inhale. **~'tore** *m* inhaler. **~zi'one** *f* inhalation

inalbe'rar|e *vt* hoist. **~si** *vr* (*cavallo*): rear [up]; (*adirarsi*) lose one's temper

inalte'ra|bile *adj* unchangeable; (*colore*) fast. **~to** *adj* unchanged

inami'da|re *vt* starch. **~to** *adj* starched

inammis'sibile *adj* inadmissible

inamovi'bile *adj* irremovable

inani'mato *adj* inanimate; (*senza vita*) lifeless

inappa'gabile *adj* unsatisfiable. **~to** *adj* unfulfilled

inappe'tenza *f* lack of appetite

inappli'cabile *adj* inapplicable

inappun'tabile *adj* faultless

inar'car|e *vt* arch; raise (sopracciglia). **~si** *vr* (*legno*): warp; (*ripiano*): sag; (*linea*): curve

inari'dir|e *vt* parch; empty of feelings (*persona*). **~si** *vr* dry up; (*persona*): become empty of feelings

inartico'lato *adj* inarticulate

inaspettata'mente *adv* unexpectedly. inaspet'tato *adj* unexpected

inaspri'mento *m* embitterment; (*di conflitto*) worsening

ina'sprir|e *vt* embitter. **~si** *vr* become embittered

inattac'cabile *adj* unassailable; (*ir-*

repensibile) irreproachable

inatten'dibile adj unreliable. **inat-**
'teso adj unexpected

inattività f inactivity. **inat'tivo** adj
inactive

inattu'abile adj impracticable

inau'dito adj unheard of

inaugu'rale adj inaugural; **viaggio**
~ maiden voyage

inaugu'ra|re vt inaugurate; open
(mostra); unveil (statua); christen
(lavastoviglie ecc). ~zi'one f inaug-
uration; (di mostra) opening; (di statua)
unveiling

inavver't|enza f inadvertence.
~ita'mente adv inadvertently

incagli'ar|e vi ground ● vt hinder.
~si vr run aground

incalco'labile adj incalculable

incal'li|rsi vr grow callous; (abituarsi)
become hardened. ~to adj callous;
(abituato) hardened

incal'za|nte adj (ritmo) driving; (ri-
chiesta) urgent. ~re vt pursue;
fig press

incame'rare vt appropriate

incammi'nar|e vt get going; (fig:
guidare) set off. ~si vr set out

incanalar|e vt canalize; fig chan-
nel. ~si vr converge on

incande'scen|te adj incandescent;
(discussione) burning

incan'ta|re vt enchant. ~rsi vr
stand spellbound; (incepparsi) jam.
~'tore, ~'trice m enchanter ●f en-
chantress

incan'tesimo m spell

incan'tevole adj enchanting

in'canto m spell; fig delight; (asta)
auction; **come per** ~ as if by magic

incanu'ti|re vt turn white. ~to
adj white

inca'pac|e adj incapable. ~ità f in-
capability

incapo'nirsi vr be set (a fare on
doing)

incap'pare vi ~ in run into

incappucci'arsi vr wrap up

incapricci'arsi vr ~ di take a
fancy to

incapsu'lare vt seal; crown (dente)

incarce'ra|re vt imprison. ~zi'one
f imprisonment

incari'ca|re vt charge. ~rsi vr take
upon oneself; **me ne incarico io** I
will see to it. ~to, -a adj in charge
●mf representative. **in'carico** m
charge; **per incarico di** on behalf of

incar'na|re vt embody. ~rsi vr be-
come incarnate

incarta'mento m documents pl.
incar'tare vt wrap [in paper]

incas'sa|re vt pack; (Mech) embed;
box in (mobile, frigo); (riscuotere)
cash; take (colpo). ~to adj set;
(fiume) deeply embanked. **in'casso**
m collection; (introito) takings pl

incasto'na|re vt set. ~'tura f set-
ting. ~to adj embedded; (anello)
inset (di with)

inca'strar|e vt fit in; (🛈: in situa-
zione) corner. ~si vr fit. **in'castro** m
joint; **a incastro** (pezzi) interlocking

incate'nare vt chain

incatra'mare vt tar

incatti'vire vt turn nasty

in'cauto adj imprudent

inca'va|re vt hollow out. ~to adj
hollow. ~'tura f hollow. **in'cavo** m
hollow; (scanalatura) groove

incendi'ar|e vt set fire to; fig in-
flame. ~si vr catch fire. ~io, -a adj
incendiary; fig: (discorso) inflamma-
tory; fig: (bellezza) sultry ●mf arson-
ist. **in'cendio** m fire. **incendio do-**
loso arson

incene'ri|re vt burn to ashes; (cre-
mare) cremate. ~rsi vr be burnt to
ashes. ~'tore m incinerator

in'censo m incense

incensu'rato adj blameless; **essere**
~ (Jur) have a clean record

incenti'vare vt motivate. **incen'tivo** m incentive

incen'trarsi vr ~ **su** centre on

incep'par|e vt block; fig hamper. ~**si** vr jam

ince'rata f oilcloth

incro'ttato adj with a plaster on

incer'tezza f uncertainty. **in'certo** adj uncertain ● m uncertainty

inces'sante adj unceasing. ~**'mente** adv incessantly

in'cest|o m incest. ~**u'oso** adj incestuous

in'cetta f buying up; **fare** ~ **di** stockpile

inchi'esta f investigation

inchi'nar|e vt, ~**si** vr bow. **in'chino** m bow; (di donna) curtsy

inchio'dare vt nail; nail down (coperchio); ~ **a letto** (malattia:) confine to bed

inchi'ostro m ink

inciam'pare vi stumble; ~ **in** (imbattersi) run into. **inci'ampo** m hindrance

inci'dentale adj incidental

inci'den|te m (episodio) incident; (infortunio) accident. ~**za** f incidence

in'cidere vt cut; (arte) engrave; (registrare) record ● vi ~ **su** (gravare) weigh upon

in'cinta adj pregnant

incipi'ente adj incipient

incipri'ar|e vt powder. ~**si** vr powder one's face

in'circa adv **all'**~ more or less

incisi'one f incision; (arte) engraving; (acquaforte) etching; (registrazione) recording

inci'sivo adj incisive ● m (dente) incisor

in'ciso m **per** ~ incidentally

incita'mento m incitement. **inci'tare** vt incite

inci'vil|e adj uncivilized; (maleducato) impolite. ~**tà** f barbarism; (maleduca-

zione) rudeness

incle'men|te adj harsh

incli'nabile adj reclining

incli'na|re vt tilt ● vi ~**re a** be inclined to. ~**rsi** vr list. ~**to** adj tilted; (terreno) sloping. ~**zi'one** f slope, inclination. **in'cline** adj inclined

in'clu|dere vt include; (allegare) enclose. ~**si'one** f inclusion. ~**sivo** adj inclusive. ~**so** pp di **includere** ● adj included; (compreso) inclusive; (allegato) enclosed

incoe'ren|te adj (contraddittorio) inconsistent. ~**za** f inconsistency

in'cognit|a f unknown quantity. ~**o** adj unknown ● m **in** ~**o** incognito

incol'lar|e vt stick; (con colla liquida) glue. ~**si** vr stick to; ~**si a qcno** stick close to sb

incolle'ri|rsi vr lose one's temper. ~**to** adj enraged

incol'mabile adj (differenza) unbridgeable; (vuoto) unfillable

incolon'nare vt line up

inco'lore adj colourless

incol'pare vt blame

in'colto adj uncultivated; (persona) uneducated

in'colume adj unhurt

incom'ben|te adj impending. ~**za** f task

in'combere vi ~ **su** hang over; ~ **a** (spettare) be incumbent on

incominci'are vt/i begin, start

incomo'dar|e vt inconvenience. ~**si** vr trouble. **in'comodo** adj uncomfortable; (inopportuno) inconvenient ● m inconvenience

incompa'rabile adj incomparable

incompe'ten|te adj incompetent. ~**za** f incompetence

incompi'uto adj unfinished

incom'pleto adj incomplete

incompren'si'bile adj incomprehensible. ~**'one** f lack of understanding; (*malinteso*) misunderstanding. **incom'preso** adj misunderstood

inconce'pibile adj inconceivable

inconclu'dente adj inconclusive; (*persona*) ineffectual

incondizio|nata'mente adv unconditionally. **~'nato** adj unconditional

inconfes'sabile adj unmentionable

inconfon'dibile adj unmistakable

incongru'ente adj inconsistent

in'congruo adj inadequate

inconsa'pevol|e adj unaware; (*inconscio*) unconscious. **~'mente** adv unwittingly

inconscia'mente adv unconsciously. **in'conscio** adj & m (*Psych*) unconscious

inconsi'sten|te adj insubstantial; (*notizia ecc*) unfounded. **~za** f (*di ragionamento, prove*) flimsiness

inconsu'eto adj unusual

incon'sulto adj rash

incontami'nato adj uncontaminated

inconte'nibile adj irrepressible

inconten'tabile adj insatiable; (*esigente*) hard to please

inconti'nen|te adj incontinent. **~za** f incontinence

incon'trar|e vt meet; encounter, meet with (difficoltà). **~si** vr meet (con qcno sb)

incon'trario: all'~ adv the other way around; (*in modo sbagliato*) the wrong way around

incontra'sta|bile adj incontrovertible. **~to** adj undisputed

in'contro m meeting; *Sport* match. **~ al vertice** summit meeting ● *prep* **~ a** towards; **andare ~ a qcno** go to meet sb; *fig* meet sb half way

inconveni'ente m drawback

incoraggi|a'mento m encouragement. **~'ante** adj encouraging.

~'are vt encourage

incornici'a|re vt frame. **~'tura** f framing

incoro'na|re vt crown. **~zi'one** f coronation

incorpo'rar|e vt incorporate; (*mescolare*) blend. **~si** vr blend; (*territori:*) merge

incorreg'gibile adj incorrigible

in'correre vi **~ in** incur; **~ nel pericolo di...** run the risk of...

incorrut'tibile adj incorruptible

incosci'en|te adj unconscious; (*irresponsabile*) reckless ● *mf* irresponsible person. **~za** f unconsciousness; recklessness

inco'stan|te adj changeable; (*persona*) fickle. **~za** f changeableness; (*di persona*) fickleness

incre'dibile adj unbelievable, incredible

incredulità f incredulity. **in'credulo** adj incredulous

incremen'tare vt increase; (*intensificare*) step up. **incre'mento** m increase. **incremento demografico** population growth

incresci'oso adj regrettable

incre'spar|e vt ruffle; wrinkle (tessuto); make frizzy (capelli); **~e la fronte** frown. **~si** vr (acqua:) ripple; (tessuto:) wrinkle; (capelli:) go frizzy

incrimi'na|re vt indict; *fig* incriminate. **~zi'one** f indictment

incri'na|re vt crack; *fig* affect (amicizia). **~rsi** vr crack; (amicizia:) be affected. **~'tura** f crack

incroci'a|re vt cross ● vi (Aeron, Naut) cruise. **~rsi** vr cross. **~'tore** m cruiser

in'crocio m crossing; (*di strade*) crossroads sg

incrol'labile adj indestructible

incro'sta|re vt encrust. **~zi'one** f encrustation

incuba'|trice f incubator. **~zi'one**

f Incubation

'**incubo** *m* nightmare

in'**cudine** *f* anvil

incu'**rabile** *adj* incurable

incu'**rante** *adj* careless

incurio'**sire** *vt* make curious. ~**si** *vr* become curious

incursi'**one** *f* raid. ~ **aerea** air raid

incurva'**mento** *m* bending

incur'**va|re** *vt*, ~**rsi** *vr* bend. ~**tura** *f* bending

in'**cusso** *pp di* incutere

incusto'**dito** *adj* unguarded

in'**cutere** *vt* arouse

'**indaco** *m* indigo

indaffa'**rato** *adj* busy

inda'**gare** *vt/i* investigate

in'**dagine** *f* research; (*giudiziaria*) investigation. ~ **di mercato** market survey

indebi'**tar|e** *vt*, ~**si** *vr* get into debt

in'**debito** *adj* undue

indeboli'**mento** *m* weakening

indebo'**li|re** *vt*, ~**rsi** *vr* weaken

inde'**cen|te** *adj* indecent; (*vergogna*) disgrace

indeci'**frabile** *adj* indecipherable

indecisi'**one** *f* indecision. inde'**ciso** *adj* undecided

inde'**fesso** *adj* tireless

indefi'**nibile** *adj* indefinable. ~**to** *adj* indefinite

indefor'**mabile** *adj* crushproof

in'**degno** *adj* unworthy

indeli'**catezza** *f* indelicacy; (*azione*) tactless act. indeli'**cato** *adj* indiscreet; (*grossolano*) indelicate

in'**denn|e** *adj* uninjured; (*da malattia*) unaffected. ~**ità** *f inv* allowance; (*per danni*) compensation. ~**ità di trasferta** travel allowance. ~**iz'zare** *vt* compensate. inden'**nizzo** *m* compensation

indero'**gabile** *adj* binding

indeside'**ra|bile** *adj* undesirable. ~**to** *adj* (*figlio, ospite*) unwanted

indetermi'**na|bile** *adj* indeterminable. ~**tezza** *f* vagueness. ~**to** *adj* indeterminate

'**India** *f* India. i~**'ano, -a** *adj* & *mf* Indian; **in fila i**~**ana** in single file

indiavo'**lato** *adj* possessed; (*vivace*) wild

indi'**ca|re** *vt* show, indicate; (*col dito*) point at; (*far notare*) point out; (*consigliare*) advise. ~**tivo** *adj* indicative • *m* (*Gram*) indicative. ~**'tore** *m* indicator; (*Techn*) gauge; (*prontuario*) directory. ~**zi'one** *f* indication; (*istruzione*) direction

'**indice** *m* (*dito*) forefinger; (*lancetta*) pointer; (*di libro, statistica*) index; (*fig: segno*) sign

indietreggi'**are** *vi* draw back; (*Mil*) retreat

indi'**etro** *adv* back, behind; **all'**~ backwards; **avanti e** ~ back and forth; **essere** ~ be behind; (*mentalmente*) be backward; (*con pagamenti*) be in arrears; (*di orologio*) be slow; **fare marcia** ~ reverse; **rimandare** ~ send back; **rimanere** ~ be left behind; **torna** ~**!** come back!

indi'**feso** *adj* undefended; (*inerme*) helpless

indiffe'**ren|te** *adj* indifferent; **mi è** ~**te** it is all the same to me. ~**za** *f* indifference

in'**digeno, -a** *adj* indigenous • *mf* native

indi'**gen|te** *adj* needy. ~**za** *f* poverty

indigesti'**one** *f* indigestion. indi'**gesto** *adj* indigestible

indi'**gna|re** *vt* make indignant. ~**rsi** *vr* be indignant. ~**to** *adj* indignant. ~**zi'one** *f* indignation

indimenti'**cabile** *adj* unforgettable

indipen'**den|te** *adj* independent.

~te'mente adv independently; **~te-mente dal tempo** regardless of the weather, whatever the weather. **~za** f independence

in'dire vt announce

indiretta'mente adv indirectly. **indi'retto** adj indirect

indiriz'zar|e vt address; (mandare) send; (dirigere) direct. **~si** vr direct one's steps. **indi'rizzo** m address; (direzione) direction

indisci'pli|na f lack of discipline. **~'nato** adj undisciplined

indi'scre|to adj indiscreet. **~zi'one** f indiscretion

indi'scusso adj unquestioned

indiscu'tibil|e adj unquestionable. **~'mente** adv unquestionably

indispen'sabile adj essential, indispensable

indispet'tir|e vt irritate. **~si** vr get irritated

indi'spo|rre vt antagonize. **~sto** pp di **indisporre** ● adj indisposed. **~sizi'one** f indisposition

indisso'lubile adj indissoluble

indistin'guibile adj indiscernible

indistinta'mente adv without exception. **indi'stinto** adj indistinct

indistrut'tibile adj indestructible

indistur'bato adj undisturbed

in'divia f endive

individu'a|le adj individual. **~'lista** mf individualist. **~lità** f individuality. **~re** vt individualize; (localizzare) locate; (riconoscere) single out

indi'viduo m individual

indivi'sibile adj indivisible. **indi'viso** adj undivided

indizi'a|re vt throw suspicion on. **~to, -a** adj suspected ● mf suspect. **in'dizio** m sign; (Jur) circumstantial evidence

'indole f nature

indolenzi'mento m stiffness

indolen'zir|si vr go stiff.

~to adj stiff

indo'lore adj painless

indo'mani m l'**~** the following day

Indo'nesia f Indonesia

indo'rare vt gild

indos'sa|re vt wear; (mettere addosso) put on. **~'tore**, **~'trice** mf model

in'dotto pp di **indurre**

indottri'nare vt indoctrinate

indovi'n|are vt guess; (predire) foretell. **~ato** adj successful; (scelta) well-chosen. **~ello** m riddle. **indo-'vino, -a** mf fortune-teller

indubbia'mente adv undoubtedly. **in'dubbio** adj undoubted

indugi'ar|e vi, **~si** vr linger. **in'dugio** m delay

indul'gen|te adj indulgent. **~za** f indulgence

in'dul|gere vi **~gere a** indulge in. **~to** pp di **indulgere** ● m (Jur) pardon

indu'mento m garment; **indumenti** pl clothes

induri'mento m hardening

indu'rir|e vt, **~si** vr harden

in'durre vt induce

in'dustri|a f industry. **~'ale** adj industrial ● mf industrialist

industrializ'za|re vt industrialize. **~to** adj industrialized. **~zi'one** f industrialization

industri|'arsi vr try one's hardest. **~'oso** adj industrious

induzi'one f induction

inebe'tito adj stunned

inebri'ante adj intoxicating, exciting

i'nedia f starvation

i'nedito adj unpublished

ineffi'cace adj ineffective

ineffici'en|te adj inefficient. **~za** f inefficiency

ineguagli'abile adj incomparable

inegu'ale adj unequal;

(superficie) uneven

inelut'tabile adj inescapable

ine'rente adj ~ a concerning

i'nerme adj unarmed; fig defenceless

inerpi'carsi vr ~ su clamber up; (pianta:) climb up

i'ner|te adj inactive; (Phys) inert. ~zia f inactivity; (Phys) inertia

inesat'tezza f inaccuracy. **ine'satto** adj inaccurate; (erroneo) incorrect; (non riscosso) uncollected

inesau'ribile adj inexhaustible

inesi'sten|te adj non-existent. ~za f non-existence

inesper'ienza f inexperience. **ine'sperto** adj inexperienced

inespli'cabile adj inexplicable

ine'sploso adj unexploded

inesti'mabile adj inestimable

inetti'tudine f ineptitude. **i'netto** adj inept; **inetto a** unsuited to

ine'vaso adj (pratiche) pending; (corrispondenza) unanswered

inevi'tabil|e adj inevitable. ~'mente adv inevitably

i'nezia f trifle

infagot'tar|e vt wrap up. ~si vr wrap [oneself] up

infal'libile adj infallible

infa'mare vt defame. ~'torio adj defamatory

in'fam|e adj infamous; (🔢: orrendo) awful, shocking. ~ia f infamy

infan'garsi vr get muddy

infan'tile adj children's; (ingenuità) childlike; pej childish

in'fanzia f childhood, (bambini) children pl; **prima** ~ infancy

infar'cire vt pepper (discorso) (di with)

infari'na|re vt flour; ~re di sprinkle with. ~'tura f fig smattering

in'farto m coronary

infasti'dir|e vt irritate. ~si vr get irritated

Infati'cabile adj untiring

in'fatti conj as a matter of fact; (veramente) indeed

infatu'a|rsi vr become infatuated (di with). ~to adj infatuated. ~zi'one f infatuation

infe'condo adj infertile

infe'del|e adj unfaithful. ~tà f unfaithfulness; ~ pl affairs

infe'lic|e adj unhappy; (inappropriato) unfortunate; (cattivo) bad. ~ità f unhappiness

infel'tri|rsi vr get matted. ~to adj matted

inferi'or|e adj (più basso) lower; (qualità) inferior • mf inferior. ~ità f inferiority

infer'meria f infirmary; (di nave) sick-bay

infermi'er|a f nurse. ~e m [male] nurse

infermità f sickness. ~ **mentale** mental illness. **in'fermo, -a** adj sick • mf invalid

infer'nale adj infernal; (spaventoso) hellish

in'ferno m hell; **va all'~!** go to hell!

infero'cirsi vr become fierce

inferri'ata f grating

infervo'rar|e vt arouse enthusiasm in. ~si vr get excited

infe'stare vt infest

infet'tar|e vt infect. ~arsi vr become infected. ~ivo adj infectious. **in'fetto** adj infected. **infezi'one** f infection

infiac'chir|e vt/i, ~si vr weaken

infiam'mabile adj [in]flammable

infiam'ma|re vt set on fire; (Med, fig) inflame. ~rsi vr catch fire; (Med) become inflamed. ~zi'one f (Med) inflammation

in'fido adj treacherous

infie'rire vi (imperversare) rage; ~ su

attack furiously

in'figger|e vt drive. ~**si** vr ~**si in** penetrate

infi'lar|e vt thread; (*mettere*) insert; (*indossare*) put on. ~**si** vr slip on (*vestito*). ~**si in** (*introdursi in*) slip into

infil'tra|rsi vr infiltrate. ~**zi'one** f infiltration; (*d'acqua*) seepage; (*Med: iniezione*) injection

infil'zare vt pierce; (*infilare*) string; (*conficcare*) stick

'infimo adj lowest

in'fine adv finally; (*insomma*) in short

infinità f infinity; **un'~ di** masses of. **infi'nito** adj infinite; (*Gram*) infinitive ● m infinite; (*Gram*) infinitive; (*Math*) infinity; **all'infinito** endlessly

infinocchi'are vt 🅣 hoodwink

infischi'arsi vr ~ **di** not care about; **me ne infischio** 🅣 I couldn't care less

in'fisso pp di **infiggere** ● m fixture; (*di porta, finestra*) frame

infit'tir|e vt/i, ~**si** vr thicken

inflazi'one f inflation

infles'sibil|e adj inflexible. ~**ità** f inflexibility

inflessi'one f inflexion

in'fli|ggere vt inflict. ~**tto** pp di **infliggere**

influ'en|te adj influential. ~**za** f influence; (*Med*) influenza

influen'za|bile adj (*mente, opinione*) impressionable. ~**re** vt influence. ~**to** adj (*malato*) with the flu

influ'ire vi ~ **su** influence

in'flusso m influence

info'carsi vr catch fire; (*viso:*) go red; (*discussione:*) become heated

infol'tire vt/i thicken

infon'dato adj unfounded

in'fondere vt instil

infor'care vt fork up; get on (*bici*); put on (*occhiali*)

infor'male adj informal

infor'ma|re vt inform. ~**rsi** vr inquire (**di** about).

infor'matic|a f computing, IT. ~**o** adj computer attrib

infor'ma|tivo adj informative. **infor'mato** adj informed; **male informato** ill-informed. ~**tore**, ~**trice** mf (*di polizia*) informer. ~**zi'one** f information (*solo sg*); **un'~zione** a piece of information

in'forme adj shapeless

infor'nare vt put into the oven

infortu'narsi vr have an accident.

infor'tu|nio m accident. ~**nio sul lavoro** industrial accident

infos'sa|rsi vr sink; (*guance, occhi:*) become hollow. ~**to** adj sunken, hollow

infradici'ar|e vt drench. ~**si** vr get drenched; (*diventare marcio*) rot

infra'dito m pl (*scarpe*) flip-flops

in'frang|ere vt break; (*in mille pezzi*) shatter. ~**ersi** vr break. ~**gibile** adj unbreakable

in'franto pp di **infrangere** ● adj shattered; (*cuore*) broken

infra'rosso adj infra-red

infrastrut'tura f infrastructure

infrazi'one f offence

infredda'tura f cold

infreddo'li|rsi vr feel cold. ~**to** adj cold

infrut'tuoso adj fruitless

infuo'ca|re vt make red-hot. ~**to** adj burning

infu'ori adv **all'~** outwards; **all'~ di** except

infuri'a|re vi rage. ~**rsi** vr fly into a rage. ~**to** adj blustering

infusi'one f infusion. **in'fuso** pp di **infondere** ● m infusion

Ing. abbr ingegnere

ingabbi'are vt cage; (*fig: mettere in prigione*) jail

ingaggi'are vt engage; sign up

(calciatori ecc); begin (lotta, battaglia). **in'gaggio** m engagement; (di calciatore) signing [up]

ingan'nar|e vt deceive; (essere infedele a) be unfaithful to. **~si** vr deceive oneself; **se non m'inganno** if I am not mistaken

ingan'nevole adj deceptive. **in 'ganno** m deceit; (frode) fraud

ingarbugli'a|re vt entangle; (confondere) confuse. **~rsi** vr get entangled; (confondersi) become confused. **~to** adj confused

inge'gnarsi vr do one's best

inge'gnere m engineer. **ingegne-'ria** f engineering

in'gegno m brains pl; (genio) genius; (abilità) ingenuity. **~sa'mente** adv ingeniously

ingelo'sir|e vt make jealous. **~si** vr become jealous

in'gente adj huge

ingenua'la'mente adv naïvely. **~ità** f naïvety, innocence. **in'genuo** adj ingenuous; (credulone) naïve

inge'renza f interference

inge'rire vt swallow

inges'sa|re vt put in plaster. **~'tura** f plaster

inghil'terra f England

inghiot'tire vt swallow

in'ghippo m trick

ingial'li|re vi, **~rsi** vr turn yellow. **~to** adj yellowed

ingigan'tir|e vt magnify ● vi, **~si** vr grow to enormous proportions

inginocchi'a|rsi vr kneel [down]. **~to** adj kneeling. **~'tolo** m prie-dieu

ingiù adv down, **all'~** downwards; **a testa ~** head downwards

ingi'un|gere vt order. **~zi'one** f injunction. **~zione di pagamento** final demand

ingi'uri|a f insult; (torto) wrong; (danno) damage. **~'are** vt insult; (fare

un torto a) wrong. **~'oso** adj insulting

ingiu'stizia f injustice. **ingi'usto** adj unjust, unfair

in'glese adj English ● m Englishman; (lingua) English ● f Englishwoman

ingoi'are vt swallow

ingol'far|e vt flood (motore). **~si** vr fig get involved; (motore): flood

ingom'bra|nte adj cumbersome. **~re** vt clutter up; fig cram (mente)

in'gombro m encumbrance; **essere d'~** be in the way

ingor'digia f greed. **in'gordo** adj greedy

ingor'gar|e vt block. **~si** vr be blocked [up]. **in'gorgo** m blockage; (del traffico) jam

ingoz'zar|e vt gobble up; (nutrire eccessivamente) stuff; fatten (animali)

ingra'naggio m gear; fig mechanism. **~re** vt fatten up ● vi be in gear

ingrandi'mento m enlargement

ingran'di|re vt enlarge; (esagerare) magnify. **~rsi** vr become larger; (aumentare) increase

ingras'sar|e vt fatten up; (Mech) grease ● vi, **~si** vr put on weight

ingrati'tudine f ingratitude. **in 'grato** adj ungrateful; (sgradevole) thankless

ingredi'ente m ingredient

in'gresso m entrance; (accesso) admittance; (sala) hall; **~ gratuito/libero** admission free; **vietato l'~** no entry; no admittance

ingros'sar|e vt make big; (gonfiare) swell ● vi, **~si** vr grow big; (gonfiare) swell

in'grosso: all'~ adv wholesale; (pressappoco) roughly

ingua'ribile adj incurable

'inguine m groin

ingurgi'tare vt gulp down

ini'bi|re vt inhibit; (vietare) forbid.

~to adj inhibited. ~zi'one f inhibition; (divieto) prohibition

iniet'tar|e vt inject. ~si vr ~si di sangue (occhi:) become bloodshot. **iniezi'one** f injection

inimi'carsi vr make an enemy of. **inimi'cizia** f enmity

inimi'tabile adj inimitable

ininter|rotta'mente adv continuously. ~'rotto adj continuous

iniquità f iniquity. **i'niquo** adj iniquitous

inizi'are vt begin; (avviare) open; ~ qcno a qcsa initiate sb in sth ● vi begin

inizia'tiva f initiative; **prendere l'~** take the initiative

inizi'a|to, -a adj initiated ● mf initiate; **gli ~ti** the initiated. ~'tore, ~'trice m initiator. ~zi'one f initiation

i'nizio m beginning, start; **dare ~ a** start; **avere ~** get under way

innaffi'a|re vt water. ~'toio m watering-can

innal'zar|e vt raise; (erigere) erect. ~si vr rise

innamo'ra|rsi vr fall in love (di with). ~ta f girl-friend. ~to adj in love ● m boy-friend

in'nanzi adv (stato in luogo) in front; (di tempo) ahead; (avanti) forward; (prima) before; **d'ora ~** from now on ● prep (prima) before; ~ **a** in front of. ~'tutto adv first of all; (soprattutto) above all

in'nato adj innate

innatu'rale adj unnatural

inne'gabile adj undeniable

innervo'sir|e vt make nervous. ~si vr get irritated

inne'scare vt prime. **in'nesco** m primer

inne'stare vt graft; (Mech) engage; (inserire) insert. **in'nesto** m graft; (Mech) clutch; (Electr) connection

inne'vato adj covered in snow

'inno m hymn. ~ **nazionale** national anthem

inno'cen|te adj innocent. ~te'mente adv innocently

in'nocuo adj innocuous

inno'va|re vt make changes in. ~'tivo adj innovative. ~'tore adj trail-blazing. ~zi'one f innovation

innume'revole adj innumerable

ino'doro adj odourless

inoffen'sivo adj harmless

inol'trar|e vt forward. ~si vr advance

inol'trato adj late

i'noltre adv besides

inon'da|re vt flood. ~zi'one f flood

inope'roso adj idle

inoppor'tuno adj untimely

inorgo'glir|e vt make proud. ~si vr become proud

inor'ridire vt horrify ● vi be horrified

inosser'vato adj unobserved; (non rispettato) disregarded; **passare ~** go unnoticed

inossi'dabile adj stainless

'inox adj inv (acciaio) stainless

inqua'dra|re vt frame; fig put in context (scrittore, problema). ~rsi vr fit into. ~'tura f framing

inqualifi'cabile adj unspeakable

inquie'tar|e vt worry. ~si get worried; (impazientirsi) get cross. **in'quieto** adj restless; (preoccupato) worried. **inqui'etudine** f anxiety

inqui'lino, -a mf tenant

inquina'mento m pollution

inqui'na|re vt pollute. ~to adj polluted

inqui'rente adj (Jur) (magistrato) examining; **commissione ~** commission of enquiry

inqui'si|re vt/i investigate. ~to adj under investigation. ~'tore, ~'trice *adj* inquiring ●*mf* inquisitor. ~z**l'one** *f* inquisition

insabbi'are *vt* shelve

insa'lat|a *f* salad. ~**a belga** endive. ~**i'era** *f* salad bowl

insa'lubre *adj* unhealthy

insa'nabile *adj* incurable

insangui'na|re *vt* cover with blood. ~**to** *adj* bloody

insa'po|re *adj* tasteless. ~**rire** *vt* flavour

insa'puta *f* all'~ **di** unknown to

insazi'abile *adj* insatiable

insce'nare *vt* stage

inscin'dibile *adj* inseparable

inse'dia'mento *m* installation

insedi'ar|e *vt* install. ~**si** *vr* install oneself

in'segna *f* sign; (*bandiera*) flag; (*decorazione*) decoration; (*emblema*) insignia *pl*; (*stemma*) symbol. ~ **luminosa** neon sign

insegna'mento *m* teaching. **inse-'gnante** *adj* teaching ●*mf* teacher

inse'gnare *vt/i* teach; ~ **qcsa a qcno** teach sb sth

insegui'mento *m* pursuit

insegu'i|re *vt* pursue. ~**tore**, ~**trice** *mf* pursuer

insemi'na|re *vt* inseminate. ~**zione** *f* insemination. ~**zione artificiale** artificial insemination

insena'tura *f* inlet

insen'sato *adj* senseless; (*folle*) crazy

insen'sibil|e *adj* insensitive; (*braccio ecc*) numb. ~**ità** *f* insensitivity

inseri'mento *m* insertion

inse'rir|e *vt* insert; place (*annuncio*); (*Electr*) connect. ~**si** *vr* ~**si in** get into. **in'serto** *m* file; (*in un film ecc*) insert

inservi'ente *mf* attendant

inserzi'o|ne *f* insertion; (*avviso*) advertisement. ~**nista** *mf* advertiser

insetti'cida *m* insecticide

in'setto *m* insect

insicu'rezza *f* insecurity. **insi'curo** *adj* insecure

in'sidi|a *f* trick; (*tranello*) snare. ~**are** *vt/i* lay a trap for. ~**oso** *adj* insidious

insi'eme *adv* together; (*contemporaneamente*) at the same time ●*prep* ~ **a** [together] with ●*m* whole; (*completo*) outfit; (*Theat*) ensemble; (*Math*) set; **nell'~** as a whole; **tutto** ~ all together; (*bere*) at one go

in'signe *adj* renowned

insignifi'cante *adj* insignificant

insi'gnire *vt* decorate

insinda'cabile *adj* final

insinu'ante *adj* insinuating

insinu'a|re *vt* insinuate. ~**rsi** *vr* penetrate; ~**rsi in** *fig* creep into

in'sipido *adj* insipid

insi'sten|te *adj* insistent. ~**te-'mente** *adv* repeatedly. ~**za** *f* insistence. **in'sistere** *vi* insist; (*perseverare*) persevere

insoddisfa'cente *adj* unsatisfactory

insoddi'sfa|tto *adj* unsatisfied; (*scontento*) dissatisfied. ~**zi'one** *f* dissatisfaction

insoffe'ren|te *adj* intolerant. ~**za** *f* intolerance

insolazi'one *f* sunstroke

inso'len|te *adj* rude, insolent. ~**za** *f* rudeness, insolence; (*commento*) insolent remark

in'solito *adj* unusual

inso'lubile *adj* insoluble

inso'luto *adj* unsolved; (*non pagato*) unpaid

insol'v|enza *f* insolvency

in'somma *adv* in short; ~! well really!; (*così così*) so so

in'sonn|e *adj* sleepless. ~**ia** *f* insomnia

insonno'lito *adj* sleepy

insonoriz'zato adj soundproofed

insoppor'tabile adj unbearable

insor'genza f onset

in'sorgere vi revolt, rise up; (sorgere) arise; (difficoltà) crop up

insormon'tabile adj (ostacolo, difficoltà) insurmountable

in'sorto pp di insorgere• adj rebellious •m rebel

insospet'tabile adj unsuspected

insospet'tir|e vt make suspicious •vi, ~si vr become suspicious

insoste'nibile adj untenable; (insopportabile) unbearable

insostitu'ibile adj irreplaceable

inspe'ra|bile adj una sua vittoria è ~bile there is no hope of him winning. ~to adj unhoped-for

inspie'gabile adj inexplicable

inspi'rare vt breathe in

in'stabil|e adj unstable; (tempo) changeable. ~ità f instability; (di tempo) changeability

instal'la|re vt install. ~rsi vr settle in. ~zi'one f installation

instau'ra|re vt found. ~rsi vr become established. ~zi'one f foundation

instra'dare vt direct

insù adv all'~ upwards

insuc'cesso m failure

insudici'ar|e vt dirty. ~si vr get dirty

insuffici'en|te adj insufficient; (inadeguato) inadequate •m (Sch) fail. ~za f insufficiency; (inadeguatezza) inadequacy; (Sch) fail. ~za cardiaca heart failure. ~za di prove lack of evidence

insu'lare adj insular

insu'lina f insulin

in'sulso adj insipid; (sciocco) silly

insul'tare vt insult. **in'sulto** m insult

insupe'rabile adj insuperable; (eccezionale) incomparable

insussi'stente adj groundless

intac'care vt nick; (corrodere) corrode; draw on (capitale); (danneggiare) damage

intagli'are vt carve. **in'taglio** m carving

intan'gibile adj untouchable

in'tanto adv meanwhile; (per ora) for the moment; (avversativo) but; ~ che while

intarsi'a|re vt inlay. ~to adj ~to di inset with. **in'tarsio** m inlay

inta'sa|re vt clog; block (traffico). ~rsi vr get blocked. ~to adj blocked

inta'scare vt pocket

in'tatto adj intact

intavo'lare vt start

inte'gra|le adj whole; **edizione ~le** unabridged edition; **pane ~le** wholemeal bread. ~**nte** adj integral. **'integro** adj complete; (retto) upright

inte'gra|re vt integrate; (aggiungere) supplement. ~rsi vr integrate. ~'tivo adj (corso) supplementary. ~zi'one f integration

integrità f integrity

intelaia'tura f framework

intel'letto m intellect

intellettu'al|e adj & mf intellectual. ~'mente adv intellectually

intelli'gen|te adj intelligent. ~te'mente adv intelligently. ~za f intelligence

intelli'gibile adj intelligible

intempe'ranza f intemperance

intem'perie fpl bad weather

inten'den|te m superintendent. ~za f ~za di finanza inland revenue office

in'tender|e vt (comprendere) understand; (udire) hear; (avere intenzione) intend; (significare) mean. ~sela con have an understanding with; ~si vr (capirsi) understand each other; ~si di (essere esperto) have a good knowledge of

intendi|'mento m understanding; (*intenzione*) intention. **~'tore**, **~'trice** mf connoisseur

intene'rir|e vt soften; (*commuovere*) touch. **~si** vr be touched

intensifi'car|e vt, **~sI** vr intensify

intensità f intensity. **inten'sivo** adj intensive. **in'tenso** adj intense

inten'tare vt start up; **~ causa contro qcno** bring o institute proceedings against sb

in'tento adj engrossed (a in) ● m purpose

intenzio'nale adj intentional. **intenzi'one** f intention; **senza ~ne** unintentionally; **avere ~ne di fare qcsa** intend to do sth, have the intention of doing sth

intenzio'nato adj **essere ~ a fare qcsa** have the intention of doing sth

intera'gire vi interact

intera'mento av completely

intera|t'tivo adj interactive. **~zi'one** f interaction

interca'lare¹ m stock phrase

interca'lare² vt insert

interckambi'abile adj interchangeable

interca'pedine f cavity

inter'ce|dere vi intercede. **~ssi'one** f intercession

intercet'tare vt intercept; tap (*telefono*). **~zi'one** f interception. **~zione telefonica** telephone tapping

inter'city m inv inter-city

intercontinen'tale adj intercontinental

inter'correre vi (*tempo:*) elapse; (*esistere*) exist

inter'detto pp di **interdire** ● adj astonished; (*proibito*) forbidden; **rimanere ~** be taken aback

inter'di|re vt forbid; (*Jur*) deprive of civil rights. **~zi'one** f prohibition

interessa'mento m interest

interes'sante adj interesting; **essere in stato ~** be pregnant

interes'sa|re vt interest; (*riguardare*) concern ● vi **~re a** matter to. **~rsi** vr **~rsi a** take an interest in. **~rsi di** take care of. **~to**, **-a** mf interested party ● adj interested; **essere ~to** pej have an interest

inte'resse m interest; **fare qcsa per ~** do sth out of self-interest

inter'faccia f (*Comput*) interface

interfe'renza f interference

interfe'r|ire vi interfere

interiezi'one f interjection

interi'ora fpl entrails

interi'ore adj interior

inter'ludio m interlude

intermedi'ario, **-a** adj & mf intermediary

inter'medio adj in-between

inter'mezzo m (*Mus, Theat*) intermezzo

intermit'ten|te adj intermittent; (*luce:*) flashing. **~za** f luce a **~za** flashing light

interna'mento m internment; (*in manicomio*) committal

inter'nare vt intern; (*in manicomio*) commit [to a mental institution]

internazio'nale adj international

'Internet f Internet, internet

in'terno adj internal; (*Geog*) inland; (*interiore*) inner; (*politica*) national; **alunno ~** boarder ● m interior; (*di condominio*) flat; (*Teleph*) extension; *Cinema* interior shot; **all'~** inside

in'tero adj whole, entire; (*intatto*) intact; (*completo*) complete; **per ~** in full

interpel'lare vt consult

inter'por|re vt place (ostacolo). **~si** vr come between

interpre'ta|re vt interpret; (*Mus*) perform. **~zi'one** f interpretation;

(*Mus*) performance. **in'terprete** *mf* interpreter; (*Mus*) performer

inter'ra|re *vt* (*seppellire*) bury; plant (*pianta*). **~to** *m* basement

interro'ga|re *vt* question; (*Sch*) test; examine (*studenti*). **~tivo** *adj* interrogative; (*sguardo*) questioning; **punto ~tivo** question mark ● *m* question. **~'torio** *adj* & *m* questioning. **~zi'one** *f* question; (*Sch*) oral [test]

inter'romper|e *vt* interrupt; (*sospendere*) stop; cut off (*collegamento*). **~si** *vr* break off

interrut'tore *m* switch

interruzi'one *f* interruption; **senza ~** non-stop. **~ di gravidanza** termination of pregnancy

interse'care *vt*, **~'carsi** *vr* intersect. **~zi'one** *f* intersection

interur'ban|a *f* long-distance call. **~o** *adj* inter-city; **telefonata ~a** long-distance call

interval'lare *vt* space out. **inter'vallo** *m* interval; (*spazio*) space; (*Sch*) break. **intervallo pubblicitario** commercial break

interve'nire *vi* intervene; (*Med: operare*) operate; **~ a** take part in. **inter'vento** *m* intervention; (*presenza*) presence; (*chirurgico*) operation; **pronto intervento** emergency services

inter'vista *f* interview

intervi'sta|re *vt* interview. **~tore, ~'trice** *mf* interviewer

in'tes|a *f* understanding; **cenno d'~a** acknowledgement. **~o** *pp di* **intendere** ● *adj* **resta ~o che...** needless to say,...; **~i!** agreed!; **~o a** meant to

inte'sta|re *vt* head; write one's name and address at the top of (*lettera*); (*Comm*) register. **~rsi** *vr* **~rsi a fare qcsa** take it into one's head to do sth. **~'tario, -a** *mf* holder. **~zi'one** *f* heading; (*su carta da lettere*)

letterhead

inte'stino *adj* (*lotte*) internal ● *m* intestine

intima'mente *adv* intimately

inti'ma|re *vt* order; **~re l'alt a qcno** order sb to stop. **~zi'one** *f* order

intimi|'dtorio *adj* threatening. **~zi'one** *f* intimidation

intimi'dire *vt* intimidate

intimità *f* cosiness. **'intimo** *adj* intimate; (*interno*) innermost; (*amico*) close ● *m* (*amico*) close friend; (*dell'animo*) heart

intimo'ri|re *vt* frighten. **~rsi** *vr* get frightened. **~to** *adj* frightened

in'tingere *vt* dip

in'tingolo *m* sauce; (*pietanza*) stew

intiriz'zi|re *vt* numb. **~rsi** *vr* grow numb. **~to** *adj* essere **~to** (*dal freddo*) be perished

intito'lar|e *vt* entitle; (*dedicare*) dedicate. **~si** *vr* be called

intolle'rabile *adj* intolerable

intona'care *vt* plaster. **in'tonaco** *m* plaster

into'na|re *vt* start to sing; tune (*strumento*); (*accordare*) match. **~rsi** *vr* match; **~rsi a** (*persona*) able to sing in tune; (*colore*) matching

intonazi'one *f* (*inflessione*) intonation; (*ironica*) tone

inton'ti|re *vt* daze; (*gas:*) make dizzy ● *vi* be dazed. **~to** *adj* dazed

intop'pare *vi* **~ in** run into

in'toppo *m* obstacle

in'torno *adv* around ● *prep* **~ a** around; (*circa*) about

intorpi'dire *vt* numb. **~rsi** *vr* become numb. **~to** *adj* torpid

intossi'ca|re *vt* poison. **~rsi** *vr* be poisoned. **~zi'one** *f* poisoning

intral'ciare *vt* hamper

in'tralcio *m* hitch; **essere d'~** be a hindrance (**a** to)

intrallaz'zare vi intrigue. **intral-'lazzo** m racket

intramon'tabile adj timeless

intransi'gen|te adj uncompromising. **~za** f intransigence

intransi'tivo adj intransitive

intrappo'lato adj rimanere ~ be trapped

intrapren'den|te adj enterprising. **~za** f initiative

intra'prendere vt undertake

intrat'tabile adj very difficult

intratte'n|ere vt entertain. **~ersi** vr linger. **~i'mento** m entertainment

intrave'dere vt catch a glimpse of; (presagire) foresee

intrecci'ar|e vt interweave; plait (capelli, corda). **~si** vr intertwine; (aggrovigliarsi) become tangled; **~e le mani** clasp one's hands

in'treccio m (trama) plot

intri'cato adj tangled

intri'gante adj scheming; (affascinante) intriguing

intri'ga|re vt entangle; (incuriosire) intrigue ● vi intrigue, scheme. **~rsi** vr meddle. **In'trigo** m plot; **intrighi** pl intrigues

in'triso adj **~ di** soaked in

intri'stirsi vr grow sad

intro'du|rre vt introduce; (inserire) insert; **~rre a** (iniziare a) introduce to. **~rsi** vr get in (**in** to). **~t'tivo** adj (pagine, discorso) introductory. **~zi'one** f introduction

in'troito m income, revenue; (incasso) takings pl

intro'metter|e vt introduce. **~si** vr interfere; (interporsi) intervene. **in'tromissi'one** f intervention

intro'vabile adj that can't be found; (prodotto) unobtainable

intro'verso, -a adj introverted ● mf introvert

intrufo'larsi vr sneak in

in'truglio m concoction

intrusi'one f intrusion. **in'truso, -a** mf intruder

intu'i|re vt perceive

intui'tivo adj intuitive. **in'tuito** m intuition. **~zi'one** f intuition

inuguagli'anza f inequality

inu'mano adj inhuman

inu'mare vt inter

inumi'dir|e vt dampen; moisten (labbra). **~si** vr become damp

l'nutil|le adj useless; (superfluo) unnecessary. **~ità** f uselessness

inutiliz'za|bile adj unusable. **~to** adj unused

inva'dente adj intrusive

in'vadere vt invade; (affollare) overrun

invali'd|are vt invalidate. **~ità** f disability; (Jur) invalidity. **in'valido, -a** adj invalid; (handicappato) disabled ● mf disabled person

in'vano adv in vain

invari'abile adj invariable

invari'ato adj unchanged

invasi'one f invasion. **in'vaso** pp di **invadere**. **inva'sore** adj invading ● m invader

invecchia'mento m (di vino) maturation

invecchi'are vt/i age

in'vece adv instead; (anzi) but; **~ di** instead of

inve'ire vi **~ contro** inveigh against

inven'd|ibile adj unsaleable. **~uto** adj unsold

inven'tare vt invent

inventari'are vt make an inventory of. **inven'tario** m inventory

inven'tivo, -a adj inventive ● f inventiveness. **~'tore, ~'trice** mf inventor. **~zi'one** f invention

inver'nale adj wintry. **in'verno** m winter

invero'simile adj improbable

inversi'one f inversion; (Mech) reversal. **in'verso** adj inverse; (opposto) opposite ● m opposite

inverte'brato adj & m invertebrate

inver'ti|re vt reverse; (capovolgere) turn upside down

investi'ga|re vt investigate. ∼**tore** m investigator. ∼**zi|one** f investigation

investi'mento m investment; (incidente) crash

inve'stire vt invest; (urtare) collide with; (travolgere) run over; ∼**qcno di** invest sb with. ∼**tura** f investiture

invi'a|re vt send. ∼**to, -a** mf envoy; (di giornale) correspondent

invidia f envy. ∼**are** vt envy. ∼**oso** adj envious

invigo'rir|e vt invigorate. ∼**si** vr become strong

invin'cibile adj invincible

in'vio m dispatch; (Comput) enter

invipe'ri|rsi vr get nasty. ∼**to** adj furious

invi'sibil|e adj invisible. ∼**ità** f invisibility

invi'tante adj (piatto, profumo) enticing

invi'ta|re vt invite. ∼**to, -a** mf guest. **in'vito** m invitation

invo'ca|re vt invoke; (implorare) beg. ∼**zi|one** f invocation

invogli'ar|e vt tempt; (indurre) induce. ∼**si** vr ∼**si di** take a fancy to

involon|taria'mente adv involuntarily. ∼**tario** adj involuntary

invol'tino m (Culin) beef olive

in'volto m parcel; (fagotto) bundle

in'volucro m wrapping

invulne'rabile adj invulnerable

inzacche'rare vt splash with mud

inzup'par|e vt soak; (intingere) dip. ∼**si** vr get soaked

'io pers pron I; **chi è? – [sono] io** who is it? – [it's] me; **l'ho fatto io**

[stesso] I did it myself ● m l'∼ the ego

l'odio m iodine

l'onio m lo ∼ the Ionian [Sea]

i'osa: a ∼ adv in abundance

iperat'tivo adj hyperactive

ipermer'cato m hypermarket

iper'metrope adj long-sighted

ipertensi'one f high blood pressure

ip'no|si f hypnosis. ∼**tico** adj hypnotic. ∼**tismo** m hypnotism. ∼**tiz'zare** vt hypnotize

ipoca'lorico adj low-calorie

ipocon'driaco, -a adj & mf hypochondriac

ipocri'sia f hypocrisy. **i'pocrita** adj hypocritical ● mf hypocrite

ipo'te|ca f mortgage. ∼**'care** vt mortgage

i'potesi f inv hypothesis; (caso, eventualità) eventuality. **ipo'tetico** adj hypothetical. **ipotiz'zare** vt hypothesize

'ippico, -a adj horse attrib ● f riding

ippoca'stano m horse-chestnut

ip'podromo m racecourse

ippo'potamo m hippopotamus

'ira f anger. ∼**'scibile** adj irascible

i'rato adj irate

'iride f (Anat) iris; (arcobaleno) rainbow

Ir'lan|da f Ireland. ∼**da del Nord** Northern Ireland. **i∼'dese** adj Irish ● m Irishman; (lingua) Irish ● f Irishwoman

iro'nia f irony. **i'ronico** adj ironic[al]

irradi'a|re vt/i radiate. ∼**zi'one** f radiation

irraggiun'gibile adj unattainable

irragio'nevole adj unreasonable; (speranza, timore) irrational; (assurdo) absurd

irrazio'nal|e adj irrational. ∼**ità** adj irrationality

irre'al|e *adj* unreal. **~'listico** *adj* unrealistic. **~'zabile** *adj* unattainable. **~ltà** *f* unreality

irrecupe'rabile *adj* irrecoverable

irrego'lar|e *adj* irregular. **~ità** *f inv* irregularity

irremo'vibile *adj* fig adamant

irrepa'rabile *adj* irreparable

irrepe'ribile *adj* not to be found; **sarò ~** I won't be contactable

irrepren'sibile *adj* irreproachable

irrepri'mibile *adj* irrepressible

irrequi'eto *adj* restless

irresi'stibile *adj* irresistible

irrespon'sabil|e *adj* irresponsible. **~ità** *f* irresponsibility

irrever'sibile *adj* irreversible

irricono'scibile *adj* unrecognizable

irri'ga|re *vt* irrigate; (fiume:) flow through. **~zi'one** *f* irrigation

irrigidi'mento *m* stiffening

irrigi'dir|e *vt*, **~si** *vr* stiffen

irrile'vante *adj* unimportant

irrimedi'abile *adj* irreparable

irripe'tibile *adj* unrepeatable

irri'sorio *adj* derisive; (differenza, particolare, somma) insignificant

irri'ta|bile *adj* irritable. **~nte** *adj* aggravating

irri'ta|re *vt* irritate. **~rsi** *vr* get annoyed. **~to** *adj* irritated; (gola) sore. **~zi'one** *f* irritation

irrobu'stir|e *vt* fortify. **~si** *vr* get stronger

ir'rompere *vi* burst (**in** into)

irro'rare *vt* sprinkle

irru'ente *adj* impetuous

irruzi'one *f* fare **~ in** burst into

i'scritto, -a *pp di* iscrivere ● *adj* registered ● *mf* member; **per ~** in writing

i'scriver|e *vt* register. **~si** *vr* **si a**

register at, enrol at (scuola); join (circolo ecc). **iscrizi'one** *f* registration; (epigrafe) inscription

i'sla|mico *adj* Islamic. **~'mismo** *m* Islam

I'slan|da *f* Iceland. **i~'dese** *adj* Icelandic ● *mf* Icelander

'isola *f* island. **le isole britanniche** the British Isles. **~ pedonale** pedestrian precinct. **~ spartitraffico** traffic island

iso'lante *adj* insulating ● *m* insulator

iso'la|re *vt* isolate; (Elettr, Mech) insulate; (acusticamente) soundproof. **~to** *adj* isolated ● *m* (di appartamenti) block

ispes'sir|e *vt*, **~si** *vr* thicken

ispet'torato *m* inspectorate. **ispet-'tore** *m* inspector. **ispezio'nare** *vt* inspect. **ispezi'one** *f* inspection

'ispido *adj* bristly

ispi'ra|re *vt* inspire; suggest (idea, soluzione). **~rsi** *vr* **~rsi a** be based on. **~to** *adj* inspired. **~zi'one** *f* inspiration; (idea) idea

Isra'el|e *m* Israel. **i~i'ano, -a** *agg* ● *mf* Israeli

istan'taneo, -a *adj* instantaneous ● *f* snapshot

i'stante *m* instant; **all'~** instantly

i'stanza *f* petition

i'sterico *adj* hysterical. **iste'rismo** *m* hysteria

isti'ga|re *vt* instigate; **~re qcno al male** incite sb to evil. **~zi'one** *f* instigation

istin'tivo *adj* instinctive. **i'stinto** *m* instinct; **d'istinto** instinctively

istitu'ire *vt* institute; (fondare) found; initiate (manifestazione)

isti'tu|to *m* institute; (universitario) department; (Sch) secondary school. **~to di bellezza** beauty salon. **~'tore, ~'trice** *mf* (insegnante) tutor;

(*fondatore*) founder

istituzio'nale *adj* institutional. **istituzi'one** *f* institution

'istrice *m* porcupine

istru'i|re *vt* instruct; (*addestrare*) train; (*informare*) inform; (*Jur*) prepare. **~to** *adj* educated

istrut't|ivo *adj* instructive. **~ore, ~rice** *mf* instructor; **giudice ~ore** examining magistrate. **~oria** *f* (*Jur*) investigation. **istruzi'one** *f* education; (*indicazione*) instruction

l'talia *f* Italy. **i~'ano, -a** *adj & mf* Italian

Italo- Descendants of those who emigrated from Italy are often referred to as *italo-americani*, *italo-brasiliani*, etc. Massive emigration started in the 1870s, mainly from the north of Italy to South America. Buenos Aires and Sao Paulo have the highest concentrations of Italians outside Italy. Subsequently more and more southern Italians emigrated to the United States.

---

itine'rario *m* route, itinerary

itte'rizia *f* jaundice

'ittico *adj* fishing *attrib*

I.V.A. *f abbr* (imposta sul valore aggiunto) VAT

Jj

jack *m inv* jack

jazz *m* jazz. **jaz'zista** *mf* jazz player

jeep *f inv* jeep

'jolly *m inv* (carta da gioco) joker

ju'niores *mfpl Sport* juniors

Kk

ka'jal *m inv* kohl

kara'oke *m inv* karaoke

kara'te *m* karate

kg *abbr* (chilogrammo) kg

km *abbr* (chilometro) km

Ll

l' *def art m/f* (before vowel) the; ▶**IL**

la *def art f* the; ▶**IL** ● *pron* (oggetto, riferito a persona) her; (riferito a cosa, animale) it; (forma di cortesia) you ● *m inv* (Mus) A

là *adv* there; **di là** (in quel luogo) in there; (da quella parte) that way; **eccolo là!** there he is!; **farsi più in là** (far largo) make way; **là dentro** in there; **là fuori** out there; **[ma] va là!** come off it!; **più in là** (nel tempo) later on; (nello spazio) further on

'labbro *m* (*pl f* (Anat) labbra) lip

labi'rinto *m* labyrinth; (di sentieri ecc) maze

labora'torio *m* laboratory; (di negozio, officina ecc) workshop

labori'oso *adj* industrious; (faticoso) laborious

labu'rista *adj* Labour ● *mf* member of the Labour Party

'lacca *f* lacquer; (per capelli) hairspray. **lac'care** *vt* lacquer

'laccio *m* noose; (lazo) lasso; (trappola) snare; (stringa) lace

lace'rante *adj* (grido) earsplitting

lace'ra|re *vt* tear; lacerate (carne).

~rsi vr tear. **~zi'one** f laceration.
'**lacero** adj torn; (cencioso) ragged
lacri|ma f tear; (goccia) drop.
~'mare vi weep. **~'mevole** adj tear-
jerking
lacri'mogeno adj gas **~** tear gas
la'cuna f gap. **lacu'noso** adj (preparazione, resoconto) incomplete
la'custre adj lake attrib

Ladino Ladin (ladino in Italian) is a direct descendant
of the Latin spoken in the
valleys in north-eastern Italy. Western Ladin is spoken in Alto Adige
alongside German, and Eastern
Ladin (also called Friulian) in Friuli-
Venezia Giulia. Numbers of speak-
ers are shrinking as gradually German or Italian predominate.

'**ladro, -a** mf thief; **al ~!** stop
thief!; **~'cinio** m theft. **la'druncolo**
m petty thief
'**lager** m inv concentration camp
laggiù adv down there; (lontano)
over there
'**lagna** f (🔊: persona) moaning Min-
nie; (film) bore
la'gna|na f complaint. **~rsi** vr
moan; (protestare) complain (**di**
about)
'**lago** m lake
la'guna f lagoon
'**laico, -a** adj lay; (vita) secular **●** m
layman **●** f laywoman
'**lama** f blade **●** m inv llama
lambic'carsi vr **~ il cervello** rack
one's brains
lam'bire vt lap
lamé m inv lamé
lamen'tar|e vt lament. **~si** vr
moan; (protestare) complain about
lamen'te|la f complaint. **~vole** adj
mournful; (pietoso) pitiful. **la'mento**
m moan
la'metta f **~ [da barba]**

razor blade
lami'era f sheet metal
'**lamina** f foil. **~ d'oro** gold leaf
lami'na|re vt laminate. **~to** adj
laminated **●** m laminate; (tessuto) lamé
'**lampa|da** f lamp. **~da abbron-
zante** sunlamp. **~da a pila** torch.
~'dario m chandelier. **~'dina** f
light bulb
lam'pante adj clear
lampeggi'a|re vi flash. **~'tore** m
(Auto) indicator
lampi'one m street lamp
'**lampo** m flash of lightning; (luce)
flash; **lampi** pl lightning sg. **~ di
genio** stroke of genius. **[cerniera]
~ zip** (fastener), zipper Am
lam'pone m raspberry
'**lana** f wool; **di ~** woollen. **~ d'acciaio** steel wool. **~ vergine** new
wool. **~ di vetro** glass wool
lan'cetta f pointer; (di orologio) hand
'**lancia** f spear; (Naut) launch
lanci'ar|e vt throw; (da un aereo)
drop; launch (missile, prodotto); give
(grido); (emettere) **~ uno sguardo a**
glance at. **~si** vr fling oneself; (intraprendere)
launch out
lanci'nante adj piercing
'**lancio** m throwing; (da aereo) drop;
(di missile, prodotto) launch. **~ del
disco** discus [throwing]. **~ del gia-
vellotto** javelin [throwing].
'**landa** f heath
lani'ero adj wool
lani'ficio m woollen mill
lan'terna f lantern; (faro)
lighthouse
la'nugine f down
lapi'dare vt stone; fig demolish
lapi'dario adj (conciso) terse
'**lapide** f tombstone; (commemorativa)
memorial tablet
'**lapis** m inv pencil
'**lapsus** m inv lapse, error

'lardo m lard

larga'mente adv widely

lar'ghezza f breadth; fig liberality. ~ **di vedute** broadmindedness

'largo adj wide; (ampio) broad; (abito) loose; (liberale) liberal; (abbondante) generous; **stare alla larga** keep away; ~ **di manica** fig generous; ~ **di spalle/vedute** broad-shouldered/-minded ●m width; **andare al** ~ (Naut) go out to sea; **fare** ~ make room; **farsi** ~ make one's way; **al** ~ **di** off the coast of

'larice m larch

la'ringe f larynx. **larin'gite** f laryngitis

'larva f larva; (persona emaciata) shadow

la'sagne fpl lasagna sg

lasciapas'sare m inv pass

lasci'ar|e vt leave; (rinunciare) give up; (rimetterci) let go [of]; (concedere) let; ~**e di fare qcsa** (smettere) stop doing sth; **lascia perdere!** forget it!; **lascialo venire** let him come. ~**si** vr (reciproco) leave each other; ~**si andare** let oneself go

'lascito m legacy

'laser adj & m inv [raggio] ~ laser [beam]

lassa'tivo adj & m laxative

'lasso m ~ **di tempo** period of time

lassù adv up there

'lastra f slab; (di ghiaccio) sheet; (Phot, di metallo) plate; (radiografia) X-ray [plate]

lastri'ca|re vt pave. ~**to**, **'lastrico** m pavement

la'tente adj latent

late'rale adj side attrib; (Med, Techn ecc) lateral; **via** ~ side street

late'rizi mpl bricks

lati'fondo m large estate

la'tino adj & m Latin

lati'tan|te adj in hiding ●mf

fugitive [from justice]

lati'tudine f latitude

'lato adj (ampio) broad; **in senso** ~ broadly speaking ●m side; (aspetto) aspect; **a** ~ **di** beside; **dal** ~ **mio** (punto di vista) for my part; **d'altro** ~ fig on the other hand

la'tra|re vi bark. ~**to** m barking

la'trina f latrine

'latta f tin, can

lat'taio, **-a** m milkman ●f milkwoman

lat'tante adj breast-fed ●mf suckling

'latt|e m milk. ~**e acido** sour milk. ~**e condensato** condensed milk. ~**e detergente** cleansing milk. ~**e in polvere** powdered milk. ~**e scremato** skimmed milk. ~**eo** adj milky. ~**e'ria** f dairy. ~**i'cini** mpl dairy products. ~**i'era** f milk jug

lat'tina f can

lat'tuga f lettuce

'laure|a f degree; **prendere la** ~**a** graduate. ~**'ando**, **-a** mf final-year student

laure'a|rsi vr graduate. ~**to**, **-a** agg & mf graduate

'lauro m laurel

'lauto adj lavish; ~ **guadagno** handsome profit

'lava f lava

la'vabile adj washable

la'vabo m wash-basin

la'vaggio m washing. ~ **automatico** (per auto) carwash. ~ **a secco** dry-cleaning

la'vagna f slate; (Sch) blackboard

la'van|da f wash; (Bot) lavender; **fare una** ~**da gastrica** have one's stomach pumped. ~**daia** f washerwoman. ~**de'ria** f laundry. ~**deria automatica** launderette

lavan'dino m sink; (fig persona) bottomless pit

lavapi'atti mf inv dishwasher

la'var|e vt wash; **~e i piatti** wash up. **~si** vr wash, have a wash; **~si i denti** brush one's teeth; **~si le mani** wash one's hands

lava'secco mf inv dry-cleaner's

lavasto'viglie f inv dishwasher

la'vata f wash; **darsi una ~** have a wash; **~ di capo** fig scolding

lava'tivo, -a mf idler

lava'trice f washing-machine

lavo'rante mf worker

lavo'ra|re vi work ● vt work; knead (pasta ecc); till (la terra); **~re a maglia** knit. **~'tivo** adj working. **~to** adj (pietra, legno) carved; (cuoio) tooled; (metallo) wrought. **~'tore, ~'trice** mf worker ● adj working. **~zi'one** f manufacture; (di terra) working; (del terreno) cultivation. **lavo'rio** m intense activity

la'voro m work; (faticoso, sociale) labour; (impiego) job; (Theat) play; **mettersi al ~** set to work (su on). **~ a maglia** knitting. **~ nero** moonlighting. **~ straordinario** overtime. **~ a tempo pieno** full-time job. **lavori** pl **di casa** housework. **lavori** pl **in corso** roadworks. **lavori** pl **stradali** roadworks

le def art fpl the; ● **=IL** ● pers pron (oggetto) them; (a lei) her; (forma di cortesia) you

le'al|e adj loyal. **~'mente** adv loyally. **~tà** f loyalty

'lebbra f leprosy

'lecca 'lecca m inv lollipop

leccapi'edi mf inv pej bootlicker

lec'ca|re vt lick; fig suck up to. **~rsi** vr lick; (fig: agghindarsi) doll oneself up; **da ~rsi i baffi** mouth-watering. **~ta** f lick

lec̄cor'nia f delicacy

'lecito adj lawful; (permesso) permissible

'ledere vt damage; (Med) injure

'lega f league; (di metalli) alloy; far **~**

con qcno take up with sb

le'gaccio m string; (delle scarpe) shoelace

le'gal|e adj legal ● m lawyer. **~ità** f legality. **~iz'zare** vt authenticate; (rendere legale) legalize. **~'mente** adv legally

le'game m tie; (amoroso) liaison; (connessione) link

lega'mento m (Med) ligament

le'gar|e vt tie; tie up (persona); tie together (due cose); (unire, rilegare) bind; alloy (metalli); (connettere) connect ● vi (far lega) get on well. **~si** vr bind oneself; **~si a qcno** become attached to sb

le'gato m legacy; (Relig) legate

lega'tura f tying; (di libro) binding

le'genda f legend

'legge f law; (parlamentare) act; **a norma di ~** by law

leg'genda f legend; (didascalia) caption. **leggen'dario** adj legendary

'leggere vt/i read

legge'r|ezza f lightness; (frivolezza) frivolity; (incostanza) fickleness. **~'mente** adv slightly

leg'gero adj light; (bevanda) weak; (lieve) slight; (frivolo) frivolous; (incostante) fickle

leg'gibile adj (scrittura) legible; (stile) readable

leg'gio m lectern; (Mus) music stand

legife'rare vi legislate

legio'nario m legionary. **legi'one** f legion

legisla'tivo adj legislative. **~'tore** m legislator. **~'tura** f legislature. **~zi'one** f legislation

legittimità f legitimacy. **le'gittimo** adj legitimate; (giusto) proper; **legit'tima difesa** self-defence

'legna f firewood

le'gname m timber

'legno m wood; **di ~** wooden. **~ compensato** plywood. **le'gnoso**

legume | liberare

adj woody

le'gume *m* pod

'lei *pers pron* (*soggetto*) she; (*oggetto, con prep*) her; (*forma di cortesia*) you; **lo ha fatto ~ stessa** she did it herself

'lembo *m* edge; (*di terra*) strip

'lena *f* vigour

le'nire *vt* soothe

lenta'mente *adv* slowly

'lente *f* lens. **~ a contatto** contact lens. **~ d'ingrandimento** magnifying glass

len'tezza *f* slowness

len'ticchia *f* lentil

len'tiggine *f* freckle

'lento *adj* slow; (*allentato*) slack; (*abito*) loose

'lenza *f* fishing-line

len'zuolo *m* (*pl* **lenzuola**) *m* sheet

le'one *m* lion; (*Astr*) Leo

leo'pardo *m* leopard

'lepre *f* hare

'lercio *adj* filthy

'lesbica *f* lesbian

lesi'nare *vt* grudge ● *vi* be stingy

lesio'nare *vt* damage. **lesi'one** *f* lesion

'leso *pp di* **ledere** ● *adj* injured

les'sare *vt* boil

'lessico *m* vocabulary

'lesso *adj* boiled ● *m* boiled meat

'lesto *adj* quick; (*mente*) sharp

le'tale *adj* lethal

le'targico *adj* lethargic. **~o** *m* lethargy; (*di animali*) hibernation

le'tizia *f* joy

'lettera *f* letter; **alla ~** literally; **~ maiuscola** capital letter; **~ minuscola** small letter; **lettere** *pl* (*letteratura*) literature *sg*; (*Univ*) Arts; **dottore in lettere** BA, Bachelor of Arts

lette'rale *adj* literal

lette'rario *adj* literary

lette'rato *adj* well-read

lettera'tura *f* literature

let'tiga *f* stretcher

let'tino *m* cot; (*Med*) couch

'letto *m* bed. **~ a castello** bunkbed. **~ a una piazza** single bed. **~ a due piazze** double bed. **~ matrimoniale** double bed

letto'rato *m* (*corso*) ≈ tutorial

let'tore, -'trice *mf* reader; (*Univ*) language assistant ● *m* (*Comput*) disk drive. **~ di CD-ROM** CD-Rom drive

let'tura *f* reading

leuce'mia *f* leukaemia

'leva *f* lever; (*Mil*) call-up; **far ~** lever. **~ del cambio** gear lever

le'vante *m* East; (*vento*) east wind

le'va|re *vt* (*alzare*) raise; (*togliere*) take away; (*rimuovere*) take off; (*estrarre*) pull out; **~re di mezzo qcsa** get sth out of the way. **~rsi** *vr* rise; (*da letto*) get up; **~rsi di mezzo, ~rsi dai piedi** get out of the way. **~ta** *f* rising; (*di posta*) collection

leva'taccia *f* **fare una ~** get up at the crack of dawn

leva'toio *adj* **ponte ~** drawbridge

levi'ga|re *vt* smooth; (*con carta vetro*) rub down. **~to** (*superficie*) polished

levri'ero *m* greyhound

lezi'one *f* lesson; (*Univ*) lecture; (*rimprovero*) rebuke

lezi'oso *adj* (*stile, modi*) affected

li *pers pron mpl* them

lì *adv* there; **fin lì** as far as there; **giù di lì** thereabouts; **lì per lì** there and then

Li'bano *m* Lebanon

'libbra *f* (*peso*) pound

li'beccio *m* south-west wind

li'bellula *f* dragon-fly

libe'rale *adj* liberal; (*generoso*) generous ● *mf* liberal

libe'ra|re *vt* free; release (*prigioniero*); vacate (*stanza*); (*salvare*) rescue. **~rsi** *vr* (*stanza*:) become va-

cant; (*Teleph*) become free; (*da impegno*) get out of it; **~rsi di** get rid of.
~'tore, **~'trice** *adj* liberating ● *mf* liberator. **~zi'one** *f* liberation, **la L~zione** Liberation Day

'liber|o *adj* free; (*strada*) clear. **~o docente** qualified university lecturer. **~o professionista** self-employed person. **~tà** *f inv* freedom; (*di prigioniero*) release. **~tà provvisoria** (*Jur*) bail; **~tà** *pl* (*confidenze*) liberties

'liberty *m & adj inv* Art Nouveau

'Libi|a *f* Libya. **l~co**, **~a** *adj & mf* Libyan

libra'in *m* bonbaclier

libre'ria *f* (*negozio*) bookshop; (*mobile*) bookcase; (*biblioteca*) library

li'bretto *m* booklet; (*Mus*) libretto. **~ degli assegni** cheque book. **~ di circolazione** logbook. **~ d'istruzioni** instruction booklet. **~ di risparmio** bankbook. **~ universitario** student record of exam results

'libro *m* book. **~ giallo** thriller. **~ paga** payroll

lice'ale *mf* secondary-school student ● *adj* secondary-school *attrib*

li'cenza *f* licence; (*permesso*) permission; (*Mil*) leave; (*Sch*) school-leaving certificate; **essere in ~** be on leave

licenzia'mento *m* dismissal

licenzi'a|re *vt* dismiss, sack [🔲]. **~rsi** *vr* (*da un impiego*) resign; (*accomiatarsi*) take one's leave

li'ceo *m* secondary school. **~ classico** *secondary school emphasizing humanities.* **~ scientifico** *secondary school emphasizing science*

Liceo There are two main types of secondary school in Italy: the *licei*, which offer an academic syllabus, and the *istituti*, which have a more vocational syllabus, offering subjects like accountancy, electronics, and catering. *Licei* may specialize in particular subjects such as science, languages, or classical studies.

'lido *m* beach

li'eto *adj* glad; (*evento*) happy; **molto ~!** pleased to meet you!

li'eve *adj* light; (*debole*) faint; (*trascurabile*) slight

lievi'tare *vi* rise ● *vt* leaven. **li'evito** *m* yeast. **lievito in polvere** baking powder

'lifting *m inv* face-lift

'ligio *adj* **essere ~ al dovere** have a sense of duty

'lilla¹ (*colore*) lilac

'lilla² *m inv* (*Bot*) lilac

'lima *f* file

limacci'oso *adj* slimy

li'mare *vt* file

li'metta *f* nail-file

limi'ta|re *m* threshold ● *vt* limit. **~rsi** *vr* **~rsi a fare qcsa** restrict oneself to doing sth; **~rsi in qcsa** cut down on sth. **~tivo** *adj* limiting. **~zi'one** *f* limitation

'limite *m* limit; (*confine*) boundary. **~ di velocità** speed limit

li'mitrofo *adj* neighbouring

limo'nata *f* (*bibita*) lemonade; (*succo*) lemon juice

li'mone *m* lemon; (*albero*) lemon tree

'limpido *adj* clear; (*occhi*) limpid

'lince *f* lynx

linci'are *vt* lynch

'lindo *adj* neat; (*pulito*) clean

'linea *f* line; (*di autobus, aereo*) route; (*di metro*) line; (*di abito*) cut; (*di auto, mobile*) design; (*fisico*) figure; **è caduta la ~** I've been cut off; **in ~** (*Comput*) on line; **mantenere la ~** keep one's figure; **mettersi in ~** line up; **nave di ~** liner; **volo di ~** scheduled flight. **~ d'arrivo** finishing line. **~ continua** unbroken line

linea'menti *mpl* features

line'are adj linear; (discorso) to the point; (ragionamento) consistent

line'etta f (tratto lungo) dash; (d'unione) hyphen

lin'gotto m ingot

'lingua f tongue; (linguaggio) language. **~'accia** f (persona) backbiter. **~'aggio** m language. **~'etta** f (di scarpa) tongue; (di strumento) reed; (di busta) flap

lingu'ist|a mf linguist. **~ica** f linguistics sg. **~ico** adj linguistic

'lino m (Bot) flax; (tessuto) linen

li'noleum m linoleum

liofiliz'za|re vt freeze-dry. **~to** adj freeze-dried

liposuzi'one f liposuction

lique'far|e vt, **~si** vi liquefy; (sciogliersi) melt

liqui'da|re vt liquidate; settle (conto); pay off (debiti); clear (merce); (ℤ: uccidere) get rid of. **~zi'one** f liquidation; (di conti) settling; (di merce) clearance sale

'liquido adj ● m liquid

liqui'rizia f liquorice

li'quore m liqueur; **liquori** pl (bevande alcoliche) liquors

'lira f lira; (Mus) lyre

'lirico, -a adj lyrical; (poesia) lyric; (cantante, musica) opera attrib ● f lyric poetry; (Mus) opera

lisci'are vt smooth; (accarezzare) stroke. **'liscio** adj smooth; (capelli) straight; (liquore) neat; (acqua minerale) still; **passarla liscia** get away with it

'liso adj worn [out]

'lista f list; (striscia) strip. **~ di attesa** waiting list; **in ~ di attesa** (Aeron) stand-by. **~ elettorale** electoral register. **~ nera** blacklist. **~ di nozze** wedding list. **li'stare** vt edge; (Comput) list

li'stino m list. **~ prezzi** price list

Lit. abbr (lire italiane) Italian lire

'lite f quarrel; (baruffa) row; (Jur) lawsuit

liti'gare vi quarrel. **li'tigio** m quarrel. **litigi'oso** adj quarrelsome

lito'rale adj coastal ● m coast

'litro m litre

li'turgico adj liturgical

li'vella f level. **~ a bolla d'aria** spirit level

livel'lar|e vt level. **~si** vr level out

li'vello m level; **passaggio a ~** level crossing; **sotto/sul ~ del mare** below/above sea level

'livido adj livid; (per il freddo) blue; (per una botta) black and blue ● m bruise

Li'vorno f Leghorn

'lizza f lists pl; **essere in ~ per qcsa** be in the running for sth

lo def art m (before s + consonant, gn, ps, z) the; ▶**IL** ● pron (riferito a persona) him; (riferito a cosa) it; **non lo so** I don't know

'lobo m lobe

lo'cal|e adj local ● m (stanza) room; (treno) local train; **~i** pl (edifici) premises. **~e notturno** night-club. **~ità** f inv locality

localiz'zare vt localize; (trovare) locate

localizzazi'one f localization

lo'canda f inn

locan'dina f bill, poster

loca'tario, -a mf tenant. **~tore, ~trice** m landlord ● f landlady. **~zi'one** f tenancy

locomo'tiva f locomotive. **~zi'one** f locomotion; **mezzi di ~zione** means of transport

'loculo m burial niche

lo'custa f locust

locuzi'one f expression

lo'dare vt praise. **'lode** f praise; **laurea con lode** first-class degree

'loden m inv (cappotto) loden coat

'lodola f lark

'loggia f loggia; (massonica) lodge

loggi'one m gallery, the gods

'logica f logic

logica'mente adv (in modo logico) logically; (ovviamente) of course

'logico adj logical

lo'gistica f logistics sg

logo'ra|re vt wear out; (sciupare) waste. **~rsi** vr wear out; (persona:) wear oneself out. **logo'rio** m wear and tear. **'logoro** adj worn-out

lom'baggine f lumbago

Lombar'dia f Lombardy

lom'bata f loin. **'lombo** m (Anat) loin

lom'brico m earthworm

'Londra f London

lon'gevo adj long-lived

longi'lineo adj tall and slim

longi'tudine f longitude

lontana'mente adv distantly; (vagamente) vaguely; **neanche ~** not for a moment

lonta'nanza f distance; (separazione) separation; **in ~** in the distance

lon'tano adj far; (distante) distant; (nel tempo) far-off; distant; (parente) distant; (vago) vague; (assente) absent; **più ~** further ● adv far [away]. **da ~** from a distance

'lontra f otter

lo'quace adj talkative

'lordo adj dirty; (somma, peso) gross

'loro¹ pron pl (soggetto) they; (oggetto) them; (forma di cortesia) you; **sta a ~** it is up to them

'loro² (il ~ m, la ~ f, i ~ mpl, le fpl) poss adj their; (forma di cortesia) your; **un ~ amico** a friend of theirs; (forma di cortesia) a friend of yours ● poss pron theirs; (forma di cortesia) yours; **i ~** (famiglia) their folk

losanga f lozenge; **a losanghe** diamond-shaped

'losco adj suspicious

'lott|a f fight, struggle; (contrasto) conflict; Sport wrestling. **lot'tare** vi fight, struggle; Sport, fig wrestle. **~'tore** m wrestler

lotte'ria f lottery

'lotto m [national] lottery; (porzione) lot; (di terreno) plot

lozi'one f lotion

lubrifi'ca|nte adj lubricating ● m lubricant. **~re** vt lubricate

luc'chetto m padlock

lucci'ca|nte adj sparkling. **~re** vi sparkle. **lucci'chio** m sparkle

'luccio m pike

'lucciola f glow worm

'luce f light; **far ~ su** shed light on; **dare alla ~** give birth to. **~ della luna** moonlight. **luci** pl **di posizione** sidelights. **~ del sole** sunlight

lu'cen|te adj shining. **~'tezza** f shine

lucer'nario m skylight

lu'certola f lizard

lucida'labbra m inv lip gloss

luci'da|re vt polish. **~'trice** f [floor-]polisher. **'lucido** adj shiny; (pavimento, scarpe) polished; (chiaro) clear; (persona, mente) lucid; (occhi) watery ● m shine. **lucido [da scarpe]** [shoe] polish

lucra'tivo adj lucrative

'luglio m July

'lugubre adj gloomy

'lui pron (soggetto) he; (oggetto, con prep) him; **lo ha fatto ~ stesso** he did it himself

lu'maca f (mollusco) snail; fig slowcoach

'lume m lamp; (luce) light; **a ~ di candela** by candlelight

luminosità f brightness. **lumi'noso** a luminous; (stanza, cielo ecc) bright

'luna f moon; **chiaro di ~** moonlight. **~ di miele** honeymoon

luna park m inv fairground

lu'nario m almanac; **sbarcare il ~** make both ends meet

lu'natico adj moody

lunedì m inv Monday

lu'netta f half-moon [shape]

lun'gaggine f slowness

lun'ghezza f length. **~ d'onda** wavelength

'lungi adv **ero [ben] ~ dall'immaginare che...** I never dreamt for a moment that...

lungimi'rante adj far-sighted

'lungo adj long; (diluito) weak; (lento) slow; **saperla lunga** be shrewd ● m length; **di gran lunga** by far; **andare per le lunghe** drag on ● prep (durante) throughout; (per la lunghezza di) along

lungofi'ume m riverside

lungo'lago m lakeside

lungo'mare m sea front

lungome'traggio m feature film

lu'notto m rear window

lu'ogo m place; (punto preciso) spot; (passo d'autore) passage; **aver ~** take place; **dar ~ a** give rise to; **del ~** (usanze) local. **~ pubblico** public place

luogote'nente m (Mil) lieutenant

lu'petto m Cub [Scout]

'lupo m wolf

'luppolo m hop

'lurido adj filthy. **luri'dume** m filth

lusin'g|are vt flatter. **~arsi** vr flatter oneself; (illudersi) fool oneself. **~hi'ero** a flattering

lus'sa|re vt, **~rsi** vr dislocate. **~zi'one** f dislocation

Lussem'burgo m Luxembourg

'lusso m luxury; **di ~** luxury attrib

lussu'oso adj luxurious

lus'suria f lust

lu'strare vt polish

'lustro adj shiny ● m sheen; fig prestige; (quinquennio) five-year period

'lutt|o m mourning; **~o stretto** deep mourning. **~u'oso** a mournful

Mm

m abbr (metro) m

ma conj but; (eppure) yet; **ma!** (dubbio) I don't know; (indignazione) really!; **ma davvero?** really?; **ma sì!** why not!; (certo che sì) of course!

'macabro adj macabre

macché int of course not!

macche'roni mpl macaroni sg

macche'ronico adj (italiano) broken

'macchia¹ f stain; (di diverso colore) spot; (piccola) speck; **senza ~** spotless

'macchia² f (boscaglia) scrub

macchi'a|re vt, **~rsi** vr stain. **~to** adj (caffè) with a dash of milk; **~to di** (sporco) stained with

'macchina f machine; (motore) engine; (automobile) car. **~ da cucire** sewing machine. **~ da presa** cine camera. **~ da scrivere** typewriter. **~ fotografica (digitale)** (digital) camera

macchinal'mente adv mechanically

macchi'nare vt plot

macchi'nario m machinery

macchi'netta f (per i denti) brace

macchi'nista m (Rail) enginedriver; (Naut) engineer; (Theat) stagehand

macchi'noso adj complicated

mace'donia f fruit salad

Mace'donia f Macedonia

macel'la|io m butcher. **~re** vt slaughter, butcher. **macelle'ria** f butcher's [shop]. **ma'cello** m (mattatoio) slaughterhouse; fig shambles sg; **andare al macello** fig go to the slaughter

mace'rar|e vt macerate; fig distress. **~si** vr be consumed

ma'cerie fpl rubble sg; (rottami) debris sg

ma'cigno m boulder

'macina f millstone

macinacaffè m inv coffee mill

macina'pepe m inv pepper mill

maci'na|re vt mill. **~to** adj ground ● m (carne) mince. **maci'nino** m mill; (hum) old banger

maciul'lare vt (stritolare) crush

macrobiotic|a f negozio di **~a** health-food shop. **~o** adj macrobiotic

macu'lato adj spotted

'madido adj **~ di** moist with

Ma'donna f Our Lady

mador'nale adj gross

'madre f mother. **~lingua** adj inv **inglese** ● lingua English native speaker. **~patria** f native land. **~perla** f mother-of-pearl

ma'drina f godmother

maestà f majesty

maestosità f majesty. **mae'stoso** adj majestic

mae'strale m northwest wind

mae'stranza f workers pl

mae'stria f mastery

ma'estro, -a mf teacher ● m master: (Mus) maestro. **~ di cerimonie** master of ceremonies ● adj (principale) chief; (di grande abilità) skilful

'mafia f Mafia. **~'oso** adj of the Mafia ● m member of the Mafia, Mafioso

Mafia The Mafia developed in Sicily in the nineteenth century, where it continues to wield considerable power in opposition to the authorities. Strictly speaking, the term Mafia applies only to Sicily, and its equivalents in other regions (Camorra in Naples and 'ndrangheta in Calabria) are separate organizations, although often working in collaboration with each other.

ma'gagna f fault

ma'gari adv (forse) maybe ● int I wish! ● conj (per esprimere desiderio) if only; (anche se!) even it

magazzini'ere m storesman, warehouseman. **magaz'zino** m warehouse; (emporio) shop; **grande magazzino** department store

'maggio m May

maggio'lino m May bug

maggio'rana f marjoram

maggio'ranza f majority

maggio'rare vt increase

maggior'domo m butler

maggi'ore adj (di dimensioni, numero) bigger, larger; (superlativo) biggest, largest; (di età) older; (superlativo) oldest; (di importanza, musica) major; (superlativo) greatest; **la maggior parte di** most; **la maggior parte del tempo** most of the time ● pron (di dimensioni) the bigger, the larger; (superlativo) the biggest, the largest; (di età) the older; (superlativo) the oldest; (di importanza) the major; (superlativo) the greatest ● m (Mil) major; (Aeron) squadron leader. **maggio'renne** adj of age ● mf adult

maggiori'tario adj (sistema) first-past-the-post attrib. **~'mente** adv [all] the more; (più di tutto) most

'Magi mpl i **re ~** the Magi

ma'gia f magic; (trucco) magic trick. **magica'mente** adv magically. **'ma-**

gico adj magic

magi'stero m (insegnamento) teaching; (maestria) skill; **facoltà di ~** arts faculty

magi'stra|le adj masterly; **istituto ~e** teachers' training college

magi'stra|to m magistrate. **~'tura** f magistrature. **la ~tura** the Bench

'magli|a f stitch; (lavoro ai ferri) knitting; (tessuto) jersey; (di rete) mesh; (di catena) link; (indumento) vest; **fare la ~a** knit. **~a diritta** knit. **~a rosa** (ciclismo) ≈ yellow jersey. **~a roverscia** purl. **~e'ria** f knitwear. **~'etta** f (tessuto) jersey

magli'one m sweater

'magma m magma

ma'gnanimo adj magnanimous

ma'gnate m magnate

ma'gnesi|a f magnesia. **~o** m magnesium

ma'gne|te m magnet. **~tico** adj magnetic. **~tismo** m magnetism

magne'tofono m tape recorder

magnifi|ca'mente adv magnificently. **~cenza** f magnificence; (generosità) munificence. **ma'gnifico** adj magnificent; (generoso) munificent

ma'gnolia f magnolia

ma'gone m avere il **~** be down; **mi è venuto il ~** I've got a lump in my throat

'magr|a f low water. **ma'grezza** f thinness. **~o** adj thin; (carne) lean; (scarso) meagre

'mai adv never; (inter, talvolta) ever; **caso ~** if anything; **caso ~ tornasse** in case he comes back; **come ~?** why?; **cosa ~?** what on earth?; **più** never again; **più che ~** more than ever; **quando ~?** whenever?; **quasi ~** hardly ever

mai'ale m pig; (carne) pork

mai'olica f majolica

maio'nese f mayonnaise

'mais m maize

mai'uscol|a f capital [letter]. **~o** adj capital

mal ▷ MALE

'mala f la **~** ⊠ the underworld

mala'fede f bad faith

malaf'fare m **gente di ~** shady characters pl

mala'lingua f backbiter

mala'mente adv (ridotto) badly

malan'dato adj in bad shape; (di salute) in poor health

ma'lanimo m ill will

ma'lanno m misfortune; (malattia) illness; **prendersi un ~** catch something

mala'pena: **a ~** adv hardly

ma'laria f malaria

mala'ticcio adj sickly

ma'lato, -a adj ill, sick; (pianta) diseased ● mf sick person. **~ di mente** mentally ill person. **malat'tia** f disease, illness; **ho preso due giorni di malattia** I had two days off sick. **malattia venerea** venereal disease

malaugu'rato adj ill-omened. **malau'gurio** m bad o ill omen

mala'vita f underworld

mala'voglia f unwillingness; **di ~** unwillingly

malcapi'tato adj wretched

malce'lato adj ill-concealed

mal'concio adj battered

malcon'tento m discontent

malco'stume m immorality

mal'destro adj awkward; (inesperto) inexperienced

maldi'cen|te adj slanderous. **~za** f slander

maldi'sposto adj ill-disposed

'male adv badly; **funzionare ~** not work properly; **star ~** be ill; **star ~ a qcno** (vestito ecc.) not suit sb; **ri-**

manerci ~ be hurt; **non c'è ~l** not bad at all ● *m* evil; (dolore) pain; (*malattia*) illness; (*danno*) harm. **distinguere il bene dal ~** know right from wrong; **andare a ~** go off; **aver ~ a** have a pain in; **dove hai ~?** where does it hurt?; **far ~ a qcno** (*provocare dolore*) hurt sb; (*cibo:*) be bad for sb; **le cipolle mi fanno ~** onions don't agree with me; **mi fa ~ la schiena** my back is hurting; **mal d'auto** car-sickness. **mal di denti** toothache. **mal di gola** sore throat. **mal di mare** sea-sickness. **avere il mal di mare** be sea-sick. **mal di pancia** stomach ache. **mal di testa** headache

male'detto *adj* cursed. (*orribile*) awful

male'di|re *vt* curse; ~**zi'one** *f* curse; ~**zione!** damn!

maledu'cato *adj* ill-mannered. ~**cazi'one** *f* rudeness

male'fatta *f* misdeed

ma'lefico *adj* (*azione*) evil; (*nocivo*) harmful

maleodo'rante *adj* foul-smelling

ma'lessere *m* indisposition; *fig* uneasiness

ma'levolo *adj* malevolent

malfa'mato *adj* of ill repute

mal'fat|to *adj* badly done; (*malformato*) ill-shaped. ~**tore** *m* wrongdoer

mal'fermo *adj* unsteady; (*salute*) poor

malfor'ma|to *adj* misshapen. ~**zi'one** *f* malformation

mal'grado *prep* in spite of ● *conj* although

ma'lia *f* spell

mali'gn|are *vi* malign. ~**ità** *f* malice; (*Med*) malignancy. **ma'ligno** *adj* malicious; (*perfido*) evil; (*Med*) malignant

malinco'ni|a *f* melancholy. **malin'conico** *adj* melancholy

malincu'ore: **a ~** *adv* reluctantly

malinfor'mato *adj* misinformed

malintenzio'nato, -a *mf* miscreant

malin'teso *adj* mistaken ● *m* misunderstanding

ma'lizi|a *f* malice; (*astuzia*) cunning; (*espediente*) trick. ~**oso** *adj* malicious; (*birichino*) mischievous

malle'abile *adj* malleable

malme'nare *vt* ill-treat

mal'messo *adj* (*vestito male*) shabbily dressed; (*casa*) poorly furnished; (*fig: senza soldi*) hard up

malnu'tri|to *adj* undernourished. ~**zi'one** *f* malnutrition

'malo *adj* **in ~ modo** badly

ma'locchio *m* evil eye

ma'lora *f* ruin; **della ~** awful; **andare in ~** go to ruin

ma'lore *m* illness; **essere colto da ~** be suddenly taken ill

mai'ri'dotto *adj* (*persona*) in a sorry state

mal'sano *adj* unhealthy

'malta *f* mortar

mal'tempo *m* bad weather

'malto *m* malt

maltrat|ta'mento *m* ill-treatment. ~**'tare** *vt* ill-treat

malu'more *m* bad mood; **di ~** in a bad mood

mal'vagi|o *adj* wicked. ~**tà** *f* wickedness

malversazi'one *f* embezzlement

mal'visto *adj* unpopular (*da* with)

malvi'vente *m* criminal

malvolenti'eri *adv* unwillingly

malvo'lere *vt* **farsi ~** make oneself unpopular

'mamma *f* mummy, mum; **~ mia!** good gracious!

mam'mella *f* breast

mam'mifero *m* mammal

'mammola *f* violet

ma'nata f handful; (colpo) slap

'manca f ▷**MANCO**

manca'mento m avere un ~ faint

man'can|te adj missing. ~**za** f lack; (assenza) absence; (insufficienza) shortage; (imperfezione) defect; **sento la sua** ~**za** I miss him

man'care vi be lacking; (essere assente) be missing; (venir meno) fail; (morire) pass away; ~ **di** be lacking in; ~ **a** fail to keep (promessa); **mi manca casa** I miss home; **mi manchi** I miss you; **mi è mancato il tempo** I didn't have [the] time; **mi manca un euro** I'm one euro short; **quanto manca alla partenza?** how long before we leave?; **è mancata la corrente** there was a power failure; **sentirsi** ~ feel faint; **sentirsi** ~ **il respiro** be unable to breathe [properly] ● vt miss (bersaglio); **è mancato poco che cadesse** he nearly fell

'manche f inv heat

man'chevole adj defective

'mancia f tip

manci'ata f handful

man'cino adj left-handed

'manco, -a adj left ● f left hand ● adv (nemmeno) not even

man'dante mf (di delitto) instigator

manda'rancio m clementine

man'dare vt send; (emettere) give off; utter (suono); ~ **a chiamare** send for; ~ **avanti la casa** run the house; ~ **giù** (ingoiare) swallow

manda'rino m (Bot) mandarin

man'data f consignment; (di serratura) turn; **chiudere a doppia** ~ double lock

man'dato m (incarico) mandate; (Jur) warrant; (di pagamento) money order. ~ **di comparizione [in giudizio]** subpoena. ~ **di perquisizione** search warrant

man'dibola f jaw

mando'lino m mandolin

'mandor|la f almond; **a** ~**la** (occhi) almond-shaped. ~**lato** m nut brittle (type of nougat). ~**lo** m almond[-tree]

'mandria f herd

maneg'gevole adj easy to handle. **maneggi'are** vt handle

ma'neggio m handling; (intrigo) plot; (scuola di equitazione) riding school

ma'netta f hand lever; **manette** pl handcuffs

man'forte m **dare** ~ **a qcno** support sb

manga'nello m truncheon

manga'nese m manganese

mange'reccio adj edible

mangia'dischi® m inv type of portable record player

mangia'fumo adj inv **candela** ~ air-purifier in the form of candle

mangia'nastri m inv cassette player

mangi'a|re vt/i eat; (consumare) eat up; (corrodere) eat away; take (scacchi, carte ecc) ● m eating; (cibo) food; (pasto) meal. ~**rsi** vr ~**rsi le parole** mumble; ~**rsi le unghie** bite one's nails

mangi'ata f big meal; **farsi una bella** ~ **di...** feast on...

man'gime m fodder

mangiucchi'are vt nibble

'mango m mango

ma'nia f mania. ~ **di grandezza** delusions of grandeur ● mf maniac

'manica f sleeve; (: gruppo) band; **a maniche lunghe** long-sleeved; **essere in maniche di camicia** be in shirt sleeves

'Manica f **la** ~ the [English] Channel

manica'retto m tasty dish

mani'chetta f hose

mani'chino m dummy

'**manico** m handle; (Mus) neck

mani'comio m mental home; (🔢: confusione) tip

mani'rotto m muɜɜ, (Mech) sleeve

mani'cure f manicure ● mf inv (persona) manicurist

mani'e|ra f manner; **in ∼ra che** so that. **∼'rato** adj affected; (stile) mannered. **∼'rismo** m mannerism

manifat'tura f manufacture; (fabbrica) factory

manife'stante mf demonstrator

manife'sta|re vt show; (esprimere) express ● vi demonstrate. **∼rsi** vr show oneself. **∼zi'one** f show; (espressione) expression; (sintomo) manifestation; (dimostrazione pubblica) demonstration

mani'festo adj evident ● m poster; (dichiarazione pubblica) manifesto

ma'niglia f handle; (sostegno, in autobus ecc) strap

manipo'la|re vt handle; (massaggiare) massage (alterare) adulterate; fig manipulate. **∼tore, ∼trice** mf manipulator. **∼zi'one** f handling; (massaggio) massage; (alterazione) adulteration; fig manipulation

mani'scalco m smith

man'naia f axe; (da macellaio) cleaver

man'naro adj lupo m ∼ werewolf

'**mano** f hand; (strato di vernice ecc) coat; **alla ∼** informal; **fuori ∼** out of the way; **man ∼** little by little; **man ∼ che** as; **sotto ∼** to hand

mano'dopera f labour

ma'nometro m gauge

mano'mettere vt tamper with; (violare) violate

ma'nopola f knob; (guanto) mitten; (su pullman) handle

mano'scritto adj handwritten ● m manuscript

mano'vale m labourer

mano'vella f handle; (Techn) crank

ma'no|vra f manoeuvre; (Rail)

shunting; **fare le ∼vre** (Auto) manoeuvre. **∼'vrabile** adj fig easy to manipulate; **∼'vrare** vt operate, fig manipulate (persona) ● vi manoeuvre

manro'vescio m slap

man'sarda f attic

mansi'one f task; (dovere) duty

mansu'eto adj meek; (animale) docile

man'tell|a f cape. **∼o** m cloak; (soprabito, di animale) coat; (di neve) mantle

mante'ner|e vt keep; (in buono stato, sostentare) maintain. **∼si in ∼si in** forma keep fit. **manteni'mento** m maintenance

'**mantice** m bellows pl; (di automobile) hood

'**manto** m cloak; (coltre) mantle

manto'vana f (di tende) pelmet

manu'al|e adj & m manual. **∼e d'uso** user manual. **∼'mente** adv manually

ma'nubrio m handle; (di bicicletta) handlebars pl; (per ginnastica) dumb bell

manu'fatto adj manufactured

manutenzi'one f maintenance

'**manzo** m steer; (carne) beef

'**mappa** f map

mappa'mondo m globe

mar ▷MARE

ma'rasma m fig decline

mara'to|na f marathon. **∼'neta** mf marathon runner

'**marca** f mark; (Comm) brand; (fabbricazione) make; (scontrino) ticket. **∼ da bollo** revenue stamp

mar'ca|re vt mark; Sport score. **∼ta'mente** adv markedly. **∼to** adj (tratto, accento) strong. **∼'tore** m (nel calcio) scorer

mar'chese, -a m marquis ● f marchioness

marchi'are vt brand

'**marchio** m brand; (caratteristica) mark. **∼ di fabbrica** trademark. **∼**

registrato registered trademark

'marcia f march; (Auto) gear; Sport walk; **mettere in ~** put into gear; **mettersi in ~** start off; **fare ~ indietro** reverse; fig back-pedal. **~ funebre** funeral march. **~ nuziale** wedding march

marciapi'ede m pavement; (di stazione) platform

marci'a|re vi march; (funzionare) go, work. **~tore**, **~trice** mf walker

'marcio adj rotten ● m rotten part; fig corruption. **mar'cire** vi go bad, rot

'marco m (moneta) mark

'mare m sea; (luogo di mare) seaside; **sul ~** (casa) at the seaside; (città) on the sea; **in alto ~** on the high seas. **~ Adriatico** Adriatic Sea. **mar Ionio** Ionian Sea. **mar Mediterraneo** Mediterranean. **mar Tirreno** Tyrrhenian Sea

ma'rea f tide; **una ~ di** hundreds of; **alta ~** high tide; **bassa ~** low tide

mareggi'ata f [sea] storm

mare'moto m tidal wave, seaquake

maresci'allo m marshal; (sottufficiale) warrantofficer

marga'rina f margarine

marghe'rita f marguerite. **margheri'tina** f daisy

margi'nale adj marginal

'margine m margin; (orlo) brink; (bordo) border. **~ di errore** margin of error. **~ di sicurezza** safety margin

ma'rina f navy; (costa) seashore; (quadro) seascape. **~ mercantile** merchant navy. **~ militare** navy

mari'naio m sailor

mari'na|re vt marinate. **~ta** f marinade. **~to** adj (Culin) marinated

ma'rino adj sea attrib, marine

mario'netta f puppet

ma'rito m husband

ma'rittimo adj maritime

mar'maglia f rabble

marmel'lata f jam; (di agrumi) marmalade

mar'mitta f pot; (Auto) silencer. **~ catalitica** catalytic converter

'marmo m marble

mar'mocchio m [I] brat

mar'mor|eo adj marble. **~iz'zato** adj marbled

mar'motta f marmot

Ma'rocco m Morocco

ma'roso m breaker

mar'rone adj brown ● m brown; (castagna) chestnut; **marroni** pl **candi** marrons glacés

mar'sina f tails pl

mar'supio m (borsa) bumbag

marte'dì m inv Tuesday. **~ grasso** Shrove Tuesday

martel'la|re vt hammer ● vi throb. **~ta** f hammer blow

martel'letto m (di giudice) gavel

mar'tello m hammer; (di battente) knocker. **~ pneumatico** pneumatic drill

marti'netto m (Mech) jack

'martire mf martyr. **mar'tirio** m martyrdom

'martora f marten

martori'are vt torment

mar'xis|mo m Marxism. **~ta** agg & mf Marxist

marza'pane m marzipan

marzi'ale adj martial

marzi'ano, -a mf Martian

'marzo m March

mascal'zone m rascal

ma'scara m inv mascara

mascar'pone m full-fat cream cheese

ma'scella f jaw

'mascher|a f mask; (costume) fancy dress; (Cinema, Theat) usher m, usherette f; (nella commedia dell'arte) stock character. **~a antigas** gas mask. **~a**

di bellezza face pack. **~ ad ossigeno** oxygen mask. **~a'mento** m masking; (*Mil*) camouflage. **masche'rare** vt mask. **~arsi** vr put on a mask; (*travestirsi*) disguise oneself; **~arsi da** dress up as. **~ata** f masquerade

maschi'accio m tomboy

ma'schi|le adj masculine; (*sesso*) male ● m masculine [gender]. **~'lista** adj sexist. **'maschio** adj male; (*virile*) manly ● m male; (*figlio*) son. **masco'lino** adj masculine

ma'scotte f inv mascot

maso'chis|mo m masochism. **~ta** adj & mf masochist

'massa f mass; (*Electr*) earth, ground Am; **comunicazioni di ~** mass media

massa'crare vt massacre. **mas'sacro** m massacre; fig mess

massaggi'a|re vt massage. **mas'saggio** m massage. **~'tore** m, **~'trice** m masseur ● f masseuse

mas'saia f housewife

masse'rizie fpl household effects

mas'siccio adj massive; (*oro* ecc) solid; (*corporatura*) heavy ● m massif

'massim|a f maxim; (*temperatura*) maximum. **~o** adj greatest; (*quantità*) maximum, greatest ● m il **~o** the maximum, **al ~o** at [the] most, as a maximum

'masso m rock

mas'sone m [Free]mason. **~'ria** f Freemasonry

ma'stello m wooden box for the grape or olive harvest

masteriz'zare vt (*Comput*) burn

masterizza'tore m (*Comput*) burner

masti'care vt chew; (*borbottare*) mumble

'mastice m mastic; (*per vetri*) putty

ma'stino m mastiff

masto'dontico adj gigantic

'mastro m master; libro **~** ledger

mastur'ba|rsi vr masturbate. **~zi'one** f masturbation

ma'tassa f skein

mate'matic|a f mathematics, maths. **~o, -a** adj mathematical ● mf mathematician

materas'sino m **~ gonfiabile** air bed

mate'rasso m mattress. **~ a molle** spring mattress

ma'teria f matter; (*materiale*) material; (*di studio*) subject. **~ prima** raw material

materi'a|le adj material; (*grossolano*) coarse ● m material. **~'lismo** m materialism. **~'lista** adj materialistic ● mf materialist. **~liz'zarsi** vr materialize. **~l'mente** adv physically

maternità f motherhood; ospedale di **~** maternity hospital

ma'terno adj maternal; lingua materna mother tongue

ma'tita f pencil

ma'trice f matrix; (*origini*) roots pl; (*Comm*) counterfoil

ma'tricola f (*registro*) register; (*Univ*) fresher

ma'trigna f stepmother

matrimoni'ale adj matrimonial; vita **~** married life. **matri'monio** m marriage; (*cerimonia*) wedding

ma'trona f matron

'matta f (*nelle carte*) joker

matta'toio m slaughterhouse

matte'rello m rolling-pin

mat'ti|na f morning; la **~na** in the morning. **~'nata** f morning; (*Theat*) matinée. **~no** m morning

'matto, -a adj mad, crazy; (*Med*) insane; (*falso*) false; (*opaco*) matt; **~ da legare** barking mad; **avere una voglia matta di** be dying for ● mf madman; madwoman

mat'tone m brick; (*libro*) bore

matto'nella f tile

mattu'tino adj morning attrib

matu'rare vt ripen. **maturità** f maturity; (Sch) school-leaving certificate. **ma'turo** adj mature; (frutto) ripe

mauso'leo m mausoleum

maxi+ pref maxi+

'mazza f club; (martello) hammer; (da baseball, cricket) bat. ~ **da golf** golfclub. **maz'zata** f blow

maz'zetta f (di banconote) bundle

'mazzo m bunch; (carte da gioco) pack

me pers pron me; **me lo ha dato** he gave it to me; **fai come me** do as I do; **è più veloce di me** he is faster than me o faster than I am

me'andro m meander

M.E.C. m abbr (Mercato Comune Europeo) EEC

mec'canica f mechanics sg

meccanica'mente adv mechanically

mec'canico adj mechanical ● m mechanic. **mecca'nismo** m mechanism

mèche fpl [farsi] fare le ~ have one's hair streaked

me'daglia f medal. ~**one** m medallion; (gioiello) locket

me'desimo adj same

'media f average; (Sch) average mark; (Math) mean; **essere nella** ~**a** be in the mid-range. **~'ano** adj middle ● m (calcio) half-back

medi'ante prep by

medi'a|re vt act as intermediary in. ~**'tore**, ~**'trice** mf mediator; (Comm) middleman

medica'mento m medicine

medi'ca|re vt treat; dress (ferita). ~**zi'one** f medication; (di ferita) dressing

medi'cina f medicine. ~**ina legale** forensic medicine. ~**i'nale** adj medicinal ● m medicine

'medico adj medical ● m doctor. ~ **generico** general practitioner. ~ **legale** forensic scientist. ~ **di turno** duty doctor

medie'vale adj medieval

'medio adj average; (punto) middle; (statura) medium ● m (dito) middle finger

medi'ocre adj mediocre; (scadente) poor

medio'evo m Middle Ages pl

medi'ta|re vt meditate; (progettare) plan; (considerare attentamente) think over ● vi meditate. ~**zi'one** f meditation

mediter'raneo adj Mediterranean; **il [mar] M**~ the Mediterranean [Sea]

me'dusa f jellyfish

me'gafono m megaphone

mega'lomane mf megalomaniac

me'gera f hag

'meglio adv better; **tanto** ~, ~ **così** so much the better ● adj better; (superlativo) best ● mf best ● f **avere la** ~ **su** have the better of; **fare qcsa alla [bell'e]** ~ do sth as best one can ● **fare del proprio** ~ do one's best; **fare qcsa il** ~ **possibile** make an excellent job of sth; **al** ~ to the best of one's ability

'mela f apple. ~ **cotogna** quince

mela'grana f pomegranate

mela'nina f melanin

melan'zana f aubergine,

eggplant *Am*

me'**lassa** *f* molasses *sg*

me'**lenso** *adj* (persona, film) dull

mel'**lifluo** *adj* (parole) honeyed; (voce) sugary

'**melma** *f* slime. **mel'moso** *adj* slimy

melo *m* apple[tree]

melo'**di|a** *f* melody. **me'lodico** *adj* melodic. **~'oso** *adj* melodious

melo'**dram|ma** *m* melodrama. **~'matico** *adj* melodramatic

melo'**grano** *m* pomegranate tree

me'**lone** *m* melon

'**membro** *m* member; (*pl* f **membra** (Anat)) limb

memo'**rabile** *adj* memorable

'**memore** *adj* mindful; (*riconoscente*) grateful

me'**mori|a** *f* memory; (*oggetto ricordo*) souvenir. **imparare a ~a** learn by heart. **~a tampone** (*Comput*) buffer. **~a volatile** (*Comput*) volatile memory; **memorie** *pl* (*biografiche*) memoirs. **~'ale** *m* memorial. **~z'zare** *vt* memorize; (*Comput*) save, store

mena'**dito**: **a ~** *adv* perfectly

me'**nare** *vt* lead; (*fam: picchiare*) hit

mendi'**cante** *mf* beggar. **~re** *vt/i* beg

me'**ningi** *fpl* spremersi le **~** rack one's brains

menin'**gite** *f* meningitis

'**meno** *adv* less; (*superlativo*) least; (*in operazioni, con temperature*) minus; **per qcsa alla ~ peggio** do sth as best one can; **fare a ~ di qcsa** do without sth; **non posso fare a ~ di ridere** I can't help laughing; **~ male!** thank goodness!; **sempre ~** less and less; **venir ~** (*svenire*) faint; **venir ~ a** (*coraggio*): fall sb; **sono le tre ~ un quarto** it's a quarter to three; **che tu venga o ~** whether you're coming or not; **quanto ~** at least ● *adj inv* less; (*con

nomi plurali) fewer ● *m* least; (*Math*) minus sign; **il ~ possibile** as little as possible; **per lo ~** at least ● *prep* except [for] ● *conj* **a ~ che** unless

~to *adj* disabled

meno'**pausa** *f* menopause

'**mensa** *f* table; (*Mil*) mess; (*Sch, Univ*) refectory

men'**sile** *adj* monthly ● *m* (*stipendio*) [monthly] salary; (*rivista*) monthly. **~ità** *f inv* monthly salary. **~'mente** *adv* monthly

'**mensola** *f* bracket; (*scaffale*) shelf

'**menta** *f* mint. **~ peperita** peppermint

men'**tale** *adj* mental. **~ità** *f inv* mentality

'**mente** *f* mind; **a ~ fredda** in cold blood; **venire in ~ a qcno** occur to sb

men'**tina** *f* mint

men'**tire** *vi* lie

'**mento** *m* chin

'**mentre** *conj* (*temporale*) while; (*invece*) whereas

menu *m inv* menu. **~ a tendina** (*Comput*) pull-down menu

menzio'**nare** *vt* mention. **menzi'one** *f* mention

men'**zogna** *f* lie

mera'**viglia** *f* wonder; **a ~** marvellously; **che ~!** how wonderful!; **con mia grande ~** much to my amazement; **mi fa ~ che...** I am surprised that...

meravigli'**ar|e** *vt* surprise. **~si** *vr* **~si di** be surprised at

meravigli'**oso** *adj* marvellous

mer'**can|te** *m* merchant. **~teggi'are** *vi* trade; (*sul prezzo*) bargain. **~'zia** *f* merchandise, goods *pl* ● *m* merchant ship

mer'**cato** *m* market; *Fin* market[-place]. **a buon ~** (*comprare*) cheap[ly]; (articolo) cheap. ~ **dei cambi** foreign exchange market. ~ **coperto** covered market. ~ **libero** free market. ~ **nero** black market

'**merce** f goods pl

mercé f **alla ~ di** at the mercy of

merce'nario adj & m mercenary

merce'ria f haberdashery; (negozio) haberdasher's

mercoledì m inv Wednesday. ~ **delle Ceneri** Ash Wednesday

mer'curio m mercury

me'renda f afternoon snack; **far ~** have an afternoon snack

meridi'ana f sundial

meridi'ano adj midday ● m meridian

meridio'nale adj southern ● mf southerner. **meridi'one** m south

me'rin|ga f meringue. ~'**gata** f meringue pie

meri'tare vt deserve. **meri'tevole** adj deserving

'**meri|to** m merit; (valore) worth; **in ~ to** a as to; **per ~ to di** thanks to. ~'**torio** adj meritorious

mer'letto m lace

'**merlo** m blackbird

mer'luzzo m cod

'**mero** adj mere

meschine'ria f meanness. **me'schino** adj wretched; (gretto) mean ● m wretch

mesco|la'mento m mixing. ~'**lanza** f mixture

mesco'la|re vt mix; shuffle (carte); (confondere) mix up; blend (tè, tabacco ecc). ~**rsi** vr mix; (immischiarsi) meddle. ~**ta** f (a carte) shuffle; (Culin) stir

'**mese** m month

me'setto m **un ~** about a month

'**messa**[1] f Mass

'**messa**[2] f (il mettere) putting. ~ **in moto** (Auto) starting. ~ **in piega** (di capelli) set. ~ **a punto** adjustment.

~ **in scena** production. ~ **a terra** earthing, grounding Am

messag'gero m messenger. **mes'saggio** m message

'**messe** f harvest

Mes'sia m Messiah

messi'cano, -a adj & mf Mexican

'**Messico** m Mexico

messin'scena f staging; fig act

'**messo** pp di **mettere** ● m messenger

mesti'ere m trade; (lavoro) job; **essere del ~** be an expert

'**mesto** adj sad

'**mestola** f (di cuoco) ladle

mestru'a|le adj menstrual. ~**zi'one** f menstruation. ~**zi'oni** pl period

'**meta** f destination; fig aim

metà f inv half; (centro) middle; **a ~ strada** half-way; **fare a ~ con** qcno go halves with sb

metabo'lismo m metabolism

meta'done m methadone

me'tafora f metaphor. **meta'forico** adj metaphorical

me'talli|co adj metallic. ~**z'zato** adj (grigio) metallic

me'tall|o m metal. ~**ur'gia** f metallurgy

metalmec'canico adj engineering ● m engineering worker

me'tano m methane. ~'**dotto** m methane pipeline

meta'nolo m methanol

me'teora f meteor. **meteo'rite** m meteorite

meteoro|lo'gia f meteorology. ~'**logico** adj meteorological

me'ticcio, -a mf half-caste

metico'loso adj meticulous

me'tod|ico adj methodical. '**metodo** m method. ~**olo'gia** f methodology

me'traggio m length (in metres)

'**metrico, -a** adj metric; (in poesia) metrical ●f metrics sg

'**metro** m metre; (nastro) tape measure ●f inv (I: metropolitana) tube Br, subway

me'**tronomo** m metronome

metro'**notte** mf inv night security guard

me'**tropoli** f inv metropolis. ~**tana** f subway, underground Br. ~**tano** adj metropolitan

'**metter|e** vt put; (indossare) put on; (I: installare) put in; ~**e al mondo** bring into the world; ~**e da parte** set aside; ~**e fiducia** inspire trust; ~**e qcsa in chiaro** make sth clear; ~**e in mostra** display; ~**e a posto** tidy up; ~**e in vendita** put up for sale; ~**e su** set up (casa, azienda); **ci ho messo un'ora** it took me an hour; **mettiamo che...** let's suppose that... ~**si** vr (indossare) put on; (diventare) turn out; ~**si a** start to; ~**si con qcno** (I: formarsi una coppia) start to go out with sb; ~**si a letto** go to bed; ~**si a sedere** sit down; ~**si in viaggio** set out

'**mezza** f è la ~ it's half past twelve; **sono le quattro e** ~ it's half past four

mezza'**luna** f half moon; (simbolo islamico) crescent; (coltello) two-handled chopping knife

mezza'**manica** f a ~ (maglia) short-sleeved

mez'**zano** adj middle

mezza'**notte** f midnight

mezz'**asta**: **a** ~ adv at half mast

'**mezzo** adj half; **di mezza età** middle-aged; ~ **bicchiere** half a glass; **una mezza idea** a vague idea; **sono le quattro e** ~ it's half past four. **mezz'ora** f half an hour. **mezza pensione** f half board. **mezza stagione** f una giacca di mezza stagione a spring/autumn jacket ●adv (a metà) half ●m (metà) half; (centro) middle; (per raggiungere un fine) means sg; **uno e** ~ one and a half; **tre anni e** ~ three and a half years; **in** ~ **a** in the middle of; **il giusto** ~ the happy medium; **levare di** ~ clear away; **per** ~ **di** by means of; **a** ~ **posta** by mail; **via di** ~ fig halfway house; (soluzione) middle way. **mezzi** pl (denaro) means pl. **mezzi pubblici** public transport. **mezzi di trasporto** [means of] transport

mezzo'**busto**: **a** ~ adj (foto, ritratto) half-length

mezzo'**fondo** m middle-distance running

mezzo'**giorno** m midday; (sud) South. **il M~** Southern Italy. ~ **in punto** high noon

mi[1] pers pron me; (refl) myself; **mi ha dato un libro** he gave me a book; **mi lavo le mani** I wash my hands; **eccomi** here I am

mi[2] m (Mus) E

'**mica**[1] f mica

'**mica**[2] adv I (per caso) by any chance; **hai** ~ **visto Paolo?** have you seen Paul, by any chance?; **non è** ~ **bello** it is not at all nice; ~ **male** not bad

'**miccia** f fuse

micidi'**ale** adj deadly

'**micio** m pussy-cat

mi'**crobo** m microbe

micro'**cosmo** m microcosm

micro'**fiche** f inv microfiche

micro'**film** m inv microfilm

mi'**crofono** m microphone

microorga'**nismo** m microorganism

microproces'**sore** m microprocessor

micro'**scopio** m microscope

micro'**solco** m (disco) long-playing record

mi'**dollo** m (pl midolla, Anat) marrow; **fino al** ~ through and through. **~ spinale** spinal cord

mi'ele m honey

'mie, mi'ei ▷ MIO

mi'et|ere vt reap. **~i'trice** f (Mech) harvester. **~i'tura** f harvest

migli'aio m (pl f **migliaia**) thousand. **a migliaia** in thousands

'miglio m (Bot) millet; (misura: pl f **miglia**) mile

miglio'ramento m improvement

miglio'rare vt/i improve

migli'ore adj better; (superlativo) the best ● mf **il/la ~** the best

'mignolo m little finger; (del piede) little toe

mi'gra|re vi migrate. **~zi'one** f migration

'mila ▷ MILLE

Mi'lano f Milan

miliar'dario, -a m millionaire; (plurimiliardario) billionaire ● f millionairess; billionairess. **mili'ardo** m billion

mili'are adj **pietra** f **~** milestone

milio'nario, -a m millionaire ● f millionairess

mili'one m million

milio'nesimo adj millionth

mili'tante adj & mf militant

mili'tare vi **~ in** be a member of (partito ecc) ● adj military ● m soldier; **fare il ~** do one's military service. **~ di leva** national serviceman

'milite m soldier. **mil'izia** f militia

'mille adj & m (pl f **mila**) a o one thousand; **due/tre mila** two/three thousand; **~ grazie!** thanks a lot!

mille'foglie m inv (Culin) vanilla slice

mil'lennio m millennium

mille'piedi m inv centipede

mil'lesimo adj & m thousandth

milli'grammo m milligram

mil'limetro m millimetre

mi'mare vt mimic (persona)

● vi mime

mi'metico adj camouflage attrib

mimetiz'zar|e vt camouflage. **~si** vr camouflage oneself

'mim|ica f mime. **~ico** adj mimic. **~o** m mime

mi'mosa f mimosa

'mina f mine; (di matita) lead

mi'naccia f threat

minacci|'are vt threaten. **~'oso** adj threatening

mi'nare vt mine; fig undermine

mina'tor|e m miner. **~io** adj threatening

mine'ra|le adj & m mineral. **~rio** adj mining attrib

mi'nestra f soup. **mine'strone** m vegetable soup; (🅵: insieme confuso) hotchpotch

mini+ pref mini+

minia'tura f miniature. **miniaturiz-'zato** adj miniaturized

mini'era f mine

mini'golf m miniature golf

mini'gonna f miniskirt

minima'mente adv minimally

mini'market m inv minimarket

minimiz'zare vt minimize

'minimo adj least, slightest; (il più basso) lowest; (salario, quantità ecc) minimum ● m minimum

mini'stero m ministry; (governo) government

mi'nistro m minister. **M~ del Tesoro** Finance Minister

mino'ranza f minority attrib

Minoranza linguistica Minoranze linguistiche (linguistic minorities) are protected by the Italian constitution. As well as dialects of Italian, and the related languages Sardinian and Ladin, other languages spoken.

i

They include German in Alto Adige; French in Valdaosta; Greek, Albanian, and Serbo-Croat in the rural south; Slovenian in the north-east and Catalan in Alghero.

mino'rato, -a adj disabled ●mf disabled person

mi'nore adj (gruppo, numero) smaller; (superlativo) smallest; (distanza) shorter; (superlativo) shortest; (prezzo) lower; (superlativo) lowest; (di età) younger; (superlativo) youngest; (di importanza) minor; (superlativo) least important ●mf younger; (superlativo) youngest; (Jur) minor; **i minori di 14 anni** children under 14. **mino'renne** adj under age ●mf minor

minori'tario adj minority attrib

minu'etto m minuet

mi'nuscolo, -a adj tiny ●f small letter

mi'nuta f rough copy

mi'nuta[1] adj minute; (persona) delicate; (ricerca) detailed, (pioggia, neve) fine; **al ~** (Comm) retail

mi'nuto[2] m (di tempo) minute; **spaccare il ~** be dead on time

mi'nuzia f trifle ●~'oso adj detailed; (persona) meticulous

'mio (il mio m, la mia f, i miei mpl, le mie fpl) adj poss my; **questa macchina è mia** this car is mine; **~ padre** my father; **un ~ amico** a friend of mine ●poss pron mine; **i miei** (genitori ecc) my folks

miope adj short-sighted. **mio'pia** f short-sightedness

'mira f aim; (bersaglio) target; **prendere la ~** take aim

mi'racolo m miracle. **~sa'mente** adv miraculously. **miraco'loso** adj miraculous

mi'raggio m mirage

mi'rare vi [take] aim, **~si** vr (guardarsi) look at oneself

mi'riade f myriad

mi'rino m sight; (Phot) view-finder

mir'tillo m blueberry

mi'santropo, -a mf misanthropist

mi'scela f mixture; (di caffè, tabacco ecc) blend. **~'tore** m (di acqua) mixer tap

miscel'lanea f miscellany

'mischia f scuffle; (nel rugby) scrum

mischi'are vt mix; shuffle (carte da gioco). **~si** vr mix; (immischiarsi) interfere

misco'noscere vt not appreciate

mi'scuglio m mixture

mise'rabile adj wretched

misera'mente adv (finire) miserably; (vivere) in abject poverty

mi'seria f poverty; (infelicità) misery; **guadagnare una ~** earn a pittance; **porca ~!** hell!

miseri'cordia f mercy. **~'oso** adj merciful

'misero adj (miserabile) wretched, (povero) poor; (scarso) paltry

mi'sfatto m misdeed

mi'sogino m misogynist

mis'saggio m video mixer

'missile m missile

missio'nario, -a mf missionary. **missi'one** f mission

misteri'oso adj mysterious. **mi'stero** m mystery

'mistica f mysticism. **~'cismo** m mysticism. **~co** adj mystic[al] ●m mystic

mistifi'care vt distort (verità). **~zi'one** f (della verità) distortion

'misto adj mixed; **scuola mista** mixed or co-educational school ●m mixture; **~ lana/cotone** wool/cotton mix

mi'sura f measure; (dimensione) measurement; (taglia) size; (limite) limit; **su ~** (abiti) made to measure; (mobile) custom-made; **a ~** (andare, calzare) perfectly. **~ di sicurezza** safety measure. **mi-**

su'rare *vt* measure; try on (indumenti); (*limitare*) limit. **misu'rarsi** *vr* **misurarsi con** (*gareggiare*) compete with. **misu'rato** *adj* measured. **misu'rino** *m* measuring spoon

'**mite** *adj* mild; (*prezzo*) moderate

'**mitico** *adj* mythical

miti'gar|e *vt* mitigate. ∼**si** *vr* calm down; (*clima:*) become mild

'**mito** *m* myth. ∼**lo'gia** *f* mythology. ∼'**logico** *adj* mythological

'**mitra** *f* (*Relig*) mitre ●*m* *inv* (*Mil*) machine-gun

mitragli'a|re *vt* machine-gun; ∼**re di domande** fire questions at. ∼'**trice** *f* machine-gun

mit'tente *mf* sender

mo' *m* **a** ∼ **di** by way of (esempio, consolazione)

'**mobbing** *m* harassment

'**mobile**[1] *adj* mobile; (*volubile*) fickle; (*che si può muovere*) movable; **beni mobili** personal estate; **squadra** ∼ flying squad

'**mobi|le**[2] *m* piece of furniture; **mobili** *pl* furniture *sg*. **mo'bilia** *f* furniture. ∼**li'ficio** *m* furniture factory

mo'bilio *m* furniture

mobili'tà *f* mobility

mobili'ta|re *vt* mobilize. ∼**zi'one** *f* mobilization

mocas'sino *m* moccasin

'**moccolo** *m* candle-end; (*moccio*) snot

'**moda** *f* fashion; **di** ∼ in fashion; **alla** ∼ (*musica, vestiti*) up-to-date; **fuori** ∼ unfashionable

modalità *f* *inv* formality; ∼ **d'uso** instruction

mo'della *f* model. **model'lare** *vt* model

model'li|no *m* model. ∼**sta** *mf* designer

mo'dello *m* model; (*stampo*) mould; (*di carta*) pattern; (*modulo*) form

'**modem** *m* *inv* modem

mode'ra|re *vt* moderate; (*diminuire*) reduce. ∼**rsi** *vr* control oneself. ∼**ta'mente** *adv* moderately ∼**to** *adj* moderate. ∼'**tore**, ∼'**trice** *mf* (*in tavola rotonda*) moderator. ∼**zi'one** *f* moderation

moderna'mente *adv* (*in modo moderno*) in a modern style. ∼**iz'zare** *vt* modernize. **mo'derno** *adj* modern

mo'dest|ia *f* modesty. ∼**o** *adj* modest

'**modico** *adj* reasonable

mo'difica *f* modification

modifi'ca|re *vt* modify. ∼**zi'one** *f* modification

mo'dista *f* milliner

'**modo** *m* way; (*garbo*) manners *pl*; (*occasione*) chance; (*Gram*) mood; **ad ogni** ∼ anyhow; **di** ∼ **che** so that; **fare in** ∼ **di** try to; **in che** ∼ (*inter*) how; **in qualche** ∼ somehow; **in questo** ∼ like this; ∼ **di dire** idiom; **per** ∼ **di dire** so to speak

modu'la|re *vt* modulate. ∼**zi'one** *f* modulation. ∼**zione di frequenza** frequency modulation

'**modulo** *m* form; (*lunare, di comando*) module. ∼ **continuo** continuous paper

mo'gano *m* mahogany

'**mogio** *adj* dejected

'**moglie** *f* wife

'**mola** *f* millstone; (*Mech*) grindstone

mo'lare *m* molar

'**mole** *f* mass; (*dimensione*) size

mo'lecola *f* molecule

mole'stare *vt* bother; (*più forte*) molest. **mo'lestia** *f* nuisance. **mo'lesto** *adj* bothersome

'**molla** *f* spring; **molle** *pl* tongs

mol'lare *vt* let go; (⬛: *lasciare*) leave; (*dare* (ceffone); (*Naut*) cast off ●*vi* cease; **mollala!** ⬛ stop that!

'**molle** *adj* soft; (*bagnato*) wet

mol'letta *f* (*per capelli*) hair-grip; (*per bucato*) clothes-peg; **mollette** *pl* (*per ghiaccio ecc*) tongs

mol'lezz|a *f* softness; **~e** *pl fig* luxury

mol'lica *f* crumb

'molo *m* pier; (*banchina*) dock

mol'teplic|e *adj* manifold; (*numeroso*) numerous. **~ità** *f* multiplicity

moltipli'ca|re *vt*, **~rsi** *vr* multiply **~tore** *m* multiplier. **~trice** *f* calculating machine. **~zi'one** *f* multiplication

molti'tudine *f* multitude

'molto
- *adj* a lot of; (*con negazione e interrogazione*) much, a lot of; (*con nomi plurali*) many, a lot of; **non ~ tempo** not much time, not a lot of time
- *adv* very; (*con verbi*) a lot; (*con avverbi*) much; **~ stupido** very stupid; **mangiare ~** eat a lot; **~ più veloce** much faster; **non mangiare ~** not eat much
- *pron* a lot; (*molto tempo*) a lot of time; (*con negazione o interrogazione*) much, a lot; (*plurale*) many; **non ne ho ~** I don't have much; **non ne ho molti** I don't have many, I don't have a lot; **non ci metterò ~** I won't be long; **fra non ~** before long; **molti** (*persone*) a lot of people; **eravamo in molti** there were a lot of us

momentanea'mente *adv* momentarily; **è ~ assente** he's not here at the moment. **momen'taneo** *adj* momentary

mo'mento *m* moment; **a momenti** (*a volte*) sometimes; (*fra un momento*) in a moment; **dal ~ che** since; **per il ~** for the time being; **da un ~ all'altro** (*cambiare idea ecc*) from one moment to the next; (*aspettare qcno ecc*) at any moment

'monac|a *f* nun. **~o m** monk

'Monaco *m* Monaco ●*f* (*di Baviera*) Munich

mo'narc|a *m* monarch. **monar'chia** *f* monarchy

mona'stero *m* (*di monaci*) monastery; (*di monache*) convent. **mo'nastico** *adj* monastic

monche'rino *m* stump

'monco *adj* maimed; (*fig: troncato*) truncated; **~ di un braccio** one-armed

mon'dano *adj* worldly; **vita mondana** social life

mondi'ale *adj* world *attrib*; **di fama ~** world-famous

'mondo *m* world; **il bel ~** fashionable society, **un ~** (*molto*) a lot

mondovisi'one *f* **in ~** transmitted worldwide

mo'nello, -a *mf* urchin

mo'neta *f* coin; (*denaro*) money; (*denaro spicciolo*) [small] change. **~ estera** foreign currency. **~ legale** legal tender. **~ unica** single currency. **mone'tario** *adj* monetary

mongolfi'era *f* hot air balloon

mo'nile *m* jewel

'monito *m* warning

moni'tore *m* monitor

monoco'lore *adj* (*Pol*) one party

mono'dose *adj inv* individually packaged

monogra'fia *f* monograph

mono'gramma *m* monogram

mono'kini *m inv* monokini

mono'lingue *adj* monolingual

monolo'cale *m* studio apartment

mo'nologo *m* monologue

mono'pattino *m* [child's] scooter

mono'poli|o *m* monopoly. **~o di Stato** state monopoly. **~z'zare** *vt* monopolize

mono'sci *m inv* monoski

monosil'labico *adj* monosyllabic. **mono'sillabo** *m* monosyllable

monoto'nia *f* monotony. **mo'no-**

m

tono adj monotonous

mono'uso adj disposable

monsi'gnore m monsignor

mon'sone m monsoon

monta'carichi m inv hoist

mon'taggio m (Mech) assembly; Cinema editing; **catena di ~** production line

mon'talgna f mountain; (zona) mountains pl. **montagne** pl **russe** big dipper. **~'gnoso** adj mountainous. **~'naro, -a** mf highlander. **~no** adj mountain attrib

mon'tante m (di finestra, porta) upright

mon'ta|re vt/i mount; get on (veicolo); (aumentare) rise; (Mech) assemble; frame (quadro); (Culin) whip; edit (film); (a cavallo) ride; **fig** blow up; **~rsi la testa** get big-headed. **~to, -a** mf poser. **~'tura** f (Mech) assembling; (di occhiali) frame; (di gioiello) mounting; fig exaggeration

'monte m mountain; **a ~** up-stream; **andare a ~** be ruined; **mandare a ~ qcsa** ruin sth. **~ di pietà** pawnshop

Monte'negro m Montenegro

monte'premi m inv jackpot

mon'tone m ram; **carne di ~** mutton

montu'oso adj mountainous

monumen'tale adj monumental. **monu'mento** m monument

mo'quette f fitted carpet

'mora f (del gelso) mulberry; (del rovo) blackberry

mo'ral|e adj moral • f morals pl; (di storia) moral • m morale. **mora'lista** mf moralist. **~ità** f morality; (condotta) morals pl. **~iz'zare** vt/i moralize. **~'mente** adv morally

morbi'dezza f softness

'morbido adj soft

mor'billo m measles sg

'morbo m disease. **~sità** f (qualità)**

morbidity

mor'boso adj morbid

mor'dente adj biting. **'mordere** vt bite; (corrodere) bite into. **mordic-chi'are** vt gnaw

mor'fina f morphine. **morfi'no-mane** mf morphine addict

mori'bondo adj dying; (istituzione) moribund

morige'rato adj moderate

mo'rire vi die; fig die out; **fa un freddo da ~** it's freezing cold, it's perishing; **~ di noia** be bored to death

mor'mone mf Mormon

mormo'r|are vt/i murmur; (brontolare) mutter. **~io** m murmuring; (lamentela) grumbling

'moro adj dark • m Moor

mo'roso adj in arrears

'morsa f vice; fig grip

'morse adj **alfabeto ~** Morse code

mor'setto m clamp

morsi'care vt bite. **'morso** m bite; (di cibo, briglia) bit; **i morsi della fame** hunger pangs

morta'della f mortadella (type of salted pork)

mor'taio m mortar

mor'tal|e adj mortal; (simile a morte) deadly; **di una noia ~e** deadly. **~ità** f mortality. **~'mente** adv (ferito) fatally; (offeso) mortally

morta'retto m firecracker

'morte f death

mortifi'ca|re vt mortify. **~rsi** vr be mortified. **~to** adj mortified. **~zi'one** f mortification

'morto, -a pp di **morire** • adj dead; **~ di freddo** frozen to death; **stanco ~** dead tired • m dead man • f dead woman

mor'torio m funeral

mo'saico m mosaic

'mosca f fly. **~ cieca** blindman's buff

'Mosca f Moscow

mo'scato adj muscat; **noce mo-scata** nutmeg ● m muscatel

mosce'rino m midge

mo'schea f mosque

moschi'cida adj fly attrib

'moscio adj limp; avere l'erre mo-scia not be able to say one's r's properly

mo'scone m bluebottle; (barca) pedalo

'mossa f movement; (passo) move, **~o** pp di **muovere** ● adj (mare) rough; (capelli) wavy; (fotografia) blurred

mo'starda f mustard

mostra f show; (d'arte) exhibition; far **~ di** pretend; in **~** on show; mettersi in **~** make oneself conspicuous

mo'stra|re vt show; (indicare) point out; (spiegare) explain; **~rsi** vr show oneself; (apparire) appear

'mostro m monster; (fig persona) genius, o sacro fig sacred cow

mostru|osa'mente adv tremendously. **~'oso** adj monstrous; (incredibile) enormous

mo'tel m inv motel

motl'va|re vt cause; (Jur) justify. **~to** adj (persona) motivated. **~zi'one** f motivation; (giustificazione) justification

mo'tivo m reason; (movente) motive; (in musica, letteratura) theme; (disegno) motif

'moto m motion; (esercizio) exercise; (gesto) movement; (sommossa) rising ● f inv (motocicletta) motor bike; mettere in **~** start (motore)

moto'carro m three-wheeler

motoci'cl|etta f motor cycle. **~ismo** m motorcycling. **~ista** mf motor cyclist

moto'cros|s m motocross. **~'sista** mf scrambler

moto'lancia f motor launch

moto'nave f motor vessel

mo'tore adj motor ● m motor, engine. **~ di ricerca** (Comput) search engine. **moto'retta** f motor scooter. **moto'rino** m moped. **motorino d'avviamento** starter

motoriz'za|to adj (Mil) motorized. **~zi'one** f (ufficio) vehicle licensing office

moto'scafo m motorboat

motove'detta f patrol vessel

'motto m motto; (facezia) witticism; (massima) saying

mouse m inv (Comput) mouse

mo'vente m motive

movimen'ta|re vt enliven. **~to** adj lively. **movi'mento** m movement; essere sempre in **movimento** be always on the go

mozi'one f motion

mozzafi'ato adj inv nail-biting

moz'zare vt cut off; dock (coda); **~ il fiato a** qcno take sb's breath away

mozza'rella f mozzarella (mild, white cheese)

mozzi'cone m (di sigaretta) stub

'mozzo m (Mech) hub; (Naut) ship's boy ● adj (coda) truncated; (testa) severed

'mucca f cow. morbo della **~ pazza** mad cow disease

'mucchio m heap, pile; un **~ di** fig lots of

'muco m mucus

'muffa f mould; fare la **~** go mouldy. **muf'fire** vi go mouldy

muf'fole fpl mittens

mug'gi|re vi (mucca:) moo, low; (toro:) bellow

mu'ghetto m lily of the valley

mugo'la|re vi whine; (persona:) moan. **mugo'lio** m whining

mulat'tiera f mule track

mu'latto, -a mf mulatto

muli'nello m (d'acqua) whirl-pool;

(di vento) eddy; (giocattolo) windmill

mu'lino m mill. ~ a vento windmill

'mulo m mule

'multa f fine. **mul'tare** vt fine

multico'lore adj multicoloured

multi'lingue adj multilingual

multi'media mpl multimedia

multimedi'ale adj multimedia attrib

multimiliar'dario, -a mf multi-millionaire

multinazio'nale f multinational

'multiplo adj & m multiple

multiproprietà f inv time-share

multi'uso adj (utensile) all-purpose

'mummia f mummy

'mungere vt milk

munici'pal|e adj municipal. ~**ità** f inv town council. **muni'cipio** m town hall

mu'nifico adj munificent

mu'nire vt fortify; ~ **di** (provvedere) supply with

munizi'oni fpl ammunition sg

'munto pp di **mungere**

mu'over|e vt move; (suscitare) arouse. ~**si** vr move

mura fpl (cinta di città) walls

mu'raglia f wall

mu'rale adj mural; (pittura) wall attrib

mur'a|re vt wall up. ~**'tore** m bricklayer; (con pietre) mason; (operaio edile) builder. ~**'tura** f (di pietra) masonry, stonework; (di mattoni) brickwork

mu'rena f moray eel

'muro m wall; (di nebbia) bank; a ~ (armadio) built-in. ~ **portante** load-bearing wall. ~ **del suono** sound barrier

'muschio m (Bot) moss

musco'la|re adj muscular. ~**'tura** f muscles pl. **'muscolo** m muscle

mu'seo m museum

museru'ola f muzzle

'musi|ca f music. ~**cal** m inv musical. ~**'cale** adj musical. ~**'cista** mf musician

'muso m muzzle; (pej: di persona) mug; (di aeroplano) nose; **fare il** ~ sulk. **mu'sone, -a** mf sulker

'mussola f muslin

musul'mano, -a m Moslem

'muta f (cambio) change; (di penne) moult; (di cani) pack; (per immersione subacquea) wetsuit

muta'mento m change

mu'tan|de fpl pants; (da donna) knickers. ~**'doni** mpl (da uomo) long johns; (da donna) bloomers

mu'tare vt change

mu'tevole adj changeable

muti'la|re vt mutilate. ~**to, -a** mf disabled person. ~**to di guerra** disabled ex-serviceman

mu'tismo m dumbness; fig obstinate silence

'muto adj dumb; (silenzioso) silent; (fonetica) mute

'mutu|a f [cassa f] ~ sickness benefit fund. ~**'ato, -a** mf ≈ NHS patient

'mutuo¹ adj mutual

'mutuo² m loan; (per la casa) mortgage; **fare un** ~ take out a mortgage. ~ **ipotecario** mortgage

Nn

n° abbr (numero) No

'nacchera f castanet

'nafta f naphtha; (per motori) diesel oil

'naia f cobra; (**☒**: servizio militare) national service

'nailon m nylon

'nano, -a adj & mf dwarf

napole'tano, -a adj & mf Neapolitan

'Napoli f Naples

'nappa f tassel; (pelle) soft leather

nar'ciso m narcissus

nar'cotico adj & m narcotic

nar'rice f nostril

nar'ra|re vt tell. ~'**tivo, -a** adj narrative ❧ fiction. ~'**tore, ~'trice** mf narrator. ~**zi'one** f narration; (racconto) story

na'sale adj nasal

nasc|ere vi (venire al mondo) be born; (germogliare) sprout; (sorgere) rise; ~**ere da** fig arise from. ~**ita** f birth. ~**i'turo** m unborn child

na'sconde|re vt hide. ~**si** vr hide

nascon'di|glio m hiding-place. ~**no** m hide-and-seek. **na'scosto** pp di **nascondere** ❧ adj hidden; **di nascosto** secretly

na'sello m (pesce) hake

'naso m nose

'nastro m ribbon; (di registratore ecc) tape. ~ **adesivo** adhesive tape. ~ **isolante** insulating tape. ~ **trasportatore** conveyor belt

na'tal|e adj (paese) of one's birth. **N~e** m Christmas; **❧ pl** parentage. ~**ità** f [number of] births. **nata'lizio** adj (del Natale) Christmas attrib; (di nascita) of one's birth

na'tante adj floating ❧ m craft

'natica f buttock

na'tio adj native

Nativ19tà f Nativity. **na'tivo, -a** agg & mf native

'nato pp di **nascere** ❧ adj born; **uno scrittore ~** a born writer; **nata Rossi** née Rossi

NATO f Nato, NATO

na'tura f nature; **pagare in ~** pay in kind. ~ **morta** still life

natu'ra|le adj natural; **al ~le** (alimento) plain, natural; **❧ le!** naturally, of course. ~**lezza** f naturalness. ~**liz'zare** vt naturalize. ~**l'mente** adv

naturally

natu'rista mf naturalist

naufra'gare vi be wrecked; (persona:) be shipwrecked. **nau'fragio** m shipwreck; fig wreck. **nau'frago, -a** mf survivor

'nause|a f nausea; **avere la ~a** feel sick. ~**ante** adj nauseating. ~**'are** vt nauseate

'nautic|a f navigation. ~**o** adj nautical

na'vale adj naval

na'vata f nave; (laterale) aisle

'nave f ship. ~ **cisterna** tanker. ~ **da guerra** warship. ~ **spaziale** spaceship

na'vetta f shuttle

navi'cella f ~ **spaziale** nose cone

navi'gabile adj navigable

navi'ga|re vi sail; ~**re in Internet** surf the Net. ~**'tore, ~'trice** mf navigator. ~**zi'one** f navigation

na'viglio m fleet; (canale) canal

nazio'na|le adj national. ~**le** f Sport national team. ~**'lismo** m nationalism. ~**lista** mf nationalist ~**lità** f inv nationality.

nazionaliz'zare vt nationalize. **nazi'one** f nation

na'zista adj & mf Nazi

N.B. abbr (nota bene) N.B.

---

ne

Spesso non si traduce: **Ne ho cinque** I've got five (of them)

● pers pron (di lui) about him; (di lei) about her; (di loro) about them; (di ciò) about it; (da ciò) from that; (di un insieme) of it; (di un gruppo) of them

····▸ **non ne conosco nessuno** I don't know any of them; **ne ho**

né | nessuno

I have some; **non ne ho più** I don't have any left

● adv from there; **ne vengo ora** I've just come from there; **me ne vado** I'm off

né conj né... né...:neither... nor...; **non ne ho il tempo né la voglia** I don't have either the time or the inclination; **né tu né io vogliamo andare** neither you nor I want to go; **né l'uno né l'altro** neither [of them/us]

ne'anche adv (neppure) not even; (senza neppure) without even ● conj (e neppure) neither... nor; **non parlo inglese, e lui ~ l** I don't speak English, neither does he o and he doesn't either

'nebbil|a f mist; (in città, su strada) fog. **~'oso** adj misty; foggy

necessaria'mente adv necessarily. **neces'sario** adj necessary

necessità f inv necessity; (bisogno) need

necessi'tare vi ~ **di** need; (essere necessario) be necessary

necro'logio m obituary

ne'fando adj wicked

ne'fasto adj ill-omened

ne'galre vt deny; (rifiutare) refuse; **essere ~to per qcsa** be no good at sth. **~'tivo, -a** adj negative ● f negative. **~zi'one** f negation; (diniego) denial; (Gram) negative

ne'gletto adj neglected

'negli = IN + GLI

negli'genl|te adj negligent. **~za** f negligence

negozi'abile adj negotiable

negozi'ante mf dealer; (bottegaio) shopkeeper

negozi'a|re vt negotiate ● vi ~**re** in trade in. **~ti** mpl negotiations

ne'gozio m shop

'negro, -a adj black ● mf black; (scrittore) ghost writer

'nei = IN + I. **nel** = IN + IL. **'nella** = IN + LA. **'nelle** = IN + LE. **'nello** = IN + LO

'nembo m nimbus

ne'mico, -a adj hostile ● mf enemy

nem'meno conj not even ●

'nenia f dirge; (per bambini) lullaby; (piagnucolio) wail

'neo+ pref neo+

neofa'scismo m neofascism

neo'litico adj Neolithic

'neon m neon

neo'nato, -a adj newborn ● mf newborn baby

neozelan'dese adj New Zealand ● mf New Zealander

nep'pure conj not even ●

'nerb|o m (forza) strength; fig backbone. **~o'ruto** adj brawny

ne'retto m (Typ) bold [type]

'nero adj black; (🅾: arrabbiato) fuming ● m black; **mettere ~ su bianco** put in writing

nerva'tura f nerves pl; (Bot) veining; (di libro) band

'nervo m nerve; (Bot) vein; **avere i nervi** be bad-tempered; **dare ai nervi a qcno** get on sb's nerves. **~'sismo** m nerviness

ner'voso adj nervous; (irritabile) bad-tempered; **avere il ~** be irritable; **esaurimento** m ~ nervous breakdown

'nespol|a f medlar. **~o** m medlar[-tree]

'nesso m link

nes'suno adj no, not... any; (qualche) any; **non ho nessun problema** I don't have any problems, I have no problems; **non lo trovo da nessuna parte** I can't find it anywhere; **in nessun modo** on no account ● pron nobody, no one, not... anybody, not... anyone; (qualcuno) anybody, anyone; **hai delle domande? – nessuna** do you have any questions? –

none; ∼ **di voi** none of you; ∼ **dei due** (di vai due) neither of you; **non ho visto** ∼ **dei tuoi amici** I haven't seen any of your friends; **c'è** ∼? is anybody there?

net'tare vt clean

net'tezza f cleanliness. ∼ **urbana** cleansing department

'netto adj clean; (chiaro) clear; (Comm) net; **di** ∼ just like that

nettur'bino m dustman

neu'tral|e adj e m neutral. ∼**ità** f neutrality. ∼**iz'zare** vt neutralize.

'neutro adj neutral; (Gram) neuter ● m (Gram) neuter

neu'trone m neutron

'neve f snow

nevi'care vi snow, ∼**ca** it is snowing. ∼**'cata** f snowfall **ne'vischio** m sleet. **ne'voso** adj snowy

nevral'gia f neuralgia

ne'vro|si f inv neurosis. ∼**tico** adj neurotic

'nibbio m kite

'nicchia f niche

nicchi'are vi shilly-shally

'nichel m nickel

nichi'lista adj e mf nihilist

nico'tina f nicotine

nidi'ata f brood. **'nido** m nest; (giardino d'infanzia) crèche

ni'ente pron nothing, not... anything; (qualcosa) anything; **non ho fatto** ∼ **di male** I didn't do anything wrong, I did nothing wrong; **grazie! –** ∼! thank you! – don't mention it!; **non serve a** ∼ it is no use; **vuoi** ∼? do you want anything?; **da** ∼ (poco importante) minor; (di poco valore) worthless ● adj inv ☐ **non ho** ∼ **fame** I'm not the slightest bit hungry ● adv **non fa** ∼ (non importa) it doesn't matter; **per** ∼ at all; (litigare) over nothing; ∼ **affatto!** no way! ● m **un bel** ∼ absolutely nothing

nientedl'meno, nlente'meno adv ∼ **che** no less than ● int fancy that!

'ninfa f nymph

nin'fea f water-lily

'ninnolo m plaything; (fronzolo) knick-knack

ni'pote m (di zii) nephew; (di nonni) grandson, grandchild ● f (di zii) niece; (di nonni) granddaughter, grandchild

'nitido adj neat; (chiaro) clear

ni'trato m nitrate

ni'tri|re vi neigh. ∼ **to** m (di cavallo) neigh

no adv no; (con congiunzione) not; **dire di no** say no; **credo di no** I don't think so, **perché no?** why not?; **io no** not me; **fa freddo, no?** it's cold, isn't it?

'nobil|e adj noble ● m noble, nobleman ● f noble, noblewoman. ∼**i'are** adj noble. ∼**tà** f nobility

'nocca f knuckle

noccl'ol|a f hazelnut. ∼**o** m (albero) hazel

'nocciolo m stone; fig heart

'noce f walnut ● m (albero, legno) walnut. ∼ **moscata** nutmeg. ∼**'pesca** f nectarine

no'civo adj harmful

'nodo m knot, fig lump; (Comput) node; **fare il** ∼ **della cravatta** do up one's tie. **no'doso** adj knotty

'noi pers pron (soggetto) we; (oggetto, con prep) us; **chi è?** ∼ **siamo** who is it? – it's us

'nola f boredom; (fastidio) bother; (persona) bore; **dar** ∼ annoy

noi'altri pers pron we

noi'oso adj boring; (fastidioso) tiresome

noleggi'are vt hire; (dare a noleggio) hire out; charter (nave, aereo). **no'leggio** m hire; (di nave, aereo) charter. **'nolo** m (Naut) freight; **a nolo** for hire

'nomade adj nomadic ● mf nomad
'nome m name; (Gram) noun; **a ~ di** in the name of; **di ~** by name. **~ di famiglia** surname. **~ da ragazza** maiden name. **no'mea** f reputation
nomencla'tura f nomenclature
no'mignolo m nickname
'nomina f appointment. **nomi'nale** adj nominal; (Gram) noun attrib
nomi'na|re vt name; (menzionare) mention; (eleggere) appoint. **~'tivo** adj nominative; (Comm) registered ● m nominative; (nome) name

non adv not; **~ ti amo** I do not love you; **~ c'è di che** not at all

Per formare il negativo dei verbi regolari si usa l'ausiliare do: **Non mi piace** I don' like it

nonché conj (tanto meno) let alone; (e anche) as well as
noncu'ran|te adj nonchalant; (negligente) indifferent. **~za** f nonchalance; (negligenza) indifference
nondi'meno conj nevertheless
'nonna f grandmother
'nonno m grandfather; **nonni** pl grandparents
non'nulla m inv trifle
'nono adj & m ninth
nono'stante prep in spite of ● conj although
nonvio'lento adj nonviolent
nord m north; **del ~** northern
nor'd-est m northeast; **a ~** north-easterly
'nordico adj northern
nordocciden'tale adj north-western
nordorien'tale adj northeastern
nor'd-ovest m northwest; **a ~** northwesterly
'norma f rule; (istruzione) instruction; **a ~ di legge** according to law; **è**

buona ~ it's advisable
nor'mal|e adj normal. **~ità** f normality. **~iz'zare** vt normalize. **~'mente** adv normally
norve'gese adj & mf Norwegian. **Nor'vegia** f Norway
nossi'gnore adv no way
nostal'gia f (di casa, patria) homesickness; (del passato) nostalgia; **aver ~** be homesick; **aver ~ di qcno** miss sb. **no'stalgico, -a** adj nostalgic ● mf reactionary
no'strano adj local; (fatto in casa) home-made
'nostro (**il nostro** m, **la nostra** f, **i nostri** mpl, **le nostre** fpl) poss adj our; **quella macchina è nostra** that car is ours; **~ padre** our father; **un ~ amico** a friend of ours ● poss pron ours
'nota f (segno) sign; (comunicazione, commento, musica) note; (conto) bill; (lista) list; **degno di ~** noteworthy; **prendere ~** take note. **note** pl caratteristiche distinguishing marks
no'tabile adj & m notable
no'taio m notary
no'ta|re vt (segnare) mark; (annotare) note down; (osservare) notice; **far ~re qcsa** point sth out. **~zi'one** f marking; (annotazione) notation
'notes m inv notepad
no'tevole adj (degno di nota) remarkable; (grande) considerable
no'tifica f notification. **notifi'care** vt notify; (Comm) advise. **~zi'one** f notification
no'tizi|a f una **~a** a piece of news; (informazione) a piece of information; **le ~e** the news sg. **~'ario** m news sg
'noto adj [well-]known; **rendere ~** (far sapere) announce
notorietà f fame; **raggiungere la ~** become famous. **no'torio** adj well-known; pej notorious
not'tambulo m night-bird

not'tata f night; **far ~ stay up all night**

notte f night; **di ~ at night; ~ bianca sleepless night. ~'tempo** adv at night

not'turno adj nocturnal; (servizio ecc) night

no'vanta adj & m ninety

novan't|enne adj & mf ninety-year-old. **~'esimo** adj ninetieth. **~ina** f about ninety. **'nove** adj & m nine. **nove'cento** adj & m nine hundred. **il Novecento** the twentieth century

no'vella f short story

novel'lino, -a adj inexperienced ● mf novice, beginner. **no'vello** adj new

no'vembre m November

novità f inv novelty; (notizie) news sg; **l'ultima ~** (moda) the latest fashion

novizi'ato m (Relig) novitiate; (tirocinio) apprenticeship

nozi'one f notion; **nozioni** nf rudimenti

'nozze fpl marriage sg; (cerimonia) wedding sg; **~ d'argento** silver wedding (anniversary); **~ d'oro** golden wedding (anniversary)

'nuble f cloud. **~e tossica** toxic cloud. **~i'fragio** m cloudburst

'nubile adj unmarried ● f unmarried woman

'nuca f nape

nucle'are adj nuclear

'nucleo m nucleus; (unità) unit

nu'di|sta mf nudist. **~tà** f inv nudity

'nudo adj naked; (spoglio) bare; **a occhio ~** to the naked eye

'nugolo m large number

'nulla pron = NIENTE

nulla'osta m inv permit

nullità f inv (persona) nonentity

'nullo adj (Jur) null and void

nume'ra|bile adj countable. **~le** adj & m numeral

nume'rare vt number. **~zi'one** f

numbering. **nu'merico** adj numerical

'numero m number; (romano, arabo) numeral; (di scarpe ecc) size; **dare i numeri** to be off one's head. **~ cardinale** cardinal [number]. **~ decimale** decimal. **~ ordinale** ordinal [number]. **~ di telefono** phone number. **~ verde** Freephone®. **nume'roso** adj numerous

'nunzio m nuncio

nu'ocere vi **~ a** harm

nu'ora f daughter-in-law

nuo'ta|re vi swim; fig wallow. **nu'oto** m swimming. **~'tore, ~'trice** mf swimmer

nu'ov|a f (notizia) news sg. **~a'mente** adv again. **~o** adj new; **di ~o** again; **rimettere a ~o** give a new lease of life to

nutri'ente adj nourishing. **~'mento** m nourishment

nu'tri|re vt nourish; harbour (sentimenti). **~rsi eat; ~rsi di** fig live on. **~'tivo** adj nourishing. **~zi'one** f nutrition

'nuvola f cloud. **nuvo'loso** adj cloudy

nuzi'ale adj nuptial; (vestito, anello ecc) wedding attrib

Oo

o conj or, **~ l'uno ~ l'altro** one or the other, either

O abbr (ovest) W

'oasi f inv oasis

obbedi'ente ecc = UBBIDIENTE ecc

obbli'ga|re vt torce, oblige; **~rsi** vr **~rsi a** undertake to. **~to** adj obliged. **~'torio** adj compulsory. **~zi'one** f obligation; (Comm) bond. **'obbligo** m obligation; (dovere) duty

avere obblighi verso be under an obligation to; **d'obbligo** be obligatory

obbligatoria'mente *adv* **fare qcsa** ~ be obliged to do sth

ob'bro|brio *m* disgrace. ~**brioso** *adj* disgraceful

obe'lisco *m* obelisk

obe'rare *vt* overburden

obesità *f* obesity. **o'beso** *adj* obese

obiet'tare *vt/i* object; ~ **su** object to

obiettivi'tà *f* objectivity. **obiet'tivo** *adj* objective ● *m* objective; (*scopo*) object

obie|t'tore *m* objector. ~**ttore di coscienza** conscientious objector. ~**zi'one** *f* objection

obi'torio *m* mortuary

o'blio *m* oblivion

o'bliquo *adj* oblique; *fig* underhand

oblite'rare *vt* obliterate

oblò *m inv* porthole

'oboe *m* oboe

obso'leto *adj* obsolete

'oca *f* (*pl* **oche**) goose

occasio'nal|e *adj* occasional. ~**'mente** *adv* occasionally

occasi'one *f* occasion; (*buon affare*) bargain; (*motivo*) cause; (*opportunità*) chance; **d'**~ secondhand

occhi'aia *f* eye socket; **occhiaie** *pl* shadows under the eyes

occhi'ali *mpl* glasses, spectacles. ~ **da sole** sunglasses. ~ **da vista** glasses, spectacles

occhi'ata *f* look; **dare un'**~ have a look at

occhieggi'are *vt* ogle ● *vi* peep

occhi'ello *m* buttonhole; (*asola*) eyelet

'occhio *m* eye; ~**!** watch out!; **a quattr'occhi** in private; **tenere d'**~ qcno keep an eye on sb; **a** ~ [e **croce**] roughly; **chiudere un'**~ turn a blind eye; **dare nell'**~ attract attention; **pagare o spendere un** ~

pay an arm and a leg. ~ **nero** (*pesto*) black eye. ~ **di pernice** (*callo*) corn. ~**lino** *m* **fare l'**~**lino a** qcno wink at sb

occiden'tale *adj* western ● *mf* westerner. **occi'dente** *m* west

oc'clu|dere *vt* obstruct. ~**si'one** *f* occlusion

occor'ren|te *adj* necessary ● *m* the necessary. ~**za** *f* need; **all'**~**za** if need be

oc'correre *vi* be necessary

occulta'mento *m* ~ **di prove** concealment of evidence

occul'ta|re *vt* hide. ~**ismo** *m* occult. **oc'culto** *adj* hidden; (*magico*) occult

occu'pante *mf* occupier; (*abusivo*) squatter

occu'pa|re *vt* occupy; spend (*tempo*); take up (*spazio*); (*dar lavoro a*) employ. ~**rsi** *vr* occupy oneself; (*trovare lavoro*) find a job; ~**rsi di** (*badare*) look after. ~**to** *adj* engaged; (*persona*) busy; (*posto*) taken. ~**zi'one** *f* occupation

o'ceano *m* ocean. ~ **Atlantico** Atlantic [Ocean]. ~ **Pacifico** Pacific [Ocean]

'ocra *f* ochre

ocu'lare *adj* ocular; (*testimone*, *bagno*) eye *attrib*

ocu'latezza *f* care. **ocu'lato** *adj* (*scelta*) wise

ocu'lista *mf* optician; (*per malattie*) ophthalmologist

od *conj* or

'ode *f* ode

odi'are *vt* hate

odi'erno *adj* of today; (*attuale*) present

'odi|o *m* hatred; **avere in** ~**o** hate. ~**'oso** *adj* hateful

odo'ra|re *vt* smell; (*profumare*) perfume ● *vi* ~**re di** smell of. ~**to** *m* sense of smell. **o'dore** *m* smell; (*pro-*

fumo) scent; **c'è odore di...** there's a smell of...; **sentire odore di** smell; **odori** pl (Culin) herbs. **odo'roso** adj fragrant

of'fender|e vt offend; (ferire) injure. **~si** vr take offence

offen'siv|a f (Mil) offensive. **~o** adj offensive

offe'rente mf offerer; (in aste) bidder

of'fert|a f offer; (donazione) donation; (Comm) supply; (nella asta) bid; **in ~a speciale** on special offer. **~o** pp di **offrire**

of'fesa f offence. **~o** pp di **offendere** ● adj offended

offi'ciare vt officiate

offi'cina f workshop; **~ [meccanica]** garage

of'frir|e vt offer. **~si** vr offer oneself; (occasione); present itself; **~si di fare qcsa** offer to do sth

offu'scar|e vt darken; fig dull (memoria, bellezza); blur (vista). **~si** vr darken; fig (memoria, bellezza) fade away; (vista): become blurred

of'talmico adj ophthalmic

oggettività f objectivity. **ogget'tivo** adj objective

og'getto m object; (argomento) subject; **oggetti** pl **smarriti** lost property, lost and found Am

'oggi adv & m today; (al giorno d'oggi) nowadays; **da ~ in poi** from today on; **a ~ a otto** week today; **dall'~ al domani** overnight; **al giorno d'~** nowadays. **~gi'orno** adv nowadays

'ogni adj inv every; (qualsiasi) any; **~ tre giorni** every three days; **ad ~ costo** at any cost; **ad ~ modo** anyway; **~ cosa** everything; **~ tanto** now and then; **~ volta che** whenever

o'gnuno pron everyone, everybody; **~ di voi** each of you

'ola f inv Mexican wave

O'lan|da f Holland. **o~'dese** adj

Dutch ● m Dutchman; (lingua) Dutch ● f Dutchwoman

ole'andro m oleander

ole'at|o adj oiled; **carta ~a** greaseproof paper

oleo'dotto m oil pipeline. **ole'oso** adj oily

ol'fatto m sense of smell

oli'are vt oil

oli'era f cruet

olim'piadi fpl Olympic Games. **o'limpico** adj Olympic. **olim'pionico** adj (primato, squadra) Olympic

'olio m oil; **sott'~** in oil; **colori a ~** oils; **quadro a ~** oil painting. **~ di mais** corn oil. **~ d'oliva** olive oil. **~ di semi** vegetable oil. **~ solare** suntan oil

o'liv|a f olive. **oli'vastro** adj olive. **oli'veto** m olive grove. **~o** m olive tree

'olmo m elm

oltraggi'are vt offend. **ol'traggio** m offence

ol'tranza f **ad ~** to the bitter end

'oltre adv (di luogo) further; (di tempo) longer ● prep (di luogo) over; (di tempo) later than; (più di) more than; (in aggiunta) besides; **~ a** (eccetto) except, apart from; **per ~ due settimane** for more than two weeks. **~'mare** adv overseas. **~'modo** adv extremely

oltrepas'sare vt go beyond; (eccedere) exceed

o'maggio m homage; (dono) gift; **in ~ con** free with; **omaggi** pl (saluti) respects

ombeli'cale adj umbilical. **ombe'lico** m navel

'ombr|a f (zona) shade; (immagine oscura) shadow; **all'~a** in the shade. **~eggi'are** vt shade

om'brello m umbrella. **ombrel'lone** m beach umbrella

om'bretto m eye-shadow

om'broso adj shady

ome'lette f inv omelette

ome'lia f (Relig) sermon

omeopa'tia f homoeopathy. **omeo'patico** adj homoeopathic. • m homoeopath

omertà f conspiracy of silence

o'messo pp di omettere

o'mettere vt omit

OMG m abbr (organismo modificato geneticamente) GMO

omi'cid|a adj murderous • mf murderer. **∼io** m murder. **∼io colposo** manslaughter

omissi'one f omission

omogeneiz'zato adj homogenized. **omo'geneo** adj homogeneous

omolo'gare vt approve

o'monimo, -a mf namesake • m (parola) homonym

omosessu'al|e adj & mf homosexual. **∼ità** f homosexuality

On. abbr (onorevole) MP

'oncia f ounce

'onda f wave; **andare in ∼** Radio go on the air. **onde** pl **corte** short wave. **onde** pl **lunghe** long wave. **onde** pl **medie** medium wave. **on'data** f wave

ondeggi'are vi wave; (barca:) roll

ondula|'torio adj undulating. **∼zi'one** f undulation; (di capelli) wave

'oner|e m burden. **∼'oso** adj onerous

onestà f honesty; (rettitudine) integrity. **o'nesto** adj honest; (giusto) just

'onice f onyx

onnipo'tente adj omnipotent

onnipre'sente adj ubiquitous; Rel omnipresent

ono'mastico m name-day

ono'ra|bile adj honourable. **∼re** vt (fare onore a) be a credit to; honour (promessa). **∼rio** adj honorary • m fee. **∼rsi** vr **∼rsi di** be proud of

o'nore m honour; **in ∼ di** (festa, ricevimento) in honour of; **fare ∼ a** do justice to (pranzo); **farsi ∼ in** excel in

ono'revole adj honourable • mf Member of Parliament

onorifi'cenza f honour; (decorazione) decoration. **ono'rifico** adj honorary

O.N.U. f abbr (Organizzazione delle Nazioni Unite) UN

o'paco adj opaque; (colori ecc) dull; (fotografia, rossetto) matt

o'pale f opal

'opera f (lavoro) work; (azione) deed; (Mus) opera; (teatro) opera house; (ente) institution; **mettere in ∼** put into effect; **mettersi all'∼** get to work; **opere** pl **pubbliche** public works. **∼ d'arte** work of art. **∼ lirica** opera

ope'raio, -a adj working • mf worker; **∼ specializzato** skilled worker

ope'ra|re vt (Med) operate on; **farsi ∼re** have an operation • vi operate; (agire) work. **∼'tivo, ∼'torio** adj operating attrib. **∼'tore, ∼'trice** mf operator; (TV) cameraman. **∼tore turistico** tour operator. **∼zi'one** f operation; (Comm) transaction

ope'retta f operetta

ope'roso adj industrious

opini'one f opinion. **∼ pubblica** public opinion, vox pop

'oppio m opium

oppo'nente adj opposing • mf opponent

op'por|re vt oppose; (obiettare) object; **∼re resistenza** offer resistance. **∼si** vr **∼si a** oppose

opportu'ni|smo m expediency. **∼sta** mf opportunist. **∼tà** f inv opportunity; (l'essere opportuno) timeliness. **oppor'tuno** adj opportune; (adeguato) appropriate; **il momento opportuno** the right moment

opposi'tore m opposer. **∼zi'one**

opposition; **d'~zione** (giornale, partito) opposition

op'posto *pp* di **opporre** ● *adj* opposite; (opinioni) opposing ● *m* opposite; **all'~** on the contrary

oppres|si'one *f* oppression. **~'sivo** *adj* oppressive. **op'presso** *pp* di **opprimere** ● *adj* oppressed. **~'sore** *m* oppressor

oppri'me|nte *adj* oppressive. **op'primere** *vt* oppress; (gravare) weigh down

op'pure *conj* otherwise, or [else]; **lunedì ~ martedì** Monday or Tuesday

op'tare *vi* **~ per** opt for

opu'lento *adj* opulent

o'puscolo *m* booklet; (pubblicitario) brochure

opzio'nale *adj* optional. **opzi'one** *f* option

'ora *f* time; (unità) hour; **di buon'~** early; **che ~ è?, che ore sono?** what time is it?; **mezz'~** half an hour; **a ore** (lavorare, pagare) by the hour; **50 km all'~** 50 km an hour; **a un'~ di macchina** one hour by car. **~ d'arrivo** arrival time. **l'~ esatta** (Teleph) speaking clock. **~ legale** daylight saving time. **~ di punta, ore di punta** peak time; (per il traffico) rush hour

'ora *adv* now; (tra poco) presently; **~ come ~** at the moment; **d'~ in poi** from now on; **per ~** for the time being, for now; **è ~ di finirla!** that's enough now! ● *conj* (dunque) now [then]; **~ che ci penso,...** now that I come to think about it,...

'orafo *m* goldsmith

o'rale *adj & m* oral; **per via ~** by mouth

ora'mai *adv* = **ORMAI**

o'rario *adj* (tariffa) hourly; (segnale) time *attrib*; (velocità) per hour ● *m* time; (tabella dell'orario) timetable, schedule *Am*; **essere in ~** be on

time; **in senso ~** clockwise. **~ di chiusura** closing time. **~ flessibile** flexitime. **~ di sportello** banking hours. **~ d'ufficio** business hours. **~ di visita** (Med) consulting hours

o'rata *f* gilthead

ora'tore, -'trice *mf* speaker

ora'torio, -a *adj* oratorical ● *m* (Mus) oratorio ● *f* oratory. **orazi'one** *f* (Relig) prayer

'orbita *f* orbit; (Anat) [eye-]socket

or'chestra *f* orchestra; (parte del teatro) pit

orche'stra|le *adj* orchestral ● *mf* member of an/the orchestra. **~re** *vt* orchestrate

or'chidea *f* orchid

'orco *m* ogre

'orda *f* horde

or'digno *m* device; (arnese) tool. **~ esplosivo** explosive device

ordi'nale *adj & m* ordinal

ordina'mento *m* order; (leggi) rules *pl*.

ordi'nanza *f* bylaw; **d'~** (soldato) on duty

ordi'nare *vt* (sistemare) arrange; (comandare) order; (prescrivere) prescribe; (Relig) ordain

ordi'nario *adj* ordinary; (grossolano) common; (professore) with tenure; **di ordinaria amministrazione** routine ● *m* ordinary; (Univ) professor

ordi'nato *adj* (in ordine) tidy

ordinazi'one *f* order; **fare un'~** place an order

'ordine *m* order; (di avvocati, medici) association; **mettere in ~** put in order; **di prim'~** first-class; **di terz'~e** (film, albergo) third- rate; **di ~ pratico/economico** of a practical/economic nature; **fino a nuovo ~** until further notice; **parola d'~** password. **~ del giorno** agenda. **ordini sacri** *pl* Holy Orders

or'dire *vt* (tramare) plot

orec'chino *m* ear-ring

o'recchi|o *m (pl f* **orecchie**) ear: **avere** ~**o** have a good ear; **mi è giunto all'**~**o che...** I've heard that...; ~'**oni** *pl (Med)* mumps *sg*

o'refice *m* jeweller. ~'**ria** *f (arte)* goldsmith's art; *(negozio)* goldsmith's [shop]

'orfano, -a *adj* orphan ● *mf* orphan. ~'**trofio** *m* orphanage

orga'netto *m* barrel-organ; *(a bocca)* mouth-organ; *(fisarmonica)* accordion

or'ganico *adj* organic ● *m* personnel

orga'nismo *m* organism; *(corpo umano)* body

orga'nista *mf* organist

organiz'za|re *vt* organize. ~**rsi** *vr* get organized. ~'**tore, -'trice** *mf* organizer. ~**zi'one** *f* organization

'organo *m* organ

or'gasmo *m* orgasm

'orgia *f* orgy

or'gogli|o *m* pride. ~'**oso** *adj* proud

orien'tale *adj* eastern; *(cinese ecc)* oriental

orienta'mento *m* orientation; **perdere l'**~ lose one's bearings; **senso dell'**~ sense of direction

orien'ta|re *vt* orientate. ~**rsi** *vr* find one's bearings; *(tendere)* tend

ori'ente *m* east. **l'Estremo O**~ the Far East. **il Medio O**~ the Middle East

o'rigano *m* oregano

origi'na|le *adj* original; *(eccentrico)* odd ● *m* original. ~**lità** *f* originality. ~**re** *vt/i* originate. ~**rio** *adj (nativo)* native

o'rigine *f* origin; **in** ~ originally; **aver** ~ **da** originate from; **dare** ~ **a** give rise to

o'rina *f* urine. **ori'nale** *m* chamberpot. **ori'nare** *vi* urinate

ori'undo *adj* native

orizzon'tale *adj* horizontal

orizzon'tare *vt* = **ORIENTARE**. **oriz'zonte** *m* horizon

or'la|re *vt* hem. ~'**tura** *f* hem. '**orlo** *m* edge; *(di vestito ecc)* hem

'orma *f* track; *(di piede)* footprint; *(impronta)* mark

or'mai *adv* by now; *(passato)* by then; *(quasi)* almost

ormeggi'are *vt* moor

ormo'nale *adj* hormonal. **or'mone** *m* hormone

ornamen'tale *adj* ornamental. **orna'mento** *m* ornament

or'na|re *vt* decorate. ~**rsi** *vr* deck oneself. ~**to** *adj (stile)* ornate

ornitolo'gia *f* ornithology

'oro *m* gold; **d'**~ gold; *fig* golden

orologi'aio, -a *mf* clockmaker, watchmaker

oro'logio *m* watch; *(da tavolo, muro ecc)* clock. ~ **a pendolo** grandfather clock. ~ **da polso** wrist-watch. ~ **a sveglia** alarm clock

o'roscopo *m* horoscope

or'rendo *adj* awful, dreadful

or'ribile *adj* horrible

orripi'lante *adj* horrifying

or'rore *m* horror; **avere qcsa in** ~ hate sth

orsacchi'otto *m* teddy bear

'orso *m* bear; *(persona scontrosa)* hermit. ~ **bianco** polar bear

or'taggio *m* vegetable

or'tensia *f* hydrangea

or'tica *f* nettle

orticol'tura *f* horticulture. '**orto** *m* vegetable plot

orto'dosso *adj* orthodox

ortogo'nale *adj* perpendicular

orto|gra'fia *f* spelling. ~'**grafico** *adj* spelling *attrib*

orto'lano m market gardener; (no gozio) greengrocer's

orto|pe'dia f orthopaedics sg. **~'pedico** adj orthopaedic ● m orthopaedist

orzai'olo m sty

or'zata f barley-water

o'sare vt/i dare; (avere audacia) be daring

oscenità f inv obscenity. **o'sceno** adj obscene

oscil'la|re vi swing; (prezzi ecc.) fluctuate; Tech oscillate, (fig: essere indeciso) vacillate. **~zi'one** f swinging; (di prezzi) fluctuation, Tech oscillation

oscura'mento m darkening; (di vista, mente) dimming; (totale) black out

oscu'r|are vt darken; fig obscure. **~arsi** vr get dark. **~ità** f darkness. **o'scuro** adj dark; (triste) gloomy; (incomprensibile) obscure

ospe'dale m hospital. **~i'ero** adj hospital attrib

ospi'ta|le adj hospitable. **~lità** f hospitality. **~re** vt give hospitality to. **'ospite** m (chi ospita) host, (chi viene ospitato) guest ● f hostess; guest

o'spizio m [old people's] home

ossa'tura f bone structure; (di romanzo) structure, framework. **'osseo** adj bone attrib

ossequi'are vt pay one's respects to. **os'sequio** m homage; ossequi pl respects. **~'oso** adj obsequious

osser'van|te adj (cattolico) practising. **~za** f observance

osser'va|re vt observe; (notare) notice; keep (ordine, silenzio). **~'tore**, **~'trice** mf observer. **~'torio** m (Astr) observatory; (Mil) observation post. **~zi'one** f observation; (rimprovero) reproach

ossessio'na|nte adj haunting; (persona) nagging. **~re** vt obsess; (infastidire) nag. **ossessi'one** f obses-

sion. **osses'sivo** adj obsessive. **os'sesso** adj obsessed

os'sia conj that is

ossi'dabile adj liable to tarnish

ossi'dar|e vt, **~si** vr oxidize

'ossido m oxide. **~ di carbonio** carbon monoxide

os'sidrico adj **fiamma ossidrica** blowlamp

ossige'na|re vt oxygenate; (decolorare) bleach; fig put back on its feet (azienda). **~si** vr **~si i capelli** dye one's hair blonde. **os'sigeno** m oxygen

'osso m (Anat: pl ossa) bone; (di frutto) stone

osso'buco m marrowbone

o'stacolare vt hinder, obstruct. **o'stacolo** m obstacle; Sport hurdle

o'staggio m hostage; **prendere in ~** take hostage

o stello m **~ della gioventù** youth hostel

osten'ta|re vt show off, **~re indifferenza** pretend to be indifferent. **~zi'one** f ostentation

oste'ria f inn

o'stetrico, -a adj obstetric ● mf obstetrician

'ostia f host; (cialda) wafer

'ostico adj tough

o'sti|le adj hostile. **~ità** f inv hostility

osti'na|rsi vr persist (a in). **~to** adj obstinate. **~zi'one** f obstinacy

'ostrica f oyster

ostru'ire vt obstruct. **~zi'one** f obstruction

otorinolaringoi'atra mf ear, nose and throat specialist

ottago'nale adj octagonal. **ot'tagono** m octagon

ot'tan|ta adj & m eighty. **~'tenne**

adj & mf eighty-year-old. **~'tesimo** adj
eightieth. **~tina** f about eighty

ot'tav|a f octave. **~o** adj eighth

otte'nere vt obtain; (più comune)
get; (conseguire) achieve

'ottico, -a adj optic[al] ● mf optician
● f (scienza) optics sg; (di lenti ecc) optics pl

otti'ma|le adj optimum. **~'mente**
adv very well

otti'mis|mo m optimism. **~ta** mf
optimist. **~tico** adj optimistic

'ottimo adj very good ● m optimum

'otto adj & m eight

ot'tobre m October

otto'cento adj & m eight hundred;
l'O**~** the nineteenth century

ot'tone m brass

ottu'ra|re vt block; fill (dente).
~rsi vr clog. **~tore** m (Phot) shutter.
~zi'one f stopping; (di dente) filling

ot'tuso pp di **ottundere** ● adj obtuse

o'vaia f ovary

o'vale adj & m oval

o'vatta f cotton wool

ovazi'one f ovation

over'dose f inv overdose

'ovest m west

o'vi|le m sheep-fold. **~no** adj sheep
attrib

ovo'via f two-seater cable car

ovulazi'one f ovulation

o'vunque adv = DOVUNQUE

ov'vero conj or; (cioè) that is

ovvia'mente adv obviously

ovvi'are vi **~ a** qcsa counter sth.
'ovvio adj obvious

ozi'are vi laze around. **'ozio** m idle-
ness. **ozi'oso** adj idle; (questione)
pointless

o'zono m ozone; buco nell'**~** hole
in the ozone layer

Pp

pa'ca|re vt quieten. **~to** adj quiet

pac'chetto m packet; (postale) parcel, package; (di sigarette) pack,
packet. **~ software** software
package

'pacchia f ① bed of roses

pacchi'ano adj garish

'pacco m parcel; (involto) bundle. **~
regalo** gift-wrapped package

paccot'tiglia f junk, rubbish

'pace f peace; **darsi ~** forget it;
fare ~ con qcno make it up with
sb; **lasciare in ~** qcno leave sb
in peace

pachi'stano, -a mf & adj Pakistani

pacifi'ca|re vt reconcile; (mettere
pace) pacify. **~zi'one** f reconciliation

pa'cifico adj pacific; (calmo) peaceful; **il P~** the Pacific

paci'fis|mo m pacifism. **~ta** mf
pacifist

pa'dano adj **pianura padana** Po
Valley

pa'del|la f frying-pan; (per malati)
bedpan

padigli'one m pavilion

'padr|e m father; **~i** pl (antenati)
forefathers. **pa'drino** m godfather.
~e'nostro m **il ~enostro** the Lord's
Prayer. **~e'terno** m God Almighty

padro'nanza f mastery. **~ di sé**
self-control

pa'drone, -a mf master; mistress;
(datore di lavoro) boss; (proprietario)
owner. **~ggi'are** vt master

pae'saggio m scenery; (pittura)
landscape. **~'gista** mf landscape
architect

pae'sano, -a adj country ● mf
villager

pa'ese m (nazione) country; (territorio) land; (villaggio) village; **il Bel P~** Italy; **va' a quel ~!** get lost!; **Paesi** pl **Bassi** Netherlands

paf'futo adj plump

'paga f pay, wages pl

pa'gabile adj payable

pa'gaia f paddle

paga'mento m payment; **a ~** (parcheggio) which you have to pay to use. **~ anticipato** (Comm) advance payment. **~ alla consegna** cash on delivery, COD

pa'gano, -a adj & mf pagan

pa'gare vt/i pay; **~ da bere a qcno** buy sb a drink

pa'gella f [school] report

'pagina f page. **Pagine** pl **Gialle®** Yellow Pages. **~ web** (Comput) web page

'paglia f straw

pagliac'cetto m (per bambini) rompers pl

pagliac'cinta f farce

pagli'accio m clown

pagli'aio m haystack

paglie'riccio m straw mattress

pagli'etta f (cappello) boater; (per pentole) stool wool

pagli'uzza f wisp of straw; (di metallo) particle

pa'gnotta f [round] loaf

pail'lette f inv sequin

'paio m (pl f **paia**) pair; **un ~** (circa due) a couple; **un ~ di** (scarpe, forbici) a pair of

Paki'stan m Pakistan

'pala f shovel; (di remo, elica) blade; (di ruota) paddle

pala'fitta f pile-dwelling

pala'sport m inv indoor sports arena

pa'late fpl **a ~** (fare soldi) hand over fist

pa'lato m palate

palaz'zetto m **~ dello sport** indoor sports arena

palaz'zina f villa

pa'lazzo m palace; (edificio) building. **~ delle esposizioni** exhibition centre. **~ di giustizia** law courts pl, courthouse. **~ dello sport** indoor sports arena

'palco m (pedana) platform; (Theat) box. **~['scenico]** m stage

pale'sare vt disclose. **~si** vr reveal oneself. **pa'lese** adj evident

Pale'stina f Palestine. **~'nese** mf Palestinian

pa'lestra f gymnasium, gym; (ginnastica) gymnastics pl

pa'letta f spade; (per focolare) shovel. **~ [della spazzatura]** dustpan

pa'letto m peg

'palio m (premio) prize. **il P~** horse-race held at Siena

paliz'zata f fence

'palla f ball; (proiettile) bullet; (🔲: bugia) porkie; **che palle** 🔲 this is a pain in the arse!. **~ di neve** snowball. **~ al piede** fig millstone round one's neck

palla'nestro f basketball

palla'mano f handball

pallanu'oto f water polo

palla'volo f volley-ball

palleggi'are vi (calcio) practise ball control; Tennis knock up

pallia'tivo m palliative

'pallido adj pale

pal'lina f (di vetro) marble

pal'lino m **avere il ~ del calcio** be crazy about football

pallon'cino m balloon; (lanterna) Chinese lantern; (🔲: etilometro) Breathalyzer®

pal'lone m ball; (calcio) football; (aerostato) balloon

pal'lore m pallor

pal'loso adj 🔲 boring

pal'lottola f pellet; (proiettile) bullet

'palm|a f (Bot) palm. **~o** m (Anat) palm; (misura) hand's-breadth; **restare con un ~o di naso** feel disappointed

pal'mare m palmtop

'palo m pole; (di sostegno) stake; (in calcio) goalpost; **fare il ~** (ladro:) keep a lookout. **~ della luce** lamppost

palom'baro m diver

pal'pare vt feel

'palpebra f eyelid

palpi'ta|re vi throb; (fremere) quiver. **~zi'one** f palpitation. **'palpito** m throb; (del cuore) beat

pa'lude f marsh, swamp

palu'doso adj marshy

pa'lustre adj marshy; (piante, uccelli) marsh attrib

'pampino m vine leaf

'panca f bench; (in chiesa) pew

pancar'ré m sliced bread

pan'cetta f (Culin) bacon; (di una certa età) paunch

pan'chetto m [foot]stool

pan'china f garden seat; (in calcio) bench

'pancia f belly; **mal di ~** stomachache; **metter su ~** develop a paunch; **a ~ in giù** lying face down

panci'olle: stare in ~ lounge about

panci'one m (persona) pot belly

panci'otto m waistcoat

pande'monio m pandemonium

pan'doro m sponge cake eaten at Christmas

'pane m bread; (pagnotta) loaf; (di burro) block. **~ a cassetta** sliced bread. **pan grattato** breadcrumbs pl. **~ di segale** rye bread. **pan di Spagna** sponge cake. **~ tostato** toast

panet|e'ria f bakery; (negozio) baker's [shop]. **~i'ere, -a** mf baker

panet'tone m kind of Christmas cake

'panfilo m yacht

pan'forte m nougat-like delicacy from Siena

'panico m panic; **lasciarsi prendere dal ~** panic

pani'ere m basket; (cesta) hamper

pani'ficio m bakery; (negozio) baker's [shop]

pa'nino m [bread] roll. **~ imbottito** filled roll. **~ al prosciutto** ham roll. **~teca** f sandwich bar

'panna f cream. **~ da cucina** [single] cream. **~ montata** whipped cream

'panne f (Mech) **in ~** broken down; **restare in ~** break down

pan'nello m panel. **~ solare** solar panel

'panno m cloth; **panni** pl (abiti) clothes

pan'nocchia f (di granoturco) cob

panno'lino m (per bambini) nappy; (da donna) sanitary towel

pano'ram|a m panorama; fig overview. **~ico** adj panoramic

pantacol'lant mpl leggings

pantalon'cini m [corti] shorts

panta'loni mpl trousers, pants Am

pan'tano m bog

pan'tera f panther; (auto della polizia) high-speed police car

pan'tofo|la f slipper

pan'zana f fib

pao'nazzo adj purple

'papa m Pope

papà m inv dad[dy]

pa'pale adj papal

papa'lina f skull-cap

papa'razzo m paparazzo

pa'pato m papacy

pa'pavero m poppy

'paper|a f (errore) slip of the tongue. **~o** m gosling

papil'lon m inv bow tie

pa'piro m papyrus

'pappa f (per bambini) pap

pappa'gallo m parrot

pappa'molle mf wimp

'para f suole fpl di ~ crêpe soles

pa'rabola f parable; (curva) parabola. ~ **satellitare** satellite dish

para'bolico adj parabolic

para'brezza m inv windscreen, windshield Am

paracadu'tar|e vt parachute. ~**si** vr parachute

paraca'du|te m inv parachute. ~**'tista** mf parachutist

para'carro m roadside post

paradi'siaco adj heavenly

para'diso m paradise. ~ **terrestre** Eden, earthly paradise

parados'sale adj paradoxical. **para'dosso** m paradox

para'fango m mudguard

paraf'fina f paraffin

parafra'sare vt paraphrase

para'fulmine m lightning-conductor

pa'raggi mpl neighbourhood sg

parago'nabile adj comparable (a to). ~**re** vt compare. **para'gone** m comparison; **a paragone di** in comparison with

pa'ragrafo m paragraph

pa'ra|lisi f inv paralysis. ~**'litico, -a** adj & mf paralytic. ~**liz'zare** vt paralyse

paral'lel|a f parallel line. ~**a'mente** adv in parallel. ~**o** agg & m parallel; ~**e** pl parallel bars. ~**o'gramma** m parallelogram

para'lume m lampshade

para'medico m paramedic

pa'rametro m parameter

para'noia f paranoia

para'occhi mpl blinkers. **parao'recchie** mpl earmuffs

Paralim'piadi fpl Paralympic Games

para'petto m parapet

para'piglia m turmoil

para'plegico, -a adj & mf paraplegic

pa'rar|e vt (addobbare) adorn; (riparare) shield; save (tiro, pallone); ward off, parry (schiaffo, pugno) ● vi (mirare) lead up to. ~**si** vr (abbigliarsi) dress up; (da pioggia, pugni) protect oneself. ~**si dinanzi a qcno** appear in front of sb

para'sole m inv parasol

paras'sita adj parasitic ● m parasite

parasta'tale adj government-controlled

pa'rata f parade; (in calcio) save; (in scherma, pugilato) parry

para'urti m inv (Auto) bumper, fender Am

para'vento m screen

par'cella f bill

parcheggi'a|re vt park. **par'cheg-gio** m parking; (posteggio) carpark, parking lot Am. ~**'tore** mf parking attendant. ~**tore abusivo** person extorting money for guarding cars

par'chimetro m parking-meter

'parco[1] adj sparing; (moderato) moderate

'parco[2] m park. ~ **a tema** theme park. ~ **di divertimenti** fun-fair. ~ **giochi** playground. ~ **naturale** wildlife park. ~ **nazionale** national park. ~ **regionale** [regional] wildlife park

pa'recchi adj a good many ● pron several

pa'recchio adj quite a lot ● pron quite a lot ● adv rather, (parecchio tempo) quite a time

pareggi'a|re vt level; (eguagliare) equal; (Comm) balance ● vi draw

pa'reggio m (Comm) balance; Sport draw

paren'tado m relatives pl; (vincolo di sangue) relationship

pa'rente mf relative. ~ **stretto**

close relation

paren'tela f relatives pl; (vincolo di sangue) relationship

pa'rentesi f inv parenthesis; (segno grafico) bracket; (fig: pausa) break. ~ pl **graffe** curly brackets. ~ **quadre** square brackets. ~ **tonde** round brackets

pa'reo m sarong

pa'rere [1] m opinion; **a mio** ~ in my opinion

pa'rere [2] vi seem; (pensare) think; **che te ne pare?** what do you think of it?; **pare di sì** it seems so

pa'rete f wall; (in alpinismo) face. ~ **divisoria** partition wall

'pari adj inv equal; (numero) even; **andare di** ~ **passo** keep pace; **arrivare** ~ draw; ~ **e patta** (copiare, ripetere) word for word ● mf inv equal; **ragazza alla** ~ au pair [girl] ● m (titolo nobiliare) peer

Pa'rigi f Paris

pa'riglia f pair

pari'tà f equality; Tennis deuce. ~'**tario** adj parity attrib

parlamen'tare adj parliamentary ● mf Member of Parliament ● vi discuss. **parla'mento** m Parliament. **Il Parlamento europeo** the European Parliament

par'la|re vt/i speak, talk; (confessare) talk; ~ **bene/male di** qcno speak well/ill of somebody; **non parliamone più** let's forget about it; **non se ne parla nemmeno!** don't even mention it!. ~**to** adj (lingua) spoken. ~'**torio** m parlour; (in prigione) visiting room

parlot'tare vi mutter. **parlot'tio** m muttering

parmigi'ano m Parmesan

paro'dia f parody

pa'rola f word; (facoltà) speech; **parole** pl (di canzone) words, lyrics; **rivolgere la** ~ **a** address; **dare a** qcno la propria ~ give sb one's

word; **in parole povere** crudely speaking. **parole** pl **incrociate** crossword [puzzle] sg. ~ **d'ordine** password. **paro'laccia** f swear-word

par'quet m inv (pavimento) parquet flooring

par'rocchi|a f parish. ~'**ale** adj parish attrib. ~'**ano, -a** mf parishioner. '**parroco** m parish priest

par'rucca f wig

parrucchi'ere, -a mf hairdresser

parruc'chino m toupée, hairpiece

parsi'moni|a f thrift

'**parso** pp di **parere**

'**parte** f part; (lato) side; (partito) party; (porzione) share; **a** ~ apart from; **in** ~ in part; **la maggior** ~ **di** the majority of; **d'altra** ~ on the other hand; **da** ~ aside; (in disparte) to one side; **farsi da** ~ stand aside; **da** ~ **di** from; (per conto di) on behalf of; **è gentile da** ~ **tua** it is kind of you; **fare una brutta** ~ **a** qcno behave badly towards sb; **da che** ~ **è...?** whereabouts is...?; **da una** ~..., **dall'altra...** on the one hand..., on the other hand...; **dall'altra** ~ **di** on the other side of; **da nessuna** ~ nowhere; **da tutte le parti** (essere) everywhere; **da questa** ~ (in questa direzione) this way; **da un anno a questa** ~ for about a year now; **essere dalla** ~ **di** qcno be on sb's side; **essere in causa** be involved; **prendere** ~ take part in. ~ **civile** plaintiff

parteci'pante mf participant

parteci'pa|re vi ~ **re a** participate in, take part in; (condividere) share in. ~**zi'one** f participation; (annuncio) announcement; Fin shareholding; (presenza) presence. **par'tecipe** adj participating

parteggi'are vi ~ **per** side with

par'tenza f departure; Sport start; **in** ~ **per** leaving for

parti'cella f particle

parti'cipio m participle

parti'colar|e adj particular; (privato) private ●m detail, particular; **fin nei minimi ~i** down to the smallest detail. **~eggi'ato** adj detailed. **~ità** f inv particularity, (dettaglio) detail

partigi'ano, -a adj & mf partisan

par'tire vi leave; (aver inizio) start, a ~ **da** (beginning) from

par'tita f game; (incontro) match; (Comm) lot; (contabilità) entry. **~ di calcio** football match. **~ a carte** game of cards

par'tito m party; (scelta) choice; (oc casione di matrimonio) match

'parto m childbirth; un ~ facile an easy birth o labour; **dolori** pl **del ~** labour pains. **~ cesareo** Caesarian section. **~rire** vt give birth to

par'venza f appearance

parzi'al|e adj partial. **~ità** f partiality. **~'mente** adv (non completamente) partially; **~mente scremato** semi-skimmed

pasco'lare vt graze. **'pascolo** m pasture

'Pasqua f Easter. **pa'squale** adj Easter attrib

'passa ~ adv (e oltre) plus

pas'sabile adj passable

pas'saggio m passage; (traversata) crossing; Sport pass; (su veicolo) lift; **essere di ~** be passing through. **~ a livello** level crossing, grade crossing Am. **~ pedonale** pedestrian crossing

pas'sante mf passer-by ●m (di cintura) loop ●adj Tennis passing

passa'porto m passport

pas'sa|re vi (attraversare) pass through; (far visita) call; (andare) go; (essere approvato) be passed; **~re alla storia** go down in history; **~re di mente** it slipped my mind; **~re per un genio/idiota** be taken for a genius/an idiot ●vt (far scorrere) pass over; (sopportare) go through; (al tele-

fono) put through; (Culin) strain; **~re di moda** go out of fashion; **le passo il signor Rossi** I'll put you through to Mr Rossi; **~rsela bene** be well off; **come te la passi?** how are you doing?. **~ta** f (di vernice) coat; (spolverata) dusting; (occhiata) look

passa'tempo m pastime

pas'sato adj past, l'anno **~** last year; **sono le tre passate** it's past o after three o'clock ●m past; (Culin) purée; (Gram) past tense. **~ prossimo** (Gram) present perfect ● re moto (Gram) [simple] past. **~ di verdure** cream of vegetable soup

passa'verdure m inv food mill

passeg'gero, -a adj passing ●mf passenger

passeggi'a|re vi walk, stroll. **~ta** f walk, stroll; (luogo) public walk; (in bicicletta) ride; **fare una ~ta** go for a walk

passeg'gino m pushchair, stroller Am

pas'seggio m walk; (luogo) promenade; **andare a ~** go for a walk; **scarpe da ~** walking shoes

passe-partout m inv master-key

passe'rella f gangway; (Aeron) boarding bridge; (per sfilate) catwalk

'passero m sparrow. **passe'rotto** m (passero) sparrow

pas'sibile adj **~ di** liable to

passio'nale adj passionate. **pas-si'one** f passion

pas'sivo adj & m passive; (Comm) liabilities pl; **in ~** (bilancio) loss-making

pass magnetico m inv swipe card

'passo m step; (orma) footprint; (andatura) pace; (brano) passage; (valico) pass; **a due passi da qui** a stone's throw away; **a ~ d'uomo** at walking pace; **fare due passi** go for a stroll; **di pari ~** fig hand in hand. **~ carrabile, ~ carraio** driveway

'past|a f (impasto per pane ecc) dough; (per dolci, pasticcino) pastry; (pastasciutta) pasta; (massa molle) paste; fig nature. **~a frolla** shortcrust pastry. **pa'stella** f batter

---

i

Pasta A popular myth says that Marco Polo brought pasta back from China. Italians like to make their own pasta for special occasions (pasta fatta in casa), usually with eggs and sometimes with various fillings. Traditional pasta varies enormously from region to region, and sometimes the same name can be used for different types.

---

pastasci'utta f pasta
pa'stello m pastel
pa'sticca f pastille; (🔢: pastiglia) pill
pasticc|e'ria f cake shop, patisserie; (pasticcini) pastries pl; (arte) confectionery
pasticci'are vi make a mess ● vt make a mess of
pasticci'ere, -a mf confectioner
pastic'cino m little cake
pa'sticci|o m (Culin) pie; (lavoro disordinato) mess. **~one, -a** mf bungler ● adj bungling
pasti'ficio m pasta factory
pa'stiglia f (Med) pill, tablet; (di menta) sweet. **~ dei freni** brake pad
'pasto m meal
pasto'rale adj pastoral. **pa'store** m shepherd; (Relig) pastor. **pastore tedesco** German shepherd
pastoriz'za|re vt pasteurize. **~zi'one** f pasteurization
pa'stoso adj doughy; fig mellow
pa'stura f pasture; (per pesci) bait
pa'tacca f (macchia) stain; (fig: oggetto senza valore) piece of junk
pa'tata f potato. **patate** pl **fritte** chips Br, French fries. **pata'tine** fpl [potato] crisps, chips Am

pata'trac m inv (crollo) crash
pâté m inv pâté
pa'tella f limpet
pa'tema m anxiety
pa'tente f licence. **~ di guida** driving licence
pater'na|le f scolding. **~'lista** m paternalist
paternità f paternity. **pa'terno** adj paternal; (affetto ecc) fatherly
pa'tetico adj pathetic. **'pathos** m pathos
pa'tibolo m gallows sg
'patina f patina; (sulla lingua) coating
pa'ti|re vt/i suffer. **~to, -a** adj suffering ●mf fanatic. **~to della musica** music lover
patolo'gia f pathology. **pato'logico** adj pathological
'patria f native land
patri'arca m patriarch
pa'trigno m stepfather
patrimoni'ale adj property attrib. **patri'monio** m estate
patri'o|ta mf patriot
pa'trizio, -a adj & mf patrician
patro|ci'nare vt support. **~'cinio** m support
patro'nato m patronage. **pa'trono** m (Relig) patron saint; (Jur) counsel
'patta¹ f (di tasca) flap
'patta² f (pareggio) draw
patteggia|'mento m bargaining. **~'are** vt/i negotiate
patti'naggio m skating. **~ su ghiaccio** ice skating. **~ a rotelle** roller skating
patti'na|re vi skate; (auto:) skid. **~'tore, ~'trice** mf skater. **'pattino** m skate; (Aeron) skid. **pattino di ghiaccio** iceskate. **pattino a rotelle** roller skate; **pattini** mpl **in linea** roller blades®.
'patto m deal; (Pol) pact; **a ~ che** on condition that

pat'tuglia f patrol. ~ **stradale** patrol car; highway patrol

pattu'ire vt negotiate

pattumi'era f dustbin, trashcan Am

pa'ura f fear; (spavento) fright; **aver** ~ **be** afraid, **mettere** ~ **a** frighten. **pau'roso** adj (che fa paura) frightening; (che ha paura) fearful; (🅱: enorme) awesome

'pausa f pause; (nel lavoro) break; **fare una** ~ pause, (nel lavoro) have a break

pavimen'ta|re vt pave (strada). ~**zi'one** f (operazione) paving. **pavi'mento** m floor

pa'vone m peacock

pazien'tare vi be patient

pazi'ente adj & mf patient. ~**'mente** adv patiently. **pazi'enza** f patience

'pazza f madwoman. ~**'mente** adv madly

paz'z|esco adj foolish; (esagerato) crazy. ~**ia** f madness, (azione) [act of] folly. **'pazzo** adj mad; fig crazy ● m madman; **essere pazzo di/per** be crazy about; **darsi alla pazza gioia** live it up. **paz'zoide** adj whacky

'pecca f fault; **senza** ~ flawless. **peccami'noso** adj sinful

pec'ca|re vi sin; ~**re di** be guilty of (ingratitudine). ~**to** m sin; ~**to che...** it's a pity that...; **[che]** ~**to!** [what a] pity!. ~**tore**, ~**trice** mf sinner

'pece f pitch

'peco|ra f sheep. ~**ra nera** black sheep. ~**raio** m shepherd. ~**rella** f **cielo a** ~**relle** sky full of fluffy white clouds. ~**rino** m (formaggio) sheep's milk cheese

pecu|li'ar|e adj ~ **di** peculiar to. ~**ità** f inv peculiarity

pe'daggio m toll

pedago'gia f pedagogy. **peda'go'gico** adj pedagogical

peda'lare vi pedal. **pe'dale** m pedal. **pedalò** m inv pedalo

pe'dana f footrest; Sport springboard

pe'dante adj pedantic. ~**'ria** f pedantry. **pedan'tesco** adj pedantic

pe'data f (in calcio) kick; (impronta) footprint

pede'rasta m pederast

pe'destre adj pedestrian

pedi'atra mf paediatrician. **pedia'tria** f paediatrics sg

pedi'cure m inv chiropodist, podiatrist Am ● m pedicure

pedi'gree m inv pedigree

pe'dina f (nella dama) piece; fig pawn. ~**'mento** m shadowing. **pedi'nare** vt shadow

pe'dofilo, -a mf paedophile

pedo'nale adj pedestrian. **pe'done, -a** mf pedestrian

peeling m inv exfoliation treatment

'peggio adv worse; ~ **per te!** too bad!; **la persona** ~ **vestita** the worst dressed person ● adj worse; **niente di** ~ nothing worse ● m il ~ **è che...** the worst of it is that..., **pensare al** ~ think the worst ● f **alla** ~ at worst; **avere la** ~ get the worst of it; **alla meno** ~ as best I can

peggiora'mento m worsening

peggio'ra|re vt make worse, worsen ● vi get worse. ~**'tivo** adj pejorative

peggi'ore adj worse; (superlativo) worst ● mf **il/la** ~ the worst

'pegno m pledge; (nei giochi di società) forfeit; fig token

pelan'drone m slob

pe'la|re vt (spennare) pluck; (spellare) skin; (sbucciare) peel; (🅱: spillare denaro) fleece. ~**rsi** vr 🅱 lose one's hair. ~**to** adj bald. ~**ti** mpl (pomodori) peeled tomatoes

pel'lame m skins pl

'pelle f skin; (cuoio) leather; (buccia) peel; **avere la ∼ d'oca** have goose-flesh

pellegri'naggio m pilgrimage. **pelle'grino, -a** mf pilgrim

pelle'rossa mf Red Indian

pellette'ria f leather goods pl

pelli'cano m pelican

pellicc|e'ria f furrier's [shop]. **pel'licc|ia** f fur; (indumento) fur coat. **∼i'aio, -a** mf furrier

pel'licola f film. **∼ [trasparente]** cling film

'pelo m hair; (di animale) coat; (di lana) pile; **per un ∼** by the skin of one's teeth. **pe'loso** adj hairy

'peltro m pewter

pe'luche m: **giocattolo di ∼** soft toy

pe'luria f down

'pelvico adj pelvic

'pena f (punizione) punishment; (sofferenza) pain; (dispiacere) sorrow; (disturbo) trouble; **a mala ∼** hardly; **mi fa ∼ l** I pity him; **vale la ∼ andare** it is worth [while] going. **∼ di morte** death sentence

pe'nal|e adj criminal; **diritto** m **∼e** criminal law. **∼ità** f inv penalty

penaliz'za|re vt penalize. **∼zi'one** f (penalità) penalty

pe'nare vi suffer; (faticare) find it difficult

pen'daglio m pendant

pen'dant m inv **fare ∼ [con]** match

pen'den|te adj hanging; (Comm) outstanding ● m (ciondolo) pendant; **∼ti** pl drop earrings. **∼za** f slope; (Comm) outstanding account

'pendere vi hang; (superficie:) slope; (essere inclinato) lean

pen'dio m slope; **in ∼** sloping

pendo'l|are adj pendulum ● mf commuter. **∼ino** m (treno) special, first class only, fast train

'pendolo m pendulum

'pene m penis

pene'trante adj penetrating; (freddo) biting

pene'tra|re vt/i penetrate; (trafiggere) pierce ● vt (odore:) get into ● vi (entrare furtivamente) steal in. **∼zi'one** f penetration

penicil'lina f penicillin

pe'nisola f peninsula

peni'ten|te adj & mf penitent. **∼za** f penitence; (in gioco) forfeit. **∼zi'ario** m penitentiary

'penna f pen; (di uccello) feather. **∼ a feltro** felt-tip[ped pen]. **∼ a sfera** ball-point [pen]

pen'nacchio m plume

penna'rello m felt-tip[ped pen]

pennel'la|re vt paint. **∼ta** f brushstroke. **pen'nello** m brush; **a pennello** (alla perfezione) perfectly

pen'nino m nib

pen'none m flagpole

pen'nuto adj feathered

pe'nombra f half-light

pe'noso adj (🄛: pessimo) painful

pen'sa|re vi think; **penso di sì l** think so; **∼re** a think of; remember to (chiudere il gas ecc); **ci penso io** I'll take care of it; **∼re di fare qcsa** think of doing sth; **∼re tra sé e sé** think to oneself ● vt think. **∼ta** f idea

pensi'e|ro m thought; (mente) mind; (preoccupazione) worry; **stare in ∼ro per** be anxious about. **∼'roso** adj pensive

'pensil|e adj hanging; **giardino ∼e** roof-garden ● m (mobile) wall unit. **∼'lina** f bus shelter

pensio'nante mf boarder; (ospite pagante) lodger

pensio'nato, -a mf pensioner ● m (per anziani) [old folks'] home; (per studenti) hostel. **pensi'one** f pension; (albergo) boarding-house; (vitto e alloggio) board and lodging; **andare in**

pensione retire; **mezza pensione** half board. **pensione completa** full board

pen'soso adj pensive

pen'tagono m pentagon

Pente'coste f Whitsun

pen'ti|rsi vr ~rsi di repent of; (rammaricarsi) regret. ~'tismo m turning informant. ~to m M☐floso turned informant

'pentola f saucepan; (contenuto) potful. ~a pressione pressure cooker

pe'nultimo adj penultimate

pe'nuria f shortage

penzol'|are vi dangle. ~oni adv dangling

pe'pa|re vt pepper. ~to adj peppery

'pepe m pepper; **grano di ~** peppercorn. ~ **in grani** whole peppercorns. ~ **macinato** ground pepper

pepero'n|ata f peppers cooked in olive oil with onion, tomato and garlic. ~'cino m chilli pepper. **pepe'rone** m pepper. **peperone verde** green pepper

pe'pita f nugget

per prep for; (attraverso) through; (stato in luogo) in, on; (distributivo) per; (mezzo, entro) by; (causa) with; (in qualità di) as; ~ **strada** on the street; ~ **la fine del mese** by the end of the month; **in fila** ~ **due** in double file; **l'ho sentito** ~ **telefono** I spoke to him on the phone, ~ **iscritto** in writing; ~ **caso** by chance; **ho aspettato** ~ **ore** I've been waiting for hours; ~ **tempo** in time; ~ **sempre** forever; ~ **scherzo** as a joke; **gridare** ~ **il dolore** scream with pain; **vendere** ~ **10 milioni** sell for 10 million; **uno** ~ **volta** one at a time; **uno** ~ **uno** one by one; **venti** ~ **cento** twenty per cent; ~ **fare qcsa** [in order to] do sth; **stare** ~ **se** about to

'pera f pear. **farsi una** ~ (☐: di eroina) shoot up

per'cento adv per cent. **percentu'ale** f percentage

perce'pibile adj perceivable; (somma) payable

perce'pi|re vt perceive; (riscuotere) cash

percet'tibile adj perceptible. ~zi'one f perception

perché conj (in interrogazioni) why; (per il fatto che) because; (affinché) so that; ~ **non vieni?** why don't you come?; **dimmi** ~ **tell me why;** no/si because!; **la ragione** ~ **l'ho fatto** the reason [that] I did it, the reason why I did it; **è troppo difficile** ~ **lo possa capire** it's too difficult for me to understand ● m inv reason [why]; **senza un** ~ without any reason

perciò conj so

per'correre vt cover (distanza); (viaggiare) travel. **per'corso** pp di **percorrere** ● m (distanza) distance; (viaggio) journey

per'cossa f blow. ~o pp di **percuotere**. **percu'otere** vt strike

percussi'o|ne f percussion; **strumenti** pl a ~ne percussion instruments. ~'nista nf percussionist

per'dente mf loser

'perder|e vt lose; (sprecare) waste; (non prendere) miss; fig. ruin; (vizio); ~e **tempo** waste time ● vi lose; (recipiente) leak; **lascia** ~**e!** forget it!. ~**si** vr get lost; (reciproco) lose touch

perdigi'orno mf inv idler

'perdita f loss; (spreco) waste; (falla) leak; **a d'occhio** as far as the eye can see. ~ **di tempo** waste of time. **perdi'tempo** m time-waster

perdo'nare vt forgive; (scusare) excuse. **per'dono** m forgiveness; (Jur) pardon

perdu'rare vi last; (perseverare) persist

perduta'mente adv hopelessly. **per'duto** pp di **perdere** ● adj lost; (rovinato) ruined

pe'renne adj everlasting; (Bot) perennial. ~'mente adv perpetually

peren'torio adj peremptory

per'fetto adj perfect ● m (Gram) perfect [tense]

perfezio'nar|e vt perfect; (migliorare) improve. ~si vr improve oneself; (specializzarsi) specialize

perfezi'o|ne f perfection; alla ~ne to perfection. ~'nista mf perfectionist

per'fidia f wickedness; (atto) wicked act. '**perfido** adj treacherous; (malvagio) perverse

per'fino adv even

perfo'ra|re vt pierce; punch (schede); (Mech) drill. ~'tore, ~'trice mf punch-card operator ● m perforator. ~zi'one f perforation; (di schede) punching

per'formance f inv performance

perga'mena f parchment

perico'lante adj precarious; (azienda) shaky

pe'rico|lo m danger; (rischio) risk; mettere in ~lo endanger. ~'loso adj dangerous

perife'ria f periphery; (di città) outskirts pl; fig fringes pl

peri'feric|a f peripheral; (strada) ring road. ~o adj (quartiere) outlying

pe'rifrasi f inv circumlocution

pe'rimetro m perimeter

peri'odico m periodical ● adj periodical; (vento, mal di testa) (Math) recurring. **pe'riodo** m period; (Gram) sentence. **periodo di prova** trial period

peripe'zie fpl misadventures

pe'rire vi perish

pe'ri|to, -a adj skilled ● mf expert

perito'nite f peritonitis

pe'rizia f skill; (valutazione) survey

'**perla** f pearl. **per'lina** f bead

perlo'meno adv at least

perlu'stra|re vt patrol. ~zi'one f patrol; **andare in** ~**zione** go on patrol

perma'loso adj touchy

perma'ne|nte adj permanent ● f perm; **farsi [fare] la** ~**nte** have a perm. ~**nza** f permanence; (soggiorno) stay; **in** ~**nza** permanently. ~**re** vi remain

perme'are vt permeate

per'messo pp di **permettere** ● m permission; (autorizzazione) permit; (Mil) leave; **[è]** ~? (posso entrare?) may I come in?; (posso passare?) excuse me. ~ **di lavoro** work permit

per'mettere vt allow, permit; **potersi** ~ **qcsa** (finanziariamente) afford sth; **come si permette?** how dare you?

permutazi'one f exchange; (Math) permutation

per'nic|e f partridge. ~i'oso adj pernicious

'**perno** m pivot

pernot'tare vi stay overnight

'**pero** m pear-tree

però conj but; (tuttavia) however

pero'rare vt plead

perpendico'lare adj & f perpendicular

perpe'trare vt perpetrate

perpetu'are vt perpetuate. **per'petuo** adj perpetual

perplessità f inv perplexity; (dubbio) doubt. **per'plesso** adj perplexed

perqui'si|re vt search. ~zi'one f search. ~**zione domiciliare** search of the premises

persecu'tore, -'trice mf persecutor. ~zi'one f persecution

persegu'ire vt pursue

persegui'tare vt persecute

perseve'ra|nza f perseverance. ~**re** vi persevere

persi'ano, -a adj Persian ● f (di finestra) shutter. '**persico** adj Persian

per'sino adv = **PERFINO**

persi'sten|te adj persistent. ~za f persistence. **per'sistere** vi persist

'perso pp di perdere ● adj lost; **a tempo ~** in one's spare time

per'sona f person; (un tale) somebody; **di ~, in ~** in person, personally; **per ~** per person, a head, per **interposta ~** through an intermediary; **persone** pl people

perso'naggio m personality; (Theat) character

perso'nal|e adj personal ● m staff. **~e di terra** ground crew. **~ità** f inv personality. **~iz'zare** vt customize (auto ecc); personalize (penna ecc)

personifi'ca|re vt personify. **~zi'one** f personification

perspi'cace adj shrewd

persua'dere vt convince; impress (critici); **~dere qcno a fare qcsa** persuade sb to do sth. **~si'one** f persuasion, **~sivo** adj persuasive. **persu'aso** pp di persuadere

per'tanto conj therefore

'pertica f pole

perti'nente adj relevant

per'tosse f whooping cough

pertur'ba|re vt perturb. **~rsi** vr be perturbed. **~zi'one** f disturbance, **~zione atmosferica** atmospheric disturbance

per'va|dere vt pervade. **~so** pp di pervadere

perven'ire vi reach; **far ~ qcsa a qcno** send sth to sb

pervers|i'one f perversion. **~ità** f perversity. **per'verso** adj perverse

perver'ti|re vt pervert. **~to** adj perverted ● m pervert

per'vinca m (colore) blue with a touch of purple

p.es. abbr (per esempio) e.g.

pesa f weighing; (bilancia) weighing machine; (per veicoli) weighbridge

pe'sante adj heavy; (stomaco) overfull ● adv (vestirsi) warmly. **~mente** adv (cadere) heavily. **pesan'tezza** f

heaviness

pe'sar|e vt/i weigh; **~e su** fig lie heavy on; **~e le parole** weigh one's words. **~si** vr weigh oneself

'pesca f (frutto) peach

'pesca² f fishing; **andare a ~ go fishing**. **~ subacquea** underwater fishing. **pe'scare** vt fish for; (prendere) catch; (fig: trovare) fish out. **~tore** m fisherman

'pesce m fish. **~ d'aprile!** April Foo!!. **~ grosso** fig big fish. **~ piccolo** fig small fry. **~ rosso** goldfish. **~ spada** swordfish. **Pesci** pl (Astr) Pisces

pesce cane m shark

pesche'reccio m fishing boat

pesche'ria f fishmonger's [shop]. **~hi'era** f fish-pond. **~i'vendolo** m fishmonger

'pesco m peach-tree

'peso m weight; **essere di ~ per qcno** be a burden to sb **di poco ~** (senza importanza) not very important

pessi'mis|mo m pessimism. **~ta** mf pessimist ● adj pessimistic. **'pessimo** adj very bad

pe'staggio m beating-up. **pe'stare** vt tread on; (schiacciare) crush; (pestare) beat; crush (aglio, prezzemolo)

'peste f plague; (persona) pest

pe'stello m pestle

pesti'cida m pesticide

pesti'len|za f pestilence; (fetore) stench. **~zi'ale** adj noxious

'pesto adj ground; **occhio ~** black eye ● m basil and garlic sauce

'petalo m petal

pe'tardo m banger

petizi'one f petition; **fare una ~** draw up a petition

petroli'era f (oil) tanker. **~lifero** adj oil-bearing. **pe'trolio** m oil

pettego'lare vi gossip. **~lezzo** m piece of gossip; **far ~lezzi** gossip

pet'tegolo, -a adj gossipy ● mf

gossip

petti'na|re vt comb. **~rsi** vr comb one's hair. **~'tura** f combing; (acconciatura) hair-style. **'pettine** m comb

'petting m petting

petti'nino m (fermaglio) comb

petti'rosso m robin

'petto m chest; (seno) breast; **a doppio ~** double-breasted

petto'rale m (in gare sportive) number. **~'rina** f (di salopette) bib. **~'ruto** adj (donna) full-breasted; (uomo) broad-chested

petu'lante adj impertinent

'pezza f cloth; (toppa) patch; (rotolo di tessuto) roll

pez'zente mf tramp; (avaro) miser

'pezzo m piece; (parte) part; **un ~** (di tempo) some time; (di spazio) a long way; **al ~** (costare) each; **fare a pezzi** tear to shreds. **~ grosso** bigwig

pia'cente adj attractive

---

pia'ce|re

● m pleasure; (favore) favour; **a ~re** as much as one likes; **per ~re!** please!; **~re [di conoscerla]!** pleased to meet you!; **con ~re** with pleasure

● vi **la Scozia mi piace** I like Scotland; **mi piacciono i dolci** I like sweets; **ti piace?** do you like it?; **faccio come mi pare e piace** I do as I please; **lo spettacolo è piaciuto** the show was a success.

Nota che il soggetto in italiano corrisponde al complemento oggetto in inglese, mentre il complemento indiretto in italiano corrisponde al soggetto in inglese: **Non mi piace** I don't like it

---

pia'vole adj pleasant

piaci'mento m **a ~ as much as you like**

pia'dina f unleavened bread

pi'aga f sore; scourge; (persona noiosa) pain; (fig: ricordo doloroso) wound

piagni'steo m whining

piagnuco'lare vi whimper

pi'alla f plane. **pial'lare** vt plane

pi'ana f plane. **pianeggi'ante** adj level

piane'rottolo m landing

pia'neta m planet

pi'angere vi cry; (disperatamente) weep ● vt (lamentare) lament; (per un lutto) mourn

pianifi'ca|re vt plan. **~zi'one** f planning

pia'nista mf (Mus) pianist

pi'ano adj flat; (a livello) flush; (regolare) smooth; (facile) easy ● adv slowly; (con cautela) gently; **andarci ~** go carefully ● m plain; (di edificio) floor; (livello) plane; (progetto) plan; (Mus) piano; **di primo ~** first-rate; **primo ~** (Phot) close-up; **in primo ~** in the foreground. **~ regolatore** town plan. **~ di studi** syllabus

piano'forte m piano. **~ a coda** grand piano

piano'terra m inv ground floor

pi'anta f plant; (del piede) sole; (disegno) plan; (di sana) (totalmente) entirely; **in ~ stabile** permanently. **~ stradale** road map. **~gi'one** f plantation

pian'tar|e vt plant; (conficcare) drive; (fam: abbandonare) dump; **piantala!** fam stop it!. **~si** vr plant oneself; (fam: lasciarsi) leave each other

pianter'reno m ground floor

pi'anto pp di piangere ● m crying; (disperato) weeping ● (lacrime) tears pl

pian|to'nare vt guard. **~'tone** m guard

pia'nura f plain

p'iastra f plate; (*lastra*) slab; (*Culin*) griddle. ~ **elettronica** circuit board. ~ **madre** (*Comput*) motherboard

pia'strella f tile

pla'strina f (*Mil*) identity disc; (*Med*) platelet; (*Comput*) chip

platta'forma f platform. ~ **di lancio** launch pad

piat'tino m saucer

pi'atto adj flat ● m plate; (*da portata, vivanda*) dish; (*portata*) course; (*parte piatta*) flat; (*di giradischi*) turntable; **piatti** pl (*Mus*) cymbals; **lavare i piatti** do the washing-up. ~ **fondo** soup plate. ~ **piano** [ordinary] plate

pi'azza f square; (*Comm*) market; **letto a una** ~ single bed; **letto a due piazze** double bed; **far** ~ **pulita** make a clean sweep. ~**forte** m stronghold. **piaz'zale** m large square. ~**'mento** m (*in classifica*) placing

piaz'za|re vt place. ~**rsi** vr Sport be placed; ~**rsi secondo** come second. ~**to** adj (*cavallo*) placed; **ben** ~**to** (*robusto*) well built

piaz'zista m salesman

piaz'zuola f ~ **di sosta** pull-in

pic'cante adj hot; (*pungente*) sharp; (*salace*) spicy

pic'carsi vr (*risentirsi*) take offence; ~ **di** (*vantarsi di*) claim to

picche fpl (*in carte*) spades

picchet'tare vt stake; (*scioperanti*) picket. **pic'chetto** m picket

picchi'a|re vt beat, hit ● vi (*bussare*) knock; (*Aeron*) nosedive; ~**re in testa** (*motore*) knock. ~**ta** f beating; (*Aeron*) nosedive; **scendere in** ~**ta** nosedive

picchlet'tare vt tap; (*punteggiare*) spot

pic'chio m woodpecker

pic'cino adj tiny; (*gretto*) mean; (*di poca importanza*) petty ● m little one, child

picci'one m pigeon

'picco m peak; **a** ~ vertically; **colare a** ~ sink

'piccolo, -a adj small, little; (*di età*) young; (*di statura*) short; (*gretto*) petty ● mf child; **da** ~ as a child

pic'cu|ne m pickaxe. ~**zza** f ice axe

pic'nic m inv picnic

pi'docchio m louse

piè m inv **a** ~ **di pagina** at the foot of the page; **saltare a** ~ **pari** skip

pi'ede m foot; **a piedi** on foot; **andare a piedi** walk; **a piedi nudi** barefoot; **a** ~ **libero** free; **in piedi** standing; **alzarsi in piedi** stand up; **ai piedi di** (*montagna*) at the foot of; **prendere** ~ (*fig*) gain ground; (*moda*) catch on; **mettere in piedi** (*allestire*) set up

piedi'stallo m pedestal

pi'ega f (*negatura*) fold; (*di gonna*) pleat; (*di pantaloni*) crease; (*grinza*) wrinkle; (*andamento*) turn; **non fare una** ~ (*ragionamento*) be flawless

pie'ga|re vt fold; (*flettere*) bend ● vi bend. ~**rsi** vr bend. ~**rsi a** fig yield to. ~**'tura** f folding

pieghet'ta|re vt pleat. ~**to** adj pleated. **pie'ghevole** adj pliable; (*tavolo*) folding ● m leaflet

piemon'tese adj Piedmontese

pi'en|a f (*di fiume*) flood; (*folla*) crowd. ~**o** adj full; (*massiccio*) solid; **in** ~**a estate** in the middle of summer; **a** ~**i voti** (*diplomarsi*) ≈ with A-grades, with first class honours ● m (*colmo*) height; (*carico*) full load; **in** ~**o** (*completamente*) fully; **fare il** ~**o** (*di benzina*) fill up

pie'none m **c'era il** ~ the place was packed

'piercing m inv body piercing

pietà f pity; (*misericordia*) mercy; **senza** ~ (*persona*) pitiless; (*spietatamente*) pitilessly; **avere** ~ **di qcno** take pity on sb; **far** ~ (*far pena*) be pitiful

pie'tanza f dish

pie'toso adj pitiful, merciful; (pes-simo) terrible

pi'etr|a f stone. ~a dura semi-precious stone. ~a preziosa precious stone. ~a dello scandalo cause of the scandal. **pie'trame** m stones pl. ~ifi'care vt petrify. **pie'trina** f flint. **pie'troso** adj stony

pigi'ama m pyjamas pl

'pigia 'pigia m inv crowd, crush. **pigi'are** vt press

pigi'one f rent; **dare a** ~ let, rent out; **prendere a** ~ rent

pigli'are vt (: afferrare) catch. **'piglio** m air

pig'mento m pigment

'pigna f cone

pi'gnolo adj pedantic

pigo'lare vi chirp. **pigo'lio** m chirping

pi'grizia f laziness. **'pigro** adj lazy; (intelletto) slow

'pila f pile; (Electr) battery; (: lampadina tascabile) torch; (vasca) basin; **a pile** battery powered

pi'lastro m pillar

'pillola f pill; **prendere la** ~ be on the pill

pi'lone m pylon; (di ponte) pier

pi'lota mf pilot ● m (Auto) driver. **pi-lo'tare** vt pilot; drive (auto)

pinaco'teca f art gallery

pi'neta f pine-wood

ping-'pong m table tennis, ping-pong :

'pingu|e adj fat. ~'edine f fatness

pingu'ino m penguin; (gelato) choc ice on a stick

'pinna f fin; (per nuotare) flipper

'pino m pine[-tree]; ~ **marittimo** cluster pine. **pi'nolo** m pine kernel

'pinta f pint

'pinza f pliers pl; (Med) forceps pl

pin'za|re vt (con pinzatrice) staple. ~'trice f stapler

pin'zette fpl tweezers pl

pinzi'monio m sauce for crudités

'pio adj pious; (benefico) charitable

pi'oggia f rain; (fig: di pietre, insulti) hail, shower; **sotto la** ~ in the rain. ~ **acida** acid rain

pi'olo m (di scala) rung

piom'ba|re vi fall heavily; ~**re su** fall upon ● vt fill (dente). ~**tura** f (di dente) filling. **piom'bino** m (sigillo) [lead] seal; (da pesca) sinker; (in gonne) weight

pi'ombo m lead; (sigillo) [lead] seal; **a** ~ plumb; **senza** ~ (benzina) lead-free

pioni'ere, -a mf pioneer

pi'oppo m poplar

pio'vano adj **acqua piovana** rainwater

pi'ov|ere vi rain; ~**e** it's raining; ~**iggi'nare** vi drizzle. **pio'voso** adj rainy

'pipa f pipe

pipì f **fare [la]** ~ **pee**

pipi'strello m bat

pi'ramide f pyramid

'piranha m inv piranha

pi'rat|a m pirate. ~**a della strada** road-hog ● adj inv pirate. ~**e'ria** f piracy

pi'rofil|a f (tegame) oven-proof dish. ~**o** adj heat-resistant

pi'romane mf pyromaniac

pi'roscafo m steamer. ~ **di linea** liner

pi'scina f swimming pool. ~ **coperta** indoor swimming pool. ~ **scoperta** outdoor swimming pool

pi'sello m pea; (: pene) willie

piso'lino m nap; **fare un** ~ have a nap

'pista f track; (Aeron) runway; (orma) footprint; (sci) slope, piste. ~ **d'atterraggio** airstrip. ~ **da ballo** dance floor. ~ **ciclabile** cycle track

pi'stacchio m pistachio

pi'stola f pistol; (per spruzzare) spray-gun. ~ a spruzzo paint spray

pi'stone m piston

pi'tone m python

pit'to|re, -'trice mf painter. ~'resco adj picturesque. **pit'torico** adj pictorial

pit'tu|ra f painting. ~'rare vt paint

più

● adv more; (superlativo) most

Il comparativo e il superlativo di aggettivi di una sillaba o che terminano in y si formano con i suffissi -er o -est: più breve shorter il più giovane the youngest

~ importante more important; il ~ importante the most important; ~ caro more expensive; il ~ caro the most expensive; di ~ more; una coperta in ~ an extra blanket, non ho ~ soldi I don't have any more money, non vive ~ a Milano he doesn't live in Milan any longer; o meno more or less; il ~ lentamente possibile as slowly as possible; mai ~! never again!; ~ di more than; sempre ~ more and more; (Math) plus

● adj more; (superlativo) most; ~ tempo more time; la classe con ~ alunni the class with most pupils; ~ volte several times

● m most; (Math) plus sign; il ~ è fatto the worst is over; parlare del ~ e del meno make small talk; i ~ the majority

piuccheper'fetto m pluperfect

pi'uma f feather. **piu'maggio** m plumage. **piu'mino** m (di cigni) down; (copriletto) eiderdown; (per cipria) powder-puff; (per spolverare) feather duster; (giacca) down jacket. **piu'mone** m ⊞ duvet

piut'tosto adv rather; (invece) instead

pl'vello m ⊞ greenhorn

'pizza f pizza; Cinema reel.

pizze'ria f pizza restaurant

pizzai'ola f slices of beef in tomato sauce, oregano and anchovies

pizzi'ca|re vt pinch; (pungere) sting; (di sapore) taste sharp; (⊞: sorprendere) catch; (Mus) pluck ● vi scratch; (cibo:) be spicy **'pizzico** m, ~otto m pinch

'pizzo m lace; (di montagna) peak

pla'ca|re vt placate; assuage (fame, dolore). ~si vr calm down

placca f plate, (commemorativa, dentale) plaque; (Med) patch

plac'ca|re vt plate. ~to adj ~to d'argento silver-plated. ~to d'oro gold-plated. ~'tura f plating

pla'centa f placenta

'placido adj placid

plagi'are vt plagiarize; pressure (persona). **'plagio** m plagiarism

plaid m inv tartan rug

pla'nare vi glide

'plancia f (Naut) bridge; (passerella) gangplank

pla'smare vt mould

'plastic|a f (arte) plastic art; (Med) plastic surgery; (materia) plastic. ~o adj plastic ● m plastic model

'platano m plane[-tree]

pla'tea f stalls pl; (pubblico) audience

'platino m platinum

plau'sibile adj plausible. ~ità f plausibility

ple'baglia f pej mob

pleni'lunio m full moon

'plettro m plectrum

pleu'rite f pleurisy

'plico m packet; **in ~ a parte** under separate cover

plissé adj inv plissé; (gonna) accordeon-pleated

plo'tone m platoon; (di ciclisti) group. ~ **d'esecuzione** firing-squad

'plumbeo adj leaden

plu'ral|e adj & m plural; **al** ~**e** in the plural. ~**ità** f majority

pluridiscipli'nare adj multidisciplinary

plurien'nale adj ~ **esperienza** many years' experience

pluripar'titico adj (Pol) multi-party

plu'tonio m plutonium

pluvi'ale adj rain attrib

pneu'matico adj pneumatic ● m tyre

pneu'monia f pneumonia

po' ▷**poco**

po'chette f inv clutch bag

po'chino m **un** ~ a little bit

'poco

● adj little; (tempo) short; (con nomi plurali) few

● adv (con verbi) not much; (con avverbi) not very; **parla** ~ he doesn't speak much; **lo conosco** ~ I don't know him very well

poco + aggettivo spesso si traduce con un aggettivo specifico: ~ **probabile** unlikely, ~ **profondo** shallow

● pron little; (poco tempo) a short time; (plurale) few

● m little; **un po'** a little [bit]; **un po' di** a little, some; **a** ~ **a** ~ little by little; **fra** ~ soon; **per** ~ (a poco prezzo) cheap; (quasi) nearly; ~ **fa** a little while ago; **sono arrivato da** ~ I have just arrived; **un bel po'** quite a lot

---

po'dere m farm

pode'roso adj powerful

'podio m dais; (Mus) podium

po'dis|mo m walking. ~**ta** mf walker

po'e|ma m poem. ~**sia** f poetry; (componimento) poem. ~**ta** m poet. ~**tessa** f poetess. ~**tico** adj poetic

poggiapi'edi m inv footrest

poggi'a|re vt lean; (posare) place ● vi ~**re su** be based on. ~**testa** m inv head-rest

poggi'olo m balcony

'poi adv (dopo) then; (più tardi) later [on]; (finalmente) finally. **d'ora in** ~ from now on; **questa** ~! well!

poiché conj since

pois m inv **a** ~ polka-dot

'poker m poker

po'lacco, -a adj Polish ● mf Pole ● m (lingua) Polish

po'lar|e adj polar. ~**iz'zare** vt polarize

'polca f polka

po'lemi|ca f controversy. ~**ca-'mente** adv controversially. ~**co** adj controversial. ~**z'zare** vi engage in controversy

po'lenta f cornmeal porridge

poli'clinico m general hospital

poli'estere m polyester

polio[mie'lite] f polio[myelitis]

'polipo m polyp

polisti'rolo m polystyrene

poli'tecnico m polytechnic

po'litic|a f politics sg; (linea di condotta) policy; **fare** ~**a** be in politics. ~**iz'zare** vt politicize. ~**o, -a** adj political ● mf politician

poliva'lente adj catch-all

poli'zi|a f police. ~**a giudiziaria** ≈ Criminal Investigation Department. ~**a stradale** traffic police. ~**esco** adj police attrib; (romanzo, film) detective attrib. ~**otto** m policeman

'polizza f policy

pol'la|io m chicken run; (▣: *luogo chiassoso*) mad house. **~me** m poultry. **~strello** m spring chicken. **~strò** m cockerel

'pollice m thumb; (*unità di misura*) inch

'polline m pollen; **allergia al ~** hay fever

polli'vendolo, -a mf poulterer

'pollo m chicken; (▣: *semplicione*) simpleton

polmo'nare adj pulmonary. **pol'mone** m lung. **~'nite** f pneumonia

'polo m pole; Sport polo, (*maglietta*) polo top. **~ nord** North Pole. **~ sud** South Pole

Po'lonia f Poland

'polpa f pulp

pol'paccio m calf

polpa'strello m fingertip

pol'pet|ta f meatball. **~tone** m meat loaf

'polpo m octopus

pol'sino m cuff

'polso m pulse; (Anat) wrist; fig authority; **avere ~** be strict

pol'tiglia f mush

pol'trire vi lie around

pol'tron|a f armchair. (Theat) seat in the stalls. **~e** adj lazy

'polve|re f dust; (*sostanza polverizzata*) powder; **in ~re** powdered; **sapone in ~re** soap powder. **~rina** f (*medicina*) powder. **~riz'zare** vt pulverize; (*nebulizzare*) atomize. **~rone** m cloud of dust. **~roso** adj dusty

po'mata f ointment, cream

po'mello m knob; (*guancia*) cheek

pomeridi'ano adj afternoon attrib; **alle tre pomeridiane** at three in the afternoon, **pome'riggio** m afternoon

'pomice f pumice

'pomo m (*oggetto*) knob. **~ d'Adamo** Adam's apple

pomo'doro m tomato

'pompa f pump; (*sfarzo*) pomp. **pompe** pl funebri (*funzione*) funeral, **pom'pare** vt pump; (*gonfiare d'aria*) pump up; (fig: *esagerare*) exaggerate; **pompare fuori** pump out

pom'pelmo m grapefruit

pom'piere m fireman; **i pompieri** the fire brigade

pom'poso adj pompous

ponde'rare vt ponder

po'nente m west

'ponte m bridge; (Naut) deck; (*impalcatura*) scaffolding; **fare il ~** make a long weekend of it

pon'tefice m pontiff

pontifi'ca|re vi pontificate. **~to** m pontificate

ponti'ficio adj papal

pon'tile m jetty

popò f inv ▣ pooh

pupo'lano adj of the people

popo'la|re adj popular; (*comune*) common ● vt populate. **~rsi** vr get crowded. **~rità** f popularity. **~zi'one** f population. **'popolo** m people. **popo'loso** adj populous

'poppa f (Naut) stern; (*mammella*) breast. **a ~** astern

pop'pa|re vt suck. **~ta** f (*pasto*) feed. **~toio** m [feeding-]bottle

popu'lista mf populist

por'cata f load of rubbish; **porcate** pl (▣: *cibo*) junk food

porcel'lana f porcelain

porcel'lino m piglet. **~ d'India** guinea-pig

porche'ria f dirt; (*cosa orrenda*) piece of filth; (*robaccia*) rubbish

por'ci|le m pigsty. **~no** adj pig attrib ● m (*fungo*) edible mushroom. **'porco** m pig; (*carne*) pork

'porgere vt give; (*offrire*) offer; **porgo distinti saluti** (*in lettera*) I remain, yours sincerely

porno'gra|fia f pornography. **~'grafico** adj pornographic

'poro m pore. **po'roso** adj porous

'porpora f purple

'por|re vt put; (collocare) place; (supporre) suppose; ask (domanda); present (candidatura); **poniamo il caso che...** let us suppose that...; **~re fine o termine a** put an end to. **~si** vr put oneself; **~si a sedere** sit down; **~si in cammino** set out

'porro m (Bot) leek; (verruca) wart

'porta f door; Sport goal; (di città) gate; (Comput) port. **~ a ~** door-to-door; **mettere alla ~** show sb the door. **~ di servizio** tradesmen's entrance

porta'bagagli m inv porter; (di treno ecc) luggage rack; (Auto) boot, trunk Am; (sul tetto di un'auto) roof rack

portabot'tiglie m inv bottle rack, wine rack

porta'cenere m inv ashtray

portachi'avi m inv keyring

porta'cipria m inv compact

portadocu'menti m inv document wallet

porta'erei f inv aircraft carrier

portafi'nestra f French window

porta'foglio m wallet; (per documenti) portfolio; (ministero) ministry

portafor'tuna m inv lucky charm
● adj inv lucky

portagi'oie m inv jewellery box

por'tale m door

porta'matite m inv pencil case

porta'mento m carriage; (condotta) behaviour

porta'mina m inv propelling pencil

portamo'nete m inv purse

portaom'brelli m inv umbrella stand

porta'pacchi m inv roof rack; (su bicicletta) luggage rack

porta'penne m inv pencil case

por'ta|re vt (verso chi parla) bring; (lontano da chi parla) take; (sorreggere) (Math) carry; (condurre) lead; (indossare)

wear; (avere) bear. **~rsi** vr (trasferirsi) move; (comportarsi) behave; **~rsi bene/male gli anni** look young/old for one's age

portari'viste m inv magazine rack

porta'sci m inv ski rack

portasiga'rette m inv cigarette-case

por'ta|ta f (di pranzo) course; (Auto) carrying capacity; (di arma) range; (fig: abilità) capability; **a ~ta di mano** within reach. **por'tatile** agg & m portable. **por'tato** adj (indumento) worn; (dotato) gifted; **essere ~to a** (tendere a) be inclined to. **~'tore, ~'trice** mf bearer; **al ~tore** to the bearer. **~'tore di handicap** disabled person

portatovagli'olo m napkin ring

porta'uovo m inv egg-cup

porta'voce m inv spokesman ● f inv spokeswoman

por'tento m marvel; (persona dotata) prodigy

'portico m portico

porti'er|a f door; (tendaggio) door curtain. **~e** m porter, doorman; Sport goalkeeper. **~e di notte** night porter

porti'n|aio, -a mf caretaker. **~e'ria** f concierge's room; (di ospedale) porter's lodge

'porto pp di porgere ● m harbour; (complesso) port; (vino) port [wine]; (spesa di trasporto) carriage; **andare in ~** succeed. **~ d'armi** gun licence

Porto'gallo m Portugal. **p~hese** adj & mf Portuguese

por'tone m main door

portu'ale m docker

porzi'one f portion

'posa f laying; (riposo) rest; (Phot) exposure; (atteggiamento) pose; **mettersi in ~** pose

po'sa|re vt put; (giù) put [down] ● vi (poggiare) rest; (per un ritratto) pose.

~rsi vr alight; (sostare) rest; (Aeron) land. **~ta** f piece of cutlery; **~te** pl cutlery sg. **~to** adj sedate

po'scritto m postscript

posi'tivo adj positive

posizio'nare vt position

posizi'one f position; **farsi una ~** get ahead

posolo'gia f dosage

po'sporre vt place after; (posticipare) postpone. **~sto** pp di posporre

posse'dere vt possess, own. **~i'mento** m possession

posses'sivo adj possessive. **pos 'sesso** m ownership; (bene) possession. **~'sore** m owner

pos'sibil|e adj possible, **il più presto ~e** as soon as possible ● m fare **[tutto]** il **~e** do one's best. **~ità** f inv possibility; (occasione) chance ● fpl (mezzi) means

possi'dente mf land-owner

'posta f post, mail; (ufficio postale) post office; (al gioco) stake; **spese di ~** postage; **per ~** by post, by mail; **a bella ~** on purpose; **Poste e Telecomunicazioni** pl (Italian) Post Office. **~ elettronica** e-mail. **~ prioritaria** ≈ first-class mail. **~ vocale** voice mail

posta'giro m postal giro

po'stale adj postal

postazi'one f position

postda'tare vt postdate (assegno)

posteggi'a|re vt/i park. **~tore, ~trice** mf parking attendant. **po 'steggio** m car-park, parking lot Am; (di taxi) taxi-rank

'posteri mpl descendants. **~ore** adj rear; (nel tempo) later **~tà** f posterity

po'sticcio adj artificial; (baffi, barba) false ● m hair-piece

postici'pare vt postpone

po'stilla f note; (Jur) rider

po'stino m postman, mailman Am

'posto pp di porre ● m place; (spazio)

room; (impiego) job; (Mil) post; (sedile) seat; **a/fuori ~** in/out of place; **prendere ~** take up room; **sul ~** on-site; **essere a ~** (casa, libri) be tidy; **fare ~** a make room for; **al ~ di** (invece di) in place of, instead of. **~ di blocco** checkpoint. **~ di guida** driving seat. **~ di lavoro** workstation. **posti** pl in piedi standing room. **~ di polizia** police station

post-'partum adj post-natal

'postumo adj posthumous ● m after-effect

po'tabile adj drinkable; **acqua ~** drinking water

po'tare vt prune

po'tassio m potassium

po'ten|te adj powerful; (efficace) effective. **~za** f power; (efficacia) potency. **~zi'ale** adj & m potential

po'tere m power; **al ~** in power ● vi can, be able to: (esser possibile) may **I come in?; posso fare qualche cosa?** can I do something?; **che tu possa essere felice!** may you be happy!; **non ne posso più** (sono stanco) I can't go on; (sono giunto) I can't take any more; **può darsi** perhaps; **può darsi che sia vero** perhaps it's true; **potrebbe aver ragione** he could be right, he might be right; **avresti potuto telefonare** you could have phoned, you might have phoned; **spero di poter venire** I hope to be able to come

potestà f inv power

'pover|o, -a adj poor; (semplice) plain ● m poor man ● f poor woman; **i ~i** the poor. **~tà** f poverty

'pozza f pool. **poz'zanghera** f puddle

'pozzo m well; (minerario) pit. **~ petrolifero** oil-well

PP.TT. abbr (Poste e Telegrafi) [Italian] Post Office

prali'nato adj (mandorla, gelato)

praline-coated

pram'matica f essere di ∼ be customary

pran'zare vi dine; (a mezzogiorno) lunch. **'pranzo m** dinner; (a mezzogiorno) lunch. **pranzo di nozze** wedding breakfast

> Pranzo Pranzo is traditonally the day's main meal and school timetables and hours of business are geared to a break between one and four o'clock. It starts with a primo (usually pasta), followed by a secondo (main course). Gradually Italians, especially city-dwellers, are adopting a more northern European timetable and making less of pranzo.

'prassi f standard procedure

prate'ria f grassland

'prati|ca f practice; (esperienza) experience; (documentazione) file; **avere ∼ca di qcsa** be familiar with sth; **far ∼ca** gain experience. ∼**'cabile** adj practicable; (strada) passable. ∼**ca'mente** adv practically. ∼**'cante** mf apprentice; (Relig) [regular] church-goer

prati'ca|re vt practise; (frequentare) associate with; (fare) make

praticità f practicality. **'pratico** adj practical; (esperto) experienced; **essere pratico di qcsa** know about sth

'prato m meadow; (di giardino) lawn

pre'ambolo m preamble

preannunci'are vt give advance notice of

preavvi'sare vt forewarn. **preav-'viso** m warning

pre'cario adj precarious

precauzi'one f precaution; (cautela) care

prece'den|te adj previous ● m precedent. ∼**te'mente** adv previously.

∼**za** f precedence; (di veicoli) right of way; **dare la** ∼ **za** give way. **pre'ce-dere** vt precede

pre'cetto m precept

precipi'ta|re vt ∼**re le cose** precipitate events ● vi fall headlong; (situazione, eventi:) come to a head. ∼**rsi** vr (gettarsi) throw oneself; (affrettarsi) rush; ∼**rsi a fare qcsa** rush to do sth. ∼**zi'one** f (fretta) haste; (atmosferica) precipitation. **precipi-'toso** adj hasty; (avventato) reckless; (caduta) headlong

preci'pizio m precipice; **a** ∼ headlong

precisa'mente adv precisely

preci'sa|re vt specify; (spiegare) clarify. ∼**zi'one** f clarification

precisi'one f precision. **pre'ciso** adj precise; (ore) sharp; (identico) identical

pre'clu|dere vt preclude. ∼**so** pp di **precludere**

pre'coc|e adj precocious; (prematuro) premature

precon'cetto adj preconceived ● m prejudice

pre'corr|ere vt ∼**ere i tempi** be ahead of one's time

precur'sore m precursor

'preda f prey; (bottino) booty; **essere in** ∼ **al panico** be panic-stricken; **in** ∼ **alle fiamme** engulfed in flames. **pre'dare** vt plunder. ∼**'tore** m predator

predeces'sore mf predecessor

pre'del|la f platform. ∼**lino** m step

predesti'na|re vt predestine. ∼**to** adj (Relig) predestined, preordained

predetermi'nato adj predetermined, preordained

pre'detto pp di **predire**

'predica f sermon; fig lecture

predi'care vt preach

predi'le|tto, -a pp di **prediligere** ● adj favourite ● mf pet. ∼**zi'one** f predilection. **predi'ligere** vt prefer

pre'dire vt foretell

predi'spo|rre vt arrange. ~**rsi** vr
~**rsi a** prepare oneself for. ~**si-**
zi'one f predisposition; (al disogno ecc)
bent (a for). ~**sto** pp di predisporre

predi'lune f prediction

predomi'na|nte adj predominant.
~**re** vi predominate. **predo'minio** m
predominance

pre'done m robber

prefabbri'cato adj prefabricated
● m prefabricated building

prefazi'one f preface

prefe'renz|a f preference; di ~ a
preferably. ~**iale** adj preferential;
corsia ~**iale** bus and taxi lane

prefe'ribile adj preferable.
~**'mente** adv preferably

prefe'ri|re vt prefer. ~**to, -a** agg &
mf favourite

pre'fet|to m prefect. ~**tura** f pre-
fecture

prefiggersi vr be determined

pre'fisso pp di prefiggere ● m pre-
fix; (Teleph) [dialling] code

pre'ga|re vt/i pray; (supplicare) beg;
farsi ~ need persuading

pre'gevole adj valuable

preghi'era f prayer; (richiesta)
request

pregi'ato adj esteemed; (prezioso)
valuable. **'pregio** m esteem; (valore)
value; (di persona) good point; **di pre-**
gio valuable

pregiudi'ca|re vt prejudice; (dan-
neggiare) harm. ~**to** adj prejudiced
● m (Jur) previous offender

pregiu'dizio m prejudice; (danno)
detriment

'prego int (non c'è di che) don't mention it!; (por favore) please; ~**?** I beg
your pardon?

pregu'stare vt look forward to

pre'lato m prelate

prela'vaggio m prewash

preleva'mento m withdrawal.
prele'vare vt withdraw (denaro); collect (merci); (Med) take. **preli'evo** m
(di soldi) withdrawal; prelievo di sangue blood sample

prelimi'nare adj preliminary ● m
preliminari pl preliminaries

pre'ludio m prelude

prema'man m inv maternity dress
● adj maternity attrib

prema'turo, -a adj premature
● mf premature baby

premedi'ta|re vt premeditate.
~**zi'one** f premeditation

'premere vt press; (Comput) hit
(tasto) ● vi ~ **a** (importare) matter to;
mi preme sapere I need to know;
~ **su** press on; push (pulsante)

pre'messa f introduction

pre'me|sso pp di premettere.
~**sso che** bearing in mind that
(mettere prima) put before.

premi'a|re vt give a prize to; (ricom-
pensare) reward. ~**zi'one** f prize
giving

premi'nente adj pre-eminent

'premio m prize; (ricompensa) reward; (Comm) premium. ~ **di conso-**
lazione booby prize

premoni'|tore adj (sogno, segno)
premonitory. ~**zi'one** f premonition

premu'nir|e vt fortify. ~**si** vr take
protective measures; ~**si di** provide
oneself with; ~**si contro** protect
oneself against

pre'mu|ra f (fretta) hurry; (cura)
care. ~**'roso** adj thoughtful

prena'tale adj antenatal

'prender|e vt take; (afferrare) seize;
catch (treno, malattia, ladro, pesce);
have (cibo, bevanda); ● (far pagare)
charge; (assumere) take on; (ottenere)
get; (occupare) take up; ~**e informa-**
zioni make inquiries; ~**e a calci/**

prendisole *m inv* sundress

preno'ta|re *vt* book, reserve. ~**si** *vr* booked, reserved ~**zi'one** *f* booking, reservation

preoccu'pante *adj* alarming

preoccu'pa|re *vt* worry. ~**rsi** *vr* ~**rsi** worry (di about); ~**rsi di fare qcsa** take the trouble to do sth. ~**to** *adj* (*ansioso*) worried. ~**zi'one** *f* worry; (*apprensione*) concern

prepa'gato *adj* prepaid

prepa'ra|re *vt* prepare. ~**rsi** *vr* get ready. ~**tivi** *mpl* preparations. ~**to** *m* (*prodotto*) preparation. ~**torio** *adj* preparatory. ~**zi'one** *f* preparation

prepensiona'mento *m* early retirement

preponde'ran|te *adj* predominant. ~**za** *f* prevalence

pre'porre *vt* place before

preposizi'one *f* preposition

pre'posto *pp di* **preporre** ● *adj* ~ **a** (*addetto a*) in charge of

prepo'ten|te *adj* overbearing ● *mf* bully

preroga'tiva *f* prerogative

'presa *f* taking; (*conquista*) capture; (*stretta*) hold; (*di cemento ecc*) setting; (*Electr*) socket; (*pizzico*) pinch; **essere alle prese con** be struggling with; **a ~ rapida** (*cemento, colla*) quick-setting; **fare ~ su qcno** influence sb. **~ d'aria** air vent. **~ multipla** adaptor

pre'sagio *m* omen. **presa'gire** *vt* foretell

'presbite *adj* long-sighted

presbi'terio *m* presbytery

pre'scelto *adj* selected

pre'scindere *vt* ~ **da** leave aside; **a ~ da** apart from

presco'lare *adj* **in età** ~ preschool

pre'scri|tto *pp di* **prescrivere**

pre'scri|vere *vt* prescribe. ~**zi'one** *f* prescription; (*norma*) rule

preselezi'one *f* **chiamare qcno in ~** call sb via the operator

presen'ta|re *vt* present; (*far conoscere*) introduce; show (*documento*); (*inoltrare*) submit. ~**rsi** *vr* present oneself; (*farsi conoscere*) introduce oneself; (*a ufficio*) attend; (*alla polizia ecc*) report; (*come candidato*) stand, run; (*occasione:*) occur; ~**rsi bene/male** (*persona:*) make a good/bad impression; (*situazione:*) look good/bad. ~**tore**, ~**trice** *m* presenter; (*di notizie*) announcer. ~**zi'one** *f* presentation; (*per conoscersi*) introduction

pre'sente *adj* present; (*attuale*) current; (*questo*) this; **aver ~** remember ● *m* present; **i presenti** those present ● *f* **allegato alla ~** (*in lettera*) enclosed

presenti'mento *m* foreboding

pre'senza *f* presence; (*aspetto*) appearance; **in ~ di, alla ~ di** in the presence of; **di bella ~** personable. **~ di spirito** presence of mind

presenzi'are *vi* ~ **a** attend

pre'sepe *m*, **pre'sepio** *m* crib

Presepe The *presepe* (also called *presepio*) is a traditional nativity scene made with ceramic or wooden figures. Most homes have small ones and large-scale models are assembled in churches during Advent. *Presepi* from Naples, sometimes made of porcelain, are particularly prized.

---

pugni kick/punch; **quanto prende?** what do you charge?; ~**e una persona per un'altra** mistake a person for someone else ● *vi* (*voltare*) turn; (*attecchire*) take root; (*rapprendersi*) set; ~**e a destra/sinistra** turn right/left; ~**e a fare qcsa** start doing sth. ~**si** *vr* ~**si a pugni** come to blows; ~**si cura di** take care of (*ammalato*)

prendi'sole *m inv* sundress

preser'va|re vt preserve; (*proteggere*) protect (**da** from). **~'tivo** m condom. **~zi'one** f preservation

'preside m headmaster; (*Univ*) dean ●f headmistress; (*Univ*) dean

presi'den|te m chairman; (*Pol*) president ●f chairwoman; (*Pol*) president. **~ del consiglio [dei ministri]** Prime Minister. **~ della repubblica** President of the Republic. **~za** f presidency; (*di assemblea*) chairmanship

presidi'are vt garrison. **pre'sidio** m garrison

presi'edere vt preside over

'preso pp di **prendere**

'pressa f (*Mech*) press

pres'sante adj urgent

pressap'poco adv about

pres'sare vt press

pressi'one f pressure. **~ del sangue** blood pressure

'presso prep near; (*a casa di*) with; (*negli indirizzi*) care of, c/o; (*lavorare*) for ●**pressi** mpl: **nei pressi di...** in the neighbourhood o vicinity of...

pressoché adv almost

pressuriz'za|re vt pressurize. **~to** adj pressurized

prestabil'li|re vt arrange in advance. **~to** adj agreed

prestam'pato adj printed ●m (*modulo*) form

pre'stante adj good-looking

pre'star|e vt lend; **~e attenzione** pay attention; **~e aiuto** lend a hand; **farsi ~e** borrow (**da** from). **~si** vr (*frase*): lend itself; (*persona*): offer

prestazi'one f performance; **prestazioni** pl (*servizi*) services

prestigia'tore, -'trice mf conjurer

pre'stigi|o m prestige; **gioco di ~o** conjuring trick. **~'oso** m pres-

tigious

'prestito m loan; **dare in ~** lend; **prendere in ~** borrow

'presto adv soon; (*di buon'ora*) early; (*in fretta*) quickly; **a ~** see you soon; **al più ~** as soon as possible; **~ o tardi** sooner or later

pre'sumere vt presume; (*credere*) think

presu'mibile adj **è ~ che...** presumably,...

pre'sunto adj (*colpevole*) presumed

presun'tu|oso adj presumptuous. **~zi'one** f presumption

presup'po|rre vt suppose; (*richiedere*) presuppose. **~sizi'one** f presupposition. **~sto** m essential requirement

'prete m priest

preten'den|te mf pretender ●m (*corteggiatore*) suitor

preten|dere vt (*pretesa*) claim; (*esigere*) demand ●vi **~dere a** claim to; **~dere di** (*esigere*) demand to. **~si'one** f pretension. **~zi'oso** adj pretentious

pre'tes|a f pretension; (*esigenza*) claim; **senza ~e** unpretentious. **~o** pp di **pretendere**

pre'testo m pretext

pre'tore m magistrate

pre'tura f magistrate's court

preva'le|nte adj prevalent. **~nte-'mente** adv primarily. **~nza** f prevalence. **~re** vi prevail

pre'valso pp di **prevalere**

preve'dere vt foresee; forecast (*tempo*); (*legge ecc:*) provide for

preve'nire vt precede; (*evitare*) prevent; (*avvertire*) forewarn

preven'ti|vare vt estimate; (*aspettarsi*) budget for. **~vo** adj preventive ●m (*Comm*) estimate

preve'nuto adj forewarned; (*mal*)

disposto) prejudiced. **~zi'one** *f* prevention; (*preconcetto*) prejudice

previ'den|te *adj* provident. **~za** *f* foresight. **~za sociale** social security, welfare *Am.* **~zi'ale** *adj* provident

'previo *adj* ~ **pagamento** on payment

previsi'one *f* forecast; **in** ~ **di** in anticipation of

pre'visto *pp di* prevedere ● *adj* foreseen ● *m* **più/meno/prima del** ~ more/less/earlier than expected

prezi'oso *adj* precious

prez'zemolo *m* parsley

'prezzo *m* price. ~ **di fabbrica** factory price. ~ **all'ingrosso** wholesale price. **[a] metà** ~ half price

prigi'on|e *f* prison; (*pena*) imprisonment. **prigio'nia** *f* imprisonment. **~i'ero, -a** *adj* imprisoned ● *mf* prisoner

'prima *adv* before; (*più presto*) earlier; (*in primo luogo*) first; ~, **finiamo questo** let's finish this first; ~ **o poi** sooner or later; **quanto** ~ as soon as possible ● *prep* ~ **di** before; ~ **d'ora** before now ● *conj* ~ **che** before ● *f* first class; (*Theat*) first night; (*Auto*) first [gear]

pri'mario *adj* primary; (*principale*) principal

pri'mat|e *m* primate. **~o** *m* supremacy; *Sport* record

prima've|ra *f* spring. **~'rile** *adj* spring *attrib*

primeggi'are *vi* excel

primi'tivo *adj* primitive; (*originario*) original

pri'mizie *fpl* early produce *sg*

'primo *adj* first; (*fondamentale*) principal; (*precedente di due*) former; (*iniziale*) early; (*migliore*) best ● *m* first; **primi** *pl* (*i primi giorni*) the beginning; **in un** ~ **tempo** at first. **prima copia** master copy

---

primordi'ale *adj* primordial

'primula *f* primrose

princi'pale *adj* main ● *m* head, boss 🔽

princi'pa|le *adj* principality. **'prin'cipe** *m* prince. **~'pessa** *f* princess

principi'ante *mf* beginner

prin'cipio *m* beginning; (*concetto*) principle; (*causa*) cause; **per** ~ on principle

pri'ore *m* prior

priori|tà *f inv* priority. **~'tario** *adj* having priority

'prisma *m* prism

pri'va|re *vt* deprive. **~rsi** *vr* deprive oneself

privatizzazi'one *f* privatization. **pri'vato, -a** *adj* private ● *mf* private citizen

privazi'one *f* deprivation

privilegi'are *vt* privilege; (*considerare più importante*) favour. **privi'legio** *m* privilege

'privo *adj* ~ **di** devoid of; (*mancante*) lacking in

pro *prep* for ● *m* advantage; **a che** ~? what's the point?

pro'babil|e *adj* probable. **~ità** *f inv* probability. **~'mente** *adv* probably

pro'ble|ma *m* problem. **~'matico** *adj* problematic

pro'boscide *f* trunk

procacci'ar|e *vt*, **~si** *vr* obtain

pro'cace (*ragazza*) provocative

pro'ced|ere *vi* proceed; (*iniziare*)

start; **~ere contro** (*Jur*) start legal proceedings against. **~i'mento** m process; (*Jur*) proceedings pl. **proce'dura** f procedure

proces'sare vt (*Jur*) try

processi'one f procession

pro'cesso m process; (*Jur*) trial

proces'sore m processor

processu'ale adj trial

pro'cinto m **essere in ~ di** be about to

pro'clama m proclamation

procla'mare vt proclaim. **~zi'one** f proclamation

procreazi'one f procreation

pro'cura f power of attorney; **per ~** by proxy

procu'rare vt/i procure; (*causare*) cause; (*cercare*) try. **~'tore** m attorney. **P~tore Generale** Attorney General. **~tore legale** lawyer. **~tore della repubblica** public prosecutor

'prode adj brave. **pro'dezza** f bravery

prodi'gare vt lavish. **~si** vr do one's best

pro'digio m prodigy. **~'oso** adj prodigious

pro'dotto pp di **produrre** ● m product. **prodotti agricoli** farm produce sg. **~ derivato** by-product. **~ interno lordo** gross domestic product. **~ nazionale lordo** gross national product

pro'durre vt produce. **~rsi** vr (*attore*) play; (*accadere*) happen. **~ttività** f productivity. **~t'tivo** adj productive. **~t'tore, ~t'trice** mf producer. **~zi'one** f production

Prof. abbr (*Professore*) Prof.

profa'nare vt desecrate

profe'rire vt utter

Prof.essa abbr (*Professoressa*) Prof.

profes'sare vt profess; practise (*professione*)

professio'nale adj professional

professi'one f profession; **libera ~ne** profession. **~'nismo** m professionalism. **~'nista** mf professional

profes'sore, -'essa mf (*Sch*) teacher; (*Univ*) lecturer; (*titolare di cattedra*) professor

pro'feta m prophet

pro'ficuo adj profitable

profi'lare vt outline; (*ornare*) border; (*Aeron*) streamline. **~si** vr stand out

profi'lattico adj prophylactic ● m condom

pro'filo m profile; (*breve studio*) outline; **di ~** in profile

profit'tare vi **~ di** (*avvantaggiarsi*) profit by; (*approfittare*) take advantage of. **pro'fitto** m profit; (*vantaggio*) advantage

profonda'mente adv deeply, profoundly. **~ità** f inv depth

pro'fondo adj deep; fig profound; (*cultura*) great

'profugo, -a mf refugee

profu'mare vt perfume. **~si** vr put on perfume

profu'mato adj (*fiore*) fragrant; (*fazzoletto ecc*) scented

profume'ria f perfumery. **pro'fumo** m perfume, scent

profusi'one f profusion; **a ~** in profusion. **pro'fuso** pp di **profondere** ● adj profuse

proget'tare vt plan. **~'tista** mf designer. **pro'getto** m plan; (*di lavoro importante*) project. **progetto di legge** bill

prog'nosi f inv prognosis; **in ~ riservata** on the danger list

pro'gramma m programme; (*Comput*) program. **~ scolastico** syllabus

program'mare vt programme; (*Comput*) program. **~'tore, ~'trice** mf [computer] programmer. **~zi'one** f programming

progre'dire vi [make] progress

progres'sione f progression.

~'sivo adj progressive. **pro'gresso** m progress

proi'bi|re vt forbid. **~'tivo** adj prohibitive. **~to** adj forbidden. **~zi'one** f prohibition

proie|t'tare vt project; show (film). **~'tore** m projector; (Auto) headlight

proi'ettile m bullet

proiezi'one f projection

'prole f offspring. **prole'tario** agg & m proletarian

prolife'rare vi proliferate. **pro'lifico** adj prolific

pro'lisso adj verbose, prolix

'prologo m prologue

pro'lunga f (Electr) extension

prolun'gar|e vt prolong; (allungare) lengthen; extend (contratto, scadenza). **~si** vr continue; **~si su** (dilungarsi) dwell upon

prome'moria m memo; (per se stessi) reminder, note; (formale) memorandum

pro'me|ssa f promise. **~sso** pp di **promettere**. **~ttere** vt/i promise

promet'tente adj promising

promi'nente adj prominent

promiscuità f promiscuity. **pro'miscuo** adj promiscuous

promon'torio m promontory

pro'mo|sso pp di **promuovere** ● adj (Sch) who has gone up a year; (Univ) who has passed an exam. **~tore**, **~trice** mf promoter

promozio'nale adj promotional. **promozi'one** f promotion

promul'gare vt promulgate

promu'overe vt promote; (Sch) move up a class

proni'pote m (di bisnonno) great-grandson; (di prozio) great-nephew ●f (di bisnonno) great-granddaughter; (di prozio) great-niece

pro'nome m pronoun

pronosti'care vt forecast. **pro'nostico** m forecast

pron'tezza f readiness; (rapidità) quickness

'pronto adj ready; (rapido) quick; **~!** (Teleph) hello!; **tenersi ~** be ready (per for); **pronti, via!** (in gara) ready! steady! go!. **~ soccorso** first aid; (in ospedale) accident and emergency

prontu'ario m handbook

pro'nuncia f pronunciation

pronunci'a|re vt pronounce; (dire) utter; deliver (discorso). **~rsi** vr (su un argomento) give one's opinion. **~to** adj pronounced; (prominente) prominent

pro'nunzia ecc = **PRONUNCIA** ecc

propa'ganda f propaganda

propa'ga|re vt propagate. **~rsi** vr spread. **~zi'one** f propagation

prope'deutico adj introductory

pro'pen|dere vi **~dere per** be in favour of. **~so** pp di **propendere** ● adj **essere ~so a fare qcsa** be inclined to do sth

propi'nare vt administer

pro'pizio adj favourable

proponi'mento m resolution

pro'por|re vt propose; (suggerire) suggest. **~si** vr set oneself (obiettivo, meta); **~si di** intend to

proporzio'na|le adj proportional. **~re** vt proportion. **proporzi'one** f proportion

pro'posito m purpose; **a ~** by the way; **a ~ di** with regard to; **di ~** (apposta) on purpose

proposizi'one f clause; (frase) sentence

pro'post|a f proposal. **~o** pp di **proporre**

proprietà f inv property; (diritto) ownership; (correttezza) propriety. **~ immobiliare** property. **~ privata** private property. **proprie'taria** f owner; (di casa affittata) landlady. **proprie'tario** m owner; (di casa affittata) landlord

'proprio adj one's [own]; (caratteristico) typical; (appropriato) proper ● adv just; (veramente) really; **non ~** not really, not exactly; (affatto) not… at all ● pron one's own ● m one's [own]; **lavorare in ~** be one's own boss; **mettersi in ~** set up on one's own

propul|si'one f propulsion. **~'sore** m propeller

'proroga f extension

proro'ga|bile adj extendable. **~re** vt extend

pro'rompere vi burst out

'prosa f prose. **pro'saico** adj prosaic

pro'scio|gliere vt release; (Jur) acquit. **~lto** pp di prosciogliere

prosciu'gare vt dry up; (bonificare) reclaim. **~si** vr dry up

prosci'utto m ham. **~ cotto** cooked ham. **~ crudo** Parma ham

pro'scri|tto, -a pp di proscrivere ● m f exile

prosecuzi'one f continuation

prosegui'mento m continuation; **buon ~!** (viaggio) have a good journey!; (festa) enjoy the rest of the party!

prosegu'ire vt continue ● vi go on, continue

prospe'r|are vi prosper. **~ità** f prosperity. **'prospero** adj prosperous; (favorevole) favourable. **~oso** adj flourishing; (ragazza) buxom

prospet'tar|e vt show. **~si** vr seem

prospet'tiva f perspective; (panorama) view; fig prospect. **pro'spetto** m (vista) view; (facciata) façade; (tabella) table

prospici'ente adj facing

prossima'mente adv soon

prossimità f proximity

'prossimo, -a adj near; (seguente) next; (molto vicino) close; **l'anno ~** next year ● m f neighbour

prosti'tu|ta f prostitute. **~zi'one** f prostitution

protago'nista mf protagonist

pro'teggere vt protect; (favorire) favour

prote'ina f protein

pro'tender|e vt stretch out. **~si** vr (in avanti) lean out. **pro'teso** pp di protendere

pro'te|sta f protest; (dichiarazione) protestation. **~'stante** adj & mf Protestant. **~'stare** vt/i protest

protet'tivo adj protective. **~tto** pp di proteggere. **~t'tore, -t'trice** mf protector; (sostenitore) patron ● m (di prostituta) pimp. **~zi'one** f protection

protocol'lare adj (visita) protocol ● vt register

proto'collo m protocol; (registro) register; **carta ~** official stamped paper

proto'tipo m prototype

pro'tra|rre vt protract; (differire) postpone. **~rsi** vr go on, continue. **~tto** pp di protrarre

protube'ran|te adj protuberant. **~za** f protuberance

'prova f test; (dimostrazione) proof; (tentativo) try; Sport heat; (Theat) rehearsal; (buzza) proof; **in ~** (assumere) for a trial period; **mettere alla ~** put to the test. **~ generale** dress rehearsal

pro'var|e vt test; (dimostrare) prove; (tentare) try; try on (abiti ecc); (sentire) feel; (Theat) rehearse. **~si** vr try

prove'nienza f origin. **prove'nire** vi provenire da come from

pro'vento m proceeds pl

prove'nuto pp di provenire

pro'verbio m proverb

pro'vetta f test-tube; **bambino in ~** test-tube baby

pro'vetto adj skilled

'provider m inv ISP, Internet Service Provider

pro'vinci|a f province; (strada) B road, secondary road. **~'ale** adj provincial; **strada ~ale** B road

pro'vino m specimen; Cinema screen test

provo'ca|nte adj provocative. **~re** vt provoke; (causare) cause. **~'tore**, **~'trice** mf trouble-maker. **~'torio** adj provocative. **~zi'one** f provocation

provve'd|ere vi **~ere** a provide for. **~i'mento** m measure; (previdenza) precaution

provvi'denz|a f providence. **~i'ale** adj providential

provvigi'one f commission

provvi'sorio adj provisional

prov'vista f supply

pro'zio, -a m great-uncle •f great-aunt

'prua f prow

pru'den|te adj prudent. **~za** f prudence; **per ~za** as a precaution

'prudere vi itch

'prugn|a f plum. **~a secca** prune. **~o** m plum[-tree]

pru'rito m itch.

pseu'donimo m pseudonym

psica'na|lisi f psychoanalysis. **~'lista** mf psychoanalyst. **~liz'zare** vt psychoanalyse

'psiche f psyche

psichi'a|tra mf psychiatrist. **~'tria** f psychiatry. **~'trico** adj psychiatric

'psichico adj mental

psico|lo'gia f psychology. **~'lo-gico** adj psychological. **psi'cologo, -a** mf psychologist

psico'patico, -a m psychopath

PT abbr (Posta e Telecomunicazioni) PO

pubbli'ca|re vt publish. **~zi'one** f publication. **~zioni** pl (di matrimonio) banns

pubbli'cista mf Journ correspondent

pubblicità f inv publicity; (annuncio) advertisement, advert; **fare ~ a qcsa** advertise sth; **piccola ~** small advertisements. **pubblici'tario** adj advertising

'pubblico adj public; **scuola pubblica** state school •m public; (spettatori) audience; **grande ~** general public. **Pubblica Sicurezza** Police. **~ ufficiale** civil servant

'pube m pubis

puber'tà f puberty

pu'dico adj modest

pue'rile adj children's; pej childish

pugi'lato m boxing. **'pugile** m boxer

pugna'la|re vt stab. **~ta** f stab. **pu'gnale** m dagger

'pugno m fist; (colpo) punch; (manciata) fistful; (numero limitato) handful; **dare un ~ a** punch

'pulce f flea; (microfono) bug

pul'cino m chick; (nel calcio) junior

pu'ledra f filly

pu'ledro m colt

pu'li|re vt clean. **~re a secco** dry-clean. **~to** adj clean. **~'tura** f cleaning. **~'zia** f (il pulire) cleaning; (l'essere pulito) cleanliness; **~zie** pl housework; **fare le ~zie** do the cleaning

'pullman m inv bus, coach; (urbano) bus

pul'mino m minibus

'pulpito m pulpit

pul'sante m button; (Electr) [push-]button. **~ di accensione** on/off switch

pul'sa|re vi pulsate. **~zi'one** f pulsation

pul'viscolo m dust

'puma m inv puma

pun'gente adj prickly; (insetto) stinging; (odore ecc) sharp

'punger|e vt prick; (insetto:) sting

pungigli'one m sting

pu'ni|re vt punish. **~'tivo** adj punitive. **~zi'one** f punishment; *Sport* tree kick

'punta f point; (*estremità*) tip; (*di monte*) peak; (*un po'*) pinch, *Sport* forward; **doppie punte** (*di capelli*) split ends

pun'tare vt point; (*spingere con forza*) push; (*scommettere*) bet; (**⚀**: *appuntare*) fasten ● vi ~ **su** fig rely on; ~ **verso** (*dirigersi*) head for; ~ **a** aspire to

punta'spilli m inv pincushion

pun'tat|a f (*di una storia*) instalment; (*televisiva*) episode; (*al gioco*) stake, bet; (*breve visita*) flying visit; **a ~e** serialized, in instalments

punteggia'tura f punctuation

pun'teggio m score

puntel'lare vt prop. **pun'tello** m prop

pun'tiglio m spite; (*ostinazione*) obstinacy. **~'oso** adj punctilious, pernickety pej

pun'tin|a f (*da disegno*) drawing pin, thumb tack Am (*di giradischi*) stylus. **~o** m dot; **a ~o** perfectly; (*cotto*) to a T

'punto m point; (*Med, in cucito*) stitch; (*in punteggiatura*) full stop; **in che ~** where, exactly?; **due punti** colon; **in ~** sharp; **mettere a ~** put right; fig fine tune; tune up (*motore*); **essere sul ~ di fare qcsa** be about to do sth, be on the point of doing sth. **~ esclamativo** exclamation mark. **~ interrogativo** question mark. **~ nero** (*Med*) blackhead. **~ di riferimento** landmark; (*per la qualità*) benchmark. **~ di vendita** point of sale. **~ e virgola** semicolon. **~ di vista** point of view

puntu'al|e adj punctual. **~ità** f punctuality. **~'mente** adv punctually

pun'tura f (*di insetto*) sting; (*di ago ecc*) prick; (*Med*) puncture; (*iniezione*) injection; (*fitta*) stabbing pain

punzecchi'are vt prick; fig tease

'pupa f doll. **pu'pazzo** m puppet.

pupazzo di neve snowman

pup'illa f (*Anat*) pupil

pu'pillo, -a mf (*di professore*) favourite

purché conj provided

'pure adv too, also; (*concessivo*) fate **~ I please do!** ● pupil (*tuttavia*) yet; (*anche se*) even if; **pur di** just to

purè m inv purée. **~ di patate** creamed potatoes

pu'rezza f purity

'purga f purge. **pur'gante** m laxative. **pur'gare** vt purge

purga'torio m purgatory

purifi'care vt purify

puri'tano, -a adj & mf Puritan

'puro adj pure; (*vino ecc*) undiluted; **per ~ caso** purely by chance

puro'sangue adj & m thoroughbred

pur'troppo adv unfortunately

pus m pus. **'pustola** f pimple

puti'ferio m uproar

putre'far|e vi, **~si** vr putrefy

'putrido adj putrid

'puzza f = PUZZO

puz'zare vi stink; **~ di bruciato** fig smell fishy

'puzzo m stink, bad smell. **~la** f polecat. **~'lente** adj stinking

p.zza abbr (piazza) Sq.

. . . .

Qq

. . . .

qua adv here; **da un anno in ~** for the last year; **da quando in ~?** since when?; **di ~** this way; **di ~ di** on this side of; **~ dentro** in here; **~ sotto** under here; **~ vicino** near here; **~ e là** here and there

qua'derno m exercise book; (*per*

appunti) notebook

quadrango'lare adj (forma) quadrangular. **qua'drangolo** m quadrangle

qua'drante m quadrant; (di orologio) dial

qua'dra|re vt square; (contabilità) balance ● vi fit in. **~to** adj square; (equilibrato) level-headed ● m square; (pugilato) ring; **al ~to** squared

quadret'tato adj squared; (carta) graph attrib. **qua'dretto** m square; (piccolo quadro) small picture; **a quadretti** (tessuto) check

quadrien'nale adj (che dura quattro anni) four-year

quadri'foglio m four-leaf clover

quadri'latero m quadrilateral

quadri'mestre m four-month period

'quadro m picture, painting; (quadrato) square; (fig: scena) sight; (tabella) table; (Theat) scene; (Comm) executive **quadri** pl (carte) diamonds; **a quadri** (tessuto, giacca, motivo) check. **quadri** pl **direttivi** senior management

quaggiù adv down here

'quaglia f quail

'qualche adj (alcuni) a few, some; (un certo) some; (in interrogazioni) any; **ho ~ problema** I have a few problems, I have some problems; **~ tempo fa** some time ago; **~ libro italiano?** have you any Italian books?; **posso pren-dere ~ libro?** can I take some books?; **in ~ modo** somehow; **in ~ posto** somewhere; **~ volta** sometimes; **~ cosa =** QUALCOSA

qual'cosa pron something; (in interrogazioni) anything; **~'altro** something else; **vuoi ~'altro?** would you like anything else?; **~a di strano** something strange; **vuoi ~a da mangiare?** would you like something to eat?

qual'cuno pron someone, somebody; (in interrogazioni) anyone, anybody; (alcuni) some; (in interrogazioni) any; **c'è ~?** is anybody in?; **qualcun altro** someone else, somebody else; **c'è qualcun altro che aspetta?** is anybody else waiting?; **ho letto ~ dei suoi libri** I've read some of his books; **conosci ~ dei suoi amici?** do you know any of his friends?

'quale adj which; (indeterminato) what; (come) as, like; **~ macchina è la tua?** which car is yours?; **~ motivo avrà di parlare così?** what reason would he have to speak like that?; **~ onore!** what an honour!; **città quali Venezia** towns like Venice; **~ che sia la tua opinione** whatever you may think ● pron inter which [one]; **~ preferisci?** which [one] do you prefer? ● pron rel **il/la ~** (persona) who; (animale, cosa) that, which; (oggetto: con prep) whom; (animale, cosa) which; **ho incontrato tua madre, la ~ mi ha detto...** I met your mother, who told me...; **l'ufficio nel ~ lavoro** the office in which I work; **l'uomo con il ~ parlavo** the man to whom I was speaking ● adv (come) as

qua'lifica f qualification; (titolo) title

qualifi'ca|re vt qualify; (definire) define. **~rsi** vr be placed. **~'tivo** adj qualifying. **~to** adj (operaio) semi-skilled. **~zi'one** f qualification

qualità f inv quality; (specie) kind; **in ~ di** in one's capacity as. **qualita'tivo** adj qualitative

qua'lora conj in case

qual'siasi, qua'lunque adj any; (non importa quale) whatever; (ordinario) ordinary; **dammi una penna ~** give me any pen [whatsoever]; **farei ~ cosa** I would do anything; **~ cosa io faccia** whatever I do; **~ persona** anyone; **in ~ caso** in any case; **una ~** any one, whichever; **l'uomo ~** lunque the man in the street

qualunqu'ismo *m* lack of political views

'quando *conj & adv* when; **da ~ ti ho visto** since I saw you; **da ~ esci con lui?** how long have you been going out with him?; **da ~ in qua?** since when?; **~... ~...** sometimes..., sometimes...

quantifi'care *vt* quantify

quantità *f inv* quantity; **una ~ di** (*gran numero*) a great deal of. **quantita'tivo** *m* amount ● *adj* quantitative

● *adj inter* how much; (*con nomi plurali*) how many; (*in esclamazione*) what a lot of; **~ tempo?** how long?; **quanti anni hai?** how old are you?

● *adj rel* as much... as; (*con nomi plurali*) as many... as; **prendi ~ denaro ti serve** take as much money as you need; **prendi quanti libri vuoi** take as many books as you like

● *pron inter* how much; (*quanto tempo*) how long; (*plurale*) how many; **quanti ne abbiamo oggi?** what date is it today?, what's the date today?

● *pron rel* as much as; (*quanto tempo*) as long as; (*plurale*) as many as; **prendine ~/quanti ne vuoi** take as much/as many as you like; **stai ~ vuoi** stay as long as you like; **questo è ~** that's it

● *adv inter* how much; (*quanto tempo*) how long; **~ sei alto?** how tall are you?; **~ hai aspettato?** how long did you wait for?; **~ costa?** how much is it?; **~ mi dispiace!** I'm so sorry!; **~ è bello!** how nice!

● *adv rel* as much as; **lavoro ~ posso** I work as much as I can; **è tanto intelligente ~ bello**

he's as intelligent as he's good-looking; **in ~** (*in qualità di*) as; (*poiché*) since; **in ~ a me** as far as I'm concerned; **per ~ however**; **per ~ ne sappia** as far as I know; **per ~ mi riguarda** as far as I'm concerned; **per ~** as for; **~ prima** (*al più presto*) as soon as possible

quan'tunque *conj* although

qua'ranta *adj & m* forty

quaran'tena *f* quarantine

quaran'tenne *adj* forty-year-old. **~io** *m* period of forty years

quaran'tesimo. ~ina *f una ~ina* about forty

qua'resima *f* Lent

quar'tetto *m* quartet

quarti'ere *m* district; (*Mil*) quarters *pl*. **~ generale** headquarters

quarto *adj* fourth ● *m* fourth; (*quarta parte*) quarter; **le sette e un ~** a quarter past seven; **quarti** *pl* **di finale** quarterfinals. **~ d'ora** quarter of an hour. **quar'tultimo, -a** *mf* fourth from the end

'quarzo *m* quartz

'quasi *adv* almost, nearly; **~ mai** hardly ever ● *conj* (*come se*) as if; **~ sto a casa** I'm tempted to stay home

quas'sù *adv* up here

'quatto *adj* crouching; (*silenzioso*) silent

quat'tordici *adj & m* fourteen

quat'trini *mpl* money *sg*

'quattro *adj & m* four; **dirne ~ a qcno** give sb a piece of one's mind; **farsi in ~** (*per qcno/per fare qcsa*) go to a lot of trouble (for sb/to do sth); **in ~ e quattr'otto** in a flash. **~ per ~** *m inv* (*Auto*) four-wheel drive [vehicle]

quat'trocchi: a ~ *adv* in private

quattro'cento *adj & m* four hundred; **il Q~cento** the fifteenth century

quattro'mila adj & m four thousand

'quell|o adj that (pl those); **quell'albero** that tree; **quegli alberi** those trees; **quel cane** that dog; **quei cani** those dogs ● pron that (pl those); ~**o** li that one over there; ~**o che** the one that; (ciò che) what; **quelli che** the ones that, those that; ~**o a destra** the one on the right

'quercia f oak

que'rela f [legal] action

quere'lare vt bring an action against

que'sito m question

questio'nario m questionnaire

quest'ione f question; (faccenda) matter; (litigio) quarrel; **in** ~ in doubt; **è fuori** ~ it's out of the question

'quest|o adj this (pl these) ● pron this [one] (pl these [ones]); ~**o qui**, ~**o qua** this one here; ~**o è quello che ha detto** that's what he said; **per** ~**o** for this or that reason. **que-st'oggi** today

que'store m chief of police

que'stura f police headquarters

qui adv here; **da** ~ **in poi** from now on; **fin** ~ (di tempo) up till now, until now; ~ **dentro** in here; ~ **sotto** under here; ~ **vicino** near here ● m ~ **pro quo** misunderstanding

quie'scienza f trattamento di ~ retirement package

quie'tanza f receipt

quie'tar|e vt calm. ~**si** vr quieten down

qui'et|e f quiet; **disturbo della** ~**e pubblica** breach of the peace. ~**o** adj quiet

'quindi adv then ● conj therefore

'quindi|ci adj & m fifteen. ~**'cina** f **una** ~**cina** about fifteen; **una** ~**cina di giorni** two weeks pl

quinquen'nale adj (che dura cinque anni) five-year. **quin'quennio** m [period of] five years

quin'tale m a hundred kilograms

'quinte fpl (Theat) wings

quin'tetto m quintet

'quinto adj fifth

quin'tuplo adj quintuple

'quota f quota; (rata) instalment; (altitudine) height; (Aeron) altitude, height; (ippica) odds pl; **perdere** ~ lose altitude; **prendere** ~ gain altitude. ~ **di iscrizione** entry fee

quo'ta|re vt (Comm) quote. ~**to** adj quoted; **essere** ~**to in Borsa** be quoted on the Stock Exchange. ~**zi'one** f quotation

quotidi'ana|mente adv daily. ~**'ano** adj (giornaliero); (ordinario) everyday ● m daily [paper]

quozi'ente m quotient. ~ **d'intelligenza** intelligence quotient, IQ

Rr

ra'barbaro m rhubarb

'rabbia f rage; (ira) anger; (Med) rabies sg; **che** ~ **!** what a nuisance!; **mi fa** ~ it makes me angry

rab'bino m rabbi

rabbiosa'mente adv furiously

rabbi'oso adj hot-tempered; (Med) rabid; (violento) violent

rabbo'nir|e vt pacify. ~**si** vr calm down

rabbrivi'dire vi shudder; (di freddo) shiver

rabbui'arsi vr become dark

raccapez'zar|e vt put together. ~**si** vr see one's way ahead

raccapricci'ante adj horrifying

raccatta'palle m inv ball boy ●f inv ball girl

raccat'tare vt pick up

rac'chetta f racket. ~ **da ping pong** table-tennis bat. ~ **da sci** ski pole. ~ **da tennis** tennis racket

racchi'udere vt contain

rac'cogli|ere vt pick; (da terra) pick up; (mietere) harvest; (collezionare) collect; (radunare) gather; win (voti ecc); (dare asilo a) take in. ~**ersi** vr gather; (concentrarsi) collect one's thoughts. ~**'mento** m concentration. ~**'tore**, ~**'trice** mf collector ● m (cartella) ring binder

rac'colto, **-a** pp di **raccogliere** ● adj (rannicchiato) hunched; (intimo) cosy; (concentrato) engrossed ● m (mietitura) harvest ●f (di scritti) compilation; (del grano ecc) harvesting; (adunata) gathering

raccoman'dabile adj recommendable; **poco** ~ (persona) shady

raccoman'da|re vt recommend; (affidare) entrust. ~**rsi** vr (implorare) beg. ~**ta** f registered letter; ~**ta con ricevuta di ritorno** recorded delivery. ~**ta-espresso** f next-day delivery of recorded items. ~**zi'one** f recommendation

raccon'tare vt tell. **rac'conto** m story

raccorci'are vt shorten

raccor'dare vt join. **rac'cordo** m connection; (stradale) feeder. **raccordo anulare** ring road. **raccordo ferroviario** siding

ra'chitico adj rickety; (poco sviluppato) stunted

racimo'lare vt scrape together

'racket m inv racket

'radar m inv radar

raddol'cir|e vt sweeten; fig soften. ~**si** vr become milder; (carattere:) mellow

raddoppi'are vt double. **rad'doppio** m doubling

raddriz'zare vt straighten

'rader|e vt shave; graze (muro); ~**e al suolo** raze. ~**si** vr shave

radi'are vt strike off; ~ **dall'albo** strike off

radia'tore m radiator. ~**zi'one** f radiation

'radica f briar

radi'cale adj radical ● m (Gram) root; (Pol) radical

ra'dicchio m chicory

ra'dice f root

'radio f inv radio; **via** ~ by radio. ~ **a transistor** transistor radio ● m (Chem) radium

radioama'tore, **-'trice** mf [radio] ham

radioascolta'tore, **-'trice** mf listener

radioat|tività f radioactivity. ~**'tivo** adj radioactive

radio'cro|naca f radio commentary; **fare la** ~**naca di** commentate on. ~**nista** mf radio reporter

radiodiffusi'one f broadcasting

radio'fonico adj radio attrib

radiogra'fare vt X-ray. ~**'fia** f X-ray [photograph]; (radiologia) radiography; **fare una** ~**fia** (paziente:) have an X-ray; (dottore:) take an X ray

radio'lina f transistor

radi'ologo, **-a** mf radiologist

radi'oso adj radiant

radio'sveglia f radio alarm

'radio'taxi m inv radio taxi

radiote'lefono m radiotelephone; (privato) cordless [phone]

radiotelevi'sivo adj broadcasting attrib

'rado adj sparse; (non frequente) rare, **di** ~ seldom

radu'nar|e vt, ~**si** vr gather [together]. **ra'duno** m meeting; Sport rally

ra'dura f clearing

r

'**rafano** m horseradish

raf'fermo adj stale

'raffica f gust; (di armi da fuoco) burst; (di domande) barrage

raffigu'ra|re vt represent. ~zi'one f representation

raffi'na|re vt refine. ~ta'mente adv elegantly. ~to adj refined. **raffine'ria** f refinery

rafforza|'mento m reinforcement; (di muscolatura) strengthening. ~re vt reinforce. ~'tivo m (Gram) intensifier

raffredda'mento m (processo) cooling

raffred'd|are vt cool. ~arsi vr get cold; (prendere un raffreddore) catch a cold. ~ore m cold. ~ore da fieno hay fever

raf'fronto m comparison

'**rafia** f raffia

Rag. abbr **ragioniere**

ra'gaz|za f girl; (fidanzata) girlfriend. ~za alla pari au pair [girl]. ~'zata f prank. ~zo m boy; (fidanzato) boyfriend

ragge'lar|e vt fig freeze. ~si vr fig turn to ice

raggi'ante adj radiant; ~ di successo flushed with success

raggi'era f a ~ with a pattern like spokes radiating from a centre

'**raggio** m ray; (Math) radius; (di ruota) spoke; ~ **d'azione** range. ~ **laser** laser beam

raggi'rare vt trick. **rag'giro** m trick

raggi'un|gere vt reach; (conseguire) achieve. ~'gibile adj (luogo) within reach

raggomito'lar|e vt wind. ~si vr curl up

raggranel'lare vt scrape together

raggrin'zir|e vt, ~si vr wrinkle

raggrup|pa'mento m (gruppo) group; (azione) grouping. ~'pare vt group together

raggu'agli|are vt compare; (informare) inform. **ragg'uaglio** m comparison; (informazione) information

ragguar'devole adj considerable

'**ragia** f resin; **acqua** ~ turpentine

ragiona'mento m reasoning; (discussione) discussion. **ragio'nare** vi reason; (discutere) discuss

ragi'one f reason; (ciò che è giusto) right; **a** ~ **o a torto** rightly or wrongly; **aver** ~ be right; **perdere la** ~ go out of one's mind

ragione'ria f accountancy

ragio'nevol|e adj reasonable. ~'mente adv reasonably

ragioni'ere, -a mf accountant

ragli'are vi bray

ragna'tela f cobweb. '**ragno** m spider

ragù m inv meat sauce

RAI f abbr (Radio Audizioni Italiane) Italian public broadcasting company

ralle'gra|re vt gladden. ~rsi vr rejoice; ~rsi con qcno congratulate sb. ~'menti mpl congratulations

rallenta'mento m slowing down

rallen'ta|re vt/i slow down; (allentare) slacken. ~rsi vr slow down. ~'tore m speed bump; **al** ~'tore in slow motion

raman'zina f reprimand

ra'marro m type of lizard

ra'mato adj copper[-coloured]

'**rame** m copper

ramifi'ca|re vi, ~rsi vr branch out; (strada:) branch. ~zi'one f ramification

rammari'carsi vr ~ **di** regret; (lamentarsi) complain (**di** about). **ram'marico** m regret

rammen'dare vt darn. **ram'mendo** m darning

rammen'tar|e vt remember; ~**e** qcsa a qcno (richiamare alla memoria) remind sb of sth. ~**si** vr remember

rammolli'i|re vt soften. ~rsi vr go

soft. ~to, -a mf wimp

'ramo m branch. ~'scello m twig

'rampa f (di scale) flight. ~ d'accesso slip road. ~ di lancio launch[ing] pad

ram'pante adj giovane ~ yuppie

rampi'cante adj climbing ● m (Bot) creeper

ram'pollo m hum brat; (discendente) descendant

ram'pone m harpoon; (per scarpe) crampon

'rana f frog; (nel nuoto) breaststroke; uomo ~ frogman

ran'core m resentment

ran'dagio adj stray

'rango m rank

rannicchi'arsi vr huddle up

rannuvo'larsi vr cloud over

ra'nocchio m frog

ranto'lare vi wheeze. 'rantolo m wheeze; (di moribondo) deathrattle

'rapa f turnip

ra'pace adj rapacious; (uccello) predatory

ra'pare vt crop

'rapida f rapids pl. ~'mente adv rapidly

rapidità f speed

'rapido adj swift ● m (treno) express [train]

rapi'mento m kidnapping

ra'pina f robbery; ~ a mano armata armed robbery; ~ in banca bank robbery. rapi'nare vt rob. ~'tore m robber

ra'pire vt abduct; (a scopo di riscatto) kidnap; (estasiare) ravish. ~'tore, ~'trice mf kidnapper

rappacifi'care vt pacify. ~rsi vr be reconciled. ~zi'one f reconciliation

rappor'tare vt reproduce (disegno); (confrontare) compare

rap'porto m report; (connessione) re-

lation; (legame) relationship; (Math, Techn) ratio; rapporti pl relationship; essere in buoni rapporti be on good terms. ~ di amicizia friendship. ~ di lavoro working relationship. rapporti pl sessuali sexual intercourse

rap'prendersi vr set; (latte:) curdle

rappre'saglia f reprisal

rappresen'tan|te mf representative. ~te di commercio sales representative. ~za f delegation; (Comm) agency; spese pl di ~za entertainment expenses; di ~za (appartamento ecc) company

rappresen'ta|re vt represent; (Theat) perform. ~'tivo adj representative. ~zi'one f representation; (spettacolo) performance

rap'preso pp di rapprendersi

rapso'dia f rhapsody

'raptus m inv fit of madness

rara'mente adv rarely, seldom

rare'fa|re vt, ~rsi vr rarefy. ~tto adj rarefied

rarità f inv rarity. 'raro adj rare

ra'sar|e vt shave; trim (siepe ecc). ~si vr shave

raschi'are vt scrape; (togliere) scrape off

rasen'tare vt go close to. ra'sente prep very close to

'raso pp di radere ● adj smooth; (colmo) full to the brim; (barba) close-cropped; ~ terra close to the ground; un cucchiaio ~ a level spoonful ● m satin

ra'solo m razor

ras'segna f review; (mostra) exhibition; (musicale, cinematografica) festival; passare in ~ review; (Mil) inspect

rasse'gna|re vt present. ~rsi vr resign oneself. ~to adj (persona, aria, tono) resigned. ~zi'one f resignation

rassere'nar|e vt clear; fig cheer up.

~si vr become clear; *fig* cheer up

rasset'tare vt tidy up; (*riparare*) mend

rassicu'ra|nte adj reassuring. **~re** vt reassure. **~zi'one** f reassurance

rasso'dare vt harden; *fig* strengthen

rassomigli'a|nza f resemblance. **~re** vi **a** resemble

rastrella'mento m (*di fieno*) raking; (*perlustrazione*) combing. **rastrel'lare** vt rake; (*perlustrare*) comb

rastrelli'era f rack; (*per biciclette*) bicycle rack; (*scolapiatti*) [plate] rack. **ra'strello** m rake

'rata f instalment; pagare a rate pay by instalments. **rate'ale** adj by instalments; pagamento rateale payment by instalments

rate'are, rateiz'zare vt divide into instalments

ra'tifica f (*Jur*) ratification

ratifi'care vt (*Jur*) ratify

'ratto m abduction; (*roditore*) rat

rattop'pare vt patch. **rat'toppo** m patch

rattrap'pir|e vt make stiff. **~si** vr become stiff

rattri'star|e vt sadden. **~si** vr become sad

rau'cedine f hoarseness. **'rauco** adj hoarse

rava'nello m radish

ravi'oli mpl ravioli sg

ravve'dersi vr mend one's ways

ravvicina'mento m reconciliation; (*Pol*) rapprochement

ravvici'nar|e vt bring closer; (*riconciliare*) reconcile. **~si** vr be reconciled

ravvi'sare vt recognize

ravvi'var|e vt revive; *fig* brighten up. **~si** vr revive

'rayon m rayon

razio'cinio m rational thought; (*buon senso*) common sense

razio'nal|e adj rational. **~ità** f (*ra-*

ziocinio) rationality; (*di ambiente*) functional nature. **~iz'zare** vt rationalize (*programmi, metodi, spazio*). **~'mente** adv rationally

razio'nare vt ration. **razi'one** f ration

'razza f race; (*di cani ecc*) breed; (*genere*) kind; **che ~ di idiota!** 🔟 what an idiot!

raz'zia f raid

razzi'ale adj racial

raz'zis|mo m racism. **~ta** adj & mf racist

'razzo m rocket. **~ da segnalazione** flare

razzo'lare vi (*polli:*) scratch about

re m inv king; (*Mus*) D

rea'gire vi react

re'ale adj real; (*di re*) royal

rea'lis|mo m realism. **~ta** mf realist; (*fautore del re*) royalist

realistica'mente adv realistically. **rea'listico** adj realistic

'reality tv f reality tv

realiz'zabile adj feasible

realiz'za|re vt (*attuare*) carry out, realize; (*Comm*) make; score (gol, canestro); (*rendersi conto di*) realize. **~rsi** vr come true; (*nel lavoro ecc*) fulfil oneself. **~zi'one** f realization; (*di sogno, persona*) fulfilment. **~zione scenica** production

rea'lizzo m (*vendita*) proceeds pl; (*riscossione*) yield

real'mente adv really

real'tà f inv reality. **~ virtuale** virtual reality

re'ato m crime

reat'tivo adj reactive

reat'tore m reactor; (*Aeron*) jet [aircraft]

reazio'nario, -a adj & mf reactionary

reazi'one f reaction. **~ a catena** chain reaction

'rebus m inv rebus; (*enigma*) puzzle

recapi'tare vt deliver. **re'capito** m address; (consegna) delivery. **recapito a domicilio** home delivery. **recapito telefonico** contact telephone number

re'car|e vt bear; (produrre) cause. **~si** vr go

re'cedere vi recede; fig give up

recens'i|one f review. **~ore** m reviewer

re'cente adj recent; **di ~** recently. **~mente** adv recently

recessi'one f recession

re'cesso m recess

re'cidere vt cut off

reci'divo, -a adj (Med) recurrent • mf repeat offender

recin'tare vt close off. **re'cinto** m enclosure; (per animali) pen; (per bambini) play-pen. **~zi'one** f (muro) wall; (rete) wire fence; (cancellata) railings pl

recipi'ente m container

re'ciproco adj reciprocal

re'ciso pp di recidere

'recita f performance. **reci'tare** vt recite; (Theat) act; play (ruolo). **~zi'one** f recitation; (Theat) acting

recla'mare vi protest • vt claim

ré'clame f inv advertising; (inserzione pubblicitaria) advertisement

re'clamo m complaint; **ufficio reclami** complaints department

recli'na|bile adj reclining; **sedile ~bile** reclining seat. **~re** vt tilt (sedile); lean (capo)

reclusi'one f imprisonment. **re'cluso, -a** adj secluded • mf prisoner

'recluta f recruit

reclu|ta'mento m recruitment. **~'tare** vt recruit

'record m inv record • adj inv (cifra) record attrib

recrimi'nare vi recriminate

recupe'rare vt recover. **re'cupero** m recovery; **corso di recupero** add-

itional classes; **minuti di recupero** Sport injury time

redargu'ire vt rebuke

re'datto pp di redigere

redat'to|re, -'trice m editor; (di testo) writer

redazi'one f (ufficio) editorial office; (di testi) editing

reddi'tizio adj profitable

'reddito m income. **~ imponibile** taxable income

re'den|to pp di redimere. **~'tore** m redeemer. **~zi'one** f redemption

re'digere vt write; draw up (documento)

re'dime|re vt redeem. **~si** vr redeem oneself

'redini fpl reins

'reduce adj **~ da** back from • mf survivor

refe'rendum m inv referendum

refe'renza f reference

refet'torio m refectory

refrat'tario adj refractory; **essere ~ a** have no aptitude for

refrige'ra|re vt refrigerate. **~zi'one** f refrigeration

refur'tiva f stolen goods pl

rega'lare vt give

re'galo m present, gift

re'gata f regatta

reg'gen|te mf regent. **~za** f regency

'regger|e vt (sorreggere) bear; (tenere in mano) hold; (dirigere) run; (governare) govern; (Gram) take • vi (resistere) hold out; (durare) last; fig stand. **~si** vr stand

'reggia f royal palace

reggi'calze m inv suspender belt

reggi'mento m regiment

reggi'petto, reggi'seno m bra

re'gia f Cinema direction; (Theat) production

re'gime m regime; (dieta) diet;

(*Mech*) speed

re'gina f queen

'regio adj royal

regio'na|le adj regional. ~'lismo m (*parola*) regionalism

regi'one f region

re'gista mf (*Cinema*) director; (*Theat, TV*) producer

regi'stra|re vt register; (*Comm*) enter; (*incidere su nastro*) tape, record; (*su disco*) record. ~'tore m recorder; (*magnetofono*) tape-recorder. ~**tore di cassa** cash register. ~**zi'one** f registration; (*Comm*) entry; (*di programma*) recording

re'gistro m register; (*ufficio*) registry. ~ **di cassa** ledger

re'gnare vi reign

'regno m kingdom; (*sovranità*) reign. **R**~ **Unito** United Kingdom

'regola f rule; **essere in** ~ be in order; (*persona*:) have one's papers in order. **rego'labile** adj (*meccanismo*) adjustable. ~'mento m regulation; (*Comm*) settlement

rego'lar|e adj regular ● vt regulate; (*ridurre, moderare*) limit; (*sistemare*) settle. ~**si** vr (*agire*) act; (*moderarsi*) control oneself. ~**ità** f regularity. ~**iz'zare** vt settle (*debito*)

rego'la|ta f **darsi una** ~**ta** pull oneself together. ~**'tore**, **-'trice** adj **piano** ~**tore** urban development plan

'regolo m ruler

regres'sivo adj regressive. **re-'gresso** m decline

reinseri'mento m (*di persona*) re-integration

reinser'irsi vr (*in ambiente*) re-integrate

reinte'grare vt restore

relativa'mente adv relatively; ~ **a** as regards. **rela'tivo** adj relative

rela'tore, **-'trice** mf (*in una conferenza*) speaker

re'lax m relaxation

relazi'one f relation[ship]; (*rapporto amoroso*) [love] affair; (*resoconto*) report; **pubbliche relazioni** pl public relations

religi'o|ne f religion. ~**so**, **-a** adj religious ●m monk ●f nun

re'liqui|a f relic. ~**'ario** m reliquary

re'litto m wreck

re'ma|re vi row. ~**'tore**, **~'trice** mf rower

remini'scenza f reminiscence

remissi'one f remission; (*sottomissione*) submissiveness. **remis'sivo** adj submissive

'remo m oar

'remora f **senza remore** without hesitation

re'moto adj remote

remune'ra|re vt remunerate. ~**zi'one** f remuneration

'render|e vt (*restituire*) return; (*esprimere*) render; (*fruttare*) yield; (*far diventare*) make. ~**si** vr become; ~**si conto di qcsa** realize sth; ~**si utile** make oneself useful

rendi'conto m report

rendi'mento m rendering; (*produzione*) yield

'rendita f income; (*dello Stato*) revenue

'rene m kidney. ~ **artificiale** kidney machine

'reni fpl (*schiena*) back

reni'tente adj **essere** ~ **a** (*consigli di qcno*) be unwilling to accept

'renna f reindeer (*pl invv*); (*pelle*) buckskin

'reo, **-a** adj guilty ● mf offender

re'parto m department; (*Mil*) unit

repel'lente adj repulsive

repen'taglio m **mettere a** ~ risk

repen'tino adj sudden

reper'ibile adj available; **non è** ~

(perduto) it's not to be found

repe'rire vt trace (fondi)

re'perto m ~ archeologico find

reper'torio m repertory; (elenco) index; **immagini** pl di ~ archive footage

'replica f reply; (obiezione) objection; (copia) replica; (Theat) repeat performance. **repli'care** vt reply; (Theat) repeat

repor'tage m inv report

repres|si'one f repression. ~'sivo adj repressive. **re'presso** pp di reprimere. **re'primere** vt repress

re'pubbli|ca f republic. ~'cano, -a adj & mf republican

repu'tare vt consider

reputazi'one f reputation

requi'sito m requirement

requisi'toria f (arringa) closing speech

'resa f surrender; (Comm) rendering ~; **dei conti** rendering of accounts

'residence m inv residential hotel

resi'den|te adj & mf resident. ~za f residence; (soggiorno) stay. ~zi'ale adj residential; **zona** ~**ziale** residential district

re'siduo adj residual ● m remainder

'resina f resin

resi'sten|te adj resistant; ~te all'acqua water-resistant. ~za f resistance; (fisica) stamina; (Electr) resistor; **la R~za** the Resistance

re'sistere vi ~ [a] resist; (a colpi, scosse) stand up to; ~ **alla pioggia/al vento** be rain-/wind-resistant

'reso pp di rendere

reso'conto m report

re'spin|gere vt repel; (rifiutare) reject; (bocciare) fail. ~**to** pp di respingere

respi'ra|re vt/i breathe. ~**tore** m respirator. ~**tore [a tubo]** snorkel; ~**torio** adj respiratory. ~**zi'one** f breathing; (Med) respiration. ~**zione**

bocca a bocca mouth-to-mouth resuscitation, kiss of life. **re'spiro** m breath; (il respirare) breathing; fig respite

respon'sabil|e adj responsible (di for); (Jur) liable ● m person responsible. ~**e della produzione** production manager. ~**ità** f inv responsibility; (Jur) liability. ~**iz'zare** vt give responsibility to

re'sponso m response

'ressa f crowd

re'stante adj remaining ● m remainder

re'stare vi = RIMANERE

restau'ra|re vt restore. ~**tore**, ~**trice** mf restorer. ~**zi'one** f restoration. **re'stauro** m (riparazione) repair

re'stio adj restive; ~ **a** reluctant to

restitu'ire vt return; (reintegrare) restore. ~**zi'one** f return; (Jur) restitution

'resto m remainder; (saldo) balance; (denaro) change; **resti** pl (avanzi) remains; **del** ~ besides

re'string|ere vt contract; take in (vestiti); (limitare) restrict; shrink (stoffa). ~**si** vr contract; (farsi più vicini) close up; (stoffa): shrink. **re'string|i'mento** m (di tessuto) shrinkage

restrit'tivo adj restrictive. ~**zi'one** f restriction

resurrezi'one f resurrection

resusci'tare vt/i revive

re'tata f round-up

'rete f net; (sistema) network; (televisiva) channel; (in calcio) goal; fig trap; (per la spesa) string bag. ~ **locale** (Comput) local [area] network. ~ **stradale** road network. ~ **televisiva** television channel

reti'cen|te adj reticent. ~**za** f reticence

retico'lato m grid; (rete metallica) wire netting. **re'ticolo** m network

re'torico, -a adj rhetorical; **domanda retorica** rhetorical question

● f rhetoric

retribu'ire vt remunerate. **∼zi'one** f remuneration.

'retro adv behind; vedi ∼ see over ● m inv back. ∼ **di copertina** outside back cover

retroat'tivo adj retroactive

retro'ce|dere vi retreat ● vt (Mil) demote; Sport relegate. **∼ssi'one** f Sport relegation

retroda'tare vt backdate

re'trogrado adj retrograde; fig old-fashioned; (Pol) reactionary

retro'guardia f (Mil) rearguard

retro'marcia f reverse [gear]

retro'scena m inv (Theat) backstage; fig background details pl

retrospet'tivo adj retrospective

retro'stante adj il palazzo ∼ the building behind

retrovi'sore m rear-view mirror

'retta¹ f (Math) straight line; (di collegio, pensionato) fee

'retta² f dar a ∼ a qcno take sb's advice

rettango'lare adj rectangular. **ret'tangolo** m rectangle

ret'tifi|ca f rectification. **∼'care** vt rectify

'rettile m reptile

retti'lineo adj rectilinear; (retto) upright ● m Sport back straight

'retto pp di reggere ● adj straight; fig upright; (giusto) correct; **angolo** ∼ right angle

ret'tore m (Relig) rector; (Univ) principal, vice-chancellor

reu'matico adj rheumatic

reuma'tismi mpl rheumatism

reve'rendo adj reverend

rever'sibile adj reversible

revisio'nare vt revise; (Comm) audit; (Auto) overhaul. **revisi'one** f revision; (Comm) audit; (Auto) overhaul. **revi'sore** m (di conti) auditor; (di bozze) proof-reader; (di traduzioni) revisor

re'vival m inv revival

'revoca f repeal. **revo'care** vt repeal

riabili'ta|re vt rehabilitate. **∼zi'one** f rehabilitation

riabitu'ar|e vt reaccustom. **∼si** vr reaccustom oneself

riac'cender|e vt rekindle (fuoco). **∼si** vr (luce): come back on

riacqui'stare vt buy back; regain (libertà, prestigio); recover (vista, udito)

riagganci'are vt replace (ricevitore); ∼ **la cornetta** hang up ● vi hang up

riallac'ciare vt refasten; reconnect (corrente); renew (amicizia)

rial'zare vt raise ● vi rise. **ri'alzo** m rise

riani'mar|e vt (Med) resuscitate; (ridare forza a) revive; (ridare coraggio a) cheer up. **∼si** vr regain consciousness; (riprendere forza) revive; (riprendere coraggio) cheer up

riaper'tura f reopening

ria'prir|e vt, **∼si** vr reopen

rias'sumere vt summarize

riassun'tivo adj summarizing. **rias'sunto** pp di riassumere ● m summary

ria'ver|e vt get back; regain (salute, vista). **∼si** vr recover

riavvicina'mento m reconciliation

riavvici'nar|e vt reconcile (paesi, persone). **∼si** vr (riconciliarsi) be reconciled, make it up

riba'dire vt (confermare) reaffirm

ri'balta f flap; (Theat) footlights pl; fig limelight

ribal'tar|e vt/i, **∼si** vr tip over; (Naut) capsize

ribas'sare vt lower ● vi fall. **ri'basso** m fall; (sconto) discount

ri'battere vt (a macchina) retype; (controbattere) deny ● vi answer back

ribel'l|arsi vr rebel. **ri'belle** adj

rebellious ● *mf* rebel. ~'**ione** *f* rebellion

'**ribes** *m inv* (*rosso*) redcurrant; (*nero*) blackcurrant

ribol'lire *vi* ferment; *fig* seethe

ri'brezzo *m* disgust, far ~ a disgust

rica'dere *vi* fall back; (*nel peccato ecc*) lapse; (*pendere*) hang [down]; ~ su (*riversarsi*) fall on. rica'duta *f* relapse

rical'care *vt* trace

rica'ma|re *vt* embroider. ~to *adj* embroidered

ri'cambi *mpl* spare parts

ricambi'are *vt* return; reciprocate (*sentimento*); ~ qcsa a qcno repay sb for sth. ri'cambio *m* replacement; (*Biol*) metabolism; **pezzo di ricambio** spare [part]

ri'camo *m* embroidery

ricapito'la|re *vt* sum up. ~zi'one *f* summary, recap 🔟

ri'carica *f* (*di sveglia*) rewinding; (*Teleph*) top-up card

ricari'care *vt* reload (*macchina fotografica, fucile, camion*); recharge (*batteria*); (*Comput*) reboot

ricat'ta|re *vt* blackmail. ~'tore, ~'trice *mf* blackmailer. ri'catto *m* blackmail

rica'va|re *vt* get; (*ottenere*) obtain; (*dedurre*) draw. ~to *m* proceeds *pl*. ri'cavo *m* proceeds *pl*

'ricca *f* rich woman. ~'mente *adv* lavishly

ric'chezza *f* wealth; *fig* richness

'riccio *adj* curly ● *m* curl; (*animale*) hedgehog. ~ di mare sea-urchin. ~lo *m* curl. ~'luto *adj* curly. ric'ciuto *adj* (*barba*) curly

'ricco *adj* rich ● *m* rich man

ri'cerca *f* search; (*indagine*) investigation; (*scientifica*) research; (*Sch*) project

ricer'ca|re *vt* search for; (*fare ricer-*

che su) research. ~ta *f* wanted woman. ~'tezza *f* refinement. ~to *adj* sought-after; (*raffinato*) refined; (*affettato*) affected ● *m* (*dalla polizia*) wanted man

ricetrasmit'tente *f* transceiver

ri'cetta *f* prescription; (*Culin*) recipe

ricet'tacolo *m* receptacle

ricet'tario *m* (*di cucina*) recipe book

ricetta'|tore, -'trice *mf* fence, receiver of stolen goods. ~zi'one *f* receiving [stolen goods]

rice'vente *adj* (*apparecchio, stazione*) receiving ● *mf* receiver

ri'cev|ere *vt* receive; (*dare il benvenuto*) welcome; (*di albergo*) accommodate. ~i'mento *m* receiving; (*accoglienza*) welcome; (*trattenimento*) reception

ricevi'tor|e *m* receiver. ~'ia *f* ~la del lotto agency authorized to sell lottery tickets

rice'vuta *f* receipt

ricezi'one *f* (*Radio, TV*) reception

richia'mare *vt* (*al telefono*) call back; (*far tornare*) recall; (*rimproverare*) rebuke; (*attirare*) draw; ~ alla mente call to mind. richi'amo *m* recall; (*attrazione*) call

richi'eder|e *vt* ask for; (*di nuovo*) ask again for; ~ a qcno di fare qcsa ask o request sb to do sth. richi'esta *f* request; (*Comm*) demand

ri'chiuder|e *vt* close again. ~si *vr* (*ferita:*) heal

rici'claggio *m* recycling

rici'clare *vt* recycle (*carta, vetro*); launder (*denaro sporco*)

'ricino *m* ollo di ~ castor oil

ricogni'zi'one *f* reconnaissance

ri'colmo *adj* full

ricomin'ciare *vt/i* start again

ricompa'rire *vi* reappear

ricom'pen|sa *f* reward. ~'sare *vt* reward

ricom'por|re *vt* (*riscrivere*) rewrite;

(ricostruire) reform; *(Typ)* reset. ∼**si** *vr* regain one's composure

riconcili'a|re *vt* reconcile. ∼**rsi** *vr* be reconciled. ∼**zi'one** *f* reconciliation

ricono'scen|te *adj* grateful. ∼**za** *f* gratitude

rico'nosc|ere *vt* recognize; *(ammettere)* acknowledge. ∼**i'mento** *m* recognition; *(ammissione)* acknowledgement; *(per la polizia)* identification. ∼**i'uto** *adj* recognized

riconside'rare *vt* rethink

rico'prire *vt* re-cover; *(rivestire)* coat; *(di insulti)* shower (**di** with); hold *(carica)*

ricor'dar|e *vt* remember; *(richiamare alla memoria)* recall; *(far ricordare)* remind; *(rassomigliare)* look like. ∼**si** *vr* ∼**si [di]** remember. **ri'cordo** *m* memory; *(oggetto)* memento; *(di viaggio)* souvenir; **ricordi** *pl (memorie)* memoirs

ricor'ren|te *adj* recurrent. ∼**za** *f* recurrence; *(anniversario)* anniversary

ri'correre *vi* recur; *(accadere)* occur; *(data:)* fall; ∼ **a** have recourse to; *(rivolgersi a)* turn to. **ri'corso** *pp di* **ricorrere ●** *m* recourse; *(Jur)* appeal

ricostitu'ente *vt* tonic

ricostitu'ire *vt* re-establish

ricostru'|ire *vt* reconstruct. ∼**zi'one** *f* reconstruction

ricove'ra|re *vt* give shelter to; ∼**re in ospedale** admit to hospital, hospitalize. ∼**to, -a** *mf* hospital patient. **ri'covero** *m* shelter; *(ospizio)* home

ricre'a|re *vt* re-create; *(ristorare)* restore. ∼**rsi** *vr* amuse oneself. ∼**tivo** *adj* recreational. ∼**zi'one** *f* recreation; *(Sch)* break

ri'credersi *vr* change one's mind

ricupe'rare *vt* recover; rehabilitate *(tossicodipendente)*; ∼ **il tempo perduto** make up for lost time. **ri'cupero** *m* recovery; *(di tossicodipendente)* rehabilitation; *(salvataggio)* res-

cue; **[minuti** *mpl* **di] ricupero** injury time

ri'curvo *adj* bent

ri'dare *vt* give back, return

ri'dente *adj (piacevole)* pleasant

'ridere *vi* laugh; ∼ **di** *(deridere)* laugh at

ri'detto *pp di* **ridire**

ridicoliz'zare *vt* ridicule. **ri'dicolo** *adj* ridiculous

ridimensio'nare *vt* reshape; *fig* see in the right perspective

ri'dire *vt* repeat; *(criticare)* find fault with

ridon'dante *adj* redundant

ri'dotto *pp di* **ridurre ●** *m (Theat)* foyer **●** *adj* reduced

ri'du|rre *vt* reduce. ∼**rsi** *vr* diminish. ∼**rsi a** be reduced to. ∼**t'tivo** *adj* reductive. ∼**zi'one** *f* reduction; *(per cinema, teatro)* adaptation

rieducazi'one *f (di malato)* rehabilitation

riem'pi|re *vt* fill [up]; fill in *(moduli ecc).* ∼**rsi** *vr* fill [up]. ∼**'tivo** *adj* filling **●** *m* filler

rien'tranza *f* recess

rien'trare *vi* go/come back in; *(tornare)* return; *(piegare indentro)* recede; ∼ **in** *(far parte)* fall within. **ri'entro** *m* return; *(di astronave)* re-entry

riepilo'gare *vt* recapitulate. **rie'pilogo** *m* roundup

riesami'nare *vt* reappraise

riesu'mare *vt* exhume

rievo'ca|re *vt* commemorate. ∼**zi'one** *f* commemoration

rifaci'mento *m* remake

ri'fa|re *vt* do again; *(creare)* make again; *(riparare)* repair; *(imitare)* imitate; make (letto). ∼**rsi** *vr* *(rimettersi)* recover; *(vendicarsi)* get even; ∼**rsi una vita/carriera** make a new life/career for oneself; ∼**rsi di** make up for. ∼**tto** *pp di* **rifare**

riferi'mento *m* reference

rife'rir|e vt report; **~e a** attribute to ● vi make a report. **~si** vr **~si a** refer to

rifi'lare vt (tagliare a filo) trim; (①: affibbiare) saddle

rifi'nir|e vt finish off. **~'tura** f finish

rifiu'tare vt refuse; (rifiuto m refusal; **rifiuti** pl (immondizie) rubbish sg. **rifiuti** pl urbani urban waste sg

riflessi'one f reflection; (osservazione) remark. **rifles'sivo** adj thoughtful; (Gram) reflexive

ri'flesso pp di **riflettere** ● m (luce) reflection; (Med) reflex; **per ~** indirectly

ri'fletter|e vt reflect ● vi think. **~si** vr be reflected

riflet'tore m reflector; (proiettore) searchlight

ri'flusso m ebb

rifocil'lar|e vt restore. **~si** vr liter, hum take some refreshment

ri'fondere vt refund

ri'forma f reform; (Relig) reformation; (Mil) medical exemption

rifor'ma|re vt re-form; (migliorare) reform; (Mil) declare unfit for military service. **~to** adj (chiesa) Reformed. **~'tore, ~'trice** mf reformer. **~'torio** m reformatory. **rifor'mista** adj reformist

riforni'mento m supply; (scorta) stock; (di combustibile) refuelling; **stazione** f **di ~** petrol station

rifor'nir|e vt **~e di** provide with. **~si** vr restock, stock up (di with)

ri'fra|ngere vt refract. **~tto** pp di **rifrangere**. **~zi'one** f refraction

rifug'gire vi **~ da** fig shun

rifugi'a|rsi vr take refuge. **~to, -a** mf refugee. **~to economico** economic refugee

ri'fugio m shelter; (nascondiglio) hideaway

'riga f line; (fila) row; (striscia) stripe; (scriminatura) parting; (regolo) rule; **a**

righe (stoffa) striped; (quaderno) ruled; **mettersi in ~** line up

ri'gagnolo m rivulet

ri'gare vt rule (foglio) ● vi **~ dritto** behave well

rigatti'ere m junk dealer

rigene'rare vt regenerate

riget'tare vt throw back; (respingere) reject; (vomitare) throw up. **ri'getto** m rejection

ri'ghello m ruler

rigid|a'mente adv rigidly. **~ità** f rigidity; (di clima) severity; (severità) strictness. **'rigido** adj rigid; (freddo) severe; (ssvoro) strict

rigi'rar|e vt turn again; (ripercorrere) go round; fig twist (argomentazione) ● vi walk about. **~si** vr turn round; (nel letto) turn over. **ri'giro** m (imbroglio) trick

'rigo m line; (Mus) staff

ri'goglio m bloom. **~'oso** adj luxuriant

ri'gonfio adj swollen

ri'gore m rigours pl; **a ~** strictly speaking; **calcio di ~** penalty [kick]; **area di ~** penalty area; **essere di ~** be compulsory

rigo'roso adj (severo) strict; (scrupoloso) rigorous

riguada'gnare vt regain (quota, velocità)

riguar'dar|e vt look at again; (considerare) regard; (concernere) concern; **per quanto riguarda** with regard to. **~si** vr take care of oneself. **ri-gu'ardo** m care; (considerazione) consideration; **nei riguardi di** towards; **riguardo a** with regard to

ri'gurgito m regurgitation

rilanci'are vt throw back (palla); (di nuovo) throw again; increase (offerta); revive (moda); relaunch (prodotto) ● vi (a carte) raise the stakes

rilasci'ar|e vt (concedere) grant; (liberare) release; issue (documento). **~si** vr relax. **ri'lascio** m release; (di documento) issue

rilassa'mento m relaxation

rilas'sa|re vt, ~**rsi** vr relax. ~**to** adj (ambiente) relaxed

rile'ga|re vt bind (libro). ~**to** adj bound. ~**tura** f binding

ri'leggere vt reread

ri'lento: a ~ adv slowly

rileva'mento m survey; (Comm) buyout

rile'van|te adj considerable

rile'va|re vt (trarre) get; (mettere in evidenza) point out; (notare) notice; (topografia) survey; (Comm) take over; (Mil) relieve. ~**zi'one** f (statistica) survey

rili'evo m relief; (Geog) elevation; (topografia) survey; (importanza) importance; (osservazione) remark; **mettere in** ~ **qcsa** point sth out

rilut'tan|te adj reluctant. ~**za** f reluctance

'rima f rhyme

riman'dare vt (posporre) postpone; (mandare indietro) send back; (mandare di nuovo) send again; (far ridare un esame) make resit an examination. **ri'mando** m return; (in un libro) cross-reference

rima'nen|te adj remaining ●m remainder. ~**za** f remainder

rima'ne|re vi stay, remain; (essere d'avanzo) be left; (venirsi a trovare) be; (restare stupito) be astonished; (restare d'accordo) agree

rimar'chevole adj remarkable

ri'mare vt/i rhyme

rimargi'nar|e vt, ~**si** vr heal

ri'masto pp di **rimanere**

rimbal'zare vi rebound; (proiettile) ricochet; **far** ~ bounce. **rim'balzo** m rebound; (di proiettile) ricochet

rimbam'bi|re vi be in one's dotage ●vt stun. ~**to** adj in one's dotage

rimboc'care vt turn up; roll up (maniche); tuck in (coperte)

rimbom'bare vi resound

rimbor'sare vt reimburse, repay. **rim'borso** m reimbursement, repayment. **rimborso spese** reimbursement of expenses

rimedi'are vi a ~ a remedy; make up for (errore); (procurare) scrape up. **ri'medio** m remedy

rimesco'lare vt mix [up]; shuffle (carte); (rivangare) rake up

ri'messa f (locale per veicoli) garage; (per aerei) hangar; (per autobus) depot; (di denaro) remittance; (di merci) consignment

ri'messo pp di **rimettere**

ri'metter|e vt put back; (restituire) return; (affidare) entrust; (perdonare) remit; (rimandare) put off; (vomitare) bring up. ~**si** vr (ristabilirsi) recover; (tempo): clear up; ~**si a** start again

'rimmel® m inv mascara

rimoder'nare vt modernize

rimon'tare vt (risalire) go up; (Mech) reassemble ●vi remount; ~ **a** (risalire) go back to

rimorchi'a|re vt tow; 🚗 pick up (ragazza). ~**tore** m tug[boat]. **ri'morchio** m tow; (veicolo) trailer

ri'morso m remorse

rimo'stranza f complaint

rimozi'one f removal; (da un incarico) dismissal. ~ **forzata** f illegally parked vehicles removed at owner's expense

rim'pasto m (Pol) reshuffle

rimpatri'are vt/i repatriate. **rim'patrio** m repatriation

rim'pian|gere vt regret. ~**to** pp di **rimpiangere** ●m regret

rimpiaz'zare vt replace

rimpiccio'lire vi become smaller

rimpinz'ar|e vt ~**e di** stuff with. ~**si** vr stuff oneself

rimprove'rare vt reproach; ~ **qcsa a qcno** reproach sb for sth.

rim'provero m reproach

rimune'rar|e vt (sostenere) remunerate. ~'tivo adj remunerative. ~zi'one f remuneration

ri'muovere vt remove

ri'nascere vi be reborn

rinascimen'tale adj Renaissance Rinasci'mento m Renaissance

ri'nascita f rebirth

rincal'zare vt (sostenere) support; (rimboccare) tuck in. rin'calzo m support; rincalzi pl (Mil) reserves

rincantucci'arsi vr hide oneself away in a corner

rinca'rare vi increase the price of ● vi become more expensive. rin'caro m price increase

rinca'sare vi return home

rinchi'uder|e vt shut up. ~si vr shut oneself up

rin'correre vt run after

rin'cors|a f run-up. ~o pp di rincorrere

rin'cresc|ere vi mi rincresce di non... I'm sorry o I regret that I can't...; se non ti ~e if you don't mind ● i'mento m regret. ~i'uto pp di rincrescere

rincreti'nire vi be stupid

rincu'lare vi (arma:) recoil; (cavallo:) shy. rin'culo m recoil

rincuo'rar|e vt encourage. ~si vr take heart

rinfacci'are vt qcsa a qcno throw sth in sb's face

rinfor'zar|e vt strengthen; (rendere più saldo) reinforce. ~si vr become stronger. rin'forzo m reinforcement; fig support

rinfran'care vt reassure

rinfre'scante adj cooling

rinfre'scar|e vt cool; (rinnovare) freshen up ● vi get cooler. ~si vr freshen [oneself] up. rin'fresco m light refreshment; (ricevimento) party

rin'fusa f alla ~ at random

ringhi'era f railing; (di scala) banisters pl

ringiova'nire vt rejuvenate (pelle, persona); (vestito:) make look younger ● vi become young again; (sembrare) look young again

ringrazia'mento m thanks pl. ~'are vt thank

rinne'gar|e vt disown. ~to, -a mf renegade

rinnova'mento m renewal; (di edifici) renovation

rinno'var|e vt renew; renovate (edifici). ~si vr be renewed; (ripetersi) recur, happen again. rin'novo m renewal

● I noce'ronte m rhinoceros

rino'mato adj renowned

rinsal'dare vt consolidate

rinsa'vire vi come to one's senses

rinsec'chi|re vi shrivel up. ~to adj shrivelled up

rinta'narsi vr hide oneself away; (animale:) retreat into its den

rinton'tire vt stun. ~ito adj dazed

rintracci'are vt trace

rintro'nare vt stun ● vi boom

ri'nuncia f renunciation

rinunci'ar|e vi ~e a renounce, give up. ~'tario adj defeatist

ri'nunzia, rinunzi'are = RINUNCIA, RINUNCIARE

rinveni'mento m (di reperti) discovery; (di refurtiva) recovery. rinve'nire vt find ● vi (riprendere i sensi) come round; (ridiventare fresco) revive

rinvi'are vt put off; (mandare indietro) return; (in libro) refer: ~ a giudizio indict

rin'vio m (in Sport) goal kick; (in libro) cross-reference; (di appuntamento) postponement; (di merce) return

rio'nale adj local. ri'one m district

riordi'nare vt tidy [up]; (ordinare di nuovo) reorder; (riorganizzare) re-organize

riorganiz'zare vt reorganize

ripa'gare vt repay

ripa'ra|re vt protect; (aggiustare) repair; (porre rimedio) remedy ● vi ~re a make up for. ~rsi vr take shelter. ~to adj (luogo) sheltered. ~zi'one f repair; fig reparation. ri'paro m shelter; (rimedio) remedy

ripar'ti|re vt (dividere) divide ● vi leave again. ~zi'one f division

ripas'sa|re vt recross; (rivedere) revise ● vi pass again. ri'passo m (di lezione) revision

ripensa'mento m second thoughts pl

ripen'sare vi change one's mind; ~ a think of; ripensaci! think again!

riper'correre vt go back over

riper'cosso pp di ripercuotere

ripercu'oter|e vt strike again. ~si vr (suono:) reverberate; ~si su (avere conseguenze) impact on. ripercussi'one f repercussion

ripe'scare vt fish out (oggetti)

ripe'tente mf student repeating a year

ripe'tet|ere vt repeat. ~ersi vr (evento:) recur. ~izi'one f repetition; (di lezione) revision; (lezione privata) private lesson. ~uta'mente adv repeatedly

ri'piano m (di scaffale) shelf; (terreno pianeggiante) terrace

ri'picc|a f fare qcsa per ~a do sth out of spite. ~o m spite

'ripido adj steep

ripie'gar|e vt refold; (abbassare) lower ● vi (indietreggiare) retreat. ~si vr bend; (sedile:) fold. ripi'ego m expedient; (via d'uscita) way out

ripi'eno adj full; (Culin) stuffed ● m filling; (Culin) stuffing

ri'porre vt put back; (mettere da parte) put away; (collocare) place; repeat (domanda)

ripor'tar|e vt (restituire) bring/take back; (riferire) report; (subire) suffer; (Math) carry; win (vittoria); transfer (disegno). ~si vr go back; (riferirsi) refer

ripo'sante adj (colore) restful, soothing

ripo'sa|re vi rest ● vt put back. ~rsi vr rest. ~to adj (mente) fresh. ri'poso m rest; andare a riposo retire; riposo! (Mil) at ease!; giorno di riposo day off

ripo'stiglio m cupboard

ri'posto pp di riporre

ri'prender|e vt take again; (prendere indietro) take back; (riconquistare) recapture; (ricuperare) recover; (ricominciare) resume; (rimproverare) reprimand; take in (cucitura); Cinema shoot. ~si vr recover; (correggersi) correct oneself

ri'presa f resumption; (ricupero) recovery; (Theat) revival; Cinema shot; (Auto) acceleration; (Mus) repeat. ~ aerea bird's-eye view

ripresen'tar|e vt resubmit (domanda, certificato). ~si vr go/come back again; (come candidato:) run again; (occasione:) arise again

ri'preso pp di riprendere

ripristi'nare vt restore

ripro'dotto pp di riprodurre

ripro'du|rre vt, ~rsi vr reproduce. ~t'tivo adj reproductive. ~zi'one f reproduction

ripro'mettersi vr intend

ri'prova f confirmation

ripudi'are vt repudiate

ripu'gnan|te adj repugnant. ~za f disgust. ripu'gnare vi ripugnare a disgust

ripu'li|re vt clean [up]; fig polish

ripuls|i'one f repulsion. ~'ivo adj repulsive

ri'quadro m square; (pannello) panel

ri'sacca f undertow

risa'lire vi go back up • vi ~ **a** (nel tempo) go back to; (essere datato a) date back to; (essere dovuto) go back to

risal'tare vi stand out. **ri'salto** m prominence; (rilievo) relief

risa'nare vt heal; (bonificare) reclaim

risa'puto adj well-known

risarci'mento m compensation. **risar'cire** vt indemnify

ri'sata f laugh

riscalda'mento m heating. ~ **autonomo** central heating (for one flat)

riscal'dar|e vt heat; warm (persona). ~**si** vr warm up

riscat'tar|e vt ransom. ~**si** vr redeem oneself. **ri'scatto** m ransom; (morale) redemption

rischia'rar|e vt light up; brighten (colore). ~**si** vr light up; (cielo:) clear up

rischi'are vt risk • vi run the risk. **'rischio** m risk. ~**'oso** adj risky

risciac'quare vt rinse

riscon'trare vt (confrontare) compare; (verificare) check; (rilevare) find. **ri'scontro** m comparison; check; (Comm: risposta) reply

ri'scossa f revolt; (riconquista) recovery

riscossi'one f collection

ri'scosso pp di **riscuotere**

riscu'oter|e vt shake; (percepire) draw; (ottenere) gain; cash (assegno). ~**si** vr rouse oneself

risen'tir|e vt hear again; (provare) feel • vi ~**re di** feel the effect of. ~**rsi** vr (offendersi) take offence. ~**to** adj resentful

ri'serbo m reserve; **mantenere il** ~ remain tight-lipped

ri'serva f reserve; (di caccia, pesca) preserve; Sport substitute, reserve. ~ **di caccia** game reserve. ~ **naturale** wildlife reserve

riser'va|re vt reserve; (prenotare)

book; (per occasione) keep. ~**rsi** vr (ripromettersi) plan for oneself (cambiamento). ~**'tezza** f reserve. ~**to** adj reserved

ri'siedere vi ~ **a** live in/at

'riso¹ m (cereale) rice

'riso² pp di **ridere** • m (pl f **risa**) laughter; (singolo) laugh. ~**'lino** m giggle

ri'solto pp di **risolvere**

risolu|'tezza f determination. **riso'luto** adj resolute, determined. ~**zi'one** f resolution

ri'solver|e vt resolve; (Math) solve. ~**si** vr (decidersi) decide; ~**si in** turn into

riso'na|nza f resonance, **aver** ~**nza** arouse great interest. ~**re** vi resound; (rimbombare) echo

ri'sorgere vi rise again

risorgi'mento m revival; (storico) Risorgimento

ri'sorsa f resource; (espediente) resort

ri'sorto pp di **risorgere**

ri'sotto m risotto

risparmi'a|re vt save (denaro), spare. ~**tore**, ~**trice** mf saver. **ri'sparmio** m saving

rispecchi'are vt reflect

rispet'tabile adj respectable. ~**ità** f respectability

rispet'tare vt respect; **farsi** ~ command respect

rispet'tivo adj respective

ri'spetto m respect; ~ **a** as regards; (in confronto a) compared to

rispet|tosa'mente adv respectfully. ~**'toso** adj respectful

risplen'dente adj shining. **ri'splendere** vi shine

rispon'den|te adj ~**te a** in keeping with. ~**za** f correspondence

ri'spondere vi answer; (rimbeccare) answer back; (obbedire) respond; ~ **a**

reply to; **~ di** (rendersi responsabile) answer for

ri'spost|a f answer, reply; (reazione) response. **~o** pp di **rispondere**

'rissa f brawl. **ris'soso** adj pugnacious

ristabi'lir|e vt re-establish. **~si** vr (in salute) recover

rista'gnare vi stagnate; (sangue:) coagulate. **ri'stagno** m stagnation

ri'stampa f reprint; (azione) reprinting. **ristam'pare** vt reprint

risto'rante m restaurant

risto'ra|re vt refresh. **~rsi** vr liter take some refreshment; (riposarsi) take a rest. **~tore**, **~trice** mf (proprietario di ristorante) restaurateur; (fornitore) caterer ● adj refreshing. **ri'storo** m refreshment; (sollievo) relief

ristret'tezza f narrowness; (povertà) poverty

ri'stretto pp di **restringere** ● adj narrow; (condensato) condensed; (limitato) restricted; **di idee ristrette** narrow-minded

ristruttu'rare vt restructure (ditta); refurbish (casa)

risucchi'are vt suck in. **ri'succhio** m whirlpool; (di corrente) undertow

risul'ta|re vi result; (riuscire) turn out. **~to** m result

risuo'nare vi echo; (Phys) resonate

risurrezi'one f resurrection

risusci'tare vt resuscitate; fig revive ● vi return to life

risvegli'ar|e vt reawaken (interesse). **~si** vr wake up; (natura:) awake; (desiderio:) be aroused. **ri'sveglio** m waking up; (dell'interesse) revival; (del desiderio) arousal

ri'svolto m lapel; (di pantaloni) turnup, cuff Am; (di manica) cuff; (di tasca) flap; (di libro) inside flap

ritagli'are vt cut out. **ri'taglio** m cutting; (di stoffa) scrap

ritar'da|re vi be late; (orologio:) be slow ● vt delay; slow down (progresso); (differire) postpone. **~'tario, -a** mf late-comer

ri'tardo m delay; **essere in ~** be late; (volo:) be delayed

ri'tegno m reserve

rite'n|ere vt retain; deduct (somma); (credere) believe. **~uta** f deduction

riti'ra|re vt throw back (palla); (prelevare) withdraw; (riscuotere) draw; collect (pacco). **~rsi** vr withdraw; (stoffa:) shrink; (da attività) retire; (marea:) recede. **~ta** f retreat; (WC) toilet. **ri'tiro** m withdrawal; (Relig) retreat; (da attività) retirement. **ritiro bagagli** baggage reclaim

'ritmo m rhythm

'rito m rite; **di ~** customary

ritoc'care vt touch up

ritor'nare vi return; (andare venire indietro) go/come back; (ricorrere) recur; (ridiventare) become again

ritor'nello m refrain

ri'torno m return

ritorsi'one f retaliation

ri'trarre vt withdraw; (distogliere) turn away; (rappresentare) portray

ritrat'ta|re vt deal with again; retract (dichiarazione). **~zi'one** f withdrawal, retraction

ritrat'tista mf portrait painter. **ri'tratto** pp di **ritrarre** ● m portrait

ri'tro|sia f shyness. **~'troso** adj backward; (timido) shy; **a ritroso** backwards; **ritroso a** reluctant to

ritro'va|re vt find [again]; regain (salute). **~rsi** vr meet; (di nuovo) meet again; (capitare) find oneself; (raccapezzarsi) see one's way. **~to** m discovery. **ri'trovo** m meeting-place; (notturno) night-club

'ritto adj upright; (diritto) straight

ritu'ale adj & m ritual

riunifi'ca|re vt reunify. **~rsi** vr be reunited. **~zi'one** f reunification

riuni'one f meeting; (fra amici) reunion

riu'nire vt (unire) join together; (radunare) gather. **~si** vr be re united, (adunarsi) meet

riusc'ire vi (aver successo) succeed (in matematica HPL) be good (in al); (aver esito) turn out; **le è riuscito simpatico** she found him likeable. **~ta** f result; (successo) success

'**riva** f shore; (di fiume) bank

ri'vale mf rival. **~ità** f inv rivalry

rivalutazi'one f revaluation

rive'dere vt see again; revise (lezione); (verificare) check

rive'lare vt reveal. **~rsi** vr (dimostrarsi) turn out. **~'tore** adj revealing ● m (Techn) detector. **~zi'one** f revelation

ri'vendere vt resell

rivendi'care vt claim. **~zi'one** f claim

ri'vendita f (negozio) shop. **~'tore**, **~'trice** mf retailer. **~tore autorizzato** authorized dealer

ri'verbero m reverberation; (bagliore) glare

rive'renza f reverence; (inchino) curtsy; (di uomo) bow

rive'rire vt respect; (ossequiare) pay one's respects to

river'sare vt pour. **~si** vr (fiume:) flow

rivesti'mento m covering

rive'stire vt (rifornire di abiti) clothe; (ricoprire) cover; (internamente) line; hold (carica). **~rsi** vr get dressed again; (per una festa) dress up

rivi'era f coast; **la ~ ligure** the Italian Riviera

ri'vincita f Sport return match; (vendetta) revenge

rivis'suto pp di **rivivere**

ri'vista f review; (pubblicazione) magazine; (Theat) revue; **passare in ~** review

ri'vivere vi come to life again; (riprendere le forze) revive ● vt relive

ri'volgere vt turn; (indirizzare) address; **~e da** (distogliere) turn away from. **~si** vr turn round; **~si a** (indirizzarsi) turn to

ri'volta f revolt

rivol'tante adj disgusting

rivol'tare vt turn [over]; (mettendo l'interno verso l'esterno) turn inside out; (sconvolgere) upset. **~si** vr (ribellarsi) revolt

rivol'tella f revolver

ri'volto pp di **rivolgere**

rivoluzio'nare vt revolutionize. **~io**, **-a** adj & mf revolutionary. **rivoluzi'one** f revolution; (fig: disordine) chaos

riz'zare vt raise; (innalzare) erect; prick up (orecchie). **~si** vr stand up; (capelli:) stand on end; (orecchie:) prick up

'**roaming** m inv (Teleph) **~** [**Internazionale**] roaming

'**roba** f stuff; (personale) belongings pl, stuff; (faccenda) thing; (❌: droga) drugs pl. **~ da mangiare** things to eat

ro'baccia f rubbish

ro'bot m inv robot. **~ da cucina** food processor

robu'stezza f sturdiness, robustness; (forza) strength. **ro'busto** adj sturdy, robust; (forte) strong

'**rocca** f fortress. **~'forte** f stronghold

roc'chetto m reel

'**roccia** f rock

ro'daggio m running in. **~re** vt run in

'**rodere** vt gnaw; (corrodere) corrode. **~si** vr **~si da** be consumed with. **rodi'tore** m rodent

rodo'dendro m rhododendron

ro'gnone m (Culin) kidney

'**rogo** m (supplizio) stake; (per

r

cadaveri) pyre

'Roma f Rome

Roma'nia f Romania

ro'manico adj Romanesque

ro'mano, -a adj & mf Roman

romanti'cismo m romanticism. **ro'mantico** adj romantic

ro'man|za f romance. **~'zato** adj romanticized. **~'zesco** adj fictional; *(stravagante)* wild, unrealistic. **~zi'ere** m novelist

ro'manzo adj Romance ● m novel. **~ giallo** thriller

'rombo m rumble; *(Math)* rhombus; *(pesce)* turbot

'romper|e vt break; break off *(relazione)*; **non ~e [le scatole]!** (🄻): *(seccare)* don't be a pain [in the neck]!. **~si** vr break; **~si una gamba** break one's leg

rompi'capo m nuisance; *(indovinello)* puzzle

rompi'collo m daredevil; **a ~** at breakneck speed

rompighi'accio m ice-breaker

rompi'scatole mf inv 🄻 pain

'ronda f rounds pl

ron'della f *(Mech)* washer

'rondine f swallow

ron'done m swift

ron'fare vi snore

ron'zino m jade

ron'zio m buzz

'rosa f rose. **~ dei venti** wind rose ● adj & m pink. **ro'saio** m rose-bush

ro'sario m rosary

ro'sato adj rosy ● m *(vino)* rosé

ro'seo m pink

ro'seto m rose garden

rosma'rino m rosemary

'roso pp di **rodere**

roso'lare vt brown

roso'lia f German measles

ro'sone m rosette; *(apertura)* rose-window

'rospo m toad

ros'setto m *(per labbra)* lipstick

'rosso adj & m red; **passare con il ~** jump a red light. **~ d'uovo** [egg] yolk. **ros'sore** m redness; *(della pelle)* flush

rostic'ce'ria f shop selling cooked meat and other prepared food

ro'tabile adj **strada ~** carriageway

ro'taia f rail; *(solco)* rut

ro'ta|re vt/i rotate. **~zi'one** f rotation

rote'are vt/i roll

ro'tella f small wheel; *(di mobile)* castor

roto'lar|e vt/i roll. **~si** vr roll [about]. **'rotolo** m roll; **andare a rotoli** go to rack and ruin

rotondità f roundness; **~ pl** *(curve femminili)* curves. **ro'tondo, -a** adj round ● f *(spiazzo)* terrace

ro'tore m rotor

'rotta¹ f *(Naut)*, *(Aeron)* course; **far ~ per** make course for; **fuori ~** off course

'rotta² f **a ~ di collo** at breakneck speed; **essere in ~ con** be on bad terms with

rot'tame m scrap; fig wreck

'rotto pp di **rompere** ● adj broken; *(stracciato)* torn

rot'tura f break

'rotula f kneecap

rou'lette f inv roulette

rou'lotte f inv caravan, trailer Am

rou'tine f inv routine; **di ~** *(operazioni, controlli)* routine

ro'vente adj scorching

'rovere m *(legno)* oak

rovesci'ar|e vt knock over; *(sottosopra)* turn upside down; *(rivoltare)* turn inside out; spill *(liquido)*; overthrow *(governo)*; reverse *(situazione)*. **~si** vr *(capovolgersi)* overturn; *(riversarsi)* pour. **ro'vescio** adj *(contrario)* reverse; **alla rovescia** *(capovolto)* upside down;

(con l'interno all'esterno) inside out ● m reverse; (nella maglia) purl; (di pioggia) downpour; *Tennis* backhand

ro'vina f ruin; (crollo) collapse

rovi'na|re vt ruin; (guastare) spoil ● vi crash. ~rsi vr be ruined. ~to adj (oggetto) ruined. rovi'noso adj ruinous

rovi'stare vt ransack

'rovo m bramble

'rozzo adj rough

R.R. abbr (ricevuta di ritorno) return receipt for registered mail

'ruba f andare a ~ sell like hot cakes

ru'bare vt steal

rubi'netto m tap, faucet Am

ru'bino m ruby

ru'brica f column; (in programma televisivo) TV report; (quaderno con indice) address book. ~ telefonica telephone and address book

'rude adj rough

'rudere m ruin

rudimen'tale adj rudimentary. rudi'menti mpl rudiments

ruffi'an|a f procuress. ~o m pimp; (adulatore) bootlicker

'ruga f wrinkle

'ruggine f rust; fare la ~ go rusty

rug'gi|re vi roar. ~to m roar

rugi'ada f dew

ru'goso adj wrinkled

rul'lare vi roll; (Aeron) taxi

rul'lino m film

rul'lio m rolling; (Aeron) taxiing

rum m inv rum

ru'meno, -a adj & mf Romanian

ru'mor|e m noise; fig rumour. ~eg-gi'are vi rumble. rumo'roso adj noisy; (sonoro) loud

ru'olo m roll; (Theat) role; di ~ on the staff

ru'ota f wheel; andare a ~ libera free-wheel. ~ di scorta spare wheel

'rupe f cliff

ru'rale adj rural

ru'scello m stream

'ruspa f bulldozer

rus'sare vi snore

'Russia f Russia. r~o, -a adj & mf Russian; (lingua) Russian

'rustico adj rural; (carattere) rough

rut'tare vi belch. 'rutto m belch

'ruvido adj coarse

ruzzo'l|are vi tumble down. ~one m tumble; cadere ruzzoloni tumble down

●●●●●●●●●●●●●●●●●●●●●●●●●●●●●●

Ss

●●●●●●●●●●●●●●●●●●●●●●●●●●●●●●

'sabato m Saturday

'sabb|ia f sand. ~ie mobili quicksand. ~i'oso a sandy

sabo'ta|ggio m sabotage. ~re vt sabotage. ~tore, ~trice mf saboteur

'sacca f sack; ~ da viaggio travelling-bag

sacca'rina f saccharin

sac'cente adj pretentious ● mf know-all

saccheggi'a|re vt sack; hum raid (frigo)

sac'chetto m bag

'sacco m sack; (Anat) sac; mettere nel ~ fly swindle; un ~ (moltissimo) a lot; un ~ di (gran quantità) lots of. ~ a pelo sleeping-bag

sacer'do|te m priest

sacra'mento m sacrament

sacrifi'ca|re vt sacrifice. ~rsi vr sacrifice oneself. ~to adj (non valorizzato) wasted. sacri'ficio m sacrifice

sa'crilego adj sacrilegious

'sacro adj sacred ● m (Anat) sacrum

sacro'santo adj sacrosanct

'sadico, -a adj sadistic ● mf sadist. **sa'dismo** m sadism

sa'etta f arrow

sa'fari m inv safari

'saga f saga

sa'gace adj shrewd

sag'gezza f wisdom

saggi'are vt test

'saggio¹ m (scritto) essay; (prova) proof; (di metallo) assay; (campione) sample; (esempio) example

'saggio² adj wise

sag'gistica f non-fiction

Sagit'tario m (Astr) Sagittarius

'sagoma f shape; (profilo) outline. **sago'mato** adj shaped

'sagra f festival

sagre'|stano m sacristan. **~'stia** f sacristy

'sala f hall; (stanza) room; (salotto) living room. **~ d'attesa** waiting room. **~ da ballo** ballroom. **~ d'imbarco** departure lounge. **~ macchine** engine room. **~ operatoria** operating theatre. **~ parto** delivery room. **~ da pranzo** dining room

sa'lame m salami

sala'moia f brine

sa'lare vt salt

sa'lario m wages pl

sa'lasso m essere un **~** fig cost a fortune

sala'tini mpl savouries (eaten with aperitifs)

sa'lato adj salty; (costoso) dear

sal'ciccia f = SALSICCIA

sal'dar|e vt weld; set (osso); pay off (debito); settle (conto); **~e a stagno** solder. **~si** vr (Med: osso:) knit

salda'trice f welder; (a stagno) soldering iron

salda'tura f weld; (azione) welding; (di osso) knitting

'saldo adj firm; (resistente) strong ● m

settlement; (svendita) sale; (Comm) balance

'sale m salt. **~ fine** table salt. **~ grosso** cooking salt. **sali** pl **e tabacchi** tobacconist's shop

'salice m willow. **~ piangente** weeping willow

sali'ente adj outstanding; **i punti salienti di un discorso** the main points of a speech

sali'era f salt-cellar

sa'lina f salt-works sg

sa'li|re vi go/come up; (levarsi) rise; (su treno ecc) get on; (in macchina) get in ● vt go/come up (scale). **~ta** f climb; (aumento) rise; **in ~ta** uphill

sa'liva f saliva

'salma f corpse

'salmo m psalm

sal'mone m & adj inv salmon

sa'lone m hall; (salotto) living room; (di parrucchiere) salon. **~ di bellezza** beauty parlour

salo'pette f inv dungarees pl

salot'tino m bower

sa'lotto m drawing room; (soggiorno) sitting room; (mobili) [three-piece] suite

sal'pare vt/i sail; **~ l'ancora** weigh anchor

'salsa f sauce

sal'sedine f saltiness

sal'siccia f sausage

sal'ta|re vi jump; (venir via) come off; (balzare) leap; (esplodere) blow up; **~r fuori** spring from nowhere; (oggetto cercato:) turn up; **è emerso che...** it emerged that...; **~re fuori con...** come out with...; **~re in mente** spring to mind ● vt jump [over]; skip (pasti, lezioni); (Culin) sauté. **~to** adj (Culin) sautéed

saltel'lare vi hop; (di gioia) skip

saltim'banco m acrobat

'salto m jump; (balzo) leap; (dislivello) drop; (omissione, lacuna) gap; **fare un**

~ **da** drop in on. ~ **in alto** high jump. ~ **con l'asta** pole-vault. ~ **in lungo** long jump. ~ **pagina** (*Comput*) page down

saltuaria'mente *adv* occasionally. **saltu'ario** *adj* desultory; **lavoro saltuario** casual work

sa'lubre *adj* healthy

salume'ria *f* delicatessen. **sa'lumi** *mpl* cold cuts

salu'tare *vt* greet; (*congedandosi*) say goodbye to; (*portare i saluti a*) give one's regards to; (*Mil*) salute ● *adj* healthy

sa'lute *f* health; ~**!** (*dopo uno starnuto*) bless you!; (*a un brindisi*) your health!

sa'luto *m* greeting; (*di addio*) goodbye; (*Mil*) salute; **saluti** *pl* (*ossequi*) regards

'salva *f* salvo; **sparare a salve** fire blanks

salvada'naio *m* money box

salva'gente *m* lifebelt; (*a giubbotto*) life-jacket; (*ciambella*) rubber ring; (*spartitraffico*) traffic island

salvaguar'dare *vt* safeguard. **salvagu'ardia** *f* safeguard

sal'vare *vt* save; (*proteggere*) protect. ~**si** *vr* save oneself

calva'clip *m in punty lincr*

salva'taggio *m* rescue; (*Naut*) salvage; (*Comput*) saving; **battello di** ~**taggio** lifeboat

sal'vezza *f* safety; (*Relig*) salvation

'salvia *f* sage

salvi'etta *f* serviette

'salvo *adj* safe ● *prep* except [for] ● *conj* ~ **che** (*a meno che*) unless; (*eccetto che*) except that

samari'tano, -a *adj & mf* Samaritan

sam'buco *m* elder

san *m* S~ **Francesco** Saint Francis

sa'nare *vt* heal

sana'torio *m* sanatorium

san'cire *vt* sanction

'sandalo *m* sandal

'sangue *m* blood; **al** ~**e** (*carne*) rare; **farsi cattivo** ~**e** per worry about. ~**e freddo** composure; **a** ~**e freddo** in cold blood. ~**igno** *adj* blood

sangui'naccio *m* (*Culin*) black pudding

sangui'nante *adj* bleeding

sangui'nar|e *vi* bleed. ~**io** *adj* bloodthirsty

sangui'noso *adj* bloody

sangui'suga *f* leech

sanità *f* soundness; (*salute*) health. ~ **mentale** mental health

sani'tario *adj* sanitary; **Servizio S~** Health Service

'sano *adj* sound; (*salutare*) healthy; ~ **di mente** sane; ~ **come un pesce** as fit as a fiddle

San Sil'vestro *m* New Year's Eve

santifi'care *vt* sanctify

'santo *adj* holy; (*con nome proprio*) saint ● *m* saint. **san'tone** *m* guru. **santu'ario** *m* sanctuary

sanzi'one *f* sanction

sa'pere *vt* know; (*essere capace di*) be able to; (*venire a sapere*) hear; **saperla lunga** know a thing or two ● *vi* ~ **di** know about; (*aver sapore di*) taste of; (*aver odore di*) smell of; **saperci fare** have the know-how ● *m* knowledge

sapi'en|te *adj* wise; (*esperto*) expert ● *m* (*uomo colto*) sage. ~**za** *f* wisdom

sa'pone *m* soap. ~ **da bucato** washing soap. **sapo'netta** *f* bar of soap

sa'pore *m* taste. **sapori'tamente** *adv* soundly. **sapo'rito** *adj* tasty

sapu'tello, -a *adj & m* ☒ know-all, know-it-all *Am*

saraci'nesca *f* roller shutter

sar'cas|mo *m* sarcasm. ~**tico** *adj* sarcastic

Sar'degna *f* Sardinia

sar'dina f sardine

'sardo, -a adj & mf Sardinian

> *i* **Sardo** *Sardo* is Sardinia's traditional language. It is considered to be an independent language because of its many differences from Italian and its long independent history. Sardinian preserves many features derived from Latin which were lost in Italian, e.g. the k-sound in words like *chelu* (Italian *cielo*).

sar'donico adj sardonic

'sarto, -a m tailor ● f dressmaker. ∼'ria f tailor's; dressmaker's; (*arte*) couture

'sasso m stone; (*ciottolo*) pebble

sassofo'nista mf saxophonist. **sas'sofono** m saxophone

sas'soso adj stony

sa'tellite adj inv & nm satellite

sati'nato adj glossy

'satira f satire. **sa'tirico** adj satirical

satu'ra|re vt saturate. ∼**zi'one** f saturation. **'saturo** adj saturated; (*pieno*) full

'sauna f sauna

savoi'ardo m (*biscotto*) sponge finger

sazi'ar|e vt satiate. ∼**si** vr ∼**si di** *fig* grow tired of

sazi'età f mangiare a ∼ eat one's fill. **'sazio** adj satiated

sbaciucchi'ar|e vt smother with kisses. ∼**si** vr kiss and cuddle

sbada'ta|ggine f carelessness; è stata una ∼**ggine** it was careless. ∼'**mente** adv carelessly. **sba'dato** adj careless

sbadigli'are vi yawn. **sba'diglio** m yawn

sba'fa|re vt sponge

'sbafo m sponging; **a** ∼ without paying

sbagli'ar|e vi make a mistake; (*aver torto*) be wrong ● vt make a mistake in; ∼**e strada** go the wrong way; ∼**e numero** get the number wrong; (*Teleph*) dial a wrong number. ∼**si** vr make a mistake. **'sbaglio** m mistake; **per sbaglio** by mistake

sbal'l|are vt unpack; 🔢 screw up (*conti*) ● vi 🔢 go crazy. ∼**ato** adj (*squilibrato*) unbalanced

sballot'tare vt toss about

sbalor'di|re vt stun ● vi be stunned. ∼'**tivo** adj amazing. ∼**to** adj stunned

sbal'zare vt throw; (*da una carica*) dismiss ● vi bounce; (*saltare*) leap. **'sbalzo** m bounce; (*sussulto*) jolt; (*di temperatura*) sudden change; **a sbalzi** in spurts; **a sbalzo** (*lavoro a rilievo*) embossed

sban'care vt bankrupt; ∼ **il banco** break the bank

sbanda'mento m (*Auto*) skid; (*Naut*) list; *fig* going off the rails

sban'da|re vi (*Auto*) skid; (*Naut*) list. ∼**rsi** vr (*disperdersi*) disperse. ∼**ta** f skid; (*Naut*) list. ∼**to, -a** adj mixed-up ● mf mixed-up person

sbandie'rare vt wave; *fig* display

sbarac'care vt/i clear up

sbaragli'are vt rout. **sba'raglio** m rout; **mettere allo sbaraglio** rout

sbaraz'zar|e vt clear. ∼**si** vr ∼**si di** get rid of

sbaraz'zino, -a adj mischievous ● mf scamp

sbar'bar|e vt, ∼**si** vr shave

sbar'care vt/i disembark; ∼ **il lunario** make ends meet. **'sbarco** m landing; (*di merci*) unloading

'sbarra f bar; (*di passaggio a livello*) barrier. ∼'**mento** m barricade. **sbar'rare** vt (*ostruire*) block; cross (*assegno*); (*spalancare*) open wide

sbatacchi'are vt/i 🔀 bang

'sbatter|e vt bang; slam, bang (*porta*); (*urtare*) knock; (*Culin*) beat;

flap (ali); shake (tappeto) ● vi hang; (porta:) slam, bang. ~**si** vr ⊠ rush around; ~**sene di qcsa** not give a damn about sth. **sbat'tuto** adj tossed; (Culin) beaten; fig run down

sba'va|re vi dribble; (colore:) smear. ~**'tura** f smear; **senza** ~**ture** fig faultless

sbelli'carsi vr ~ **dalle risa** split one's sides [with laughter]

'sberla f slap

sbia'di|re vt/i, ~**rsi** vr fade. ~**to** adj faded; fig colourless

sbian'ca|re vt/i, ~**si** vr whiten

sbi'eco adj slanting; **di** ~ on the slant; (guardare) sidelong; **guardare qcno di** ~ look askance at sb; **ta-gliare di** ~ cut on the bias

sbigot'ti|re vt dismay ● vi, ~**rsi** vr be dismayed. ~**to** adj dismayed

sbilanci'ar|e vt unbalance ● vi (per-dere l'equilibrio) overbalance. ~**si** vr lose one's balance

sbizzar'rirsi vr satisfy one's whims

sbloc'care vt unblock; (Mech) re-lease; decontrol (prezzi)

sboc'care vi ~ **in** (fiume:) flow into; (strada:) lead to; (folla:) pour into

sboc'cato adj foul-mouthed

sbocci'are vi blossom

'sbocco m flowing; (foce) mouth; (Comm) outlet

sbolo'gnare vt ⊞ get rid of

'sbornia f **prendere una** ~ get drunk

sbor'sare vt pay out

sbot'tare vi burst out

sbotto'nar|e vt unbutton. ~**si** vr (⊞: confidarsi) open up; ~**si la cami-cia** unbutton one's shirt

sbra'carsi vr put on something more comfortable; ~ **dalle risate** ⊞ kill oneself laughing

sbracci'a|rsi vr wave one's arms. ~**to** adj bare-armed; (abito)

sleeveless

sbrai'tare vi bawl

sbra'nare vt tear to pieces

sbricio'lar|e vt, ~**si** vr crumble

sbri'ga|re vt expedite; (occuparsi di) attend to. ~**rsi** vr be quick. ~**tivo** adj quick

sbrindel'lare vt tear to shreds. ~**to** adj in rags

sbrodo'l|are vt stain

'sbronz|a f **prendersi una** ~ get tight. **sbron'zarsi** vr get tight. ~**o** adj (ubriaco) tight

sbruffo'na|ta f boast. **sbruf'tone**, **-a** mf boaster

sbu'care vi come out

sbucci'ar|e vt peel; shell (piselli). ~**si** vr graze oneself

sbuf'fare vi snort; (per impazienza) fume. **'sbuffo** m puff

'scabbia f scabies; fig

scac'ciare vt chase away

'scacco m check; ~**hi** pl (gioco) chess; (pezzi) chessmen; **dare** ~**o matto** a checkmate; **dare** ~ **a** (tessuto) checked. ~**hi'era** f chess-board

sca'dente adj shoddy

sca'de|nza f expiry; (Comm) matur-ity; (di progetto) deadline; **a breve/lunga** ~**nza** short-/long-term. ~**re** vi expire; (trattato) expire; (debito:) be due. **sca'duto** adj out-of-date

sca'fandro m diving suit; (di astro-nauta) spacesuit

scaf'fale m shelf; (libreria) bookshelf

sca'fista m motor-boat operator; (pej) refugee smuggler (using motorboat)

'scafo m hull

scagion'are vt exonerate

'scaglia f scale; (di sapone) flake; (scheggia) chip

scagli'ar|e vt fling. ~**si** vr fling oneself; ~**si contro** fig rail against

scaglio'nare vt space out. **~'one** m group; **a ~oni** in groups. **~one di reddito** tax bracket

'scala f staircase; (*portatile*) ladder; (*Mus, misura, fig*) scale; **scale** pl stairs. **~ mobile** escalat-or; (*dei salari*) cost of living index

sca'la|re vt climb; layer (*capelli*); (*detrarre*) deduct. **~ta** f climb; (*dell'Everest ecc*) ascent; **fare delle ~te** go climbing. **~'tore, ~'trice** mf climber

scalca'gnato adj down at heel

scalci'are vi kick

scalci'nato adj shabby

scalda'bagno m water heater

scalda'muscoli m inv leg-warmer

scal'dar|e vt heat. **~si** vr warm up; (*eccitarsi*) get excited

scal'fi|re vt scratch. **~t'tura** f scratch

scali'nata f flight of steps. **sca'lino** m step; (*di scala a pioli*) rung

scalma'narsi vr get worked up

'scalo m slipway; (*Aeron, Naut*) port of call; **fare ~ a** call at; (*Aeron*) land at

sca'lo|gna f bad luck. **~'gnato** adj unlucky

scalop'pina f escalope

scal'pello m chisel

'scalpo m scalp

scal'pore m noise; **far ~** fig cause a sensation

scal'trezza f shrewdness. **'scaltro** adj shrewd

scal'zare vt bare the roots of (*albero*); fig undermine; (*da una carica*) oust

'scalzo adj & adv barefoot

scambi'|are vt exchange; **~are** qcno per qualcun altro mistake sb for somebody else. **~'evole** adj reciprocal

'scambio m exchange; (*Comm*) trade; **libero ~** free trade

scamosci'ato adj suede

scampa'gnata f trip to the country

scampa'nato adj (*gonna*) flared

scampanel'lata f [loud] ring

scam'pare vt save; (*evitare*) escape. **'scampo** m escape

'scampolo m remnant

scanala'tura f groove

scandagli'are vt sound

scanda'listico adj sensational

scandaliz'zare vt scandalize. **~iz'zarsi** vr be scandalized

'scanda|lo m scandal. **~'loso** adj (*somma*) ecc scandalous; (*fortuna*) outrageous

Scandi'navia f Scandinavia. **scandi'navo, -a** adj & mf Scandi-navian

scan'dire vt scan (*verso*); pronounce clearly (*parole*)

scan'nare vt slaughter

'scanner m inv scanner

scanneriz'zare vt (*Comput*) scan

scan'sar|e vt shift; (*evitare*) avoid. **~si** vr get out of the way

scansi'one f (*Comput*) scanning

'scanso m **a ~ di** in order to avoid; **a ~ di equivoci** to avoid any misunderstanding

scanti'nato m basement

scanto'nare vi turn the corner; (*svignarsela*) sneak off

scanzo'nato adj easy-going

scapacci'one m smack

scape'strato adj dissolute

'scapito m loss

'scapola f shoulder-blade

'scapolo m bachelor

scappa'mento m (*Auto*) exhaust

scap'pa|re vi escape; (*andarsene*) dash [off]; (*sfuggire*) slip; **mi ~ da ridere!** I want to burst out laughing. **~ta** f short visit. **~'tella** f escapade; (*infedeltà*) fling. **~'toia** f way out

scappel'lotto m cuff

scarabocchi'are vt scribble

scara'bocchio m scribble

scara'faggio m cockroach

scara'muccia f skirmish

scaraven'tare vt hurl

scarce'rare vt release [from prison]

scardi'nare vt unhinge

'scarica f discharge; (di arma da fuoco) volley; fig shower

scari'care vt discharge; unload (arma, merci); (Comput) download; fig unburden. **~rsi** r (fiume:) flow; (orologio, batteria:) run down, fig unwind. **~tore** m loader; (di porto) docker. **'scarico** adj unloaded; (vuoto) empty; (orologio) run-down; (batteria) flat; fig untroubled ● m unloading; (di rifiuti) dumping; (di acqua) draining; (di sostanze inquinanti) discharge; (luogo) [rubbish] dump; (Auto) exhaust; (idraulico) drain; (tubo) waste pipe

scarlat'tina f scarlet fever

scar'latto adj scarlet

'scarno adj thin; (viso) bare

sca'rogna f [1] bad luck **~'gnato** adj [1] unlucky

'scarpa f shoe. **scarpe** pl da ginnastica trainers, gym shoes

scar'pata f slope; (burrone) escarpment

scarpi'nare vi hike

scar'pone m boot. **scarponi** pl da sci ski boot. **scarponi** pl da trekking walking boots

scarroz'zare vt/i drive around

scarseggi'are vi be scarce; **~ di** (mancare) be short of

scar'sezza f scarcity, shortage. **scarsità** f shortage. **'scarso** adj scarce; (manchevole) short

scarta'mento m (Rail) gauge. **~ ridotto** narrow gauge

scar'tare vt discard; unwrap (pacco); (respingere) reject ● vi (deviare) swerve. **'scarto** m scrap; (in carte) discard; (deviazione) swerve; (distacco) gap

scas'sare vt break. **~to** adj [1] clapped out

scassi'nare vt force open

scassina'tore, -'trice mf burglar. **'scasso** m (furto) house-breaking

scate'naire vt fig stir up. **~rsi** vr break out; fig (temporale:) break; (**[1]**: infiammarsi) get excited. **~to** adj crazy

'scatola f box, (di latta) can, tin Br; **in ~** (cibo) canned, tinned Br

scat'tare vi go off; (balzare) spring up; (adirarsi) lose one's temper; take (foto). **'scatto** m (blico) spring; (d'ira) outburst; (di telefono) unit; (dispositivo) release; **a scatti** jerkily; **di scatto** suddenly

scatu'rire vi spring

scaval'care vt jump over (muretto); climb over (muro); (fig: superare) overtake

sca'vare vt dig (buca); dig up (tesoro); excavate (città sepolta). **'scavo** m excavation

'scegliere vt choose, select

scelle'rato adj wicked

'scelta f choice; (di articoli) range; **...a ~** (in menu) choice of...; **prendine uno a ~a** take your choice o pick; **di prima ~a** top-grade, choice. **~o** pp di **scegliere** ● adj select; (merce ecc) choice

sce'mare vt/i diminish

sce'menza f silliness; (azione) silly thing to do/say. **'scemo** adj silly

'scempio m havoc; (fig: di paesaggio) ruination; **fare ~ di** play havoc with

'scena f scene; (palcoscenico) stage; **entrare in ~** go/come on; fig enter the scene; **fare ~** put on an act; **fare una ~** make a scene; **andare in ~** (Theat) be staged, be put on **sce'nario** m scenery

sce'nata f row, scene

'scendere vi go/come down; (da treno, autobus) get off; (da macchina) get out; (strada:) slope; (notte, prezzi:)

fall ● vt go/come down (scale)

sceneggi'a|re vt dramatize. **~to m** television serial. **~'tura** f screenplay

'scenico adj scenic

scervel'la|rsi vr rack one's brains. **~to** adj brainless

'sceso pp di **scendere**

scetti'cismo m scepticism. **'scettico, -a** adj sceptical ● mf sceptic

'scheda f card. **~ elettorale** ballot-paper. **~ di espansione** (Comput) expansion card. **~ telefonica** phone-card. **sche'dare** vt file. **sche'dario** m file; (mobile) filing cabinet

sche'dina f ≈ pools coupon; **giocare la ~** do the pools

scheggi'a| f fragment; (di legno) splinter. **~'arsi** vr chip; (legno:) splinter

'scheletro m skeleton

'schema m diagram; (abbozzo) outline. **sche'matico** adj schematic

'scherma f fencing

scher'mirsi vr protect oneself

'schermo m screen; **grande ~** big screen

scher'nire vt mock. **'scherno** m mockery

scher'zare vi joke; (giocare) play

'scherzo m joke; (trucco) trick; (effetto) play; (Mus) scherzo; **fare uno ~ a qcno** play a joke on sb. **scher'zoso** adj playful

schiaccia'noci m inv nutcrackers pl

schiacci'ante adj damning

schiacci'are vt crush; Sport smash; press (pulsante); crack (noce)

schiaffeggi'are vt slap. **schi'affo** m slap; **dare uno schiaffo a** slap

schiamaz'zare vi make a racket; (galline:) cackle

schian'ta|re vt break. **~si** vr crash ● vi **schianto dalla fatica** I'm wiped out. **'schianto** m crash; ⚡ knock-out; (divertente) scream

schia'rir|e vt clear; (sbiadire) fade

● vi, **~si** vr brighten up; **~si la gola** clear one's throat

schiavitù f slavery. **schi'avo, -a** mf slave

schi'ena f back; **mal di ~** back-ache. **schi'enale** m (di sedia) back

schi'er|a f (Mil) rank; (moltitudine) crowd. **~a'mento** m lining up

schie'ra|re vt draw up. **~si** vr draw up; **~si con** (parteggiare) side with

schiet'tezza f frankness. **schi'etto** adj frank; (puro) pure

schi'fezza f una ~ rubbish. **schifil'toso** adj fussy. **'schifo** m disgust; **mi fa schifo** it makes me sick. **schi'foso** adj disgusting; (di cattiva qualità) rubbishy

schioc'care vt crack; snap (dita). **schi'occo** m (di frusta) crack; (di bacio) smack; (di dita, lingua) click

schi'uder|e vt, **~si** vr open

schi'u|ma f foam; (di sapone) lather; (feccia) scum. **~ma da barba** shaving foam. **~'mare** vt skim ● vi foam

schi'uso pp di **schiudere**

schi'vare vt avoid. **'schivo** adj bashful

schizo'frenico adj schizophrenic

schiz'zare vt squirt; (inzaccherare) splash; (abbozzare) sketch ● vi spurt; **~ via** scurry away

schizzi'noso adj squeamish

'schizzo m squirt; (di fango) splash; (abbozzo) sketch

sci m inv ski; (sport) skiing. **~ d'acqua** water-skiing

'scia f wake; (di fumo ecc) trail

sci'abola f sabre

scia'callo m jackal; fig profiteer

sciac'quar|e vt rinse. **~si** vr rinse oneself; **sci'acquo** m mouthwash

scia'gu|ra f disaster. **~'rato** adj unfortunate; (scellerato) wicked

scialac'quare vt squander

scia'lare vi squander

sci'albo adj pale; fig dull

sci'alle m shawl

scia'luppa f dinghy. **~ di salva-taggio** lifeboat

sci'ame m swarm

sci'ampo m shampoo

scian'cato adj lame

sci'are vi ski

sci'arpa f scarf

sci'atica f (Med) sciatica

scia'tore, -'trice mf skier

sci'atto adj slovenly; (stile) careless. **sciat'tone, -a** mf slovenly person

scienti'fico adj scientific

sci'enz|a f science; (sapere) know-ledge. **~i'ato, -a** mf scientist

'scimmi|a f monkey. **~ot'tare** vt ape

scimpanzé m inv chimpan-zee, chimp

scimu'nito adj idiotic

'scinder|e vt. **~si** vr split

scin'tilla f spark. **scintil'lante** adi sparkling. **scintil'lare** vi sparkle

scioc'ca|nte adj shocking. **~re** vt shock

scioc'chezza f foolishness; (assur-dità) nonsense. **sci'occo** adj foolish

sci'oglier|e vt (liberare) re-lease; (liquefare) melt; dissolve (con-trailo, qesa nell'acqua); loosen up (muscoli). **~si** vr release oneself; (liquefarsi) melt; (contratto:) be dis-solved; (pastiglia:) dissolve

sciogli'lingua m inv tongue-twister

scio'lina f wax

sciol'tezza f agility, (disinvol-tura) ease

sci'olto pp di **sciogliere ●** adj loose; (agile) agile; (disinvolto) easy; **versi sciolti** blank verse og

sciope'ra|nte mf striker. **~re** vi go on strike, strike. **sci'opero** m strike. **sciopero a singhiozzo** on-off strike

sciori'nare vt fig show off

scip'pare vt snatch. **~'tore, ~'trice** mf bag snatcher. **'scippo** m bag-snatching

sci'rocco m sirocco

scirop'pato adj (frutta) in syrup. **sci'roppo** m syrup

'scisma m schism

scissi'one f division

'scisso pp di **scindere**

sciu'par|e vt spoil; (sperperare) waste. **~si** vr get spoiled; (deperire) wear oneself out. **sciu'pio** m waste

scivo'l|are vi slide, (involontariamente) slip. **'scivolo** m slide; (Techn) chute. **~oso** adj slippery

scoc'care vt shoot ● vi (scintilla:) shoot out; (ora:) strike

scocci'a|re vt (dare noia a) bother. **~rsi** vr be bothered. **~to** adj ① narked. **~'tore, ~'trice** mf bore. **~'tura** f nuisance

sco'della f bowl

scodinzo'lare vi wag its tail

scogli'era f cliff; (a fior d'acqua) reef. **'scoglio** m rock; (fig: ostacolo) stum-bling block

scoi'attolo m squirrel

scola'pasta m inv colander. **~pi'atti** m inv dish drainer

sco'lara f schoolgirl

sco'lare vt drain; strain (pasta, ver-dura) ● vi drip

sco'la|ro m schoolboy. **~resca** f pupils pl. **~stico** adj school attrib

scol'la|re vt cut away the neck of (abito); (staccare) unstick. **~to** adj low-necked. **~'tura** f neckline

'scolo m drainage

scolo'ri|re vt, **~rsi** vr fade. **~to** adj faded

scol'pire vi carve; (imprimere) engrave

scombi'nare vt upset

scombusso'lare vt muddle up

scom'mess|a f bet. **~o** pp di

scommettere. scom'mettere vt bet

scomo'dar|e, vt, ~si vr trouble. **scomodità** f discomfort. **'scomodo** adj uncomfortable

scompa'rire vi disappear; (morire) pass on. **scom'parsa** f disappearance; (morte) passing, death. **scom-'parso, -a** pp di **scomparire** ● mf departed

scomparti'mento m compartment. **scom'parto** f compartment

scom'penso m imbalance

scompigli'are vt disarrange. **scom'piglio** m confusion

scom'po|rre vt take to pieces; (fig: turbare) upset. ~**rsi** vr get flustered. ~**sto** pp di **scomporre** ● adj (sguaiato) unseemly; (disordinato) untidy

sco'muni|ca f excommunication. ~**'care** vt excommunicate

sconcer'ta|re vt disconcert; (rendere perplesso) bewilder. ~**to** adj disconcerted; bewildered

scon'cezza f obscenity. **'sconcio** adj dirty ● m è uno sconcio che... it's a disgrace that...

sconclusio'nato adj incoherent

scon'dito adj unseasoned; (insalata) with no dressing

sconfes'sare vt disown

scon'figgere vt defeat

sconfi'na|re vi cross the border; (in proprietà privata) trespass. ~**to** adj unlimited

scon'fitt|a f defeat. ~**o** pp di **sconfiggere**

scon'forto m dejection

sconge'lare vt thaw out (cibo), defrost

scongiu'rare vt beseech; (evitare) avert. ~**'uro** m fare gli scongiuri touch wood, knock on wood Am

scon'nesso pp di **sconnettere** ● adj fig incoherent. **scon'nettere** vt disconnect

sconosci'uto, -a adj unknown

● mf stranger

sconquas'sare vt smash; (sconvolgere) upset

conside'rato adj inconsiderate

sconsigli'a|bile adj not advisable. ~**re** vt advise against

sconso'lato adj disconsolate

scon'ta|re vt discount; (dedurre) deduct; (pagare) pay off; serve (pena). ~**to** adj discount; (ovvio) expected; ~**to del 10%** with 10% discount

scon'tento adj displeased ● m discontent

'sconto m discount; **fare uno** ~ give a discount

scon'trarsi vr clash; (urtare) collide

scon'trino m ticket; (di cassa) receipt

'scontro m clash; (urto) collision

scon'troso adj unsociable

sconveni'ente adj unprofitable; (scorretto) unseemly

sconvol'gente adj mind-blowing

sconvol'gere vt upset; (mettere in disordine) disarrange. ~**gi'mento** m upheaval. ~**to** pp di **sconvolgere** ● adj distraught

'scopa f broom. **sco'pare** vt sweep

scoperchi'are vt take the lid off (pentola); take the roof off (casa)

sco'pert|a f discovery. ~**o** pp di **scoprire** ● adj uncovered; (senza riparo) exposed; (conto) overdrawn; (spoglio) bare

'scopo m aim; **allo** ~ **di** in order to

scoppi'are vi burst; fig break out. **scoppiet'tare** vi crackle. **'scoppio** m burst; (di guerra) outbreak; (esplosione) explosion

sco'prire vt discover; (togliere la copertura a) uncover

scoraggi'a|re vt discourage. ~**rsi** vr lose heart

scor'butico adj peevish

scorcia'toia f short cut

'scorcio m (di epoca) end; (di cielo)

patch; (in arte) foreshortening; **di ~** (vedere) from an angle. **~ panoramico** panoramic view

scor'da|re vt, **~rsi** vr forget. **~to** adj (Mus) out of tune

'scorgere vt make out; (notare) notice

'scoria f waste; (di metallo, carbone) slag; **scorie** pl **radioattive** radioactive waste

scor'nato adj fig hangdog. **'scorno** m humiliation

scorpi'one m scorpion; (Astr) **S ~** Scorpio

scorraz'zare vi run about

'scorrere vt (dare un'occhiata) glance through ● vi run; (scivolare) slide; (fluire) flow; (Comput) scroll. **scorrevole** adj **porta scorrevole** sliding door

scorre'ria f raid

scorret'tezza f (mancanza di educazione) bad manners pl. **scor'retto** adj incorrect; (sconveniente) improper

scorri'banda f raid; fig excursion

'scorsa f glance. **~o** pp di **scorrere** ● adj last

scor'soio adj **nodo ~** noose

'scor|ta f escort; (provvista) supply. **~'tare** vt escort

scor'te|se adj discourteous. **~'sia** f discourtesy

scorti'ca|re vt skin. **~'tura** f graze

'scorto pp di **scorgere**

'scorza f peel; (crosta) crust; (corteccia) bark

sco'sceso adj steep

'scossa f shake; (Electr, fig) shock; **prendere la ~** get an electric shock. **~ elettrica** electric shock. **~ sismica** earth tremor

'scosso pp di **scuotere** ● adj shaken; (sconvolto) upset

sco'stante adj off-putting

sco'sta|re vt push away. **~rsi** vr stand aside

scostu'mato adj dissolute; (maleducato) ill-mannered

scot'tante adj dangerous

scot'ta|re vt scald ● vi burn; (bevanda:) be too hot; (sole, pentola:) be very hot. **~rsi** vr burn oneself; (al sole) get sunburnt; fig get one's fingers burnt. **~'tura** f burn; (da liquido) scald; **~tura solare** sunburn; fig painful experience

'scotto adj overcooked

sco'vare vt (scoprire) discover

'Scozia f Scotland. **~'zese** adj Scottish ● mf Scot

scredi'tare vt discredit

scre'mare vt skim

screpo'la|re vt, **~rsi** vr crack. **~to** adj (labbra) chapped. **~'tura** f crack

screzi'ato adj speckled

'screzio m disagreement

scribac|chi'are vt scribble. **~'chino, -a** mf scribbler; (impiegato) penpusher

scricchio'l|are vi creak. **~io** m creaking

scricciolo m wren

'scrigno m casket

scrimina'tura f parting

'scrit|ta f writing; (su muro) graffiti. **~to** pp di **scrivere** ● adj written ● m writing; (lettera) letter. **~'toio** m writing-desk. **~'tore, ~'trice** mf writer. **~'tura** f writing; (Relig) scripture

scrittu'rare vt engage

scriva'nia f desk

'scrivere vt write; (descrivere) write about; **~ a macchina** type

scroc'c|are vt **~are a sponge off. 'scrocco** m **1** a **scrocco 1** without paying. **~one, -a** mf sponger

'scrofa f sow

scrol'la|re vt shake; **~e le spalle** shrug one's shoulders. **~si** vr shake oneself; **~si qcsa di dosso** shake sth off

S

scrosci'are vi roar; (pioggia:) pelt down. **'scroscio** m roar; (di pioggia) pelting

scro'star|e vt scrape. **~si** vr peel off

'scrupo|lo m scruple; (diligenza) care; **senza scrupoli** unscrupulous, without scruples. **~loso** adj scrupulous

scru'ta|re vt scan; (indagare) search. **~'tore** m (alle elezioni) returning officer

scruti'nare vt scrutinize. **scru'tinio** m (di voti alle elezioni) poll; (Sch) assessment of progress

scu'cire vt unstitch

scude'ria f stable

scu'detto m Sport championship shield

'scudo m shield

sculacci'a|re vt spank. **~'ata** f spanking. **~'one** m spanking

sculet'tare vi wiggle one's hips

scul'to|re, -'trice m sculptor • f sculptress. **~'tura** f sculpture

scu'ola f school. **~ elementare** primary school. **~ guida** driving school. **~ materna** day nursery. **~ media [inferiore]** secondary school (10-13). **~ [media] superiore** secondary school (13-18)

scu'oter|e vt shake. **~si** vr (destarsi) rouse oneself; **~si di dosso** shake off

'scure f axe

scu'reggia f 🗓 fart. **scureggi'are** vi 🗓 fart

scu'rire vt/i darken

'scuro adj dark • m darkness; (imposta) shutter

'scusa f excuse; (giustificazione) apology; **chiedere ~** apologize; **chiedo ~!** I'm sorry!

scu'sar|e vt excuse. **~si** vr **~si apologize (di** for); **[mi] scusi!** excuse me!; (chiedendo perdono) [I'm] sorry!

sdebi'tarsi vr repay a kindness

sde'gna|re vt despise. **~rsi** vr get angry. **~to** adj indignant. **'sdegno** m disdain. **sde'gnoso** adj disdainful

sdolci'nato adj sentimental

sdoppi'are vt halve

sdrai'arsi vr lie down. **'sdraio** m [sedia a] sdraio deckchair

sdrammatiz'zare vi provide some comic relief

sdruccio'levole adj slippery

---

se

● conj if; (interrogativo) whether, if; **se mai** (caso mai) if need be; **se mai telefonasse,...** should he call,..., if he calls,...; **se no** otherwise, or else; **se non altro** at least, if nothing else; **se pure** (sebbene) even though; (anche se) even if; **non so se sia vero** I don't know whether it's true, I don't know if it's true; **come se** as if; **se lo avessi saputo prima!** if only I had known before!; **e se andassimo fuori a cena?** how about going out for dinner?

● m inv if

---

sé pers pron oneself; (lui) himself; (lei) herself; (esso, essa) itself; (loro) themselves; **l'ha fatto da sé** he did it himself; **ha preso i soldi con sé** he took the money with him; **si sono tenuti le notizie per sé** they kept the news to themselves

seb'bene conj although

'secca f shallows pl; **in ~** (nave) aground

sec'cante adj annoying

sec'ca|re vt dry; (importunare) annoy • vi dry up. **~rsi** vr dry up; (irritarsi) get annoyed; (annoiarsi) get bored. **~'tore, ~'trice** mf nuisance. **~'tura** f bother

secchi'ello m pail

'secchio m bucket. ~ **della spazzatura** rubbish bin, trash can Am

'secco, -a adj dry; (*dissecato*) dried; (*magro*) thin; (*brusco*) curt; (*preciso*) sharp ● m (*siccità*) drought; **lavare a ~** dry-clean

secessi'one f secession

seco'lare adj age-old; (*laico*) secular. **'secolo** m century; (*epoca*) age

se'cond|a f (*Rail, Sch*) second class; (*Auto*) second [gear]. ~o adj second ● m second; (*secondo piatto*) main course ● prep according to, ~o **me** in my opinion

secrezi'one f secretion

'sedano m celery

seda'tivo adj & m sedative

'sede f seat; (*centro*) centre; (*Relig*) see; (*Comm*) head office. ~ **sociale** registered office

seden'tario adj sedentary

se'der|e vi sit ● ~**si** vr sit down ● m (*deretano*) bottom

'sedia f chair. ~ **a dondolo** rocking chair. ~ **a rotelle** wheelchair

sedi'cente adj self-styled

'sedici adj & m sixteen

se'dile m seat

sedizi'o|ne f sedition. ~**so** adj seditious

se'dotto pp di **sedurre**

sedu'cente adj seductive

se'durre vt seduce

se'duta f session; (*di posa*) sitting. ~ **stante** adv here and now

seduzi'one f seduction

'sega f saw

'segala f rye

se'gare vt saw

'seggio m seat. ~ **elettorale** polling station

seg'gio|la f chair. ~**lino** m seat; (*da bambino*) child's seat. ~**lone** m (*per bambini*) high chair

seggio'via f chair lift

seghe'ria f sawmill

se'ghetto m hacksaw

seg'mento m segment

segna'lar|e vt signal; (*annunciare*) announce; (*indicare*) point out. ~**si** vr distinguish oneself

se'gna|le m signal; (*stradale*) sign. ~**le acustico** beep. ~**le orario** time signal. ~**letica** f signals pl. ~**letica stradale** road signs pl

se'gnare vt mark; (*prendere nota*) note; (*indicare*) indicate; Sport score. ~**si** vr cross oneself. **'segno** m sign; (*traccia, limite*) mark; (*bersaglio*) target; **far segno** (*col capo*) nod; (*con la mano*) beckon. **segno zodiacale** birth sign

segre'ga|re vt segregate. ~**zi'one** f segregation

segretari'ato m secretariat

segre'tario, -a mf secretary. ~ **comunale** town clerk

segrete'ria f [administrative] office; (*segretariato*) secretariat. ~ **telefonica** answering machine

segre'tezza f secrecy

se'greto adj & m secret; **in ~** in secret

segu'ace mf follower

segu'ente adj following, next

se'gugio m bloodhound

segu'ire vt/i follow; (*continuare*) continue

segui'tare vt/i continue

'seguito m retinue; (*sequela*) series; (*continuazione*) continuation; **di ~** in succession; **in ~** later on; **in ~ a** following; **al ~** owing to; **fare ~ a** follow up

'sei adj & m six. **sei'cento** adj & m six hundred; **il Seicento** the seventeenth century. **sei'mila** adj & m six thousand

sel'ciato m paving

selet'tivo adj selective. **selezio'nare** vt select. **selezi'one** f selection '**sella** f saddle. **sel'lare** vt saddle

seltz m soda water

'**selva** f forest

selvag'gina f game

sel'vaggio, -a adj wild; (primitivo) savage • mf savage

sel'vatico adj wild

se'maforo m traffic lights pl

se'mantica f semantics sg

sem'brare vi seem; (assomigliare) look like; **che te ne sembra?** what do you think?; **mi sembra che...** I think...

'**seme** m seed; (di mela) pip; (di carte) suit; (sperma) semen

se'mestre m half-year

semi'cerchio m semicircle

semifi'nale f semifinal

semi'freddo m ice cream and sponge dessert

'**semina** f sowing

semi'nare vt sow; ⊞ shake off (inseguitori)

semi'nario m seminar; (Relig) seminary

seminter'rato m basement

se'mitico adj Semitic

sem'mai conj in case • adv è lui, ~, che... if anyone, it's him who...

'**semola** f bran. **semo'lino** m semolina

'**semplic|e** adj simple; **in parole semplici** in plain words. **~'cemente** adv simply. **~cità** f simplicity. **~fi'care** vt simplify

'**sempre** adv always; (ancora) still; **per ~** for ever

sempre'verde adj & m evergreen

'**senape** f mustard

se'nato m senate. **sena'tore** m senator

se'nil|e adj senile. **~ità** f senility

'**senno** m sense

'**seno** m breast; (Math) sine

sen'sato adj sensible

sensazi|o'nale adj sensational. **~'one** f sensation

sen'sibil|e adj sensitive; (percepibile) perceptible; (notevole) considerable. **~ità** f sensitivity. **~iz'zare** vt make more aware (**a** of)

sensi'tivo, -a adj sensory • mf sensitive person; (medium) medium

'**senso** m sense; (significato) meaning; (direzione) direction; **non ha ~** it doesn't make sense; **perdere i sensi** lose consciousness. **~ dell'umorismo** sense of humour. **~ unico** (strada) one-way; **~ vietato** no entry

sensu'al|e adj sensual. **~ità** f sensuality

sen'tenz|a f sentence; (massima) saying. **~i'are** vi pass judgment

senti'ero m path

sentimen'tale adj sentimental. **senti'mento** m feeling

senti'nella f sentry

sen'ti|re vt feel; (udire) hear; (ascoltare) listen to; (gustare) taste; (odorare) smell • vi feel; (udire) hear; **~re caldo/freddo** feel hot/cold. **~rsi** vr feel; **~rsi di fare qcsa** feel like doing sth; **~rsi bene** feel well; **~rsi poco bene** feel unwell. **~to** adj sincere

sen'tore m inkling

'**senza** prep without; **~ correre** without running; **senz'altro** certainly; **~ ombrello** without an umbrella

senza'tetto m inv i **~** the homeless

sepa'ra|re vt separate. **~rsi** vr separate; (amici) part; **~rsi da** be separated from. **~ta'mente** adv separately. **~zi'one** f separation

se'pol|cro m sepulchre. **~to** pp di **seppellire**. **~'tura** f burial

seppel'lire vt bury

'**seppia** f cuttle fish; **nero di ~** sepia

sep'pure conj even if

se'quenza f sequence

seque'strare vt (rapire) kidnap; (Jur) impound; (confiscare) confiscate. **se'questro** m impounding; (di persona) kidnap[ping]

'sera f evening; **di** ∼ in the evening. **se'rale** adj evening. **se'rata** f evening; (ricevimento) party

ser'bare vt keep; harbour (odio); cherish (speranza)

serba'toio m tank. ∼ **d'acqua** water tank; (per una città) reservoir

'Serbia f Serbia

'serbo, -a adj & mf Serbian ● m (lingua) Serbian

sere'nata f serenade

serenità f serenity. **se'reno** adj serene; (cielo) clear

ser'gente m sergeant

seria'mente adv seriously

'serie f inv series; (complesso) set; Sport division; **fuori** ∼ custom-built; **produzione in** ∼ mass production; **di** ∼ **B** second-rate

serietà f seriousness. **'serio** adj serious; (degno di fiducia) reliable; **sul serio** seriously; (davvero) really

ser'mone m sermon

'serpe f liter viper. ∼**ggiare** vi meander; (diffondersi) spread

ser'pente m snake

'serra f greenhouse; **effetto** ∼ greenhouse effect

ser'randa f shutter

ser'ra|re vt shut; (stringere) tighten; (incalzare) press on. ∼**tura** f lock

'server m inv (Comput) server

ser'vir|e vt serve; (al ristorante) wait on ● vi serve; (essere utile) be of use; **non serve** it's no good. ∼**si** vr (di cibo) help oneself; ∼**si da** buy from; ∼**si di** use

servitù f servitude; (personale di servizio) servants pl

ser'vizio m service; (da caffè ecc) set;

(di cronaca, sportivo) report; **servizi** pl bathroom; **essere di** ∼ be on duty; **fare** ∼ (autobus ecc) run; **fuori** ∼ (bus) not in service; (ascensore) out of order; ∼ **compreso** service charge included. ∼ **in camera** room service. ∼ **civile** civilian duties done instead of national service. ∼ **militare** military service. ∼ **pubblico** utility company. ∼ **al tavolo** waiter service

'servo, -a mf servant

servo'sterzo m power steering

ses'san|ta adj & m sixty. ∼**tina** f **una** ∼**tina** about sixty

sessi'one f session

'sesso m sex

sessu'al|e adj sexual. ∼**ità** f sexuality

'sesto¹ adj sixth

'sesto² m (ordine) order

'seta f silk

setacci'are vt sieve. **se'taccio** m sieve

'sete f thirst; **avere** ∼ be thirsty

'setta f sect

set'tan|ta adj & m seventy. ∼**tina** f **una** ∼**tina** about seventy

'sette adj & m seven. ∼**cento** agg & m seven hundred; **il S**∼**cento** the eighteenth century

set'tembre m September

settentri|o'nale adj northern ● mf northerner. ∼**'one** m north

setti'ma|na f week. ∼**'nale** agg & m weekly

'settimo adj seventh

set'tore m sector

severità f severity. **se'vero** adj severe; (rigoroso) strict

se'vizi|a f torture; **se'vizie** pl torture sg. ∼**are** vt torture

sezio'nare vt divide; (Med) dissect. **sezi'one** f section; (reparto) department; (Med) dissection

sfaccen'dato adj idle

sfacchi'na|re vi toil. ∼**ta** f

drudgery

sfaccia'taggine f insolence. **∼'ato** adj cheeky, fresh Am

sfa'celo m ruin; **in ∼** in ruins

sfal'darsi vr flake off

sfa'mar|e vt feed. **∼si** vr satisfy one's hunger

sfar'zoso adj sumptuous

sfa'sato adj ① confused; (motore) which needs tuning

sfasci'a|re vt unbandage; (fracassare) smash. **∼rsi** vr fall to pieces. **∼to** adj beat-up

sfa'tare vt explode

sfati'cato adj lazy

sfavil'lare vi sparkle

sfavo'revole adj unfavourable

sfavo'rire vt disadvantage

'sfer|a f sphere. **∼ico** adj spherical

sfer'rare vt unshoe (cavallo); (scagliare) land

sfer'zare vt whip

sfian'carsi vr wear oneself out

sfi'bra|re vt exhaust. **∼to** adj exhausted

sfida f challenge. **sfi'dare** vt challenge

sfi'duci|a f mistrust. **∼'ato** adj discouraged

sfigu'rare vt disfigure ● vi (far cattiva figura) look out of place

sfilacci'ar|e vt, **∼si** vr fray

sfi'la|re vt unthread; (togliere di dosso) take off ● vi (truppe:) march past; (in parata) parade. **∼rsi** vr come unthreaded; (collant:) ladder; take off (pantaloni). **∼ta** f parade; (sfilza) series. **∼ta di moda** fashion show

'sfilza f (di errori) string

'sfinge f sphinx

sfi'nito adj worn out

sfio'rare vt skim; touch on (argomento)

sfio'rire vi wither; (bellezza:) fade

'sfitto adj vacant

'sfizio m whim, fancy; **togliersi uno ∼** satisfy a whim

sfo'cato adj out of focus

sfoci'are vi **∼ in** flow into

sfode'ra|re vt draw (pistola, spada). **∼to** adj unlined

sfo'gar|e vt vent. **∼si** vr give vent to one's feelings

sfoggi'are vt/i show off. **'sfoggio** m show, display; **fare sfoggio di** show off

'sfoglia f sheet of pastry; **pasta ∼** puff pastry

sfogli'are vt leaf through

'sfogo m outlet; fig outburst; (Med) rash; **dare ∼ a** give vent to

sfol'gorare vi blaze

sfol'lare vt clear ● vi (Mil) be evacuated

sfol'tire vt thin [out]

sfon'dare vt break down ● vi (aver successo) make a name for oneself

'sfondo m background

sfor'ma|re vt pull out of shape (tasche). **∼rsi** vr lose its shape; (persona:) lose one's figure. **∼to m** (Culin) flan

sfor'nito adj **∼ di** (negozio) out of

sfor'tuna f bad luck. **∼ta'mente** adv unfortunately. **sfortu'nato** adj unlucky

sfor'zar|e vt force. **∼si** vr try hard. **'sforzo** m effort; (tensione) strain

sfot'tere vt ① tease

sfracel'larsi vr smash

sfrat'tare vt evict. **'sfratto** m eviction

sfrecci'are vi flash past

sfregi'a|re vt slash. **∼to** adj scarred

'sfregio m slash

sfre'na|rsi vr run wild. **∼to** adj wild

sfron'tato adj shameless

sfrutta'mento m exploitation.

sfrut'tare vt exploit

sfug'gente adj elusive; (mento) receding

sfug'gi|re vi escape; ~**re a** escape [from]; **mi sfugge** it escapes me; **mi è sfuggito di mano** I lost hold of it ● vt avoid. ~**ta / di** ~**ta** in passing

sfu'ma|re vi (svanire) vanish; (colore:) shade off ● vt soften (colore). ~**'tura** f shade

sfuri'ata f outburst [of anger]

sga'bello m stool

sgabuz'zino m cupboard

sgambet'tare vi kick one's legs, (camminare) trot. **sgam'betto** m **fare lo sgambetto a qcno** trip sb up

sganasci'arsi vr ~ **dalle risa** roar with laughter

sganci'ar|e vt unhook; (Rail) uncouple; drop (bombe); ▢ cough up (denaro). ~**si** vr become unhooked; fig get away

sganghe'rato adj ramshackle

sgar'bato adj rude. **'sgarbo** m discourtesy

sgargi'ante adj garish

sgar'rare vi be wrong; (da regola) stray from the straight and narrow, **sgarro** m mistake, slip

sgattaio'lare vi sneak away; ~ **via** decamp

sghignaz'zare vi laugh scornfully, sneer

sgoccio'lare vi drip

sgo'larsi vr shout oneself hoarse

sgomb[e]'rare vt clear [out]. **'sgombro** adj clear ● m (trasloco) removal; (pesce) mackerel

sgomen'tar|e vt dismay. ~**si** vr be dismayed. **sgo'mento** m dismay

sgomi'nare vt defeat

sgom'mata f screech of tyres

sgonfi'ar|e vt deflate. ~**si** vr go down. **'sgonfio** adj flat

'sgorbio m scrawl; (fig: vista sgradevole) sight

sgor'gare vi gush [out] ● vt flush out, unblock (lavandino)

sgoz'zare vt ~ **qcno** cut sb's throat

sgra'd|evole adj disagreeable. ~**ito** adj unwelcome

sgrammati'cato adj ungrammatical

sgra'nare vt shell (piselli); open wide (occhi)

sgran'chir|e vt, ~**si** vr stretch

sgranocchi'are vt munch

sgras'sare vt remove the grease from

sgrazi'ato adj ungainly

sgreto'lar|e vt, ~**si** vr crumble

sgri'da|re vt scold. ~**ta** f scolding

sgros'sare vt rough-hew (marmo); fig polish

sguai'ato adj coarse

sgual'cire vt crumple

sgu'ardo m look; (breve) glance

squaz'zare vi splash; (nel fango) wallow

sguinzagli'are vt unleash

sgusci'ar|e vt shell ● vi (sfuggire) slip away; ~ **fuori** slip out

shake'rare vt shake

---

si

● pers pron (riflessivo) oneself; (lui) himself; (lei) herself; (esso, essa) itself; (loro) themselves; (reciproco) each other; (tra più di due) one another; (impersonale) you, one; **lavarsi** wash [oneself]; **si è lavata** she washed [herself]; **lavarsi le mani** wash one's hands; **si è lavata le mani** she washed her hands; **si è mangiato un pollo intero** he ate an entire chicken by himself; **incontrarsi** meet each other; **la gente si aiuta a vicenda** people help one another; **non**

si sa mai you never know, one never knows *fml*; **queste cose si dimenticano facilmente** these things are easily forgotten ● *m* (*chiave*, *nota*) B

sì *adv* yes

'sia¹ ▷ESSERE

'sia² *conj* **~...~...** (*entrambi*) both...and...; (*o l'uno o l'altro*) either...or...; **~ che venga**, **~ che non venga** whether he comes or not; **scegli ~ questo ~ quello** choose either this one or that one; **voglio ~ questo che quello** I want both this one and that one

sia'mese *adj* Siamese

sibi'lare *vi* hiss

si'cario *m* hired killer

sicché *conj* (*perciò*) so [that]; (*allora*) then

sic'come *conj* as

siccità *f* drought

Si'cilia *f* Sicily. **s~'ano, -a** *adj & mf* Sicilian

si'cura *f* safety catch; (*di portiera*) child-proof lock. **~'mente** *adv* definitely

sicu'rezza *f* certainty; (*salvezza*) safety; **uscita di ~** emergency exit. **~ delle frontiere** homeland security

si'curo *adj* safe; (*certo*) sure; (*saldo*) steady; (*Comm*) sound ● *adv* certainly ● *m* safety; **al ~** safe; **andare sul ~** play [it] safe; **di ~** definitely; **di ~**, **sarà arrivato** he must have arrived

siderur'gia *f* iron and steel industry

'sidro *m* cider

si'epe *f* hedge

si'ero *m* serum

sieroposi'tivo *adj* HIV positive

si'esta *f* afternoon nap

si'fone *m* siphon

Sig. *abbr* (*signore*) Mr

Sig.a *abbr* (*signora*) Mrs, Ms

siga'retta *f* cigarette

'sigaro *m* cigar

Sigg. *abbr* (*signori*) Messrs

sigil'lare *vt* seal. **si'gillo** *m* seal

'sigla *f* initials *pl.* **~ musicale** signature tune. **si'glare** *vt* initial

Sig.na *abbr* (*signorina*) Miss, Ms

signifi'ca|re *vt* mean. **~'tivo** *adj* significant. **~to** *m* meaning

si'gnora *f* lady; (*davanti a nome proprio*) Mrs; (*non sposata*) Miss; (*in lettere ufficiali*) Dear Madam; **il signor Vené e ~** Mr and Mrs Vené

si'gnore *m* gentleman; (*Relig*) lord; (*davanti a nome proprio*) Mr; (*in lettere ufficiali*) Dear Sir. **signo'rile** *adj* gentlemanly; (*di lusso*) luxury

signo'rina *f* young lady; (*seguito da nome proprio*) Miss

silenzia'tore *m* silencer

si'lenzi|o *m* silence. **~'oso** *adj* silent

silhou'ette *f* silhouette

si'licio *m* piastrina di **~** silicon chip

sili'cone *m* silicone

'sillaba *f* syllable

silu'rare *vt* torpedo. **si'luro** *m* torpedo

simboleggi'are *vt* symbolize

sim'bolico *adj* symbolic[al]

'simbolo *m* symbol

similarità *f inv* similarity

'simil|e *adj* similar; (*tale*) such; **~e a** like **~** *m* (*il prossimo*) fellow man. **~'mente** *adv* similarly. **~'pelle** *f* Leatherette®

simme'tria *f* symmetry. **sim'metrico** *adj* symmetric[al]

simpa'ti|a *f* liking; (*compenetrazione*) sympathy; **prendere qcno in ~a** take a liking to sb. **sim'patico** *adj* nice. **~iz'zante** *mf* well-wisher. **~iz'zare** *vi* **~izzare con** take a liking to; **~izzare per qcsa/qcno** lean towards sth/sb

sim'posio m symposium

simu'la|re vt simulate; feign (amicizia, interesse). **~zl'one** f simulation

simul'taneo adj simultaneous

sina'goga f synagogue

sincerità f sincerity. **sin'cero** adj sincere

'sincope f syncopation; (Med) fainting fit

sincron'ia f synchronization

sincroniz'zare vt synchronize

sinda'ca|le adj trade] union, [labor] union Am. **~lista** mf trade unionist, labor union member Am. **~re** vt inspect. **~to** m [trade] union, [labor] union Am; (associazione) syndicate

'sindaco m mayor

'sindrome f syndrome

sinto'nia f symphony. **sin'fonico** adj symphonic

singhioz'zare vi (di pianto) sob; (di hiccup) hiccup; (di pianto) sob

singo'lar|e adj singular ●m singular. **~mente** adv individually; (stranamente) peculiarly

'singolo adj single ●m individual; Tennis singles pl

si'nistra f left; a ~ on the left; girare a ~ turn to the left; con la guida a ~ (auto) with left-hand drive

sini'strato adj injured

si'nistr|o, -a adj left[-hand]; (avverso) sinister ●m accident ●f left [hand]; (Pol) left [wing]

'sino prep = FINO

si'nonimo adj synonymous ●m synonym

sin'tassi f syntax

'sintesi f inv synthesis; (riassunto) summary

sin'teti|co adj synthetic; (conciso) summary. **~z'zare** vt summarize

sintetiz'za'tore m synthesizer

sinto'matico adj symptomatic.

'sintomo m symptom

sinto'nia f tuning; **in ~** on the same wavelength

sinu'oso adj (strada) winding

si'pario m curtain

si'rena f siren

'Siria f Syria. **s~ano, -a** adj & mf Syrian

si'ringa f syringe

'sismico adj seismic

si'stem|a m system. **~a operativo** (Comput) operating system

siste'ma|re vt (mettere) put, tidy up (casa, camera); (risolvere) sort out; (procurare lavoro a) fix up with a job; (trovare alloggio a) find accommodation for; (sposare) marry off; (fam: punire) sort out. **~rsi** vr settle down; (trovare un lavoro) find a job; (trovare alloggio) find accommodation; (sposarsi) marry. **~tico** adj systematic. **~zi'one** f arrangement; (di questione) settlement; (lavoro) job; (alloggio) accommodation; (matrimonio) marriage

'sito m site. **~ web** web site

situ'are vt place

situazi'one f situation

ski-'lift m inv ski tow

slacci'are vt unfasten

slanci'a|rsi vr hurl oneself. **~to** adj slender. **'slancio** m impetus; (impulso) impulse

sla'vato adj fair

'slavo adj Slav[onic]

sle'al|e adj disloyal. **~tà** f disloyalty

sle'gare vt untie

'slitta f sledge, sleigh. **~'mento** m (di macchina) skid; (fig: di riunione) postponement

slit'ta|re vi (Auto) skid; (riunione:) be put off. **~ta** f skid

slit'tino m toboggan

'slogan m inv slogan

slo'ga|re vt dislocate. **~rsi** vr **~rsi una caviglia** sprain one's ankle. **~tura** f dislocation

sloggi'a|re vi move out

Slo'vacchia f Slovakia

Slo'venia f Slovenia

smacchi'a|re vt clean. **~tore** m stain remover

'smacco m humiliating defeat

smagli'ante adj dazzling

smagli'a|rsi vr (calza:) run. **~'tura** f run

smalizi'ato adj cunning

smal'ta|re vt enamel; glaze (ceramica); varnish (unghie). **~to** adj enamelled

smalti'mento m disposal; (di merce) selling off. **~ rifiuti** waste disposal; (di grassi) burning off

smal'tire vt burn off; (merce) sell off; fig get through (corrispondenza); **~ la sbornia** sober up

'smalto m enamel; (di ceramica) glaze; (per le unghie) nail varnish

smantel|la'mento m dismantling. **~'lare** vt dismantle

smarri'mento m loss; (psicologico) bewilderment

smar'ri|re vt lose; (temporaneamente) mislay. **~rsi** vr get lost; (turbarsi) be bewildered

smasche'rar|e vt unmask. **~si** vr (tradirsi) give oneself away

smemo'rato, -a adj forgetful ● mf scatterbrain

smen'ti|re vt deny. **~ta** f denial

sme'raldo m & adj emerald

smerci'are vt sell off

smerigli'ato adj emery; vetro **~** frosted glass. **sme'riglio** m emery

'smesso pp di **smettere** ● adj (abiti) cast-off

'smett|ere vt stop; stop wearing (abiti); **~ila!** stop it!

smi'dol'lato adj spineless

sminu'ir|e vt diminish. **~si** vr fig belittle oneself

sminuz'zare vt crumble; (fig: analizzare) analyse in detail

smista'mento m clearing; (postale) sorting. **smi'stare** vt sort; (Mil) post

smisu'rato adj boundless; (esorbitante) excessive

smobili'ta|re vt demobilize. **~zi'one** f demobilization

smo'dato adj immoderate

smog m smog

'smoking m inv dinner jacket, tuxedo Am

smon'ta|re vt take to pieces; (scoraggiare) dishearten ● vi (da veicolo) get off; (da cavallo) dismount; (dal servizio) go off duty. **~si** vr lose heart

'smorfi|a f grimace; (moina) simper; **fare ~e** make faces. **~'oso** adj affected

'smorto adj pale; (colore) dull

smor'zare vt dim (luce); tone down (colori); deaden (suoni); quench (sete)

'smosso pp di **smuovere**

smotta'mento m landslide

sms m inv (short message service) text message

'smunto adj emaciated

smu'over|e vt shift; (commuovere) move. **~si** vr move; (commuoversi) be moved

smus'sar|e vt round off; (fig: attenuare) tone down. **~si** vr go blunt

snatu'rato adj inhuman

snel'lir|e vt slim down. **~si** vr slim [down]. **'snello** adj slim

sner'va|re vt enervate. **~rsi** vr get exhausted

sni'dare vt drive out

snif'fare vt snort

snob'bare vt snub. **sno'bismo** m snobbery

snoccio'lare vt stone; fig blurt out

sno'da|re vt untie; (sciogliere) loosen. **~rsi** vr come untied; (strada:) wind. **~to** adj (persona) double-jointed; (dita) flexible

so'ave adj gentle

sobbal'zare vi jerk; (trasalire) start. **sob'balzo** m jerk; (trasalimento) start

sobbar'carsi vr ~ a undertake

sob'borgo m suburb

sobil'la|re vt stir up

'sobrio adj sober

soc'chiu|dere vt half-close. **~so** pp di socchiudere ● adj (occhi) half-closed; (porta) ajar

soc'cor|rere vt assist. **~so** pp di soccorrere ● m assistance; **soccorsi** pl rescuers; (dopo disastro) relief workers. **~so stradale** breakdown service

socialdemo'cra|tico, -a adj Social Democratic ● mf Social Democrat. **~'zia** f Social Democracy

soci'ale adj social

socia'li|smo m Socialism. **~sta** agg & mf Socialist. **~z'zare** vi socialize

società f inv society; (Comm) company. **~ per azioni** plc. **~ a responsabilità limitata** limited liability company

soci'evole adj sociable

'socio, -a mf member; (Comm) partner

sociolo'gia f sociology. **socio'logico** adj sociological

'soda f soda

soddisfa'cente adj satisfactory

soddi'sfa|re vt/i satisfy; meet (richiesta); make amends for (offesa). **~tto** pp di soddisfare ● adj satisfied. **~zi'one** f satisfaction

'sodo adj hard; fig firm; (uovo) hard-boiled ● adv hard; **dormire ~** sleep soundly

sofà m inv sofa

soffe'ren|te adj ill

soffer'marsi vr pause; **~ su** dwell on

sof'ferto pp di soffrire

soffi'a|re vt blow; reveal (segreto); (rubare) pinch 🗉 ● vi blow. **~ta** f fig 🗉 tip-off

'soffice adj soft

'soffio m puff; (Med) murmur

sof'fitt|a f attic. **~o** m ceiling

soffo'ca'mento m suffocation

soffo'ca|nte adj suffocating. **~re** vt/i suffocate; (con cibo) choke; fig stifle

sof'friggere vt fry lightly

sof'frire vt/i suffer; (sopportare) bear; **~ di** suffer from

sof'fritto pp di soffriggere

sof'fuso adj (luce) soft

sofisti'ca|re vt (adulterare) adulterate ● vi (sottilizzare) quibble. **~to** adj sophisticated

sugget'tivo adj subjective

sog'getto m subject ● adj subject; **essere ~ a** be subject to

soggezi'one f subjection; (rispetto) awe

sogghi'gnare vi sneer

soggio'gare vt subdue

soggior'nare vi stay. **soggi'orno** m stay; (stanza) living room

soggi'ungere vt add

'soglia f threshold

sogli'ola f sole

so'gna|re vt/i dream; **~re a occhi aperti** daydream. **~'tore, ~'trice** mf dreamer. **'sogno** m dream: **fare un sogno** have a dream; **neanche per sogno!** not at all!

'soia f soya

sol m (Mus) G

so'laio m attic

sola'mente adv only

so'lar|e adj (energia, raggi) solar; (crema) sun attrib. **~ium** m inv solarium

sol'care vt plough. **'solco** m furrow; (di ruota) track; (di nave) wake; (di disco) groove

sol'dato m soldier

'soldo m **non ha un ~** he hasn't got a penny; **senza un ~** penniless;

soldi pl (denaro) money sg

'sole m sun; (luce del sole) sun[light]; **al ~** in the sun; **prendere il ~** sunbathe

soleg'giato adj sunny

so'lenn|e adj solemn. **~ità** f solemnity

so'lere vi be in the habit of; **come si suol dire** as they say

sol'fato m sulphate

soli'da|le adj in agreement. **~rietà** f solidarity

solidifi'car|e vt/i, **~si** vr solidify

solidità f solidity; (di colori) fastness. **'solido** adj solid; (robusto) sturdy; (colore) fast ● m solid

so'lista adj solo ● mf soloist

solita'mente adv usually

soli'tario adj solitary; (isolato) lonely ● m (brillante) solitaire; (gioco di carte) patience, solitaire

'solito adj usual; **essere ~ fare qcsa** be in the habit of doing sth ● m usual; **di ~** usually

soli'tudine f solitude

solleci'ta|re vt speed up; urge (persona). **~zi'one** f (richiesta) request; (preghiera) entreaty

sol'leci|to adj prompt ● m reminder. **~tudine** f promptness; (interessamento) concern

solle'one m noonday sun; (periodo) dog days of summer

solleti'care vt tickle

solleva'mento m **~ pesi** weightlifting

solle'var|e vt lift; (elevare) raise; (confortare) comfort. **~si** vr rise; (riaversi) recover

solli'evo m relief

'solo, -a adj alone; (isolato) lonely; (unico) only; (Mus) solo; **da ~** by myself/yourself/himself etc ● m **il ~, la sola** the only one ● m (Mus) solo ● adv only

sol'stizio m solstice

sol'tanto adv only

so'lubile adj soluble; (caffè) instant

soluzi'one f solution; (Comm) payment

sol'vente adj & m solvent; **~ per unghie** nail polish remover

so'maro m ass; (Sch) dunce

so'matico adj somatic

somigli'an|te adj similar. **~za** f resemblance

somigli'ar|e vi **~e a** resemble. **~si** vr be alike

'somma f sum; (Math) addition

som'mare vt add; (totalizzare) add up

som'mario adj & m summary

som'mato adj **tutto ~** all things considered

sommeli'er m inv wine waiter

som'mer|gere vt submerge. **~gibile** m submarine. **~so** pp di sommergere

som'messo adj soft

sommini'stra|re vt administer. **~zi'one** f administration

sommità f inv summit

'sommo adj highest; fig supreme ● m summit

som'mossa f rising

sommozza'tore m frogman

so'naglio m bell

so'nata f sonata; fig 🔟 beating

'sonda f (Mech) drill; (Med, spaziale). **son'daggio** m drilling; (Med, spaziale) probe; (indagine) survey. **sondaggio d'opinioni** opinion poll. **son'dare** vt sound; (investigare) probe

sonnambu'lismo m sleepwalking. **son'nambulo, -a** mf sleepwalker

sonnecchi'are vi doze

son'nifero m sleeping-pill

'sonno m sleep; **aver ~** be sleepy. **~lenza** f sleepiness

so'noro adj resonant; (rumoroso) loud; (onde, scheda) sound attrib

sontu'oso adj sumptuous

sopo'rifero adj soporific

sop'palco m platform

soppe'rire vi **a ~ a qcsa** provide for sth

soppe'sare vt weigh up

soppor'ta|re vt support, (tollerare) stand; bear (dolore)

soppressi'one f removal; (di legge) abolition; (di diritti, pubblicazione) suppression; (annullamento) cancellation. **sop'presso** pp di **sopprimere**

sop'primere vt get rid of: abolish (legge); suppress (diritti, pubblicazione); (annullare) cancel

'sopra adv on top; (più in alto) higher [up]; (al piano superiore) upstairs; (in testo) above; **mettilo lì ~** put it up there; **di ~** upstairs; **pensarci ~** think about it; **vedi ~** see above • prep **~ [a]** on; (senza contatto, oltre) over; (riguardo a) about; **è ~ al tavolo, è ~ il tavolo** it's on the table; **il quadro è appeso ~ al camino** the picture is hanging over the fireplace; **il ponte passa ~ all'autostrada** the bridge crosses over the motorway; **è caduto ~ il tetto** it fell on the roof; **l'uno ~ l'altro** one on top of the other; (senza contatto) one above the other; **abita ~ di me** he lives upstairs from me; **i bambini ~ i dieci anni** children over ten; **20° ~ lo zero** 20° above zero; **~ il livello del mare** above sea level; **rifletti ~ quello che è successo** think about what happened • m **il [di] ~** the top

so'prabito m overcoat

soprac'ciglio m (pl f **sopracciglia**) eyebrow

sopracco'per|ta f bedspread; (di libri) [dust-]jacket. **~'tina** f book jacket

soprad'detto adj above-mentioned

sopraele'vata f elevated railway

sopraf'fa|re vt overwhelm. **~tto** pp di **sopraffare**. **~zi'one** f abuse of power

sopraf'fino adj excellent; (gusto, udito) highly refined

sopraggi'ungere vi (persona:) turn up; (accadere) happen

soprallu'ogo m inspection

sopram'mobile m ornament

soprannatu'rale adj & m supernatural

sopran'nome m nickname

so'prano mf soprano

soprappensi'ero adv lost in thought

sopras'salto m **di ~** with a start

soprasse'dere vi **~ a** postpone

soprat'tutto adv above all

sopravvalu'tare vt overvalue

sopravve'nire vi turn up; (accadere) happen. **~'vento** m fig upper hand

sopravvi|s'suto pp di **sopravvivere**. **~'venza** f survival. **sopravvi'vere** vi survive; **sopravvivere a** outlive (persona)

soprinten|den|te mf supervisor; (di museo ecc) keeper. **~za** f supervision; (ente) board

so'pruso m abuse of power

soq'quadro m **mettere a ~** turn upside down

sor'betto m sorbet

'sordido adj sordid; (avaro) stingy

sor'dina f mute; **in ~** on the quiet

sor'dità f deafness. **'sordo, -a** adj deaf; (rumore, dolore) dull • mf deaf person. **sordo'muto, -a** adj deaf-and-dumb

so'rel|la f sister. **~'lastra** f step-sister

sor'gente f spring; (fonte) source

'sorgere vi rise; fig arise

sormon'tare vt surmount

sorni'one adj sly

sorpas'sa|re vt surpass; (*eccedere*) exceed; (*veicolo*) overtake. **~to** adj old-fashioned. **sor'passo** m overtaking

sorpren'dente adj surprising; (*straordinario*) remarkable

sor'prendere vt surprise; (*cogliere in flagrante*) catch

sor'pre|sa f surprise; **di ~a** by surprise. **~o** pp di **sorprendere**

sor're|ggere vt support; (*tenere*) hold up. **~ggersi** vr support oneself. **~tto** pp di **sorreggere**

sor'ri|dere vi smile. **~so** pp di **sorridere** ● m smile

sorseggi'are vt sip. **'sorso** m sip; (*piccola quantità*) drop

'sorta f sort; **di ~** whatever; **ogni ~ di** all sorts of

'sorte f fate; (*caso imprevisto*) chance; **tirare a ~** draw lots. **sor'teggio** m draw

sorti'legio m witchcraft

sor'ti|re vi come out. **~ta** f (*Mil*) sortie; (*battuta*) witticism

'sorto pp di **sorgere**

sorvegli'an|te mf keeper; (*controllore*) overseer. **~za** f watch; (*Mil ecc*) surveillance

sorvegli'are vt watch over; (*controllare*) oversee; (*polizia:*) keep under surveillance

sorvo'lare vt fly over; fig skip

'sosia m inv double

sos'pen|dere vt hang; (*interrompere*) stop; (*privare di una carica*) suspend. **~si'one** f suspension

so'speso pp di **sospendere** ● adj (*impiegato, alunno*) suspended; **~ a** hanging from; **~ a un filo** fig hanging by a thread ● m **in ~** pending; (*emozionato*) in suspense

sospet'tare vt suspect. **so'spetto** adj suspicious; **persona sospetta** suspicious person ● m suspicion; (*persona*) suspect. **~'toso** adj suspicious

so'spin|gere vt drive. **~to** pp di **sospingere**

sospi'rare vi sigh ● vt long for. **so'spiro** m sigh

'sosta f stop; (*pausa*) pause; **senza ~** non-stop; **"divieto di ~"** "no parking"

sostan'tivo m noun

so'stanz|a f substance; **~e** pl (*patrimonio*) property sg. **~i'oso** adj substantial; (*cibo*) nourishing

so'stare vi stop; (*fare una pausa*) pause

so'stegno m support

soste'ner|e vt support; (*sopportare*) bear; (*resistere*) withstand; (*affermare*) maintain; (*nutrire*) sustain; sit (*esame*); **~e le spese** meet the costs. **~si** vr support oneself

sosteni'tore, -'trice mf supporter

sostenta'mento m maintenance

soste'nuto adj (*stile*) formal; (*prezzi, velocità*) high

sostitu'ir|e vt substitute (a for), replace (con with). **~si** vr **~si a** replace

sostitu|to, -ta mf replacement, stand-in ● m (*surrogato*) substitute. **~zi'one** f substitution

sot'tana f petticoat; (*di prete*) cassock

sotter'raneo adj underground ● m cellar

sotter'rare vt bury

sottigli'ezza f slimness; fig subtlety

sot'tile adj thin; (*udito, odorato*) keen; (*osservazione, distinzione*) subtle. **~iz'zare** vi split hairs

sottin'te|ndere vt imply. **~so** pp di **sottintendere** ● m allusion; **senza ~si** openly ● adj implied

'sotto adv below; (*più in basso*) lower [down]; (*al di sotto*) underneath; (*al piano di sotto*) downstairs; **è lì ~** it's underneath; ~ ~ deep down; (di nascosto) on the quiet; (di ~ down-stairs; **mettersi** ~ fig get down to it; **mettere** ~ (🗖: investire) knock down ● prep ~ [a] under; (al di sotto di) underneath; **abita** ~ **di me** he lives downstairs from me; **i bambini** ~ **i dieci anni** children under ten; 20° ~ zero 20° below zero; ~ **il livello del mare** below sea level; ~ **la pioggia** in the rain; ~ **calmante** under sedation; ~ **condizione che...** on condition that...; ~ **giuramento** under oath; ~ **sorveglianza** under surveillance; ~ **Natale/gli esami** around Christmas/exam time; **al di** ~ **di** under; **andare** ~ **I 50 all'ora** do less than 50km an hour ● m **il [di]** ~ the bottom

sotto'banco adv under the counter

sottobicchi'ere m coaster

sotto'bosco m undergrowth

sotto'braccio adv arm in arm

sotto'fondo m background

sottoline'are vt underline; fig stress

sot'tolio adv in oil

sotto'mano adv within reach

sottoma'rino adj & m submarine

sotto'messo pp di **sottomettere**

sotto'mettere vt submit; subdue (popolo), ~**si** vr submit **sottomissi'one** f submission

sottopas'saggio m underpass; (pedonale) subway

sotto'por|re vt submit; (costringere) subject, ~**si** vr submit oneself; ~**si a** undergo. **sotto'posto** pp di **sottoporre**

sotto'scala m cupboard under the stairs

sotto'scritto pp di **sottoscrivere** ● m undersigned

sotto'scri|vere vt sign; (approvare) sanction, subscribe to. ~**zi'one** f (petizione) petition; (approvazione) sanction; (raccolta di denaro) appeal

sotto'sopra adv upside down

sotto'stante adj **la strada** ~ the road below

sottosu'olo m subsoil

sottosvilup'pato adj under-developed

sotto'terra adv underground

sotto'titolo m subtitle

sottovalu'tare vt underestimate

sotto'veste f slip

sotto'voce adv in a low voice

sottovu'oto adj vacuum-packed

sot'tra|rre vt remove; embezzle (fondi); (Math) subtract; ~**rsi** vr ~**rsi a** escape from; avoid (responsabilità). ~**rto** pp di **sottrarre**. ~**zi'one** f removal; (di fondi) embezzlement; (Math) subtraction

sottuffici'ale m non-commissioned officer; (Naut) petty officer

sou'brette f inv showgirl

so'vietico, -a adj & mf Soviet

sovraccari'care vt overload. **sovrac'carico** adj overloaded (**di** with) ● m overload

sovrannatu'rale adj & m = SO-PRANNATURALE

so'vrano, -a adj sovereign; fig su preme ● mf sovereign

sovrap'por|re vt superimpose. ~**si** vr overlap

sovra'stare vt dominate; fig: (pericolo:) hang over

sovrinten'den|te, ~za = SO-PRINTENDENTE, SUPRINTENDENZA

sovru'mano adj superhuman

sovvenzi'one f subsidy

sovver'sivo adj subversive

'sozzo adj filthy

S.p.A. abbr (società per azioni) plc

spac'ca|re vt split; chop (legna). ~**rsi** vr split. ~**'tura** f split

spacci'a|re vt deal in, push (droga); ~**re qcsa per qcsa** pass sth off as sth. ∼**rsi** vr ∼**rsi per** pass oneself off as. ∼'**tore,** ∼'**trice** mf (di droga) pusher; (di denaro falso) distributor of forged bank notes. ∼'**spaccio** m (di droga) dealing; (negozio) shop

'**spacco** m split

spac'**cone, -a** mf boaster

'**spada** f sword. ∼**c'cino** m swordsman

spae'**sato** adj disorientated

spa'**ghetti** mpl spaghetti sg

spa'**ghetto** m (🔲: spavento) fright

'**Spagna** f Spain

spa'**gnolo, -a** adj Spanish ● mf Spaniard ● m (lingua) Spanish

'**spago** m string; **dare** ∼ **a qcno** encourage sb

spai'**ato** adj odd

spalan'**ca|re** vt, ∼**rsi** vr open wide. ∼**to** adj wide open

spa'**lare** vt shovel

spall'**a** f shoulder; (di comico) straight man; ∼**e** pl (schiena) back; **alle** ∼**e di qcno** (ridere) behind sb's back. ∼**eggi'are** vt back up

spal'**letta** f parapet

spalli'**era** f back; (di letto) headboard; (ginnastica) wall bars pl

spal'**lina** f strap; (imbottitura) shoulder pad

spal'**mare** vt spread

'**spander|e** vt spread; (versare) spill. ∼**si** vr spread

spappo'**lare** vt crush

spa'**ra|re** vt/i shoot; ∼**rle grosse** talk big. ∼**toria** f shooting

sparecchi'**are** vt clear

spa'**reggio** m (Comm) deficit; Sport play-off

'**sparg|ere** vt scatter; (diffondere) spread; shed (lacrime, sangue). ∼**ersi** vr spread. ∼**i'mento** m scattering; ∼**imento di sangue** bloodshed

spa'**ri|re** vi disappear; ∼**sci!** get lost!. ∼**zi'one** f disappearance

spar'**lare** vi ∼ **di** run down

'**sparo** m shot

sparpagli'**ar|e** vt, ∼**si** vr scatter

'**sparso** pp di spargere ● adj scattered; (sciolto) loose

spar'**tire** vt share out; (separare) separate

sparti'**traffico** m inv traffic island; (di autostrada) central reservation, median strip Am

spartizi'**one** f division

spa'**ruto** adj gaunt; (gruppo) small; (peli, capelli) sparse

sparvi'**ero** m sparrow-hawk

'**spasimo** m spasm

spa'**smodico** adj spasmodic

spas'**sar|si** vr amuse oneself; ∼**sela** have a good time

spassio'**nato** adj dispassionate

'**spasso** m fun; **essere uno** ∼ be hilarious; **andare a un** ∼ go for a walk. spas'**soso** adj hilarious

'**spatola** f spatula

spau'**racchio** m scarecrow; fig bugbear. spau'**rire** vt frighten

spa'**valdo** adj defiant

spaventa'**passeri** m inv scarecrow

spaven'**tar|e** vt frighten. ∼**si** vr be frightened. spa'**vento** m fright. spa-ven'**toso** adj frightening; (🔲: enorme) incredible

spazi'**ale** adj spatial; (cosmico) space attrib

spazi'**are** vt space out ● vi range

spazien'**tirsi** vr lose patience

'**spazio** m space. ∼**'oso** adj spacious

spaz'**z|are** vt sweep; ∼**are via** sweep away; (🔲: mangiare) devour. ∼**a'tura** f rubbish. ∼**ino** m road sweeper; (netturbino) dustman

'**spazzol|a** f brush; (di tergicristallo) blade. ∼**'lare** vt brush. ∼**'lino** m small brush. ∼**'lino da denti** toothbrush. ∼**'lone** m scrubbing brush

specchi'arsi vr look at oneself in the mirror; (riflettersi) be mirrored; ~ **in qcno** model oneself on sb

specchi'etto m ~ **retrovisore** driving mirror

'specchio m mirror

speci'ale adj special ●m (TV) special [programme]. ~**lista** mf specialist. ~**lità** f inv specialty

specializ'zare vt, ~**rsi** vr specialize. ~**to** adj skilled

special'mente adv especially

'specie f inv species; (tipo) kind; **fare ~ a** surprise

specifi'care vt specify. **spe'cifico** adj specific

specu'lare[1] vi speculate; ~ **su** (indagare) speculate on; (Fin) speculate in

specu'lare[2] adj mirror attrib

specula'tore, -'trice mf speculator. ~**zi'one** f speculation

spe'dire vt send. ~**to** pp di **spedire** ●adj quick; (parlata) fluent. ~**zi'one** f dispatch; (Comm) consignment; (scientifica) expedition

'spegnere vt put out; turn off (gas, luce); switch off (motore), slake (sete). ~**si** vr go out; (morire) pass away

spelacchi'ato (tappeto) threadbare; (cane) mangy

spe'lare vt skin (coniglio). ~**si** vr (cane) moult

speleolo'gia f potholing

spel'lare vt skin; fig fleece. ~**si** vr peel off

spe'lonca f cave; fig hole

spendacci'one, -a mf spendthrift

'spendere vt spend; ~ **fiato** waste one's breath

spen'nare vt pluck; 🔄 fleece (cliente)

spennel'lare vt brush

spensie|ra'tezza f lightheartedness. ~**'rato** adj carefree

'spento pp di **spegnere** ●adj off; (gas) out; (smorto) dull

spe'ranza f hope; **pieno di ~** hopeful; **senza ~** hopeless

spe'rare vt hope for; (aspettarsi) expect ●vi ~ **in** trust in; **spero di sì** I hope so

'sperdersi vr get lost. ~**'duto** adj lost; (isolato) secluded

spergi'uro, -a mf perjurer ●m perjury

sperimen'tale adj experimental. ~**re** vt experiment with; test (resistenza, capacità, teoria). ~**zi'one** f experimentation

'sperma m sperm

spe'rone m spur

sperpe'rare vt squander. **'sperpero** m waste

'spesa f expense; (acquisto) purchase; **andare a far ~e** go shopping; **fare la ~a** do the shopping; **fare le ~e di** pay for; ~**e bancarie** bank charges. ~**e a carico del destinatario** carriage forward. **spe'sato** adj all-expenses-paid. ~**o** pp di **spendere**

'spesso[1] adj thick

'spesso[2] adv often

spes'sore m thickness; (fig: consistenza) substance

spet'tabile adj (Comm) abbr (**Spett.**) **S~ ditta Rossi** Messrs Rossi

spettaco'lare adj spectacular. **spet'tacolo** m spectacle; (rappresentazione) show. ~**loso** adj spectacular

spet'tare vi ~ **a** be up to; (diritto:) be due to

spetta'tore, -'trice mf spectator; **spettatori** pl audience sg

spettego'lare vi gossip

spet'trale adj ghostly. **'spettro** m ghost; (Phys) spectrum

'spezie fpl spices

spez'zare vt, ~**si** vr break

spezza'tino m stew

spez'zato m coordinated jacket and trousers

spezzet'tare vt break into small pieces

'spia f spy; (della polizia) informer; (di porta) peep-hole; **fare la ~** sneak. **~ [luminosa]** light. **~ dell'olio** oil [warning] light

spiacci'care vt squash

spia'ce|nte adj sorry. **~vole** adj unpleasant

spi'aggia f beach

spia'nare vt level; (rendere liscio) smooth; roll out (pasta); raze to the ground (edificio)

spian'tato adj fig penniless

spi'are vt spy on; wait for (occasione ecc)

spiattel'lare vt blurt out; shove (oggetto)

spi'azzo m (radura) clearing

spic'ca|re vt **~re un salto** jump; **~re il volo** take flight ● vi stand out. **~to** adj marked

'spicchio m (di agrumi) segment; (di aglio) clove

spicci'a|rsi vr hurry up. **~tivo** adj speedy

'spicciolo adj (comune) banal; (denaro, 5 euro) in change. **spiccioli** pl change sg

'spicco m relief; **fare ~** stand out

'spider f inv open-top sports car

spie'dino m kebab. **spiedo** m spit; **allo spiedo** on a spit, spit-roasted

spie'ga|re vt explain; open out (cartina); unfurl (vele). **~rsi** vr explain oneself; (vele, bandiere:) unfurl. **~zi'one** f explanation

spiegaz'zato adj crumpled

spie'tato adj ruthless

spiffe'rare vt blurt out ● vi (vento:) whistle. **'spiffero** m draught

'spiga f spike; (Bot) ear

spigli'ato adj self-possessed

'spigolo m edge; (angolo) corner

'spilla f brooch. **~ da balia** safety pin. **~ di sicurezza** safety pin

spil'lare vt tap

'spillo m pin. **~ di sicurezza** safety pin; (in arma) safety catch

spi'lorcio adj stingy

'spina f thorn; (di pesce) bone; (Electr) plug. **~ dorsale** spine

spi'naci mpl spinach

spi'nale adj spinal

spi'nato adj (filo) barbed; (pianta) thorny

spi'nello m Ⓘ joint

'spinger|e vt push; fig drive. **~si** vr (andare) proceed

spi'noso adj thorny

'spint|a f push; (violenta) thrust; fig spur. **~o** pp di **spingere**

spio'naggio m espionage

spio'vente adj sloping

spi'overe vi liter stop raining; (ricadere) fall; (scorrere) flow down

'spira f coil

spi'raglio m small opening; (soffio d'aria) breath of air; (raggio di luce) gleam of light

spi'rale adj spiral ● f spiral; (negli orologi) hairspring; (anticoncezionale) coil

spi'rare vi (soffiare) blow; (morire) pass away

spiri't|ato adj possessed; (espressione) wild. **spirito** m spirit; (arguzia) wit; (intelletto) mind; **fare dello spirito** be witty; **sotto spirito** in brandy. **~o'saggine** f witticism. **spi'ritoso** adj witty

spiritu'ale adj spiritual

'splen|dere vi shine. **~dido** adj splendid. **~'dore** m splendour

'spoglia f (di animale) skin; **spoglie** pl (salma) mortal remains; (bottino) spoils

spogli'a|re vt strip; (svestire) undress; (fare lo spoglio di) go through. **~rello** m strip-tease. **~rsi** vr strip, undress. **~toio** m dressing room; Sport changing room; (guardaroba) cloakroom, checkroom *Am.* '**spoglio** *adj* undressed; (albero, muro) bare ● *m* (scrutinio) perusal

'**spola** *f* shuttle; **fare la ~** shuttle

spol'**pare** *vt* flesh; *fig* fleece

spolve'rare *vt* dust, 🔲 devour (cibo)

'**sponda** *f* shore; (di fiume) bank; (bordo) edge

sponsoriz'zare *vt* sponsor

spon'taneo *adj* spontaneous

spopo'lar|e *vt* depopulate ● *vi* (avere successo) draw the crowds. **~si** *vr* become depopulated

sporadica'mente *adv* sporadically. **spo'radico** *adj* sporadic

spor'clare *vt* dirty; (macchiare) soil. **~arsi** *vr* get dirty. **~izla** *f* dirt. '**sporco** *adj* dirty; **avere la coscienza sporca** have a guilty conscience ● *m* dirt

spor'gen|te *adj* jutting. ● **za** *f* projection

'**sporger|e** *vt* stretch out; **~e querela contro** take legal action against ● *vi* jut out. **~si** *vr* lean out

sport *m inv* sport

'**sporta** *f* shopping basket

spor'tello *m* door; (di banca ecc) window. **~ automatico** cash dispenser

spor'tivo, -a *adj* sports *attrib*; (persona) sporty ● *m* sportsman ● *f* sportswoman

'**sporto** *pp di* sporgere

'**sposa** *f* bride. **~'lizio** *m* wedding

spo'sar|e *vt* marry; *fig* espouse. **~rsi** *vr* get married; (vino:) go (con with). **~to** *adj* married. '**sposo** *m* bridegroom; **sposi** *pl* (novelli) newlyweds

spossa'tezza *f* exhaustion. **spos'sato** *adj* exhausted, worn out

spo'star|e *vt* move; (differire) postpone; (cambiare) change. **~rsi** *vr* move. **~to, -a** *adj* ill-adjusted ● *mf*

(disadattato) misfit

'**spranga** *f* bar. **spran'gare** *vt* bar

'**sprazzo** *m* (di colore) splash; (di luce) flash; *fig* glimmer

spre'care *vt* waste. '**spreco** *m* waste

spre'gevole *adj* despicable. **~la'tivo** *adj* pejorative. '**spregio** *m* contempt

spregiudi'cato *adj* unscrupulous

spremer|e *vt* squeeze. **~si** *vr* **~si le meningi** rack one's brains

spremia'grumi *m* lemon squeezer

spre'muta *f* juice. **~ d'arancia** fresh orange [juice]

sprez'zante *adj* contemptuous

sprigio'nar|e *vt* emit. **~si** *vr* burst out

spriz'zare *vt/i* spurt; be bursting with (salute, gioia)

sprofon'dar|e *vi* sink; (crollare) collapse. **~si** *vr* **~si in** sink into; *fig* be engrossed in

'**sprone** *m* spur; (sartoria) yoke

sproporzio'nato *adj* disproportionate. **~'one** *f* disproportion

sproposi'tato *adj* full of blunders; (enorme) huge. **spro'posito** *m* blunder; (eccesso) excessive amount

sprovve'duto *adj* unprepared; **~ di** lacking in

sprov'visto *adj* **~ di** out of; lacking in (fantasia, pazienza); **alla sprovvista** unexpectedly

spruz'za|re *vt* sprinkle; (vaporizzare) spray; (inzaccherare) spatter. **~'tore** *m* spray; '**spruzzo** *m* spray; (di fango) splash

spudo'ratezza *f* shamelessness. **~'rato** *adj* shameless

'**spugna** *f* sponge; (tessuto) towelling. **spu'gnoso** *adj* spongy

'**spuma** *f* foam; (schiuma) froth; (Culin) mousse. **spu'mante** *m* sparkling wine. **spumeg'giare** *vi* foam

spun'ta|re *vt* break the point of;

trim (capelli); **~rla** fig win ● vi
(pianta:) sprout; (capelli:) begin to
grow; (sorgere) rise; (apparire) appear.
~rsi vr get blunt. **~ta** f trim

spun'tino m snack

'spunto m cue; fig starting point;
dare ~ a give rise to

spur'gar|e vt purge. **~si** vr (Med)
expectorate

spu'tare vt/i spit; **~ sentenze** pass
judgment. **'sputo** m spit

'squadra f team, squad; (di polizia
ecc) squad; (da disegno) square. **squa-
'drare** vt square; (guardare) look up
and down

squa'dr|iglia f, **~one** m squadron

squagli'ar|e vt, **~si** vr melt; (~sela
(⊤): svignarsela) steal out

squalifi|ca f disqualification.
~'care vt disqualify

'squallido adj squalid. **squal'lore** m
squalor

'squalo m shark

'squama f scale; (di pelle) flake

squa'm|are vt scale. **~arsi** vr
(pelle:) flake off. **~'moso** adj scaly;
(pelle) flaky

squarcia'gola: a ~ adv at the top
of one's voice

squarci'are vt rip. **'squarcio** m rip;
(di ferita, in nave) gash; (di cielo) patch

squattri'nato adj penniless

squilib'ra|re vt unbalance. **~to, -a**
adj unbalanced ● mf lunatic. **squi'li-
brio** m imbalance

squil'la|nte adj shrill. **~re** vi (cam-
pana:) peal; (tromba:) blare; (telefono:) ring. **'squillo** m blare; (Teleph)
ring ● f (ragazza) call girl

squi'sito adj exquisite

sradi'care vt uproot; eradicate
(vizio, male)

sragio'nare vi rave

srego'lato adj inordinate; (dissoluto)
dissolute

s.r.l. abbr (società a responsabilità li-

mitata) Ltd

sroto'lare vt uncoil

SS abbr (strada statale) national road

'stabile adj stable; (permanente) lasting; (saldo) steady; **compagnia ~**
(Theat) repertory company ● m (edificio) building

stabili'mento m factory; (industriale) plant; (edificio) establishment.
~ balneare lido

stabi'li|re vt establish; (decidere) de-
cide. **~rsi** vr settle. **~tà** f stability

stabiliz'zar|e vt stabilize. **~rsi** vr
stabilize. **~'tore** m stabilizer

stac'car|e vt detach; pronounce
clearly (parole); (separare) separate;
turn off (corrente) ● vi (⊤: finire di lavorare) knock off. **~si** vr come off;
~si da break away from (partito, famiglia)

stacci'onata f fence

'stacco m gap

'stadio m stadium

'staffa f stirrup

staf'fetta f dispatch rider

stagio'nale adj seasonal

stagio'na|re vt season (legno);
mature (formaggio). **~to** adj (legno)
seasoned; (formaggio) matured

stagi'one f season; **alta/bassa ~**
high/low season

stagli'arsi vr stand out

sta'gna|nte adj stagnant. **~re** vt
(saldare) solder; (chiudere ermeticamente)
seal ● vi stagnate. **'stagno** adj water-
tight ● m pond; (metallo) tin

sta'gnola f tinfoil

'stall|a f stable; (per buoi) cowshed.
~i'ere m groom

stal'lone m stallion

sta'mani, stamat'tina adv this
morning

stam'becco m ibex

stam'berga f hovel

'stampa f (Typ) printing; (giornali,
giornalisti) press; (riproduzione) print

stam'pa|nte f printer. **~nte laser** laser printer. **~re** vt print. **~'tello** m block letters pl

stam'pella f crutch

'stampo m mould; **di vecchio ~** (persona) of the old school

sta'nare vt drive out

stan'car|e vt tire; (annoiare) bore. **~si** vr get tired

stan'chezza f tiredness. **'stanco** adj tired; **stanco di** fed up with. **stanco morto** dead tired, exhausted

'standard adj & m inv standard. **~iz'zare** vt standardize

'stan|ga f bar; (persona) beanpole. **~'gata** f fig blow; (🅵: nel calcio) big kick. **stan'ghetta** f (di occhiali) leg

sta'notte adv tonight; (la notte scorsa) last night

'stante prep on account of; **a se ~** separate

stan'tio adj stale

stan'tuffo m piston

'stanza f room; (metrica) stanza

stanzi'are vt allocate

stap'pare vt uncork

■ stare

● vi (rimanere) stay; (abitare) live; (con gerundio) be; **sto solo cinque minuti** I'll stay only five minutes; **sto in piazza Peyron** I live in Peyron Square; **sta dormendo** he's sleeping; **~ a** (attenersi) keep to; (spettare) be up to; **~ bene** (economicamente) be well off; (di salute) be well; (addirsi) suit; **~ dietro a** (seguire) follow; (sorvegliare) keep an eye on; (corteggiare) run after; **~ in piedi** stand; **~ per** be about to; **come stai/sta?** how are you?; **lasciar ~** leave alone; **starci** (essere contenuto) go into; (essere d'accordo) agree; **il 3 nel 12 ci sta 4 volte** 3 into 12

goes 4; **non sa ~ agli scherzi** he can't take a joke; **~ sulle proprie** keep oneself to oneself.

● **starsene** vr (rimanere) stay

---

starnu'tire vi sneeze. **star'nuto** m sneeze

sta'sera adv this evening, tonight

sta'tale adj state attrib ● mf state employee ● f main road

'statico adj static

sta'tista m statesman

sta'tistic|a f statistics sg. **~o** adj statistical

'stato pp di essere, stare ● m state; (posizione sociale) position; (Jur) status. **~ d'animo** frame of mind. **~ civile** marital status. S**~ Maggiore** (Mil) General Staff. **Stati** pl **Uniti [d'America]** United States [of America]

'statua f statue

statuni'tense adj United States attrib, US attrib ● mf citizen of the United States, US citizen

sta'tura f height; **di alta ~** tall; **di bassa ~** short

sta'tuto m statute

stazio'nario adj stationary

stazi'one f station; (città) resort. **~ balneare** seaside resort. **~ ferroviaria** train station. **~ di servizio** service station. **~ termale** spa

'stecca f stick; (di ombrello) rib; (da biliardo) cue; (Med) splint; (di sigarette) carton; (di reggiseno) stiffener

stec'cato m fence

stec'chito adj skinny; (rigido) stiff; (morto) stone cold dead

'stella f star; **salire alle stelle** (prezzi) rise sky-high. **~ alpina** edelweiss. **~ cadente** shooting star. **~ filante** streamer. **~ di mare** starfish

stel'lare adj stellar

'stelo m stem; **lampada** f **a ~**

standard lamp

'stemma m coat of arms

stempi'ato adj bald at the temples

sten'dardo m standard

'stender|e vt spread out; (*appendere*) hang out; (*distendere*) stretch [out]; (*scrivere*) write down. ~**si** vr stretch out

stendibianche'ria m inv, **sten-di'toio** m clothes horse

stenodatti|logra'fia f shorthand typing

stenogra'f|are vt take down in shorthand. ~**ia** f shorthand

sten'ta|re vi ~**re** a find it hard to. ~**to** adj laboured. **'stento** m effort; **a stento** with difficulty; **stenti** pl hardships, privations

'sterco m dung

'stereo['fonico] adj stereo- [phonic]

stereoti'pato adj stereotyped; (*sorriso*) insincere. **stere'otipo** m stereotype

steril|e adj sterile; (*terreno*) barren. ~**ità** f sterility. ~**iz'zare** vt sterilize. ~**izzazi'one** f sterilization

ster'lina f pound; **lira** ~ [pound] sterling

stermi'nare vt exterminate

stermi'nato adj immense

ster'minio m extermination

ste'roide m steroid

ster'zare vi steer. **'sterzo** m steering

'steso pp di **stendere**

'stesso adj same; **io** ~ myself; **tu** ~ yourself; **me** ~ myself; **se** ~ himself; **in quel momento** ~ at that very moment; **dalla stessa regina** by the Queen herself; **coi miei stessi occhi** with my own eyes ●pron **lo** ~ the same one; (*la stessa cosa*) the same; **fa lo** ~ it's all the same; **ci vado lo** ~ I'll go just the same

ste'sura f drawing up; (*documento*) draft

stick m **colla a** ~ glue stick; **deodorante a** ~ stick deodorant

'stigma m stigma. ~**te** fpl stigmata

sti'lare vt draw up

'stil|e m style. **sti'lista** mf stylist. ~**iz'zato** adj stylized

stil'lare vi ooze

stilo'grafica f fountain pen. ~**o** adj **penna** ~**a** fountain pen

'stima f esteem; (*valutazione*) estimate. **sti'mare** vt esteem; (*valutare*) estimate; (*ritenere*) consider

stimo'la|nte adj stimulating ●m stimulant. ~**re** vt stimulate; (*incitare*) incite

'stimolo m stimulus; (*fitta*) pang

'stinco m shin

'stinger|e vt/i fade. ~**si** vr fade. **'stinto** pp di **stingere**

sti'par|e vt cram. ~**si** vr crowd together

stipendi'ato adj salaried ●m salaried worker. **sti'pendio** m salary

'stipite m doorpost

stipu'la|re vt stipulate. ~**zi'one** f stipulation; (*accordo*) agreement

stira'mento m sprain

sti'ra|re vt iron; (*distendere*) stretch. ~**rsi** vr (*distendersi*) stretch; pull (*muscolo*). ~**tura** f ironing. **'stiro** m **ferro da stiro** iron

'stirpe f stock

stiti'chezza f constipation. **'stitico** adj constipated

'stiva f (*Naut*) hold

sti'vale m boot. **stivali** pl di **gomma** Wellington boots

'stizza f anger

stiz'zi|re vt irritate. ~**rsi** vr become irritated. ~**to** adj irritated. **stiz'zoso** adj peevish

stocca'fisso m stockfish

stoc'cata f stab; (*battuta pungente*) gibe

'stoffa f material; fig stuff

'stola f stole

'stolto adj foolish

stoma'chevole adj revolting

'stomaco m stomach; **mal di ∼** stomach-ache

sto'na|re vt/i sing/play out of tune ● vi (non intonarsi) clash. **∼to** adj out of tune; (discordante) clashing; (confuso) bewildered. **∼'tura** f false note; (discordanza) clash

'stoppia f stubble

'stop|pino m wick

'stop'poso adj tough

'storcer|e vt, **∼si** vr twist

stor'dire vt stun; (intontire) daze. **∼rsi** vr dull one's senses. **∼to** adj stunned; (intontito) dazed; (sventato) heedless

'storia f history; (racconto, bugia) story; (pretesto) excuse; **fare [delle] storie** make a fuss

'storico, -a adj historical; (di importanza storica) historic ● mf historian

stori'one m sturgeon

'stormo m flock

'storno m starling

storpi'a|re vt cripple; mangle (parole). **∼'tura** f deformation. **'stor-pio, -a** adj crippled ● mf cripple

'stort|a f (distorsione) sprain; **prendere una ∼a alla caviglia** sprain one's ankle. **∼o** pp di **storcere** ● adj crooked; (ritorto) twisted; (gambe) bandy; fig wrong

sto'viglie fpl crockery sg

'strabico, -a adj cross-eyed

strabili'ante adj astonishing

stra'bismo m squint

straboc'care vi overflow

stra'carico adj overloaded

strac'ci|are vt tear; (🄸: vincere) thrash. **∼'ato** adj torn; (persona) in rags; (prezzi) slashed; **a un prezzo ∼ato** dirt cheap. **'straccio, -a** adj torn ● m rag; (strofinaccio) cloth. **∼'one**

m tramp

stra'cotto adj overdone; (🄸: innamorato) head over heels ● m stew

'strada f road; (di città) street; **essere fuori ∼** be on the wrong track; **fare ∼** lead the way, **farsi ∼** make one's way. **∼ maestra** main road. **∼ a senso unico** one-way street. **∼ senza uscita** blind alley. **stra'dale** adj road attrib

strafalci'one m blunder

stra'fare vi overdo things

stra'foro: di ∼ adv on the sly

strafot'ten|te adj arrogant. **∼za** f arrogance

'strage f slaughter

'stralcio m (parte) extract

stralu'na|re vt **∼re gli occhi** open one's eyes wide. **∼to** adj (occhi) staring; (persona) distraught

stramaz'zare vi fall heavily

stram'beria f oddity. **'strambo** adj strange

strampa'lato adj odd

stra'nezza f strangeness

strango'lare vt strangle

strani'ero, -a adj foreign ● mf foreigner

'strano adj strange

straordi|naria'mente adv extraordinarily. **∼'nario** adj extraordinary; (notevole) remarkable; (edizione) special; **lavoro ∼nario** overtime; **treno ∼nario** special train

strapaz'zar|e vt ill-treat; scramble (uova). **∼si** vr tire oneself out. **stra-'pazzo** m strain; **da strapazzo** fig worthless

strapi'eno adj overflowing

strapi'ombo m projection; **a ∼** sheer

strap'par|e vt tear; (per distruggere) tear up; pull out (dente, capelli); (sradicare) pull up; (estorcere) wring. **∼si** vr get torn; (allontanarsi) tear oneself away. **'strappo** m tear; (strattone) jerk; (🔲: *passaggio*) lift; **fare uno strappo alla regola** make an exception to the rule. ∼ **muscolare** muscle strain

strapun'tino m folding seat

strari'pare vi flood

strasci'c|are vt trail; shuffle (piedi); drawl (parole). ∼**strascico** m train; *fig* after-effect

strass m inv rhinestone

strata'gemma m stratagem

strate'gia f strategy. **stra'tegico** adj strategic

'strato m layer; (*di vernice ecc*) coat; (*roccioso, sociale*) stratum. ∼**sfera** f stratosphere. ∼**sferico** adj stratospheric

stravac'carsi vr 🔲 slouch

strava'gan|te adj extravagant; (*eccentrico*) eccentric. ∼**za** f extravagance; (*eccentricità*) eccentricity

stra'vecchio adj ancient

strave'dere vt ∼ **per** worship

stravizi'are vi indulge oneself. **stra'vizio** m excess

stra'volg|ere vt twist; (*turbare*) upset. ∼**i'mento** m twisting. **stra'volto** adj distraught; (🔲: *stanco*) done in

strazi'a|nte adj heartrending; (*dolore*) agonizing. ∼**re** vt grate on (orecchie); break (cuore). **'strazio** m agony; **che strazio!** 🔲 it's awful!

'strega f witch. **stre'gare** vt bewitch. **stre'gone** m wizard

'stregua f alla ∼ **di** like

stre'ma|re vt exhaust. ∼**to** adj exhausted

'strenuo adj strenuous

strepi'tare vi make a din. **'strepito** m noise. ∼**'toso** adj noisy; *fig* resounding

stres'sa|nte adj (lavoro, situazione) stressful. ∼**to** adj stressed [out]

'stretta f grasp; (*dolore*) pang; **essere alle strette** be in dire straits.

∼ **di mano** handshake

stret'tezza f narrowness; **stret'tezze** pl (*difficoltà finanziarie*) financial difficulties

'stret|to pp di **stringere** ● adj narrow; (*serrato*) tight; (*vicino*) close; (*dialetto*) broad; (*rigoroso*) strict; **lo** ∼ **to necessario** the bare minimum ● m (Geog) strait. ∼**toia** f bottleneck; (🔲: *difficoltà*) tight spot

stri'a|to adj striped. ∼**'tura** f streak

stri'dente adj strident

'stridere vi squeak; *fig* clash. **stri'dore** m screech

'stridulo adj shrill

strigli'a|re vt groom. ∼**ta** f grooming; *fig* dressing down

stril'l|are vi t scream. **'strillo** m scream

strimin'zito adj skimpy; (*magro*) skinny

strimpel'lare vt strum

'strin|ga f lace; (Comput) string. ∼**'gato** adj *fig* terse

'stringer|e vt press; (*serrare*) squeeze; (*tenere stretto*) hold tight; take in (abito); (*comprimere*) be tight; (*restringere*) tighten; ∼ **la mano a** shake hands with ● vi (*premere*) press. ∼**si** vr (*accostarsi*) draw close (**a** to); (*avvicinarsi*) squeeze up

'striscia f strip; (riga) stripe. **strisce** pl [**pedonali**] zebra crossing sg

strisci'ar|e vi crawl; (*sfiorare*) graze ● vt drag (piedi). ∼**si** vr ∼**si a** rub against. **'striscio** m graze; (Med) smear; **colpire di striscio** graze

strisci'one m banner

strito'lare vt grind

striz'zare vt squeeze; (*torcere*) wring [out]; ∼ **l'occhio** wink

'strofa f strophe

strofi'naccio m cloth; (*per spolverare rare*) duster

strofi'nare vt rub

strombaz'zare vt boast about ●vi hoot

strombaz'zata f hoot

stron'care vt cut off; (reprimere) crush; (criticare) tear to shreds

stropicci'are vt rub; crumple (vestito)

stroz'za|re vt strangle. **~tura** f strangling; (di strada) narrowing

strozzi'naggio m loan-sharking

stroz'zino m pej usurer; (truffatore) shark

strug'gente adj all-consuming

strumen'tale adj instrumental

strumentaliz'zare vt make use of

stru'mento m instrument; (arnese) tool. **~ a corda** string instrument. **~ musicale** musical instrument

strusci'are vt rub

'strutto m lard

strut'tura f structure. **struttu'rale** adj structural

struttu'rare vt structure

strutturazi'one f structuring

'struzzo m ostrich

stuc'ca|re vt stucco

stuc'chevole adj nauseating

'stucco m stucco

stu'den|te, -t'essa mf student; (di scuola) schoolboy; schoolgirl. **~tesco** adj student; (di scolaro) school attrib

studi'ar|e vt study. **~si** vr **~si di** try to

'studi|o m studying; (stanza, ricerca) study; (di artista, TV ecc) studio; (di professionista) office. **~'oso, -a** adj studious ●mf scholar

'stufa f stove. **~ elettrica** electric fire

stu'fa|re vt (Culin) stew; (dare fastidio) bore. **~rsi** vr get bored. **~to** m stew

'stufo adj bored; **essere ~ di** be fed up with

stu'oia f mat

stupefa'cente adj amazing ●m drug

stu'pendo adj stupendous

stupi'd'aggine f (azione) stupid thing; (cosa da poco) nothing. **~ata** f stupid thing. **~ità** f stupidity. **'stupido** adj stupid

stu'pir|e vt astonish ●vi, **~si** vr be astonished. **stu'pore** m amazement

stu'pra|re vt rape. **~tore** m rapist. **'stupro** m rape

sturalavan'dini m inv plunger

stu'rare vt uncork; unblock (lavandino)

stuzzi'care vt prod [at]; pick (denti); poke (fuoco); (molestare) tease; whet (appetito)

stuzzi'chino m (Culin) appetizer

su prep on; (senza contatto) over; (riguardo a) about; (circa, intorno a) about, around; **le chiavi sono sul tavolo** the keys are on the table; **il quadro è appeso sul camino** the picture is hanging over the fireplace; **un libro sull'antico Egitto** a book on o about Ancient Egypt; **costa sul 25 euro** it costs about 25 euros; **decidere sul momento** decide at the time; **su commissione** on commission; **su due piedi** on the spot; **uno su dieci** one out of ten ●adv (sopra) up; (al piano di sopra) upstairs; (addosso) on; **ho su il cappotto** I've got my coat on; **in su** (guardare) up; **dalla vita in su** from the waist up; **su!** come on!

su'bacqueo adj underwater

subaffit'tare vt sublet. **subaf'fitto** m sublet

subal'terno adj & m subordinate

sub'buglio m turmoil

sub'conscio adj & m subconscious

'subdolo adj devious

suben'trare vi (circostanze:) come up; **~ a** take the place of

su'bire vt undergo; (patire) suffer

subis'sare vt fig ~ **di** overwhelm with

'subito adv at once; ~ **dopo** straight after

su'blime adj sublime

subodo'rare vt suspect

subordi'nato, -a adj & mf subordinate

subur'bano adj suburban

suc'cedere vi (accadere) happen; ~**e a** succeed; (venire dopo) follow; ~**e al trono** succeed to the throne. ~**si** vr happen one after the other

successi'one f succession; **in** ~ **in** succession

succes|siva'mente adv subsequently. ~**'sivo** adj successive

suc'ces|so pp di **succedere** ●m success; (esito) outcome; (disco ecc) hit

succes'sore m successor

succhi'are vt suck [up]

suc'cinto adj (conciso) concise; (abito) scanty

'succo m juice; fig essence; ~ **di frutta** fruit juice. **suc'coso** adj juicy

succu'lento adj succulent

succur'sale f branch [office]

sud m south; **del** ~ southern

su'da|re vi sweat; (faticare) sweat blood; ~**re freddo** be in a cold sweat. ~**ta** f sweat. ~**'ticcio** adj sweaty. ~**to** adj sweaty

sud'detto adj above-mentioned

'suddito, -a mf subject

suddi'vi|dere vt subdivide. ~**si'o-ne** f subdivision

su'd-est m southeast

'sudici|o adj filthy. ~**'ume** m filth

su'dore m sweat; fig sweat

su'd-ovest m southwest

suffici'en|te adj sufficient; (presuntuoso) conceited ●m bare essentials pl; (Sch) pass mark. ~**za** f sufficiency; (presunzione) conceit; (Sch) pass; **a** ~**za** enough

suf'fisso m suffix

suf'fragio m vote. ~ **universale** universal suffrage

suggeri'mento m suggestion

sugge'ri|re vt suggest; (Theat) prompt. ~**'tore**, ~**'trice** m (Theat) prompter

suggestiona'bile adj suggestible

suggestio'na|re vt influence suggesti'one f influence

sugge'stivo adj suggestive; (musica ecc) evocative

'sughero m cork

'sugli = **su** + **GLI**

'sugo m (di frutta) juice; (di carne) gravy; (salsa) sauce; (sostanza) substance

'sui = **su** + **I**

sui'cid|a adj suicidal ●mf suicide. **suici'darsi** vr commit suicide. ~**io** m suicide

su'ino adj **carne suina** pork ●m swine

sul = **su** + **IL**. **'sullo** = **su** + **LO**. **'sulla** = **su** + **LA**. **'sulle** = **su** + **LE**

sul'ta|na f sultana. ~**'nina** adj **uva** ~**nina** sultana. ~**no** m sultan

'sunto m summary

'suo, -a poss adj **il** ~, **i suoi** his; (di cosa, animale) its; (forma di cortesia) your; **la sua, le sue** her; (di cosa, animale) its; (forma di cortesia) your; **questa macchina è sua** this car is his/hers; ~ **padre** his/her/your father; **un** ~ **amico** a friend of his/hers/ yours ●poss pron **il** ~, **i suoi** his; (di cosa, animale) its; (forma di cortesia) yours; **la sua, le sue** hers; (di cosa animale) its; (forma di cortesia) yours; **i suoi** his/her folk

su'ocera f mother-in-law

su'ocero m father-in-law

su'ola f sole

su'olo m ground; (terreno) soil

suo'na|re vt/i (Mus) play; ring (campanello); sound (allarme, clacson);

(orologio) strike. ~'tore, ~'trice mf player. suone'ria f alarm. su'ono m sound

su'ora f nun; Suor Maria Sister Maria

superal'colico m spirit ● adj bevande pl superalcoliche spirits

supera'mento m (di timidezza) overcoming, (di esame) success (di in)

supe'rare vt surpass; (vincere) exceed; (vincere) overcome, overtake (veicolo); pass (esame)

su'perbo adj haughty; (magnifico) superb

superdo'tato adj highly gifted

superfici'ale adj superficial ● mf superficial person. ~ità f superficiality. super'ficie f surface; (area) area

su'perfluo adj superfluous

superi'ore adj superior; (di grado) senior; (più elevato) higher; (sovrastante) upper; (al di sopra) above ● mf superior. ~ità f superiority

superla'tivo adj & m superlative

supermer'cato m supermarket

super'sonico adj supersonic

su'perstite adj surviving ● mf survivor

superstizi'one f superstition. ~so adj superstitious

super'strada f toll-free motorway

supervisi'one f supervision. ~sore m supervisor

su'pino adj supine

suppel'lettili fpl furnishings

suppergiù adv about

supplemen'tare adj supplementary

supple'mento m supplement; ~ rapido express train supplement

sup'plen|te adj temporary ● mf (Sch) supply teacher. ~za f temporary post

'suppli|ca f plea; (domanda) petition. ~'care vt beg

sup'plire vt replace ● vi ~ a (compensare) make up for

sup'plizio m torture

sup'porre vt suppose

sup'porto m support

supposizi'one f supposition

sup'posta f suppository

sup'posto pp di supporre

supre'mazia f supremacy. su'premo adj supreme

sur'fare vi ~ in Internet surf the Net

surge'la|re vt deep-freeze. ~ti mpl frozen food sg. ~to adj frozen

surrea'lismo m surrealism. ~ta mf surrealist

surriscal'dare vt overheat

surro'gato m substitute

suscet'tibile adj touchy. ~ità f touchiness

susci'tare vt stir up; arouse (ammirazione ecc)

su'sina f plum. ~o m plumtree

su'spense f suspense

sussegu'ente adj subsequent. ~irsi vr follow one after the other

sussidi'ar|e vt subsidize. ~io adj subsidiary. sus'sidio m subsidy, (aiuto) aid. sussidio di disoccupazione unemployment benefit

sussi'ego m haughtiness

sussi'sten|za f subsistence. sus'sistere vi subsist; (essere valido) hold good

sussul'tare vi start. sus'sulto m start

sussur'rare vt whisper. sus'surro m whisper

sva'gar|e vt amuse. ~si vr amuse oneself. 'svago m relaxation; (divertimento) amusement

svaligi'are vt rob; burgle (casa)

svalu'ta|re vt devalue; fig underestimate. ~rsi vr lose value. ~zi'one f devaluation

svam'pito adj absent-minded

sva'nire vi vanish

svantaggi|'ato adj at a disadvantage; (bambino, paese) disadvantaged. **svan'taggio** m disadvantage; **essere in svantaggio** Sport be losing; **∼oso** adj disadvantageous

svapo'rare vi evaporate

svari'ato adj varied

sva'sato adj flared

'svastica f swastika

sve'dese adj & m (lingua) Swedish ● mf Swede

'sveglia f (orologio) alarm [clock]; **∼!** get up!; **mettere la ∼** set the alarm [clock]

svegli'ar|e vt wake up; fig awaken. **∼si** vr wake up. **'sveglio** adj awake; (di mente) quick-witted

sve'lare vt reveal

svel'tezza f speed; fig quick-wittedness

svel'tir|e vt quicken. **∼si** vr (persona:) liven up. **'svelto** adj quick; (slanciato) svelte; **alla svelta** quickly

svend|ere vt undersell. **∼ita** f [clearance] sale

sve'nire vi faint

sven'ta|re vt foil. **∼to** adj thoughtless ● mf thoughtless person

'sventola f slap

svento'lare vt/i wave

sven'trare vt disembowel; fig demolish (edificio)

sven'tura f misfortune. **sventu'rato** adj unfortunate

sve'nuto pp di svenire

svergo'gnato adj shameless

sver'nare vi winter

sve'stir|e vt undress

'Svezia f Sweden

svez'zare vt wean

svi'ar|e vt divert; (corrompere) lead astray. **∼si** vr fig go astray

svico'lare vi turn down a side street; (dalla questione ecc) evade the issue; (da una persona) dodge out of the way

svi'gnarsela vr slip away

svi'lire vt debase

svilup'par|e vt, **∼si** vr develop. **svi'luppo** m development; **paese in via di sviluppo** developing country

svinco'lare vt release; clear (merce). **∼si** vr free oneself. **'svincolo** m clearance; (di autostrada) exit

svisce'ra|re vt gut; fig dissect. **∼to** adj passionate; (ossequioso) obsequious

'svista f oversight

svi'ta|re vt unscrew. **∼to** adj (fig: matto) cracked, nutty

'Svizzer|a f Switzerland. **s∼o, -a** adj & mf Swiss

> Svizzera Italian is one of the four national languages of Switzerland, but is spoken widely only in the canton of Ticino in the south of the country, and to a lesser extent in Grisons. Around half a million people in Switzerland have Italian as their first language. Their language rights are protected by the Swiss constitution.

svogli|a'tezza f half-hearted-ness. **∼'ato** adj lazy

svolaz'za|nte adj (capelli) windswept. **∼re** vi flutter

'svolger|e vt unwind; unwrap (pacco); (risolvere) solve; (portare a termine) carry out; (sviluppare) develop. **∼si** vr (accadere) take place. **svolgi'mento** m course; (sviluppo) development

'svolta f turning; fig turning-point. **svol'tare** vi turn

'svolto pp di svolgere

svuo'tare vt empty [out]

Tt

tabac'r|aio, -a mf tobacconist. **~he'ria** f tobacconist's. **ta'bacco** m tobacco

Tabaccheria By law, cigarettes and other tobacco products can be sold only in *tabaccherie*, which must be licensed by the State. They can be recognized by a sign with a large T. As well as tobacco, *tabaccherie* have a monopoly on postage stamps, lottery tickets, and other items controlled by the State.

ta'bel|la f table; (*lista*) list. **~la dei prezzi** price list. **~'lina** f (*Math*) multiplication table. **~'lone** m wall chart. **~'lone del canestro** backboard

taber'nacolo m tabernacle

tabù adj & m inv taboo

tabu'lato m [data] printout

'tacca f notch; **di mezza ~** (*attore, giornalista*) second-rate

tac'cagno adj 1 stingy

tac'cheggio m shoplifting

tac'chetto m Sport stud

tac'chino m turkey

tacci'are vt **~ qcno di qcsa** accuse sb of sth

'tacco m heel; **alzare i tacchi** take to one's heels; **scarpe senza ~** flat shoes. **tacchi** pl a spillo stiletto heels

taccu'ino m notebook

ta'cere vi be silent ● vt say nothing about; **mettere a ~ qcsa** (*scandalo*) hush sth up

ta'chimetro m speedometer

'tacito adj silent; (*inespresso*) tacit.

taci'turno adj taciturn

ta'fano m horsefly

taffe'ruglio m scuffle

'taglia f (*riscatto*) ransom; (*ricompensa*) reward; (*statura*) height; (*misura*) size. **~ unica** one size

taglia'carte m inv paperknife

taglia'erba m inv lawn-mower

tagliafu'oco adj inv **porta ~** fire door; **striscia ~** fire break

tagli'ando m coupon; **fare il ~** ≈ put one's car in for its MOT

tagli'ar|e vt cut; (*attraversare*) cut across; (*interrompere*) cut off; (*togliere*) cut out; carve (*carne*); mow (*erba*); **farsi ~ e i capelli** have a haircut ● vi cut. **~si** vr cut oneself; **~si i capelli** have a haircut

taglia'telle fpl tagliatelle sg, thin, flat strips of egg pasta

taglieggi'are vt extort money from

tagli'ente adj sharp ● m cutting edge. **~re** m chopping board

'taglio m cut; (*il tagliare*) cutting; (*di stoffa*) length; (*parte tagliente*) edge. **~ cesareo** Caesarean section

tagli'ola f trap

tagliuz'zare vt cut

tail'leur m inv [lady's] suit

'talco m talcum powder

'tale adj such a; (*con nomi plurali*) such; **c'è un ~ disordine** there is such a mess; **non accetto tali scuse** I won't accept such excuses; **il rumore era ~ che non si sentiva nulla** there was so much noise you couldn't hear yourself think; **il ~ giorno** on such and such a day; **quel tal signore** that gentleman; **il ~ quale** just like ● pron un ~ someone; **quel ~ man.** **Il tal dei tali** such and such a person

ta'lento m talent

tali'smano m talisman

tallo'nare vt be hot on the heels of

tallon'cino m coupon

tal'lone m heel

tal'mente adv so

ta'lora adv = TALVOLTA

'talpa f mole

tal'volta adv sometimes

tamburel'lare vi (con le dita); drum; (pioggia): beat, drum. **tambu'rello** m tambourine. **tambu'rino** m drummer. **tam'buro** m drum

tampona'mento m (Auto) collision; (di ferita) dressing; (di falla) plugging. **~ a catena** pile-up. **tampo'nare** vt (urtare) crash into; (otturare) plug. **tam'pone** m swab; (per timbri) pad; (per mestruazioni) tampon; (Comput) (per treni) buffer

'tana f den

'tanfo m stench

'tanga m inv tanga

tan'gen|te adj tangent ● f tangent; (somma) bribe. **~'topoli** f widespread corruption in Italy in the early 90s. **~zi'ale** f orbital road

tan'gibile adj tangible

'tango m tango

tan'tino un ~ adv a little [bit]

'tanto adj [so] much; (con nomi plurali) [so] many, [such] a lot of; ~ **tempo** [such] a long time; **non ha tanta pazienza** he doesn't have much patience; ~ **tempo quanto ti serve** as much time as you need; **non è ~ intelligente quanto suo padre** he's not as intelligent as his father; **tanti amici quanti parenti** as many friends as relatives ● pron much; (plurale) many; (tanto tempo) a long time; **è un uomo come tanti** he's just an ordinary man; **tanti** (molte persone) many people; **non ci vuole così ~** it doesn't take that long; ~ **quanto** as much as; **tanti quanti** as many as ● conj (comunque) anyway, in any case ● adv (così) so; (con verbi) so much; ~ **debole** so weak; **è ~ ingenuo da crederle** he's naive enough to be-

lieve her; **di ~ in ~** every now and then; ~ **l'uno come l'altro** both; ~ **quanto** as much as; **tre volte ~** three times as much; **una volta ~** once in a while; **tant'è** so much so; ~ **per cambiare** for a change

'tappa f stop; (parte di viaggio) stage

tappa'buchi m inv stopgap

tap'par|e vt plug; cork (bottiglia); ~**e la bocca a qcno** 🆎 shut sb up. ~**si** vr ~**gli occhi** cover one's eyes; ~**si il naso** hold one's nose

tappa'rella f 🆎 roller blind

tappe'tino m mat; (Comput) mouse mat

tap'peto m carpet; (piccolo) rug; **mandare qcno al** ~ knock sb down

tappez'z|are vt paper (pareti); (rivestire) cover. ~**e'ria** f tapestry; (di carta) wallpaper; (arte) upholstery. ~**i'ere** m upholsterer; (imbianchino) decorator

'tappo m plug; (di sughero) cork; (di metallo, per penna) top; (🆎: persona piccola) dwarf. ~ **di sughero** cork

'tara f (difetto) flaw; (ereditaria) hereditary defect; (peso) tare

ta'rantola f tarantula

ta'ra|re vt calibrate (strumento). ~**to** adj (Comm) discounted; (Techn) calibrated; (Med) with a hereditary defect; 🆎 crazy

tarchi'ato adj stocky

tar'dare vi be late ● vt delay

'tard|i adv late; **al più** ~**i** at the latest; **più** ~**i** later [on]; **sul** ~**i** late in the day; **far** ~**i** (essere in ritardo) be late; (con gli amici) stay up late; **a più** ~**i** I see you later. **tar'divo** adj late; (bambino) retarded. ~**o** adj slow; (tempo) late

'targ|a f plate; (Auto) numberplate. ~**a di circolazione** numberplate. **tar'gato** adj **un'auto targata** ... with the registration number.... ~**'hetta** f (su porta) nameplate; (sulla *valigia)* name tag

ta'rif|fa *f* rate, tariff. ~**'fario** *m* price list

'tarlo *m* woodworm

'tarma *f* moth

ta'rocco *m* tarot; **ta'rocchi** *pl* tarot

tartagli'are *vi* stutter

'tartaro *adj* & *m* tartar

tarta'ruga *f* tortoise; *(di mare)* turtle; *(per pettine ecc)* tortoiseshell

tartas'sare *vt* harass

tar'tina *f* canapé

tar'tufo *m* truffle

'tasca *f* pocket; *(in borsa)* compartment; **da ~** pocket *attrib*.; **~ da pasticciere** icing bag

ta'scabile *adj* pocket *attrib* ● *m* paperback

tasca'pane *m inv* haversack

ta'schino *m* breast pocket

'tassa *f* tax; *(d'iscrizione ecc)* fee; *(doganale)* duty. **~ di circolazione** road tax. **~ d'iscrizione** registration fee

tas'sametro *m* taximeter

tas'sare *vt* tax

tassa|tiva'mente *adv* without question

tassazi'one *f* taxation

tas'sello *m* wedge; *(di stoffa)* gusset

tassì *m inv* taxi. **tas'sista** *mf* taxi driver

'tasso[1] *m* yew; *(animale)* badger

'tasso[2] *m* rate. **~ di cambio** exchange rate. **~ di interesse** interest rate

la'stare *vt* feel; *(sondare)* sound; **~ il terreno** *fig* test the water

tasti'e|ra *f* keyboard. **~'rista** *mf* keyboarder

'tasto *m* key; *(tatto)* touch. **~ delicato** *fig* touchy subject. **~ funzione** *(Comput)* function key. **~ tabulatore** tab key

'tattica *f* tactics *pl*

'tattico *adj* tactical

'tatto *m (senso)* touch; *(accortezza)* tact; **aver ~** be tactful

tatu'a|ggio *m* tattoo. **~re** *vt* tattoo

'tavola *f* table; *(illustrazione)* plate; *(asse)* plank. **~ calda** snackbar

tavo'lato *m* boarding; *(pavimento)* wood floor

tavo'letta *f* bar; *(medicinale)* tablet; **andare a ~** *(Auto)* drive flat out

tavo'lino *m* small table

'tavolo *m* table. **~ operatorio** *(Med)* operating table

tavo'lozza *f* palette

'tazza *f* cup; *(del water)* bowl. **~ da caffè/tè** coffee-cup/teacup

taz'zina *f* **~ da caffè** espresso coffee cup

T.C.I. *abbr* (Touring Club Italiano) Italian Touring Club

te *pers pron* you; **te l'ho dato** I gave it to you

tè *m inv* tea

tea'trale *adj* theatrical

te'atro *m* theatre. **~ all'aperto** open-air theatre. **~ di posa** *Cinema* set. **~ tenda** marquee for theatre performances

'tecnico, -a *adj* technical ● *mf* technician ● *f* technique

tec'nigrafo *m* drawing board

tecno|lo'gia *f* technology. **~'logico** *adj* technological

te'desco, -a *adj* & *mf* German

te'dioso *adj* tedious

te'game *m* saucepan

'teglia *f* baking tin

'tegola *f* tile; *fig* blow

tei'era *f* teapot

tek *m* teak

'tela *f* cloth; *(per quadri, vele)* canvas; *(Theat)* curtain. **~ cerata** oilcloth. **~ di lino** linen

te'laio *m (di bicicletta, finestra)* frame; *(Auto)* chassis; *(per tessere)* loom

tele'camera f television camera

teleco'man'dato adj remote-controlled, remote control attrib. **~'mando** m remote control

Telecom Italia f Italian State telephone company

telecomunicazi'oni fpl telecommunications

tele'cro|naca f [television] commentary. **~naca diretta** live [television] coverage. **~'nista** mf television commentator

tele'ferica f cableway

telefo'na|re vt/i [tele]phone, ring. **~ta** f call. **~ta interurbana** long-distance call

telefonica'mente adv by [tele-]phone

tele'fo|nico adj [tele]phone attrib. **~'nino** m mobile [phone]. **~'nista** mf operator

te'lefono m [tele]phone. **~ senza filo** cordless [phone]. **~ interno** internal telephone. **~ satellitare** satphone. **~ a schede** cardphone

telegior'nale m television news sg

tele'grafico adj telegraphic; (risposta) monosyllabic; **sii telegrafico** keep it brief

tele'gramma m telegram

telela'voro m teleworking

tele'matica f data communications, telematics

teleno'vela f soap opera

teleobiet'tivo m telephoto lens

telepa'tia f telepathy

telero'manzo m television serial

tele'scopio m telescope

teleselezi'one f subscriber trunk dialling, STD; **chiamare in ~** dial direct

telespetta'tore, -'trice mf viewer

tele'text® m Teletext®

televisi'one f television; **guardare la ~** watch television

televi'sivo adj television attrib; **operatore ~** television cameraman; **apparecchio ~** television set

televi'sore m television [set]

'tema m theme; (Sch) essay. **te'matica** f main theme

teme'rario adj reckless

te'mere vt be afraid of, fear ● vi be afraid, fear

temperama'tite m inv pencil-sharpener

tempera'mento m temperament

tempe'ra|re vt temper; sharpen (matita). **~to** adj temperate. **~'tura** f temperature. **~tura ambiente** room temperature

tempe'rino m penknife

tem'pe|sta f storm. **~sta di neve** snowstorm. **~sta di sabbia** sandstorm

tempe'stiva'mente adv quickly. **~'stivo** adj timely. **~'stoso** adj stormy

'tempia f (Anat) temple

'tempio m (Relig) temple

tem'pismo m timing

'tempo m time; (atmosferico) weather; (Mus) tempo; (Gram) tense; (di film) part; (di partita) half; **a suo ~** in due course; **~ fa** some time ago; **un ~** once; **ha fatto il suo ~** it's superannuated. **~ supplementare** Sport extra time, overtime Am. **~'rale** adj temporal ● m [thunder] storm. **~ranea'mente** adv temporarily. **~raneo** adj temporary. **~reg-gi'are** vi play for time

tem'prare vt temper

te'nac|e adj tenacious. **~ia** f tenacity

te'naglia f pincers pl

'tenda f curtain; (per campeggio) tent; (tendone) awning. **~ a ossigeno** oxygen tent

ten'denz|a f tendency. **~ial'mente** adv by nature

'**tendere** vt (allargare) stretch [out]; (tirare) tighten; (porgere) hold out; fig lay (trappola) ● vi ~ **a** aim at; (essere portato a) tend to

ten'dine m tendon

ten'do|**ne** m awning; (di circo) tent. **~poli** f inv tent city

te'nebroso adj gloomy

te'nente m lieutenant

tenera'mente adv tenderly

te'ner|**e** vt hold; (mantenere) keep; (gestire) run; (prendere) take; (seguire) follow; (considerare) consider ● vi hold; **~ci a**, **~e a** be keen on; **~e per** support (squadra). **~si** vr hold on (**a** to); (in una condizione) keep oneself; (seguire) stick to; **~si indietro** stand back

tene'rezza f tenderness. '**tenero** adj tender

te'nia f tapeworm

'**tennis** m tennis. **~ da tavolo** table tennis. **ten'nista** mf tennis player

te'nore m standard; (Mus) tenor; **~ di legge** by law. **~ di vita** standard of living

tensi'one f tension; (Electr) voltage; **alta ~** high voltage

ten'tacolo m tentacle

ten'ta|**re** vt attempt; (sperimentare) try; (indurre in tentazione) tempt. **~'tivo** m attempt. **~zi'one** f temptation

tenten'nare vi waver

'**tenue** adj fine; (debole) weak; (esiguo) small; (leggero) slight

te'nuta f (capacità) capacity; (Sport: resistenza) stamina; (possedimento) estate; (divisa) uniform; (abbigliamento) clothes pl; **a ~ d'aria** airtight. **~ di strada** road holding

teolo'gia f theology, **teo'logico** adj theological. **te'ologo** m theologian

teo'rema m theorem

teo'ria f theory

teorica'mente adv theoretically.

te'orico adj theoretical

te'pore m warmth

'**teppa** f mob. **tep'pismo** m hooliganism **tep'pista** m hooligan

tera'peutico adj therapeutic. **tera'pia** f therapy

tergicri'stallo m windscreen wiper, windshield wiper Am

tergilu'notto m rear windscreen wiper

tergiver'sare vi hesitate

'**tergo** m **a ~** behind

ter'ma|**le** adj thermal, **stazione ~** spa. '**terme** fpl thermal baths

'termico adj thermal

termi'na|**le** adj & m terminal; **malato ~le** terminally ill person. **~re** vt/i finish, end. '**termine** m (limite) limit; (fine) end; (condizione, espressione) term

terminolo'gia f terminology

ter'mite f termite

termoco'perta f electric blanket

ter'mometro m thermometer

'**termos** m inv thermos®

termosi'fone m radiator; (sistema) central heating

ter'mostato m thermostat

'**terra** f earth; (regione) land; (terreno) ground; (argilla) clay; (cosmetico) dark face powder (for impression of tan); **a ~** (sulla costa) ashore; (installazioni) onshore; **per ~** on the ground; **sotto ~** underground. **~'cotta** f terracotta; **vasellame di ~cotta** earthenware. **~pi'eno** m embankment

ter'razza f, **~o** m balcony

terremo'tato, -a adj (zona) affected by an earthquake ● mf earthquake victim. **terre'moto** m earthquake

ter'reno adj earthly ● m ground; (suolo) soil; (proprietà terriera) land; **perdere/guadagnare ~** lose/gain ground. **~ di gioco** playing field

t

ter'restre adj terrestrial; **esercito** ~ land forces pl

ter'ribil|e adj terrible. ~'mente adv terribly

ter'riccio m potting compost

terrifi'cante adj terrifying

territori'ale adj territorial. **terri'torio** m territory

ter'rore m terror

terro'ris|mo m terrorism. ~ta mf terrorist

terroriz'zare vt terrorize

'terso adj clear

ter'zetto m trio

terzi'ario adj tertiary

'terzo adj third; **di terz'ordine** (locale, servizio) third-rate; **la terza età** the third age ● m third; **terzi** pl (Jur) third party sg. **terz'ultimo, -a** agg & mf third from last

'tesa f brim

'teschio m skull

'tesi f inv thesis

'teso pp di **tendere** ● adj taut; fig tense

tesor|e'ria f treasury. ~i'ere m treasurer

te'soro m treasure; (tesoreria) treasury

'tessera f card; (abbonamento all'autobus) season ticket

'tessere vt weave; hatch (complotto)

tesse'rino m travel card

'tessile adj textile. **tessili** mpl textiles; (operai) textile workers

tessi'tore, -'trice mf weaver

tes'suto m fabric; (Anat) tissue

'testa f head; (cervello) brain; **essere in** ~ **a** be ahead of; **in** ~ Sport in the lead; ~ **o croce?** heads or tails?

'testa-'coda m inv **fare un** ~ spin right round

testa'mento m will; **T**~ (Relig) Testament

testar'daggine f stubbornness. **te'stardo** adj stubborn

te'stata f head; (intestazione) heading; (colpo) butt

'teste mf witness

te'sticolo m testicle

testi'mon|e mf witness. ~e **oculare** eye witness

testi'monial mf inv celebrity promoting brand of cosmetics

testimoni'anza f testimony. ~'are vt testify to ● vi give evidence

'testo m text; **far** ~ be an authority

te'stone, -a mf blockhead

testu'ale adj textual

'tetano m tetanus

'tetro adj gloomy

tetta'rella f teat

'tetto m roof. ~ **apribile** sunshine roof. **tet'toia** f roofing. **tet'tuccio** m tettuccio **apribile** sun-roof

'Tevere m Tiber

ti pers pron you; (riflessivo) yourself; **ti ha dato un libro** he gave you a book; **lavati le mani** wash your hands; **eccoti!** here you are!; **sbrigati!** hurry up!

ti'ara f tiara

ticchet't|are vi tick. ~io m ticking

'ticchio m tic; (ghiribizzo) whim

'ticket m inv (per farmaco, esame) amount paid by National Health patients

tiepida'mente adv half-heartedly. **ti'epido** adj lukewarm

ti'fare vi ~ **per** shout for. **'tifo** m (Med) typhus; **fare il tifo per** fig be a fan of

tifol'dea f typhoid

ti'fone m typhoon

ti'foso, -a mf fan

'tiglio m lime

ti'grato adj **gatto** ~ **tabby** [cat]

'tigre f tiger

'tilde mf tilde

tim'ballo m (Culin) pie

tim'brare vt stamp; ~ **il cartellino** clock in/out

'timbro m stamp; (di voce) tone

timida'mente adv timidly, shyly. **timi'dezza** f timidity, shyness. **'timido** adj timid, shy

'timo m thyme

ti'mon|e m rudder. ~**i'ere** m helmsman

ti'more m fear; (soggezione) awe

'timpano m eardrum; (Mus) kettledrum

ti'nello m dining-room

'tinger|e vt dye; (macchiare) stain. ~**si** vi (viso, cielo) be tinged (**di** with); ~**si i capelli** have one's hair dyed; (da solo) dye one's hair

'tino m, **ti'nozza** f tub

'tint|a f dye; (colore) colour; **in** ~**a unita** plain. ~**a'rella** f ⚫ suntan

tintin'nare vi tinkle

'tinto pp di tingere. ~**'ria** f (negozio) cleaner's. **tin'tura** f dyeing; (colorante) dye

'tipico adj typical

'tipo m type; (individuo) guy

tipogra'fia f printery; (arte) typography. **tipo'grafico** adj typographic[al]. **ti'pografo** m printer

tip tap m tap dancing

ti'raggio m draught

tiramisù m inv dessert made of coffee-soaked sponge, eggs, Marsala, cream and cocoa powder

tiran'nia f tyranny. **ti'ranno, -a** adj tyrannical ⚫ mf tyrant

ti'rar|e vt pull; (gettare) throw; kick (palla); (sparare) fire; (tracciare) draw; (stampare) print ⚫ vi pull; (vento): blow; (abito): be tight; (sparare) fire; ~**e avanti** get by; ~**e su** (crescere) bring up; (da terra) pick up; ~**si indietro** fig back out

tiras'segno m target shooting; (alla fiera) rifle range

ti'rata f tug; **in una** ~ in one go

tira'tore m shot. ~ **scelto** marksman

tira'tura f printing; (di giornali) circulation; (di libri) [print] run

'tirchio adj mean

tiri'tera f spiel

'tiro m (traino) draught; (lancio) throw; (sparo) shot; (scherzo) trick. ~ **con l'arco** archery. ~ **alla fune** tug-of-war. ~ **a segno** rifle-range

tiro'cinio m apprenticeship

ti'roide f thyroid

Tir'reno m **il [mar]** ~ the Tyrrhenian Sea

ti'sana f herb[al] tea

tito'lare adj regular ⚫ mf principal; (proprietario) owner; (calcio) regular player

'titolo m title; (accademico) qualification; (Comm) security; **a** ~ **di** as; **a** ~ **di favore** as a favour. **titoli** pl di studio qualifications

titu'ba|nte adj hesitant. ~**nza** f hesitation. ~**re** vi hesitate

tivù f inv ⊤ TV, telly

'tizio m fellow

tiz'zone m brand

toc'cante adj touching

toc'ca|re vt touch; touch on (argomento); (tastare) feel; (riguardare) concern ⚫ vi ~**re a** (capitare) happen to; **mi tocca aspettare** I'll have to wait; **tocca a te** it's your turn; (pagare da bere) it's your round

tocca'sana m inv cure-all

'tocco m touch; (di pennello, orologio) stroke; (di pane ecc) chunk ⚫ adj ⊤ crazy, touched

'toga f toga; (accademica, di magistrato) gown

'toglier|e vt take off (coperta); take away (bambino da scuola, sete) (Math); take out, remove (dente); ~**e qcsa di mano a qcno** take sth away from sb; ~**e qcno dei guai** get sb out of trouble; **ciò non toglie**

che... nevertheless... **~si** vr take off (abito); **~si la vita** take one's [own] life

toilette f inv, **to'letta** f toilet; (mobile) dressing table

tolle'ra|nte adj tolerant. **~nza** f tolerance. **~re** vt tolerate

'tolto pp di **togliere**

to'maia f upper

'tomba f grave, tomb

tom'bino m manhole cover

'tombola f bingo; (caduta) tumble

'tomo m tome

'tonaca f habit

tonalità f inv (Mus) tonality

'tondo adj round ● m circle

'tonico adj & m tonic

tonifi'care vt brace

tonnel'la|ggio m tonnage. **~ta** f ton

'tonno m tuna [fish]

'tono m tone

ton'sil|la f tonsil. **~lite** f tonsillitis

'tonto adj ① thick

top m inv (indumento) sun-top

to'pazio m topaz

'topless m inv in **~** topless

'topo m mouse. **~ di biblioteca** fig bookworm

to'ponimo m place name

'toppa f patch; (serratura) keyhole

to'race m chest

'torba f peat

'torbido adj cloudy; fig troubled

'torcer|e vt twist; wring [out] (biancheria). **~si** vr twist

'torchio m press

'torcia f torch

torci'collo m stiff neck

'tordo m thrush

to'rero m bullfighter

To'rino f Turin

tor'menta f snowstorm

tormen'tare vt torment.

tor'mento m torment

torna'conto m benefit

tor'nado m tornado

tor'nante m hairpin bend

tor'nare vi return, go/come back; (ridiventare) become again; (conto:) add up; **~ a sorridere** become happy again

tor'neo m tournament

'tornio m lathe

'torno m **togliersi di ~** get out of the way

'toro m bull; (Astr) **T~**Taurus

tor'pedin|e f torpedo

tor'pore m torpor

'torre f tower; (scacchi) castle. **~ di controllo** control tower

torrefazi'one f roasting

tor'ren|te m torrent, mountain stream; (fig: di lacrime) flood. **~zi'ale** adj torrential

tor'retta f turret

'torrido adj torrid

torri'one m keep

tor'rone m nougat

'torso m torso; (di mela, pera) core; **a ~ nudo** bare-chested

'torsolo m core

'torta f cake; (crostata) tart

tortel'lini mpl tortellini, small packets of pasta stuffed with pork, ham, Parmesan and nutmeg

torti'era f baking tin

tor'tino m pie

'torto pp di **torcere** ● adj twisted ● m wrong; (colpa) fault; **aver ~** be wrong; **a ~** wrongly

'tortora f turtle-dove

tortu'oso adj winding; (ambiguo) tortuous

tor'tu|ra f torture. **~rare** vt torture

'torvo adj grim

to'sare vt shear

tosa'tura f shearing

To'scana f Tuscany

'**tosse** f cough

'**tossico** adj toxic ● m poison. **tossi-'comane** mf drug addict

tos'sire vi cough

tosta'pane m inv toaster

to'stare vt toast (pane); roast (caffè)

'**tosto** adv (subito) soon ● adj **I** cool

tot adj inv una cifra ~ such and such a figure ● m un ~ so much

to'tal|e adj & m total. ~**ità** f entirety; **la** ~**ità dei presenti** all those present

totali'tario adj totalitarian

totaliz'zare vt total; score (punti)

total'mente adv totally

'**totano** m squid

toto'calcio m ≈ (football) pools pl

tournée f inv tour

to'vaglia f tablecloth. ~**etta** f ~**etta** [all'americana] place mat. ~**olo** m napkin

'**tozzo** adj squat

tra = FRA

traballa|nte adj staggering; (sedia) rickety. ~**re** vi stagger; (veicolo:) jolt

tra'biccolo m **I** contraption, (auto) jalopy

traboc'care vi overflow

traboc'chetto m trap

tracan'nare vt gulp down

'**tracc|ia** f shoulder; (orma) footstep; (striscia) trail; (residuo) trace; fig sign. ~**'are** vt trace; sketch out (schema); draw (linea). ~**'ato** m (schema) layout

tra'chea f windpipe

tra'colla f shoulder-strap; **borsa a** ~ shoulder-bag

tra'collo m collapse

tradi'mento m betrayal

tra'di|re vt betray; be unfaithful to (moglie, marito). ~**tore**, ~**trice** mf traitor

tradizio'na|le adj traditional.

~**lista** mf traditionalist. ~**l'mente** adv traditionally. **tradizi'one** f tradition

tra'dotto pp di tradurre

tra'du|rre vt translate. ~**ttore**, ~**trice** mf translator. ~**ttore elettronico** electronic phrasebook. ~**zi'one** f translation

tra'ente mf (Comm) drawer

trafe'lato adj breathless

traffi'ca|nte mf dealer. ~**nte di droga** [drug] pusher. ~**re** vi (affaccendarsi) busy oneself; ~**re in** pej trafficking. **'traffico** m traffic; (Comm) trade

tra'figgere vt stab; (straziare) pierce

tra'fila f fig rigmarole

trafo'rare vt bore, drill. **tra'foro** m boring; (galleria) tunnel

trafu'gare vt steal

tra'gedia f tragedy

traghet'tare vt ferry, **tra'ghetto** m ferrying, (nave) ferry

tragica'mente adv tragically. '**tragico** adj tragic

tra'gitto m journey; (per mare) crossing

tra'guardo m finishing post; (meta) goal

traiet'toria f trajectory

trai'nare vt drag; (rimorchiare) tow

tralasci'are vt interrupt; (omettere) leave out

'**tralcio** m (Bot) shoot

tra'liccio m trellis

tram m inv tram, streetcar Am

'**trama** f weft; (di film ecc) plot

traman'dare vt hand down

tra'mare vt weave; (macchinare) plot

tram'busto m turmoil

trame'stio m bustle

tramez'zino m sandwich

tra'mezzo m partition

'tramite prep through ● m link; **fare da** ~ act as go-between

tramon'tana f north wind

tramon'tare vi set; (declinare) decline. **tra'monto** m sunset; (declino) decline

tramor'tire vt stun ● vi faint

trampo'lino m springboard; (per lo sci) ski-jump

'trampolo m stilt

tramu'tare vt transform

'trancia f shears pl; (fetta) slice

tra'nello m trap

trangugi'are vt gulp down

tranne prep except

tranquilla'mente adv peacefully

tranquil'lante m tranquillizer

tranquil'lità f calm; (di spirito) tranquillity. **∼z'zare** vt reassure. **tran'quillo** adj quiet; (pacifico) peaceful; (coscienza) easy

transat'lantico adj transatlantic ● m ocean liner

tran'sa|tto pp di transigere. **∼zi'one** f (Comm) transaction

tran'senna f (barriera) barrier

trans'genico adj genetically modified, transgenic

tran'sigere vi reach an agreement; (cedere) yield

transi'ta|bile adj passable. **∼re** vi pass

transi'tivo adj transitive

'transi|to m transit; diritto di **∼to** right of way; **"divieto di ∼to"** "no thoroughfare". **∼'torio** adj transitory. **∼zi'one** f transition

tranvi'ere m tram driver

'trapano m drill

trapas'sare vt go [right] through ● vi (morire) pass away

tra'passo m passage

tra'pezio m trapeze; (Math) trapezium

trapi|an'tare vt transplant. **∼'anto** m transplant

'trappola f trap

tra'punta f quilt

'trarre vt draw; (ricavare) obtain; **∼ in inganno** deceive

trasa'lire vi start

trasan'dato adj shabby

trasbor'dare vt transfer; (Naut) tran[s]ship ● vi change. **tra'sbordo** m trans[s]hipment

tra'scendere vt transcend ● vi (eccedere) go too far

trasci'nar|e vt drag; (entusiasmo:) carry away. **∼si** vr drag oneself

tra'scorrere vt spend ● vi pass

tra'scri|tto pp di trascrivere. **∼vere** vt transcribe. **∼zi'one** f transcription

trascu'ra|bile adj negligible. **∼re** vt neglect; (non tenere conto di) disregard. **∼'tezza** f negligence. **∼to** adj negligent; (curato male) neglected; (nel vestire) slovenly

traseco'lato adj amazed

trasferi'mento m transfer; (trasloco) move

trasfe'ri|re vt transfer. **∼rsi** vr move

tra'sferta f transfer; (indennità) subsistence allowance; Sport away match; **giocare in ∼** play away

trasfigu'rare vt transfigure

trasfor'ma|re vt transform; (in rugby) convert. **∼tore** m transformer. **∼zi'one** f transformation; (in rugby) conversion

trasfor'mista mf quick-change artist

trasfusi'one f transfusion

trasgre'dire vt disobey; (Jur) infringe

trasgredi'trice f transgressor

trasgres|si'one f infringement. **∼'sore** m transgressor

tra'slato adj metaphorical

traslo'car|e vt move ● vi, **∼si** vr move house. **tra'sloco** m removal

tra'smesso pp di trasmettere

tra'smett|ere vt pass on; (Radio, TV) broadcast; (Med, Techn) transmit. ~i'tore m transmitter

trasmis'si|bile adj transmissible. ~'one f transmission; (Radio, TV) programme

trasmit'tente m transmitter •f broadcasting station

traso'gnа|re vi day-dream

traspa'ren|te adj transparent. ~za f transparency; in ~za against the light. traspa'rire vi show [through]

traspi'ra|re vi perspire; fig transpire. ~zi'one f perspiration

tra'sporre vt transpose

traspor'tare vt transport; lasciarsi ~ da get carried away by. tra'sporto m transport; (passione) passion

trastul'lar|e vt amuse. ~si vr amuse oneself

trasu'dare vt ooze with •vi sweat

trasver'salе adj transverse

trasvo'la|re vt fly over •vi ~re su fig skim over. ~ta f crossing [by air]

'tratta f illegal trade; (Comm) draft

trat'tabile adj or near offer

tratta'mento m treatment. ~ di riquardo special treatment

trat'ta|re vt treat; (commerciare in) deal in; (negoziare) negotiate •vi ~re di deal with. ~rsi vr di che si tratta? what is it about?; si tratta di... it's about.... ~'tive fpl negotiations. ~to m treaty; (opera scritta) treatise

tratteggi'are vt outline; (descrivere) sketch

tratte'ner|e vt (far restare) keep; hold (respiro, in questura); hold back (lacrime, riso); (frenare) restrain; (da paga) withhold; sono stato trattenuto I got held up. ~rsi vr restrain oneself; (fermarsi) stay; ~si su (indugiare) dwell on. tratteni'mento m entertainment; (ricevimento) party

tratte'nuta f deduction

trat'tino m dash; (in parole composte) hyphen

'tratto pp di trarre •m (di spazio, tempo) stretch; (di penna) stroke; (linea) line; (brano) passage; tratti pl features; a tratti at intervals; ad un ~ suddenly

trat'tore m tractor

tratto'ria f restaurant

'trauma m trauma. trau'matico adj traumatic

tra'vaglio m labour; (angoscia) anguish

trava'sare vt decant

'trave f beam

tra'versa f crossbar; è una ~ di Via Roma it's off Via Roma

traver'sa|re vt cross. ~ta f crossing

traver'sie fpl misfortunes

tra'versina f (Rail) sleeper

tra'verso adj crosswise •adv di ~o crossways; andare di ~o (cibo:) go down the wrong way; camminare di ~o not walk in a straight line. ~one m (in calcio) cross

travesti'mento m disguise

trave'sti|re vt disguise. ~rsi vr disguise oneself. ~to adj disguised •m transvestite

travi'are vt lead astray

travi'sare vt distort

tra'vol|gere vt sweep away; (soprafare) overwhelm. ~to pp di travolgere

trazi'one f traction. ~ anteriore/posteriore front-/rear-wheel drive

tre adj & m three

trebbi'are vt thresh

'treccia f plait, braid

tre'cento adj & m three hundred; Il T~ the fourteenth century

tredi'cesima f Christmas bonus of one month's pay

'**tredici** adj & m thirteen

'**tregua** f truce; fig respite

tre'**mare** vi tremble; (di freddo) shiver

tremenda'**mente** adv terribly. tre'**mendo** adj terrible; **ho una fame tremenda** I'm very hungry

tremen'**tina** f turpentine

tre'**mila** adj & m three thousand

'**tremito** m tremble

tremo'**lare** vi shake; (luce:) flicker. tre'**more** m trembling

tre'**nino** m miniature railway

'**treno** m train

'**tren**|**ta** adj & m thirty; ~**ta e lode** top marks. ~**tatré giri** m inv LP. ~'**tenne** adj & mf thirty-year-old. ~'**tesimo** adj & m thirtieth. ~'**tina** f **una** ~**tina di** about thirty

trepi'**dare** vi be anxious. '**trepido** adj anxious

treppi'**ede** m tripod

'**tresca** f intrigue; (amorosa) affair

tri'**angolo** m triangle

tri'**bale** adj tribal

tribo'**la|re** vi suffer; (fare fatica) go through trials and tribulations. ~**zi'one** f tribulation

tribù f inv tribe

tri'**buna** f tribune; (per uditori) gallery; Sport stand. ~ **coperta** stand

tribu'**nale** m court

tribu'**tare** vt bestow

tribu'**tario** adj tax attrib. tri'**buto** m tribute; (tassa) tax

tri'**checo** m walrus

tri'**ciclo** m tricycle

trico'**lore** adj three-coloured ● m (bandiera) tricolour

tri'**dente** m trident

trien'**nale** adj (ogni tre anni) three-yearly; (lungo tre anni) three-year. tri'**ennio** m three-year period

tri'**foglio** m clover

trifo'**lato** adj sliced and cooked with olive oil, parsley and garlic

'**triglia** f mullet

trigonome'**tria** f trigonometry

tri'**mestre** m quarter; (Sch) term

'**trina** f lace

trin'**cea** f trench

trincia'**pollo** m inv poultry shears pl

trinci'**are** vt cut up

Trini'**tà** f Trinity

'**trio** m trio

trion'**fa|le** adj triumphal. ~**nte** adj triumphant. ~**re** vi triumph; ~**re su** triumph over. tri'**onfo** m triumph

tripli'**care** vt triple. '**triplice** adj triple; **in triplice [copia]** in triplicate. '**triplo** adj treble ● m **il triplo (di)** three times as much (as)

'**trippa** f tripe; (﹅: pancia) belly

'**trist**|**e** adj sad; (luogo) gloomy. tri'**stezza** f sadness. ~**o** adj wicked; (meschino) miserable

trita'**carne** m inv mincer

tri'**ta|re** vt mince. '**trito** adj **trito e ritrito** well-worn, trite

'**trittico** m triptych

tritu'**rare** vt chop finely

triumvi'**rato** m triumvirate

tri'**vella** f drill. trivel'**lare** vt drill

trivi'**ale** adj vulgar

tro'**feo** m trophy

'**trogolo** m (per maiali) trough

'**troia** f sow; (﹅: donna) whore

'**tromba** f trumpet; (Auto) horn; (delle scale) well. ~ **d'aria** whirlwind

trom'**b**|**etta** m toy trumpet. ~**one** m trombone

trom'**bosi** f thrombosis

tron'**care** vt sever; truncate (parola)

'**tronco** adj truncated; **licenziare in** ~ fire on the spot ● m trunk; (di strada) section. tron'**cone** m stump

troneggi'**are** vi ~ **su** tower over

'**trono** m throne

tropi'cale adj tropical. **'tropico** m tropic

'troppo adj too much; (con nomi plurali) too many ● pron too much; (plurale) too many; (troppo tempo) too long; **troppi** (troppa gente) too many people ● adv too; (con verbi) too much; **~ stanco** too tired; **ho mangiato ~** I ate too much; **hai fame? – non ~** are you hungry? – not very

'trota f trout

trot'tare vi trot. **trotterel'lare** vi trot along; (bimbo.) toddle

'trotto m trot; **andare al ~.** trot

'trottola f [spinning] top; (movimento) spin

'troupe f inv **~ televisiva** camera crew

tro'vare vt find; (scoprire) find out; (incontrare) meet; (ritenere) think; **andare a ~re** go and see. **~rsi** vr find oneself; (luogo:) be; (sentirsi) feel. **~ta** f bright idea. **~ta pubblicitaria** advertising gimmick

truc'care vt make up; (falsificare) fix ⊞. **~rsi** vr make up

'trucco m (cosmetico) make-up; (imbroglio) trick

'truce adj fierce; (delitto) appalling

truci'dare vt slay

'truciolo m shaving

truci'lento adj truculent

'truffa f fraud. **truf'fare** vt swindle. **~tore, ~trice** mf swindler

'truppa f troops pl; (gruppo) group

tu pers pron you; **sei tu?** is that you?; **l'hai fatto tu?** did you do it yourself?; **a tu per tu** in private; **darsi del tu** use the familiar tu

'tuba f tuba; (cappello) top hat

tuba'tura f piping

tubazi'oni fpl piping sg, pipes

tuberco'losi f tuberculosis

tu'betto m tube

tu'bino m (vestito) shift

'tubo m pipe; (Anat) canal; **non ho** capito un **~** ⊞ I understood zilch. **~ di scappamento** exhaust [pipe]

tuf'fare vt plunge. **~rsi** vr dive. **~tore, ~trice** mf diver

'tuffo m dive; (angolo) dip; **ho avuto un ~ al cuore** my heart missed a beat. **~ di testa** dive

'tufo m tufa

tu'gurio m hovel

tuli'pano m tulip

'tulle m tulle

tume'fatto adj swollen. **~zi'one** f swelling. **'tumido** adj swollen

tu'more m tumour

tumulazi'one f burial

tu'multo m turmoil; (sommossa) riot. **~u'oso** adj uproarious

'tunica f tunic

Tuni'sia f Tunisia

'tunnel m inv tunnel

'tuo (il **~** m, la tua f, i **~i** mpl, le tue fpl) poss adj your, è tua questa **macchina?** is this car yours?; **un ~** **amico** a friend of yours; **~ padre** your father ● poss pron yours; **i tuoi** your folks

tuo'nare vi thunder. **tu'ono** m thunder

tu'orlo m yolk

tu'racciolo m stopper; (di sughero) cork

tu'rar|e vt stop; cork (bottiglia). **~si** vr become blocked; **~si il naso** hold one's nose

turba'mento m disturbance; (sconvolgimento) upsetting. **~ della quiete pubblica** breach of the peace

tur'bante m turban

tur'ba|re vt upset. **~rsi** vr get upset. **~to** adj upset

tur'bina f turbine

turbi'nare vi whirl. **'turbine** m whirl. **turbine di vento** whirlwind

turbo'lenza f turbulence

turboreat'tore m turbo-jet

tur'chese adj & mf turquoise

Tur'chia f Turkey

tur'chino adj & m deep blue

'turco, -a adj Turkish • mf Turk • m (lingua) Turkish; fig double Dutch; **fumare come un ~** smoke like a chimney

tu'rismo m tourism. **~ culturale** heritage tourism. **~ta** mf tourist. **~tico** adj tourist attrib

'turno m turn; **a ~** in turn; **di ~** on duty; **fare a ~** take turns. **~ di notte** night shift

'turpe adj base

'tuta f overalls pl; Sport tracksuit. **~ da lavoro** overalls pl. **~ mimetica** camouflage. **~ spaziale** spacesuit. **~ subacquea** wetsuit

tu'tela f (Jur) guardianship; (protezione) protection. **tute'lare** vt protect

tu'tina f sleepsuit; (da danza) leotard

tu'tore, -'trice mf guardian

'tutta f **mettercela ~ per fare qcsa** go flat out for sth

tutta'via conj nevertheless

'tutto adj whole; (con nomi plurali) all; (ogni) every; **tutta la classe** the whole class, all the class; **tutti gli alunni** all the pupils; **a tutta velocità** at full speed; **ho aspettato ~ il giorno** I waited all day [long]; **in ~ il mondo** all over the world; **noi tutti** all of us; **era tutta contenta** she was delighted; **tutti e due** both; **tutti e tre** all three • pron all; (tutta la gente) everybody; (tutte le cose) everything; (qualunque cosa) anything; **l'ho mangiato ~** I ate it all; **le ho lavate tutte** I washed them all; **raccontami ~** tell me everything; **lo sanno tutti** everybody knows; **è capace di ~** he's capable of anything; **~ compreso** all in; **del ~** quite; **in ~** altogether • adv completely; **tutt'a un tratto** all at once; **tutt'altro** not at all; **tutt'altro** che anything but • m whole. **~'fare** a inv & nmf [impiegato] **~** general handyman; **donna**

~ general maid

tut'tora adv still

tutù m inv tutu, ballet dress

tv f inv TV

* * *

Uu

* * *

ubbidi'en|te adj obedient. **~za** f obedience. **ubbi'dire** vi **~ (a)** obey

ubi'cato adj located. **~zi'one** f location

ubria'car|e vt get drunk. **~si** vr get drunk; **~si di** fig become intoxicated with

ubria'chezza f drunkenness; **in stato di ~** inebriated

ubri'aco, -a adj drunk • mf drunk

ubria'cone m drunkard

uccel'liera f aviary. **uc'cello** m bird; (≡: pene) cock

uc'cider|e vt kill. **~si** vr kill oneself

ucci|si'one f killing. **uc'ciso** pp di **uccidere. ~sore** m killer

u'dente adj **i non udenti** the hearing-impaired

u'dibile adj audible

udi'enza f audience; (colloquio) interview; (Jur) hearing

u'di|re vt hear. **~tivo** adj auditory. **~to** m hearing. **~tore, ~trice** mf listener; (Sch) unregistered student (allowed to attend lectures). **~torio** m audience

uffici'al|e adj official • m officer; (funzionario) official; **pubblico ~e** public official. **~iz'zare** vt make official

uf'ficio m office; (dovere) duty. **~ di collocamento** employment office. **~ informazioni** information office. **~ del personale** personnel department. **~sa'mente** adv unofficially

uffici'oso *adj* unofficial

'ufo[1] *m inv* ufo

'ufo[2]: a ~ *adv* without paying

uggi'oso *adj* boring

uguagli'anza *f* equality. ~**re** *vt* make equal; (*essere uguale*) equal; (*livellare*) level. ~**rsi** *vr* ~**rsi a** compare oneself to

ugu'ale *adj* equal; (*lo stesso*) the same; (*simile*) like. ~**mente** *adv* equally; (*malgrado tutto*) all the same

'ulcera *f* ulcer

uli'veto *m* olive grove

ulteri'ore *adj* further. ~**mente** *adv* further

ultima'mente *adv* lately

ulti'mare *vt* complete. ~**tum** *m inv* ultimatum

ulti'missime *fpl* stop press *sg*

'ultimo *adj* last; (*notizie ecc*) latest; (*più lontano*) farthest; *fig* ultimate ● *m* last; **fino all'**~ to the last; **per** ~ at the end; **l'**~ **piano** the top floor

ultrà *mf inv* sport fanatical supporter

ultramo'derno *adj* ultramodern

ultra'rapido *adj* extra-fast

ultrasen'sibile *adj* ultrasensitive

ultra'sonico *adj* ultrasonic. ~**u'o-no** *m* ultrasound

ultravio'letto *adj* ultraviolet

ulu'lare *vi* howl. ~**to** *m* howling

umana'mente *adv* (*trattare*) humanely; ~ **impossibile** not humanly possible

uma'nesimo *m* humanism

umanità *f* humanity. **umani'tario** *adj* humanitarian. **u'mano** *adj* human; (*benevolo*) humane

umidifica'tore *m* humidifier

umidità *f* dampness; (*di clima*) humidity. **'umido** *adj* damp; (*clima*) humid; (*mani, occhi*) moist ● *m* dampness; **in umido** (*Culin*) stewed

'umile *adj* humble

umili'ante *adj* humiliating. ~**re** *vt* humiliate. ~**rsi** *vr* humble oneself

~**zi'one** *f* humiliation. **umil'mente** *adv* humbly. **umiltà** *f* humility

u'more *m* humour; (*stato d'animo*) mood; **di cattivo/buon** ~ in a bad/good mood

umo'rismo *m* humour. ~**ta** *mf* humorist. ~**tico** *adj* humorous

---

un *in def art*

> Un/una si traduce con *uno* quando si tratta di un numero

a;

····▶ (*davanti a vocale o h muta*) an; ▷**UNO**

una *indef art* *f* a; ▷**UN**

u'nanime *adj* unanimous. ~**e'mente** *adv* unanimously. ~**ità** *f* unanimity; **all'**~**ità** unanimously

unci'nato *adj* hooked; (*parentesi*) angle

un'cino *m* hook

'undici *adj* & *m* eleven

'ungere *vt* grease; (*sporcare*) get greasy; (*Relig*) anoint; (*blandire*) flatter. ~**si** *vr* (*con olio solare*) oil oneself; ~**si le mani** get one's hands greasy

unghe'rese *adj* & *mf* Hungarian. **Unghe'ria** *f* Hungary

'unghia *f* nail; (*di animale*) claw. ~**'ata** *f* (*graffio*) scratch

ungu'ento *m* ointment

unica'mente *adv* only. **'unico** *adj* only; (*singolo*) single; (*incomparabile*) unique

unifi'care *vt* unify. ~**zi'one** *f* unification

unifor'mare *vt* level. ~**si** *vr* conform (a to)

uni'forme *adj* & *f* uniform. ~**ità** *f* uniformity

unilate'rale *adj* unilateral

uni'one *f* union; (*armonia*) unity. **U~ Europea** European Union. **U~ Mo-**

netaria Europea European Monetary Union. **~ sindacale** trade union

u'ni|re *vt* unite; (*collegare*) join; blend (colori ecc). **~rsi** *vr* unite; (*collegarsi*) join

'unisex *adj inv* unisex

unità *f inv* unity; (*Math, Mil*) unit; (*Comput*) drive. **~rio** *adj* unitary

u'nito *adj* united; (*tinta*) plain

univer'sal|e *adj* universal. **~'mente** *adv* universally

università *f inv* university. **~rio, -a** *adj* university *attrib* • *mf* (*insegnante*) university lecturer; (*studente*) undergraduate

Università Italy's first university was founded in Bologna in 1088, and they are still run on traditional lines. Oral exams are the norm. Students study for a number of exams, which can be taken in a flexible order. For this reason Italian students often combine study with a job. The drop-out rate is high.

uni'verso *m* universe

uno, -a *indef art* (*before s + consonant, gn, ps, z*) a
• *pron* one; **a ~ a ~** one by one; **l'~ e l'altro** both [of them]; **né l'~ né l'altro** neither [of them]; **~ di noi** one of us; **~ fa quello che può** you do what you can
• *adj* a, one
• *m* (*numerale*) one; (*un tale*) some man;
• *f* some woman

'unt|o *pp di* ungere • *adj* greasy • *m* grease. **~u'oso** *adj* greasy. **unzi'one** *f* l'Estrema Unzione Extreme Unction

u'omo *m* (*pl* uomini) man. **~ d'affari** business man. **~ di fiducia** right-hand man. **~ di Stato** statesman

u'ovo *m* (*pl f* uova) egg. **~ in camicia** poached egg. **~ alla coque** boiled egg. **~ di Pasqua** Easter egg. **~ sodo** hard-boiled egg. **~ strapazzato** scrambled egg

ura'gano *m* hurricane

u'ranio *m* uranium

urba'n|esimo *m* urbanization. **~ista** *mf* town planner. **~istica** *f* town planning. **~istico** *adj* urban. **urbanizzazi'one** *f* urbanization. **ur'bano** *adj* urban; (*cortese*) urbane

ur'gen|te *adj* urgent. **~te'mente** *adv* urgently. **~za** *f* urgency; **in caso d'~za** in an emergency; **d'~za** (*misura, chiamata*) emergency

'urgere *vi* be urgent

u'rina *f* urine. **uri'nare** *vi* urinate

ur'lare *vi* yell; (*cane, vento*): howl. **'urlo** *m* (*pl m* urli, *f* urla) shout; (*di cane, vento*) howling

'urna *f* urn; (*elettorale*) ballot box; **andare alle urne** go to the polls

urrà *int* hurrah!

ur'tar|e *vt* knock against; (*scontrarsi*) bump into; *fig* irritate. **~si** *vr* collide; *fig* clash

'urto *m* knock; (*scontro*) crash; (*contrasto*) conflict; *fig* clash; **d'~** (*misure, terapia*) shock

usa e getta *adj inv* (rasoio, siringa) disposable

u'sanza *f* custom; (*moda*) fashion

u'sa|re *vt* use; (*impiegare*) employ; (*esercitare*) exercise; **~ fare qcsa** be in the habit of doing sth • *vi* (*essere di moda*) be fashionable; **non si usa più** it is out of fashion; it's not used any more. **~to** *adj* used; (*non nuovo*) second-hand

u'scente *adj* (presidente) outgoing

usci'ere *m* usher. **'uscio** *m* door

u'sci|re *vi* come out; (*andare fuori*) go out; (*sfuggire*) get out; (*essere sorteggiato*) come up; (*giornale*:) come out; **~re da** (*Comput*) exit from, quit; **~re di strada** leave the road. **~ta** *f* exit, way out; (*spesa*) outlay; (*di auto-*

strada) junction; (*battuta*) witty remark; **essere in libera ~ta** be off duty. **~ta di servizio** back door. **~ta di sicurezza** emergency exit

usi'gnolo *m* nightingale

'uso *m* use; (*abitudine*) custom; (*usanza*) usage; **fuori ~** out of use; **per ~ esterno** for external use only

U.S.S.L. *f abbr* (Unità Socio-Sanitaria Locale) local health centre

ustio'na|rsi *vr* burn oneself ● *adj* burnt. **usti'one** *f* burn

usu'ale *adj* usual

usufru'ire *vi* **~ di** take advantage of

u'sura *f* usury

usur'pare *vt* usurp

u'tensile *m* tool; (*Culin*) utensil; **cassetta degli utensili** tool box

u'tente *mf* user. **~ finale** end user

u'tenza *f* use; (*utenti*) users *pl*. **~ finale** end users

ute'rino *adj* uterine. **'utero** *m* womb

'utile *adj* useful ● *m* (*Comm*) profit. **~ità** *f* usefulness; (*Comput*) utility. **~i'taria** *f* (*Auto*) small car. **~i'tario** *adj* utilitarian

utiliz'za|re *vt* utilize. **~zi'one** *f* utilization. **uti'lizzo** *m* use

utu'pistico *adj* Utopian

'uva *f* grapes *pl*; **chicco d'~** grape. **~ passa** raisins *pl*. **~ sultanina** currants *pl*

Vv

va'cante *adj* vacant

va'canza *f* holiday; (*posto vacante*) vacancy. **essere in ~** be on holiday

'vacca *f* cow. **~ da latte** dairy cow

vacci'nare *vt* vaccinate. **~na·zi'one** *f* vaccination. **vac'cino** *m*

---

vaccine

vacil'la|nte *adj* tottering; (*oggetto*) wobbly; (*luce*) flickering; *fig* wavering. **~re** *vi* totter; (*oggetto:*) wobble; (*luce:*) flicker; *fig* waver

'vacuo *adj* (*vano*) vain; *fig* empty ● *m* vacuum

vagabon'dare *vi* wander. **vaga-'bondo, -a** *adj* (*cane*) stray; **gente vagabonda** tramps *pl* ● *mf* tramp

va'gare *vi* wander

vagheggi'are *vt* long for

va'gi|na *f* vagina. **~'nale** *adj* vaginal

va'gi|re *vi* whimper

'vaglia *m inv* money order. **~ ban·cario** bank draft. **~ postale** postal order

vagli'are *vt* sift; *fig* weigh

'vago *adj* vague

vagon'cino *m* (*di funivia*) car

va'gone *m* (*per passeggeri*) carriage; (*per merci*) wagon. **~ letto** sleeper. **~ ristorante** restaurant car

vai'olo *m* smallpox

va'langa *f* avalanche

va'lente *adj* skilful

va'le|re *vi* be worth; (*contare*) count; (*regola:*) apply (**per** to); (*essere valido*) be valid; **far ~ i propri diritti** assert one's rights; **farsi ~** assert oneself; **non vale!** that's not fair! ● *vt* **~re qcsa a qcno** (*procurare*) earn sb sth; **~ne la pena** be worth it; **vale la pena di vederlo** it's worth seeing; **~si di** avail oneself of

valeri'ana *f* valerian

va'levole *adj* valid

vali'care *vt* cross. **'valico** *m* pass

validità *f* validity; **con ~ illimitata** valid indefinitely

'valido *adj* valid; (*efficace*) efficient; (*contributo*) valuable

valige'ria *f* (*fabbrica*) leather factory; (*negozio*) leather goods shop

va'ligia f suitcase; **fare le valigie** pack one's bags. **∼ diplomatica** diplomatic bag

val'lata f valley. **'valle** f valley; **a valle** downstream

val'lett|a f (TV) assistant. **∼o** m valet; (TV) assistant

val'lone m (valle) deep valley

va'lor|e m value; (merito) merit; (coraggio) valour; **∼i** pl (Comm) securities; **di ∼e** (oggetto) valuable; **oggetti** pl **di ∼e** valuables; **senza ∼e** worthless. **∼iz'zare** vt (mettere in valore) use to advantage; (aumentare di valore) increase the value of; (migliorare l'aspetto di) enhance

valo'roso adj courageous

'valso pp di **valere**

va'luta f currency. **∼ estera** foreign currency

valu'ta|re vt value; weigh up (situazione). **∼rio** adj (mercato, norme) currency. **∼zi'one** f valuation

'valva f valve. **'valvola** f valve; (Electr) fuse

vam'pata f blaze; (di calore) blast; (al viso) flush

vam'piro m vampire

vana'mente adv in vain

van'da|lico adj atto **∼lico** act of vandalism. **∼'lismo** m vandalism. **'vandalo** m vandal

vaneggi'are vi rave

'vanga f spade. **van'gare** vt dig

van'gelo m Gospel; (🄸: verità) gospel [truth]

vanifi'care vt nullify

va'niglia f vanilla. **∼'ato** adj (zucchero) vanilla attrib

vanità f vanity. **vani'toso** adj vain

'vano adj vain **● m** (stanza) room; (spazio vuoto) hollow

van'taggi|o m advantage; Sport lead; Tennis advantage; **trarre ∼o da qcsa** derive benefit from sth. **∼'oso** adj advantageous

van't|are vt praise; (possedere) boast. **∼arsi** vr boast. **∼e'ria** f boasting. **'vanto** m boast

va'nvera f **a ∼** at random; **parlare a ∼** talk nonsense

va'por|e m steam; (di benzina, cascata) vapour; **a ∼e** steam attrib; **al ∼e** (Culin) steamed. **∼e acqueo** steam, water vapour; **battello a ∼e** steamboat. **vapo'retto** m ferry. **∼i'era** f steam engine

vaporiz'za|re vt vaporize. **∼'tore** m spray

vapo'roso adj (vestito) filmy; **capelli vaporosi** big hair sg

va'rare vt launch

var'care vt cross. **'varco** m passage; **aspettare al varco** lie in wait

vari'abil|e adj variable **● f** variability. **∼ità** f variability

vari'a|nte f variant. **∼re** vt/i vary; **∼re di umore** change one's mood. **∼zi'one** f variation

va'rice f varicose vein

vari'cella f chickenpox

vari'coso adj varicose

varie'gato adj variegated

varietà f inv variety **● m** inv variety show

'vario adj varied; (al pl, parecchi) various; **vari** pl (molti) several; **varie ed eventuali** any other business

vario'pinto adj multicoloured

'varo m launch

va'saio m potter

'vasca f tub; (piscina) pool; (lunghezza) length. **∼ da bagno** bath

va'scello m vessel

va'schetta f tub

vase'lina f Vaseline®

vasel'lame m china. **∼ d'oro/ d'argento** gold/silver plate

'vaso m pot; (da fiori) vase; (Anat) vessel; (per cibi) jar. **∼ da notte** chamber pot

vas'soio m tray

vastità f vastness. **'vasto** adj vast; **di vaste vedute** broad-minded

Vati'cano m Vatican

ve pers pron you; **ve l'ho dato** I gave it to you

vecchia f old woman. **vecchi'aia** f old age. **'vecchio** adj old ●mf old man; **i vecchi** old people

'vece f in ~ **di** in place of; **fare le veci di qcno** take sb's place

ve'dente adj **i non vedenti** the visually handicapped

ve'der|e vt/i see; **far ~e** show; **farsi ~e** show one's face; **non vedo l'ora di...** I can't wait to...; **~si** vr see oneself; (reciproco) see each other

ve'detta f lookout; (Naut) patrol vessel

'vedovo, -a m widower ●f widow

ve'duta f view

vee'mente adj vehement

vege'tale adj & m vegetable. **~i'ano** adj & mf vegan. **~are** vi vegetate. **~ri'ano, -a** adj & mf vegetarian. **~zi'one** f vegetation

'vegeto adj ▷**vivo**

veg'gente mf clairvoyant

'veglia f watch; **fare la ~** keep watch. **~ funebre** vigil

vegli'|are vi be awake; **~are su** watch over. **~'one** m ~ **di Capodanno** New Year's Eve celebration

ve'icolo m vehicle

'vela f sail; (Sport) sailing; **far ~** set sail

ve'la|re vt veil; (fig: nascondere) hide. **~rsi** vr (vista:) mist over; (voce:) go husky. **~ta'mente** adv indirectly. **~to** adj veiled; (occhi:) misty; (collant) sheer

'velcro® m velcro®

veleggi'are vi sail

ve'leno m poison. **vele'noso** adj poisonous

veli'ero m sailing ship

ve'lina f (carta) ~ **tissue paper**;

(copia) carbon copy

ve'lista m yachtsman ●f yachtswoman

ve'livolo m aircraft

vellei'tario adj unrealistic

'vello m fleece

vellu'tato adj velvety. **vel'luto** m velvet. **velluto a coste** corduroy

'velo m veil; (di zucchero, cipria) dusting; (tessuto) voile

ve'loc|e adj fast. **~e'mente** adv quickly. **velo'cista** mf (Sport) sprinter. **~ità** f inv speed; (Auto: marcia) gear. **~iz'zare** vt speed up

ve'lodromo m cycle track

'vena f vein; **essere in ~ di** be in the mood for

ve'nale adj venal; (persona) mercenary, venal

ve'nato adj grainy

vena'torio adj hunting attrib

vena'tura f (di legno) grain; (di foglia, marmo) vein

ven'demmia f grape harvest. **~'are** vt harvest

'vender|e vt sell. **~si** vr sell oneself; **"vendesi"** "for sale"

ven'detta f revenge

vendi'car|e vt avenge. **~rsi** vr get one's revenge. **~'tivo** adj vindictive

'vendi|ta f sale; **in ~ta** on sale. **~ta all'asta** sale by auction. **~ta al dettaglio** retailing. **~ta all'ingrosso** wholesaling. **~ta al minuto** retailing. **~'tore, ~'trice** mf seller. **~tore ambulante** hawker, pedlar

vene'ra|bile, ~ndo adj venerable

vene'ra|re vt revere

venerdì m inv Friday. **V~ Santo** Good Friday

'Venere f Venus, **ve'nereo** adj venereal

Ve'nezi|a f Venice. **v~'ano, -a** agg & mf Venetian ●f (persiana) Venetian blind; (Culin) sweet bun

veni'ale adj venial

ve'nire vi come; (riuscire) turn out; (costare) cost; (in passivi) be; **~ a sapere** learn; **~ in mente** occur; **~ meno** (svenire) faint; **~ meno a un contratto** go back on a contract; **~ via** come away; (staccarsi) come off; **vieni a prendermi** come and pick me up

ven'taglio m air.

ven'tata f gust [of wind]; fig breath

ven'te|nne adj & mf twenty-year-old. **~simo** adj & m twentieth. **'venti** adj & m twenty

venti'la|re vt air. **~'tore** m fan. **~zi'one** f ventilation

ven'tina f una **~** (circa venti) about twenty

ventiquat'trore f inv (valigia) overnight case

'vento m wind; **farsi ~** fan oneself

ven'tosa f sucker

ven'toso adj windy

'ventre m stomach. **ven'triloquo** m ventriloquist

ven'tura f fortune

ven'turo adj next

ve'nuta f coming

vera'mente adv really

ve'randa f veranda

ver'bal|e adj verbal ● m (di riunione) minutes pl. **~'mente** adv verbally

'verbo m verb. **~ ausiliare** auxiliary [verb]

'verde adj green ● m green; (vegetazione) greenery; (semaforo) green light. **~ oliva** olive green. **~'rame** m verdigris

ver'detto m verdict

ver'dura f vegetables pl; **una ~** a vegetable

'verga f rod

vergi'n|ale adj virginal. **'vergine** f virgin; (Astr) V**~** Virgo ● adj virgin; (cassetta) blank. **~ità** f virginity

ver'gogna f shame; (timidezza) shyness

vergo'gn|arsi vr feel ashamed; (essere timido) feel shy. **~oso** adj ashamed; (timido) shy; (disonorevole) shameful

ve'rifica f check. **verifi'cabile** adj verifiable

verifi'car|e vt check. **~si** vr come true

ve'rismo m realism

verit|à f truth. **~i'ero** adj truthful

'verme m worm. **~ solitario** tapeworm

ver'miglio adj & m vermilion

'vermut m inv vermouth

ver'nacolo m vernacular

ver'nic|e f paint; (trasparente) varnish; (pelle) patent leather; fig veneer; **"vernice fresca"** "wet paint". **~i'are** vt paint; (con vernice trasparente) varnish. **~ia'tura** f painting; (strato) paintwork; fig veneer

'vero adj true; (autentico) real; (perfetto) perfect; **è ~?** is that so?; **sei stanca, ~?** you're tired, aren't you ● m truth; (realtà) life

verosimigli'anza f probability. **vero'simile** adj probable

ver'ruca f wart; (sotto la pianta del piede) verruca

versa'mento m payment; (in banca) deposit

ver'sante m slope

ver'sa|re vt pour; (spargere) shed; (rovesciare) spill; pay (denaro). **~rsi** vr spill; (sfociare) flow

ver'satil|e adj versatile. **~ità** f versatility

ver'setto m verse

versi'one f version; (traduzione) translation; **"~ integrale"** "unabridged version"

'verso[1] m verse; (grido) cry; (gesto) gesture; (senso) direction; (modo) manner; **non c'è ~ di** there is no way of

'verso[2] prep towards; (nei pressi di)

round about; ~ **dove?** which way?

'vertebra f vertebra

'vertere vi ~ **su** focus on

verti'cal|e adj vertical; (in parole crociate) down ● m vertical ● f handstand. ~'**mente** adv vertically

'vertice m summit; (Math) vertex; **conferenza al** ~ summit conference

ver'tigine f dizziness; (Med) vertigo. **vertigini** pl giddy spells

vertigi'nosa'mente adv dizzily. ~'**noso** adj dizzy; (velocità) breakneck; (prezzi) sky-high; (scollatura) plunging

ve'scica f bladder; (sulla pelle) blister

'vescovo m bishop

'vespa f wasp

vespasi'ano m urinal

'vespro m vespers pl

ves'sillo m standard

ve'staglia f dressing gown

'vest|e f dress, (rivestimento) covering; **in** ~ **di** in the capacity of. ~'**iario** m clothing

ve'stibolo m hall

ve'stigio m (pl m vestigi, pl f vestigia) trace

ve'stire vt dress. ~**rsi** vr get dressed. ~**ti** pl clothes. ~**to** adj dressed ● m (da uomo) suit; (da donna) dress

vete'rano, -a adj & mf veteran

veteri'naria f veterinary science

veteri'nario adj veterinary ● m veterinary surgeon

'veto m inv veto

ve'traio m glazier. ~**ta** f big window; (in chiesa) stained-glass window; (porta) glass door. ~**to** adj glazed. **vetre'ria** f glass works

vetri'olo m vitriol

'vetro m glass; (di finestra, porta) pane. ~'**resina** f fibreglass

'vetta f peak

vet'tore m vector

vetto'vaglie fpl provisions

vet'tura f coach; (ferroviaria) carriage; (Auto) car. **vettu'rino** m coachman

vezzeggi'a|re vt fondle. ~'**tivo** m pet name. **'vezzo** m habit; (attrattiva) charm; **vezzi** pl (moine) affectation sg. **vez'zoso** adj charming; pej affected

vi pers pron you; (riflessivo) yourselves; (reciproco) each other; (tra più persone) one another; **vi ho dato un libro** I gave you a book; **lavatevi le mani** wash your hands; **essevi** here you are! ● adv = **ci**

via¹ f street, road; fig way; (Anat) tract; **in** ~ **di** in the course of; **per** ~ **di** on account of; ~ ~ **che** as; **per** ~ **aerea** by airmail

via² adv away; (fuori) out; **andar** ~ go away; **e così** ~ and so on; **e** ~ **dicendo** and whatnot ● **int** ~**! go away!, Sport go!; (andiamo) come on! ● m starting signal

viabilità f road conditions pl; (rete) road network; (norme) road and traffic laws pl

via'card f inv motorway card

viaggi'a|re vi travel. ~'**tore, ~'trice** m traveller

vi'aggio m journey; (breve) trip; **buon** ~! safe journey!, have a good trip!; **fare un** ~ go on a journey. ~ **di nozze** honeymoon

vi'ale m avenue; (privato) drive

vi'bra|nte adj vibrant. ~**re** vi vibrate; (fremere) quiver. ~**zi'one** f vibration

vi'cario m vicar

'vice mf deputy. ~**diret'tore** m assistant manager

vi'cenda f event; **a** ~ (fra due) each other; (a turno) in turn[s]

vice'versa adv vice versa

vici'na|nza f nearness; ~**nze** pl (paraggi) neighbourhood. ~**to** m

v

neighbourhood; (*vicini*) neighbours *pl*

vi'cino, -a *adj* near; (*accanto*) next ● *adv* near, close. ~ **a** *prep* near [to] ● *mf* neighbour. ~ **di casa** nextdoor neighbour

'vicolo *m* alley

'video *m* video. ~**'camera** *f* camcorder. ~**cas'setta** *f* video cassette

videoci'tofono *m* video entry phone

video'clip *m inv* video clip

videogi'oco *m* video game

videoregistra'tore *m* videorecorder

video'teca *f* video library

video'tel® *m* ≈ Videotex®

videote'lefono *m* videophone

videotermi'nale *m* visual display unit, VDU

vidi'mare *vt* authenticate

vie'ta|re *vt* forbid; **sosta** ~**ta** no parking; ~**to fumare** no smoking

vi'gente *adj* in force. **'vigere** *vi* be in force

vigi'la|nte *adj* vigilant. ~**nza** *f* vigilance. ~**re** *vt* keep an eye on ● *vi* keep watch

'vigile *adj* watchful ● *m* ~ **[urbano]** policeman. ~ **del fuoco** fireman

vi'gilia *f* eve

vigliacche'ria *f* cowardice. **vi-gli'acco, -a** *adj* cowardly ● *mf* coward

'vigna *f*, **vi'gneto** *m* vineyard

vi'gnetta *f* cartoon

vi'gore *m* vigour; **entrare in** ~ come into force. **vigo'roso** *adj* vigorous

'vile *adj* cowardly; (*abietto*) vile

'villa *f* villa

vil'laggio *m* village. ~ **turistico** holiday village

vil'lano *adj* rude ● *m* boor; (*contadino*) peasant

villeggi'a|nte *mf* holiday-maker. ~**re** *vi* spend one's holidays. ~**'tura** *f*

holiday[s] [*pl*]

vil'l|etta *f* small detached house. ~**ino** *m* detached house

viltà *f* cowardice

'vimine *m* wicker

'vinc|ere *vt* win; (*sconfiggere*) beat; (*superare*) overcome. ~**ita** *f* win; (*somma vinta*) winnings *pl*. ~**i'tore**, ~**i'trice** *mf* winner

vinco'lante *adj* binding. ~**re** *vt* bind; (*Comm*) tie up. **'vincolo** *m* bond

vi'nicolo *adj* wine *attrib*

vinil'pelle® *f* Leatherette®

'vino *m* wine. ~ **spumante** sparkling wine. ~ **da taglio** blending wine. ~ **da tavola** table wine

'vinto *pp di* **vincere**

vi'ola *f* (*Bot*) violet; (*Mus*) viola. **viola** *adj & m inv* purple

vio'la|re *vt* violate. ~**zi'one** *f* violation. ~**zione di domicilio** breaking and entering

violen'tare *vt* rape

vio'len|to *adj* violent. ~**za** *f* violence. ~**za carnale** rape

vio'letta *f* violet

vio'letto *adj & m* (*colore*) violet

violi'nista *mf* violinist. **vio'lino** *m* violin. **violon'cello** *m* cello

vi'ottolo *m* path

'vipera *f* viper

vi'ra|ggio *m* (*Phot*) toning; (*Aeron, Naut*) turn. ~**re** *vi* turn

'virgola *f* comma. ~**ette** *fpl* inverted commas

vi'ril|e *adj* virile; (*da uomo*) manly. ~**ità** *f* virility; manliness

virtù *f inv* virtue; **in** ~ **di** (*legge*) under. **virtu'ale** *adj* virtual. **virtu'oso** *adj* virtuous ● *m* virtuoso

viru'lento *adj* virulent

'virus *m inv* virus

visa'gista *mf* beautician

visce'rale *adj* visceral; (*odio*) deep-seated; (*reazione*) gut

'viscere m internal organ ● fpl **guts**

'vischio m mistletoe. **∼'oso** adj viscous; (appiccicoso) **sticky**

vi'sconte m viscount. **∼'essa** f viscountess

vi'scoso adj viscous

vi'sibile adj visible

visi'bilio m profusion; **andare in ∼** go into ecstasies

visibilità f visibility

visi'era f (di elmo) visor; (di berretto) peak

visio'nare vt examine; Cinema screen. **visi'one** f vision; **prima vi'sione** Cinema first showing

'visita f visit; (breve) call; (Med) examination; (di controllo (Med)) checkup. **visi'tare** vt visit; (brevemente) call on; (Med) examine; **∼a'tore, ∼a'trice** mf visitor

vi'sivo adj visual

'viso m face

vi'sone m mink

'vispo adj lively

vis'suto pp di **vivere** ● adj experienced

'vista f sight; (veduta) view; **a ∼ d'occhio** (crescere) visibly; (restando) dersi) as far as the eye can see; **in ∼ di** in view of. **∼o** pp di **vedere** ● m visa. **vi'stoso** adj showy; (notevole) considerable

visu'ale adj visual. **∼izza'tore** m (Comput) display, VDU. **∼izzazi'one** f (Comput) display

'vita f life; (durata della vita) lifetime; (Anat) waist; **a ∼** for life; **essere in ∼** be alive

vi'tale adj vital. **∼ità** f vitality

vita'lizio adj life attrib ● m [life] annuity

vita'min|a f vitamin. **∼iz'zato** adj vitamin-enriched

'vite f (Mech) screw; (Bot) vine

vi'tello m calf; (Culin) veal; (pelle) calfskin

vi'ticcio m tendril

viticol'tore m wine grower. **∼ura** f wine growing

'vitreo adj vitreous; (sguardo) glassy

'vittima f victim

'vitto m food; (pasti) board ∼ **e alloggio** board and lodging

vit'toria f victory

vittori'oso adj victorious

vi'uzza f narrow lane

'viva int hurrah!; **∼ la Regina!** long live the Queen!

vi'vac|e adj vivacious; (mente) lively; (colore) bright. **∼ità** f (di mente) liveliness; (di colore) brightness. **∼iz'zare** vt liven up

vi'vaio m nursery; (per pesci) pond; fig breeding ground

viva'mente adv (ringraziare) warmly

vi'vanda f food; (piatto) dish

vi'vente adj living ● mpl **i viventi** the living

'vivere vi live; **∼ di** live on ● vt (passare) go through ● m life

'viveri mpl provisions

'vivido adj vivid

vivisezi'one f vivisection

'vivo adj alive; (vivente) living; (vivace) lively; (colore) bright; **∼ e vegeto** alive and kicking; **farsi ∼** keep in touch; (arrivare) turn up ● m dal ∼ (trasmissione) live; (disegnare) from life; **i vivi** the living

vizi'are vt spoil (bambino ecc); (guastare) vitiate. **∼'ato** adj spoilt; (aria) stale. **'vizio** m vice; (cattiva abitudine) bad habit; (difetto) flaw. **∼'oso** adj dissolute; (difettoso) faulty; **circolo ∼oso** vicious circle

vocabo'lario m dictionary; (lessico) vocabulary. **vo'cabolo** m word

vo'cale adj vocal ● f vowel. **vo'calico** adj (corde) vocal; (suono) vowel attrib

vocazi'one f vocation

'voce f voice; (diceria) rumour; (di bilancio, dizionario) entry

voci'are vi (spettegolare) gossip ● m buzz of conversation

vocife'rare vi shout

'vog|a f rowing; (lena) enthusiasm; (moda) vogue; **essere in ~a** be in fashion. **vo'gare** vi row. **~a'tore** m oarsman; (attrezzo) rowing machine

'vogli|a f desire; (volontà) will; (della pelle) birthmark; **aver ~a di fare qcsa** feel like doing sth

'voi pers pron you; **siete ~?** is that you?; **l'avete fatto ~?** did you do it yourself?. **~a'ltri** pers pron you

vo'lano m shuttlecock; (Mech) flywheel

vo'lante adj flying; (foglio) loose ● m steering-wheel

volan'tino m leaflet

vo'la|re vi fly. **~ta** f Sport final sprint; **di ~ta** in a rush

vo'latile adj (liquido) volatile ● m bird

volée f inv Tennis volley

vo'lente adj **~ o nolente** whether you like it or not

volenti'eri adv willingly; **~!** with pleasure!

vo'lere vt want; (chiedere di) ask for; (aver bisogno di) need; **vuole che io faccia io** he wants me to do it; **fai come vuoi** do as you like; **se tuo padre vuole, ti porto al cinema** if your father agrees, I'll take you to the cinema; **vorrei un caffè** I'd like a coffee; **la vuoi smettere?** will you stop that!; **senza ~** without meaning to; **voler bene/male a qcno** love/have something against sb; **voler dire** mean; **ci vuole il latte** we need milk; **ci vuole tempo/pazienza** it takes time/patience; **volerne a** have a grudge against; **vuoi ... vuoi...** either... or... ● m will; **vo'leri** pl wishes

vol'gar|e adj vulgar; (popolare) common. **~ità** f inv vulgarity. **~iz'zare** vt popularize. **~'mente** adv (grossolanamente) vulgarly, coarsely; (comunemente) commonly

'volger|e vt/i turn. **~si** vr turn [round]; **~si a** (dedicarsi) take up

voli'era f aviary

voli'tivo adj strong-minded

'volo m flight; **al ~** (fare qcsa) quickly; (prendere qcsa) in mid-air; **alzarsi in ~** (uccello) take off; **in ~** airborne. **~ di linea** scheduled flight. **~ nazionale** domestic flight. **~ a vela** gliding.

volontà f inv will; (desiderio) wish; **a ~** (mangiare) as much as you like. **volontaria'mente** adv voluntarily. **volon'tario** adj voluntary ● m volunteer

volon'teroso adj willing

'volpe f fox

volt m inv volt

'volta f time; (turno) turn; (curva) bend; (Archit) vault; **4 volte** 4 4 times 4; a volte sometimes; **c'era una ~...** once upon a time, there was...; **una ~** once; **due volte** twice; **tre/quattro volte** three/four times; **una ~ per tutte** once and for all; **uno per ~** one at a time; **uno alla ~** one at a time; **alla ~ di** in the direction of

volta'faccia m inv volte-face

vol'taggio m voltage

vol'ta|re vt/i turn; (rigirare) turn round; (rivoltare) turn over. **~rsi** vr turn [round]

volta'stomaco m nausea

volteggi'are vi circle; (ginnastica) vault

'volto pp di **volgere** ● m face; **mi ha mostrato il suo vero ~** he revealed his true colours

vo'lubile adj fickle

vo'lum|e m volume. **~i'noso** adj voluminous

voluta'mente adv deliberately

voluttu'osità f voluptuousness. **~'oso** adj voluptuous

vomi'tare vt vomit, be sick. **'vomito** m vomit

'vongola f clam

vo'race adj voracious

vo'ragine f abyss

'vortice m whirl; (gorgo) whirlpool; (di vento) whirlwind

'vostro (il **~** m, la vostra f, i vostri mpl, le vostre fpl) poss adj your; è vostra questa macchina? is this car yours?; un **~** amico a friend of yours; **~** padre your father ● poss pron yours; i vostri your folks

vo'ta|nte mf voter. **~re** vi vote. **~zi'one** f voting; (Sch) marks pl. **'voto** m vote; (Sch) mark; (Relig) vow

vs. abbr (Comm) (vostro) yours

vul'canico adj volcanic. **vul'cano** m volcano

vulne'rabile adj vulnerable, **~ità** f vulnerability

vuo'tare vt, **vuo'tarsi** vr empty

vu'oto adj empty; (non occupato) vacant; **~ di** (sprovvisto) devoid of ● m empty space; (Phys) vacuum; fig void; assegno a **~** dud cheque; sotto **~** (prodotto) vacuum-packed; **~ a** perdere no deposit **~ d'aria** air pocket

---

'webmaster m webmaster

'western adj inv cowboy attrib ● m cinema western

Xx

X, x adj raggi pl X X-rays; il giorno X D-day

xeno'fobia f xenophobia. **xe'nofobo, -a** adj xenophobic ● mf xenophobe

xi'lofono m xylophone

Yy

yacht m inv yacht

yen m inv Fin yen

'yoga m yoga; (praticante) yogi

'yogurt m inv yoghurt. **~i'era** f yoghurt-maker

Zz

zaba[gl]i'one m zabaglione (dessert made from eggs, wine or marsala and sugar)

zaf'fata f whiff; (di fumo) cloud

zaffe'rano m saffron

zaf'firo m sapphire

'zaino m rucksack

'zampa f leg; a quattro zampe (animale) four-legged; (carponi) on

Ww

W abbr (viva) long live

'wafer m inv (biscotto) wafer

walkie-'talkie m inv walkie-talkie

watt m inv watt

WC m WC

'Web m inv Web

v
w
x
y
z

all four s

zampil'la|nte adj spurting. ~re vi spurt. **zam'pillo** m spurt

zam'pogna f bagpipe

zam'pone fpl stuffed pig's trotter with lentils

'zanna f fang; (di elefante) tusk

zan'zar|a f mosquito. ~i'era f (velo) mosquito net; (su finestra) insect screen

'zappa f hoe. **zap'pare** vt hoe

'zattera f raft

zatte'roni mpl (scarpe) wedge shoes

za'vorra f ballast; fig dead wood

'zazzera f mop of hair

'zebra f zebra; **zebre** pl (passaggio pedonale) zebra crossing

'zecca[1] f mint; **nuovo di ~** brand-new

'zecca[2] f (parassita) tick

zec'chino m sequin; **oro ~** pure gold

ze'lante adj zealous. **'zelo** m zeal

'zenit m zenith

'zenzero m ginger

'zeppa f wedge

'zeppo m packed full; **pieno ~ di** crammed o packed with

zer'bino m doormat

'zero m zero, nought; (in calcio) nil; Tennis love; **due a ~** (in partite) two nil

'zeta f zed, zee Am

'zia f aunt

zibel'lino m sable

'zigomo m cheek-bone

zig'zag m inv zigzag; **andare a ~** zigzag

zim'bello m decoy; (oggetto di scherno) laughing-stock

'zinco m zinc

'zingaro, -a mf gypsy

'zio m uncle

zi'tel|la f spinster; pej old maid. ~'lona f pej old maid

zit'tire vi fall silent ● vt silence. **'zitto** adj silent; **sta' zitto!** keep quiet!

ziz'zania f (discordia) discord

'zoccolo m clog; (di cavallo) hoof; (di terra) clump; (di parete) skirting board, baseboard Am; (di colonna) base

zodia'cale adj of the zodiac. **zo-'diaco** m zodiac

'zolfo m sulphur

'zolla f clod; (di zucchero) lump

zol'letta f sugar lump

'zombi mf inv fig zombi

'zona f zone; (area) area. **~ di depressione** area of low pressure. **~ disco** area for parking discs only. **~ pedonale** pedestrian precinct. **~ verde** green belt

'zonzo adv andare a ~ stroll about

zoo m inv zoo

zoolo'gia f zoology. **zoo'logico** adj zoological. **zo'ologo, -a** mf zoologist

zoo sa'fari m inv safari park

zoppi'ca|nte adj limping; fig shaky. **~re** vi limp; (essere debole) be shaky. **'zoppo, -a** adj lame ● mf cripple

zoti'cone m boor

'zucca f marrow; (fig: testa) head; (fig: persona) thickie

zucche'r|are vt sugar. **~i'era** f sugar bowl. **~i'ficio** m sugar refinery. **zucche'rino** adj sugary ● m sugar lump

'zucchero m sugar. **~ di canna** cane sugar. **~ vanigliato** vanilla sugar. **~ a velo** icing sugar. **zucche-'roso** adj honeyed

zuc'chin|a f, **~o** m courgette, zucchini Am

'zuffa f scuffle

zufo'lare vt/i whistle

zu'mare vi zoom

'zuppa f soup. **~ inglese** trifle

zup'petta f fare **~ [con]** dunk

zup'piera f soup tureen

'zuppo adj soaked

Phrasefinder

Useful phrases

yes, please
no, thank you
sorry
excuse me
you're welcome
I'm sorry, I don't understand

Meeting people
hello/goodbye
how do you do?
how are you?
nice to meet you

Asking questions
do you speak English/Italian?
what's your name?
where are you from?
where is...?
can I have...?
would you like...?
do you mind if...?

Statements about yourself
my name is...
I'm English/Italian
I don't speak Italian/English
very well
I'm here on holiday
I live near York/Pisa

Emergencies
can you help me, please?
I'm lost
I'm ill
call an ambulance/the Police
watch out!

Frasi utili

sì, grazie
no, grazie
scusa
mi scusi
prego
scusi, non capisco

Incontri
ciao/arrivederci
come sta?
come stai?
piacere

Fare domande
parli inglese/italiano?
come ti chiami?
di dove sei?
dov'è...?
posso avere...?
vuoi...?
le dispiace se...?

Presentarsi
mi chiamo...
sono inglese/italiano
non parlo molto bene
l'italiano/l'inglese
sono qui in vacanza
abito vicino a York/Pisa

Emergenze
mi può aiutare, per favore?
mi sono perso
sto male
chiami un'ambulanza/la polizia
attenzione!

❶ Going Places

On the road

where's the nearest garage/
petrol station (*US* filling station)?

what's the best way to get there?

I've got a puncture

I'd like to hire a bike/car

I'm looking for somewhere to park

there's been an accident

my car's broken down

the car won't start

By rail

where can I buy a ticket?

what time is the next train to
York/Milan?

do I have to change?

can I take my bike on the train?

which platform for the train to
Bath/Florence?

there's a train to London at 10 o'clock

a single/return to Birmingham/
Turin, please

I'd like a cheap day-return/
an all-day ticket

I'd like to reserve a seat

Sulla strada

dov'è la stazione di servizio
più vicina?

qual è la strada migliore per
arrivarci?

ho bucato

vorrei noleggiare una bicicletta/
una macchina

sto cercando parcheggio

c'è stato un incidente

ho la macchina in panne

la macchina non parte

In treno

dove si fanno i biglietti?

a che ora è il prossimo treno per
York/Milano?

devo cambiare?

posso portare la bicicletta sul treno?

da quale binario parte il treno per
Bath/Firenze?

c'è un treno per Londra alle 10

un biglietto di sola andata/
di andata e ritorno per
Birmingham/Torino, per
favore

vorrei un biglietto giornaliero di
andata e ritorno a tariffa ridotta

vorrei prenotare un posto

At the airport

when's the next flight to Paris/Rome?

what time do I have to check in?

where do I check in?

I'd like to confirm my flight

I'd like a window seat/an aisle seat

I want to change/cancel my reservation

All'aeroporto

quand'è il prossimo volo per Parigi/Roma?

a che ora si fa il check-in?

dov'è il check-in?

vorrei confermare il mio volo

vorrei un posto accanto al finestrino/di corridoio

voglio cambiare/annullare la mia prenotazione

Getting there

could you tell me the way to the castle?

how long will it take to get there?

how far is it from here?

which bus do I take for the cathedral?

can you tell me where to get off?

how much is the fare to the town centre (US center)?

what time is the last bus?

how do I get to the airport?

where's the nearest underground (US subway) station?

can you call me a taxi, please?

take the first turning right

turn left at the traffic lights/ just past the church

I'll take a taxi

Chiedere e dare indicazioni

può indicarmi la strada per il castello?

quanto ci vuole per arrivarci?

quanto dista da qui?

quale autobus devo prendere per andare al duomo?

può dirmi dove devo scendere?

quant'è la tariffa per il centro?

a che ora è l'ultimo autobus?

come si arriva all'aeroporto?

dov'è la metropolitana più vicina?

può chiamarmi un taxi, per favore?

prenda la prima svolta a destra

al semaforo giri a sinistra/ appena dopo la chiesa

prenderò un taxi

❷ Keeping in touch

On the phone	Al telefono
where can I buy a phone card?	dove si comprano le schede telefoniche?
may I use your phone?	posso usare il telefono?
do you have a mobile?	ha il telefonino?
what is the code for Venice/Sheffield?	qual è il prefisso di Venezia/Sheffield?
I want to make a phone call	vorrei fare una telefonata
I'd like to reverse the charges (US call collect)	vorrei fare una telefonata a carico del destinatario
the line's engaged (US busy)	è occupato
there's no answer	non risponde nessuno
hello, this is Natalie	pronto, sono Natalie
is Richard there, please?	c'è Richard, per favore?
who's calling?	chi parla?
sorry, wrong number	ha sbagliato numero
just a moment, please	un attimo, prego
would you like to hold?	vuole attendere in linea?
please tell him/her I called	gli/le dica che ho chiamato, per favore
I'd like to leave a message for him/her	vorrei lasciare un messaggio
I'll try again later	riproverò più tardi
please tell her that Clare called	le dica che ha chiamato Clare
can he/she ring me back?	mi può richiamare?
my home number is...	il mio numero è...
my business number is...	il mio numero al lavoro è...
my fax number is...	il mio numero di fax è...
we were cut off	è caduta la linea

Writing	Corrispondenza
what's your address?	qual è il tuo indirizzo?
here's my business card	questo è il mio biglietto da visita
where is the nearest post office?	dov'è l'ufficio postale più vicino?
could I have a stamp for the UK/Italy, please?	mi dà un francobollo per la Gran Bretagna/l'Italia, per favore?
I'd like stamps for two postcards to the USA, please	vorrei due francobolli per cartolina per gli Stati Uniti, per favore
I'd like to send a parcel/a telegram	vorrei spedire un pacco/ mandare un telegramma

On line	Internet
are you on the Internet?	sei su Internet?
what's your e-mail address?	qual è il tuo indirizzo di posta elettronica?
we could send it by e-mail	possiamo spedirlo con la posta elettronica
I'll e-mail it to you on Thursday	te lo mando per posta elettronica giovedì
I looked it up on the Internet	l'ho cercato su Internet
the information is on their website	le informazioni si trovano sul sito web

Meeting up	Appuntamenti
what shall we do this evening?	cosa facciamo stasera?
where shall we meet?	dove ci diamo appuntamento?
I'll see you outside the café at 6 o'clock	ci vediamo davanti al bar alle 6
see you later	a più tardi
I can't today, I'm busy	oggi non posso, sono impegnato

❸ Food and Drink

Booking a restaurant

can you recommend a good restaurant?

I'd like to reserve a table for four

a reservation for tomorrow evening at eight o'clock

I booked a table for two

Prenotare un ristorante

può consigliarmi un buon ristorante?

vorrei prenotare un tavolo per quattro

una prenotazione per domani sera alle otto

ho prenotato un tavolo per due

Ordering

could we see the menu/wine list, please?

do you have a vegetarian menu?

could we have some more bread/wine?

could I have the bill (US check)?

What would you recommend?

I'd like a black/white coffee

... an espresso

... a decaffeinated coffee

... a liqueur

Per Ordinare

possiamo avere il menù/la carta dei vini, per favore?

avete un menù vegetariano?

possiamo avere dell'altro pane/vino?

il conto, per favore

Che cosa consiglia?

Vorrei un caffè/un caffè macchiato

... un espresso

... un decaffeinato

... un liquore

You will hear ...

Prendete un aperitivo?

Volete ordinare?

Prendete un antipasto?

Che cosa prendete come secondo?

Posso consigliare ...

Prendete un dolce?

Prendete un caffè/un liquore?

Altro?

Buon appetito!

Il servizio non è compreso.

Il cameriere chiede ...

Would you like an aperitif?

Are you ready to order?

Would you like a starter?

What will you have for the main course?

I can recommend ...

Would you like a dessert?

Would you like some coffee/a liqueur?

Anything else?

Enjoy your meal!

Service is not included.

The menu		Il menu	
starters/antipasti		**antipasti/starters**	
melon	melone	antipasto di mare	seafood starter
omelette	frittata	antipasto di terra	assorted hams etc
soup	zuppa	prosciutto crudo	cured ham
salad	insalata	zuppa	soup
fish/pesce		**pesce/fish**	
cod	merluzzo	acciughe	anchovies
hake	nasello	calamari	squid
halibut	ippoglosso	cozze	mussels
herring	aringa	dentice	sea bream
monk fish	squadro	frutti di mare	seafood
mussels	cozze	gamberetti	shrimp
oysters	ostriche	gamberi	prawns
plaice	platessa	merluzzo	cod
prawns	gamberi	nasello	hake
red mullet	triglie	ostriche	oysters
salmon	salmone	pesce spada	swordfish
seafood	frutti di mare	platessa	plaice
sea bass	spigola	rombo	turbot
shrimp	gamberetti	salmone	salmon
sole	sogliola	sogliola	sole
squid	calamari	spigola	sea bass
trout	trota	tonno	tuna
tuna	tonno	triglie	red mullet
turbot	rombo	trota	trout
meat/carne		**carne/meat**	
beef	manzo	agnello	lamb
chicken	pollo	anatra	duck
duck	anatra	bistecca	steak
goose	oca	cinghiale	wild boar
hare	lepre	coniglio	rabbit
lamb	agnello	fegato	liver
liver	fegato	lepre	hare
pork	maiale	maiale	pork
rabbit	coniglio	manzo	beef
steak	bistecca	oca	goose
veal	vitello	pollo	chicken
wild boar	cinghiale	vitello	veal

❸ Food and Drink

vegetables/verdure

artichokes	carciofi
asparagus	asparagi
aubergines	melanzane
beans	fagioli
cabbage	cavolo
carrots	carote
cauliflower	cavolfiore
celery	sedano
courgettes	zucchini
green beans	fagiolini
mushrooms	funghi
onions	cipolle
peas	piselli
peppers	peperoni
potatoes	patate
salad	insalata

verdure/vegetables

asparagi	asparagus
carciofi	artichokes
carote	carrots
cavolfiore	cauliflower
cavolo	cabbage
cipolle	onions
fagioli	beans
fagiolini	green beans
funghi	mushrooms
insalata	salad
melanzane	aubergines
patate	potatoes
peperoni	peppers
piselli	peas
sedano	celery
zucchini	courgettes

how it's cooked/cottura

boiled	lesso
fried	fritto
grilled	alla griglia
griddled	alla piastra
puree	purè
roast	arrosto
stewed	in umido
rare	al sangue
medium	cotta al punto giusto
well done	ben cotta

cottura/how it's cooked

al forno	cooked in the oven
al pomodoro	in tomato sauce
al ragù	in a meat sauce
al sangue	rare
alla griglia	grilled
arrosto	roast
ben cotta	well done
cotta al punto giusto	medium
fritto	fried
in umido	stewed
lesso	boiled

desserts/dolci

cream	panna
fruit	frutta
ice cream	gelato
pie	torta
tart	crostata

dolci/desserts

crostata	tart
frutta	fruit
gelato	ice cream
panna	cream
torta	pie

accompaniments/
contorni, salse, ecc.

bread	pane
butter	burro
cheese	formaggio
herbs	erbe
mayonnaise	maionese
mustard	senape
olive oil	olio d'oliva
pepper	pepe
rice	riso
salt	sale
sauce	salsa
seasoning	condimento
vinegar	aceto

drinks/bevande

beer	birra
bottle	bottiglia
carbonated	gassato
half-bottle	mezza bottiglia
liqueur	liquore
mineral water	acqua minerale
red wine	vino rosso
soft drinks	bibite
	analcoliche
sparkling wine	spumante
still	naturale
table wine	vino da tavola
white wine	vino bianco
wine	vino

contorni, salse, ecc./
accompaniments

aceto	vinegar
burro	butter
condimento	seasoning
erbe	herbs
formaggio	cheese
maionese	mayonnaise
olio d'oliva	olive oil
pane	bread
pepe	pepper
riso	rice
sale	salt
salsa	sauce
senape	mustard

bevande/drinks

acqua minerale	mineral water
bibite analcoliche	soft drinks
birra	beer
bottiglia	bottle
gassato	carbonated
liquore	liqueur
mezza bottiglia	half-bottle
naturale	still
spumante	sparkling wine
vino	wine
vino bianco	white wine
vino da tavola	table wine
vino rosso	red wine

##

☆☆☆

❹ Places to stay

Camping

Camping	In campeggio
can we pitch our tent here?	possiamo montare la tenda qui?
can we park our caravan here?	possiamo parcheggiare la roulotte qui?
what are the facilities like?	che attrezzature ci sono?
how much is it per night?	quant'è a notte?
where do we park the car?	dov'è il parcheggio?
we're looking for a campsite	stiamo cercando un campeggio
this is a list of local campsites	questo è l'elenco dei campeggi della zona
we go on a camping holiday every year	andiamo in campeggio tutti gli anni

At the hotel

At the hotel	In albergo
I'd like a double/single room with bath	vorrei una camera doppia/singola con bagno
we have a reservation in the name of Morris	abbiamo prenotato a nome Morris
we'll be staying three nights, from Friday to Sunday	ci fermiamo tre notti, da venerdì a domenica
how much does the room cost?	quant'è la camera?
I'd like to see the room, please	vorrei vedere la camera, per favore
what time is breakfast?	a che ora è la colazione?
can I leave this in your safe?	posso lasciare questo nella cassaforte?
bed and breakfast	camera e prima colazione
we'd like to stay another night	vorremmo fermarci un'altra notte
please call me at 7:30	mi chiami alle 7:30, per favore
are there any messages for me?	ci sono messaggi per me?

Hostels

could you tell me where the youth hostel is?

what time does the hostel close?

I'm staying in a hostel

the hostel we're staying in is great value

I know a really good hostel in Dublin

I'd like to go backpacking in Australia

Ostelli

mi sa dire dov'è l'ostello della gioventù?

a che ora chiude l'ostello?

alloggio in un ostello

l'ostello in cui alloggiamo è molto conveniente

conosco un ottimo ostello a Dublino

mi piacerebbe girare l'Australia con zaino e sacco a pelo

Rooms to let

I'm looking for a room with a reasonable rent

I'd like to rent an apartment for a few weeks

where do I find out about rooms to let?

what's the weekly rent?

I'm staying with friends at the moment

I rent an apartment on the outskirts of town

the room's fine—I'll take it

the deposit is one month's rent in advance

In affitto

vorrei affittare una camera a prezzo modico

vorrei affittare un appartamento per qualche settimana

dove posso informarmi su camere in affitto?

quant'è l'affitto alla settimana?

al momento alloggio presso amici

affitto un appartamento in periferia

la camera mi piace, la prendo

la caparra è di un mese d'affitto

❺ Shopping and money

At the bank

I'd like to change some money	vorrei cambiare dei soldi
I want to change some lire into pounds	vorrei cambiare delle lire in sterline
do you take Eurocheques?	accettate Eurochèque?
what's the exchange rate today?	quant'è il tasso di cambio oggi?
I prefer traveller's cheques (*US* traveler's checks) to cash	preferisco i traveller's cheque al contante
I'd like to transfer some money from my account	vorrei fare un bonifico
I'll get some money from the cash machine	prenderò dei soldi dal bancomat®
I'm with another bank	ho il conto in un'altra banca

Finding the right shop

Il negozio giusto

where's the main shopping district?	dov'è la zona commerciale principale?
where's a good place to buy sunglasses/shoes?	qual è il posto migliore per comprare occhiali da sole/scarpe?
where can I buy batteries/postcards?	dove posso comprare pile/cartoline?
where's the nearest chemist/bookshop?	dov'è la farmacia/libreria più vicina?
is there a good food shop around here?	c'è un buon negozio di generi alimentari qui vicino?
what time do the shops open/close?	a che ora aprono/chiudono i negozi?
where can I hire a car?	dove posso noleggiare una macchina?
where did you get those?	dove le/li hai comprate?
I'm looking for presents for my family	sto cercando dei regalini per la mia famiglia
we'll do all our shopping on Saturday	faremo la spesa sabato
I love shopping	adoro fare spese

Are you boing served?	Nei negozi
how much does that cost?	quanto costa quello?
can I try it on?	posso provarlo?
can you keep it for me?	me lo mette da parte?
could you wrap it for me, please?	me lo incarta, per favore?
can I pay by credit card/cheque (US check)?	posso pagare con la carta di credito/ un assegno?
do you have this in another colour (US color)?	c'è in altri colori?
could I have a bag, please?	mi dà un sacchetto, per favore?
I'm just looking	sto solo dando un'occhiata
I'll think about it	ci devo pensare
I'd like a receipt, please	mi dà lo scontrino, per favore?
I need a bigger/smaller size	mi serve la taglia più grande/piccola
I take a size 10/a medium	porto la 42/la media
it doesn't suit me	non mi sta bene
I'm sorry, I don't have any change/anything smaller	mi dispiace, non ho spiccioli/ biglietti più piccoli
that's all, thank you	nient'altro, grazie

Changing things	Cambiare un acquisto
can I have a refund?	rimborsate i soldi?
can you mend it for me?	può ripararlo?
can I speak to the manager?	posso parlare con il direttore?
it doesn't work	non funziona
I'd like to change it, please	vorrei cambiarlo, per favore
I bought this here yesterday	l'ho comprato qui ieri

❻ Good timing

Telling the time	Dire l'ora
could you tell me the time?	mi dice che ore sono?
what time is it?	che ora è?
it's 2 o'clock	sono le due
at about 8 o'clock	verso le otto
at 9 o'clock tomorrow	domani mattina alle nove
from 10 o'clock onwards	dalle dieci in poi
at 8 a.m./p.m.	alle otto di mattina/di sera
at 5 o'clock in the morning/afternoon	alle cinque del mattino/di sera
it's five past/quarter past/half past one	è l'una e cinque/e un quarto/e mezza
it's twenty-five to/quarter to/five to one	è l'una meno venticinque/meno un quarto/meno cinque
a quarter /three quarters of an hour	un quarto/tre quarti d'ora

Days and dates	Giorni, mesi e date
Sunday, Monday, Tuesday, Wednesday, Thursday, Friday, Saturday	domenica, lunedì, martedì, mercoledì, giovedì, venerdì, sabato
January, February, March, April, May, June, July, August, September, October, November, December	gennaio, febbraio, marzo, aprile, maggio, giugno, luglio, agosto, settembre, ottobre, novembre, dicembre
what's the date?	quanti ne abbiamo oggi?
it's the second of June	è il due giugno
we meet up every Monday	ci incontriamo ogni lunedì
she comes on Tuesdays	viene di martedì
we're going away in August	saremo via ad agosto
it was the first of April	era il primo aprile
on November 8th	l'otto novembre

Public holidays and special days	Festività
Bank holiday	festa civile
Bank holiday Monday	festa civile che cade di lunedì
long weekend	ponte
New Year's Day (Jan 1)	Capodanno (1 gennaio)
Epiphany (Jan 6)	Epifania (la Befana. 6 gennaio)
St Valentine's Day (Feb 14)	San Valentino (14 febbraio)
Shrove Tuesday/Pancake Day	martedì grasso
Ash Wednesday	mercoledì delle Ceneri
St Joseph's Day (Mar 19)	San Giuseppe (19 marzo)
Mother's Day	Festa della mamma
Palm Sunday	domenica delle Palme
Maundy Thursday	giovedì grasso
Good Friday	venerdì santo
Easter Day	Pasqua
Easter Monday	lunedì dell'Angelo (pasquetta)
Anniversary of the liberation of Italy in 1945	anniversario della Liberazione (25 aprile)
May Day (May 1)	festa del lavoro (1 maggio)
Father's Day	Festa del papà
Independence Day (Jul 4)	anniversario dell'Indipendenza (4 luglio)
Assumption (Aug 15)	Assunzione (ferragosto: 15 agosto)
Halloween (Oct 31)	vigilia d'Ognissanti
All Saints' Day (Nov 1)	Ognissanti (1 novembre)
Thanksgiving	giorno del Ringraziamento
Christmas Eve (Dec 24)	vigilia di Natale (24 dicembre)
Christmas Day (Dec 25)	Natale (25 dicembre)
Boxing Day (Dec 26)	Santo Stefano (26 dicembre)
New Year's Eve (Dec 31)	San Silvestro (31 dicembre)

❼ Conversion charts/Tabelle di conversione

Length/Lunghezze

inches/pollici	0.39	3.9	7.8	11.7	15.6	19.7	39
cm/centimetri	1	10	20	30	40	50	100

Distance/Distanze

miles/miglia	0.62	6.2	12.4	18.6	24.9	31	62
km/kilometri	1	10	20	30	40	50	100

Weight/Pesi

pounds/libbre	2.2	22	44	66	88	110	220
kg/kilogrammi	1	10	20	30	40	50	100

Capacity/Capacità

gallons/galloni	0.22	2.2	4.4	6.6	8.8	11	22
litres/litri	1	10	20	30	40	50	100

Temperature/Temperature

°C	0	5	10	15	20	25	30	37	38	40
°F	32	41	50	59	68	77	86	98.4	100	104

Clothing and shoe sizes/Taglie e numeri di scarpe

Women's clothing sizes/Abbigliamento femminile

UK	8	10	12	14	16	18
US	6	8	10	12	14	16
Continent	36	38	40	42	44	46

Men's clothing sizes/Abbigliamento maschile

UK/US	36	38	40	42	44	46
Continent	46	48	50	52	54	56

Men's and women's shoes/Scarpe da uomo e da donna

UK women	4	5	6	7	7.5	8				
UK men				6	7	8	9	10	11
US	6.5	7.5	8.5	9.5	10.5	11.5	12.5	13.5	14.5
Italy	37	38	39	40	41	42	43	44	45

Aa

/ʌ/, accented /eɪ/ indef art; davanti a una vocale **an**

➤➤➤ un *m*, una *f*; (before s + consonant, gn, ps and z) uno; (before feminine noun starting with a vowel) un'; **a tiger is a feline** la tigre è un felino; **a knife and fork** un coltello e una forchetta; **a Mr Smith is looking for you** un certo signor Smith ti sta cercando

➤➤➤ (each) a; **£2 a kilo/a head** due sterline al chilo/a testa

when a refers to professions, it is not translated: **I am a lawyer** sono avvocato

A /eɪ/ n (Mus) la m inv

aback /ə'bæk/ adv **be taken ~** essere preso in contropiede

abandon /ə'bændən/ vt abbandonare; (give up) rinunciare a ● n abbandono m. **~ed** adj abbandonato

abashed /ə'bæʃt/ adj imbarazzato

abate /ə'beɪt/ vi calmarsi

abattoir /'æbətwɑː(r)/ n mattatoio m

abbey /'æbɪ/ n abbazia f

abbreviate /ə'briːvɪeɪt/ vt abbreviare. **~ion** n abbreviazione f

abdicate /'æbdɪkeɪt/ vi abdicare ● vt rinunciare a. **~ion** n abdicazione f

abdomen /'æbdəmən/ n addome m. **~inal** adj addominale

abduct /əb'dʌkt/ vt rapire. **~ion** n rapimento m

abhor /əb'hɔː(r)/ vt (pt/pp abhorred) aborrire. **~rence** n orrore m

abide /ə'baɪd/ vt (pt/pp abided) (tolerate) sopportare ● **abide by** vi rispettare. **~ing** adj perpetuo

ability /ə'bɪlətɪ/ n capacità f inv

abject /'æbdʒekt/ adj (poverty) degradante; (apology) umile; (coward) abietto

ablaze /ə'bleɪz/ adj in fiamme; **be ~ with light** risplendere di luci

able /'eɪbl/ adj capace, abile; **be ~ to do sth** poter fare qcsa; **were you ~ to...?** sei riuscito a...? **~-'bodied** adj robusto; (Mil) abile

ably /'eɪblɪ/ adv abilmente

abnormal /æb'nɔːml/ adj anormale. **~ity** n anormalità f inv. **~ly** adv in modo anormale

aboard /ə'bɔːd/ adv & prep a bordo

abolish /ə'bɒlɪʃ/ vt abolire. **~ition** n abolizione f

abominable /ə'bɒmɪnəbl/ adj abominevole

abort /ə'bɔːt/ vt fare abortire; fig annullare. **~ion** n aborto m; **have an ~ion** abortire. **~ive** adj (attempt) infruttuoso

abound /ə'baʊnd/ vi abbondare; **~ in** abbondare di

about /ə'baʊt/ adv (here and there) [di] qua e [di] là; (approximately) circa; **be ~** (illness, tourists:) essere in giro; **be up and ~** essere alzato; **leave sth lying ~** lasciare in giro qcsa ● prep (concerning) su; (in the region of) intorno a; (here and there in) per; **what is the book/the film ~?** di cosa parla il libro/il film?; **he wants to see you – what ~?** ti vuole vedere – a che proposito?; **talk/know ~** parlare/sapere di; **I know nothing ~ it** non ne so niente; **~ 5**

o'clock intorno alle 5; **travel** the ~ **world** viaggiare per il mondo; **be ~ to do sth** stare per fare qcsa; **how ~ going to the cinema?** e se andassimo al cinema?

about: ~-'**face** n, ~-'**turn** n dietro front m inv

above /ə'bʌv/ adv & prep sopra; ~ **all** soprattutto

above: ~-'**board** adj onesto. ~-'**mentioned** adj suddetto

abrasive /ə'breɪsɪv/ adj abrasivo; (remark) caustico ● n abrasivo m

abreast /ə'brest/ adv fianco a fianco; **come ~ of** allinearsi con; **keep ~ of** tenersi al corrente di

abroad /ə'brɔːd/ adv all'estero

abrupt /ə'brʌpt/ adj brusco

abscess /'æbses/ n ascesso m

abscond /əb'skɒnd/ vi fuggire

absence /'æbsəns/ n assenza f; (lack) mancanza f

absent[1] /'æbsənt/ adj assente

absent[2] /æb'sent/ vt ~ **oneself** essere assente

absentee /æbsən'tiː/ n assente mf

absent-minded /æbsənt'maɪndɪd/ adj distratto

absolute /'æbsəluːt/ adj assoluto; **an ~ idiot** un perfetto idiota. ~**ly** adv assolutamente; (: indicating agreement) esattamente

absolve /əb'zɒlv/ vt assolvere

absorb /əb'sɔːb/ vt assorbire; ~**ed in** assorto in. ~**ent** adj assorbente

absorption /əb'sɔːpʃn/ n assorbimento m; (in activity) concentrazione f

abstain /əb'steɪn/ vi astenersi (from da)

abstemious /əb'stiːmɪəs/ adj moderato

abstention /əb'stenʃn/ n (Pol) astensione f

abstract /'æbstrækt/ adj astratto ● n astratto m; (summary) estratto m

absurd /əb'sɜːd/ adj assurdo. ~**ity** n

assurdità f inv

abundan|ce /ə'bʌndəns/ n abbondanza f. ~**t** adj abbondante

abuse[1] /ə'bjuːz/ vt (misuse) abusare di; (insult) insultare; (ill-treat) maltrattare

abuse[2] /ə'bjuːs/ n abuso m; (verbal) insulti mpl; (ill-treatment) maltrattamento m. ~**ive** adj offensivo

abysmal /ə'bɪzml/ adj 🔲 pessimo; (ignorance) abissale

abyss /ə'bɪs/ n abisso m

academic /ækə'demɪk/ adj teorico; (qualifications, system) scolastico; **be ~** (person:) avere predisposizione allo studio ● n docente mf universitario, -a

academy /ə'kædəmɪ/ n accademia f; (of music) conservatorio m

accelerat|e /ək'seləreɪt/ vt/i accelerare. ~**ion** n accelerazione f. ~**or** n (Auto) acceleratore m

accent /'æksənt/ n accento m

accept /ək'sept/ vt accettare. ~**able** adj accettabile. ~**ance** n accettazione f

access /'ækses/ n accesso m. ~**ible** adj accessibile

accession /ək'seʃn/ n (to throne) ascesa f al trono

accessory /ək'sesərɪ/ n accessorio m; (Jur) complice mf

accident /'æksɪdənt/ n incidente m; (chance) caso m; **by ~** per caso; (unintentionally) senza volere; **I'm sorry, it was an ~** mi dispiace, non l'ho fatto apposta. ~**al** adj (meeting) casuale; (death) incidentale; (unintentional) involontario. ~**ally** adv per caso; (unintentionally) inavvertitamente

acclaim /ə'kleɪm/ n acclamazione f ● vt acclamare (**as** come)

accolade /'ækəleɪd/ n riconoscimento m

accommodat|e /ə'kɒmədeɪt/ vt ospitare; (oblige) favorire. ~**ing** adj accomodante. ~**ion** n (place to stay) sistemazione f

accompan|iment /əˈkʌmpənɪmənt/ n accompagnamento m. **~ist** n (Mus) accompagnatore, -trice mf

accompany /əˈkʌmpənɪ/ vt (pt/pp -ied) accompagnare

accomplice /əˈkʌmplɪs/ n complice mf

accomplish /əˈkʌmplɪʃ/ vt (achieve) concludere; realizzare (aim). **~ed** adj dotato; (fact) compiuto. **~ment** n realizzazione f; (achievement) risultato m; (talent) talento m

accord /əˈkɔːd/ n (treaty) accordo m; **with one ~** tutti d'accordo; **of his own ~** di sua spontanea volontà. **~ance** n **in ~ance with** in conformità di o a

according /əˈkɔːdɪŋ/ adv **~ to** secondo. **~ly** adv di conseguenza

accordion /əˈkɔːdɪən/ n fisarmonica f

accost /əˈkɒst/ vt abbordare

account /əˈkaʊnt/ n conto m; (description) descrizione f; (of eye-witness) resoconto m; **~s** pl (Comm) conti mpl; **on ~ of** a causa di; **on no ~** per nessun motivo; **on this ~** per questo motivo; **on my ~** per causa mia; **of no ~** importanza; **take into ~** tener conto di ● **account for** v (explain) spiegare; (person) render conto di; (constitute) costituire. **~ability** n responsabilità f inv. **~able** adj responsabile (**for** di)

accountant /əˈkaʊntənt/ n (bookkeeper) contabile mf; (consultant) commercialista mf

accumulat|e /əˈkjuːmjʊleɪt/ vt accumulare ● vi accumularsi. **~ion** n accumulazione f

accura|cy /ˈækjʊrəsɪ/ n precisione f. **~te** adj preciso. **~tely** adv con precisione

accusation /ækjʊˈzeɪʃn/ n accusa f

accuse /əˈkjuːz/ vt accusare; **~ sb of doing sth** accusare qcno di fare

qcsa. **~d** n **the ~d** l'accusato m, l'accusata f

accustom /əˈkʌstəm/ vt abituare (**to** a); **grow** or **get ~ed to** abituarsi a. **~ed** adj abituato

ace /eɪs/ n (Cards) asso m; (tennis) ace m inv

ache /eɪk/ n dolore m ● vi dolere, far male; **~ all over** essere tutto indolenzito

achieve /əˈtʃiːv/ vt ottenere (success); realizzare (goal, ambition). **~ment** n (feat) successo m

acid /ˈæsɪd/ adj acido ● n acido m. **~ity** n acidità f. **~ rain** n pioggia f acida

acknowledge /əkˈnɒlɪdʒ/ vt riconoscere; rispondere a (greeting); far cenno di aver notato (sb's presence); **~ receipt of** accusare ricevuta di. **~ment** n riconoscimento m; **send an ~ment of a letter** confermare il ricevimento di una lettera

acne /ˈæknɪ/ n acne f

acorn /ˈeɪkɔːn/ n ghianda f

acoustic /əˈkuːstɪk/ adj acustico. **~s** npl acustica fsg

acquaint /əˈkweɪnt/ vt **~ sb with** metter qcno a corrente di; **be ~ed with** conoscere (person); essere a conoscenza di (fact). **~ance** n (person) conoscente mf; **make sb's ~ance** fare la conoscenza di qcno

acquiesce /ækwɪˈes/ vi acconsentire (**to, in** a). **~nce** n acquiescenza f

acquire /əˈkwaɪə(r)/ vt acquisire

acquisit|ion /ækwɪˈzɪʃn/ n acquisizione f. **~ive** adj avido

acquit /əˈkwɪt/ vt (pt/pp **acquitted**) assolvere; **~ oneself well** cavarsela bene. **~tal** n assoluzione f

acre /ˈeɪkə(r)/ n acro m (= 4 047 m²)

acrid /ˈækrɪd/ adj acre

acrimon|ious /ækrɪˈməʊnɪəs/ adj aspro. **~y** n asprezza f

acrobat /ˈækrəbæt/ n acrobata mf. **~ic** adj acrobatico

a

across /ə'krɒs/ adv dall'altra parte; (wide) in larghezza; (not lengthwise) attraverso; (in crossword) orizzontale; **come** ~ **sth** imbattersi in qcsa; **go** ~ attraversare ● prep (crosswise) di traverso su; (on the other side of) dall'altra parte di

act /ækt/ n atto m; (in variety show) numero m; **put on an** ~ 🔲 fare scena ● vi agire; (behave) comportarsi; (Theat) recitare; (pretend) fingere; ~ **as** fare da ● vt recitare (role). ~**ing** adj (deputy) provvisorio ● n (Theat) recitazione f; (profession) teatro m. ~**ing profession** n professione f dell'attore

action /'ækʃn/ n azione f; (Mil) combattimento m; (Jur) azione f legale; **out of** ~ (machine:) fuori uso; **take** ~ agire. ~ **'replay** n replay m inv

activ|e /'æktıv/ adj attivo. ~**ely** adv attivamente. ~**ity** n attività f inv

act|or /'æktə(r)/ n attore m. ~**ress** n attrice f

actual /'æktʃʊəl/ adj (real) reale. ~**ly** adv in realtà

acute /ə'kju:t/ adj acuto; (shortage, hardship) estremo

ad /æd/ n 🔲 pubblicità f inv

AD abbr (Anno Domini) d.C.

adapt /ə'dæpt/ vt adattare (play) ● vi adattarsi. ~**ability** n adattabilità f. ~**able** adj adattabile

adaptation /ædæp'teıʃn/ n (Theat) adattamento m

adapter, adaptor /ə'dæptə(r)/ n adattatore m; (two-way) presa f multipla

add /æd/ vt aggiungere; (Math) addizionare ● vi addizionare; ~ **to** (fig: increase) aggravare. ~ **up** vt addizionare (figures) ● vi addizionare; ~ **up to** ammontare a; **it doesn't** ~ **up** fig non quadra

adder /'ædə(r)/ n vipera f

addict /'ædıkt/ n tossicodipendente

mf; fig fanatico, -a mf

addict|ed /ə'dıktıd/ adj assuefatto (**to** a); ~**ed to drugs** tossicodipendente; **he's** ~**ed to television** è videodipendente. ~**ion** n dipendenza f; (to drugs) tossicodipendenza f. ~**ive** adj **be** ~**ive** dare assuefazione

addition /ə'dıʃn/ n (Math) addizione f; (thing added) aggiunta f; **in** ~ in aggiunta. ~**al** adj supplementare. ~**ally** adv in più

additive /'ædıtıv/ n additivo m

address /ə'dres/ n indirizzo m; (speech) discorso m; **form of** ~ formula f di cortesia ● vt indirizzare; (speak to) rivolgersi a (person); tenere un discorso a (meeting). ~**ee** n destinatario, -a mf

adept /'ædept/ adj & n esperto, -a mf (**at** in)

adequate /'ædıkwət/ adj adeguato. ~**ly** adv adeguatamente

adhere /əd'hıə(r)/ vi aderire; ~ **to** attenersi a (principles, rules)

adhesive /əd'hi:sıv/ adj adesivo ● n adesivo m

adjacent /ə'dʒeısənt/ adj adiacente

adjective /'ædʒıktıv/ n aggettivo m

adjourn /ə'dʒɜ:n/ vt/i aggiornare (**until** a). ~**ment** n aggiornamento m

adjust /ə'dʒʌst/ vt modificare; regolare (focus, sound etc) ● vi adattarsi. ~**able** adj regolabile. ~**ment** n adattamento m; (Techn) regolamento m

administer /əd'mınıstə(r)/ vt amministrare; somministrare (medicine)

administrat|ion /ədmını'streıʃn/ n amministrazione f; (Pol) governo m. ~**or** n amministratore, -trice mf

admirable /'ædmərəbl/ adj ammirevole

admiral /'ædmərəl/ n ammiraglio m

admiration /ædmə'reıʃn/ n ammirazione f

admire /əd'maıə(r)/ vt ammirare. ~**r**

~r n ammiratore, -trice mf

admission /əd'mɪʃn/ n ammissione f; (to hospital) ricovero m; (entry) ingresso m

admit /əd'mɪt/ vt (pt/pp admitted) (let in) far entrare; (to hospital) ricoverare; (acknowledge) ammettere. ~ **to sth** ammettere qcsa. ~**tance** n ammissione f; **'no ~tance'** 'vietato l'ingresso'. ~**tedly** adv bisogna riconoscerlo

admonish /əd'mɒnɪʃ/ vt ammonire

ado /ə'du:/ n **without more ~** senza ulteriori indugi

adolescen|ce /ædə'lesns/ n adolescenza f. ~**t** adj & n adolescente mf

adopt /ə'dɒpt/ vt adottare; (Pol) scegliere (candidate). ~**ion** n adozione f. ~**ive** adj adottivo

ador|able /ə'dɔːrəbl/ adj adorabile. ~**ation** n adorazione f

adore /ə'dɔː(r)/ vt adorare

adrenalin /ə'drenəlɪn/ n adrenalina f

Adriatic /eɪdrɪ'ætɪk/ adj & n **the ~** [Sea] il mare Adriatico, l'Adriatico m

adrift /ə'drɪft/ adj alla deriva; **be ~** andare alla deriva; **come ~** staccarsi

adult /'ædʌlt/ n adulto, -a mf

adultery /ə'dʌltərɪ/ n adulterio m

advance /əd'vɑːns/ n avanzamento m; (Mil) avanzata f; (payment) anticipo m; **in ~** in anticipo ● vi avanzare; (make progress) fare progressi ● vt avanzare (theory); promuovere (cause); anticipare (money). ~ **booking** n prenotazione f [in anticipo]. ~**d** adj avanzato. ~**ment** n promozione f

advantage /əd'vɑːntɪdʒ/ n vantaggio m; **take ~ of** approfittare di. ~**ous** adj vantaggioso

advent /'ædvent/ n avvento m

adventur|e /əd'ventʃə(r)/ n avventura f. ~**ous** adj avventuroso

adverb /'ædvɜːb/ n avverbio m

adversary /'ædvəsərɪ/ n avversario, -a mf

advers|e /'ædvɜːs/ adj avverso. ~**ity** n avversità f

advert /'ædvɜːt/ n [t] = **advertisement**

advertise /'ædvətaɪz/ vt reclamizzare; mettere un annuncio per (job, flat) ● vi fare pubblicità; (for job, flat) mettere un annuncio

advertisement /əd'vɜːtɪsmənt/ n pubblicità f inv; (in paper) inserzione f, annuncio m

advertis|er /'ædvətaɪzə(r)/ n (in newspaper) inserzionista mf. ~**ing** n pubblicità f ● attrib pubblicitario

advice /əd'vaɪs/ n consigli mpl; **piece of ~** consiglio m

advisable /əd'vaɪzəbl/ adj consigliabile

advis|e /əd'vaɪz/ vt consigliare; (inform) avvisare; ~**e sb to do sth** consigliare a qcno di fare qcsa; ~**e sb against sth** sconsigliare qcsa a qcno. ~**er** n consulente mf. ~**ory** adj consultivo

advocate[1] /'ædvəkət/ n (supporter) fautore, -trice mf

advocate[2] /'ædvəkeɪt/ vt propugnare

aerial /'eərɪəl/ adj aereo ● n antenna f

aerobics /eə'rəʊbɪks/ n aerobica fsg

aero|drome /'eərədrəʊm/ n aerodromo m. ~**plane** n aeroplano m

aerosol /'eərəsɒl/ n bomboletta f spray

aesthetic /iːs'θetɪk/ adj estetico

afar /ə'fɑː(r)/ adv **from ~** da lontano

affable /'æfəbl/ adj affabile

affair /ə'feə(r)/ n affare m; (scandal) caso m; (sexual) relazione f

affect /ə'fekt/ vt influire su; (emotionally) colpire; (concern) riguardare.

a

~**ation** n affettazione f. ~**ed** adj affettato

affection /əˈfekʃn/ n affetto m. ~**ate** adj affettuoso

affirm /əˈfɜːm/ vt affermare; (Jur) dichiarare solennemente

affirmative /əˈfɜːmətɪv/ adj affermativo ● n **in the** ~ affermativamente

afflict /əˈflɪkt/ vt affliggere. ~**ion** n afflizione f

affluen|ce /ˈæfluəns/ n agiatezza f. ~**t** adj agiato

afford /əˈfɔːd/ vt **be able to** ~ **sth** potersi permettere qcsa. ~**able** adj abbordabile

affront /əˈfrʌnt/ n affronto m

afield /əˈfiːld/ adv **further** ~ più lontano

afloat /əˈfləʊt/ adj a galla

afraid /əˈfreɪd/ adj **be** ~ aver paura; **I'm** ~ **not** purtroppo no; **I'm** ~ **so** temo di sì; **I'm** ~ **I can't help you** mi dispiace, ma non posso esserle d'aiuto

afresh /əˈfreʃ/ adv da capo

Africa /ˈæfrɪkə/ n Africa f. ~**n** adj & n africano, -a mf

after /ˈɑːftə(r)/ adv dopo; **the day** ~ il giorno dopo; **be** ~ cercare ● prep dopo; ~ **all** dopotutto; **the day** ~ **tomorrow** dopodomani ● conj dopo che

after-: ~-effect n conseguenza f. ~**math** /-mɑːθ/ n conseguenze fpl; **the** ~**math of war** il dopoguerra; **in the** ~**math of** nel periodo successivo a. ~'**noon** n pomeriggio m; **good** ~'**noon!** buon giorno!. ~**shave** n [lozione f] dopobarba m inv. ~**thought** n added as an ~**thought** aggiunto in un secondo momento; ~**wards** adv in seguito

again /əˈgeɪn/ adv di nuovo; [then] ~ (besides) inoltre; (on the other hand) d'altra parte; ~ **and** ~ conti-

nuamente

against /əˈgeɪnst/ prep contro

age /eɪdʒ/ n età f inv; (era) era f; ~**s** 🔢 secoli; **what** ~ **are you?** quanti anni hai?; **be under** ~ non avere l'età richiesta; **he's two years of** ~ ha due anni ● vt/i (pres p **ageing**) invecchiare

aged[1] /eɪdʒd/ adj ~ **two** di due anni

aged[2] /ˈeɪdʒɪd/ adj anziano ● n **the** ~ pl gli anziani

agency /ˈeɪdʒənsɪ/ n agenzia f; **have the** ~ **for** essere un concessionario di

agenda /əˈdʒendə/ n ordine m del giorno; **on the** ~ all'ordine del giorno; fig in programma

agent /ˈeɪdʒənt/ n agente mf

aggravat|e /ˈægrəveɪt/ vt aggravare; (annoy) esasperare. ~**ion** n aggravamento m; (annoyance) esasperazione f

aggress|ion /əˈgreʃn/ n aggressione f. ~**ive** adj aggressivo. ~**iveness** n aggressività f. ~**or** n aggressore m

aghast /əˈgɑːst/ adj inorridito

agil|e /ˈædʒaɪl/ adj agile. ~**ity** n agilità f

agitat|e /ˈædʒɪteɪt/ vt mettere in agitazione; (shake) agitare ● vi fig ~**e for** creare delle agitazioni per. ~**ed** adj agitato. ~**ion** n agitazione f. ~**or** n agitatore m, -trice m

ago /əˈgəʊ/ adv fa; **a long time/a month** ~ molto tempo/un mese fa

agoniz|e /ˈægənaɪz/ vi angosciarsi (over per). ~**ing** adj angosciante

agony /ˈægənɪ/ n agonia f; (mental) angoscia f; **be in** ~ avere dei dolori atroci

agree /əˈgriː/ vt accordarsi su; ~ **to do sth** accettare di fare qcsa; ~ **that** essere d'accordo [sul fatto] che ● vi essere d'accordo; (figures): concordare; (reach agreement) mettersi d'accordo; (get on) andare d'accordo; (consent) acconsentire (to a); it doesn't ~ with me mi fa male: ~ with sth (approve of) approvare qcsa

agreeable /ə'gri:əbl/ adj gradevole; (willing) d'accordo

agreed /ə'gri:d/ adj convenuto

agreement /ə'gri:mənt/ n accordo m; in ~ d'accordo

agricultural /ægrɪ'kʌltʃərəl/ adj agricolo. ~e n agricoltura f

aground /ə'graʊnd/ adv run ~ (ship:) arenarsi

ahead /ə'hed/ adv avanti; be ~ of essere davanti a; fig essere avanti rispetto a; draw ~ passare davanti (of a); get ~ (in life) riuscire; go ~! fai pure!; look ~ pensare all'avvenire; plan ~ fare progetti per l'avvenire

aid /eɪd/ n aiuto m; in ~ of a favore di ● vt aiutare

Aids /eɪdz/ n AIDS m

aim /eɪm/ n mira f; fig scopo m; take ~ prendere la mira ● vt puntare (gun) (at contro) ● vi mirare; ~ to do sth aspirare a fare qcsa. ~less adj, ~lessly adv senza scopo

air /eə(r)/ n aria f; be on the ~ (programme:) essere in onda; put on ~s darsi delle arie; by ~ in aereo; (airmail) per via aerea ● vt arieggiare; far conoscere (views)

air: ~-conditioned adj con aria condizionata. ~-conditioning n aria f condizionata. ~craft n aereo m. ~craft carrier n portaerei f inv. ~field n campo m d'aviazione. ~ force n aviazione f. ~ freshener n deodorante m per l'ambiente. ~gun n fucile m pneumatico. ~ hostess n hostess f inv. ~line n compagnia f aerea. ~mail n posta f aerea. ~plane n Am aereo m. ~port n aeroporto m. ~tight adj ermetico. ~-traffic controller n controllore m

di volo

airy /'eərɪ/ adj (-ier, -iest) arieggiato; (manner) noncurante

aisle /aɪl/ n corridoio m; (in supermarket) corsia f; (in church) navata f

ajar /ə'dʒɑ:(r)/ adj socchiuso

alarm /ə'lɑ:m/ n allarme m; set the ~ (of alarm clock) mettere la sveglia ● vt allarmare. ~ clock n sveglia f

Albania /æl'beɪnɪə/ n Albania f

album /'ælbəm/ n album m inv

alcohol /'ælkəhɒl/ n alcol m. ~ic adj alcolico ● n alcolizzato, -a mf. ~ism n alcolismo m

alcove /'ælkəʊv/ n alcova f

alert /ə'lɜ:t/ adj sveglio; (watchful) vigile ● n segnale m d'allarme; be on the ~ stare allerta ● vt allertare

algebra /'ældʒɪbrə/ n algebra f

Algeria /æl'dʒɪərɪə/ n Algeria f. ~n adj & n algerino, -a mf

alias /'eɪlɪəs/ n pseudonimo m ● adv alias

alibi /'ælɪbaɪ/ n alibi m inv

alien /'eɪlɪən/ adj straniero; fig estraneo ● n straniero, -a mf; (from space) alieno, -a mf

alienate /'eɪlɪəneɪt/ vt alienare. ~ion n alienazione f

alight[1] /ə'laɪt/ vi scendere; (bird:) posarsi

alight[2] /ə'laɪt/ adj be ~ essere in fiamme; set ~ dar fuoco a

align /ə'laɪn/ vt allineare. ~ment n allineamento m; out of ~ment non allineato

alike /ə'laɪk/ adj simile; be ~ rassomigliarsi ● adv in modo simile; look ~ rassomigliarsi; summer and winter ~ sia d'estate che d'inverno

alimony /'ælɪmənɪ/ n alimenti mpl

alive /ə'laɪv/ adj vivo; ~ with brulicante di; ~ to sensibile a; ~ and kicking vivo e vegeto

alkali /'ælkəlaɪ/ n alcali m

a

all /ɔːl/
● adj tutto; ~ **the children**, ~ **children** tutti i bambini; ~ **day** tutto il giorno; **he refused** ~ **help** ha rifiutato qualsiasi aiuto; **for** ~ **that** (nevertheless) ciononostante; **in** ~ **sincerity** in tutta sincerità; **be** ~ **for** essere favorevole a
● pron tutto; ~ **of you/them** tutti voi/loro; ~ **of it** tutto; ~ **of the town** tutta la città; **in** ~ in tutto; ~ **in** ~ tutto sommato; **most of** ~ più di ogni altra cosa; **once and for** ~ una volta per tutte
● adv completamente; ~ **but** quasi; ~ **at once** (at the same time) tutto in una volta; ~ **at once**, ~ **of a sudden** all'improvviso; ~ **too soon** troppo presto; ~ **the same** (nevertheless) ciononostante; ~ **the better** meglio ancora; **she's not** ~ **that good an actress** non è poi così brava come attrice; ~ **in** tutto; ⚽ esausto; **thirty/three** ~ (in sport) trenta/tre pari; ~ **over** (finished) tutto finito; (everywhere) dappertutto; **it's** ~ **right** (I don't mind) non fa niente; **I'm** ~ **right** (not hurt) non ho niente; ~ **right!** va bene!

allay /əˈleɪ/ vt placare (suspicions, anger)

allegation /ælɪˈɡeɪʃn/ n accusa f

allege /əˈledʒ/ vt dichiarare. ~**d** adj presunto. ~**dly** adv a quanto si dice

allegiance /əˈliːdʒəns/ n fedeltà f

allerg|ic /əˈlɜːdʒɪk/ adj allergico. ~**y** n allergia f

alleviate /əˈliːvɪeɪt/ vt alleviare

alley /ˈælɪ/ n vicolo m; (for bowling) corsia f

alliance /əˈlaɪəns/ n alleanza f

alligator /ˈælɪɡeɪtə(r)/ n alligatore m

allocat|e /ˈæləkeɪt/ vt assegnare; distribuire (resources). ~**ion** n assegnazione f. (of resources) distribuzione f

allot /əˈlɒt/ vt (pt/pp allotted) distribuire. ~**ment** n distribuzione f; (share) parte f; (land) piccolo lotto di terreno

allow /əˈlaʊ/ vt permettere; (grant) accordare; (reckon on) contare; (agree) ammettere; ~ **for** tener conto di; ~ **sb to do sth** permettere a qcno di fare qcsa; **you are not** ~**ed to...** è vietato...

allowance /əˈlaʊəns/ n sussidio m; (Am: pocket money) paghetta f; (for petrol etc) indennità f inv; (of luggage, duty free) limite m; **make** ~**s for** essere indulgente verso (sb); tener conto di (sth)

alloy /ˈælɔɪ/ n lega f

allusion /əˈluːʒn/ n allusione f

ally[1] /ˈælaɪ/ n alleato, -a mf

ally[2] /əˈlaɪ/ vt (pt/pp -ied) alleare; ~ **oneself with** allearsi con

almighty /ɔːlˈmaɪtɪ/ adj (⚽: big) mega inv ● n **the A~** l'Onnipotente m

almond /ˈɑːmənd/ n mandorla f; (tree) mandorlo m

almost /ˈɔːlməʊst/ adv quasi

alone /əˈləʊn/ adj solo; **leave me** ~**!** lasciami in pace!; **let** ~ (not to mention) figuriarsi ● adv da solo

along /əˈlɒŋ/ prep lungo ● adv ~ **with** assieme a; **all** ~ tutto il tempo; **come** ~**!** (hurry up) vieni qui; **I'll be** ~ **in a minute** arrivo tra un attimo; **move** ~ spostarsi; **move** ~**!** circolare!

along'side adv lungo bordo ● prep lungo; **work** ~ **sb** lavorare fianco a fianco con qcno

aloof /əˈluːf/ adj distante

aloud /əˈlaʊd/ adv ad alta voce

alphabet /ˈælfəbet/ n alfabeto m. ~**ical** adj alfabetico

Alps /ælps/ npl Alpi fpl

already /ɔːlˈredɪ/ adv già

Alsatian /ælˈseɪʃn/ n (dog) pastore m tedesco

also /ˈɔːlsəʊ/ adv anche; ~, I need... [e] inoltre, ho bisogno di...

altar /ˈɔːltə(r)/ n altare m

alter /ˈɔːltə(r)/ vt cambiare; aggiustare (clothes) ● vi cambiare. ~**ation** n modifica f

alternate[1] /ˈɔːltəneɪt/ vi alternarsi ● vt alternare

alternate[2] /ɔːlˈtɜːnət/ adj alterno; on ~ days a giorni alterni

alternative /ɔːlˈtɜːnətɪv/ adj alternativo ● n alternativa f. ~**ly** adv alternativamente

although /ɔːlˈðəʊ/ conj benché, sebbene

altitude /ˈæltɪtjuːd/ n altitudine f

altogether /ɔːltəˈgeðə(r)/ adv (in all) in tutto; (completely) completamente; I'm not ~ sure non sono del tutto sicuro

aluminium /æljʊˈmɪnɪəm/ n, Am **aluminum** /əˈluːmɪnəm/ n alluminio m

always /ˈɔːlweɪz/ adv sempre

am /æm/ ▷ **BE**

a.m. abbr (ante meridiem) del mattino

amalgamate /əˈmælgəmeɪt/ vt fondere ● vi fondersi

amass /əˈmæs/ vt accumulare

amateur /ˈæmətə(r)/ n non professionista m; pej dilettante m ● attrib dilettante; ~ **dramatics** filodrammatica f. ~**ish** adj dilettantesco

amaze /əˈmeɪz/ vt stupire. ~**d** adj stupito. ~**ment** n stupore m

amazing /əˈmeɪzɪŋ/ adj incredibile

ambassador /æmˈbæsədə(r)/ n ambasciatore, -trice mf

ambigu|ity /æmbɪˈgjuːətɪ/ n ambiguità f inv. ~**ous** adj ambiguo

ambiti|on /æmˈbɪʃn/ n ambizione

f; (aim) aspirazione f. ~**ous** adj ambizioso

ambivalent /æmˈbɪvələnt/ adj ambivalente

amble /ˈæmbl/ vi camminare senza fretta

ambulance /ˈæmbjʊləns/ n ambulanza f

ambush /ˈæmbʊʃ/ n imboscata f ● vt tendere un'imboscata a

amend /əˈmend/ vt modificare. ~**ment** n modifica f. ~**s** npl **make ~s** fare ammenda (**for** di, per)

amenities /əˈmiːnətɪz/ npl comodità fpl

America /əˈmerɪkə/ n America f. ~**n** adj & n americano, -a mf

American dream Il cosiddetto 'sogno americano' è la convinzione che negli Stati Uniti chiunque sia disposto a lavorare sodo possa migliorare la propria posizione economica e sociale. Per gli immigrati e le minoranze il concetto di American dream significa anche libertà e uguaglianza di diritti

amiable /ˈeɪmɪəbl/ adj amabile

amicable /ˈæmɪkəbl/ adj amichevole

ammonia /əˈməʊnɪə/ n ammoniaca f

ammunition /æmjʊˈnɪʃn/ n munizioni fpl

amnesty /ˈæmnəstɪ/ n amnistia f

among[st] /əˈmʌŋ[st]/ prep tra, fra

amount /əˈmaʊnt/ n quantità f inv; (sum of money) importo m ● vi ~ **to** ammontare a; fig equivalere a

amphibi|an /æmˈfɪbɪən/ n anfibio m. ~**ous** adj anfibio

amphitheatre /ˈæmfɪ-/ n anfiteatro m

amp|le /ˈæmpl/ adj (large) grande; (proportions) ampio; (enough)

a

largamente sufficiente

amplif|ier /ˈæmplɪfaɪə(r)/ n amplificatore m. **~y** vt (pt/pp **-ied**) amplificare (sound)

amputat|e /ˈæmpjuteɪt/ vt amputare. **~ion** n amputazione f

amuse /əˈmjuːz/ vt divertire. **~ment** n divertimento m. **~ment arcade** n sala f giochi

amusing /əˈmjuːzɪŋ/ adj divertente

an /ən/, accentato /æn/ ▸**A**

anaem|ia /əˈniːmɪə/ n anemia f. **~ic** adj anemico

anaesthetic /ænəsˈθetɪk/ n anestesia f

anaesthet|ist /əˈniːsθətɪst/ n anestesista mf

analogy /əˈnælədʒɪ/ n analogia f

analyse /ˈænəlaɪz/ vt analizzare

analysis /əˈnæləsɪs/ n analisi f inv

analyst /ˈænəlɪst/ n analista mf

analytical /ænəˈlɪtɪkl/ adj analitico

anarch|ist /ˈænəkɪst/ n anarchico, -a mf. **~y** n anarchia f

anatom|ical /ænəˈtɒmɪkl/ adj anatomico. **~ically** adv anatomicamente. **~y** n anatomia f

ancest|or /ˈænsestə(r)/ n antenato, -a mf. **~ry** n antenati mpl

anchor /ˈæŋkə(r)/ n ancora f ● vi gettar l'ancora ● vt ancorare

anchovy /ˈæntʃəvɪ/ n acciuga f

ancient /ˈeɪnʃənt/ adj antico. 🔟 vecchio

ancillary /ænˈsɪlərɪ/ adj ausiliario

and /ænd/, /ənd/, accentato /ænd/ conj e; **two ~ two** due più due; **six hundred ~ two** seicentodue; **more ~ more** sempre più; **nice ~ warm** bello caldo; **try ~ come** cerca di venire; **go ~ get** vai a prendere

anecdote /ˈænɪkdəʊt/ n aneddoto m

anew /əˈnjuː/ adv di nuovo

angel /ˈeɪndʒl/ n angelo m. **~ic** adj angelico

anger /ˈæŋɡə(r)/ n rabbia f ● vt far arrabbiare

angle[1] /ˈæŋɡl/ n angolo m; fig angolazione f; **at an ~** storto

angle[2] vi pescare con la lenza; **~ for** fig cercare di ottenere. **~r** n pescatore, -trice mf

Anglican /ˈæŋɡlɪkən/ adj & n anglicano, -a mf

angr|y /ˈæŋɡrɪ/ adj (**-ier, -iest**) arrabbiato; **get ~y** arrabbiarsi; **~y with** or **at sb** arrabbiato con qcno; **~y at** or **about sth** arrabbiato per qcsa. **~ily** adv rabbiosamente

anguish /ˈæŋɡwɪʃ/ n angoscia f

animal /ˈænɪml/ adj & n animale m

animate[1] /ˈænɪmət/ adj animato

animat|e[2] /ˈænɪmeɪt/ vt animare. **~ed** adj animato; (person) vivace. **~ion** n animazione f

animosity /ænɪˈmɒsətɪ/ n animosità f inv

ankle /ˈæŋkl/ n caviglia f

annihilat|e /əˈnaɪəleɪt/ vt annientare. **~ion** n annientamento m

anniversary /ænɪˈvɜːsərɪ/ n anniversario m

announce /əˈnaʊns/ vt annunciare. **~ment** n annuncio m. **~r** n annunciatore, -trice mf

annoy /əˈnɔɪ/ vt dare fastidio a; **get ~ed** essere infastidito. **~ance** n seccatura f; (anger) irritazione f. **~ing** adj fastidioso

annual /ˈænjʊəl/ adj annuale; (income) annuo ● n (Bot) pianta f annua; (children's book) almanacco m

annul /əˈnʌl/ vt (pt/pp **annulled**) annullare

anonymous /əˈnɒnɪməs/ adj anonimo

anorak /ˈænəræk/ n giacca f a vento

another /əˈnʌðə(r)/ adj & pron; **~ [one]** un altro, un'altra; **in ~ way** diversamente; **one ~** l'un l'altro

answer /'ɑːnsə(r)/ n risposta f; (solution) soluzione f ● vt rispondere a (person, question, letter); esaudire (prayer); ~ **the door** aprire la porta; ~ **the telephone** rispondere al telefono ● vi rispondere; ~ **back** ribattere; ~ **for** rispondere di. ~**able** adj responsabile; **be** ~**able to sb** rispondere a qcno. ~**ing machine** n (Teleph) segreteria f telefonica

ant /ænt/ n formica f

antagonis|m /æn'tægənɪzm/ n antagonismo m. ~**tic** adj antagonistico

antagonize /æn'tægənaɪz/ vt provocare l'ostilità di

Antarctic /æn'tɑːktɪk/ n Antartico m ● adj antartico

antenatal /æntɪ'neɪtl/ adj prenatale

antenna /æn'tenə/ n antenna f

anthem /'ænθəm/ n inno m

anthology /æn'θɒlədʒɪ/ n antologia f

anthropology /ænθrə'pɒlədʒɪ/ n antropologia f

anti-'aircraft /æntɪ-/ adj antiaereo

antibiotic /æntɪbaɪ'ɒtɪk/ n antibiotico m

anticipat|e /æn'tɪsɪpeɪt/ vt prevedere, (forestall) anticipare. ~**ion** /-'peɪʃn/ n anticipo m; (excitement) attesa f

anti'climax n delusione f

anti'clockwise adj & adv in senso antiorario

antidote /'æntɪdəʊt/ n antidoto m

'antifreeze n antigelo m

antiquated /'æntɪkweɪtɪd/ adj antiquato

antique /æn'tiːk/ adj antico ● n antichità f inv. ~ **dealer** n antiquario, -a mf

antiquity /æn'tɪkwətɪ/ n antichità f

anti'septic adj & n antisettico m

anti'social adj (behaviour) antisociale; (person) asociale

antlers /'æntləz/ npl corna fpl

anus /'eɪnəs/ n ano m

anxiety /æŋ'zaɪətɪ/ n ansia f

anxious /'æŋkʃəs/ adj ansioso. ~**ly** adv con ansia

any /'enɪ/

● adj (no matter which) qualsiasi, qualunque; ~ **colour/number you like** qualsiasi colore/numero ti piaccia; **we don't have** ~ **wine/biscuits** non abbiamo vino/biscotti; **for** ~ **reason** per qualsiasi ragione

any is often not translated: **have we** ~ **wine/biscuits?** abbiamo del vino/dei biscotti?

● pron (some) ne; (no matter which) uno qualsiasi; **I don't want** ~ [**of it**] non ne voglio [nessuno]; **there aren't** ~ non ce ne sono; **have we** ~**?** ne abbiamo?; **have you read** ~ **of her books?** hai letto qualcuno dei suoi libri?

● adv **I can't go** ~ **quicker** non posso andare più in fretta; **is it** ~ **better?** va un po' meglio?; **would you like** ~ **more?** ne vuoi ancora?; **I can't eat** ~ **more** non posso mangiare più niente

'anybody pron chiunque; (after negative) nessuno; **I haven't seen** ~ non ho visto nessuno

'anyhow adv ad ogni modo, comunque; (badly) non importa come

'anyone pron = anybody

'anything pron qualche cosa, qualcosa; (no matter what) qualsiasi cosa; (after negative) niente; **take/buy you like** prendi/compra quello che vuoi, **I don't remember** ~ non mi ricordo niente; **he's** ~ **but stupid** è tutto, ma non stupido; **I'll do** ~ **but that** farò qualsiasi cosa, tranne quello

a 'anyway adv ad ogni modo, comunque

'anywhere adv dovunque; (after negative) da nessuna parte; put it ~ mettilo dove vuoi; I can't find it ~ non lo trovo da nessuna parte; ~ else da qualch'altra parte; (after negative) da nessun'altra parte; I don't want to go ~ else non voglio andare da nessun'altra parte

apart /ə'pɑːt/ adv lontano; live ~ vivere separati; 100 miles ~ lontani 100 miglia; ~ from a parte; you can't tell them ~ non si possono distinguere; joking ~ scherzi a parte

apartment /ə'pɑːtmənt/ n (Am: flat) appartamento m; in my ~ a casa mia

apathy /'æpəθɪ/ n apatia f

ape /eɪp/ n scimmia ● vt scimmiottare

aperitif /ə'perətiːf/ n aperitivo m

aperture /'æpətʃə(r)/ n apertura f

apex /'eɪpeks/ n vertice m

apologetic /əpɒlə'dʒetɪk/ adj (air, remark) di scusa; be ~ essere spiacente

apologize /ə'pɒlədʒaɪz/ vi scusarsi (for per)

apology /ə'pɒlədʒɪ/ n scusa f; fig an ~ for a dinner una sottospecie di cena

apostle /ə'pɒsl/ n apostolo m

apostrophe /ə'pɒstrəfɪ/ n apostrofo m

appal /ə'pɔːl/ vt (pt/pp appalled) sconvolgere. ~ling adj sconvolgente

apparatus /æpə'reɪtəs/ n apparato m

apparent /ə'pærənt/ adj evidente; (seeming) apparente. ~ly adv apparentemente

apparition /æpə'rɪʃn/ n apparizione f

appeal /ə'piːl/ n appello m; (attraction) attrattiva f ● vi fare appello; ~

to (be attractive to) attrarre. ~ing adj attraente

appear /ə'pɪə(r)/ vi apparire; (seem) sembrare; (publication): uscire; (Theat) esibirsi. ~ance n apparizione f; (look) aspetto m; to all ~ances a giudicare dalle apparenze; keep up ~ances salvare le apparenze

appease /ə'piːz/ vt placare

appendicitis /əpendɪ'saɪtɪs/ n appendicite f

appendix /ə'pendɪks/ n (pl -ices /-ɪsiːz/) (of book) appendice f; (pl -es) (Anat) appendice f

appetite /'æpɪtaɪt/ n appetito m

applaud /ə'plɔːd/ vt/i applaudire. ~se n applauso m

apple /'æpl/ n mela f. ~-tree n melo m

appliance /ə'plaɪəns/ n attrezzo m; [electrical] ~ elettrodomestico m

applicable /'æplɪkəbl/ adj be ~ to essere valido per; not ~ (on form) non applicabile

applicant /'æplɪkənt/ n candidato, -a mf

application /æplɪ'keɪʃn/ n applicazione f; (request) domanda f; (for job) candidatura f. ~ form n modulo m di domanda

applied /ə'plaɪd/ adj applicato

apply /ə'plaɪ/ vt (pt/pp -ied) applicare; ~ oneself applicarsi ● vi applicarsi; (law:) essere applicabile; ~ to (ask) rivolgersi a; ~ for fare domanda (job etc)

appoint /ə'pɔɪnt/ vt nominare; fissare (time). ~ment n appuntamento m; (to job) nomina f; (job) posto m

appraisal /ə'preɪz(ə)l/ n valutazione f

appreciable /ə'priːʃəbl/ adj sensibile

appreciat|e /ə'priːʃɪeɪt/ vt apprezzare; (understand) comprendere ● vi (increase in value) aumentare di valore.

~ion n (gratitude) riconoscenza f; (enjoyment) apprezzamento m; (understanding) comprensione f; (in value) aumento m. **~ive** adj riconoscente

apprehens|ion /æprɪˈhenʃn/ n arresto m; (fear) apprensione f. **~ive** adj apprensivo

apprentice /əˈprentɪs/ n apprendista mf. **~ship** n apprendistato m

approach /əˈprəʊtʃ/ n avvicinamento m; (to problem) approccio m; (access) accesso m; **make ~es to** fare degli approcci con ● vt avvicinarsi ● vt avvicinarsi a; (with request) rivolgersi a; affrontare (problem). **~able** adj accessibile

appropriate¹ /əˈprəʊprɪət/ adj appropriato

appropriate² /əˈprəʊprɪeɪt/ vt appropriarsi di

approval /əˈpruːvl/ n approvazione f; **on ~** in prova

approv|e /əˈpruːv/ vt approvare ● vi **~e of** approvare (sth); avere una buona opinione di (sb). **~ing** adj (smile, nod) d'approvazione

approximate /əˈprɒksɪmət/ adj approssimativo. **~ly** adv approssimativamente

approximation /əprɒksɪˈmeɪʃn/ n approssimazione f

apricot /ˈeɪprɪkɒt/ n albicocca f

April /ˈeɪprəl/ n aprile m; **~ Fool's Day** il primo d'aprile

apron /ˈeɪprən/ n grembiule m

apt /æpt/ adj appropriato; **be ~ to do sth** avere tendenza a fare qcsa

aptitude /ˈæptɪtjuːd/ n disposizione f. **~ test** n test n inv attitudinale

aquarium /əˈkweərɪəm/ n acquario m

Aquarius /əˈkweərɪəs/ n (Astr) Acquario m

aquatic /əˈkwætɪk/ adj acquatico

Arab /ˈærəb/ adj & n arabo, -a mf. **~ian** adj arabo

Arabic /ˈærəbɪk/ adj arabo; **~ numerals** numeri npl arabici ● n arabo m

arable /ˈærəbl/ adj coltivabile

arbitrary /ˈɑːbɪtrəri/ adj arbitrario

arbitrat|e /ˈɑːbɪtreɪt/ vi arbitrare. **~ion** n arbitraggio m

arc /ɑːk/ n arco m

arcade /ɑːˈkeɪd/ n portico m; (shops) galleria f

arch /ɑːtʃ/ n arco m; (of foot) dorso m del piede

archaeological /ɑːkɪəˈlɒdʒɪkl/ adj archeologico

archaeolog|ist /ɑːkɪˈɒlədʒɪst/ n archeologo, -a mf. **~y** n archeologia f

archaic /ɑːˈkeɪɪk/ adj arcaico

arch'bishop /ɑːtʃ-/ n arcivescovo m

architect /ˈɑːkɪtekt/ n architetto m. **~ural** adj architettonico

architecture /ˈɑːkɪtektʃə(r)/ n architettura f

archives /ˈɑːkaɪvz/ npl archivi mpl

archway /ˈɑːtʃweɪ/ n arco m

Arctic /ˈɑːktɪk/ adj artico ● n **the ~** l'Artico

ardent /ˈɑːdənt/ adj ardente

arduous /ˈɑːdjuəs/ adj arduo

are /ɑː(r)/ ▷ BE

area /ˈeərɪə/ n area f; (region) zona f; (fig: field) campo m. **~ code** n prefisso m [telefonico]

arena /əˈriːnə/ n arena f

Argentina /ɑːdʒənˈtiːnə/ n Argentina f

Argentinian /-ˈtɪnɪən/ adj & n argentino, -a mf

argu|e /ˈɑːgjuː/ vi litigare (about su); (debate) dibattere; **don't ~!** non discutere! ● vt (debate) dibattere; **~e that** sostenere che

argument /ˈɑːgjʊmənt/ n argomento m; (reasoning) ragionamento m; **have an ~** litigare. **~ative** adj polemico

a

arid /'ærɪd/ adj arido

Aries /'eəri:z/ n (Astr) Ariete m

arise /ə'raɪz/ vi (pt arose, pp arisen) (opportunity, need, problem:) presentarsi; (result) derivare

aristocracy /ærɪ'stɒkrəsɪ/ n aristocrazia f

aristocrat /'ærɪstəkræt/ n aristocratico, -a mf. **~ic** adj aristocratico

arithmetic /ə'rɪθmətɪk/ n aritmetica f

arm /ɑːm/ n braccio m; (of chair) bracciolo m; **~s** pl (weapons) armi fpl; **~ in ~** a braccetto; **up in ~s** [] furioso (about per) ● vt armare

'armchair n poltrona f

armed /ɑːmd/ adj armato; **~ forces** forze fpl armate; **~ robbery** rapina f a mano armata

armour /'ɑːmə(r)/ n armatura f. **~ed** adj (vehicle) blindato

'armpit n ascella f

army /'ɑːmɪ/ n esercito m; **join the ~** arruolarsi

aroma /ə'rəʊmə/ n aroma f. **~tic** adj aromatico

arose /ə'rəʊz/ ▷ARISE

around /ə'raʊnd/ adv intorno; **all ~** tutt'intorno; **I'm not from ~ here** non sono di qui; **he's not ~** non c'è ● prep intorno a; in giro per (room, shops, world)

arouse /ə'raʊz/ vt svegliare; (sexually) eccitare

arrange /ə'reɪndʒ/ vt sistemare (furniture, books); organizzare (meeting); fissare (date, time); **~ to do sth** combinare di fare qcsa. **~ment** n (of furniture) sistemazione f; (Mus) arrangiamento m; (agreement) accordo; (of flowers) composizione f; **make ~ments** prendere disposizioni

arrears /ə'rɪəz/ npl arretrati mpl; **be in ~** essere in arretrato; **paid in ~** pagato a lavoro eseguito

arrest /ə'rest/ n arresto m; **under ~** in stato d'arresto ● vt arrestare

arrival /ə'raɪvl/ n arrivo m; **new ~s** pl nuovi arrivati mpl

arrive /ə'raɪv/ vi arrivare; **~ at** fig raggiungere

arrogan|ce /'ærəgəns/ n arroganza f. **~t** adj arrogante

arrow /'ærəʊ/ n freccia f

arse /ɑːs/ n [] culo m

arsenic /'ɑːsənɪk/ n arsenico m

arson /'ɑːsn/ n incendio m doloso. **~ist** n incendiario, -a mf

art /ɑːt/ n arte f; **~s and crafts** pl artigianato m; **the A~s** pl l'arte f; **A~s degree** (Univ) laurea f in Lettere

artery /'ɑːtərɪ/ n arteria f

'art gallery n galleria f d'arte

arthritis /ɑː'θraɪtɪs/ n artrite f

artichoke /'ɑːtɪtʃəʊk/ n carciofo m

article /'ɑːtɪkl/ n articolo m; **~ of clothing** capo m d'abbigliamento

articulate[1] /ɑː'tɪkjʊlət/ adj (speech) chiaro; **be ~** esprimersi bene

articulate[2] /ɑː'tɪkjʊleɪt/ vt scandire (words). **~d lorry** n autotreno m

artificial /ɑːtɪ'fɪʃl/ adj artificiale. **~ly** adv artificialmente; (smile) artificiosamente

artillery /ɑː'tɪlərɪ/ n artiglieria f

artist /'ɑːtɪst/ n artista mf

as /æz/ conj come; (since) siccome; (while) mentre; **as he grew older** diventando vecchio; **as you get to know her** conoscendola meglio; **young as she is** per quanto sia giovane ● prep come; **as a friend** come amico; **as a child** da bambino; **as a foreigner** in quanto straniero; **disguised as** travestito da ● adv as well (also) anche; **as soon as I get home** [non] appena arrivo a casa; **as quick as you** veloce quanto te; **as quick as you can** più veloce che puoi; **as far as** (distance) fino a; **as far as I'm concerned** per quanto mi riguarda; **as long as** finché; (provided that) purché

asbestos /æz'bestɒs/ n amianto m

ascend /ə'send/ vi salire ● vt salire a (throne)

Ascension /ə'senʃn/ n (Relig) Ascensione f

ascent /ə'sent/ n ascesa f

ascertain /æsə'teɪn/ vt accertare

ash¹ /æʃ/ n (tree) frassino m

ash² n cenere f

ashamed /ə'ʃeɪmd/ adj be/feel ~ vergognarsi

ashore /ə'ʃɔ:(r)/ adv a terra; go ~ sbarcare

ash: ~tray n portacenere m A-**Wednesday** n mercoledì m inv delle Ceneri

Asia /'eɪʒə/ n Asia f. **~n** adj & n asiatico, -a mf. **~tic** adj asiatico

aside /ə'saɪd/ adv take sth ~ prendere qcno a parte; **put sth** ~ mettere qcsa da parte; ~ **from you** Am a parte te

ask /ɑ:sk/ vt fare (question); (invite) invitare; ~ **sb** sth domandare or chiedere qcsa a qcno; ~ **sb to do sth** domandare or chiedere a qcno di fare qcsa ● vi ~ **about** sth informarsi su qcsa; ~ **after** chiedere notizie) di; ~ **for** chiedere (sth); chiedere di (sb); ~ **for trouble** ① andare in cerca di guai. □ ~ **in** vt ~ **sb in** invitare qcno ad entrare. □ ~ **out** vt ~ **sb out** chiedere a qcno di uscire

askew /ə'skju:/ adj & adv di traverso

asleep /ə'sli:p/ adj be ~ dormire; **fall** ~ addormentarsi

asparagus /ə'spærəgəs/ n asparagi mpl

aspect /'æspekt/ n aspetto m

asphalt /'æsfælt/ n asfalto m

aspire /ə'spaɪə(r)/ vi ~ **to** aspirare a

ass /æs/ n asino m

assassin /ə'sæsɪn/ n assassino, -a m

assassin: ~ate vt assassinare. **~ation** n as-

sassino m

assault /ə'sɔ:lt/ n (Mil) assalto m; (Jur) aggressione f ● vt aggredire

assemble /ə'sembl/ vi radunarsi ● vt radunare; (Techn) montare

assembly /ə'semblɪ/ n assemblea f; (Sch) assemblea f giornaliera di alunni o professori di una scuola; (Techn) montaggio m. ~ **line** n catena f di montaggio

assent /ə'sent/ n assenso m ● vi acconsentire

assert /ə'sɜ:t/ vt asserire; far valere (one's rights), ~ **oneself** farsi valere. **~ion** n asserzione f. **~ive** adj be ~ive farsi valere

assess /ə'ses/ vt valutare; (for tax purposes) stabilire l'imponibile di. **~ment** n valutazione f; (of tax) accertamento m

asset /'æset/ n (advantage) vantaggio m; (person) elemento m prezioso. **~s** pl beni mpl, (on balance sheet) attivo msg

assign /ə'saɪn/ vt assegnare. **~ment** n (task) incarico m

assimilate /ə'sɪmɪleɪt/ vt assimilare; integrare (person)

assist /ə'sɪst/ vt/i assistere. ~ **sb to do sth** assistere qcno nel fare qcsa. **~ance** n assistenza f. **~ant** adj assistente; ~ant **manager** vicedirettore, -trice mf ● n assistente mf; (in shop) commesso, -a mf

associat|e¹ /ə'səʊʃɪeɪt/ vt associare (with a); be **~ed with** sth (involved in) essere coinvolto in qcsa ● vi ~e **with** frequentare. **~ion** n associazione f. **A~ion 'Football** n [gioco m del] calcio m

associate² /ə'səʊʃɪət/ adj associato ● n collega mf; (member) socio, -a mf

assort|ed /ə'sɔ:tɪd/ adj assortito. **~ment** n assortimento m

assum|e /ə'sju:m/ vt presumere; assumere (control); **~e office** entrare in carica; **~ing that you're right,...**

ammettendo che tu abbia ragione,...

assumption /ə'sʌmpʃn/ n supposizione f; **on the ~ that** partendo dal presupposto che; **the A~** (Relig) l'Assunzione f

assurance /ə'ʃʊərəns/ n assicurazione f; (confidence) sicurezza f

assure /ə'ʃʊə(r)/ vt assicurare. **~d** adj sicuro

asterisk /'æstərɪsk/ n asterisco m

asthma /'æsmə/ n asma f. **~tic** adj asmatico

astonish /ə'stɒnɪʃ/ vt stupire. **~ing** adj stupefacente. **~ment** n stupore m

astound /ə'staʊnd/ vt stupire

astray /ə'streɪ/ adv **go ~** smarrirsi; (morally) uscire dalla retta via; **lead ~** traviare

astronaut /'æstrənɔ:t/ n astronauta mf

astronom|er /ə'strɒnəmə(r)/ n astronomo, -a mf. **~ical** adj astronomico. **~y** n astronomia f

astute /ə'stju:t/ adj astuto

asylum /ə'saɪləm/ n [political] **~** asilo m politico; [lunatic] **~** manicomio m

at /ət/, accentato /æt/ prep a; **at the station/the market** alla stazione/al mercato; **at the office/the bank** in ufficio/banca; **at the beginning** all'inizio; **at John's** da John; **at the hairdresser's** dal parrucchiere; **at home** a casa; **at work** al lavoro; **at school** a scuola; **at a party/wedding** a una festa/un matrimonio; **at 1 o'clock** all'una; **at 50 km an hour** a 50 all'ora; **at Christmas/Easter** a Natale/Pasqua; **at times** talvolta; **two at a time** due alla volta; **good at languages** bravo nelle lingue; **at sb's request** su richiesta di qcno; **are you at all worried?** sei preoccupato?

ate /et/ ▷**EAT**

atheist /'eɪθɪɪst/ n ateo, -a mf

athlet|e /'æθli:t/ n atleta mf. **~ic** adj atletico. **~ics** n atletica fsg

Atlantic /ət'læntɪk/ adj & n **the ~ [Ocean]** l'[Oceano m] Atlantico m

atlas /'ætləs/ n atlante m

atmosphere /'ætməsfɪə(r)/ n atmosfera f. **~ic** adj atmosferico

atom /'ætəm/ n atomo m. **~ bomb** n bomba f atomica

atomic /ə'tɒmɪk/ adj atomico

atrocious /ə'trəʊʃəs/ adj atroce; (meal, weather) abominevole

atrocity /ə'trɒsətɪ/ n atrocità f inv

attach /ə'tætʃ/ vt attaccare; attribuire (importance); **be ~ed to** fig essere attaccato a

attachment /ə'tætʃmənt/ n (affection) attaccamento m; (accessory) accessorio m

attack /ə'tæk/ n attacco m; (physical) aggressione f • vt attaccare; (physically) aggredire. **~er** n assalitore, -trice mf; (critic) detrattore, -trice mf

attain /ə'teɪn/ vt realizzare (ambition); raggiungere (success, age, goal)

attempt /ə'tempt/ n tentativo m • vt tentare

attend /ə'tend/ vt essere presente a; (go regularly to) frequentare; (doctor:) avere in cura • vi essere presente; (pay attention) prestare attenzione. **□ ~ to** vt occuparsi di; (in shop) servire. **~ance** n presenza f. **~ant** n guardiano, -a mf

attention /ə'tenʃn/ n attenzione f; **~!** (Mil) attenti!; **pay ~** prestare attenzione; **need ~** aver bisogno di attenzioni; (skin, hair, plant:) dover essere curato; (car, tyres:) dover essere riparato; **for the ~ of** all'attenzione di

attentive /ə'tentɪv/ adj (pupil, audience) attento

attic /'ætɪk/ n soffitta f

attitude /'ætɪtju:d/ n atteggiamento m

attorney /əˈtɜːnɪ/ n (Am: lawyer) avvocato m; **power of ~** delega f

attract /əˈtrækt/ vt attirare; **~ion** n attrazione f; (feature) attrattiva f; **~ive** adj (person) attraente; (proposal, price) allettante

attribute¹ /ˈætrɪbjuːt/ n attributo m

attribute² /əˈtrɪbjuːt/ vt attribuire

aubergine /ˈəʊbəʒiːn/ n melanzana f

auction /ˈɔːkʃn/ n asta f ● vt vendere all'asta. **~eer** n banditore m

audacious /ɔːˈdeɪʃəs/ adj sfacciato; (daring) audace. **~ty** n sfacciataggine f; (daring) audacia f

audible /ˈɔːdəbl/ adj udibile

audience /ˈɔːdɪəns/ n (Theat) pubblico m; (TV) telespettatori mpl; (Radio) ascoltatori mpl; (meeting) udienza f

audit /ˈɔːdɪt/ n verifica f del bilancio ● vt verificare

audition /ɔːˈdɪʃn/ n audizione f ● vi fare un'audizione

auditor /ˈɔːdɪtə(r)/ n revisore m di conti

auditorium /ɔːdɪˈtɔːrɪəm/ n sala f

augment /ɔːɡˈment/ vt aumentare

augur /ˈɔːɡə(r)/ vi **~ well/ill** essere di buon/cattivo augurio

August /ˈɔːɡəst/ n agosto m

aunt /ɑːnt/ n zia f

au pair /əʊˈpeə(r)/ n **~ [girl]** ragazza f alla pari

aura /ˈɔːrə/ n aura f

auster|e /ɒˈstɪə(r)/ adj austero. **~ity** n austerità f

Australia /ɒˈstreɪlɪə/ n Australia f. **~n** adj & n australiano, -a mf

Austria /ˈɒstrɪə/ n Austria f. **~n** adj & n austriaco, -a mf

authentic /ɔːˈθentɪk/ adj autentico. **~ate** vt autenticare. **~ity** n autenticità f

author /ˈɔːθə(r)/ n autore m

authoritative /ɔːˈθɒrɪtətɪv/ adj autorevole; (manner) autoritario

authority /ɔːˈθɒrətɪ/ n autorità f; (permission) autorizzazione f; **be in ~ over** avere autorità su

authorization /ɔːθəraɪˈzeɪʃn/ n autorizzazione f

authorize /ˈɔːθəraɪz/ vt autorizzare

autobi'ography /ɔːtə-/ n autobiografia f

autograph /ˈɔːtə-/ n autografo m

automate /ˈɔːtəmeɪt/ vt automatizzare

automatic /ɔːtəˈmætɪk/ adj automatico ● n (car) macchina f col cambio automatico; (washing machine) lavatrice f automatica. **~ally** adv automaticamente

automation /ɔːtəˈmeɪʃn/ n automazione f

automobile /ˈɔːtəməbiːl/ n automobile f

autonom|ous /ɔːˈtɒnəməs/ adj autonomo. **~y** n autonomia f

autopsy /ˈɔːtɒpsɪ/ n autopsia f

autumn /ˈɔːtəm/ n autunno m. **~al** adj autunnale

auxiliary /ɔːɡˈzɪlɪərɪ/ adj ausiliario ● n ausiliare m

avail /əˈveɪl/ n **to no ~** invano ● vi **~ oneself of** approfittare di

available /əˈveɪləbl/ adj disponibile; (book, record etc) in vendita

avalanche /ˈævəlɑːnʃ/ n valanga f

avarice /ˈævərɪs/ n avidità f

avenue /ˈævənjuː/ n viale m; fig strada f

average /ˈævərɪdʒ/ adj medio; (mediocre) mediocre ● n media f; **on ~** in media ● vt (sales, attendance) etc: raggiungere una media di. □ **~ out at** vt risultare in media

avers|e /əˈvɜːs/ adj **not be ~e to** sth non essere contro qcsa. **~ion** n avversione f (**to** per)

avert /əˈvɜːt/ vt evitare (crisis); di-

stogliere (eyes)
aviation /eɪvɪˈeɪʃn/ n aviazione f
avid /ˈævɪd/ adj avido (**for** di); (reader) appassionato
avocado /ævəˈkɑːdəʊ/ n avocado m
avoid /əˈvɔɪd/ vt evitare. **~able** adj evitabile
await /əˈweɪt/ vt attendere
awake /əˈweɪk/ adj sveglio; **wide ~** completamente sveglio ● vi (pt awoke, pp awoken) svegliarsi
awaken /əˈweɪkn/ vt svegliare. **~ing** n risveglio m
award /əˈwɔːd/ n premio m; (medal) riconoscimento m; (of prize) assegnazione f ● vt assegnare; (hand over) consegnare
aware /əˈweə(r)/ adj **be ~ of** (sense) percepire; (know) essere conscio di; **become ~ of** accorgersi di; (learn) venire a sapere di; **be ~ that** rendersi conto che. **~ness** n percezione f; (knowledge) consapevolezza f
awash /əˈwɒʃ/ adj inondato (**with** di)
away /əˈweɪ/ adv via; **go/stay ~** andare/stare via; **he's ~ from his desk/the office** non è alla sua scrivania/in ufficio; **far ~** lontano; **four kilometres ~** a quattro chilometri; **play ~** (Sport) giocare fuori casa. **~ game** n partita f fuori casa
awe /ɔː/ n soggezione f
awful /ˈɔːfl/ adj terribile. **~ly** adv terribilmente; (pretty) estremamente
awkward /ˈɔːkwəd/ adj (movement) goffo; (moment, situation) imbarazzante; (time) scomodo. **~ly** adv (move) goffamente; (say) con imbarazzo
awning /ˈɔːnɪŋ/ n tendone m
awoke(n) /əˈwəʊk (ən)/ ▷ **AWAKE**
axe /æks/ n scure f ● vt (pres p axing) fare dei tagli a (budget); sopprimere (jobs); annullare (project)
axis /ˈæksɪs/ n (pl axes /-siːz/) asse m

axle /ˈæksl/ n (Techn) asse m

Bb

BA n abbr Bachelor of Arts
babble /ˈbæbl/ vi farfugliare; (stream:) gorgogliare
baby /ˈbeɪbɪ/ n bambino, -a mf; (🇮: darling) tesoro m
baby: **~ carriage** n Am carrozzina f. **~ish** adj bambinesco. **~-sit** vi fare da baby-sitter. **~-sitter** n baby-sitter mf
bachelor /ˈbætʃələ(r)/ n scapolo m; **B~ of Arts/Science** laureato, -a mf in lettere/in scienze
back /bæk/ n schiena f; (of horse, hand) dorso m; (of chair) schienale m; (of house, cheque, page) retro m; (in football) difesa f; **at the ~** in fondo; **in the ~** (Auto) dietro; **~ to front** (sweater) il davanti di dietro; **at the ~ of beyond** in un posto sperduto ● adj posteriore; (taxes, payments) arretrato ● adv indietro; (returned) di ritorno; **turn/move ~** tornare/ spostarsi indietro; **put it ~ here/ there** rimettilo qui/là; **~ at home** di ritorno a casa; **I'll be ~ in five minutes** torno fra cinque minuti; **I'm just ~** sono appena tornato; **when do you want the book ~?** quando rivuoi il libro?; **pay ~** ripagare (sb); restituire (money); **~ in power** di nuovo al potere ● vt (support) sostenere; (with money) finanziare; puntare su (horse); (cover the back of) rivestire il retro di ● vi (Auto) fare retromarcia. **□ ~ down** vi battere in ritirata. **□ ~ in** vi (Auto) entrare in retromarcia; (person:) entrare camminando all'indietro. **□ ~ out** vi (Auto) uscire in retromarcia; (person:) uscire cammi-

nando all'indietro; *fig* tirarsi indietro (of da). □ **~ up** *vt* sostenere; confermare (person's alibi); (*Comput*) fare una copia di salvataggio di, **be ~ed up** (traffic) essere congestionato ● *vi* (*Auto*) fare retromarcia

back: **~ache** *n* mal *m* di schiena. **~bone** *n* spina *f* dorsale. **~date** *vt* retrodatare (cheque). **~ 'door** *n* porta *f* di servizio

backer /'bækə(r)/ *n* sostenitore, -trice *mf*; (with money) finanziatore, -trice *mf*

back: **~ 'fire** *vi* (*Auto*) avere un ritorno di fiamma; (fig: plan) fallire. **~ ground** *n* sfondo *m*; (environment) ambiente *m*. **~hand** *n* (tennis) rovescio *m*

backing /'bækɪŋ/ *n* (support) supporto *m*; (material) riserva *f*; (*Mus*) accompagnamento *m*; **~ group** gruppo *m* d'accompagnamento

back: **~lash** *n* *fig* reazione *f* opposta. **~log** *n* **~log of work** lavoro *m* arretrato. **~side** *n* [] fondoschiena *m inv*. **~slash** *n* (*Typ*) barra *f* retroversa. **~stage** *adj* & *adv* dietro le quinte. **~stroke** *n* dorso *m*. **~-up** *n* rinforzi *mpl*; (*Comput*) riserva *f*

backward /'bækwəd/ *adj* (step) in dietro; (child) lento nell'apprendimento; (country) arretrato ● *adv* **~s** (also Am: **~**) indietro; (fall, walk) all'indietro; **~s and forwards** avanti e indietro

back: **~water** *n* *fig* luogo *m* di scarto. **~ 'yard** *n* cortile *m*

bacon /'beɪkn/ *n* pancetta *f*

bacteria /bæk'tɪərɪə/ *npl* batteri *mpl*

bad /bæd/ *adj* (**worse**, **worst**) cattivo; (weather, habit, news, accident) brutto; (apple etc) marcio; **the light is ~** non c'è una buona luce; **use ~ language** dire delle parolacce; **feel ~** sentirsi male; (feel guilty) sentirsi in colpa; **have a ~ back** avere dei problemi alla schiena; **smoking is ~ for you** fumare fa male; **go ~** an-

dare a male; **that's just too ~!** pazienza!; **not ~** niente male

bade /bæd/ **▷ BID**

badge /bædʒ/ *n* distintivo *m*

badger /'bædʒə(r)/ *n* tasso *m* ● *vt* tormentare

badly /'bædlɪ/ *adv* male; (hurt) gravemente; **~ off** povero; **~ behaved** maleducato; **need ~** aver estremamente bisogno di

bad-'mannered *adj* maleducato

badminton /'bædmɪntən/ *n* badminton *m*

bad-'tempered *adj* irascibile

baffle /'bæfl/ *vt* confondere

bag /bæg/ *n* borsa *f*; (of paper) sacchetto *m*; **old ~** [] megera *f*; **~s under the eyes** occhiaie *fpl*; **~s of** [] un sacco di

baggage /'bægɪdʒ/ *n* bagagli *mpl*

baggy /'bægɪ/ *adj* (clothes) ampio

'bagpipes *npl* cornamusa *fsg*

bail /beɪl/ *n* cauzione *f*; **on ~** su cauzione ● **bail out** *vt* (*Naut*) aggottare; **~ sb out** (*Jur*) pagare la cauzione per qcno ● *vi* (*Aeron*) paracadutarsi

bait /beɪt/ *n* esca *f* ● *vt* innescare; (fig: torment) tormentare

bake /beɪk/ *vt* cuocere al forno; (make) fare ● *vi* cuocersi al forno

baker /'beɪkə(r)/ *n* fornaio, -a *mf*, panettiere, -a *mf*; **~'s [shop]** panetteria *f*. **~y** *n* panificio *m*, forno *m*

balance /'bæləns/ *n* equilibrio *m*; (*Comm*) bilancio *m*; (outstanding sum) saldo *m*; [**bank**] **~** saldo *m*; **be or hang in the ~** *fig* essere in sospeso ● *vt* bilanciare; equilibrare (budget); (*Comm*) fare il bilancio di (books) ● *vi* bilanciarsi; (*Comm*) essere in pareggio. **~d** *adj* equilibrato. **~ sheet** *n* bilancio *m* [d'esercizio]

balcony /'bælkənɪ/ *n* balcone *m*

bald /bɔːld/ *adj* (person) calvo; (tyre) liscio; (statement) nudo e crudo; **go ~**

bale | bar

~ perdere i capelli

bale /beɪl/ n balla f

ball¹ /bɔːl/ n palla f; (football) pallone m; (of yarn) gomitolo m; **on the ~** 🔢 sveglio

ball² n (dance) ballo m

ballad /'bæləd/ n ballata f

ballast /'bæləst/ n zavorra f

ball-'bearing n cuscinetto m a sfera

ballerina /bælə'riːnə/ n ballerina f [classica]

ballet /'bæleɪ/ n balletto m; (art form) danza f; **~ dancer** n ballerino, -a mf [classico, -a]

balloon /bə'luːn/ n pallone m; (Aeron) mongolfiera f

ballot /'bælət/ n votazione f. **~-box** n urna f. **~-paper** n scheda f di votazione

ball: ~-point ['pen] n penna f a sfera. **~room** n sala f da ballo

Baltic /'bɔːltɪk/ adj & n **the ~ [Sea]** il [mar] Baltico

bamboo /bæm'buː/ n bambù m inv

ban /bæn/ n proibizione f ● vt (pt/pp banned) proibire; **~ from** espellere da (club); **she was ~ned from driving** le hanno ritirato la patente

banal /bə'nɑːl/ adj banale. **~ity** n banalità f inv

banana /bə'nɑːnə/ n banana f

band /bænd/ n banda f; (stripe) nastro m; (Mus: pop group) complesso m; (Mus: brass ~) banda f; (Mil) fanfara f ● **band together** vi riunirsi

bandage /'bændɪdʒ/ n benda f ● vt fasciare (limb)

b. & b. abbr bed and breakfast

bandit /'bændɪt/ n bandito m

band: ~stand n palco m coperto [dell'orchestra]. **~wagon** n **jump on the ~wagon** fig seguire la corrente

bandy¹ /'bændɪ/ vt (pt/pp -ied)

scambiarsi (words). □ **~ about** vt far circolare

bandy² adj (-ier, -iest) **be ~** avere le gambe storte

bang /bæŋ/ n (noise) fragore m; (of gun, firework) scoppio m; (blow) colpo m ● **adv ~ in the middle of** 🔢 proprio nel mezzo di; **go ~** (gun:) sparare; (balloon:) esplodere ● int bum! ● vt battere (fist); battere su (table); sbattere (door, head) ● vi scoppiare; (door:) sbattere

banger /'bæŋə(r)/ n (firework) petardo m; (🔢: sausage) salsiccia f; **old ~** (🔢: car) macinino m

bangle /'bæŋgl/ n braccialetto m

banish /'bænɪʃ/ vt bandire

banisters /'bænɪstəz/ npl ringhiera fsg

bank¹ /bæŋk/ n (of river) sponda f; (slope) scarpata f ● vi (Aeron) inclinarsi in virata

bank² n banca f ● vt depositare in banca ● vi **~ with** avere un conto [bancario] presso. □ **~ on** vt contare su

bank card n carta f assegno.

banker /'bæŋkə(r)/ n banchiere m

bank: ~ 'holiday n giorno m festivo. **~ing** n bancario m. **~note** n banconota f

bankrupt /'bæŋkrʌpt/ adj fallito; **go ~** fallire ● n persona f che ha fatto fallimento ● vt far fallire. **~cy** n bancarotta f

banner /'bænə(r)/ n stendardo m; (of demonstrators) striscione m

banquet /'bæŋkwɪt/ n banchetto m

banter /'bæntə(r)/ n battute fpl di spirito

baptism /'bæptɪzm/ n battesimo m

Baptist /'bæptɪst/ adj & n battista mf

baptize /bæp'taɪz/ vt battezzare

bar /bɑː(r)/ n sbarra f; (Jur) ordine m degli avvocati; (of chocolate) tavoletta

barbarian | bass

f; (café) bar m inv; (counter) banco m; (Mus) battuta f; (fig: obstacle) ostacolo m; ~ **of soap/gold** saponetta f/lingotto m; **behind** ~**s** 🔲 dietro le sbarre ● vt (pt/pp **barred**) sbarrare (way); sprangare (door); escludere (person) ● prep tranne; ~ **none** in assoluto

barbarian /bɑː'beərɪən/ n barbaro, -a mf

barbar|ic /bɑː'bærɪk/ adj barbarico. ~**ity** n barbarie f inv. ~**ous** adj barbaro

barbecue /'bɑːbɪkjuː/ n barbecue m inv, (party) grigliata f, barbecue m inv ● vt arrostire sul barbecue

barber /'bɑːbə(r)/ n barbiere m

bare /beə(r)/ adj nudo; (tree, room) spoglio; (floor) senza moquette ● vt scoprire; mostrare (teeth)

bare: ~**back** adv senza sella. ~**faced** adj sfacciato. ~**foot** adv scalzo. ~**headed** adj a capo scoperto

barely /'beəlɪ/ adv appena

bargain /'bɑːgɪn/ n (agreement) patto m; (good buy) affare m; **into the** ~ per di più ● vi contrattare; (haggle) trattare; ~ **for** (expect) aspettarsi

barge /bɑːdʒ/ n barcone m ● **barge in** vi 🔲 (to room) piombare dentro; (into conversation) interrompere bruscamente. ~ **into** vt piombare dentro a (room); venire addosso a (person)

baritone /'bærɪtəʊn/ n baritono m

bark[1] /bɑːk/ n (of tree) corteccia f

bark[2] n abbaiamento m ● vi abbaiare

barley /'bɑːlɪ/ n orzo m

bar: ~**maid** n barista f. ~**man** n barista m

barmy /'bɑːmɪ/ adj 🔲 strampalato

barn /bɑːn/ n granaio m

barometer /bə'rɒmɪtə(r)/ n barometro m

baron /'bærn/ n barone m. ~**ess** n

baronessa f

baroque /bə'rɒk/ adj & n barocco m

barracks /'bærəks/ npl caserma fsg

barrage /'bærɑːʒ/ n (Mil) sbarramento m; (fig: of criticism) sfilza f

barrel /'bærl/ n barile m, botte f; (of gun) canna f. ~**-organ** n organetto m [a cilindro]

barren /'bærən/ adj sterile; (landscape) brullo

barricade /bærɪ'keɪd/ n barricata f ● vt barricare

barrier /'bærɪə(r)/ n barriera f; (Rail) cancello m; fig ostacolo m

barrister /'bærɪstə(r)/ n avvocato m

barter /'bɑːtə(r)/ vi barattare (for con)

base /beɪs/ n base f ● adj vile ● vt basare; **be** ~**d on** basarsi su

base: ~**ball** n baseball m. ~**ment** n seminterrato m

bash /bæʃ/ n colpo m [violento] ● vt colpire [violentemente]; (dent) ammaccare; ~**ed in** ammaccato

bashful /'bæʃfl/ adj timido

basic /'beɪsɪk/ adj di base, (conditon, requirement) basilare, (living conditions) povero; **my Italian is pretty** ~ il mio italiano è abbastanza rudimentale; **the** ~**s** (of language, science) i rudimenti; (essentials) l'essenziale m. ~**ally** adv fondamentalmente

basil /'bæzɪl/ n basilico m

basin /'beɪsn/ n bacinella f; (wash-hand) lavabo m; (for food) recipiente m; (Geog) bacino m

basis /'beɪsɪs/ n (pl -**ses** /-siːz/) base f

bask /bɑːsk/ vi crogiolarsi

basket /'bɑːskɪt/ n cestino m. ~**ball** n pallacanestro f

bass /beɪs/ adj basso; ~ **voice** voce f di basso ● n basso m

bastard /'bɑːstəd/ n (*illegitimate child*) bastardo, -a mf; ✗ figlio m di puttana

bat¹ /bæt/ n mazza f; (*for table tennis*) racchetta f; **off one's own ~** 🆃 tutto da solo ● vt (pt/pp **batted**) battere; **she didn't ~ an eyelid** fig non ha battuto ciglio

bat² n (*Zool*) pipistrello m

batch /bætʃ/ n gruppo m; (*of goods*) partita f; (*of bread*) infornata f

bated /'beɪtɪd/ adj **with ~ breath** col fiato sospeso

bath /bɑːθ/ n (pl **~s** /bɑːðz/) bagno m; (*tub*) vasca f da bagno; **~s** pl piscina f; **have a ~** fare un bagno ● vt fare il bagno a

bathe /beɪð/ n bagno m ● vi fare il bagno ● vt lavare (*wound*). **~r** n bagnante mf

bathing /'beɪðɪŋ/ n bagni mpl. **~-cap** n cuffia f. **~-costume** n costume m da bagno

bathroom n bagno m

battalion /bə'tæliən/ n battaglione m

batter /'bætə(r)/ n (*Culin*) pastella f; **~ed** adj (*car*) malandato; (*wife, baby*) maltrattato

battery /'bætəri/ n batteria f; (*of torch, radio*) pila f

battle /'bætl/ n battaglia f; fig lotta f ● vi fig lottare

battle: ~field n campo m di battaglia. **~ship** n corazzata f

bawl /bɔːl/ vt/i urlare

bay¹ /beɪ/ n (*Geog*) baia f

bay² n **keep at ~** tenere a bada

bay³ n (*Bot*) alloro m. **~-leaf** n foglia f d'alloro

bayonet /'beɪənɪt/ n baionetta f

bay 'window n bay window f inv (*grande finestra sporgente*)

bazaar /bə'zɑː(r)/ n bazar m inv

BC abbr (*before Christ*) a.C.

be /biː/

● vi (*pres* **am**, **are**, **is**, **are**; *pt* **was**, **were**; *pp* **been**) essere; **he is a teacher** è insegnante, fa l'insegnante; **what do you want to be?** cosa vuoi fare?; **be quiet!** sta' zitto!; **I am cold/hot** ho freddo/caldo; **it's cold/hot, isn't it?** fa freddo/caldo, vero?; **how are you?** come stai?; **I am well** sto bene; **there is** c'è; **there are** ci sono; **I have been to Venice** sono stato a Venezia; **has the postman been?** è passato il postino?; **you're coming too, aren't you?** vieni anche tu, no?; **it's yours, is it?** è tuo, vero?; **was John there?** – **yes, he was** c'era John? – sì, c'era; **John wasn't there** – **yes he was** John non c'era – sì che c'era!; **three and three are six** tre più tre fanno sei; **he is five** ha cinque anni; **that will be £10, please** fanno 10 sterline, per favore; **how much is it?** quanto costa?; **that's £5 you owe me** mi devi 5 sterline

● v aux **I am coming/reading** sto venendo/leggendo; **I'm staying** (*not leaving*) resto; **I am being lazy** sono pigro; **I was thinking of you** stavo pensando a te; **you are not to tell him** non devi dirgielo; **you are to do that immediately** devi farlo subito

● *passive* essere; **I have been robbed** sono stato derubato

beach /biːtʃ/ n spiaggia f. **~wear** n abbigliamento m da spiaggia

bead /biːd/ n perlina f

beak /biːk/ n becco m

beaker /'biːkə(r)/ n coppa f

beam /biːm/ n trave f; (*of light*) raggio m ● vi irradiare; (*person:*) essere raggiante. **~ing** adj raggiante

bean /biːn/ n fagiolo m; (of coffee) chicco m

bear¹ /beə(r)/ n orso m

bear² v (pt **bore**, pp **borne**) ● vt (endure) sopportare; mettere al mondo (child); (carry) portare; ~ **in mind** tenere presente ● vi ~ **left/right** andare a sinistra/a destra. □~ **with** vt aver pazienza con. ~**able** adj sopportabile

beard /bɪəd/ n barba f. ~**ed** adj barbuto

bearer /'beərə(r)/ n portatore, -trice mf; (of passport) titolare mf

bearing /'beərɪŋ/ n portamento m; (Techn) cuscinetto m [a sfera]; have a ~ **on** avere attinenza con; **get one's** ~**s** orientarsi

beast /biːst/ n bestia f; (☐: person) animale m

beat /biːt/ n battito m; (rhythm) battuta f; (of policeman) giro m d'ispezione ● v (pt **beat**, pp **beaten**) ● vt battere; picchiare (person); ~ **it** ☐ darsela a gambe!; **it** ~**s me why...** ☐ non capisco proprio perché... **beat up** vt picchiare

beating /'biːtɪŋ/ n bastonata f; **get a** ~**ing** (with fists) essere preso a pugni; (team, player): prendere una batosta

beautician /bjuː'tɪʃn/ n estetista mf

beauti|ful /'bjuːtɪfl/ adj bello. ~**fully** adv splendidamente

beauty /'bjuːtɪ/ n bellezza f. ~ **parlour** n istituto m di bellezza. ~ **spot** n neo m; (place) luogo m pittoresco

beaver /'biːvə(r)/ n castoro m

became /bɪ'keɪm/ ▷BECOME

because /bɪ'kɒz/ conj perché; ~ **you didn't tell me, I...** poiché non me lo hai detto.... ● adv ~ **of** a causa di

beckon /'bekn/ vt/i ~ **[to]** chiamare con un cenno

becom|e /bɪ'kʌm/ v (pt **became**, pp **become**) ● vt diventare ● vi diventare; **what has** ~**e of her?** che ne è di lei? ~**ing** adj (clothes) bello

bed /bed/ n letto m; (of sea, lake) fondo m; (layer) strato m; (of flowers) aiuola f; **in** ~ a letto; **go to** ~ andare a letto; ~ **and breakfast** pensione f familiare in cui il prezzo della camera comprende la prima colazione. ~**clothes** npl lenzuola fpl e coperte fpl. ~**ding** n biancheria f per il letto, materasso e guanciali

bed: ~**room** n camera f da letto. ~**sitter** n = camera f ammobiliata fornita di cucina. ~**spread** n copriletto m. ~**time** n l'ora f di andare a letto

bee /biː/ n ape f

beech /biːtʃ/ n faggio m

beef /biːf/ n manzo m. ~**burger** n hamburger m inv

bee: ~**hive** n alveare m. ~**line** n **make a** ~**line for** ☐ precipitarsi verso

been /biːn/ ▷BE

beer /bɪə(r)/ n birra f

beetle /'biːtl/ n scarafaggio m

beetroot /'biːtruːt/ n barbabietola f

before /bɪ'fɔː(r)/ prep prima di; **the day** ~ **yesterday** ieri l'altro; ~ **long** fra poco ● adv prima; **never** ~ **have I seen...** non ho mai visto prima...; ~ **that** prima; ~ **going** prima di andare ● conj (time) prima che; ~ **you go** prima che tu vada. ~**hand** adv in anticipo

befriend /bɪ'frend/ vt trattare da amico

beg /beg/ v (pt/pp **begged**) ● vi mendicare ● vt pregare; chiedere (favour, forgiveness)

began /bɪ'gæn/ ▷BEGIN

beggar /'begə(r)/ n mendicante mf; **poor** ~**!** povero cristo!

begin /bɪ'gɪn/ vt/i (pt **began**, pp **begun**, pres p **beginning**) cominciare. ~**ner** n principiante mf. ~**ning**

n principio *m*

b **begrudge** /brɪˈɡrʌdʒ/ *vt* (*envy*) essere invidioso di; dare malvolentieri (money)

begun /brɪˈɡʌn/ ▷BEGIN

behalf /brɪˈhɑːf/ *n* on ~ of a nome di; on my ~ a nome mio

behave /brɪˈheɪv/ *vi* comportarsi; ~ [oneself] comportarsi bene

behaviour /brɪˈheɪvjə(r)/ *n* comportamento *m*; (*of prisoner, soldier*) condotta *f*

behead /brɪˈhed/ *vt* decapitare

behind /brɪˈhaɪnd/ *prep* dietro; be ~ sth *fig* stare dietro qcsa ● *adv* dietro, indietro; (*late*) in ritardo; **a long way** ~ molto indietro ● *n* [I] didietro *m*. ~hand *adv* indietro

beige /beɪʒ/ *adj* & *n* beige *m inv*

being /ˈbiːɪŋ/ *n* essere *m*; come into ~ nascere

belated /brɪˈleɪtɪd/ *adj* tardivo

belch /beltʃ/ *vi* ruttare ● *vt* ~ [out] eruttare (smoke)

belfry /ˈbelfrɪ/ *n* campanile *m*

Belgian /ˈbeldʒən/ *adj* & *n* belga *mf*

Belgium /ˈbeldʒəm/ *n* Belgio *m*

belief /brɪˈliːf/ *n* fede *f*; (*opinion*) convinzione *f*

believe /brɪˈliːv/ *vt/i* credere. ~r *n* (*Relig*) credente *mf*; be a great ~r in credere fermamente in

belittle /brɪˈlɪtl/ *vt* sminuire (person, achievements)

bell /bel/ *n* campana *f*; (on door) campanello *m*

belligerent /brɪˈlɪdʒərənt/ *adj* belligerante; (*aggressive*) bellicoso

bellow /ˈbeləʊ/ *vi* gridare a squarciagola; (animal:) muggire

bellows /ˈbeləʊz/ *npl* (for fire) soffietto *msg*

belly /ˈbelɪ/ *n* pancia *f*

belong /brɪˈlɒŋ/ *vi* appartenere (to a); (*be member*) essere socio (to di). ~ings *npl* cose *fpl*

beloved /brɪˈlʌvɪd/ *adj* & *n* amato, -a *mf*

below /brɪˈləʊ/ *prep* sotto; (with numbers) al di sotto di ● *adv* sotto, di sotto; (*Naut*) sotto coperta; see ~ guardare qui di seguito

belt /belt/ *n* cintura *f*; (area) zona *f*; (*Techn*) cinghia *f* ● *vi* ~ along ([I]: rush) filare velocemente ● *vt* ([I]: hit) picchiare

bench /bentʃ/ *n* panchina *f*; (work~) piano *m* da lavoro; the B~ (Jur) la magistratura

bend /bend/ *n* curva *f*; (of river) ansa *f* ● *v* (pt/pp bent) ● *vt* piegare ● *vi* piegarsi; (road:) curvare; ~ [down] chinarsi. □ ~ over *vi* inchinarsi

beneath /brɪˈniːθ/ *prep* sotto, al di sotto di; he thinks it's ~ him *fig* pensa che sia sotto al suo livello ● *adv* giù

beneficial /benɪˈfɪʃl/ *adj* benefico

beneficiary /benɪˈfɪʃərɪ/ *n* beneficiario, -a *mf*

benefit /ˈbenɪfɪt/ *n* vantaggio *m*; (allowance) indennità *f inv* ● *v* (pt/pp -fited, pres p -fiting) ● *vt* giovare a ● *vi* trarre vantaggio (from da)

benign /brɪˈnaɪn/ *adj* benevolo; (Med) benigno

bent /bent/ ▷BEND ● *adj* (person) ricurvo; (distorted) curvato; ([I]: dishonest) corrotto; be ~ on doing sth essere ben deciso a fare qcsa ● *n* predisposizione *f*

bereave|d /brɪˈriːvd/ *n* the ~d *pl* i familiari del defunto. ~ment *n* lutto *m*

beret /ˈbereɪ/ *n* berretto *m*

berry /ˈberɪ/ *n* bacca *f*

berserk /bəˈsɜːk/ *adj* go ~ diventare una belva

berth /bɜːθ/ *n* (bed) cuccetta *f*; (anchorage) ormeggio *m* ● *vi* ormeggiare

beside /brɪˈsaɪd/ *prep* accanto a; ~ oneself fuori di sé

besides /brɪˈsaɪdz/ *prep* oltre a

● *adv* inoltre

besiege /bɪˈsiːdʒ/ *vt* assediare

best /best/ *adj* migliore; **the ~ part of a day** la maggior parte dell'anno; ~ **before** (Comm) preferibilmente prima di ● *n* **the ~** il meglio; (person) il/la migliore; **at ~** a tutt'al più; **all the ~!** tanti auguri!; **do one's ~** fare del proprio meglio; **to the ~ of my knowledge** per quel che ne so; **make the ~ of it** cogliere il lato buono della cosa ● *adv* meglio, nel modo migliore; **as ~ I could** meglio che potevo. ~ **'man** *n* testimone *m*

bestow /bɪˈstəʊ/ *vt* conferire (**on** a)

best'seller *n* bestseller *m inv*

bet /bet/ *n* scommessa *f* ● *vt/i* (pt/pp **bet** or **betted**) scommettere

betray /bɪˈtreɪ/ *vt* tradire. ~**al** *n* tradimento *m*

better /ˈbetə(r)/ *adj* migliore, meglio; **get** ~ migliorare; (after illness) rimettersi ● *adv* meglio; ~ **off** meglio; (wealthier) più ricco; **all the** ~ tanto meglio; **the sooner the** ~ prima è, meglio è; **I've thought** ~ **of it** ci ho ripensato; **you'd** ~ **stay** faresti meglio a restare; **I'd** ~ **not** è meglio che non lo faccia ● *vt* migliorare; ~ **oneself** migliorare le proprie condizioni

between /bɪˈtwiːn/ *prep* fra, tra; ~ **you and me** detto fra di noi; ~ **us** (together) tra me e te ● *adv* [**in**] ~ in mezzo; (time) frattempo

beverage /ˈbevərɪdʒ/ *n* bevanda *f*

beware /bɪˈweə(r)/ *vi* guardarsi (**of** da); ~ **of the dog!** attenti al cane!

bewilder /bɪˈwɪldə(r)/ *vt* disorientare; ~**ed** perplesso. ~**ment** *n* perplessità *f*

beyond /bɪˈjɒnd/ *prep* oltre; ~ **reach** irraggiungibile; ~ **doubt** senza alcun dubbio; ~ **belief** di non credere; **it's** ~ **me** 𝕚 non riesco proprio a capire ● *adv* più in là

bias /ˈbaɪəs/ *n* (preference) preferenza *f*; pej pregiudizio *m* ● *vt* (pt/pp **biased**) (influence) influenzare. ~**ed** *adj* parziale

bib /bɪb/ *n* bavaglino *m*

Bible /ˈbaɪbl/ *n* Bibbia *f*

biblical /ˈbɪblɪkl/ *adj* biblico

biceps /ˈbaɪseps/ *n* bicipite *m*

bicker /ˈbɪkə(r)/ *vi* litigare

bicycle /ˈbaɪsɪkl/ *n* bicicletta *f* ● *vi* andare in bicicletta

bid[1] /bɪd/ *n* offerta *f*; (attempt) tentativo *m* ● *vt/i* (pt/pp **bid**, pres p **bidding**) offrire, (in cards) dichiarare

bid[2] *vt* (pt **bade** or **bid**, pp **bidden** or **bid**, pres p **bidding**) liter (command) comandare; ~ **sb welcome** dare il benvenuto a qcno

bidder /ˈbɪdə(r)/ *n* offerente *mf*

bide /baɪd/ *vt* ~ **one's time** aspettare il momento buono

bifocals /baɪˈfəʊklz/ *npl* occhiali *mpl* bifocali

big /bɪg/ *adj* (**bigger**, **biggest**) grande; (brother, sister) più grande; (🇮🇹: generous) generoso ● *adv* **talk** ~ 🇮🇹 spararle grosse

bigamist /ˈbɪgəmɪst/ *n* bigamo, -a *mf*. ~**y** *n* bigamia *f*

big-headed *adj* 🇮🇹 gasato

bigot /ˈbɪgət/ *n* fanatico, -a *mf*. ~**ed** *adj* di mentalità ristretta

bike /baɪk/ *n* 🇮🇹 bici *f inv*

bikini /bɪˈkiːnɪ/ *n* bikini *m inv*

bile /baɪl/ *n* bile *f*

bilingual /baɪˈlɪŋgwəl/ *adj* bilingue

bill[1] /bɪl/ *n* fattura *f*; (in restaurant etc) conto *m*; (poster) manifesto *m*; (Pol) progetto *m* di legge; (Am: note) biglietto *m* di banca ● *vt* fatturare

bill[2] *n* (beak) becco *m*

'billfold *n* Am portafoglio *m*

billiards /ˈbɪljədz/ *n* biliardo *m*

billion /ˈbɪljən/ *n* (thousand million) miliardo *m*; (old-fashioned Br: million million) mille miliardi *mpl*

bin /bɪn/ n bidone m

bind /baɪnd/ vt (pt/pp **bound**) legare (to a); (bandage) fasciare; (Jur) obbligare. ~**ing** adj (promise, contract) vincolante ● n (of book) rilegatura f; (on ski) attacco m [di sicurezza]

binge /bɪndʒ/ n 🔢 have a ~ fare baldoria; (eat a lot) abbuffarsi ● vi abbuffarsi (on di)

binoculars /bɪˈnɒkjʊləz/ npl **[pair of]** ~ binocolo msg

biograph|er /baɪˈɒgrəfə(r)/ n biografo, -a mf. ~**y** n biografia f

biological /baɪəˈlɒdʒɪkl/ adj biologico

biolog|ist /baɪˈɒlədʒɪst/ n biologo, -a mf. ~**y** n biologia f

birch /bɜːtʃ/ n (tree) betulla f

bird /bɜːd/ n uccello m; (🔢: girl) ragazza f

Biro® /ˈbaɪrəʊ/ n biro® f inv

birth /bɜːθ/ n nascita f

birth: ~ **certificate** n certificato m di nascita. ~**-control** n controllo m delle nascite. ~**day** n compleanno m. ~**mark** n voglia f. ~**rate** n natalità f

biscuit /ˈbɪskɪt/ n biscotto m

bisect /baɪˈsekt/ vt dividere in due [parti]

bishop /ˈbɪʃəp/ n vescovo m; (in chess) alfiere m

bit¹ /bɪt/ n pezzo m; (smaller) pezzetto m; (for horse) morso m; (Comput) bit m inv; **a** ~ **of** un pezzo di (cheese, paper); un po' di (time, rain, silence); ~ **by** ~ poco a poco; **do one's** ~ fare la propria parte

bit² ▷BITE

bitch /bɪtʃ/ n cagna f; (🔣) stronza f. ~**y** adj velenoso

bit|e /baɪt/ n morso m; (insect ~) puntura f; (mouthful) boccone m ● vt (pt **bit**, pp **bitten**) mordere; (insect:) pungere; ~**e one's nails** mangiarsi le unghie ● vi mordere; (insect:) pungere. ~**ing** adj (wind, criticism) pun-

gente; (remark) mordace

bitter /ˈbɪtə(r)/ adj amaro ● n Br birra f amara. ~**ly** adv amaramente; **it's** ~**ly cold** c'è un freddo pungente. ~**ness** n amarezza f

bizarre /bɪˈzɑː(r)/ adj bizzarro

black /blæk/ adj nero; **be** ~ **and blue** essere pieno di lividi ● n negro, -a mf ● vt boicottare (goods). □ ~ **out** vt cancellare ● vi (lose consciousness) perdere coscienza

black: ~**berry** n mora f. ~**bird** n merlo m. ~**board** n (Sch) lavagna f. ~**'currant** n ribes m nero; nero; ~**'eye** n occhio m nero. ~ **ice** n ghiaccio m (sulla strada). ~**leg** n Br crumiro m. ~**list** vt mettere sulla lista nera. ~**mail** n ricatto m ● vt ricattare. ~**mailer** n ricattatore, -trice mf. ~**-out** n blackout m inv; **have a** ~**-out** (Med) perdere coscienza. ~**smith** n fabbro m

bladder /ˈblædə(r)/ n (Anat) vescica f

blade /bleɪd/ n lama f; (of grass) filo m

blame /bleɪm/ n colpa f ● vt dare la colpa a; ~ **sb for doing sth** dare la colpa a qcno per aver fatto qcsa; **no one is to** ~ non è colpa di nessuno. ~**less** adj innocente

bland /blænd/ adj (food) insipido; (person) insulso

blank /blæŋk/ adj bianco; (look) vuoto ● n spazio m vuoto; (cartridge) a salve. ~ **'cheque** n assegno m in bianco

blanket /ˈblæŋkɪt/ n coperta f

blare /bleə(r)/ vi suonare a tutto volume. □ ~ **out** vt far risuonare ● vi (music, radio:) strillare

blaspheme /blæsˈfiːm/ vi bestemmiare

blasphem|ous /ˈblæsfəməs/ adj blasfemo. ~**y** n bestemmia f

blast /blɑːst/ n (gust) raffica f; (sound) scoppio m ● vt (with explosive) far saltare ● int ⊠ maledizioni. **~ed** adj ⊠ maledetto

blast-off n (of missile) lancio m

blatant /'bleɪtənt/ adj sfacciato

blaze /bleɪz/ n incendio m; a **~ of** colour un'esplosione f di colori ● vi ardere

blazer /'bleɪzə(r)/ n blazer m inv

bleach /bliːtʃ/ n decolorante m; (for cleaning) candeggina f ● vt sbiancare; ossigenare (hair)

bleak /bliːk/ adj desolato; (fig: prospects, future) tetro

bleat /bliːt/ vi belare ● n belato m

bleed /bliːd/ v (pt/pp bled) ● vi sanguinare ● vt spurgare (brakes, radiator)

bleep /bliːp/ n bip m ● vi suonare ● vt chiamare (col cercapersone) (doctor). **~er** n cercapersone m inv

blemish /'blemɪʃ/ n macchia f

blend /blend/ n (of tea, coffee, whisky) miscela f; (of colours) insieme m ● vt mescolare ● vi (colours, sounds:) fondersi (with con). **~er** n (Culin) frullatore m

bless /bles/ vt benedire. **~ed** adj also ⊠ benedetto. **~ing** n benedizione f

blew /bluː/ ▷BLOW²

blight /blaɪt/ n (Bot) ruggine f ● vt far avvizzire (plants)

blind¹ /blaɪnd/ adj cieco; **the ~** npl i ciechi mpl; **~ man/woman** cieco/ cieca ● vt accecare

blind² n [roller] **~** avvolgibile m; [Venetian] **~** veneziana f

blind| **~ 'alley** n vicolo m cieco. **~fold** adj **be ~fold** avere gli occhi bendati ● n benda f ● vt bendare gli occhi a. **~ly** adv ciecamente. **~ness** n cecità f

blink /blɪŋk/ vi sbattere le palpebre; (light:) tremolare

blinkers /'blɪŋkəz/ npl paraocchi m

bliss /blɪs/ n (Rel) beatitudine f; (happiness) felicità f. **~ful** adj beato;

(happy) meraviglioso

blister /'blɪstə(r)/ n (Med) vescica f; (in paint) bolla f ● vi (paint:) formare una bolla/delle bolle

blizzard /'blɪzəd/ n tormenta f

bloated /'bləʊtɪd/ adj gonfio

blob /blɒb/ n goccia f

bloc /blɒk/ n (Pol) blocco m

block /blɒk/ n blocco m; (building) isolato m; (building ~) cubo m (per giochi di costruzione); **~ of flats** palazzo m ● vt bloccare. **~ up** vt bloccare

blockade /blɒ'keɪd/ n blocco m ● vt bloccare

blockage /'blɒkɪdʒ/ n ostruzione f

block| **~head** n ① testone, -a mf. **~ 'letters** npl stampatello m

bloke /bləʊk/ n ① tizio m

blonde /blɒnd/ adj biondo ● n bionda f

blood /blʌd/ n sangue m

blood| **~ bath** n bagno m di sangue. **~ group** n gruppo m sanguigno. **~hound** n segugio m. **~ pressure** n pressione f del sangue. **~shed** n spargimento m di sangue. **~shot** adj iniettato di sangue. **~stream** n sangue m. **~thirsty** adj assetato di sangue

bloody /'blʌdɪ/ adj (-ier, -iest) insanguinato; ⊠ maledetto ● adv ⊠ **~ easy/difficult** facile/difficile da matti. **~-minded** adj scorbutico

bloom /bluːm/ n fiore m; **in ~** (flower:) sbocciato; (tree:) in fiore ● vi fiorire; fig essere in forma smagliante

blossom /'blɒsəm/ n fiori mpl (d'albero); (single one) fiore m ● vi sbocciare

blot /blɒt/ n also fig macchia f ● **blot out** vt (pt/pp blotted) fig cancellare

blotch /blɒtʃ/ n macchia f. **~y** adj chiazzato

'blotting-paper n carta f assorbente

blouse /blaʊz/ n camicetta f

blow¹ /bləʊ/ n colpo m

blow² v (pt **blew**, pp **blown**) ● vi (wind): soffiare; (fuse): saltare ● vt (ⓘ: squander) sperperare; ~ **one's nose** soffiarsi il naso. ◻ ~ **away** vt far volar via (papers) ● vi (papers): volare via. ◻ ~ **down** vt abbattere ● vi abbattersi al suolo. ◻ ~ **out** vt (extinguish) spegnere. ◻ ~ **over** vi (storm): passare; (fuss, trouble): dissiparsi. ◻ ~ **up** vt (inflate) gonfiare; (enlarge) ingrandire (photograph); (by explosion) far esplodere ● vi esplodere

blow: ~**-dry** vt asciugare col fon. ~**lamp** n fiamma f ossidrica

'blowtorch n fiamma f ossidrica

blue /bluː/ adj (pale) celeste; (navy) blu inv; (royal) azzurro; ~ **with cold** livido per il freddo ● n blu m inv; **have the ~s** essere giù (di tono); **out of the ~** inaspettatamente

blue: ~**bell** n giacinto m di bosco. ~**berry** n mirtillo m. ~**bottle** n moscone m. ~**print** n film m inv a luci rosse. ~**print** n fig riferimento m

bluff /blʌf/ n bluff m inv ● vi bluffare

blunder /'blʌndə(r)/ n gaffe f inv ● vi fare una/delle gaffe

blunt /blʌnt/ adj spuntato; (person) reciso. ~**ly** adv schiettamente

blur /blɜː(r)/ n **it's all a** ~ fig è tutto un insieme confuso ● vt (pt/pp **blurred**) rendere confuso. ~**red** adj (vision, photo) sfocato

blurb /blɜːb/ n soffietto m editoriale

blurt /blɜːt/ vt ~ **out** spifferare

blush /blʌʃ/ n rossore m ● vi arrossire

boar /bɔː(r)/ n cinghiale m

board /bɔːd/ n tavola f; (for notices) tabellone m; (committee) assemblea f; (of directors) consiglio m; **full** ~ Br pensione f completa; **half** ~ Br mezza pensione f; **~ and lodging** vitto e alloggio m; **go by the** ~ ⓘ andare a monte ● vt (Naut, Aeron) sa-

lire a bordo di ● vi (passengers:) salire a bordo. ◻ ~ **up** vt sbarrare con delle assi. ◻ ~ **with** vt stare a pensione da.

boarder /'bɔːdə(r)/ n pensionante mf; (Sch) convittore, -trice mf

board: ~**ing-house** n pensione f. ~**ing-school** n collegio m

boast /bəʊst/ vi vantarsi (about di). ~**ful** adj vanaglorioso

boat /bəʊt/ n barca f; (ship) nave f. ~**er** n (hat) paglietta f

bob /bɒb/ n (hairstyle) caschetto m ● vi (pt/pp **bobbed**) (also ~ **up and down**) andare su e giù

'bob-sleigh n bob m inv

bode /bəʊd/ vi ~ **well/ill** essere di buono/cattivo augurio

bodily /'bɒdɪlɪ/ adj fisico ● adv (forcibly) fisicamente

body /'bɒdɪ/ n corpo m; (organization) ente m; (amount: of poems etc) quantità f. ~**guard** n guardia f del corpo. ~**part** n pezzo m del corpo. ~**work** n (Auto) carrozzeria f

bog /bɒg/ n palude f ● vt (pt/pp **bogged**) **get** ~**ged down** impantanarsi

boggle /'bɒgl/ vi **the mind** ~**s** non posso neanche immaginarlo

bogus /'bəʊgəs/ adj falso

boil¹ /bɔɪl/ n (Med) foruncolo m

boil² n **bring/come to the** ~ portare/arrivare ad ebollizione ● vi [far] bollire ● vt bollire; (fig: with anger) ribollire; **the water** o **kettle's** ~**ing** l'acqua bolle. **boil down to** vt fig ridursi a. ◻ ~ **over** vi straboccare (bollendo). ◻ ~ **up** vt far bollire

boiler /'bɔɪlə(r)/ n caldaia f. ~**suit** n tuta f

boisterous /'bɔɪstərəs/ adj chiassoso

bold /bəʊld/ adj audace ● n (Typ) neretto m. ~**ness** n audacia f

bolster /'bəʊlstə(r)/ n cuscino m (lungo e rotondo) ● vt ~ **[up]** sostenere

bolt /bəʊlt/ n (for door) catenaccio m; (for fixing) bullone m ● vt fissare (con i bulloni) (**to** a); chiudere col chiavistello (door); ingurgitare (food) ● vi svignarsela; (horse:) scappar via ● vi ~ **upright** diritto come un fuso

bomb /bɒm/ n bomba f ● vt bombardare

bombard /bɒm'bɑːd/ vt also fig bombardare

bomb|er /'bɒmə(r)/ n (Aeron) bombardiere m; (person) dinamitardo m. ~**er jacket** giubbotto m, bomber m inv. ~**shell** n (fig: news) bomba f

bond /bɒnd/ n fig legame m; (Comm) obbligazione f ● vt (glue:) attaccare

bondage /'bɒndɪdʒ/ n schiavitù f

bone /bəʊn/ n osso m; (of fish) spina f ● vt disossare (meat); togliere le spine da (fish). ~-**'dry** adj secco

bonfire /'bɒn-/ n falò m inv. ~ **night** festa celebrata la notte del 5 novembre con fuochi d'artificio e falò

bonnet /'bɒnɪt/ n cuffia f; (of car) cofano m

bonus /'bəʊnəs/ n (individual) gratifica f; (production ~) premio m; (life insurance) dividendo m; **a** ~ fig qualcosa in più

bony /'bəʊnɪ/ adj (**-ier, -iest**) ossuto; (fish) pieno di spine

boo /buː/ interj (to surprise or frighten) bu! ● vt/i fischiare

boob /buːb/ n [1] (mistake) gaffe f inv; (breast) tetta f ● vi [1] fare una gaffe

book /bʊk/ n libro m; (of tickets) blocchetto m; **keep the** ~**s** (Comm) tenere la contabilità; **be in sb's bad/good** ~**s** essere nel libro nero/nelle grazie di qualcuno ● vt (reserve) prenotare; (for offence) multare ● vt (reserve) prenotare

book|case n libreria f. ~**ing-office** n biglietteria f. ~**keeping** n contabilità f. ~**let** n opuscolo m. ~**maker** n allibratore m. ~**mark** n segnalibro m. ~**seller** n libraio, -a mf.

~**shop** n libreria f. ~**worm** n topo m di biblioteca

boom /buːm/ n (Comm) boom m inv; (upturn) impennata f; (of thunder, gun) rimbombo m ● vi (thunder, gun:) rimbombare; fig prosperare

boost /buːst/ n spinta f ● vt stimolare (sales); sollevare (morale); far crescere (hopes). ~**er** n (Med) dose f supplementare

boot /buːt/ n stivale m; (up to ankle) stivaletto m; (football) scarpetta f; (climbing) scarpone m; (Auto) portabagagli m inv ● vt (Comput) inizializzare

booth /buːð/ n (telephone, voting) cabina f; (at market) bancarella f

booze /buːz/ [1] n alcolici mpl. ~**-up** n bella bevuta f

border /'bɔːdə(r)/ n bordo m; (frontier) frontiera f; (in garden) bordura f ● vi ~ **on** confinare con; fig essere ai confini di (madness). ~**line** n linea f di demarcazione. ~ **line case** caso m dubbio

bore¹ /bɔː(r)/ ▷**BEAR²**

bore² vt (Techn) forare

bor|e³ n (of gun) calibro m; (person) seccatore, -trice mf; (thing) seccatura f ● vt annoiare. ~**edom** n noia f. **be ~ed** (to tears or to death) annoiarsi (da morire). ~**ing** adj noioso

born /bɔːn/ pp **be** ~ nascere; **I was** ~ **in 1966** sono nato nel 1966 ● adj nato; **a** ~ **liar/actor** un bugiardo/attore nato

borne /bɔːn/ ▷**BEAR²**

borough /'bʌrə/ n municipalità f inv

borrow /'bɒrəʊ/ vt prendere a prestito (**from** da); **can I** ~ **your pen?** mi presti la tua penna?

boss /bɒs/ n direttore, -trice mf ● vt (also ~ **about**) comandare a bacchetta. ~**y** adj autoritario

botanical /bə'tænɪkl/ adj botanico

botan|ist /'bɒtənɪst/ n botanico, -a mf. ~**y** n botanica f

both /bəʊθ/ adj & pron tutti e due,

entrambi ● *adv* ~ **men and women** entrambi uomini e donne; ~ **[of] the children** tutti e due i bambini; **they are** ~ **dead** sono morti entrambi; ~ **of them** tutti e due

bother /ˈbɒðə(r)/ *n* preoccupazione *f*; (*minor trouble*) fastidio *m*: **it's no** ~ non c'è problema ● *int* **[!]** che seccatura! ● *vt* (*annoy*) dare fastidio a; (*disturb*) disturbare ● *vi* preoccuparsi (**about** di); **don't** ~ lascia perdere

bottle /ˈbɒtl/ *n* bottiglia *f*; (*baby's*) biberon *m inv* ● *vt* imbottigliare. □ ~ **up** *vt fig* reprimere

bottle: ~-**neck** *n fig* ingorgo *m*. ~-**opener** *n* apribottiglie *m inv*

bottom /ˈbɒtm/ *adj* ultimo; **the** ~ **shelf** l'ultimo scaffale in basso ● *n* (*of container*) fondo *m*; (*of river*) fondale *m*; (*of hill*) piedi *mpl*; (*buttocks*) sedere *m*; **at the** ~ **of the page** in fondo alla pagina; **get to the** ~ **of** *fig* vedere cosa c'è sotto. ~**less** *adj* senza fondo

bough /baʊ/ *n* ramoscello *m*

bought /bɔːt/ *▷BUY*

boulder /ˈbəʊldə(r)/ *n* masso *m*

bounce /baʊns/ *vi* rimbalzare; (**□**: *cheque*) essere respinto ● *vt* far rimbalzare (*ball*)

bound¹ /baʊnd/ *n* balzo *m* ● *vi* balzare

bound² *▷BIND* ● *adj* ~ **for** (*ship*) diretto a; **be** ~ **to do** (*likely*) dovere fare per forza; (*obliged*) essere costretto a fare

boundary /ˈbaʊndərɪ/ *n* limite *m*

bouquet /bʊˈkeɪ/ *n* mazzo *m* da fiori; (*of wine*) bouquet *m*

bout /baʊt/ *n* (*Med*) attacco *m*; (*Sport*) incontro *m*

bow¹ /bəʊ/ *n* (*weapon*) arco *m*; (*Mus*) archetto *m*; (*knot*) nodo *m*

bow² /baʊ/ *n* inchino *m* ● *vi* inchinarsi ● *vt* piegare (*head*)

bow³ /baʊ/ *n* (*Naut*) prua *f*

bowl¹ /bəʊl/ *n* (*for soup, cereal*) scodella *f*; (*of pipe*) fornello *m*

bowl² *n* (*ball*) boccia *f* ● *vt* lanciare ● *vi* (*Cricket*) servire; (*in bowls*) lanciare. □ ~ **over** *vt* buttar giù; (*fig: leave speechless*) lasciar senza parole

bowler¹ /ˈbəʊlə(r)/ *n* (*Cricket*) lanciatore *m*; (*Bowls*) giocatore *m* di bocce

bowler² *n* ~ **[hat]** bombetta *f*

bowling /ˈbəʊlɪŋ/ *n* gioco *m* delle bocce. ~-**alley** *n* pista *f* da bowling

bow-'tie /bəʊ-/ *n* cravatta *f* a farfalla

box¹ /bɒks/ *n* scatola *f*; (*Theat*) palco *m*

box² *vi* (*Sport*) fare il pugile ● *vt* ~ **sb's ears** dare uno scappaccione a qcno

box|er /ˈbɒksə(r)/ *n* pugile *m*. ~**ing** *n* pugilato *m*. **B**~**ing Day** *n* [giorno *m* di] Santo Stefano *m*

box: ~-**office** *n* (*Theat*) botteghino *m*. ~-**room** *n* Br sgabuzzino *m*

boy /bɔɪ/ *n* ragazzo *m*; (*younger*) bambino *m*

'boy band *n* boy band *f inv*

boycott /ˈbɔɪkɒt/ *n* boicottaggio *m* ● *vt* boicottare

boy: ~**friend** *n* ragazzo *m*. ~**ish** *adj* da ragazzino

bra /brɑː/ *n* reggiseno *m*

brace /breɪs/ *n* sostegno *m*; (*dental*) apparecchio *m*. ~**s** *npl* bretelle *fpl* ● *vt* ~ **oneself** *fig* farsi forza (**for** per affrontare)

bracelet /ˈbreɪslɪt/ *n* braccialetto *m*

bracken /ˈbrækn/ *n* felce *f*

bracket /ˈbrækɪt/ *n* mensola *f*; (*group*) categoria *f*; (*Typ*) parentesi *f inv* ● *vt* mettere fra parentesi

brag /bræg/ *vi* (*pt/pp* **bragged**) vantarsi (**about** di)

braid /breɪd/ *n* (*edging*) passamano *m*

brain /breɪn/ *n* cervello *m*. ~**s** *pl fig* testa *f sg*

brain: ~**child** *n* invenzione *f* personale. ~**wash** *vt* fare il lavaggio del cervello a. ~**wave** *n* lampo *m* di genio

brainy /'breɪnɪ/ adj (-ier, -iest) intelligente

broke /brəʊk/ n freno m ● vt frenare. **~light** n stop m inv

bramble /'bræmbl/ n rovo m; (fruit) mora f

bran /bræn/ n crusca f

branch /brɑːntʃ/ n also fig ramo m; (Comm) succursale f ● vi (road:) biforcarsi. □ ~ **off** vi biforcarsi. □ ~ **out** vi ~ out into allargare le proprie attività nel ramo di

brand /brænd/ n marca f; (on animal) marchio m ● vt marcare (animal); fig tacciare (as di)

brandish /'brændɪʃ/ vt brandire

brandy /'brændɪ/ n brandy m inv

brash /bræʃ/ adj sfrontato

brass /brɑːs/ n ottone m; **the ~** (Mus) gli ottoni mpl; **top ~** 🔲 pezzi mpl grossi. **~ band** n banda f (di soli ottoni)

brassiere /'bræzɪə(r)/ n fml, Am reggipetto m

brat /bræt/ n pej marmocchio, -a mf

bravado /brə'vɑːdəʊ/ n bravata f

brave /breɪv/ adj coraggioso ● vt affrontare. **~ry** n coraggio m

brawl /brɔːl/ n rissa f ● vi azzuffarsi

brazen /'breɪzn/ adj sfrontato

Brazil /brə'zɪl/ n Brasile m. **~ian** adj & n brasiliano, -a mf. **~ nut** n noce f del Brasile

breach /briːtʃ/ n (of law) violazione f; (gap) breccia f; (fig: in party) frattura f; **~ of contract** inadempienza f di contratto; **~ of the peace** violazione f della quiete pubblica ● vt recedere (contract)

bread /bred/ n pane m; **a slice of ~ and butter** una fetta di pane imburrato

breadcrumbs npl briciole fpl; (Culin) pangrattato m

breadth /bredθ/ n larghezza f

'bread-winner n quello, -a mf che porta i soldi a casa

break /breɪk/ n rottura f; (interval) intervallo m, (interruption) interruzione f; (🔲: chance) opportunità f inv ● v (pt broke, pp broken) ● vt rompere; (interrupt) interrompere; ~ **one's arm** rompersi un braccio ● vi rompersi; (day:) spuntare; (storm:) scoppiare; (news:) diffondersi; (boy's voice:) cambiare. □ ~ **away** vi scappare; fig chiudere (from con). □ ~ **down** vi (machine, car:) guastarsi; (emotionally) cedere (psicologicamente) ● vt sfondare (door); ripartire (figures). □ ~ **into** vt introdursi (con la forza) in; forzare (car). □ ~ **off** vt rompere (engagement) ● vi (part of whole:) rompersi. □ ~ **out** vi (fight, war:) scoppiare. □ ~ **up** vt far cessare (fight); disperdere (crowd) ● vi (crowd:) disperdersi; (couple:) separarsi; (Sch) iniziare le vacanze

'break|able /'breɪkəbl/ adj fragile. **~age** n rottura f. **~down** n (of car, machine) guasto m; (Med) esaurimento m nervoso; (of figures) analisi f inv. **~er** n (wave) frangente m

breakfast /'brekfəst/ n [prima] colazione f

break: **~through** n scoperta f. **~water** n frangiflutti m inv

breast /brest/ n seno m. **~feed** vt allattare (al seno). **~stroke** n nuoto m a rana

breath /breθ/: **~less** adj senza fiato. **~taking** adj mozzafiato. **~ test** n prova [etilica] del palloncino

breathalyse /'breθəlaɪz/ vt sottoporre alla prova [etilica] del palloncino. **~r®** n Br alcoltest m inv

breathe /briːð/ vt/i respirare. □ ~ **in** vi inspirare ● vt respirare (scent, air). □ ~ **out** vt/i espirare

breath|er /'briːðə(r)/ n pausa f. **~ing** n respirazione f

bred /bred/ ▷ BREED

breed /briːd/ n razza f ● v (pt/pp

bred ● vt allevare; (give rise to) generare ● vi riprodursi. ~er n allevatore, -trice mf. ~ing n allevamento m; fig educazione f

breez|e /briːz/ n brezza f. ~y adj ventoso

brew /bruː/ n infuso m ● vt mettere in infusione (tea); produrre (beer) ● vi fig (trouble): essere nell'aria. ~er n birraio m. ~ery n fabbrica f di birra

bribe /braɪb/ n (money) bustarella f; (large sum of money) tangente f ● vt corrompere. ~ry n corruzione f

brick /brɪk/ n mattone m. '~layer n muratore ● **brick up** vt murare

bridal /'braɪdl/ adj nuziale

bride /braɪd/ n sposa f. ~groom n sposo m. ~smaid n damigella f d'onore

bridge¹ /brɪdʒ/ n ponte m; (of nose) dorso m; (of spectacles) ponticello m ● vt fig colmare (gap)

bridge² n (Cards) bridge m

bridle /'braɪdl/ n briglia f

brief¹ /briːf/ adj breve

brief² n istruzioni fpl; (Jur: case) causa f ● vt dare istruzioni a; (Jur) affidare la causa a. ~case n cartella f

briefs /briːfs/ npl slip m inv

brigade /brɪ'geɪd/ n brigata f. ~ier n generale m di brigata

bright /braɪt/ adj (metal, idea) brillante; (day, room, future) luminoso; (clever) intelligente; ~ **red** rosso m acceso

bright|en /'braɪtn/ v ~en [up] ● vt ravvivare; rallegrare (person) ● vi (weather:) schiarirsi; (face:) illuminarsi; (person:) rallegrarsi. ~ly adv (shine) intensamente; (smile) allegramente. ~ness n luminosità f; (intelligence) intelligenza f

brilliance /'brɪljəns/ n luminosità f; (of person) genialità f

brilliant /'brɪljənt/ adj (very good) eccezionale; (very intelligent) brillante; (sunshine) splendente

brim /brɪm/ n bordo m; (of hat) tesa f ● **brim over** vi (pt/pp **brimmed**) traboccare

brine /braɪn/ n salamoia f

bring /brɪŋ/ vt (pt/pp **brought**) portare (person, object). □ ~ **about** vt causare. □ ~ **along** vt portare [con sé]. □ ~ **back** vt restituire (sth borrowed); reintrodurre (hanging); fare ritornare in mente (memories). □ ~ **down** vt portare giù; fare cadere (government); fare abbassare (price). □ ~ **off** vt ~ **sth off** riuscire a fare qcsa. □ ~ **on** vt (cause) provocare. □ ~ **out** vt (emphasize) mettere in evidenza; pubblicare (book). □ ~ **round** vt portare; (persuade) convincere; far rinvenire (unconscious person). □ ~ **up** vt (vomit) rimettere; allevare (children); tirare fuori (question, subject)

brink /brɪŋk/ n orlo m

brisk /brɪsk/ adj svelto; (person) sbrigativo; (trade, business) redditizio; (walk) a passo spedito

brist|le /'brɪsl/ n setola f ● vi ~ling **with** pieno di. ~ly adj (chin) ispido

Brit|ain /'brɪtn/ n Gran Bretagna f. ~ish adj britannico; (ambassador) della Gran Bretagna ● npl **the** ~ish il popolo britannico. ~on n cittadino, -a britannico, -a mf

brittle /'brɪtl/ adj fragile

broach /brəʊtʃ/ vt toccare (subject)

broad /brɔːd/ adj ampio; (hint) chiaro; (accent) marcato. **two metres** ~ largo due metri; **in** ~ **daylight** in pieno giorno. ~ **band** n banda f larga. ~ **beans** npl fave fpl

'broadcast n trasmissione f ● v/i (pt/pp **-cast**) trasmettere. ~er n giornalista mf radiotelevisivo. ~ing n diffusione f radiotelevisiva; **be in** ~ing lavorare per la televisione/radio

broaden /'brɔːdn/ vt allargare ● vi allargarsi

broadly /'brɔːdlɪ/ adv largamente; ~ **[speaking]** generalmente

broad'minded adj di larghe vedute

broccoli /'brɒkəlɪ/ n inv broccoli mpl

brochure /'brəʊʃə(r)/ n opuscolo m; (travel ~) dépliant m inv

broke /brəʊk/ ▷**BREAK** ● adj 🔢 al verde

broken /'brəʊkn/ ▷**BREAK** ● adj rotto; (fig: marriage) fallito. ~ **English** inglese m stentato. ~**-hearted** adj affranto

broker /'brəʊkə(r)/ n broker m inv

brolly /'brɒlɪ/ n 🔢 ombrello m

bronchitis /brɒŋ'kaɪtɪs/ n bronchite f

bronze /brɒnz/ n bronzo m ● attrib di bronzo

brooch /brəʊtʃ/ n spilla f

brood /bruːd/ n covata f; (hum: children) prole f ● vi fig rimuginare

brook /brʊk/ n ruscello m

broom /bruːm/ n scopa f. ~**stick** n manico m di scopa

broth /brɒθ/ n brodo m

brothel /'brɒθl/ n bordello m

brother /'brʌðə(r)/ n fratello m

brother|**-in-law** n (pl ~**s-in-law**) cognato m. ~**ly** adj fraterno

brought /brɔːt/ ▷**BRING**

brow /braʊ/ n fronte f; (of hill) cima f

'browbeat vt (pt **-beat**, pp **-beaten**) intimidire

brown /braʊn/ adj marrone; castano (hair) ● n marrone m ● vt rosolare (meat) ● vi (meat:) rosolarsi. ~ **'paper** n carta f da pacchi

browse /braʊz/ vi (read) leggicchiare; (in shop) curiosare

bruise /bruːz/ n livido m; (on fruit) ammaccatura f ● vt ammaccare (fruit); ~ **one's arm** farsi un livido sul braccio. ~**d** adj contuso

brunette /bruː'net/ n bruna f

brunt /brʌnt/ n **bear the** ~ **of sth** subire maggiormente qcsa

brush /brʌʃ/ n spazzola f; (with long handle) spazzolone m; (for paint) pennello m; (bushes) boscaglia f; (fig: conflict) breve scontro m ● vt spazzolare (hair); lavarsi (teeth); scopare (stairs, floor). □ ~ **against** vt sfiorare. □ ~ **aside** vt fig ignorare. □ ~ **off** vt spazzolare; (with hands) togliere; ignorare (criticism). □ ~ **up** vt/i fig ~ **up [on]** rinfrescare

brusque /brʊsk/ adj brusco

Brussels /'brʌslz/ n Bruxelles f. ~ **sprouts** npl cavoletti mpl di Bruxelles

brutal /'bruːtl/ adj brutale. ~**ity** n brutalità f inv

brute /bruːt/ n bruto m. ~ **force** n forza f bruta

BSc n abbr Bachelor of Science

BSE n abbr (bovine spongiform encephalitis) encefalite f bovina spongiforme

bubble /'bʌbl/ n bolla f; (in drink) bollicina f

buck¹ /bʌk/ n maschio m del cervo; (rabbit) maschio m del coniglio ● vi (horse:) saltare a quattro zampe. □ ~ **up** vt 🔢 tirarsi su; (hurry) sbrigarsi

buck² n Am 🔢 dollaro m

buck³ n **pass the** ~ scaricare la responsabilità

bucket /'bʌkɪt/ n secchio m

buckle /'bʌkl/ n fibbia f ● vt allacciare ● vi (shelf:) piegarsi; (wheel:) storcersi

bud /bʌd/ n bocciolo m

Buddhis|**m** /'bʊdɪzm/ n buddismo m. ~**t** adj & n buddista mf

buddy /'bʌdɪ/ n 🔢 amico, -a mf

budge /bʌdʒ/ vt spostare ● vi spostarsi

budgerigar /'bʌdʒərɪgɑː(r)/ n cocorita f

budget /'bʌdʒɪt/ n bilancio m; (allot-

ted to specific activity) budget m inv ● vi _(pt/pp_ **budgeted)** prevedere le spese; ~ **for sth** includere qcsa nelle spese previste

buffalo /'bʌfələʊ/ n _(inv or pl_ **-es)** bufalo m

buffer /'bʌfə(r)/ n _(Rail)_ respingente m; **old** ~ ① vecchio bacucco m; ~ **zone** n cuscinetto

buffet¹ /'bʊfeɪ/ n buffet m inv

buffet² /'bʌfɪt/ vt _(pt/pp_ **buffeted)** sferzare

bug /bʌg/ n _(insect)_ insetto m; _(Comput)_ bug m inv; (①: _device)_ cimice f ● vt _(pt/pp_ **bugged)** ① installare delle microspie in _(room);_ mettere sotto controllo _(telephone);_ (①: _annoy)_ scocciare

buggy /'bʌgɪ/ n _[baby]_ ~ passeggino m

bugle /'bju:gl/ n tromba f

build /bɪld/ n _(of person)_ corporatura f ● vt/i _(pt/pp_ **built)** costruire. □ ~ **on** vt aggiungere _(extra storey);_ sviluppare _(previous work)._ □ ~ **up** vt ~ **up one's strength** rimettersi in forza ● vi _(pressure, traffic:)_ aumentare; _(excitement, tension:)_ crescere

builder /'bɪldə(r)/ n _(company)_ costruttore m; _(worker)_ muratore m

building /'bɪldɪŋ/ n edificio m. ~ **site** n cantiere m _[di costruzione]._ ~ **society** n istituto m di credito immobiliare

'**build-up** n _(of gas etc)_ accumulo m; _fig_ battage m inv pubblicitario

built /bɪlt/ ▶**BUILD**. ~**-in** adj _(unit)_ a muro; _(fig: feature)_ incorporato. ~**-up area** n _(Auto)_ centro m abitato

bulb /bʌlb/ n bulbo m; _(Electr)_ lampadina f

Bulgaria /bʌl'geərɪə/ n Bulgaria f

bulge /bʌldʒ/ n rigonfiamento m ● vi _sverare_ (with) **with** dis); _(stomach, wall:)_ sporgere; _(eyes, with surprise:)_ uscire dalle orbite. ~**ing** adj gonfio; _(eyes)_ sporgente

bulk /bʌlk/ n volume m; _(greater part)_ grosso m; **in** ~ in grande quantità; _(loose)_ sfuso. ~**y** adj voluminoso

bull /bʊl/ n toro m.

'**bulldog** n bulldog m inv

bulldozer /'bʊldəʊzə(r)/ n bulldozer m inv

bullet /'bʊlɪt/ n pallottola f

bulletin /'bʊlɪtɪn/ n bollettino m. ~ **board** n _(Comput)_ bacheca f elettronica

'**bullet-proof** adj antiproiettile inv; _(vehicle)_ blindato

'**bullfight** n corrida f. ~**er** n torero m

bull: **~ring** n arena f. ~**'s-eye** n centro m del bersaglio; **score a** ~**'s-eye** fare centro

bully /'bʊlɪ/ n prepotente mf ● vt fare il/la prepotente con. ~**ing** n prepotenze pl

bum¹ /bʌm/ n ✕ sedere m

bum² n Am ① vagabondo, -a mf ● **bum around** vi ① vagabondare

bumble-bee /'bʌmbl-/ n calabrone m

bump /bʌmp/ n botta f; _(swelling)_ bozzo m, gonfiore m; _(in road)_ protuberanza f ● vt sbattere. □ ~ **into** vt sbattere contro; _(meet)_ imbattersi in. □ ~ **off** vt ① far fuori

bumper /'bʌmpə(r)/ n _(Auto)_ paraurti m inv ● adj abbondante

bun /bʌn/ n focaccina f _(dolce);_ _(hair)_ chignon m inv

bunch /bʌntʃ/ n _(of flowers, keys)_ mazzo m; _(of bananas)_ casco m; _(of people)_ gruppo m; ~ **of grapes** grappolo m d'uva

bundle /'bʌndl/ n fascio m; _(of money)_ mazzetta f; **a** ~ **of nerves** ① un fascio di nervi ● vt ~ **[up]** affastellare

bungalow /'bʌŋgələʊ/ n bungalow m inv

bungle /'bʌŋgl/ vt fare un

pasticcio di

bunk /bʌŋk/ n cuccetta f. **~-beds** npl letti mpl a castello

bunny /'bʌnɪ/ n 🔢 coniglietto m

buoy /bɔɪ/ n boa f

burden /'bɜːdn/ n carico m ● vt caricare, **~some** adj gravoso

bureau /'bjʊərəʊ/ n (pl **-x** /-əʊz/ or **~s**) (desk) scrivania f; (office) ufficio m

bureaucracy /bjʊə'rɒkrəsɪ/ n burocrazia f

bureaucrat /'bjʊərəkræt/ n burocrate mf. **~ic** adj burocratico

burger /'bɜːgə(r)/ n hamburger m inv

burglar /'bɜːglə(r)/ n svaligiatore, -trice mf. **~ alarm** n antifurto m inv

burgle /'bɜːgl/ vt svaligiare

burial /'berɪəl/ n sepoltura f. **~-ground** n cimitero m

burly /'bɜːlɪ/ adj (-ier, -iest) corpulento

burn /bɜːn/ n bruciatura f ● v (pt/pp burnt or burned) 🔢 vt bruciare ● vi bruciare. **□ ~ down** vt/i bruciare. **□ ~ out** vi fig esaurirsi. **~er** n (on stove) bruciatore m ● (Comput) masterizzatore m

burnt /bɜːnt/ ▷ **burn**

burp /bɜːp/ n 🔢 rutto m ● vi 🔢 ruttare

burrow /'bʌrəʊ/ n tana f ● vt scavare (hole)

bursar /'bɜːsə(r)/ n economo, -a mf. **~y** n borsa f di studio

burst /bɜːst/ n (of gunfire, energy, laughter) scoppio m; (of speed) scatto m ● v (pt/pp burst) 🔢 vt far scoppiare ● vi scoppiare, **~ into tears** scoppiare in lacrime; **she ~ into the room** ha fatto irruzione nella stanza. **□ ~ out** vi **~ out laughing/crying** scoppiare a ridere/piangere

bury /'berɪ/ vt (pt/pp **-ied**) seppellire; (hide) nascondere

bus /bʌs/ n autobus m inv, pullman m

inv; (long distance) pullman m inv, corriera f

bush /bʊʃ/ n cespuglio m; (land) boscaglia f. **~y** adj (-ier, -iest) folto

business /'bɪznɪs/ n affare m; (Comm) affari mpl; (establishment) attività f di commercio; **on ~** per affari; **he has no ~ to** non ha alcun diritto di; **mind one's own ~** farsi gli affari propri; **that's none of your ~** non sono affari tuoi. **~-like** adj efficiente. **~man** n uomo m d'affari. **~woman** n donna f d'affari

busker /'bʌskə(r)/ n suonatore, -trice mf ambulante

'bus station n stazione f degli autobus

'bus-stop n fermata f d'autobus

bust[1] /bʌst/ n busto m; (chest) petto m

bust[2] /bʌst/ adj 🔢 rotto; **go ~** fallire ● v (pt/pp busted or bust) 🔢 ● vt far scoppiare ● vi scoppiare. **'bust-up** n 🔢 lite f

busy /'bɪzɪ/ adj (-ier, -iest) occupato; (day, time) intenso; (street) affollato; (with traffic) pieno di traffico; **be ~ doing** essere occupato a fare ● vt **~ oneself** darsi da fare

'busybody n ficcanaso mf inv

but /bʌt/, atono /bət/ conj ma ● prep eccetto, tranne; **nobody ~ you** nessuno tranne te; **~ for** (without) se non fosse stato per; **the last ~ one** il penultimo; **the next ~ one** il secondo ● adv (only) soltanto; **there were ~ two** ce n'erano soltanto due

butcher /'bʊtʃə(r)/ n macellaio m; **~'s [shop]** macelleria f ● vt macellare; fig massacrare

butler /'bʌtlə(r)/ n maggiordomo m

butt /bʌt/ n (of gun) calcio m; (of cigarette) mozzicone m; (for water) barile m; (fig: target) bersaglio m ● vt dare una testata a; (goat:) dare una cornata a. **□ ~ in** vi interrompere

butter /'bʌtə(r)/ n burro m ● vt imburrare. □~ **up** vt 🔢 aruffianarsi

butter: ~**cup** n ranuncolo m. ~**fingers** nsg 🔢 be a ~**fingers** avere le mani di pasta frolla. ~**fly** n farfalla f

button /'bʌtn/ n bottone m ● vt ~ **[up]** abbottonare ● vi abbottonarsi. ~**hole** n occhiello m, asola f

buy /baɪ/ n good/bad ~ buon/cattivo acquisto m ● vt (pt/pp **bought**) comprare; ~ **sb a drink** pagare da bere a qcno; **I'll** ~ **this one** (drink) questo, lo offro io. ~**er** n compratore, -trice mf

buzz /bʌz/ n ronzio m; **give sb a** ~ 🔢 (on phone) dare un colpo di telefono a qcno; (excite) mettere in fermento qcno ● vt ~ **sb** chiamare qcno col cicalino. □~ **off** vi 🔢 levarsi di torno

buzzer /'bʌzə(r)/ n cicalino m

by /baɪ/
● prep (near, next to) vicino a; (at the latest) per; **by Mozart** di Mozart; **he was run over by a bus** è stato investito da un autobus; **by oneself** da solo; **by the sea** al mare; **by sea** via mare; **by car/bus** in macchina/autobus; **by day/night** di giorno/notte; **by the hour/metre** a ore/metri; **six metres by four** sei metri per quattro; **he won by six metres** ha vinto di sei metri; **I missed the train by a minute** ho perso il treno per un minuto; **I'll be home by six** sarò a casa per le sei; **by this time next week** a quest'ora tra una settimana; **he rushed by me** mi è passato accanto di corsa
● adv **she'll be here by and by** sarà qui fra poco; **by and large** in complesso

bye[-bye] /baɪ['baɪ]/ int 🔢 ciao

by: ~**-election** n elezione f straordinaria indetta per coprire una carica rimasta vacante in Parlamento. ~**-law** n legge f locale. ~**pass** n circonvallazione f; (Med) by-pass m inv ● vt evitare. ~**-product** n sottoprodotto m. ~**stander** n spettatore, -trice mf

••••••••••••••••••••••••••••••

Cc

••••••••••••••••••••••••••••••

cab /kæb/ n taxi m inv; (of lorry, train) cabina f

cabaret /'kæbəreɪ/ n cabaret m inv

cabbage /'kæbɪdʒ/ n cavolo m

cabin /'kæbɪn/ n (of plane, ship) cabina f; (hut) capanna f

cabinet /'kæbɪnɪt/ n armadietto m; [display] ~ vetrina f; **C**~ (Pol) consiglio m dei ministri. ~**-maker** n ebanista mf

cable /'keɪbl/ n cavo m. ~ '**railway** n funicolare f. ~ '**television** n televisione f via cavo

cackle /'kækl/ vi ridacchiare

cactus /'kæktəs/ n (pl -**ti** /-taɪ/ or -**tuses**) cactus m inv

caddie /'kædɪ/ n portabastoni m inv

caddy /'kædɪ/ n [**tea**-]~ barattolo m del tè

cadet /kə'det/ n cadetto m

cadge /kædʒ/ vt/i 🔢 scroccare

café /'kæfeɪ/ n caffè m inv

cafeteria /kæfə'tɪərɪə/ n tavola f calda

caffeine /'kæfiːn/ n caffeina f

cage /keɪdʒ/ n gabbia f

cake /keɪk/ n torta f; (small) pasticcino m. ~**d** adj incrostato (**with** di)

calamity /kə'læmətɪ/ n calamità f inv

calcium /'kælsɪəm/ n calcio m

calculat|e /'kælkjʊlɪt/ vt calcolare. **~ing** adj fig calcolatore. **~ion** n calcolo m. **~or** n calcolatrice f

calendar /'kælɪndə(r)/ n calendario m

calf¹ /kɑːf/ n (pl **calves**) vitello m

calf² n (pl **calves**) (Anat) polpaccio m

calibre /'kælɪbə(r)/ n calibro m

call /kɔːl/ n grido m; (Teleph) telefonata f; (visit) visita f; **be on ~** (doctor) essere di guardia ● vt chiamare; (visit) visitare ● vi (telephone) chiamare; **~ [in** or **round]** passare. **□ ~ back** vt richiamare. **□ ~ for** vt (ask for) chiedere; (require) richiedere; (fetch) passare a prendere. **□ ~ off** vt richiamare (dog); disdire (meeting); revocare (strike). **□ ~ on** vt chiamare; (appeal to) fare un appello a; (visit) visitare. **□ ~ out** vt chiamare ad alta voce (names) ● vi chiamare ad alta voce. **□ ~ together** vt riunire. **□ ~ up** vt (Mil) chiamare alle armi; (Teleph) chiamare

call: **~-box** n cabina f telefonica. **~ centre** n call centre m inv. **~er** n visitatore, -trice mf; (Teleph) persona f che telefona. **~ing** n vocazione f

callous /'kæləs/ adj insensibile

calm /kɑːm/ adj calmo ● n calma f. **□ ~ down** vt calmare ● vi calmarsi. **~ly** adv con calma

calorie /'kælərɪ/ n caloria f

calves /kɑːvz/ npl see **calf¹** & **2**

camcorder /'kæmkɔːdə(r)/ n videocamera f

came /keɪm/ ▷COME

camel /'kæml/ n cammello m

camera /'kæmərə/ n macchina f fotografica; (TV) telecamera f. **~man** n operatore m [televisivo], cameraman m inv

camouflage /'kæməflɑːʒ/ n mimetizzazione f ● vt mimetizzare

camp /kæmp/ n campeggio f; (Mil) campo m ● vi campeggiare; (Mil) accamparsi

campaign /kæm'peɪn/ n campagna f ● vi fare una campagna

camp: **~-bed** n letto m da campo. **~er** n campeggiatore, -trice mf; (Auto) camper m inv. **~ing** n campeggio m. **~site** n campeggio m

campus /'kæmpəs/ n (pl **-puses**) (Univ) città f universitaria, campus m inv

can¹ /kæn/ n (for petrol) latta f; (tin) scatola f; **~ of beer** lattina f di birra ● vt mettere in scatola

can² /kæn/, atono /kən/ v aux (pres **can**; pt **could**) (be able to) potere; (know how to) sapere; **I cannot** or **can't go** non posso andare; **he could not** or **couldn't go** non poteva andare; **she can't swim** non sa nuotare; **I ~ smell something burning** sento odor di bruciato

Canada /'kænədə/ n Canada m. **~ian** adj & n canadese mf

canal /kə'næl/ n canale m

Canaries /kə'neərɪz/ npl Canarie fpl

canary /kə'neərɪ/ n canarino m

cancel /'kænsl/ v (pt/pp **cancelled**) ● vt disdire (meeting, newspaper); revocare (contract, order); annullare (reservation, appointment, stamp). **~lation** n (of meeting, contract) revoca f; (in hotel, restaurant, for flight) cancellazione f

cancer /'kænsə(r)/ n cancro m; **C~** (Astr) Cancro m. **~ous** adj canceroso

candid /'kændɪd/ adj franco

candidate /'kændɪdət/ n candidato, -a mf

candle /'kændl/ n candela f. **~stick** n portacandele m inv

candour /'kændə(r)/ n franchezza f

candy /'kændɪ/ n Am caramella f; **a [piece of] ~** una caramella. **~floss** n zucchero m filato

cane /keɪn/ n (stick) bastone m; (Sch)

bacchetta f ● vt prendere a bacchettate (pupil)

canister /ˈkænɪstə(r)/ n barattolo m (di metallo)

cannabis /ˈkænəbɪs/ n cannabis f

cannibal /ˈkænɪbl/ n cannibale mf. **~ism** n cannibalismo m

cannon /ˈkænən/ n inv cannone m. **~-ball** n palla f di cannone

cannot /ˈkænɒt/ ▷CAN²

canoe /kəˈnuː/ n canoa f ● vi andare in canoa

'can-opener n apriscatole m inv

canopy /ˈkænəpɪ/ n baldacchino f; (of parachute) calotta f

cantankerous /kænˈtæŋkərəs/ adj stizzoso

canteen /kænˈtiːn/ n mensa f; **~** of cutlery servizio m di posate

canter /ˈkæntə(r)/ vi andare a piccolo galoppo

canvas /ˈkænvəs/ n tela f; (painting) dipinto m su tela

canvass /ˈkænvəs/ vi (Pol) fare propaganda elettorale. **~ing** n sollecitazione f di voti

canyon /ˈkænjən/ n canyon m inv

cap /kæp/ n berretto m; (nurse's) cuffia f; (top, lid) tappo m ● vt (pt/pp capped) (fig: do better than) superare

capability /keɪpəˈbɪlətɪ/ n capacità f

capable /ˈkeɪpəbl/ adj capace; (skilful) abile; **be ~e of doing sth** essere capace di fare qcsa. **~y** adv con abilità

capacity /kəˈpæsətɪ/ n capacità f; (function) qualità f; in my **~** as in qualità di

cape¹ /keɪp/ n (cloak) cappa f

cape² n (Geog) capo m

capital /ˈkæpɪtl/ n (town) capitale f; (money) capitale m; (letter) lettera f maiuscola. **~ city** n capitale f

capital|ism /ˈkæpɪtəlɪzm/ n capitalismo m. **~ist** adj & n capitalista mf.

~ize vi **~ize on** fig trarre vantaggio da. **~ 'letter** n lettera f maiuscola. **~ 'punishment** n pena f capitale

capitulat|e /kəˈpɪtjʊleɪt/ vi capitolare. **~ion** n capitolazione f

Capricorn /ˈkæprɪkɔːn/ n (Astr) Capricorno m

capsize /kæpˈsaɪz/ vi capovolgersi ● vt capovolgere

capsule /ˈkæpsjʊl/ n capsula f

captain /ˈkæptɪn/ n capitano m ● vt comandare (team)

caption /ˈkæpʃn/ n intestazione f; (of illustration) didascalia f

captivate /ˈkæptɪveɪt/ vt incantare

captiv|e /ˈkæptɪv/ adj prigioniero; **hold/take ~e** tenere/fare prigioniero ● n prigioniero, -a mf. **~ity** n prigionia f; (animals) cattività f

capture /ˈkæptʃə(r)/ n cattura f ● vt catturare; attirare (attention)

car /kɑː(r)/ n macchina f; **by ~** in macchina

carafe /kəˈræf/ n caraffa f

caramel /ˈkærəmel/ n (sweet) caramella f al mou; (Culin) caramello m

caravan /ˈkærəvæn/ n roulotte f inv; (horse-drawn) carovana f

carbohydrate /kɑːbəˈhaɪdreɪt/ n carboidrato m

carbon /ˈkɑːbən/ n carbonio m

carbon di'oxide n anidride f carbonica

carburettor /kɑːbjʊˈretə(r)/ n carburatore m

carcass /ˈkɑːkəs/ n carcassa f

card /kɑːd/ n (for birthday, Christmas etc) biglietto m di auguri; (playing ~)

carta f [da gioco]; (membership ~) tessera f; (business ~) biglietto m da visita; (credit ~) carta f di credito; (Comput) scheda f

'cardboard n cartone m. ~ **'box** n scatola f di cartone; (large) scatolone m

cardigan /'kɑːdɪɡən/ n cardigan m inv

cardinal /'kɑːdɪnl/ adj cardinale; ~ **number** numero m cardinale ● n (Relig) cardinale m

care /keə(r)/ n cura f; (caution) attenzione f; (worry) preoccupazione f; ~ **of** (on letter abbr c/o) presso; **take** ~ (be cautious) fare attenzione; **bye, take** ~ ciao, stammi bene; **take** ~ **of** occuparsi di, **be taken into** ~ essere preso in custodia da un ente assistenziale ● vi ~ **about** interessarsi di; ~ **for** (feel affection for) volere bene a; (look after) aver cura di; **I don't** ~ **for chocolate** non mi piace il cioccolato; **I don't** ~ non me ne importa, **who** ~s? chi se ne frega?

career /kə'rɪə(r)/ n carriera f; (profession) professione f ● vi andare a tutta velocità

care: ~**free** adj spensierato. ~**ful** adj attento, (driver) prudente. ~**fully** adv con attenzione. ~**less** adj irresponsabile; (in work) trascurato; (work) fatto con poca cura; (driver) distratto. ~**lessly** adv negligentemente. ~**lessness** n trascuratezza f. ~**r** n persona f che accudisce a un anziano o a un malato

caress /kə'res/ n carezza f ● vt accarezzare

'caretaker n custode m/f; (in school) bidello m

'car ferry n traghetto m (per il trasporto di auto)

cargo /'kɑːɡəʊ/ n (pl -es) carico m

Caribbean /kærɪ'biːən/ n **the** ~ (sea) il Mar dei Caraibi ● adj caraibico

caricature /'kærɪkətjʊə(r)/ n caricatura f

carnage /'kɑːnɪdʒ/ n carneficina f

carnation /kɑː'neɪʃn/ n garofano m

carnival /'kɑːnɪvl/ n carnevale m

carol /'kærəl/ n [**Christmas**] ~ canto m natalizio

carp[1] /kɑːp/ n inv carpa f

carp[2] vi ~ **at** trovare da ridire su

'car park n parcheggio m

carpenter /'kɑːpɪntə(r)/ n falegname m. ~**ry** n falegnameria f

carpet /'kɑːpɪt/ n tappeto m; (wall-to-wall) moquette f inv ● vt mettere la moquette in (room)

carriage /'kærɪdʒ/ n carrozza f; (of goods) trasporto m; (cost) spese fpl di trasporto; (bearing) portamento m; ~**way** n strada f carrozzabile; **north-bound** ~**way** carreggiata f nord

carrier /'kærɪə(r)/ n (company) impresa f di trasporti; (Aeron) compagnia f di trasporto aereo; (of disease) portatore m. ~ **bag** n borsa f [per la spesa]

carrot /'kærət/ n carota f

carry /'kærɪ/ vt (pt/pp -ied) ● vt portare; (transport) trasportare; **get carried away** [fig] lasciarsi prender la mano ● vi (sound) trasmettersi. □ ~ **off** vt portare via, vincere (prize). □ ~ **on** vi continuare; (fam: make scene) fare delle storie; ~ **on with** sth continuare a; ~ **on with sb** [fam] intendersela con qcno ● vt mantenere (business). □ ~ **out** vt portare fuori, eseguire (instructions, task); mettere in atto (threat); effettuare (experiment, survey)

'carry-cot n porte-enfant m inv

cart /kɑːt/ n carretto m ● vt ([fam]: carry) portare

carton /'kɑːtn/ n scatola f di cartone; (for drink) cartone m; (of cream, yoghurt) vasetto m; (of cigarettes) stecca f

cartoon /kɑːˈtuːn/ n vignetta f; (strip) vignette fpl; (film) cartone m animato; (in art) bozzetto m. **~ist** n vignettista mf; (for films) disegnatore, -trice mf di cartoni animati

cartridge /ˈkɑːtrɪdʒ/ n cartuccia f; (for film) bobina f; (of record player) testina f

carve /kɑːv/ vt scolpire; tagliare (meat)

case¹ /keɪs/ n caso m; **in any ~** in ogni caso; **in that ~** in questo caso; **just in ~** per sicurezza; **in ~ he comes** nel caso in cui venisse

case² n (container) scatola f; (crate) cassa f; (for spectacles) astuccio m; (suitcase) valigia f; (for display) vetrina f

cash /kæʃ/ n denaro m contante; (🔲: money) contanti mpl; **pay [in] ~** pagare in contanti; **~ on delivery** pagamento alla consegna ● vt incassare (cheque). **~ desk** n cassa f

cashier /kæˈʃɪə(r)/ n cassiere, -a mf

casino /kəˈsiːnəʊ/ n casinò m inv

casket /ˈkɑːskɪt/ n scrigno m; (Am: coffin) bara f

casserole /ˈkæsərəʊl/ n casseruola f; (stew) stufato m

cassette /kəˈset/ n cassetta f. **~ recorder** n registratore m (a cassette)

cast /kɑːst/ n (mould) forma f; (Theat) cast m inv; (plaster) ~ (Med) ingessatura f ● vt (pt/pp **cast**) dare (vote); (Theat) assegnare le parti di (play); fondere (metal); (throw) gettare; **~ an actor as** dare ad un attore il ruolo di; **~ a glance at** lanciare uno sguardo a. **□ ~ off** vi (Naut) sganciare gli ormeggi ● vt (in knitting) diminuire. **□ ~ on** vt (in knitting) avviare

castaway /ˈkɑːstəweɪ/ n naufrago, -a mf

caster /ˈkɑːstə(r)/ n (wheel) rotella f. **~ sugar** n zucchero m raffinato

cast 'iron n ghisa f

cast-'iron adj di ghisa; fig solido

castle /ˈkɑːsl/ n castello m;

(in chess) torre f

'cast-offs npl abiti mpl smessi

castrat|e /kæˈstreɪt/ vt castrare. **~ion** n castrazione f

casual /ˈkæʒʊəl/ adj (chance) casuale; (remark) senza importanza; (glance) di sfuggita; (attitude, approach) disinvolto; (chat) informale; (clothes) casual inv; (work) saltuario. **~ wear** abbigliamento m casual. **~ly** adv (dress) casual; (meet) casualmente

casualty /ˈkæʒʊəltɪ/ n (injured person) ferito m; (killed) vittima f. **~ [department]** n pronto soccorso m

cat /kæt/ n gatto m; pej arpia f

catalogue /ˈkætəlɒg/ n catalogo m ● vt catalogare

catalyst /ˈkætəlɪst/ n (Chem) & fig catalizzatore m

catapult /ˈkætəpʌlt/ n catapulta f; (child's) fionda f ● vt fig catapultare

catarrh /kəˈtɑː(r)/ n catarro m

catastroph|e /kəˈtæstrəfɪ/ n catastrofe f. **~ic** adj catastrofico

catch /kætʃ/ n (of fish) pesca f; (fastener) fermaglio m; (on door) fermo m; (on window) gancio m; (🔲: snag) tranello m ● v t (pt/pp **caught**) ● vt acchiappare (ball); (grab) afferrare; prendere (illness, fugitive, train); **~ a cold** prendersi un raffreddore; **~ sight of** scorgere; **I caught him stealing** l'ho sorpreso mentre rubava; **~ one's finger in the door** chiudersi il dito nella porta; **~ sb's eye** or **attention** attirare l'attenzione di qcno ● vt (fire): prendere; (get stuck) impigliarsi. **□ ~ on** vi 🔲 (understand) afferrare; (become popular) diventare popolare. **□ ~ up** vt raggiungere ● vi recuperare; (runner:) riguadagnare terreno; **~ up with** raggiungere (sb); mettersi in pari con (work)

catching /ˈkætʃɪŋ/ adj contagioso

catchphrase n tormentone m

catchy /ˈkætʃɪ/ adj (**-ier, -iest**)

orecchiabile

categor|ical /kætɪˈgɒrɪkl/ adj categorico. **~y** n categoria f

cater /ˈkeɪtə(r)/ vi **~ for** provvedere a (needs); fig venire incontro alle esigenze di. **~ing** n (trade) ristorazione f. (food) rinfresco m

caterpillar /ˈkætəpɪlə(r)/ n bruco m

cathedral /kəˈθiːdrl/ n cattedrale f

Catholic /ˈkæθəlɪk/ adj & n cattolico, -a mf. **~ism** n cattolicesimo m

cat's eyes npl catarifrangente msg (inserito nell'asfalto)

cattle /ˈkætl/ npl bestiame msg

catwalk /ˈkætwɔːk/ n passerella f

caught /kɔːt/ ▸CATCH

cauliflower /ˈkɒlɪ-/ n cavolfiore m

cause /kɔːz/ n causa f ● vt causare; **~ sb to do sth** far fare qcsa a qcno

caution /ˈkɔːʃn/ n cautela f; (warning) ammonizione f ● vt mettere in guardia; (Jur) ammonire

cautious /ˈkɔːʃəs/ adj cauto

cavalry /ˈkævlrɪ/ n cavalleria f

cave /keɪv/ n caverna f ● **cave in** vi (roof:) crollare; (fig: give in) capitolare

cavern /ˈkævən/ n caverna f

caviare /ˈkævɪɑː(r)/ n caviale m

cavity /ˈkævətɪ/ n cavità f inv; (in tooth) carie f inv

CD n CD m inv. **~ player** n lettore m [di] compact

CD-Rom /siːdiːˈrɒm/ n CD-Rom m inv. **~ drive** n lettore m [di] CD-Rom

cease /siːs/ vt/i cessare. **~-fire** n cessate il fuoco m inv. **~less** adj incessante

cedar /ˈsiːdə(r)/ n cedro m

ceiling /ˈsiːlɪŋ/ n soffitto m; fig tetto m [massimo]

celebrat|e /ˈselɪbreɪt/ vt festeggiare (birthday, victory) ● vi far festa. **~ed** adj celebre (for per). **~ion** n celebrazione f

celebrity /sɪˈlebrətɪ/ n celebrità f inv

celery /ˈselərɪ/ n sedano m

cell /sel/ n cella f; (Biol) cellula f

cellar /ˈselə(r)/ n scantinato m; (for wine) cantina f

cello /ˈtʃeləʊ/ n violoncello m

Cellophane® /ˈseləfeɪn/ n cellofan m inv

cellphone /ˈselfəʊn/ n cellulare m

cellular phone /seljʊləˈfəʊn/ n [telefono m] cellulare m

celluloid /ˈseljʊlɔɪd/ n celluloide f

Celsius /ˈselsɪəs/ adj Celsius m

cement /sɪˈment/ n cemento m; (adhesive) mastice m ● vt cementare; fig consolidare

cemetery /ˈsemətrɪ/ n cimitero m

censor /ˈsensə(r)/ n censore m ● vt censurare. **~ship** n censura f

censure /ˈsenʃə(r)/ vt biasimare

census /ˈsensəs/ n censimento m

cent /sent/ n (of dollar) centesimo m; (of euro) cent m inv, centesimo m

centenary /senˈtiːnərɪ/ n, Am **centennial** /senˈtenɪəl/ n centenario m

center /ˈsentə(r)/ n Am = centre

centi|grade /ˈsentɪ-/ adj centigrado. **~metre** n centimetro m. **~pede** n centopiedi m inv

central /ˈsentrl/ adj centrale. **~ 'heating** n riscaldamento m autonomo. **~ize** vt centralizzare. **~ly** adv al centro; **~ly heated** con riscaldamento autonomo. **~ reser'vation** n (Auto) banchina f spartitraffico

centre /ˈsentə(r)/ n centro m ● v (pt/pp **centred**) vt centrare ● vi **~ on** fig incentrarsi su. **~-'forward** n centravanti m inv

century /ˈsentʃərɪ/ n secolo m

cereal /ˈsɪərɪəl/ n cereale m

ceremon|ial /serɪˈməʊnɪəl/ adj & n cerimonia f ● cerimoniale m. **~ious** adj cerimonioso

ceremony /ˈserɪmənɪ/ n

cerimonia f

certain /'sɜːtn/ adj certo; **for ~** di sicuro; **make ~** accertarsi ; **he is ~ to win** è certo di vincere; **it's not ~ whether** he'll come non è sicuro che venga. **~ly** adv certamente; **~ly not!** no di certo! **~ty** n certezza f; **it's a ~ty** è una cosa certa

certificate /sə'tɪfɪkət/ n certificato m

certify /'sɜːtɪfaɪ/ vt (pt/pp -ied) certificare; (declare insane) dichiarare malato di mente

chafe /tʃeɪf/ vt irritare

chain /tʃeɪn/ n catena f ● vt incatenare (prisoner); attaccare con la catena (dog) (to a). □ ~ up vt legare alla catena (dog)

chain: ~ re'action n reazione f a catena. ~-smoker n fumatore, -trice mf accanito, -a. ~ store n negozio m appartenente a una catena

chair /tʃeə(r)/ n sedia f; (Univ) cattedra f ● vt presiedere. ~-lift n seggiovia f. ~man n presidente m

chalet /'ʃæleɪ/ n chalet m inv; (in holiday camp) bungalow m inv

chalk /tʃɔːk/ n gesso m. ~y adj gessoso

challeng|e /'tʃælɪndʒ/ n sfida f; (Mil) intimazione f ● vt sfidare; (Mil) intimare il chi va là a; fig mettere in dubbio (statement). ~er n sfidante mf. ~ing adj (job) impegnativo

chamber /'tʃeɪmbə(r)/ n **C~ of Commerce** camera f di commercio

chambermaid n cameriera f [d'albergo]

champagne /ʃæm'peɪn/ n champagne m inv

champion /'tʃæmpɪən/ n (Sport) campione m; (of cause) difensore, difenditrice mf ● vt (defend) difendere. ~ship n (Sport) campionato m

chance /tʃɑːns/ n caso m; (possibility) possibilità f inv; (opportunity) occasione

f; **by ~** per caso; **take a ~** correre un rischio; **give sb a second ~** dare un'altra possibilità a qcno ● attrib fortuito ● vt **I'll ~ it** [] corro il rischio

chancellor /'tʃɑːnsələ(r)/ n cancelliere m; (Univ) rettore m; **C~ of the Exchequer** ≈ ministro m del tesoro

chandelier /ʃændə'lɪə(r)/ n lampadario m

change /tʃeɪndʒ/ n cambiamento m; (money) resto m; (small coins) spiccioli mpl; **for a ~** tanto per cambiare; **a ~ of clothes** un cambio di vestiti; **the ~ [of life]** la menopausa ● vt cambiare; (substitute) scambiare (for con); ~ **one's clothes** cambiarsi [i vestiti]; ~ **trains** cambiare treno ● vi cambiare; (~ clothes) cambiarsi; **all ~!** stazione terminale!

changeable /'tʃeɪndʒəbl/ adj mutevole; (weather) variabile

'**changing-room** n camerino m, (for sports) spogliatoio m

channel /'tʃænl/ n canale m; **the [English] C~** la Manica; **the C~ Islands** le Isole del Canale ● vt (pt/pp channelled) ~ **one's energies into sth** convogliare le proprie energie in qcsa

chant /tʃɑːnt/ n cantilena f; (of demonstrators) slogan m inv di protesta ● vt cantare; (demonstrators:) gridare

chao|s /'keɪɒs/ n caos m. ~**tic** adj caotico

chap /tʃæp/ n [] tipo m

chapel /'tʃæpl/ n cappella f

chaperon /'ʃæpərəʊn/ n chaperon f inv ● vt fare da chaperon a (sb)

chapter /'tʃæptə(r)/ n capitolo m

char¹ /tʃɑː(r)/ n [] donna f delle pulizie

char² vt (pt/pp charred) (burn) carbonizzare

character /'kærɪktə(r)/ n carattere m; (in novel, play) personaggio m; **quite a ~** [] un tipo particolare

characteristic /kærɪktə'rɪstɪk/ adj

caratteristico ● n caratteristica f.
~ally adv tipicamente

characterize /'kærɪktəraɪz/ vt caratterizzare

charade /ʃə'rɑːd/ n farsa f

charcoal /'tʃɑː/ n carbonella f

charge /tʃɑːdʒ/ n (cost) prezzo m; (Electr, Mil) carica f; (Jur) accusa f; free of ~ gratuito; **be in** ~ essere responsabile (of di); **take** ~ assumersi la responsabilità; **take** ~ **of** occuparsi di ● vt far pagare (fee); far pagare a (person); (Electr, Mil) caricare; (Jur) accusare (**with** di); ~ **sb for sth** far pagare qcsa a qcno; ~ **it to my account** lo addebiti sul mio conto ● vi (attack) caricare

charitable /'tʃærɪtəbl/ adj caritatevole; (kind) indulgente

charity /'tʃærətɪ/ n carità f; (organization) associazione f di beneficenza; **concert given for** ~ concerto m di beneficenza; **live on** ~ vivere di elemosina

charm /tʃɑːm/ n fascino m; (object) ciondolo m ● vt affascinare. **~ing** adj affascinante

chart /tʃɑːt/ n carta f nautica; (table) tabella f

charter /'tʃɑːtə(r)/ n ~ **[flight]** [volo m] charter m inv ● vt noleggiare. **~ed accountant** n commercialista mf

chase /tʃeɪs/ n inseguimento m ● vt inseguire. **chase away** or **off** vt cacciare via

chassis /'ʃæsɪ/ n (pl chassis /-sɪz/) telaio m

chastity /'tʃæstətɪ/ n castità f

chat /tʃæt/ n chiacchierata f; **have a** ~ **with** fare quattro chiacchiere con ● vi (pt/pp chatted) chiacchierare; (Comput) chattare. ~ **show** n talk show m inv

chatter /'tʃætə(r)/ n chiacchiere fpl ● vi chiacchierare; (teeth:) battere. **~box** n 🄸 chiacchierone, -a mf

chauffeur /'ʃəʊfə(r)/ n autista mf

chauvin|ism /'ʃəʊvɪnɪzm/ n sciovinismo m. **~ist** n sciovinista mf. **male ~ist** n 🄸 maschilista m

cheap /tʃiːp/ adj a buon mercato; (rate) economico; (vulgar) grossolano; (of poor quality) scadente ● adv a buon mercato. **~ly** adv a buon mercato

cheat /tʃiːt/ n imbroglione, -a mf; (at cards) baro m ● vt imbrogliare; ~ **sb out of sth** sottrarre qcsa a qcno con l'inganno ● vi imbrogliare; (at cards) barare. ~ **on** vt 🄸 tradire (wife)

check[1] /tʃek/ adj (pattern) a quadri ● n disegno m a quadri

check[2] n verifica f; (of tickets) controllo m; (in chess) scacco m; (Am: bill) conto m; (Am: cheque) assegno m; (Am: tick) segnetto m; **keep a** ~ **on** controllare; **keep in** ~ tenere sotto controllo ● vt verificare; controllare (tickets); (restrain) contenere; (stop) bloccare ● vi controllare; ~ **on sth** controllare qcsa. ● ~ **in** vi registrarsi all'arrivo (in albergo); (Aeron) fare il check-in ● vt registrare all'arrivo (in albergo). ● ~ **out** vi (of hotel) saldare il conto ● vt (🄸: investigate) controllare. ● ~ **up** vi accertarsi; ~ **up on** prendere informazioni su

check: ~-**in** n (in airport: place) banco m accettazione, check-in m inv; ~-**mate** int scacco matto! ● ~-**out** n (in supermarket) cassa f. ● ~-**up** n (Med) visita f di controllo, check-up m inv

cheek /tʃiːk/ n guancia f; (impudence) sfacciataggine f. **~y** adj sfacciato

cheep /tʃiːp/ vi pigolare

cheer /tʃɪə(r)/ n evviva m inv; **three** ~**s** tre urrà; ~**s!** salute!; (goodbye) arrivederci!; (thanks) grazie! ● vt/i acclamare. ● ~ **up** vt tirare su [di morale] ● vi tirarsi su [di morale]; ~ **up!** su con la vita!. **~ful** adj allegro. **~fulness** n allegria f. **~ing** n acclamazione f

cheerio /tʃɪərɪ'əʊ/ int 🄸 arrivederci

'**cheerless** /tʃɪərlɪs/ adj triste, tetro

cheese /tʃiːz/ n formaggio m.
~**cake** n dolce m al formaggio

chef /ʃef/ n cuoco, -a mf, chef mf inv

chemical /ˈkemɪkl/ adj chimico ● n
prodotto m chimico

chemist /ˈkemɪst/ n (pharmacist) farmacista mf; (scientist) chimico, -a mf;
~'**s** [**shop**] farmacia f. ~**ry** n chimica f

cheque /tʃek/ n assegno m.
~-**book** n libretto m degli assegni.
~ **card** n carta f assegni

cherish /ˈtʃerɪʃ/ vt curare teneramente; (love) avere caro; nutrire (hope)

cherry /ˈtʃerɪ/ n ciliegia f; (tree) ciliegio m

chess /tʃes/ n scacchi mpl

chessboard n scacchiera f

chest /tʃest/ n petto m; (box) cassapanca f

chestnut /ˈtʃesnʌt/ n castagna f;
(tree) castagno m

chest of ˈdrawers n cassettone m

chew /tʃuː/ vt masticare. ~**inggum**
n gomma f da masticare

chic /ʃiːk/ adj chic inv

chick /tʃɪk/ n pulcino m; (🔲: girl) ragazza f

chicken /ˈtʃɪkɪn/ n pollo m ● adj attrib
(soup) di pollo ● **chicken out** vi 🔲
he ~**ed out** gli è venuta fifa. ~**pox**
n varicella f

chicory /ˈtʃɪkərɪ/ n cicoria f

chief /tʃiːf/ adj principale ● n capo m.
~**ly** adv principalmente

chilblain /ˈtʃɪlbleɪn/ n gelone m

child /tʃaɪld/ n (pl ~**ren**) bambino,
-a mf; (son/daughter) figlio, -a mf

child: ~**birth** n parto m. ~**hood** n
infanzia f. ~**ish** adj infantile. ~**less**
adj senza figli. ~**like** adj ingenuo

Chile /ˈtʃɪlɪ/ n Cile m. ~**an** adj & n cileno, -a mf

chill /tʃɪl/ n freddo m; (illness) infreddatura f ● vt raffreddare

chilli /ˈtʃɪlɪ/ n (pl -**es**) ~ [**pepper**]
peperoncino m

chilly /ˈtʃɪlɪ/ adj freddo

chime /tʃaɪm/ vi suonare

chimney /ˈtʃɪmnɪ/ n camino m.
~-**pot** n comignolo m. ~-**sweep** n
spazzacamino m

chimpanzee /tʃɪmpænˈziː/ n scimpanzé m inv

chin /tʃɪn/ n mento m

china /ˈtʃaɪnə/ n porcellana f

China n Cina f. ~**ese** adj & n cinese
mf; (language) cinese m; **the** ~**ese** pl i
cinesi

chink[1] /tʃɪŋk/ n (slit) fessura f

chink[2] n (noise) tintinnio m

chip /tʃɪp/ n (fragment) scheggia f; (in
china, paintwork) scheggiatura f;
(Comput) chip m inv; (in gambling) fiche f
inv; ~**s** pl Br (Culin) patatine fpl fritte;
Am (Culin) patatine fpl ● vt (pt/pp
chipped) (damage) scheggiare. ~ □ ~
in vi 🔲 intromettersi; (with money)
contribuire. ~**ped** adj (damaged)
scheggiato

chiropodist /kɪˈrɒpədɪst/ n podiatra mf inv. ~**y** n podiatria f

chirp /tʃɜːp/ vi cinguettare; (cricket:)
fare cri cri. ~**y** adj 🔲 pimpante

chisel /ˈtʃɪzl/ n scalpello m

chivalrous /ˈʃɪvlrəs/ adj cavalleresco. ~**ry** n cavalleria f

chives /tʃaɪvz/ npl erba f cipollina

chlorine /ˈklɔːriːn/ n cloro m

chock-a-block /tʃɒkəˈblɒk/,
chock-full /tʃɒkˈfʊl/ adj pieno zeppo

chocolate /ˈtʃɒkələt/ n cioccolato
m; (drink) cioccolata f; **a** ~ un cioccolatino

choice /tʃɔɪs/ n scelta f ● adj scelto

choir /ˈkwaɪə(r)/ n coro m. ~**boy** n
corista m

choke /tʃəʊk/ n (Auto) aria f ● vt/i
soffocare

cholera /ˈkɒlərə/ n colera m

cholesterol /kəˈlestərɒl/ n colesterolo m

choose /tʃuːz/ vt/i (pt **chose**, pp **chosen**) scegliere; **as you ~** come vuoi

chop /tʃɒp/ n (blow) colpo m (d'ascia); (Culin) costata f ● vt (pt/pp **chopped**) tagliare. **~ down** vt abbattere (tree). **~ off** vt spaccare

chop|per /ˈtʃɒpə(r)/ n accetta f; 🔲 elicottero m. **~py** adj increspato

chord /kɔːd/ n (Mus) corda f

chore /tʃɔː(r)/ n corvé f inv; **[household] ~s** faccende fpl domestiche

chorus /ˈkɔːrəs/ n coro m; (of song) ritornello m

chose, chosen /tʃəʊz/, /ˈtʃəʊzn/ ▷**CHOOSE**

Christ /kraɪst/ n Cristo m

christen /ˈkrɪsn/ vt battezzare. **~ing** n battesimo m

Christian /ˈkrɪstʃən/ adj & n cristiano, -a mf. **~ity** n cristianesimo m. **~ name** n nome m di battesimo

Christmas /ˈkrɪsməs/ n Natale m ● attrib di Natale. **'~ card** n biglietto m d'auguri di Natale. **~ 'Day** n il giorno di Natale. **~ 'Eve** n la vigilia di Natale. **~ present** n regalo m di Natale. **'~ pudding** dolce m natalizio a base di frutta candita e liquore. **'~ tree** n albero m di Natale

chrome /krəʊm/ n, **chromium** /ˈkrəʊmɪəm/ n cromo m

chromosome /ˈkrəʊməsəʊm/ n cromosoma m

chronic /ˈkrɒnɪk/ adj cronico

chronicle /ˈkrɒnɪkl/ n cronaca f

chronological /krɒnəˈlɒdʒɪkl/ adj cronologico. **~ly** adv (ordered) in ordine cronologico

chubby /ˈtʃʌbɪ/ adj (**-ier, -iest**) paffuto

chuck /tʃʌk/ vt 🔲 buttare. □ **~ out**

vt 🔲 buttare via (object); buttare fuori (person)

chuckle /ˈtʃʌkl/ vi ridacchiare

chug /tʃʌg/ vi (pt/pp **chugged**) **the train ~ged out of the station** il treno è uscito dalla stazione sbuffando

chum /tʃʌm/ n amico, -a mf. **~my** adj 🔲 **be ~my with** essere amico di

chunk /tʃʌŋk/ n grosso pezzo m

church /tʃɜːtʃ/ n chiesa f. **~yard** n cimitero m

churn /tʃɜːn/ vt churn out sfornare

chute /ʃuːt/ n scivolo m; (for rubbish) canale m di scarico

cider /ˈsaɪdə(r)/ n sidro m

cigar /sɪˈgɑː(r)/ n sigaro m

cigarette /sɪgəˈret/ n sigaretta f

cine-camera /ˈsɪnɪ-/ n cinepresa f

cinema /ˈsɪnɪmə/ n cinema m inv

cinnamon /ˈsɪnəmən/ n cannella f

circle /ˈsɜːkl/ n cerchio m; (Theat) galleria f; **in a ~** in cerchio ● vt girare intorno a; cerchiare (mistake) ● vi descrivere dei cerchi

circuit /ˈsɜːkɪt/ n circuito m; (lap) giro m; **~ board** n circuito m stampato. **~ous** adj **~ous route** percorso m lungo e indiretto

circular /ˈsɜːkjʊlə(r)/ adj circolare ● n circolare f

circulat|e /ˈsɜːkjʊleɪt/ vt far circolare ● vi circolare. **~ion** n circolazione f; (of newspaper) tiratura f

circumcis|e /ˈsɜːkəmsaɪz/ vt circoncidere. **~ion** n circoncisione f

circumference /səˈkʌmfərəns/ n conconferenza f

circumstance /ˈsɜːkəmstəns/ n circostanza f; **~s** pl (financial) condizioni fpl finanziarie

circus /ˈsɜːkəs/ n circo m

cistern /ˈsɪstən/ n (tank) cisterna f; (of WC) serbatoio m

cite /saɪt/ vt citare

citizen /ˈsɪtɪzn/ n cittadino, -a mf;

(of town) abitante mf. **~ship** n cittadinanza f

citrus /ˈsɪtrəs/ n **[fruit]** agrume m

city /ˈsɪtɪ/ n città f inv; **the C~** la City (di Londra)

> **City** La City è quella parte del centro di Londra dove un tempo si trovava l'antica città. Oggi è il centro finanziario della capitale britannica dove numerose banche e istituti finanziari hanno la propria sede centrale; molto spesso the City indica infatti le istituzioni finanziarie oltre che la zona della città.

civic /ˈsɪvɪk/ adj civico

civil /ˈsɪvɪl/ adj civile

civilian /sɪˈvɪljən/ adj civile; **in ~ clothes** in borghese ● n civile mf

civilization /sɪvɪlaɪˈzeɪʃn/ n civiltà f inv. **~e** vt civilizzare

civil: **~ 'servant** n impiegato, -a mf statale. **C~ 'Service** n pubblica amministrazione f

clad /klæd/ adj vestito (**in** di)

claim /kleɪm/ n richiesta f; (right) diritto m; (assertion) dichiarazione f; **lay ~ to sth** rivendicare qcsa ● vt richiedere; reclamare (lost property); rivendicare (ownership); **~ that** sostenere che. **~ant** n richiedente mf

clairvoyant /kleəˈvɔɪənt/ n chiaroveggente mf

clam /klæm/ n (Culin) vongola f ● **clam up** vi (pt/pp **clammed**) zittirsi

clamber /ˈklæmbə(r)/ vi arrampicarsi

clammy /ˈklæmɪ/ adj (-ier, -iest) appiccicaticcio

clamour /ˈklæmə(r)/ n (protest) rimostranza f ● vi **~ for** chiedere a gran voce

clamp /klæmp/ n morsa f ● vt am-

morsare; (Auto) mettere i ceppi bloccaruote a. ● **~ down** vi T essere duro; **~ down on** reprimere

clan /klæn/ n clan m inv

clang /klæŋ/ n suono m metallico. **~er** n T gaffe f inv

clap /klæp/ n colpo m; **give sb a ~** applaudire qcno; **~ of thunder** tuono m ● vt/i (pt/pp **clapped**) applaudire; **~ one's hands** applaudire. **~ping** n applausi mpl

clarification /klærɪfɪˈkeɪʃn/ n chiarimento m. **~fy** vt/i (pt/pp **-ied**) chiarire

clarinet /klærɪˈnet/ n clarinetto m

clarity /ˈklærətɪ/ n chiarezza f

clash /klæʃ/ n scontro m; (noise) fragore m ● vi scontrarsi; (colours:) stonare; (events:) coincidere

clasp /klɑːsp/ n chiusura f ● vt agganciare; (hold) stringere

class /klɑːs/ n classe f; (lesson) corso m ● vt classificare

classic /ˈklæsɪk/ adj classico ● n classico m; **~s** pl (Univ) lettere fpl classiche. **~al** adj classico

classification /klæsɪfɪˈkeɪʃn/ n classificazione f. **~fy** vt (pt/pp **-ied**) classificare

classroom n aula f

classy /ˈklɑːsɪ/ adj (-ier, -iest) T d'alta classe

clatter /ˈklætə(r)/ n fracasso m ● vi far fracasso

clause /klɔːz/ n clausola f; (Gram) proposizione f

claustrophobia /klɔːstrəˈfəʊbɪə/ n claustrofobia f

claw /klɔː/ n artiglio m; (of crab, lobster & (Techn)) tenaglia f ● vt (cat:) graffiare

clay /kleɪ/ n argilla f

clean /kliːn/ adj pulito, lindo ● adv completamente ● vt pulire (shoes, windows); **~ one's teeth** lavarsi i denti; **have a coat ~ed** portare un

cleaner | clock

cappotto in lavanderia. **clean up** vt pulire ● vi far pulizia

cleaner /'kli:nə(r)/ n uomo m/donna f delle pulizie; (substance) detersivo m, [dry] **~'s** lavanderia f, tintoria f

cleanliness /'klenlinis/ n pulizia f

cleanse /klenz/ vt pulire. **~r** n detergente m

cleansing cream /'klenz-/ n latte m detergente

clear /klɪə(r)/ adj chiaro; (conscience) pulito; (road) libero; (profit, advantage, majority) netto; (sky) sereno; (water) limpido; (glass) trasparente; **make sth ~** mettere qcsa in chiaro; **have I made myself ~?** mi sono fatto capire?; **five ~ days** cinque giorni buoni ● adv **stand ~ of** allontanarsi da; **keep ~ of** tenersi alla larga da ● vt sgombrare (room, street); sparecchiare (table); (acquit) scagionare; (authorize) autorizzare; scavalcare senza toccare (fence, wall); guadagnare (sum of money); passare (Customs); **~ one's throat** schiarirsi la gola ● vi (face, sky:) rasserenarsi; (fog:) dissiparsi **~ away** vt metter via, **~ off** vi [Ii] filar via **~ out** vt sgombrare ● vi [Ii] filar via, **~ up** vt (tidy) mettere a posto; chiarire (mystery) ● vi (weather:) schiarirsi

clearance /'klɪərəns/ n (space) spazio m libero; (authorization) autorizzazione f; (Customs) sdoganamento m. **~ sale** n liquidazione f

clear|ing /'klɪərɪŋ/ n radura f. **~ly** adv chiaramente. **~way** n (Auto) strada f con divieto di sosta

cleavage /'kli:vɪdʒ/ n (woman's) décolleté m inv

clench /klentʃ/ vt serrare

clergy /'klɜ:dʒɪ/ npl clero m. **~man** n ecclesiastico m

cleric /'klerɪk/ n ecclesiastico m. **~al** adj impiegatizio; (Relig) clericale

clerk /klɑ:k/, Am /klɜ:k/ n impiegato, -a mf; (Am: shop assistant) commesso, -a mf

clever /'klevə(r)/ adj intelligente; (skilful) abile

cliché /'kli:ʃeɪ/ n cliché m inv

click /klɪk/ vi scattare; (Comput) cliccare ● n (Comput) click m. **click on** vt (Comput) cliccare su

client /'klaɪənt/ n cliente mf

cliff /klɪf/ n scogliera f

climat|e /'klaɪmət/ n clima f. **~ic** adj climatico

climax /'klaɪmæks/ n punto m culminante

climb /klaɪm/ n salita f ● vt scalare (mountain); arrampicarsi su (ladder, tree) ● vi arrampicarsi; (rise) salire; (road:) salire. **~ down** vi scendere; (from ladder, tree) scendere; fig tornare sui propri passi

climber /'klaɪmə(r)/ n alpinista mf; (plant) rampicante m

clinch /klɪntʃ/ vt [II] concludere (deal) ● n (in boxing) clinch m inv

cling /klɪŋ/ vi (pt/pp clung) aggrapparsi; (stick) aderire. **~ film** n pellicola f trasparente

clinic /'klɪnɪk/ n ambulatorio m. **~al** adj clinico

clink /klɪŋk/ n tintinnio m; (II: prison) galera f ● vi tintinnare

clip¹ /klɪp/ n fermaglio m; (jewellery) spilla f ● vt (pt/pp clipped) attaccare

clip² n (extract) taglio m ● vt obliterare (ticket). **~board** n fermabloc m inv. **~pers** npl (for hair) rasoio m; (for hedge) tosasiepi m inv; (for nails) tronchesina f. **~ping** n (from newspaper) ritaglio m

cloak /kləʊk/ n mantello m. **~room** n guardaroba m inv; (toilet) bagno m

clock /klɒk/ n orologio m; (II: speedometer) tachimetro m. **~ in** vi attaccare. **~ out** vi staccare

clock: ~wise adj & adv in senso orario. **~work** n meccanismo m

clog /klɒg/ n zoccolo m ● vt (pt/pp **clogged**) ~ [up] intasare (drain); inceppare (mechanism) ● vi (drain): intasarsi

cloister /'klɔɪstə(r)/ n chiostro m

clone /kləʊn/ n clone m

close¹ /kləʊs/ adj vicino; (friend) intimo; (weather) afoso; **have a ~ shave** 𝕀 scamparla bella; **be ~ to sb** essere unito a qcno ● adv vicino; ~ **by** vicino; ~ **on five o'clock** quasi le cinque

close² /kləʊz/ n fine f ● vt chiudere ● vi chiudersi; (shop:) chiudere. □ ~ **down** vt chiudere ● vi (TV station:) interrompere la trasmissione; (factory:) chiudere

closely /'kləʊslɪ/ adv da vicino; (watch, listen) attentamente

closet /'klɒzɪt/ n Am armadio m

close-up /'kləʊs-/ n primo piano m

closure /'kləʊʒə(r)/ n chiusura f

clot /klɒt/ n grumo m; (𝕀: idiot) tonto, -a mf ● vi (pt/pp **clotted**) (blood:) coagularsi

cloth /klɒθ/ n (⊳ fabric) tessuto m; (duster etc) straccio m

clothe /kləʊð/ vt vestire

clothes /kləʊðz/ npl vestiti mpl, abiti mpl. ~**brush** n spazzola f per abiti. ~**line** n corda f stendibiancheria

clothing /'kləʊðɪŋ/ n abbigliamento m

cloud /klaʊd/ n nuvola f ● **cloud over** vi rannuvolarsi. ~**burst** n acquazzone m

cloudy /'klaʊdɪ/ adj (**-ier, -iest**) nuvoloso; (liquid) torbido

clout /klaʊt/ n 𝕀 colpo m; (influence) impatto m (**with** su) ● vt 𝕀 colpire

clove /kləʊv/ n chiodo m di garofano; ~ **of garlic** spicchio m d'aglio

clover /'kləʊvə(r)/ n trifoglio m

clown /klaʊn/ n pagliaccio m ● vi ~ [**about**] fare il pagliaccio

club /klʌb/ n club m inv; (weapon)

clava f; (Sport) mazza f; ~**s** pl (Cards) fiori mpl ● v (pt/pp **clubbed**) ● vt bastonare. □ ~ **together** vi unirsi

cluck /klʌk/ vi chiocciare

clue /kluː/ n indizio m; (in crossword) definizione f; **I haven't a ~** 𝕀 non ne ho idea

clump /klʌmp/ n gruppo m

clumsiness /'klʌmzɪnɪs/ n goffaggine f

clumsy /'klʌmzɪ/ adj (**-ier, -iest**) maldestro; (tool) scomodo; (remark) senza tatto

clung /klʌŋ/ ▷ **CLING**

cluster /'klʌstə(r)/ n gruppo m ● vi raggrupparsi (**round** intorno a)

clutch /klʌtʃ/ n stretta f; (Auto) frizione f; **be in sb's ~es** essere in balia di qcno ● vt stringere; (grab) afferrare ● vi ~ **at** afferrare

clutter /'klʌtə(r)/ n caos m ● vt ~ [up] ingombrare

coach /kəʊtʃ/ n pullman m inv; (Rail) vagone m; (horse-drawn) carrozza f; (Sport) allenatore, -trice mf ● vt fare esercitare; (Sport) allenare

coal /kəʊl/ n carbone m

coalition /kəʊə'lɪʃn/ n coalizione f

coarse /kɔːs/ adj grossolano; (joke) spinto

coast /kəʊst/ n costa f ● vi (free-wheel) scendere a ruota libera ~**al** adj costiero. ~**er** n (mat) sottobicchiere m inv

coast: ~**guard** n guardia f costiera. ~**line** n litorale m

coat /kəʊt/ n cappotto m; (of animal) manto m; (of paint) mano f; ~ **of arms** stemma f ● vt coprire; (with paint) ricoprire. ~**-hanger** n gruccia f. ~**-hook** n gancio m [appendiabiti]

coating /'kəʊtɪŋ/ n rivestimento m; (of paint) stato m

coax /kəʊks/ vt convincere con le moine

cobweb /'kɒb-/ n ragnatela f

cocaine | colour

cocaine /kəˈkeɪn/ n cocaina f

cock /kɒk/ n gallo m; (any male bird) maschio m • vt sollevare il grilletto di (gun); ~ **its ears** (animal:) drizzare le orecchie

cockerel /ˈkɒkərəl/ n galletto m

cock-'eyed adj ⓘ storto; (absurd) assurdo

cockney /ˈkɒknɪ/ n (dialect) dialetto m londinese; (person) abitante mf dell'est di Londra

cock: ~**pit** n (Aeron) cabina f. ~**roach** /-rəʊtʃ/ n scarafaggio m. ~**tail** n cocktail m inv. ~**-up** n ⓧ **make a** ~**-up** fare un casino (of con)

cocky /ˈkɒkɪ/ adj (-ier, -iest) ⓘ presuntuoso

cocoa /ˈkəʊkəʊ/ n cacao m

coconut /ˈkəʊkənʌt/ n noce f di cocco

cocoon /kəˈkuːn/ n bozzolo m

cod /kɒd/ n inv merluzzo m

COD abbr (cash on delivery) pagamento m alla consegna

code /kəʊd/ n codice m. ~**d** adj codificato

coeducational /kəʊ-/ adj misto

coerc|e /kəʊˈɜːs/ vt costringere. ~**ion** n coercizione f

coffee /ˈkɒfɪ/ n caffè m inv

coffeepot n caffettiera f

coffin /ˈkɒfɪn/ n bara f

cog /kɒɡ/ n (Techn) dente m (di ruota)

coherent /kəʊˈhɪərənt/ adj coerente; (when speaking) logico

coil /kɔɪl/ n rotolo m; (Electr) bobina f; ~**s** pl spire fpl • vt ~ [**up**] avvolgere

coin /kɔɪn/ n moneta f • vt coniare (word)

coincide /kəʊɪnˈsaɪd/ vi coincidere

coinciden|ce /kəʊˈɪnsɪdəns/ n coincidenza f. ~**tal** adj casuale. ~**tally** adv casualmente

coke /kəʊk/ n [carbone m] coke m

Coke® n Coca[-cola]® f

cold /kəʊld/ adj freddo; **I'm** ~ ho freddo • n freddo m; (Med) raffreddore m

cold 'blooded adj spietato

coleslaw /ˈkəʊlslɔː/ n insalata f di cavolo crudo, cipolle e carote in maionese

collaborat|e /kəˈlæbəreɪt/ vi collaborare; ~**e on sth** collaborare in qcsa. ~**ion** n collaborazione f; (with enemy) collaborazionismo m. ~**or** n collaboratore, -trice mf; (with enemy) collaborazionista f

collaps|e /kəˈlæps/ n crollo m • vi (person:) svenire; (roof, building:) crollare. ~**ible** adj pieghevole

collar /ˈkɒlə(r)/ n colletto m; (for animal) collare m. ~**-bone** n clavicola f

colleague /ˈkɒliːɡ/ n collega mf

collect /kəˈlekt/ vt andare a prendere (person); ritirare (parcel, tickets); riscuotere (taxes); raccogliere (rubbish), (as hobby) collezionare • vi riunirsi • adv **call** ~ Am telefonare a carico del destinatario. ~**ed** adj controllato

collection /kəˈlekʃn/ n collezione f; (in church) questua f; (of rubbish) raccolta f; (of post) levata f

collector /kəˈlektə(r)/ n (of stamps etc) collezionista mf

college /ˈkɒlɪdʒ/ n istituto m parauniversitario; **C~ of ...** Scuola f di ...

collide /kəˈlaɪd/ vi scontrarsi

collision /kəˈlɪʒn/ n scontro m

colloquial /kəˈləʊkwɪəl/ adj colloquiale. ~**ism** n espressione f colloquiale

colon /ˈkəʊlən/ n due punti mpl; (Anat) colon m inv

colonel /ˈkɜːnl/ n colonnello m

colonial /kəˈləʊnɪəl/ adj coloniale

coloniz|e /ˈkɒlənaɪz/ vt colonizzare. ~**y** n colonia f

colossal /kəˈlɒsl/ adj colossale

colour /ˈkʌlə(r)/ n colore m; (complexion) colorito m; **~s** pl (flag) bandiera fsg; **off ~** 🔲 giù di tono ● vt colorare; **~ [in]** colorare ● vi (blush) arrossire

colour: **~-blind** adj daltonico. **~ed** adj (coloured); (person) di colore ● n (person) persona f di colore. **~ful** adj pieno di colore. **~less** adj incolore

column /ˈkɒləm/ n colonna f. **~ist** n giornalista mf che cura una rubrica

coma /ˈkəʊmə/ n coma m inv

comb /kəʊm/ n pettine m; (for wearing) pettinino m ● vt pettinare; (fig: search) setacciare; **~ one's hair** pettinarsi i capelli

combat /ˈkɒmbæt/ n combattimento m ● vt (pt/pp combated) combattere

combination /kɒmbɪˈneɪʃn/ n combinazione f

combine¹ /kəmˈbaɪn/ vt unire; **~ a job with being a mother** conciliare il lavoro con il ruolo di madre ● vi (chemical elements:) combinarsi

combine² /ˈkɒmbaɪn/ n (Comm) associazione f. **~ harvester** n mietitrebbia f

combustion /kəmˈbʌstʃn/ n combustione f

come /kʌm/ vi (pt came, pp come) venire; **where do you ~ from?** da dove vieni?; **~ to** (reach) arrivare a; **that ~s to £10** fanno 10 sterline; **~ into money** ricevere dei soldi; **~ true/open** verificarsi/aprirsi; **~ first** arrivare primo; fig venire prima di tutto; **~ in two sizes** esistere in due misure; **the years to ~** gli anni a venire; **how ~?** 🔲 come mai? **come about** vi succedere. **~ across** vi ~ across as being 🔲 dare l'impressione di essere ● vt (find) imbattersi in. **~ along** vi venire; (job, opportunity:) presentarsi; (progress) andare bene. **~ apart** vi smontarsi; (break) rompersi. **~ away** vi venir via; (button, fastener:) staccarsi. **~ back** vi ritornare. **~ by**

vi passare ● vt (obtain) avere. **~ down** vi scendere; **~ down to** (reach) arrivare a. **come in** vi entrare; (in race) arrivare; (tide:) salire. **~ in for** vt **~ in for criticism** essere criticato. **~ off** vi staccarsi; (take place) esserci; (succeed) riuscire. **~ on** vi (make progress) migliorare; **~ on!** (hurry) dai!; (indicating disbelief) ma va là!. **~ out** vi venir fuori; (book, sun:) uscire; (stain:) andar via. **~ over** vi venire. **~ round** vi venire; (after fainting) riaversi; (change one's mind) farsi convincere. **~ to** vi (after fainting) riaversi. **~ up** vi salire; (sun:) sorgere; (plant:) crescere; **something came up** (I was prevented) ho avuto un imprevisto. **~ up with** vt tirar fuori

'come-back n ritorno m

comedian /kəˈmiːdɪən/ n comico m

comedy /ˈkɒmədɪ/ n commedia f

comet /ˈkɒmɪt/ n cometa f

comfort /ˈkʌmfət/ n benessere m; (consolation) conforto m ● vt confortare

comfortabl|e /ˈkʌmfətəbl/ adj comodo; **be ~e** (person:) stare comodo; (fig: in situation) essere a proprio agio; (financially) star bene. **~y** adv comodamente

'comfort station n Am bagno m pubblico

comic /ˈkɒmɪk/ adj comico ● n comico, -a mf; (periodical) fumetto m. **~al** adj comico. **~ strip** n striscia f di fumetti

coming /ˈkʌmɪŋ/ n venuta f; **~s and goings** viavai m

comma /ˈkɒmə/ n virgola f

command /kəˈmɑːnd/ n comando m; (order) ordine m; (mastery) padronanza f ● vt ordinare; comandare (army)

commandeer /kɒmənˈdɪə(r)/ vt requisire

command|er /kəˈmɑːndə(r)/ n comandante m. **~ing** adj (view) imponente; (lead) dominante. **~ing** officer *n* comandante m. **~ment** *n* comandamento m

commemorat|e /kə'meməreɪt/ *vt* commemorare. **~ion** *n* commemorazione *f*. **~ive** *adj* commemorativo

commence /kə'mens/ *vt/i* cominciare. **~ment** *n* inizio m

commend /kə'mend/ *vt* complimentarsi con (**on** per); (*recommend*) raccomandare (**to** a). **~able** *adj* lodevole

comment /'kɒment/ *n* commento m ● *vi* fare commenti (**on** su)

commentary /'kɒməntrɪ/ *n* commento m; [**running**] **~** (**on** radio, (TV)) cronaca *f* diretta

commentat|e /'kɒmənteɪt/ *vt* **~e on** (TV, Radio) fare la cronaca di. **~or** *n* cronista *mf*

commerce /'kɒmɜ:s/ *n* commercio m

commercial /kə'mɜ:ʃl/ *adj* commerciale ● *n* (TV) pubblicità *f inv*. **~ize** *vt* commercializzare

commiserate /kə'mɪzəreɪt/ *vi* esprimere il proprio rincrescimento (**with** a)

commission /kə'mɪʃn/ *n* commissione *f*; **receive one's ~** (Mil) essere promosso ufficiale; **out of ~** fuori uso ● *vt* commissionare

commissionaire /kəmɪʃə'neə(r)/ *n* portiere m

commit /kə'mɪt/ *vt* (*pt/pp* committed) commettere; (*to prison, hospital*) affidare (**to** a); impegnare (funds); **~ oneself** impegnarsi. **~ment** *n* impegno m; (*involvement*) compromissione *f*. **~ted** *adj* impegnato

committee /kə'mɪtɪ/ *n* comitato m

commodity /kə'mɒdətɪ/ *n* prodotto m

common /'kɒmən/ *adj* comune; (*vulgar*) volgare ● *n* prato m pubblico; **have in ~** avere in comune; **House of C~s** Camera *f* dei Comuni. **~er** *n*

persona f non nobile

common: **~ law** *n* diritto m consuetudinario. **~ly** *adv* comunemente. **C~ 'Market** *n* Mercato m Comune. **~place** *adj* banale. **~room** *n* sala *f* dei professori/degli studenti. **~ 'sense** *n* buon senso m

>
> **Commonwealth** Il *Commonwealth*, fondato nel 1931, è l'insieme delle ex colonie e possedimenti dell'ex impero britannico. I paesi membri, oggi stati indipendenti, sono legati da legami economici e culturali. I vari capi di stato si incontrano con scadenza biennale, e progetti educativi internazionali vengono promossi regolarmente. Ogni quattro anni, inoltre, si tengono i *Commonwealth Games*, manifestazioni sportive cui partecipano atleti dei vari paesi.

commotion /kə'məʊʃn/ *n* confusione *f*

communicate /kə'mju:nɪkeɪt/ *vt/i* comunicare

communication /kəmju:nɪ'keɪʃn/ *n* comunicazione *f*; (*of disease*) trasmissione *f*; **be in ~ with sb** essere in contatto con qcno; **~s** *pl* (*technology*) telecomunicazioni *fpl*. **~ cord** *n* fermata *f* d'emergenza

communicative /kə'mju:nɪkətɪv/ *adj* comunicativo

Communion /kə'mju:nɪən/ *n* [**Holy**] **~** comunione *f*

Communis|m /'kɒmjʊnɪzm/ *n* comunismo m. **~t** *adj* & *n* comunista *mf*

community /kə'mju:nətɪ/ *n* comunità *f*. **~ centre** *n* centro m sociale

commute /kə'mju:t/ *vi* fare il pendolare ● *vt* (Jur) commutare. **~r** *n* pendolare *mf*

compact[1] /kəm'pækt/ *adj* compatto

compact[2] /'kɒmpækt/ *n* portacipria f inv. • ~ **disc** n compact disc m inv

companion /kəm'pænjən/ n compagno, -a mf. ~ **ship** n compagnia f

company /'kʌmpəni/ n compagnia f; (guests) ospiti mpl. ~ **car** n macchina f della ditta

comparable /'kɒmpərəbl/ adj paragonabile

comparative /kəm'pærətɪv/ adj comparativo; (relative) relativo • n (Gram) comparativo m. ~ **ly** adv relativamente

compare /kəm'peə(r)/ vt paragonare (**with/to** a) • vi essere paragonato

comparison /kəm'pærɪsn/ n paragone m

compartment /kəm'pɑ:tmənt/ n compartimento m; (Rail) scompartimento m

compass /'kʌmpəs/ n bussola f. ~**es** npl, **pair of** ~**es** compasso msg

compassion /kəm'pæʃn/ n compassione f. ~**ate** adj compassionevole

compatible /kəm'pætəbl/ adj compatibile

compel /kəm'pel/ vt (pt/pp **compelled**) costringere. ~**ling** (reason) inconfutabile

compensat|e /'kɒmpənseɪt/ vt risarcire • vi ~ **for** fig compensare di. ~**ion** n risarcimento m; (fig: comfort) consolazione f

compère /'kɒmpeə(r)/ n presentatore, -trice mf

compete /kəm'pi:t/ vi competere; (take part) gareggiare

competen|ce /'kɒmpɪtəns/ n competenza f. ~**t** adj competente

competition /kɒmpə'tɪʃn/ n concorrenza f; (contest) gara f

competitive /kəm'petɪtɪv/ adj competitivo; ~ **prices** prezzi mpl concorrenziali

competitor /kəm'petɪtə(r)/ n

concorrente mf

complacen|cy /kəm'pleɪsənsɪ/ n compiacimento m. ~**t** adj compiaciuto

complain /kəm'pleɪn/ vi lamentarsi (**about** di); (formally) reclamare; ~ **of** (Med) accusare. ~**t** n lamentela f; (formal) reclamo m; (Med) disturbo m

complement¹ /'kɒmplɪmənt/ n complemento m

complement² /'kɒmplɪment/ vt complementare; ~ **each other** complementarsi a vicenda. ~**ary** adj complementare

complete /kəm'pli:t/ adj completo; (utter) finito • vt completare; compilare (form). ~**ly** adv completamente

completion /kəm'pli:ʃn/ n fine f

complex /'kɒmpleks/ adj complesso • n complesso m

complexion /kəm'plekʃn/ n carnagione f

complexity /kəm'pleksətɪ/ n complessità f inv

complicat|e /'kɒmplɪkeɪt/ vt complicare. ~**ed** adj complicato. ~**ion** n complicazione f

compliment /'kɒmplɪmənt/ n complimento m; ~**s** pl omaggi mpl • vt complimentare. ~**ary** adj complimentoso; (given free) in omaggio

comply /kəm'plaɪ/ vi (pt/pp **-ied**) ~ **with** conformarsi a

component /kəm'pəʊnənt/ adj & n ~ [**part**] componente m

compose /kəm'pəʊz/ vt comporre; ~ **oneself** ricomporsi; **be** ~**d of** essere composto da. ~**d** adj (calm) composto. ~**r** n compositore, -trice mf

composition /kɒmpə'zɪʃn/ n composizione f; (essay) tema m

compost /'kɒmpɒst/ n composta f

composure /kəm'pəʊzə(r)/ n calma f

compound /'kɒmpaʊnd/ adj composto. ~ **fracture** n frattura f espostd. **~ 'interest** n interesse m com posto •n (Chem) composto •n (Gram) parola f composta; (enclosure) recinto m

comprehen|d /komprɪ'hend/ vt comprendere. **~sible** adj comprensibile. **~sion** n comprensione f

comprehensive /komprɪ'hensɪv/ adj & n comprensivo; **~ [school]** scuola f media in cui gli allievi hanno capacità d'apprendimento diverse. **~ insurance** n (Auto) polizza f casco

compress[1] /'kompres/ n compressa f

compress[2] /kəm'pres/ vt comprimere; **~ed air** aria f compressa

comprise /kəm'praɪz/ vt comprendere; (form) costituire

compromise /'komprəmaɪz/ n compromesso m •vt compromettere •vi fare un compromesso

compuls|ion /kəm'pʌlʃn/ n desiderio m irresistibile. **~ive** adj (Psych) patologico; **~ive eating** mania f nervosa di mangiare. **~ory** adj obbligatorio

compute /kəm'pjuːt/ vt calcolare

comput|er /kəm'pjuːtə(r)/ n computer m inv. **~erize** vt computerizzare. **~ing** n informatica f

comrade /'komreɪd/ n camerata m; (Pol) compagno, -a mf. **~ship** n cameratismo m

con[1] /kon/ ▷ **PRO**

con[2] n 1 fregatura f •vt (pt/pp conned) 1 fregare

concave /'koŋkeɪv/ adj concavo

conceal /kən'siːl/ vt nascondere

concede /kən'siːd/ vt (admit) ammettere; (give up) rinunciare a; lasciar fare (goal)

conceit /kən'siːt/ n presunzione f. **~ed** adj presuntuoso

conceivable /kən'siːvəbl/ adj concepibile

conceive /kən'siːv/ vt (Biol) concepire •vi aver figli. □ **~ of** vt fig concepire

concentrat|e /'konsəntreɪt/ vt concentrare •vi concentrarsi. **~ion** n concentrazione f. **~ion camp** n campo m di concentramento

concept /'konsept/ n concetto m. **~ion** n concezione f; (idea) idea f

concern /kən'sɜːn/ n preoccupazione f; (Comm) attività f inv •vt (be about, affect) riguardare; (worry) preoccupare; **be ~ed about** essere preoccupato per; **~ oneself with** preoccuparsi di; **as far as I am ~ed** per quanto mi riguarda. **~ing** prep riguardo a

concert /'konsət/ n concerto m. **~ed** adj collettivo

concertina /konsə'tiːnə/ n piccola fisarmonica f

concerto /kən'tʃeətəʊ/ n concerto m

concession /kən'seʃn/ n concessione f, (reduction) sconto m. **~ary** adj (reduced) scontato

concise /kən'saɪs/ adj conciso

conclu|de /kən'kluːd/ vt concludere •vi concludersi. **~ding** adj finale

conclusion /kən'kluːʒn/ n conclusione f; **in ~** per concludere

conclusive /kən'kluːsɪv/ adj definitivo. **~ly** adv in modo definitivo

concoct /kən'kokt/ vt confezionare; fig inventare. **~ion** n mistura f; (drink) intruglio m

concrete /'koŋkriːt/ adj concreto •n calcestruzzo m

concussion /kən'kʌʃn/ n commozione f cerebrale

condemn /kən'dem/ vt condannare; dichiarare inagibile (building). **~ation** n condanna f

condensation /konden'seɪʃn/ n condensazione f

condense /kən'dens/ vt condensare; (Phys) condensare •vi condensarsi. **~d milk** n latte m condensato

condescend /kɒndɪ'send/ vi degnarsi. ~**ing** adj condiscendente

condition /kən'dɪʃn/ n condizione f; **on** ~ **that** a condizione che ●vt (Psych) condizionare. ~**al** adj (acceptance) condizionato; (Gram) condizionale ●n (Gram) condizionale m. ~**er** n balsamo m; (for fabrics) ammorbidente m

condolences /kən'dəʊlənsɪz/ npl condoglianze fpl

condom /'kɒndəm/ n preservativo m

condo[minium] /'kɒndə ('mɪnɪəm)/ n Am condominio m

condone /kən'dəʊn/ vt passare sopra a

conduct¹ /'kɒndʌkt/ n condotta f

conduct² /kən'dʌkt/ vt condurre; dirigere (orchestra). ~**or** n direttore m d'orchestra; (of bus) bigliettaio m; (Phys) conduttore m. ~**ress** n bigliettaia f

cone /kəʊn/ n cono m; (Bot) pigna f; (Auto) birillo m ● **cone off** vt **be** ~**d off** (Auto) essere chiuso da birilli

confederation /kənfedə'reɪʃn/ n confederazione f

conference /'kɒnfərəns/ n conferenza f

confess /kən'fes/ vt confessare ● vi confessare; (Relig) confessarsi. ~**ion** n confessione f. ~**ional** n confessionale m. ~**or** n confessore m

confetti /kən'fetɪ/ n coriandoli mpl

confide /kən'faɪd/ vt confidare. □ ~ **in** ~ **in sb** fidarsi di qcno

confidence /'kɒnfɪdəns/ n (trust) fiducia f; (self-assurance) sicurezza f di sé; (secret) confidenza f; **in** ~ in confidenza. ~ **trick** n truffa f

confident /'kɒnfɪdənt/ adj fiducioso; (self-assured) sicuro di sé. ~**ly** adv con aria fiduciosa

confidential /kɒnfɪ'denʃl/ adj confidenziale

configur|ation /kənfɪgə'reɪʃn/ n configurazione f. ~**e** vt configurare

confine /kən'faɪn/ vt rinchiudere; (limit) limitare; **be** ~**d to bed** essere confinato a letto. ~**d** adj (space) limitato. ~**ment** n detenzione f; (Med) parto m

confirm /kən'fɜːm/ vt confermare; (Relig) cresimare. ~**ation** n conferma f; (Relig) cresima f. ~**ed** adj incallito; ~**ed bachelor** scapolo m impenitente

confiscat|e /'kɒnfɪskeɪt/ vt confiscare. ~**ion** n confisca f

conflict¹ /'kɒnflɪkt/ n conflitto m

conflict² /kən'flɪkt/ vi essere in contraddizione. ~**ing** adj contraddittorio

conform /kən'fɔːm/ vi (person:) conformarsi; (thing:) essere conforme (**to** a). ~**ist** n conformista mf

confounded /kən'faʊndɪd/ adj 🔳 maledetto

confront /kən'frʌnt/ vt affrontare; **the problems** ~**ing us** i problemi che dobbiamo affrontare. ~**ation** n confronto m

confus|e /kən'fjuːz/ vt confondere. ~**ing** adj che confonde. ~**ion** n confusione f

congeal /kən'dʒiːl/ vi (blood:) coagularsi

congest|ed /kən'dʒestɪd/ adj congestionato. ~**ion** n congestione f

congratulat|e /kən'grætjʊleɪt/ vt congratularsi con (**on** per). ~**ions** npl radunarsi f

congregat|e /'kɒŋgrɪgeɪt/ vi radunarsi. ~**ion** n (Relig) assemblea f

congress /'kɒŋgres/ n congresso m. ~**man** n Am (Pol) membro m del congresso

conifer /'kɒnɪfə(r)/ n conifera f

conjugat|e /'kɒndʒʊgeɪt/ vt coniugare. ~**ion** n coniugazione f

conjunction /kən'dʒʌŋkʃn/ n congiunzione f; **in** ~ **with** insieme a

conjur|e /'kʌndʒə(r)/ vi ~**ing**

tricks npl giochi mpl di prestigio. **~or** n prestigiatore, -trice mf. □ **~ up** vt evocare (image); tirar fuori dal nulla (meal)

conk /kɒŋk/ vi **~ out** 🔢 (machine:) guastarsi; (person:) crollare

'con-man n 🔢 truffatore m

connect /kə'nekt/ vt collegare; **be ~ed with** avere legami con; (be related to) essere imparentato con; **be well ~ed** aver conoscenze influenti ● vi essere collegato (**with** a); (train:) fare coincidenza

connection /tə'nekʃn/ n (between ideas) nesso m; (in travel) coincidenza f; (Electr) collegamento m; **in ~ with** con riferimento a. **~s** pl (people) conoscenze fpl

connoisseur /kɒnə'sɜː(r)/ n intenditore, -trice mf

conquer /'kɒŋkə(r)/ vt conquistare; fig superare (fear). **~or** n conquistatore m

conquest /'kɒŋkwest/ n conquista f

conscience /'kɒnʃəns/ n coscienza f

conscientious /kɒnʃɪ'enʃəs/ adj coscienzioso. **~ objector** n obiettore m di coscienza

conscious /'kɒnʃəs/ adj conscio; (decision) meditato; **[fully] ~** cosciente; **be/become ~ of sth** rendersi conto di qcsa. **~ly** adv consapevolmente. **~ness** n consapevolezza f; (Med) conoscenza f

conscript¹ /'kɒnskrɪpt/ n coscritto m

conscript² /kən'skrɪpt/ vt (Mil) chiamare alle armi. **~ion** n coscrizione f, leva f

consecrate /'kɒnsɪkreɪt/ vt consacrare. **~ion** n consacrazione f

consecutive /kən'sekjʊtɪv/ adj consecutivo

consensus /kən'sensəs/ n consenso m

consent /kən'sent/ n consenso m ● vi acconsentire

consequen|ce /'kɒnsɪkwəns/ n conseguenza f; (importance) importanza f. **~t** adj conseguente. **~tly** adv di conseguenza

conservation /kɒnsə'veɪʃn/ n conservazione f. **~ist** n fautore, -trice mf della tutela ambientale

conservative /kən'sɜːvətɪv/ adj conservativo; (estimate) ottimistico. **C~** (Pol) adj conservatore ● n conservatore, -trice mf

conservatory /kən'sɜːvətrɪ/ n spazio m chiuso da vetrata adiacente alla casa

conserve /kən'sɜːv/ vt conservare

consider /kən'sɪdə(r)/ vt considerare; **~ doing sth** considerare la possibilità di fare qcsa. **~able** adj considerevole. **~ably** adv considerevolmente

considerate /kən'sɪdərət/ adj pieno di riguardo. **~ately** adv con riguardo. **~ation** n considerazione f; (thoughtfulness) attenzione f; (respect) riguardo m; (payment) compenso m; **take sth into ~ation** prendere in considerazione. **~ing** prep considerando

consign /kən'saɪn/ vt affidare. **~ment** n consegna f

consist /kən'sɪst/ vi **~ of** consistere di

consisten|cy /kən'sɪstənsɪ/ n coerenza f; (density) consistenza f. **~t** adj coerente; (loyalty) costante. **~tly** adv coerentemente; (late, loyal) costantemente

consolation /kɒnsə'leɪʃn/ n consolazione f. **~ prize** n premio m di consolazione

console /kən'saɪl/ vt consolare

consolidate /kən'sɒlɪdeɪt/ vt consolidare

consonant /'kɒnsənənt/ n consonante f

c

conspicuous /kən'spɪkjʊəs/ adj facilmente distinguibile

conspiracy /kən'spɪrəsɪ/ n cospirazione f

conspire /kən'spaɪə(r)/ vi cospirare

constable /'kʌnstəbl/ n agente m [di polizia]

constant /'kɒnstənt/ adj costante. **~ly** adv costantemente

constellation /kɒnstə'leɪʃn/ n costellazione f

consternation /kɒnstə'neɪʃn/ n costernazione f

constipat|ed /'kɒnstɪpeɪtɪd/ adj stitico. **~ion** n stitichezza f

constituency /kən'stɪtjʊənsɪ/ n area f elettorale di un deputato nel Regno Unito

constituent /kən'stɪtjʊənt/ n costituente m; (Pol) elettore, -trice mf

constitut|e /'kɒnstɪtjuːt/ vt costituire. **~ion** n costituzione f. **~ional** adj costituzionale

construct /kən'strʌkt/ vt costruire. **~ion** n costruzione f; **under ~ion** in costruzione. **~ive** adj costruttivo

consul /'kɒnsl/ n console m. **~ar** adj consolare. **~ate** n consolato m

consult /kən'sʌlt/ vt consultare. **~ant** n consulente mf; (Med) specialista mf. **~ation** n consultazione f; (Med) consulto m

consume /kən'sjuːm/ vt consumare. **~r** n consumatore, -trice mf. **~r goods** npl beni mpl di consumo. **~r organization** n organizzazione f per la tutela dei consumatori

consummate /'kɒnsəmeɪt/ vt consumare

consumption /kən'sʌmpʃn/ n consumo m

contact /'kɒntækt/ n contatto m; (person) conoscenza f ● vt mettersi in contatto con. **~ 'lenses** npl lenti fpl a contatto

contagious /kən'teɪdʒəs/ adj contagioso

contain /kən'teɪn/ vt contenere; **~ oneself** controllarsi. **~er** n recipiente m; (for transport) container m inv

contaminat|e /kən'tæmɪneɪt/ vt contaminare. **~ion** n contaminazione f

contemplat|e /'kɒntəmpleɪt/ vt contemplare; (consider) considerare; **~e doing sth** considerare di fare qcsa. **~ion** n contemplazione f

contemporary /kən'tempərərɪ/ adj & n contemporaneo, -a mf

contempt /kən'tempt/ n disprezzo m; **beneath ~** più che vergognoso; **~ of court** oltraggio m alla Corte. **~ible** adj spregevole. **~uous** adj sprezzante

contend /kən'tend/ vi **~ with** occuparsi di ● vt (assert) sostenere. **~er** n concorrente mf

content¹ /'kɒntent/ n contenuto m

content² /kən'tent/ adj soddisfatto ● vt **~ oneself** accontentarsi (with di). **~ed** adj soddisfatto. **~edly** adv con aria soddisfatta

contentment /kən'tentmənt/ n soddisfazione f

contents /'kɒntents/ npl contenuto m

contest¹ /'kɒntest/ n gara f

contest² /kən'test/ vt contestare (statement); impugnare (will); (Pol) (candidates:) contendersi; (candidate:) aspirare a. **~ant** n concorrente mf

context /'kɒntekst/ n contesto m

continent /'kɒntɪnənt/ n continente m; **the C~** l'Europa f continentale

continental /kɒntɪ'nentl/ adj continentale. **~ breakfast** n prima colazione f a base di pane, marmellata, croissant, ecc. **~ quilt** n piumone m

contingency /kən'tɪndʒənsɪ/ n eventualità f inv

continual /kən'tɪnjʊəl/ adj

continuo

continuation /kəntɪnjʊˈeɪʃn/ n
continuazione f

continue /kənˈtɪnjuː/ vt continuare;
~ doing or **to do sth** continuare a
fare qcsa; **to be ~d** continua ● vi
continuare. **~d** adj continuo

continuity /kɒntɪˈnjuːətɪ/ n continuità f

continuous /kənˈtɪnjʊəs/ adj
continuo

contort /kənˈtɔːt/ vt contorcere.
~ion n contorsione f. **~ionist**
n contorsionista mf

contour /ˈkɒntʊə(r)/ n contorno m;
(line) curva f di livello

contraband /ˈkɒntrəbænd/ n contrabbando m

contracep|tion /kɒntrəˈsepʃn/ n
contraccezione f. **~tive** n contraccettivo m

contract¹ /ˈkɒntrækt/ n contratto m

contract² /kənˈtrækt/ vt (get smaller)
contrarsi ● vt contrarre (illness).
~ion n contrazione f. **~or** n imprenditore, -trice mf

contradict /kɒntrəˈdɪkt/ vt
contraddire. **~ion** n contraddizione f.
~ory adj contraddittorio

contraption /kənˈtræpʃn/ n 🔲
aggeggio m

contrary¹ /ˈkɒntrərɪ/ adj contrario
● adv **~ to** contrariamente a ● n
contrario m; **on the ~** al contrario

contrary² /kənˈtreərɪ/ adj disobbediente

contrast¹ /ˈkɒntrɑːst/ n contrasto m

contrast² /kənˈtrɑːst/ vt confrontare ● vi contrastare. **~ing** adj contrastante

contraven|e /kɒntrəˈviːn/ vt trasgredire. **~tion** n trasgressione f

contribut|e /kənˈtrɪbjuːt/ vt/i contribuire. **~ion** n contribuzione f;
(what is contributed) contributo m. **~or**

n contributore, -trice mf

contrive /kənˈtraɪv/ vt escogitare;
~ to do sth riuscire a fare qcsa

control /kənˈtrəʊl/ n controllo m;
~s pl (of car, plane) comandi mpl; **get
out of ~** sfuggire al controllo ● vt
(pt/pp **controlled**) controllare; **~
oneself** controllarsi

controvers|ial /kɒntrəˈvɜːʃl/ adj
controverso. **~y** n controversia f

convalesce /kɒnvəˈles/ vi essere in
convalescenza

convector /kənˈvektə(r)/ n **~
[heater]** convettore m

convene /kənˈviːn/ vt convocare
● vi riunirsi

convenience /kənˈviːnɪəns/ n
convenienza f; [public] **~** gabinetti
mpl pubblici; **with all modern ~s**
con tutti i comfort

convenient /kənˈviːnɪənt/ adj comodo; **be ~ for sb** andar bene per
qcno; **if it is ~ [for you]** se ti va
bene. **~ly** adv comodamente, **~ly
located** in una posizione comoda

convent /ˈkɒnvənt/ n convento m

convention /kənˈvenʃn/ n convenzione f; (assembly) convegno m. **~al**
adj convenzionale

converge /kənˈvɜːdʒ/ vi convergere

conversation /kɒnvəˈseɪʃn/ n
conversazione f. **~al** adj di conversazione. **~alist** n conversatore,
-trice mf

converse¹ /kənˈvɜːs/ vi conversare

converse² /ˈkɒnvɜːs/ n inverso m.
~ly adv viceversa

conversion /kənˈvɜːʃn/ n conversione f

convert¹ /ˈkɒnvɜːt/ n convertito,
-a mf

convert² /kənˈvɜːt/ vt convertire
(into); sconsacrare (church).
~ible adj convertibile ● n (Auto) macchina f decappottabile

convex /ˈkɒnveks/ adj convesso

convey /kən'veɪ/ vt portare; trasmettere (idea, message). **∼or belt** n nastro m trasportatore

convict¹ /'kɒnvɪkt/ n condannato, -a mf

convict² /kən'vɪkt/ vt giudicare colpevole. **∼ion** n condanna f; (belief) convinzione f; **previous ∼ion** precedente m penale

convinc|e /kən'vɪns/ vt convincere. **∼ing** adj convincente

convoluted /'kɒnvəluːtɪd/ adj contorto

convoy /'kɒnvɔɪ/ n convoglio m

convuls|e /kən'vʌls/ vt sconvolgere; **be ∼ed with laughter** contorcersi dalla risa. **∼ion** n convulsione f

coo /kuː/ vi tubare

cook /kʊk/ n cuoco, -a mf • vt cucinare; **is it ∼ed?** è cotto?; **∼ the books** 🅣 truccare i libri contabili • vi (food:) cuocere; (person:) cucinare. **∼book** n libro m di cucina

cooker /'kʊkə(r)/ n cucina f; (apple) mela f da cuocere. **∼y** n cucina f. **∼y book** n libro m di cucina

cookie /'kʊkɪ/ n Am biscotto m

cool /kuːl/ adj fresco; (calm) calmo; (unfriendly) freddo • n fresco m • vt rinfrescare • vi rinfrescarsi. **∼box** n borsa f termica. **∼ness** n freddezza f

coop /kuːp/ n stia f • vt **∼ up** rinchiudere

co-operat|e /kəʊ'ɒpəreɪt/ vi cooperare. **∼ion** n cooperazione f

co-operative /kəʊ'ɒpərətɪv/ adj cooperativo • n cooperativa f

co-opt /kəʊ'ɒpt/ vt eleggere

co-ordinat|e /kəʊ'ɔːdɪneɪt/ vt coordinare. **∼ion** n coordinazione f

cop /kɒp/ n 🅣 poliziotto m

cope /kəʊp/ v 🅣 farcela; **can she ∼ by herself?** ce la fa da sola?; **∼ with** farcela con

copious /'kəʊpɪəs/ adj abbondante

copper¹ /'kɒpə(r)/ n rame m; **∼s** pl

monete fpl da uno o due pence • attrib di rame

copper² n 🅣 poliziotto m

copy /'kɒpɪ/ n copia f • vt (pt/pp -ied) copiare

copyright n diritti mpl d'autore

coral /'kɒrəl/ n corallo m

cord /kɔːd/ n corda f; (thinner) cordoncino m; (fabric) velluto m a coste; **∼s** pl pantaloni mpl di velluto a coste

cordial /'kɔːdɪəl/ adj cordiale • n analcolico m

cordon /'kɔːdn/ n cordone m (di persone) **• cordon off** vt mettere un cordone (di persone) intorno a

core /kɔː(r)/ n (of apple, pear) torsolo m; (fig: of organization) cuore m; (of problem, theory) nocciolo m

cork /kɔːk/ n sughero m; (for bottle) turacciolo m. **∼screw** n cavatappi m inv

corn¹ /kɔːn/ n grano m; (Am: maize) granturco m

corn² n (Med) callo m

corned beef /kɔːnd'biːf/ n manzo m sotto sale

corner /'kɔːnə(r)/ n angolo m; (football) calcio m d'angolo, corner m inv • vt fig bloccare; (Comm) accaparrarsi (market)

cornet /'kɔːnɪt/ n (Mus) cornetta f; (for ice-cream) cono m

corn: ∼flour n, Am **∼starch** n farina f di granturco

corny /'kɔːnɪ/ adj (-ier, -iest) (🅣: joke, film) scontato; (person) banale; (sentimental) sdolcinato

coronary /'kɒrənərɪ/ adj coronario • n **∼ [thrombosis]** trombosi f coronarica

coronation /kɒrə'neɪʃn/ n incoronazione f

coroner /'kɒrənə(r)/ n coroner m inv (nel diritto britannico, ufficiale incaricato delle indagini su morti sospette)

corporal¹ /'kɔːpərəl/ n (Mil)

caporale *m*

corporal² *adj* corporale; ~ **punishment** punizione *f* corporale

corporate /'kɔːpərət/ *adj* (decision, policy, image) aziendale; ~ **life** la vita in un'azienda

corporation /kɔːpə'reɪʃn/ *n* ente *m*; (of town) consiglio *m* comunale

corps /kɔː(r)/ *n* (*pl* **corps** /kɔːz/) corpo *m*

corpse /kɔːps/ *n* cadavere *m*

corpulent /'kɔːpjʊlənt/ *adj* corpulento

correct /kə'rekt/ *adj* corretto; **be** ~ (person:) aver ragione; ~**!** esatto! ●*vt* correggere. ~**ion** *n* correzione *f*. ~**ly** *adv* correttamente

correspond /kɒrɪ'spɒnd/ *vi* corrispondere (**to** a); (two things:) corrispondere; (write) scriversi. ~**ence** *n* corrispondenza *f*. ~**ent** *n* corrispondente *mf*. ~**ing** *adj* corrispondente. ~**ingly** *adv* in modo corrispondente

corridor /'kɒrɪdɔː(r)/ *n* corridoio *m*

corro|de /kə'rəʊd/ *vt* corrodere ●*vi* corrodersi. ~**sion** *n* corrosione *f*

corrugated /'kɒrəgeɪtɪd/ *adj* ondulato. ~ **iron** *n* lamiera *f* ondulata

corrupt /kə'rʌpt/ *adj* corrotto ●*vt* corrompere. ~**ion** *n* corruzione *f*

corset /'kɔːsɪt/ *n* **& -s** *pl* busto *m*

Corsica /'kɔːsɪkə/ *n* Corsica *f*. ~**n** *adj & n* corso, -a *mf*

cosmetic /kɒz'metɪk/ *adj* cosmetico ●*n* ~**s** *pl* cosmetici *mpl*

cosmic /'kɒzmɪk/ *adj* cosmico

cosmopolitan /kɒzmə'pɒlɪtən/ *adj* cosmopolita

cosmos /'kɒzmɒs/ *n* cosmo *m*

cosset /'kɒsɪt/ *vt* coccolare

cost /kɒst/ *n* costo *m*; ~**s** *pl* (*Jur*) spese *fpl* processuali; **at all** ~**s** a tutti i costi; **I learnt to my** ~ ho imparato a mie spese ●*vt* (*pt/pp* **cost**) costare; **it** ~ **me £20** mi è costato 20 sterline ●*vt* (*pt/pp* **costed**)

~ **[out]** stabilire il prezzo di

costly /'kɒstlɪ/ *adj* (**-ier, -iest**) costoso

costume /'kɒstjuːm/ *n* costume *m*. ~ **jewellery** *n* bigiotteria *f*

cosy /'kəʊzɪ/ *adj* (**-ier, -iest**) (pub, chat) intimo; **it's nice and** ~ **in here** si sta bene qui

cot /kɒt/ *n* lettino *m*; (*Am: camp-bed*) branda *f*

cottage /'kɒtɪdʒ/ *n* casetta *f*. ~ **'cheese** *n* fiocchi *mpl* di latte

cotton /'kɒtn/ *n* cotone *m* ●*attrib* di cotone ●*vi* **cotton on** *vi* 1 capire

cotton 'wool *n* cotone *m* idrofilo

couch /kaʊtʃ/ *n* divano *m*. ~ **po-tato** *n* pantofolaio, -a *mf*

cough /kɒf/ *n* tosse *f* ●*vi* tossire. □ ~ **up** *vt/i* sputare; (1: pay) sborsare

'cough mixture *n* sciroppo *m* per la tosse

council /'kaʊnsl/ *n* consiglio *m*. ~ **house** *n* casa *f* popolare

councillor /'kaʊnsələ(r)/ *n* consigliere, -a *mf*

counsel /'kaʊnsl/ *n* consigli *mpl*; (*Jur*) avvocato *m* ●*vt* (*pt/pp* **coun-selled**) consigliare a (person). ~**lor** *n* consigliere, -a *mf*

count¹ /kaʊnt/ *n* (nobleman) conte *m*

count² *n* conto *m*; **keep** ~ tenere il conto ●*vt/i* contare. □ ~ **on** *vt* contare su

countdown /'kauntdaun/ n conto m alla rovescia

counter[1] /'kauntə(r)/ n banco m; (in games) gettone m

counter[2] adv ~ **to** contro, in contrasto a; **go** ~ **to sth** andare contro qcsa ● vt/i opporre (measure, effect); parare (blow)

counter'act vt neutralizzare

'counter-attack n contrattacco m

'counterfeit /-fɪt/ adj contraffatto ● n contraffazione f ● vt contraffare

'counterfoil n matrice f

counter-pro'ductive adj controproduttivo

countess /'kauntɪs/ n contessa f

countless /'kauntlɪs/ adj innumerevole

country /'kʌntrɪ/ n nazione f, paese m; (native land) patria f; (countryside) campagna f; **in the** ~ in campagna; **go to the** ~ andare in campagna; (Pol) indire le elezioni politiche. ~**man** n uomo m di campagna; (fellow ~man) compatriota m. ~**side** n campagna f

county /'kaunti/ n contea f (unità amministrativa britannica)

coup /ku:/ n (Pol) colpo m di stato

couple /'kʌpl/ n coppia f; **a** ~ **of** un paio di

coupon /'ku:pɒn/ n tagliando m; (for discount) buono m sconto

courage /'kʌrɪdʒ/ n coraggio m. ~**ous** adj coraggioso

courgette /kuə'ʒet/ n zucchino m

courier /'kurɪə(r)/ n corriere m; (for tourists) guida f

course /kɔ:s/ n (Sch) corso m; (Naut) rotta f; (Culin) portata f; (for golf) campo m; ~ **of treatment** (Med) serie f inv di cure; **of** ~ naturalmente; **in the** ~ **of** durante; **in due** ~ a tempo debito

court /kɔ:t/ n tribunale m; (Sport)

campo m; **take sb to** ~ citare qcno in giudizio ● vt fare la corte a (woman); sfidare (danger); ~**ing couples** coppiette fpl

courteous /'kɜ:tɪəs/ adj cortese

courtesy /'kɜ:təsɪ/ n cortesia f

court: ~ '**martial** n (pl ~**s martial**) corte f marziale ~**-martial** vt (pt ~**-martialled**) portare davanti alla corte marziale; ~**yard** n cortile m

cousin /'kʌzn/ n cugino, -a mf

cove /kəuv/ n insenatura f

cover /'kʌvə(r)/ n (of cushion, to protect sth) fodera f; (of book, magazine) copertina f; **take** ~ mettersi al riparo; **under separate** ~ a parte ● vt coprire; foderare (cushion); (Journ) fare un servizio su. □ ~ **up** vt coprire; fig soffocare (scandal)

coverage /'kʌvərɪdʒ/ n (Journ) **it got a lot of** ~ i media gli hanno dedicato molto spazio

cover: ~ **charge** n coperto m. ~**ing** n copertura f; (for floor) rivestimento m; ~**ing letter** lettera f d'accompagnamento

covet /'kʌvɪt/ vt bramare

cow /kau/ n vacca f, mucca f

coward /'kauəd/ n vigliacco, -a mf. ~**ice** n vigliaccheria f. ~**ly** adj da vigliacco

'cowboy n cowboy m inv; 🔲 buffone m

cower /'kauə(r)/ vi acquattarsi

coy /kɔɪ/ adj falsamente timido; (flirtatiously) civettuolo; **be** ~ **about sth** essere evasivo su qcsa

crab /kræb/ n granchio m

crack /kræk/ n (in wall) crepa f; (in china, glass, bone) incrinatura f; (noise) scoppio m; 🔲 (joke) battuta f; **have a** ~ (try) fare un tentativo ● adj 🔲 (best) di prim'ordine ● vt incrinare (china, glass); schiacciare (nut); decifrare (code); 🔲 risolvere (problem); ~ **a joke** 🔲 fare una battuta ● vi (china, glass:) incrinarsi; (whip:) schioccare. □ ~ **down** vi 🛈 prendere seri provvedimenti. □ ~ **down on** vt 🛈 prendere seri provvedimenti contro

cracker /'krækə(r)/ n (biscuit) cracker m inv; (firework) petardo m; [**Christmas**] ~ tubo m di cartone colorato contenente una sorpresa

crackle /'krækl/ vi crepitare

cradle /'kreɪdl/ n culla f

craft¹ /krɑːft/ n inv (boat) imbarcazione f

craft² /krɑːft/ n mestiere m; (technique) arte f. ~**sman** n artigiano m

crafty /'krɑːftɪ/ adj (-ier, -iest) astuto

cram /kræm/ v (pt/pp **crammed**) ● vt stipare (**into** in) ● vi (for exams) sgobbare

cramp /kræmp/ n crampo m. ~**ed** adj (room) stretto; (handwriting) appiccicato

cranberry /'krænbərɪ/ n (Culin) mirtillo m rosso

crane /kreɪn/ n (at docks, bird) gru f inv ● vt ~ **one's neck** allungare il collo

crank¹ /kræŋk/ n tipo, -a mf strampalato, -a

crank² n (Techn) manovella f. ~**shaft** n albero m a gomiti

cranky /'kræŋkɪ/ adj strampalato; (Am: irritable) irritabile

cranny /'krænɪ/ n fessura f

crash /kræʃ/ n (noise) fragore m; (Aeron, Auto) incidente m; (Comm) crollo m ● vi schiantarsi (**into** contro); (plane:) precipitare ● vt schiantare (car)

crash: ~ **course** n corso m intensivo. ~ **helmet** n casco m

crate /kreɪt/ n (for packing) cassa f

crater /'kreɪtə(r)/ n cratere m

crav|e /kreɪv/ vt morire dalla voglia di. ~**ing** n voglia f smodata

crawl /krɔːl/ n (swimming) stile m libero; **do the** ~ nuotare a stile libero; **at a** ~ a passo di lumaca ● vi andare carponi, ~ **with** brulicare di. ~**er lane** n (Auto) corsia f riservata al traffico lento

crayon /'kreɪən/ n pastello m a cera; (pencil) matita f colorata

craze /kreɪz/ n mania f

crazy /'kreɪzɪ/ adj (-ier, -iest) matto; **be** ~ **about** andar matto per

creak /kriːk/ n scricchiolio m ● vi scricchiolare

cream /kriːm/ n crema f; (fresh) panna f ● adj (colour) [bianco] panna inv ● vt (Culin) sbattere. ~ **cheese** n formaggio m cremoso. ~**y** adj cremoso

crease /kriːs/ n piega f ● vt stropicciare ● vi stropicciarsi. ~**-resistant** adj che non si stropiccia

creat|e /kriː'eɪt/ vt creare. ~**ion** n creazione f. ~**ive** adj creativo. ~**or** n creatore, -trice mf

creature /'kriːtʃə(r)/ n creatura f

crèche /kreʃ/ n asilo m nido

credibility /kredə'bɪlətɪ/ n credibilità f

credible /'kredəbl/ adj credibile

credit /'kredɪt/ n credito m; (honour) merito m; **take the** ~ **for** prendersi il merito di ● vt (pt/pp **credited**) accreditare; ~ **sb with sth** (Comm) accreditare qcsa a qcno; fig attribuire qcsa a qcno. ~**able** adj lodevole

credit: ~ **card** n carta f di credito. ~**or** n creditore, -trice mf

creed /kriːd/ n credo m inv

creek /kriːk/ n insenatura f; (Am: stream) torrente m

creep /kriːp/ vi (pt/pp **crept**) muoversi furtivamente ● n 🛈 tipo m viscido. ~**er** n pianta f rampicante. ~**y** adj che fa venire i brividi

cremat|e /krɪ'meɪt/ vt cremare. ~**ion** n cremazione f

crematorium /kremə'tɔːrɪəm/ n

crematorio m

crept /krept/ ▷**CREEP**

crescent /'kresənt/ n mezzaluna f

crest /krest/ n cresta f; (coat of arms) cimiero m

Crete /kriːt/ n Creta f

crevice /'krevis/ n crepa f

crew /kruː/ n equipaggio m; (gang) équipe f inv. ~ **cut** n capelli mpl a spazzola. ~ **neck** n girocollo m

crib¹ /krɪb/ n (for baby) culla f

crib² vt/i (pt/pp **cribbed**) 🄵 copiare

crick /krɪk/ n ~ **in the neck** torcicollo m

cricket¹ /'krɪkɪt/ n (insect) grillo m

cricket² n cricket m. ~**er** n giocatore m di cricket

crime /kraɪm/ n crimine m; (criminality) criminalità f

criminal /'krɪmɪnl/ adj criminale; (law, court) penale ● n criminale mf

crimson /'krɪmzn/ adj cremisi inv

cringe /krɪndʒ/ vi (cower) acquattarsi; (at bad joke etc) fare una smorfia

crinkle /'krɪŋkl/ vt spiegazzare ● vi spiegazzarsi

cripple /'krɪpl/ n storpio, -a mf ● vt storpiare; fig danneggiare. ~**d** adj (person) storpio; (ship) danneggiato

crisis /'kraɪsɪs/ n (pl **-ses** /-siːz/) crisi f inv

crisp /krɪsp/ adj croccante; (air) frizzante; (style) incisivo. ~**bread** n crostini mpl di pane. ~**s** npl patatine fpl

criterion /kraɪ'tɪərɪən/ n (pl **-ria** /-rɪə/) criterio m

critic /'krɪtɪk/ n critico, -a mf. ~**al** adj critico. ~**ally** adv in modo critico; ~**ally ill** gravemente malato

criticism /'krɪtɪsɪzm/ n critica f; **he doesn't like** ~ non ama le critiche

criticize /'krɪtɪsaɪz/ vt criticare

croak /krəʊk/ vi gracchiare; (frog:) gracidare

Croatia /krəʊ'eɪʃə/ n Croazia f

crochet /'krəʊʃeɪ/ n lavoro m all'uncinetto ● vt fare all'uncinetto. ~**hook** n uncinetto m

crockery /'krɒkərɪ/ n terrecotte fpl

crocodile /'krɒkədaɪl/ n coccodrillo m. ~ **tears** lacrime fpl di coccodrillo

crocus /'krəʊkəs/ n (pl **-es**) croco m

crook /krʊk/ n (🄵: criminal) truffatore, -trice mf

crooked /'krʊkɪd/ adj storto; (limb) storpiato; (🄵: dishonest) disonesto

crop /krɒp/ n raccolto m; fig quantità f inv ● v (pt/pp **cropped**) ● vt coltivare. □ ~ **up** vi 🄵 presentarsi

croquet /'krəʊkeɪ/ n croquet m

croquette /krəʊ'ket/ n crocchetta f

cross /krɒs/ adj (annoyed) arrabbiato; **talk at** ~ **purposes** fraintendersi ● n croce f; (Bot, Zool) incrocio m ● vt sbarrare (cheque); incrociare (road, animals); ~ **oneself** farsi il segno della croce; ~ **one's arms** incrociare le braccia; ~ **one's legs** accavallare le gambe; **keep one's fingers** ~**ed for sb** tenere le dita incrociate per qcno; **it's** ~**ed my mind** mi è venuto in mente ● vi (go across) attraversare; (lines:) incrociarsi. □ ~ **out** vt depennare

cross: ~**bar** n (of goal) traversa f; (on bicycle) canna f. ~**ex'amine** vt sottoporre a controinterrogatorio. ~**-'eyed** adj strabico. ~**fire** n fuoco m incrociato. ~**ing** n (for pedestrians) passaggio m pedonale; (sea journey) traversata f. ~**-'reference** n rimando m. ~**roads** n incrocio m. ~**'section** n sezione f; (of community) campione m. ~**word** n ~**word [puzzle]** parole fpl crociate

crouch /kraʊtʃ/ vi accovacciarsi

crow /krəʊ/ n corvo m; **as the** ~ **flies** in linea d'aria ● vi cantare. ~**bar** n piede m di porco

crowd /kraʊd/ n folla f ● vt affollare ● vi affollarsi. ~**ed** adj affollato

crown /kraʊn/ n corona f ● vt incoronare; incapsulare (tooth)

crucial /'kruːʃl/ *adj* cruciale

crucifix /'kruːsɪfɪks/ *n* crocifisso *m*

crucif|ixion /kruːsɪ'fɪkʃn/ *n* crocifissione *f*. **~y** *vt* (*pt/pp* **-ied**) crocifiggere

crude /kruːd/ *adj* (oil) greggio; (language) crudo; (person) rozzo

cruel /kruːəl/ *adj* (**crueller, cruellest**) crudele (**to** verso). **~ly** *adv* con crudeltà. **~ty** *n* crudeltà *f*

cruis|e /kruːz/ *n* crociera *f* ● *vi* fare una crociera; (car) andare a velocità di crociera. **~er** *n* (Mil) incrociatore *m*; (motor boat) motoscafo *m*. **~ing speed** *n* velocità *f* in *inv* di crociera

crumb /krʌm/ *n* briciola *f*

crumb|le /'krʌmbl/ *vt* sbriciolare ● *vi* sbriciolarsi; (building, society) sgretolarsi. **~ly** *adj* friabile

crumple /'krʌmpl/ *vt* spiegazzare ● *vi* spiegazzarsi

crunch /krʌntʃ/ *n* 🔲 **when it comes to the ~** quando si viene al dunque ● *vt* sgranocchiare ● *vi* (snow) scricchiolare

crusade /kruː'seɪd/ *n* crociata *f*. **~r** *n* crociato *m*

crush /krʌʃ/ *n* (crowd) calca *f*; **have a ~ on sb** essersi preso una cotta per qcno ● *vt* schiacciare; sgualcire (clothes)

crust /krʌst/ *n* crosta *f*

crutch /krʌtʃ/ *n* gruccia *f*; (Anat) inforcatura *f*

crux /krʌks/ *n* *fig* punto *m* cruciale

cry /kraɪ/ *n* grido *m*; **have a ~** farsi un pianto; **a far ~ from** *fig* tutta un'altra cosa rispetto a ● *vi* (*pt/pp* **cried**) (weep) piangere; (call) gridare

crypt /krɪpt/ *n* cripta *f*. **~ic** *adj* criptico

crystal /'krɪstl/ *n* cristallo *m*; (glassware) cristalli *mpl*. **~lize** *vi* (become clear) concretizzarsi

cub /kʌb/ *n* (animal) cucciolo *m*; **C~**

[Scout] lupetto *m*

Cuba /'kjuːbə/ *n* Cuba *f*

cubby-hole /'kʌbɪ-/ *n* (compartment) scomparto *m*; (room) ripostiglio *m*

cub|e /kjuːb/ *n* cubo *m*. **~ic** *adj* cubico

cubicle /'kjuːbɪkl/ *n* cabina *f*

cuckoo /'kʊkuː/ *n* cuculo *m*. **~ clock** *n* orologio *m* a cucù

cucumber /'kjuːkʌmbə(r)/ *n* cetriolo *m*

cuddl|e /'kʌdl/ *vt* coccolare ● *vi* **~e up to** starsene accoccolato insieme a ● *n* **have a ~e** (child). **~e** farsi coccolare; (lovers) abbracciarsi. **~y** *adj* tenerone; (animal cuddly) coccolone. **~y toy** *n* peluche *m*

cue¹ /kjuː/ *n* segnale *m*; (Theat) battuta *f* d'entrata

cue² /kjuː/ *n* (in billiards) stecca *f*. **~ ball** *n* pallino *m*

cuff /kʌf/ *n* polsino *m*; (Am: turn-up) orlo *m*; (blow) scapaccione *m*; **off the ~** improvvisando ● *vi* dare una pacca a. **~-link** *n* gemello *m*

cul-de-sac /'kʌldəsæk/ *n* vicolo *m* cieco

culinary /'kʌlɪnərɪ/ *adj* culinario

cull /kʌl/ *vt* scegliere (flowers); (kill) selezionare e uccidere

culminat|e /'kʌlmɪneɪt/ *vi* culminare. **~ion** *n* culmine *m*

culprit /'kʌlprɪt/ *n* colpevole *mf*

cult /kʌlt/ *n* culto *m*

cultivate /'kʌltɪveɪt/ *vt* coltivare; *fig* coltivarsi (person)

cultural /'kʌltʃərəl/ *adj* culturale

culture /'kʌltʃə(r)/ *n* cultura *f*. **~d** *adj* colto

cumbersome /'kʌmbəsəm/ *adj* ingombrante

cunning /'kʌnɪŋ/ *adj* astuto ● *n* astuzia *f*

cup /kʌp/ *n* tazza *f*; (prize, of bra) coppa *f*

cupboard /'kʌbəd/ *n* armadio *m*

~**love** 🔢 amore m interessato

curator /kjʊəˈreɪtə(r)/ n direttore, -trice mf (di museo)

curb /kɜːb/ vt tenere a freno

curdle /ˈkɜːdl/ vi coagularsi

cure /kjʊə(r)/ n cura f ● vt curare; (salt) mettere sotto sale; (smoke) affumicare

curfew /ˈkɜːfjuː/ n coprifuoco m

curiosity /kjʊərɪˈɒsəti/ n curiosità f

curious /ˈkjʊərɪəs/ adj curioso. ~**ly** adv (strangely) curiosamente

curl /kɜːl/ n ricciolo m ● vt arricciare ● vi arricciarsi. □ ~ **up** vi raggomitolarsi

curler /ˈkɜːlə(r)/ n bigodino m

curly /ˈkɜːli/ adj (-ier, -iest) riccio

currant /ˈkʌrənt/ n (dried) uvetta f

currency /ˈkʌrənsi/ n valuta f; (of word) ricorrenza f; **foreign** ~ valuta f estera

current /ˈkʌrənt/ adj corrente ● n corrente f. ~ **affairs** or **events** npl attualità fsg. ~**ly** adv attualmente

curriculum /kəˈrɪkjʊləm/ n programma m di studi. ~ **vitae** n curriculum vitae m

curry /ˈkʌri/ n curry m inv; (meal) piatto m cucinato nel curry ● vt (pt/pp -ied) ~ **favour** with sb cercare d'ingraziarsi qcno

curse /kɜːs/ n maledizione f; (oath) imprecazione f ● vt maledire ● vi imprecare

cursory /ˈkɜːsəri/ adj sbrigativo

curt /kɜːt/ adj brusco

curtain /ˈkɜːtn/ n tenda f; (Theat) sipario m

curtsy /ˈkɜːtsi/ n inchino m ● vi (pt/pp -ied) fare l'inchino

curve /kɜːv/ n curva f ● vi curvare; ~ **to the right/left** curvare a destra/sinistra. ~**d** adj curvo

cushion /ˈkʊʃn/ n cuscino m ● vt attutire; (protect) proteggere

cushy /ˈkʊʃi/ adj (-ier, -iest) 🔢

facile

custard /ˈkʌstəd/ n (liquid) crema f pasticciera

custody /ˈkʌstədi/ n (of child) custodia f; (imprisonment) detenzione f preventiva

custom /ˈkʌstəm/ n usanza f; (Jur) consuetudine f; (Comm) clientela f. ~**ary** adj (habitual) abituale; **it's** ~**ary to...** è consuetudine.... ~**er** n cliente mf

customs /ˈkʌstəmz/ npl dogana f. ~ **officer** n doganiere m

cut /kʌt/ n (with knife etc, of clothes) taglio m; (reduction) riduzione f; (in public spending) taglio m ● vt/i (pt/pp cut, pres p cutting) tagliare; (reduce) ridurre; ~ **one's finger** tagliarsi il dito; ~ **sb's hair** tagliare i capelli a qcno ● vi (with cards) alzare. □ ~ **back** vt tagliare (hair); potare (hedge); (reduce) ridurre. □ ~ **down** vt abbattere (tree); (reduce) ridurre. □ ~ **off** vt tagliar via; (disconnect) interrompere; fig isolare; **I was** ~ **off** (Teleph) la linea è caduta. □ ~ **out** vt ritagliare; (delete) eliminare; **be** ~ **out for** 🔢 essere tagliato per; ~ **it out!** 🔢 dacci un taglio!. □ ~ **up** vt (slice) tagliare a pezzi

cute /kjuːt/ adj 🔢 (in appearance) carino; (clever) acuto

cutlery /ˈkʌtləri/ n posate fpl

cutlet /ˈkʌtlɪt/ n cotoletta f

'**cut-price** adj a prezzo ridotto; (shop) che fa prezzi ridotti

'**cut-throat** adj spietato

cutting /ˈkʌtɪŋ/ adj (remark) tagliente ● n (from newspaper) ritaglio m; (of plant) talea f

CV n abbr curriculum vitae

cycl|e /ˈsaɪkl/ n ciclo m; (bicycle) bicicletta f, bici f inv 🔢 ● vi andare in bicicletta. ~**ing** n ciclismo m. ~**ist** n ciclista mf

cylind|er /ˈsɪlɪndə(r)/ n cilindro m. ~**rical** adj cilindrico

cynic /'smɪk/ n cinico, -a mf. **~al** adj cinico. **~ism** n cinismo m

Cyprus /'saɪprəs/ n Cipro m

Czech /tʃek/ adj ceco; **~ Republic** Repubblica f Ceca ● n ceco, -a mf

Dd

dab /dæb/ n colpetto m, a **~** of un pochino di ● vt (pt/pp **dabbed**) toccare leggermente (eyes). □ **~ on** vt mettere un po' di (paint etc)

daddy-'long-legs n zanzarone m [dei boschi]; (Am: spider) ragno m

daffodil /'dæfədɪl/ n giunchiglia f

daft /dɑːft/ adj sciocco

dagger /'dægə(r)/ n stiletto m

dahlia /'deɪlɪə/ n dalia f

Dáil Éireann Dáil Éireann è la camera bassa del Parlamento della Reppublica di Irlanda. È composto di 166 deputati (o TD) in rappresentanza di 41 collegi elettorali. I deputati sono infatti eletti col sistema proporzionale e la Costituzione ne prevede uno per ogni 20.000-30.000 cittadini.

daily /'deɪlɪ/ adj giornaliero ● adv giornalmente ● n (newspaper) quotidiano m; (🂠: cleaner) donna f delle pulizie

dainty /'deɪntɪ/ adj (**-ier, -iest**) grazioso; (movement) delicato

dairy /'deərɪ/ n caseificio m; (shop) latteria f. **~ cow** n mucca f da latte. **~ products** npl latticini mpl

daisy /'deɪzɪ/ n margheritina f; (larger) margherita f

dam /dæm/ n diga f ● vt (pt/pp dammed) costruire una diga su

damage /'dæmɪdʒ/ n danno m (**to** a); **~es** pl (Jur) risarcimento msg ● vt danneggiare; fig nuocere a. **~ing** adj dannoso

dame /deɪm/ n liter dama f; Am 🂠 donna f

damn /dæm/ adj 🂠 maledetto ● adv (lucky, late) maledettamente ● n I don't give a **~** 🂠 non me ne frega un accidente ● vt dannare. **~ation** n dannazione f ● int 🂠 accidenti!

damp /dæmp/ adj umido ● n umidità f ● vt inumidire

dance /dɑːns/ n ballo m ● vt/i ballare. **~-hall** n sala f da ballo. **~ music** n musica f da ballo

dancer /'dɑːnsə(r)/ n ballerino, -a mf

dandelion /'dændɪlaɪən/ n dente m di leone

dandruff /'dændrʌf/ n forfora f

Dane /deɪn/ n danese mf; **Great ~** danese m

danger /'deɪndʒə(r)/ n pericolo m; in/out of **~** fuori pericolo. **~ous** adj pericoloso. **~ously** adv pericolosamente; **~ously ill** in pericolo di vita

dangle /'dæŋgl/ vi penzolare ● vt far penzolare

Danish /'deɪnɪʃ/ adj & n danese m. **~ 'pastry** n dolce m a base di pasta sfoglia contenente pasta di mandorle, mele ecc

dare /deə(r)/ vt/i (venture); (challenge) sfidare (**to** a); **~ [to] do sth** osare fare qcsa; **I ~ say!** molto probabile! ● n sfida f. **~devil** n spericolato, -a mf

daring /'deərɪŋ/ adj audace ● n audacia f

dark /dɑːk/ adj buio; **~ blue/brown** blu/marrone scuro; **it's getting ~** sta cominciando a fare buio; **~ horse** fig (in race, contest) vincitore m imprevisto; (not much known about) misterioso m; **keep sth ~** fig tenere qcsa nascosto ● n **after ~** col buio;

in the ~ al buio; **keep sb in the ~** fig tenere qcno all'oscuro

dark|en /'dɑːkn/ vt oscurare ● vi oscurarsi. ~**ness** n buio m

'**dark-room** n camera f oscura

darling /'dɑːlɪŋ/ adj adorabile; **my ~ Joan** carissima Joan ● n tesoro m

darn /dɑːn/ vt rammendare. ~**ing-needle** n ago m da rammendo

dart /dɑːt/ n dardo m; (in sewing) pince f inv; ~**s** sg (game) freccette fpl ● vi lanciarsi

dartboard /'dɑːtbɔːd/ n bersaglio m [per freccette]

dash /dæʃ/ n (Typ) trattino m; (in Morse) linea f; **a ~ of milk** un goccio di latte; **make a ~ for** lanciarsi verso ● vt **I must ~** devo scappare ● vt far svanire (hopes). ~ **off** vi scappar via ● vt (write quickly) buttare giù. ~ **out** vi uscire di corsa

'**dashboard** n cruscotto m

data /'deɪtə/ npl & sg dati mpl. ~**base** n base [di] dati f, database m inv. ~**comms** n telematica f. ~ **process-ing** n elaborazione f [di] dati

date[1] /deɪt/ n (fruit) dattero m

date[2] /deɪt/ n (meeting) appunta-mento m; **to ~** fino ad oggi; **out of ~** (not fashionable) fuori moda; (ex-pired) scaduto; (information) non ag-giornato; **make a ~ with sb** dare un appuntamento a qcno; **be up to ~** essere aggiornato ● vt/i datare; (go out with) uscire con. □ ~ **back to** vi risalire a

dated /'deɪtɪd/ adj fuori moda; (lan-guage) antiquato

daub /dɔːb/ vt imbrattare (walls)

daughter /'dɔːtə(r)/ n figlia f. ~-**in-law** n (pl ~**s-in-law**) nuora f

dawdle /'dɔːdl/ vi bighellonare; (over work) cincischiarsi

dawn /dɔːn/ n alba f; **at ~** all'alba ● vi albeggiare; **it ~ed on me** fig mi è apparso chiaro

day /deɪ/ n giorno m; (whole day) gior-

nata f; (period) epoca f; **these ~s** oggigiorno; **in those ~s** a quei tempi; **it's had its ~** ▣ ha fatto il suo tempo

day: ~**break** n at ~**break** allo spuntar del giorno. ~**dream** n sogno m ad occhi aperti ● vi sognare ad occhi aperti. ~**light** n luce f del giorno. ~**time** n giorno m; **in the ~time** di giorno

daze /deɪz/ n **in a ~** stordito; fig sbalordito. ~**d** adj stordito; fig sba-lordito

dazzle /'dæzl/ vt abbagliare

dead /ded/ adj morto; (numb) intorpi-dito; ~ **body** morto m; ~ **centre** pieno centro m ● adv ~ **tired** stanco morto; ~ **slow/easy** lentissimo/ facilissimo; **you're ~ right** hai per-fettamente ragione; **stop ~** fermarsi di colpo; **be ~ on time** essere in perfetto orario ● n **the ~** pl i morti; **in the ~ of night** nel cuore della notte

deaden /'dedn/ vt attutire (sound); calmare (pain)

dead: ~ **'end** n vicolo m cieco. ~**line** n scadenza f. ~**lock** n reach ~**lock** fig giungere a un punto morto

deadly /'dedlɪ/ adj (-ier, -iest) mor-tale; (▣: dreary) barboso; ~ **sins** peccati mpl capitali

deaf /def/ adj sordo; ~ **and dumb** sordomuto. ~-**aid** n apparecchio m acustico

deaf|en /'defn/ vt assordare; (per-manently) render sordo. ~**ening** adj assordante. ~**ness** n sordità f

deal /diːl/ n (agreement) patto m; (in business) accordo m; **whose ~?** (in cards) a chi tocca dare le carte?; **a good** or **great ~** molto; **get a raw ~** ▣ ricevere un trattamento ingiu-sto ● vt (pt/pp **dealt** /delt/) (in cards) dare; ~ **sb a blow** dare un colpo a qcno. □ ~ **in** vi trattare in. □ ~ **out** vt (hand out) distribuire. □ ~ **with** vt (handle) occuparsi di; trattare con (company); (be about) trattare di; **that's been ~t with** è stato risolto

dealer /'di:lə(r)/ n commerciante mf; (in drugs) spacciatore, -trice mf. **~ings** npl **have ~ings with** avere a che fare con

dean /di:n/ n decano m; (Univ) ≈ preside mf di facoltà

dear /dɪə(r)/ adj caro; (in letter) Caro; (formal) Gentile ● n caro, -a mf ● int **oh ~!** Dio mio!. **~ly** adv (love) profondamente; (pay) profumatamente

death /deθ/ n morte f. **~ certificate** n certificato m di morte. **~ duty** n tassa f di successione

death trap n trappola f mortale

debatable /dɪ'beɪtəbl/ adj discutibile

debate /dɪ'beɪt/ n dibattito m ● vt discutere; (in formal debate) dibattere ● vi **~ whether to...** considerare se...

debauchery /dɪ'bɔːtʃərɪ/ n dissolutezza f

debit /'debɪt/ n debito m ● vt (pt/pp debited) (Comm) addebitare (sum)

debris /'debri:/ n macerie fpl

debt /det/ n debito m; **be in ~** avere dei debiti. **~or** n debitore, -trice mf

decade /'dekeɪd/ n decennio m

decaden|ce /'dekədəns/ n decadenza f. **~t** adj decadente

decay /dɪ'keɪ/ n (also fig) decadenza f; (rot) decomposizione f; (of teeth) carie f inv ● vi imputridire; (rot) decomporsi; (tooth:) cariarsi

deceased /dɪ'si:st/ adj defunto ● n **the ~d** il defunto, la defunta

deceit /dɪ'si:t/ n inganno m. **~ful** adj falso

deceive /dɪ'si:v/ vt ingannare

December /dɪ'sembə(r)/ n dicembre m

decency /'di:sənsɪ/ n decenza f

decent /'di:sənt/ adj decente; (respectable) rispettabile; **very ~ of you** molto gentile da parte tua. **~ly** adv decentemente; (kindly) gentilmente

decept|ion /dɪ'sepʃn/ n inganno m. **~ive** adj ingannevole. **~ively** adv ingannevolmente; **it looks ~ively easy** sembra facile, ma non lo è

decibel /'desɪbel/ n decibel m inv

decide /dɪ'saɪd/ vt decidere ● vi decidere (on di)

decided /dɪ'saɪdɪd/ adj risoluto. **~ly** adv risolutamente; (without doubt) senza dubbio

decimal /'desɪml/ adj decimale ● n numero m decimale. **~ point** n virgola f

decipher /dɪ'saɪfə(r)/ vt decifrare

decision /dɪ'sɪʒn/ n decisione f

decisive /dɪ'saɪsɪv/ adj decisivo

deck¹ /dek/ vt abbigliare

deck² n (Naut) ponte m; **on ~** in coperta; **top ~** (of bus) piano m di sopra; **~ of cards** mazzo m. **~-chair** n [sedia f a] sdraio f inv

declaration /deklə'reɪʃn/ n dichiarazione f

declare /dɪ'kleə(r)/ vt dichiarare; **anything to ~?** niente da dichiarare?

decline /dɪ'klaɪn/ n declino m ● vt also (Gram) declinare ● vi (decrease) diminuire; (health:) deperire; (say no) rifiutare

decode /di:'kəʊd/ vt decifrare; (Comput) decodificare

decompose /di:kəm'pəʊz/ vi decomporsi

décor /'deɪkɔ:(r)/ n decorazione f; (including furniture) arredamento m

decorat|e /'dekəreɪt/ vt decorare; (paint) pitturare; (wallpaper) tappezzare. **~ion** n decorazione f. **~ive** adj decorativo. **~or** n painter and **~or** n imbianchino m

decoy¹ /'di:kɔɪ/ n esca f

decoy² /dɪˈkɔɪ/ vt adescare

decrease¹ /ˈdiːkriːs/ n diminuzione f

decrease² /dɪˈkriːs/ vt/i diminuire

decree /dɪˈkriː/ n decreto m ● vt (pt/pp **decreed**) decretare

decrepit /dɪˈkrepɪt/ adj decrepito

dedicat|e /ˈdedɪkeɪt/ vt dedicare. **~ed** adj (person) scrupoloso. **~ion** n dedizione f; (in book) dedica f

deduce /dɪˈdjuːs/ vt dedurre (**from** da)

deduct /dɪˈdʌkt/ vt dedurre

deduction /dɪˈdʌkʃn/ n deduzione f

deed /diːd/ n azione f; (Jur) atto m di proprietà

deem /diːm/ vt ritenere

deep /diːp/ adj profondo; **go off the ~ end** 🛈 arrabbiarsi

deepen /ˈdiːpn/ vt approfondire; scavare più profondamente (trench) ● vi approfondirsi; (fig: mystery:) infittirsi

deep-'freeze n congelatore m

deeply /ˈdiːplɪ/ adv profondamente

deer /dɪə(r)/ n inv cervo m

deface /dɪˈfeɪs/ vt sfigurare (picture); deturpare (monument)

default /dɪˈfɔːlt/ n (non-payment) morosità f; (failure to appear) contumacia f; **win by ~** (Sport) vincere per abbandono dell'avversario; **in ~ of** per mancanza di ● a **~ drive** (Comput) lettore m di default ● vi (not pay) venir meno a un pagamento

defeat /dɪˈfiːt/ n sconfitta f ● vt sconfiggere; (frustrate) vanificare (attempts); **that ~s the object** questo fa fallire l'obiettivo

defect¹ /dɪˈfekt/ vi (Pol) fare defezione

defect² /ˈdiːfekt/ n difetto m. **~ive** adj difettoso

defence /dɪˈfens/ n difesa f. **~less** adj indifeso

defend /dɪˈfend/ vt difendere; (justify) giustificare. **~ant** n (Jur) imputato, -a mf

defensive /dɪˈfensɪv/ adj difensivo ● n difensiva f; **on the ~** sulla difensiva

defer /dɪˈfɜː(r)/ v (pt/pp **deferred**) ● vt (postpone) rinviare ● vi **to ~ to sb** rimettersi a qcno

deferen|ce /ˈdefərəns/ n deferenza f. **~tial** adj deferente

defian|ce /dɪˈfaɪəns/ n sfida f; **in ~ce of** sfidando. **~t** adj (person) ribelle; (gesture, attitude) di sfida. **~tly** adv con aria di sfida

deficien|cy /dɪˈfɪʃənsɪ/ n insufficienza f. **~t** adj insufficiente; **be ~t in** mancare di

deficit /ˈdefɪsɪt/ n deficit m inv

define /dɪˈfaɪn/ vt definire

definite /ˈdefɪnɪt/ adj definito; (certain) (answer, yes) definitivo; (improvement, difference) netto; **he was ~ about it** è stato chiaro in proposito. **~ly** adv sicuramente

definition /defɪˈnɪʃn/ n definizione f

definitive /dɪˈfɪnətɪv/ adj definitivo

deflat|e /dɪˈfleɪt/ vt sgonfiare. **~ion** n (Comm) deflazione f

deflect /dɪˈflekt/ vt deflettere

deform|ed /dɪˈfɔːmd/ adj deforme. **~ity** n deformità f inv

defrost /diːˈfrɒst/ vt sbrinare (fridge); scongelare (food)

deft /deft/ adj abile

defuse /diːˈfjuːz/ vt disinnescare; calmare (situation)

defy /dɪˈfaɪ/ vt (pt/pp **-ied**) (challenge) sfidare; resistere a (attempt); (not obey) disobbedire a

degenerate¹ /dɪˈdʒenəreɪt/ vi degenerare; **~ into** fig degenerare in

degenerate² /dɪˈdʒenərət/ adj degenerato

degree /dɪˈgriː/ n grado m; (Univ)

laurea f; **20 ~s** 20 gradi; **not to the same** ~ non allo stesso livello

deign /deɪn/ vi ~ **to do sth** degnarsi di fare qcsa

deity /ˈdiːɪtɪ/ n divinità f inv

dejected /dɪˈdʒektɪd/ adj demoralizzato

delay /dɪˈleɪ/ n ritardo m; **without** ~ senza indugio ● vt ritardare; **be ~ed** (person:) essere trattenuto; (train, aircraft:) essere in ritardo ● vi indugiare

delegate¹ /ˈdelɪgət/ n delegato, -a inf

delegate² /ˈdelɪgeɪt/ vt delegare. ~**ion** n delegazione f

delete /dɪˈliːt/ vt cancellare. ~**ion** n cancellatura f

deliberate¹ /dɪˈlɪbərət/ adj deliberato; (slow) posato. ~**ly** adv deliberatamente; (slowly) in modo posato

deliberate² /dɪˈlɪbəreɪt/ vt/i deliberare. ~**ion** n deliberazione f

delicacy /ˈdelɪkəsɪ/ n delicatezza f; (food) prelibatezza f

delicate /ˈdelɪkət/ adj delicato

delicatessen /delɪkəˈtesn/ n negozio m di specialità gastronomiche

delicious /dɪˈlɪʃəs/ adj delizioso

delight /dɪˈlaɪt/ n piacere m ● vt deliziare ● vi ~ **in** dilettarsi con. ~**ed** adj lieto. ~**ful** adj delizioso

delirious /dɪˈlɪrɪəs/ adj **be ~rious** delirare; (fig: very happy) essere pazzo di gioia. ~**rium** n delirio m

deliver /dɪˈlɪvə(r)/ vt consegnare; recapitare (post, newspaper); tenere (speech); dare (message); tirare (blow); (set free) liberare; ~ **a baby** far nascere un bambino. ~**ance** n liberazione f. ~**y** n consegna f; (of post) distribuzione f; (Med) parto m; **cash on ~y** pagamento m alla consegna

delude /dɪˈluːd/ vt ingannare; ~ **oneself** illudersi

deluge /ˈdeljuːdʒ/ n diluvio m ● vt

(fig: with requests etc) inondare

delusion /dɪˈluːʒn/ n illusione f

de luxe /dəˈlʌks/ adj di lusso

delve /delv/ vi ~ **into** (into pocket etc) frugare in; (into notes, the past) fare ricerche in

demand /dɪˈmɑːnd/ n richiesta f; (Comm) domanda f; **in ~** richiesto; **on ~** a richiesta ● vt esigere (**of**/**from** da). ~**ing** adj esigente

demented /dɪˈmentɪd/ adj demente

demister /diːˈmɪstə(r)/ n (Auto) sbrinatore m

demo /ˈdeməʊ/ n (pl ~s) 🔲 manifestazione f; ~ **disk** (Comput) demo disk m inv

democracy /dɪˈmɒkrəsɪ/ n democrazia f

democrat /ˈdeməkræt/ n democratico, -a mf. ~**ic** adj democratico

demolish /dɪˈmɒlɪʃ/ vt demolire. ~**lition** n demolizione f

demon /ˈdiːmən/ n demonio m

demonstrate /ˈdemənstreɪt/ vt dimostrare; fare una dimostrazione sull'uso di (appliance) ● vi (Pol) manifestare. ~**ion** n dimostrazione f; (Pol) manifestazione f

demonstrator /ˈdemənstreɪtə(r)/ n (Pol) manifestante mf; (for product) dimostratore, -trice mf

demoralize /dɪˈmɒrəlaɪz/ vt demoralizzare

demote /dɪˈməʊt/ vt retrocedere di grado; (Mil) degradare

demure /dɪˈmjʊə(r)/ adj schivo

den /den/ n tana f; (room) rifugio m

denial /dɪˈnaɪəl/ n smentita f

denim /ˈdenɪm/ n [tessuto m] jeans m; ~**s** pl [blue]jeans mpl

Denmark /ˈdenmɑːk/ n Danimarca f

denounce /dɪˈnaʊns/ vt denunciare

dense /dens/ adj denso; (crowd, forest) fitto; (stupid) ottuso. ~**ely** adv (populated) densamente; **~ely wooded** fittamente ricoperto di alberi. **~ity** n densità f inv; (of forest) fittezza f

dent /dent/ n ammaccatura f ● vt ammaccare; **~ed** adj ammaccato

dental /'dentl/ adj dei denti; (treatment) dentistico; (hygiene) dentale. **~ surgeon** n odontoiatra mf, medico m dentista

dentist /'dentist/ n dentista mf. **~ry** n odontoiatria f

dentures /'dentʃəz/ npl dentiera fsg

deny /dɪ'naɪ/ vt (pt/pp -ied) negare; (officially) smentire; **~ sb sth** negare qcsa a qcno

deodorant /di:'əʊdərənt/ n deodorante m

depart /dɪ'pɑ:t/ vi (plane, train:) partire; (liter: person) andare via; (deviate) allontanarsi (**from** da)

department /dɪ'pɑ:tmənt/ n reparto m; (Pol) ministero m; (of company) sezione f; (Univ) dipartimento m. **~ store** n grande magazzino m

departure /dɪ'pɑ:tʃə(r)/ n partenza f; (from rule) allontanamento m; **new ~** svolta f

depend /dɪ'pend/ vi dipendere (**on** da); (rely) contare (**on** su); **it all ~s** dipende; **~ing on what he says** a seconda di quello che dice. **~able** adj fidato. **~ant** n persona f a carico. **~ence** n dipendenza f. **~ent** adj dipendente (**on** da)

depict /dɪ'pɪkt/ vt (in writing) dipingere; (with picture) rappresentare

deplete /dɪ'pli:t/ vt ridurre; **totally ~d** completamente esaurito

deplor|able /dɪ'plɔ:rəbl/ adj deplorevole. **~e** vt deplorare

deploy /dɪ'plɔɪ/ vt (Mil) spiegare ● vi schierarsi

deport /dɪ'pɔ:t/ vt deportare. **~ation** n deportazione f

depose /dɪ'pəʊz/ vt deporre

deposit /dɪ'pɒzɪt/ n deposito m;

(against damage) cauzione f; (first instalment) acconto m ● vt (pt/pp **deposited**) depositare. **~ account** n libretto m di risparmio; (without instant access) conto m vincolato

depot /'depəʊ/ n deposito m; Am (Rail) stazione f ferroviaria

depress /dɪ'pres/ vt deprimere; (press down) premere. **~ed** adj depresso; **~ed area** zona f depressa. **~ing** adj deprimente. **~ion** n depressione f

deprivation /deprɪ'veɪʃn/ n privazione f

deprive /dɪ'praɪv/ vt **~ sb of sth** privare qcno di qcsa. **~d** adj (area, childhood) disagiato

depth /depθ/ n profondità f inv; **in ~** (study, analyse) in modo approfondito; **in the ~s of winter** in pieno inverno; **be out of one's ~** (in water) non toccare il fondo; fig sentirsi in alto mare

deputize /'depjʊtaɪz/ vi **~ for** fare le veci di

deputy /'depjʊtɪ/ n vice mf; (temporary) sostituto, -a mf ● attrib **~ leader** ≈ vicesegretario, -a mf; **~ chairman** vicepresidente mf

derail /dɪ'reɪl/ vt **be ~ed** (train:) essere deragliato. **~ment** n deragliamento m

derelict /'derəlɪkt/ adj abbandonato

deri|de /dɪ'raɪd/ vt deridere. **~sion** n derisione f

derisory /dɪ'raɪsərɪ/ adj (laughter) derisorio; (offer) irrisorio

derivation /derɪ'veɪʃn/ n derivazione f

derivative /dɪ'rɪvətɪv/ adj derivato ● n derivato m

derive /dɪ'raɪv/ vt (obtain) derivare; **be ~d from** (word:) derivare da

derogatory /dɪ'rɒgətrɪ/ adj (comments) peggiorativo

descend /dɪ'send/ vi scendere ● vt scendere da; **be ~ed from** discendere da. ~ant n discendente mf

descent /dɪ'sent/ n discesa f; (lineage) origine f

describe /dɪ'skraɪb/ vt descrivere

descrip|tion /dɪ'skrɪpʃn/ n descrizione f; **they had no help of any ~tion** non hanno avuto proprio nessun aiuto. ~**tive** adj descrittivo; (vivid) vivido

desecrat|e /'desɪkreɪt/ vt profanare. ~**ion** n profanazione f

desert[1] /'dezət/ n deserto m ● adj deserto; ~ **island** isola f deserta

desert[2] /dɪ'zɜ:t/ vt abbandonare ● vi disertare. ~**ed** adj deserto. ~**er** n (Mil) disertore m. ~**ion** n (Mil) diserzione f; (of family) abbandono m

deserts /dɪ'zɜ:ts/ npl **get one's just ~** ottenere ciò che ci si merita

deserv|e /dɪ'zɜ:v/ vt meritare. ~**ing** adj meritevole; ~**ing cause** opera f meritoria

design /dɪ'zaɪn/ n progettazione f; (fashion ~, appearance) design m inv; (pattern) modello m; (aim) proposito m ● vt progettare; disegnare (clothes, furniture, model); **be ~ed for** essere fatto per

designat|e /'dezɪɡneɪt/ vt designare. ~**ion** n designazione f

designer /dɪ'zaɪnə(r)/ n progettista mf; (of clothes) stilista mf; (Theat: of set) scenografo, -a m

desirable /dɪ'zaɪərəbl/ adj desiderabile

desire /dɪ'zaɪə(r)/ n desiderio m ● vt desiderare

desk /desk/ n scrivania f; (in school) banco m; (in hotel) reception f inv; (cash ~) cassa f. ~**top 'publishing** n desktop publishing f da tavolo

desolat|e /'desələt/ adj desolato. ~**ion** n desolazione f

despair /dɪ'speə(r)/ n disperazione f; **in ~** disperato; (say) per disperazione ● vi **I ~ of that boy** quel ra-

gazzo mi fa disperare

desperat|e /'despərət/ adj disperato; **be ~e** (criminal:) essere un disperato; **be ~e for** sth morire dalla voglia di. ~**ely** adv disperatamente; **he said ~ely** ha detto, disperato. ~**ion** n disperazione f; **in ~ion** per disperazione

despicable /dɪ'spɪkəbl/ adj disprezzevole

despise /dɪ'spaɪz/ vt disprezzare

despite /dɪ'spaɪt/ prep malgrado

despondent /dɪ'spɒndənt/ adj abbattuto

despot /'despɒt/ n despota m

dessert /dɪ'zɜ:t/ n dolce m. ~**spoon** n cucchiaio m da dolce

destination /destɪ'neɪʃn/ n destinazione f

destiny /'destɪnɪ/ n destino m

destitute /'destɪtju:t/ adj bisognoso

destroy /dɪ'strɔɪ/ vt distruggere. ~**er** n (Naut) cacciatorpediniere m

destruc|tion /dɪ'strʌkʃn/ n distruzione f. ~**tive** adj distruttivo; (fig: criticism) negativo

detach /dɪ'tætʃ/ vt staccare. ~**able** adj separabile. ~**ed** adj fig distaccato; ~**ed house** villetta f

detachment /dɪ'tætʃmənt/ n distacco m; (Mil) distaccamento m

detail /'di:teɪl/ n particolare m, dettaglio m; **in ~** particolareggiatamente ● vt esporre con tutti i particolari; (Mil) assegnare. ~**ed** adj particolareggiato, dettagliato

detain /dɪ'teɪn/ vt (police:) trattenere; (delay) far ritardare. ~**ee** n detenuto, -a mf

detect /dɪ'tekt/ vt individuare; (perceive) percepire. ~**ion** n scoperta f

detective /dɪ'tektɪv/ n investigatore, -trice mf. ~ **story** n racconto m poliziesco

detector /dɪ'tektə(r)/ n (for metal) metal detector m inv

detention /dɪˈtenʃn/ n detenzione f; (Sch) punizione f

deter /dɪˈtɜː(r)/ vt (pt/pp deterred) impedire; ~ sb from doing sth impedire a qcno di fare qcsa

detergent /dɪˈtɜːdʒənt/ n detersivo m

deteriorat|e /dɪˈtɪərɪəreɪt/ vi deteriorarsi. ~ion n deterioramento m

determination /dɪtɜːmɪˈneɪʃn/ n determinazione f

determine /dɪˈtɜːmɪn/ vt (ascertain) determinare; ~ to (resolve) decidere di. ~d adj deciso

deterrent /dɪˈterənt/ n deterrente m

detest /dɪˈtest/ vt detestare. ~able adj detestabile

detonat|e /ˈdetəneɪt/ vt far detonare • vi detonare. ~or n detonatore m

detour /ˈdiːtʊə(r)/ n deviazione f

detract /dɪˈtrækt/ vi ~ from sminuire (merit); rovinare (pleasure, beauty)

detriment /ˈdetrɪmənt/ n to the ~ of a danno di. ~al adj dannoso

de'value vt svalutare (currency)

devastat|e /ˈdevəsteɪt/ vt devastare. ~ed adj 🔢 sconvolto. ~ing adj devastante; (news) sconvolgente. ~ion n devastazione f

develop /dɪˈveləp/ vt sviluppare; contrarre (illness); (add to value of) valorizzare (area) • vi svilupparsi. ~ into divenire. ~er n [property] ~er imprenditore, -trice mf edile

development /dɪˈveləpmənt/ n sviluppo m; (of vaccine etc) messa f a punto

deviant /ˈdiːvɪənt/ adj deviato

deviat|e /ˈdiːvɪeɪt/ vi deviare. ~ion n deviazione f

device /dɪˈvaɪs/ n dispositivo m

devil /ˈdevl/ n diavolo m

devious /ˈdiːvɪəs/ adj (person) sub-

dolo; (route) tortuoso

devise /dɪˈvaɪz/ vt escogitare

devoid /dɪˈvɔɪd/ adj ~ of privo di

devolution /diːvəˈluːʃn/ n (of power) decentramento m

devot|e /dɪˈvəʊt/ vt dedicare. ~ed adj (daughter etc) affezionato; be ~ed to sth consacrarsi a qcsa. ~ee n appassionato, -a mf

devotion /dɪˈvəʊʃn/ n dedizione f; ~s pl (Relig) devozione fsg

devour /dɪˈvaʊə(r)/ vt divorare

devout /dɪˈvaʊt/ adj devoto

dew /djuː/ n rugiada f

dexterity /dekˈsterətɪ/ n destrezza f

diabet|es /daɪəˈbiːtiːz/ n diabete m. ~ic adj diabetico • n diabetico, -a mf

diabolical /daɪəˈbɒlɪkl/ adj diabolico

diagnose /daɪəgˈnəʊz/ vt diagnosticare

diagnosis /daɪəgˈnəʊsɪs/ n (pl -oses /-siːz/) diagnosi f inv

diagonal /daɪˈægənl/ adj diagonale • n diagonale f

diagram /ˈdaɪəgræm/ n diagramma m

dial /ˈdaɪəl/ n (of clock, machine) quadrante m; (Teleph) disco m combinatore • v (pt/pp dialled) • vi (Teleph) fare il numero; ~ direct chiamare in teleselezione • vt fare (number)

dialect /ˈdaɪəlekt/ n dialetto m

dialling: ~ code n prefisso m. ~ tone n segnale m di linea libera

dialogue /ˈdaɪəlɒg/ n dialogo m

'dial tone n Am (Teleph) segnale m di linea libera

diameter /daɪˈæmɪtə(r)/ n diametro m

diamond /ˈdaɪəmənd/ n diamante m, brillante m; (shape) losanga f; ~s pl (in cards) quadri mpl

diaper /ˈdaɪəpə(r)/ n Am pannolino m

diaphragm /ˈdaɪəfræm/ n diaframma m

diarrhoea /daɪəˈriːə/ n diarrea f

diary /ˈdaɪərɪ/ n (for appointments) agenda f; (for writing in) diario m

dice /daɪs/ n inv dadi mpl ● vt (Culin) tagliare a dadini

dictate /dɪkˈteɪt/ vt/i dettare. ~**ion** n dettato m

dictator /dɪkˈteɪtə(r)/ n dittatore m. ~**ial** adj dittatoriale. ~**ship** n dittatura f

dictionary /ˈdɪkʃənrɪ/ n dizionario m

did /dɪd/ ▷DO

didn't /ˈdɪdnt/ = did not

die /daɪ/ vi (pres p dying) morire (of di); **be dying to do sth** 🗓 morire dalla voglia di fare qcsa. ~ **down** vi calmarsi; (fire, flames:) spegnersi. ~ **out** vi estinguersi; (custom:) morire

diesel /ˈdiːzl/ n diesel m

diet /ˈdaɪət/ n regime m alimentare; (restricted) dieta f; **be on a** ~ essere a dieta ● vi essere a dieta

differ /ˈdɪfə(r)/ vi differire; (disagree) non essere d'accordo

difference /ˈdɪfrəns/ n differenza f; (disagreement) divergenza f

different /ˈdɪfrənt/ adj diverso, differente; (various) diversi; **be** ~ **from** essere diverso da

differently /ˈdɪfrəntlɪ/ adv in modo diverso; ~ **from** diversamente da

difficult /ˈdɪfɪkəlt/ adj difficile. ~**y** n difficoltà f inv

diffuse[1] /dɪˈfjuːs/ adj diffuso; (wordy) prolisso

diffuse[2] /dɪˈfjuːz/ vt (Phys) diffondere

dig /dɪg/ n (poke) spinta f; (remark) frecciata f; (Archaeol) scavo m; ~**s** pl 🗓 camera fsg ammobiliata ● vt/i (pt/ pp **dug**, pres p **digging**) scavare

(hole); vangare (garden); (thrust) conficcare; ~ **sb in the ribs** dare una gomitata a qcno. □ ~ **out** vt fig tirar fuori. □ ~ **up** vt scavare (garden, street, object); sradicare (plant); (fig find) scovare

digest[1] /ˈdaɪdʒest/ n compendio m

digest[2] /daɪˈdʒest/ vt digerire. ~**ible** adj digeribile. ~**ion** n digestione f

digger /ˈdɪgə(r)/ n (Techn) scavatrice f

digit /ˈdɪdʒɪt/ n cifra f; (finger) dito m

digital /ˈdɪdʒɪtl/ adj digitale; ~ **camera** fotocamera f digitale. ~ **clock** orologio m digitale

digitize /ˈdɪdʒɪtaɪz/ vt digitalizzare

dignified /ˈdɪgnɪfaɪd/ adj dignitoso

dignitary /ˈdɪgnɪtərɪ/ n dignitario m

dignity /ˈdɪgnɪtɪ/ n dignità f

digress /daɪˈgres/ vi divagare. ~**ion** n digressione f

dike /daɪk/ n diga f

dilapidated /dɪˈlæpɪdeɪtɪd/ adj cadente

dilate /daɪˈleɪt/ vi dilatarsi

dilemma /dɪˈlemə/ n dilemma m

dilute /daɪˈluːt/ vt diluire

dim /dɪm/ adj (dimmer, dimmest) debole (light); (dark) scuro; (prospect, chance) scarso; (indistinct) impreciso; (🗓 stupid) tonto ● vt/i (pt/pp dimmed) affievolire. ~**ly** adv (see, remember) indistintamente; (shine) debolmente

dime /daɪm/ n Am moneta f da dieci centesimi

dimension /daɪˈmenʃn/ n dimensione f

diminish /dɪˈmɪnɪʃ/ vt/i diminuire

dimple /ˈdɪmpl/ n fossetta f

din /dɪn/ n baccano m

dine /daɪn/ vi pranzare. ~**r** n (Am: restaurant) tavola f calda; **the last** ~**r in the restaurant** l'ultimo cliente nel ristorante

dinghy /'dɪŋɡɪ/ n dinghy m; (inflatable) canotto m pneumatico

dingy /'dɪndʒɪ/ adj (-ier, -iest) squallido e tetro

dinner /'dɪnə(r)/ n cena f; (at midday) pranzo m. **~-jacket** n smoking m inv

dinosaur /'daɪnəsɔː(r)/ n dinosauro m

dint /dɪnt/ n **by ~ of** a forza di

dip /dɪp/ n (in ground) inclinazione f; (Culin) salsina f; **go for a ~** andare a fare una nuotata ● v (pt/pp **dipped**) ● vt (in liquid) immergere; abbassare (head, headlights) ● vi (land): formare un avvallamento. □ **~ into** vt scorrere (book)

diphthong /'dɪfθɒŋ/ n dittongo m

diploma /dɪ'pləʊmə/ n diploma m

diplomacy /dɪ'pləʊməsɪ/ n diplomazia f

diplomat /'dɪpləmæt/ n diplomatico, -a mf. **~ic** adj diplomatico. **~ically** adv con diplomazia

'dip-stick n (Auto) astina f dell'olio

dire /'daɪə(r)/ adj (situation, consequences) terribile

direct /dɪ'rekt/ adj diretto ● adv direttamente ● vt (aim) rivolgere (attention, criticism); (control) dirigere; fare la regia di (film, play); **~ sb** (show the way) indicare la strada a qcno; **~ sb to do sth** ordinare a qcno di fare qcsa. **~ 'current** n corrente m continua

direction /dɪ'rekʃn/ n direzione f; (of play, film) regia f; **~s** pl indicazioni fpl

directly /dɪ'rektlɪ/ adv direttamente; (at once) immediatamente ● conj [non] appena

director /dɪ'rektə(r)/ n (Comm) direttore, -trice mf; (of play, film) regista m

directory /dɪ'rektərɪ/ n elenco m; (Teleph) elenco m [telefonico]; (of streets) stradario m

dirt /dɜːt/ n sporco m; **~ cheap** 🄵 [un] prezzo stracciato

dirty /'dɜːtɪ/ adj (-ier, -iest) sporco; **~ trick** brutto scherzo m; **~ word** parolaccia f ● vt (pt/pp -ied) sporcare

dis|a'bility /dɪs-/ n infermità f inv. **~abled** adj invalido

disad'vantage n svantaggio m; **at a ~tage** in una posizione di svantaggio. **~taged** adj svantaggiato. **~tageous** adj svantaggioso

disa'gree vi non essere d'accordo, **~ with** (food): far male a

disa'greeable adj sgradevole

disa'greement n disaccordo m; (quarrel) dissidio m

disap'pear vi scomparire. **~ance** f scomparsa f

disap'point vt deludere; **I'm ~ed** sono deluso. **~ing** adj deludente. **~ment** n delusione f

disap'proval n disapprovazione f

disap'prove vi disapprovare; **~ of** sb/sth disapprovare qcno/qcsa

dis'arm vt disarmare ● vi (Mil) disarmarsi. **~ament** n disarmo m. **~ing** adj (frankness etc) disarmante

disar'ray n in **~** in disordine

disaster /dɪ'zɑːstə(r)/ n disastro m. **~rous** adj disastroso

dis'band vt smobilitare; sbandare (troops) ● vi sciogliersi; (regiment): essere smobilitato

disbe'lief n incredulità f; **in ~** con incredulità

disc /dɪsk/ n disco m; (CD) compact disc m inv

discard /dɪ'skɑːd/ vt scartare; (throw away) eliminare; scaricare (boyfriend)

discern /dɪ'sɜːn/ vt discernere. **~ible** adj discernibile. **~ing** adj perspicace

'discharge[1] n (Electr) scarica f; (dismissal) licenziamento m; (Mil) congedo m; (Med: of blood) emissione f; (of cargo) scarico m

dis'charge² vt scaricare (battery, cargo); (dismiss) licenziare; (Mil) congedare; (Jur) assolvere (accused); dimettere (patient) ● vi (Electr) scaricarsi

disciple /dɪˈsaɪpl/ n discepolo m

disciplinary /ˈdɪsɪplɪnərɪ/ adj disciplinare

discipline /ˈdɪsɪplɪn/ n disciplina f ● vt disciplinare; (punish) punire

disc jockey n disc jockey m inv

dis'claim vt disconoscere. ~er n rifiuto m

dis'close vt svelare. ~ure n rivelazione f

disco /ˈdɪskəʊ/ n discoteca f

dis'colour vt scolorire ● vi scolorirsi

dis'comfort n scomodità f; fig disagio m

disconcert /dɪskənˈsɜːt/ vt sconcertare

discon'nect vt disconnettere

disconsolate /dɪsˈkɒnsələt/ adj sconsolato

discon'tent n scontentezza f. ~ed adj scontento

discon'tinue vt cessare, smettere; (Comm) sospendere la produzione di; ~d line fine f serie

discord n discordia f; (Mus) dissonanza f. ~ant adj ~ant note nota f discordante

discount¹ n sconto m

dis'count² vt (not believe) non credere a; (leave out of consideration) non tener conto di

dis'courage vt scoraggiare. (dissuade) dissuadere

dis'courteous adj scortese

discover /dɪsˈkʌvə(r)/ vt scoprire. ~y n scoperta f

dis'credit n discredito m ● vt (pt/pp discredited) screditare

discreet /dɪsˈkriːt/ adj discreto

discrepancy /dɪsˈkrepənsɪ/ n discrepanza f

discretion /dɪsˈkreʃn/ n discrezione f

discriminat|e /dɪsˈkrɪmɪneɪt/ vi discriminare (against contro); ~e between distinguere tra. ~ing adj esigente. ~ion n discriminazione f; (quality) discernimento m

discus /ˈdɪskəs/ n disco m

discuss /dɪsˈkʌs/ vt discutere; (examine critically) esaminare. ~ion n discussione f

disdain /dɪsˈdeɪn/ n sdegno f ● vt sdegnare. ~ful adj sdegnoso

disease /dɪˈziːz/ n malattia f. ~d adj malato

disem'bark vi sbarcare

disen'tangle vt districare

dis'figure vt deformare

dis'grace n vergogna f; i am in ~ sono caduto in disgrazia; it's a ~ è una vergogna ● vt disonorare. ~ful adj vergognoso

disgruntled /dɪsˈɡrʌntld/ adj malcontento

disguise /dɪsˈɡaɪz/ n travestimento m; in ~ travestito ● vt contraffare (voice); dissimulare (emotions); ~d as travestito da

disgust /dɪsˈɡʌst/ n disgusto m; in ~ con aria disgustata ● vt disgustare. ~ing adj disgustoso

dish /dɪʃ/ n piatto m; do the ~es lavare i piatti ● **dish out** vt (serve) servire; (distribute) distribuire. □ ~ **up** vt servire

dishcloth n strofinaccio m

dis'honest adj disonesto. ~y n disonestà f

dis'honour n disonore m ● vt disonorare (family); non onorare (cheque). ~able adj disonorevole. ~ably adv in modo disonorevole

dishwasher n lavapiatti f inv

disil'lusion vt disilludere. ~ment n disillusione f

disin'fect vt disinfettare. ~ant n

d

disinfettante *m*

dis'integrate *vi* disintegrarsi

dis'interested *adj* disinteressato

dis'jointed *adj* sconnesso

disk /dɪsk/ *n* (Comput) disco *m*; (diskette) dischetto *m*

dis'like *n* avversione *f*; **your likes and ~s** i tuoi gusti ● vt I ~ **him/it** non mi piace; **I don't ~ him/it** non mi dispiace

dis'locate /'dɪsləkeɪt/ vt slogare; ~ **one's shoulder** slogarsi una spalla

dis'lodge vt sloggiare

dis'loyal adj sleale. ~**ty** n slealtà *f*

dismal /'dɪzməl/ adj (person) abbacchiato; (news, weather) deprimente; (performance) mediocre

dismantle /dɪs'mæntl/ vt smontare (tent, machine); fig smantellare

dis'may n sgomento *m*. ~**ed** adj sgomento

dis'miss vt licenziare (employee); (reject) scartare (idea, suggestion). ~**al** n licenziamento *m*

dis'mount vi smontare

diso'bedien|ce n disubbidienza *f*. ~**t** adj disubbidiente

diso'bey vt disubbidire a (rule) ● vi disubbidire

dis'order n disordine *m*; (Med) disturbo *m*. ~**ly** adj disordinato; (crowd) turbolento; ~**ly conduct** turbamento *m* della quiete pubblica

dis'organized adj disorganizzato

dis'orientate vt disorientare

dis'own vt disconoscere

disparaging /dɪ'spærɪdʒɪŋ/ adj sprezzante

dispatch /dɪ'spætʃ/ n (Comm) spedizione *f*; (Mil, report) dispaccio *m*; **with ~** con prontezza ● vt spedire; (kill) spedire al creatore

dispel /dɪ'spel/ vt (pt/pp dispelled) dissipare

dispensable /dɪ'spensəbl/ adj dispensabile

dispense /dɪ'spens/ vt distribuire; ~ **with** fare a meno di; **dispensing chemist** farmacista *mf*; (shop) farmacia *f*. ~**r** n (device) distributore *m*

dispers|al /dɪ'spɜːsl/ n dispersione *f*. ~**e** vt disperdere ● vi disperdersi

dispirited /dɪ'spɪrɪtɪd/ adj scoraggiato

display /dɪ'spleɪ/ n mostra *f*; (Comm) esposizione *f*; (of feelings) manifestazione *f*; pej ostentazione *f*; (Comput) display *m* inv ● vt mostrare; esporre (goods); manifestare (feeling); (Comput) visualizzare

dis'please vt non piacere a; **be ~d with** essere scontento di

dis'pleasure n malcontento *m*

disposable /dɪ'spəʊzəbl/ adj (throwaway) usa e getta; (income) disponibile

disposal /dɪ'spəʊzl/ n (getting rid of) eliminazione *f*; **be at sb's ~** essere a disposizione di qcno

disproportionate /dɪsprə'pɔːʃə-nət/ adj sproporzionato

dis'prove vt confutare

dispute /dɪ'spjuːt/ n disputa *f*; (industrial) contestazione *f* ● vt contestare (statement)

disqualifi'cation n squalifica *f*; (from driving) ritiro *m* della patente

dis'qualify vt (pt/pp -ied) escludere; (Sport) squalificare; ~ **sb from driving** ritirare la patente a qcno

disre'gard n mancanza *f* di considerazione ● vt ignorare

dis'reputable adj malfamato

disre'spect n mancanza *f* di rispetto. ~**ful** adj irrispettoso

disrupt /dɪs'rʌpt/ vt creare scompiglio in; sconvolgere (plans). ~**ion** n scompiglio *m*; (of plans) sconvolgimento *m*. ~**ive** adj (person, behaviour) indisciplinato

dissatis'faction n malcontento *m*

dis'satisfied adj scontento

dissect /dɪ'sekt/ vt sezionare. **~ion** n dissezione f

dissent /dɪ'sent/ n dissenso m ● vi dissentire

dissertation /dɪsə'teɪʃn/ n tesi f inv

dissident /'dɪsɪdənt/ n dissidente mf

dis'similar adj dissimile (**to** da)

dissolute /'dɪsəluːt/ adj dissoluto

dissolve /dɪ'zɒlv/ vt dissolvere ● vi dissolversi

dissuade /dɪ'sweɪd/ vt dissuadere

distance /'dɪstəns/ n distanza f. **it's a short ~ from here to the station** la stazione non è lontana da qui; **in the ~** in lontananza; **from a ~** da lontano

distant /'dɪstənt/ adj distante; (relative) lontano

dis'taste n avversione f. **~ful** adj spiacevole

distil /dɪ'stɪl/ vt (pt/pp **distilled**) distillare. **~lation** n distillazione f. **~lery** n distilleria f

distinct /dɪ'stɪŋkt/ adj chiaro; (different) distinto. **~ion** n distinzione f; (Sch) massimo m dei voti. **~ive** adj caratteristico. **~ly** adv chiaramente

distinguish /dɪ'stɪŋgwɪʃ/ vt/i distinguere; **~ oneself** distinguersi. **~ed** adj rinomato; (appearance) distinto; (career) brillante

distort /dɪ'stɔːt/ vt distorcere. **~ion** n distorsione f

distract /dɪ'strækt/ vt distrarre. **~ed** adj assente; (🄘: worried) preoccupato. **~ing** adj che distoglie. **~ion** n distrazione f; (despair) disperazione f. **drive sb to ~** portare qcno alla disperazione

distraught /dɪ'strɔːt/ adj sconvolto

distress /dɪ'stres/ n angoscia f; (pain) sofferenza f; (danger) difficoltà f ● vt sconvolgere; (sadden) affliggere. **~ing** adj penoso; (shocking) sconvolgente. **~ signal** n segnale m di richiesta di soccorso

distribute /dɪ'strɪbjuːt/ vt distribuire. **~ion** n distribuzione f. **~or** n distributore m

district /'dɪstrɪkt/ n regione f, (Admin) distretto m ● **~ nurse** n infermiera, -a mf che fa visite a domicilio

dis'trust n sfiducia f ● vt non fidarsi di. **~ful** adj diffidente

disturb /dɪ'stɜːb/ vt disturbare; (emotionally) turbare; spostare (papers). **~ance** n disturbo m; **~ances** (pl: rioting etc) disordini mpl. **~ed** adj turbato; (mentally) **~ed** malato di mente. **~ing** adj inquietante

dis'used adj non utilizzato

ditch /dɪtʃ/ n fosso m ● vt (🄘: abandon) abbandonare (plan, car); piantare (lover)

dither /'dɪðə(r)/ vi titubare

divan /dɪ'væn/ n divano m

dive /daɪv/ n tuffo m; (Aeron) picchiata f, (🄘: place) bettola f ● vi tuffarsi; (when in water) immergersi; (Aeron) scendere in picchiata; (🄘: rush) precipitarsi

diver /'daɪvə(r)/ n (from board) tuffatore, -trice mf; (scuba) sommozzatore, -trice mf; (deep sea) palombaro m

diverge /daɪ'vɜːdʒ/ vi divergere. **~gent** adj divergente

diverse /daɪ'vɜːs/ adj vario

diversify /daɪ'vɜːsɪfaɪ/ vt/i (pt/pp -**ied**) diversificare

diversion /daɪ'vɜːʃn/ n deviazione f; (distraction) diversivo m

diversity /daɪ'vɜːsəti/ n varietà f

divert /daɪ'vɜːt/ vt deviare (traffic); distogliere (attention)

divide /dɪ'vaɪd/ vt dividere (**by** per); **six ~d by two** sei diviso due ● vi dividersi

dividend /'dɪvɪdend/ n dividendo m; **pay ~s** fig ripagare

divine /dɪ'vaɪn/ adj divino

diving /'daɪvɪŋ/ n (from board) tuffi mpl; (scuba) immersione f. ~**board** n trampolino m. ~**mask** n maschera f [subacquea]. ~**suit** n muta f; (deep sea) scafandro m

division /dɪ'vɪʒn/ n divisione f; (in sports league) serie f

divorce /dɪ'vɔːs/ n divorzio m ● vt divorziare da. ~**d** adj divorziato; **get** ~**d** divorziare

divorcee /dɪvɔː'siː/ n divorziato, -a mf

divulge /daɪ'vʌldʒ/ vt rendere pubblico

DIY n abbr do-it-yourself

dizziness /'dɪzɪnɪs/ n giramenti mpl di testa

dizzy /'dɪzɪ/ adj (-ier, -iest) vertiginoso; **I feel** ~ mi gira la testa

do¹ /duː/

3 sing pres tense **does**; past tense **did**; past participle **done**

● vt fare; (🗓: cheat) fregare; **be done** (Culin) essere cotto; **well done** (Culin) ben cotto; **do the flowers** sistemare i fiori; **do the washing up** lavare i piatti; **do one's hair** farsi i capelli

● vi (be suitable) andare; (be enough) bastare; **this will do** questo va bene; **that will do!** basta così!; **do well/badly** cavarsela bene/male; **how is he doing?** come sta?

● v aux (used to form questions and negatives; often not translated) **do you speak Italian?** parli italiano?; **you don't like him, do you?** non ti piace, vero?; (expressing astonishment) non dirmi che ti piace!; **yes, I do** sì; (emphatic) invece sì; **no, I don't** no, **I don't smoke** non fumo; **don't**

you/doesn't he? vero?; **so do I** anch'io; **do come in, John** entra, John; **how do you do?** piacere. □ ~ **away with** vt abolire (rule). □ ~ **for** vt done for 🗓 rovinato. □ ~ **in** vt (🗓: kill) uccidere; farsi male a (back); **done in** 🗓 esausto. □ ~ **up** vt (fasten) abbottonare; (renovate) rimettere a nuovo; (wrap) avvolgere. □ ~ **with** vt **I could do with a spanner** mi ci vorrebbe una chiave inglese. □ ~ **without** vt fare a meno di

do² /duː/ n (pl **dos** or **do's**) 🗓 festa f

docile /'dəʊsaɪl/ adj docile

dock¹ /dɒk/ n (Jur) banco m degli imputati

dock² n (Naut) bacino m ● vi entrare in porto; (spaceship:) congiungersi. ~**er** n portuale m. ~**s** npl porto m. ~**yard** n cantiere m navale

doctor /'dɒktə(r)/ n dottore m, dottoressa f ● vt alterare (drink); castrare (cat). ~**ate** n dottorato m

doctrine /'dɒktrɪn/ n dottrina f

document /'dɒkjʊmənt/ n documento m. ~**ary** adj documentario ● n documentario m

dodge /dɒdʒ/ n 🗓 trucco m ● vt schivare (blow); evitare (person) ● vi scansarsi. □ ~ **out of the way** scansarsi

dodgems /'dɒdʒəmz/ npl autoscontro msg

dodgy /'dɒdʒɪ/ adj (-ier, -iest) (🗓: dubious) sospetto

doe /dəʊ/ n femmina f (di daino, renna, lepre); (rabbit) coniglia f

does /dʌz/ ▷ **DO**

doesn't /'dʌznt/ = does not

dog /dɒg/ n cane m ● vt (pt/pp dogged) (illness, bad luck:) perseguitare

dogged /'dɒgɪd/ adj ostinato

'**dog house** n in the ~ 🗓 in disgrazia

dogma | dove

dogma /'dɒgmə/ n dogma m. **~tic**
adj dogmatico

do-it-yourself /du:ɪtʃə'self/ n fai
da te m, bricolage m. **~ shop** n negozio m di bricolage

dole /dəʊl/ n sussidio m di disoccupazione; **be on the ~** essere disoccupato ● **dole out** vt distribuire

doleful /'dəʊlfl/ adj triste

doll /dɒl/ n bambola f ● **doll oneself
up** vt 🅸 mettersi in ghingheri

dollar /'dɒlə(r)/ n dollaro m

dollop /'dɒləp/ n 🅸 cucchiaiata f

dolphin /'dɒlfɪn/ n delfino m

dome /dəʊm/ n cupola f

domestic /də'mestɪk/ adj domestico; (Pol) interno; (Comm) nazionale

domesticated /də'mestɪkeɪtɪd/ adj
(animal) addomesticato

domestic flight n volo m nazionale

dominant /'dɒmɪnənt/ adj do-
minante

dominat|e /'dɒmɪneɪt/ vt/i domi-
nare. **~ion** n dominio m

domineering /dɒmɪ'nɪərɪŋ/ adj
autoritario

Dominion /də'mɪnjən/ n Br (Pol)
dominion m inv

donat|e /dəʊ'neɪt/ vt donare. **~ion**
n donazione f

done /dʌn/ ▷ **DO**

donkey /'dɒŋkɪ/ n asino m; **~'s
years** 🅸 secoli mpl. **~-work** n sgobbata f

donor /'dəʊnə(r)/ n donatore,
-trice mf

doodle /'du:dl/ vi scarabocchiare

doom /du:m/ n fato m; (ruin) rovina f
● vt be **~ed [to failure]** essere destinato al fallimento; **~ed** (ship) destinato ad affondare

door /dɔ:(r)/ n porta f; (of car) portiera f; **out of ~s** all'aperto

door: **~mat** n zerbino m. **~step** n
gradino m della porta. **~way** n vano

m della porta

dope /dəʊp/ n 🅸 (drug) droga f leggera; (information) indiscrezioni fpl;
(idiot) idiota mf ● vt drogare; (Sport)
dopare

dormant /'dɔ:mənt/ adj latente;
(volcano) inattivo

dormitory /'dɔ:mɪtərɪ/ n dormitorio m

dormouse /'dɔ:-/ n ghiro m

dosage /'dəʊsɪdʒ/ n dosaggio m

dose /dəʊs/ n dose f

dot /dɒt/ n punto m; **at 8 o'clock on
the ~** alle 8 in punto

dot-com /dɒt'kɒm/ n azienda f le-
gata a internet

dote /dəʊt/ vi **~ on** stravedere per

dotty /'dɒtɪ/ adj (-ier, -iest) 🅸
(idea) folle

double /'dʌbl/ adj doppio ● adv cost
~ costare il doppio; **see ~** vedere
doppio; **~ the amount** la quantità
doppia ● n doppio m; (person) sosia m
inv. **~s** pl (Tennis) doppio m; **at the ~**
di corsa ● vt raddoppiare; (fold) piegare in due ● vi raddoppiare. **~ back**
vi (go back) fare dietro front.
~ up vi (bend) piegarsi in due
(with per); (share) dividere una
stanza

double: **~-bass** n contrabbasso m.
~-bed n letto m matrimoniale.
~-chin n doppio mento m. **~-click**
vt/i cliccare due volte, fare doppio
clic (on su). **~-cross** vt ingannare.
~-decker n autobus m inv a due
piani. **~ Dutch** n 🅸 ostrogoto m.
~-glazing n doppiovetro m

doubly /'dʌblɪ/ adv doppiamente

doubt /daʊt/ n dubbio m ● vt dubi-
tare di. **~ful** adj dubbio; (having
doubts) in dubbio. **~fully** adv con aria
dubbiosa. **~less** adv indubbiamente

dough /dəʊ/ n pasta f; (for bread)
impasto m; (🅸 money) quattrini mpl.
~nut n bombolone m, krapfen m inv

dove /dʌv/ n colomba f. **~tail** n

(Techn) incastro m a coda di rondine

down¹ /daʊn/ n (feathers) piumino m

down² adv giù; go/come ∼ scendere; ∼ there laggiù; sales are ∼ le vendite sono diminuite; £50 ∼ 50 sterline d'acconto; ∼ 10% ridotto del 10%; ∼ with...! abbasso...! • prep walk ∼ the road camminare per strada; ∼ the stairs per le scale; fall ∼ the stairs cadere giù dalle scale; get that ∼ you! 🅸 butta giù!; be ∼ the pub 🅸 essere al pub • vt bere tutto d'un fiato (drink)

down: ∼-and-'out n spiantato, -a mf. ∼cast adj abbattuto. ∼fall n caduta f; (of person) rovina f. ∼-'hearted adj scoraggiato. ∼'hill adv in discesa; go ∼hill essere in declino. ∼load vt scaricare. ∼'payment n deposito m. ∼pour n acquazzone m. ∼right adj (absolute) totale; (lie) bell'e buono; (idiot) perfetto • adv (completely) completamente. ∼stairs adv al piano di sotto • adj del piano di sotto. ∼'stream adv a valle. ∼-to-'earth adj (person) con i piedi per terra. ∼town adv Am in centro. ∼ward[s] adj verso il basso; (slope) in discesa • adv verso il basso

dowry /'daʊrɪ/ n dote f

doze /dəʊz/ n sonnellino m • vi sonnecchiare. ▫ ∼ off vi assopirsi

dozen /'dʌzn/ n dozzina f; ∼s of books libri a dozzine

Dr abbr doctor

drab /dræb/ adj spento

draft¹ /drɑːft/ n abbozzo m; (Comm) cambiale f; Am (Mil) leva f • vt abbozzare; Am (Mil) arruolare

draft² n Am = draught

drag /dræg/ n 🅸 scocciatura f; in ∼ 🅸 (man) travestito da donna • vt (pt/pp dragged) trascinare; dragare (river). ▫ ∼ on vi (time, meeting) trascinarsi

dragon /'drægən/ n drago m. ∼-fly n libellula f

drain /dreɪn/ n tubo m di scarico; (grid) tombino m; the ∼s pl le fognature; be a ∼ on sb's finances prosciugare le finanze di qcno • vt drenare (land, wound); scolare (liquid, vegetables); svuotare (tank, glass, person) • vi ∼ [away] andar via

drama /'drɑːmə/ n arte f drammatica; (play) opera f teatrale; (event) dramma m

dramatic /drə'mætɪk/ adj drammatico

dramat|ist /'dræmətɪst/ n drammaturgo, -a mf. ∼ize vt adattare per il teatro; fig drammatizzare

drank /dræŋk/ ▷DRINK

drape /dreɪp/ n Am tenda f • vt appoggiare (over su)

drastic /'dræstɪk/ adj drastico; ∼ally adv drasticamente

draught /drɑːft/ n corrente f [d'aria]; ∼s sg (game) [gioco m della] dama fsg

'draught beer n birra f alla spina

draughty /'drɑːftɪ/ adj pieno di correnti d'aria; it's ∼ c'è corrente

draw /drɔː/ n (attraction) attrazione f; (Sport) pareggio m; (in lottery) sorteggio m • v (pt drew, pp drawn) • vt tirare; attirare (attract); disegnare (picture); tracciare (line); ritirare (money); ∼ lots tirare a sorte • vi (tea:) essere in infusione; (Sport) pareggiare; **~ near** vi avvicinarsi. □ **~ back** vt tirare indietro; ritirare (hand); tirare (curtains) vi (recoil) tirarsi indietro. □ **~ in** vi ritrarre (claws etc) ● vi (train) arrivare; (days:) accorciarsi. □ **~ out** vt (pull out) tirar fuori; ritirare (money) ● vi (train) partire; (days:) allungarsi. □ **~ up** vt redigere (document) ● vi (stop) fermarsi; **~ oneself up to one's full height** farsi grande ● vi (stop) fermarsi

draw: **~back** n inconveniente m. **~bridge** n ponte m levatoio

drawer /drɔː(r)/ n cassetto m

drawing /'drɔːɪŋ/ n disegno m

drawing: **~-pin** n puntina f. **~room** n salotto m

drawl /drɔːl/ n pronuncia f strascicata

drawn /drɔːn/ ▷DRAW

dread /dred/ n terrore m ● vt aver il terrore di

dreadful /'dredfʊl/ adj terribile. **~ly** adv terribilmente

dream /driːm/ n sogno m ● attrib di sogno ● vt/i (pt/pp dreamt /dremt/ or dreamed) sognare (**about/of** di)

dreary /'drɪərɪ/ adj (-ier, -iest) tetro; (boring) monotono

dredge /dredʒ/ vt/i dragare

dregs /dregz/ npl feccia fsg

drench /drentʃ/ vt get **~ed** inzupparsi; **~ed** zuppo

dress /dres/ n (woman's) vestito m; (clothing) abbigliamento m ● vt vestire; (decorate) adornare; (Culin) condire; (Med) fasciare; **~ oneself, get ~ed** vestirsi ● vi vestirsi. □ **~ up** vi mettersi elegante; (in disguise) travestirsi (**as** da)

dress circle n (Theat) prima galleria f

dressing /'dresɪŋ/ n (Culin) condimento m; (Med) fasciatura f

dressing: **~-gown** n vestaglia f.

~-room n (in gym) spogliatoio m; (Theat) camerino m. **~-table** n toilette f inv

dress: **~maker** n sarta f. **~ rehearsal** n prova f generale

drew /druː/ ▷DRAW

dribble /'drɪbl/ vi gocciolare; (baby:) sbavare; (Sport) dribblare

dried /draɪd/ adj (food) essiccato

drier /draɪə(r)/ n asciugabiancheria m inv

drift /drɪft/ n movimento m lento; (of snow) cumulo m; (meaning) senso m ● vi (off course) andare alla deriva; (snow:) accumularsi; (fig: person:) procedere a tentoni. □ **~ apart** vi (people:) allontanarsi l'uno dall'altro

drill /drɪl/ n trapano m; (Mil) esercitazione f ● vt trapanare; (Mil) fare esercitare ● vi (Mil) esercitarsi; **~ for oil** trivellare in cerca di petrolio

drink /drɪŋk/ n bevanda f; (alcoholic) bicchierino m; **have a ~** bere qualcosa; **a ~ of water** un po' d'acqua ● vt/i (pt drank, pp drunk) bere. □ **~ up** vt finire ● vi finire il bicchiere

drink|able /'drɪŋkəbl/ adj potabile. **~er** n bevitore, -trice mf

'drinking-water n acqua f potabile

drip /drɪp/ n gocciolamento m; (drop) goccia f; (Med) flebo f inv; (🔲: person) mollaccione, -a mf ● vi (pt/pp dripped) gocciolare. **~-dry** adj che non si stira. **~ping** n (from meat) grasso m d'arrosto ● adj **~ping** [**wet**] fradicio

drive /draɪv/ n (in car) giro m; (entrance) viale m; (energy) grinta f; (Psych) pulsione f; (organized effort) operazione f; (Techn) motore m; (Comput) lettore m ● v (pt drove, pp driven) ● vt guidare (car); (Sport: hit) mandare; (Techn) far funzionare; **~ sb mad** far diventare matto qcno ● vi guidare. □ **~ at** vt **what are you driving at?** dove vuoi arrivare? **drive away**

portare via in macchina; (chase) cacciare ● vi andare via in macchina. □ ~ **in** vt piantare (nail) ● vi arrivare [in macchina]. □ ~ **off** vt portare via in macchina; (chase) cacciare ● vi andare via in macchina. □ ~ **on** vi proseguire (in macchina). □ ~ **up** vi arrivare (in macchina)

drivel /'drɪvl/ n 🔁 sciocchezze fpl

driver /'draɪvə(r)/ n guidatore, -trice mf; (of train) conducente mf

driving /'draɪvɪŋ/ adj (rain) violento; (force) motore ● n guida f

driving: ~ **licence** n patente f di guida. ~ **test** n esame m di guida

drizzle /'drɪzl/ n pioggerella f ● vi piovigginare

drone /drəʊn/ n (bee) fuco m; (sound) ronzio m

droop /druːp/ vi abbassarsi; (flowers:) afflosciarsi

drop /drɒp/ n (of liquid) goccia f; (fall) caduta f; (in price, temperature) calo m ● v (pt/pp **dropped**) ● vt far cadere; sganciare (bomb); (omit) omettere; (give up) abbandonare ● vi cadere; (price, temperature, wind:) calare; (ground:) essere in pendenza. □ ~ **in** vi passare. □ ~ **off** vt depositare (person) ● vi cadere; (fall asleep) assopirsi. □ ~ **out** vi cadere; (of race, society) ritirarsi; ~ **out of school** lasciare la scuola

'**drop-out** n persona f contro il sistema sociale

drought /draʊt/ n siccità f

drove /drəʊv/ ▷ **DRIVE**

drown /draʊn/ vi annegare ● vt annegare; coprire (noise); **he was** ~**ed** è annegato

drowsy /'draʊzɪ/ adj sonnolento

drudgery /'drʌdʒərɪ/ n lavoro m pesante e noioso

drug /drʌg/ n droga f; (Med) farmaco m; **take** ~ **s** drogarsi ● v (pt/pp **drugged**) drogare

drug: ~ **addict** n tossicomane, -a

mf. ~ **dealer** n spacciatore, -trice mf [di droga]. ~**gist** n Am farmacista mf. ~**store** n Am negozio m di generi vari, inclusi medicinali, che funge anche da bar; (dispensing) farmacia f

drum /drʌm/ n tamburo m; (for oil) bidone m; ~**s** (pl: in pop-group) batteria f ● v (pt/pp **drummed**) ● vi suonare il tamburo; (in pop-group) suonare la batteria ● vt ~ **sth into sb** ripetere qcsa a qcno cento volte. ~**mer** n percussionista mf; (in pop-group) batterista mf. ~**stick** n bacchetta f; (of chicken, turkey) coscia f

drunk /drʌŋk/ ▷ **DRINK** ● adj ubriaco; **get** ~ ubriacarsi ● n ubriaco, -a mf

drunk|ard /'drʌŋkəd/ n ubriacone, -a mf. ~**en** adj ubriaco; ~**en driving** guida f in stato di ebbrezza

dry /draɪ/ adj (**drier**, **driest**) asciutto; (climate, country) secco ● vt/i (pt/pp **dried**) asciugare; ~ **one's eyes** asciugarsi le lacrime. □ ~ **up** vi seccarsi; (fig: source:) prosciugarsi; (🔁: be quiet) stare zitto; (do dishes) asciugare i piatti

dry: ~'**clean** vt pulire a secco. ~'**cleaner's** n (shop) tintoria f. ~**ness** n secchezza f

DTD n abbr (digital type definition) DTD f

dual /'djuːəl/ adj doppio

dual '**carriageway** n strada f a due carreggiate

dub /dʌb/ vt (pt/pp **dubbed**) doppiare (film); (name) soprannominare

dubious /'djuːbɪəs/ adj dubbio; **be** ~ **about** avere dei dubbi riguardo

duchess /'dʌtʃɪs/ n duchessa f

duck /dʌk/ n anatra f ● vt (in water) immergere; ~ **one's head** abbassare la testa ● vi abbassarsi. ~**ling** n anatroccolo m

duct /dʌkt/ n condotto m; (Anat) dotto m

dud /dʌd/ 🔁 adj (Mil) disattivato; (coin) falso; (cheque) a vuoto ● n

(*banknote*) banconota *f* falsa

due /dju:/ *adj* dovuto; **be ~** (*train:*) essere previsto; **the baby is ~ next week** il bambino dovrebbe nascere la settimana prossima; **~ to** (*owing to*) a causa di; **be ~ to** (*causally*) essere dovuto a; **I'm ~ to...** dovrei...; **in ~ course** a tempo debito ● *adv* **~ north** direttamente a nord

duel /dju:əl/ *n* duello *m*

dues /dju:z/ *npl* quota *f* [di iscrizione]

duet /dju:'et/ *n* duetto *m*

dug /dʌg/ ▷ DIG

duke /dju:k/ *n* duca *m*

dull /dʌl/ *adj* (*overcast, not bright*) cupo; (*not shiny*) opaco; (*sound*) soffocato; (*boring*) monotono; (*stupid*) ottuso ● *vt* intorpidire (*mind*); attenuare (*pain*)

dumb /dʌm/ *adj* muto; (fam *stupid*) ottuso. **~founded** *adj* sbigottito. □ **~ down** *vt* semplificare il livello di

dummy /dʌmi/ *n* (*tailor's*) manichino *m*; (*for baby*) succhiotto *m*; (*model*) riproduzione *f*

dump /dʌmp/ *n* (*for refuse*) scarico *m*; (fam *town*) mortorio *m*; **be down in the** ~s fam essere depresso ● *vt* scaricare; (fam *put down*) lasciare; (fam *get rid of*) liberarsi di

dumpling /dʌmplɪŋ/ *n* gnocco *m*

dunce /dʌns/ *n* zuccone, -a *mf*

dung /dʌŋ/ *n* sterco *m*

dungarees /dʌŋgə'ri:z/ *npl* tuta *fsg*

dungeon /dʌndʒən/ *n* prigione *f* sotterranea

duplicate¹ /dju:plɪkət/ *adj* doppio ● *n* duplicato *m*; (*document*) copia *f*; **in ~** in duplicato

duplicate² /dju:plɪkeɪt/ *vt* fare un duplicato di; (*research:*) essere una ripetizione di (*work*)

durable /djuərəbl/ *adj* resistente; durevole (*basis, institution*)

duration /djuə'reɪʃn/ *n* durata *f*

duress /djuə'res/ *n* costrizione *f*; **under ~** sotto minaccia

during /djuərɪŋ/ *prep* durante

dusk /dʌsk/ *n* crepuscolo *m*

dust /dʌst/ *n* polvere *f* ● *vt* spolverare; (*sprinkle*) cospargere (*cake*) (**with** di) ● *vi* spolverare

dust: **~bin** *n* pattumiera *f*. **~er** *n* strofinaccio *m*. **~-jacket** *n* sopraccoperta *f*. **~man** *n* spazzino *m*. **~pan** *n* paletta *f* per la spazzatura

dusty /dʌsti/ *adj* (**-ier**, **-iest**) polveroso

Dutch /dʌtʃ/ *adj* olandese; **go ~** fare alla romana ● *n* (*language*) olandese *m*; **the ~** *pl* gli olandesi. **~man** *n* olandese *m*

duty /dju:ti/ *n* dovere *m*; (*task*) compito *m*; (*tax*) dogana *f*; **be on ~** essere di servizio. **~-free** *adj* esente da dogana

duvet /du:veɪ/ *n* piumone *m*

dwarf /dwɔ:f/ *n* (*pl* -**s** *or* **dwarves**) nano, -a *mf* ● *vt* rimpicciolire

dwell /dwel/ *vi* (*pt/pp* **dwelt**) liter di morare. □ **~ on** *vt* fig soffermarsi su. **~ing** *n* abitazione *f*

dwindle /dwɪndl/ *vi* diminuire

dye /daɪ/ *n* tintura *f* ● *vt* (*pres p* **dyeing**) tingere

dying /daɪɪŋ/ ▷ DIE²

dynamic /daɪ'næmɪk/ *adj* dinamico

dynamite /daɪnəmaɪt/ *n* dinamite *f*

dynamo /daɪnəməʊ/ *n* dinamo *f* inv

dynasty /dɪnəsti/ *n* dinastia *f*

Ee

each /i:tʃ/ *adj* ogni ● *pron* ognuno, £1 **~** una sterlina ciascuno; **they love/hate ~ other** si amano/ odiano; **we lend ~ other money** ci prestiamo i soldi

eager /'i:gə(r)/ adj ansioso (**to do** di fare); (pupil) avido di sapere. **~ly** adv (wait) ansiosamente; (offer) premurosamente. **~ness** n premura f

eagle /'i:gl/ n aquila f

ear[1] /ɪə(r)/ n (of corn) spiga f

ear[2] n orecchio m. **~ache** n mal m d'orecchi. **~drum** n timpano m

earl /ɜ:l/ n conte m

early /'ɜ:lɪ/ adj (-ier, -iest) (before expected time) in anticipo; (spring) prematuro; (reply) pronto; (works, writings) primo; **be here ~!** sii puntuale!; **you're ~!** sei in anticipo!; **~ morning walk** passeggiata f mattutina; **in the ~ morning** la mattina presto; **in the ~ spring** all'inizio della primavera; **~ retirement** prepensionamento m ● adv presto; (ahead of time) in anticipo; **~ in the morning** la mattina presto

earn /ɜ:n/ vt guadagnare; (deserve) meritare

earnest /'ɜ:nɪst/ adj serio ● n **in ~** sul serio. **~ly** adv con aria seria

earnings /'ɜ:nɪŋz/ npl guadagni mpl; (salary) stipendio m

ear: **~phones** npl cuffia fsg. **~ring** n orecchino m. **~shot** n **within ~shot** a portata d'orecchio; **he is out of ~shot** non può sentire

earth /ɜ:θ/ n terra f; **where/what on ~?** dove/che diavolo? ● vt (Electr) mettere a terra

'earthquake n terremoto m

earwig /'ɪəwɪg/ n forbicina f

ease /i:z/ n **at ~** a proprio agio; **at ~!** (Mil) riposo!; **ill at ~** a disagio; **with ~** con facilità ● vt calmare (pain); alleviare (tension, shortage); (slow down) rallentare; (loosen) allentare ● vi (pain, situation, wind:) calmarsi

easel /'i:zl/ n cavalletto m

easily /'i:zɪlɪ/ adv con facilità; **~ the best** certamente il meglio

east /i:st/ n est m; **to the ~ of** est

di ● adj dell'est ● adv verso est

Easter /'i:stə(r)/ n Pasqua f. **~ egg** n uovo m di Pasqua

east|erly /'i:stəlɪ/ adj di levante. **~ern** adj orientale. **~ward[s]** /-wəd[z]/ adv verso est

easy /'i:zɪ/ adj (-ier, -iest) facile; **take it** or **things ~** prendersela con calma; **take it ~!** (don't get excited) calma!; **go ~ with** non andarci piano con

easy: **~ chair** n poltrona f. **~'going** adj conciliante; **too ~going** troppo accomodante

eat /i:t/ vt/i (pt ate, pp eaten) mangiare. **~ into** vt intaccare. □ **~ up** vt mangiare tutto (food); fig inghiottire (profits)

eaves /i:vz/ npl cornicione msg. **~drop** vi (pt/pp **~dropped**) origliare; **~drop on** ascoltare di nascosto

ebb /eb/ n (tide) riflusso m; **at a low ~** fig a terra ● vi rifluire; fig declinare

ebony /'ebənɪ/ n ebano m

eccentric /ɪk'sentrɪk/ adj & n eccentrico, -a mf

echo /'ekəʊ/ n (pl -es) eco f or m ● vt (pt/pp echoed, pres p echoing) ● vt echeggiare; ripetere (words) ● vi risuonare (with di)

eclipse /ɪ'klɪps/ n (Astr) eclissi f inv ● vt fig eclissare

ecolog|ical /i:kə'lɒdʒɪkl/ adj ecologico. **~y** n ecologia f

e-commerce /'i:'kɒmɜ:s/ n e-commerce m inv, commercio m elettronico

economic /i:kə'nɒmɪk/ adj economico; **~ refugee** rifugiato, -a mf economico, -a. **~al** adj economico. **~ally** adv economicamente; (thriftily) in economia. **~s** n economia f

economist /ɪ'kɒnəmɪst/ n economista mf

economize /ɪ'kɒnəmaɪz/ vi economizzare (**on** su)

economy /ɪˈkɒnəmɪ/ n economia f

ecstasy /ˈekstəsɪ/ n estasi f inv; (drug) ecstasy f

eczema /ˈeksɪmə/ n eczema m

edge /edʒ/ n bordo m; (of knife) filo m; (of road) ciglio m; **on** ~ con i nervi tesi; **have the** ~ **on** 🔲 avere un vantaggio su ● vt bordare. □ ~ **forward** vi avanzare lentamente

edgeways /ˈedʒweɪz/ adv di fianco; **I couldn't get a word in** ~ non ho potuto infilare neanche mezza parola nel discorso

edgy /ˈedʒɪ/ adj nervoso

edible /ˈedɪbl/ adj commestibile; **this pizza's not** ~ questa pizza è immangiabile

---

Edinburgh Festival La più importante manifestazione culturale britannica, fondata nel 1947 e tenuta annualmente nella capitale scozzese, in agosto. Il festival offre spettacoli di musica, teatro, danza, ecc. e attira ogni anno moltissimi visitatori. Un settore sempre molto interessante è quello del cosiddetto *Fringe*, ossia gli eventi fuori dal programma ufficiale

---

edit /ˈedɪt/ vt (pt/pp edited) fare la revisione di (text); curare l'edizione di (anthology, dictionary); dirigere (newspaper); montare (film); editare (tape); ~**ed by** (book) a cura di

edition /ɪˈdɪʃn/ n edizione f

editor /ˈedɪtə(r)/ n (of anthology, dictionary) curatore, -trice mf; (of newspaper) redattore, -trice mf; (of film) responsabile mf del montaggio

editorial /edɪˈtɔːrɪəl/ adj redazionale ● n (Journ) editoriale m

educate /ˈedjʊkeɪt/ vt istruire; educare (public, mind); **be** ~**d at Eton** essere educato a Eton. ~**d** adj istruito

education /edjʊˈkeɪʃn/ n istru-

zione f; (culture) cultura f, educazione f. ~**al** adj istruttivo; (visit) educativo; (publishing) didattico

eel /iːl/ n anguilla f

eerie /ˈɪərɪ/ adj (**-ier, -iest**) inquietante

effect /ɪˈfekt/ n effetto m; **in** ~ in effetti; **take** ~ (law:) entrare in vigore; (medicine:) fare effetto ● vt effettuare

effective /ɪˈfektɪv/ adj efficace; (striking) che colpisce; (actual) di fatto; ~ **from** in vigore a partire da. ~**ly** adv efficacemente; (actually) di fatto. ~**ness** n efficacia f

effeminate /ɪˈfemɪnət/ adj effeminato

efficiency /ɪˈfɪʃənsɪ/ n efficienza f; (of machine) rendimento m

efficient /ɪˈfɪʃənt/ adj efficiente. ~**ly** adv efficientemente

effort /ˈefət/ n sforzo m; **make an** ~ sforzarsi. ~**less** adj facile. ~**lessly** adv con facilità

e.g. abbr (exempli gratia) per es.

egg[1] /eg/ vt ~ **on** 🔲 incitare

egg[2] n uovo m. ~**cup** n portauovo m inv. ~**head** n 🔲 intellettuale mf ● **shell** n guscio m d'uovo. ~**timer** n clessidra f per misurare il tempo di cottura delle uova

ego /ˈiːgəʊ/ n ego m. ~**centric** adj egocentrico. ~**ism** n egoismo m. ~**ist** n egoista mf. ~**tism** n egotismo m. ~**tist** n egotista mf

Egypt /ˈiːdʒɪpt/ n Egitto m. ~**ian** adj & n egiziano, -a mf

eiderdown /ˈaɪdə-/ n (quilt) piumino m

eight /eɪt/ adj otto ● n otto m. ~**teen** adj diciotto. ~**'teenth** adj diciottesimo

eighth /eɪtθ/ adj ottavo ● n ottavo m

eightieth /ˈeɪtɪɪθ/ adj ottantesimo

eighty /ˈeɪtɪ/ adj ottanta

either /ˈaɪðə(r)/ adj & pron ~ [of

them] l'uno o l'altro; **I don't like ~ [of them]** non mi piace né l'uno né l'altro; **on ~ side** da tutte e due le parti ● *adv* **I don't ~** nemmeno io; **I don't like John or his brother ~** non mi piace John e nemmeno suo fratello ● *conj* **~ John or his brother will be there** o saranno o John o suo fratello; **I don't like ~ John or his brother** non mi piacciono né John né suo fratello; **~ you go to bed or else...** o vai a letto o altrimenti ...

eject /ɪ'dʒekt/ *vt* eiettare (pilot); espellere (tape, drunk)

eke /iːk/ *vt* **~ out** far bastare; (*increase*) arrotondare; **~ out a living** arrangiarsi

elaborate¹ /ɪ'læbərət/ *adj* elaborato

elaborate² /ɪ'læbəreɪt/ *vi* entrare nei particolari (**on** di)

elapse /ɪ'læps/ *vi* trascorrere

elastic /ɪ'læstɪk/ *adj* elastico ● *n* elastico *m*. **~ 'band** n elastico *m*

elated /ɪ'leɪtɪd/ *adj* esultante

elbow /'elbəʊ/ *n* gomito *m*

elder¹ /'eldə(r)/ *n* (*tree*) sambuco *m*

eld|er² *adj* maggiore ● **the ~** il/la maggiore. **~erly** *adj* anziano. **~est** *adj* maggiore ● **the ~est** il/la maggiore

elect /ɪ'lekt/ *adj* **the president ~** il futuro presidente ● *vt* eleggere; **~ to do sth** decidere di fare qcsa. **~ion** n elezione *f*

elector /ɪ'lektə(r)/ *n* elettore, -trice *mf*. **~al** *adj* elettorale; **~al roll** liste *fpl* elettorali. **~ate** n elettorato *m*

electric /ɪ'lektrɪk/ *adj* elettrico

electrical /ɪ'lektrɪkl/ *adj* elettrico; **~ engineering** elettrotecnica *f*

electric 'blanket n termocoperta *f*

electrician /ɪlek'trɪʃn/ *n* elettricista *m*

electricity /ɪlek'trɪsəti/ *n*

elettricità *f*

electrify /ɪ'lektrɪfaɪ/ *vt* (*pt/pp* -**ied**) elettrificare; *fig* elettrizzare. **~ing** *adj fig* elettrizzante

electrocute /ɪ'lektrəkjuːt/ *vt* fulminare; (*execute*) giustiziare sulla sedia elettrica

electrode /ɪ'lektrəʊd/ *n* elettrodo *m*

electron /ɪ'lektrɒn/ *n* elettrone *m*

electronic /ɪlek'trɒnɪk/ *adj* elettronico. **~ mail** n posta *f* elettronica. **~s** n elettronica *f*

elegance /'elɪgəns/ *n* eleganza *f*

elegant /'elɪgənt/ *adj* elegante

element /'elɪmənt/ *n* elemento *m*. **~ary** *adj* elementare

elephant /'elɪfənt/ *n* elefante *m*

elevat|e /'elɪveɪt/ *vt* elevare. **~ion** n elevazione *f*; (*height*) altitudine *f*; (*angle*) alzo *m*

elevator /'elɪveɪtə(r)/ *n Am* ascensore *m*

eleven /ɪ'levn/ *adj* undici ● *n* undici *m*. **~th** *adj* undicesimo; **at the ~th hour** 🔟 all'ultimo momento

elf /elf/ *n* (*pl* **elves**) elfo *m*

eligible /'elɪdʒəbl/ *adj* eleggibile; **be ~ for** aver diritto a

eliminate /ɪ'lɪmɪneɪt/ *vt* eliminare

élite /er'liːt/ *n* fior fiore *m*

ellip|se /ɪ'lɪps/ *n* ellisse *f*. **~tical** *adj* ellittico

elm /elm/ *n* olmo *m*

elope /ɪ'ləʊp/ *vi* fuggire [per sposarsi]

eloquen|ce /'eləkwəns/ *n* eloquenza *f*. **~t** *adj* eloquente. **~tly** *adv* con eloquenza

else /els/ *adv* altro; **who ~?** e chi altro?; **he did of course, who ~?** l'ha fatto lui e chi, se no?; **nothing ~** nient'altro; **or ~** altrimenti; **someone ~** qualcun altro; **somewhere ~** da qualche altra parte; **anyone ~** chiunque altro; (*as ques-*

tion) nessun'altro?; (*anything* ~ qualunque altra cosa; (*as question*) altro?. ~**where** *adv* altrove

elude /ɪˈluːd/ *vt* eludere; (*avoid*) evitare; **the name ~s me** il nome mi sfugge

elusive /ɪˈluːsɪv/ *adj* elusivo

emaciated /ɪˈmeɪsɪeɪtɪd/ *adj* emaciato

e-mail /ˈiːmeɪl/ *n* posta *f* elettronica ● *vt* spedire via posta elettronica. ~ **address** *n* indirizzo *m* e-mail

embankment /ɪmˈbæŋkmənt/ *n* argine *m*; (*Rail*) massicciata *f*

embargo /emˈbɑːɡəʊ/ *n* (*pl* **-es**) embargo *m*

embark /ɪmˈbɑːk/ *vi* imbarcarsi; ~ **on** intraprendere. ~**ation** *n* imbarco *m*

embarrass /emˈbærəs/ *vt* imbarazzare. ~**ed** *adj* imbarazzato. ~**ing** *adj* imbarazzante. ~**ment** *n* imbarazzo *m*

embassy /ˈembəsɪ/ *n* ambasciata *f*

embedded /ɪmˈbedɪd/ *adj* (*in concrete*) cementato; (*traditions, feelings*) radicato

embellish /ɪmˈbelɪʃ/ *vt* abbellire

embers /ˈembəz/ *npl* braci *fpl*

embezzle /ɪmˈbezl/ *vt* appropriarsi indebitamente di. ~**ment** *n* appropriazione *f* indebita

emblem /ˈembləm/ *n* emblema *m*

embrace /ɪmˈbreɪs/ *n* abbraccio *m* ● *vt* abbracciare ● *vi* abbracciarsi

embroider /ɪmˈbrɔɪdə(r)/ *vt* ricamare (*design*); *fig* abbellire. ~**y** *n* ricamo *m*

embryo /ˈembrɪəʊ/ *n* embrione *m*

emerald /ˈemərəld/ *n* smeraldo *m*

emerge /ɪˈmɜːdʒ/ *vi* emergere; (*come into being: nation*) nascere; (*sun, flowers*) spuntare fuori. ~**gence** *n* emergere *m*; (*of new country*) nascita *f*

emergency /ɪˈmɜːdʒənsɪ/ *n* emergenza *f*; **in an** ~ in caso di emergenza. ~ **exit** *n* uscita *f* di sicurezza

emigrant /ˈemɪɡrənt/ *n* emigrante *mf*

emigrat|e /ˈemɪɡreɪt/ *vi* emigrare. ~**ion** *n* emigrazione *f*

eminent /ˈemɪnənt/ *adj* eminente. ~**ly** *adv* eminentemente

emission /ɪˈmɪʃn/ *n* emissione *f*; (*of fumes*) esalazione *f*

emit /ɪˈmɪt/ *vt* (*pl/pp* **emitted**) emettere; esalare (*fumes*)

emotion /ɪˈməʊʃn/ *n* emozione *f*. ~**al** *adj* denso di emozione; (*person, reaction*) emotivo; **become ~al** avere una reazione emotiva

emotive /ɪˈməʊtɪv/ *adj* emotivo

emperor /ˈempərə(r)/ *n* imperatore *m*

emphasis /ˈemfəsɪs/ *n* enfasi *f*; **put the** ~ **on sth** accentuare qcsa

emphasize /ˈemfəsaɪz/ *vt* accentuare (*word, syllable*); sottolineare (*need*)

emphatic /ɪmˈfætɪk/ *adj* categorico

empire /ˈempaɪə(r)/ *n* impero *m*

empirical /ɪmˈpɪrɪkl/ *adj* empirico

employ /emˈplɔɪ/ *vt* impiegare; *fig* usare (*tact*). ~**ee** *n* impiegato, -a *mf*. ~**er** *n* datore *m* di lavoro. ~**ment** *n* occupazione *f*; (*work*) lavoro *m*. ~**ment agency** *n* ufficio *m* di collocamento

empower /ɪmˈpaʊə(r)/ *vt* autorizzare; (*enable*) mettere in grado

empress /ˈemprɪs/ *n* imperatrice *f*

empty /ˈemptɪ/ *adj* vuoto; (*promise, threat*) vano ● *v* (*pt/pp* **-ied**) ● *vt* vuotare (*container*) ● *vi* vuotarsi

emulate /ˈemjʊleɪt/ *vt* emulare

emulsion /ɪˈmʌlʃn/ *n* emulsione *f*

enable /ɪˈneɪbl/ *vt* ~ **sb to** mettere qcno in grado di

enact /ɪˈnækt/ *vt* (*Theat*) rappresentare; decretare (*law*)

enamel /ɪˈnæml/ *n* smalto *m* ● *vt* (*pt/pp* **enamelled**) smaltare

enchant /ɪnˈtʃɑːnt/ vt incantare.
~ing adj incantevole. ~ment n incanto m

encircle /ɪnˈsɜːkl/ vt circondare

enclave /ˈenkleɪv/ n enclave f inv; fig territorio m

enclos|e /ɪnˈkləʊz/ vt circondare (land); (in letter) allegare (with a). ~ed adj (space) chiuso; (in letter) allegato. ~ure n (at zoo) recinto m; (in letter) allegato m

encore /ˈɒŋkɔː(r)/ n & int bis m inv

encounter /ɪnˈkaʊntə(r)/ n incontro m; (battle) scontro m ● vt incontrare

encourag|e /ɪnˈkʌrɪdʒ/ vt incoraggiare; promuovere (the arts, independence). ~ement n incoraggiamento m; (of the arts) promozione f. ~ing adj incoraggiante; (smile) di incoraggiamento

encroach /ɪnˈkrəʊtʃ/ vi ~ on invadere (land, privacy); abusare di (time); interferire con (rights)

encyclop[a]ed|ia /ɪnsaɪkləˈpiː-dɪə/ n enciclopedia f. ~ic adj enciclopedico

end /end/ n fine f; (of box, table, piece of string) estremità f; (of town, room) parte f; (purpose) fine m; **in the ~** alla fine; **at the ~ of May** alla fine di maggio; **at the ~ of the street/garden** in fondo alla strada/al giardino; **on ~** (upright) in piedi; **for days on ~** per giorni e giorni; **for six days on ~** per sei giorni di fila; **put an ~ to** sth mettere fine a qcsa; **make ~s meet** Ⅰ sbarcare il lunario; **no ~ of** Ⅰ un sacco di ● vt/i finire. **a ~ up** vi finire; ~ **up doing sth** finire col fare qcsa

endanger /ɪnˈdeɪndʒə(r)/ vt rischiare (one's life); mettere a repentaglio (sb else, success of sth)

endear|ing /ɪnˈdɪərɪŋ/ adj accattivante. ~ment n term of ~ment vezzeggiativo m

endeavour /ɪnˈdevə(r)/ n tentativo m ● vi sforzarsi (**to** di)

ending /ˈendɪŋ/ n fine f; (Gram) desinenza f

endless /ˈendlɪs/ adj interminabile; (patience) infinito. ~ly adv continuamente; (patient) infinitamente

endorse /enˈdɔːs/ vt girare (cheque); (sports personality:) fare pubblicità a (product); approvare (plan). ~ment n (of cheque) girata f; (of plan) conferma f; (on driving licence) registrazione f su patente di un'infrazione

endur|e /ɪnˈdjʊə(r)/ vt sopportare ● vi durare. ~ing adj duraturo

enemy /ˈenəmɪ/ n nemico, -a mf ● attrib nemico

energetic /enəˈdʒetɪk/ adj energico

energy /ˈenədʒɪ/ n energia f

enforce /ɪnˈfɔːs/ vt far rispettare (law). ~d adj forzato

engage /ɪnˈɡeɪdʒ/ vt assumere (staff), (Theat) ingaggiare; (Auto) ingranare (gear) ● vi (Techn) ingranare; ~ **in** impegnarsi in. ~d adj (in use, busy) occupato; (person) impegnato; (to be married) fidanzato; **get ~d** fidanzarsi (**to** con); ~d **tone** (Teleph) segnale m di occupato. ~ment n fidanzamento m; (appointment) appuntamento m; (Mil) combattimento m; ~ment **ring** anello m di fidanzamento

engine /ˈendʒɪn/ n motore m; (Rail) locomotrice f. ~-**driver** n macchinista m

engineer /endʒɪˈnɪə(r)/ n ingegnere m; (service, installation) tecnico m; (Naut, Am Rail) macchinista m ● vt fig architettare. ~ing n ingegneria f

England /ˈɪŋɡlənd/ n Inghilterra f

English /ˈɪŋɡlɪʃ/ adj inglese; **the ~ Channel** la Manica f ● n (language) inglese m; **the ~** pl gli inglesi. ~**man** n inglese m. ~**woman** n inglese f

engrav|e /ɪnˈɡreɪv/ vt incidere.

~ing n incisione f

engulf /ɪnˈgʌlf/ vt (fire, waves:) inghiottire

enhance /ɪnˈhɑːns/ vt accrescere (beauty, reputation); migliorare (performance)

enigma /ɪˈnɪgmə/ n enigma m. **~tic** adj enigmatico

enjoy /ɪnˈdʒɔɪ/ vt godere di (good health); **~ oneself** divertirsi; **I ~ cooking/painting** mi piace cucinare/dipingere; **~ your meal** buon appetito. **~able** adj piacevole. **~ment** n piacere m

enlarge /ɪnˈlɑːdʒ/ vt ingrandire ● vi **~ upon** dilungarsi su. **~ment** n ingrandimento m

enlighten /ɪnˈlaɪtn/ vt illuminare. **~ed** adj progressista. **~ment** n The E**~ment** l'Illuminismo m

enlist /ɪnˈlɪst/ vt (Mil) reclutare; **~ sb's help** farsi aiutare da qcno ● vi (Mil) arruolarsi

enliven /ɪnˈlaɪvn/ vt animare

enormity /ɪˈnɔːmətɪ/ n enormità f

enormous /ɪˈnɔːməs/ adj enorme. **~ly** adv estremamente; (grateful) infinitamente

enough /ɪˈnʌf/ adj & n abbastanza; **I didn't bring ~ clothes** non ho portato abbastanza vestiti; **have you had ~?** (to eat/drink) hai mangiato/bevuto abbastanza?; **is that ~?** ne ho abbastanza!; **is that ~?** basta?; **that's ~** I basta così!; **£50 isn't ~** 50 sterline non sono sufficienti ● adv abbastanza; **you're not working fast ~** non lavori abbastanza in fretta; **funnily ~** stranamente

enquir|e /ɪnˈkwaɪə(r)/ vi domandare; **~e about** chiedere informazioni su. **~y** n domanda f; (investigation) inchiesta f

enrage /ɪnˈreɪdʒ/ vt fare arrabbiare

enrol /ɪnˈrəʊl/ vi (pt/pp **-rolled**) (for exam, in club) iscriversi (**for, in** a).

~ment n iscrizione f

ensu|e /ɪnˈsjuː/ vi seguire; **the ~ing discussion** la discussione che ne è seguita

ensure /ɪnˈʃʊə(r)/ vt assicurare; **~ that** (person:) assicurarsi che; (measure:) garantire che

entail /ɪnˈteɪl/ vt comportare; **what does it ~?** in che cosa consiste?

entangle /ɪnˈtæŋgl/ vt **get ~d in** rimanere impigliato in; fig rimanere coinvolto in

enter /ˈentə(r)/ vt entrare in; iscrivere (name, runner in race); cominciare (university); partecipare a (competition); (Comput) immettere (data); (write down) scrivere ● vi entrare; (Theat) entrare in scena; (register as competitor) iscriversi; (take part) partecipare (**in** a)

enterprise /ˈentəpraɪz/ n impresa f; (quality) iniziativa f. **~ing** adj intraprendente

entertain /entəˈteɪn/ vt intrattenere; (invite) ricevere; nutrire (ideas, hopes); prendere in considerazione (possibility) ● vi intrattenersi; (have guests) ricevere. **~er** n artista m/f. **~ing** adj (person) di gradevole compagnia; (evening, film, play) divertente. **~ment** n (amusement) intrattenimento m

enthral /ɪnˈθrɔːl/ vt (pt/pp **enthralled**) **be ~led** essere affascinato (**by** da)

enthusias|m /ɪnˈθjuːzɪæzm/ n entusiasmo m. **~t** n entusiasta m/f. **~tic** adj entusiastico

entice /ɪnˈtaɪs/ vt attirare. **~ment** n incentivo m

entire /ɪnˈtaɪə(r)/ adj intero. **~ly** adv del tutto; **I'm not ~ly satisfied** non sono completamente soddisfatto. **~ty** n in its **~ty** nell'insieme

entitle /ɪnˈtaɪtl/ vt intitolare; **be ~d** (book:) intitolarsi; **be ~d to sth** avere diritto a qcsa. **~ment** n diritto m

entity /ˈentətɪ/ n entità f

entrance[1] /'entrəns/ n entrata f; (Theat) entrata f in scena; (right to enter) ammissione f. **'no ~'** 'ingresso vietato'. **~ examination** n esame m di ammissione. **~ fee** n how much is the **~ fee?** quanto costa il biglietto di ingresso?

entrance[2] /ın'trɑːns/ vt estasiare

entrant /'entrənt/ n concorrente mf

entreat /ın'triːt/ vt supplicare

entrenched /ın'trentʃt/ adj (ideas, views) radicato

entrust /ın'trʌst/ vt ~ sb with sth, ~ sth to sb affidare qcsa a qcno

entry /'entrı/ n ingresso m; (way in) entrata f; (in directory etc) voce f; (in appointment diary) appuntamento m; no ~ ingresso vietato; (Auto) accesso vietato. **~ form** n modulo m di ammissione. **~ visa** n visto m di ingresso

enumerate /ı'njuːməreıt/ vt enumerare

envelop /ın'veləp/ vt (pt/pp enveloped) avviluppare

envelope /'envələup/ n busta f

enviable /'envıəbl/ adj invidiabile

envious /'envıəs/ adj invidioso. **~ly** adv con invidia

environment /ın'vaırənmənt/ n ambiente m

environmental /ınvaırən'mentl/ adj ambientale. **~ist** n ambientalista mf. **~ly** adv **~ly friendly** che rispetta l'ambiente

envisage /ın'vızıdʒ/ vt prevedere

envoy /'envɔı/ n inviato, -a mf

envy /'envı/ n invidia f ● vt (pt/pp -ied) ~ sb sth invidiare qcno per qcsa

enzyme /'enzaım/ n enzima m

epic /'epık/ adj epico ● n epopea f

epidemic /epı'demık/ n epidemia f

epilep|sy /'epılepsı/ n epilessia f. **~tic** adj & n epilettico, -a mf

epilogue /'epılɒg/ n epilogo m

episode /'epısəud/ n episodio m

epitaph /'epıtɑːf/ n epitaffio m

epitom|e /ı'pıtəmı/ n epitome f. **~ize** vt essere il classico esempio di

epoch /'iːpɒk/ n epoca f

equal /'iːkwl/ adj (parts, amounts) uguale; of ~ **height** della stessa altezza; be ~ to the task essere a l'altezza del compito ● n pari m inv ● vt (pt/pp equalled) (be same in quantity as) essere pari a; (rival) uguagliare; **5 plus 5 ~s 10** 5 più 5 [è] uguale a 10. **~ity** n uguaglianza f

equalize /'iːkwəlaız/ vi (Sport) pareggiare. **~r** n (Sport) pareggio m

equally /'iːkwəlı/ adv (divide) in parti uguali; ~ **intelligent** della stessa intelligenza; **~,...** allo stesso tempo...

equator /ı'kweıtə(r)/ n equatore m

equilibrium /iːkwı'lıbrıəm/ n equilibrio m

equinox /'iːkwınɒks/ n equinozio m

equip /ı'kwıp/ vt (pt/pp equipped) equipaggiare; attrezzare (kitchen, office). **~ment** n attrezzatura f

equivalent /ı'kwıvələnt/ adj equivalente; be ~ to equivalere a ● n equivalente m

equivocal /ı'kwıvəkl/ adj equivoco

era /'ıərə/ n età f; (geological) era f

eradicate /ı'rædıkeıt/ vt eradicare

erase /ı'reız/ vt cancellare. **~r** n gomma f [da cancellare]; (for blackboard) cancellino m

erect /ı'rekt/ adj eretto ● vt erigere. **~ion** n erezione f

ero|de /ı'rəud/ vt (water:) erodere; (acid:) corrodere. **~sion** n erosione f; (by acid) corrosione f

erotic /ı'rɒtık/ adj erotico.

err /ɜː(r)/ vi errare; (sin) peccare

errand /'erənd/ n commissione f

erratic /ı'rætık/ adj irregolare; (person, moods) imprevedibile; (exchange rate) incostante

erroneous /ɪ'rəʊnɪəs/ adj erroneo

error /'erə(r)/ n errore m; **in ~** per errore

erudit|e /'erʊdaɪt/ adj erudito.
~ion n erudizione f

erupt /ɪ'rʌpt/ vi eruttare; (spots:) spuntare; (fig: in anger) dare in escandescenze. **~ion** n eruzione f; fig scoppio m

escalat|e /'eskəleɪt/ vi intensificarsi
● vt intensificare. **~ion** n escalation f
inv. **~or** n scala f mobile

escapade /'eskəpeɪd/ n scappatella f

escape /ɪ'skeɪp/ n fuga f; (from prison) evasione f; **have a narrow ~** cavarsela per un pelo ● vi (prisoner:) evadere (**from** da); sfuggire (**from** sb alla sorveglianza di qcno); (animal:) scappare; (gas:) fuoriuscire ● vt ~ **notice** passare inosservato; **the name ~s me** mi sfugge il nome

escapism /ɪ'skeɪpɪzm/ n evasione f [dalla realtà]

escort[1] /'eskɔt/ n accompagnatore, -trice mf; (Mil etc) scorta f

escort[2] /ɪ'skɔt/ vt accompagnare; (Mil etc) scortare

Eskimo /'eskɪməʊ/ n esquimese mf

especial /ɪ'speʃl/ adj speciale. **~ly** adv specialmente; (kind) particolarmente

espionage /'espɪənɑːʒ/ n spionaggio m

essay /'eseɪ/ n saggio m; (Sch) tema f

essence /'esns/ n essenza f; **in ~** in sostanza

essential /ɪ'senʃl/ adj essenziale
● npl **the ~s** l'essenziale m. **~ly** adv essenzialmente

establish /ɪ'stæblɪʃ/ vt stabilire (contact, lead); fondare (firm); (prove) accertare; **~ oneself as** offermarsi come. **~ment** n (firm) azienda f; **the E~ment** l'ordine m costituito

estate /ɪ'steɪt/ n tenuta f; (possessions) patrimonio m; (housing) quartiere m residenziale. **~ agent** n agente m immobiliare. **~ car** n giardiniera f

esteem /ɪ'stiːm/ n stima f ● vt stimare; (consider) giudicare

estimate[1] /'estɪmət/ n valutazione f; (Comm) preventivo m; **at a rough ~** a occhio e croce

estimat|e[2] /'estɪmeɪt/ vt stimare. **~ion** n (esteem) stima f; **in my ~ion** (judgement) a mio giudizio

estuary /'estjʊərɪ/ n estuario m

etc /et'setərə/ abbr (et cetera) ecc

etching /'etʃɪŋ/ n acquaforte f

eternal /ɪ'tɜːnl/ adj eterno

eternity /ɪ'tɜːnətɪ/ n eternità f

ethic /'eθɪk/ n etica f. **~al** adj etico.
~s n etica f

ethnic /'eθnɪk/ adj etnico

etiquette /'etɪket/ n etichetta f

EU n abbr (European Union) UE f

euphemis|m /'juːfəmɪzm/ n eufemismo m. **~tic** adj eufemistico

euphoria /juː'fɔːrɪə/ n euforia f

euro /'jʊərəʊ/ n euro m inv

Euro- /'jʊərəʊ/ pref **~cheque** n eurochèque m inv. **~dollar** n eurodollaro m

Europe /'jʊərəp/ n Europa f

European /jʊərə'piːən/ adj europeo.
~ Union Unione f Europea ● n europeo, -a mf

Euro-sceptic /jʊərəʊ'skeptɪk/ adj eurocettico ● n euroscettico, -a mf

evacuate /ɪ'vækjʊeɪt/ vt evacuare (building, area). **~ion** n evacuazione f

evade /ɪ'veɪd/ vt evadere (taxes); evitare (the enemy, authorities); **~ the issue** evitare l'argomento

evaluate /ɪ'væljʊeɪt/ vt valutare.
~ion /-'eɪʃn/ n valutazione f

evangelical /iːvæn'dʒelɪkl/ adj evangelico. **~list** n evangelista m

evaporat|e /ɪ'væpəreɪt/ vi evaporare; fig svanire. **~ion** n evaporazione f

evasion /ɪ'veɪʒn/ n evasione f

evasive /ɪ'veɪsɪv/ adj evasivo

eve /iːv/ n liter vigilia f

even /'iːvn/ adj (level) piatto; (same, equal) uguale; (regular) regolare; (number) pari; **get ~ with** vendicarsi di; **now we're ~** adesso siamo pari ● adv anche, ancora; **~ if** anche se; **~ so** con tutto ciò; **not ~** nemmeno; **~ bigger/hotter** ancora più grande/caldo ● vt **~ the score** (Sport) pareggiare. **□ ~ out** vi livellarsi. **□ ~ up** vt livellare

evening /'iːvnɪŋ/ n sera f; (whole evening) serata f; **this ~** stasera; **in the ~** la sera; **~ class** n corso m serale. **~ dress** n abito m scuro; (woman's) abito m da sera

event /ɪ'vent/ n avvenimento m; (function) manifestazione f; (Sport) gara f; **in the ~ of** nell'eventualità di; **in the ~ that...** alla fine. **~ful** adj movimentato

eventual /ɪ'ventjʊəl/ adj **the ~ winner was...** alla fine il vincitore è stato.... **~ity** n eventualità f. **~ly** adv alla fine; **~ly!** finalmente!

ever /'evə(r)/ adv mai; **I haven't ~...** non ho mai...; **for ~** per sempre; **hardly ~** quasi mai; **~ since** da quando; (since that time) da allora; **~ so** 🗓 veramente

'evergreen n sempreverde m

ever'lasting adj eterno

every /'evrɪ/ adj ogni; **~ one** ciascuno; **~ other day** un giorno sì un giorno no

every: ~body pron tutti pl. **~day** adj quotidiano, di ogni giorno. **~one** pron tutti pl; **~thing** pron tutto; **~where** adv dappertutto; (wherever) dovunque

evict /ɪ'vɪkt/ vt sfrattare. **~ion** n sfratto m

eviden|ce /'evɪdəns/ n evidenza f; (Jur) testimonianza f; **give ~ce** te-

stimoniare. **~t** adj evidente. **~tly** adv evidentemente

evil /'iːvl/ adj cattivo ● n male m

evocative /ɪ'vɒkətɪv/ adj evocativo; **be ~ of** evocare

evoke /ɪ'vəʊk/ vt evocare

evolution /iːvə'luːʃn/ n evoluzione f

evolve /ɪ'vɒlv/ vt evolvere ● vi evolversi

ewe /juː/ n pecora f

exact /ɪg'zækt/ adj esatto ● vt esigere. **~ing** adj esigente. **~itude** n esattezza f. **~ly** adv esattamente; **not ~ly** non proprio. **~ness** n precisione f

exaggerat|e /ɪg'zædʒəreɪt/ vt/i esagerare. **~ion** n esagerazione f

exam /ɪg'zæm/ n esame m

examination /ɪgzæmɪ'neɪʃn/ n esame m; (of patient) visita f

examine /ɪg'zæmɪn/ vt esaminare; visitare (patient). **~r** n (Sch) esaminatore, -trice mf

example /ɪg'zɑːmpl/ n esempio m; **for ~** per esempio; **make an ~ of sb** punire qcno per dare un esempio; **be an ~ to sb** dare il buon esempio a qcno

exasperat|e /ɪg'zæspəreɪt/ vt esasperare. **~ion** n esasperazione f

excavat|e /'ekskəveɪt/ vt scavare; (Archaeol) fare gli scavi di. **~ion** n scavo m

exceed /ɪk'siːd/ vt eccedere. **~ingly** adv estremamente

excel /ɪk'sel/ v (pt/pp **excelled**) ● vi eccellere ● vt **~ oneself** superare se stessi

excellen|ce /'eksələns/ n eccellenza f. **E~cy** n (title) Eccellenza f. **~t** adj eccellente

except /ɪk'sept/ prep eccetto, tranne; **~ for** eccetto, tranne; **~ that...** eccetto che.... ● vt eccettuare. **~ing** prep eccetto, tranne

exception | exist

exception /ɪkˈsepʃn/ n eccezione f; **take ~ to** fare obiezioni a. **~al** adj eccezionale. **~ally** adv eccezionalmente

excerpt /ˈeksɜːpt/ n estratto m

excess /ɪkˈses/ n eccesso m; **in ~ of** oltre. **~ baggage** n bagaglio m in eccedenza. **~ fare** n supplemento m

excessive /ɪkˈsesɪv/ adj eccessivo. **~ly** adv eccessivamente

exchange /ɪksˈtʃeɪndʒ/ n scambio m; (Teleph) centrale f; (Comm) cambio m; **in ~** in cambio (for di) ● vt scambiare (for con); cambiare (money). **~ rate** n tasso m di cambio

excise[1] /ˈeksaɪz/ n dazio m; **~ duty** dazio m

excise[2] /ɪkˈsaɪz/ vt recidere

excitable /ɪkˈsaɪtəbl/ adj eccitabile

excit|e /ɪkˈsaɪt/ vt eccitare. **~ed** adj eccitato; **get ~ed** eccitarsi. **~edly** adv tutto eccitato. **~ement** n eccitazione f. **~ing** adj eccitante; (story, film) appassionante; (holiday) entusiasmante

exclaim /ɪkˈskleɪm/ vt/i esclamare

exclamation /ekskləˈmeɪʃn/ n esclamazione f. **~ mark** n, Am **~ point** n punto m esclamativo

exclu|de /ɪkˈskluːd/ vt escludere. **~ding** pron escluso. **~sion** n esclusione f

exclusive /ɪkˈskluːsɪv/ adj (rights, club) esclusivo; (interview) in esclusiva; **~ of...** ...escluso. **~ly** adv esclusivamente

excruciating /ɪkˈskruːʃɪeɪtɪŋ/ adj atroce (pain); (fam: very bad) spaventoso

excursion /ɪkˈskɜːʃn/ n escursione f

excusable /ɪkˈskjuːzəbl/ adj perdonabile

excuse[1] /ɪkˈskjuːs/ n scusa f

excuse[2] /ɪkˈskjuːz/ vt scusare; **~ from** esonerare da; **~ me!** (to get attention) scusi!; (to get past) permesso!,

scusi!; (indignant) come ha detto?

ex-di'rectory adj be **~** non figurare sull'elenco telefonico

execute /ˈeksɪkjuːt/ vt eseguire; (put to death) giustiziare; attuare (plan)

execution /eksɪˈkjuːʃn/ n esecuzione f; (of plan) attuazione f. **~er** n boia m inv

executive /ɪgˈzekjʊtɪv/ adj esecutivo ● n dirigente mf; (Pol) esecutivo m

executor /ɪgˈzekjʊtə(r)/ n (Jur) esecutore, -trice mf

exempt /ɪgˈzempt/ adj esente ● vt esentare (from da). **~ion** n esenzione f

exercise /ˈeksəsaɪz/ n esercizio m; (Mil) esercitazione f; physical **~s** ginnastica f; **take ~** fare del moto ● vt esercitare (muscles, horse); portare a spasso (dog); mettere in pratica (skills) ● vi esercitarsi. **~ book** n quaderno m

exert /ɪgˈzɜːt/ vt esercitare; **~ oneself** sforzarsi. **~ion** n sforzo m

exhale /eksˈheɪl/ vt/i esalare

exhaust /ɪgˈzɔːst/ n (Auto) scappamento m; (pipe) tubo m di scappamento; **~ fumes** fumi mpl di scarico m ● vt esaurire. **~ed** adj esausto. **~ing** adj estenuante; (climate, person) sfibrante. **~ion** n esaurimento m. **~ive** adj fig esauriente

exhibit /ɪgˈzɪbɪt/ n oggetto m esposto; (Jur) reperto m ● vt esporre; fig dimostrare

exhibition /eksɪˈbɪʃn/ n mostra f; (of strength, skill) dimostrazione f. **~ist** n esibizionista mf

exhibitor /ɪgˈzɪbɪtə(r)/ n espositore, -trice mf

exhort /ɪgˈzɔːt/ vt esortare

exile /ˈeksaɪl/ n esilio m; (person) esule mf ● vt esiliare

exist /ɪgˈzɪst/ vi esistere. **~ence** n esistenza f; **in ~** esistente; **be in**

~ence esistere. ~ing adj attuale

exit /ˈeksɪt/ n uscita f; (Theat) uscita f di scena ● vi (Theat) uscire di scena; (Comput) uscire

exorbitant /ɪgˈzɔːbɪtənt/ adj esorbitante

exotic /ɪgˈzɒtɪk/ adj esotico

expand /ɪkˈspænd/ vt espandere ● vi espandersi; (Comm) svilupparsi; (metal:) dilatarsi; ~ **on** (fig: explain better) approfondire

expanse /ɪkˈspæns/ n estensione f. ~ion n espansione f; (Comm) sviluppo m; (of metal) dilatazione f. ~ive adj espansivo

expatriate /eksˈpætrɪət/ n espatriato, -a mf

expect /ɪkˈspekt/ vt aspettare (letter, baby); (suppose) pensare; (demand) esigere; I ~ **so** penso di sì; **be** ~**ing** essere in stato interessante

expectan|cy /ɪkˈspektənsɪ/ n aspettativa f. ~**t** adj in attesa; ~**t mother** donna f incinta. ~**tly** adv con impazienza

expectation /ekspekˈteɪʃn/ n aspettativa f, speranza f

expedient /ɪkˈspiːdɪənt/ adj conveniente ● n espediente m

expedition /ekspɪˈdɪʃn/ n spedizione f. ~**ary** adj (Mil) di spedizione

expel /ɪkˈspel/ vt (pt/pp expelled) espellere

expend /ɪkˈspend/ vt consumare. ~**able** adj sacrificabile

expenditure /ɪkˈspendɪtʃə(r)/ n spesa f

expense /ɪkˈspens/ n spesa f; **business** ~**s** pl spese fpl; **at my** ~ a mie spese; **at the** ~ **of** fig a spese di

expensive /ɪkˈspensɪv/ adj caro, costoso. ~**ly** adv costosamente

experience /ɪkˈspɪərɪəns/ n esperienza f ● vt provare (sensation); avere (problem). ~**d** adj esperto

experiment /ɪkˈsperɪmənt/ n esperimento ● vi sperimentare. ~**al**

adj sperimentale

expert /ˈekspɜːt/ adj & n esperto, -a mf. ~**ly** adv abilmente

expertise /ekspɜːˈtiːz/ n competenza f

expire /ɪkˈspaɪə(r)/ vi scadere

expiry /ɪkˈspaɪərɪ/ n scadenza f. ~ **date** n data f di scadenza

explain /ɪkˈspleɪn/ vt spiegare

explana|tion /ekspləˈneɪʃn/ n spiegazione f. ~**tory** adj esplicativo

explicit /ɪkˈsplɪsɪt/ adj esplicito. ~**ly** adv esplicitamente

explode /ɪkˈspləʊd/ vi esplodere ● vt fare esplodere

exploit[1] /ˈeksplɔɪt/ n impresa f

exploit[2] /ɪkˈsplɔɪt/ vt sfruttare. ~**ation** n sfruttamento m

explora|tion /ekspləˈreɪʃn/ n esplorazione f. ~**tory** adj esplorativo

explore /ɪkˈsplɔː(r)/ vt esplorare; fig studiare (implications). ~**r** n esploratore, -trice mf

explos|ion /ɪkˈspləʊʒn/ n esplosione f. ~**ive** adj & n esplosivo m

export /ˈekspɔːt/ n esportazione f ● vt /-ˈspɔːt/ esportare. ~**er** n esportatore, -trice mf

expos|e /ɪkˈspəʊz/ vt esporre; (reveal) svelare; smascherare (traitor etc). ~**ure** n esposizione f; (Med) esposizione f prolungata al freddo/caldo; (of crimes) smascheramento m; **24** ~**ures** (Phot) 24 pose

express /ɪkˈspres/ adj espresso ● adv (send) per espresso ● n (train) espresso ● vt esprimere; ~ **oneself** esprimersi. ~**ion** n espressione f. ~**ive** adj espressivo. ~**ly** adv espressamente

expulsion /ɪkˈspʌlʃn/ n espulsione f

exquisite /ekˈskwɪzɪt/ adj squisito

extend /ɪkˈstend/ vt prolungare (visit, road); prorogare (visa, contract); ampliare (building, knowledge); (*stretch out*) allungare; tendere (hand); ● vi (garden, knowledge) estendersi

extension /ɪkˈstenʃn/ n prolungamento m; (*of visa, contract*) proroga f; (*of treaty*) ampliamento m; (*part of building*) annesso m; (*length of cable*) prolunga f; (*Teleph*) interno m; ~ 226 interno 226

extensive /ɪkˈstensɪv/ adj ampio, vasto. ~ly adv ampiamente

extent /ɪkˈstent/ n (scope) portata f; to a certain ~ fino a un certo punto; to such an ~ that... fino al punto che...

exterior /ɪkˈstɪərɪə(r)/ adj & n esterno m

exterminat|e /ɪkˈstɜːmɪneɪt/ vt sterminare. ~ion n sterminio m

external /ɪkˈstɜːnl/ adj esterno; for ~ use only (Med) per uso esterno. ~ly adv esternamente

extinct /ɪkˈstɪŋkt/ adj estinto. ● ion n estinzione f

extinguish /ɪkˈstɪŋgwɪʃ/ vt estinguere. ~er n estintore m

extort /ɪkˈstɔːt/ vt estorcere. ~ion n estorsione f

extortionate /ɪkˈstɔːʃənət/ adj esorbitante

extra /ˈekstrə/ adj in più; (train) straordinario; an ~ £10 10 sterline extra, 10 sterline in più ● adv in più; (especially) più; **pay** ~ pagare in più, pagare extra; **strong/busy** fortissimo/occupatissimo ● n (Theat) comparsa f; ~s pl extra mpl

extract¹ /ˈekstrækt/ n estratto m

extract² /ɪkˈstrækt/ vt estrarre (tooth, oil); strappare (secret); ricavare (truth). ~or n [fan] m aspiratore m

extradit|e /ˈekstrədaɪt/ vt (Jur) estradare. ~ion n estradizione f

extraordinar|y /ɪkˈstrɔːdɪnərɪ/ adj straordinario. ~ily adv straordinariamente

extravagan|ce /ɪkˈstrævəgəns/ n (with money) prodigalità f; (of behaviour) stravaganza f. ~t adj spendaccione; (bizarre) stravagante; (claim) esagerato

extrem|e /ɪkˈstriːm/ adj estremo. ● n estremo m; in the ~e al massimo. ~ely adv estremamente. ~ist n estremista mf

extricate /ˈekstrɪkeɪt/ vt districare

extrovert /ˈekstrəvɜːt/ n estroverso, -a mf

exuberant /ɪgˈzjuːbərənt/ adj esuberante

exude /ɪgˈzjuːd/ vt also fig trasudare

exult /ɪgˈzʌlt/ vi esultare

eye /aɪ/ n occhio m; (of needle) cruna f; **keep an ~ on** tener d'occhio; **see ~ to ~** aver le stesse idee ● vt (pt/pp eyed, pres p ey[e]ing) guardare

eye: ~**ball** n bulbo m oculare. ~**brow** n sopracciglio m (pl sopracciglia f). ~**lash** n ciglio m (pl ciglia f). ~**lid** n palpebra f. ~**opener** n rivelazione f. ~**shadow** n ombretto m. ~**sight** n vista f. ~**sore** n 🔟 pugno m nell'occhio. ~**witness** n testimone mf oculare

Ff

fable /ˈfeɪbl/ n favola f

fabric /ˈfæbrɪk/ n also fig tessuto m

fabulous /ˈfæbjʊləs/ adj 🔟 favoloso

façade /fəˈsɑːd/ n (of building, person) facciata f

face /feɪs/ n faccia f, viso m; (grimace) smorfia f; (surface) faccia f; (of clock) quadrante m; **pull** ~s far boccacce; **in the** ~ **of** di fronte a; **on the** ~ **of it** in apparenza ● vt essere di fronta a; (confront) affrontare; ~

north (house:) dare a nord; **~ the fact that** arrendersi al fatto che. □ **~ up to** *vt* accettare (facts); affrontare (person)

face: **~-flannel** $n \approx$ guanto *m* di spugna. **~less** *adj* anonimo. **~-lift** *n* plastica *f* facciale

facetious /fə'si:ʃəs/ *adj* spiritoso. ~ **remarks** spiritosaggini *mpl*

facial /'feɪʃl/ *adj* facciale ●*n* trattamento *m* di bellezza al viso

facile /'fæsaɪl/ *adj* semplicistico

facilitate /fə'sɪlɪteɪt/ *vt* rendere possibile; (make easier) facilitare

facility /fə'sɪlətɪ/ *n* facilità *f*; **~ies** *pl* (of area, in hotel etc) attrezzature *fpl*

fact /fækt/ *n* fatto *m*; **in ~** infatti

faction /'fækʃn/ *n* fazione *f*

factor /'fæktə(r)/ *n* fattore *m*

factory /'fæktərɪ/ *n* fabbrica *f*

factual /'fæktʃʊəl/ *adj* **be ~** attenersi ai fatti. **~ly** *adv* (inaccurate) dal punto di vista dei fatti

faculty /'fækəltɪ/ *n* facoltà *f inv*

fad /fæd/ *n* capriccio *m*

fade /feɪd/ *vi* sbiadire; (sound, light:) affievolirsi; (flower:) appassire. □ **~ in** *vt* cominciare in dissolvenza (picture). □ **~ out** *vt* finire in dissolvenza (picture)

fag /fæg/ *n* (chore) fatica *f*; (🄸: cigarette) sigaretta *f*; (Am 🅇: homosexual) frocio *m*. **~ end** *n* 🄸 cicca *f*

Fahrenheit /'færənhaɪt/ *adj* Fahrenheit

fail /feɪl/ *n* **without ~** senz'altro ●*vi* (attempt:) fallire; (eyesight, memory:) indebolirsi; (engine, machine:) guastarsi; (marriage:) andare a rotoli; (in exam) essere bocciato; **~ to do sth** non fare qcsa; **I tried but I ~ed** ho provato ma non ci sono riuscito ●*vt* non superare (exam); bocciare (candidate); (disappoint) deludere; **words ~ me** mi mancano le parole

failing /'feɪlɪŋ/ *n* difetto *m* ●*prep* **~ that** altrimenti

failure /'feɪljə(r)/ *n* fallimento *m*; (mechanical) guasto *m*; (person) incapace *mf*

faint /feɪnt/ *adj* leggero; (memory) vago; **feel ~** sentirsi mancare ●*n* svenimento *m* ●*vi* svenire

faint: **~-'hearted** *adj* timido. **~ly** *adv* (slightly) leggermente

fair[1] /feə(r)/ *n* fiera *f*

fair[2] *adj* (hair, person) biondo; (skin) chiaro; (weather) bello; (just) giusto; (quite good) discreto; (Sch) abbastanza bene; **a ~ amount** abbastanza ●**play ~** fare un gioco pulito. **~ly** *adv* con giustizia; (rather) discretamente, abbastanza. **~ness** *n* giustizia *f*. **~ play** *n* fair play *m inv*

fairy /'feərɪ/ *n* fata *f*; **~ story**, **~-tale** *n* fiaba *f*

faith /feɪθ/ *n* fede *f*; (trust) fiducia *f*; **in good/bad ~** in buona/mala fede

faithful /'feɪθfl/ *adj* fedele. **~ly** *adv* fedelmente; **yours ~ly** distinti saluti. **~ness** *n* fedeltà *f*

fake /feɪk/ *adj* falso ●*n* falsificazione *f*; (person) impostore *m* ●*vt* falsificare; (pretend) fingere

falcon /'fɔ:lkən/ *n* falcone *m*

fall /fɔ:l/ *n* caduta *f*; (in prices) ribasso *m*; (Am: autumn) autunno *m*; **have a ~** fare una caduta ●*vi* (pt **fell**, pp **fallen**) cadere; (night:) scendere; **~ in love** innamorarsi. □ **~ about** *vi* (with laughter) morire dal ridere. □ **~ back on** *vt* ritornare su. □ **~ for** *vt* 🄸 innamorarsi di (person); cascarci (sth, trick). □ **~ down** *vi* cadere; (building:) crollare. □ **~ in** *vi* caderci dentro; (collapse) crollare; (Mil) mettersi in riga; **~ in with** concordare con (suggestion, plan). □ **~ off** *vi* cadere; (diminish) diminuire. □ **~ out** *vi* (quarrel) litigare; **his hair is ~ing out** perde i capelli. □ **~ over** *vi* cadere. □ **~ through** *vi* (plan:) andare a monte

fallacy /'fæləsɪ/ *n* errore *m*

fallible /ˈfæləbl/ adj fallibile

'fall-out n pioggia f radioattiva

false /fɔːls/ adj falso; ~ **bottom** doppio fondo m; ~ **start** (Sport) falsa partenza f. ~**hood** n menzogna f. ~**ness** n falsità f

false 'teeth npl dentiera f

falsify /ˈfɔːlsɪfaɪ/ vt (pt/pp -ied) falsificare

falter /ˈfɔːltə(r)/ vi vacillare; (making speech) esitare

fame /feɪm/ n fama f

familiar /fəˈmɪlɪə(r)/ adj familiare; **be ~ with** (know) conoscere. ~**ity** /-lɪˈærətɪ/ n familiarità f. ~**ize** vt familiarizzare; ~**ize oneself with** familiarizzarsi con

family /ˈfæməlɪ/ n famiglia f

family: ~ **'planning** n pianificazione f familiare. ~ **'tree** n albero m genealogico

famine /ˈfæmɪn/ n carestia f

famished /ˈfæmɪʃt/ adj fam **be ~** avere una fame da lupo

famous /ˈfeɪməs/ adj famoso

fan[1] /fæn/ n ventilatore m; (handheld) ventaglio m ● vt (pt/pp **fanned**) far vento a; ~ **oneself** sventagliarsi; fig ~ **the flames** soffiare sul fuoco.
□ ~ **out** vi spiegarsi a ventaglio

fan[2] n (admirer) ammiratore, -trice mf; (Sport) tifoso m; (of Verdi etc) appassionato, -a mf

fanatic /fəˈnætɪk/ n fanatico, -a mf. ~**al** adj fanatico. ~**ism** n fanatismo m

'fan belt n cinghia f per ventilatore

fanciful /ˈfænsɪfl/ adj fantasioso

fancy /ˈfænsɪ/ n fantasia f; **I've taken a real ~ to him** mi è molto simpatico; **as the ~ takes you** come ti pare ● adj lussuoso ● vt (pt/pp **ied**) (believe) credere; (⊡: want) aver voglia di; **he fancies you** ⊡ gli piaci; ~ **that!** ma guarda un po'! ~ **'dress** n costume m (per maschera)

fanfare /ˈfænfeə(r)/ n fanfara f

fang /fæŋ/ n zanna f; (of snake) dente m

fantasize /ˈfæntəsaɪz/ vi fantasticare. ~**tic** adj fantastico. ~**y** n fantasia f

far /fɑː(r)/ adv lontano; (much) molto; **by ~** di gran lunga; ~ **away** lontano; **as ~ as the church** fino alla chiesa; **how ~ is it from here?** quanto dista da qui?; **as ~ as I know** per quanto io sappia ● adj (end, side) altro; **the F~ East** l'Estremo Oriente m

farc|e /fɑːs/ n farsa f. ~**ical** adj ridicolo

fare /feə(r)/ n tariffa f; (food) vitto m. ~**-dodger** n passeggero, -a mf senza biglietto

farewell /feəˈwel/ int liter addio! ● n addio m

far-'fetched adj improbabile

farm /fɑːm/ n fattoria f ● vi fare il contadino ● vt coltivare (land). ~**er** n agricoltore m

farm: ~**house** n casa f colonica. ~**ing** n agricoltura f. ~**yard** n aia f

far: ~**-reaching** adj di larga portata. ~**-'sighted** adj fig prudente; (Am: long-sighted) presbite

farther /ˈfɑːðə(r)/ adv più lontano ● adj **at the ~ end of** all'altra estremità di

fascinat|e /ˈfæsɪneɪt/ vt affascinare. ~**ing** adj affascinante. ~**ion** n fascino m

fascis|m /ˈfæʃɪzm/ n fascismo m. ~**t** n fascista mf ● adj fascista

fashion /ˈfæʃn/ n moda f; (manner) maniera f ● vt modellare. ~**able** adj di moda; **be ~able** essere alla moda. ~**ably** adv alla moda

fast[1] /fɑːst/ adj veloce; (colour) indelebile; **be ~** (clock:) andare avanti ● adv velocemente; (firmly) saldamente; ~**er!** più in fretta!; **be ~ asleep** dormire profondamente

fast² /fɑːst/ n digiuno m ● vi digiunare

fasten /'fɑːsn/ vt allacciare; chiudere (window); (stop flapping) mettere un fermo a ● vi allacciarsi. **~er** n, **~ing** n chiusura f

fat /fæt/ adj (fatter, fattest) (person, cheque) grasso ● n grasso m

fatal /'feɪtl/ adj mortale; (error) fatale. **~ism** n fatalismo m. **~ist** n fatalista mf. **~ity** n morte f. **~ly** adv mortalmente

fate /feɪt/ n destino m. **~ful** adj fatidico

father /'fɑːðə(r)/ n padre m; F~ Christmas Babbo m Natale ● vt generare (child)

father: ~hood n paternità f. **~-in-law** n (pl **~s-in-law**) suocero m. **~ly** adj paterno

fathom /'fæð(ə)m/ n (Naut) braccio m ● vt **[out]** comprendere

fatigue /fə'tiːg/ n fatica f.

fatten /'fætn/ vt ingrassare (animal). **~ing** adj **cream** is **~ing** la panna fa ingrassare

fatty /'fætɪ/ adj grasso ● n ① ciccione, -a mf

fatuous /'fætjʊəs/ adj fatuo

faucet /'fɔːsɪt/ n Am rubinetto m

fault /fɔːlt/ n difetto m; (Geol) faglia f; (Tennis) fallo m; **be at ~** avere torto; **find ~ with** trovare da ridire su; **it's your ~** è colpa tua ● vt criticare. **~less** adj impeccabile

faulty /'fɔːltɪ/ adj difettoso

favour /'feɪvə(r)/ n favore m; **be in ~ of sth** essere a favore di qcsa; **do sb a ~** fare un piacere a qcno ● vt (prefer) preferire. **~able** adj favorevole

favourit|e /'feɪvərɪt/ adj preferito ● n preferito, -a mf; (Sport) favorito, -a mf. **~ism** n favoritismo m

fawn /fɔːn/ adj fulvo ● n (animal) cerbiatto m

fax /fæks/ n (document, machine) fax m inv; **by ~** per fax ● vt faxare. **~ ma-**

chine n fax m inv. **~-modem** n modem-fax m inv, fax-modem m inv

fear /fɪə(r)/ n paura f; **no ~!** ① vai tranquillo! ● vt temere ● vi **~ for sth** temere per qcsa

fear|ful /'fɪəfl/ adj pauroso; (awful) terribile. **~less** adj impavido. **~some** adj spaventoso

feas|ibility /fiːzɪ'bɪlɪtɪ/ n praticabilità f. **~ible** adj fattibile; (possible) probabile

feast /fiːst/ n festa f; (banquet) banchetto m ● vi banchettare; **~ on** godersi

feat /fiːt/ n impresa f

feather /'feðə(r)/ n piuma f

feature /'fiːtʃə(r)/ n (quality) caratteristica f; (Journ) articolo m; **~s** (pl: of face) lineamenti mpl ● vt (film:) avere come protagonista ● vi (on a list etc) comparire. **~ film** n lungometraggio m

February /'febrʊərɪ/ n febbraio m

fed /fed/ ▷**FEED** ● adj **be ~ up** ① essere stufo (**with** di)

federal /'fed(ə)rəl/ adj federale

federation /fedə'reɪʃn/ n federazione f

fee /fiː/ n tariffa f; (lawyer's, doctor's) onorario m; (for membership, school) quota f

feeble /'fiːbl/ adj debole; (excuse) fiacco

feed /fiːd/ n mangiare m; (for baby) pappa f ● v (pt/pp **fed**) ● vt dar da mangiare a (animal); (support) nutrire; **~ sth into sth** inserire qcsa in qcsa ● vi mangiare

¹feedback n controreazione f; (of information) reazione f, feedback m

feel /fiːl/ v (pt/pp **felt**) ● vt sentire; (experience) provare; (think) pensare; (touch: searching) tastare; (touch: for texture) toccare ● vi **~ soft/hard** essere duro/morbido al tatto; **~ hot/hungry** aver caldo/fame; **~ ill** sentirsi male; **I don't ~ like it** non ne ho voglia: **how do you ~ about it?** (opinion) che te ne pare?; **it doesn't ~ right** non mi sembra giusto. **~er** n (of animal) antenna f; **put out ~ers** fig tastare il terreno. **~ing** n sentimento m; (awareness) sensazione f

feel /fiːl/ ▷FEEL

feign /feɪn/ vt simulare

fell¹ /fel/ vt (knock down) abbattere

fell² ▷FALL

fellow /ˈfeləʊ/ n (of society) socio m; (🔲 man) tipo m

fellow 'countryman n compatriota m

felony /ˈfeləni/ n delitto m

felt¹ /felt/ ▷FEEL

felt² n feltro m. **~[-tipped] 'pen** /-tɪpt/ n pennarello m

female /ˈfiːmeɪl/ adj femminile; **the ~ antelope** l'antilope femmina ● n femmina f

femin|ine /ˈfemɪnɪn/ adj femminile ● n (Gram) femminile m. **~inity** /-ˈnɪnəti/ n femminilità f. **~ist** adj & n femminista mf

fence /fens/ n recinto m; (🔲 person) ricettatore m ● vi (Sport) tirar di scherma; **~ in** vt chiudere in un recinto. **~er** n schermidore m. **~ing** n steccato m; (Sport) scherma f

fend /fend/ vi **~ for oneself** badare a se stesso. **~ off** vt parare; difendersi da (criticisms)

fender /ˈfendə(r)/ n parafuoco m inv; (Am: on car) parafango m

fennel /ˈfenl/ n finocchio m

ferment¹ /ˈfɜːment/ n fermento m

ferment² /fəˈment/ vi fermentare ● vt far fermentare. **~ation** n fermentazione f

fern /fɜːn/ n felce f

feroc|ious /fəˈrəʊʃəs/ adj feroce. **~ity** n ferocia f

ferret /ˈferɪt/ n furetto m ● **ferret out** vt scovare

ferry /ˈferi/ n traghetto m ● vt

traghettare

fertil|e /ˈfɜːtaɪl/ adj fertile. **~ity** n fertilità f

fertilize /ˈfɜːtɪlaɪz/ vt fertilizzare (land, ovum). **~r** n fertilizzante m

fervent /ˈfɜːvənt/ adj fervente

fervour /ˈfɜːvə(r)/ n fervore m

fester /ˈfestə(r)/ vi suppurare

festival /ˈfestɪvl/ n (Mus, Theat) festival m; (Relig) festa f

festive /ˈfestɪv/ adj festivo. **~e season** periodo m delle feste natalizie. **~ities** vt andare/venire a prendere, (be sold for) raggiungere [il prezzo di]

fetch /fetʃ/ vt andare/venire a prendere; (be sold for) raggiungere [il prezzo di]

fetching /ˈfetʃɪŋ/ adj attraente

fête /feɪt/ n festa f ● vt festeggiare

fetish /ˈfetɪʃ/ n feticcio m

fetter /ˈfetə(r)/ n incatenare

feud /fjuːd/ n faida f

feudal /ˈfjuːdl/ adj feudale

fever /ˈfiːvə(r)/ n febbre f. **~ish** adj febbricitante; fig febbrile

few /fjuː/ adj pochi; **every ~ days** ogni due o tre giorni; **a ~ people** alcuni; **~er reservations** meno prenotazioni; **the ~est number** il numero più basso ● pron pochi; **~ of us** pochi di noi; **a ~** alcuni; **quite a ~** parecchi; **~er than last year** meno dell'anno scorso

fiancé /fɪˈɒnseɪ/ n fidanzato m. **~e** n fidanzata f

fiasco /fɪˈæskəʊ/ n fiasco m

fib /fɪb/ n storia f; **tell a ~** raccontare una storia

fibre /ˈfaɪbə(r)/ n fibra f. **~glass** n fibra f di vetro

fickle /ˈfɪkl/ adj incostante

fiction /ˈfɪkʃn/ n (works of) ~ narrativa f; (fabrication) finzione f. **~al** adj immaginario

fictitious /fɪkˈtɪʃəs/ adj fittizio

fiddle /ˈfɪdl/ n 🎻 violino m; (cheating) imbroglio m ● vi gingillarsi (**with** con) ● vt 🎻 truccare (accounts)

fidget /ˈfɪdʒɪt/ vi agitarsi. **~y** adj agitato

field /fiːld/ n campo m

field: **~-glasses** npl binocolo msg. **F~** '**Marshal** n feldmaresciallo m. **~work** n ricerche fpl sul terreno

fiend /fiːnd/ n demonio m

fierce /fɪəs/ adj feroce. **~ness** n ferocia f

fiery /ˈfaɪərɪ/ adj (-ier, -iest) focoso

fifteen /fɪfˈtiːn/ adj & n quindici m. **~th** adj quindicesimo

fifth /fɪfθ/ adj quinto

fiftieth /ˈfɪftɪɪθ/ adj cinquantesimo

fifty /ˈfɪftɪ/ adj cinquanta

fig /fɪg/ n fico m

fight /faɪt/ n lotta f; (brawl) zuffa f; (argument) litigio m; (boxing) incontro m ● v (pt/pp **fought**) ● vt also fig combattere ● vi combattere; (brawl) azzuffarsi; (argue) litigare. **~er** n combattente mf; (Aeron) caccia m inv. **~ing** n combattimento m

figment /ˈfɪgmənt/ n **it's a ~ of your imagination** questa è tutta una tua invenzione

figurative /ˈfɪgjərətɪv/ adj (sense) figurato; (art) figurativo

figure /ˈfɪgə(r)/ n (digit) cifra f; (carving, sculpture, illustration, form) figura f; (body shape) linea f; **~ of speech** modo m di dire ● vi (appear) figurare ● vt (Am: think) pensare. **□ ~ out** vt dedurre; capire (person)

figurehead n figura f simbolica

file¹ /faɪl/ n scheda f; (set of documents) incartamento m; (folder) cartellina f; (Comput) file m inv ● vt archiviare (documents)

file² /faɪl/ n (line) fila f; **in single ~** in fila

file³ /faɪl/ n (Techn) lima f ● vt limare

filing cabinet /ˈfaɪlɪŋkæbɪnət/ n schedario m, classificatore m

fill /fɪl/ n **eat one's ~** mangiare a sazietà ● vt riempire; otturare (tooth) ● vi riempirsi. **□ ~ in** vt compilare (form). **□ ~ out** vt compilare (form). **□ ~ up** vi (room, tank:) riempirsi; (Auto) far il pieno ● vt riempire

fillet /ˈfɪlɪt/ n filetto m ● vt (pt/pp **filleted**) disossare

filling /ˈfɪlɪŋ/ n (Culin) ripieno m; (of tooth) piombatura f. **~ station** n stazione f di rifornimento

film /fɪlm/ n (Cinema) film m inv; (Phot) pellicola f; [**cling**] **~** pellicola f per alimenti ● vt/i filmare. **~ star** n star f inv, divo, -a mf

filter /ˈfɪltə(r)/ n filtro m ● vt filtrare. **□ ~ through** vi (news:) trapelare. **~ tip** n filtro m; (cigarette) sigaretta f col filtro

filth /fɪlθ/ n sudiciume m. **~y** adj (-ier, -iest) sudicio; (word) sconcio

fin /fɪn/ n pinna f

final /ˈfaɪnl/ adj finale; (conclusive) decisivo ● n (Sport) finale f. **~s** pl (Univ) esami mpl finali

finale /fɪˈnɑːlɪ/ n finale m

final|ist /ˈfaɪnəlɪst/ n finalista mf. **~ity** n finalità f

final|ize /ˈfaɪnəlaɪz/ vt mettere a punto (text); definire (agreement). **~ly** adv (at last) finalmente; (at the end) alla fine; (to conclude) per finire

finance /ˈfaɪnæns/ n finanza f ● vt finanziare

financial /faɪˈnænʃl/ adj finanziario

find /faɪnd/ n scoperta f ● vt (pt/pp **found**) trovare; (establish) scoprire; **~ sb guilty** (Jur) dichiarare qcno colpevole. **□ ~ out** vt scoprire ● vi (enquire) informarsi

findings /ˈfaɪndɪŋz/ npl conclusioni fpl

fine¹ /faɪn/ n (penalty) multa f ● vt multare

fine² /faɪn/ adj bello; (slender) fine; **he's ~** (in health) sta bene. **~ arts** npl belle arti fpl. ● adv bene; **that's cutting it**

~ non ci lascia molto tempo ● int [va] bene. ~**ly** adv (cut) finemente

finger /'fɪŋɡə(r)/ n dito m (pl dita f) ● vt tastare

finger: ~**nail** n unghia f. ~**print** n impronta f digitale. ~**tip** n punta f del dito: **have sth at one's ~tips** sapere qcsa a menadito; (close at hand) avere qcsa a portata di mano

finish /'fɪnɪʃ/ n fine f; (finishing line) traguardo m; (of product) finitura f; **have a good ~** (runner:) avere un buon finale ● vt finire; ~ **reading** finire di leggere ● vi finire

finite /'faɪnaɪt/ adj limitato

Finland /'fɪnlənd/ n Finlandia f

Finn /fɪn/ n finlandese mf. ~**ish** adj finlandese ● n (language) finnico m

fiord /fjɔːd/ n fiordo m

fir /fɜː(r)/ n abete m

fire /'faɪə(r)/ n fuoco m; (forest, house) incendio m; **be on ~** bruciare; **catch ~** prendere fuoco; **set ~ to** dar fuoco a; **under ~** sotto il fuoco ● vt cuocere (pottery); sparare (shot); tirare (gun); (⬜ dismiss) buttar fuori ● vi sparare (**at** a)

fire: ~ **alarm** n allarme m antincendio. ~**arm** n arma f da fuoco. ~ **brigade** n vigili mpl del fuoco. ~**engine** n autopompa f. ~**escape** n uscita f di sicurezza. ~ **extinguisher** n estintore m. ~**man** n pompiere m, vigile m del fuoco. ~**place** n caminetto m. ~**side** n **by** or **at the ~side** accanto al fuoco. ~**wood** n legna f (da ardere). ~**work** n fuoco m d'artificio

firm¹ /fɜːm/ n ditta f, azienda f

firm² adj fermo; (soil) compatto; (stable, properly fixed) solido; (resolute) risoluto. ~**ly** adv (hold) stretto; (say) con fermezza

first /fɜːst/ adj & n primo, -a mf; **at ~** all'inizio; **who's ~?** chi è il primo; **from the ~** (fin) dall'inizio ● adv (arrive, leave) per primo; (beforehand)

prima, (in listing) prima di tutto, innanzitutto

first: ~ **aid** n pronto soccorso m. ~-**aid kit** n cassetta f di pronto soccorso. ~-**class** adj di prim'ordine; (Rail) di prima classe ● adv (travel) in prima classe. ~ **floor** n primo piano m; (Am: ground floor) pianterreno m. ~**ly** adv in primo luogo. ~ **name** n nome m di battesimo. ~-**rate** adj ottimo

fish /fɪʃ/ n pesce m ● vt/i pescare. n ~ **out** vt tirar fuori

fish: ~**erman** n pescatore m. ~ **finger** n bastoncino m di pesce

fishing /'fɪʃɪŋ/ n pesca f. ~ **boat** n peschereccio m. ~-**rod** n canna f da pesca

fish: ~**monger** /-mʌŋɡə(r)/ n pescivendolo m. ~**y** adj (⬜: suspicious) sospetto

fission /'fɪʃn/ n (Phys) fissione f

fist /fɪst/ n pugno m

fit¹ n (attack) attacco m; (of rage) accesso m; (of generosity) slancio m

fit² adj (fitter, fittest) (suitable) adatto; (healthy) in buona salute; (Sport) in forma; **be ~ to do** essere in grado di fare qcsa; ~ **to eat** buono da mangiare; **keep ~** tenersi in forma

fit³ n (of clothes) taglio m; **it's a good ~** (coat) etc. sta bene ● v (pt/pp **fitted**) ● vi (be the right size) andare bene; **it doesn't ~** (no room) non ci sta ● vt (fix) applicare (**to** a); (install) installare: **it doesn't ~ me** (coat etc:) non mi va bene; ~ **with** fornire di. n ~ **in** vi (person:) adattarsi; **it won't ~ in** (no room) non ci sta ● vt (in schedule, vehicle) trovare un buco per

fitful /'fɪtfl/ adj irregolare. ~**fully** adv (sleep) a sprazzi. ~**ments** npl (in house) impianti mpl fissi. ~**ness** n (suitability) capacità f; (physical) ~**ness** forma f, fitness m

fitting /'fɪtɪŋ/ adj appropriato ●n (of clothes) prova f; (Techn) montaggio m; ~s pl accessori mpl. ~ **room** n camerino m

five /faɪv/ adj & n cinque m. ~r n □ biglietto m da cinque sterline

fix /fɪks/ n (▣: drugs) pera f; **be in a** ~ □ essere nei guai ●vt fissare; (repair) aggiustare; preparare (meal). □ ~ **up** vt fissare (meeting)

fixed /fɪkst/ adj fisso

fixture /'fɪkstʃə(r)/ n (Sport) incontro m; ~s **and fittings** impianti mpl fissi

fizz /fɪz/ vi frizzare

fizzle /'fɪzl/ vi ~ **out** finire in nulla

fizzy /'fɪzɪ/ adj gassoso. ~ **drink** n bibita f gassata

flabbergasted /'flæbəga:stɪd/ adj **be** ~ rimanere a bocca aperta

flabby /'flæbɪ/ adj floscio

flag[1] /flæg/ n bandiera f ●**flag down** vt (pt/pp **flagged**) far segno di fermarsi a (taxi)

flag[2] vi (pt/pp **flagged**) cedere

'flag-pole n asta f della bandiera

flagrant /'fleɪgrənt/ adj flagrante

flair /fleə(r)/ n (skill) talento m; (style) stile m

flake /fleɪk/ n fiocco m ●vi ~ [**off**] cadere in fiocchi

flaky /'fleɪkɪ/ adj a scaglie. ~ **pastry** n pasta f sfoglia

flamboyant /flæm'bɔɪənt/ adj (personality) brillante; (tie) sgargiante

flame /fleɪm/ n fiamma f

flammable /'flæməbl/ adj infiammabile

flan /flæn/ n [**fruit**] ~ crostata f

flank /flæŋk/ n fianco m ●vt fiancheggiare

flannel /'flænl/ n flanella f; (for washing) ≈ guanto m di spugna; ~**s** (trousers) pantaloni mpl di flanella

flap /flæp/ n (of pocket, envelope) ri-

svolto m; (of table) ribalta f; **in a** ~ □ in grande agitazione ●v (pt/pp **flapped**) ●vi sbattere; □ agitarsi ●vt ~ **its wings** battere le ali

flare /fleə(r)/ n fiammata f; (device) razzo m ●**flare up** vi (rash:) venire fuori; (fire:) fare una fiammata; (person, situation:)) esplodere. ~**d** adj (garment) svasato

flash /flæʃ/ n lampo m; **in a** ~ □ in un attimo ●vi lampeggiare; ~ **past** passare come un bolide ●vt lanciare (smile); ~ **one's head-lights** lampeggiare; ~ **a torch** at puntare una torcia su

flash: ~**back** n scena f retrospettiva. ~**light** n (Phot) flash m inv; (Am: torch) torcia f [elettrica]. ~**y** adj vistoso

flask /flɑːsk/ n fiasco m; (vacuum ~) termos m inv

flat /flæt/ adj (flatter, flattest) piatto; (refusal) reciso; (beer) sgassato; (battery) scarico; (tyre) a terra; **A** ~ (Mus) la bemolle ●n appartamento m; (Mus) bemolle m; (puncture) gomma f a terra

flat: ~**ly** adv (refuse) categoricamente. ~ **rate** n tariffa f unica

flatten /'flætn/ vt appiattire

flatter /'flætə(r)/ vt adulare. ~**ing** adj (comments) lusinghiero; (colour, dress) che fa sembrare più bello. ~**y** n adulazione f

flaunt /flɔːnt/ vt ostentare

flavour /'fleɪvə(r)/ n sapore m ●vt condire; **chocolate-~ed** al sapore di cioccolato. ~**ing** n condimento m

flaw /flɔː/ n difetto m. ~**less** adj perfetto

flea /fliː/ n pulce m. ~ **market** n mercato m delle pulci

fleck /flek/ n macchiolina f

fled /fled/ ▷**FLEE**

flee /fliː/ vt/i (pt/pp **fled**) fuggire (**from** da)

fleec|e /fliːs/ n pelliccia f ●vt □

spennare. **~y** *adj* (lining) felpato

fleet /fliːt/ *n* flotta *f*; (*of cars*) parco *m*

fleeting /ˈfliːtɪŋ/ *adj* **catch a ~ glance of sth** intravedere qcsa; **for a ~ moment** per un attimo

flesh /fleʃ/ *n* carne *f*; **in the ~** in persona. **~y** *adj* carnoso

flew /fluː/ ▷ **FLY**[1]

flex[1] /fleks/ *vt* flettere (muscle)

flex[2] *n* (Electr) filo *m*

flexibility /fleksɪˈbɪlətɪ/ *n* flessibilità *f*. **~le** *adj* flessibile

flexitime /ˈfleksɪtaɪm/ *n* orario *m* flessibile

flick /flɪk/ *vt* dare un buffetto a; **~ sth off sth** togliere qcsa da qcsa con un colpetto. **□ ~ through** *vt* sfogliare

flicker /ˈflɪkə(r)/ *vi* tremolare

flight[1] /flaɪt/ *n* (fleeing) fuga *f*; **take ~** darsi alla fuga

flight[2] *n* (flying) volo *m*; **~ of stairs** rampa *f*

flight recorder *n* registratore *m* di volo

flimsy /ˈflɪmzɪ/ *adj* (**-ier, -iest**) (material) leggero; (shelves) poco robusto; (excuse) debole

flinch /flɪntʃ/ *vi* (wince) sussultare; (draw back) ritirarsi; **~ from a task** *fig* sottrarsi a un compito

fling /flɪŋ/ *n* **have a ~** (*fam*: affair) aver un'avventura ● *vt* (*pt/pp* **flung**) gettare

flint /flɪnt/ *n* pietra *f* focaia; (*for lighter*) pietrina *f*

flip /flɪp/ *v* (*pt/pp* **flipped**) ● *vt* dare un colpetto a; buttare in aria (coin) ● *vi* 🔲 uscire dai gangheri; (go mad) impazzire. **□ ~ through** *vt* sfogliare

flippant /ˈflɪpənt/ *adj* irriverente

flipper /ˈflɪpə(r)/ *n* pinna *f*

flirt /flɜːt/ *n* civetta *f* ● *vi* flirtare

float /fləʊt/ *n* galleggiante *m*; (in procession) carro *m*; (money) riserva *f* di cassa ● *vi* galleggiare; (Fin) fluttuare

flock /flɒk/ *n* gregge *m*; (of birds) stormo *m* ● *vi* affollarsi

flog /flɒg/ *vt* (*pt/pp* **flogged**) bastonare; (🔲: sell) vendere

flood /flʌd/ *n* alluvione *f*; (fig: of replies, letters, tears) diluvio *m*; **be in ~** (river): essere straripato ● *vt* allagare ● *vi* (river): straripare

floodlight *n* riflettore *m* ● *vt* (*pt/pp* **floodlit**) illuminare con riflettori

floor /flɔː(r)/ *n* pavimento *m*; (storey) piano *m*; (for dancing) pista *f* ● *vt* (baffle) confondere; (knock down) stendere (person)

floor polish *n* cera *f* per il pavimento

flop /flɒp/ *n* 🔲 (failure) tonfo *m*; (Theat) fiasco *m* ● *vi* (*pt/pp* **flopped**) (🔲: fail) far fiasco. **n ~ down** *vi* accasciarsi

floppy /ˈflɒpɪ/ *adj* floscio. **~ 'disk** *n* floppy disk *m inv*. **~ [disk] drive** *n* lettore di floppy *m*

floral /ˈflɔːrəl/ *adj* floreale

florid /ˈflɒrɪd/ *adj* (complexion) florido; (style) troppo ricercato

florist /ˈflɒrɪst/ *n* fioraio, -a *mf*

flounder[1] /ˈflaʊndə(r)/ *vi* dibattersi; (speaker:) impappinarsi

flounder[2] *n* (fish) passera *f* di mare

flour /ˈflaʊə(r)/ *n* farina *f*

flourish /ˈflʌrɪʃ/ *n* gesto *m* drammatico; (scroll) ghirigoro *m* ● *vi* prosperare ● *vt* brandire

flout /flaʊt/ *vt* fregarsene di (rules)

flow /fləʊ/ *n* flusso *m* ● *vi* scorrere; (hang loosely) ricadere

flower /ˈflaʊə(r)/ *n* fiore *m* ● *vi* fiorire

flower: ~bed *n* aiuola *f*. **~y** *adj* fiorito

flown /fləʊn/ ▷ **FLY**[2]

flu /fluː/ *n* influenza *f*

fluctuat|e /ˈflʌktjʊeɪt/ vi fluttuare. **~ion** n fluttuazione f

fluent /ˈfluːənt/ adj spedito; **speak ~ Italian** parlare correntemente l'italiano. **~ly** adv speditamente

fluff /flʌf/ n peluria f. **~y** adj (-ier, -iest) vaporoso; (toy) di peluche

fluid /ˈfluːɪd/ adj fluido● n fluido m

flung /flʌŋ/ ▷FLING

fluorescent /flʊəˈresnt/ adj fluorescente

flush /flʌʃ/ n (blush) [vampata f di] rossore m ● vi arrossire ● vt lavare con un getto d'acqua; **~ the toilet** tirare l'acqua ● adj a livello (**with** di); (🔲: affluent) a soldi

flute /fluːt/ n flauto m

flutter /ˈflʌtə(r)/ n battito m ● vi svolazzare

flux /flʌks/ n **in a state of ~** in uno stato di flusso

fly[1] /flaɪ/ n (pl **flies**) mosca f

fly[2] v (pt **flew**, pp **flown**) vi volare; (go by plane) andare in aereo; (flag:) sventolare; (rush) precipitarsi; **~ open** spalancarsi ● vt pilotare (plane); trasportare [in aereo] (troops, supplies); volare con (Alitalia etc)

fly[3] n & **flies** pl (on trousers) patta f

flying /ˈflaɪɪŋ/: **~ 'buttress** n arco m rampante. **~ 'colours: with ~ colours** a pieni voti. **~ 'saucer** n disco m volante. **~ 'start** n **get off to a ~ start** fare un'ottima partenza. **~ 'visit** n visita f lampo

fly: **~leaf** n risguardo m. **~over** n cavalcavia m inv

foal /fəʊl/ n puledro m

foam /fəʊm/ n schiuma f; (synthetic) gommapiuma® f ● vi spumare; **~ at the mouth** fare la bava alla bocca. **~ 'rubber** n gommapiuma® f

fob /fɒb/ vt (pt/pp **fobbed**) **~ sth off** affibbiare qcsa (**on sb** a qcno); **~ sb off** liquidare qcno

focal /ˈfəʊkl/ adj focale

focus /ˈfəʊkəs/ n fuoco m; **in ~** a fuoco; **out of ~** sfocato ● v (pt/pp **focused** or **focussed**) ● vt fig concentrare (**on su**) vi (Phot) ~ on mettere a fuoco; fig concentrarsi (**on su**)

fodder /ˈfɒdə(r)/ n foraggio m

foe /fəʊ/ n nemico, -a mf

foetus /ˈfiːtəs/ n (pl **-tuses**) feto m

fog /fɒg/ n nebbia f

foggy /ˈfɒgɪ/ adj (**foggier, foggiest**) nebbioso; **it's ~** c'è nebbia

'fog-horn n sirena f da nebbia

foil[1] /fɔɪl/ n lamina f di metallo

foil[2] vt (thwart) frustrare

foil[3] n (sword) fioretto m

foist /fɔɪst/ vt appioppare (**on sb** a qcno)

fold[1] /fəʊld/ n (for sheep) ovile m

fold[2] n piega f● vt piegare; **~ one's arms** incrociare le braccia ● vi piegarsi; (fail) crollare. □ **~ up** vt ripiegare (chair) ● vi essere pieghevole; (business:) collassare

fold|er /ˈfəʊldə(r)/ n cartella f. **~ing** adj pieghevole

folk /fəʊk/ npl gente f; **my ~s** (family) i miei; **hello there ~s** ciao a tutti

folklore n folclore m

follow /ˈfɒləʊ/ vt/i seguire; **it doesn't ~** non è necessariamente così; **~ suit** fig fare lo stesso; **as ~s** come segue. □ **~ up** vt fare seguito a (letter)

follow|er /ˈfɒləʊə(r)/ n seguace mf. **~ing** adj seguente ● n seguito m; (supporters) seguaci mpl ● prep in seguito a

folly /ˈfɒlɪ/ n follia f

fond /fɒnd/ adj affezionato; (hope) vivo; **be ~ of** essere appassionato di (music); **I'm ~ of...** (food, person) mi piace moltissimo...

fondle /ˈfɒndl/ vt coccolare

fondness /ˈfɒndnɪs/ n affetto m; (for things) amore m

font /font/ n fonte f battesimale; (Typ) carattere m di stampa

food /fuːd/ n cibo m; (for animals, groceries) mangiare m; **let's buy some ~** compriamo qualcosa da mangiare

food processor n tritatutto m inv elettrico

fool[1] /fuːl/ n sciocco, -a mf; **she's no ~** non è una stupida; **make a ~ of oneself** rendersi ridicolo ● vt prendere in giro ● vi **~ around** giocare; (husband, wife) avere l'amante

fool[2] n (Culin) crema f

fool|hardy adj temerario, ~**ish** adj stolto, ~**ishly** adv scioccamente. ~**ishness** n sciocchezza f. ~**proof** adj facilissimo

foot /fut/ n (pl **feet**) piede m; (of animal) zampa f; (measure) piede m (= 30,48 cm); **on ~** a piedi; **on one's feet** in piedi; **put one's ~ in it** fig fare una gaffe

foot: ~-and-mouth disease n afta f epizootica. ~**ball** n calcio m; (ball) pallone m. ~**baller** n giocatore m di calcio. ~**bridge** n passerella f. ~**hills** npl colline fpl pedemontane. ~**hold** n punto m d'appoggio. ~**ing** n lose one's ~**ing** perdere l'appiglio; **on an equal ~ing** in condizioni di parità. ~**man** n valletto m. ~**note** n nota f a piè di pagina. ~**path** n sentiero m. ~**print** n orma f. ~**step** n passo m; **follow in sb's ~steps** fig seguire l'esempio di qcno. ~**wear** n calzature fpl

for /fə(r)/, accentato /fɔː(r)/
● prep per; ~ **this reason** per questa ragione; **I have lived here ~ ten years** vivo qui da dieci anni; ~ **supper** per cena; ~ **all that** nonostante questo; **what ~?** che scopo?; **send ~ à doctor** chiamare un dottore; **fight ~ a cause** lottare per una causa; **go ~ a walk** andare a fare una passeggiata; **there's no need ~ you to go** non c'è bisogno che tu vada. **It's not ~ me to say** non sta a me dirlo; **now you're ~ it** ora sei nei pasticci
● conj poiché, perché

forage /ˈforidʒ/ n foraggio m ● vi ~ **for** cercare

forbade /fəˈbæd/ ▷ **FORBID**

forbear|ance /fɔːˈbeərəns/ n pazienza f. ~**ing** adj tollerante

forbid /fəˈbɪd/ vt (pt **forbade**, pp **forbidden**) proibire. ~**ding** adj (prospect) che spaventa; (stern) severo

force /fɔːs/ n forza f; **in** ~ in vigore; (in large numbers) in massa; **come into** ~ entrare in vigore; **the** [**armed**] ~**s** pl le forze armate ● vt forzare; ~ **sth on sb** (decision) imporre qcsa a qcno; (drink) costringere qcno a fare qcsa

forced /fɔːst/ adj forzato

force: ~-feed vt (pt/pp **-fed**) nutrire a forza. ~**ful** adj energico

forceps /ˈfɔːseps/ npl forcipe m

forcible /ˈfɔːsɪbl/ adj forzato

ford /fɔːd/ n guado m ● vt guadare

fore /fɔː(r)/ n **to the** ~ in vista; **come to the** ~ salire alla ribalta

fore: ~arm n avambraccio m. ~**boding** /-ˈbəʊdɪŋ/ n presentimento m. ~**cast** n previsione f ● vt (pt/pp ~**cast**) prevedere. ~**court** n cortile m anteriore. ~**finger** n [dito m] indice m. ~**front** n **be in the ~front** essere all'avanguardia. ~**gone** adj **be a ~gone conclusion** essere una cosa scontata. ~**ground** n primo piano m. ~**head** /ˈfɔːhed/, /ˈforid/ n fronte f

foreign /ˈforən/ adj straniero; (trade) estero; (not belonging) estraneo; **he is** ~ è uno straniero. ~**currency** n valuta f estera. ~**er** n straniero, -a mf. ~ **language** n lingua f straniera

fore: ∼**man** n caporeparto m. ∼**most** adj principale ● adv first and ∼most in primo luogo

'forerunner n precursore m

fore'see vt (pt -saw, pp -seen) prevedere. ∼**able** adj in the ∼**able future** in futuro per quanto si possa prevedere

'foresight n previdenza f

forest /'fɒrɪst/ n foresta f. ∼**er** n guardia f forestale

fore'stall vt prevenire

forestry /'fɒrɪstrɪ/ n silvicoltura f

'foretaste n pregustazione f

fore'tell vt (pt/pp -told) predire

forever /fə'revə(r)/ adv per sempre; he's ∼ complaining si lamenta sempre

fore'warn vt avvertire

foreword /'fɔːwɜːd/ n prefazione f

forfeit /'fɔːfɪt/ n (in game) pegno m; (Jur) penalità f ● vt perdere

forgave /fə'geɪv/ ▶ **FORGIVE**

forge[1] /fɔːdʒ/ vi ∼ **ahead** (runner:) lasciarsi indietro gli altri; fig farsi strada

forge[2] n fucina f ● vt fucinare; (counterfeit) contraffare. ∼**r** n contraffattore m. ∼**ry** n contraffazione f

forget /fə'get/ vt/i (pt -got, pp -gotten, pres p -getting) dimenticare; dimenticarsi di (language, skill). ∼**ful** adj smemorato. ∼**fulness** n smemoratezza f. ∼**-me-not** n nonti-scordar-dimé m inv. ∼**table** adj (day, film) da dimenticare

forgive /fə'gɪv/ vt (pt -gave, pp -given) ∼ **sb** for **sth** perdonare qcno per qcsa. ∼**ness** n perdono m

forgo /fɔː'gəʊ/ vt (pt -went, pp -gone) rinunciare a

forgot(ten) /fə'gɒt(n)/ ▶ **FORGET**

fork /fɔːk/ n forchetta f; (for digging) forca f; (in road) bivio m ● vi (road:) biforcarsi; ∼ **right** prendere a de-

stra. □ ∼ **out** vt 🔟 sborsare

fork-lift 'truck n elevatore m

forlorn /fə'lɔːn/ adj (look) perduto; (place) derelitto; ∼ **hope** speranza f vana

form /fɔːm/ n forma f; (document) modulo m; (Sch) classe f ● vt formare; formulare (opinion) ● vi formarsi

formal /'fɔːml/ adj formale. ∼**ity** n formalità f inv. ∼**ly** adv in modo formale; (officially) ufficialmente

format /'fɔːmæt/ n formato m ● vt formattare (disk, page)

formation /fɔː'meɪʃn/ n formazione f

former /'fɔːmə(r)/ adj precedente; (PM, colleague) ex; the ∼, the latter il primo, l'ultimo. ∼**ly** adv precedentemente; (in olden times) in altri tempi

formidable /'fɔːmɪdəbl/ adj formidabile

formula /'fɔːmjʊlə/ n (pl -ae /-liː/ or -s) formula f

formulate /'fɔːmjʊleɪt/ vt formulare

forsake /fə'seɪk/ vt (pt -sook /-sʊk/, pp -saken) abbandonare

fort /fɔːt/ n (Mil) forte m

forth /fɔːθ/ adv back and ∼ avanti e indietro; and so ∼ e così via

forth: ∼**coming** adj prossimo; (communicative) comunicativo; no response was ∼ non arrivava nessuna risposta. ∼**right** adj schietto. ∼**with** adv immediatamente

fortieth /'fɔːtɪɪθ/ adj quarantesimo

fortnight /'fɔːt-/ Br n quindicina f. ∼**ly** adj bimensile ● adv ogni due settimane

fortress /'fɔːtrɪs/ n fortezza f

fortunate /'fɔːtʃənət/ adj fortunato; that's ∼! meno male!. ∼**ly** adv fortunatamente

fortune /'fɔːtʃuːn/ n fortuna f. ∼**-teller** n indovino, -a mf

forty /ˈfɔːtɪ/ adj & n quaranta m

forum /ˈfɔːrəm/ n foro m

forward /ˈfɔːwəd/ adv avanti; (towards the front) in avanti ● adj (presumptuous) sfacciato ● n (Sport) attaccante m ● vt inoltrare (letter); spedire (goods). **~s** adv avanti

fossil /ˈfɒsl/ n fossile m. **~ized** adj fossile; (ideas) fossilizzato

foster /ˈfɒstə(r)/ vt allevare (child). **~-child** n figlio, -a m/ in affidamento. **~-mother** n madre f affidataria

fought /fɔːt/ ▷FIGHT

foul /faʊl/ adj (smell, taste) cattivo, (air) viziato; (language) osceno (blood, weather) orrendo; **~ play** (Jur) delitto m ● n (Sport) fallo m ● vt inquinare (water); (Sport) commettere un fallo contro; (nets, rope) impigliarsi in. **~-smelling** adj puzzo

found¹ /faʊnd/ ▷FIND

found² vt fondare

foundation /faʊnˈdeɪʃn/ n (basis) fondamento m; (charitable) fondazione f. **~s** pl (of building) fondamenta fpl; **lay the ~-stone** porre la prima pietra

founder¹ /ˈfaʊndə(r)/ n fondatore, -trice m

founder² vi (ship:) affondare

fountain /ˈfaʊntɪn/ n fontana f. **~-pen** n penna f stilografica

four /fɔː(r)/ adj & n quattro m

four: ~some /ˈfɔːsəm/ n quartetto m. **~teen** adj & n quattordici m. **~'teenth** adj quattordicesimo

fourth /fɔːθ/ adj quarto

fowl /faʊl/ n pollame m

fox /fɒks/ n volpe f ● vt (puzzle) ingannare

foyer /ˈfɔɪeɪ/ n (Theat) ridotto m; (in hotel) salone m d'ingresso

fraction /ˈfrækʃn/ n frazione f

fracture /ˈfræktʃə(r)/ n frattura f ● vt fratturare ● vi fratturarsi

fragile /ˈfrædʒaɪl/ adj fragile

fragment /ˈfrægmənt/ n frammento m. **~ary** adj frammentario

fragrance /ˈfreɪgrəns/ n fragranza f. **~t** adj fragrante

frail /freɪl/ adj gracile

frame /freɪm/ n (of picture, door, window) cornice f; (of spectacles) montatura f; (Anat) ossatura f; (structure, of bike) telaio m; **~ of mind** stato m d'animo ● vt incorniciare (picture); fig formulare; (🔲) incriminate. **~work** n struttura f

France /frɑːns/ n Francia f

frank¹ /fræŋk/ vt affrancare (letter)

frank² adj franco. **~ly** adv francamente

frantic /ˈfræntɪk/ adj frenetico; **be ~ with worry** essere agitatissimo. **~ally** adv freneticamente

fraternal /frəˈtɜːnl/ adj fraterno

fraud /frɔːd/ n frode f; (person) impostore m. **~ulent** adj fraudolento

fraught /frɔːt/ adj **~ with** pieno di

fray¹ /freɪ/ n mischia f

fray² vi sfilacciarsi

freak /friːk/ n fenomeno m; (person) scherzo m di natura; (🔲) weird person tipo m strambo ● adj anormale. **~ish** adj strambo

freckle /ˈfrekl/ n lentiggine f. **~d** adj lentigginoso

free /friː/ adj (freer, freest) libero; (ticket, copy) gratuito; (lavish) generoso; **~ of charge** gratuito; **set ~** liberare ● vt (pt/pp **freed**) liberare

free: ~dom n libertà f. **~hold** n proprietà f (fondiaria) assoluta. **~ kick** n calcio m di punizione. **~lance** adj & adv indipendente. **~ly** adv liberamente; (generously) generosamente; **I ~ly admit that...** devo ammettere che... **f~mason** n massone m. **~range** adj **~-range egg** uovo m di gallina ruspante. **~style** n stile m libero. **~way** n Am autostrada f

freez|e /fri:z/ vt (pt **froze**, pp **frozen**) gelare; bloccare (wages) ● vi (water:) gelare; **it's ~ing** si gela; **my hands are ~ing** ho le mani congelate

freez|er /'fri:zə(r)/ n freezer m inv, congelatore m. **~ing** adj gelido ● n **below ~ing** sotto zero

freight /freit/ n carico m. **~er** n nave f da carico. **~ train** n Am treno m merci

French /frentʃ/ adj francese ● n (language) francese m; **the ~** pl i francesi mpl

French: **~ 'fries** npl patate fpl fritte. **~man** n francese m. **~ 'window** n porta-finestra f. **~woman** n francese f

frenzied /'frenzid/ adj frenetico

frenzy /'frenzi/ n frenesia f

frequency /'fri:kwənsi/ n frequenza f

frequent¹ /'fri:kwənt/ adj frequente. **~ly** adv frequentemente

frequent² /fri'kwent/ vt frequentare

fresh /freʃ/ adj fresco; (new) nuovo; (Am: cheeky) sfacciato. **~ly** adv di recente

freshen /'freʃn/ vi (wind:) rinfrescare. □ **~ up** vt dare una rinfrescata a ● vi rinfrescarsi

freshness /'freʃnis/ n freschezza f

fret /fret/ vi (pt/pp **fretted**) inquietarsi. **~ful** adj irritabile

friction /'frikʃn/ n frizione f

Friday /'fraidei/ n venerdì m inv

fridge /fridʒ/ n frigo m

fried /fraid/ ▷**FRY** ● adj fritto; **~ egg** uovo m fritto

friend /frend/ n amico, -a mf. **~ly** adj (-ier, -iest) (relations, meeting, match) amichevole; (neighbourhood, smile) piacevole; (software) di facile uso; **be ~ly with** essere amico di. **~ship** n amicizia f

frieze /fri:z/ n fregio m

fright /frait/ n paura f; **take ~** spaventarsi

frighten /'fraitn/ vt spaventare. **~ed** adj spaventato; **be ~ed** aver paura (of di). **~ing** adj spaventoso

frightful /'fraitfl/ adj terribile

frigid /'fridʒid/ adj frigido. **~ity** n freddezza f; (Psych) frigidità f

frill /fril/ n volant m inv. **~y** adj (dress) con tanti volant

fringe /frindʒ/ n frangia f; (of hair) frangetta f; (fig: edge) margine m. **~ benefits** npl benefici mpl supplementari

fritter /'fritə(r)/ n frittella f ● **fritter away** vt sprecare

frivol|ity /fri'vɒləti/ n frivolezza f. **~ous** adj frivolo

fro /frəʊ/ ▷**TO**

frock /frɒk/ n abito m

frog /frɒg/ n rana f. **~man** n uomo m rana

frolic /'frɒlik/ vi (pt/pp **frolicked**) (lambs:) sgambettare; (people:) folleggiare

from /frɒm/ prep da; **~ Monday** da lunedì; **~ that day** da quel giorno; **he's ~ London** è di Londra; **this is a letter ~ my brother** questa è una lettera di mio fratello; **documents ~ the 16th century** documenti del XVI secolo; **made ~** fatto con; **she felt ill ~ fatigue** si sentiva male dalla stanchezza; **~ now on** d'ora in poi

front /frʌnt/ n parte f anteriore; (fig: organization etc) facciata f; (of garment) davanti m; (sea~) lungomare m; (Mil, Pol, Meteorol) fronte m; **in ~ of** davanti a; **in** or **at the ~** davanti; **to the ~** avanti ● adj davanti; (page, row, wheel) anteriore

frontal /'frʌntl/ adj frontale

front 'door n porta f d'entrata

frontier /'frʌntiə(r)/ n frontiera f

frost /frɒst/ n gelo m; (hoar~) brina f

~**bite** n congelamento m, ~**bitten** adj congelato

frost|ed /'frɒstɪd/ adj ~**ed glass** vetro m smerigliato. ~**ily** adv gelidamente. ~**ing** n Am (Culin) glassa f. ~**y** adj also fig gelido

froth /frɒθ/ n schiuma f ● vi far schiuma. ~**y** adj schiumoso

frown /fraʊn/ n cipiglio m ● vi aggrottare le sopraciglia. n ~ **on** vt disapprovare

froze /frəʊz/ ▷FREEZE

frozen /'frəʊzn/ ▷FREEZE ● adj (corpse, hand) congelato; (waste) gelido; (Culin) surgelato; **I'm** ~ sono gelato. ~ **food** n surgelati mpl

frugal /'fru:gl/ adj frugale

fruit /fru:t/ n frutto m; (collectively) frutta f; **eat more** ~ mangia più frutta ● vi far frutti. ~ **cake** n dolce m con frutta candita

fruition /fru:'ɪʃn/ n **come to** ~ dare dei frutti

fruit: ~**less** adj infruttuoso. ~ **salad** n macedonia f [di frutta]

frustrat|e /frʌ'streɪt/ vt frustrare; rovinare (plans). ~**ing** adj frustrante. ~**ion** n frustrazione f

fry /fraɪ/ vt/i (pt/pp **fried**) friggere

fry² /fraɪ/ n inv **small** ~ fig pesce m piccolo

frying pan n padella f

fudge /fʌdʒ/ n caramella f a base di zucchero, burro e latte

fuel /'fju:əl/ n carburante m; fig nutrimento m ● vt fig alimentare

fugitive /'fju:dʒɪtɪv/ n fuggiasco, a mf

fulfil /fʊl'fɪl/ vt (pt/pp **-filled**) soddisfare (conditions, need); realizzare (dream, desire); ~ **oneself** realizzarsi. ~**ling** adj soddisfacente. ~**ment** n **sense of** ~**ment** senso m di appagamento

full /fʊl/ adj pieno (**of** di); (detailed) esauriente; (bus, hotel) completo;

(skirt) ampio; **at** ~ **speed** a tutta velocità; **in** ~ **swing** in pieno fervore ● n **in** ~ per intero

full: ~ **moon** n luna f piena. ~**-scale** adj (model) in scala reale; (alert) di massima gravità ● ~ **stop** n punto m. ~**-time** adj & adv a tempo pieno

fully /'fʊlɪ/ adv completamente; (in detail) dettagliatamente; ~ **booked** (hotel, restaurant) tutto prenotato

fumble /'fʌmbl/ vi ~ **in** rovistare in; ~ **with** armeggiare con; ~ **for one's keys** rovistare alla ricerca delle chiavi

fume /fju:m/ vi (be angry) essere furioso

fumes /fju:mz/ npl fumi mpl; (from car) gas mpl di scarico

fumigate /'fju:mɪgeɪt/ vt suffumicare

fun /fʌn/ n divertimento m; **for** ~ per ridere; **make** ~ **of** prendere in giro; **have** ~ divertirsi

function /'fʌŋkʃn/ n funzione f; (event) cerimonia f ● vi funzionare; ~ **as** (serve as) funzionare da. ~**al** adj funzionale

fund /fʌnd/ n fondo m; fig pozzo m; ~**s** pl fondi mpl ● vt finanziare

fundamental /fʌndə'mentl/ adj fondamentale

funeral /'fju:nərəl/ n funerale m

funeral directors n impresa f di pompe funebri

funfair /'fʌnfeə/ n luna park m inv

fungus /'fʌŋgəs/ n (pl **-gi** /-gaɪ/) fungo m

funnel /'fʌnl/ n imbuto m; (on ship) ciminiera f

funnily /'fʌnɪlɪ/ adv comicamente; (oddly) stranamente; ~ **enough** strano a dirsi

funny /'fʌnɪ/ adj (**-ier, -iest**) buffo; (odd) strano. ~ **business** n affare m losco

fur /fɜː(r)/ n pelo m; (for clothing) pelliccia f; (in kettle) deposito m. ~ **'coat** n pelliccia f

furious /ˈfjʊərɪəs/ adj furioso

furnace /ˈfɜːnɪs/ n fornace f

furnish /ˈfɜːnɪʃ/ vt ammobiliare (flat); fornire (supplies). ~**ed** adj ~**ed room** stanza f ammobiliata. ~**ings** npl mobili mpl

furniture /ˈfɜːnɪtʃə(r)/ n mobili mpl

furrow /ˈfʌrəʊ/ n solco m

furry /ˈfɜːrɪ/ adj (animal) peloso; (toy) di peluche

further /ˈfɜːðə(r)/ adj (additional) ulteriore; **at the ~ end** all'altra estremità; **until ~ notice** fino a nuovo avviso ● adv più lontano; ~,... inoltre,...; ~ **off** più lontano ● vt promuovere

further'more adv per di più

furthest /ˈfɜːðɪst/ adj più lontano ● adv più lontano

furtive /ˈfɜːtɪv/ adj furtivo

fury /ˈfjʊərɪ/ n furore m

fuse¹ /fjuːz/ n (of bomb) detonatore m; (cord) miccia f

fuse² n (Electr) fusibile m ● vt fondere; (Electr) far saltare ● vi fondersi; (Electr) saltare; **the lights have ~d** sono saltate le luci. ~**-box** n scatola f dei fusibili

fuselage /ˈfjuːzəlɑːʒ/ n (Aeron) fusoliera f

fusion /ˈfjuːʒn/ n fusione f

fuss /fʌs/ n storie fpl; **make a ~** fare storie; **make a ~ of** colmare di attenzioni ● vi fare storie

fussy /ˈfʌsɪ/ adj (-ier, -iest) (person) difficile da accontentare; (clothes etc) pieno di fronzoli

futile /ˈfjuːtaɪl/ adj inutile. ~**ity** n futilità f

future /ˈfjuːtʃə(r)/ adj & n futuro; **in ~** in futuro. ~ **perfect** futuro m anteriore

futuristic /fjuːtʃəˈrɪstɪk/ adj futuristico

fuzz /fʌz/ n **the ~** (✺: police) la pula

fuzzy /ˈfʌzɪ/ adj (-ier, -iest) (hair) crespo; (photo) sfuocato

....

Gg

....

gab /gæb/ n ⚠ **have the gift of the ~** avere la parlantina

gabble /ˈgæb(ə)l/ vi parlare troppo in fretta

gad /gæd/ vi (pt/pp gadded) ~ **about** andarsene in giro

gadget /ˈgædʒɪt/ n aggeggio m

Gaelic /ˈgeɪlɪk/ adj & n gaelico m

gaffe /gæf/ n gaffe f inv

gag /gæg/ n bavaglio m; (joke) battuta f ● vt (pt/pp gagged) imbavagliare

gaily /ˈgeɪlɪ/ adv allegramente

gain /geɪn/ n guadagno m; (increase) aumento m ● vt acquisire; ~ **weight** aumentare di peso; ~ **access** accedere ● vi (clock): andare avanti. ~**ful** adj ~**ful employment** lavoro m remunerativo

gait /geɪt/ n andatura f

gala /ˈgɑːlə/ n gala f; **swimming ~** manifestazione f di nuoto ● attrib di gala

galaxy /ˈgæləksɪ/ n galassia f

gale /geɪl/ n bufera f

gall /gɔːl/ n (impudence) impudenza f

gallant /ˈgælənt/ adj coraggioso; (chivalrous) galante. ~**ry** n coraggio m

'gall-bladder n cistifellea f

gallery /ˈgælərɪ/ n galleria f

galley /ˈgælɪ/ n (ship's kitchen) cambusa f; ~ **[proof]** bozza f in colonna

gallivant /'gælɪvænt/ vi andare in giro

gallon /'gælən/ n gallone m (= 4,5 l; Am = 3,7 l)

gallop /'gæləp/ n galoppo m ● vi galoppare

gallows /'gæləʊz/ n forca f

galore /gə'lɔː(r)/ adv a bizzeffe

galvanize /'gælvənaɪz/ vt (Techn) galvanizzare; fig stimolare (into a)

gambl|e /'gæmbl/ n (risk) azzardo m ● vi giocare; (on Stock Exchange) speculare; ~e on (rely) contare su. ~er n giocatore, -trice mf [d'azzardo]. ~ing n gioco m [d'azzardo]

game /geɪm/ n gioco m; (match) partita f; (animals, birds) selvaggina f; ~s (Sch) ≈ ginnastica f ● adj (brave) coraggioso; are you ~? ti va?, be ~ for essere pronto per. ~keeper n guardacaccia m inv

gammon /'gæmən/ n coscia f di maiale

gamut /'gæmət/ n fig gamma f

gander /'gændə(r)/ n oca f maschio

gang /gæŋ/ n banda f; (of workmen) squadra f ● **gang up** vi far comunella (on contro)

gangling /'gæŋglɪŋ/ adj spilungone

gangmaster /'gæŋmɑːstə(r)/ n caporale m (di manodopera abusiva)

gangrene /'gæŋgriːn/ n cancrena f

gangster /'gæŋstə(r)/ n gangster m inv

gangway /'gæŋweɪ/ n passaggio m; (Aeron, Naut) passerella f

gaol /dʒeɪl/ n carcere m ● vt incarcerare. ~er n carceriere m

gap /gæp/ n spazio m; (in ages, between teeth) scarto m; (in memory) vuoto m; (in story) punto m oscuro

gap|e /geɪp/ vi stare a bocca aperta; (be wide open) spalancarsi; ~e at guardare a bocca aperta. ~ing adj aperto

garage /'gærɑːʒ/ n garage m inv; (for repairs) meccanico m; (for petrol) stazione f di servizio

garbage /'gɑːbɪdʒ/ n immondizia f; (nonsense) idiozie fpl. ~ can n Am bidone m dell'immondizia

garden /'gɑːdn/ n giardino m; [public] ~s giardini mpl pubblici ● vi fare giardinaggio. ~ centre n negozio m di piante e articoli da giardinaggio. ~er n giardiniere, -a mf. ~ing n giardinaggio m

gargle /'gɑːgl/ n gargarismo m ● vi fare gargarismi

gargoyle /'gɑːgɔɪl/ n garguglia f inv

garish /'geərɪʃ/ adj sgargiante

garland /'gɑːlənd/ n ghirlanda f

garlic /'gɑːlɪk/ n aglio m. ~ bread n pane m condito con aglio

garment /'gɑːmənt/ n indumento m

garnish /'gɑːnɪʃ/ n guarnizione f ● vt guarnire

garrison /'gærɪsn/ n guarnigione f

garter /'gɑːtə(r)/ n giarrettiera f; (for socks) reggicalze m inv da uomo

gas /gæs/ n gas m inv; (Am: petrol) benzina f ● v (pt/pp gassed) ● vt asfissiare ● vi fam blaterare. ~ cooker n cucina f a gas. ~ fire n stufa f a gas

gash /gæʃ/ n taglio m ● vt tagliare

gasket /'gæskɪt/ n (Techn) guarnizione f

gas: ~ **mask** n maschera f antigas. ~**-meter** n contatore m del gas

gasoline /'gæsəli:n/ n Am benzina f

gasp /gɑ:sp/ vi avere il fiato mozzato

'gas station n Am distributore m di benzina

gastric /'gæstrɪk/ adj gastrico. ~ **'flu** n influenza f gastro-intestinale. ~ **'ulcer** n ulcera f gastrica

gate /geɪt/ n cancello m; (at airport) uscita f

gate: ~**crash** vt entrare senza invito a. ~**crasher** n intruso, -a mf. ~**way** n ingresso m

gather /'gæðə(r)/ vt raccogliere; (conclude) dedurre; (in sewing) arricciare; ~ **speed** acquistare velocità; ~ **together** radunare (people, belongings); (obtain gradually) acquistare ● vi (people:) radunarsi. ~**ing** n family ~**ing** ritrovo m di famiglia

gaudy /'gɔ:dɪ/ adj (**-ier, -iest**) pacchiano

gauge /geɪdʒ/ n calibro m; (Rail) scartamento m; (device) indicatore m ● vt misurare; fig stimare

gaunt /gɔ:nt/ adj (thin) smunto

gauze /gɔ:z/ n garza f

gave /geɪv/ ▷GIVE

gawky /'gɔ:kɪ/ adj (**-ier, -iest**) sgraziato

gawp /gɔ:p/ vi ~ [**at**] 🔢 guardare con aria da ebete

gay /geɪ/ adj gaio; (homosexual) omosessuale; (bar, club) gay

gaze /geɪz/ n sguardo m fisso ● vi guardare; ~ **at** fissare

GB abbr (Great Britain) GB

gear /gɪə(r)/ n equipaggiamento m; (Techn) ingranaggio m; (Auto) marcia f; **in** ~ con la marcia innestata; **change** ~ cambiare marcia ● vt finalizzare (**to** a)

gearbox n (Auto) scatola f del cambio

geese /gi:s/ ▷GOOSE

gel /dʒel/ n gel m inv

gelatine /'dʒelətɪn/ n gelatina f

gelignite /'dʒelɪgnaɪt/ n gelatina esplosiva f

gem /dʒem/ n gemma f

Gemini /'dʒemɪnaɪ/ n (Astr) Gemelli mpl

gender /'dʒendə(r)/ n (Gram) genere m

gene /dʒi:n/ n gene m

genealogy /dʒi:nɪ'ælədʒɪ/ n genealogia f

general /'dʒenrəl/ adj generale ● n generale m; **in** ~ in generale. ~ **e'lection** n elezioni fpl politiche

generaliz|ation /dʒenrəlaɪ'zeɪʃn/ n generalizzazione f. ~**e** vi generalizzare

generally /'dʒenrəlɪ/ adv generalmente

general prac'titioner n medico m generico

generate /'dʒenəreɪt/ vt generare

generation /dʒenə'reɪʃn/ n generazione f

generator /'dʒenəreɪtə(r)/ n generatore m

generosity /dʒenə'rɒsɪtɪ/ n generosità f

generous /'dʒenərəs/ adj generoso. ~**ly** adv generosamente

genetic /dʒɪ'netɪk/ adj genetico. ~ **engineering** n ingegneria f genetica. ~**s** n genetica f

Geneva /dʒɪ'ni:və/ n Ginevra f

genial /'dʒi:nɪəl/ adj gioviale

genitals /'dʒenɪtlz/ npl genitali mpl

genitive /'dʒenɪtɪv/ adj & n ~ [**case**] genitivo m

genius /'dʒi:nɪəs/ n (pl **-uses**) genio m

genocide /'dʒenəsaɪd/ n genocidio m

genre /'ʒɑ:ig.rə/ n genere m [letterario]

gent /dʒent/ n 🔢 signore m; **the** ~**s**

sg il bagno per uomini

genteel /dʒen'tiːl/ adj raffinato

gentle /'dʒentl/ adj delicato; (breeze, tap, slope) leggero

gentleman /'dʒentlmən/ n signore m; (well-mannered) gentiluomo m

gentle|ness /'dʒentlnɪs/ n delicatezza f. **~ly** adv delicatamente

genuine /'dʒenjʊɪn/ adj genuino. **~ly** adv (sorry) sinceramente

geograph|ical /dʒɪə'græfɪkl/ adj geografico. **~y** n geografia f

geological /dʒɪə'lɒdʒɪkl/ adj geologico

geolog|ist /dʒɪ'ɒlədʒɪst/ n geologo, -a m/f. **~y** n geologia f

geranium /dʒə'reɪnɪəm/ n geranio m

geriatric /dʒerɪ'ætrɪk/ adj geriatrico; **~ ward** n reparto m geriatria. **~s** n geriatria f

germ /dʒɜːm/ n germe m; ● s pl microbi mpl

German /'dʒɜːmən/ n & adj tedesco, -a m/f; (language) tedesco m

Germanic /dʒɜː'mænɪk/ adj germanico

German 'measles n rosolia f

Germany /'dʒɜːmənɪ/ n Germania f

germinate /'dʒɜːmɪneɪt/ vi germogliare

gesticulate /dʒe'stɪkjʊleɪt/ vi gesticolare

gesture /'dʒestʃə(r)/ n gesto m

---

get /get/ verb

past tense/past participle **got**, past participle Am **gotten**, pres participle **getting**

● vt (receive) ricevere; (obtain) ottenere; trovare (job); (buy, catch, fetch) prendere; (transport, deliver to airport etc) portare; (reach on telephone) trovare; (**I**: understand) comprendere; preparare (meal); **~ sb to do sth** far fare qcsa a qcno

● vi (become) **~ tired/bored/angry** stancarsi/annoiarsi/arrabbiarsi; **I'm ~ting hungry** mi sta venendo fame; **~ dressed/married** vestirsi/sposarsi; **~ sth ready** preparare qcsa; **~ nowhere** non concludere nulla; **this is ~ting us nowhere** questo non ci è di nessun aiuto, **~ to** (reach) arrivare a. **□ ~ at** vt (criticize) criticare; **I see what you're ~ting at** ho capito cosa vuoi dire; **what are you ~ting at?** dove vuoi andare a parare? **□ ~ away** vi (leave) andarsene; (escape) scappare. **□ ~ back** vi tornare ● vt (recover) riavere; **~ one's own back** rifarsi. **□ ~ by** vi passare; (manage) cavarsela. **□ ~ down** vi scendere; **~ down to work** mettersi al lavoro ● vt (depress) buttare giù. **□ ~ in** vi entrare ● vt mettere dentro (washing); far venire (plumber). **□ ~ off** vi scendere; (from work) andarsene; (Jur) essere assolto; **~ off the bus/one's bike** scendere dal pullman/dalla bici ● vt (remove) togliere. **□ ~ on** vi salire; (be on good terms) andare d'accordo; (make progress) andare avanti; (in life) riuscire; **~ on the bus/one's bike** salire sul pullman/sulla bici; **how are you ~ting on?** come va?. **□ ~ out** vi uscire; (of car) scendere; **~ out!** fuori!; **~ out of** (avoid doing) evitare ● vt togliere (cork, stain). **□ ~ over** vi andare al di là ● vt (recover from) riprendersi da (illness). **□ ~ round** vt aggirare (rule); rigirare (person) ● vi **I never ~ round to it** non mi sono mai deciso a farlo. **□ ~ through** vi (on telephone) prendere la linea. □~ **up** vi alzarsi; (climb) salire; ~ **up a hill** salire su una collina

geyser /'gi:zə(r)/ n scaldabagno m; (Geol) geyser m inv

ghastly /'gɑ:stlɪ/ adj (-ier, -iest) terribile; **feel** ~ sentirsi da cani

gherkin /'gɜ:kɪn/ n cetriolino m

ghetto /'getəʊ/ n ghetto m

ghost /'ɡəʊst/ n fantasma m. ~**ly** adj spettrale

giant /'dʒaɪənt/ n gigante m ● adj gigante

gibberish /'dʒɪbərɪʃ/ n stupidaggini fpl

gibe /dʒaɪb/ n malignità f inv

giblets /'dʒɪblɪts/ npl frattaglie fpl

giddiness /'gɪdɪnɪs/ n vertigini fpl

giddy /'gɪdɪ/ adj (-ier, -iest) vertiginoso; **feel** ~ avere le vertigini

gift /gɪft/ n dono m; (to charity) donazione f. ~**ed** adj dotato. ~-**wrap** vt impacchettare in carta da regalo

gig /gɪg/ n (Mus) [i] concerto m

gigantic /dʒaɪ'gæntɪk/ adj gigantesco

giggle /'gɪgl/ n risatina f ● vi ridacchiare

gild /gɪld/ vt dorare

gills /gɪlz/ npl branchia fsg

gilt /gɪlt/ adj dorato ● n doratura f. ~-**edged stock** n investimento m sicuro

gimmick /'gɪmɪk/ n trovata f

gin /dʒɪn/ n gin m inv

ginger /'dʒɪndʒə(r)/ adj rosso fuoco inv; (cat) rosso ● n zenzero m. ~ **ale** n, ~ **beer** n bibita f allo zenzero. ~**bread** n panpepato m

gipsy /'dʒɪpsɪ/ n = gypsy

giraffe /dʒɪ'rɑ:f/ n giraffa f

girder /'gɜ:də(r)/ n (Techn) trave f

girl /gɜ:l/ n ragazza f; (female child) femmina f. ~ **band** n girl band f inv. ~**friend** n amica f; (of boy) ragazza f.

~**ish** adj da ragazza

giro /'dʒaɪərəʊ/ n bancogiro m; (cheque) sussidio m di disoccupazione

girth /gɜ:θ/ n circonferenza f

gist /dʒɪst/ n **the** ~ la sostanza

give /gɪv/ n elasticità f ● v (pt gave, pp given) ● vt dare; (as present) regalare (to a); fare (lecture, present, shriek); donare (blood); ~ **birth** partorire ● vi (to charity) fare delle donazioni; (yield) cedere; □ ~ **away** vt dar via; (betray) tradire; (distribute) assegnare; ~ **away the bride** portare la sposa all'altare. □ ~ **back** vt restituire. □ ~ **in** vt consegnare ● vi (yield) arrendersi. □ ~ **off** vt emanare. □ ~ **over** vi ~ **over!** piantala!. □ ~ **up** vt rinunciare a; ~ **oneself up** arrendersi ● vi rinunciare. □ ~ **way** vi cedere; (Auto) dare la precedenza; (collapse) crollare

given /'gɪvn/ ▷**GIVE** ● adj ~ **name** nome m di battesimo

glacier /'glæsɪə(r)/ n ghiacciaio m

glad /glæd/ adj contento (**of** di). ~**den** vt rallegrare

gladly /'glædlɪ/ adv volentieri

glamour /'glæmə(r)/ n fascino m

glance /glɑ:ns/ n sguardo m ● vi ~ **at** dare un'occhiata a. □ ~ **up** vi alzare gli occhi

gland /glænd/ n glandola f

glare /gleə(r)/ n bagliore m; (look) occhiataccia f ● vi ~ **at** dare un'occhiataccia a

glaring /'gleərɪŋ/ adj sfolgorante; (mistake) madornale

glass /glɑ:s/ n vetro m; (for drinking) bicchiere m; ~**es** (pl: spectacles) occhiali mpl. ~**y** adj vitreo

glaze /gleɪz/ n smalto m ● vt mettere i vetri a (door, window); smaltare (pottery); (Culin) spennellare. ~**d** adj (eyes) vitreo

gleam /gliːm/ n luccichio m • vi luccicare

glean /gliːn/ vt racimolare (information)

glee /gliː/ n gioia f. **~ful** adj gioioso

glib /glɪb/ adj pej insincero

glide /glaɪd/ vi scorrere; (through the air) planare. **~er** n aliante m

glimmer /ˈglɪmə(r)/ n barlume m • vi emettere un barlume

glimpse /glɪmps/ n **catch a ~ of** intravedere • vt intravedere

glint /glɪnt/ vi luccicare

glisten /ˈglɪsn/ vi luccicare

glitter /ˈglɪtə(r)/ vi brillare

gloat /gləʊt/ vi gongolare (**over** su)

global /ˈgləʊbl/ adj mondiale. **~ization** n globalizzazione f

globe /gləʊb/ n globo m; (map) mappamondo m

gloom /gluːm/ n oscurità f; (sadness) tristezza f. **~ily** adv (sadly) con aria cupa

gloomy /ˈgluːmɪ/ adj (-ier, -iest) cupo

glorify /ˈglɔːrɪfaɪ/ vt (pt/pp -ied) glorificare; **a ~ied waitress** niente più che una cameriera

glorious /ˈglɔːrɪəs/ adj splendido; (deed, hero) glorioso

glory /ˈglɔːrɪ/ n gloria f; (splendour) splendore m; (cause for pride) vanto m • vi (pt/pp -ied) **~ in** vantarsi di

gloss /glɒs/ n lucentezza f. **~ paint** n vernice f lucida • **gloss over** vt sorvolare su

glossary /ˈglɒsərɪ/ n glossario m

glossy /ˈglɒsɪ/ adj (-ier, -iest) lucido; **~ [magazine]** rivista f femminile

glove /glʌv/ n guanto m. **~ compartment** n (Auto) cruscotto m

glow /gləʊ/ n splendore m; (in cheeks) rossore m; (of candle) luce f soffusa • vi risplendere; (candle:) brillare; (person:) avvampare. **~ing** adj ardente; (account) entusiastico

~-worm n lucciola f

glucose /ˈgluːkəʊs/ n glucosio m

glue /gluː/ n colla f • vt (pres p gluing) incollare

glum /glʌm/ adj (glummer, glummest) tetro

glutton /ˈglʌtn/ n ghiottone, -a mf. **~ous** adj ghiotto. **~y** n ghiottoneria f

gnarled /nɑːld/ adj nodoso

gnash /næʃ/ vt **~ one's teeth** digrignare i denti

gnaw /nɔː/ vt rosicchiare

go¹ /gəʊ/ n (pl goes) energia f; (attempt) tentativo m; **on the go** in movimento; **at one go** in una sola volta; **it's your go** tocca a te; **make a go of it** riuscire

go² /gəʊ/

3 sing pres tense **goes**, past tense **went**, past participle **gone**

• vi andare; (leave) andar via; (vanish) sparire; (become) diventare; (be sold) vendersi; **go and see** andare a vedere; **go swimming/shopping** andare a nuotare/fare spese; **where's the time gone?** come ha fatto il tempo a volare così?; **it's all gone** è finito; **be going to do** stare per fare; **I'm not going to** non ne ho nessuna intenzione; **to go** (T) hamburgers etc) da asporto; **a coffee to go** un caffè da portar via. □ **~ about** vi andare in giro. □ **~ away** vi andarsene. □ **~ back** vi ritornare. □ **~ by** vi passare. □ **~ down** vi scendere; (sun:) tramontare; (ship:) affondare; (swelling:) diminuire. □ **~ for** vt andare a prendere; andare a cercare (doctor); (choose) optare per; (T: attack) aggredire; **he's** not the kind I go for non è il genere che mi attira. ▫ ~ **in** vi entrare. ▫ ~ **in for** vt partecipare a (competition); darsi a (tennis). ▫ ~ **off** vi andarsene; (alarm:) scattare; (gun, bomb:) esplodere; (food, milk:) andare a male; **go off well** riuscire. ▫ ~ **on** vi andare avanti; **what's going on?** cosa succede? **go on at** vt **I** scocciare. ▫ ~ **out** vi uscire; (light, fire:) spegnersi. ▫ ~ **over** vi andare ▫ vt (check) controllare. ▫ ~ **round** vi andare in giro; (visit) andare; (turn) girare; **is there enough to go round?** ce n'è abbastanza per tutti? **go through** vi (bill, proposal:) passare ● vt (suffer) subire; (check) controllare; (read) leggere. ▫ ~ **under** vi passare sotto; (ship, swimmer:) andare sott'acqua; (fail) fallire. ▫ ~ **up** vi salire; (Theat: curtain:) aprirsi. ▫ ~ **with** vt accompagnare. ▫ ~ **without** vt fare a meno di (supper, sleep) ● vi fare senza

goad /gəʊd/ vt spingere (**into** a); (taunt) speronare

'**go-ahead** adj (person, company) intraprendente ● n okay m

goal /gəʊl/ n porta f; (point scored) gol m inv; (in life) obiettivo m; **score a** ~ segnare. ~**ie** **I**, ~**keeper** n portiere m. ~**-post** n palo m

goat /gəʊt/ n capra f

gobble /'gɒbl/ vt ~ [**down, up**] tranguiare

God, god /gɒd/ n Dio m, dio m

god: ~**child** n figlioccio, -a f. ~**-daughter** n figlioccia f. ~**dess** n dea f. ~**father** n padrino m. ~**forsaken** adj dimenticato da Dio. ~**mother** n madrina f. ~**send** n manna f. ~**son** n figlioccio m

going /'gəʊɪŋ/ adj (price, rate) corrente; ~ **concern** azienda f florida

● n **it's hard** ~ è una faticaccia; **while the** ~ **is good** finché si può. ~**s-'on** npl avvenimenti mpl

gold /gəʊld/ n oro m ● adj d'oro

golden /'gəʊldn/ adj dorato. ~**handshake** n buonuscita f (al termine di un rapporto di lavoro). ~ **mean** n giusto mezzo m. ~ **wedding** n nozze fpl d'oro

gold: ~**fish** n inv pesce m rosso. ~**-mine** n miniera f d'oro. ~**-plated** adj placcato d'oro. ~**smith** n orefice m

golf /gɒlf/ n golf m

golf: ~**-club** n circolo m di golf; (implement) mazza f da golf. ~**-course** n campo m di golf. ~**er** n giocatore, -trice mf di golf

gondo|la /'gɒndələ/ n gondola f. ~**lier** n gondoliere m

gone /gɒn/ ▷**go**

gong /gɒŋ/ n gong m inv

good /gʊd/ adj (better, best) buono; (child, footballer, singer) bravo; (holiday, film) bello; ~ **at** bravo in; **a ~ deal of** anger molta rabbia; **as** ~ **as** (almost) quasi; ~ **morning**, ~ **afternoon** buon giorno; ~ **evening** buona sera; ~ **night** buonanotte; **have a ~ time** divertirsi ● n bene m; **for** ~ per sempre; **do** ~ far del bene; **do sb** ~ far bene a qcno; **it's no** ~ è inutile; **be up to no** ~ combinare qualcosa

goodbye /gʊd'baɪ/ int arrivederci

good: ~**-for-nothing** n buono, -a mf a nulla. **G~ 'Friday** n Venerdì m Santo

good-'looking adj bello

goodness /'gʊdnɪs/ n bontà f; **my** ~**!** santo cielo!; **thank** ~**!** grazie al cielo!

goods /gʊdz/ npl prodotti mpl. ~ **train** n treno m merci

good'will n buona volontà f; (Comm) avviamento m

goody /'gʊdɪ/ n ([T]: person) buono m. **~-goody** n santarellino, -a mf

gooey /'gu:ɪ/ adj [T] appiccicaticcio; fig sdolcinato

google /'gu:gl/ vt/i googlare

goose /gu:s/: **~ flesh** n, **~-pimples** npl pelle fsg d'oca

gooseberry /'gʊzbərɪ/ n uva f spina

gore[1] /gɔ:(r)/ n sangue m

gore[2] vt incornare

gorge /gɔ:dʒ/ n (Geog) gola f ● vt **~ oneself** ingozzarsi

gorgeous /'gɔ:dʒəs/ adj stupendo

gorilla /gə'rɪlə/ n gorilla m inv

gorse /gɔ:s/ n ginestrone m

gory /'gɔ:rɪ/ adj (-ier, -iest) cruento

gosh /gɒʃ/ int [T] caspita

gospel /'gɒspl/ n vangelo m. **~ truth** n sacrosanta verità f

gossip /'gɒsɪp/ n pettegolezzi mpl; (person) pettegolo, -a mf ● vi pettegolare. **~y** adj pettegolo

got /gɒt/ ▷GET: **have ~** avere; **have ~ to do** sth dover fare qcsa

gotten /'gɒtn/ Am see get

gouge /gaʊdʒ/ vt **~ out** cavare

gourmet /'gʊəmeɪ/ n buongustaio -a mf

govern /'gʌv(ə)n/ vt/i governare; (determine) determinare

government /'gʌvnmənt/ n governo m. **~al** adj governativo

governor /'gʌvənə(r)/ n governatore m; (of school) membro m del consiglio di istituto; (of prison) direttore, -trice mf; ([T]: boss) capo m

gown /gaʊn/ n vestito m; (Jur, Univ) toga f

GP n abbr general practitioner

GPS abbr (Global Positioning System) GPS m

grab /græb/ vt (pt/pp grabbed) **~ [hold of]** afferrare

grace /greɪs/ n grazia f; (before meal)

benedicite m inv; **with good ~** volentieri; **three days' ~** tre giorni di proroga. **~ful** adj aggraziato. **~fully** adv con grazia

gracious /'greɪʃəs/ adj cortese; (elegant) lussuoso

grade /greɪd/ n livello m; (Comm) qualità f; (Sch) voto m; (Am Sch: class) classe f; Am **= gradient** ● vt (Comm) classificare; (Sch) dare il voto a. **~ crossing** n Am passaggio m a livello

gradient /'greɪdɪənt/ n pendenza f

gradual /'grædʒʊəl/ adj graduale. **~ly** adv gradualmente

graduate[1] /'grædʒʊət/ n laureato, -a mf

graduate[2] /'grædʒʊeɪt/ vi (Univ) laurearsi

graduation /grædʒʊ'eɪʃn/ n laurea f

graffiti /grə'fi:tɪ/ npl graffiti mpl

graft /grɑ:ft/ n (Bot, Med) innesto m; (Med: organ) trapianto m; ([T]: hard work) duro lavoro m; ([T]: corruption) corruzione f ● vt innestare; trapiantare (organ)

grain /greɪn/ n (of sand, salt) granello m; (of rice) chicco m; (cereals) cereali mpl; (in wood) venatura f; **it goes against the ~** fig è contro la mia/sua natura

gram /græm/ n grammo m

grammar /'græmə(r)/ n grammatica f. **~ school** n ≈ liceo m

grammatical /grə'mætɪkl/ adj grammaticale

grand /grænd/ adj grandioso; [T] eccellente

'grandchild n nipote mf

'granddaughter n nipote f

'grandeur /'grændʒə(r)/ n grandiosità f

'grandfather n nonno m. **~ clock** n pendolo m (che poggia a terra)

grandiose /'grændɪəʊs/ adj

grandioso

grand: ∼**mother** n nonna f. ∼**parents** npl nonni mpl. ∼ **pi'ano** n pianoforte m a coda. ∼**son** n nipote m. ∼**stand** n tribuna f

granite /'grænɪt/ n granito m

granny /'grænɪ/ n fam nonna f

grant /grɑːnt/ n (money) sussidio m; (Univ) borsa f di studio • vt accordare; (admit) ammettere; **take sth for** ∼**ed** dare per scontato qcsa

granule /'grænjuːl/ n granello m

grape /greɪp/ n acino m; ∼**s** pl uva fsg

grapefruit /'greɪp-/ n inv pompelmo m

graph /grɑːf/ n grafico m

graphic /'græfɪk/ adj grafico; (vivid) vivido. ∼**s** n grafica f

grapple /'græpl/ vi ∼ **with** also fig essere alle prese con

grasp /grɑːsp/ n stretta f; (understanding) comprensione f • vt afferrare. ∼**ing** adj avido

grass /grɑːs/ n erba f; **at the** ∼ **roots** alla base. ∼**hopper** n cavalletta f. ∼**land** n prateria f

grassy /'grɑːsɪ/ adj erboso

grate[1] /greɪt/ n grata f

grate[2] vt (Culin) grattugiare • vi stridere

grateful /'greɪtfl/ adj grato. ∼**ly** adv con gratitudine

grater /'greɪtə(r)/ n (Culin) grattugia f

gratify /'grætɪfaɪ/ vt (pt/pp -**ied**) appagare. ∼**ied** adj appagato. ∼**ying** adj appagante

grating /'greɪtɪŋ/ n grata f

gratitude /'grætɪtjuːd/ n gratitudine f

gratuitous /grə'tjuːɪtəs/ adj gratuito

gratuity /grə'tjuːɪtɪ/ n gratifica f

grave[1] /greɪv/ adj grave

grave[2] n tomba f

gravel /'grævl/ n ghiaia f

grave: ∼**stone** n lapide f. ∼**yard** n cimitero m

gravitate /'grævɪteɪt/ vi gravitare

gravity /'grævɪtɪ/ n gravità f

gravy /'greɪvɪ/ n sugo m della carne

gray /greɪ/ adj Am = **grey**

graze[1] /greɪz/ vi (animal): pascolare

graze[2] n escoriazione f • vt (touch lightly) sfiorare; (scrape) escoriare; sbucciarsi (knee)

grease /griːs/ n grasso m • vt ungere. ∼**-proof 'paper** n carta f oleata

greasy /'griːsɪ/ adj (-**ier**, -**iest**) untuoso; (hair, skin) grasso

great /greɪt/ adj grande; (fam: marvellous) eccezionale

great: **G**∼ **'Britain** n Gran Bretagna f. ∼**'grandfather** n bisnonno m. ∼**'grandmother** n bisnonna f

great|ly /'greɪtlɪ/ adv enormemente. ∼**ness** n grandezza f

Greece /griːs/ n Grecia f

greed /griːd/ n avidità f; (for food) ingordigia f

greedy /'griːdɪ/ adj (-**ier**, -**iest**) avido; (for food) ingordo

Greek /griːk/ adj n greco, -a mf; (language) greco m

green /griːn/ adj verde; (fig: inexperienced) immaturo • n verde m; ∼**s** pl verdura f; **the G**∼**s** pl (Pol) i verdi. ∼ **belt** n zona f verde intorno a una città. ∼ **card** n (Auto) carta f verde

---

Green Card Negli Stati
Uniti è un documento ufficiale che concede a qual-
siasi persona priva della cittadinanza americana il permesso di
risiedere e lavorare indefinitiva-
mente negli Stati Uniti. Nel Regno
Unito, invece, è un documento che
i conducenti o proprietari di

autoveicoli devono richiedere alla propria compagnia di assicurazione per convalidare la polizza in occasione di viaggi all'estero.

greenery /ˈɡriːnəri/ n verde m

green: ~**grocer** n fruttivendolo, -a mf ~**house** n serra f. ~**house effect** n effetto m serra. ~ **light** n [I] verde m

greet /ɡriːt/ vt salutare; (welcome) accogliere. ~**ing** n saluto m; (welcome) accoglienza f. ~**ings card** n biglietto m d'auguri

gregarious /ɡrɪˈɡeəriəs/ adj gregario; (person) socievole

grenade /ɡrɪˈneɪd/ n granata f

grew /ɡruː/ ▷**GROW**

grey /ɡreɪ/ adj grigio; (hair) bianco ● n grigio m. ~**hound** n levriero m

grid /ɡrɪd/ n griglia f; (on map) reticolato m; (Electr) rete f

grief /ɡriːf/ n dolore m; **come to** ~ (plans) naufragare

grievance /ˈɡriːvəns/ n lamentela f

grieve /ɡriːv/ vt addolorare ● vi essere addolorato

grill /ɡrɪl/ n graticola f, (for grilling) griglia f; **mixed** ~ grigliata f mista ● vt/i cuocere alla griglia; (interrogate) sottoporre a terzo grado

grille /ɡrɪl/ n grata f

grim /ɡrɪm/ adj (grimmer, grimmest) arcigno; (determination) accanito

grimace /ɡrɪˈmeɪs/ n smorfia f ● vi fare una smorfia

grime /ɡraɪm/ n sudiciume m

grimy /ˈɡraɪmi/ adj (-ier, -iest) sudicio

grin /ɡrɪn/ n sorriso m ● vi (pt/pp grinned) fare un gran sorriso

grind /ɡraɪnd/ n ([I]: hard work) sfacchinata f ● vt (pt/pp ground) macinare; affilare (knife); (Am: mince) tritare; ~ **one's teeth** digrignare

i denti

grip /ɡrɪp/ n presa f; fig controllo m; (bag) borsone m; **get a** ~ **on oneself** controllarsi ● vt (pt/pp gripped) afferrare; (tyres:) far presa su; tenere avvinto (attention)

grisly /ˈɡrɪzli/ adj (-ier, -iest) raccapricciante

gristle /ˈɡrɪsl/ n cartilagine f

grit /ɡrɪt/ n graniglia f; (for roads) sabbia f; (courage) coraggio m ● vt (pt/pp gritted) spargere sabbia su (road); ~ **one's teeth** serrare i denti

groan /ɡrəʊn/ n gemito m ● vi gemere

grocer /ˈɡrəʊsə(r)/ n droghiere, -a mf; ~**'s [shop]** drogheria f. ~**ies** npl generi mpl alimentari

groggy /ˈɡrɒɡi/ adj (-ier, -iest) stordito; (unsteady) barcollante

groin /ɡrɔɪn/ n (Anat) inguine m

groom /ɡruːm/ n sposo m; (for horse) stalliere m ● vt strigliare (horse); fig preparare; **well-~ed** ben curato

groove /ɡruːv/ n scanalatura f

grope /ɡrəʊp/ vi brancolare; ~ **for** cercare a tastoni

gross /ɡrəʊs/ adj (coarse) volgare; (glaring) grossolano; (salary, weight) lordo ● n inv grossa f. ~**ly** adv (very) enormemente

grotesque /ɡrəʊˈtesk/ adj grottesco

ground[1] /ɡraʊnd/ ▷**GRIND**

ground[2] n terra f; (Sport) terreno m; (reason) ragione f; ~**s** pl (park) giardini mpl; (of coffee) fondi mpl ● vi (ship:) arenarsi ● vt bloccare a terra (aircraft); (Am Electr) mettere a terra

ground: ~ **floor** n pianterreno m. ~**ing** n base f. ~**less** adj infondato. ~**sheet** n telone m impermeabile. ~**work** n lavoro m di preparazione

group /ɡruːp/ n gruppo m ● vt raggruppare ● vi raggrupparsi

grouse[1] /ɡraʊs/ n inv gallo m

cedrone

grouse² /graʊs/ n **1** brontolare

grovel /ˈɡrɒvl/ vi (pt/pp **grovelled**) strisciare. ~**ling** adj leccapiedi inv

grow /ɡrəʊ/ v (pt **grew**, pp **grown**) • vi crescere; (become) diventare; (unemployment, fear:) aumentare; (town:) ingrandirsi • vt coltivare; ~ **one's hair** farsi crescere i capelli. □ ~ **up** vi crescere; (town:) svilupparsi

growl /graʊl/ n grugnito m • vi ringhiare

grown /ɡrəʊn/ ▷**GROW** • adj adulto. ~**up** adj & n adulto, -a mf

growth /ɡrəʊθ/ n crescita f; (increase) aumento m; (Med) tumore m

grub /ɡrʌb/ n larva f; (**1**: food) mangiare m

grubby /ˈɡrʌbɪ/ adj (**-ier, -iest**) sporco

grudg|e /ɡrʌdʒ/ n rancore m; **bear sb a** ~**e** portare rancore a qcno • vt dare a malincuore. ~**ing** adj reluttante. ~**ingly** adv a malincuore

gruelling /ˈɡruːəlɪŋ/ adj estenuante

gruesome /ˈɡruːsəm/ adj macabro

gruff /ɡrʌf/ adj burbero

grumble /ˈɡrʌmbl/ vi brontolare (**at** contro)

grumpy /ˈɡrʌmpɪ/ adj (**-ier, -iest**) scorbutico

grunt /ɡrʌnt/ n grugnito m • vi fare un grugnito

guarant|ee /ɡærənˈtiː/ n garanzia f • vt garantire. ~**or** n garante mf

guard /ɡɑːd/ n guardia f; (security) guardiano m; (on train) capotreno m; (Techn) schermo m protettivo; **be on** ~ essere di guardia • vt sorvegliare; (protect) proteggere. □ ~ **against** vt guardarsi da. ~**dog** n cane m da guardia

guarded /ˈɡɑːdɪd/ adj guardingo

guardian /ˈɡɑːdɪən/ n (of minor) tutore, -trice mf

guerrilla /ɡəˈrɪlə/ n guerrigliero, -a mf. ~ **warfare** n guerriglia f

guess /ɡes/ n supposizione f • vt indovinare • vi supporre; (Am: suppose) supporre. ~**work** n supposizione f

guest /ɡest/ n ospite mf; (in hotel) cliente mf. ~**house** n pensione f

guffaw /ɡʌˈfɔː/ n sghignazzata f • vi sghignazzare

guidance /ˈɡaɪdəns/ n guida f; (advice) consigli mpl

guide /ɡaɪd/ n guida f; [**Girl**] **G**~ giovane esploratrice f • vt guidare. ~**book** n guida f turistica

guide: ~**dog** n cane m per ciechi. ~**lines** npl direttive fpl

guild /ɡɪld/ n corporazione f

guile /ɡaɪl/ n astuzia f

guillotine /ˈɡɪlətiːn/ n ghigliottina f; (for paper) taglierina f

guilt /ɡɪlt/ n colpa f. ~**ily** adv con aria colpevole

guilty /ˈɡɪltɪ/ adj (**-ier, -iest**) colpevole; **have a** ~ **conscience** avere la coscienza sporca

guinea-pig /ˈɡɪnɪ-/ n porcellino m d'India; (fig: used for experiments) cavia f

guitar /ɡɪˈtɑː(r)/ n chitarra f. ~**ist** n chitarrista mf

gulf /ɡʌlf/ n (Geog) golfo m; fig abisso m

gull /ɡʌl/ n gabbiano m

gullet /ˈɡʌlɪt/ n esofago m; (throat) gola f

gullible /ˈɡʌlɪbl/ adj credulone

gully /ˈɡʌlɪ/ n burrone m; (drain) canale m di scolo

gulp /ɡʌlp/ n azione f di deglutire; (of food) boccone m; (of liquid) sorso m • vi deglutire. □ ~ **down** vt trangugiare (food); scolarsi (liquid)

gum¹ /ɡʌm/ n (Anat) gengiva f

gum² /ɡʌm/ n gomma f; (chewing gum) gomma f da masticare, chewing gum m inv • vt (pt/pp **gummed**) ingommare (**to** a)

gun /gʌn/ n pistola f; (*rifle*) fucile m; (*cannon*) cannone m ● **gun down** vt (*pt/pp* **gunned**) freddare

gun: **~fire** n spari mpl; (*of cannon*) colpi mpl [di cannone]. **~man** uomo m armato

gun: **~powder** n polvere f da sparo. **~shot** n colpo m [di pistola]

gurgle /ˈgɜːgl/ vi gorgogliare; (*baby:*) fare degli urletti

gush /gʌʃ/ vi sgorgare; (*enthuse*) parlare con troppo entusiasmo (**over** di). **~ out** vi sgorgare. **~ing** adj eccessivamente entusiasta

gust /gʌst/ n (*of wind*) raffica f

gusto /ˈgʌstəʊ/ n **with ~** con trasporto

gusty /ˈgʌstɪ/ adj ventoso

gut /gʌt/ n intestino m; **~s** pl pancia f; (**fig**: *courage*) fegato m ● vt (*pt/pp* **gutted**) (*Culin*) svuotare delle interiora; **~ted by fire** sventrato da un incendio

gutter /ˈgʌtə(r)/ n canale m di scolo; (*on roof*) grondaia f; fig bassifondi mpl

guttural /ˈgʌtərəl/ adj gutturale

guy /gaɪ/ n ⨐ tipo m, tizio m

guzzle /ˈgʌzl/ vt ingozzarsi con (*food*); **he's ~d the lot** si è sbafato tutto

gym /dʒɪm/ n ⨐ palestra f; (*gymnastics*) ginnastica f

gymnasium /dʒɪmˈneɪzɪəm/ n palestra f

gymnast /ˈdʒɪmnæst/ n ginnasta mf. **~ics** n ginnastica f

gymslip /n (*Sch*) ≈ grembiule m (da bambina)

gynaecolog|ist /gaɪnɪˈkɒlədʒɪst/ n ginecologo, -a mf. **~y** n ginecologia f

gypsy /ˈdʒɪpsɪ/ n zingaro, -a mf

gyrate /dʒaɪˈreɪt/ vi roteare

gun | hair

Hh

haberdashery /hæbəˈdæʃərɪ/ n merceria f; Am negozio m d'abbigliamento da uomo

habit /ˈhæbɪt/ n abitudine f; (*Relig:* *costume*) tonaca f; **be in the ~ of doing sth** avere l'abitudine di fare qcsa

habitable /ˈhæbɪtəbl/ adj abitabile

habitat /ˈhæbɪtæt/ n habitat m inv

habitation /hæbɪˈteɪʃn/ n **unfit for human ~** inabitabile

habitual /həˈbɪtjʊəl/ adj abituale; (*smoker, liar*) inveterato. **~ly** adv regolarmente

hack¹ /hæk/ n (*writer*) scribacchino, -a mf

hack² vt tagliare; **~ to pieces** tagliare a pezzi

hackneyed /ˈhæknɪd/ adj trito [e ritrito]

had /hæd/ ▷HAVE

haddock /ˈhædək/ n inv eglefino m

haemorrhage /ˈhemərɪdʒ/ n emorragia f

haemorrhoids /ˈhemərɔɪdz/ npl emorroidi fpl

hag /hæg/ n **old ~** vecchia befana f

haggard /ˈhægəd/ adj sfatto

hail¹ /heɪl/ vt salutare; far segno a (*taxi*) ● vi **~ from** provenire da

hail² /heɪl/ n grandine f ● vi grandinare. **~stone** n chicco m di grandine. **~storm** n grandinata f

hair /heə(r)/ n capelli mpl; (*on body, of animal*) pelo m

hair: **~brush** n spazzola f per capelli. **~cut** n taglio m di capelli; **have a ~cut** farsi tagliare i capelli. **~do** n ⨐ pettinatura f. **~dresser** n parrucchiere, -a mf. **~dryer** n fon m *inv*; (*with hood*) casco m [asciugaca-pelli]. **~-grip** n molletta f. **~pin** n forcina f. **~pin 'bend** n tornante m, curva f a gomito. **~-raising** adj terri-ficante. **~-style** n acconciatura f

hairy /'heərɪ/ adj (**-ier, -iest**) peloso; (囗: *frightening*) spaventoso

half /hɑ:f/ n (pl **halves**) metà f inv; **cut in ~** tagliare a metà; **one and a ~** uno e mezzo; **a dozen** mezza dozzina; **~ an hour** mezz'ora ● adj mezzo; [at] **~ price** [a] metà prezzo ● adv a metà; **~ past two** le due e mezza

half: **~-'hearted** adj esitante. **~ 'mast** n at **~** a mast a mezz'asta. **~-'term** n vacanza f di metà trime-stre. **~'time** n (*Sport*) intervallo m. **~'way** adj the **~way mark/stage** il livello intermedio ● adv a metà strada; **get ~way** fig arrivare a metà

hall /hɔ:l/ n (*entrance*) ingresso m; (*room*) sala f; (*mansion*) residenza f di campagna; **~ of residence** (*Univ*) casa f dello studente

'hallmark n marchio m di garanzia; fig marchio m

hallo /hə'ləʊ/ int ciao!; (*on telephone*) pronto!; **say ~ to** salutare

Hallowe'en /hæləʊ'i:n/ n vigilia f d'Ognissanti e notte delle streghe, celebrata soprattutto dai bambini

hallucination /həlu:sɪ'neɪʃn/ n al-lucinazione f

halo /'heɪləʊ/ n (pl **-es**) aureola f; (*Astr*) alone m

halt /hɔ:lt/ n alt m inv; **come to a ~** fermarsi; (*traffic:*) bloccarsi ● vi fer-marsi; **~!** alt! ● vt fermare. **~ing** adj esitante

halve /hɑ:v/ vt dividere a metà; (*re-duce*) dimezzare

ham /hæm/ n prosciutto m; (*Theat*) attore, -trice mf da strapazzo

hamburger /'hæmbɜ:gə(r)/ n hamburger m inv

hammer /'hæmə(r)/ n martello m

● vt martellare ● vi **~ at/on** pic-chiare a

hammock /'hæmək/ n amaca f

hamper[1] /'hæmpə(r)/ n cesto m; [gift] **~** cestino m

hamper[2] vt ostacolare

hamster /'hæmstə(r)/ n criceto m

hand /hænd/ n mano f; (*of clock*) lancetta f; (*writing*) scrittura f; (*worker*) manovale m; **at ~, to ~** a portata di mano; **on the one ~** da un lato; **on the other ~** d'altra parte; **out of ~** incontrollabile; (*summarily*) su due piedi; **give sb a ~** dare una mano a qcno ● vt porgere. **~ down** vt tramandare. **~ in** vt con-segnare. **~ out** vt distribuire. **~ over** vt passare; (*to police*) consegnare

hand: **~bag** n borsa f (*da signora*). **~brake** n freno m a mano. **~cuffs** npl manette fpl. **~ful** n manciata f; **be [quite] a ~ful** fig essere difficile da tenere a freno

handicap /'hændɪkæp/ n handicap m inv. **~ped** adj **mentally/physically ~ped** mentalmente/fisicamente handicappato

handi|craft /'hændɪkrɑ:ft/ n arti-gianato m. **~work** n opera f

handkerchief /'hæŋkətʃɪf/ n (pl **~s &** -**chieves**) fazzoletto m

handle /'hændl/ n manico m; (*of door*) maniglia f; **fly off the ~** 囗 perdere le staffe ● vt maneggiare; occuparsi di (problem, customer); prendere (difficult person); trattare (subject). **~bars** npl manubrio m

hand: **~out** n (*at lecture*) foglio m informativo; (囗: *money*) elemosina f. **~shake** n stretta f di mano

handsome /'hænsəm/ adj bello; (fig: *generous*) generoso

handwriting n calligrafia f

handy /'hændɪ/ adj (**-ier, -iest**) utile; (*person*) abile; **have/keep ~** avere/ tenere a portata di mano. **~man** n tuttofare m inv

hang /hæŋ/ vt (pt/pp hung) appendere (picture); (pt/pp hanged) impiccare (criminal). ~ **oneself** impiccarsi ● vi (pt/pp hung) pendere; (hair:) scendere ● n **get the ~ of it** (fam) afferrare. □ ~ **about** vi gironzolare. □ ~ **on** vi tenersi stretto; (fam: wait) aspettare; (Teleph) restare in linea. □ ~ **on to** vt tenersi stretto a; (keep) tenere. □ ~ **out** vi spuntare; **where does he usually ~ out?** (fam) dove bazzica di solito? ● vt stendere (washing). □ ~ **up** vt appendere; (Teleph) riattaccare ● vi essere appeso; (Teleph) riattaccare

hangar /'hæŋə(r)/ n (Aeron) hangar m inv

hanger /'hæŋə(r)/ n gruccia f. **~-on** n leccapiedi mf

hang: ~**-glider** n deltaplano m. **~over** n (fam) postumi mpl da sbornia. **~ up** n (fam) complesso m

hanky /'hæŋki/ n (fam) fazzoletto m

haphazard /hæp'hæzəd/ adj a casaccio

happen /'hæpn/ vi capitare, succedere; **as it ~s** per caso; **I ~ed to meet him** mi è capitato di incontrarlo; **what has ~ed to him?** cosa gli è capitato? (become of) che fine ha fatto? **~ing** n avvenimento m

happi|ly /'hæpɪli/ adv felicemente; (fortunately) fortunatamente. **~ness** n felicità f

happy /'hæpi/ adj (-ier, -iest) contento, felice. **~-go-'lucky** adj spensierato

harass /'hærəs/ vt perseguitare. **~ed** adj stressato. **~ment** n persecuzione f; **sexual ~ment** molestie fpl sessuali

harbour /'ha:bə(r)/ n porto m ● vt dare asilo a; nutrire (grudge)

hard /ha:d/ adj duro, (question, problem) difficile; ~ **of hearing** duro d'orecchi; **be ~ on sb** (person:) essere duro con qcno ● adv (work) duramente; (pull, hit, rain, snow) forte; ~ **hit by unemployment** duramente colpito dalla disoccupazione; **take sth ~** non accettare qcsa; **think ~!** pensaci bene!; **try ~** mettercela tutta; **try ~er** metterci più impegno; ~ **done by** (fam) trattato ingiustamente

hard: hard-boiled adj (egg) sodo. ~ **disk** n hard disk m inv, disco m rigido

harden /'ha:dn/ vi indurirsi

hard: ~**-headed** adj (businessman) dal sangue freddo. **~line** adj duro

hard|ly /'ha:dli/ adv appena; ~ **ever** quasi mai. **~ness** n durezza f. **~ship** n avversità f inv

hard: ~ **'shoulder** n (Auto) corsia f d'emergenza. **~ware** n ferramenta fpl; (Comput) hardware m inv. ~**'working** adj **be ~-working** essere un gran lavoratore

hardy /'ha:di/ adj (-ier, -iest) dal fisico resistente; (plant) che sopporta il gelo

hare /heə(r)/ n lepre f. **~-brained** adj (fam) (scheme) da scervellati

hark /ha:k/ vi ~ **back to** (fig) ritornare su

harm /ha:m/ n male m; (damage) danni mpl; **out of ~'s way** in un posto sicuro; **it won't do any ~** non farà certo male ● vt far male a; (damage) danneggiare. **~ful** adj dannoso. **~less** adj innocuo

harmonica /ha:'mɒnɪkə/ n armonica f [a bocca]

harmonious /ha:'məʊniəs/ adj armonioso. **~ly** adv in armonia

harness /'ha:nɪs/ n finimenti mpl; (of parachute) imbracatura f ● vt bardare (horse); sfruttare (resources)

harp /ha:p/ n arpa f ● **harp on** vi (fam) insistere (about su). **~ist** n arpista mf

harpoon /ha:'pu:n/ n arpione m

harpsichord /'ha:psikɔ:d/ n clavicembalo m

harrowing /'hærəʊɪŋ/ adj straziante

harsh /hɑːʃ/ adj duro; (light) abbagliante. **~ness** n durezza f

harvest /'hɑːvɪst/ n raccolta f; (of grapes) vendemmia f; (crop) raccolto m ● vt raccogliere

has /hæz/ ▷**HAVE**

hassle /'hæsl/ n rottura f ● vt rompere le scatole a

haste /heɪst/ n fretta f

hast|y /'heɪsti/ adj (-ier, -iest) frettoloso; (decision) affrettato. **~ily** adv frettolosamente

hat /hæt/ n cappello m

hatch[1] /hætʃ/ n (for food) sportello m passavivande; (Naut) boccaporto m

hatch[2] vi **~[out]** rompere il guscio; (egg:) schiudersi ● vt covare; tramare (plot)

'**hatchback** n tre/cinque porte m inv; (door) porta f del bagagliaio

hatchet /'hætʃɪt/ n ascia f

hate /heɪt/ n odio m ● vt odiare. **~ful** adj odioso

hatred /'heɪtrɪd/ n odio m

haught|y /'hɔːti/ adj (-ier, -iest) altezzoso. **~ily** adv altezzosamente

haul /hɔːl/ n (fish) pescata f; (loot) bottino m; (pull) tirata f ● vt tirare; trasportare (goods) ● vi **~ on** tirare. **~age** n trasporto m. **~ier** n autotrasportatore m

haunt /hɔːnt/ n ritrovo m ● vt frequentare; (linger in the mind) perseguitare: **this house is ~ed** questa casa è abitata da fantasmi

have /hæv/

● vt (3 sg pres tense **has**; pt/pp **had**) avere; fare (breakfast, bath, walk etc); **~ a drink** bere qualcosa; **~ lunch/dinner** pranzare/cenare; **~ a rest** riposarsi; **I had my hair cut** mi sono tagliata i capelli; **we had the**

house painted abbiamo fatto tinteggiare la casa; **I had it made** l'ho fatto fare; **~ to do sth** dover fare qcsa; **~ him telephone me tomorrow** digli di telefonarmi domani; **he has** or **he's got two houses** ha due case; **you've got the money, ~n't you?** hai i soldi, no?

● v aux avere; (with verbs of motion & some others) essere; **I ~ seen him** l'ho visto; **he has never been there** non ci è mai stato. □ **~ on** vt (be wearing) portare; (dupe) prendere in giro; **I've got something on tonight** ho un impegno stasera. □ **~ out** vt **~ it out with sb** chiarire le cose con qcno

● npl **the ~s and the ~-nots** i ricchi e i poveri

haven /'heɪvn/ n fig rifugio m

haversack /'hævə-/ n zaino m

havoc /'hævək/ n strage f; **play ~ with** fig scombussolare

hawk /hɔːk/ n falco m

hay /heɪ/ n fieno m. **~ fever** n raffreddore m da fieno. **~stack** n pagliaio m

'**haywire** adj **I** **go ~** dare i numeri; (plans:) andare all'aria

hazard /'hæzəd/ n (risk) rischio m ● vt rischiare; **~ a guess** azzardare un'ipotesi. **~ous** adj rischioso. **~ [warning] lights** npl (Auto) luci fpl d'emergenza

haze /heɪz/ n foschia f

hazel /'heɪz(ə)l/ n nocciolo m; (colour) [color m] nocciola m. **~-nut** n nocciola f

hazy /'heɪzi/ adj (-ier, -iest) nebbioso; (fig: person) confuso; (memories) vago

he /hiː/ pron lui; **he's tired** è stanco; **I'm going but he's not** io vengo, ma lui no

head /hed/ n testa f; (of firm) capo

m; (of primary school) direttore, -trice *mf*; (of secondary school) preside *mf*; (on beer) schiuma *f*; **be off one's** ~ essere fuori di testa; **have a good** ~ **for business** avere il senso degli affari; **have a good** ~ **for heights** non soffrire di vertigini; **10 pounds a** ~ 10 sterline a testa; **20** ~ **of cattle** 20 capi di bestiame; ~ **first** a capofitto; ~ **over heels in love** innamorato pazzo; ~**s or tails?** testa o croce? ● *vt* essere a capo di; essere in testa a (list); colpire di testa (ball) ● *vi* ~ **for** dirigersi verso.

head: ~**ache** *n* mal *m* di testa. ~**er** /'hedə(r)/ *n* rinvio *m* di testa; (dive) tuffo *m* di testa. ~**ing** *n* (in list etc) titolo *m*. ~**lamp** *n* (Auto) fanale *m*. ~**land** *n* promontorio *m*. ~**line** *n* titolo *m*. ~**long** *adj* & *adv* a capofitto. ~**'master** *n* (of primary school) direttore *m*; (of secondary school) preside *m*. ~**'mistress** *n* (of primary school) direttrice *f*; (of secondary school) preside *f*. ~**-on** *adj* (collision) frontale ● *adv* frontalmente. ~**phones** *npl* cuffie *fpl*. ~**quarters** *npl* sede *fsg*; (Mil) quartier *m* generale *msg*. ~**strong** *adj* testardo.

heady /'hedɪ/ *adj* che dà alla testa.

heal /hiːl/ *vt/i* guarire.

health /helθ/ *n* salute *f*.

health|y /'helθɪ/ *adj* (-ier, -iest) sano. ~**ily** *adv* in modo sano.

heap /hiːp/ *n* mucchio *m*; ~**s of** [T] un sacco di. ● *vt* ~ [**up**] ammucchiare; ~**ed teaspoon** un cucchiaino abbondante.

hear /hɪə(r)/ *vt/i* (*pt/pp* heard) sentire; ~, ~! bravo! ~ **from** *vi* aver notizie di. ~ **of** *vi* sentir parlare di; **he would not** ~ **of it** non ne ha voluto sentir parlare.

hearing /'hɪərɪŋ/ *n* udito *m*; (Jur) udienza *f*. ~**-aid** *n* apparecchio *m* acustico.

'hearsay *n* **from** ~ per sentito dire.

hearse /hɜːs/ *n* carro *m* funebre.

heart /hɑːt/ *n* cuore *m*; ~**s** *pl* (in cards) cuori *mpl*; **by** ~ a memoria.

heart: ~**ache** *n* pena *f*. ~ **attack** *n* infarto *m*. ~**-break** *n* afflizione *f*. ~**breaking** *adj* straziante. ~**burn** *n* mal *m* di stomaco. ~**felt** *adj* di cuore.

hearth /hɑːθ/ *n* focolare *m*.

heart|ily /'hɑːtɪlɪ/ *adv* di cuore; (eat) con appetito; **be** ~**ily sick of sth** non poterne più di qcsa. ~**less** *adj* spietato. ~**searching** *n* esame *m* di coscienza. ~**to-** ~ *n* conversazione *f* a cuore aperto ● *adj* a cuore aperto. ~**y** *adj* caloroso; (meal) copioso; (person) gioviale.

heat /hiːt/ *n* calore *m*; (Sport) prova *f* eliminatoria ● *vt* scaldare ● *vi* scaldarsi. ~**ed** *adj* (swimming pool) riscaldato; (discussion) animato. ~**er** *n* (for room) stufa *f*; (for water) boiler *m* inv; (Auto) riscaldamento *f*.

heath /hiːθ/ *n* brughiera *f*.

heathen /'hiːðn/ *adj* & *n* pagano, -a *mf*.

heather /'heðə(r)/ *n* erica *f*.

heating /'hiːtɪŋ/ *n* riscaldamento *m*.

heat: ~**-stroke** *n* colpo *m* di sole. ~ **wave** *n* ondata *f* di calore.

heave /hiːv/ *vt* tirare; (lift) tirare su; (F: throw) gettare; emettere (sigh) ● *vi* tirare.

heaven /'hevn/ *n* paradiso *m*; ~ **help you if...** Dio ti scampi se...; **H**~**s!** santo cielo!; ~**ly** *adj* celeste; (T) delizioso.

heav|y /'hevɪ/ *adj* (-ier, -iest) pesante; (traffic) intenso; (rain, cold) forte; **be a** ~**y smoker/drinker** essere un gran fumatore/bevitore. ~**ily** *adv* pesantemente (smoke, drink etc) molto. ~**yweight** *n* peso *m* massimo

Hebrew /'hiːbruː/ *adj* ebreo

heckle /'hekl/ *vt* interrompere di continuo. ~**r** *n* disturbatore, -trice *mf*

hectic /'hektɪk/ *adj* frenetico

hedge /hedʒ/ *n* siepe *f* ● *vi fig* essere

evasivo. **~hog** n riccio m

heed /hiːd/ n **pay ~ to** prestare ascolto a. ● vt prestare ascolto a. **~less** adj noncurante

heel[1] /hiːl/ n tallone m; (of shoe) tacco m; **take to one's ~s** 🔟 darsela a gambe

heel[2] vi **~ over** (Naut) inclinarsi

hefty /ˈheftɪ/ adj (**-ier, -iest**) massiccio

heifer /ˈhefə(r)/ n giovenca f

height /haɪt/ n altezza f; (of plane) altitudine f; (of season, fame) culmine m. **~en** vt fig accrescere

heir /eə(r)/ n erede mf. **~ess** n ereditiera f. **~loom** n cimelio m di famiglia

held /held/ ▷**HOLD**[2]

helicopter /ˈhelɪkɒptə(r)/ n elicottero m

hell /hel/ n inferno m; **go to ~!** 🗵 va' al diavolo! ● int porca miseria!

hello /həˈləʊ/ int & n = **hallo**

helm /helm/ n timone m; **at the ~** fig al timone

helmet /ˈhelmɪt/ n casco m

help /help/ n aiuto m; (employee) aiuto m domestico; **that's no ~** non è d'aiuto ● vt aiutare; **~ oneself to sth** servirsi di qcsa; **~ yourself** (at table) serviti pure; **I could not ~ laughing** non ho potuto trattenermi dal ridere; **it cannot be ~ed** non c'è niente da fare; **I can't ~ it** non ci posso far niente ● vi aiutare

help|er /ˈhelpə(r)/ n aiutante mf. **~ful** adj (person) di aiuto; (advice) utile. **~ing** n porzione f. **~less** adj (unable to manage) incapace; (powerless) impotente

hem /hem/ n orlo m ● vt (pt/pp **hemmed**) orlare. □ **~ in** vt intrappolare

hemisphere /ˈhemɪ-/ n emisfero m

hen /hen/ n gallina f; (any female bird) femmina f

hence /hens/ adv (for this reason) quindi. **~ˈforth** adv d'ora innanzi

henpecked adj tiranneggiato dalla moglie

her /hɜː(r)/ poss adj il suo m, la sua f, i suoi mpl, le sue fpl; **~ mother/father** sua madre/suo padre ● pers pron (direct object) la; (indirect object) le; (after prep) lei; **I know ~** la conosco; **give ~ the money** dalle i soldi; **give it to ~** dagliele; **I came with ~** sono venuto con lei; **it's ~** è lei; **I've seen ~** l'ho vista; **I've seen ~, but not him** ho visto lei, ma non lui

herb /hɜːb/ n erba f

herbal /ˈhɜːb(ə)l/ adj alle erbe; **~ tea** tisana f

herd /hɜːd/ n gregge m ● vt (tend) sorvegliare; (drive) far muovere; fig ammassare

here /hɪə(r)/ adv qui, qua; **in ~** qui dentro; **come/bring ~** vieni/porta qui; **~ is... , ~ are...** ecco...; **~ you are!** ecco qua!. **~ˈafter** adv in futuro. **~ˈby** adv con la presente

heredit|ary /həˈredɪtərɪ/ adj ereditario. **~y** n eredità f

here|sy /ˈherəsɪ/ n eresia f. **~tic** n eretico, -a m f

here·with adv (Comm) con la presente

heritage /ˈherɪtɪdʒ/ n eredità f. **~ tourism** n turismo m culturale

hernia /ˈhɜːnɪə/ n ernia f

hero /ˈhɪərəʊ/ n (pl **-es**) eroe m

heroic /hɪˈrəʊɪk/ adj eroico

heroin /ˈherəʊɪn/ n eroina f (droga)

hero|ine /ˈherəʊɪn/ n eroina f. **~ism** n eroismo m

heron /ˈherən/ n airone m

herring /ˈherɪŋ/ n aringa f

hers /hɜːz/ poss pron il suo m, la sua f, i suoi mpl, le sue fpl; **a friend of ~** un suo amico; **friends of ~** suoi amici; **that is ~** quello è suo; (as opposed to mine) quello è il suo

her'self *pers pron (riflessivo)* si; *(om phatic)* lei stessa; *(after prep)* sé, se stessa; **she poured a ~ drink** si è versata da bere; **she told me so ~** me lo ha detto lei stessa; **she's proud of ~** è fiera di sé; **by ~** da sola

hesitant /ˈhezɪtənt/ *adj* esitante. **~ly** *adv* con esitazione

hesitat|e /ˈhezɪteɪt/ *vi* esitare. **~ion** *n* esitazione *f*

hetero'sexual /hetərəʊ-/ *adj* eterosessuale

hexagon /ˈheksəgən/ *n* esagono *m*. **~al** *adj* esagonale

hey /heɪ/ *int* ehi

heyday /ˈheɪ/ *n* tempi *mpl* d'oro

hi /haɪ/ *int* ciao!

hibernat|e /ˈhaɪbəneɪt/ *vi* andare in letargo. **~ion** *n* letargo *m*

hiccup /ˈhɪkʌp/ *n* singhiozzo *m*; (![hitch]) intoppo *m* ● *vi* fare un singhiozzo

hide[1] /haɪd/ *n (leather)* pelle *f (di animale)*

hide[2] *vt (pt hid, pp hidden)* nascondere ● *vi* nascondersi. **~-and-'seek** *n* play **~-and-seek** giocare a nascondino

hideous /ˈhɪdɪəs/ *adj* orribile

'hide-out *n* nascondiglio *m*

hiding[1] /ˈhaɪdɪŋ/ *n* (![beating]) bastonata *f*; *(defeat)* batosta *f*

hiding[2] *n* go into **~** sparire dalla circolazione

hierarchy /ˈhaɪərɑːkɪ/ *n* gerarchia *f*

hieroglyphics /haɪərəˈglɪfɪks/ *npl* geroglifici *mpl*

hi-fi /ˈhaɪfaɪ/ *n* ![] stereo *m*, hi-fi *m inv* ● *adj* ![] ad alta fedeltà

high /haɪ/ *adj* alto; *(meat)* che comincia ad andare a male; *(wind)* forte; *(on drugs)* fatto; **it's ~ time we did something about it** è ora che facciamo qualcosa in proposito ● *adv* in alto; **~ and low** in lungo e in largo

● *n* massimo *m*; *(temperature)* massima *f*; **be on a ~** ![] essere fatto

high: **~er education** *n* formazione *f* universitaria. **~-handed** *adj* dispotico. **~ heels** *npl* tacchi *mpl* alti

highlight /ˈhaɪlaɪt/ *n* fig momento *m* clou; **~s** *pl (in hair)* mèche *fpl* ● *vt (emphasize)* evidenziare. **~er** *n (marker)* evidenziatore *m*

highly /ˈhaɪlɪ/ *adv* molto; **speak ~ of** lodare; **think ~ of** avere un'alta opinione di. **~-strung** *adj* nervoso

high: **~ rise** *adj (building)* molto alto ● *n* edificio *m* molto alto. **~ school** *n* ≈ scuola *f* superiore. **~ street** *n* strada *f* principale. **~way code** *n* codice *m* stradale

High School Negli Stati Uniti indica la scuola superiore, generalmente per studenti di età compresa tra i 14 e i 18 anni. In Gran Bretagna il termine è usato solo nella denominazione di alcune scuole.

hijack /ˈhaɪdʒæk/ *vt* dirottare ● *n* dirottamento *m*. **~er** *n* dirottatore, trice *mf*

hike /haɪk/ *n* escursione *f* a piedi ● *vi* fare un'escursione a piedi. **~r** *n* escursionista *mf*

hilarious /hɪˈleərɪəs/ *adj* esilarante

hill /hɪl/ *n* collina *f*; *(mound)* collinetta *f*; *(slope)* altura *f*

hill: **~side** *n* pendio *m*. **~y** *adj* collinoso

hilt /hɪlt/ *n* impugnatura *f*; **to the ~** *(support)* fino in fondo; *(mortgaged)* fino al collo

him /hɪm/ *pers pron (direct object)* lo; *(indirect object)* gli; *(with prep)* lui; **I know ~** lo conosco; **give ~ the money** dagli i soldi; **give it to ~** daglielo; **I spoke to ~** gli ho parlato; **it's ~** è lui; **she loves ~** lo ama; **she loves ~, not you** ama lui, non te. **~'self** *pers pron (reflexive)* si;

(emphatic) lui stesso; (after prep) sé, se stesso; **he poured ~ a drink** si è versato da bere; **he told me so ~self** me lo ha detto lui stesso; **he's proud of ~self** è fiero di sé; **by ~self** da solo

hind|er /'hɪndə(r)/ vt intralciare. **~rance** n intralcio m

hindsight /'haɪnd-/ n with ~ con il senno del poi

Hindu /'hɪnduː/ n indù mf inv ● adj indù. **~ism** n induismo m

hinge /hɪndʒ/ n cardine m ● vi ~ **on** fig dipendere da

hint /hɪnt/ n (clue) accenno m; (advice) suggerimento m; (indirect suggestion) allusione f; (trace) tocco m ● vt ~ **that...** far capire che... ● vi ~ **at** alludere a

hip /hɪp/ n fianco m

hippie /'hɪpɪ/ n hippy mf inv

hippopotamus /hɪpə'pɒtəməs/ n (pl **-muses** or **-mi** /-maɪ/) ippopotamo m

hire /'haɪə(r)/ vt affittare; assumere (person); ~ **[out]** affittare ● n noleggio m; **'for ~'** 'affittasi'. ~ **car** n macchina f a noleggio. ~ **purchase** n acquisto m a rateale

his /hɪz/ poss adj il suo, la sua f, i suoi mpl, le sue fpl; ~ **mother/father** sua madre/suo padre ● poss pron il suo m, la sua f, i suoi mpl, le sue fpl; **a friend of** ~ un suo amico; **friends of** ~ dei suoi amici; **that is** ~ questo è suo; (as opposed to mine) questo è il suo

hiss /hɪs/ n sibilo m; (of disapproval) fischio m ● vt fischiare ● vi sibilare; (in disapproval) fischiare

historian /hɪ'stɔːrɪən/ n storico, -a mf

history /'hɪstərɪ/ n storia f; **make** ~ passare alla storia

hit /hɪt/ n (blow) colpo m; (🔊: success) successo m; **score a direct** ~ (missile) colpire in pieno ● vt/i (pt/pp **hit**,

pres p **hitting**) colpire; ~ **one's head on the table** battere la testa contro il tavolo; **the car** ~ **the wall** la macchina ha sbattuto contro il muro; ~ **the roof** 🔊 perdere le staffe. ~ **off** vt ~ **it off** andare d'accordo. □ ~ **on** vt fig trovare

hitch /hɪtʃ/ n intoppo m; **technical** ~ problema m tecnico ● vt attaccare; ~ **a lift** chiedere un passaggio. □ ~ **up** vt tirarsi su (trousers). ~ **hike** vi fare l'autostop. ~ **-hiker** n autostoppista mf

hither /'hɪðə(r)/ adv ~ **and thither** di qua e di là. ~ **'to** adv finora

hit-or-'miss adj on a very ~ **basis** all'improvvista

hive /haɪv/ n alveare m; ~ **of industry** fucina f di lavoro ● **hive off** vt (Comm) separare

hoard /hɔːd/ n provvista f; (of money) gruzzolo m ● vt accumulare

hoarding /'hɔːdɪŋ/ n palizzata f; (with advertisements) tabellone m per manifesti pubblicitari

hoarse /hɔːs/ adj rauco. ~ **ly** adv con voce rauca. ~ **ness** n raucedine f

hoax /həʊks/ n scherzo m; (false alarm) falso allarme m. ~ **er** n burlone, -a mf

hob /hɒb/ n piano m di cottura

hobble /'hɒbl/ vi zoppicare

hobby /'hɒbɪ/ n hobby m inv. ~ **horse** n fig fissazione f

hockey /'hɒkɪ/ n hockey m

hoe /həʊ/ n zappa f

hog /hɒg/ n maiale m ● vt (pt/pp **hogged**) 🔊 monopolizzare

hoist /hɔɪst/ n montacarichi m inv; (🔊: push) spinta f in su ● vt sollevare; innalzare (flag); levare (anchor)

hold¹ /həʊld/ n (Aeron, Naut) stiva f

hold² n presa f; (fig: influence) ascendente m; **get** ~ **of** trovare; procurarsi (information) ● v (pt/pp **held**) ● vt tenere; (container) contenere; essere titolare di (licence, passport);

trattenere (breath, suspect); mantenere vivo (interest); (civil servant etc): occupare (position); (retain) mantenere; **~ sb's hand** tenere qcno per mano; **~ one's tongue** tenere la bocca chiusa; **~ sb responsible** considerare qcno responsabile; **~ that** (believe) ritenere che ●vi tenere; (weather, luck): durare; (offer): essere valido; (Teleph) restare in linea; **I don't ~ with the idea that...** 🔲 non sono d'accordo sul fatto che... □~ **back** vt rallentare ●vi esitare. □~ **down** vt tenere a bada (sb). □~ **on** vi (wait) attendere; (Teleph) restare in linea. □~ **on to** vt aggrapparsi a; (keep) tenersi. □~ **out** vt porgere (hand); fig offrire (possibility) ●vi (resist) resistere. □~ **up** vt tenere su; (delay) rallentare; (rob) assalire; **~ one's head up** fig tenere la testa alta

'hold: **~all** n borsone m. **~er** n titolare mf; (of record) detentore, -trice mf; (container) astuccio m. **~-up** n ritardo m (attack) rapina f a mano armata

hole /həʊl/ n buco m

holiday /'hɒlɪdeɪ/ n vacanza f; (public) giorno m festivo; (day off) giorno m di ferie; **go on ~** andare in vacanza. **~-maker** n vacanziere mf

holiness /'həʊlɪnɪs/ n santità f; **Your H~** Sua Santità

Holland /'hɒlənd/ n Olanda f

hollow /'hɒləʊ/ adj cavo; (promise) a vuoto; (voice) assente; (cheeks) infossato ●n cavità f inv; (in ground) affossamento m

holly /'hɒlɪ/ n agrifoglio m

holocaust /'hɒləkɔːst/ n olocausto m

holster /'həʊlstə(r)/ n fondina f

holy /'həʊlɪ/ adj (-ier, -est) santo; (water) benedetto. **H~ Ghost** or **Spirit** n Spirito m Santo. **H~ Scriptures** npl sacre scritture fpl. **H~ Week** n settimana f santa

homage /'hɒmɪdʒ/ n omaggio m; **pay ~ to** rendere omaggio a

home /həʊm/ n casa f; (for children) istituto m; (for old people) casa f di riposo; (native land) patria f ●adv at ~ a casa; (football) in casa; **feel at ~** sentirsi a casa propria; **come/go ~** venire/andare a casa; **drive a nail ~** piantare un chiodo a fondo ●adj domestico; (movie, video) casalingo; (team) ospitante; (Pol) nazionale

home: **~ ad'dress** n indirizzo m di casa. **~land** n patria f; **~land security** n sicurezza f delle frontiere. **~less** adj senza tetto

homely /'həʊmlɪ/ adj (-ier, -iest) semplice; (atmosphere) familiare; (Am: ugly) bruttino

home: **~made** adj fatto in casa. **H~ Office** n Br ministero m degli interni. **~sick** adj be **~sick** avere nostalgia (for di). **~ town** n città f inv natia. **~work** n (Sch) compiti mpl

homicide /'hɒmɪsaɪd/ n (crime) omicidio m

homoeopath|ic /həʊmɪə'pæθɪk/ adj omeopatico. **~y** n omeopatia f

homogeneous /hɒmə'dʒiːnɪəs/ adj omogeneo

homo'sexual adj & n omosessuale f

honest /'ɒnɪst/ adj onesto; (frank) sincero. **~ly** adv onestamente; (frankly) sinceramente; **~ly!** ma insommal. **~y** n onestà f; (frankness) sincerità f

honey /'hʌnɪ/ n miele m; (🔲: darling) tesoro m

honey: **~comb** n favo m. **~moon** n luna f di miele. **~suckle** n caprifoglio m

honorary /'ɒnərərɪ/ adj onorario

honour /'ɒnə(r)/ n onore m ●vt onorare. **~able** adj onorevole. **~ably** adv con onore. **~s degree** n ≈ diploma m di laurea

hood /hʊd/ n cappuccio m; (of pram)

tettuccio *m*; (*over cooker*) cappa *f*; Am (*Auto*) cofano *m*

hoodlum /'huːdləm/ *n* teppista *m*

'hoodwink *vt* 🔲 infinocchiare

hoof /huːf/ *n* (*pl* ~s *or* **hooves**) zoccolo *m*

hook /huk/ *n* gancio *m*; (*for fishing*) amo *m*; **off the** ~ (*Teleph*) staccato; *fig* fuori pericolo ● *vt* agganciare ● *vi* agganciarsi

hook|ed /hukt/ *adj* (*nose*) adunco ~**ed on** (🔲: *drugs*) dedito a; **be** ~**ed on skiing** essere un fanatico dello sci. ~**er** *n* Am 🔲 battona *f*

hookey /'huki/ *n* **play** ~ Am 🔲 marinare la scuola

hooligan /'huːlɪgən/ *n* teppista *mf*. ~**ism** *n* teppismo *m*

hoop /huːp/ *n* cerchio *m*

hooray /hu'reɪ/ *int* & *n* = **hurrah**

hoot /huːt/ *n* colpo *m* di clacson; (*of siren*) ululato *m*; (*of owl*) grido *m* ● *vi* (*owl*) gridare; (*car*:) clacsonare; (*siren*:) ululare; (*jeer*) fischiare. ~**er** *n* (*of factory*) sirena *f*; (*Auto*) clacson *m inv*

hoover® /'huːvə(r)/ *n* aspirapolvere *m inv* ● *vt* passare l'aspirapolvere su (*carpet*); passare l'aspirapolvere in (*room*)

hop /hɒp/ *n* saltello *m* ● *vi* (*pt/pp* **hopped**) saltellare; ~ **it!** 🔲 tela!, □~ **in** *vi* 🔲 saltar su

hope /həʊp/ *n* speranza *f* ● *vi* sperare (**for** in); **I** ~ **so/not** spero di sì/ no ● *vt* ~ **that** sperare che

hope|ful /'həʊpfl/ *adj* pieno di speranza; (*promising*) promettente; **be** ~**ful that** avere buone speranze che. ~**fully** *adv* con speranza; (*it is hoped*) se tutto va bene. ~**less** *adj* senza speranze; (*useless*) impossibile; (*incompetent*) incapace. ~**lessly** *adv* disperatamente; (*inefficient, lost*) completamente. ~**lessness** *n* disperazione *f*

horde /hɔːd/ *n* orda *f*

horizon /hə'raɪzn/ *n* orizzonte *m*

horizontal /hɒrɪ'zɒntl/ *adj* orizzontale

hormone /'hɔːməʊn/ *n* ormone *m*

horn /hɔːn/ *n* corno *m*; (*Auto*) clacson *m inv*

horoscope /'hɒrəskəʊp/ *n* oroscopo *m*

horribl|e /'hɒrɪbl/ *adj* orribile. ~**y** *adv* spaventosamente

horrid /'hɒrɪd/ *adj* orrendo

horrific /hə'rɪfɪk/ *adj* raccapricciante; (*accident, prices, story*) terrificante

horrify /'hɒrɪfaɪ/ *vt* (*pt/pp* **-ied**) far inorridire; **I was horrified** ero sconvolto. ~**ing** *adj* terrificante

horror /'hɒrə(r)/ *n* orrore *m*. ~ **film** *n* film *m* dell'orrore

horse /hɔːs/ *n* cavallo *m*.

horse: ~**back** *n* **on** ~**back** a cavallo. ~**power** *n* cavallo *m* [vapore]. ~**-racing** *n* corse *fpl* di cavalli. ~**shoe** *n* ferro *m* di cavallo

horti'cultural /hɔːtɪ-/ *adj* di orticoltura

'horticulture *n* orticoltura *f*

hose /həʊz/ *n* (*pipe*) manichetta *f* ● **hose down** *vt* lavare con la manichetta

hospice /'hɒspɪs/ *n* (*for the terminally ill*) ospedale *m* per i malati in fase terminale

hospitabl|e /hɒ'spɪtəbl/ *adj* ospitale. ~**y** *adv* con ospitalità

hospital /'hɒspɪtl/ *n* ospedale *m*

hospitality /hɒspɪ'tælətɪ/ *n* ospitalità *f*

host[1] /həʊst/ *n* **a** ~ **of** una moltitudine di

host[2] *n* ospite *m*

host[3] *n* (*Relig*) ostia *f*

hostage /'hɒstɪdʒ/ *n* ostaggio *m*; **hold sb** ~ tenere qcno in ostaggio

hostel /'hɒstl/ *n* ostello *m*

hostess /'həʊstɪs/ *n* padrona *f* di

casa; *(Aeron)* hostess *f inv*

hostile /'hɒstaɪl/ *adj* ostile

hostility /hɒ'stɪlətɪ/ *n* ostilità *f*; **~ies** *pl* ostilità *fpl*

hot /hɒt/ *adj* **(hotter, hottest)** caldo; *(spicy)* piccante; **I am** or **feel ~** ho caldo; **it is ~** fa caldo

'hotbed *n fig* focolaio *m*

hotchpotch /'hɒtʃpɒtʃ/ *n* miscuglio *m*

'hot-dog *n* hot dog *m inv*

hotel /həʊ'tel/ *n* albergo *m*. **~ier** *n* albergatore, -trice *m*

hot: ~house *n* serra *f*. **~plate** *n* piastra *f* riscaldante **~-'water bottle** *n* borsa *f* dell'acqua calda

hound /haʊnd/ *n* cane *m* da caccia
● *vt fig* perseguire

hour /'aʊə(r)/ *n* ora *f*. **~ly** *adj* ad ogni ora; *(pay, rate)* a ora ● *adv* ogni ora

house¹ /haʊs/ *n*: **~boat** *n* casa *f* galleggiante. **~breaking** *n* furto *m* con scasso. **~hold** *n* casa *f*, famiglia *f*. **~holder** *n* capo *m* di famiglia. **~keeper** *n* governante *f* di casa. **~keeping** *n* governo *m* della casa; *(money)* soldi *mpl* per le spese di casa. **~plant** *n* pianta *f* da appartamento. **~trained** *adj* che non sporca in casa. **~warming party** *n* festa *f* di inaugurazione della nuova casa. **~wife** *n* casalinga *f*. **~work** *n* lavoro *m* domestico

house¹ /haʊs/ *n* casa *f*; *(Pol)* camera *f*; *(Theat)* sala *f*; **at my ~** a casa mia, da me

house² /haʊz/ *vt* alloggiare *(person)*

housing /'haʊzɪŋ/ *n* alloggio *m*. **~ estate** *n* zona *f* residenziale

hovel /'hɒvl/ *n* tugurio *m*

hover /'hɒvə(r)/ *vi* librarsi; *(linger)* indugiare. **~craft** *n* hovercraft *m inv*

how /haʊ/ *adv* come; **~ are you?** come stai?; **~ about a coffee/going on holiday?** che ne diresti di un caffè/di andare in vacanza?; **~**

do you do? molto lieto!; **~ old are you?** quanti anni hai?; **~ long** quanto tempo; **~ many** quanti; **~ much** quanto, **~ often** ogni quanto; **and ~!** eccome!; **~ odd!** che strano!

how'ever *adv (nevertheless)* comunque; **~ small** per quanto piccolo

howl /haʊl/ *n* ululato *m* ● *vi* ululare; *(cry, with laughter)* singhiozzare. **~er** *n* 🇮🇹 strafalcione *m*

HP *n abbr* hire purchase; *n abbr* (horse power) C.V.

hub /hʌb/ *n* mozzo *m; fig* centro *m*

'hub-cap *n* coprimozzo *m*

huddle /'hʌdl/ *vi* **~ together** rannicchiarsi

hue¹ /hjuː/ *n* colore *m*

hue² *n* **~ and cry** clamore *m*

huff /hʌf/ *n* be in/go into a **~** fare il broncio

hug /hʌg/ *n* abbraccio *m* ● *vt (pt/pp hugged)* abbracciare; *(keep close to)* tenersi vicino a

huge /hjuːdʒ/ *adj* enorme

hull /hʌl/ *n* (Naut) scafo *m*

hullo /hə'ləʊ/ *int* = **hello**

hum /hʌm/ *n* ronzio *m* ● *v (pt/pp hummed)* *vt* canticchiare ● *vi* (motor:) ronzare; *fig* fervere *(di attività)*. **~** and **haw** esitare

human /'hjuːmən/ *adj* umano ● *n* essere *m* umano. **~ 'being** *n* essere *m* umano

humane /hjuː'meɪn/ *adj* umano

humanitarian /hjuːmænɪ'teəriən/ *adj* & *n* umanitario, -a *mf*

humanit|y /hjuː'mænətɪ/ *n* umanità *f*; **~ies** *pl* (Univ) dottrine *fpl* umanistiche

humble /'hʌmbl/ *adj* umile ● *vt* umiliare

'humdrum *adj* noioso

humid /'hjuːmɪd/ *adj* umido. **~ifier** *n* umidificatore *m*. **~ity** /-'mɪdətɪ/ *n* umidità *f*

humiliat|e /hjuːˈmɪlɪeɪt/ *vt* umiliare. **∼ion** *n* umiliazione *f*

humility /hjuːˈmɪlɪtɪ/ *n* umiltà *f*

humorous /ˈhjuːmərəs/ *adj* umoristico. **∼ly** *adv* con spirito

humour /ˈhjuːmə(r)/ *n* umorismo *m*; (*mood*) umore *m*; **have a sense of ∼** avere il senso dell'umorismo. ● *vt* compiacere

hump /hʌmp/ *n* protuberanza *f*; (*of camel, hunchback*) gobba *f*

hunch /hʌntʃ/ *n* (*idea*) intuizione *f*

'hunch|back *n* gobbo, -a *mf*. **∼ed** *adj* **∼ed up** incurvato

hundred /ˈhʌndrəd/ *adj* **one/a ∼** cento ● *n* cento *m*; **∼s of** centinaia di. **∼th** *adj* centesimo ● *n* centesimo *m*. **∼weight** *n* cinquanta chili *m*

hung /hʌŋ/ ▷HANG

Hungarian /hʌŋˈgeərɪən/ *n & adj* ungherese *mf*; (*language*) ungherese *m*

Hungary /ˈhʌŋgərɪ/ *n* Ungheria *f*

hunger /ˈhʌŋgə(r)/ *n* fame *f*. **∼-strike** *n* sciopero *m* della fame *m*

hungr|y /ˈhʌŋgrɪ/ *adj* (-ier, -iest) affamato; **be ∼y** aver fame. **∼ily** *adv* con appetito

hunk /hʌŋk/ *n* (grosso) pezzo *m*

hunt /hʌnt/ *n* caccia *f* ● *vt* andare a caccia di (*animal*); dare la caccia a (*criminal*) ● *vi* andare a caccia; **∼ for** cercare. **∼er** *n* cacciatore *m*. **∼ing** *n* caccia *f*

hurl /hɜːl/ *vt* scagliare

hurrah /hʊˈrɑː/, **hurray** /hʊˈreɪ/ *int* urrà! ● *n* urrà *m*

hurricane /ˈhʌrɪkən/ *n* uragano *m*

hurried /ˈhʌrɪd/ *adj* affrettato; (*job*) fatto in fretta. **∼ly** *adv* in fretta

hurry /ˈhʌrɪ/ *n* fretta *f*; **be in a ∼** aver fretta ● *vi* (*pt/pp* -ied) affrettarsi. □ **∼ up** *vi* sbrigarsi ● *vt* fare sbrigare (*person*); accelerare (*things*)

hurt /hɜːt/ *v* (*pt/pp* hurt) ● *vt* far male a; (*offend*) ferire ● *vi* far male; **my leg ∼s** mi fa male la gamba.

∼ful *adj fig* offensivo

hurtle /ˈhɜːtl/ *vi* **∼ along** andare a tutta velocità

husband /ˈhʌzbənd/ *n* marito *m*

hush /hʌʃ/ *n* silenzio *m*. ● **hush up** *vt* mettere a tacere. **∼ed** *adj* (*voice*) sommesso. **∼-'hush** *adj* 🔲 segretissimo

husky /ˈhʌskɪ/ *adj* (-ier, -iest) (*voice*) rauco

hustle /ˈhʌsl/ *vt* affrettare ● *n* attività *f* incessante; **∼ and bustle** trambusto *m*

hut /hʌt/ *n* capanna *f*

hybrid /ˈhaɪbrɪd/ *adj* ibrido ● *n* ibrido *m*

hydrant /ˈhaɪdrənt/ *n* [**fire**] **∼** idrante *m*

hydraulic /haɪˈdrɔːlɪk/ *adj* idraulico

hydroe'lectric /haɪdrəʊ-/ *adj* idroelettrico

hydrofoil /ˈhaɪdrə-/ *n* aliscafo *m*

hydrogen /ˈhaɪdrədʒən/ *n* idrogeno *m*

hyena /haɪˈiːnə/ *n* iena *f*

hygien|e /ˈhaɪdʒiːn/ *n* igiene *f*. **∼ic** *adj* igienico

hymn /hɪm/ *n* inno *m*. **∼-book** *n* libro *m* dei canti

hypermarket /ˈhaɪpəmɑːkɪt/ *n* ipermercato *m*

hyphen /ˈhaɪfn/ *n* lineetta *f*. **∼ate** *vt* unire con lineetta

hypno|sis /hɪpˈnəʊsɪs/ *n* ipnosi *f*. **∼tic** *adj* ipnotico

hypno|tism /ˈhɪpnətɪzm/ *n* ipnotismo *m*. **∼tist** *n* ipnotizzatore, -trice *mf*. **∼tize** *vt* ipnotizzare

hypochondriac /haɪpə-kɒndrɪæk/ *adj* ipocondriaco ● *n* ipocondriaco, -a *mf*

hypocrisy /hɪˈpɒkrəsɪ/ *n* ipocrisia *f*

hypocrit|e /ˈhɪpəkrɪt/ *n* ipocrita *mf*. **∼ical** *adj* ipocrita

hypodermic /haɪpəˈdɜːmɪk/ *adj & n* **∼** [**syringe**] siringa *f* ipodermica

hypothe|sis /har'pɒθəsɪs/ n ipotesi f inv. ~**tical** /-'θetɪkl/ adj ipotetico. ~**tically** adv in teoria; (speak) per ipotesi

hyster|ia /hɪ'stɪərɪə/ n isterismo m. ~**ical** adj isterico. ~**ically** adv istericamente; ~**ically funny** da morir dal ridere. ~**ics** npl attacco m isterico

• • • • • • • • • • • • • • • • • • • •

Ii

• • • • • • • • • • • • • • • • • • • •

I /aɪ/ pron io; **I'm tired** sono stanco; **he's going, but I'm not** lui va, ma io no

ice /aɪs/ n ghiaccio m • vt glassare (cake). □ ~ **over/up** vi ghiacciarsi

ice: ~**-axe** n piccozza f per il ghiaccio. ~**berg** /-bɜːg/ n iceberg m inv. ~**box** n Am frigorifero m. ~**-cream** n gelato m. ~**cube** n cubetto m di ghiaccio

Iceland /'aɪslənd/ n Islanda f. ~**er** n islandese mf. ~**ic** /-'lændɪk/ adj & n islandese m

ice: ~**-lolly** n ghiacciolo m. ~**-rink** n pista f di pattinaggio. ~ **skater** pattinatore, trice mf sul ghiaccio. ~ **skating** pattinaggio m su ghiaccio

icicle /'aɪsɪkl/ n ghiacciolo m

icing /'aɪsɪŋ/ n glassa f. ~ **sugar** n zucchero m a velo

icon /'aɪkɒn/ n icona f

ic|y /'aɪsɪ/ adj (-ier, -iest) ghiacciato; fig gelido. ~**ily** adv gelidamente

idea /aɪ'dɪə/ n idea f; **I've no** ~! non ne ho idea!

ideal /aɪ'dɪəl/ adj ideale • n ideale m. ~**ism** n idealismo m. ~**ist** n idealista mf. ~**istic** adj idealistico. ~**ize** vt idealizzare. ~**ly** adv idealmente

identical /aɪ'dentɪkl/ adj identico

identi|fication /aɪdentɪfɪ'keɪʃn/ n

identificazione f; (proof of identity) documento m di riconoscimento. ~**fy** vt (pt/pp -ied) identificare

identity /aɪ'dentətɪ/ n identità f inv. ~ **card** n carta f d'identità. ~ **theft** n furto m d'identità

ideological /aɪdɪə'lɒdʒɪkl/ adj ideologico. ~**y** n ideologia f

idiom /'ɪdɪəm/ n idioma f. ~**atic** adj idiomatico

idiot /'ɪdɪət/ n idiota mf. ~**ic** adj idiota

idl|e /'aɪd(ə)l/ adj (lazy) pigro, ozioso; (empty) vano; (machine) fermo • vi oziare; (engine:) girare a vuoto. ~**eness** n ozio m. ~**y** adv oziosamente

idol /'aɪdl/ n idolo m. ~**ize** vt idolatrare

idyllic /ɪ'dɪlɪk/ adj idillico

i.e. abbr (id est) cioè

if /ɪf/ conj così **as if** come se

ignite /ɪg'naɪt/ vt dar fuoco a • vi prender fuoco

ignition /ɪg'nɪʃn/ n (Auto) accensione f. ~ **key** n chiave f d'accensione

ignoramus /ɪgnə'reɪməs/ n ignorante mf

ignoran|ce /'ɪgnərəns/ n ignoranza f. ~**t** adj (lacking knowledge) ignaro; (rude) ignorante

ignore /ɪg'nɔː(r)/ vt ignorare

ill /ɪl/ adj ammalato; **feel** ~ **at ease** sentirsi a disagio • adv male • n male m. ~**-advised** adj avventato. ~ **bred** adj maleducato

illegal /ɪ'liːgl/ adj illegale

illegibl|e /ɪ'ledʒɪbl/ adj illeggibile

illegitima|cy /ɪlɪ'dʒɪtɪməsɪ/ n illegittimità f. ~**te** adj illegittimo

illitera|cy /ɪ'lɪtərəsɪ/ n analfabetismo m. ~**te** adj & n analfabeta mf

illness /'ɪlnɪs/ n malattia f

illogical /ɪ'lɒdʒɪkl/ adj illogico

illuminat|e /ɪˈluːmɪneɪt/ vt illuminare. **∼ing** adj chiarificatore. **∼ion** n illuminazione f

illusion /ɪˈluːʒn/ n illusione f; **be under the ∼ that** avere l'illusione che

illustrat|e /ˈɪləstreɪt/ vt illustrare. **∼ion** n illustrazione f. **∼or** n illustratore, -trice mf

illustrious /ɪˈlʌstrɪəs/ adj illustre

ill 'will n malanimo m

image /ˈɪmɪdʒ/ n immagine f; (exact likeness) ritratto m

imagin|able /ɪˈmædʒɪnəbl/ adj immaginabile. **∼ary** adj immaginario

imaginat|ion /ɪmædʒɪˈneɪʃn/ n immaginazione f, fantasia f; **it's your ∼ion** è solo una tua idea. **∼ive** adj fantasioso. **∼ively** adv con fantasia or immaginazione

imagine /ɪˈmædʒɪn/ vt immaginare; (wrongly) inventare

im'balance n squilibrio m

imbecile /ˈɪmbəsiːl/ n imbecille mf

imitat|e /ˈɪmɪteɪt/ vt imitare. **∼ion** n imitazione f. **∼or** n imitatore, -trice mf

immaculate /ɪˈmækjʊlət/ adj immacolato. **∼ly** adv immacolatamente

imma'ture adj immaturo

immediate /ɪˈmiːdɪət/ adj immediato; (relative) stretto; **in the ∼ vicinity** nelle immediate vicinanze. **∼ly** adv immediatamente; **∼ly next to** subito accanto a ● conj [non] appena

immense /ɪˈmens/ adj immenso

immers|e /ɪˈmɜːs/ vt immergere; **be ∼ed in** fig essere immerso in. **∼ion** n immersione f. **∼ion heater** n scaldabagno m elettrico

immigrant /ˈɪmɪɡrənt/ n immigrante mf

imminent /ˈɪmɪnənt/ adj imminente

immobil|e /ɪˈməʊbaɪl/ adj immo-

bile. **∼ize** vt immobilizzare

immoderate /ɪˈmɒdərət/ adj smodato

immoral /ɪˈmɒrəl/ adj immorale. **∼ity** n immoralità f

immortal /ɪˈmɔːtl/ adj immortale. **∼ity** n immortalità f. **∼ize** vt immortalare

immune /ɪˈmjuːn/ adj immune (**to**/**from** da). **∼ system** n sistema m immunitario

immunity /ɪˈmjuːnəti/ n immunità f

immuniz|e /ˈɪmjʊnaɪz/ vt immunizzare

imp /ɪmp/ n diavoletto m

impact /ˈɪmpækt/ n impatto m

impair /ɪmˈpeə(r)/ vt danneggiare

impale /ɪmˈpeɪl/ vt impalare

impart /ɪmˈpɑːt/ vt impartire

im'parti|al adj imparziale. **∼'ality** n imparzialità f

im'passable adj impraticabile

im'passive adj impassibile

im'patien|ce n impazienza f. **∼t** adj impaziente. **∼tly** adv impazientemente

impeccabl|e /ɪmˈpekəbl/ adj impeccabile. **∼y** adv in modo impeccabile

impede /ɪmˈpiːd/ vt impedire

impediment /ɪmˈpedɪmənt/ n impedimento m; (in speech) difetto m

impending /ɪmˈpendɪŋ/ adj imminente

impenetrable /ɪmˈpenɪtrəbl/ adj impenetrabile

imperative /ɪmˈperətɪv/ adj imperativo ● n (Gram) imperativo m

imper'ceptible adj impercettibile

im'perfect adj imperfetto; (faulty) difettoso ● n (Gram) imperfetto m. **∼ion** n imperfezione f

imperial /ɪmˈpɪərɪəl/ adj imperiale. **∼ism** n imperialismo m. **∼ist** n imperialista mf

im'personal adj impersonale

impersonate /ɪmˈpɜːsəneɪt/ vt impersonare. **~or** n imitatore, -trice mf

impertinen|ce /ɪmˈpɜːtɪnəns/ n impertinenza f. **~t** adj impertinente

impervious /ɪmˈpɜːvɪəs/ adj **~ to** fig indifferente a

impetuous /ɪmˈpetjʊəs/ adj impetuoso. **~ly** adv impetuosamente

impetus /ˈɪmpɪtəs/ n impeto m

implacable /ɪmˈplækəbl/ adj implacabile

im'plant¹ vt trapiantare; fig inculcare

'implant² n trapianto m

implement¹ /ˈɪmplɪmənt/ n attrezzo m

implement² /ˈɪmplɪment/ vt mettere in atto. **~ation** /-ˈeɪʃn/ n attuazione f

implicat|e /ˈɪmplɪkeɪt/ vt implicare. **~ion** n implicazione f; **by ~ion** implicitamente

implicit /ɪmˈplɪsɪt/ adj implicito; (absolute) assoluto

implore /ɪmˈplɔː(r)/ vt implorare

imply /ɪmˈplaɪ/ vt (pt/pp -ied) implicare; **what do you ~ing?** che cosa vorresti insinuare?

impo'lite adj sgarbato

import¹ /ˈɪmpɔːt/ n (Comm) importazione f

import² /ɪmˈpɔːt/ vt importare

importan|ce /ɪmˈpɔːtəns/ n importanza f. **~t** adj importante

importer /ɪmˈpɔːtə(r)/ n importatore, -trice mf

impos|e /ɪmˈpəʊz/ vt Imporre (on a) ● vi imporsi; **~e on** abusare di. **~ing** adj imponente. **~ition** /ɪmpəˈzɪʃn/ n imposizione f

impossi'bility n impossibilità f

im'possibl|e adj impossibile

impostor /ɪmˈpɒstə(r)/ n impostore, -trice mf

impoten|ce /ˈɪmpətəns/ n impotenza f. **~t** adj impotente

impound /ɪmˈpaʊnd/ vt confiscare

impoverished /ɪmˈpɒvərɪʃt/ adj impoverito

im'practical adj non pratico

impregnable /ɪmˈpregnəbl/ adj imprendibile

impregnate /ˈɪmpregneɪt/ vt impregnare (with di); (Biol) fecondare

im'press vt imprimere; fig colpire (positivamente); **~ sth on sb** fare capire qcsa a qcno

impression /ɪmˈpreʃn/ n impressione f; (imitation) imitazione f. **~able** adj (child, mind) influenzabile. **~ism** n impressionismo m. **~ist** n imitatore, -trice mf; (artist) impressionista mf

impressive /ɪmˈpresɪv/ adj imponente

'imprint¹ n impressione f

im'print² vt imprimere; **~ed on my mind** impresso nella mia memoria

im'prison vt incarcerare. **~ment** n reclusione f

im'probable adj improbabile

impromptu /ɪmˈprɒmptjuː/ adj improvvisato

im'proper adj (use) improprio; (behaviour) scorretto. **~ly** adv scorrettamente

improve /ɪmˈpruːv/ vt/i migliorare. **improve on** vt perfezionare. **~ment** n miglioramento m

improvis|e /ˈɪmprəvaɪz/ vt/i improvvisare

impuden|ce /ˈɪmpjʊdəns/ n sfrontatezza f. **~t** adj sfrontato

impulse /ˈɪmpʌls/ n impulso m; **on [an] ~e** impulsivamente. **~ive** adj impulsivo

im'pur|e adj impuro. **~ity** n impurità f inv; **~ities** pl impurità fpl

in /ɪn/ prep in; (with names of towns) a;

in the garden in giardino; **in the street** in or per strada; **in bed/hospital** a letto/all'ospedale; **in the world** nel mondo; **in the rain** sotto la pioggia; **in the sun** al sole; **in this heat** con questo caldo; **in summer/winter** in estate/inverno; **in 1995** nel 1995; **in the evening** la sera; **he's arriving in two hours time** arriva fra due ore; **deaf in one ear** sordo da un orecchio; **in the army** nell'esercito; **in English/Italian** in inglese/italiano; **in ink/pencil** a penna/matita; **in red** (dressed, circled) di rosso; **the man in the raincoat** l'uomo con l'impermeabile; **in a soft/loud voice** a voce bassa/alta; **one in ten people** una persona su dieci; **in doing this, he...** nel far questo,...; **in itself** in sé; **in that** in quanto ● *adv* (*at home*) a casa; (*indoors*) dentro; **he's not in yet** non è ancora arrivato; **in there/here** lì/qui dentro; **ten in all** dieci in tutto; **day in, day out** giorno dopo giorno; **have it in for sb** [I] avercela con qcno; **send him in** fallo entrare; **come in** entrare; **bring in the washing** portare dentro i panni ● *adj* ([I]: *in fashion*) di moda ● *n* **the ins and outs** i dettagli

ina'bility *n* incapacità *f*

inac'cessible *adj* inaccessibile

in'accuracy /ɪnˈækjʊrəsɪ/ *n* inesattezza *f*. **~te** *adj* inesatto

in'active *adj* inattivo. **~tivity** *n* inattività *f*

in'adequate *adj* inadeguato. **~ly** *adv* inadeguatamente

inadvertently /ɪnədˈvɜːtəntlɪ/ *adv* inavvertitamente

inad'visable *adj* sconsigliabile

inane /ɪˈneɪn/ *adj* stupido

in'animate *adj* esanime

inap'propriate *adj* inadatto

inar'ticulate *adj* inarticolato

inat'tentive *adj* disattento

in'audible *adj* impercettibile

inaugurate /ɪˈnɔːɡjʊreɪt/ *vt* inaugurare. **~ion** *n* inaugurazione *f*

inborn /ˈɪnbɔːn/ *adj* innato

inbred /ɪnˈbred/ *adj* congenito

incalculable /ɪnˈkælkjʊləbl/ *adj* incalcolabile

in'capable *adj* incapace

incapacitate /ɪnkəˈpæsɪteɪt/ *vt* rendere incapace

incarnate /ɪnˈkɑːnət/ *adj* **the devil ~e** il diavolo in carne e ossa

incendiary /ɪnˈsendɪərɪ/ *adj* incendiario

incense¹ /ˈɪnsens/ *n* incenso *m*

incense² /ɪnˈsens/ *vt* esasperare

incentive /ɪnˈsentɪv/ *n* incentivo *m*

incessant /ɪnˈsesənt/ *adj* incessante

incest /ˈɪnsest/ *n* incesto *m*

inch /ɪntʃ/ *n* pollice *m* (= 2.54 cm) ● *vi* **~ forward** avanzare gradatamente

inciden|ce /ˈɪnsɪdəns/ *n* incidenza *f*. **~t** *n* incidente *m*

incidental /ɪnsɪˈdentl/ *adj* incidentale; **~ expenses** spese *fpl* accessorie. **~ly** *adv* incidentalmente; (*by the way*) a proposito

incinerat|e /ɪnˈsɪnəreɪt/ *vt* incenerire. **~or** *n* inceneritore *m*

incision /ɪnˈsɪʒn/ *n* incisione *f*

incite /ɪnˈsaɪt/ *vt* incitare. **~ment** *n* incitamento *m*

inclination /ɪnklɪˈneɪʃn/ *n* inclinazione *f*

incline¹ /ɪnˈklaɪn/ *vt* inclinare; **be ~d to do sth** essere propenso a fare qcsa

incline² /ˈɪnklaɪn/ *n* pendio *m*

inclu|de /ɪnˈkluːd/ *vt* includere. **~ding** *prep* incluso. **~sion** *n* inclusione *f*

inclusive /ɪnˈkluːsɪv/ *adj* incluso; **~ of** comprendente; **be ~ of** comprendere ● *adv* incluso

incognito /ɪnkɒɡˈniːtəʊ/ *adv* incognito

inco'herent *adj* incoerente; (*be-*

cause drunk etc) incomprensibile

income /ˈɪŋkʌm/ n reddito m. ~ **tax** n imposta f sul reddito

'incoming adj in arrivo. ~ **tide** n marea f montante

in'comparable adj incomparabile

incom'patible adj incompatibile

in'competen|ce n incompetenza f. ~**t** adj incompetente

incom'plete adj incompleto

incompre'hensible adj incomprensibile

incon'ceivable adj inconcepibile

incon'clusive adj inconcludente

incongruous /ɪnˈkɒŋgrʊəs/ adj contrastante

incon'siderate adj trascurabile

incon'sistency n incoerenza f

incon'sistent adj incoerente; **be ~ with** non essere coerente con. ~**ly** adv in modo incoerente

incon'spicuous adj non appariscente. ~**ly** adv modestamente

incon'venien|ce n scomodità f; (drawback) inconveniente m; **put sb to ~ce** dare disturbo a qcno. ~**t** adj scomodo; (time, place) inopportuno. ~**tly** adv in modo inopportuno

incorporate /ɪnˈkɔːpəreɪt/ vt incorporare; (contain) comprendere

incor'rect adj incorretto. ~**ly** adv scorrettamente

increase¹ /ˈɪŋkriːs/ n aumento m; **on the ~** in aumento

increas|e² /ɪnˈkriːs/ vt/i aumentare. ~**ing** adj (impatience etc) crescente; (numbers) in aumento. ~**ingly** adv sempre più

in'credible adj incredibile

incredulous /ɪnˈkredjʊləs/ adj incredulo

incriminate /ɪnˈkrɪmɪneɪt/ vt (Jur) incriminare

incubat|e /ˈɪŋkjʊbeɪt/ vt incubare. ~**ion** n incubazione f. ~**ion period** n (Med) periodo m di incubazione.

~**or** n (for baby) incubatrice f

incur /ɪnˈkɜː(r)/ vt (pt/pp incurred) incorrere; contrarre (debts)

in'curable adj incurabile

indebted /ɪnˈdetɪd/ adj obbligato (to verso)

in'decent adj indecente

inde'cision n indecisione f

inde'cisive adj indeciso. ~**ness** n indecisione f

indeed /ɪnˈdiːd/ adv (in fact) difatti; **yes ~!** sì, certamente!; **~ I am/do** veramente!; **very much ~** moltissimo; **thank you very much ~** grazie infinite; **~?** davvero?

inde'finable adj indefinibile

in'definite adj indefinito. ~**ly** adv indefinitamente; (postpone) a tempo indeterminato

indelible /ɪnˈdelɪbl/ adj indelebile

indemnity /ɪnˈdemnɪti/ n indennità f inv

indent¹ /ˈɪndent/ n (Typ) rientranza f dal margine

indent² /ɪnˈdent/ vt (Typ) fare rientrare dal margine. ~**ation** n (notch) intaccatura f

inde'penden|ce n indipendenza f. ~**t** adj indipendente. ~**tly** adv indipendentemente

indescribable /ɪndɪˈskraɪbəbl/ adj indescrivibile

indestructible /ɪndɪˈstrʌktəbl/ adj indistruttibile

indeterminate /ɪndɪˈtɜːmɪnət/ adj indeterminato

index /ˈɪndeks/ n indice m

index: ~ **finger** n dito m indice. ~**-linked** adj (pension) legato al costo della vita

India /ˈɪndɪə/ n India f. ~**n** adj indiano; (American) indiano [d'America] ● n indiano, -a mf; (American) indiano, -a mf [d'America]

indicat|e /ˈɪndɪkeɪt/ vt indicare; (register) segnare ● vi (Auto) mettere la freccia. **~ion** n indicazione f.

indicative /ɪnˈdɪkətɪv/ adj **be ~ of** essere indicativo di ●n (Gram) indicativo m

indicator /ˈɪndɪkeɪtə(r)/ n (Auto) freccia f

indict /ɪnˈdaɪt/ vt accusare. **~ment** n accusa f

in'differen|ce n indifferenza f. **~t** adj indifferente; (not good) mediocre

indi'gest|ible adj indigesto. **~ion** n indigestione f

indigna|nt /ɪnˈdɪɡnənt/ adj indignato. **~ntly** adv con indignazione. **~tion** n indignazione f

indi'rect adj indiretto. **~ly** adv indirettamente

indi'screet adj indiscreto

indis'cretion n indiscrezione f

indiscriminate /ɪndɪˈskrɪmɪnət/ adj indiscriminato. **~ly** adv senza distinzione

indi'spensable adj indispensabile

indisposed /ɪndɪˈspəʊzd/ adj indisposto

indis'putable /ɪndɪˈspjuːtəbl/ adj indisputabile

indistinguishable /ɪndɪˈstɪŋɡwɪʃəbl/ adj indistinguibile

individual /ɪndɪˈvɪdʒʊəl/ adj individuale ●n individuo m. **~ity** n individualità f

indoctrinate /ɪnˈdɒktrɪneɪt/ vt indottrinare

indomitable /ɪnˈdɒmɪtəbl/ adj indomito

indoor /ˈɪndɔː(r)/ adj interno; (shoes) per casa; (plant) da appartamento; (swimming pool etc) coperto. **~s** adv dentro

induce /ɪnˈdjuːs/ vt indurre (**to** a); (produce) causare. **~ment** n (incentive) incentivo m

indulge /ɪnˈdʌldʒ/ vt soddisfare; viziare (child) ●vi **~ in** concedersi. **~nce** n lusso m; (leniency) indulgenza

f. **~nt** adj indulgente

industrial /ɪnˈdʌstrɪəl/ adj industriale; **take ~ action** scioperare. **~ist** n industriale mf. **~ized** adj industrializzato

industri|ous /ɪnˈdʌstrɪəs/ adj industrioso. **~y** n industria f; (zeal) operosità f

inebriated /ɪˈniːbrɪeɪtɪd/ adj ebbro

in'edible adj immangiabile

inef'fective adj inefficace

ineffectual /ɪnɪˈfektʃʊəl/ adj inutile; (person) inconcludente

inef'ficien|cy n inefficienza f. **~t** adj inefficiente

in'eligible adj inadatto

inept /ɪˈnept/ adj inetto

ine'quality n ineguaglianza f

inert /ɪˈnɜːt/ adj inerte. **~ia** n inerzia f

inescapable /ɪnɪˈskeɪpəbl/ adj inevitabile

inevitabl|e /ɪnˈevɪtəbl/ adj inevitabile. **~y** adv inevitabilmente

ine'xact adj inesatto

inex'cusable adj imperdonabile

inex'pensive adj poco costoso

inex'perience n inesperienza f. **~d** adj inesperto

inexplicable /ɪnɪkˈsplɪkəbl/ adj inesplicabile

in'fallible adj infallibile

infam|ous /ˈɪnfəməs/ adj infame; (person) famigerato. **~y** n infamia f

infan|cy /ˈɪnfənsɪ/ n infanzia f; **in its ~cy** fig agli inizi. **~t** n bambino, -a mf piccolo, -a. **~tile** adj infantile

infantry /ˈɪnfəntrɪ/ n fanteria f

infatuat|ed /ɪnˈfætʃʊeɪtɪd/ adj infatuato (**with** di). **~ion** n infatuazione f

infect /ɪnˈfekt/ vt infettare; **become ~ed** (wound:) infettarsi. **~ion** adj infettivo

infer /ɪnˈfɜː(r)/ vt (pt/pp **inferred**) dedurre (**from** da); (imply) implicare.

~ence n deduzione f

inferior /m'frərıə(r)/ adj inferiore; (goods) scadente; (in rank) subalterno ● n inferiore mf; (in rank) subalterno, -a mf

inferiority /mfıərı'ɒrəti/ n inferiorità f. **~ complex** n complesso m di inferiorità

in'fertile adj sterile. **~'tility** n sterilità f

infest /m'fest/ vt **be ~ed with** essere infestato di

infidelity n infedeltà f

infiltrate /'ınfıltreıt/ vt infiltrare; (Pol) infiltrarsi in

infinite /'ınfınət/ adj infinito

infinitive /m'fınətıv/ n (Gram) infinito m

infinity /m'fınətı/ n infinità f

infirm /m'fɜːm/ adj debole. **~ary** n infermeria f. **~ity** n debolezza f

inflame /m'fleım/ vt infiammare. **~d** adj infiammato; **become ~d** infiammarsi

in'flammable adj infiammabile

inflammation /ınflə'meıʃn/ n infiammazione f

inflate /m'fleıt/ vt gonfiare. **~ion** n inflazione f. **~ionary** adj inflazionario

in'flexible adj inflessibile

inflict /m'flıkt/ vt infliggere (**on** a)

influence /'ınfluəns/ n influenza f ● vt influenzare. **~tial** adj influente

influenza /ınflu'enzə/ n influenza f

influx /'ınflʌks/ n affluenza f

inform /m'fɔːm/ vt informare; **keep sb ~ed** tenere qcno al corrente ● vi **~ against** denunziare

in'formal adj informale; (agreement) ufficioso. **~ally** adv in modo informale. **~mality** n informalità f inv

information /ınfə'meıʃn/ n informazioni fpl; **a piece of ~ion** un'informazione. **~ion highway** n autostrada f telematica. **~ion**

technology n informatica f. **~ive** adj informativo; (film, book) istruttivo

informer /m'fɔːmə(r)/ n informatore, -trice mf; (Pol) delatore, -trice mf

infra-red /ınfrə-/ adj infrarosso

infringe /m'frındʒ/ vt **~ on** usurpare. **~ment** n violazione f

infuriate /m'fjʊərıeıt/ vt infuriare. **~ing** adj esasperante

ingenious /m'dʒiːnıəs/ adj ingegnoso

ingenuity /ındʒı'njuːətı/ n ingegnosità f

ingot /'ıŋgət/ n lingotto m

ingrained /m'greınd/ adj (in person) radicato; (dirt) incrostato

ingratiate /m'greıʃıeıt/ vt **~ oneself with sb** ingraziarsi qcno

in'gratitude n ingratitudine f

ingredient /m'griːdıənt/ n ingrediente m

ingrowing /'ıŋgrəʊıŋ/ adj (nail) incarnito

inhabit /m'hæbıt/ vt abitare. **~ant** n abitante mf

inhale /m'heıl/ vt aspirare; (Med) inalare ● vi inspirare; (when smoking) aspirare. **~r** n (device) inalatore m

inherent /m'hıərənt/ adj inerente

inherit /m'herıt/ vt ereditare. **~ance** n eredità f inv

inhibit /m'hıbıt/ vt inibire. **~ed** adj inibito. **~ion** n inibizione f

inho'spitable adj inospitale

initial /ı'nıʃl/ adj iniziale ● n iniziale f ● vt (pt/pp **initialled**) siglare. **~ly** adv all'inizio

initiate /ı'nıʃıeıt/ vt iniziare. **~ion** n iniziazione f

initiative /ı'nıʃətıv/ n iniziativa f

inject /m'dʒekt/ vt iniettare. **~ion** n iniezione f

injure /'ındʒə(r)/ vt ferire; (wrong) nuocere. **~y** n ferita f; (wrong) torto m

in'justice n ingiustizia f; **do sb an ~** giudicare qcno in modo sbagliato

ink /ɪŋk/ n inchiostro m

inland /'ɪnlənd/ adj interno ● adv all'interno. **I~ Revenue** n fisco m

in-laws /'ɪnlɔːz/ npl 🅸 parenti mpl acquisiti

inlay /'ɪnleɪ/ n intarsio m

inlet /'ɪnlet/ n insenatura f; (Techn) entrata f

inmate /'ɪnmeɪt/ n (of hospital) degente mf; (of prison) carcerato, -a mf

inn /ɪn/ n locanda f

innate /ɪ'neɪt/ adj innato

inner /'ɪnə(r)/ adj interno. **~most** adj il più profondo. **~ tube** camera f d'aria

innocen|ce /'ɪnəsəns/ n innocenza f. **~t** adj innocente

innocuous /ɪ'nɒkjʊəs/ adj innocuo

innovat|e /'ɪnəveɪt/ vi innovare. **~ion** n innovazione f. **~ive** adj innovativo. **~or** n innovatore, -trice mf

innuendo /ɪnjʊ'endəʊ/ n (pl -es) insinuazione f

innumerable /ɪ'njuːmərəbl/ adj innumerevole

inoculat|e /ɪ'nɒkjʊleɪt/ vt vaccinare. **~ion** n vaccinazione f

inof'fensive adj inoffensivo

in'opportune adj inopportuno

input /'ɪnpʊt/ n input m inv, ingresso m

inquest /'ɪnkwest/ n inchiesta f

inquir|e /ɪn'kwaɪə(r)/ vi informarsi (about su); **~e into** far indagini su ● vt domandare. **~y** n domanda f; (investigation) inchiesta f

inquisitive /ɪn'kwɪzətɪv/ adj curioso

in'sane adj pazzo; fig insensato

in'sanity n pazzia f

insatiable /ɪn'seɪʃəbl/ adj insaziabile

inscri|be /ɪn'skraɪb/ vt iscrivere. **~ption** n iscrizione f

inscrutable /ɪn'skruːtəbl/ adj impenetrabile

insect /'ɪnsekt/ n insetto m. **~icide** n insetticida m

inse'cur|e adj malsicuro; (fig: person) insicuro. **~ity** n mancanza f di sicurezza

in'sensitive adj insensibile

in'separable adj inseparabile

insert¹ /'ɪnsɜːt/ n inserto m

insert² /ɪn'sɜːt/ vt inserire. **~ion** n inserzione f

inside /ɪn'saɪd/ n interno m. **~s** npl 🅸 pancia f ● attrib (Auto) **~ lane** n corsia f interna ● adv dentro; **~ out** a rovescio; (thoroughly) a fondo ● prep dentro; (of time) entro

insight /'ɪnsaɪt/ n intuito m (into per); **an ~ into** un quadro di

insig'nificant adj insignificante

insin'cer|e adj poco sincero. **~ity** n mancanza f di sincerità

insinuat|e /ɪn'sɪnjʊeɪt/ vt insinuare. **~ion** n insinuazione f

insipid /ɪn'sɪpɪd/ adj insipido

insist /ɪn'sɪst/ vi insistere (on per) ● vt **~ that** insistere che. **~ence** n insistenza f. **~ent** adj insistente

insolen|ce /'ɪnsələns/ n insolenza f. **~t** adj insolente

in'soluble adj insolubile

insomnia /ɪn'sɒmnɪə/ n insonnia f

inspect /ɪn'spekt/ vt ispezionare; controllare (ticket). **~ion** n ispezione f; (of ticket) controllo m. **~or** n ispettore, -trice mf; (of tickets) controllore m

inspiration /ɪnspə'reɪʃn/ n ispirazione f

inspire /ɪn'spaɪə(r)/ vt ispirare

insta'bility n instabilità f

install /ɪn'stɔːl/ vt installare. **~ation** n installazione f

instalment /ɪn'stɔːlmənt/ n (Comm) rata f; (of serial) puntata f; (of publication) fascicolo m

instance /'ɪnstəns/ n (case) caso m; (example) esempio m; **in the first ~** in primo luogo; **for ~** per esempio

instant /'ɪnstənt/ adj immediato; (Culin) espresso ● n istante m. **~aneous** adj istantaneo

instead /ɪn'sted/ adv invece; **~ of doing** anziché fare; **~ of me** al mio posto; **~ of going** invece di andare

instigate /'ɪnstɪgeɪt/ vt istigare. **~ion** n istigazione f; **at his ~ion** dietro suo suggerimento. **~or** n istigatore, -trice mf

instinct /'ɪnstɪŋkt/ n istinto m. **~ive** adj istintivo

institute /'ɪnstɪtjuːt/ n istituto m ● vt istituire (scheme); iniziare (search); intentare (legal action). **~ion** n istituzione f; (home for elderly) istituto m per anziani; (for mentally ill) istituto m per malati di mente

instruct /ɪn'strʌkt/ vt istruire; (order) ordinare. **~ion** n istruzione f; **~s** (orders) ordini mpl. **~ive** adj istruttivo. **~or** n istruttore, -trice mf

instrument /'ɪnstrʊmənt/ n strumento m. **~al** adj strumentale; **be ~al in** contribuire a. **~alist** n strumentista mf

insubordinate adj insubordinato. **~nation** n insubordinazione f

in'sufferable adj insopportabile

insuf'ficient adj insufficiente

insular /'ɪnsjʊlə(r)/ adj fig gretto

insulate /'ɪnsjʊleɪt/ vt isolare. **~ing tape** n nastro m isolante. **~ion** n isolamento m

insulin /'ɪnsjʊlɪn/ n insulina f

insult[1] /'ɪnsʌlt/ n insulto m

insult[2] /ɪn'sʌlt/ vt insultare

insurance /ɪn'ʃʊərəns/ n assicurazione f. **~e** vt assicurare

intact /ɪn'tækt/ adj intatto

integral /'ɪntɪgrəl/ adj integrale

integrate /'ɪntɪgreɪt/ vt integrare ● vi integrarsi. **~ion** n integrazione f

integrity /ɪn'tegrətɪ/ n integrità f

intellect /'ɪntəlekt/ n intelletto m. **~ual** adj n intellettuale mf

intelligence /ɪn'telɪdʒəns/ n intelligenza f; (Mil) informazioni fpl. **~t** adj intelligente

intelligible /ɪn'telɪdʒəbl/ adj intelligibile

intend /ɪn'tend/ vt destinare; (have in mind) aver intenzione di; **be ~ed for** essere destinato a. **~ed** adj (effect) voluto ● **my ~ed** ① il mio/la mia fidanzata, -a

intense /ɪn'tens/ adj intenso; (person) dai sentimenti intensi. **~ly** adv intensamente; (very) estremamente

intensity /ɪn'tensətɪ/ n intensità f

intensive /ɪn'tensɪv/ adj intensivo. **~ care** (for people in coma) rianimazione f; **~ care [unit]** terapia f intensiva

intent /ɪn'tent/ adj intento; **~ on** (absorbed in) preso da; **be ~ on doing sth** essere intento a fare qcsa ● n intenzione f; **to all ~s and purposes** a tutti gli effetti. **~ly** adv attentamente

intention /ɪn'tenʃn/ n intenzione f. **~al** adj intenzionale. **~ally** adv intenzionalmente

inter'action n cooperazione f. **~ve** adj Interattivo

intercept /ɪntə'sept/ vt intercettare

'interchange n scambio m; (Auto) raccordo m [autostradale]

inter'changeable adj interscambiabile

'intercourse n (sexual) rapporti mpl [sessuali]

interest /'ɪntrəst/ n interesse m; **have an ~ in** (Comm) essere cointeressato in; **be of ~** essere interessante; **~ rate** n tasso m di interesse ● vt interessare. **~ed** adj interessato. **~ing** adj interessante

interface /'ɪntəfeɪs/ n interfaccia f ● vt interfacciare ● vi interfacciarsi

interfere /ɪntəˈfɪə(r)/ vi interferire; **∼ with** interferire con. **∼nce** n interferenza f

interior /ɪnˈtɪərɪə(r)/ adj interiore ● n interno m. **∼ designer** n arredatore, -trice mf

interlude /ˈɪntəluːd/ n intervallo m

intermediary /ɪntəˈmiːdɪərɪ/ n intermediario, -a mf

interminable /ɪnˈtɜːmɪnəbl/ adj interminabile

intermittent /ɪntəˈmɪtənt/ adj intermittente

intern /ɪnˈtɜːn/ vt internare

internal /ɪnˈtɜːnl/ adj interno. **I∼ 'Revenue** (Am) n fisco m. **∼ly** adv internamente; (deal with) all'interno

inter'national adj internazionale ● n (game) incontro m internazionale; (player) competitore, -trice mf in gare internazionali. **∼ly** adv internazionalmente

Internet /ˈɪntənet/ n Internet m

interpret /ɪnˈtɜːprɪt/ vt interpretare ● vi fare l'interprete. **∼ation** n interpretazione f. **∼er** n interprete mf

interrogate /ɪnˈterəgeɪt/ vt interrogare. **∼ion** n interrogazione f; (by police) interrogatorio m

interrogative /ɪntəˈrɒgətɪv/ adj & n [**pronoun**] interrogativo m

interrupt /ɪntəˈrʌpt/ vt/i interrompere. **∼ion** n interruzione f

intersect /ɪntəˈsekt/ vi intersecarsi ● vt intersecare. **∼ion** n intersezione f; (of street) incrocio m

inter'twine vi attorcigliarsi

interval /ˈɪntəvl/ n intervallo m; **bright ∼s** pl schiarite fpl

interven|e /ɪntəˈviːn/ vi intervenire. **∼tion** n intervento m

interview /ˈɪntəvjuː/ n (Journ) intervista f; (for job) colloquio m [di lavoro] ● vt intervistare. **∼er** n intervistatore, -trice mf

intestine /ɪnˈtestɪn/ n intestino m.

∼al adj intestinale

intimacy /ˈɪntɪməsɪ/ n intimità f

intimate¹ /ˈɪntɪmət/ adj intimo. **∼ly** adv intimamente

intimate² /ˈɪntɪmeɪt/ vt far capire; (imply) suggerire

intimidat|e /ɪnˈtɪmɪdeɪt/ vt intimidire. **∼ion** n intimidazione f

into /ˈɪntə/, di fronte a una vocale /ˈɪntʊ/ prep dentro, in; **go ∼ the house** andare dentro [casa] o in casa; **be ∼** (🄵: like) essere appassionato di; **I'm not ∼ that** questo non mi piace; **7 ∼ 21 goes 3** il 7 nel 21 ci sta 3 volte; **translate ∼ French** tradurre in francese; **get ∼ trouble** mettersi nei guai

in'tolerable adj intollerabile

in'toleran|ce n intolleranza f. **∼t** adj intollerante

intoxicat|ed /ɪnˈtɒksɪkeɪtɪd/ adj inebriato. **∼ion** n ebbrezza f

in'transitive adj intransitivo

intravenous /ɪntrəˈviːnəs/ adj endovenoso. **∼ly** adv per via endovenosa

intrepid /ɪnˈtrepɪd/ adj intrepido

intricate /ˈɪntrɪkət/ adj complesso

intrigu|e /ɪnˈtriːg/ n intrigo m ● vt intrigare ● vi tramare. **∼ing** adj intrigante

intrinsic /ɪnˈtrɪnsɪk/ adj intrinseco

introduce /ɪntrəˈdjuːs/ vt presentare; (bring in, insert) introdurre

introduct|ion /ɪntrəˈdʌkʃn/ n introduzione f; (to person) presentazione f; (to book) prefazione f. **∼ory** adj introduttivo

introvert /ˈɪntrəvɜːt/ n introverso, -a mf

intru|de /ɪnˈtruːd/ vi intromettersi. **∼der** n intruso, -a mf. **∼sion** n intrusione f

intuit|ion /ɪntjʊˈɪʃn/ n intuito m. **∼ive** adj intuitivo

inundate /ˈɪnʌndeɪt/ vt (flood)

inondare (**with** di)

invade /ɪnˈveɪd/ vt invadere. **~r** n invasore m

invalid[1] /ˈɪnvəlɪd/ n invalido, -a mf

invalid[2] /ɪnˈvælɪd/ adj non valido. **~ate** vt invalidare

in'valuable adj prezioso; (priceless) inestimabile

in'variab|le adj invariabile. **~y** adv invariabilmente

invasion /ɪnˈveɪʒn/ n invasione f

invent /ɪnˈvent/ vt inventare. **~ion** n invenzione f. **~ive** adj inventivo. **~or** n inventore, trice mf

inventory /ˈɪnvəntrɪ/ n inventario m

invest /ɪnˈvest/ vt investire ● vi fare investimenti; **~ in** (🔟: buy) comprarsi

investigat|e /ɪnˈvestɪɡeɪt/ vt investigare. **~ion** n investigazione f

invest|ment /ɪnˈvestmənt/ n investimento m. **~or** n investitore, -trice mf

inveterate /ɪnˈvetərət/ adj inveterato

invidious /ɪnˈvɪdɪəs/ adj ingiusto; (position) antipatico

invincible /ɪnˈvɪnsəbl/ adj invincibile

in'visible adj invisibile

invitation /ɪnvɪˈteɪʃn/ n invito m

invit|e /ɪnˈvaɪt/ vt invitare; (attract) attirare. **~ing** adj invitante

invoice /ˈɪnvɔɪs/ n fattura ● vt **~** sb emettere una fattura a qcno

in'voluntar|y adj involontaria

involve /ɪnˈvɒlv/ vt comportare; (affect, include) coinvolgere; (entail) implicare; **get ~d with sb** legarsi a qcno; (romantically) legarsi sentimentalmente a qcno. **~d** adj complesso. **~ment** n coinvolgimento m

inward /ˈɪnwəd/ adj interno; (thoughts etc) interiore; **~ invest-ment** (Comm) investimento m stra-

niero. **~ly** adv interiormente. **~[s]** adv verso l'interno

iodine /ˈaɪədiːn/ n iodio m

iota /aɪˈəʊtə/ n briciolo m

IOU n abbr (I owe you) pagherò m inv

IQ n abbr (intelligence quotient) Q.I.

Iran /ɪˈrɑːn/ n Iran m. **~ian** adj & n iraniano, -a mf

Iraq /ɪˈrɑːk/ n Iraq m. **~i** adj & n iracheno, -a mf

irate /aɪˈreɪt/ adj adirato

Ireland /ˈaɪələnd/ n Irlanda f

iris /ˈaɪrɪs/ n (Anat) iride f; (Bot) iris f inv

Irish /ˈaɪrɪʃ/ adj irlandese ● n the **~** pl gli irlandesi mpl. **~man** n irlandese m. **~woman** n irlandese f

iron /ˈaɪən/ adj di ferro. I**~ Curtain** n cortina f di ferro ● n ferro m; (appliance) ferro m [da stiro] ● vt/i stirare. □ **~ out** vt eliminare stirando; fig appianare

ironmonger /-mʌŋɡə(r)/ n **~'s [shop]** negozio m di ferramenta

irony /ˈaɪrənɪ/ n ironia f

irrational /ɪˈræʃənl/ adj irrazionale

irrefutable /ɪrɪˈfjuːtəbl/ adj irrefu-tabile

irregular /ɪˈreɡjʊlə(r)/ adj irrego-lare. **~ity** n irregolarità f inv

irrelevant /ɪˈreləvənt/ adj non per-tinente

irreparab|le /ɪˈrepərəbl/ adj irrepa-rabile. **~y** adv irreparabilmente

irreplaceable /ɪrɪˈpleɪsəbl/ adj in-sostituibile

irresistible /ɪrɪˈzɪstəbl/ adj irresi-stibile

irrespective /ɪrɪˈspektɪv/ adj **~ of** senza riguardo per

irresponsible /ɪrɪˈspɒnsɪbl/ adj ir-responsabile

irreverent /ɪˈrevərənt/ adj irre-verente

irrevocab|le /ɪˈrevəkəbl/ adj irre-vocabile. **~y** adv irrevocabilmente

irrigat|e /ˈɪrɪgeɪt/ vt irrigare. **~ion** n irrigazione f

irritable /ˈɪrɪtəbl/ adj irritabile

irritat|e /ˈɪrɪteɪt/ vt irritare. **~ing** adj irritante. **~ion** n irritazione f

is /ɪz/ ▷BE

Islam /ˈɪzlɑːm/ n Islam m. **~ic** adj islamico

island /ˈaɪlənd/ n isola f; (in road) isola f spartitraffico. **~er** n isolano, -a mf

isolat|e /ˈaɪsəleɪt/ vt isolare. **~ed** adj isolato. **~ion** n isolamento m

Israel /ˈɪzreɪl/ n Israele m. **~i** adj & n israeliano, -a mf

issue /ˈɪʃuː/ n (outcome) risultato m; (of magazine) numero m; (of stamps etc) emissione f; (offspring) figli mpl; (matter, question) questione f; **at** ~ in questione; **take** ~ **with sb** prendere posizione contro qcno ● vt distribuire (supplies); rilasciare (passport); emettere (stamps, order); pubblicare (book); **be** ~**d with sth** ricevere qcsa ● vi ~ **from** uscire da

it /ɪt/ pron (direct object) lo m, la f; (indirect object) gli m, le f; **it's broken** è rotto/rotta; **will it be enough?** basterà?; **it's hot** fa caldo; **it's raining** piove; **it's me** sono io; **who is it?** chi è?; **it's two o'clock** sono le due; **I doubt it** ne dubito; **take it with you** prendilo con te; **give it a wipe** dagli una pulita

Italian /ɪˈtæljən/ adj & n italiano, -a mf; (language) italiano m

Italy /ˈɪtəlɪ/ n Italia f

itch /ɪtʃ/ n prurito m ● vi avere prurito, prudere; **be** ~**ing to** 🅸 avere una voglia matta di. **~y** adj dà prude; **my foot is** ~**y** ho prurito al piede

item /ˈaɪtəm/ n articolo m; (on agenda, programme) punto m; (on invoice) voce f; ~ **[of news]** notizia f. **~ize** vt dettagliare (bill)

itinerary /aɪˈtɪnərərɪ/ n itinerario m

itself /ɪtˈself/ pron (reflexive) si; (emphatic) essa stessa; **the baby looked at** ~ **in the mirror** il bambino si è guardato nello specchio; **by** ~ da solo; **the machine in** ~ **is simple** la macchina di per sé è semplice

ITV n abbr (Independent Television) stazione f televisiva privata britannica

ivory /ˈaɪvərɪ/ n avorio m

ivy /ˈaɪvɪ/ n edera f

The Ivy League Il gruppo delle più antiche e rinomate università statunitensi, situate nel nordest del paese: Harvard, Yale, Columbia University, Cornell University, Dartmouth College, Brown University, Princeton University e la University of Pennsylvania. L'espressione deriva dall'edera che cresce sugli antichi edifici universitari.

Jj

jab /dʒæb/ n colpo m secco; (🅸: injection) puntura f ● vt (pt/pp jabbed) punzecchiare

jack /dʒæk/ n (Auto) cric m inv; (in cards) fante m, jack m inv ● **jack up** vt (Auto) sollevare [con il cric]

jackdaw /ˈdʒækdɔː/ n taccola f

jacket /ˈdʒækɪt/ n giacca f; (of book) sopraccoperta f. ~ **po¹tato** n patata f cotta al forno con la buccia

¹jackpot n premio m (di una lotteria); **win the** ~ vincere alla lotteria; **hit the** ~ fig fare un colpo grosso

jade /dʒeɪd/ n giada f ● attrib di giada

jagged /ˈdʒægɪd/ adj dentellato

jail /dʒeɪl/ = gaol

jam[1] /dʒæm/ n marmellata f

jam[2] n (Auto) ingorgo m; (🔲: difficulty) guaio m ● v (pt/pp **jammed**) ● vt (cram) pigiare; disturbare (broadcast); inceppare (mechanism, drawer etc); be ~med (roads:) essere congestionato ● vi (mechanism:) incepparsi; (window, drawer:) incastrarsi

Jamaica /dʒə'meɪkə/ n Giamaica f. ~n adj & n giamaicano, -a mf

jangle /'dʒæŋgl/ vt far squillare ● vi squillare

janitor /'dʒænɪtə(r)/ n (caretaker) custode m; (in school) bidello, -a mf

january /'dʒænjʊərɪ/ n gennaio m

japan /dʒə'pæn/ n Giappone m. ~ese adj & n giapponese mf; (language) giapponese m

jar[1] /dʒɑː(r)/ n (glass) barattolo m

jar[2] vi (pt/pp jarred) (sound:) stridere

jargon /'dʒɑːgən/ n gergo m

jaundice /'dʒɔːndɪs/ n itterizia f. ~d fig inacidito

jaunt /dʒɔːnt/ n gita f

jaunty /'dʒɔːntɪ/ adj (-ier, -iest) sbarazzino

jaw /dʒɔː/ n mascella f; (bone) mandibola f

jay-walker /'dʒeɪwɔːkə(r)/ n pedone m distratto

jazz /dʒæz/ n jazz m ● jazz up vt ravvivare. ~y adj vistoso

jealous /'dʒeləs/ adj geloso. ~y n gelosia f

jeans /dʒiːnz/ npl [blue] jeans mpl

jeep /dʒiːp/ n jeep f inv

jeer /dʒɪə(r)/ n scherno m ● vi schernire; ~ at prendersi gioco di ● vt (boo) fischiare

jelly /'dʒelɪ/ n gelatina f. ~fish n medusa f

jeopar|dize /'dʒepədaɪz/ vt mettere in pericolo. ~dy n in ~dy in pericolo

jerk /dʒɜːk/ n scatto m, scossa f ● vt scattare ● vi sobbalzare; (limb,

muscle:) muoversi a scatti. ~ily adv a scatti. ~y adj traballante

jersey /'dʒɜːzɪ/ n maglia f; (Sport) maglietta f; (fabric) jersey m

jest /dʒest/ n scherzo m; in ~ per scherzo ● vi scherzare

Jesus /'dʒiːzəs/ n Gesù m

jet[1] /dʒet/ n (stone) giaietto m

jet[2] n (of water) getto m; (nozzle) becco m; (plane) aviogetto m, jet m inv

jet: ~-black adj nero ebano. ~lag n scombussolamento m da fuso orario. ~-pro'pelled adj a reazione

jettison /'dʒetɪsn/ vt gettare a mare; fig abbandonare

jetty /'dʒetɪ/ n molo m

Jew /dʒuː/ n ebreo m

jewel /'dʒuːəl/ n gioiello m. ~ler n gioielliere m; ~ler's [shop] gioielleria f. ~lery n gioielli mpl

Jewess /'dʒuːɪs/ n ebrea f

Jewish /'dʒuːɪʃ/ adj ebreo

jiffy /'dʒɪfɪ/ n 🔲 in a ~ in un batter d'occhio

jigsaw /'dʒɪgsɔː/ n ~ [puzzle] puzzle m inv

jilt /dʒɪlt/ vt piantare

jingle /'dʒɪŋgl/ n (rhyme) canzoncina f pubblicitaria ● vi tintinnare

job /dʒɒb/ n lavoro m; this is going to be quite a ~ 🔲 [questa] non sarà un'impresa facile; it's a good ~ that... meno male che.... ~ centre n ufficio m statale di collocamento. ~less adj senza lavoro

jockey /'dʒɒkɪ/ n fantino m

jocular /'dʒɒkjʊlə(r)/ adj scherzoso

jog /dʒɒg/ n colpetto m; at a ~ a fare jogging ● v (pt/pp jogged) ● vt (hit) urtare; ~ sb's memory farlo ritornare in mente a qcno ● vi (Sport) fare jogging. ~ging n jogging m

join /dʒɔɪn/ n giuntura f ● vt raggiungere, unire; raggiungere (person); (become member of) iscriversi a; entrare in (firm) ● vi (roads:) congiungersi. □ ~ **in** vi partecipare. □ ~ **up** vi (*Mil*) arruolarsi ● vt unire

joiner /'dʒɔɪnə(r)/ n falegname m

joint /dʒɔɪnt/ adj comune ● n articolazione f; (*in wood, brickwork*) giuntura f; (*Culin*) arrosto m; (**I:** *bar*) bettola f; (**▣:***drug*) spinello m. ~**ly** adv unitamente

joist /dʒɔɪst/ n travetto m

jok|e /dʒəʊk/ n (*trick*) scherzo m; (*funny story*) barzelletta f ● vi scherzare. ~**er** n burlone, -a m f; (*in cards*) jolly m inv. ~**ing** n ~**ing apart** scherzi a parte. ~**ingly** adv per scherzo

jolly /'dʒɒlɪ/ adj (**-ier, -iest**) allegro ● adv **I** molto

jolt /dʒəʊlt/ n scossa f, sobbalzo m ● vt far sobbalzare ● vi sobbalzare

jostle /'dʒɒsl/ vt spingere

jot /dʒɒt/ n nulla f ● **jot down** vt (pt/pp jotted) annotare. ~**ter** n taccuino m

journal /'dʒɜːnl/ n giornale m; (*diary*) diario m. ~**ese** n gergo m giornalistico. ~**ism** n giornalismo m. ~**ist** n giornalista m f

journey /'dʒɜːnɪ/ n viaggio m

jovial /'dʒəʊvɪəl/ adj gioviale

joy /dʒɔɪ/ n gioia f. ~**ful** adj gioioso. ~**ride** n **I** giro m con una macchina rubata. ~**stick** n (*Comput*) joystick m inv

jubil|ant /'dʒuːbɪlənt/ adj giubilante. ~**ation** n giubilo m

jubilee /'dʒuːbɪliː/ n giubileo m

judge /dʒʌdʒ/ n giudice m ● vt giudicare; (*estimate*) valutare; (*consider*) ritenere ● vi giudicare (**by** da). ~**ment** n giudizio m; (*Jur*) sentenza f

judic|ial /dʒuː'dɪʃl/ adj giudiziario. ~**iary** n magistratura f. ~**ious** adj giudizioso

judo /'dʒuːdəʊ/ n judo m

jug /dʒʌg/ n brocca f; (*small*) bricco m

juggernaut /'dʒʌgənɔːt/ n **I**

grosso autotreno m

juggle /'dʒʌgl/ vi fare giochi di destrezza. ~**r** n giocoliere, -a m f

juice /dʒuːs/ n succo m

juicy /'dʒuːsɪ/ adj (**-ier, -iest**) succoso; (**I:** *story*) piccante

juke-box /'dʒuːk-/ n juke-box m inv

July /dʒʊ'laɪ/ n luglio m

jumble /'dʒʌmbl/ n accozzaglia f ● vt ~ **[up]** mischiare. ~ **sale** n vendita f di beneficenza

jumbo /'dʒʌmbəʊ/ n ~ **[jet]** jumbo jet m inv

jump /dʒʌmp/ n salto m; (*in prices*) balzo m; (*in horse racing*) ostacolo m ● vi saltare; (*with fright*) sussultare; (*prices*): salire rapidamente; ~ **to conclusions** saltare alle conclusioni ● vt saltare; ~ **the gun** fig precipitarsi; ~ **the queue** non rispettare la fila. □ ~ **at** vt fig accettare con entusiasmo (*offer*). □ ~ **up** vi rizzarsi in piedi

jumper /'dʒʌmpə(r)/ n (*sweater*) golf m inv

jumpy /'dʒʌmpɪ/ adj nervoso

junction /'dʒʌŋkʃn/ n (*of roads*) incrocio m; (*of motorway*) uscita f; (*Rail*) nodo m ferroviario

June /dʒuːn/ n giugno m

jungle /'dʒʌŋgl/ n giungla f

junior /'dʒuːnɪə(r)/ adj giovane; (*in rank*) subalterno; (*Sport*) junior inv ● n **the** ~**s** (*Sch*) i più giovani. ~ **school** n scuola f elementare

junk /dʒʌŋk/ n cianfrusaglie fpl. ~ **food** n **I** cibo m poco sano, porcherie fpl. ~ **mail** posta f spazzatura

junkie /'dʒʌŋkɪ/ n **▣** tossico, -a m f

'junk-shop n negozio m di rigattiere

jurisdiction /dʒʊərɪs'dɪkʃn/ n giurisdizione f

juror /'dʒʊərə(r)/ n giurato, -a m f

jury /'dʒʊərɪ/ n giuria f

just /dʒʌst/ adj giusto ● adv (*barely*)

appena; (*simply*) solo; (*exactly*) esattamente; **~ as tall** altrettanto alto; **~ as I was leaving** proprio quando stavo andando via; **I've ~ seen** her l'ho appena vista; **it's ~ as well** meno male; **~ at that moment** proprio in quel momento; **~ listen!** ascolta!; **I'm ~ going** sto andando proprio ora

justice /'dʒʌstɪs/ n giustizia f; **do ~ to** rendere giustizia a; **J~ of the Peace** giudice m conciliatore

justifiabl|e /'dʒʌstɪfaɪəbl/ adj giustificabile

justi|fication /dʒʌstɪfɪ'keɪʃn/ n giustificazione f. **~fy** vt (*pt/pp* -**ied**) giustificare

jut /dʒʌt/ vi (*pt/pp* jutted) **~ out** sporgere

juvenile /'dʒu:vənaɪl/ adj giovanile; (*childish*) infantile; (*for the young*) per i giovani ●n giovane mf. **~ delinquency** n delinquenza f giovanile

Kk

kangaroo /kæŋgə'ru:/ n canguro m

karate /kə'rɑ:tɪ/ n karate m

keel /ki:l/ n chiglia f ●**keel over** vi capovolgersi

keen /ki:n/ adj (*intense*) acuto; (*interest*) vivo; (*eager*) entusiastico; (*competition*) feroce; (*wind, knife*) tagliente; **~ on** entusiasta di; **she's ~ on him** le piace molto; **be ~ to do sth** avere voglia di fare qcsa. **~ness** n entusiasmo m

keep /ki:p/ n (*maintenance*) mantenimento m; (*of castle*) maschio m; **for ~s** per sempre ● vt (*pt/pp* kept) ●vt tenere; (*not throw away*) conservare; (*detain*) trattenere; mantenere (family,

promise); avere (shop); allevare (animals); rispettare (law, rules); **~ sth hot** tenere qcsa in caldo; **~ sb from doing sth** impedire a qcno di fare qcsa.; **~ sb waiting** far aspettare qcno; **~ sth to oneself** tenere qcsa per sé; **~ sth from sb** tenere nascosto qcsa a qcno ● vi (*remain*) rimanere; (*food*) conservarsi; **~ calm** rimanere calmo; **~ left/right** tenere la destra/la sinistra; **~ [on] doing sth** continuare a fare qcsa. □ **~ back** vt trattenere (person); **~ sth back from sb** tenere nascosto qcsa a qcno ● vi tenersi indietro. □ **~ in with** vt mantenersi in buoni rapporti con. □ **~ on** vi [F] assillare (**at sb** qcno). □ **~ up** vi stare al passo ● vt (*continue*) continuare

kennel /'kenl/ n canile m; **~s** pl (*boarding*) canile m; (*breeding*) allevamento m di cani

Kenya /'kenjə/ n Kenia m. **~n** adj & n keniota mf

kept /kept/ ▷ **KEEP**

kerb /kɜ:b/ n bordo m del marciapiede

kerosene /'kerəsi:n/ n Am cherosene m

ketchup /'ketʃʌp/ n ketchup m

kettle /'ketl/ n bollitore m; **put the ~ on** mettere l'acqua a bollire

key /ki:/ n chiave f; (*of piano, typewriter*) tasto m ● vt **~ [in]** digitare (character); **could you ~ this?** puoi battere questo?

key:~board n (*Comput, Mus*) tastiera f. **~hole** n buco m della serratura. **~ring** n portachiavi m inv

khaki /'kɑ:kɪ/ adj cachi inv ●n cachi m

kick /kɪk/ n calcio m; (F: *thrill*) piacere m; **for ~s** [F] per spasso ● vt dar calci a; **~ the bucket** [F] crepare ● vi (animal): scalciare; (person): dare calci. □ **~ off** vi (Sport) dare il calcio d'inizio; [F] iniziare. □ **~ up** vt **~ up**

a row fare una scenata

'kick-off n (Sport) calcio m d'inizio

kid /kɪd/ n capretto m; (🔲: child) ragazzino, -a mf ● v (pt/pp **kidded**) ● vt 🔲 prendere in giro ● vi 🔲 scherzare

kidnap /'kɪdnæp/ vt (pt/pp **-napped**) rapire, sequestrare. **~per** n sequestratore, -trice mf, rapitore, -trice mf. **~ping** n rapimento m, sequestro m [di persona]

kidney /'kɪdnɪ/ n rene m; (Culin) rognone m. **~ machine** rene m artificiale

kill /kɪl/ vt uccidere; fig mettere fine a; ammazzare (time). **~er** n assassino, -a mf. **~ing** n uccisione f; (murder) omicidio m; **make a ~ing** fig fare un colpo grosso

kiln /kɪln/ n fornace f

kilo /'kiːlə/ n chilo m. **~byte** n kilobyte m inv. **~gram** n chilogrammo m. **~metre** /'kɪləmiːtə(r)/ n chilometro m. **~watt** n chilowatt m inv

kilt /kɪlt/ n kilt m inv (gonnellino degli scozzesi)

kin /kɪn/ n congiunti mpl; **next of ~** parente m stretto; parenti mpl stretti

kind¹ /kaɪnd/ n genere m, specie f; (brand, type) tipo m; **~ of** 🔲 alquanto; **two of a ~** due della stessa specie

kind² adj gentile, buono; **~ to animals** amante degli animali; **~ regards** cordiali saluti

kindergarten /'kɪndəgɑːtn/ n asilo m infantile

kindle /'kɪndl/ vt accendere

kind|ly /'kaɪndlɪ/ adj (-ier, -iest) benevolo ● adv gentilmente; (if you please) per favore. **~ness** n gentilezza f

king /kɪŋ/ n re m inv. **~dom** n regno m

king: ~fisher n martin m inv pescatore. **~-sized** adj (cigarette) king-size inv, lungo; (bed) matrimoniale

grande

kink /kɪŋk/ n nodo m. **~y** adj 🔲 bizzarro

kiosk /'kiːɒsk/ n chiosco m; (Teleph) cabina f telefonica

kipper /'kɪpə(r)/ n aringa f affumicata

kiss /kɪs/ n bacio m; **~ of life** respirazione f bocca a bocca ● vt baciare ● vi baciarsi

kit /kɪt/ n equipaggiamento m, kit m inv; (tools) attrezzi mpl; (construction ~) pezzi mpl da montare, kit m inv ● **kit out** vt (pt/pp **kitted**) equipaggiare. **~bag** n sacco m a spalla

kitchen /'kɪtʃɪn/ n cucina f ● attrib di cucina. **~ette** n cucinino m

kitchen towel Scottex® m inv

kite /kaɪt/ n aquilone m

kitten /'kɪtn/ n gattino m

knack /næk/ n tecnica f; **have the ~ for doing sth** avere la capacità di fare qcsa

knead /niːd/ vt impastare

knee /niː/ n ginocchio m. **~cap** n rotula f

kneel /niːl/ vi (pt/pp **knelt**) **~ [down]** inginocchiarsi; **be ~ing** essere inginocchiato

knelt /nelt/ ▷ **KNEEL**

knew /njuː/ ▷ **KNOW**

knickers /'nɪkəz/ npl mutandine fpl

knife /naɪf/ n (pl **knives**) coltello m ● vt 🔲 accoltellare

knight /naɪt/ n cavaliere m; (in chess) cavallo m ● vt nominare cavaliere

knit /nɪt/ vt/i (pt/pp **knitted**) lavorare a maglia; **~ one, purl one** un diritto, un rovescio. **~ting** n lavorare m a maglia; (work) lavoro m a maglia. **~ting-needle** n ferro m da calza. **~wear** n maglieria f

knives /naɪvz/ ▷ **KNIFE**

knob /nɒb/ n pomello m; (of stick) pomo m; (of butter) noce f. **~bly** adj nodoso; (bony) spigoloso

knock /nɒk/ n colpo m; **there was a ~ at the door** hanno bussato alla porta ● vt bussare a (door); (□: criticize) denigrare; **~ a hole in sth** fare un buco in qcsa; **~ one's head against** battere la testa (**on** contro) ● vi (at door) bussare. **□ ~ about** vt malmenare ● vi girovagare. **□ ~ down** vt far cadere; (with fist) stendere con un pugno; (in car) investire; (□: reduce) ribassare (price). **□ ~ off** vt (□: steal) fregare; (□: complete quickly) fare alla bell'e meglio ● vi (□: cease work) staccare. **□ ~ out** vt eliminare; (make unconscious) mettere K.O.; (□: anaesthetize) addormentare. **□ ~ over** vt rovesciare; (in car) investire

knock: **~er** n battente m. **~-kneed** /-'niːd/ adj con gambe storte. **~-out** n (in boxing) knock-out m inv

knot /nɒt/ n nodo m ● vt (pt/pp knotted) annodare

know /nəʊ/ v (pt knew, pp known) ● vt sapere; conoscere (person, place); (recognize) riconoscere; **get to ~ sb** conoscere qcno; **~ how to swim** sapere nuotare ● vi sapere; **did you ~ about this?** lo sapevi? ● n **in the ~** □ al corrente

know: **~-all** n □ sapientone, -a mf. **~-how** n abilità f. **~-ingly** adv (intentionally) consapevolmente; (smile etc) con un'aria d'intesa

knowledge /'nɒlɪdʒ/ n conoscenza f. **~able** adj ben informato

known /nəʊn/ ▷ KNOW ● adj noto

knuckle /'nʌkl/ n nocca f ● **knuckle down** vi darci sotto (**to** con). **□ ~ under** vi sottomettersi

Koran /kə'rɑːn/ n Corano m

Korea /kə'rɪə/ n Corea f. **~n** adj & n coreano, -a mf

kosher /'kəʊʃə(r)/ adj kasher inv

kudos /'kjuːdɒs/ n □ gloria f

L l

lab /læb/ n laboratorio m

label /'leɪbl/ n etichetta f ● vt (pt/pp labelled) mettere un'etichetta a; fig etichettare (person)

laboratory /lə'bɒrətri/ n laboratorio m

laborious /lə'bɔːrɪəs/ adj laborioso

labour /'leɪbə(r)/ n lavoro m; (workers) manodopera f; (Med) doglie fpl; **be in ~** avere le doglie; **L~** (Pol) partito m laburista ● attrib (Pol) laburista ● vi lavorare ● vt ~ **the point** fig ribadire il concetto. **~er** n manovale m

lace /leɪs/ n pizzo m; (of shoe) laccio m ● attrib di pizzo ● vt allacciare (shoes); correggere (drink)

lacerate /'læsəreɪt/ vt lacerare

lack /læk/ n mancanza f ● vt mancare di; **I ~ the time** mi manca il tempo ● vi **be ~ing** mancare; **he ~ing in sth** mancare di qcsa

lad /læd/ n ragazzo m

ladder /'lædə(r)/ n scala f; (in tights) sfilatura f

laden /'leɪdn/ adj carico (**with** di)

ladle /'leɪdl/ n mestolo m ● vt ~ **[out]** versare (col mestolo)

lady /'leɪdɪ/ n signora f; (title) Lady; **ladies [room]** bagno m per donne

lady: **~bird** n, Am **~bug** n coccinella f. **~-like** adj signorile

lag[1] /læg/ vi (pt/pp lagged) ~ **behind** restare indietro

lag[2] vt (pt/pp lagged) isolare (pipes)

lager /'lɑːgə(r)/ n birra f chiara

lagoon /lə'guːn/ n laguna f

laid /leɪd/ ▷ LAY[3]

lain /leɪn/ ▷ LIE[2]

lair /leə(r)/ n tana f

lake /leɪk/ n lago m

lamb /læm/ n agnello m

lame /leɪm/ adj zoppo; fig (argument) zoppicante; (excuse) traballante

lament /lə'ment/ n lamento m ● vt lamentare ● vi lamentarsi

lamentable /'læməntəbl/ adj deplorevole

lamp /læmp/ n lampada f; (in street) lampione m. ~**post** n lampione m. ~**shade** n paralume m

lance /lɑːns/ n fiocina f ● vt (Med) incidere. ~**-'corporal** n appuntato m

land /lænd/ n terreno m; (country) paese m; (as opposed to sea) terra f; **plot of ~** pezzo m di terreno ● vt (Naut) sbarcare; (fam: obtain) assicurarsi; **be ~ed with sth** 🔟 ritrovarsi fra capo e collo qcsa ● vi (Aeron) atterrare; (fall) cadere. □ **~ up** vi 🔟 finire

landing /'lændɪŋ/ n (Naut) sbarco m; (Aeron) atterraggio m; (top of stairs) pianerottolo m. ~**-stage** n pontile m da sbarco. ~ **strip** n pista f d'atterraggio di fortuna

land: ~**lady** n proprietaria f; (of flat) padrona f di casa. ~**lord** n proprietario m; (of flat) padrone m di casa. ~**mark** n punto m di riferimento; fig pietra f miliare. ~**scape** /-skeɪp/ n paesaggio m. ~**slide** n frana f; (Pol) valanga f di voti

lane /leɪn/ n sentiero m; (Auto, Sport) corsia f

language /'læŋgwɪdʒ/ n lingua f; (speech, style) linguaggio m. ~ **laboratory** n laboratorio m linguistico

lank /læŋk/ adj (hair) diritto

lanky /'læŋkɪ/ adj (-ier, -iest) allampanato

lantern /'læntən/ n lanterna f

lap¹ /læp/ n grembo m

lap² /læp/ n (of journey) tappa f; (Sport) giro m ● v (pt/pp lapped) ● vi (water:) ~ **against** lambire ● vt (Sport) doppiare

lap³ vt (pt/pp lapped) ~ **up** bere avidamente; bersi completamente (lies); credere ciecamente a (praise)

lapel /lə'pel/ n bavero m

lapse /læps/ n sbaglio m; (moral) sbandamento m [morale]; (of time) intervallo m ● vi (expire) scadere; (morally) scivolare; ~ **into** cadere in

laptop /'læptɒp/ n ~ **[computer]** computer m inv portabile, laptop m inv

lard /lɑːd/ n strutto m

larder /'lɑːdə(r)/ n dispensa f

large /lɑːdʒ/ adj grande; (number, amount) grande, grosso; **by and ~** in complesso; **at ~** in libertà; (in general) ampiamente. ~**ly** adv ampiamente; ~**ly because of** in gran parte a causa di

lark¹ /lɑːk/ n (bird) allodola f

lark² /lɑːk/ n (joke) burla f ● **lark about** vi giocherellare

larva /'lɑːvə/ n (pl **-vae** /-viː/) larva f

laser /'leɪzə(r)/ n laser m inv. ~ **printer** n stampante f laser

lash /læʃ/ n frustata f; (eyelash) ciglio m ● vt (whip) frustare; (tie) legare fermamente. □ ~ **out** vi attaccare; (spend) sperperare (on in)

lashings /'læʃɪŋz/ npl ~ **of** 🔟 una marea di

lass /læs/ n ragazzina f

lasso /lə'suː/ n lazo m

last /lɑːst/ adj (final) ultimo; (recent) scorso; ~ **year** l'anno scorso; ~ **night** ieri sera; **at ~** alla fine; **at ~!** finalmente!; **that's the ~ straw** 🔟 questa è l'ultima goccia ● n ultimo, -a m f; **the ~ but one** il penultimo ● adv per ultimo; (last time) l'ultima volta ● vi durare. ~**ing** adj durevole. ~**ly** adv infine

late /leɪt/ adj (delayed) in ritardo; (at a late hour) tardo; (deceased) defunto; **it's ~** è tardi; **in ~ November** alla fine di Novembre ● adv tardi; **stay up ~** stare alzati fino a tardi.

~comer n ritardatario, -a mf; (to political party etc) nuovo, -a arrivato, -a mf. **~ly** adv recentemente. **~ness** n ora f tarda; (delay) ritardo m

latent /'leɪtnt/ adj latente

later /'leɪtə(r)/ adj (train) che parte più tardi; (edition) più recente ● adv più tardi; **~ on** più tardi, dopo

lateral /'lætərəl/ adj laterale

latest /'leɪtɪst/ adj ultimo; (most recent) più recente; **the ~ [news]** le ultime notizie ● n **six o'clock at the ~** alle sei al più tardi

lathe /leɪð/ n tornio m

lather /'lɑːðə(r)/ n schiuma f ● vt insaponare ● vi far schiuma

Latin /'lætɪn/ adj latino ● n latino m. **~ America** n America f Latina. **~ American** adj & n latino-americano, -a mf

latitude /'lætɪtjuːd/ n (Geog) latitudine f; fig libertà f d'azione

latter /'lætə(r)/ adj ultimo. **~ly** adv ultimamente

Latvia /'lætvɪə/ n Lettonia f. **~n** adj & n lettone mf

laugh /lɑːf/ n risata f ● vi ridere (at/about di); **~ at sb** (mock) prendere in giro qcno. **~able** adj ridicolo. **~ing-stock** n zimbello m

laughter /'lɑːftə(r)/ n risata f

launch[1] /lɔːntʃ/ n (boat) varo m

launch[2] n lancio m; (of ship) varo m ● vt lanciare (rocket, product); varare (ship); sferrare (attack)

launder /'lɔːndə(r)/ vt lavare e stirare; **~ money** fig riciclare denaro sporco. **~ette** n lavanderia f automatica

laundry /'lɔːndrɪ/ n lavanderia f; (clothes) bucato m

lava /'lɑːvə/ n lava f

lavatory /'lævətrɪ/ n gabinetto m

lavish /'lævɪʃ/ adj copioso; (wasteful) prodigo; **on a ~ scale** su vasta scala

● vt **~ sth on sb** ricoprire qcno di qcsa. **~ly** adv copiosamente

law /lɔː/ n legge f; **study ~** studiare giurisprudenza, studiare legge; **~ and order** ordine m pubblico

lawcourt n tribunale m

lawn /lɔːn/ n prato m [all'inglese]. **~-mower** n tosaerbe m inv

'law suit n causa f

lawyer /'lɔːjə(r)/ n avvocato m

lax /læks/ adj negligente; (morals etc) lassista

laxative /'læksətɪv/ n lassativo m

lay[1] /leɪ/ adj laico; fig profano

lay[2] ▷LIE[2]

lay[3] vt (pt/pp **laid**) porre, mettere; apparecchiare (table) ● vi (hen): fare le uova. □ **~ down** vt posare; stabilire (rules, conditions). □ **~ off** vt licenziare (workers) ● vi (⚠: stop): **~ off!** smettila! **lay out** vt (display, set forth) esporre; (plan) pianificare (garden); (spend) sborsare; (Typ) impaginare

lay: ~about n fannullone, -a mf. **~-by** n corsia f di sosta

layer /'leɪə(r)/ n strato m

lay: ~man n profano m. **~out** n disposizione f; (Typ) impaginazione f, layout m inv

laze /leɪz/ vi [**about**] oziare

laziness /'leɪzɪnɪs/ n pigrizia f

lazy /'leɪzɪ/ adj (-ier, -iest) pigro. **~-bones** n poltrone, -a mf

lead[1] /led/ n piombo m; (of pencil) mina f

lead[2] /liːd/ n guida f; (leash) guinzaglio m; (flex) filo m; (clue) indizio m; (Theat) parte f principale; (distance ahead) distanza f (over su); **in the ~** in testa ● v (pt/pp **led**) vt condurre; dirigere (expedition, party etc); (induce) indurre. **~ the way** mettersi in testa ● vi (be in front) condurre; (in race, competition) essere in testa; (at cards) giocare (per primo). □ **~ away** vt portar via. □ **~ to** vt portare a.

□ **~ up to** vt preludere; **what's this ~ing up to?** dove porta questo?

leader /'liːdə(r)/ n capo m; (of orchestra) primo violino m; (in newspaper) articolo m di fondo. **~ship** n direzione f, leadership f; (in management) show **~ship** mostrare capacità di comando

leading /'liːdɪŋ/ adj principale; **~ lady/man** attrice f/attore m principale; **~ question** domanda f tendenziosa

leaf /liːf/ n (pl **leaves**) foglia f; (of table) asse f. **leaf through** vt sfogliare. **~let** n dépliant m inv; (advertising) dépliant m inv pubblicitario; (political) manifestino m

league /liːg/ n lega f; (Sport) campionato m; **be in ~ with** essere in combutta con

leak /liːk/ n (hole) fessura f; (Naut) falla f; (of gas & fig) fuga f ● vi colare; (ship:) fare acqua; (liquid, gas:) fuoriuscire ● vt **~ sth to sb** fig far trapelare qcsa a qcno. **~y** adj che perde; (Naut) che fa acqua

lean¹ /liːn/ adj magro

lean² /liːn/ v (pt/pp **leaned** or **leant** /lent/) ● vt appoggiare (**against**/**on** contro/su) ● vi appoggiarsi (**against**/**on** contro/su); (not be straight) pendere; **be ~ing against** essere appoggiato contro; **~ on sb** (depend on) appoggiarsi a qcno; (⊡: exert pressure on) stare alle calcagne di qcno. □ **~ back** vi sporgersi indietro. □ **~ forward** vi piegarsi in avanti. □ **~ out** vi sporgersi. □ **~ over** vi piegarsi

leaning /'liːnɪŋ/ adj pendente; **the L~ Tower of Pisa** la torre di Pisa, la torre pendente ● n tendenza f

leap /liːp/ n salto m ● vi (pt/pp **leapt** /lept/ or **leaped**) saltare; **he leapt at it** ⊡ l'ha preso al volo. **~-frog** n cavallina f. **~ year** n anno m bisestile

learn /lɜːn/ v (pt/pp **learnt** or **learned**) ● vt imparare; **~ to swim** imparare a nuotare; **I have ~ed that...** (heard) sono venuto a sapere

che... ● vi imparare

learn|ed /'lɜːnɪd/ adj colto. **~er** n also (Auto) principiante mf. **~ing** n cultura f. **~ing curve** n curva f d'apprendimento

lease /liːs/ n contratto m d'affitto; (rental) affitto m ● vt affittare

leash /liːʃ/ n guinzaglio m

least /liːst/ adj più piccolo; (amount) minore; **you've got ~ luggage** hai meno bagagli di tutti ● n the **~** il meno; **at ~** almeno; **not in the ~** niente affatto ● adv meno; **the ~ expensive wine** il vino meno caro

leather /'leðə(r)/ n pelle f; (of soles) cuoio m ● attrib di pelle/cuoio. **~y** adj (meat, skin) duro

leave /liːv/ n (holiday) congedo m; (Mil) licenza f; **on ~** in congedo/licenza ● v (pt/pp **left**) ● vt lasciare; uscire da (house, office); (forget) dimenticare; **there is nothing left** non è rimasto niente ● vi andare via; (train, bus:) partire. □ **~ behind** vt lasciare; (forget) dimenticare. □ **~ out** vt omettere; (not put away) lasciare fuori

leaves /liːvz/ ▷**LEAF**

Leban|on /'lebənən/ n Libano m. **~ese** /-'niːz/ adj & n libanese mf

lecture /'lektʃə(r)/ n conferenza f; (Univ) lezione f; (reproof) ramanzina f ● vi fare una conferenza (**on** su); (Univ) insegnare (**on sth** qcsa) ● vt **~ sb** rimproverare qcno. **~r** n conferenziere, -a mf; (Univ) docente mf universitario, -a

led /led/ ▷**LEAD²**

ledge /ledʒ/ n cornice f; (of window) davanzale m

leek /liːk/ n porro m

leer /lɪə(r)/ n sguardo m libidinoso ● vi **~ [at]** guardare in modo libidinoso

left¹ /left/ ▷**LEAVE**

left² adj sinistro ● adv a sinistra ● n also (Pol) sinistra f; **on the ~**

a sinistra;

left: **~-handed** adj mancino. **~-'luggage office** n deposito m bagagli. **~-overs** npl rimasugli mpl. **~-wing** adj (Pol) di sinistra

leg /leg/ n gamba f; (of animal) zampa f; (of journey) tappa f; (Culin: of chicken) coscia f; (: of lamb) cosciotto m

legacy /'legəsɪ/ n lascito m

legal /'liːgl/ adj legale; **take ~ action** intentare un'azione legale. **~ly** adv legalmente

legality /lɪ'gælətɪ/ n legalità f

legalize /'liːgəlaɪz/ vt legalizzare

legend /'ledʒənd/ n leggenda f. **~ary** adj leggendario

legib|le /'ledʒəbl/ adj leggibile. **~ly** adv in modo leggibile

legislat|e /'ledʒɪsleɪt/ vi legiferare. **~ion** n legislazione f

legitimate /lɪ'dʒɪtɪmət/ adj legittimo; (excuse) valido

leisure /'leʒə(r)/ n tempo m libero; **at your ~** con comodo. **~ly** adj senza fretta

lemon /'lemən/ n limone m. **~ade** n limonata f

lend /lend/ vt (pt/pp lent) prestare; **~ a hand** fig dare una mano. **~ing library** n biblioteca f per il prestito

length /leŋθ/ n lunghezza f; (piece) pezzo m; (of wallpaper) parte f; (of visit) durata f; **at ~** a lungo; (at last) alla fine

length|en /'leŋθən/ vt allungare ● vi allungarsi. **~ways** adv per lungo

lengthy /'leŋθɪ/ adj (-ier, -iest) lungo

lens /lenz/ n lente f; (Phot) obiettivo m; (of eye) cristallino m

lent /lent/ ▷ LEND

Lent n Quaresima f

Leo /'liːəʊ/ n (Astr) Leone m

leopard /'lepəd/ n leopardo m

leotard /'liːətɑːd/ n body m inv

lesbian /'lezbɪən/ adj lesbico ● n lesbica f

less /les/ adj meno di; **~ and ~** sempre meno ● adv & prep meno ● n meno m

lessen /'lesn/ vt/i diminuire

lesson /'lesn/ n lezione f

lest /lest/ conj liter per timore che

let /let/ vt (pt/pp let, pres p letting) lasciare, permettere; (rent) affittare; **~ alone** (not to mention) tanto meno; **'to ~'** 'affittasi'; **~ us go** andiamo; **~ sb do sth** lasciare fare qcsa a qcno, permettere a qcno di fare qcsa; **~ me know** fammi sapere; **just ~ him try!** che ci provi solamente!; **~ oneself in for sth** ⨂ impelagarsi in qcsa. **~ down** vt sciogliere (hair); abbassare (blinds); (lengthen) allungare; (disappoint) deludere; **don't ~ me down** conta su di te. **~ in** vt far entrare. **~ off** vt far partire; (not punish) perdonare; **~ sb off doing sth** abbonare qcsa a qcno. **~ out** vt far uscire; (make larger) allargare; emettere (scream, groan). **~ through** vt far passare. **~ up** vi ⨂ diminuire

'let-down n ⨂ delusione f

lethal /'liːθl/ adj letale

letharg|ic /lɪ'θɑːdʒɪk/ adj apatico. **~y** n apatia f

letter /'letə(r)/ n lettera f. **~-box** n buca f per le lettere. **~-head** n carta f intestata. **~ing** n caratteri mpl

lettuce /'letɪs/ n lattuga f

'let-up n ⨂ pausa f

leukaemia /luːˈkiːmɪə/ n leucemia f

level /'levl/ adj piano; (in height, competition) allo stesso livello; (spoonful) raso; **draw ~ with sb** affiancare qcno ● n livello m; **on the ~** ⨂ giusto ● vt (pt/pp levelled) livellare; (aim) puntare (at su)

level 'crossing n passaggio m a livello

lever /'liːvə(r)/ n leva f ● **lever up** vt sollevare (con una leva). **~age** ~n azione f di una leva; fig influenza f

levy /'levi/ vt (pt/pp levied) imporre (tax)

lewd /ljuːd/ adj osceno

liabilit|y /laɪə'bɪlətɪ/ n responsabilità f; (🔲: burden) peso m; **~ies** pl debiti mpl

liable /'laɪəbl/ adj responsabile (for di); **be ~ to** (rain, brake etc) rischiare di; (tend to) tendere a

liaise /lɪ'eɪz/ vi 🔲 essere in contatto

liaison /lɪ'eɪzɒn/ n contatti mpl; (Mil) collegamento m; (affair) relazione f

liar /'laɪə(r)/ n bugiardo, -a mf

libel /'laɪbl/ n diffamazione f ● vt (pt/pp libelled) diffamare. **~lous** adj diffamatorio

liberal /'lɪb(ə)rəl/ adj (tolerant) di larghe vedute; (generous) generoso. **L~** adj (Pol) liberale ● n liberale m/f

liberat|e /'lɪbəreɪt/ vt liberare. **~ed** adj (woman) emancipata. **~ion** n liberazione f; (of women) emancipazione f. **~or** n liberatore, -trice mf

liberty /'lɪbətɪ/ n libertà f; **take the ~ of doing** sth prendersi la libertà di fare qcsa; **be at ~ to do** sth essere libero di fare qcsa

Libra /'liːbrə/ n (Astr) Bilancia f

librarian /laɪ'breərɪən/ n bibliotecario, -a mf

library /'laɪbrərɪ/ n biblioteca f

Libya /'lɪbɪə/ n Libia f. **~n** adj & n libico, -a mf

lice /laɪs/ ▷ **LOUSE**

licence /'laɪsns/ n licenza f; (for TV) canone m televisivo; (for driving) patente f; (freedom) sregolatezza f. **~-plate** n targa f

license /'laɪsns/ vt autorizzare; **be ~d** (car:) avere il bollo; (restaurant:) essere autorizzato alla vendita di alcolici

lick /lɪk/ n leccata f; **a ~ of paint**

una passata leggera di pittura ● vt leccare; (🔲: defeat) battere; leccarsi (lips)

lid /lɪd/ n coperchio m; (of eye) palpebra f

lie¹ /laɪ/ n bugia f; **tell a ~** mentire ● vi (pt/pp lied, pres p lying) mentire

lie² vi (pt lay, pp lain, pres p lying) (person:) sdraiarsi; (object:) stare; (remain) rimanere; **leave** sth **lying about** or **around** lasciare qcsa in giro. □ **~ down** vi sdraiarsi

lie-in n 🔲 **have a ~** restare a letto fino a tardi

lieutenant /lef'tenənt/ n tenente m

life /laɪf/ n (pl **lives**) vita f

life: **~belt** n salvagente m. **~boat** n lancia f di salvataggio; (on ship) scialuppa f di salvataggio. **~buoy** n salvagente m. **~coach** n life coach m/f inv. **~guard** n bagnino m. **~jacket** n giubbotto m di salvataggio. **~less** adj inanimato. **~like** adj realistico. **~long** adj di tutta la vita. **~size[d]** adj in grandezza naturale. **~time** n vita f; **the chance of a ~time** un'occasione unica

lift /lɪft/ n ascensore m; (Auto) passaggio m ● vt sollevare; revocare (restrictions); (🔲: steal) rubare ● vi (fog:) alzarsi. □ **~ up** vt sollevare

'lift-off n decollo m (di razzo)

light¹ /laɪt/ adj (not dark) luminoso; **~ green** verde chiaro ● n luce f; (lamp) lampada f; **in the ~ of** fig alla luce di; **have you got a ~?** ha da accendere?; **come to ~** essere rivelato ● vt (pt/pp **lit** or **lighted**) accendere; (illuminate) illuminare. □ **~ up** vi (face:) illuminarsi

light² adj (not heavy) leggero ● adv **travel ~** viaggiare con poco bagaglio

'light-bulb n lampadina f

lighten¹ /'laɪtn/ vt illuminare

lighten² vt alleggerire (load)

lighter /'laɪtə(r)/ n accendino m

light: ~**-hearted** adj spensierato. ~**house** n faro m. ~**ly** adv leggermente; (accuse) con leggerezza; (without concern) senza dare importanza alla cosa; **get off** ~**ly** cavarsela a buon mercato

lightning /'laɪtnɪŋ/ n lampo m, fulmine m. ~**-conductor** n para fulmine m

lightweight adj leggero ●n (in boxing) peso m leggero

like[1] /laɪk/ adj simile ● prep come; ~ **this/that** così; **what's he** ~? com'è? ● conj (fam: as) come; (Am: as if) come se

like[2] vt piacere, gradire; **I should/ would** ~ vorrei, gradirei; **I** ~ **him** mi piace; **I** ~ **this car** mi piace questa macchina; **I** ~ **dancing** mi piace ballare; **I** ~ **that!** [1] questa mi è piaciuta! ●n ~**s and dislikes** pl gusti mpl

like|able /'laɪkəbl/ adj simpatico. ~**lihood** n probabilità f. ~**ly** adj (-ier, -iest) probabile ● adv probabilmente; **not** ~**ly!** [1] neanche per sogno!

liken /'laɪkn/ vt paragonare (**to** a)

like|ness /'laɪknɪs/ n somiglianza f. ~**wise** adv lo stesso

liking /'laɪkɪŋ/ n gusto m; **is it to your** ~? è di suo gusto?; **take a** ~ **to sb** prendere qcno in simpatia

lilac /'laɪlək/ n lillà m ● adj color lillà

lily /'lɪlɪ/ n giglio m. ~ **of the valley** n mughetto m

limb /lɪm/ n arto m

lime[1] /laɪm/ n (fruit) cedro m; (tree) tiglio m

lime[2] n calce f. ~**light** n **be in the** ~**light** essere molto in vista. ~**stone** n calcare m

limit /'lɪmɪt/ n limite m; **that's the** ~! [1] questo è troppo! ● vt limitare (**to** a). ~**ation** n limite m. ~**ed** adj ristretto; ~**ed company** società f

anonima

limousine /'lɪməziːn/ n limousine f inv

limp[1] /lɪmp/ n andatura f zoppicante; **have a** ~ zoppicare ● vi zoppicare

limp[2] adj floscio

line[1] /laɪn/ n linea f; (length of rope, cord) filo m; (of writing) riga f; (of poem) verso m; (row) fila f; (wrinkle) ruga f; (of business) settore m; (Am: queue) coda f; **in** ~ **with** in conformità con ● vt segnare; fiancheggiare (street). □ ~ **up** vi allinearsi ● vt allineare

line[2] vt foderare (garment)

lined[1] /laɪnd/ adj (face) rugoso; (paper) a righe

lined[2] adj (garment) foderato

linen /'lɪnɪn/ n lino m; (articles) biancheria f ● attrib di lino

liner /'laɪnə(r)/ n nave f di linea

linger /'lɪŋɡə(r)/ vi indugiare

lingerie /'læ̃əʒəriː/ n biancheria f intima (da donna)

linguist /'lɪŋɡwɪst/ n linguista mf

linguistic /lɪŋ'ɡwɪstɪk/ adj linguistico. ~**s** n linguistica fsg

lining /'laɪnɪŋ/ n (of garment) fodera f; (of brakes) guarnizione f

link /lɪŋk/ n (of chain) anello m; fig legame m ● vt collegare. □ ~ **up** vi unirsi (**with** a); (TV) collegarsi

lino /'laɪnəʊ/ n, **linoleum** /lɪ'nəʊlɪəm/ n linoleum m

lint /lɪnt/ n garza f

lion /'laɪən/ n leone m. ~**ess** n leonessa f

lip /lɪp/ n labbro m (pl labbra f); (edge) bordo m

lip: ~**read** vi leggere le labbra; ~**service** n **pay** ~**service** to approvare soltanto a parole. ~**salve** n burro m [di] cacao. ~**stick** n rossetto m

liqueur /lɪ'kjʊə(r)/ n liquore m

liquid /'lɪkwɪd/ n liquido m ● adj

liquido

liquidat|e /'lɪkwɪdeɪt/ vt liquidare. **~ion** n liquidazione f; (Comm) **go into ~ion** andare in liquidazione

liquidize /'lɪkwɪdaɪz/ vt rendere liquido. **~r** n (Culin) frullatore m

liquor /'lɪkə(r)/ n bevanda f alcoolica

liquorice /'lɪkərɪs/ n liquirizia f

liquor store n Am negozio m di alcolici

lisp /lɪsp/ n pronuncia f con la lisca ● vi parlare con la lisca

list¹ /lɪst/ n lista f ● vt elencare

list² vi (ship:) inclinarsi

listen /'lɪsn/ vi ascoltare; **~ to** ascoltare. **~er** n ascoltatore, -trice mf

listless /'lɪstlɪs/ adj svogliato

lit /lɪt/ ▷ LIGHT¹

literacy /'lɪtərəsɪ/ n alfabetizzazione f

literal /'lɪtərəl/ adj letterale. **~ly** adv letteralmente

literary /'lɪtərərɪ/ adj letterario

literate /'lɪtərət/ adj **be ~** saper leggere e scrivere

literature /'lɪtrətʃə(r)/ n letteratura f

Lithuania /lɪθjʊ'eɪnɪə/ n Lituania f. **~n** adj e n lituano, -a mf

litre /'li:tə(r)/ n litro m

litter /'lɪtə(r)/ n immondizie fpl; (Zool) figliata f ● vt **be ~ed with** essere ingombrato di. **~-bin** n bidone m della spazzatura

little /'lɪtl/ adj piccolo; (not much) poco ● adv & n poco m; **a ~** un po'; **a ~ water** un po' d'acqua; **a ~ better** un po' meglio; **~ by ~** a poco a poco

live¹ /laɪv/ adj vivo; (ammunition) carico; **~ broadcast** trasmissione f in diretta; **be ~d** (Electr) essere sotto tensione; **~ wire** n fig persona f dinamica ● adv (broadcast) in diretta

live² /lɪv/ vi vivere; (reside) abitare; **~ with** convivere con. **□ ~ down** vt far dimenticare. **□ ~ off** vt vivere alle spalle di. **□ ~ on** vt vivere di ● vi sopravvivere. **□ ~ up** vt **~ it up** fare la bella vita. **□ ~ up to** vt essere all'altezza di

liveli|hood /'laɪvlɪhʊd/ n mezzi mpl di sostentamento. **~ness** n vivacità f

lively /'laɪvlɪ/ adj (-ier, -iest) vivace

liver /'lɪvə(r)/ n fegato m

lives /laɪvz/ ▷ LIFE

livestock /'laɪv-/ n bestiame m

livid /'lɪvɪd/ adj lividо

living /'lɪvɪŋ/ adj vivo ● n **earn one's ~** guadagnarsi da vivere; **the ~** pl i vivi. **~-room** n soggiorno m

lizard /'lɪzəd/ n lucertola f

load /ləʊd/ n carico m; **~s of** un sacco di ● vt caricare. **~ed** adj carico; (②: rich) ricchissimo

loaf¹ /ləʊf/ n (pl loaves) pagnotta f

loaf² vi oziare

loan /ləʊn/ n prestito m; **on ~** in prestito ● vt prestare

loath|e /ləʊð/ vt detestare. **~ing** n disgusto m. **~some** adj disgustoso

lobby /'lɒbɪ/ n atrio m; (Pol) gruppo m di pressione, lobby f inv

lobster /'lɒbstə(r)/ n aragosta f

local /'ləʊkl/ adj locale; **I'm not ~** non sono del posto ● n abitante mf del luogo; (②: public house) pub m locale. **□ au'thority** n autorità f locale. **□ call** n (Teleph) telefonata f urbana. **□ government** n autorità f inv locale

locality /ləʊ'kælətɪ/ n zona f

local|ization /ləʊklaɪ'zeɪʃn/ n localizzazione f. **~ized** adj localizzato

locally /'ləʊkəlɪ/ adv localmente; (live, work) nei paraggi

locat|e /ləʊ'keɪt/ vt situare; trovare (person); **be ~ed** essere situato. **~ion** n posizione f; **filmed**

on ∼ion girato in esterni

lock¹ /lɒk/ n (hair) ciocca f

lock² n (on door) serratura f; (on canal) chiusa f ● vt chiudere a chiave; bloccare (wheels) ● vi chiudersi. □ ∼ **in** vt chiudere dentro. □ ∼ **out** vt chiudere fuori. □ ∼ **up** vt (in prison) mettere dentro ● vi chiudere

locker /'lɒkə(r)/ n armadietto m

locket /'lɒkɪt/ n medaglione m

lock: ∼**out** n serrata f. ∼**smith** n fabbro m

locomotive /ləʊkə'məʊtɪv/ n locomotiva f

lodge /lɒdʒ/ n (porter's) portineria f; (masonic) loggia f ● vt presentare (claim, complaint); (with bank, solicitor) depositare; be ∼d essersi conficcato ● vi essere a pensione (**with** da); (become fixed) conficcarsi. ∼**r** n inquilino, -a mf

lodgings /'lɒdʒɪŋz/ npl camere fpl in affitto

loft /lɒft/ n soffitta f

lofty /'lɒftɪ/ adj (-ier, -iest) alto; (haughty) altezzoso

log /lɒg/ n ceppo m; (Auto) libretto m di circolazione; (Naut) giornale m di bordo ● vt (pt **logged**) registrare. □ ∼ **on to** vt (Comput) connettersi a

logarithm /'lɒgərɪðm/ n logaritmo m

'log-book n (Naut) giornale m di bordo; (Auto) libretto m di circolazione

loggerheads /'lɒgə-/ npl **be at** ∼ [i] essere in totale disaccordo

logic /'lɒdʒɪk/ n logica f. ∼**al** adj logico. ∼**ally** adv logicamente

logistics /lə'dʒɪstɪks/ npl logistica f

logo /'ləʊgəʊ/ n logo m inv

loin /lɔɪn/ n (Culin) lombata f

loiter /'lɔɪtə(r)/ vi gironzolare

lollipop /'lɒlɪpɒp/ n lecca-lecca m inv. ∼**y** n lecca-lecca m; ([i]: money)

quattrini mpl

London /'lʌndən/ n Londra f ● attrib londinese, di Londra. ∼**er** n londinese mf

lone /ləʊn/ adj solitario. ∼**liness** n solitudine f

lonely /'ləʊnlɪ/ adj (-ier, -iest) solitario; (person) solo

lone|r /'ləʊnə(r)/ n persona f solitaria. ∼**some** adj solo

long¹ /lɒŋ/ adj lungo; a ∼ **time** molto tempo; a ∼ **way** distante; **in the** ∼ **run** a lungo andare; (in the end) alla fin fine ● adv a lungo, lungamente; **how** ∼ **is?** quanto è lungo?; (in time) quanto dura?; **all day** ∼ tutto il giorno; **not** ∼ **ago** non molto tempo fa; **before** ∼ fra breve; **he's no** ∼**er here** non è più qui; **or so** ∼**as** finché; (provided that) purché; **so** ∼**!** [i] ciao!; **will you be** ∼**?** [ti] ci vuole molto?

long² vi ∼ **for** desiderare ardentemente

long-'distance adj a grande distanza; (Sport) di fondo; (call) interurbano

longing /'lɒŋɪŋ/ adj desideroso ● n brama f. ∼**ly** adv con desiderio

longitude /'lɒŋgɪtjuːd/ n (Geog) longitudine f

long: ∼ **jump** n salto m in lungo. ∼**-range** adj (Aeron, Mil) a lunga portata; (forecast) a lungo termine. ∼**-sighted** adj presbite. ∼**-term** adj a lunga scadenza. ∼**-winded** /-'wɪndɪd/ adj prolisso

loo /luː/ n [i] gabinetto m

look /lʊk/ n occhiata f; (appearance) aspetto m; [**good**] ∼**s** pl bellezza f; **have a** ∼ **at** dare un'occhiata a ● vi guardare; (seem) sembrare; ∼ **here!** ml ascolti bene!; ∼ **at** guardare; ∼ **for** cercare; ∼ **like** (resemble) assomigliare a. □ ∼ **after** vt badare a. ∼ **down** vi guardare in basso; ∼ **down on sb** fig guardare dall'alto in basso qcno. ◻ ~ **forward to** vt essere impaziente di. ◻ ~ **in on** vt passare da. ◻ ~ **into** (examine) esaminare. ◻ ~ **on to** vt (room): dare su. ◻ ~ **out** vi guardare fuori; (take care) fare attenzione; ~ **out for** cercare; ~ **out** vt attento! **look round** vi girarsi; (in shop, town etc) dare un'occhiata a. ◻ ~ **through** vt dare un'occhiata a (script, notes). ◻ ~ **up** vi guardare in alto; ~ **up to sb** fig rispettare qcno ● vt cercare [nel dizionario] (word); (visit) andare a trovare

'**look-out** n guardia f; (prospect) prospettiva f; **be on the ~ for** tenere gli occhi aperti per

loom /luːm/ vi apparire; fig profilarsi

loony /'luːnɪ/ adj & n 🖪 matto. ~a. mf. ~ **bin** n manicomio m

loop /luːp/ n cappio m; (in garment) passante m. ~**hole** n (in the law) scappatoia f

loose /luːs/ adj libero; (knot) allentato; (page) staccato; (clothes) largo; (morals) dissoluto; (inexact) vago; **be at a ~ end** non sapere cosa fare; **come ~** (knot): sciogliersi; **set ~** liberare. ~ **change** n spiccioli mpl. ~**ly** adv scorrevolmente; (defined) vagamente

loosen /'luːsn/ vt sciogliere

loot /luːt/ n bottino m ● vt/i depredare. ~**er** n predatore, -trice mf. ~**ing** n saccheggio m

lop /lɒp/ ~ **off** vt (pt/pp lopped) potare

lop'sided adj sbilenco

lord /lɔːd/ n signore m; (title) Lord m; **House of L~s** Camera f dei Lords; **the L~'s Prayer** il Padrenostro; **good L~!** Dio mio!

lorry /'lɒrɪ/ n camion m inv; ~ **driver** n camionista mf

lose /luːz/ v (pt/pp lost) ● vt perdere ● vi perdere; (clock): essere indietro; **get lost** perdersi; **get lost!** 🖪 va a quel paese! ~**r** n perdente mf

loss /lɒs/ n perdita f; (Comm) ~**es** perdite fpl; **be at a ~** essere perplesso; **be at a ~ for words** non trovare le parole

lost /lɒst/ ▷**LOSE** ● adj perduto. ~ '**property office** n ufficio m oggetti smarriti

lot[1] /lɒt/ (at auction) lotto m; **draw** ~**s** tirare a sorte

lot[2] n **the** ~ il tutto; **a ~ of**, ~**s of** molto/i; **the** ~ **of you** tutti voi; **it has changed a ~** è cambiato molto

lotion /'ləʊʃn/ n lozione f

lottery /'lɒtərɪ/ n lotteria f. ~ **ticket** n biglietto m della lotteria

loud /laʊd/ adj sonoro, alto; (colours) sgargiante ● adv forte; **out** ~ ad alta voce. ~'**hailer** n megafono m. ~**ly** adv forte. ~'**speaker** n altoparlante m

lounge /laʊndʒ/ n salotto m; (in hotel) salone m ● vi poltrire. ~ **suit** n vestito m da uomo, completo m da uomo

louse /laʊs/ n (pl lice) pidocchio m

lousy /'laʊzɪ/ adj (-ier, -iest) 🖪 schifoso

lout /laʊt/ n zoticone m. ~**ish** adj rozzo

lovable /'lʌvəbl/ adj adorabile

love /lʌv/ n amore m; (Tennis) zero m; **in** ~ innamorato (with di) ● vt amare (person, country); **I** ~ **watching tennis** mi piace molto guardare il tennis. ~**affair** n relazione f [sentimentale]. ~ **letter** n lettera f d'amore

lovely /'lʌvlɪ/ adj (-ier, -iest) bello; (in looks) bello, attraente; (in character) piacevole; (meal) delizioso; **have a ~ time** divertirsi molto

lover /'lʌvə(r)/ n amante mf

loving /'lʌvɪŋ/ adj affettuoso

low /ləʊ/ adj basso; (depressed) giù inv ● adv basso; **feel** ~ sentirsi giù ● n minimo m; (Meteorol) depressione f

at an all-time ∼ (prices *etc*) al livello minimo

lower /'ləʊə(r)/ *adj & adv* ▷**LOW** ● *vt* abbassare: ∼ **oneself** abbassarsi

loyal /'lɔɪəl/ *adj* leale. ∼**ty** *n* lealtà *f*; ∼ **card** carta *f* fedeltà

lozenge /'lɒzɪndʒ/ *n* losanga *f*; (*tablet*) pastiglia *f*

LP *n abbr* long-playing record

Ltd *abbr* (Limited) s.r.l.

lubricat|e /'lu:brɪkeɪt/ *vt* lubrificare. ∼**ion** *n* lubrificazione *f*

lucid /'lu:sɪd/ *adj* (explanation) chiaro; (*sane*) lucido. ∼**ity** *n* lucidità *f*; (*of explanation*) chiarezza *f*

luck /lʌk/ *n* fortuna *f*; **bad** ∼ sfortuna *f*; **good** ∼! buona fortuna! ∼**ily** *adv* fortunatamente

lucky /'lʌkɪ/ *adj* (**-ier, -iest**) fortunato; **be** ∼ essere fortunato; (*thing:*) portare fortuna. ∼ **'charm** *n* portafortuna *m inv*

lucrative /'lu:krətɪv/ *adj* lucrativo

ludicrous /'lu:dɪkrəs/ *adj* ridicolo. ∼**ly** *adv* (expensive, complex) eccessivamente

lug /lʌɡ/ *vt* (*pt/pp* **lugged**) 🔲 trascinare

luggage /'lʌɡɪdʒ/ *n* bagaglio *m*; ∼**-rack** *n* portabagagli *m inv*. ∼ **trolley** *n* carrello *m* portabagagli. ∼**-van** *n* bagagliaio *m*

lukewarm /'lu:k-/ *adj* tiepido; *fig* poco entusiasta

lull /lʌl/ *n* pausa *f* ● *vt* ∼ **to sleep** cullare

lullaby /'lʌləbaɪ/ *n* ninna nanna *f*

lumber /'lʌmbə(r)/ *n* cianfrusaglie *fpl*; (*Am: timber*) legname *m* ● *vt* 🔲 ∼ **sb with sth** affibbiare qcsa a qcno. ∼ **jack** *n* tagliaboschi *m inv*

luminous /'lu:mɪnəs/ *adj* luminoso

lump¹ /lʌmp/ *n* (*of sugar*) zolletta *f*; (*swelling*) gonfiore *m*; (*in breast*) nodulo *m*; (*in sauce*) grumo *m* ● *vt* ∼

together ammucchiare

lump² *vt* ∼ **it** 🔲 **you'll just have to** ∼ **it** che ti piaccia o no è così

lump sum *n* somma *f* globale

lumpy /'lʌmpɪ/ *adj* (**-ier, -iest**) grumoso

lunacy /'lu:nəsɪ/ *n* follia *f*

lunar /'lu:nə(r)/ *adj* lunare

lunatic /'lu:nətɪk/ *n* pazzo, -a *mf*

lunch /lʌntʃ/ *n* pranzo *m* ● *vi* pranzare

luncheon /'lʌntʃn/ *n* (*formal*) pranzo *m*. ∼ **meat** *n* carne *f* in scatola. ∼ **voucher** *n* buono *m* pasto

lung /lʌŋ/ *n* polmone *m*. ∼ **cancer** *n* cancro *m* al polmone

lunge /lʌndʒ/ *vi* lanciarsi (**at** su)

lurch¹ /lɜ:tʃ/ *n* **leave in the** ∼ 🔲 lasciare nei guai

lurch² *vi* barcollare

lure /lʊə(r)/ *n* esca *f*; *fig* lusinga *f* ● *vt* adescare

lurid /'lʊərɪd/ *adj* (*gaudy*) sgargiante; (*sensational*) sensazionalistico

lurk /lɜ:k/ *vi* appostarsi

luscious /'lʌʃəs/ *adj* saporito; *fig* sexy *inv*

lush /lʌʃ/ *adj* lussureggiante

lust /lʌst/ *n* lussuria *f* ● *vi* ∼ **after** desiderare [fortemente]. ∼**ful** *adj* lussurioso

lute /lu:t/ *n* liuto *m*

luxuriant /lʌɡ'ʒʊərɪənt/ *adj* lussureggiante

luxurious /lʌɡ'ʒʊərɪəs/ *adj* lussuoso

luxury /'lʌkʃərɪ/ *n* lusso *m* ● *attrib* di lusso

lying /'laɪɪŋ/ ▷**LIE¹** & **²** ● *n* mentire *m*

lynch /lɪntʃ/ *vt* linciare

lyric /'lɪrɪk/ *adj* lirico. ∼**al** *adj* lirico; (🔲: *enthusiastic*) entusiasta. ∼**s** *npl* parole *fpl*

Mm

mac /mæk/ n 🔲 impermeabile m

macaroni /mækə'rəʊnɪ/ n maccheroni mpl

mace¹ /meɪs/ n (staff) mazza f

mace² n (spice) macis m o f

machine /mə'ʃiːn/ n macchina f
● vt (sew) cucire a macchina; (Techn) lavorare a macchina. ~-gun n mitragliatrice f

machinery /mə'ʃiːnərɪ/ n macchinario m

mackerel /'mækr(ə)l/ n inv sgombro m

mackintosh /'mækɪntɒʃ/ n impermeabile m

mad /mæd/ adj (madder, maddest) pazzo, matto; (🔲: angry) furioso (at con); like ~ 🔲 come un pazzo; be ~ about sb/sth (🔲: keen on) andare matto per qcno/qcsa

madam /'mædəm/ n signora f

mad cow disease n morbo m della mucca pazza

madden /'mædn/ vt (make angry) far diventare matto

made /meɪd/ ▷ MAKE; ~ to measure [fatto] su misura

mad|ly /'mædlɪ/ adv 🔲 follemente; ~ly in love innamorato follemente. ~man n pazzo m. ~ness n pazzia f

madonna /mə'dɒnə/ n madonna f

magazine /mægə'ziːn/ n rivista f; (Mil, Phot) magazzino m

maggot /'mægət/ n verme m

magic /'mædʒɪk/ n magia f; (tricks) giochi mpl di prestigio ● adj magico; (trick) di prestigio. ~al adj magico

magician /mə'dʒɪʃn/ n mago, -a mf; (entertainer) prestigiatore, -trice mf

magistrate /'mædʒɪstreɪt/ n

magistrato m

magnet /'mægnɪt/ n magnete m, calamita f. ~ic adj magnetico. ~ism n magnetismo m

magnification /mægnɪfɪ'keɪʃn/ n ingrandimento m

magnificen|ce /mæg'nɪfɪsəns/ n magnificenza f. ~t adj magnifico

magnify /'mægnɪfaɪ/ vt (pt/pp -ied) ingrandire; (exaggerate) ingigantire. ~ing glass n lente f d'ingrandimento

magnitude /'mægnɪtjuːd/ n grandezza f; (importance) importanza f

magpie /'mægpaɪ/ n gazza f

mahogany /mə'hɒgənɪ/ n mogano m ● attrib di mogano

maid /meɪd/ n cameriera f; old ~ pej zitella f

maiden /'meɪdn/ n (liter) fanciulla f ● adj (speech, voyage) inaugurale. ~ 'aunt n zia f zitella. ~ name n nome m da ragazza

mail /meɪl/ n posta f ● vt impostare. ~-bag n sacco m postale. ~box n Am cassetta f delle lettere; (e-mail) casella f di posta elettronica. ~ing list n elenco m d'indirizzi per un mailing. ~man n Am postino m. ~ order n vendita f per corrispondenza. ~-order firm n ditta f di vendita per corrispondenza. ~shot n mailing m inv

maim /meɪm/ vt menomare

main¹ /meɪn/ n (water, gas, electricity) conduttura f principale

main² adj principale; the ~ thing is to... la cosa essenziale è di... ● n in the ~ in complesso

main:~land /-lænd/ n continente m. ~ly adv principalmente. ~ street n via f principale

maintain /meɪn'teɪn/ vt mantenere; (keep in repair) curare la manutenzione di; (claim) sostenere

maintenance /'meɪntənəns/ n mantenimento m; (care) manutenzione f; (allowance) alimenti mpl

maisonette /meɪzəˈnet/ n appartamento m a due piani

majestic /məˈdʒestɪk/ adj maestoso

majesty /ˈmædʒəstɪ/ n maestà f; His/Her M~ Sua Maestà

major /ˈmeɪdʒə(r)/ adj maggiore; ~ road strada f con diritto di precedenza ●n (Mil, Mus) maggiore m ●vi Am ~ in specializzarsi in

Majorca /məˈjɔːkə/ n Maiorca f

majority /məˈdʒɒrɪtɪ/ n maggioranza f; be in the ~ avere la maggioranza

make /meɪk/ n (brand) marca f ●v (pt/pp made) ●vt fare; (earn) guadagnare; rendere (happy, clear); prendere (decision); ~ sb laugh far ridere qcno; ~ sb do sth far fare qcsa a qcno; ~ it (to party, top of hill etc) farcela; **what time do you ~ it?** che ore fai? ●vi ~ as if to fare per. □~ **do** vi arrangiarsi. □~ **for** vi dirigersi verso. □~ **off** vi fuggire. □~ **out** vt (distinguish) distinguere; (write out) rilasciare (cheque); compilare (list); (claim) far credere. □~ **over** vt cedere. □~ **up** vt (constitute) comporre; (complete) completare; (invent) inventare; (apply cosmetics to) truccare; fare (parcel); ~ **up one's mind** decidersi; ~ **it up** (after quarrel) riconciliarsi ●vi (after quarrel) fare la pace; ~ **up for** compensare; ~ **up for lost time** recuperare il tempo perso

'make-believe n finzione f

maker /ˈmeɪkə(r)/ n fabbricante mf; M~ Creatore m

make: ~**shift** adj di fortuna ●n espediente m. ~**-up** n trucco m; (character) natura f

making /ˈmeɪkɪŋ/ n **have the ~s of** aver la stoffa di

maladjust|ed /mæləˈdʒʌstɪd/ adj disadattato

malaria /məˈleərɪə/ n malaria f

Malaysia /məˈleɪzɪə/ n Malesia f

male /meɪl/ adj maschile ●n maschio m. ~ **nurse** n infermiere m

malfunction /mælˈfʌŋkʃn/ n funzionamento m imperfetto ●vi funzionare male

malice /ˈmælɪs/ n malignità f; **hear sb** ~ voler del male a qcno

malicious /məˈlɪʃəs/ adj maligno

mallet /ˈmælɪt/ n martello m di legno

malnu'trition /mæl-/ n malnutrizione f

mal'practice n negligenza f

malt /mɔːlt/ n malto m

Malta /ˈmɔːltə/ n Malta f. ~**ese** adj & n maltese mf

mammal /ˈmæml/ n mammifero m

mammoth /ˈmæməθ/ adj mastodontico ●n mammut m inv

man /mæn/ n (pl **men**) uomo m; (chess, draughts) pedina f ●vt (pt/pp **manned**) equipaggiare; essere di servizio a (counter, telephone)

manage /ˈmænɪdʒ/ vt dirigere; gestire (shop, affairs); (cope with) farcela; ~ **to do sth** riuscire a fare qcsa ●vi riuscire; (cope) farcela (**on** con). ~**able** adj (hair) docile; (size) maneggevole. ~**ment** n gestione f; the ~**ment** la direzione

manager /ˈmænɪdʒə(r)/ n direttore m; (of shop, bar) gestore m; (Sport) manager m inv. ~**ess** n direttrice f. ~**ial** adj ~**ial staff** personale m direttivo

mandat|e /ˈmændeɪt/ n mandato m. ~**ory** adj obbligatorio

mane /meɪn/ n criniera f

mangle /ˈmæŋgl/ vt (damage) maciullare

man: ~**'handle** vt malmenare. ~**hole** n botola f. ~**hood** n età f adulta; (quality) virilità f. ~**-hour** n ora f lavorativa. ~**-hunt** n caccia f all'uomo

man|ia /ˈmeɪnɪə/ n mania f. ~**iac** n maniaco, -a mf

manicure /ˈmænɪkjʊə(r)/ n manicure f • vt fare la manicure a

manifest /ˈmænɪfest/ adj manifesto • vt ~ **itself** manifestarsi. ~ly adv palesemente

manifesto /mænɪˈfestəʊ/ n manifesto m

manipulat|e /məˈnɪpjʊleɪt/ vt manipolare. ~ion n manipolazione f

man'kind n genere m umano

manly /ˈmænlɪ/ adj virile

'man-made adj artificiale. ~ **fibre** n fibra f sintetica

manner /ˈmænə(r)/ n maniera f; **in this** ~ in questo modo; **have no** ~s avere dei pessimi modi; **good/bad** ~s buone/cattive maniere fpl. ~ism n affettazione f

manor /ˈmænə(r)/ n maniero m

'manpower n manodopera f

mansion /ˈmænʃn/ n palazzo m

'manslaughter n omicidio m colposo

mantelpiece /ˈmæntl-/ n mensola f di caminetto

manual /ˈmænjʊəl/ adj manuale • n manuale m

manufacture /mænjʊˈfæktʃə(r)/ vt fabbricare • n manifattura f. ~r n fabbricante m

manure /məˈnjʊə(r)/ n concime m

manuscript /ˈmænjʊskrɪpt/ n manoscritto m

many /ˈmenɪ/ adj & pron molti; **there are as** ~ **boys as girls** ci sono tanti ragazzi quante ragazze; **as** ~ **as 500** ben 500; **as** ~ **as that** così tanti; **as** ~ altrettanti; **very** ~, **a good/great** ~ moltissimi; ~ **a time** molte volte

map /mæp/ n carta f geografica; (of town) mappa f • **map out** vt (pt/pp **mapped**) fig programmare

mar /mɑː(r)/ vt (pt/pp **marred**) rovinare

marathon /ˈmærəθən/ n maratona f

marble /ˈmɑːbl/ n marmo m; (for game) pallina f • attrib di marmo

march n marcia f; (protest) dimostrazione f • vi marciare • vt far marciare; ~ **sb off** scortare qcno fuori

March /mɑːtʃ/ n marzo m

mare /meə(r)/ n giumenta f

margarine /mɑːdʒəˈriːn/ n margarina f

margin /ˈmɑːdʒɪn/ n margine m. ~al adj marginale. ~ally adv marginalmente

marijuana /mærɪˈwɑːnə/ n marijuana f

marina /məˈriːnə/ n porticciolo m

marine /məˈriːn/ adj marino • n (sailor) soldato m di fanteria marina

marionette /mærɪəˈnet/ n marionetta f

mark¹ /mɑːk/ n (currency) marco m

mark² n (stain) macchia f; (sign, indication) segno m; (Sch) voto m • vt segnare; (stain) macchiare; (Sch) correggere; (Sport) marcare; ~ **time** (Mil) segnare il passo; fig non far progressi; ~ **my words** ricordati quello che dico. □ ~ **out** vt delimitare; fig designare

marked /mɑːkt/ adj marcato. ~ly adv notevolmente

marker /ˈmɑːkə(r)/ n (for highlighting) evidenziatore m; (Sport) marcatore m; (of exam) esaminatore, -trice mf

market /ˈmɑːkɪt/ n mercato m • vt vendere al mercato; (launch) commercializzare; **on the** ~ sul mercato. ~ing n marketing m. ~ **re'search** n ricerca f di mercato

marksman /ˈmɑːksmən/ n tiratore m scelto

marmalade /ˈmɑːməleɪd/ n marmellata f d'arance

maroon /məˈruːn/ adj marrone rossastro

marquee /mɑːˈkiː/ n tendone m

marriage /ˈmærɪdʒ/ n

matrimonio m

married /'mærɪd/ adj sposato; (life) coniugale

marrow /'mærəʊ/ n (Anat) midollo m; (vegetable) zucca f

marr|y /'mærɪ/ vt (pt/pp married) sposare; get ~ied sposarsi • vi sposarsi

marsh /mɑːʃ/ n palude f

marshal /'mɑːʃl/ n (steward) cerimoniere m • vt (pt/pp marshalled) fig organizzare (arguments)

marshy /'mɑːʃɪ/ adj paludoso

martial /'mɑːʃl/ adj marziale

martyr /'mɑːtə(r)/ n martire mf • vt martoriare. ~ed adj 🇮🇹 da martire

marvel /'mɑːvl/ n meraviglia f • vi (pt/pp marvelled) meravigliarsi (at di). ~lous adj meraviglioso

Marxis|m /'mɑːksɪzm/ n marxismo m. ~t adj & n marxista mf

marzipan /'mɑːzɪpæn/ n marzapane m

mascara /mæ'skɑːrə/ n mascara m inv

mascot /'mæskət/ n mascotte f inv

masculin|e /'mæskjʊlɪn/ adj maschile • n (Gram) maschile m. ~ity n mascolinità f

mash /mæʃ/ vt impastare. ~ed potatoes npl purè m inv di patate

mask /mɑːsk/ n maschera f • vt mascherare

masochis|m /'mæsəkɪzm/ n masochismo m. ~t n masochista mf

mason /'meɪsn/ n muratore m

Mason n massone m. ~ic adj massonico

masonry /'meɪsnrɪ/ n massoneria f

masquerade /mɑːskə'reɪd/ n fig mascherata f • vi ~ as (pose) farsi passare per

mass¹ /mæs/ n (Relig) messa f

mass² n massa f; ~es of 🇮🇹 un sacco di • vi ammassarsi

massacre /'mæsəkə(r)/ n massacro m • vt massacrare

massage /'mæsɑːʒ/ n massaggio m • vt massaggiare, fig manipolare (statistics)

masseu|r /mæ'sɜː/ n massaggiatore m. ~se n massaggiatrice f

massive /'mæsɪv/ adj enorme

mass: ~ media n comunicazione di massa, mass media mpl. ~-pro'duce vt produrre in serie

mast /mɑːst/ n (Naut) albero m; (for radio) antenna f

master /'mɑːstə(r)/ n maestro m, padrone m; (teacher) professore m; (of ship) capitano m; M~ (boy) signorino m

master: ~-key n passe-partout m inv. ~-mind n cervello m • vt ideare e dirigere. ~piece n capolavoro m. ~-stroke n colpo m da maestro. ~y n (of subject) padronanza f

masturbat|e /'mæstəbeɪt/ vi masturbarsi. ~ion n masturbazione f

mat /mæt/ n stuoia f; (on table) sottopiatto m

match¹ /mætʃ/ n (Sport) partita f; (equal) uguale mf; (marriage) matrimonio m; (person to marry) partito m; **be a good** ~ (colours:) intonarsi bene; **be no** ~ **for** non essere dello stesso livello di • vt (equal) uguagliare; (be like) andare bene con • vi intonarsi

match² n fiammifero m. ~box n scatola f di fiammiferi

matching /'mætʃɪŋ/ adj intonato

mate¹ /meɪt/ n compagno, -a mf; (assistant) aiuto m; (Naut) secondo m; (🇮🇹: friend) amico, -a mf • vi accoppiarsi • vt accoppiare

mate² n (in chess) scacco m matto

material /mə'tɪərɪəl/ n materiale m; (fabric) stoffa f; **raw** ~s materie fpl prime • adj materiale

maternal /mə'tɜːnl/ adj materno

maternity /mə'tɜːnɪtɪ/ n maternità f. ~ clothes npl abiti mpl premaman.

~ ward n maternità f inv

mathematic|al /mæðə'mætɪkl/ adj matematico. **~ian** n matematico, -a mf

mathematics /mæθə'mætɪks/ n matematica fsg

maths /mæθs/ n 🔢 matematica fsg

matinée /'mætɪneɪ/ n (Theat) matinée m

matriculat|e /mə'trɪkjʊlət/ vi immatricolarsi. **~ion** n immatricolazione f

matrix /'meɪtrɪks/ n (pl matrices /-siːz/) matrice f

matted /'mætɪd/ adj ~ hair capelli mpl tutti appiccicati tra loro

matter /'mætə(r)/ n (affair) faccenda f; (question) questione f; (pus) pus m; (phys: substance) materia f; **as a ~ of fact** a dire la verità; **what is the ~?** che cosa c'è? ● vi importare; **~ to sb** essere importante per qcno; **it doesn't ~** non importa. **~-of-fact** adj pratico

mattress /'mætrɪs/ n materasso m

matur|e /mə'tʃʊə(r)/ adj maturo; (Comm) in scadenza ● vi maturare ● vt far maturare. **~ity** n maturità f; (Fin) maturazione f

maul /mɔːl/ vt malmenare

mauve /məʊv/ adj malva

maxim /'mæksɪm/ n massima f

maximum /'mæksɪməm/ adj massimo; **ten minutes ~** dieci minuti al massimo ● n (pl -ima) massimo m

may /meɪ/ v aux (solo al presente) potere; **~ I come in?** posso entrare?; **if I ~ say so** se mi posso permettere; **~ you both be very happy** siate felici!; **I ~ as well stay** potrei anche rimanere; **it ~ be true** potrebbe esser vero; **she ~ be old, but...** sarà anche vecchia, ma...

May /meɪ/ n maggio m

maybe /'meɪbiː/ adv forse, può darsi

'May Day n il primo maggio

mayonnaise /meɪə'neɪz/ n maionese f

mayor /'meə(r)/ n sindaco m. **~ess** n sindaco m; (wife of mayor) moglie f del sindaco

maze /meɪz/ n labirinto m

me /miː/ pron (object) mi; (with preposition) me; **she called me** mi ha chiamato; **she called me, not you** ha chiamato me, non te; **give me the money** dammi i soldi; **give it to me** dammelo; **he gave it to me** me lo ha dato; **it's ~** sono io

meadow /'medəʊ/ n prato m

meagre /'miːgə(r)/ adj scarso

meal¹ n pasto m

meal² n (grain) farina f

mean¹ /miːn/ adj avaro; (unkind) meschino

mean² adj medio ● n (average) media f; **Greenwich ~ time** ora f media di Greenwich

mean³ vt (pt/pp meant) voler dire; (signify) significare; (intend) intendere; **I ~ it** lo dico seriamente; **~ well** avere buone intenzioni; **be ~ for** (present:) essere destinato a; (remark:) essere riferito a

meander /mɪ'ændə(r)/ vi vagare

meaning /'miːnɪŋ/ n significato m. **~ful** adj significativo. **~less** adj senza senso

means /miːnz/ n mezzo m; **~ of transport** mezzo m di trasporto; **by ~ of** per mezzo di; **by all ~** certamente!; **by no ~** niente affatto ● npl (resources) mezzi mpl

meant /ment/ ▷ **MEAN³**

'meantime n **in the ~** nel frattempo ● adv intanto

'meanwhile adv intanto

measles /'miːzlz/ n morbillo m

measly /'miːzli/ adj 🔢 misero

measure /'meʒə(r)/ n misura f ● vt/i misurare. □ ~ **up to** vt fig essere all'altezza di. **~d** adj misurato.

m

~ment n misura f

meat /miːt/ n carne f. ~ **ball** n (Culin) polpetta f di carne. ~ **loaf** n polpettone m

mechanic /mɪˈkænɪk/ n meccanico m. ~**ical** adj meccanico; ~**ical engineering** ingegneria f meccanica. ~**ically** adv meccanicamente. ~**ics** n meccanica f ● npl meccanismo msg

mechanism /ˈmekənɪzm/ n meccanismo m. ~**ize** vt meccanizzare

medal /ˈmedl/ n medaglia f

medallist /ˈmedəlɪst/ n vincitore, -trice mf di una medaglia

meddle /ˈmedl/ vi immischiarsi (**in** di); (tinker) armeggiare (**with** con)

media /ˈmiːdɪə/ ▶**MEDIUM** ● npl the ~ i mass media

mediate /ˈmiːdɪeɪt/ vi fare da mediatore. ~**ion** n mediazione f. ~**or** n mediatore, -trice mf

medical /ˈmedɪkl/ adj medico ● n visita f medica. ~ **insurance** n assicurazione f sanitaria. ~ **student** n studente, -essa mf di medicina

medicated /ˈmedɪkeɪtɪd/ adj medicato. ~**ion** n (drugs) medicinali mpl

medicinal /mɪˈdɪsɪnl/ adj medicinale

medicine /ˈmedsən/ n medicina f

medieval /medɪˈiːvl/ adj medievale

mediocre /miːdɪˈəʊkə(r)/ adj mediocre. ~**ity** n mediocrità f

meditate /ˈmedɪteɪt/ vi meditare (**on** su). ~**ion** n meditazione f

Mediterranean /medɪtəˈreɪnɪən/ n the ~ [Sea] il [mare m] Mediterraneo m ● adj mediterraneo

medium /ˈmiːdɪəm/ adj medio; (Culin) di media cottura ● n (pl **media**) mezzo m; (pl -s) (person) medium mf inv

medium-sized adj di taglia media

medley /ˈmedlɪ/ n miscuglio m; (Mus) miscellanea f

meek /miːk/ adj mite, mansueto.

~**ly** adv docilmente

meet /miːt/ v (pt/pp **met**) ● vt incontrare; (at station, airport) andare incontro a; (for first time) fare la conoscenza di; pagare (bill); soddisfare (requirements) ● vi incontrarsi; (committee:) riunirsi; ~ **with** incontrare (problem); incontrarsi con (person) ● n raduno m [sportivo]

meeting /ˈmiːtɪŋ/ n riunione f, meeting m inv; (large) assemblea f; (by chance) incontro m

megabyte /ˈmegəbaɪt/ n megabyte m

megaphone /ˈmegəfəʊn/ n megafono m

melancholy /ˈmelənkəlɪ/ adj malinconico ● n malinconia f

mellow /ˈmeləʊ/ adj (wine) generoso; (sound, colour) caldo; (person) dolce ● vi (person:) addolcirsi

melodrama /ˈmelə-/ n melodramma m. ~**tic** adj melodrammatico

melody /ˈmelədɪ/ n melodia f

melon /ˈmelən/ n melone m

melt /melt/ vt sciogliere ● vi sciogliersi. ~ **down** vt fondere. ~**ing-pot** n fig crogiuolo m

member /ˈmembə(r)/ n membro m; ~ **countries** paesi mpl membri; **M~ of Parliament** deputato, -a mf; **M~ of the European Parliament** eurodeputato, -a mf. ~**ship** n iscrizione f; (members) soci mpl

membrane /ˈmembreɪn/ n membrana f

memo /ˈmeməʊ/ n promemoria m inv

memorable /ˈmemərəbl/ adj memorabile

memorandum /meməˈrændəm/ n promemoria m inv

memorial /mɪˈmɔːrɪəl/ n monumento m. ~ **service** n funzione f commemorativa

memorize /ˈmeməraɪz/ vt

memorizzare

memory /'meməri/ n also (Comput) memoria f; (thing remembered) ricordo m; **from** ~ a memoria; **in** ~ **of** in ricordo di

men /men/ ▷**MAN**

menac|e /'menəs/ n minaccia f; (nuisance) piaga f ● vt minacciare. ~**ing** adj minaccioso

mend /mend/ vt riparare; (darn) rammendare ● n **on the** ~ in via di guarigione

'**menfolk** n uomini mpl

menial /'mi:nɪəl/ adj umile

meningitis /menɪn'dʒaɪtɪs/ n meningite f

menopause /'menə-/ n menopausa f

menstruat|e /'menstrʊeɪt/ vi mestruare. ~**ion** n mestruazione f

mental /'mentl/ adj mentale; (Ⅱ: mad) pazzo. ~ **a'rithmetic** n calcolo m mentale. ~ '**illness** n malattia f mentale

mental|ity /men'tælətɪ/ n mentalità f inv. ~**ly** adv mentalmente; ~**ly ill** malato di mente

mention /'menʃn/ n menzione f ● vt menzionare; **don't** ~ **it** non c'è di che

menu /'menju:/ n menu m inv

MEP n abbr Member of the European Parliament

mercenary /'mɜːsɪnərɪ/ adj mercenario ● n mercenario m

merchandise /'mɜːtʃəndaɪz/ n merce f

merchant /'mɜːtʃənt/ n commerciante mf. ~ **bank** n banca f d'affari. ~ '**navy** n marina f mercantile

merci|ful /'mɜːsɪfʊl/ adj misericordioso. ~**fully** adv Ⅱ grazie a Dio. ~**less** adj spietato

mercury /'mɜːkjʊrɪ/ n mercurio m

mercy /'mɜːsɪ/ n misericordia f; **be at sb's** ~ essere alla mercè di qcno,

essere in balìa di qcno. ~**ly** adv solamente

mere /mɪə(r)/ adj solo. ~**ly** adv solamente

merge /mɜːdʒ/ vi fondersi

merger /'mɜːdʒə(r)/ n fusione f

meringue /mə'ræŋ/ n meringa f

merit /'merɪt/ n merito m; (advantage) qualità f inv ● vt meritare

mermaid /'mɜːmeɪd/ n sirena f

merri|ly /'merɪlɪ/ adv allegramente. ~**ment** n baldoria f

merry /'merɪ/ adj (-ier, -iest) allegro; ~ **Christmas!** Buon Natale! **merry-**-**go-round** n giostra f. ~-**making** n festa f

mesh /meʃ/ n maglia f

mesmerize /'mezməraɪz/ vt ipnotizzare. ~**d** adj fig ipnotizzato

mess /mes/ n disordine m, casino m Ⅱ; (trouble) guaio m; (something spilt) sporco m; (Mil) mensa f; **make a** ~ **of** (botch) fare un pasticcio di ● **mess about** vi perder tempo; ~ **about with** armeggiare con ● vt prendere in giro (person). □ ~ **up** vt mettere in disordine, incasinare Ⅱ; (botch) mandare all'aria

message /'mesɪdʒ/ n messaggio m

messenger /'mesɪndʒə(r)/ n messaggero m

Messiah /mɪ'saɪə/ n Messia m

Messrs /'mesəz/ npl (on letter) ~ Smith Spett. ditta Smith

messy /'mesɪ/ adj (-ier, -iest) disordinato; (in dress) sciatto

met /met/ ▷**MEET**

metal /'metl/ n metallo m ● adj di metallo. ~**lic** adj metallico

metaphor /'metəfə(r)/ n metafora f. ~**ical** adj metaforico

meteor /'mi:tɪə(r)/ n meteora f. ~**ic** adj fig fulmineo

meteorological /mi:tɪərə'lɒdʒɪkl/ adj meteorologico

meteo|rologist /mi:tɪə'rɒlədʒɪst/ n meteorologo, -a mf. ~**rology** n meteorologia f

meter[1] /'miːtə(r)/ n contatore m

meter[2] n Am = **metre**

method /'meθəd/ n metodo m

methodical /mɪ'θɒdɪkl/ adj metodico. **~ly** adv metodicamente

methylated /'meθɪleɪtɪd/ adj **~ spirit[s]** alcol m denaturato

meticulous /mɪ'tɪkjʊləs/ adj meticoloso. **~ly** adv meticolosamente

metre /'miːtə(r)/ n metro m

metric /'metrɪk/ adj metrico

metropolis /mɪ'trɒpəlɪs/ n metropoli f inv

mew /mjuː/ n miao m ● vi miagolare

Mexican /'meksɪkən/ adj & n messicano, -a mf. **Mexico** n Messico m

miaow /mɪ'aʊ/ n miao m ● vi miagolare

mice /maɪs/ ▷MOUSE

mickey /'mɪkɪ/ n **take the ~ out of** prendere in giro

micro /'maɪkrəʊ/: **~chip** n microchip m. **~computer** n microcomputer m. **~film** n microfilm m. **~phone** n microfono m. **~processor** n microprocessore m. **~scope** n microscopio m. **~scopic** adj microscopico. **~wave** n microonda f, (oven) forno m a microonde

microbe /'maɪkrəʊb/ n microbo m

mid /mɪd/ adj **~ May** metà maggio; **in ~ air** a mezz'aria

midday /mɪd'deɪ/ n mezzogiorno m

middle /'mɪdl/ adj di centro; **the M~ Ages** il medioevo; **the ~ class[es]** la classe media; **the M~ East** il Medio Oriente ● n mezzo m; **in the ~ of** (room, floor etc) In mezzo a; **in the ~ of the night** nel pieno della notte, a notte piena

middle: ~-aged adj di mezza età, **~-class** adj borghese. **~man** n (Comm) intermediario m

middling /'mɪdlɪŋ/ adj discreto

midge /mɪdʒ/ n moscerino m

midget /'mɪdʒɪt/ n nano, -a mf

Midlands /'mɪdləndz/ npl **the ~** l'Inghilterra fsg centrale

midnight /'mɪdnaɪt/ n mezzanotte f

midriff /'mɪdrɪf/ n diaframma m

midst /mɪdst/ n **in the ~ of** in mezzo a, in mezzo a; **in our ~** fra di noi, in mezzo a noi

mid: ~summer n mezza estate f. **~way** adv a metà strada. **~wife** n ostetrica f. **~'winter** n pieno inverno m

might[1] /maɪt/ v aux **I ~** potrei; **will you come?** – **I ~** vieni? – può darsi; **it ~ be true** potrebbe essere vero; **I ~ as well stay** potrei anche restare; **you ~ have drowned** avresti potuto affogare; **you ~ have said so!** avresti potuto dirlo!

might[2] n potere m

mighty /'maɪtɪ/ adj (**-ier, -iest**) potente ● adv ⊞ molto

migraine /'miːɡreɪn/ n emicrania f

migrant /'maɪɡrənt/ adj migratore ● n (bird) migratore, -trice mf; (person: for work) emigrante mf

migrat|e /maɪ'ɡreɪt/ vi migrare. **~ion** n migrazione f

Milan /mɪ'læn/ n Milano f

mild /maɪld/ adj (weather) mite; (person) dolce; (flavour) delicato; (illness) leggero

mildew /'mɪldjuː/ n muffa f

mild|ly /'maɪldlɪ/ adv moderatamente; (say) dolcemente; **to put it ~ly** a dir poco, senza esagerazione. **~ness** n (of person, words) dolcezza f; (of weather) mitezza f

mile /maɪl/ n miglio m (= 1,6 km); **~s nicer** ⊞ molto più bello

mile|age /-ɪdʒ/ n chilometraggio m. **~stone** n pietra f miliare

militant /'mɪlɪtənt/ adj & n militante mf

military /'mɪlɪtrɪ/ adj militare. **~ service** n servizio m militare

militia /mɪˈlɪʃə/ n milizia f

milk /mɪlk/ n latte m ● vt mungere

milk: ~**man** n lattaio m. ~ **shake** n frappé m inv

milky /ˈmɪlkɪ/ adj (-ier, -iest) latteo; (tea etc) con molto latte. **M~ Way** n (Astr) Via f Lattea

mill /mɪl/ n mulino m; (factory) fabbrica f; (for coffee etc) macinino m ● vt macinare (grain). **mill about, mill around** n brulicare

millennium /mɪˈlenɪəm/ n millennio m

miller /ˈmɪlə(r)/ n mugnaio m

million /ˈmɪljən/ n milione m; **a** ~ **pounds** un milione di sterline. ~**aire** n miliardario, -a mf

'millstone n fig peso m

mime /maɪm/ n mimo m ● vt mimare

mimic /ˈmɪmɪk/ n imitatore, -trice mf ● vt (pt/pp **mimicked**) imitare. ~**ry** n mimetismo m

mince /mɪns/ n carne f tritata ● vt (Culin) tritare; **not** ~ **one's words** parlare senza mezzi termini

mince 'pie n pasticcino m a base di frutta secca

mincer /ˈmɪnsə(r)/ n tritacarne m inv

mind /maɪnd/ n mente f; (sanity) ragione f; **to my** ~ a mio parere; **give sb a piece of one's** ~ dire chiaro e tondo a qcno quello che si pensa; **make up one's** ~ decidersi; **have sth in** ~ avere qcsa in mente; **bear sth in** ~ tenere presente qcsa; **have something on one's** ~ essere preoccupato; **have a good** ~ **to** avere una grande voglia di; **I have changed my** ~ ho cambiato idea; **in two** ~**s** indeciso; **are you out of your** ~? sei diventato matto? ● vt (look after) occuparsi di; **I don't** ~ **the noise** il rumore non mi dà fastidio; **I don't** ~ **what we do** non mi importa che facciamo; ~ **the**

step! attenzione al gradino! ● vi **I don't** ~ non mi importa; **never** ~! non importa!; **do you** ~ **if...?** ti dispiace se...? **mind out** vi ~ **out!** [fai] attenzione!

mind|ful adj ~**ful of** attento a. ~**less** adj noncurante

mine¹ /maɪn/ poss pron il mio m, la mia f, i miei mpl, le mie fpl; **a friend of** ~ un mio amico; **friends of** ~ dei miei amici; **that is** ~ questo è mio; (as opposed to yours) questo è il mio

mine² n miniera f; (explosive) mina f ● vt estrarre; (Mil) minare. ~ **detector** n rivelatore m di mine. ~**field** n campo m minato

mineral /ˈmɪnərəl/ n minerale m ● adj minerale. ~ **water** n acqua f minerale

mingle /ˈmɪŋgl/ vi ~ **with** mescolarsi a

mini /ˈmɪnɪ/ n (skirt) mini f

miniature /ˈmɪnɪtʃə(r)/ adj in miniatura ● n miniatura f

mini|bus /ˈmɪnɪ-/ n minibus m, pulmino m. ~**cab** n taxi m inv

minim|al /ˈmɪnɪməl/ adj minimo. ~**ize** vt minimizzare. ~**um** n (pl -ima) minimo m ● adj minimo; **ten minutes** ~**um** minimo dieci minuti

mining /ˈmaɪnɪŋ/ n estrazione f ● adj estrattivo

miniskirt /ˈmɪnɪ-/ n minigonna f

minist|er /ˈmɪnɪstə(r)/ n ministro m; (Relig) pastore m. ~**erial** adj ministeriale

ministry /ˈmɪnɪstrɪ/ n (Pol) ministero m; **the** ~ (Relig) il ministero sacerdotale

mink /mɪŋk/ n visone m

minor /ˈmaɪnə(r)/ adj minore ● n minorenne mf

minority /maɪˈnɒrətɪ/ n minoranza f; (age) minore età f

mint¹ /mɪnt/ n ① patrimonio m ● adj **in** ~ **condition** in condizione perfetta

mint² n (herb) menta f

minus /'maməs/ prep meno; (⊞: without) senza ● n ~ **[sign]** meno m

minute¹ /'mɪnɪt/ n minuto m; **in a** ~ (shortly) in un minuto; ~s pl (of meeting) verbale msg

minute² /mar'njuːt/ adj minuto; (precise) minuzioso

miracle /'mɪrəkl/ n miracolo m. ~ulous adj miracoloso

mirage /'mɪrɑːʒ/ n miraggio m

mirror /'mɪrə(r)/ n specchio m ● vt rispecchiare

mirth /mɜːθ/ n ilarità f

misapprehension n malinteso m; **be under a** ~ avere frainteso

misbehave vi comportarsi male

miscalculate vt/i calcolare male. ~lation n calcolo m sbagliato

miscarriage n aborto m spontaneo; ~ **of justice** errore m giudiziario. **miscarry** vi abortire

miscellaneous /mɪsə'leɪnɪəs/ adj assortito

mischief /'mɪstʃɪf/ n malefatta f; (harm) danno m

mischievous /'mɪstʃɪvəs/ adj (naughty) birichino; (malicious) dannoso

misconception n concetto m erroneo

misconduct n cattiva condotta f

misdemeanour n reato m

miser /'maɪzə(r)/ n avaro m

miserable /'mɪzrəbl/ adj (unhappy) infelice; (wretched) miserabile; (fig: weather) deprimente. ~ly adv (live, fail) miseramente; (say) tristemente

miserly /'maɪzəlɪ/ adj avaro; (amount) ridicolo

misery /'mɪzərɪ/ n miseria f; (⊞: person) piagnone, -a mf

misfire vi (gun:) far cilecca; (plan etc:) non riuscire

'misfit n disadattato, -a mf

misfortune n sfortuna f

misguided adj fuorviato

mishap /'mɪshæp/ n disavventura f

misinterpret vt fraintendere

misjudge vt giudicar male; (estimate wrongly) valutare male

mislay vt (pt/pp laid) smarrire

mislead vt (pt/pp -led) fuorviare. ~ing adj fuorviante

mismanage vt amministrare male. ~ment n cattiva amministrazione f

'misprint n errore m di stampa

miss /mɪs/ n colpo m mancato ● vt (fail to hit or find) mancare; perdere (train, bus, class); (feel the loss of) sentire la mancanza di; **I** ~ed that **part** (failed to notice) mi è sfuggita quella parte ● vi **but he** ~ed (failed to hit) ma l'ha mancato. □ ~ **out** vt saltare, omettere

Miss n (pl -es) signorina f

misshapen /mɪs'ʃeɪpən/ adj malformato

missile /'mɪsaɪl/ n missile m

missing /'mɪsɪŋ/ adj mancante; (person) scomparso; (Mil) disperso; **be** ~ essere introvabile

mission /'mɪʃn/ n missione f

missionary /'mɪʃənrɪ/ n missionario, -a mf

mist /mɪst/ n (fog) foschia f ● **mist up** vi appannarsi, annebbiarsi

mistake /mɪ'steɪk/ n sbaglio m; **by** ~ per sbaglio ● vt (pt mistook, pp mistaken) sbagliare (road, house); fraintendere (meaning, words); ~ **for** prendere per

mistaken /mɪ'steɪkən/ adj sbagliato; **be** ~ sbagliarsi; ~ **identity** errore m di persona. ~ly adv erroneamente

mistletoe /'mɪsltəʊ/ n vischio m

mistress /'mɪstrɪs/ n padrona f; (teacher) maestra f; (lover) amante f

mistrust n sfiducia f ● vt non aver fiducia in

misty /'mɪstɪ/ adj (-ier, -iest) nebbioso

misunder'stand vt (pt/pp -**stood**) fraintendere. ~**ing** n malinteso m

misuse¹ /mɪs'juːz/ vt usare male

misuse² /mɪs'juːs/ n cattivo uso m

mite /maɪt/ n (child) piccino, -a m

mitten /'mɪtn/ n manopola f, muffola m

mix /mɪks/ n (combination) mescolanza f; (Culin) miscuglio m; (ready-made) preparato m ● vt mischiare ● vi mischiarsi; (person): inserirsi; ~ **with** (associate with) frequentare. ~ **up** vt mescolare (papers); (confuse, mistake for) confondere

mixed /mɪkst/ adj misto; ~ **up** (person) confuso

mixer /'mɪksə(r)/ n (Culin) frullatore m, mixer m inv; **he's a good** ~ è un tipo socievole

mixture /'mɪkstʃə(r)/ n mescolanza f; (medicine) sciroppo m; (Culin) miscela f

'mix-up n (confusion) confusione f; (mistake) pasticcio m

moan /məʊn/ n lamento m ● vi lamentarsi; (complain) lagnarsi

moat /məʊt/ n fossato m

mob /mɒb/ n folla f; (rabble) gentaglia f; (☐: gang) banda f ● vt (pt/pp mobbed) assalire

mobile /'məʊbaɪl/ adj mobile ● n composizione f mobile. ~ '**home** n casa f roulotte. ~ [**phone**] n [telefono m] cellulare m, telefonino m

mock /mɒk/ adj finto ● vt canzonare. ~**ery** n derisione f

model /'mɒdl/ n modello m; [**fashion**] ~ indossatore, -trice mf, modello, -a mf ● adj (yacht, plane) in miniatura; (pupil, husband) esemplare, modello ● v (pt/pp **modelled**) ● vt indossare (clothes) ● vi fare il/l'indossatore, -trice m f; (for artist) posare

modem /'məʊdem/ n modem m inv

moderate¹ /'mɒdəreɪt/ vt moderare ● vi moderarsi

moderate² /'mɒdərət/ adj moderato ● n (Pol) moderato, -a mf. ~**ly** adv (drink, speak etc) moderatamente; (good, bad etc) relativamente

moderation /mɒdə'reɪʃn/ n moderazione f; **in** ~ con moderazione

modern /'mɒdn/ adj moderno. ~**ize** vt modernizzare

modest /'mɒdɪst/ adj modesto. ~**y** n modestia f

modif|ication /mɒdɪfɪ'keɪʃn/ n modificazione f. ~**y** vt (pt/pp -**fied**) modificare

module /'mɒdjuːl/ n modulo m

moist /mɔɪst/ adj umido

moisten /'mɔɪsn/ vt inumidire

moistur|e /'mɔɪstʃə(r)/ n umidità f. ~**izer** n [crema f] idratante m

mole¹ /məʊl/ n (on face etc) neo m

mole² n (Zool) talpa f

molecule /'mɒlɪkjuːl/ n molecola f

molest /mə'lest/ vt molestare

mollycoddle /'mɒlɪkɒdl/ vt tenere nella bambagia

molten /'məʊltən/ adj fuso

mom /mɒm/ n Am ☐ mamma f

moment /'məʊmənt/ n momento m; **at the** ~ in questo momento. ~**arily** adv momentaneamente. ~**ary** adj momentaneo

momentous /mə'mentəs/ adj molto importante

momentum /mə'mentəm/ n impeto m

monarch /'mɒnək/ n monarca m. ~**y** n monarchia f

monast|ery /'mɒnəstrɪ/ n monastero m. ~**ic** adj monastico

Monday /'mʌndeɪ/ n lunedì m inv

money /'mʌnɪ/ n denaro m

money-box n salvadanaio m

mongrel /'mʌŋɡrəl/ n bastardo m

monitor /'mɒnɪtə(r)/ n (Techn) monitor m inv ● vt controllare

monk /mʌŋk/ n monaco m

monkey /'mʌŋkɪ/ n scimmia f.
~-nut n nocciolina f americana.
~-wrench n chiave f inglese a
rullino

mono /'mɒnəʊ/ n mono m

monologue /'mɒnəlɒg/ n mono-
logo m

monopol|ize /mə'nɒpəlaɪz/ vt mo-
nopolizzare. **~y** n monopolio m

monotone /'mɒnətəʊn/ n speak
in a ~ parlare con tono monotono

monoton|ous /mə'nɒtənəs/ adj
monotono. **~y** n monotonia f

monsoon /mɒn'suːn/ n monsone m

monster /'mɒnstə(r)/ n mostro m

monstrous /'mɒnstrəs/ adj mo-
struoso

Montenegro /mɒntɪ'niːgrəʊ/ n
Montenegro m

month /mʌnθ/ n mese m. **~ly** adj
mensile ● adv mensilmente ● n (periodical) mensile m

monument /'mɒnjʊmənt/ n monumento m. **~al** adj fig monumentale

moo /muː/ n muggito m ● vi (pt/pp
mooed) muggire

mood /muːd/ n umore m; **be in a
good/bad** ~ essere di buon/cattivo
umore; **be in the** ~ **for** essere in
vena di

moody /'muːdɪ/ adj (-ier, -iest) (variable) lunatico; (bad-tempered) di ma-
lumore

moon /muːn/ n luna f; **over the** ~
🄵 al settimo cielo

moon: **~light** n chiaro m di luna
● vi 🄵 lavorare in nero. **~lit** adj illu-
minato dalla luna

moor[1] /mʊə(r)/ n brughiera f

moor[2] vt (Naut) ormeggiare

mop /mɒp/ n straccio m (per i
pavimenti); ~ **of hair** zazzera f ● vt
(pt/pp mopped) lavare con lo straccio. □ ~ **up** vt (dry) asciugare con lo

straccio; (clean) pulire con lo straccio

mope /məʊp/ vi essere depresso

moped /'məʊped/ n ciclomotore m

moral /'mɒrəl/ adj morale ● n morale f. **~ly** adv moralmente. **~s** pl
moralità f

morale /mə'rɑːl/ n morale m

morality /mə'rælətɪ/ n moralità f

more /mɔː(r)/ adj più; a few ~
books un po' più di libri; some ~
tea? ancora un po' di tè?; there's
no ~ bread non c'è più pane; there
are no ~ apples non ci sono più
mele; one ~ word and ... ancora
una parola e... ● pron di più; would
you like some ~? ne vuoi ancora?;
no ~, thank you non ne voglio più,
grazie ● adv più; ~ interesting più
interessante; ~ and ~ quickly sempre più veloce; ~ than più di; I
don't love him any ~ non lo amo
più; once ~ ancora una volta; ~ or
less più o meno; the ~ I see him,
the ~ I like him più lo vedo, più
mi piace

moreover /mɔː'rəʊvə(r)/ adv
inoltre

morgue /mɔːg/ n obitorio m

morning /'mɔːnɪŋ/ n mattino m,
mattina f; **in the** ~ del mattino; (tomorrow) domani mattina

Morocc|o /mə'rɒkəʊ/ n Marocco m
● adj **~an** adj & n marocchino, -a mf

moron /'mɔːrɒn/ n 🄵 deficiente mf

morose /mə'rəʊs/ adj scontroso

Morse /mɔːs/ n ~ [code] [codice
m] Morse m

morsel /'mɔːsl/ n (food) boccone m

mortal /'mɔːtl/ adj & n mortale mf.
~ity n mortalità f. **~ly** adv
(wounded, offended) a morte;
(afraid) da morire

mortar /'mɔːtə(r)/ n mortaio m

mortgage /'mɔːgɪdʒ/ n mutuo m;
(on property) ipoteca f ● vt ipotecare

mortuary /'mɔːtjʊərɪ/ n camera f
mortuaria

m

mosaic /məʊˈzeɪɪk/ n mosaico m

Moslem /ˈmʊzlɪm/ adj & n musulmano, -a mf

mosque /mɒsk/ n moschea f

mosquito /mɒsˈkiːtəʊ/ n (pl -es) zanzara f

moss /mɒs/ n muschio m. ~y adj muschioso

most /məʊst/ adj (majority) la maggior parte di; **for the ~ part** per lo più ● adv più, maggiormente; (very) estremamente, molto; **the ~ interesting day** la giornata più interessante; **a ~ interesting day** una giornata estremamente interessante; **the ~ beautiful woman in the world** la donna più bella del mondo; **~ unlikely** veramente improbabile ● pron ~ **of them** la maggior parte di loro; **at [the] ~** al massimo; **make the ~ of** sfruttare al massimo; **~ of the time** la maggior parte del tempo. ~**ly** adv per lo più

MOT n revisione f obbligatoria di autoveicoli

motel /məʊˈtel/ n motel m inv

moth /mɒθ/ n falena f; [**clothes-**] ~ tarma f

mother /ˈmʌðə(r)/ n madre f; **M~'s Day** la festa della mamma ● vt fare da madre a

mother: ~-**in-law** n (pl ~**s-in-law**) suocera f. ~**ly** adj materno. ~-**of-pearl** n madreperla f. ~-**to-be** n futura mamma f. ~ **tongue** n madrelingua f

motif /məʊˈtiːf/ n motivo m

motion /ˈməʊʃn/ n moto m; (proposal) mozione f; (gesture) gesto m ● vt/i ~ [**to**] **sb to come in** fare segno a qcno di entrare. ~**less** adj immobile. ~**lessly** adv senza alcun movimento

motivate /ˈməʊtɪveɪt/ vt motivare. ~**ion** n motivazione f

motive /ˈməʊtɪv/ n motivo m

motley /ˈmɒtlɪ/ adj disparato

motor /ˈməʊtə(r)/ n motore m; (car) macchina f ● adj a motore; (Anat) motore ● vi andare in macchina

motor: ~ **bike** n $\boxed{\mathbb{F}}$ moto f inv. ~ **boat** n motoscafo m. ~ **car** n automobile f. ~ **cycle** n motocicletta f. ~-**cyclist** n motociclista mf. ~**ing** n automobilismo m. ~**ist** n automobilista mf. ~**way** n autostrada f

motto /ˈmɒtəʊ/ n (pl -es) motto m

mould[1] /məʊld/ n (fungus) muffa f

mould[2] n stampo m ● vt foggiare; fig formare. ~**ing** n (Archit) cornice f

mouldy /ˈməʊldɪ/ adj ammuffito; ($\boxed{\mathbb{F}}$: worthless) ridicolo

moult /məʊlt/ vi (bird:) fare la muta; (animal:) perdere il pelo

mound /maʊnd/ n mucchio m; (hill) collinetta f

mount /maʊnt/ n (horse) cavalcatura f; (of jewel, photo, picture) montatura f ● vt montare a (horse); salire su (bicycle); incastonare (jewel); incorniciare (photo, picture) ● vi aumentare. □ ~ **up** vi aumentare

mountain /ˈmaʊntɪn/ n montagna f; ~ **bike** n mountain bike f inv

mountaineer /maʊntɪˈnɪə(r)/ n alpinista mf. ~**ing** n alpinismo m

mountainous /ˈmaʊntɪnəs/ adj montagnoso

mourn /mɔːn/ vt lamentare ● vi ~ **for** piangere la morte di. ~**er** n persona f che partecipa a un funerale. ~**ful** adj triste. ~**ing** n **in** ~**ing** in lutto

mouse /maʊs/ n (pl mice) topo m; (Comput) mouse m inv. ~**trap** n trappola f [per topi]

mousse /muːs/ n (Culin) mousse f inv

moustache /məˈstɑːʃ/ n baffi mpl

mouth[1] /maʊð/ vt ~ **sth** dire qcsa silenziosamente muovendo solamente le labbra

mouth[2] /maʊθ/ n bocca f; (of river) foce f

mouth: ~**ful** n boccone m

~-organ n armonica f [a bocca].
~-wash n acqua f dentifricia

move /muːv/ n mossa f; (moving
house) trasloco m; **on the ~** in movimento; **get a ~ on** 🔲 darsi una
mossa ● vt muovere; (emotionally)
commuovere; spostare (car, furniture); (transfer) trasferire; (propose)
proporre; **~ house** traslocare ● vi
muoversi; (move house) traslocare.
□ **~ along** vi andare avanti ● vt
muovere in avanti. □ **~ away** vi allontanarsi; (move house) trasferirsi ● vt
allontanare. □ **~ forward** vi avanzare ● vt spostare avanti. □ **~ in** vi
(to a house) trasferirsi. □ **~ off** vi
(vehicle): muoversi. □ **~ out** vi (of
house) andare via. □ **~ over** vi spostarsi ● vt spostare. □ **~ up** vi muoversi; (advance, increase) avanzare

movement /'muːvmənt/ n movimento m

movie /'muːvɪ/ n film m inv; **go to
the ~s** andare al cinema

moving /'muːvɪŋ/ adj mobile; (touching) commovente

mow /məʊ/ vt (pt **mowed**, pp
mown or **mowed**) tagliare (lawn).
□ **~ down** vt (destroy) sterminare

mower /'məʊə(r)/ n tosaerbe m inv

MP n abbr Member of Parliament

Mr /'mɪstə(r)/ n (pl **Messrs**) Signor m

Mrs /'mɪsɪz/ n Signora f

Ms /mɪz/ n Signora f (modo di formale di
rivolgersi ad una donna quando non si vuole
connotarla come sposata o nubile)

much /mʌtʃ/ adj, adv & pron molto;
~ as per quanto; **I love you just as
~ as before/him** ti amo quanto
prima/lui; **as ~ as £5 million** ben
cinque milioni di sterline; **as ~ as
that** così tanto; **very ~** tantissimo,
moltissimo; **~ the same** quasi
uguale

muck /mʌk/ n (dirt) sporcizia f;
(farming) letame m; (🔲: filth) porcheria
f. □ **~ about** vi 🔲 perder tempo; **~**

about with trafficare con. □ **~ up** vt
🔲 rovinare; (make dirty) sporcare

mud /mʌd/ n fango m

muddle /'mʌdl/ n disordine m; (mixup) confusione f ● vt **~ [up]** confondere (dates)

muddy /'mʌdɪ/ adj (**-ier**, **-iest**)
(path) fangoso; (shoes) infangato

muesli /'mjuːzlɪ/ n muesli m inv

muffle /'mʌfl/ vt smorzare (sound).
muffle up vt (for warmth) imbaccuccare

muffler /'mʌflə(r)/ n sciarpa f; Am
(Auto) marmitta f

mug[1] /mʌg/ n tazza f; (for beer) boccale m; (🔲: face) muso m; (🔲: simpleton) pollo m

mug[2] vt (pt/pp **mugged**) aggredire e
derubare. **~ger** n assalitore, -trice
mf. **~ging** n aggressione f per strada

muggy /'mʌgɪ/ adj (**-ier**, **-iest**) afoso

mule /mjuːl/ n mulo m

mull /mʌl/ vt **~ over** rimuginare su

multiple /'mʌltɪpl/ adj multiplo

multiplication /mʌltɪplɪ'keɪʃn/ n
moltiplicazione f

multiply /'mʌltɪplaɪ/ v (pt/pp **-ied**)
● vt moltiplicare (**by** per) ● vi moltiplicarsi

mum[1] /mʌm/ adj **keep ~** 🔲 non
aprire bocca

mum[2] n 🔲 mamma f

mumble /'mʌmbl/ vt/i borbottare

mummy[1] /'mʌmɪ/ n 🔲 mamma f

mummy[2] n (Archaeol) mummia f

mumps /mʌmps/ n orecchioni mpl

munch /mʌntʃ/ vt/i sgranocchiare

mundane /mʌn'deɪn/ adj (everyday)
banale

municipal /mjuː'nɪsɪpl/ adj municipale

mural /'mjʊərəl/ n dipinto m murale

murder /'mɜːdə(r)/ n assassinio m
● vt assassinare; (🔲: ruin) massacrare.
~er n assassino m, -a mf. **~ous**
adj omicida

m

murky /'mɜ:kɪ/ adj (**-ier, -iest**)
oscuro

murmur /'mɜ:mə(r)/ n mormorio m
● vt/i mormorare

muscle /'mʌsl/ n muscolo m
● **muscle in** vi ⊞ intromettersi
(**on** in)

muscular /'mʌskjʊlə(r)/ adj muscolare; (strong) muscoloso

muse /mju:z/ vi meditare (**on** su)

museum /mju:'zɪəm/ n museo m

mushroom /'mʌʃrʊm/ n fungo m
● vi fig spuntare come funghi

music /'mju:zɪk/ n musica f; (written)
spartito m.

musical /'mju:zɪkl/ adj musicale;
(person) dotato di senso musicale
● n commedia f musicale. ~ **box** n
carillon m inv. ~ **instrument** n strumento m musicale

musician /mju:'zɪʃn/ n musicista m

Muslim /'mʊzlɪm/ adj & n musulmano, -a mf

mussel /'mʌsl/ n cozza f

must /mʌst/ v aux (solo al presente)
dovere; **you ~ not be late** non devi
essere in ritardo; **she ~ have finished by now** (probability) deve aver
finito ormai ● n a **~** una cosa da
non perdere

mustard /'mʌstəd/ n senape f

musty /'mʌstɪ/ adj (**-ier, -iest**)
stantio

mutation /mju:'teɪʃn/ n (Biol) mutazione f

mute /mju:t/ adj muto

mutilat|e /'mju:tɪleɪt/ vt mutilare.
~**ion** n mutilazione f

mutter /'mʌtə(r)/ vt/i borbottare

mutton /'mʌtn/ n carne f di
montone

mutual /'mju:tjʊəl/ adj reciproco;
(⊞: common) comune. ~**ly** adv reciprocamente

muzzle /'mʌzl/ n (of animal) muso
m; (of firearm) bocca f; (for dog) muse-

ruola f ● vt fig mettere il bavaglio a

my /maɪ/ adj il mio m, la mia f, i miei
mpl, le mie fpl; **my mother/father**
mia madre/mio padre

myself /maɪ'self/ pron (reflexive) mi;
(emphatic) me stesso; (after prep) me;
I've seen it ~ l'ho visto io stesso;
by ~ da solo; **I thought to ~** ho
pensato tra me e me; **I'm proud of
~** sono fiero di me

mysterious /mɪ'stɪərɪəs/ adj misterioso. ~**ly** adv misteriosamente

mystery /'mɪstərɪ/ n mistero m; ~
[**story**] racconto m del mistero

mysti|c[al] /'mɪstɪk[l]/ adj mistico.
~**cism** n misticismo m

mystify /'mɪstɪfaɪ/ vt (pt/pp **-ied**)
disorientare

mystique /mɪ'sti:k/ n mistica f

myth /mɪθ/ n mito m. ~**ical** adj
mitico

mythology /mɪ'θɒlədʒɪ/ n mitologia f

Nn

nab /næb/ vt (pt/pp **nabbed**) ⊞
beccare

nag¹ /næg/ n (horse) ronzino m

nag² (pt/pp **nagged**) vt assillare ● vi
essere insistente ● n (person) brontolone, -a mf. ~**ging** adj (pain) persistente

nail /neɪl/ n chiodo m; (of finger, toe)
unghia f ● **nail down** vt inchiodare;
~ **sb down to a time/price** far fissare a qcno un'ora/un prezzo

nail polish n smalto m [per
unghie]

naked /'neɪkɪd/ adj nudo; **with the
~ eye** a occhio nudo

name /neɪm/ n nome m; **what's**

your ~? come ti chiami?; my ~ is Matthew mi chiamo Matthew; I know her by ~ la conosco di nome; by the ~ of Bates di nome Bates; call sb ~s ① insultare qcno ● vi (to position) nominare; chiamare (baby), (identify) citare; be ~d after essere chiamato col nome di. ~less adj senza nome. ~ly adv cioè

namesake n omonimo, -a mf

nanny /'næni/ n bambinaia f. ~-goat n capra f

nap /næp/ n pisolino m; **have a ~** fare un pisolino ● vi (pt/pp napped). **catch sb ~ping** cogliere qcno alla sprovvista

napkin /'næpkin/ n tovagliolo m

Naples /'neiplz/ n Napoli f

nappy /'næpi/ n pannolino m

narcotic /nɑː'kɒtik/ adj & n narcotico m

narrate /nə'reit/ vt narrare. ~ion n narrazione f

narrative /'nærətiv/ adj narrativo ● n narrazione f

narrator /nə'reitə(r)/ n narratore, -trice mf

narrow /'nærəʊ/ adj stretto; (fig: views) ristretto; (margin, majority) scarso ● vi restringersi. ~ly adv ~ly escape death evitare la morte per un pelo. ~-minded adj di idee ristrette

nasal /'neizl/ adj nasale

nasty /'nɑːsti/ adj (-ier, -iest) (smell, person, remark) cattivo; (injury, situation, weather) brutto; **turn ~** (person) diventare cattivo

nation /'neiʃn/ n nazione f

national /'næʃənl/ adj nazionale ● n cittadino, -a mf

national 'anthem n inno m nazionale

nationalism /'næʃənəlizm/ n nazionalismo m

nationality /næʃə'næləti/ n nazionalità f inv

'nation-wide adj su scala nazionale

native /'neitiv/ adj nativo; (innate) innato ● n nativo, -a mf; (local inhabitant) abitante m del posto; (outside Europe) indigeno, -a mf; **she's a ~ of Venice** è originaria di Venezia

native: ~ **land** n paese m natìo. ● **language** n lingua f madre

Nativity /nə'tivəti/ n the ~ la Natività f. ~ **play** n rappresentazione f sulla nascita di Gesù

natter /'nætə(r)/ vi ① chiacchierare

natural /'nætʃrəl/ adj naturale

natural 'history n storia f naturale

naturalist /'nætʃ(ə)rəlist/ n naturalista mf

naturally /'nætʃ(ə)rəli/ adv (of course) naturalmente; (by nature) per natura

nature /'neitʃə(r)/ n natura f, **by ~** per natura. ~ **reserve** n riserva f naturale

naughty /'nɔːti/ adj (-ier, -iest) monello; (slightly indecent) spinto

nausea /'nɔːziə/ n nausea f

nautical /'nɔːtikl/ adj nautico. ~ **mile** n miglio m marino

naval /'neivl/ adj navale

nave /neiv/ n navata f centrale

navel /'neɪvl/ n ombelico m

navigable /'nævɪgəbl/ adj navigabile

navigat|e /'nævɪgeɪt/ vi navigare; (Auto) fare da navigatore • vt navigare su (river). **~ion** n navigazione f. **~or** n navigatore m

navy /'neɪvɪ/ n marina f • **~ [blue]** adj blu marine inv • n blu m inv marine

Neapolitan /nɪə'pɒlɪtən/ adj & n napoletano, -a mf

near /nɪə(r)/ a vicino; (future) prossimo; the **~est bank** la banca più vicina • adv vicino; **draw ~** avvicinarsi; **~ at hand** a portata di mano • prep vicino a; **he was ~ to tears** aveva le lacrime agli occhi • vt avvicinarsi a

near: ~by adj & adv vicino. **~ly** adv quasi; **it's not ~ly enough** non è per niente sufficiente. **~-sighted** adj Am miope

neat /niːt/ adj (tidy) ordinato; (clever) efficace; (undiluted) liscio. **~ly** adv ordinatamente; (cleverly) efficacemente. **~ness** n (tidiness) ordine m

necessarily /nesə'serɪlɪ/ adv necessariamente

necessary /'nesəsərɪ/ adj necessario

necessit|ate /nɪ'sesɪteɪt/ vt rendere necessario. **~y** n necessità f inv

neck /nek/ n collo m; (of dress) colletto m; **~ and ~** testa a testa

necklace /'neklɪs/ n collana f

neckline n scollatura f

need /niːd/ n bisogno m; **be in ~ of** avere bisogno di; **if ~ be** se ce ne fosse bisogno; **there is a ~ for** c'è bisogno di; **there is no ~ for that** non ce n'è bisogno; **there is no ~ for you to go** non c'è bisogno che tu vada • vt aver bisogno di; **I ~ to know** devo saperlo; **it ~s to be done** bisogna farlo • v aux **you ~ not go** non c'è bisogno che tu vada;

~ I come? devo [proprio] venire?

needle /'niːdl/ n ago m; (for knitting) uncinetto m; (of record player) puntina f • vt ([1]: annoy) punzecchiare

needless /'niːdlɪs/ adj inutile

'needlework n cucito m

needy /'niːdɪ/ adj (-ier, -iest) bisognoso

negative /'negatɪv/ adj negativo • n negazione f; (Phot) negativo m; **in the ~** (Gram) alla forma negativa

neglect /nɪ'glekt/ n trascuratezza f; **state of ~** stato m di abbandono • vt trascurare; **he ~ed to write** non si è curato di scrivere. **~ed** adj trascurato. **~ful** adj negligente; **be ~ful of** trascurare

negligen|ce /'neglɪdʒəns/ n negligenza f. **~t** adj negligente

negligible /'neglɪdʒəbl/ adj trascurabile

negotiable /nɪ'gəʊʃəbl/ adj (road) transitabile; (Comm) negoziabile; **not ~** (cheque) non trasferibile

negotiat|e /nɪ'gəʊʃɪeɪt/ vt negoziare; (Auto) prendere (bend) • vi negoziare. **~ion** n negoziato m. **~or** n negoziatore, -trice mf

neigh /neɪ/ vi nitrire

neighbour /'neɪbə(r)/ n vicino, -a mf. **~hood** n vicinato m; **in the ~hood of** nei dintorni di; fig circa. **~ing** adj vicino. **~ly** adj amichevole

neither /'naɪðə(r)/ adj & pron nessuno dei due, né l'uno né l'altro • adv **~... nor** né... né • conj nemmeno, neanche; **~ do/did I** nemmeno io

neon /'niːɒn/ n neon m. **~ light** n luce f al neon

nephew /'nevjuː/ n nipote m

nerve /nɜːv/ n nervo m; ([1]: courage) coraggio m; ([1]: impudence) faccia f tosta; **lose one's ~** perdersi d'animo. **~-racking** adj logorante

nervous /'nɜːvəs/ adj nervoso; **he makes me ~** mi mette in agitazione; **he a ~ wreck** avere i nervi a pezzi. **~ breakdown** n esaurimento m nervoso. **~ly** adv nervosamente. **~ness** n nervosismo m; (before important event) tensione f

nervy /'nɜːvɪ/ adj (-ier, -iest) nervoso; (Am: impudent) sfacciato

nest /nest/ n nido m ● vi fare il nido. **~-egg** n gruzzolo m

nestle /'nesl/ vi accoccolarsi

net[1] /net/ n rete f ● vt (pt/pp netted) (catch) prendere (con la rete)

net[2] adj netto ● vt (pt/pp netted) incassare un utile netto di

netball n sport m inv femminile, simile a pallacanestro

Netherlands /'neðələndz/ npl **the ~** i Paesi mpl Bassi

netting /'netɪŋ/ n [wire] ~ reticolato m

nettle /'netl/ n ortica f

network n rete f

neurosis /njʊə'rəʊsɪs/ n (pl -oses /-siːz/) nevrosi f inv. **~otic** adj nevrotico

neuter /'njuːtə(r)/ adj (Gram) neutro ● n (Gram) neutro m ● vt sterilizzare

neutral /'njuːtrəl/ adj neutro; (country, person) neutrale ● n in (Auto) in folle. **~ity** n neutralità f. **~ize** vt neutralizzare

never /'nevə(r)/ adv [non...] mai; (I: expressing disbelief) ma va; **~ again** mai più; **well I ~!** chi l'avrebbe detto!. **~-ending** adj interminabile

nevertheless /nevəðə'les/ adv tuttavia

new /njuː/ adj nuovo

new: **~born** adj neonato. **~comer** n nuovo, -a arrivato, -a mf. **~fangled** /-'fæŋgld/ adj pej modernizzante

newly adv (recently) di recente; **~built** costruito di recente; **~-weds** npl sposini mpl

news /njuːz/ n notizie fpl; (TV) tele-

giornale m; (Radio) giornale m radio; **piece of ~** notizia f

news: **~agent** n giornalaio, -a mf. **~caster** n giornalista mf televisivo, -a/radiofonico, -a. **~flash** n notizia f flash. **~letter** n bollettino m d'informazione. **~paper** n giornale m; (material) carta f di giornale. **~reader** n giornalista mf televisivo, -a/radiofonico, -a

new: **~ year** n (next year) anno m nuovo; **N~ Year's Day** n Capodanno m. **N~ Year's Eve** n vigilia f di Capodanno. **N~ Zealand** /'ziːlənd/ n Nuova Zelanda f

next /nekst/ adj prossimo; (adjoining) vicino; **who's ~?** a chi tocca?; **~ door** accanto; **~ to nothing** quasi niente; **the ~ day** il giorno dopo; **~ week** la settimana prossima, **the week after ~** fra due settimane ● adv dopo; **when will you see him ~?** quando lo rivedi la prossima volta?; **~ to** accanto a ● n seguente mf; **~ of kin** parente m prossimo

nib /nɪb/ n pennino m

nibble /'nɪbl/ vt/i mordicchiare

nice /naɪs/ adj (day, weather, holiday) bello; (person) gentile, simpatico; (food) buono; **it was ~ meeting you** è stato un piacere conoscerla. **~ly** adv gentilmente; (well) bene. **~ties** n nicchia f

niche /niːʃ/ n nicchia f

nick /nɪk/ n tacca f; (on chin etc) taglietto m; (I: prison) galera f; (I: police station) centrale f [di polizia]; **in the ~ of time** I appena in tempo ● vt intaccare; (I: steal) fregare; (I: arrest) beccare; **~ one's chin** farsi un taglietto nel mento

nickel /'nɪkl/ n nichel m; Am moneta f da cinque centesimi

nickname n soprannome m ● vt soprannominare

nicotine /'nɪkətiːn/ n nicotina f

niece /niːs/ n nipote f

niggling /'nɪglɪŋ/ *adj* (detail) insignificante; (pain) fastidioso; (doubt) persistente

night /naɪt/ *n* notte *f*; (evening) sera *f*; **at ∼** la notte, di notte; (in the evening) la sera, di sera; **Monday ∼** lunedì notte/sera ● *adj* di notte

night: **∼cap** *n* papalina *f*; (drink) bicchierino *m* bevuto prima di andare a letto. **∼-club** *n* locale *m* notturno, night[-club] *m* inv. **∼-dress** *n* camicia *f* da notte. **∼-fall** *n* crepuscolo *m*. **∼-gown**, [] **∼-ie** /'naɪtɪ/ *n* camicia *f* da notte

night: **∼-life** *n* vita *f* notturna. **∼ly** *adj* di notte, di sera ● *adv* ogni notte, ogni sera. **∼mare** *n* incubo *m*. **∼-school** *n* scuola *f* serale. **∼-time** *n* **at ∼-time** di notte, la notte. **∼-watchman** *n* guardiano *m* notturno

nil /nɪl/ *n* nulla *m*; (Sport) zero *m*

nimbl|e /'nɪmbl/ *adj* agile. **∼y** *adv* agilmente

nine /naɪn/ *adj* nove *inv* ● *n* nove *m*. **∼teen** *adj* diciannove *inv* ● *n* diciannove. **∼'teenth** *adj* & *n* diciannovesimo, -a *mf*

ninetieth /'naɪntɪɪθ/ *adj* & *n* novantesimo, -a

ninety /'naɪntɪ/ *adj* novanta *inv* ● *n* novanta *m*

ninth /naɪnθ/ *adj* & *n* nono, -a *mf*

nip /nɪp/ *n* pizzicotto *m*; (bite) morso *m* ● *vt* pizzicare; (bite) mordere; **∼ in the bud** *fig* stroncare sul nascere ● *vi* ([] run) fare un salto

nipple /'nɪpl/ *n* capezzolo *m*; (Am: on bottle) tettarella *f*

nippy /'nɪpɪ/ *adj* (-ier, -iest) [] (cold) pungente; (quick) svelto

nitrogen /'naɪtrədʒn/ *n* azoto *m*

no /nəʊ/ *adv* no ● *n* (*pl* **noes**) no *m* inv ● *adj* nessuno; **I have no time** non ho tempo; **in no time** in un baleno; **'no parking'** 'sosta vietata'; **'no smoking'** 'vietato fumare'; **no one**

nessuno *v.* **nobody**

noble /'nəʊbl/ *adj* nobile. **∼man** *n* nobile *m*

nobody /'nəʊbədɪ/ *pron* nessuno; **he knows ∼** non conosce nessuno ● *n* **he's a ∼** non è nessuno

nocturnal /nɒk'tɜːnl/ *adj* notturno

nod /nɒd/ *n* cenno *m* del capo ● *vi* (*pt/pp* **nodded**) fare un cenno col capo; (in agreement) fare di sì col capo ● *vt* **∼ one's head** fare di sì col capo. □ **∼ off** *vi* assopirsi

noise /nɔɪz/ *n* rumore *m*; (loud) rumore *m*, chiasso *m*. **∼less** *adj* silenzioso. **∼lessly** *adv* silenziosamente

noisy /'nɔɪzɪ/ *adj* (-ier, -iest) rumoroso

nomad /'nəʊmæd/ *n* nomade *mf*. **∼ic** *adj* nomade

nominat|e /'nɒmɪneɪt/ *vt* proporre come candidato; (appoint) designare. **∼ion** *n* nomina *f*; (person nominated) candidato, -a *mf*

nonchalant /'nɒnʃələnt/ *adj* disinvolto

non-com'mittal *adj* che non si sbilancia

nondescript /'nɒndɪskrɪpt/ *adj* qualunque

none /nʌn/ *pron* (person) nessuno; (thing) niente; **∼ of us** nessuno di noi; **∼ of this** niente di questo; **there's ∼ left** non ce n'è più ● *adv* **she's ∼ too pleased** non è per niente soddisfatta; **I'm ∼ the wiser** non ne so più di prima

nonentity /nɒ'nentɪtɪ/ *n* nullità *f*

non-ex'istent *adj* inesistente

nonplussed /nɒn'plʌst/ *adj* perplesso

nonsens|e /'nɒnsəns/ *n* sciocchezze *fpl.* **∼ical** *adj* assurdo

non-'smoker *n* non fumatore, -trice *mf*; (compartment) scompartimento *m* non fumatori

non-'stop *adj* **∼ 'flight** volo *m* diretto ● *adv* senza sosta; (fly) senza scalo

noodles /'nuːdlz/ npl taglierini mpl

nook /nʊk/ n cantuccio m

noon /nuːn/ n mezzogiorno m; **at ~** a mezzogiorno

noose /nuːs/ n nodo m scorsoio

nor /nɔː(r)/ adv & conj né; **~ do I** neppure io

norm /nɔːm/ n norma f.

normal /'nɔːml/ adj normale. **~ity** n normalità f. **~ly** adv (usually) normalmente

north /nɔːθ/ n nord m; **to the ~ of** a nord di ● adj del nord, settentrionale ● adv a nord

north: N~ America n America f del Nord. **~-east** adj di nord-est, nordorientale ● n nord-est m ● adv a nord-est; (travel) verso nord-est

norther|ly /'nɔːðəlɪ/ adj (direction) nord; (wind) del nord. **~n** adj del nord, settentrionale. **N~n Ireland** n Irlanda f del Nord

north: N~ 'Sea n Mare m del Nord. **~ward[s]** /-wəd(z)/ adv verso nord. **~-west** adj di nord-ovest, nordoccidentale ● n nord-ovest m ● adv a nord-ovest; (travel) verso nord-ovest

Nor|way /'nɔːweɪ/ n Norvegia f. **~wegian** adj & n norvegese mf

nose /nəʊz/ n naso m

nose: ~bleed n emorragia f nasale. **~dive** n (Aeron) picchiata f

nostalg|ia /nɒ'stældʒɪə/ n nostalgia f. **~ic** adj nostalgico

nostril /'nɒstrəl/ n narice f

nosy /'nəʊzɪ/ adj (-ier, -iest) I ficcanaso inv

not /nɒt/ adv non; **he is ~** Italian non è italiano; **I hope ~** spero di no; **~ all of us** have been invited non siamo stati tutti invitati; **if ~** se no; **~ at all** niente affatto; **~ a bit** per niente; **~ even** neanche; **~ yet** non ancora; **~ only... but also...** non solo... ma anche...

notabl|e /'nəʊtəbl/ adj (remarkable) notevole. **~y** adv (in particular) in particolare

notary /'nəʊtərɪ/ n notaio m; **~ 'public** notaio m

notch /nɒtʃ/ n tacca f ● **notch up** vt (score) segnare

note /nəʊt/ n nota f; (short letter, banknote) biglietto m; (memo, written comment etc) appunto m; **of ~** (person) di spicco; (comments, event) degno di nota; **make a ~ of** prendere nota di; **take ~ of** (notice) prendere nota di ● vt (notice) notare; (write) annotare. **~ ~ down** vt annotare

'notebook n taccuino m; (Comput) notebook m inv

noted /'nəʊtɪd/ adj noto, celebre (for per)

notepaper n carta f da lettere

nothing /'nʌθɪŋ/ pron niente, nulla ● adv niente affatto. **for ~** (free, in vain) per niente; (with no reason) senza motivo; **~ but** nient'altro che; **~ much** poco o nulla; **~ interesting** niente di interessante; **it's ~ to do with you** non ti riguarda

notice /'nəʊtɪs/ n (on board) avviso m; (review) recensione f; (termination of employment) licenziamento m; |**advance|** ~ preavviso m; **two months ~** due mesi di preavviso; **at short ~** con breve preavviso; **until further ~** fino a nuovo avviso; **hand in one's ~** (employee) dare le dimissioni; **give an employee ~** dare il preavviso a un impiegato; **take no ~ of** non fare caso a; **take no ~!** non farci caso! ● vt notare. **~able** adj evidente. **~ably** adv sensibilmente. **~-board** n bacheca f

noti|fication /nəʊtɪfɪ'keɪʃn/ n notifica f. **~fy** vt (pt/pp -ied) notificare

notion /'nəʊʃn/ n idea f, nozione f; **~s** pl (Am: haberdashery) merceria f

notorious /nəʊ'tɔːrɪəs/ adj famigerato; **be ~ for** essere tristemente famoso per

n

notwith'standing /prep malgrado
● *abbr* ciononostante

nougat /'nu:ga:/ *n* torrone *m*

nought /nɔ:t/ *n* zero *m*

noun /naʊn/ *n* nome *m*, so-
stantivo *m*

nourish /'nʌrɪʃ/ *vt* nutrire. **~ing** *adj*
nutriente. **~ment** *n* nutrimento *m*

novel /'nɒvl/ *adj* insolito ● *n* romanzo *m*. **~ist** *n* romanziere, -a *mf*.
~ty *n* novità *f*; **~ties** *pl (objects)* og-
gettini *mpl*

November /nəʊ'vembə(r)/ *n* novembre *m*

novice /'nɒvɪs/ *n* novizio, -a *mf*

now /naʊ/ *adv* ora, adesso; **by ~**
ormai; **just ~** proprio ora; **right ~**
subito; **~ and again**, **~ and then**
ogni tanto; **~, ~!** su! ● *conj* **~**
[**that**] ora che, adesso che

'nowadays *adv* oggigiorno

nowhere /'nəʊ-/ *adv* in nessun
posto, da nessuna parte

nozzle /'nɒzl/ *n* bocchetta *f*

nuance /'nju:ɑ̃:ns/ *n* sfumatura *f*

nuclear /'nju:klɪə(r)/ *adj* nucleare

nucleus /'nju:klɪəs/ *n* (*pl* **-lei** /-lɪaɪ/)
nucleo *m*

nude /nju:d/ *adj* nudo ● *n* nudo *m*;
in the ~ nudo

nudge /nʌdʒ/ *n* colpetto *m* di gomito ● *vt* dare un colpetto col gomito a

nudism /'nju:dɪzm/ *n* nudismo *m*

nud|ist /'nju:dɪst/ *n* nudista *mf*.
~ity *n* nudità *f*

nuisance /'nju:sns/ *n* seccatura *f*;
(*person*) piaga *f*; **what a ~!** che seccatura!

null /nʌl/ *adj* **~ and void** nullo

numb /nʌm/ *adj* intorpidito; **~ with
cold** intirizzito dal freddo

number /'nʌmbə(r)/ *n* numero *m*; **a
~ of people** un certo numero di
persone ● *vt* numerare; (*include*) annoverare. **~-plate** *n* targa *f*

numeral /'nju:mərəl/ *n* numero *m*,
cifra *f*

numerical /nju:'merɪkl/ *adj* numerico; **in ~ order** in ordine numerico

numerous /'nju:mərəs/ *adj* nu-
meroso

nun /nʌn/ *n* suora *f*

nurse /nɜ:s/ *n* infermiere, -a *mf*;
children's ~ bambinaia *f* ● *vt* curare

nursery /'nɜ:səri/ *n* stanza *f* dei
bambini; (*for plants*) vivaio *m*; [**day**]
~ asilo *m*. **~ rhyme** *n* filastrocca *f*. **~
school** *n* scuola *f* materna

nut /nʌt/ *n* noce *f*; (*Techn*) dado *m*;
(☐: *head*) zucca *f*; **~s** *npl* frutta *f*
secca; **be ~s** ☐ essere svitato.
~crackers *npl* schiaccianoci *m inv.*
~meg *n* noce *f* moscata

nutrit|ion /nju:'trɪʃn/ *n* nutrizione
f. **~ious** *adj* nutriente

'nutshell *n* **in a ~** *fig* in parole
povere

nylon /'naɪlɒn/ *n* nailon *m*; **~s** *pl*
calze *fpl* di nailon ● *attrib* di nailon

Oo

oaf /əʊf/ *n* (*pl* **oafs**) zoticone, -a *mf*

oak /əʊk/ *n* quercia *f* ● *attrib* di
quercia

OAP *n abbr* (old-age pensioner) pensionato, -a *mf*

oar /ɔ:(r)/ *n* remo *m*. **~sman** *n* voga-
tore *m*

oasis /əʊ'eɪsɪs/ *n* (*pl* **oases** /-si:z/)
oasi *f inv*

oath /əʊθ/ *n* giuramento *m*; (*swear-
word*) bestemmia *f*

oatmeal /'əʊt-/ *n* farina *f* d'avena

oats /əʊts/ *npl* avena *fsg*; (*Culin*)
[**rolled**] **~** fiocchi *mpl* di avena

obedien|ce /əˈbiːdɪəns/ n ubbidienza f. **~t** adj ubbidiente

obes|e /əˈbiːs/ adj obeso. **~ity** n obesità f

obey /əˈbeɪ/ vt ubbidire a; osservare (instructions, rules) ● vi ubbidire

obituary /əˈbɪtjʊərɪ/ n necrologio m

object¹ /ˈɒbdʒɪkt/ n oggetto m; (Gram) complemento m oggetto; **money is no ~** i soldi non sono un problema

object² /əbˈdʒekt/ vi (be against) opporsi (**to** a); **~ that...** obiettare che...

objection /əbˈdʒekʃn/ n obiezione f; **have no ~** non avere niente in contrario. **~able** adj discutibile; (person) sgradevole

objectiv|e /əbˈdʒektɪv/ adj oggettivo ● n obiettivo m. **~ely** adv obiettivamente. **~ity** n oggettività f

obligation /ɒblɪˈɡeɪʃn/ n obbligo m; **be under an ~** avere un obbligo, **without ~** senza impegno

obligatory /əˈblɪɡətrɪ/ adj obbligatorio

oblig|e /əˈblaɪdʒ/ vt (compel) obbligare; **much ~ed** grazie mille. **~ing** adj disponibile

oblique /əˈbliːk/ adj obliquo; fig indiretto ● n [stroke] barra f

obliterate /əˈblɪtəreɪt/ vt obliterare

oblivion /əˈblɪvɪən/ n oblio m

oblivious /əˈblɪvɪəs/ adj **be ~** essere dimentico (**of, to** di)

oblong /ˈɒblɒŋ/ adj oblungo ● n rettangolo m

obnoxious /əbˈnɒkʃəs/ adj detestabile

oboe /ˈəʊbəʊ/ n oboe m inv

obscen|e /əbˈsiːn/ adj osceno; (profits, wealth) vergognoso. **~ity** n oscenità f inv

obscur|e /əbˈskjʊə(r)/ adj oscuro ● vt oscurare; (confuse) mettere in ombra. **~ity** n oscurità f

obsequious /əbˈsiːkwɪəs/ adj ossequioso

observatory /əbˈzɜːvətrɪ/ n osservatorio m

observe /əbˈzɜːv/ vt osservare; (notice) notare; (keep, celebrate) celebrare. **~r** n osservatore, -trice mf

obsess /əbˈses/ vt **be ~ed by** essere fissato con. **~ion** n fissazione f. **~ive** adj ossessivo

obsolete /ˈɒbsəliːt/ adj obsoleto; (word) desueto

obstacle /ˈɒbstəkl/ n ostacolo m

obstina|cy /ˈɒbstɪnəsɪ/ n ostinazione f. **~te** adj ostinato

obstruct /əbˈstrʌkt/ vt ostruire; (hinder) ostacolare. **~ion** n ostruzione f; (obstacle) ostacolo m. **~ive** adj **be ~ive** (person:) creare dei problemi

obtain /əbˈteɪn/ vt ottenere. **~able** adj ottenibile

obtrusive /əbˈtruːsɪv/ adj (object) stonato

obtuse /əbˈtjuːs/ adj ottuso

obvious /ˈɒbvɪəs/ adj ovvio. **~ly** adv ovviamente

occasion /əˈkeɪʒn/ n occasione f; (event) evento m; **on ~** talvolta; **on the ~ of** in occasione di

occasional /əˈkeɪʒənl/ adj saltuario; **he has the ~ glass of wine** ogni tanto beve un bicchiere di vino. **~ly** adv ogni tanto

occult /ɒˈkʌlt/ adj occulto

occupant /ˈɒkjʊpənt/ n occupante mf; (of vehicle) persona f a bordo

occupation /ɒkjʊˈpeɪʃn/ n occupazione f; (job) professione f. **~al** adj professionale

occupier /ˈɒkjʊpaɪə(r)/ n residente mf

occupy /ˈɒkjʊpaɪ/ vt (pt/pp occupied) occupare; (keep busy) tenere occupato

occur /əˈkɜː(r)/ vi (pt/pp occurred)

accadere; (*exist*) trovarsi; **it ~red to me that** mi è venuto in mente che. **~rence** n (*event*) fatto m

ocean /ˈəʊʃn/ n oceano m

octave /ˈɒktɪv/ n (*Mus*) ottava f

October /ɒkˈtəʊbə(r)/ n ottobre m

octopus /ˈɒktəpəs/ n (*pl* **-puses**) polpo m

odd /ɒd/ adj (*number*) dispari; (*not of set*) scompagnato; (*strange*) strano; **forty ~** quaranta e rotti; **~ jobs** lavoretti mpl; **the ~ one out** l'eccezione; **at ~ moments** a tempo perso; **have the ~ glass of wine** avere un bicchiere di vino ogni tanto

odd|ity /ˈɒdɪtɪ/ n stranezza f. **~ly** adv stranamente; **~ly enough** stranamente. **~ment** n (*of fabric*) scampolo m

odds /ɒdz/ npl (*chances*) probabilità fpl; **at ~** in disaccordo; **~ and ends** cianfrusaglie fpl; **it makes no ~** non fa alcuna differenza

odour /ˈəʊdə(r)/ n odore m. **~less** adj inodore

of /ɒv/, /əv/ prep di; **a cup of tea/ coffee** una tazza di tè/caffè; **the hem of my skirt** l'orlo della mia gonna; **the summer of 1989** l'estate del 1989; **the two of us** noi due; **made of** di; **that's very kind of you** è molto gentile da parte tua; **a friend of mine** un mio amico; **a child of three** un bambino di tre anni; **the fourth of January** il quattro gennaio; **within a year of their divorce** a circa un anno dal loro divorzio; **half of it** la metà; **the whole of the room** tutta la stanza

off /ɒf/ prep da; (*distant from*) lontano da; **take £10 ~ the price** ridurre il prezzo di 10 sterline; **~ the coast** presso la costa; **a street ~ the main road** una traversa della via principale; (*near*) una strada vicino alla via principale; **get ~ the ladder** scendere dalla scala; **get off the bus** uscire dall'autobus; **leave the lid ~**

the saucepan lasciare la pentola senza il coperchio ● adv (*button, handle*) staccato; (*light, machine*) spento; (*brake*) tolto; (*tap*) chiuso; **'off'** (*on appliance*) 'off'; **2 kilometres ~** a due chilometri di distanza; **a long way ~** molto distante; (*time*) lontano; **~ and on** di tanto in tanto; **with his hat/coat ~** senza il cappello/cappotto; **with the light ~** a luce spenta; **20% ~** 20% di sconto; **be ~** (*leave*) andar via;° (*Sport*) essere partito; (*food*:) essere andato a male; (*all gone*) essere finito; (*wedding, engagement*:) essere cancellato; **I'm ~ alcohol** ho smesso di bere; **be ~ one's food** non avere appetito; **she's ~ today** (*on holiday*) è in ferie oggi; (*ill*:) è malata oggi; **I'm ~ home** vado a casa; **you'd be better ~ doing...** faresti meglio a fare...; **have a day ~** avere un giorno di vacanza; **drive/sail ~** andare via

'off-beat adj insolito

'off-chance n possibilità f remota

offence /əˈfens/ n (*illegal act*) reato m; **give ~** offendere; **take ~** offendersi (**at** per)

offend /əˈfend/ vt offendere. **~er** n (*Jur*) colpevole mf

offensive /əˈfensɪv/ adj offensivo ● n offensiva f

offer /ˈɒfə(r)/ n offerta f ● vt offrire; opporre (*resistance*); **~ sb sth** offrire qcsa a qcno; **~ to do sth** offrirsi di fare qcsa. **~ing** n offerta f

off'hand adj (*casual*) spiccio ● adv su due piedi

office /ˈɒfɪs/ n ufficio m; (*post, job*) carica f. **~ hours** pl orario m d'ufficio

officer /ˈɒfɪsə(r)/ n ufficiale m; (*police*) agente m [di polizia]

official /əˈfɪʃl/ adj ufficiale ● n funzionario, -a mf; (*Sport*) dirigente m. **~ly** adv ufficialmente

'offing n **in the ~** in vista

'off-licence n negozio m per la vendita di alcolici

'off-putting adj 🔲 scoraggiante

offset vt (pt/pp -set, pres p -setting) controbilanciare

offshore ●adj (wind) di terra; (company, investment) offshore. ● adv (sail) al largo; (relocate) all'estero (in paesi dove la manodopera costa meno); **to move jobs ~** delocalizzare gli impieghi. **~ rig** n piattaforma f petrolifera, off-shore m inv

off'side adj (Sport) [in] fuori gioco; (wheel etc.) (left) sinistro; (right) destro

'offspring n prole m

off'stage adv dietro le quinte

off-'white adj bianco sporco

often /'ɒfn/ adv spesso; **how ~** ogni quanto; **every so ~** una volta ogni tanto

ogle /'əʊgl/ vt mangiarsi con gli occhi

oh /əʊ/ int oh!; **~ dear** oh Dio!

oil /ɔɪl/ n olio m; (petroleum) petrolio m; (for heating) nafta f ● vt oliare

oil: **~field** n giacimento m di petrolio. **~painting** n pittura f a olio. **~ refinery** n raffineria f di petrolio. **~ rig** piattaforma f per trivellazione subacquea

oily /'ɔɪli/ adj (-ier, -iest) unto; fig untuoso

ointment /'ɔɪntmənt/ n pomata f

OK /əʊ'keɪ/ int va bene, o.k. ● adj **if that's OK with you** se ti va bene; **she's OK** (well) sta bene; **is the milk still OK?** il latte è ancora buono? ● adv (well) bene ● vt (anche **okay**) (pt/pp **okayed**) dare l'o.k.

old /əʊld/ adj vecchio; (girlfriend) ex; **how ~ is she?** quanti anni ha?; **she is ten years ~** ha dieci anni

old: **~ age** n vecchiaia f. **~fashioned** adj antiquato

olive /'ɒlɪv/ n (fruit, colour) oliva f; (tree) olivo m ● adj d'oliva; (colour) olivastro. **~ branch** n fig ramoscello m

d'olivo. **~ 'oil** n olio m di oliva

Olympic /ə'lɪmpɪk/ adj olimpico; **~s, ~ Games** Olimpiadi fpl

omelette /'ɒmlɪt/ n omelette f inv

omen /'əʊmən/ n presagio m

omission /ə'mɪʃn/ n omissione f

omit /ə'mɪt/ vt (pt/pp **omitted**) omettere; **~ to do sth** tralasciare di fare qcsa

once /wʌns/ adv una volta; (formerly) un tempo; **~ upon a time there was** c'era una volta; **at ~** subito; (at the same time) contemporaneamente; **~ and for all** una volta per tutte ● conj [non] appena. **~-over** n 🔲 **give sb/sth the ~-over** (look, check) dare un'occhiata veloce a qcno/qcsa

---

one /wʌn/

● adj uno, una; **not ~ person** nemmeno una persona

● n uno m

● pron uno; (impersonal) si; **~ another** l'un l'altro; **~ by ~** [a] uno a uno; **~ never knows** non si sa mai

one: **~self** pron (reflexive) si; (emphatic) sé, se stesso; **by ~self** da solo; **be proud of ~self** essere fieri di sé. **~-way** adj (street) a senso unico; (ticket) di sola andata

onion /'ʌnjən/ n cipolla f

on-line adj/adv su Internet; **you are now ~** ora sei in linea

'onlooker n spettatore, -trice mf

only /'əʊnlı/ adj solo; **~ child** figlio, -a mf unico, -a ● adv & conj solo, solamente; **~ just** appena

'onset n (beginning) inizio m

on-shore adj (on land) di terra; (breeze) di mare

onslaught /'ɒnslɔːt/ n attacco m

onus /'əʊnəs/ n **the ~ is on me** spetta a me la responsabilità (**to** di)

ooze /uːz/ vi fluire

opaque /əʊˈpeɪk/ adj opaco

open /ˈəʊpən/ adj aperto; (free to all) pubblico; (job) vacante; **in the ~ air** all'aperto ● n **in the ~** all'aperto; (fig) alla luce del sole ● vt aprire ● vi aprirsi; (shop;) aprire; (flower:) sbocciare. □ **~ up** vt aprire ● vi aprirsi

opening /ˈəʊpənɪŋ/ n apertura f; (beginning) inizio m; (job) posto m libero; **~ hours** npl orario m d'apertura

openly /ˈəʊpənlɪ/ adv apertamente

open: **~-ˈminded** adj aperto; (broadminded) di vedute larghe. **~-plan** adj a pianta aperta

Open University Fondata nel 1969, è il sistema di università a distanza del Regno Unito. L'insegnamento viene impartito con vari mezzi: per corrispondenza, attraverso programmi radiotelevisivi trasmessi dalla BBC e anche via Internet. Gli studenti inviano per posta i compiti svolti a un tutore. Generalmente si seguono corsi part time della durata di quattro o cinque anni, anche se non ci sono limiti di tempo per completare gli studi.

opera /ˈɒpərə/ n opera f

opera-house n teatro m lirico

operate /ˈɒpəreɪt/ vt far funzionare (machine, lift); azionare (lever, brake); mandare avanti (business) ● vi (Techn) funzionare; (be in action) essere in funzione; (Mil, fig) operare; **~ on** (Med) operare

operatic /ɒpəˈrætɪk/ adj lirico, operistico

operation /ɒpəˈreɪʃn/ n operazione f; (Techn) funzionamento m; **in ~** (Techn) in funzione; **come into ~** fig entrare in funzione; (law:) entrare in vigore; **have an ~** (Med) subire un'operazione. **~al** adj operativo; (law etc) in vigore

operative /ˈɒpərətɪv/ adj operativo

operator /ˈɒpəreɪtə(r)/ n (user) operatore, -trice mf; (Teleph) centralinista m

opinion /əˈpɪnjən/ n opinione f; **in my ~** secondo me. **~ated** adj dogmatico

opponent /əˈpəʊnənt/ n avversario, -a mf

opportune /ˈɒpətjuːn/ adj opportuno. **~ist** n opportunista mf. **~istic** adj opportunistico

opportunity /ɒpəˈtjuːnəti/ n opportunità f inv

oppose /əˈpəʊz/ vt opporsi a; **be ~ed to sth** essere contrario a qcsa; **as ~ed to** al contrario di. **~ing** adj avversario; (opposite) opposto

opposite /ˈɒpəzɪt/ adj opposto; (house) di fronte; **~ number** fig controparte f; **the ~ sex** l'altro sesso ● n contrario m ● adv di fronte ● prep di fronte a

opposition /ɒpəˈzɪʃn/ n opposizione f

oppress /əˈpres/ vt opprimere. **~ion** n oppressione f. **~ive** adj oppressivo; (heat) opprimente. **~or** n oppressore m

opt /ɒpt/ vi **~ for** optare per; **~ out** dissociarsi (of da)

optical /ˈɒptɪkl/ adj ottico; **~ illusion** illusione f ottica

optician /ɒpˈtɪʃn/ n ottico, -a mf

optimism /ˈɒptɪmɪzm/ n ottimismo m. **~t** n ottimista mf. **~tic** adj ottimistico

option /ˈɒpʃn/ n scelta f; (Comm) opzione f. **~al** adj facoltativo; **~al extras** pl optional m inv

or /ɔː(r)/ conj o, oppure; (after negative) né; or [else] se no; **in a year or two** fra un anno o due

oral /ˈɔːrəl/ adj orale ● n 🛈 esame m orale. **~ly** adv oralmente

orange /ˈɒrɪndʒ/ n arancia f; (colour) arancione m ● adj arancione. **~ade** n aranciata f. **~ juice** n succo m d'arancia

orbit /'ɔːbɪt/ n orbita f ● vt orbitare. **~al** adj **~al road** tangenziale f

orchard /'ɔːtʃəd/ n frutteto m

orchestra /'ɔːkɪstrə/ n orchestra f. **~al** adj orchestrale. **~trate** vt orchestrare

orchid /'ɔːkɪd/ n orchidea f

ordain /ɔː'deɪn/ vt decretare; (Relig) ordinare

ordeal /ɔː'diːl/ n fig terribile esperienza f

order /'ɔːdə(r)/ n ordine m; (Comm) ordinazione f; **out of ~** (machine) fuori servizio; **in ~ that** affinché; **in ~ to** per ● vt ordinare

orderly /'ɔːdəlɪ/ adj ordinato ● n (Mil) attendente m; (Med) inserviente m

ordinary /'ɔːdɪnərɪ/ adj ordinario

ore /ɔː(r)/ n minerale m grezzo

organ /'ɔːgən/ n (Anat, Mus) organo m

organic /ɔː'gænɪk/ adj organico; (without chemicals) biologico. **~ally** adv organicamente; **~ally grown** coltivato biologicamente

organism /'ɔːgənɪzm/ n organismo m

organist /'ɔːgənɪst/ n organista mf

organization /ɔːgənaɪ'zeɪʃn/ n organizzazione f

organize /'ɔːgənaɪz/ vt organizzare. **~r** n organizzatore, -trice mf

orgasm /'ɔːgæzm/ n orgasmo m

orgy /'ɔːdʒɪ/ n orgia f

Orient /'ɔːrɪənt/ n Oriente m. **o~al** adj orientale ● n orientale mf

orient|ate /'ɔːrɪentet/ vt **~ate** oneself orientarsi. **~ation** n orientamento m

origin /'ɒrɪdʒɪn/ n origine f

original /ə'rɪdʒən(ə)l/ adj originario; (not copied, new) originale ● n originale m; **in the ~** in versione originale.

~ity n originalità f. **~ly** adv originariamente

originate /ə'rɪdʒɪnet/ vi **~e in** avere origine in. **~or** n ideatore, -trice mf

ornament /'ɔːnəmənt/ n ornamento m; (on mantelpiece etc) soprammobile m. **~al** adj ornamentale. **~ation** n decorazione f

ornate /ɔː'neɪt/ adj ornato

orphan /'ɔːfn/ n orfano, -a mf ● vt rendere orfano; **be ~ed** rimanere orfano. **~age** n orfanotrofio m

orthodox /'ɔːθədɒks/ adj ortodosso

oscillate /'ɒsɪleɪt/ vi oscillare

osteopath /'ɒstɪəpæθ/ n osteopata mf

ostracize /'ɒstrəsaɪz/ vt bandire

ostrich /'ɒstrɪtʃ/ n struzzo m

other /'ʌðə(r)/ adj, pron ● n altro, -a mf; **the ~ [one]** l'altro, -a mf; **the ~ two** gli altri due; **two ~s** altri due; **~ people** gli altri; **any ~ questions?** altre domande?; **every ~ day** (alternate days) a giorni alterni; **the ~ day** l'altro giorno; **the ~ evening** l'altra sera; **someone/ something or ~** qualcuno/qualcosa ● adv **~ than him** tranne lui; **somehow or ~** in qualche modo; **somewhere or ~** da qualche parte

'otherwise adv altrimenti; (differently) diversamente

otter /'ɒtə(r)/ n lontra f

ouch /aʊtʃ/ int ahi!

ought /ɔːt/ v aux I/we **~ to stay** dovrei/dovremmo rimanere; **he ~ not to have done it** non avrebbe dovuto farlo; **that ~ to be enough** questo dovrebbe bastare

ounce /aʊns/ n oncia f (= 28,35 g)

our /'aʊə(r)/ adj il nostro m, la nostra f, i nostri mpl, le nostre fpl. **mother/father** nostra madre/ nostro padre

ours /'aʊəz/ poss pron il nostro m, la nostra f, i nostri mpl, le nostre fpl; **a**

friend of ~ un nostro amico; **friends of** ~ dei nostri amici; **that is** ~ quello è nostro; (as opposed to yours) quello è il nostro

ourselves /aʊəˈselvz/ pron (reflexive) ci; (emphatic) noi, noi stessi; **we poured** ~ **a drink** ci siamo versati da bere; **we heard it** ~ l'abbiamo sentito noi stessi; **we are proud of** ~ siamo fieri di noi; **by** ~ da soli

out /aʊt/ adv fuori; (not alight) spento; **be** ~ (flower:) essere sbocciato; (workers:) essere in sciopero; (calculation:) essere sbagliato; (Sport) essere fuori; (unconscious) aver perso i sensi; (fig: not feasible) fuori questione; **the sun is** ~ è uscito il sole; ~ **and about** in piedi; ~ **...!** 🔟 fuori!; **you should get** ~ **more** dovresti uscire più spesso; ~ **with it!** 🔟 sputa il rospo!; ● prep ~ **of** fuori da; ~ **of date** non aggiornato; (passport) scaduto; ~ **of order** guasto; ~ **of print/stock** esaurito; ~ **of bed/the room** fuori dal letto/dalla stanza; ~ **of breath** senza fiato; ~ **of danger** fuori pericolo; ~ **of work** disoccupato; **nine** ~ **of ten** nove su dieci; **be** ~ **of sugar/bread** rimanere senza zucchero/pane; **go** ~ **of the room** uscire dalla stanza

'outbreak n (of war) scoppio m; (of disease) insorgenza f

'outburst n esplosione f

'outcome n risultato m

'outcry n protesta f

out'dated adj sorpassato

out'do vt (pt -did, pp -done) superare

'outdoor adj (life, sports) all'aperto; ~ **clothes** pl vestiti per uscire; ~ **swimming pool** piscina f scoperta

out'doors adv all'aria aperta; **go** ~ uscire [all'aria aperta]

'outer adj esterno

'outfit n equipaggiamento m; (clothes) completo m; (🔟: organization)

organizzazione. ~**ter** n men's ~**ter's** negozio m di abbigliamento maschile

'outgoing adj (president) uscente; (mail) in partenza; (sociable) estroverso. ~**s** npl uscite fpl

out'grow vi (pt -grew, pp -grown) diventare troppo grande per

outing /'aʊtɪŋ/ n gita f

outlandish /aʊtˈlændɪʃ/ adj stravagante

'outlaw n fuorilegge mf inv ● vt dichiarare illegale

'outlay n spesa f

'outlet n sbocco m; fig sfogo m; (Comm) punto m [di] vendita

'outline n contorno m; (summary) sommario m ● vt tracciare il contorno di; (describe) descrivere

out'live vt sopravvivere a

'outlook n vista f; (future prospect) prospettiva f; (attitude) visione f

'outlying adj ~ **areas** pl zone fpl periferiche

out'number vt superare in numero

'out-patient n paziente mf esterno, -a; ~**s' department** ambulatorio m

'output n produzione f

'outright¹ adj completo; (refusal) netto

out'right² adv completamente; (at once) immediatamente; (frankly) francamente

'outset n inizio m; **from the** ~ fin dall'inizio

'outside¹ adj esterno ● n esterno m; **from the** ~ dall'esterno; **at the** ~ al massimo

out'side² adv all'esterno, fuori; (of doors) fuori; **go** ~ andare fuori ● prep fuori da; (in front of) davanti a

'outskirts npl sobborghi mpl

out'spoken adj schietto

out'standing adj eccezionale;

(landmark) prominente; (not settled) in sospeso

out'stretched adj allungato

out'strip vt (pt/pp **-stripped**) superare

outward /-wəd/ adj esterno; (journey) di andata ● adv verso l'esterno. **~ly** adv esternamente. **~s** adv verso l'esterno

out'weigh vt aver maggior peso di

out'wit vt (pt/pp **-witted**) battere in astuzia

oval /'əʊvl/ adj ovale ● n ovale m

ovary /'əʊvərɪ/ n (Anat) ovaia f

ovation /əʊ'veɪʃn/ n ovazione f

oven /'ʌvn/ n forno m. **~-ready** adj pronto da mettere in forno

over /'əʊvə(r)/ prep sopra; (across) al di là di; (during) durante; (more than) più di; **~ the phone** al telefono; **~ the page** alla pagina seguente; **all ~ Italy** in tutta [l']Italia; (travel) per l'Italia ● adv (above) col resto giù; (ended) finito; **~ again** un'altra volta; **~ and ~** più volte; **~ and above** oltre a; **~ here/there** qui/là; all **~** (everywhere) dappertutto; **it's all ~** è tutto finito; **I ache all ~** ho male dappertutto; **come/bring ~** venire/ portare; **turn ~** girare

over- pref (too) troppo

overall[1] /'əʊvərɔ:l/ n grembiule m; **~s** pl tuta fsg [da lavoro]

overall[2] /əʊvər'ɔ:l/ adj complessivo; (general) generale ● adv complessivamente

over'balance vi perdere l'equilibrio

over'bearing adj prepotente

overboard adv (Naut) in mare

overcast adj coperto

over'charge vt **~ sb** far pagare più del dovuto a qcno ● vi far pagare più del dovuto

overcoat n cappotto m

over'come vt (pt **-came**, pp **-come**)

vincere; **be ~ by** essere sopraffatto da

over'crowded adj sovraffollato

over'do vt (pt **-did**, pp **-done**) esagerare; (cook too long) stracuocere; **~ it** (fam: do too much) strafare

overdose n overdose f inv

overdraft n scoperto m; **have an ~** avere il conto scoperto

over'draw vt (pt **-drew**, pp **-drawn**) **~ one's account** andare allo scoperto; **be ~n by** (account:) essere [allo] scoperto di

over'due adj in ritardo

over'estimate vt sopravvalutare

overflow[1] n (water) acqua f che deborda; (people) pubblico m in eccesso; (outlet) scarico m; **~ car park** parcheggio m supplementare

over'flow[2] vi debordare

over'grown adj (garden) coperto di erbacce

overhaul[1] n revisione f

over'haul[2] vt (Techn) revisionare

over'head[1] adv in alto

overhead[2] adj aereo; (railway) sopraelevato; (lights) da soffitto. **~s** npl spese fpl generali

over'hear vt (pt/pp **-heard**) sentire per caso (conversation)

over'joyed adj felicissimo

over'land adj & adv via terra; **~ route** via f terrestre

over'lap v (pt/pp **-lapped**) ● vi sovrapporsi ● vt sovrapporre

over'leaf adv sul retro

over'load vt sovraccaricare

over'look vt dominare; (fail to see, ignore) lasciarsi sfuggire

over'night[1] adv per la notte; **stay ~** fermarsi a dormire

overnight[2] adj notturno; **~ bag** piccola borsa f da viaggio; **~ stay** sosta f per la notte

overpass n cavalcavia m inv

over'pay vt (pt/pp **-paid**) strapagare

over'power vt sopraffare. ~ing adj insostenibile

over'priced adj troppo caro

overre'act vi avere una reazione eccessiva. ●~ion f reazione f eccessiva

over'rid|e vt (pt -rode, pp -ridden) passare sopra a. ~ing adj prevalente

over'rule vt annullare (decision)

over'run vt (pt -ran, pp -ran, pres p -running) invadere; oltrepassare (time); **be ~ with** essere invaso da

over'seas[1] adv oltremare

'overseas[2] adj d'oltremare

over'see vt (pt -saw, pp -seen) sorvegliare

over'shadow vt adombrare

over'shoot vt (pt/pp -shot) oltrepassare

'oversight n disattenzione f; **an ~** una svista

over'sleep vi (pt/pp -slept) svegliarsi troppo tardi

over'step vt (pt/pp -stepped) ~ **the mark** oltrepassare ogni limite

overt /əʊˈvɜːt/ adj palese

over'tak|e vt/i (pt -took, pp -taken) sorpassare. ~ing n sorpasso m; **no ~ing** divieto di sorpasso

'overthrow[1] n (Pol) rovesciamento m

over'throw[2] vt (pt -threw, pp -thrown) (Pol) rovesciare

'overtime n lavoro m straordinario ● adv **work ~** fare lo straordinario

overture /ˈəʊvətjʊə(r)/ n (Mus) preludio m; ~s pl fig approccio msg

over'turn vt ribaltare ● vi ribaltarsi

over'weight adj sovrappeso

overwhelm /-ˈwelm/ vt sommergere (**with** di); (with emotion) confondere. ~ing adj travolgente; (victory, majority) schiacciante

over'work n lavoro m eccessivo ● vt far lavorare eccessivamente ● vi lavorare eccessivamente

ow|e /əʊ/ vt also fig dovere ([to] sb a qcno); ~**e sb sth** dovere qcsa a qcno. ~**ing** adj **be ~ing** (money:) essere da pagare ● prep ~**ing to** a causa di

owl /aʊl/ n gufo m

own[1] /əʊn/ adj proprio ● pron **a car of my ~** una macchina per conto mio; **on one's ~** da solo; **hold one's ~ with** tener testa a; **get one's ~ back** 🖪 prendersi una rivincita

own[2] vt possedere; (confess) ammettere; **I don't ~ it** non mi appartiene. □ ~ **up** vi confessare (**to sth** qcsa)

owner /ˈəʊnə(r)/ n proprietario, -a mf. ~**ship** n proprietà f

oxygen /ˈɒksɪdʒən/ n ossigeno m; ~ **mask** maschera f a ossigeno

oyster /ˈɔɪstə(r)/ n ostrica f

ozone /ˈəʊzəʊn/ n ozono m. ~**-'friendly** adj che non danneggia l'ozono. ~ **layer** n fascia f d'ozono

Pp

pace /peɪs/ n passo m; (speed) ritmo m; **keep ~ with** camminare di pari passo con ● vi ~ **up and down** camminare avanti e indietro. ~**-maker** n (Med) pacemaker m; (runner) battistrada m

Pacific /pəˈsɪfɪk/ adj & n **the ~ [Ocean]** l'oceano m Pacifico, il Pacifico

pacifist /ˈpæsɪfɪst/ n pacifista mf

pacify /ˈpæsɪfaɪ/ vt (pt/pp -ied) placare (person); pacificare (country)

pack /pæk/ n (of cards) mazzo m; (of hounds) muta f; (of wolves, thieves) branco m; (of cigarettes etc) pacchetto

m; a ~ of lies un mucchio di bugie
● vt impacchettare (article); fare
(suitcase); mettere in valigia (swim-
suit etc); (press down) comprimere;
~ed [out] (crowded) pieno zeppo ● vi
fare i bagagli; send sb ~ing 🔲
mandare qcno a stendere. □ ~ up vt
impacchettare ● vi 🔲 (machine:)
piantare in asso

package /'pækɪdʒ/ n pacco m,
impacchettare. ~ **deal** offerta f
tutto compreso. ~ **holiday** n vacanza f organizzata. ~ **tour** viaggio m
organizzato

packet /'pækɪt/ n pacchetto m; **cost
a** ~ 🔲 costare un sacco

pact /pækt/ n patto m

pad¹ /pæd/ n imbottitura f; (for writing) bloc-notes m, taccuino m; (🔲:
home) [piccolo] appartamento m ● vt
(pt/pp padded) imbottire. □ ~ **out** vt
gonfiare

pad² vi (pt/pp padded) camminare
con passo felpato

paddle¹ /'pæd(ə)l/ n pagaia f ● vt
(row) spingere remando

paddle² vi (wade) sguazzare

paddock /'pædək/ n recinto m

padlock /'pædlɒk/ n lucchetto m
● vt chiudere con lucchetto

paediatrician /piːdɪə'trɪʃn/ n pe-
diatra mf

page¹ /peɪdʒ/ n pagina f

page² n (boy) paggetto m; (in hotel)
fattorino m ● vt far chiamare (person)

pager /'peɪdʒə(r)/ n cercapersone
m inv

paid /peɪd/ ▷PAY ● adj ~ **employment** lavoro m remunerato; **put** ~
to mettere un termine a

pail /peɪl/ n secchio m

pain /peɪn/ n dolore m; **be in** ~ soffrire; **take** ~s darsi un gran d'affare;
~ **in the neck** 🔲 spina f nel fianco

pain: ~**ful** adj doloroso; (laborious)
penoso. ~**killer** n calmante m.
~**less** adj indolore

painstaking /'peɪnzteɪkɪŋ/ adj minuzioso

paint /peɪnt/ n pittura f; ~**s** colori
mpl ● vt/i pitturare; (artist:) dipingere.
~**brush** n pennello m. ~**er** n pittore m,
-trice mf; (decorator) imbianchino m.
~**ing** n pittura f; (picture) dipinto m.
~**work** n pittura f

pair /peə(r)/ n paio m; (of people)
coppia f; ~ **of trousers** paio m di
pantaloni; ~ **of scissors** paio m di
forbici

pajamas /pə'dʒɑːməz/ npl Am pigiama msg

Pakistan /pɑːkɪ'stɑːn/ n Pakistan m.
~**i** adj pakistano ● n pakistano, -a mf

pal /pæl/ n 🔲 amico, -a mf

palace /'pælɪs/ n palazzo m

palatable /'pælətəbl/ adj gradevole
(al gusto)

palate /'pælət/ n palato m

pale /peɪl/ adj pallido

Palestin|e /'pælɪstaɪn/ n Palestina
f. ~**ian** adj palestinese ● n palestinese mf

palette /'pælɪt/ n tavolozza f

palm /pɑːm/ n palmo m; (tree) palma
f; P~ **Sunday** n Domenica f delle
Palme ● **palm off** vt ~ **sth off on sb**
rifilare qcsa a qcno

palpable /'pælpəbl/ adj palpabile;
(perceptible) tangibile

palpitat|e /'pælpɪteɪt/ vi palpitare.
~**ions** npl palpitazioni fpl

pamper /'pæmpə(r)/ vt viziare

pamphlet /'pæmflɪt/ n opuscolo m

pan /pæn/ n tegame m, pentola f;
(for frying) padella f; (of scales) piatto
m ● vt (pt/pp panned) (🔲: criticize)
stroncare

pancake n crêpe f inv, frittella f

panda /'pændə/ n panda m inv. ~
car n macchina f della polizia

pandemonium /pændɪ'məʊnɪəm/ n pandemonio m

pander /'pændə(r)/ vi ~ **to sb**

compiacere qcno

pane /peɪn/ n **~ [of glass]** vetro m

panel /ˈpænl/ n pannello m; (group of people) giuria f; **~ of experts** gruppo m di esperti. **~ling** n pannelli mpl

pang /pæŋ/ n **~s of hunger** morsi mpl della fame; **~s of conscience** rimorsi mpl di coscienza

panic /ˈpænɪk/ n panico m ● vi (pt/pp **panicked**) lasciarsi prendere dal panico. **~-stricken** adj in preda al panico

panoram|a /pænəˈrɑːmə/ n panorama m. **~ic** adj panoramico

pansy /ˈpænzɪ/ n viola f del pensiero; (🔢: effeminate man) finocchio m

pant /pænt/ vi ansimare

panther /ˈpænθə(r)/ n pantera f

panties /ˈpæntɪz/ npl mutandine fpl

pantomime /ˈpæntəmaɪm/ n pantomima f

pantry /ˈpæntrɪ/ n dispensa f

pants /pænts/ npl (underwear) mutande fpl; (woman's) mutandine fpl; (trousers) pantaloni mpl

'pantyhose n Am collant m inv

paper /ˈpeɪpə(r)/ n (also wallpaper) carta f da parati; (newspaper) giornale m; (exam) esame m; (treatise) saggio m; **~s** pl (documents) documenti mpl; (for identification) documento m [d'identità]; **on ~** in teoria; **put down on ~** mettere per iscritto ● attrib di carta ● vt tappezzare

paper: ~back n edizione f economica. **~-clip** n graffetta f. **~weight** n fermacarte m inv. **~work** n lavoro m d'ufficio

parable /ˈpærəbl/ n parabola f

parachut|e /ˈpærəʃuːt/ n paracadute m ● vi lanciarsi col paracadute. **~ist** n paracadutista mf

parade /pəˈreɪd/ n (military) parata f militare ● vi sfilare ● vt (show off) far sfoggio di

paradise /ˈpærədaɪs/ n paradiso m

paraffin /ˈpærəfɪn/ n paraffina f

paragraph /ˈpærəgrɑːf/ n paragrafo m

parallel /ˈpærəlel/ adj & adv parallelo. **~ bars** npl parallele fpl. **~ port** n (Comput) porta f parallela ● n (Geog), fig parallelo m; (line) parallela f ● vt essere paragonabile a

Paralympics /pærəˈlɪmpɪks/ npl **the P~** le Paraolimpiadi fpl

paralyse /ˈpærəlaɪz/ vt also fig paralizzare

paralysis /pəˈræləsɪs/ n (pl **-ses** /-siːz/) paralisi f inv

paramedic /pærəˈmedɪk/ n paramedico, -a mf

parameter /pəˈræmɪtə(r)/ n parametro m

paranoia /pærəˈnɔɪə/ n paranoia f

paranoid /ˈpærənɔɪd/ adj paranoico, -a mf

paraphernalia /pærəfəˈneɪlɪə/ n armamentario m

paraplegic /pærəˈpliːdʒɪk/ adj raplegico ● n paraplegico, -a mf

parasite /ˈpærəsaɪt/ n parassita m

paratrooper /ˈpærətruːpə(r)/ n paracadutista m

parcel /ˈpɑːsl/ n pacco m

parch /pɑːtʃ/ vt disseccare; **be ~ed** (person): morire dalla sete

pardon /ˈpɑːdn/ n perdono m; (Jur) grazia f; **~?** prego?; **I beg your ~?** fml chiedo scusa?; **I do beg your ~** (sorry) chiedo scusa! ● vt perdonare; (Jur) graziare

parent /ˈpeərənt/ n genitore, -trice mf; **~s** pl genitori mpl. **~al** adj dei genitori

parenthesis /pəˈrenθəsɪs/ n (pl **-ses** /-siːz/) parentesi m inv

Paris /ˈpærɪs/ n Parigi f

parish /ˈpærɪʃ/ n parrocchia f. **~ioner** n parrocchiano, -a mf

park /pɑːk/ n parco m ● vt/i (Auto) posteggiare, parcheggiare; **~ one-self** 🔢 installarsi

park-and-'ride n park

and ride *m inv*

parking /ˈpɑːkɪŋ/ *n* parcheggio *m*, posteggio *m*; **'no ~'** 'divieto di sosta'. **~-lot** *n Am* posteggio *m*, parcheggio *m*. **~-meter** *n* parchimetro *m* ~ **space** *n* posteggio *m* parcheggio *m*

parliament /ˈpɑːləmənt/ *n* parlamento *m*. **~ary** *adj* parlamentare

Parliament Il Parlamento britannico è l'organo legislativo del paese, suddiviso in due Camere: *House of Commons* e *House of Lords*. La prima è composta di 650 parlamentari, o MPs (*Members of Parliament*), eletti a suffragio popolare; la seconda è formata da oltre 1000 membri, tra i quali esponenti dell'aristocrazia, ex primi ministri e cittadini che si sono in qualche modo distinti. Ogni anno è il capo della monarchia ad aprire ufficialmente il Parlamento e l'anno legislativo.

parlour /ˈpɑːlə(r)/ *n* salotto *m*

parochial /pəˈrəʊkɪəl/ *adj* parrocchiale; *fig* ristretto

parody /ˈpærədɪ/ *n* parodia *f* ⬦ *vt* (*pt/pp* **-ied**) parodiare

parole /pəˈrəʊl/ *n* on ~ in libertà condizionale ⬦ *vt* mettere in libertà condizionale

parrot /ˈpærət/ *n* pappagallo *m*

parsley /ˈpɑːslɪ/ *n* prezzemolo *m*

parsnip /ˈpɑːsnɪp/ *n* pastinaca *f*

part /pɑːt/ *n* parte *f*; (*of machine*) pezzo *m*; **for my ~** per quanto mi riguarda; **on the ~ of** da parte di, **take sb's ~** prendere le parti di qcno; **take ~ in** prendere parte a ⬦ *adv* in parte ⬦ *vt* ~ **one's hair** farsi la riga ⬦ *vi* (*people*) separarsi; **~ with** separarsi da

partial /ˈpɑːʃl/ *adj* parziale; **be ~ to** aver un debole per. **~ly** *adv* parzialmente

participant /pɑːˈtɪsɪpənt/ *n* parte cipante *m*. **~ate** *vi* partecipare (**in** a). **~ation** *n* partecipazione *f*

particle /ˈpɑːtɪkl/ *n* (*Gram, Phys*) particella *f*

particular /pəˈtɪkjʊlə(r)/ *adj* particolare; (*precise*) meticoloso; *pej* noioso; **in ~** in particolare. **~ly** *adv* particolarmente. **~s** *npl* particolari *mpl*

parting /ˈpɑːtɪŋ/ *n* separazione *f*; (*in hair*) scriminatura *f* ⬦ *attrib* di commiato

partisan /pɑːtɪˈzæn/ *n* partigiano, -a *mf*

partition /pɑːˈtɪʃn/ *n* (*wall*) parete *f*; *(Pol)* divisione *f* ⬦ *vt* dividere (*in parti*). □ ~ **off** *vt* separare

partly /ˈpɑːtlɪ/ *adv* in parte

partner /ˈpɑːtnə(r)/ *n* (*Comm*) socio, -a *mf*; (*sport, in relationship*) compagno, -a *mf*. **~ship** *n* (*Comm*) società *f*

partridge /ˈpɑːtrɪdʒ/ *n* pernice *f*

part-time *adj* & *adv* part time; **be ~** or **work ~** lavorare part time

party /ˈpɑːtɪ/ *n* ricevimento *m*, festa *f*; (*group*) gruppo *m*; (*Pol*) partito *m*; (*Jur*) parte *f* (*in causa*); **be ~ to** essere parte attiva in

pass /pɑːs/ *n* lasciapassare *m inv*; (*in mountains*) passo *m*, (*Sport*) passaggio *m*; (*Sch: mark*) [voto *m*] sufficiente *m*; **make a ~ at** 🄛 fare delle avances a ⬦ *vt* passare; (*overtake*) sorpassare; (*approve*) far passare; fare (*remark*); (*Jur*) pronunciare (*sentence*); ~ **the time** passare il tempo ⬦ *vi* passare; (*in exam*) essere promosso. □ ~ **away** *vi* mancare. □ ~ **down** *vt* passare; *fig* trasmettere. □ ~ **out** *vi* 🄛 svenire. □ ~ **round** *vt* far passare. □ ~ **through** *vt* attraversare. □ ~ **up** *vt* passare, (🄛 *miss*) lasciarsi scappare

passable /ˈpɑːsəbl/ *adj* (*road*) praticabile; (*satisfactory*) passabile

passage /ˈpæsɪdʒ/ *n* passaggio *m*; (*corridor*) corridoio *m*; (*voyage*) traversata f

passenger /'pæsɪndʒə(r)/ n passeggero, -a mf. ~ **seat** n posto m accanto al guidatore

passer-by /pɑːsə'baɪ/ n (pl ~sby) passante m

passion /'pæʃn/ n passione f. ~**ate** adj appassionato

passive /'pæsɪv/ adj passivo ●n passivo m. ~**ness** n passività f

Passover /'pɑːsəʊvə(r)/ n Pasqua f ebraica

pass: ~**port** n passaporto m. ~**word** n parola f d'ordine

past /pɑːst/ adj passato; (former) ex; in the ~ few days nei giorni scorsi; that's all ~ tutto questo è passato; the ~ week la settimana scorsa ●n passato m ●prep oltre; at ten ~ two alle due e dieci ●adv oltre; go/come ~ passare

pasta /'pæstə/ n pasta[sciutta] f

paste /peɪst/ n pasta f; (dough) impasto m; (adhesive) colla f ● vt incollare

pastel /'pæstl/ n pastello m ● attrib pastello

pasteurize /'pɑːstʃəraɪz/ vt pastorizzare

pastime /'pɑːstaɪm/ n passatempo m

pastry /'peɪstrɪ/ n pasta f; ~ies pasticcini mpl

pasture /'pɑːstʃə(r)/ n pascolo m

pasty[1] /'pæstɪ/ n ≈ pasticcio m

pasty[2] /'peɪstɪ/ adj smorto

pat /pæt/ n buffetto m; (of butter) pezzetto m ● adv have sth off ~ conoscere qcsa a menadito ● vt (pt/pp patted) dare un buffetto a; ~ sb on the back fig congratularsi con qcno

patch /pætʃ/ n toppa f; (spot) chiazza f; (period) periodo m; not a ~ on fig molto inferiore a ● vt mettere una toppa su. ~ **up** vt riparare alla bell'e meglio; appianare (quarrel)

pâté /'pæteɪ/ n pâté m inv

patent /'peɪtnt/ adj palese ● n brevetto m ● vt brevettare. ~ **leather shoes** npl scarpe fpl di vernice. ~**ly** adv in modo palese

patern|al /pə'tɜːnl/ adj paterno. ~**ity** n paternità f inv

path /pɑːθ/ n (pl ~s /pɑːðz/) sentiero m; (orbit) traiettoria m; fig strada f

pathetic /pə'θetɪk/ adj patetico; (◻: very bad) penoso

patience /'peɪʃns/ n pazienza f; (game) solitario m

patient /'peɪʃnt/ adj paziente ● n paziente mf. ~**ly** adv pazientemente

patio /'pætɪəʊ/ n terrazza f

patriot /'pætrɪət/ n patriota mf. ~**ic** adj patriottico. ~**ism** n patriottismo m

patrol /pə'trəʊl/ n pattuglia f ● vt/i pattugliare. ~ **car** n autopattuglia f

patron /'peɪtrən/ n patrono m; (of charity) benefattore, -trice mf; (of the arts) mecenate mf; (customer) cliente mf

patroniz|e /'pætrənaɪz/ vt frequentare abitualmente; fig trattare con condiscendenza. ~**ing** adj condiscendente. ~**ingly** adv con condiscendenza

pattern /'pætn/ n disegno m (stampato); (for knitting, sewing) modello m

paunch /pɔːntʃ/ n pancia f

pause /pɔːz/ n pausa f ● vi fare una pausa

pave /peɪv/ vt pavimentare; ~ the way preparare la strada (for a). ~**ment** n marciapiede m

paw /pɔː/ n zampa f ● vt ◻ mettere le zampe addosso a

pawn[1] /pɔːn/ n (in chess) pedone m; fig pedina f

pawn[2] vt impegnare ● n in ~ in pegno. ~**broker** n prestatore, -trice mf su pegno. ~**shop** n monte m di pietà

pay /peɪ/ n paga f; **in the ~ of** al soldo di ● v (*pt/pp* **paid**) ● vt pagare; prestare (attention); fare (compliment, visit); **~ cash** pagare in contanti ● vi pagare; (*be profitable*) rendere; **It doesn't ~** to..., *fig* è fatica sprecata...; **~ for sth** pagare per qcsa. □ **~ back** vt ripagare. □ **~ in** vt versare. □ **~ off** vt saldare (debt) ● vi *fig* dare dei frutti. □ **~ up** vi pagare

payable /'peɪəbl/ adj pagabile; **make ~ to** intestare a

payment /'peɪmənt/ n pagamento m

PC n *abbr* (personal computer) PC m *inv*

pea /piː/ n pisello m

peace /piːs/ n pace f; **~ of mind** tranquillità f

peach /piːtʃ/ n pesca f; (tree) pesco m

peacock /'piːkɒk/ n pavone m

peak /piːk/ n picco m; *fig* culmine m. **~ed 'cap** n berretto m a punta. **~ hours** npl ore fpl di punta

peal /piːl/ n (*of bells*) scampanio m; **~s of laughter** fragore m di risate

'peanut n nocciolina f [americana]. **~s** [I] miseria f

pear /peə(r)/ n pera f; (tree) pero m

pearl /pɜːl/ n perla f

peasant /'peznt/ n contadino, -a mf

pebble /'pebl/ n ciottolo m

peck /pek/ n beccata f; (*kiss*) bacetto m ● vt beccare; (*kiss*) dare un bacetto a. **~ing order** n gerarchia f. **~ at** vt beccare

peculiar /pɪ'kjuːlɪə(r)/ adj strano; (*special*) particolare; **~ to** tipico di. **~ity** n stranezza f; (*feature*) particolarità f *inv*

pedal /'pedl/ n pedale m ● vi pedalare. **~ bin** n pattumiera f a pedale

pedantic /pɪ'dæntɪk/ adj pedante

pedestal /'pedɪstl/ n piedistallo m

pedestrian /pɪ'destrɪən/ n pedone m ● adj *fig* scadente. **~ 'crossing** n passaggio m pedonale. **~ 'precinct** n zona f pedonale

pedigree /'pedɪgriː/ n pedigree m *inv*; (*of person*) lignaggio m ● attrib (animal) di razza, con pedigree

peek /piːk/ vi [I] sbirciare

peel /piːl/ n buccia f ● vt sbucciare ● vi (nose) etc: spellarsi; (paint) staccarsi

peep /piːp/ n sbirciata f ● vi sbirciare

peer¹ /pɪə(r)/ vi **~ at** scrutare

peer² n nobile m; **his ~s** pl (*in rank*) i suoi pari mpl; (*in age*) i suoi coetanei mpl. **~age** n nobiltà f

peg /peg/ n (hook) piolo m; (*for tent*) picchetto m; (*for clothes*) molletta f; **off the ~** [I] prêt-à-porter

pejorative /pɪ'dʒɒrətɪv/ adj peggiorativo

pelican /'pelɪkən/ n pellicano m

pellet /'pelɪt/ n pallottola f

pelt /pelt/ n bombarda ● vi ([I]: run fast) catapultarsi; **~ down** (rain): venir giù a fiotti

pelvis /'pelvɪs/ n (Anat) bacino m

pen¹ /pen/ n (*for animals*) recinto m

pen² n penna f; (ball-point) penna f a sfera

penal /'piːnl/ adj penale. **~ize** vt penalizzare

penalty /'penltɪ/ n sanzione f; (fine) multa f; (*in football*) **[kick]** [calcio m di] rigore m; **~ area** o **box** area f di rigore

penance /'penəns/ n penitenza f

pence /pens/ ▷**PENNY**

pencil /'pensl/ n matita f. **~sharpener** n temperamatite m *inv*

pendulum /'pendjʊləm/ n pendolo m

penetrat|e /'penɪtreɪt/ vt/i penetrare. **~ing** adj acuto; (*sound, stare*) penetrante. **~ion** n penetrazione f

penguin /'pengwɪn/ n pinguino m

penicillin /penɪˈsɪlɪn/ n penicillina f

peninsula /pɪˈnɪnsjʊlə/ n penisola f

penis /ˈpiːnɪs/ n pene m

pen: ~**knife** n temperino m.
~**name** n pseudonimo m

penniless /ˈpenɪlɪs/ adj senza
un soldo

penny /ˈpenɪ/ n (pl **pence**; single
coins **pennies**) penny m; Am centesimo m; **spend a** ~ 🚽 andare
in bagno

pension /ˈpenʃn/ n pensione f. ~**er**
n pensionato, -a mf

pensive /ˈpensɪv/ adj pensoso

Pentecost /ˈpentɪkɒst/ n Pentecoste f

pent-up /ˈpentʌp/ adj represso

penultimate /pɪˈnʌltɪmət/ adj penultimo

people /ˈpiːpl/ npl persone fpl, gente
fsg; (citizens) popolo msg; **a lot of** ~
una marea di gente; **the** ~ la gente;
English ~ gli inglesi; ~ **say** si dice;
for four ~ per quattro ● vt popolare

pepper /ˈpepə(r)/ n pepe m; (vegetable) peperone m ● vt (season) pepare

pepper: ~**corn** n grano m di pepe.
~ **mill** n macinapepe m inv. ~**mint** n
menta f peperita; (sweet) caramella f
alla menta. ~**pot** n pepiera f

per /pɜː(r)/ prep per; ~ **annum** al-
l'anno; ~ **cent** percento

perceive /pəˈsiːv/ vt percepire; (interpret) interpretare

percentage /pəˈsentɪdʒ/ n percen-
tuale f

perceptible /pəˈseptəbl/ adj per-
cettibile; (difference) sensibile

percept|ion /pəˈsepʃn/ n perce-
zione f. ~**ive** adj perspicace

perch /pɜːtʃ/ n pertica f ● vi (bird:)
appollaiarsi

percolator /ˈpɜːkəleɪtə(r)/ n caffettiera f a filtro

percussion /pəˈkʌʃn/ n percussione f. ~ **instrument** n strumento

m a percussione

perfect¹ /ˈpɜːfɪkt/ adj perfetto ● n
(Gram) passato m prossimo

perfect² /pəˈfekt/ vt perfezionare.
~**ion** n perfezione f; **to** ~**ion** alla
perfezione. ~**ionist** n perfezio-
nista mf

perfectly /ˈpɜːfɪktlɪ/ adv perfet-
tamente

perform /pəˈfɔːm/ vt compiere,
fare; eseguire (operation, sonata);
recitare (role); mettere in scena
(play) ● vi (Theat) recitare; (Techn) funzionare. ~**ance** n esecuzione f; (at
theatre, cinema) rappresentazione f;
(Techn) rendimento m. ~**er** n artista mf

perfume /ˈpɜːfjuːm/ n profumo m

perhaps /pəˈhæps/ adv forse

peril /ˈperɪl/ n pericolo m. ~**ous** adj
pericoloso

perimeter /pəˈrɪmɪtə(r)/ n perime-
tro m

period /ˈpɪərɪəd/ n periodo m; (men-
struation) mestruazioni fpl; (Sch) ora f
di lezione; (full stop) punto m fermo
● attrib (costume) d'epoca; (furniture)
in stile. ~**ic** adj periodico. ~**ical** n
periodico m, rivista f

peripher|al /pəˈrɪfərəl/ adj perife-
rico. ~**y** n periferia f

perish /ˈperɪʃ/ vi (rot) deteriorarsi;
(die) perire. ~**able** adj deteriorabile

perjur|e /ˈpɜːdʒə(r)/ vt ~**e** oneself
spergiurare. ~**y** n spergiuro m

perk /pɜːk/ n 🔁 vantaggio m

perm /pɜːm/ n permanente f ● vt ~
sb's hair fare la permanente a qcno

permanent /ˈpɜːmənənt/ adj permanente; (job, address) stabile. ~**ly**
adv stabilmente

permissible /pəˈmɪsəbl/ adj am-
missibile

permission /pəˈmɪʃn/ n permesso m

permit¹ /pəˈmɪt/ vt (pt/pp -**mitted**)
permettere; ~ **sb to do sth** permet-

tere a qcno di fare qcsa

permit² /'pɜːmɪt/ n autorizzazione f

perpendicular /pɜːpən'dɪkjʊlə(r)/ adj perpendicolare ● n perpendicolare f

perpetual /pə'petjʊəl/ adj perenne. **~ly** adv perennemente

perpetuate /pə'petjʊeɪt/ vt perpetuare

perplex /pə'pleks/ vt lasciare perplesso. **~ed** adj perplesso. **~ity** n perplessità f inv

persecut|e /'pɜːsɪkjuːt/ vt perseguitare. **~ion** n persecuzione f

perseverance /pɜːsɪ'vɪərəns/ n perseveranza f

persever|e /pɜːsɪ'vɪə(r)/ vi perseverare. **~ing** adj assiduo

Persian /'pɜːʃn/ adj persiano

persist /pə'sɪst/ vi persistere; **~ in doing sth** persistere nel fare qcsa. **~ence** n persistenza f. **~ent** adj persistente. **~ently** adv persistentemente

person /'pɜːsn/ n persona f; **in ~** di persona

personal /'pɜːsənl/ adj personale. **~ hygiene** n igiene f personale. **~ organizer** n (Comput) agenda f elettronica. **~ly** adv personalmente

personality /pɜːsə'nælətɪ/ n personalità f inv; (on TV) personaggio m

personnel /pɜːsə'nel/ n personale m

perspective /pə'spektɪv/ n prospettiva f

perspiration /pɜːspɪ'reɪʃn/ n sudore m. **~ire** vi sudare

persuade /pə'sweɪd/ vt persuadere. **~sion** n persuasione f; (belief) convinzione f

persuasive /pə'sweɪsɪv/ adj persuasivo. **~ly** adv in modo persuasivo

pertinent /'pɜːtɪnənt/ adj pertinente (to a)

perturb /pə'tɜːb/ vt perturbare

peruse /pə'ruːz/ vt leggere

perverse /pə'vɜːs/ adj irragionevole. **~ion** n perversione f

pervert /'pɜːvɜːt/ n pervertito, -a mf

pessimis|m /'pesɪmɪzm/ n pessimismo m. **~t** n pessimista mf. **~tic** adj pessimistico. **~tically** adv in modo pessimistico

pest /pest/ n piaga f; (fam: person) peste f

pester /'pestə(r)/ vt molestare

pesticide /'pestɪsaɪd/ n pesticida m

pet /pet/ n animale m domestico; (favourite) cocco, -a mf ● adj prediletto ● v (pt/pp petted) ● vt coccolare ● vi (couple:) praticare il petting

petal /'petl/ n petalo m

petition /pə'tɪʃn/ n petizione f

pet 'name n vezzeggiativo m

petrol /'petrəl/ n benzina f

petroleum /pɪ'trəʊlɪəm/ n petrolio m

petrol: ~-pump n pompa f di benzina. **~ station** n stazione f di servizio. **~ tank** n serbatoio m della benzina

petticoat /'petɪkəʊt/ n sottoveste f

petty /'petɪ/ adj (-ier, -iest) insignificante; (mean) meschino. **~ 'cash** n cassa f per piccole spese

petulant /'petjʊlənt/ adj petulante

pew /pjuː/ n banco m (di chiesa)

phantom /'fæntəm/ n fantasma m

pharmaceutical /fɑːmə'sjuːtɪkl/ adj farmaceutico

pharmac|ist /'fɑːməsɪst/ n farmacista mf. **~y** n farmacia f

phase /feɪz/ n fase f ● vt **phase in/out** introdurre/eliminare gradualmente

pheasant /'feznt/ n fagiano m

phenomen|al /fɪ'nɒmɪnl/ adj fenomenale; (incredible) incredibile. **~ally** adv incredibilmente. **~on** n (pl -na) fenomeno m

philistine /'fɪlɪstaɪn/ n filisteo, -a mf

P

philosoph|er /fɪˈlɒsəfə(r)/ n filosofo, -a mf. **~ical** adj filosofico. **~ically** adv con filosofia. **~y** n filosofia f

phlegm /flem/ n (Med) flemma f

phlegmatic /fleɡˈmætɪk/ adj flemmatico

phobia /ˈfəʊbɪə/ n fobia f

phone /fəʊn/ n telefono m; **be on the ~** avere il telefono; (be phoning) essere al telefono ● vt telefonare a ● vi telefonare. □ **~ back** vt/i richiamare. **~ book** n guida f del telefono. **~ box** n cabina f telefonica. **~ call** telefonata f. **~ card** n scheda f telefonica. **~in** n trasmissione f con chiamate in diretta. **~ number** n numero m telefonico

phonetic /fəˈnetɪk/ adj fonetico. **~s** n fonetica f

phoney /ˈfəʊnɪ/ adj (**-ier, -iest**) fasullo

phosphorus /ˈfɒsfərəs/ n fosforo m

photo /ˈfəʊtəʊ/ n foto f; **~ album** n album m inv di fotografie. **~copier** n fotocopiatrice f. **~copy** n fotocopia f ● vt fotocopiare

photogenic /fəʊtəʊˈdʒenɪk/ adj fotogenico

photograph /ˈfəʊtəɡrɑːf/ n fotografia f ● vt fotografare

photograph|er /fəˈtɒɡrəfə(r)/ n fotografo, -a mf. **~ic** adj fotografico. **~y** n fotografia f

phrase /freɪz/ n espressione f ● vt esprimere. **~-book** n libro m di fraseologia

physical /ˈfɪzɪkl/ adj fisico. **~ edu'cation** n educazione f fisica. **~ly** adv fisicamente

physician /fɪˈzɪʃn/ n medico m

physic|ist /ˈfɪzɪsɪst/ n fisico, -a mf. **~s** n fisica f

physiology /fɪzɪˈɒlədʒɪ/ n fisiologia f

physio'therap|ist /fɪzɪəʊ-/ n fisioterapista mf. **~y** n fisioterapia f

physique /fɪˈziːk/ n fisico m

pianist /ˈpɪənɪst/ n pianista mf

piano /pɪˈænəʊ/ n piano m

pick¹ /pɪk/ n (tool) piccone m

pick² /pɪk/ n scelta f; **take your ~** prendi quello che vuoi ● vt (select) scegliere; cogliere (flowers); scassinare (lock); borseggiare (pockets); **~ and choose** fare il difficile; **~ one's nose** mettersi le dita nel naso; **~ a quarrel** attaccar briga; **~ holes in** [] criticare; **~ at one's food** spilluzzicare. □ **~ on** vt ([]: nag) assillare; **he always ~s on me** ce l'ha con me. □ **~ out** vt (identify) individuare. □ **~ up** vt sollevare; (off the ground, information) raccogliere; prendere in braccio (baby); imparare; prendersi (illness); (buy) comprare; captare (signal); (collect) andare/venire a prendere; prendere (passengers, habit); (police:) arrestare (criminal); [] rimorchiare (girl); **~ oneself up** riprendersi ● vi (improve) recuperare; (weather:) rimettersi

'pickaxe n piccone m

picket /ˈpɪkɪt/ n picchettista mf ● vt picchettare. **~ line** n picchetto m

pickle /ˈpɪkl/ n **~s** pl sottaceti mpl; **in a ~** fig nei pasticci ● vt mettere sottaceto

pick: ~pocket n borsaiolo m. **~-up** n (truck) furgone m; (on record-player) pickup m inv

picnic /ˈpɪknɪk/ n picnic m ● vi (pt/pp -nicked) fare un picnic

picture /ˈpɪktʃə(r)/ n (painting) quadro m; (photo) fotografia f; (drawing) disegno m; (film) film m inv; **put sb in the ~** fig mettere qcno al corrente; **the ~s** n il cinema ● vt (imagine) immaginare. **~sque** adj pittoresco

pie /paɪ/ n torta f

piece /piːs/ n pezzo m; (in game) pedina f; **a ~ of bread/paper** un

pezzo di pane/carta; **a ~ of news/
advice** una notizia/un consiglio; **take
to ~s** smontare. **~meal** adv un po'
alla volta. **~work** n il lavoro m a cottimo ● **piece together** vt montare;
fig ricostruire

pier /pɪə(r)/ n molo m; (pillar) pilastro m

pierce /pɪəs/ vt perforare; **~e a
hole in sth** fare un buco in qcsa.
~ing n [body] ~ piercing m inv ● adj
penetrante

pig /pɪg/ n maiale m

pigeon /'pɪdʒɪn/ n piccione m,
~hole n casella f

piggy /'pɪgɪ/ **~back** n give sb a
~back portare qcno sulle spalle. **~
bank** n salvadanaio m

pig'headed adj 🇮🇹 cocciuto

pigtail /(plait) treccina f

pile /paɪl/ n (heap) pila f ● vt ~ **sth on to
sth** appilare qcsa su qcsa. □ **~ up** vt
accatastare ● vi ammucchiare

piles /paɪlz/ npl emorroidi fpl

'pile-up n tamponamento m a
catena

pilgrim /'pɪlgrɪm/ n pellegrino, -a
mf. **~age** n pellegrinaggio m

pill /pɪl/ n pillola f

pillar /'pɪlə(r)/ n pilastro m. **~box**
n buca f delle lettere

pillow /'pɪləʊ/ n guanciale m.
~case n federa f

pilot /'paɪlət/ n pilota mf ● vt pilotare. **~light** n fiamma f di sicurezza

pimple /'pɪmpl/ n foruncolo m

pin /pɪn/ n spillo m; (Electr) spinotto
m; (Med) chiodo m; **I have ~s and
needles in my leg** 🇮🇹 mi formicola
una gamba ● vt (pt/pp **pinned**) appuntare (**to/on** su); (sewing) fissare
con gli spilli; (hold down) immobilizzare; **~ sb down to a date** ottenere
un appuntamento da qcno; **~ sth
on sb** 🇮🇹 addossare a qcno la colpa
di qcsa. □ **~ up** vt appuntare; (on
wall) affiggere

pinafore /'pɪnəfɔː(r)/ n grembiule
m. **~ dress** n scamiciato m

pincers /'pɪnsəz/ npl tenaglie fpl

pinch /pɪntʃ/ n pizzicotto m; (of salt)
presa f; **at a ~** 🇮🇹 in caso di bisogno ● vt pizzicare; (🇮🇹: steal) fregare
● vi (shoe:) stringere

pine¹ /paɪn/ n (tree) pino m

pine² vi **she is pining for you** le
manchi molto. □ **~ away** vi deperire

pineapple /'paɪn/ n ananas m inv

'ping-pong n ping-pong m

pink /pɪŋk/ adj rosa m

pinnacle /'pɪnəkl/ n guglia f

PIN number n codice m segreto

pin: **~point** vt definire con precisione. **~stripe** adj gessato

pint /paɪnt/ n pinta f (= 0,571, Am:
0,47 l); **a ~** 🇮🇹 una birra media

pioneer /paɪə'nɪə(r)/ n pioniere, -a
mf ● vt essere un pioniere di

pious /'paɪəs/ adj pio

pip /pɪp/ n (seed) seme m

pipe /paɪp/ n tubo m; (for smoking)
pipa f; **the ~s** (Mus) la cornamusa
● vt far arrivare con tubature (water,
gas etc). □ **~ down** vi 🇮🇹 abbassare
la voce

pipe: **~dream** n illusione f. **~line**
n conduttura f; **in the ~line** 🇮🇹 in
cantiere

piping /'paɪpɪŋ/ adj **~ hot** bollente

pirate /'paɪrət/ n pirata m

Pisces /'paɪsiːz/ n (Astr) Pesci mpl

piss /pɪs/ vi 🔞 pisciare

pistol /'pɪstl/ n pistola f

piston /'pɪstn/ n (Techn) pistone m

pit /pɪt/ n fossa f; (mine) miniera f;
(for orchestra) orchestra f ● vt (pt/pp
pitted) fig opporre (**against** a)

pitch¹ /pɪtʃ/ n (tone) tono m; (level)
altezza f; (in sport) campo m; (fig: degree) grado m ● vt montare (tent).
□ **~ in** vi 🇮🇹 mettersi sotto

pitch² n **~-black** adj nero come la
pece. **~-dark** adj buio pesto

'pitfall n fig trabocchetto m

pith /pɪθ/ n (of lemon, orange) interno m della buccia

piti|ful /'pɪtɪfl/ adj pietoso. **~less** adj spietato

pittance /'pɪtns/ n miseria f

pity /'pɪtɪ/ n pietà f; **what a ~!** che peccato!; **take ~ on** avere compassione di ● vt aver pietà di

pivot /'pɪvət/ n perno m; fig fulcro m ● vi imperniarsi (**on** su)

pizza /'piːtsə/ n pizza f

placard /'plækɑːd/ n cartellone m

placate /plə'keɪt/ vt placare

place /pleɪs/ n posto m; (🏠: house) casa f; (in book) segno m; **feel out of ~** sentirsi fuori posto; **take ~** aver luogo; **all over the ~** dappertutto ● vt collocare; (remember) identificare; **~ an order** fare un'ordinazione; **be ~d** (in race) piazzarsi. **~-mat** n sottopiatto m

placid /'plæsɪd/ adj placido

plague /pleɪg/ n peste f

plaice /pleɪs/ n inv platessa f

plain /pleɪn/ adj chiaro; (simple) semplice; (not pretty) scialbo; (not patterned) normale; (chocolate) fondente; **in ~ clothes** in borghese ● adv (simply) semplicemente ● n pianura f. **~ly** adv francamente; (simply) semplicemente; (obviously) chiaramente

plaintiff /'pleɪntɪf/ n (Jur) parte f lesa

plait /plæt/ n treccia f ● vt intrecciare

plan /plæn/ n progetto m, piano m ● vt (pt/pp **planned**) progettare; (intend) prevedere

plane¹ /pleɪn/ n (tree) platano m

plane² n aeroplano m

plane³ /pleɪn/ n (tool) pialla f ● vt piallare

planet /'plænɪt/ n pianeta m

plank /plæŋk/ n asse f

planning /'plænɪŋ/ n pianificazione f. **~ permission** n licenza f edilizia

plant /plɑːnt/ n pianta f; (machinery) impianto m; (factory) stabilimento m ● vt piantare. **~ation** n piantagione f

plaque /plɑːk/ n placca f

plasma /'plæzmə/ n plasma m

plaster /'plɑːstə(r)/ n intonaco m; (Med) gesso m; (sticking ~) cerotto m; **~ of Paris** gesso m ● vt intonacare (wall); (cover) ricoprire. **~ed** adj 🅰 sbronzo. **~er** n intonacatore m

plastic /'plæstɪk/ n plastica f ● adj plastico

plastic surgery n chirurgia f plastica

plate /pleɪt/ n piatto m; (flat sheet) placca f; (gold and silverware) argenteria f; (in book) tavola f [fuori testo] ● vt (cover with metal) placcare

platform /'plætfɔːm/ n (stage) palco m; (Rail) marciapiede m; (Pol) piattaforma f; **~ 5** binario 5

platinum /'plætɪnəm/ n platino m ● attrib di platino

platitude /'plætɪtjuːd/ n luogo m comune

platonic /plə'tɒnɪk/ adj platonico

plausible /'plɔːzəbl/ adj plausibile

play /pleɪ/ n gioco m; (Theat), (TV) rappresentazione f; (Radio) sceneggiato m radiofonico; **~ on words** gioco m di parole ● vt giocare a; (act) recitare; suonare (instrument); giocare (card) ● vi giocare; (Mus) suonare; **~ safe** non prendere rischi. **□ ~ down** vt minimizzare. **□ ~ up** vi 🅰 fare i capricci

play: **~er** n giocatore, -trice mf. **~ful** adj scherzoso. **~ground** n (Sch) cortile m (per la ricreazione). **~group** n asilo m

playing: **~-card** n carta f da gioco. **~-field** n campo m da gioco

play: **~-pen** n box m inv. **~wright** /-raɪt/ n drammaturgo, -a mf

plc n abbr (public limited company) s.r.l.

plea /pliː/ n richiesta f; **make a ~**

for fare un appello a

plead /pli:d/ vi fare appello (**for** a); ~ **guilty** dichiararsi colpevole; ~ **with** sb implorare qcno

pleasant /'plez(ə)nt/ adj piacevole. ~**ly** adv piacevolmente; (say, smile) cordialmente

pleas|e /pli:z/ adv per favore; ~**e do** prego ● vt far contento; ~**e oneself** fare il proprio comodo; ~**e yourself!** come vuoi!; pej fai come ti pare!. ~**ed** adj lieto; ~**ed with/ about** contento di. ~**ing** adj gradevole

pleasure /'pleʒə(r)/ n piacere m, **with** ~ con piacere, volentieri

pleat /pli:t/ n piega f ● vt pieghettare. ~**ed 'skirt** n gonna f a pieghe

pledge /pledʒ/ n pegno m; (promise) promessa f ● vt impegnarsi a; (pawn) impegnare

plentiful /'plentifl/ adj abbondante

plenty /'plenti/ n abbondanza; ~ **of money** molti soldi; ~ **of people** molta gente; **I've got** ~ ne ho in abbondanza

pliable /'plaɪəbl/ adj flessibile

pliers /'plaɪəz/ npl pinze fpl

plight /plaɪt/ n condizione f

plimsolls /'plɪmsəlz/ npl scarpe fpl da ginnastica

plod /plɒd/ vi (pt/pp **plodded**) trascinarsi; (work hard) sgobbare

plot /plɒt/ n complotto m; (of novel) trama f; ~ **of land** appezzamento m [di terreno] ● vt/i complottare

plough /plaʊ/ n aratro m; ~**man's lunch** piatto m di formaggi e sottaceti, servito con pane. ● vt/i arare. □ ~ **back** vt (Comm) reinvestire

ploy /plɔɪ/ n [1] manovra f

pluck /plʌk/ n fegato m ● vt strappare, depilare (eyebrows); spennare (bird); cogliere (flower). □ ~ **up courage** farsi coraggio

plucky /'plʌkɪ/ adj (**-ier, -iest**) coraggioso

plug /plʌg/ n tappo m; (Electr) spina f; (Auto) candela f; ([1]: advertisement) pubblicità f inv ● vt (pt/pp **plugged**) tappare; ([1]: advertise) pubblicizzare con insistenza. □ ~ **in** vt (Electr) inserire la spina di

plum /plʌm/ n prugna f; (tree) prugno m

plumage /'plu:mɪdʒ/ n piumaggio m

plumb|er /'plʌmə(r)/ n idraulico m. ~**ing** n impianto m idraulico

plume /plu:m/ n piuma f

plump /plʌmp/ adj paffuto ● **plump for** vt scegliere

plunge /plʌndʒ/ n tuffo m; **take the** ~ [1] buttarsi ● vt tuffare; fig sprofondare ● vi tuffarsi

plural /'plʊərəl/ adj plurale ● n plurale m

plus /plʌs/ prep più ● adj in più; **500** ~ più di 500 ● n più m; (advantage) extra m inv

plush /plʌʃ[ɪ]/ adj lussuoso

plutonium /plu'təʊnɪəm/ n plutonio m

ply /plaɪ/ vt (pt/pp **plied**) ~ sb **with drink** continuare a offrire da bere a qcno. ~**wood** n compensato m

p.m. abbr (post meridiem) del pomeriggio

PM n abbr Prime Minister

pneumonia /nju:'məʊnɪə/ n polmonite f

P.O. abbr Post Office

poach /pəʊtʃ/ vt (Culin) bollire; cacciare di frodo (deer); pescare di frodo (salmon). ~**ed egg** uovo m in camicia. ~**er** n bracconiere m

pocket /'pɒkɪt/ n tasca f; **be out of** ~ rimetterci ● vt intascare. ~**-book** n taccuino m. ~**-money** n denaro m per le piccole spese

pod /pɒd/ n baccello m

poem /'pəʊɪm/ n poesia f

poet /'pəʊɪt/ n poeta m. **~ic** adj poetico

poetry /'pəʊɪtrɪ/ n poesia f

poignant /'pɔɪnjənt/ adj emozionante

point /pɔɪnt/ n punto m; (sharp end) punta f; (meaning, purpose) senso m; (Electr) presa f [di corrente]; **~s** pl (Rail) scambio m; **~ of view** punto di vista; **good/bad ~s** aspetti mpl positivi/negativi; **what is the ~?** a che scopo?; **the ~ is** il fatto è; **I don't see the ~** non vedo il senso; **up to a ~** fino a un certo punto; **be on the ~ of doing sth** essere sul punto di fare qcsa ● vt puntare (at verso) ● vi (with finger) puntare il dito; **~ at/to** (person): mostrare col dito; (indicator): indicare. □ **~ out** vt far notare (fact); **~ sth out to sb** far notare qcsa a qcno

point-'blank adj a bruciapelo

point|ed /'pɔɪntɪd/ adj appuntito; (question) diretto. **~ers** npl (advice) consigli mpl. **~less** adj inutile

poise /pɔɪz/ n padronanza f. **~d** adj in equilibrio. **~d to** sul punto di

poison /'pɔɪzn/ n veleno m ● vt avvelenare. **~ous** adj velenoso

poke /pəʊk/ n (piccola) spinta f ● vt spingere; (fire) attizzare; (put) ficcare; **~ fun at** prendere in giro. □ **~ about** vi frugare

poker[1] /'pəʊkə(r)/ n attizzatoio m

poker[2] n (Cards) poker m

poky /'pəʊkɪ/ adj (-ier, -iest) angusto

Poland /'pəʊlənd/ n Polonia f

polar /'pəʊlə(r)/ adj polare. **~ 'bear** n orso m bianco. **~ize** vt polarizzare

pole[1] n palo m

pole[2] n (Geog, Electr) polo m

Pole /pəʊl/ n polacco, -a mf

police /pə'liːs/ npl polizia f ● vt pattugliare (area)

police: **~man** n poliziotto m. **~ station** n commissariato m.

~woman n donna f poliziotto

policy[1] /'pɒlɪsɪ/ n politica f

policy[2] n (insurance) polizza f

polio /'pəʊlɪəʊ/ n polio f

polish /'pɒlɪʃ/ n (shine) lucentezza f; (substance) lucido m; (for nails) smalto m; fig raffinatezza f ● vt lucidare; fig smussare. □ **~ off** vt [I] finire in fretta; spazzolare (food)

Polish /'pəʊlɪʃ/ adj polacco ● n (language) polacco m

polished /'pɒlɪʃt/ adj (manner) raffinato; (performance) senza sbavature

polite /pə'laɪt/ adj cortese. **~ly** adv cortesemente. **~ness** n cortesia f

politic|al /pə'lɪtɪkl/ adj politico. **~ally** adv dal punto di vista politico. **~ian** n politico m

politics /'pɒlɪtɪks/ n politica f

poll /pəʊl/ n votazione f; (election) elezioni fpl; (opinion ~) sondaggio m d'opinione; **go to the ~s** andare alle urne ● vt ottenere (votes)

pollen /'pɒlən/ n polline m

pollut|e /pə'luːt/ vt inquinare. **~ion** n inquinamento m

polo /'pəʊləʊ/ n polo m. **~-neck** n collo m alto. **~ shirt** n dolcevita f

polythene /'pɒlɪθiːn/ n politene m. **~ bag** n sacchetto m di plastica

polyun'saturated adj polinsaturo

pomp /pɒmp/ n pompa f

pompous /'pɒmpəs/ adj pomposo

pond /pɒnd/ n stagno m

ponder /'pɒndə(r)/ vt/i ponderare

pony /'pəʊnɪ/ n pony m. **~-tail** n coda f di cavallo. **~-trekking** n escursioni fpl col pony

poodle /'puːdl/ n barboncino m

pool[1] /puːl/ n (of water, blood) pozza f; [swimming] ~ piscina f

pool[2] n (common fund) cassa f comune; (in cards) piatto m; (game) biliardo m a buca. **~s** npl ≈ totocalcio msg ● vt mettere insieme

poor /pʊə(r)/ *adj* povero; (*not good*) scadente; **in ~ health** in cattiva salute ● *npl* **the ~ i** poveri. **~ly** *adj* be **~ly** non stare bene ● *adv* male

pop¹ /pɒp/ *n* botto *m*, (*drink*) bibita *f* gasata ● *v* (*pt/pp* **popped**) ● *vt* (①: *put*) mettere; (*burst*) far scoppiare ● *vi* (*burst*) scoppiare. □ **~ in/out** *vi* ① fare un salto/un salto fuori

pop² *n* ① musica *f* pop ● *attrib* pop

popcorn /ˈpɒpkɔːn/ *n* popcorn *m inv*

pope /pəʊp/ *n* papa *m*

poplar /ˈpɒplə(r)/ *n* pioppo *m*

poppy /ˈpɒpɪ/ *n* papavero *m*

popular /ˈpɒpjʊlə(r)/ *adj* popolare; (*belief*) diffuso. **~ity** *n* popolarità *f inv*

populat|e /ˈpɒpjʊleɪt/ *vt* popolare. **~ion** *n* popolazione *f*

'pop-up *n* popup *m inv*

porcelain /ˈpɔːsəlɪn/ *n* porcellana *f*

porch /pɔːtʃ/ *n* portico *m*; Am veranda *f*

porcupine /ˈpɔːkjʊpaɪn/ *n* porcospino *m*

pore¹ /pɔː(r)/ *n* poro *m*

pore² *vi* **~ over** immergersi in

pork /pɔːk/ *n* carne *f* di maiale

porn /pɔːn/ *n* ① porno *m*. **~o** *adj* ① porno *inv*

pornograph|ic /pɔːnəˈɡræfɪk/ *adj* pornografico. **~y** *n* pornografia *f*

porpoise /ˈpɔːpəs/ *n* focena *f*

porridge /ˈpɒrɪdʒ/ *n* farinata *f* di fiocchi d'avena

port¹ /pɔːt/ *n* porto *m*

port² *n* (*Naut: side*) babordo *m*

port³ *n* (*wine*) porto *m*

portable /ˈpɔːtəbl/ *adj* portatile

porter /ˈpɔːtə(r)/ *n* portiere *m*; (*for luggage*) facchino *m*

'porthole *n* oblò *m inv*

portion /ˈpɔːʃn/ *n* parte *f*, (*of food*) porzione *f*

portrait /ˈpɔːtrɪt/ *n* ritratto *m*

portray /pɔːˈtreɪ/ *vt* ritrarre; (*represent*) descrivere; (*actor:*) impersonare. **~al** *n* ritratto *m*

Portug|al /ˈpɔːtjʊɡl/ *n* Portogallo *m*. **~uese** *adj* portoghese ● *n* portoghese *mf*

pose /pəʊz/ *n* posa *f* ● *vt* porre (*problem, question*) ● *vi* (*for painter*) posare; **~ as** atteggiarsi a

posh /pɒʃ/ *adj* ① lussuoso; (*people*) danaroso

position /pəˈzɪʃn/ *n* posizione *f*; (*job*) posto *m*; (*status*) ceto *m* [sociale] ● *vt* posizionare

positive /ˈpɒzɪtɪv/ *adj* positivo; (*certain*) sicuro; (*progress*) concreto ● *n* positivo *m*. **~ly** *adv* positivamente; (*decidedly*) decisamente

possess /pəˈzes/ *vt* possedere. **~ion** *n* possesso *m*; **~ions** *pl* beni *mpl*

possess|ive /pəˈzesɪv/ *adj* possessivo. **~iveness** *n* carattere *m* possessivo. **~or** *n* possessore, ditrice *mf*

possibility /pɒsəˈbɪlɪti/ *n* possibilità *f inv*

possib|le /ˈpɒsɪbl/ *adj* possibile. **~ly** *adv* possibilmente; **I couldn't ~ly** accept non mi è possibile accettare; **he can't ~ly be right** non è possibile che abbia ragione; **could you ~ly...?** potrebbe per favore...?

post¹ /pəʊst/ *n* (*pole*) palo *m* ● *vt* affiggere (*notice*)

post² *n* (*place of duty*) posto *m* ● *vt* appostare; (*transfer*) assegnare

post³ *n* (*mail*) posta *f*; **by ~** per posta ● *vt* spedire; (*put in letter-box*) imbucare; (*as opposed to fax*) mandare per posta; **keep sb ~ed** tenere qcno al corrente

post- *pref* dopo

postage /ˈpəʊstɪdʒ/ *n* affrancatura *f*. **~ stamp** *n* francobollo *m*

postal /ˈpəʊstl/ *adj* postale. **~ order** *n* vaglia *m* postale

post: ~box *n* cassetta *f* delle lettere. **~card** *n* cartolina *f*. **~code** *n* codice m postale

poster /'pəʊstə(r)/ n poster m inv; (advertising, election) cartellone m

posterity /pɒ'sterətɪ/ n posterità f

posthumous /'pɒstjʊməs/ adj postumo. ~ly adv dopo la morte

post: ~man n postino m. ~mark n timbro m postale

post-mortem /-'mɔːtəm/ n autopsia f

'post office n ufficio m postale

postpone /pəʊst'pəʊn/ vt rimandare. ~ment n rinvio m

posture /'pɒstʃə(r)/ n posizione f

pot /pɒt/ n vaso m; (for tea) teiera f; (for coffee) caffettiera f; (for cooking) pentola f; ~s of money [] un sacco di soldi; go to ~ [] andare in malora

potato /pə'teɪtəʊ/ n (pl -es) patata f

poten|t /'pəʊtənt/ adj potente. ~tate n potentato m

potential /pə'tenʃl/ adj potenziale ● n potenziale m. ~ly adv potenzialmente

pot: ~hole n cavità f inv; (in road) buca f. ~shot n take a ~shot at sparare a casaccio a

potter[1] /'pɒtə(r)/ vi ~ about gingillarsi

potter[2] n vasaio, -a mf. ~y n lavorazione f della ceramica; (articles) ceramiche fpl; (place) laboratorio m di ceramiche

potty /'pɒtɪ/ adj (-ier, -iest) [] matto ● n vasino m

pouch /paʊtʃ/ n marsupio m

poultry /'pəʊltrɪ/ n pollame m

pounce /paʊns/ vi balzare; ~ on saltare su

pound[1] /paʊnd/ n vasaio, n libbra f (= 0,454 kg); (money) sterlina f

pound[2] vt battere ● vi (heart:) battere forte; (run heavily) correre pesantemente

pour /pɔː(r)/ vt versare ● vi riversarsi;

(with rain) piovere a dirotto. □ ~ out vi riversarsi fuori ● vt versare (drink); sfogare (troubles)

pout /paʊt/ vi fare il broncio ● n broncio m

poverty /'pɒvətɪ/ n povertà f

powder /'paʊdə(r)/ n polvere f; (cosmetic) cipria f ● vt polverizzare; (face) incipriare. ~y adj polveroso

power /'paʊə(r)/ n potere m; (Electr) corrente f [elettrica]; (Math) potenza f. ~ cut n interruzione f di corrente. ~ed adj ~ed by electricity dotato di corrente [elettrica]. ~ful adj potente. ~less adj impotente. ~-station n centrale f elettrica

PR n abbr public relations

practicable /'præktɪkəbl/ adj praticabile

practical /'præktɪkl/ adj pratico. ~ 'joke n burla f. ~ly adv praticamente

practice /'præktɪs/ n pratica f; (custom) usanza f; (habit) abitudine f; (exercise) esercizio m; (Sport) allenamento m; in ~ (in reality) in pratica; out of ~ fuori esercizio; put into ~ mettere in pratica

practise /'præktɪs/ vt fare pratica in; (carry out) mettere in pratica; esercitare (profession) ● vi esercitarsi; (doctor:) praticare. ~d adj esperto

praise /preɪz/ n lode f ● vt lodare. ~worthy adj lodevole

pram /præm/ n carrozzella f

prank /præŋk/ n tiro m

prawn /prɔːn/ n gambero m. ~ 'cocktail n cocktail m inv di gamberetti

pray /preɪ/ vi pregare. ~er n preghiera f

preach /priːtʃ/ vt/i predicare. ~er n predicatore, -trice mf

pre-ar'range /priː-/ vt predisporre

precarious /prɪ'keərɪəs/ adj precario. ~ly adv in modo precario

precaution /prɪ'kɔːʃn/ n precauzione f; as a ~ per precauzione.

~ary adj preventivo

precede /prɪˈsiːd/ vt precedere

preceden|ce /ˈpresɪdəns/ n precedenza f. **~t** n precedente m

preceding /prɪˈsiːdɪŋ/ adj precedente

precinct /ˈpriːsɪŋkt/ n (traffic-free) zona f pedonale; (Am: district) circoscrizione f

precious /ˈpreʃəs/ adj prezioso, (style) ricercato ● adv **①** **~ little** ben poco

precipice /ˈpresɪpɪs/ n precipizio m

precipitate /prɪˈsɪpɪteɪt/ vt precipitare

precis|e /prɪˈsaɪs/ adj preciso. **~ely** adv precisamente. **~ion** n precisione f

precursor /priːˈkɜːsə(r)/ n precursore m

predator /ˈpredətə(r)/ n predatore, -trice mf. **~y** adj rapace

predecessor /ˈpriːdɪsesə(r)/ n predecessore m

predicament /prɪˈdɪkəmənt/ n situazione f difficile

predict /prɪˈdɪkt/ vt predire. **~able** adj prevedibile. **~ion** n previsione f

preen /priːn/ vt lisciarsi; **~ oneself** fig farsi bello

pre|fab /ˈpriːfæb/ n **①** casa f prefabbricata. **~'fabricated** adj prefabbricato

preface /ˈprefɪs/ n prefazione f

prefect /ˈpriːfekt/ n (Sch) studente, -tessa mf della scuola superiore con responsabilità disciplinari, ecc

prefer /prɪˈfɜː(r)/ vt (pt/pp preferred) preferire

prefera|ble /ˈprefərəbl/ adj preferibile (to a). **~bly** adv preferibilmente

preferen|ce /ˈprefərəns/ n preferenza f. **~tial** adj preferenziale

pregnan|cy /ˈpregnənsi/ n gravidanza f. **~t** adj incinta

prehi'storic /priː-/ adj preistorico

prejudice /ˈpredʒʊdɪs/ n pregiudizio m ● vt influenzare (**against** contro); (harm) danneggiare. **~d** adj prevenuto

preliminary /prɪˈlɪmɪnəri/ adj preliminare

prelude /ˈpreljuːd/ n preludio m

premature /ˈpremətjʊə(r)/ adj prematuro

pre'meditated /priː-/ adj premeditato

premier /ˈpremɪə(r)/ adj primario ● n (Pol) primo ministro m, premier m inv

première /ˈpremɪeə(r)/ n prima f

premises /ˈpremɪsɪz/ npl locali mpl; **on the ~** sul posto

premium /ˈpriːmɪəm/ n premio m; **be at a ~** essere una cosa rara

premonition /preməˈnɪʃn/ n presentimento m

preoccupied /priːˈɒkjʊpaɪd/ adj preoccupato

preparation /prepəˈreɪʃn/ n preparazione f. **~s** preparativi mpl

preparatory /prɪˈpærətri/ adj preparatorio ● adv **~ to** per

prepare /prɪˈpeə(r)/ vt preparare ● vi prepararsi (**for** per); **~d to** disposto a

preposition /prepəˈzɪʃn/ n preposizione f

preposterous /prɪˈpɒstərəs/ adj assurdo

prerequisite /priːˈrekwɪzɪt/ n condizione f sine qua non

prescribe /prɪˈskraɪb/ vt prescrivere

prescription /prɪˈskrɪpʃn/ n (Med) ricetta f

presence /ˈprezns/ n presenza f; **~ of mind** presenza f di spirito

present¹ /ˈpreznt/ adj presente ● n presente m; **at ~** attualmente

present² n (gift) regalo m; **give sb sth as a ~** regalare qcsa a qcno

P

present³ /prɪˈzent/ vt presentare; ~ sb with an award consegnare un premio a qcno. **~able** adj be **~able** essere presentabile

presentation /preznˈteɪʃn/ n presentazione f

presently /ˈprezntlɪ/ adv fra poco; (Am: now) attualmente

preservation /prezəˈveɪʃn/ n conservazione f

preservative /prɪˈzɜːvətɪv/ n conservante m

preserve /prɪˈzɜːv/ vt preservare; (maintain, Culin) conservare ● vt (in hunting & fig) riserva f; (jam) marmellata f

preside /prɪˈzaɪd/ vi presiedere (over a)

presidency /ˈprezɪdənsɪ/ n presidenza f

president /ˈprezɪdənt/ n presidente m. **~ial** adj presidenziale

press /pres/ n (machine) pressa f; (newspapers) stampa f ● vt premere (flower); (iron) stirare; (squeeze) stringere ● vi (urge) incalzare. □ ~ **for** vi fare pressione per; be ~**ed** for essere a corto di. □ ~ **on** vi andare avanti

press: ~ **conference** n conferenza f stampa. **~ cutting** n ritaglio m di giornale. **~ing** adj urgente. **~-up** n flessione f

pressure /ˈpreʃə(r)/ n pressione f ● vt = pressurize. **~-cooker** n pentola f a pressione. **~ group** n gruppo m di pressione

pressurize /ˈpreʃəraɪz/ vt far pressione su. **~d** adj pressurizzato

prestige /preˈstiːʒ/ n prestigio m. **~ious** adj prestigioso

presumably /prɪˈzjuːməblɪ/ adv presumibilmente

presume /prɪˈzjuːm/ vt presumere; ~ **to do sth** permettersi di fare qcsa

presup'pose /priː-/ vt presupporre

pretence /prɪˈtens/ n finzione f; (pretext) pretesto m; **it's all** ~ è tutta una scena

pretend /prɪˈtend/ vt fingere; (claim) pretendere ● vi fare finta

pretentious /prɪˈtenʃəs/ adj pretenzioso

pretext /ˈpriːtekst/ n pretesto m

pretty /ˈprɪtɪ/ adj (-ier, -iest) carino ● adv (🔟: fairly) abbastanza

prevail /prɪˈveɪl/ vi prevalere; ~ **on** sb to do sth convincere qcno a fare qcsa. **~ing** adj prevalente

prevalen|ce /ˈprevələns/ n diffusione f. **~t** adj diffuso

prevent /prɪˈvent/ vt impedire; ~ sb [from] doing impedire a qcno di fare qcsa. **~ion** n prevenzione f. **~ive** adj preventivo

preview /ˈpriːvjuː/ n anteprima f

previous /ˈpriːvɪəs/ adj precedente. **~ly** adv precedentemente

prey /preɪ/ n preda f; **bird of** ~ uccello m rapace ● vi ~ **on** far preda di; ~ **on sb's mind** attanagliare qcno

price /praɪs/ n prezzo m ● vt (Comm) fissare il prezzo di. **~less** adj inestimabile; (🔟: amusing) spassosissimo. **~y** adj 🔟 caro

prick /prɪk/ n puntura f ● vt pungere. □ ~ **up** vt ~ **up one's ears** rizzare le orecchie

prick|le /ˈprɪkl/ n spina f; (sensation) formicolio m. **~ly** adj pungente; (person) irritabile

pride /praɪd/ n orgoglio m ● vt ~ **oneself on** vantarsi di

priest /priːst/ n prete m

prim /prɪm/ adj (primmer, primmest) perbenino

primarily /ˈpraɪmərɪlɪ/ adv in primo luogo

primary /ˈpraɪmərɪ/ adj primario; (chief) principale. ~ **school** n scuola f elementare

prime[1] /praɪm/ adj principale, primo; (first-rate) eccellente ● **be in one's ~** essere nel fiore degli anni

prime[2] vt preparare (surface, person)

Prime Minister n Primo m Ministro

primeval /praɪˈmiːvl/ adj primitivo

primitive /ˈprɪmɪtɪv/ adj primitivo

primrose /ˈprɪmrəʊz/ n primula f

prince /prɪns/ n principe m

princess /prɪnˈses/ n principessa f

principal /ˈprɪnsəpl/ adj principale ● n (Sch) preside m

principally /ˈprɪnsəplɪ/ adv principalmente

principle /ˈprɪnsəplɪ/ n principio m; **in ~** in teoria; **on ~** per principio

print /prɪnt/ n (mark, trace) impronta f; (Phot) copia f; (picture) stampa f; **in ~** (printed out) stampato; (book) in commercio; **out of ~** esaurito ● vt stampare; (write in capitals) scrivere in stampatello. **~ed matter** n stampe fpl

print|er /ˈprɪntə(r)/ n stampante f; (Typ) tipografo, -a mf. **~er port** n (Comput) porta f per la stampante. **~ing** n tipografia f

'printout n (Comput) stampa f

prior /ˈpraɪə(r)/ adj precedente. **~ to** prep prima di

priority /praɪˈɒrətɪ/ n precedenza f; (matter) priorità f inv

prise /praɪz/ vt **~ open/up** forzare

prison /ˈprɪz(ə)n/ n prigione f. **~er** n prigioniero, -a mf

privacy /ˈprɪvəsɪ/ n privacy f inv

private /ˈpraɪvət/ adj privato; (car, secretary, letter) personale; in (Mil) soldato m semplice; **in ~** in privato. **~ly** adv (funded, educated etc) privatamente; (in secret) in segreto; (confidentially) in privato; (inwardly) interiormente

privation /praɪˈveɪʃn/ n privazione

f; **~s** npl stenti mpl

privilege /ˈprɪvəlɪdʒ/ n privilegio m. **~d** adj privilegiato

prize /praɪz/ n premio m ● adj (idiot etc) perfetto ● vt apprezzare. **giving** n premiazione f. **~-winner** n vincitore, -trice mf. **~-winning** adj vincente

pro /prəʊ/ n (Ⅱ: professional) professionista mf; **the ~s and cons** il pro e il contro

probability /prɒbəˈbɪlətɪ/ n probabilità f inv

probable /ˈprɒbəbl/ adj probabile. **~y** adv probabilmente

probation /prəˈbeɪʃn/ n prova f; (Jur) libertà f vigilata. **~ary** adj in prova; **~ary period** periodo m di prova

probe /prəʊb/ n sonda f; (fig: investigation) indagine f ● vt sondare; (investigate) esaminare a fondo

problem /ˈprɒbləm/ n problema m ● adj problematico. **~atic** adj problematico

procedure /prəˈsiːdʒə(r)/ n procedimento m

proceed /prəˈsiːd/ vi procedere ● vt **~ to do sth** proseguire facendo qcsa

proceedings /prəˈsiːdɪŋz/ npl (report) atti mpl; (Jur) azione f legale

proceeds /ˈprəʊsiːdz/ npl ricavato msg

process /ˈprəʊses/ n processo m; (procedure) procedimento m; **in the ~** nel far ciò ● vt trattare; (Admin) occuparsi di; (Phot) sviluppare

procession /prəˈseʃn/ n processione f

processor /ˈprəʊsesə(r)/ n (Comput) processore m; (for food) robot m inv da cucina

proclaim /prəˈkleɪm/ vt proclamare

procure /prəˈkjʊə(r)/ vt ottenere

prod /prɒd/ n colpetto m ● vt (pt/pp **prodded**) punzecchiare; fig incitare

produce[1] /'prɒdjuːs/ n prodotti mpl; ~ **of Italy** prodotto in Italia

produce[2] /prə'djuːs/ vt produrre; (bring out) tirar fuori; (cause) causare; (☐: give birth to) fare. ~**r** n produttore m

product /'prɒdʌkt/ n prodotto m. ~**ion** n produzione f; (Theat) spettacolo m

productiv|e /prə'dʌktɪv/ adj produttivo. ~**ity** n produttività f

profession /prə'feʃn/ n professione f. ~**al** adj professionale; (not amateur) professionista; (piece of work) da professionista; (man) di professione ●n professionista mf. ~**ally** adv professionalmente

professor /prə'fesə(r)/ n professore m [universitario]

proficien|cy /prə'fɪʃnsɪ/ n competenza f. ~**t** adj **be** ~**t** in essere competente in

profile /'prəʊfaɪl/ n profilo m

profit /'prɒfɪt/ n profitto m ●vi ~ **from** trarre profitto da. ~**able** adj proficuo. ~**ably** adv in modo proficuo

profound /prə'faʊnd/ adj profondo. ~**ly** adv profondamente

profus|e /prə'fjuːs/ adj ~**e apologies/flowers** una profusione di scuse/fiori. ~**ion** n profusione f; **in** ~**ion** in abbondanza

prognosis /prɒg'nəʊsɪs/ n (pl -**oses**) prognosi f inv

program /'prəʊgræm/ n programma m ●vt (pt/pp **programmed**) programmare

programme /'prəʊgræm/ n Br programma m. ~**r** n (Comput) programmatore, -trice mf

progress[1] /'prəʊgres/ n progresso m; **in** ~ in corso; **make** ~ fig fare progressi

progress[2] /prə'gres/ vi progredire; fig fare progressi

progressive /prə'gresɪv/ adj progressivo; (reforming) progressista. ~**ly** adv progressivamente

prohibit /prə'hɪbɪt/ vt proibire. ~**ive** adj proibitivo

project[1] /'prɒdʒekt/ n progetto m; (Sch) ricerca f

project[2] /prə'dʒekt/ vt proiettare (film, image) ●vi (jut out) sporgere

projector /prə'dʒektə(r)/ n proiettore m

prolific /prə'lɪfɪk/ adj prolifico

prologue /'prəʊlɒg/ n prologo m

prolong /prə'lɒŋ/ vt prolungare

promenade /prɒmə'nɑːd/ n lungomare m inv

prominent /'prɒmɪnənt/ adj prominente; (conspicuous) di rilievo

promiscu|ity /prɒmɪ'skjuːətɪ/ n promiscuità f. ~**ous** adj promiscuo

promis|e /'prɒmɪs/ n promessa f ●vt promettere; ~**e sb that** promettere a qcno che; **I** ~**ed to** l'ho promesso. ~**ing** adj promettente

promot|e /prə'məʊt/ vt promuovere; **be** ~**ed** (Sport) essere promosso. ~**ion** n promozione f

prompt /prɒmpt/ adj immediato; (punctual) puntuale ●adv in punto ●vt incitare (**to** a); (Theat) suggerire a ●vi suggerire. ~**er** n suggeritore, -trice mf. ~**ly** adv puntualmente

Proms /prɒmz/ npl rassegna f di concerti estivi di musica classica presso l'Albert Hall a Londra

---

Proms I Proms sono una serie di concerti di musica classica che ogni estate, per otto settimane, si tengono giornalmente all'Albert Hall di Londra. Istituiti nel 1895 per iniziativa di Sir Henry Wood, il loro nome è l'abbreviazione di promenade concerts, concerti durante i quali a parte del pubblico in sala sono riservati posti in piedi.

prone /prəʊn/ adj be ~ to do sth essere incline a fare qcsa

pronoun /ˈprəʊnaʊn/ n pronome m

pronounce /prəˈnaʊns/ vt pronunciare; (declare) dichiarare. ~d adj (noticeable) pronunciato

pronunciation /prənʌnsɪˈeɪʃn/ n pronuncia f

proof /pruːf/ n prova f; (Typ) bozza f, prova f ● adj ~ against a prova di

propaganda /prɒpəˈɡændə/ n propaganda f

propel /prəˈpel/ vt (pt/pp propelled) spingere. ~ler n elica f

proper /ˈprɒpə(r)/ adj corretto; (suitable) adatto; (🔲: real) vero [e proprio]. ~ly adv correttamente. ~ 'name, ~ 'noun n nome m proprio

property /ˈprɒpətɪ/ n proprietà f inv. ~ developer n agente m immobiliare. ~ market n mercato m immobiliare

prophecy /ˈprɒfəsɪ/ n profezia f

prophesy /ˈprɒfɪsaɪ/ vt (pt/pp -ied) profetizzare

prophet /ˈprɒfɪt/ n profeta m. ~ic adj profetico

proportion /prəˈpɔːʃn/ n proporzione f; (share) parte f; ~s pl (dimensions) proporzioni fpl. ~al adj proporzionale. ~ally adv in proporzione

proposal /prəˈpəʊzl/ n proposta f; (of marriage) proposta f di matrimonio

propose /prəˈpəʊz/ vt proporre; (intend) proporsi ● vi fare una proposta di matrimonio

proposition /prɒpəˈzɪʃn/ n proposta f; (🔲: task) impresa f

proprietor /prəˈpraɪətə(r)/ n proprietario, -a mf

prose /prəʊz/ n prosa f

prosecute /ˈprɒsɪkjuːt/ vt intentare azione contro. ~ion n azione f giudiziaria. the ~ion l'accusa f. ~or n [Public] P~or il Pubblico Ministero m

prospect[1] /ˈprɒspekt/ n (expectation) prospettiva f

prospect[2] /prəˈspekt/ vi ~ for cercare

prospect|ive /prəˈspektɪv/ adj (future) futuro; (possible) potenziale. ~or n cercatore m

prospectus /prəˈspektəs/ n prospetto m

prosper /ˈprɒspə(r)/ vi prosperare, (person:) stare bene finanziariamente. ~ity n prosperità f

prosperous /ˈprɒspərəs/ adj prospero

prostitut|e /ˈprɒstɪtjuːt/ n prostituta f. ~ion n prostituzione f

prostrate /ˈprɒstreɪt/ adj prostrato; ~ with grief fig prostrato dal dolore

protagonist /prəʊˈtæɡənɪst/ n protagonista mf

protect /prəˈtekt/ vt proteggere (from da). ~ion n protezione f, ~ive adj protettivo. ~or n protettore, -trice mf

protein /ˈprəʊtiːn/ n proteina f

protest[1] /ˈprəʊtest/ n protesta f

protest[2] /prəˈtest/ vt/i protestare

Protestant /ˈprɒtɪstənt/ adj protestante ● n protestante mf

protester /prəˈtestə(r)/ n contestatore, -trice mf

protocol /ˈprəʊtəkɒl/ n protocollo m

protrude /prəˈtruːd/ vi sporgere

proud /praʊd/ adj fiero (of di). ~ly adv fieramente

prove /pruːv/ vt provare ● vi ~ to be a lie rivelarsi una bugia. ~n adj dimostrato

proverb /ˈprɒvɜːb/ n proverbio m. ~ial adj proverbiale

provide /prəˈvaɪd/ vt fornire; ~ sb with sth fornire qcsa a qcno ● vi ~ for (law:) prevedere

provided /prəˈvaɪdɪd/ conj ~ [that] purché

providen|ce /'prɒvɪdəns/ n provvidenza f. ~**tial** adj provvidenziale

providing /prə'vaɪdɪŋ/ conj = provided

provinc|e /'prɒvɪns/ n provincia f; fig campo m. ~**ial** adj provinciale

provision /prə'vɪʒn/ n (of food, water) approvvigionamento m (of di); (of law) disposizione f; ~s pl provviste fpl. ~**al** adj provvisorio

provocat|ion /prɒvə'keɪʃn/ n provocazione f. ~**ive** adj provocatorio; (sexually) provocante. ~**ively** adv in modo provocatorio

provoke /prə'vəʊk/ vt provocare

prow /praʊ/ n prua f

prowess /'praʊɪs/ n abilità f inv

prowl /praʊl/ vi aggirarsi ●on the ~ in cerca di preda. ~**er** n tipo m sospetto

proximity /prɒk'sɪmətɪ/ n prossimità f

proxy /'prɒksɪ/ n procura f; (person) persona f che agisce per procura

prude /pruːd/ n be a ~ essere eccessivamente pudico

pruden|ce /'pruːdəns/ n prudenza f. ~**t** adj prudente; (wise) oculatezza f

prudish /'pruːdɪʃ/ adj eccessivamente pudico

prune[1] /pruːn/ n prugna f secca

prune[2] vt potare

pry /praɪ/ vi (pt/pp **pried**) ficcare il naso

psalm /sɑːm/ n salmo m

psychiatric /saɪkɪ'ætrɪk/ adj psichiatrico

psychiatr|ist /saɪ'kaɪətrɪst/ n psichiatra mf. ~**y** n psichiatria f

psychic /'saɪkɪk/ adj psichico; **I'm not** ~ non sono un indovino

psychological /saɪkə'lɒdʒɪkl/ adj psicologico

psycholog|ist /saɪ'kɒlədʒɪst/ n psicologo, -a mf. ~**y** n psicologia f

pub /pʌb/ n 🔲 pub m inv

> **Pub** In Gran Bretagna, molti **pubs** (abbreviazione di **public house**) fanno parte di catene e sono proprietà di grandi birrerie, altri invece sono indipendenti (**free houses**). Oltre che per bere, si va al **pub** per socializzare e giocare a freccette, biliardo, ecc.; alcuni organizzano serate di quiz a gruppi. L'orario di apertura è deciso a seconda della licenza dell'esercizio, ma quello più comune va dalle 11 alle 23.

puberty /'pjuːbətɪ/ n pubertà f

public /'pʌblɪk/ adj pubblico ●in the ~ il pubblico; in ~ in pubblico. ~**ly** adv pubblicamente

publican /'pʌblɪkən/ n gestore, -trice mf/proprietario, -a mf di un pub

publication /pʌblɪ'keɪʃn/ n pubblicazione f

public: ~ **'holiday** n festa f nazionale. ~ **'house** n pub m

publicity /pʌb'lɪsətɪ/ n pubblicità f

publicize /'pʌblɪsaɪz/ vt pubblicizzare

public: ~ **relations** fpl. relazioni fpl. ~ **'school** n scuola f privata; Am scuola f pubblica

> **public schools** In Inghilterra sono, al contrario di quanto il nome farebbe pensare, scuole secondarie private a pagamento, in cui spesso gli allievi risiedono in collegio.

publish /'pʌblɪʃ/ vt pubblicare. ~**er** n editore m; (firm) editore m, casa f editrice. ~**ing** n editoria f

pudding /'pʊdɪŋ/ n dolce m cotto al vapore; (course) dolce m

puddle /'pʌdl/ n pozzanghera f

puff /pʌf/ n (of wind) soffio m; (of

smoke) tirata f; (for powder) piumino m ● vt sbuffare. **puff at** vt tirare boccate da (pipe). **~ out** vt lasciare senza fiato (person); spegnere (candle). **~ed** adj (out of breath) senza fiato. **~ pastry** n pasta f sfoglia

puffy /'pʌfɪ/ adj gonfio

pull /pol/ n trazione f; (fig: attraction) attrazione f; (🄸: influence) influenza f ● vt tirare; estrarre (tooth); stirarsi (muscle); **~ faces** far boccacce; **~ oneself together** cercare di controllarsi; **~ one's weight** mettercela tutta; **~ sb's leg** 🄸 prendere in giro qcno. **□ ~ down** vt (demolish) demolire. **□ ~ in** vi (Auto) accostare. **□ ~ off** vt togliere; 🄸 azzeccare. **□ ~ out** vt tirar fuori ● vi (Auto) spostarsi; (of competition) ritirarsi. **□ ~ through** vi (recover) farcela. **□ ~ up** vt sradicare (plant); (reprimand) rimproverare ● vi (Auto) fermarsi

pullover /'polaova(r)/ n pullover m

pulp /pʌlp/ n poltiglia f; (of fruit) polpa f; (for paper) pasta f

pulpit /'polpit/ n pulpito m

pulse /pʌls/ n polso m

pummel /'pʌml/ vt (pt/pp **pummelled**) prendere a pugni

pump /pʌmp/ n pompa f ● vt pompare; 🄸 cercare di estorcere da. **□ ~ up** vt (inflate) gonfiare

pumpkin /'pʌmpkin/ n zucca f

pun /pʌn/ n gioco m di parole

punch[1] /pʌntʃ/ n pugno m; (device) pinza f per forare ● vt dare un pugno a; forare (ticket); perforare (hole)

punch[2] n (drink) ponce m inv

punctual /'pʌŋktjʊal/ adj puntuale. **~ity** n puntualità f. **~ly** adv puntualmente

punctuat|e /'pʌŋktjʊeit/ vt punteggiare. **~ion** n punteggiatura f. **~ion mark** n segno m di interpunzione

puncture /'pʌŋktʃə(r)/ n foro m;

(tyre) foratura f ● vt forare

punish /'pʌnɪʃ/ vt punire. **~able** adj punibile. **~ment** n punizione f

punk /pʌŋk/ n punk m inv

punt /pʌnt/ n (boat) barchino m

punter /'pʌntə(r)/ n (gambler) scommettitore, -trice m/f; (client) consumatore, -trice m/f

puny /'pjuːnɪ/ adj (**-ier, -iest**) striminzito

pup /pʌp/ n = **puppy**

pupil /'pjuːpl/ n alunno, -a m/f; (of eye) pupilla f

puppet /'pʌpit/ n marionetta f; (glove ~, fig) burattino m

puppy /'pʌpi/ n cucciolo m

purchase /'pɜːtʃəs/ n acquisto m; (leverage) presa f ● vt acquistare. **~r** n acquirente mf

pure /pjʊə(r)/ adj puro. **~ly** adv puramente

purgatory /'pɜːɡətri/ n purgatorio m

purge /pɜːdʒ/ (Pol) n epurazione f ● vt epurare

puri|fication /pjʊərɪfɪ'keɪʃn/ n purificazione f. **~fy** vt (pt/pp **ied**) purificare

puritan /'pjʊəritən/ n puritano. **~ical** adj puritano

purity /'pjʊərɪtɪ/ n purità f

purple /'pɜːpl/ adj viola

purpose /'pɜːpəs/ n scopo m; (determination) fermezza f; **on ~** apposta. **~-built** adj costruito ad hoc. **~ful** adj deciso. **~fully** adv con decisione. **~ly** adv apposta

purr /pɜː(r)/ vi (cat:) fare le fusa

purse /pɜːs/ n borsellino m; (Am: handbag) borsa f ● vt increspare (lips)

pursue /pə'sjuː/ vt inseguire, fig seguire. **~r** n inseguitore, -trice mf

pursuit /pə'sjuːt/ n inseguimento m; (fig: of happiness) ricerca f; (pastime) attività f inv; **in ~** all'inseguimento

pus /pʌs/ n pus m

push /pʊʃ/ n spinta f; (fig: effort) sforzo m; (drive) iniziativa f; **at a ~** in caso di bisogno; **get the ~** 🔲 essere licenziato ● vt spingere; premere (button); (pressurize) far pressione su; **be ~ed for time** 🔲 non avere tempo ● vi spingere. □ **~ aside** vt scostare. □ **~ back** vt respingere. □ **~ off** vt togliere ● vi (🔲: leave) levarsi dai piedi. □ **~ on** vi (continue) continuare. □ **~ up** vt alzare (price)

push: **~-chair** n passeggino m. **~-up** n flessione f

pushy /ˈpʊʃɪ/ adj 🔲 troppo intraprendente

put /pʊt/ vt (pt/pp put, pres p putting) mettere; **~ the cost of sth at** valutare il costo di qcsa ● vi **~ to sea** salpare. □ **~ aside** vt mettere da parte. □ **~ away** vt mettere via. □ **~ back** vt rimettere; mettere indietro (clock). □ **~ by** vt mettere da parte. □ **~ down** vt mettere giù; (suppress) reprimere; (kill) sopprimere; (write) annotare; **~ one's foot down** 🔲 essere fermo; (Auto) dare un'accelerata; **~ down to** (attribute) attribuire. □ **~ forward** vt avanzare; mettere avanti (clock). □ **~ in** vt (insert) introdurre; (submit) presentare ● vi **~ in for** far domanda di. □ **~ off** vt spegnere (light); (postpone) rimandare; **~ sb off** tenere a bada qcno; (deter) smontare qcno; (disconnect) distrarre qcno; **~ sb off sth** (disgust) disgustare qcno di qcsa. □ **~ on** vt mettersi (clothes); mettere (brake); (Culin) mettere su; accendere (light); mettere in scena (play); prendere (accent); **~ on weight** mettere su qualche chilo. □ **~ out** vt spegnere (fire, light); tendere (hand); (inconvenience) creare degli inconvenienti a. □ **~ through** vt far passare; (Teleph) **I'll ~ you through to him** glielo passo. □ **~ up** vt alzare; erigere (building); montare (tent); aprire

(umbrella); affiggere (notice); aumentare (price); ospitare (guest); **~ sb up to sth** mettere qcsa in testa a qcno ● vi (at hotel) stare; **~ up with** sopportare ● adj **stay ~!** rimani lì!

puzz|**le** /ˈpʌzl/ n enigma m; (jigsaw) puzzle m inv ● vt lasciare perplesso ● vi **~e over** scervellarsi su. **~ing** adj inspiegabile

pygmy /ˈpɪgmɪ/ n pigmeo, -a mf

pyjamas /pəˈdʒɑːməz/ npl pigiama msg

pylon /ˈpaɪlən/ n pilone m

pyramid /ˈpɪrəmɪd/ n piramide f

python /ˈpaɪθn/ n pitone m

Qq

quack[1] /kwæk/ n qua qua m inv ● vi fare qua qua

quack[2] n (doctor) ciarlatano m

quadrangle /ˈkwɒdræŋgl/ n quadrangolo m; (court) cortile m quadrangolare

quadruped /ˈkwɒdrʊped/ n quadrupede m

quadruple /ˈkwɒdrʊpl/ adj quadruplo ● vt quadruplicare ● vi quadruplicarsi. **~ts** npl quattro gemelli mpl

quagmire /ˈkwɒgmaɪə(r)/ n pantano m

quaint /kweɪnt/ adj pittoresco; (odd) bizzarro

quake /kweɪk/ n 🔲 terremoto m ● vi tremare

qualif|**ication** /kwɒlɪfɪˈkeɪʃn/ n qualifica f. **~ied** adj qualificato; (limited) con riserva

qualify /ˈkwɒlɪfaɪ/ v (pt/pp -ied) ● vt (course:) dare la qualifica a (as di); (entitle) dare diritto a; (limit) precisare

● vi ottenere la qualifica; (Sport) qualificarsi

quality /'kwɒlətɪ/ n qualità f inv

qualm /kwɑ:m/ n scrupolo m

quandary /'kwɒndərɪ/ n dilemma m

quantity /'kwɒntətɪ/ n quantità f inv; **in ~** in grande quantità

quarantine /'kwɒrəntiːn/ n quarantena f

quarrel /'kwɒrəl/ n lite f ● vi (pt/pp quarrelled) litigare. **~some** adj litigioso

quarry[1] /'kwɒrɪ/ n (prey) preda f

quarry[2] n (Mining) cava f

quart /kwɔːt/ n 1.14 litro

quarter /'kwɔːtə(r)/ n quarto m; (of year) trimestre m; Am 25 centesimi mpl; **~s** pl (Mil) quartiere msg; **at [a] ~ to six** alle sei meno un quarto ● vt dividere in quattro. **~-final** n quarto m di finale

quarterly /'kwɔːtəlɪ/ adj trimestrale ● adv trimestralmente

quartz /kwɔːts/ n quarzo m. **~ watch** n orologio m al quarzo

quay /kiː/ n banchina f

queasy /'kwiːzɪ/ adj **I feel ~** ho la nausea

queen /kwiːn/ n regina f. **~ mother** n regina f madre

queer /kwɪə(r)/ adj strano; (dubious) sospetto; (I : homosexual) finocchio ● n I finocchio m

quench /kwentʃ/ vt **~ one's thirst** dissetarsi

query /'kwɪərɪ/ n domanda f; (question mark) punto m interrogativo ● vt (pt/pp -ied) interrogare; (doubt) mettere in dubbio

quest /kwest/ n ricerca f (for di)

question /'kwestʃn/ n domanda f; (for discussion) questione f; **out of the ~** fuori discussione; **without ~** senza dubbio; **in ~** in questione ● vt

interrogare; (doubt) mettere in dubbio. **~able** adj discutibile. **~ mark** n punto m interrogativo

questionnaire /kwestʃə'neə(r)/ n questionario m

queue /kjuː/ n coda f, fila f ● vi **~ [up]** mettersi in coda (for per)

quick /kwɪk/ adj veloce; **be ~** sbrigati!; **have a ~ meal** fare un spuntino ● adv in fretta ● n **be cut to the ~** fig essere punto sul vivo. **~ly** adv in fretta. **~-tempered** adj collerico

quid /kwɪd/ n inv I sterlina f

quiet /'kwaɪət/ adj (calm) tranquillo; (silent) silenzioso; (voice, music) basso; **keep ~ about** I non raccontare a nessuno; **on the ~** di nascosto. **~ly** adv (peacefully) tranquillamente; (say) a bassa voce

quiet|en /'kwaɪətn/ vt calmare. □ **~ down** vi calmarsi. **~ness** n quiete f

quilt /kwɪlt/ n piumino m. **~ed** adj trapuntato

quintet /kwɪn'tet/ n quintetto m

quirk /kwɜːk/ n stranezza f

quit /kwɪt/ v (pt/pp quitted, quit) ● vt lasciare; (give up) smettere (doing di fare) ● vi (I : resign) andarsene; (Comput) uscire; **give sb notice to ~** (landlord) dare a qcno il preavviso di sfratto

quite /kwaɪt/ adv (fairly) abbastanza; (completely) completamente; (really) veramente; **~ [so]!** proprio così!; **~ a few** parecchi

quits /kwɪts/ adj pari

quiver /'kwɪvə(r)/ vi tremare

quiz /kwɪz/ n (game) quiz m inv ● vt (pt/pp quizzed) interrogare

quota /'kwəʊtə/ n quota f

quotation /kwəʊ'teɪʃn/ n citazione f; (price) preventivo m; (of shares) quota f. **~ marks** npl virgolette fpl

quote /kwəʊt/ n I = quotation; **in ~s** tra virgolette ● vt citare; quotare (price)

Rr

rabbi /'ræbaɪ/ n rabbino m; (title) rabbi

rabbit /'ræbɪt/ n coniglio m

rabies /'reɪbiːz/ n rabbia f

race[1] /reɪs/ n (people) razza f

race[2] n corsa f ● vi correre ● vt gareggiare con; fare correre (horse)

race: ~**course** n ippodromo m. ~**horse** n cavallo m da corsa. ~**track** n pista m

racial /'reɪʃl/ adj razziale. ~**ism** n razzismo m

racing /'reɪsɪŋ/ n corse fpl; (horse-) corse fpl dei cavalli. ~ **car** n macchina f da corsa. ~ **driver** n corridore m automobilistico

racis|m /'reɪsɪzm/ n razzismo m. ~**t** adj razzista ● n razzista mf

rack[1] /ræk/ n (for bikes) rastrelliera f; (for luggage) portabagagli m inv; (for plates) scolapiatti m inv ● vt ~ one's brains scervellarsi

rack[2] n go to ~ and ruin andare in rovina

racket[1] /'rækɪt/ n (Sport) racchetta f

racket[2] n (din) chiasso m; (swindle) truffa f; (crime) racket m inv, giro m

radar /'reɪdɑː(r)/ n radar m inv

radian|ce /'reɪdɪəns/ n radiosità f inv. ~**t** adj raggiante

radiat|e /'reɪdɪeɪt/ vt irradiare ● vi (heat:) irradiarsi. ~**ion** n radiazione f

radiator /'reɪdɪeɪtə(r)/ n radiatore m

radical /'rædɪkl/ adj radicale ● n radicale mf. ~**ly** adv radicalmente

radio /'reɪdɪəʊ/ n radio f inv

radio|active /reɪdɪəʊ'æktɪv/ adj radioattivo. ~**activity** n radioattività f

radish /'rædɪʃ/ n ravanello m

radius /'reɪdɪəs/ n (pl -**dii** /-dɪaɪ/) raggio m

raffle /'ræfl/ n lotteria f

raft /rɑːft/ n zattera f

rafter /'rɑːftə(r)/ n trave f

rag /ræg/ n straccio m; (pej: newspaper) giornalaccio m; **in** ~**s** straccciato

rage /reɪdʒ/ n rabbia f; **all the** ~ ▣ all'ultima moda ● vi infuriarsi; (storm:) infuriare; (epidemic:) imperversare

ragged /'rægɪd/ adj logoro; (edge) frastagliato

raid /reɪd/ n (by thieves) rapina f; (Mil) incursione f, raid m inv; (police) irruzione f ● vt (Mil) fare un'incursione in; (police, burglars:) fare irruzione in. ~**er** n (of bank) rapinatore, -trice mf

rail /reɪl/ n ringhiera f; (hand-) ringhiera f; (Naut) parapetto m; **by** ~ per ferrovia

'railroad n Am = **railway**

'railway n ferrovia f. ~**man** n ferroviere m. ~ **station** n stazione f ferroviaria

rain /reɪn/ n pioggia f ● vi piovere

rain: ~**bow** n arcobaleno m. ~**coat** n impermeabile m. ~**fall** n precipitazione f [atmosferica]

rainy /'reɪnɪ/ adj (-ier, -iest) piovoso

raise /reɪz/ n Am aumento m ● vt alzare; levarsi (hat); allevare (children, animals); sollevare (question); ottenere (money)

raisin /'reɪzn/ n uva f passa

rake /reɪk/ n rastrello m ● vt rastrellare. □ ~ **up** vt raccogliere col rastrello; ▣ rivangare

rally /'rælɪ/ n raduno m; (Auto) rally m inv; (Tennis) scambio m ● vt (pt/pp -**ied**) radunare ● vi radunarsi; (recover strength) riprendersi

ram /ræm/ n montone m; (Astr) Ariete m ● vt (pt/pp **rammed**) cozzare contro

RAM /ræm/ n [memoria f] RAM f

ramble /ˈræmbl/ n escursione f e vi gironzolare; (in speech) divagare. **~er** n escursionista m; (rose) rosa f rampicante. **~ing** adj (in speech) sconnesso; (club) escursionistico

ramp /ræmp/ n rampa f; (Aeron) scaletta f mobile (di aerei)

rampage /ˈræmpeɪdʒ/ n be/go on the ~ scatenarsi e vi ~ through the streets scatenarsi per le strade

ramshackle /ˈræmʃækl/ adj sgangherato

ran /ræn/ ▷ **RUN**

ranch /rɑːntʃ/ n ranch m

random /ˈrændəm/ adj casuale; ~ sample campione m a caso e n at ~ a casaccio

rang /ræŋ/ ▷ **RING²**

range /reɪndʒ/ n serie f; (Comm, Mus) gamma f; (of mountains) catena f; (distance) raggio m; (for shooting) portata f; (stove) cucina f economica; at a ~ of a una distanza di e vi estendersi; ~ from... to... andare da... a.... **~r** n guardia f forestale

rank /ræŋk/ n (row) riga f; (Mil) grado m; (social position) rango m; the ~ and file la base f; the ~s (Mil) i soldati mpl semplici e vt (place) annoverare (among tra) e vi (be placed) collocarsi

ransack /ˈrænsæk/ vt rovistare; (pillage) saccheggiare

ransom /ˈrænsəm/ n riscatto m; hold sb to ~ tenere qcno in ostaggio (per il riscatto)

rant /rænt/ vi ~ [and rave] inveire; what's he **~ing** on about? cosa sta blaterando?

rap /ræp/ n colpo m [secco]; (Mus) rap m e vi (pt/pp **rapped**) e vt dare colpetti a e vi ~ at bussare a

rape /reɪp/ n (sexual) stupro m e vt violentare, stuprare

rapid /ˈræpɪd/ adj rapido. **~ity** n rapidità f. **~ly** adv rapidamente

rapids /ˈræpɪdz/ npl rapida fsg

rapist /ˈreɪpɪst/ n violentatore m

rapture /ˈræptʃə(r)/ n estasi f. **~ous** adj entusiastico

rare¹ /reə(r)/ adj raro. **~ly** adv raramente

rare² adj (Culin) al sangue

rarefied /ˈreərɪfaɪd/ adj rarefatto

rarity /ˈreərɪtɪ/ n rarità f inv

rascal /ˈrɑːskl/ n mascalzone m

rash¹ /ræʃ/ n (Med) eruzione f

rash² adj avventato. **~ly** adv avventatamente

rasher /ˈræʃə(r)/ n fetta f di pancetta

rasp /rɑːsp/ n (noise) stridio m. **~ing** adj stridente

raspberry /ˈrɑːzbərɪ/ n lampone m

rat /ræt/ n topo m; (fig: person) carogna f; **smell a** ~ fig sentire puzzo di bruciato

rate /reɪt/ n (speed) velocità f; (of payment) tariffa f; (of exchange) tasso m; **~s** pl (taxes) imposte fpl comunali sui beni immobili; **at any** ~ in ogni caso; **at this** ~ di questo passo e vt stimare; ~ **among** annoverare tra e vi ~ **as** essere considerato

rather /ˈrɑːðə(r)/ adv piuttosto; ~! eccomi; ~ **too**... un po' troppo...

rating /ˈreɪtɪŋ/ n indice m; ~s pl (Radio, TV) indice m d'ascolto, audience f inv

ratio /ˈreɪʃɪəʊ/ n rapporto m

ration /ˈræʃn/ n razione f e vt razionare

rational /ˈræʃənl/ adj razionale. **~ize** vt/i razionalizzare

rattle /ˈrætl/ n tintinnio m; (toy) sonaglio m e vi tintinnare e vt (shake) scuotere; (fig) innervosire. □ ~ **off** vt (fig) sciorinare

raucous /ˈrɔːkəs/ adj rauco

rave /reɪv/ vi vaneggiare; ~ **about** andare in estasi per

raven /ˈreɪvn/ n corvo m imperiale

ravenous /ˈrævənəs/ adj (person)

affamato

ravine /rə'vi:n/ n gola f

raving /'reivin/ adj ~ **mad** ① matto da legare

ravishing /'ræviʃiŋ/ adj incantevole

raw /rɔ:/ adj crudo; (not processed) grezzo; (weather) gelido; (inexperienced) inesperto; **get a ~ deal** ① farsi fregare. ~ **ma'terials** npl materie fpl prime

ray /rei/ n raggio m; ~ **of hope** barlume m di speranza

raze /reiz/ vt ~ **to the ground** radere al suolo

razor /'reizə(r)/ n rasoio m. ~ **blade** n lametta f da barba

re /ri:/ prep con riferimento a

reach /ri:tʃ/ n portata f; **within** ~ a portata di mano; **out of** ~ **of** fuori dalla portata di; **within easy** ~ facilmente raggiungibile ● vt arrivare a (place, decision); (contact) contattare; (pass) passare; **I can't** ~ **it** non ci arrivo ● vi arrivare (to a); ~ **for** allungare la mano per prendere

re'act /rı-/ vi reagire

re'action /rı-/ n reazione f. ~**ary** adj reazionario, -a mf

reactor /rı'æktə(r)/ n reattore m

read /ri:d/ vt (pt/pp **read** /red/) leggere; (Univ) studiare ● vi leggere; (instrument:) indicare. □ ~ **out** vt leggere ad alta voce

readable /'ri:dəbl/ adj piacevole a leggersi; (legible) leggibile

reader /'ri:də(r)/ n lettore, -trice mf; (book) antologia f

readily /'redılı/ adv volentieri; (easily) facilmente. ~**ness** n disponibilità f inv; **in** ~**ness** pronto

reading /'ri:diŋ/ n lettura f

rea'djust /ri:-/ vt regolare di nuovo ● vi riabituarsi (to a)

ready /'redı/ adj (-ier, -iest) pronto; (quick) veloce; **get** ~ prepararsi

ready-'made adj confezionato

real /ri:l/ adj vero; (increase) reale ● adv Am ① veramente. ~ **estate** n beni mpl immobili

realis|m /'rıəlızm/ n realismo m. ~**t** n realista mf. ~**tic** adj realistico

reality /rı'ælətı/ n realtà f inv; ~ **TV** n reality TV f

realization /rıəlaı'zeıʃn/ n realizzazione f

realize /'rıəlaız/ vt realizzare

really /'rıəlı/ adv davvero

realm /relm/ n regno m

realtor /'rıəltə(r)/ n Am agente mf immobiliare

reap /ri:p/ vt mietere

reap'pear /ri:-/ vi riapparire

rear¹ /rıə(r)/ adj posteriore; (Auto) di dietro; ~ **end** ① didietro m ● n the ~ (of building) il retro m; (of bus, plane) la parte f posteriore; **from the** ~ da dietro

rear² vt allevare ● vi ~ [**up**] (horse:) impennarsi

rear'range /ri:-/ vt cambiare la disposizione di

reason /'ri:zn/ n ragione f; **within** ~ nei limiti del ragionevole ● vi ragionare; ~ **with** cercare di far ragionare. ~**able** adj ragionevole. ~**ably** adv (in reasonable way, fairly) ragionevolmente

reas'sur|ance /ri:-/ n rassicurazione f. ~**e** vt rassicurare; ~**e sb of sth** rassicurare qcno su qcsa. ~**ing** adj rassicurante

rebate /'ri:beit/ n rimborso m; (discount) deduzione f

rebel¹ /'rebl/ n ribelle mf

rebel² /rı'bel/ vi (pt/pp **rebelled**) ribellarsi. ~**lion** n ribellione f. ~**lious** adj ribelle

re'bound¹ /rı-/ vi rimbalzare; fig ricadere

'rebound² /ri:-/ n rimbalzo m

rebuff /rı'bʌf/ n rifiuto m

re'build /riː-/ vt (pt/pp **-built**) ricostruire

rebuke /rɪ'bjuːk/ vt rimproverare

re'call /rɪ-/ vt richiamo m; beyond ~ irrevocabile ● vt richiamare, riconvocare (diplomat, parliament); (remember) rievocare

recap /'riːkæp/ vt/i 🔟 = recapitulate ● n ricapitolazione f

recapitulate /riːkə'pɪtjʊleɪt/ vt/i ricapitolare

re'capture /riː-/ vt riconquistare; ricatturare (person, animal)

reced|e /rɪ'siːd/ vi allontanarsi. ~ing adj (forehead, chin) sfuggente; have ~ing hair essere stempiato

receipt /rɪ'siːt/ n ricevuta f; (receiving) ricezione f; ~s pl (Comm) entrate fpl

receive /rɪ'siːv/ vt ricevere. ~r n (Teleph) ricevitore m; (Radio, TV) apparecchio m ricevente; (of stolen goods) ricettatore, -trice mf

recent /'riːsnt/ adj recente. ~ly adv recentemente

reception /rɪ'sepʃn/ n ricevimento m; (welcome) accoglienza f; (Radio) ricezione f; ~ |desk| (in hotel) reception f inv. ~ist n persona f che fa reception

receptive /rɪ'septɪv/ adj ricettivo

recess /rɪ'ses/ n rientranza f; (holiday) vacanza f; Am (Sch) intervallo m

recession /rɪ'seʃn/ n recessione f

re'charge /riː-/ vt ricaricare

recipe /'resəpɪ/ n ricetta f

recipient /rɪ'sɪpɪənt/ n (of letter) destinatario, -a mf; (of money) beneficiario, -a mf

recital /rɪ'saɪtl/ n recital m inv

recite /rɪ'saɪt/ vt recitare; (list) elencare

reckless /'reklɪs/ adj (action, decision) sconsiderato; be a ~ driver guidare in modo spericolato. ~ly adv in modo sconsiderato. ~ness n

sconsideratezza f

reckon /'rekən/ vt calcolare; (consider) pensare. □ ~ **on/with** vt fare i conti con

re'claim /rɪ-/ vt reclamare, bonificare (land)

reclin|e /rɪ'klaɪn/ vi sdraiarsi. ~ing adj (seat) reclinabile

recluse /rɪ'kluːs/ n recluso, -a mf

recognition /rekəg'nɪʃn/ n riconoscimento m; beyond ~ irriconoscibile

recognize /'rekəgnaɪz/ vt riconoscere

re'coil /rɪ-/ vi (in fear) indietreggiare

recollect /rekə'lekt/ vt ricordare. ~ion n ricordo m

recommend /rekə'mend/ vt raccomandare. ~ation n raccomandazione f

recon|cile /'rekənsaɪl/ vt riconciliare; conciliare (facts). ~cile oneself to rassegnarsi a. ~ciliation n riconciliazione f

reconnaissance /rɪ'kɒnɪsns/ n (Mil) ricognizione f

reconnoitre /rekə'nɔɪtə(r)/ vi (pres p -tring) fare una ricognizione

recon'sider /riː-/ vt riconsiderare

recon'struct /riː-/ vt ricostruire. ~ion n ricostruzione f

record¹ /rɪ'kɔːd/ vt registrare; (make a note of) annotare

record² /'rekɔːd/ n (file) documentazione f; (Mus) disco m; (Sport) record m inv; ~s pl (files) schedario msg; keep a ~ of tener nota di; off the ~ in via ufficiosa; have a [criminal] ~ avere la fedina penale sporca

recorder /rɪ'kɔːdə(r)/ n (Mus) flauto m dolce

recording /rɪ'kɔːdɪŋ/ n registrazione f

'record-player n giradischi m inv

recount /rɪ'kaʊnt/ vt raccontare

re-'count¹ /riː-/ vt ricontare

're-count[2] /'ri:-/ n (Pol) nuovo conteggio m

recover /rɪ'kʌvə(r)/ vt/i recuperare. **~y** n recupero m; (of health) guarigione m

re-'cover /ri:-/ vt rifoderare

recreation /rekrɪ'eɪʃn/ n ricreazione f. **~al** adj ricreativo

recruit /rɪ'kru:t/ n (Mil) recluta f; **new ~** (member) nuovo -a adepto, -a mf; (worker) neoassunto, -a mf ● vt assumere (staff). **~ment** n assunzione f

rectang|le /'rektæŋgl/ n rettangolo m. **~ular** adj rettangolare

rectify /'rektɪfaɪ/ vt (pt/pp -ied) rettificare

recuperate /rɪ'ku:pəreɪt/ vi ristabilirsi

recur /rɪ'kɜ:(r)/ vi (pt/pp recurred) ricorrere; (illness:) ripresentarsi

recurren|ce /rɪ'kʌrəns/ n ricorrenza f; (of illness) ricomparsa f. **~t** adj ricorrente

recycle /ri:'saɪkl/ vt riciclare

red /red/ adj (redder, reddest) rosso ● n rosso m; **in the ~** (account) scoperto. R**~ Cross** n Croce f rossa

redd|en /'redn/ vt arrossare ● vi arrossire. **~ish** adj rossastro

re'decorate /ri:-/ vt (paint) ridipingere; (wallpaper) ritappezzare

redeem /rɪ'di:m/ vt **~ing quality** unico aspetto m positivo

redemption /rɪ'dempʃn/ n riscatto m

red: **~-haired** adj con i capelli rossi. **~-'handed** adj **catch sb ~-handed** cogliere qcno con le mani nel sacco. **~ herring** n diversione f. **~-hot** adj rovente

red: **~ light** n (Auto) semaforo m rosso

re'double /ri:-/ vt raddoppiare

red 'tape n Ⓘ burocrazia f

reduc|e /rɪ'dju:s/ vt ridurre; (Culin)

far consumare. **~tion** n riduzione f

redundan|cy /rɪ'dʌndənsɪ/ n licenziamento m; (payment) cassa f integrazione. **~t** adj superfluo; **make ~t** licenziare; **be made ~t** essere licenziato

reed /ri:d/ n (Bot) canna f

reef /ri:f/ n scogliera f

reek /ri:k/ vi puzzare (of di)

reel /ri:l/ n bobina f ● vi (stagger) vacillare. □ **~ off** vt fig snocciolare

refectory /rɪ'fektərɪ/ n refettorio m; (Univ) mensa f universitaria

refer /rɪ'fɜː(r)/ v (pt/pp referred) ● vt rinviare (matter) (**to** a); indirizzare (person) ● vi **~ to** fare allusione a; (consult) rivolgersi a (book)

referee /refə'ri:/ n arbitro m; (for job) garante mf ● vt/i (pt/pp refereed) arbitrare

reference /'refərəns/ n riferimento m; (in book) nota f bibliografica; (for job) referenza f; (Comm) **'your ~'** 'riferimento'; **with ~ to** con riferimento a; **make [a] ~ to** fare riferimento a. **~ book** n libro m di consultazione. **~ number** n numero m di riferimento

referendum /refə'rendəm/ n referendum m inv

re'fill[1] /ri:-/ vt riempire di nuovo; ricaricare (pen, lighter)

'refill[2] /'ri:-/ n (for pen) ricambio m

refine /rɪ'faɪn/ vt raffinare. **~d** adj raffinato. **~ment** n raffinatezza f; (Techn) raffinazione f. **~ry** n raffineria f

reflect /rɪ'flekt/ vt riflettere; **be ~ed in** essere riflesso in ● vi (think) riflettere (**on su**); **~ badly on sb** fig mettere in cattiva luce qcno. **~ion** n riflessione f; (image) riflesso m; **on ~ion** dopo riflessione. **~ive** adj riflessivo. **~or** n riflettore m

reflex /'ri:fleks/ n riflesso m ● attrib di riflesso

reflexive /rɪ'fleksɪv/ adj riflessivo

reform | relate

reform /rɪ'fɔːm/ n riforma f • vt riformare • vi correggersi. **R~ation** n (*Relig*) riforma f • **~er** n riformatore, -trice mf

refrain¹ /rɪ'freɪn/ n ritornello m

refrain² vi astenersi (**from** da)

refresh /rɪ'freʃ/ vt rinfrescare. **~ing** adj rinfrescante. **~ments** npl rinfreschi mpl

refrigerat|e /rɪ'frɪdʒəreɪt/ vt conservare in frigo. **~or** n frigorifero m

re'fuel /riː-/ v (pt/pp **-fuelled**) • vt rifornire (*di carburante*) • vi fare rifornimento

refuge /'refjuːdʒ/ n rifugio m; **take ~** rifugiarsi

refugee /refjʊ'dʒiː/ n rifugiato, -a mf

'refund¹ n rimborso m

re'fund² /rɪ-/ vt rimborsare

refusal /rɪ'fjuːzl/ n rifiuto m

refuse¹ /rɪ'fjuːz/ vt/i rifiutare; **~ to do sth** rifiutar di fare qcsa

refuse² /'refjuːs/ n rifiuti mpl. **~ collection** n raccolta f dei rifiuti

refute /rɪ'fjuːt/ vt confutare

re'gain /rɪ-/ vt riconquistare

regal /'riːgl/ adj regale

regard /rɪ'gɑːd/ n (*heed*) riguardo m; (*respect*) considerazione f; **~s** pl saluti mpl, **send/give my ~s to your brother** salutami tuo fratello • vt (*consider*) considerare (**as** come); **as ~s** riguardo a. **~ing** prep riguardo a. **~less** adv lo stesso; **~less of** senza badare a

regatta /rɪ'gætə/ n regata f

regime /reɪ'ʒiːm/ n regime m

regiment /'redʒɪmənt/ n reggimento m. **~al** adj reggimentale. **~ation** n irregimentazione f

region /'riːdʒən/ n regione f; **in the ~ of** fig approssimativamente. **~al** adj regionale

register /'redʒɪstə(r)/ n registro m • vt registrare; mandare per raccomandata (*letter*); assicurare (*luggage*); immatricolare (*vehicle*); mostrare (*feeling*) • vi (*instrument*) funzionare; (*student:*) iscriversi (**for** a); **~ with** iscriversi nella lista di (*doctor*)

registrar /redʒɪ'strɑː(r)/ n ufficiale m di stato civile

registration /redʒɪ'streɪʃn/ n (*of vehicle*) immatricolazione f; (*of letter*) raccomandazione f; (*of luggage*) assicurazione f; (*for course*) iscrizione f. **~ number** n (*Auto*) targa f

registry office /'redʒɪstrɪ-/ n anagrafe f

regret /rɪ'gret/ n rammarico m • vt (pt/pp **regretted**) rimpiangere; **I ~ that** mi rincresce che. **~fully** adv con rammarico

regrettab|le /rɪ'gretəbl/ adj spiacevole. **~ly** adv spiacevolmente; (*before adjective*) deplorevolmente

regular /'regjʊlə(r)/ adj regolare; (*usual*) abituale • n cliente mf abituale. **~ity** n regolarità f. **~ly** adv regolarmente

regulat|e /'regjʊleɪt/ vt regolare. **~ion** n (*rule*) regolamento m

rehearsal /rɪ'hɜːsl/ n (*Theat*) prova f. **~e** vt/i provare

reign /reɪn/ n regno m • vi regnare

reinforce /riːɪn'fɔːs/ vt rinforzare. **~d 'concrete** n cemento m armato. **~ment** n rinforzo m

reiterate /riː'ɪtəreɪt/ vt reiterare

reject /rɪ'dʒekt/ vt rifiutare. **~ion** n rifiuto m; (*Med*) rigetto m

rejoic|e /rɪ'dʒɔɪs/ vi liter rallegrarsi. **~ing** n gioia f

rejuvenate /rɪ'dʒuːvəneɪt/ vt ringiovanire

relapse /rɪ'læps/ n ricaduta f • vi ricadere

relate /rɪ'leɪt/ vt (*tell*) riportare; (*connect*) collegare • vi ~ **to** riferirsi a; identificarsi con (*person*). **~d** adj imparentato (**to** a); (*ideas* etc) affine

relation /rɪˈleɪʃn/ n rapporto m; (person) parente mf. ~**ship** n rapporto m (blood tie) parentela f; (affair) relazione f

relative /ˈrelətɪv/ n parente mf ● adj relativo. ~**ly** adv relativamente

relax /rɪˈlæks/ vt rilassare; allentare (pace, grip) ● vi rilassarsi. ~**ation** n rilassamento m, relax m inv; (recreation) svago m. ~**ing** adj rilassante

relay[1] /riːˈleɪ/ vt ritrasmettere; (Radio, TV) trasmettere

relay[2] /ˈriːleɪ/ n (Electr) relais m inv; **work in** ~**s** fare i turni. ~ [race] n [corsa f a] staffetta f

release /rɪˈliːs/ n rilascio m; (of film) distribuzione f ● vt liberare; lasciare (hand); togliere (brake); distribuire (film); rilasciare (information etc)

relegate /ˈrelɪgeɪt/ vt relegare; **be** ~**d** (Sport) essere retrocesso

relent /rɪˈlent/ vi cedere. ~**less** adj inflessibile; (unceasing) incessante. ~**lessly** adv incessantemente

relevance /ˈrelɪvəns/ n pertinenza f. ~**t** adj pertinente (to a)

reliability /rɪlaɪəˈbɪlətɪ/ n affidabilità f. ~**le** adj affidabile a. ~**ly** adv in modo affidabile; **be** ~**ly informed** sapere da fonte certa

reliance /rɪˈlaɪəns/ n fiducia f (on in). ~**t** adj fiducioso (on in)

relic /ˈrelɪk/ n (Relig) reliquia f; ~**s** npl resti mpl

relief /rɪˈliːf/ n sollievo m; (assistance) soccorso m; (distraction) diversivo m; (replacement) cambio m; (in art) rilievo m; **in** ~ in rilievo. ~ **map** n carta f in rilievo. ~ **train** n treno m supplementare

relieve /rɪˈliːv/ vt alleviare; (take over from) dare il cambio a; ~ **of** liberare da (burden)

religion /rɪˈlɪdʒən/ n religione f

religious /rɪˈlɪdʒəs/ adj religioso. ~**ly** adv (conscientiously) scrupolosamente

relinquish /rɪˈlɪŋkwɪʃ/ vt abbandonare; ~ **sth to sb** rinunciare a qcsa in favore di qcno

relish /ˈrelɪʃ/ n gusto m; (Culin) salsa f ● vt fig apprezzare

reluctance /rɪˈlʌktəns/ n riluttanza f. ~**t** adj riluttante. ~**tly** adv a malincuore

rely /rɪˈlaɪ/ vi (pt/pp -ied) ~ **on** dipendere da; (trust) contare su

remain /rɪˈmeɪn/ vi restare. ~**der** n resto m. ~**ing** adj restante. ~**s** npl resti mpl; (dead body) spoglie fpl

remand /rɪˈmɑːnd/ n **on** ~ in custodia cautelare ● vt ~ **in custody** rinviare con detenzione provvisoria

remark /rɪˈmɑːk/ n osservazione f ● vt osservare. ~**able** adj notevole. ~**ably** adv notevolmente

remarry /riː-/ vi risposarsi

remedy /ˈremədɪ/ n rimedio m (for contro) ● vt (pt/pp -ied) rimediare a

remember /rɪˈmembə(r)/ vt ricordare, ricordarsi; ~ **to do sth** ricordarsi di fare qcsa; ~ **me to him** salutamelo ● vi ricordarsi

remind /rɪˈmaɪnd/ vt ~ **sb of sth** ricordare qcsa a qcno. ~**er** n ricordo m; (memo) promemoria m; (letter) lettera f di sollecito

reminisce /remɪˈnɪs/ vi rievocare il passato. ~**nces** npl reminiscenze fpl. ~**nt** adj **be** ~ **of** richiamare alla memoria

remnant /ˈremnənt/ n resto m; (of material) scampolo m; (trace) traccia f

remorse /rɪˈmɔːs/ n rimorso m. ~**ful** adj pieno di rimorso. ~**less** adj spietato. ~**lessly** adv senza pietà

remote /rɪˈməʊt/ adj remoto; (slight) minimo. ~ **access** n (Comput) accesso m remoto. ~ **control** n telecomando m. ~**controlled** adj telecomandato. ~**ly** adv lontanamente; **be not** ~**ly...** non essere lontanamente...

re'movable /rɪ-/ adj rimovibile

removal /rɪˈmuːvl/ n rimozione f;

remove | reproduce

(*from house*) trasloco *m*. **~ van** *n* camion *m inv* da trasloco

remove /rɪ'muːv/ *vt* togliere; togliersi (*clothes*); eliminare (*stain, doubts*)

render /'rendə(r)/ *vt* rendere (*service*)

renegade /'renɪgeɪd/ *n* rinnegato, -a *mf*

renew /rɪ'njuː/ *vt* rinnovare (*contract*). **~al** *n* rinnovo *m*

renounce /rɪ'naʊns/ *vt* rinunciare a

renovat|e /'renəveɪt/ *vt* rinnovare. **~ion** *n* rinnovo *m*

renown /rɪ'naʊn/ *n* fama *f*. **~ed** *adj* rinomato

rent /rent/ *n* affitto *m* ● *vt* affittare; **~ [out]** dare in affitto. **~al** *n* affitto *m*

renunciation /rɪnʌnsɪ'eɪʃn/ *n* rinuncia *f*

re'open /riː-/ *vt/i* riaprire

re'organize /riː-/ *vt* riorganizzare

rep /rep/ *n* (*Comm*) rappresentante *mf*. (*Theat*) ≈ teatro *m* stabile

repair /rɪ'peə(r)/ *n* riparazione *f*; **in good/bad ~** in cattive/buone condizioni ● *vt* riparare

repatriat|e /riː'pætrɪeɪt/ *vt* rimpatriare. **~ion** *n* rimpatrio *m*

re'pay /riː-/ *vt* (*pt/pp* **-paid**) ripagare. **~ment** *n* rimborso *m*

repeal /rɪ'piːl/ *n* abrogazione *f* ● *vt* abrogare

repeat /rɪ'piːt/ *n* (*TV*) replica *f* ● *vt/i* ripetere; **~ oneself** ripetersi. **~ed** *adj* ripetuto. **~edly** *adv* ripetutamente

repel /rɪ'pel/ *vt* (*pt/pp* **repelled**) respingere; *fig* ripugnare. **~lent** *adj* ripulsivo

repent /rɪ'pent/ *vi* pentirsi. **~ance** *n* pentimento *m*. **~ant** *adj* pentito

repertoire /'repətwɑː(r)/ *n* repertorio *m*

repetit|ion /repɪ'tɪʃn/ *n* ripetizione

f. **~ive** *adj* ripetitivo

re'place /riː-/ *vt* (*put back*) rimettere a posto; (*take the place of*) sostituire; **~ sth with sth** sostituire qcsa con qcsa. **~ment** *n* sostituzione *f*; (*person*) sostituto, -a *mf* ● **ment part** *n* pezzo *m* di ricambio

'replay /riː-/ *n* (*Sport*) partita *f* ripetuta; [**action**] **~** replay *m inv*

replenish /rɪ'plenɪʃ/ *vt* rifornire (*stocks*); (*refill*) riempire di nuovo

replica /'replɪkə/ *n* copia *f*

reply /rɪ'plaɪ/ *n* risposta *f* (**to** a) ● *vt/i* (*pt/pp* **replied**) rispondere

report /rɪ'pɔːt/ *n* rapporto *m*; (*TV, Radio*) servizio *m*; (*Journ*) cronaca *f*; (*Sch*) pagella *f*; (*rumour*) diceria *f* ● *vt* riportare; **~ sb to the police** denunciare qcno alla polizia ● *vi* riportare; (*present oneself*) presentarsi (**to** a). **~edly** *adv* secondo quanto si dice. **~er** *n* cronista *mf*, reporter *mf inv*

reprehensible /reprɪ'hensəbl/ *adj* riprovevole

represent /reprɪ'zent/ *vt* rappresentare

representative /reprɪ'zentətɪv/ *adj* rappresentativo ● *n* rappresentante *mf*

repress /rɪ'pres/ *vt* reprimere. **~ion** *n* repressione *f*. **~ive** *adj* repressivo

reprieve /rɪ'priːv/ *n* commutazione *f* della pena capitale; (*postponement*) sospensione *f* della pena capitale; *fig* tregua *f* ● *vt* sospendere la sentenza a; *fig* risparmiare

reprimand /'reprɪmɑːnd/ *n* rimprovero *m* ● *vt* rimproverare

reprisal /rɪ'praɪzl/ *n* rappresaglia *f*; **in ~ for** per rappresaglia contro

reproach /rɪ'prəʊtʃ/ *n* ammonimento *m* ● *vt* ammonire. **~ful** *adj* di rimprovero. **~fully** *adv* con aria di rimprovero

repro'duc|e /riː-/ *vt* riprodurre ● *vi*

riprodursi. **~tion** n riproduzione f.
~tive adj riproduttivo

reprove /rɪ'pruːv/ vt rimproverare

reptile /'reptaɪl/ n rettile m

republic /rɪ'pʌblɪk/ n repubblica f.
~an adj repubblicano ● n repubblicano, -a f

repugnan|ce /rɪ'pʌgnəns/ n ripu-
gnanza f. **~t** adj ripugnante

repuls|ion /rɪ'pʌlʃn/ n repulsione f.
~ive adj ripugnante

reputable /'repjʊtəbl/ adj affidabile

reputation /repjʊ'teɪʃn/ n reputazione f

request /rɪ'kwest/ n richiesta f ● vt
richiedere. **~ stop** n fermata f a richiesta

require /rɪ'kwaɪə(r)/ vt (need) ne-
cessitare di; (demand) esigere. **~d** adj
richiesto; **I am ~d to do** si esige
che lo faccia. **~ment** n esigenza f;
(condition) requisito m

rescue /'reskjuː/ n salvataggio m
● vt salvare. **~r** n salvatore, -trice mf

research /rɪ'sɜːtʃ/ n ricerca f ● vt
fare ricerche su; (Journ) fare un'inchiesta su ● vi **~ into** fare ricerche
su. **~er** n ricercatore, -trice mf

resem|blance /rɪ'zembləns/ n ras-
somiglianza f. **~ble** vt rassomi-
gliare a

resent /rɪ'zent/ vt risentirsi per.
~ful adj pieno di risentimento.
~fully adv con risentimento. **~ment**
n risentimento m

reservation /rezə'veɪʃn/ n (booking) prenotazione f; (doubt, enclosure)
riserva f

reserve /rɪ'zɜːv/ n riserva f; (shyness) riserbo m ● vt riservare; riser-
varsi (right). **~d** adj riservato

reservoir /'rezəvwɑː(r)/ n bacino m
idrico

re'shuffle /riː-/ n (Pol) rimpasto m
● vt (Pol) rimpastare

residence /'rezɪdəns/ n residenza f;
(stay) soggiorno m. **~ permit** n per-

messo m di soggiorno

resident /'rezɪdənt/ adj residente
● n residente mf. **~ial** adj residenziale

residue /'rezɪdjuː/ n residuo m

resign /rɪ'zaɪn/ vt dimettersi da; **~
oneself to** rassegnarsi a ● vi dare le
dimissioni. **~ation** n rassegnazione
f; (from job) dimissioni fpl. **~ed** adj
rassegnato

resilient /rɪ'zɪlɪənt/ adj elastico; fig
con buone capacità di ripresa

resin /'rezɪn/ n resina f

resist /rɪ'zɪst/ vt resistere a ● vi resistere. **~ance** n resistenza f. **~ant** adj
resistente

resolut|e /'rezəluːt/ adj risoluto.
~ely adv con risolutezza. **~ion** n risolutezza f

resolve /rɪ'zɒlv/ vt **~ to do** decidere di fare

resort /rɪ'zɔːt/ n (place) luogo m di
villeggiatura; **as a last ~** come ultima risorsa ● vi **~ to** ricorrere a

resource /rɪ'sɔːs/ n **~s** pl risorse
fpl. **~ful** adj pieno di risorse; (solution) ingegnoso. **~fulness** n ingegnosità f inv

respect /rɪ'spekt/ n rispetto m; (aspect) aspetto m; **with ~ to** per
quanto riguarda ● vt rispettare

respect|able /rɪ'spektəbl/ adj ri-
spettabile. **~ably** adv rispettabil-
mente. **~ful** adj rispettoso

respective /rɪ'spektɪv/ adj rispet-
tivo. **~ly** adv rispettivamente

respiration /respɪ'reɪʃn/ n respirazione f

respite /'respaɪt/ n respiro m

respond /rɪ'spɒnd/ vi rispondere;
(react) reagire (to a); (patient:) rispondere (to a)

response /rɪ'spɒns/ n risposta f;
(reaction) reazione f

responsibility /rɪspɒnsɪ'bɪlɪtɪ/ n
responsabilità f inv

responsib|le /rɪ'spɒnsəbl/ adj responsabile; (job) impegnativo

responsive /rɪ'spɒnsɪv/ adj be ~ (audience etc:) reagire; (brakes:) essere sensibile

rest¹ /rest/ n riposo m; (Mus) pausa f; **have a ~** riposarsi ● **at rest** riposare; (lean) appoggiare (on su); (place) appoggiare ● vi riposarsi; (elbows:) appoggiarsi; (hopes:) riposare

rest² n the ~ il resto m; (people) gli altri mpl ● vi it ~s with you sta a te

restaurant /'restərɒnt/ n ristorante m. ~ **car** n vagone m ristorante

restful /'restfl/ adj riposante

restive /'restɪv/ adj irrequieto

restless /'restlɪs/ adj nervoso

restoration /restə'reɪʃn/ n (of building) restauro m

restore /rɪ'stɔː(r)/ vt ristabilire; restaurare (building); (give back) restituire

restrain /rɪ'streɪn/ vt trattenere; ~ **oneself** controllarsi. ~**ed** adj controllato. ~**t** n restrizione f; (moderation) ritegno m

restrict /rɪ'strɪkt/ vt limitare; ~ **to** limitarsi a. ~**ion** n limite m; (restraint) restrizione f. ~**ive** adj limitativo

'rest room n Am toilette f inv

result /rɪ'zʌlt/ n risultato m; **as a ~** a causa (of di) ● vi ~ **from** risultare da; ~ **in** portare a

resume /rɪ'zjuːm/ vt/i riprendere

résumé /'rezjʊmeɪ/ n riassunto m; Am curriculum vitae m inv

resurrect /rezə'rekt/ vt fig risuscitare. ~**ion** n the R~**ion** (Relig) la Risurrezione

resuscitat|e /rɪ'sʌsɪteɪt/ vt rianimare. ~**ion** n rianimazione f

retail /'riːteɪl/ n vendita f al minuto o al dettaglio ● adj & adv al minuto ● vt vendere al minuto ● vi ~ **at** essere venduto al pubblico al prezzo di. ~**er** n dettagliante mf

retain /rɪ'teɪn/ vt conservare; (hold back) trattenere

retaliat|e /rɪ'tælɪeɪt/ vi vendicarsi. ~**ion** n rappresaglia f; **in ~ion for** per rappresaglia contro

retarded /rɪ'tɑːdɪd/ adj ritardato

rethink /riː'θɪŋk/ vt (pt/pp rethought) ripensare

reticen|ce /'retɪsəns/ n reticenza f. ~**t** adj reticente

retina /'retɪnə/ n retina f

retinue /'retɪnjuː/ n seguito m

retire /rɪ'taɪə(r)/ vi andare in pensione; (withdraw) ritirarsi ● vt mandare in pensione (employee). ~**d** adj in pensione. ~**ment** n pensione f; **since my ~ment** da quando sono andato in pensione

retiring /rɪ'taɪərɪŋ/ adj riservato

retort /rɪ'tɔːt/ n replica f ● vt ribattere

re'trace /riː-/ vt ripercorrere; ~ **one's steps** ritornare sui propri passi

retract /rɪ'trækt/ vt ritirare; ritrattare (statement, evidence) ● vi ritrarsi

re'train /riː-/ vt riqualificare ● vi riqualificarsi

retreat /rɪ'triːt/ n ritirata f; (place) ritiro m ● vi ritirarsi; (Mil) battere in ritirata

re'trial /riː-/ n nuovo processo m

retrieval /rɪ'triːvl/ n recupero m

retrieve /rɪ'triːv/ vt recuperare

retrograde /'retrəgreɪd/ adj retrogrado

retrospect /'retrəspekt/ n in ~ guardando indietro. ~**ive** adj retrospettivo; (legislation) retroattivo ● n retrospettiva f

return /rɪ'tɜːn/ n ritorno m; (giving back) restituzione f; (Comm) profitto m; (ticket) biglietto m di andata e ritorno; **by ~** [**of post**] a stretto giro di posta; **in ~** in cambio (**for** di); **many happy ~s!** cento di questi giorni; ● vi ritornare ● vt (give back) restituire; ricambiare (affection, invitation); (put back) rimettere; (send back) mandare indietro; (elect) eleggere

return: ~ **match** n rivincita f. ~ **ticket** n biglietto m di andata e ritorno

reunion /riːˈjuːnɪən/ n riunione f

reunite /riːjuˈnaɪt/ vt riunire

rev /rev/ n (Auto), ① giro m (di motore) ● v (pt/pp **revved**) ● vt ~ [**up**] far andare su di giri ● vi andare su di giri

reveal /rɪˈviːl/ vt rivelare; (dress:) scoprire. ~**ing** adj rivelatore; (dress) osé

revel /revl/ vi (pt/pp **revelled**) ~ **in** sth godere di qcsa

revelation /revəˈleɪʃn/ n rivelazione f

revelry /ˈrevlrɪ/ n baldoria f

revenge /rɪˈvendʒ/ n vendetta f; (Sport) rivincita f; **take** ~ vendicarsi ● vt vendicare

revenue /ˈrevənjuː/ n reddito m

revere /rɪˈvɪə(r)/ vt riverire. ~**nce** n riverenza f

Reverend /ˈrevərənd/ adj reverendo

reverent /ˈrevərənt/ adj riverente

reverse /rɪˈvɜːs/ adj opposto; **in** ~ **order** in ordine inverso ● n contrario m; (back) rovescio m; (Auto) marcia m indietro ● vt invertire; ~ **the car into the garage** entrare in garage a marcia indietro; ~ **the charges** (Teleph) fare una telefonata a carico ● vi (Auto) fare marcia indietro

revert /rɪˈvɜːt/ vi ~ **to** tornare a

review /rɪˈvjuː/ n (survey) rassegna f; (re-examination) riconsiderazione f; (Mil) rivista f; (of book, play) recensione f ● vt riesaminare (situation); (Mil) passare in rivista; recensire (book, play). ~**er** n critico, -a m f

revis|e /rɪˈvaɪz/ vt rivedere; (for exam) ripassare. ~**ion** n revisione f;

(for exam) ripasso m

revive /rɪˈvaɪv/ vt resuscitare; rianimare (person) ● vi riprendersi; (person:) rianimarsi

revolt /rɪˈvəʊlt/ n rivolta f ● vi ribellarsi ● vt rivoltare. ~**ing** adj rivoltante

revolution /revəˈluːʃn/ n rivoluzione f; (Auto) ~**s per minute** giri mpl al minuto. ~**ary** adj & n rivoluzionario, -a m f. ~**ize** vt rivoluzionare

revolve /rɪˈvɒlv/ vi ruotare; ~ **around** girare intorno

revolv|er /rɪˈvɒlvə(r)/ n rivoltella f, revolver m inv. ~**ing** adj ruotante

revue /rɪˈvjuː/ n rivista f

revulsion /rɪˈvʌlʃn/ n ripulsione f

reward /rɪˈwɔːd/ n ricompensa f ● vt ricompensare. ~**ing** adj gratificante

re'write /riː-/ vt (pt **rewrote**, pp **rewritten**) riscrivere

rhetoric /ˈretərɪk/ n retorica f. ~**al** adj retorico

rhinoceros /raɪˈnɒsərəs/ n rinoceronte m

rhubarb /ˈruːbɑːb/ n rabarbaro m

rhyme /raɪm/ n rima f; (poem) filastrocca f ● vi rimare

rhythm /ˈrɪðm/ n ritmo m. ~**ic[al]** adj ritmico. ~**ically** adv con ritmo

rib /rɪb/ n costola f

ribbon /ˈrɪbən/ n nastro m; **in** ~**s** a brandelli

rice /raɪs/ n riso m

rich /rɪtʃ/ adj ricco; (food) pesante ● n **the** ~ pl i ricchi mpl; ~**es** pl ricchezze fpl. ~**ly** adv riccamente; (deserve) largamente

ricochet /ˈrɪkəʃeɪ/ n rimbalzare ● n rimbalzo m

rid /rɪd/ vt (pt/pp **rid**, pres p **ridding**) sbarazzare (**of** di); **get** ~ **of** sbarazzarsi di

riddance /ˈrɪdns/ n **good** ~! che liberazione!

ridden /ˈrɪdn/ ▷RIDE

riddle /ˈrɪdl/ n enigma m

ride /raɪd/ n (on horse) cavalcata f; (in vehicle) giro m; (journey) viaggio m; **take sb for a ~** 🔲 prendere qcno in giro ● v (pt **rode**, pp **ridden**) ● vt montare (horse); andare su (bicycle) ● vi andare a cavallo; (jockey, showjumper;) cavalcare; (cyclist:) andare in bicicletta; (in vehiclo) viaggiare. **~r** n cavallerizzo, -a m f; (in race) fantino m; (on bicycle) ciclista mf; (in document) postilla f

ridge /rɪdʒ/ n spigolo m; (on roof) punta f; (of mountain) cresta f

ridicule /'rɪdɪkjuːl/ n ridicolo m ● vt mettere in ridicolo

ridiculous /rɪ'dɪkjʊləs/ adj ridicolo

rife /raɪf/ adj be ~ essere diffuso; ~ **with** pieno di

rifle /'raɪfl/ n fucile m; **~-range** tiro m al bersaglio ● vt ~ **[through]** mettere a soqquadro

rift /rɪft/ n fessura f; fig frattura f

rig¹ /rɪg/ n equipaggiamento m; (of sea) piattaforma f per trivellazioni subacquee ● vt **rig out** vt (pt/pp **rigged**) equipaggiare. □ ~ **up** vt allestire

rig² vt (pt/pp **rigged**) manovrare (election)

right /raɪt/ adj giusto; (not left) destro; **be ~** (person:) aver ragione; (clock:) essere giusto; **put ~** mettere all'ora (clock); correggere (person); rimediare a (situation); **that's ~!** proprio così! ● adv (correctly) bene; (not left) a destra; (directly) proprio; (completely) completamente; **~ away** immediatamente ● n giusto m; (not left) destra f; (what is due) diritto m; **on/to the ~** a destra; **be in the ~** essere nel giusto; **know ~ from wrong** distinguere il bene dal male; **by ~s** secondo giustizia; **the R~** (Pol) la destra f ● vt raddrizzare; **~ a wrong** fig riparare a un torto. **~ angle** n angolo m retto

rightful /'raɪtfl/ adj legittimo

right: **~-'handed** adj che usa la mano destra. **~-hand 'man** n fig

braccio m destro

rightly /'raɪtlɪ/ adv giustamente

right: **~ of way** n diritto m di transito; (path) passaggio m; (Auto) precedenza f. **~-'wing** adj (Pol) di destra ● n (Sport) ala f destra

rigid /'rɪdʒɪd/ adj rigido. **~ity** n rigidità f inv

rigorous /'rɪgərəs/ adj rigoroso

rim /rɪm/ n bordo m; (of wheel) cerchione m

rind /raɪnd/ n (on fruit) scorza f; (on cheese) crosta f; (on bacon) cotenna f

ring¹ /rɪŋ/ n (circle) cerchio m; (on finger) anello m; (boxing) ring m inv; (for circus) pista f; **stand in a ~** essere in cerchio

ring² n suono m; **give sb a ~** (Teleph) dare un colpo di telefono a qcno ● v (pt **rang**, pp **rung**) ● vt suonare; ~ **[up]** (Teleph) telefonare a ● vi suonare; (Teleph) ~ **[up]** telefonare. □ ~ **back** vt/i (Teleph) richiamare. □ ~ **off** vi (Teleph) riattaccare

ring: **~leader** n capobanda m. **~ road** n circonvallazione f

rink /rɪŋk/ n pista f di pattinaggio

rinse /rɪns/ n risciacquo m; (hair colour) cachet m inv ● vt sciacquare

riot /'raɪət/ n rissa f; (of colour) accozzaglia f; **~s** pl disordini mpl; **run ~** impazzare ● vi creare disordini. **~er** n dimostrante m. **~ous** adj sfrenato

rip /rɪp/ n strappo m ● vt (pt/pp **ripped**) strappare; ~ **open** aprire con uno strappo. □ ~ **off** vt 🔲 fregare

ripe /raɪp/ adj maturo; (cheese) stagionato

ripen /'raɪpn/ vi maturare; (cheese:) stagionarsi ● vt far maturare; stagionare (cheese)

'rip off n 🔲 frode f

ripple /'rɪpl/ n increspatura f; (sound) mormorio m

rise /raɪz/ n (of sun) levata f; (fig: to fame, power) ascesa f; (increase) aumento m; **give ~ to** dare adito a ● vi (pt **rose**, pp **risen**) alzarsi; (sun:) sorgere; (dough:) lievitare; (prices, water level:) aumentare; (to power, position) arrivare (**to** a). **~r** n early **~r** persona f mattiniera

rising /'raɪzɪŋ/ adj (sun) levante; **~ generation** nuova generazione f ● n (revolt) sollevazione f

risk /rɪsk/ n rischio m; **at one's own ~** a proprio rischio e pericolo ● vt rischiare

risky /'rɪskɪ/ adj (**-ier, -iest**) rischioso

rite /raɪt/ n rito m; **last ~s** estrema unzione f

ritual /'rɪtjʊəl/ adj rituale ● n rituale m

rival /'raɪvl/ adj rivale ● n rivale mf; **~s** pl (Comm) concorrenti mpl ● vt (pt/pp **rivalled**) rivaleggiare con. **~ry** n rivalità f inv; (Comm) concorrenza f

river /'rɪvə(r)/ n fiume m. **~-bed** n letto m del fiume

rivet /'rɪvɪt/ n rivetto m ● vt rivettare; **~ed by** fig inchiodato da

road /rəʊd/ n strada f, via f; **be on the ~** viaggiare

road: **~-map** n carta f stradale. **~side** n bordo m della strada. **~-works** npl lavori mpl stradali. **~worthy** adj sicuro

roam /rəʊm/ vi girovagare

roar /rɔː(r)/ n ruggito m; **~s of laughter** scroscio msg di risa ● vi ruggire; (lorry, thunder:) rombare; **with laughter** ridere fragorosamente. **~ing** adj do a **~ing trade** 🔼 fare affari d'oro

roast /rəʊst/ adj arrosto; **~ pork** arrosto m di maiale ● n arrosto m ● vt arrostire (meat) ● vi arrostirsi

rob /rɒb/ vt (pt/pp **robbed**) derubare (**of** di); svaligiare (bank). **~ber** n rapinatore m. **~bery** n rapina f

robe /rəʊb/ n tunica f; (Am: bathrobe) accappatoio m

robin /'rɒbɪn/ n pettirosso m

robot /'rəʊbɒt/ n robot m inv

robust /rəʊ'bʌst/ adj robusto

rock¹ /rɒk/ n roccia f; (in sea) scoglio m; (sweet) zucchero m candito. **on the ~s** (ship) incagliato; (marriage) finito; (drink) con ghiaccio

rock² vt cullare (baby); (shake) far traballare; (shock) scuotere ● vi dondolarsi

rock³ n (Mus) rock m inv

rock-'bottom adj bassissimo ● n livello m più basso

rocket /'rɒkɪt/ n razzo m ● vi salire alle stelle

rocky /'rɒkɪ/ adj (**-ier, -iest**) roccioso; fig traballante

rod /rɒd/ n bacchetta f; (for fishing) canna f

rode /rəʊd/ ▷RIDE

rodent /'rəʊdnt/ n roditore m

rogue /rəʊg/ n farabutto m

role /rəʊl/ n ruolo m

roll /rəʊl/ n rotolo m; (bread) panino m; (list) lista f; (of ship, drum) rullio m ● vi rotolare; **be ~ing in money** 🔼 nuotare nell'oro ● vt spianare (lawn, pastry). □ **~ over** vi rigirarsi. □ **~ up** vt arrotolare; rimboccarsi (sleeves) ● vi 🔼 arrivare

'roll-call n appello m

roller /'rəʊlə(r)/ n rullo m; (for hair) bigodino m. **~ blades** npl pattini npl in linea. **~-blind** n tapparella f. **~-coaster** n montagne fpl russe. **~-skate** n pattino m a rotelle

'rolling-pin n mattarello m

Roman /'rəʊmən/ adj romano ● n romano, -a mf. **~ Catholic** adj cattolico ● n cattolico, -a mf

romance /rəʊ'mæns/ n (love affair) storia f d'amore; (book) romanzo m rosa

Romania /rəʊ'meɪnɪə/ n Romania f. **~n** adj rumeno ● n rumeno, -a mf

romantic /rəʊ'mæntɪk/ adj roman-

tlco. **~ally** adv romanticamente.
~ism n romanticismo m

Rome /rəʊm/ n Roma f

romp /rɒmp/ n gioco m rumoroso
● vi giocare rumorosamente. **~ers**
npl pagliaccetto msg

roof /ruːf/ n tetto m; (of mouth) palato m ● vt mettere un tetto su.
~-rack n portabagagli m inv. **~-top**
n tetto m

rook /rʊk/ n corvo m; (in chess)
torre f

room /ruːm/ n stanza f; (bedroom)
camera f; (for functions) sala f; (space)
spazio m ~ay adj spazioso
(clothes) ampio

roost /ruːst/ vi appollaiarsi

root¹ /ruːt/ n radice f; **take ~** metter radici ● **root out** vt fig scovare

root² vi **~ about** grufolare; **~ for**
sb Am 🔢 fare il tifo per qcno

rope /rəʊp/ n corda f; **know the ~s**
🔢 conoscere i trucchi del mestiere
● **rope in** vt 🔢 coinvolgere

rose¹ /rəʊz/ n rosa f; (of watering-can)
bocchetta f

rose² ▷RISE

rosé /ˈrəʊzeɪ/ n [vino m] rosé m inv

rot /rɒt/ n marciume m; (🔢: nonsense) sciocchezze fpl ● vi (pt/pp rotted) marcire

rota /ˈrəʊtə/ n tabella f dei turni

rotary /ˈrəʊtərɪ/ adj rotante

rotat|e /rəʊˈteɪt/ vt far ruotare; avvicendare (crops) ● vi ruotare. **~ion**
n rotazione f; **in ~ion** a turno

rote /rəʊt/ n **by ~** meccanicamente

rotten /ˈrɒtn/ adj marcio; 🔢 schifoso; (person) penoso

rough /rʌf/ adj (not smooth) ruvido;
(ground) accidentato; (behaviour) rozzo;
(sport) violento; (area) malfamato;
(crossing, time) brutto; (estimate)
approssimativo ● adv (play) grossolanamente; **sleep ~** dormire sotto i

ponti ● vt **~ it** vivere senza confort.
□ **~ out** vt abbozzare

roughage /ˈrʌfɪdʒ/ n fibre fpl

rough|ly /ˈrʌflɪ/ adv rozzamente;
(more or less) pressappoco. **~ness** n
ruvidità f; (of behaviour) rozzezza f

roulette /ruːˈlet/ n roulette f inv

round /raʊnd/ adj rotondo ● n
tondo m; (slice) fetta f; (of visits, drinks)
giro m; (of competition) partita f; (boxing) ripresa f, round m inv; **do one's
~s** (doctor:) fare il giro delle visite
● prep intorno a; **open ~ the clock**
aperto ventiquattr'ore ● adv **all ~**
tutt'intorno; **ask sb ~** invitare qcno;
go/come ~ to (a friend etc) andare
da; **turn/look ~** girarsi. **~ about** adv
(approximately) intorno a ● vt arrotondare; girare (corner). □ **~ down** vt
arrotondare (per difetto). □ **~ off** vt
(end) terminare. □ **~ on** vt aggredire.
□ **~ up** vt radunare; arrotondare
(prices)

roundabout /ˈraʊndəbaʊt/ adj indiretto ● n giostra f; (for traffic) rotonda f

round: **~ 'trip** n viaggio m di andata e ritorno

rous|e /raʊz/ vt svegliare; risvegliare
(suspicion, interest). **~ing** adj di incoraggiamento

route /ruːt/ n itinerario m; (Aeron,
Naut) rotta f; (of bus) percorso m

routine /ruːˈtiːn/ adj di routine ● n
routine f; (Theat) numero m

row¹ /rəʊ/ n (line) fila f; **three years
in a ~** tre anni di fila

row² vi (in boat) remare

row³ /raʊ/ n 🔢 (quarrel) litigata f;
(noise) baccano m ● vi 🔢 litigare

rowdy /ˈraʊdɪ/ adj (-ier, -iest)
chiassoso

rowing boat /ˈrəʊɪŋ-/ n barca f
a remi

royal /ˈrɔɪəl/ adj reale

royalt|y /ˈrɔɪəltɪ/ n appartenenza f

alla famiglia reale; (*persons*) i membri *mpl* della famiglia reale. **~ies** *npl* (*payments*) diritti *mpl* d'autore

rub /rʌb/ *n* give sth a ~ dare una sfregata a qcsa ● *vt* (*pt/pp* **rubbed**) sfregare. □ ~ **in** *vt* don't ~ **it in** ⒤ non rigirare il coltello nella piaga. □ ~ **off** *vt* mandar via sfregando (stain); (*from blackboard*) cancellare ● *vi* andar via; ~ **off on** essere trasmesso a. □ ~ **out** *vt* cancellare

rubber /ˈrʌbə(r)/ *n* gomma *f*; (*eraser*) gomma *f* [da cancellare]. ~ **band** *n* elastico *m*. **~y** *adj* gommoso

rubbish /ˈrʌbɪʃ/ *n* immondizie *fpl*; (⒤: *nonsense*) idiozie *fpl*; (⒤: *junk*) robaccia *f* ● *vt* ⒤ fare a pezzi. ~ **bin** *n* pattumiera *f*. ~ **dump** *n* discarica *f*; (*official*) discarica *f* comunale

rubble /ˈrʌbl/ *n* macerie *fpl*

ruby /ˈruːbɪ/ *n* rubino *m* ● *attrib* di rubini; (lips) scarlatta

rucksack /ˈrʌksæk/ *n* zaino *m*

rudder /ˈrʌdə(r)/ *n* timone *m*

rude /ruːd/ *adj* scortese; (*improper*) spinto. **~ly** *adv* scortesemente. **~ness** *n* scortesia *f*

ruffian /ˈrʌfɪən/ *n* farabutto *m*

ruffle /ˈrʌfl/ *n* gala *f* ● *vt* scompigliare (hair)

rug /rʌg/ *n* tappeto *m*; (*blanket*) coperta *f*

rugby /ˈrʌgbɪ/ *n* ~ [**football**] rugby *m*

rugged /ˈrʌgɪd/ *adj* (*coastline*) roccioso

ruin /ˈruːɪn/ *n* rovina *f*; **in ~s** in rovina ● *vt* rovinare. **~ous** *adj* estremamente costoso

rule /ruːl/ *n* regola *f*; (*control*) ordinamento *m*; (*for measuring*) metro *m*; **~s** regolamento *msg*; **as a** ~ generalmente ● *vt* governare; dominare (colony, behaviour); that stabilire (line ● *vi* governare. □ ~ **out** *vt* escludere

ruler /ˈruːlə(r)/ *n* capo *m* di Stato;

(*sovereign*) sovrano, -a *mf*; (*measure*) righello *m*, regolo *m*

ruling /ˈruːlɪŋ/ *adj* (class) dirigente; (party) di governo ● *n* decisione *f*

rum /rʌm/ *n* rum *m* *inv*

rumble /ˈrʌmbl/ *n* rombo *m*; (*of stomach*) brontolio *m* ● *vi* rombare; (stomach:) brontolare

rummage /ˈrʌmɪdʒ/ *vi* rovistare (in/through in)

rumour /ˈruːmə(r)/ *n* diceria *f* ● *vt* **it is ~ed that** si dice che

run /rʌn/ *n* (on foot) corsa *f*; (*distance to be covered*) tragitto *m*; (*outing*) giro *m*; (*Theat*) rappresentazioni *fpl*; (*in skiing*) pista *f*; (*Am: ladder*) smagliatura *f* (in calze); **at a ~** di corsa; ~ **of bad luck** periodo *m* sfortunato; **on the ~** in fuga; **have the ~ of** avere a disposizione; **in the long ~** a lungo termine ● *v* (*pt* **ran**, *pp* **run**, *pres p* **running**) ● *vi* correre; (river:) scorrere; (nose, make-up:) colare; (bus:) fare servizio; (play:) essere in cartellone; (colours:) sbiadire; (*in election*) presentarsi [come candidato] ● *vt* (*manage*) dirigere; tenere (house); (*drive*) dare un passaggio a; correre (risk); (*Comput*) lanciare; (*Journ*) pubblicare (article); (*pass*) far scorrere (eyes, hand); ~ **a bath** far scorrere l'acqua per il bagno. □ ~ **across** *vi* imbattersi in. □ ~ **away** *vi* scappare [via]. □ ~ **down** *vi* scaricarsi; (clock:) scaricarsi; (stocks:) esaurirsi ● *vt* (*Auto*) investire; (*reduce*) esaurire; (⒤: *criticize*) denigrare. □ ~ **in** *vi* entrare di corsa. □ ~ **into** *vi* (*meet*) imbattersi in; (knock against) urtare. □ ~ **off** *vi* andare via di corsa ● *vt* stampare (copies). □ ~ **out** *vi* uscire di corsa; (supplies, money:) esaurirsi; ~ **out of** rimanere senza. □ ~ **over** *vi* correre; (overflow) traboccare ● *vt* (*Auto*) investire. □ ~ **through** *vi* scorrere. □ ~ **up** *vi* salire di corsa; (*towards*) arrivare di corsa ● *vt* accumulare (debts, bill);

529 **runaway | saga**

(sew) cucire

'runaway n fuggitivo, -a mf

run-'down adj (area) in abbandono; (person) esaurito ● n analisi f

rung¹ /rʌŋ/ n (of ladder) piolo m

rung² ▷RING²

runner /'rʌnə(r)/ n podista mf, (in race) corridore, -trice mf; (on sledge) pattino m. ~ **bean** n fagiolino m. ~**up** n secondo, -a mf classificato, -a

running /'rʌnɪŋ/ adj in corsa; (water) corrente; **four times** ~ quattro volte di seguito ● n corsa f; (management) direzione f; **be in the** ~ essere in lizza. ~ **'commentary** n cronaca f

runny /'rʌnɪ/ adj semiliquido; ~ **nose** naso che cola

runway n pista f

rupture /'rʌptʃə(r)/ n rottura f; (Med) ernia f ● vt rompere; ~ **oneself** farsi venire l'ernia ● vi rompersi

rural /'rʊərəl/ adj rurale

ruse /ruːz/ n astuzia f

rush¹ /rʌʃ/ n (Bot) giunco m

rush² n fretta f; **in a** ~ di fretta ● vi precipitarsi ● vt far premura a; ~ **sb to hospital** trasportare qcsa di corsa all'ospedale. ~**hour** n ora f di punta

Russia /'rʌʃə/ n Russia f. ~**n** adj & n russo, -a mf; (language) russo m

rust /rʌst/ n ruggine f ● vi arrugginirsi

rustle /'rʌsl/ vi frusciare ● vt far frusciare; Am rubare (cattle) □ ~ **up** vt 𝕀 rimediare

'rustproof adj a prova di ruggine

rusty /'rʌstɪ/ adj (-ier, -iest) arrugginito

rut /rʌt/ n solco m; **in a** ~ 𝕀 nella routine

ruthless /'ruːθlɪs/ adj spietato. ~**ness** n spietatezza f

rye /raɪ/ n segale f

Ss

sabotage /'sæbətɑːʒ/ n sabotaggio m ● vt sabotare. ~**eur** n sabotatore, -trice mf

saccharin /'sækərɪn/ n saccarina f

sachet /'sæʃeɪ/ n bustina f; (scented) sacchetto m profumato

sack¹ /sæk/ vt (plunder) saccheggiare

sack² n sacco m; **get the** ~ 𝕀 essere licenziato ● vt 𝕀 licenziare. ~**ing** n tela f per sacchi; (𝕀: dismissal) licenziamento m

sacrament /'sækrəmənt/ n sacramento m

sacred /'seɪkrɪd/ adj sacro

sacrifice /'sækrɪfaɪs/ n sacrificio m ● vt sacrificare

sacrilege /'sækrɪlɪdʒ/ n sacrilegio m

sad /sæd/ adj (**sadder, saddest**) triste. ~**den** vt rattristare

saddle /'sædl/ n sella f ● vt sellare; **I've been ~d with...** fig mi hanno affibbiato...

sad|ly /'sædlɪ/ adv tristemente; (unfortunately) sfortunatamente. ~**ness** n tristezza f

safe /seɪf/ adj sicuro; (out of danger) salvo; (object) al sicuro; ~ **and sound** sano e salvo ● n cassaforte f. ~**guard** n protezione f ● vt proteggere. ~**ly** adv in modo sicuro; (arrive) senza incidenti; (assume) con certezza

safety /'seɪftɪ/ n sicurezza f. ~**belt** n cintura f di sicurezza. ~**deposit box** n cassetta f di sicurezza. ~**pin** n spilla f per sicurezza o da balia. ~**valve** n valvola f di sicurezza

sag /sæg/ vi (pt/pp **sagged**) abbassarsi

saga /'sɑːgə/ n saga f

sage /seɪdʒ/ n (herb) salvia f

Sagittarius /sædʒɪˈteərɪəs/ n Sagittario m

said /sed/ ▷SAY

sail /seɪl/ n vela f; (trip) giro m in barca a vela ● vi navigare; (Sport) praticare la vela; (leave) salpare ● vt pilotare

sailing /ˈseɪlɪŋ/ n vela f. **~-boat** n barca f a vela. **~-ship** n veliero m

sailor /ˈseɪlə(r)/ n marinaio m

saint /seɪnt/ n santo, -a mf. **~ly** adj da santo

sake /seɪk/ n for the ~ of (person) per il bene di; (peace) per amor di; for the ~ of it per il gusto di farlo

salad /ˈsæləd/ n insalata f. **~ bowl** n insalatiera f. **~ cream** n salsa f per condire l'insalata. **~-dressing** n condimento m per insalata

salary /ˈsælərɪ/ n stipendio m

sale /seɪl/ n vendita f (at reduced prices) svendita f; for/on ~ in vendita

sales|man /ˈseɪlzmən/ n venditore m; (traveller) rappresentante m. **~woman** n venditrice f

saliva /səˈlaɪvə/ n saliva f

salmon /ˈsæmən/ n salmone m

saloon /səˈluːn/ n (Auto) berlina f; (Am: bar) bar m

salt /sɔːlt/ n sale m ● adj salato; (fish, meat) sotto sale ● vt salare; (cure) mettere sotto sale. **~-cellar** n saliera f. **~'water** n acqua f di mare. **~y** adj salato

salute /səˈluːt/ n (Mil) saluto m ● vt salutare ● vi fare il saluto

salvage /ˈsælvɪdʒ/ n (Naut) recupero m ● vt recuperare

salvation /sælˈveɪʃn/ n salvezza f. **S~ Army** n Esercito m della Salvezza

same /seɪm/ adj stesso (as di) ● pron the ~ lo stesso; be all the ~ essere tutti uguali ● adv the ~ nello stesso

modo; all the ~ (however) lo stesso; the ~ to you altrettanto

sample /ˈsɑːmpl/ n campione m ● vt testare

sanction /ˈsæŋkʃn/ n (approval) autorizzazione f; (penalty) sanzione f ● vt autorizzare

sanctuary /ˈsæŋktjʊərɪ/ n (Relig) santuario m; (refuge) asilo m; (for wildlife) riserva f

sand /sænd/ n sabbia f ● vt ~ [down] carteggiare

sandal /ˈsændl/ n sandalo m

sandpaper /ˈsændpeɪpə(r)/ n carta f vetrata ● vt cartavetrare

sandwich /ˈsænwɪdʒ/ n tramezzino m ● vt ~ed between schiacciato tra

sandy /ˈsændɪ/ adj (-ier, -iest) (beach, soil) sabbioso; (hair) biondiccio

sane /seɪn/ adj (not mad) sano di mente; (sensible) sensato

sang /sæŋ/ ▷SING

sanitary /ˈsænɪtərɪ/ adj igienico; (system) sanitario. **~ napkin** n Am, **~ towel** n assorbente m igienico

sanitation /sænɪˈteɪʃn/ n impianti mpl igienici

sanity /ˈsænətɪ/ n sanità f inv di mente; (common sense) buon senso m

sank /sæŋk/ ▷SINK

sapphire /ˈsæfaɪə(r)/ n zaffiro m ● adj blu zaffiro

sarcas|m /ˈsɑːkæzm/ n sarcasmo m. **~tic** adj sarcastico

sardine /sɑːˈdiːn/ n sardina f

sash /sæʃ/ n fascia f; (for dress) fusciacca f

sat /sæt/ ▷SIT

satchel /ˈsætʃl/ n cartella f

satellite /ˈsætəlaɪt/ n satellite m. **~ dish** n antenna f parabolica. **~ television** n televisione f via satellite

satin /ˈsætɪn/ n raso m ● attrib di raso

satire /ˈsætaɪə(r)/ n satira f

satirical /səˈtɪrɪkl/ adj satirico

satisfaction /sætɪsˈfækʃn/ n soddisfazione f; **be to sb's ~** soddisfare qcno

satisfactor|y /sætɪsˈfæktərɪ/ adj soddisfacente. **~ily** adv in modo soddisfacente

satisf|y /ˈsætɪsfaɪ/ vt (pt/pp -fied) soddisfare; (convince) convincere; **be ~ied** essere soddisfatto. **~ying** adj soddisfacente

satphone /ˈsætfəʊn/ n telefono m satellitare

saturate /ˈsætʃəreɪt/ vt inzuppare (with di); (Chem), fig saturare (with di). **~d** adj saturo

Saturday /ˈsætədeɪ/ n sabato m

sauce /sɔːs/ n salsa f; (cheek) impertinenza f. **~pan** n pentola f

saucer /ˈsɔːsə(r)/ n piattino m

saucy /ˈsɔːsɪ/ adj (-ier, -iest) impertinente

Saudi Arabia /saʊdɪ əˈreɪbɪə/ n Arabia f Saudita

sauna /ˈsɔːnə/ n sauna f

saunter /ˈsɔːntə(r)/ vi andare a spasso

sausage /ˈsɒsɪdʒ/ n salsiccia f; (dried) salame m

savage /ˈsævɪdʒ/ adj feroce; (tribe, custom) selvaggio ● n selvaggio, -a mf ● vt fare a pezzi. **~ry** n ferocia f

save /seɪv/ n (Sport) parata f ● vt salvare (from da); (keep, collect) tenere; risparmiare (time, money); (avoid) evitare; (Sport) parare (goal); (Comput) salvare, memorizzare ● vi ~ [**up**] risparmiare ● prep salvo

saver /ˈseɪvə(r)/ n risparmiatore, -trice mf

savings /ˈseɪvɪŋz/ npl (money) risparmi mpl. **~ account** n libretto m di risparmio. **~ bank** n cassa f di risparmio

saviour /ˈseɪvjə(r)/ n salvatore m

savour /ˈseɪvə(r)/ n sapore m ● vt

assaporare. **~y** adj salato; fig rispettabile

saw[1] /sɔː/ see see[1]

saw[2] n sega f ● vt/i (pt **sawed**, pp **sawn** or **sawed**) segare. **~dust** n segatura f

saxophone /ˈsæksəfəʊn/ n sassofono m

say /seɪ/ n have one's ~ dire la propria; **have a ~** avere voce in capitolo ● vt/i (pt/pp **said**) dire; **that is to ~** cioè; that goes without **~ing** questo è ovvio; **when all is said and done** alla fine dei conti. **~ing** n proverbio m

scab /skæb/ n crosta f; pej crumiro m

scald /skɔːld/ vt scottare; (milk) scaldare ● n scottatura f

scale[1] /skeɪl/ n (of fish) scaglia f

scale[2] n scala f; **on a grand ~** su vasta scala ● vt (climb) scalare. □ **~ down** vt diminuire

scales /skeɪlz/ npl (for weighing) bilancia f sg

scalp /skælp/ n cuoio m capelluto

scamper /ˈskæmpə(r)/ vi ~ **away** sgattaiolare via

scan /skæn/ n (Med) scanning m inv, scansiografia f ● vt (pt/pp **scanned**) scrutare; (quickly) dare una scorsa a; (Med) fare uno scanning di

scandal /ˈskændl/ n scandalo m; (gossip) pettegolezzi mpl. **~ize** vt scandalizzare. **~ous** adj scandaloso

Scandinavia /skændɪˈneɪvɪə/ n Scandinavia f. **~n** adj & n scandinavo, -a mf

scanner /ˈskænə(r)/ n (Comput) scanner m inv

scant /skænt/ adj scarso

scant|y /ˈskæntɪ/ adj (-ier, -iest) scarso; (clothing) succinto. **~ily** adv scarsamente; (clothed) succintamente

scapegoat /ˈskeɪp-/ n capro m

espiatorio

scar /skɑ:(r)/ n cicatrice f • vt (pt/pp scarred) lasciare una cicatrice a

scarc|e /skeəs/ adj scarso; fig raro; **make oneself ~e** 🄸 svignarsela. **~ely** adv appena; **~ely anything** quasi niente. **~ity** n scarsezza f

scare /skeə(r)/ n spavento m; (panic) panico m • vt spaventare; **be ~d** aver paura (of di)

'scarecrow n spaventapasseri m inv

scarf /skɑ:f/ n (pl scarves) sciarpa f; (square) foulard m inv

scarlet /'skɑ:lət/ adj scarlatto. **~ fever** n scarlattina f

scary /'skeərɪ/ adj **be ~** far paura

scathing /'skeɪðɪŋ/ adj mordace

scatter /'skætə(r)/ vt spargere; (disperse) disperdere • vi disperdersi. **~-brained** adj 🄸 scervellato. **~ed** adj sparso

scavenge /'skævɪndʒ/ vi frugare nella spazzatura. **~r** n persona f che fruga nella spazzatura

scenario /sɪ'nɑ:rɪəʊ/ n scenario m

scene /si:n/ n scena f; (quarrel) scenata f; **behind the ~s** dietro le quinte

scenery /'si:nərɪ/ n scenario m

scenic /'si:nɪk/ adj panoramico

scent /sent/ n odore m; (trail) scia f; (perfume) profumo m. **~ed** adj profumato (with di)

sceptic|al /'skeptɪkl/ adj scettico. **~ism** n scetticismo m

schedule /'ʃedju:l/ n piano m, programma m; (of work) programma m; (timetable) orario m; **behind ~** indietro; **on ~** nei tempi previsti; **according to ~** secondo i tempi previsti • vt prevedere. **~d flight** n volo m di linea

scheme /ski:m/ n (plan) piano m; (plot) macchinazione f • vi pej macchinare

scholar /'skɒlə(r)/ n studioso, -a mf. **~ly** adj erudito. **~ship** n erudizione f; (grant) borsa f di studio

school /sku:l/ n scuola f; (in university) facoltà f; (of fish) branco m

school: **~boy** n scolaro m. **~girl** n scolara f. **~ing** n istruzione f. **~teacher** n insegnante mf

sciatica /saɪ'ætɪkə/ n sciatica f

scien|ce /'saɪəns/ n scienza f; **~ce fiction** fantascienza f. **~tific** adj scientifico. **~tist** n scienziato, -a mf

scissors /'sɪzəz/ npl forbici fpl

scoff¹ /skɒf/ vi **~ at** schernire

scoff² vt 🄸 divorare

scold /skəʊld/ vt sgridare. **~ing** n sgridata f

scoop /sku:p/ n paletta f; (Journ) scoop m inv • **scoop out** vt svuotare. □ **~ up** vt tirare su

scope /skəʊp/ n portata f; (opportunity) opportunità f inv

scorch /skɔ:tʃ/ vt bruciare. **~er** n 🄸 giornata f torrida. **~ing** adj caldissimo

score /skɔ:(r)/ n punteggio m; (individual) punteggio m; (Mus) partitura f; (for film, play) musica f; **a ~** [of] (twenty) una ventina [di]; **keep [the] ~** tenere il punteggio; **on that ~** a questo proposito • vt segnare (goal); (cut) incidere • vi far punti; (in football etc) segnare; (keep score) tenere il punteggio. **~r** n segnapunti m inv; (of goals) giocatore, -trice mf che segna

scorn /skɔ:n/ n disprezzo m • vt disprezzare. **~ful** adj sprezzante

Scorpio /'skɔ:pɪəʊ/ n Scorpione m

scorpion /'skɔ:pɪən/ n scorpione m

Scot /skɒt/ n scozzese mf

scotch vt far cessare

Scotch /skɒtʃ/ adj scozzese • n (whisky) whisky m [scozzese]

Scot|land /'skɒtlənd/ n Scozia f. **~s, ~tish** adj scozzese

scoundrel /ˈskaʊndrəl/ n mascalzone m

scour[1] /ˈskaʊə(r)/ vt (search) perlustrare

scour[2] (clean) strofinare

scourge /skɜːdʒ/ n flagello m

scout /skaʊt/ n (Mil) esploratore m ● vi ● for andare in cerca di

Scout n [Boy] ~ [boy]scout m inv

scowl /skaʊl/ n sguardo m torvo ● vi guardare [di] storto

scram /skræm/ vi [I] levarsi dai piedi

scramble /ˈskræmbl/ n (climb) arrampicata f ● vi (clamber) arrampicarsi; ~ **for** azzuffarsi per ● vt (Teleph) creare delle interferenze in; (eggs) strapazzare

scrap[1] /skræp/ n (I: fight) litigio m

scrap[2] n pezzetto m; (metal) ferraglia f; ~s pl (of food) avanzi mpl ● vt (pt/pp scrapped) buttare via

'scrap-book n album m inv

scrape /skreɪp/ vt raschiare; (damage) graffiare. ◻ ~ **through** vi passare per un pelo. ◻ ~ **together** vt racimolare

scraper /ˈskreɪpə(r)/ n raschietto m

'scrap-yard n deposito m di ferraglia; (for cars) cimitero m delle macchine

scratch /skrætʃ/ n graffio m; (to relieve itch) grattata f; **start from ~**

partire da zero; **up to ~** (work) all'altezza ● vt graffiare; (to relieve itch) grattare ● vi grattarsi. (to relieve itch) ● **card** n gratta e vinci m inv

scrawl /skrɔːl/ n scarabocchio m ● vt/i scarabocchiare

scream /skriːm/ n strillo m ● vt/i strillare

screech /skriːtʃ/ n stridore m ● vi stridere ● vt strillare

screen /skriːn/ n paravento m; (Cinema, TV) schermo m ● vt proteggere; (conceal) riparare; proiettare (film); (candidates) passare al setaccio; (Med) sottoporre a visita medica. **~ing** n (Med) visita f medica; (of film) proiezione f. **~play** n sceneggiatura f

screw /skruː/ n vite f ● vt avvitare. ◻ ~ **up** vt (crumple) accartocciare; strizzare (eyes); storcere (face); (I: bungle) mandare all'aria. **~driver** n cacciavite m

scribble /ˈskrɪbl/ n scarabocchio m ● vt/i scarabocchiare

script /skrɪpt/ n scrittura f (a mano); (of film) sceneggiatura f

scroll /skrəʊl/ n rotolo m (di pergamena); (decoration) voluta f. ◻ ~ **down** vi scorrere in giù

scrounge /skraʊndʒ/ vt/i scroccare. **~r** n scroccone, -a mf

scrub[1] /skrʌb/ n (land) boscaglia f

scrub[2] vt/i (pt/pp scrubbed) strofinare; (I: cancel) cancellare (plan)

scruff /skrʌf/ n **by the ~ of the neck** per la collottola

scruffy /ˈskrʌfi/ adj (-ier, -iest) trasandato

scruple /ˈskruːpl/ n scrupolo m

scrupulous /ˈskruːpjʊləs/ adj scrupoloso

scrutinize /ˈskruːtɪnaɪz/ vt scrutinare. **~y** n (look) esame m minuzioso

scuffle /ˈskʌfl/ n tafferuglio m

sculpt /skʌlpt/ vt/i scolpire. **~or** n scultore m. **~ure** n scultura f

s

scum /skʌm/ n schiuma f; (people) feccia f

scurry /'skʌrɪ/ vi (pt/pp -ied) affrettare il passo

scuttle /'skʌtl/ vi (hurry) ~ **away** correre via

sea /siː/ n mare m; **at** ~ in mare; fig confuso; **by** ~ via mare. ~**board** n costiera f. ~**food** n frutti mpl di mare. ~**gull** n gabbiano m

seal¹ /siːl/ n (Zool) foca f

seal² /siːl/ n sigillo m; (Techn) chiusura f ermetica ● vt sigillare; (Techn) chiudere ermeticamente. □ ~ **off** vt bloccare (area)

'sea-level n livello m del mare

seam /siːm/ n cucitura f; (of coal) strato m

'seaman n marinaio m

seamy /'siːmɪ/ adj sordido; (area) malfamato

seance /'seɪɑːns/ n seduta f spiritica

search /sɜːtʃ/ n ricerca f; (official) perquisizione f; **in** ~ **of** alla ricerca di ● vt frugare (**for** alla ricerca di); perlustrare (area); (officially) perquisire ● vi ~ **for** cercare. ~**ing** adj penetrante

search: ~**light** n riflettore m. ~**-party** n squadra f di ricerca

sea: ~**sick** adj be/get ~ avere il mal di mare. ~**side** n at/to the ~**side** al mare

season /'siːzn/ n stagione f ● vt (flavour) condire. ~**able** adj, ~**al** adj stagionale. ~**ing** n condimento m

'season ticket n abbonamento m

seat /siːt/ n (chair) sedia f; (in car) sedile m; (place to sit) posto m [a sedere]; (bottom) dietro m; (of government) sede f; **take a** ~ sedersi ● vt mettere a sedere; (have seats for) aver posti [a sedere] per; **remain** ~**ed** mantenere il proprio posto. ~**-belt** n cintura f di sicurezza

sea: ~**weed** n alga f marina. ~**worthy** adj in stato di navigare

seclu|ded /sɪ'kluːdɪd/ adj appartato. ~**sion** n isolamento m

second¹ /sɪ'kɒnd/ vt (transfer) distaccare

second² /'sekənd/ adj secondo; **on** ~ **thoughts** ripensandoci meglio ● n secondo m; ~**s** pl (goods) merce fsg di seconda scelta; **have** ~**s** (at meal) fare il bis; **John the S**~ Giovanni Secondo ● adv (in race) al secondo posto ● vt assistere; appoggiare (proposal)

secondary /'sekəndrɪ/ adj secondario. ~ **school** n ≈ scuola f media (inferiore e superiore)

second: ~ **'class** adv (travel, send) in seconda classe. ~**-class** adj di seconda classe

'second hand n (on clock) lancetta f dei secondi

second-'hand adj & adv di seconda mano

secondly /'sekəndlɪ/ adv in secondo luogo

second-'rate adj di second'ordine

secrecy /'siːkrəsɪ/ n segretezza f; **in** ~ in segreto

secret /'siːkrɪt/ adj segreto ● n segreto m

secretarial /sekrə'teərɪəl/ adj (work, staff) di segreteria

secretary /'sekrətərɪ/ n segretario, -a mf

secretive /'siːkrətɪv/ adj riservato. ~**ness** n riserbo m

sect /sekt/ n setta f. ~**arian** adj settario

section /'sekʃn/ n sezione f

sector /'sektə(r)/ n settore m

secular /'sekjʊlə(r)/ adj secolare; (education) laico

secure /sɪ'kjʊə(r)/ adj sicuro ● vt proteggere; chiudere bene (door); rendere stabile (ladder); (obtain) assicurarsi. ~**ly** adv saldamente

securit|y /sɪ'kjʊərətɪ/ n sicurezza f;

(*for loan*) garanzia *f*. **~ies** *npl* titoli *mpl*

sedate¹ /sɪˈdeɪt/ *adj* posato

sedate² *vt* somministrare sedativi a

sedation /sɪˈdeɪʃn/ *n* somministrazione *f* di sedativi: **be under ~** essere sotto l'effetto di sedativi

sedative /ˈsedətɪv/ *adj* sedativo ● *n* sedativo *m*

sediment /ˈsedɪmənt/ *n* sedimento *m*

seduce /sɪˈdjuːs/ *vt* sedurre

seduct|ion /sɪˈdʌkʃn/ *n* seduzione *f*, **~ive** *adj* seducente

see /siː/ *v* (*pt* **saw**, *pp* **seen**) ● *vt* vedere; (*understand*) capire; (*escort*) accompagnare; **go and ~** andare a vedere; (*visit*) andare a trovare; **~ you!** ci vediamo!; **~ you later!** a più tardi!; **~ing that** visto che ● *vi* vedere; (*understand*) capire; **~ that** (*make sure*) assicurarsi che; **~ about** occuparsi di. ● **~ off** *vt* vedere partire; (*chase away*) mandar via. □ **~ through** *vi* vedere attraverso; *fig* non farsi ingannare da ● *vt* portare a buon fine. □ **~ to** *vi* occuparsi di

seed /siːd/ *n* seme *m*; (*Tennis*) testa *f* di serie; **go to ~** fare seme; *fig* lasciarsi andare. ● **ed player** *n* (*Tennis*) testa *f* di serie. **~ling** *n* pianticella *f*

seedy /ˈsiːdɪ/ *adj* (**-ier, -iest**) squallido

seek /siːk/ *vt* (*pt/pp* **sought**) cercare

seem /siːm/ *vi* sembrare. **~ingly** *adv* apparentemente

seen /siːn/ ▷**see¹**

see-saw /ˈsiːsɔː/ *n* altalena *f*

seethe /siːð/ *vi* **~ with anger** ribollire di rabbia

'see-through *adj* trasparente

segment /ˈsegmənt/ *n* segmento *m*, (*of orange*) spicchio *m*

segregat|e /ˈsegrɪgeɪt/ *vt* segregare. **~ion** *n* segregazione *f*

seize /siːz/ *vt* afferrare; (*Jur*) confi-

scare. □ **~ up** *vi* (*Techn*) bloccarsi

seizure /ˈsiːʒə(r)/ *n* (*Jur*) confisca *f*; (*Med*) colpo *m* [apoplettico]

seldom /ˈseldəm/ *adv* raramente

select /sɪˈlekt/ *adj* scelto; (*exclusive*) esclusivo ● *vt* scegliere, selezionare (team). **~ion** *n* selezione *f*. **~ive** *adj* selettivo. **~or** *n* (*Sport*) selezionatore, -trice *mf*

self /self/ *n* Io *m*

self: **~-ad'dressed** *adj* con il proprio indirizzo. **~-'catering** *n* in appartamento attrezzato di cucina. **~-'centred** *adj* egocentrico **~-'confidence** *n* fiducia *f* in se stesso. **~-'confident** *adj* sicuro di sé. **~-'conscious** *adj* impacciato. **~-con'tained** *adj* (flat) con ingresso indipendente. **~-con'trol** *n* autocontrollo *m*. **~-de'fence** *n* autodifesa *f*; (*Jur*) legittima difesa *f*. **~-em'ployed** *adj* che lavora in proprio. **~-'evident** *adj* ovvio. **~-in'dulgent** *adj* indulgente con se stesso. **~-'interest** *n* interesse *m* personale

self|ish /ˈselfɪʃ/ *adj* egoista. **~ishness** *n* egoismo *m*. **~less** *adj* disinteressato

self: **~-'pity** *n* autocommiserazione *f*. **~-'portrait** *n* autoritratto *m*. **~-re'spect** *n* amor *m* proprio. **~-'righteous** *adj* presuntuoso. **~-'sacrifice** *n* abnegazione *f*. **~-'satisfied** *adj* compiaciuto di sé. **~-'service** *n* self-service *m inv* ● *attrib* self-service. **~-suf'ficient** *adj* autosufficiente

sell /sel/ *v* (*pt/pp* **sold**) ● *vt* vendere; **be sold out** essere esaurito ● *vi* vendersi. □ **~ off** *vt* liquidare

seller /ˈselə(r)/ *n* venditore, -trice *mf*

Sellotape® /ˈseləʊ-/ *n* nastro *m* adesivo, scotch® *m*

'sell-out *n* (**Ⅰ**: *betrayal*) tradimento *m*; **be a ~** (concert:) fare il tutto esaurito

semblance /'sembləns/ n parvenza f

semester /si'mestə(r)/ n Am semestre m

semi /'semɪ/: **~breve** /'semibri:v/ n semibreve f. **~circle** n semicerchio m. **~'circular** adj semicircolare. **~colon** n punto e virgola m. **~de'tached** adj gemella • n casa f gemella. **~'final** n semifinale f

seminar /'semɪnɑ:(r)/ n seminario m. **~y** n seminario m

senate /'senət/ n senato m. **~or** n senatore m

send /send/ vt/i (pt/pp sent) mandare; **~ for** mandare a chiamare (person); far venire (thing). **~er** n mittente m. **~off** n commiato m

senil|e /'si:naɪl/ adj arteriosclerotico; (Med) senile. **~ity** n senilismo m

senior /'si:nɪə(r)/ adj più vecchio; (in rank) superiore • n (in rank) superiore mf; (in sport) senior mf; **she's two years my ~** è più vecchia di me di due anni. **~ 'citizen** n anziano, -a mf

seniority /si:nɪ'ɒrɪtɪ/ n anzianità f inv di servizio

sensation /sen'seɪʃn/ n sensazione f. **~al** adj sensazionale. **~ally** adv in modo sensazionale

sense /sens/ n senso m; (common ~) buon senso m; **in a ~** in un certo senso; **make ~** aver senso • vt sentire. **~less** adj insensato; (unconscious) privo di sensi

sensibl|e /'sensəbl/ adj sensato; (suitable) appropriato. **~y** adv in modo appropriato

sensitiv|e /'sensətɪv/ adj sensibile; (touchy) suscettibile. **~ely** adv con sensibilità. **~ity** n sensibilità f inv

sensual /'sensjʊəl/ adj sensuale. **~ity** n sensualità f inv

sensuous /'sensjʊəs/ adj voluttuoso

sent /sent/ ▷SEND

sentence /'sentəns/ n frase f; (Jur) sentenza f; (punishment) condanna f • vt **~ to** condannare a

sentiment /'sentɪmənt/ n sentimento m; (opinion) opinione f; (sentimentality) sentimentalismo m. **~al** adj sentimentale; pej sentimentalista. **~ality** n sentimentalità f inv

sentry /'sentrɪ/ n sentinella f

separable /'sepərəbl/ adj separabile

separate¹ /'sepərət/ adj separato. **~ly** adv separatamente

separat|e² /'sepəreɪt/ vt separare • vi separarsi. **~ion** n separazione f

September /sep'tembə(r)/ n settembre m

septic /'septɪk/ adj settico; **go ~** infettarsi. **~ tank** n fossa f biologica

sequel /'si:kwəl/ n seguito m

sequence /'si:kwəns/ n sequenza f

Serbia /'sɜ:bɪə/ n Serbia f

serenade /serə'neɪd/ n serenata f • vt fare una serenata a

seren|e /sɪ'ri:n/ adj sereno. **~ity** n serenità f inv

sergeant /'sɑ:dʒənt/ n sergente m

serial /'sɪərɪəl/ n racconto m a puntate; (TV) sceneggiato m a puntate; (Radio) commedia f radiofonica. **~ize** vt pubblicare a puntate; (Radio, TV) trasmettere a puntate. **~ killer** n serial killer mf inv. **~ number** n numero m di serie. **~ port** n (Comput) porta f seriale

series /'sɪəri:z/ n serie f inv

serious /'sɪərɪəs/ adj serio; (illness, error) grave. **~ly** adv seriamente; (ill) gravemente; **take ~ly** prendere sul serio. **~ness** n serietà f inv; (of situation) gravità f inv

sermon /'sɜ:mən/ n predica f

serum /'sɪərəm/ n siero m

servant /'sɜ:vənt/ n domestico, -a mf

serve /sɜ:v/ n (Tennis) servizio m • vt servire; scontare (sentence); **its purpose** servire al proprio scopo; **it ~s you right!** ben ti sta!; **~s two**

per due persone ● vi prestare servizio; (Tennis) servire; **~ as** servire da. **~r** n (Comput) server m inv

service /'sɜːvɪs/ n servizio m; (Relig) funzione f; (maintenance) revisione f; **~s** pl forze fpl armate; (on motorway) area f di servizio: **in the ~s** sotto le armi; **of ~ to** utile a; **out of ~** (machine:) guasto ● vt (Techn) revisionare. **~able** adj utilizzabile; (hard-wearing) resistente; (practical) pratico

service: **~ charge** n servizio m. **~ station** n stazione f di servizio

serviette /sɜːvɪ'et/ n tovagliolo m

servile /'sɜːvaɪl/ adj servile

session /'seʃn/ n seduta f; (Jur) sessione f; (Univ) anno m accademico

set /set/ n serie f, set m inv; (of crockery, cutlery) servizio m; (Radio, TV) apparecchio m; (Math) insieme m; (Theat) scenario m; (Cinema, Tennis) set m inv; (of people) circolo m; (of hair) messa f in piega ● adj (ready) pronto; (rigid) fisso; (book) in programma: **be ~ on doing sth** essere risoluto a fare qcsa; **be ~ in one's ways** essere abitudinario ● v (pt/pp **set**, pres p **setting**) ● vt mettere, porre; mettere (alarm clock); assegnare (task, homework); fissare (date, limit); chiedere (questions); montare (gem); assestare (bone); apparecchiare (table); **~ fire to** dare fuoco a; **~ free** liberare ● vi (sun:) tramontare; (jelly, concrete:) solidificare; **about doing sth** mettersi a fare qcsa. □ **~ back** vt mettere indietro; (hold up) ritardare; (⊟: cost) costare a. □ **~ off** vi partire ● vt avviare; mettere (alarm); fare esplodere (bomb). □ **~ out** vi partire; **~ out to do sth** proporsi di fare qcsa ● vt disporre; (state) esporre. **~ ~ to** vi mettersi all'opera. □ **~ up** vt fondare (company); istituire (committee)

'set-back n passo m indietro

settee /se'tiː/ n divano m

setting /'setɪŋ/ n scenario m; (pos-

ition) posizione f; (of sun) tramonto m; (of jewel) montatura f

settle /'setl/ vt (decide) definire; risolvere (argument); fissare (date); calmare (nerves); saldare (bill) ● vi (to live) stabilirsi; (snow, dust, bird:) posarsi; (subside) assestarsi; (sediment:) depositarsi. □ **~ down** vi sistemarsi; (stop making noise) calmarsi. □ **~ for** vt accontentarsi di. □ **~ up** vi regolare i conti

settlement /'setlmənt/ n (agreement) accordo m; (of bill) saldo m; (colony) insediamento m

settler /'setlə(r)/ n colonizzatore, -trice mf

'set-to n ⊟ zuffa f; (verbal) batti becco m

'set-up n situazione f

seven /'sevn/ adj sette. **~teen** adj diciassette. **~teenth** adj diciassettesimo

seventh /'sevnθ/ adj settimo

seventieth /'sevntɪəθ/ adj settantesimo

seventy /'sevntɪ/ adj settanta

sever /'sevə(r)/ vt troncare (relations)

several /'sevrəl/ adj & pron parecchi

sever|e /sɪ'vɪə(r)/ adj severo; (pain) violento; (illness) grave; (winter) rigido. **~ely** adv severamente; (ill) gravemente. **~ity** n severità f inv; (of pain) violenza f; (of illness) gravità f; (of winter) rigore m

sew /səʊ/ vt/i (pt sewed, pp sewn or sewed) cucire. □ **~ up** vt ricucire

sewage /'suːɪdʒ/ n acque fpl di scolo

sewer /'suːə(r)/ n fogna f

sewing /'səʊɪŋ/ n cucito m; (work) lavoro m di cucito. **~ machine** n macchina f da cucire

sewn /səʊn/ ▷**SEW**

sex /seks/ n sesso m; **have ~** avere rapporti sessuali. **~ist** adj sessista. **~ offender** n colpevole mf di delitti a sfondo sessuale

sexual /ˈseksjʊəl/ adj sessuale. ~ **'intercourse** n rapporti mpl sessuali. ~**ity** n sessualità f inv. ~**ly** adv sessualmente

sexy /ˈseksɪ/ adj (-ier, -iest) sexy

shabbily /ˈʃæbɪlɪ/ adv (-ier, -iest) scialbo; (treatment) meschino. ~**iness** n trasandatezza f; (of treatment) meschinità f inv

shack /ʃæk/ n catapecchia f ● **shack up with** vt ① vivere con

shade /ʃeɪd/ n ombra f; (of colour) sfumatura f; (for lamp) paralume m; (Am: for window) tapparella f; a ~ **better** un tantino meglio ● vt riparare dalla luce; (draw lines on) ombreggiare. ~**s** npl ① occhiali mpl da sole

shadow /ˈʃædəʊ/ n ombra f; S~ **Cabinet** governo m ombra ● vt (follow) pedinare. ~**y** adj ombroso

shady /ˈʃeɪdɪ/ adj (-ier, -iest) ombroso; (①: disreputable) losco

shaft /ʃɑːft/ n (Techn) albero m; (of light) raggio m; (of lift, mine) pozzo m; ~**s** pl (of cart) stanghe fpl

shaggy /ˈʃægɪ/ adj (-ier, -iest) irsuto; (animal) dal pelo arruffato

shake /ʃeɪk/ n scrollata f ● v (pt shook, pp shaken) ● vt scuotere; agitare (bottle); far tremare (building); ~ **hands with** stringere la mano a ● vi tremare. ~**up** n (Pol) rimpasto m; (Comm) ristrutturazione f

shaky /ˈʃeɪkɪ/ adj (-ier, -iest) tremante; (table etc) traballante; (unreliable) vacillante

shall /ʃæl/ v aux I ~ **go** andrò; we ~ **see** vedremo; **what I do?** cosa faccio?; **I'll come too, ~ I?** vengo anch'io, no?; **thou shalt not kill** liter non uccidere

shallow /ˈʃæləʊ/ adj basso, poco profondo; (dish) poco profondo; fig superficiale

sham /ʃæm/ adj falso ● n finzione f;

(person) spaccone, -a mf ● vt (pt/pp shammed) simulare

shambles /ˈʃæmblz/ n baraonda fsg

shame /ʃeɪm/ n vergogna f; **it's a ~** that è un peccato che; **what a ~!** che peccato! ~**-faced** adj vergognoso

shame|ful /ˈʃeɪmfl/ adj vergognoso. ~**less** adj spudorato

shampoo /ʃæmˈpuː/ n shampoo m inv ● vt fare uno shampoo a

shape /ʃeɪp/ n forma f; (figure) ombra f; **take ~** prendere forma; **get back in** ~ ritornare in forma ● vt dare forma a (into) ● vi ~ [up] mettere la testa e posto; ~ **up nicely** mettersi bene. ~**less** adj informe

share /ʃeə(r)/ n porzione f; (Comm) azione f ● vt dividere; condividere (views) ● vi dividere. ~**holder** n azionista mf

shark /ʃɑːk/ n squalo m, pescecane m; fig truffatore, -trice mf

sharp /ʃɑːp/ adj (knife etc) tagliente; (pencil) appuntito; (drop) a picco; (reprimand) severo; (outline) marcato; (alert) acuto; (unscrupulous) senza scrupoli; ~ **pain** fitta f ● adv in punto; (Mus) fuori tono; **look ~!** sbrigati! ● n (Mus) diesis m inv. ~**en** vt affilare (knife); appuntire (pencil)

shatter /ˈʃætə(r)/ vt frantumare; fig mandare in frantumi. ~**ed** (①: exhausted) a pezzi ● vi frantumarsi

shav|e /ʃeɪv/ n rasatura f; **have a ~e** farsi la barba ● vt radere ● vi radersi. ~**er** n rasoio m elettrico. ~**ing-brush** n pennello m da barba; ~**ing foam** n schiuma f da barba; ~**ing soap** n sapone m da barba

shawl /ʃɔːl/ n scialle m

she /ʃiː/ pron lei

sheaf /ʃiːf/ n (pl sheaves) fascio m

shear /ʃɪə(r)/ vt (pt sheared, pp shorn o sheared) tosare

shears /ʃɪəz/ npl (for hedge) cesoie fpl

shed¹ /ʃed/ n baracca f; (for cattle) stalla f

shed² vt (pt/pp shed, pres p shedding) perdere; versare (blood, tears); ~ light on far luce su

sheep /ʃiːp/ n inv pecora f. ~ **dog** n cane m da pastore

sheepish /ˈʃiːpɪʃ/ adj imbarazzato. ~ly adv con aria imbarazzata

sheer /ʃɪə(r)/ adj puro; (steep) a picco; (transparent) trasparente ● adv a picco

sheet /ʃiːt/ n lenzuolo m; (of paper) foglio m; (of glass, metal) lastra f

shelf /ʃelf/ n (pl shelves) ripiano m; (set of shelves) scaffale m

shell /ʃel/ n conchiglia f; (of egg, snail, tortoise) guscio m; (of crab) corazza f; (of unfinished building) ossatura f; (Mil) granata f ● vt sgusciare (peas); (Mil) bombardare. □ ~ **out** vt 🗓 sborsare

'shellfish n inv mollusco m; (Culin) frutti mpl di mare

shelter /ˈʃeltə(r)/ n rifugio m; (air raid ~) rifugio m antiaereo ● vt riparare (from da); fig mettere al riparo; (give lodging to) dare asilo a ● vi ripararsi. ~ed adj (spot) riparato; (life) ritirato

shelve /ʃelv/ vt accantonare (project)

shelving /ˈʃelvɪŋ/ n (shelves) ripiani mpl

shepherd /ˈʃepəd/ n pastore m ● vt guidare. ~'s **pie** n pasticcio m di carne tritata o patato

sherry /ˈʃerɪ/ n sherry m

shield /ʃiːld/ n scudo m; (for eyes) maschera f; (Techn) schermo m ● vt proteggere (from da)

shift /ʃɪft/ n cambiamento m; (in position) spostamento m; (at work) turno m ● vt spostare; (take away) togliere; riversare (blame) ● vi spostarsi; (wind:) cambiare; (🗓: move quickly) darsi una mossa

shifty /ˈʃɪftɪ/ adj (-ier, -iest) pej losco; (eyes) sfuggente

shimmer /ˈʃɪmə(r)/ n luccichio m ● vi luccicare

shin /ʃɪn/ n stinco m

shine /ʃaɪn/ n lucentezza f; give sth a ~ dare una lucidata a qcsa ● v (pt/pp shone) ● vi splendere; (reflect light) brillare; (shoes:) essere lucido ● vt ~ a light on puntare una luce su

shingle /ˈʃɪŋgl/ n (pebbles) ghiaia f

shiny /ˈʃaɪnɪ/ adj (-ier, -iest) lucido

ship /ʃɪp/ n nave f ● vt (pt/pp shipped) spedire; (by sea) spedire via mare

ship: ~**ment** n spedizione f; (consignment) carico m. ~**ping** n trasporto m; (traffic) imbarcazioni fpl. ~**shape** adj & adv in perfetto ordine. ~**wreck** n naufragio m. ~**wrecked** adj naufragato. ~**yard** n cantiere m navale

shirk /ʃɜːk/ vt scansare. ● er n scansafatiche m inv

shirt /ʃɜːt/ n camicia f; in ~**sleeves** in maniche di camicia

shit /ʃɪt/ 🗓 n & int merda f ● vi (pt/pp shit) cagare

shiver /ˈʃɪvə(r)/ n brivido m ● vi rabbrividire

shoal /ʃəʊl/ n (of fish) banco m

shock /ʃɒk/ n (impact) urto m; (Electr) scossa f [elettrica]; fig colpo m, shock m inv; (Med) shock m inv; get a ~ (Electr) prendere la scossa ● vt scioccare. ~**ing** adj scioccante; (🗓: weather, handwriting etc) tremendo

shod /ʃɒd/ ▷SHOE

shoddy /ˈʃɒdɪ/ adj (-ier, -iest) scadente

shoe /ʃuː/ n scarpa f; (of horse) ferro m ● vt (pt/pp shod, pres p shoeing) ferrare (horse)

shoe: ~**horn** n calzante m. ~**lace** n laccio m da scarpa

shone /ʃɒn/ ▷SHINE

shoo /ʃuː/ vt ~ **away** cacciar via ● *int* sciò

shook /ʃʊk/ ▷ SHAKE

shoot /ʃuːt/ n (Bot) germoglio m; (hunt) battuta f di caccia ● v (pt/pp **shot**) ● vt sparare; girare (film) ● vi (hunt) andare a caccia. □ ~ **down** vt abbattere. □ ~ **out** vi (rush) precipitarsi fuori. □ ~ **up** vi (grow) crescere in fretta; (prices:) salire di colpo

shop /ʃɒp/ n negozio m; (workshop) officina f; **talk** ~ 🔢 parlare di lavoro ● vi (pt/pp **shopped**) far compere; **go** ~**ping** andare a far compere. □ ~ **around** vi confrontare i prezzi

shop: ~**assistant** n commesso, -a mf. ~**keeper** n negoziante mf. ~**lifter** n taccheggiatore, -trice mf. ~**lifting** n taccheggio m. ~**per** n compratore, -trice mf

shopping /ʃɒpɪŋ/ n compere fpl; (articles) acquisti mpl; **do the** ~ fare la spesa. ~ **bag** n borsa f per la spesa. ~ **centre** n centro m commerciale. ~ **trolley** n carrello m

shop: ~**steward** n rappresentante mf sindacale. ~**'window** n vetrina f

shore /ʃɔː(r)/ n riva f

shorn /ʃɔːn/ ▷ SHEAR

short /ʃɔːt/ adj corto; (not lasting) breve; (person) basso; (curt) brusco; **a** ~ **time ago** poco tempo fa; **be** ~ **of sth** essere a corto di; **be in** ~ **supply** essere scarso; fig essere raro; **Mick is** ~ **for Michael** Mick è il diminutivo di Michael ● adv bruscamente; **in** ~ in breve; ~ **of doing** a meno di fare; **go** ~ essere privato (of di); **stop** ~ **of doing sth** non arrivare fino a fare qcsa; **cut** ~ interrompere (meeting, holiday); **to cut a long story** ~ per farla breve

shortage /ʃɔːtɪdʒ/ n scarsità f inv

short: ~**bread** n biscotto m di pasta frolla. ~'**circuit** n corto m circuito. ~'**coming** n difetto m. ~'**cut** n scorciatoia f

shorten /ʃɔːtn/ vt abbreviare; accorciare (garment)

shorthand n stenografia f

short|ly /ʃɔːtlɪ/ adv presto; ~**ly before/after** poco prima/dopo. ~**ness** n brevità f inv; (of person) bassa statura f

shorts /ʃɔːts/ npl calzoncini mpl corti

short-'sighted adj miope

shot /ʃɒt/ ▷ SHOOT ● n colpo m; (person) tiratore m; (Phot) foto f; (injection) puntura f; (🔢 attempt) prova f; **like a** ~ 🔢 come un razzo. ~**gun** n fucile m da caccia

should /ʃʊd/ v aux **I** ~ **go** dovrei andare; **I** ~ **have seen him** avrei dovuto vederlo; **I** ~ **like** mi piacerebbe; **this** ~ **be enough** questo dovrebbe bastare; **if he** ~ **come** se dovesse venire

shoulder /ʃəʊldə(r)/ n spalla f ● vt mettersi in spalla; fig accollarsi. ~**bag** n borsa f a tracolla. ~**blade** n scapola f. ~**strap** n spallina f; (of bag) tracolla f

shout /ʃaʊt/ n grido m ● vt/i gridare. □ ~ **at** vi alzar la voce con. □ ~ **down** vt azzittire gridando

shove /ʃʌv/ n spintone m ● vt spingere; (🔢 put) ficcare ● vi spingere. □ ~ **off** vi 🔢 togliersi di torno

shovel /ʃʌvl/ n pala f ● vt (pt/pp **shovelled**) spalare

show /ʃəʊ/ n (display) manifestazione f; (exhibition) mostra f; (ostentation) ostentazione f; (Theat, TV) spettacolo m; (programme) programma m; **on** ~ esposto ● v (pt **showed**, pp **shown**) ● vt mostrare; (put on display) esporre; proiettare (film) ● vi (film:) essere proiettato; **your slip is** ~**ing** ti si vede la sottoveste. □ ~ **in** vt fare accomodare. □ ~ **off** vi 🔢 mettersi in mostra ● vt mettere in mostra. □ ~ **up** vi risaltare; (🔢 arrive) farsi vedere ● vt (🔢 embarrass) far fare una brutta figura a

'**show-down** n regolamento m dei conti

shower /ʃaʊə(r)/ n doccia f; (of rain) acquazzone m; **have a** ~ fare la doccia ● vt ~ **with** coprire di ● vi fare la doccia. ~**proof** adj impermeabile. ~**y** adj da acquazzoni

'**show-jumping** n concorso m ippico

shown /ʃəʊn/ ▷ SHOW

'**show-off** n esibizionista mf

showy /'ʃəʊi/ adj appariscente

shrank /ʃræŋk/ ▷ SHRINK

shred /ʃred/ n brandello m; fig briciolo m ● vt (pt/pp **shredded**) fare a brandelli; (Culin) tagliuzzare. ~**der** n distruttore m di documenti

shrewd /ʃruːd/ adj accorto. ~**ness** n accortezza f

shriek /ʃriːk/ n strillo m ● vt/i strillare

shrift /ʃrɪft/ n **give sb short** ~ liquidare qcno rapidamente

shrill /ʃrɪl/ adj penetrante

shrimp /ʃrɪmp/ n gamberetto m

shrine /ʃraɪn/ n (place) santuario m

shrink /ʃrɪŋk/ v (pt **shrank**, pp **shrunk**) restringersi; (draw back) ritrarsi (**from** da)

shrivel /'ʃrɪvl/ vi (pt/pp **shrivelled**) raggrinzare

shroud /ʃraʊd/ n sudario m; fig manto m

Shrove /ʃrəʊv/ n ~ '**Tuesday** martedì m grasso

shrub /ʃrʌb/ n arbusto m

shrug /ʃrʌg/ n scrollata f di spalle ● vt/i (pt/pp **shrugged**) ~ **one's shoulders** scrollare le spalle

shrunk /ʃrʌŋk/ ▷ SHRINK. ~**en** adj rimpicciolito

shudder /'ʃʌdə(r)/ n fremito m ● vi fremere

shuffle /'ʃʌfl/ vi strascicare i piedi ● vt mescolare (cards)

shun /ʃʌn/ vt (pt/pp **shunned**)

rifuggire

shunt /ʃʌnt/ vt smistare

shush /ʃʊʃ/ int zitto!

shut /ʃʌt/ v (pt/pp **shut**, pres p **shutting**) ● vt chiudere ● vi chiudersi; (shop) chiudere. □ ~ **down** vt/i chiudere. □ ~ **up** vt chiudere; (!) far tacere ● vi (!) stare zitto; (!) ~ **up!** stai zitto!

shutter /'ʃʌtə(r)/ n serranda f; (Phot) otturatore m

shuttle /'ʃʌtl/ n navetta f ● vi far la spola

shuttle: ~**cock** n volano m. ~ **service** n servizio m pendolare

shy /ʃaɪ/ adj (timid) timido. ~**ness** n timidezza f

Sicily /'sɪsɪlɪ/ n Sicilia f. ~**ian** adj & n siciliano, -a mf

sick /sɪk/ adj ammalato; (humour) macabro; **be** ~ (vomit) vomitare; **be** ~ **of sth** ① essere stufo di qcsa; **feel** ~ aver la nausea

sick|ly /'sɪklɪ/ adj (-**ier**, -**iest**) malaticcio. ~**ness** n malattia f; (vomiting) nausea f. ~**ness benefit** n indennità f di malattia

side /saɪd/ n lato m; (of person, mountain) fianco m; (of road) bordo m; on **the** ~ (as sideline) come attività secondaria; ~ **by** ~ fianco a fianco; **take** ~**s** immischiarsi; **take sb's** ~ prendere le parti di qcno; **be on the safe** ~ andare sul sicuro ● attrib laterale ● vi ~ **with** parteggiare per

side: ~**board** n credenza f. ~**-effect** n effetto m collaterale. ~**lights** npl luci fpl di posizione. ~**line** n attività f inv complementare. ~**-show** n attrazione f. ~**-step** vt schivare. ~**-track** vt sviare. ~**walk** n Am marciapiede m. ~**ways** adv obliquamente

siding /'saɪdɪŋ/ n binario m di raccordo

sidle /'saɪdl/ vi camminare furtivamente (**up to** verso)

siege /siːdʒ/ n assedio m

sieve /sɪv/ n setaccio m ● vt setacciare

sift /sɪft/ vt setacciare; ~ **[through]** fig passare al setaccio

sigh /saɪ/ n sospiro m ● vi sospirare

sight /saɪt/ n vista f; (on gun) mirino m; **the** ~**s** pl le cose da vedere; **at first** ~ a prima vista; **be within/out of** ~ essere/non essere in vista; **lose** ~ **of** perdere di vista; **know by** ~ conoscere di vista. **have bad** ~ vederci male ● vt avvistare

'sightseeing n **go** ~ andare a visitare posti

sign /saɪn/ n segno m; (notice) insegna f ● vt/i firmare. □ ~ **on** vi (as unemployed) presentarsi all'ufficio di collocamento; (Mil) arruolarsi

signal /ˈsɪɡnl/ n segnale m ● v (pt/pp signalled) ● vt segnalare ● vi fare segnali; ~ **to sb** far segno a qcno (**to** di). ~**box** n cabina f di segnalazione

signature /ˈsɪɡnətʃə(r)/ n firma f. ~ **tune** n sigla f [musicale]

significan|ce /sɪɡˈnɪfɪkəns/ n significato m. ~**t** adj significativo

signify /ˈsɪɡnɪfaɪ/ vt (pt/pp -ied) indicare

signpost /ˈsaɪn-/ n segnalazione f stradale

silence /ˈsaɪləns/ n silenzio m ● vt far tacere. ~**r** n (on gun) silenziatore m; (Auto) marmitta f

silent /ˈsaɪlənt/ adj silenzioso; (film) muto; **remain** ~ rimanere in silenzio. ~**ly** adv silenziosamente

silhouette /sɪluˈet/ n sagoma f, silhouette f inv ● vt **be** ~**d** profilarsi

silicon /ˈsɪlɪkən/ n silicio m. ~ **chip** n piastrina f di silicio

silk /sɪlk/ n seta f ● attrib di seta. ~**worm** n baco m da seta

silky /ˈsɪlkɪ/ adj (-ier, -iest) come la seta

silly /ˈsɪlɪ/ adj (-ier, -iest) sciocco

silt /sɪlt/ n melma f

silver /ˈsɪlvə(r)/ adj d'argento; (paper) argentato ● n argento m; (silverware) argenteria f

silver: ~**-plated** adj placcato d'argento. ~**ware** n argenteria f

similar /ˈsɪmɪlə(r)/ adj simile. ~**ity** n somiglianza f. ~**ly** adv in modo simile

simile /ˈsɪmɪlɪ/ n similitudine f

simmer /ˈsɪmə(r)/ vi bollire lentamente ● vt far bollire lentamente. □ ~ **down** vi calmarsi

simple /ˈsɪmpl/ adj semplice; (person) sempliciotto. ~**-'minded** adj sempliciotto

simplicity /sɪmˈplɪsətɪ/ n semplicità f inv

simply /ˈsɪmplɪ/ adv semplicemente

simulat|e /ˈsɪmjʊleɪt/ vt simulare. ~**ion** n simulazione f

simultaneous /sɪmlˈteɪnɪəs/ adj simultaneo

sin /sɪn/ n peccato m ● vi (pt/pp sinned) peccare

---

since /sɪns/

● prep da **I've been waiting** ~ **Monday** aspetto da lunedì

● adv da allora

● conj da quando; (because) siccome

---

sincere /sɪnˈsɪə(r)/ adj sincero. ~**ly** adv sinceramente; **Yours** ~**ly** distinti saluti

sincerity /sɪnˈserətɪ/ n sincerità f inv

sinful /ˈsɪnfl/ adj peccaminoso

sing /sɪŋ/ vt/i (pt sang, pp sung) cantare

singe /sɪndʒ/ vt (pres p singeing) bruciacchiare

singer /ˈsɪŋə(r)/ n cantante mf

single /ˈsɪŋɡl/ adj solo; (not double) semplice; (unmarried) celibe; (woman) nubile; (room) singolo; (bed) a una piazza ● n (ticket) biglietto m di sola andata; (record) singolo m; ~s pl (Tennis) singolo m ● **single out** vt scegliere; (distinguish) distinguere

single-handed adj & adv da solo

singular /'sɪŋgjʊlə(r)/ adj (Gram) singolare ● n singolare m. ~**ly** adv singolarmente

sinister /'sɪnɪstə(r)/ adj sinistro

sink /sɪŋk/ n lavandino m ● v (pt sank, pp sunk) ● vi affondare ● vt affondare (ship); scavare (shaft); investire (money). □ ~ **in** vi penetrare; it took a while to ~ **in** (fig: be understood) c'è voluto un po' a capirlo

sinner /'sɪnə(r)/ n peccatore, -trice mf

sip /sɪp/ n sorso m ● vt (pt/pp sipped) sorseggiare

siphon /'saɪfn/ n (bottle) sifone m ● **siphon off** vt travasare (con sifone)

sir /sɜ:(r)/ n signore m; S~ (title) Sir m; Dear S ~ Spettabile ditta

siren /'saɪrən/ n sirena f

sister /'sɪstə(r)/ n sorella f; (nurse) [infermiera f] caposala f. ~**-in-law** (pl ~s-in-law) cognata f. ~**ly** adj da sorella

sit /sɪt/ v (pt/pp sat, pres p sitting) ● vi essere seduto; (sit down) sedersi; (committee): riunirsi ● vt sostenere (exam). □ ~ **back** vi fig starsene con le mani in mano. □ ~ **down** vi mettersi a sedere. □ ~ **up** vi mettersi seduto; (not slouch) stare seduto diritto; (stay up) stare alzato

site /saɪt/ n posto m; (Archaeol) sito m; (building ~) cantiere m ● vt collocare

sit-in /'sɪtɪn/ n occupazione f (di fabbrica, ecc.)

sitting /'sɪtɪŋ/ n seduta f; (for meals) turno m. ~**room** n salotto m

situate /'sɪtjʊeɪt/ vt situare. ~**d** adj situato. ~**ion** n situazione f; (location) posizione f; (job) posto m

six /sɪks/ adj sei. ~**teen** adj sedici.

~**teenth** adj sedicesimo

sixth /sɪksθ/ adj sesto

sixtieth /'sɪkstɪɪθ/ adj sessantesimo

sixty /'sɪkstɪ/ adj sessanta

size /saɪz/ n dimensioni fpl; (of clothes) taglia f, misura f; (of shoes) numero m; what ~ **is the room?** che dimensioni ha la stanza? ● **size up** vt
🔟 valutare

sizzle /'sɪzl/ vi sfrigolare

skate[1] /skeɪt/ n inv (fish) razza f

skate[2] n pattino m ● vi pattinare

skateboard /'skeɪtbɔ:d/ n skateboard m inv

skater /'skeɪtə(r)/ n pattinatore, -trice mf

skating /'skeɪtɪŋ/ n pattinaggio m. ~**-rink** n pista f di pattinaggio

skeleton /'skelɪtn/ n scheletro m. ~ **key** n passe-partout m inv. ~ **staff** n personale m ridotto

sketch /sketʃ/ n schizzo m; (Theat) sketch m inv ● vt fare uno schizzo di

sketch|y /'sketʃɪ/ adj (-ier, -iest) abbozzato. ~**ily** adv in modo abbozzato

ski /ski:/ n sci m inv ● vi (pt/pp skied, pres p skiing) sciare; go ~**ing** andare a sciare

skid /skɪd/ n slittata f ● vi (pt/pp skidded) slittare

skier /'ski:ə(r)/ n sciatore, -trice mf

skiing /'ski:ɪŋ/ n sci m

skilful /'skɪlfl/ adj abile

'**ski-lift** n impianto m di risalita

skill /skɪl/ n abilità f inv. ~**ed** adj dotato; (worker) specializzato

skim /skɪm/ vt (pt/pp skimmed) schiumare; scremare (milk). □ ~ **off** vt togliere. □ ~ **through** vt scorrere

skimp /skɪmp/ vi ~ **on** lesinare su

skimpy /'skɪmpɪ/ adj (-ier, -iest) succinto

skin /skɪn/ n pelle f; (on fruit) buccia f ● vt (pt/pp skinned) spellare

skin: ~-deep adj superficiale.

~-diving n nuoto m subacqueo

skinny /'skɪnɪ/ adj (**-ier, -iest**) molto magro

skip¹ /skɪp/ n (container) benna f

skip² n salto m ● v (pt/pp **skipped**) ● vi saltellare; (with rope) saltare la corda ● vt omettere.

skipper /'skɪpə(r)/ n skipper m inv

skipping-rope /'skɪpɪŋrəʊp/n corda f per saltare

skirmish /'skɜːmɪʃ/ n scaramuccia f

skirt /skɜːt/ n gonna f ● vt costeggiare

skittle /'skɪtl/ n birillo m

skulk /skʌlk/ vi aggirarsi furtivamente

skull /skʌl/ n cranio m

sky /skaɪ/ n cielo m. **~light** n lucernario m. **~ marshal** n guardia f armata a bordo di un aereo. **~scraper** n grattacielo m

slab /slæb/ n lastra f; (slice) fetta f; (of chocolate) tavoletta f

slack /slæk/ adj lento; (person) fiacco ● vi fare lo scansafatiche. □ **~ off** vi rilassarsi

slacken /'slækn/ vi allentare; **~ [off]** (trade): rallentare; (speed, rain:) diminuire ● vt allentare; diminuire (speed)

slain /sleɪn/ ▷**SLAY**

slam /slæm/ v (pt/pp **slammed**) ● vt sbattere; (🔢: criticize) stroncare ● vi sbattere

slander /'slɑːndə(r)/ n diffamazione f ● vt diffamare. **~ous** adj diffamatorio

slang /slæŋ/ n gergo m. **~y** adj gergale

slant /slɑːnt/ n pendenza f; (point of view) angolazione f; **on the ~** in pendenza ● vt pendere; fig distorcere (report) ● vi pendere

slap /slæp/ n schiaffo m ● vt (pt/pp **slapped**) schiaffeggiare; (put) schiaffare ● adv in pieno

slap-: ~dash adj 🔢 frettoloso

slash /slæʃ/ n taglio m ● vt tagliare; ridurre drasticamente (prices)

slat /slæt/ n stecca f

slate /sleɪt/ n ardesia f ● vt 🔢 fare a pezzi

slaughter /'slɔːtə(r)/ n macello m; (of people) massacro m ● vt macellare; massacrare (people). **~house** n macello m

slave /sleɪv/ n schiavo, -a mf ● vi **~ [away]** lavorare come un negro. **~-driver** n schiavista mf

slav|ery /'sleɪvərɪ/ n schiavitù f inv. **~ish** adj servile

slay /sleɪ/ vt (pt slew, pp slain) ammazzare

sleazy /'sliːzɪ/ adj (**-ier, -iest**) sordido

sledge /sledʒ/ n slitta f. **~-hammer** n martello m

sleek /sliːk/ adj liscio, lucente; (well-fed) pasciuto

sleep /sliːp/ n sonno m; **go to ~** addormentarsi; **put to ~** far addormentare ● v (pt/pp **slept**) ● vi dormire ● vt **~s six** ha sei posti letto. **~er** n (Rail) treno m con vagoni letto; (compartment) vagone m letto; **be a light/heavy ~er** avere il sonno leggero/pesante

sleeping-: ~bag n sacco m a pelo. **~-car** n vagone m letto. **~-pill** n sonnifero m

sleepless adj insonne

sleepy /'sliːpɪ/ adj (**-ier, -iest**) assonnato; **be ~** aver sonno

sleet /sliːt/ n nevischio m ● vi **it is ~ing** nevischia

sleeve /sliːv/ n manica f; (for record) copertina f. **~less** adj senza maniche

sleigh /sleɪ/ n slitta f

slender /'slendə(r)/ adj snello; (fingers, stem) affusolato; fig scarso; (chance) magro

slept /slept/ ▷**SLEEP**

slew¹ /slu:/ *vi* girare

slew² ▷**SLAY**

slice /slaɪs/ *n* fetta *f* ● *vt* affettare;
~**d bread** pane *m* a cassetta

slick /slɪk/ *adj* liscio; (cunning) astuto
● *n* (*oil slick*) chiazza *f* di petrolio

slide /slaɪd/ *n* (*in playground*) scivolo *m*; (*for hair*) fermaglio
m (*per capelli*); (*Phot*) diapositiva *f* ● *v*
(*pt/pp* **slid**) ● *vi* scivolare ● *vt* far scivolare. ~**-rule** *n* regolo *m* calcolatore. ~**ing** *adj* scorrevole; (*door, seat*) scorrevole; ~**ing scale** scala *f* mobile

slight /slaɪt/ *adj* leggero; (*importance*) poco; (*slender*) esile; **not in the** ~**est** niente affatto ● *vt* offendere ● *n* offesa *f*. ~**ly**
adv leggermente

slim /slɪm/ *adj* (**slimmer, slimmest**)
snello; *fig* scarso; (*chance*) magro ● *vi*
dimagrire

slime /slaɪm/ *n* melma *f*. ~**y** *adj*
melmoso; *fig* viscido

sling /slɪŋ/ *n* (*Med*) benda *f* al collo
● *vt* (*pt/pp* **slung**) ⚪ lanciare

slip /slɪp/ *n* scivolata *f*; (*mistake*) lieve
errore *m*; (*petticoat*) sottoveste *f*; (*for
pillow*) federa *f*; (*paper*) scontrino *m*;
give sb the ~ ⚪ sbarazzarsi di
qcno; ~ **of the tongue** lapsus *m inv*
● *v* (*pt/pp* **slipped**) ● *vi* scivolare; (*go
quickly*) sgattaiolare; (*decline*) retrocedere ● *vt* **he** ~**ped it into his
pocket** se l'è infilato in tasca; ~
away *vi* sgusciar via; (*time*):
sfuggire. ~ **into** *vi* infilarsi
(*clothes*). ~ **up** *vi* ⚪ sbagliare

slipper /ˈslɪpə(r)/ *n* pantofola *f*

slippery /ˈslɪpərɪ/ *adj* scivoloso

slip-road *n* bretella *f*

slipshod /ˈslɪpʃɒd/ *adj* trascurato

slip-up *n* ⚪ sbaglio *m*

slit /slɪt/ *n* spacco *m*; (*tear*) strappo *m*;
(*hole*) fessura *f* ● *vt* (*pt/pp* **slit**) tagliare

slither /ˈslɪðə(r)/ *vi* scivolare

slobber /ˈslɒbə(r)/ *vi* sbavare

slog /slɒg/ *n* [*hard*] ~ sgobbata *f*
● *vi* (*pt/pp* **slogged**) (*work*) sgobbare

slogan /ˈsləʊgən/ *n* slogan *m inv*

slop /slɒp/ *v* (*pt/pp* **slopped**) ● *vt* versare. ~ **over** *vi* versarsi

slope /sləʊp/ *n* pendenza *f*; (*ski*-) pista *f* ● *vi* essere inclinato, inclinarsi.
~**ing** *adj* in pendenza

sloppy /ˈslɒpɪ/ *adj* (*work*) trascurato; (*worker*) negligente; (*in dress*) sciatto; (*sentimental*)
sdolcinato

slosh /slɒʃ/ *vi* ⚪ (*person, feet*:)
squazzare; (*water*:) scrosciare ● *vt*
(⚪: *hit*) colpire

slot /slɒt/ *n* fessura *f*; (*time*-) spazio
m ● *v* (*pt/pp* **slotted**) ● *vt* infilare. □ ~
in *vi* incastrarsi

'slot-machine *n* distributore *m* automatico; (*for gambling*) slot-machine
f inv

slouch /slaʊtʃ/ *vi* (*in chair*) stare
scomposto

Slovakia /sləˈvækɪə/ *n* Slovacchia *f*

Slovenia /sləˈviːnɪə/ *n* Slovenia *f*

slovenly /ˈslʌvnlɪ/ *adj* sciatto.
~**iness** *n* sciatteria *f*

slow /sləʊ/ *adj* lento; **be** ~ (*clock*:)
essere indietro; **in** ~ **motion** al rallentatore ● *adv* lentamente ● *vt* ~
down/up *vt/vi* rallentare

slowly *adv* lentamente

sludge /slʌdʒ/ *n* fanghiglia *f*

slug /slʌg/ *n* lumacone *m*; (*bullet*) pallottola *f*. ~**gish** *adj* lento

slum /slʌm/ *n* (*house*) tugurio *m*; ~**s**
pl bassifondi *mpl*

slumber /ˈslʌmbə(r)/ *vi* dormire

slump /slʌmp/ *n* crollo *m*; (*economic*)
depressione *f* ● *vi* crollare

slung /slʌŋ/ ▷**SLING**

slur /slɜ:(r)/ *n* (*discredit*) calunnia *f* ● *vt*
(*pt/pp* **slurred**) biascicare

slush /slʌʃ/ *n* pantano *m* nevoso; *fig*
sdolcinatezza *f*. ~ **fund** *n* fondi *mpl*

s

neri. ~y adj fangoso; (sentimental) sdolcinato

sly /slaɪ/ adj (-er, -est) scaltro ● on the ~ di nascosto

smack¹ /smæk/ n (on face) schiaffo m; (on bottom) sculaccione m ● vt (on face) schiaffeggiare; (on bottom) sculacciare; ~ one's lips far schioccare le labbra ● adv 🔁 in pieno

smack² vi ~ of fig sapere di

small /smɔːl/ adj piccolo; be out/ work ~ until the ~ hours fare le ore piccole ● adv chop up ~ fare a pezzettini ● the ~ of the back la parte bassa della schiena fpl

small: ~ ads npl annunci mpl [commerciali]. ~ 'change n spiccioli mpl. ~pox n vaiolo m. ~ talk n chiacchiere fpl

smart /smɑːt/ adj elegante; (clever) intelligente; (brisk) svelto; be ~ (🔁: cheeky) fare il furbo ● vi (hurt) bruciare

smash /smæʃ/ n fragore m; (collision) scontro m; (Tennis) schiacciata f ● vt spaccare; (Tennis) schiacciare ● vi spaccarsi; (crash) schiantarsi (into contro). ~ [hit] n successo m. ~ing adj 🔁 fantastico

smattering /'smætərɪŋ/ n infarinatura f

smear /smɪə(r)/ n macchia f; (Med) striscio m ● vt imbrattare; (coat) spalmare (with di); fig calunniare

smell /smel/ n odore m; (sense) odorato m ● v (pt/pp smelt o smelled) ● vt odorare; (sniff) annusare ● vi odorare (of di)

smelly /'smelɪ/ adj (-ier, -iest) puzzolente

smelt¹ /smelt/ ▷SMELL

smelt² vt fondere

smile /smaɪl/ n sorriso m ● vi sorridere; ~ at sorridere a (sb); sorridere di (sth)

smirk /smɜːk/ n sorriso m compiaciuto

smithereens /smɪðə'riːnz/ npl

to/in ~ in mille pezzi

smock /smɒk/ n grembiule m

smog /smɒg/ n smog m inv

smoke /sməʊk/ n fumo m ● vt/i fumare. ~less adj senza fumo; (fuel) che non fa fumo

smoker /'sməʊkə(r)/ n fumatore, -trice mf; (Rail) vagone m fumatori

smoky /'sməʊkɪ/ adj (-ier, -iest) fumoso; (taste) di fumo

smooth /smuːð/ adj liscio; (movement) scorrevole; (sea) calmo; (manners) mellifluo ● vt lisciare. □ ~ out vt lisciare. ~ly adv in modo scorrevole

smother /'smʌðə(r)/ vt soffocare

smoulder /'sməʊldə(r)/ vi fumare; (with rage) consumarsi

smudge /smʌdʒ/ n macchia f ● vt/i imbrattare

smug /smʌg/ adj (smugger, smuggest) compiaciuto. ~ly adv con aria compiaciuta

smuggl|e /'smʌgl/ vt contrabbandare. ~er n contrabbandiere, a, mf. ~ing n contrabbando m

snack /snæk/ n spuntino m. ~-bar n snack bar m inv

snag /snæg/ n (problem) intoppo m

snail /sneɪl/ n lumaca f; at a ~'s pace a passo di lumaca

snake /sneɪk/ n serpente m

snap /snæp/ n colpo m secco; (photo) istantanea f ● attrib (decision) istantaneo ● v (pt/pp snapped) ● vi (break) spezzarsi; ~ at (dog) cercare di azzannare; (person:) parlare seccamente a ● vt (break) spezzare; (say) dire seccamente; far un'istantanea di. □ ~ up vt afferrare

snappy /'snæpɪ/ adj (-ier, -iest) scorbutico; (smart) elegante; make it ~! sbrigati!

'snapshot n istantanea f

snare /sneə(r)/ n trappola f

snarl /snɑːl/ n ringhio m ● vi

ringhiare

snatch /snætʃ/ n strappo m; (*fragment*) brano m; (*theft*) scippo m; **make a ~ at** cercare di afferrare qcsa ● vt strappare [di mano] (from a); (*steal*) scippare; rapire (child)

sneak /sniːk/ n 🔢 spia mf ● vi (🔢 *tell tales*) fare la spia ● vt (*take*) rubare; **~ a look at** dare una sbirciata a. □ **~ in/out** vi sgattaiolare dentro/fuori

sneakers /ˈsniːkəz/ npl Am scarpe fpl da ginnastica

sneaky /ˈsniːkɪ/ adj sornione

sneer /snɪə(r)/ n ghigno m ● vi sogghignare; (*mock*) ridere di

sneeze /sniːz/ n starnuto m ● vi starnutire

snide /snaɪd/ adj 🔢 insinuante

sniff /snɪf/ n (*of dog*) annusata f ● vi tirare su col naso ● vt odorare (flower); sniffare (glue, cocaine); (dog:) annusare

snigger /ˈsnɪɡə(r)/ n risatina f soffocata ● vi ridacchiare

snip /snɪp/ n taglio m; (🔢 *bargain*) affare m ● vt/i (*pt/pp* snipped) **~ [at]** tagliare

snippet /ˈsnɪpɪt/ n **a ~ of information/news** una breve notizia/informazione

snivel /ˈsnɪvl/ vi (*pt/pp* snivelled) piagnucolare. **~ling** adj piagnucoloso

snob /snɒb/ n snob mf. **~bery** n snobismo m. **~bish** adj da snob

snooker /ˈsnuːkə(r)/ n snooker m

snoop /snuːp/ n spia f ● vi 🔢 curiosare

snooze /snuːz/ n sonnellino m ● vi fare un sonnellino

snore /snɔː(r)/ vi russare

snorkel /ˈsnɔːkl/ n respiratore m

snort /snɔːt/ n sbuffo m ● vi sbuffare

snout /snaʊt/ n grugno m

snow /snəʊ/ n neve f ● vi nevicare; **~ed under with** fig sommerso di

snow: ~ball n palla f di neve ● vi fare a palle di neve. **~board** n snowboard m. **~drift** n cumulo m di neve. **~fall** n nevicata f. **~flake** n fiocco m di neve. **~man** n pupazzo m di neve. **~plough** n spazzaneve m. **~storm** n tormenta f. **~y** adj nevoso

snub /snʌb/ n sgarbo m ● vt (*pt/pp* snubbed) snobbare

'snub-nosed adj dal naso all'insù

snug /snʌɡ/ adj (snugger, snuggest) comodo; (*tight*) aderente

---

so /səʊ/

● *adv* così; **so far** finora; **so am I** anch'io; **so I see** così pare; **that is so** è così; **so much** così tanto; **so much the better** tanto meglio; **so it is** è proprio così; **if so se** è così; **so as to** in modo da; **so long!** 🔢 a presto!

● *pron* **I hope/think/am afraid so** spero/penso/temo di sì; **I told you so** te l'ho detto; **because I say so** perché te lo dico io; **I did so!** è vero!; **so saying/doing,...** così dicendo/facendo,...; **or so** circa; **very much so** sì, molto; **and so forth** o **on** e così via

● *conj* (*therefore*) perciò; (*in order that*) così; **so that** affinché; **so there!** ecco!; **so what!** e allora!; **so where have you been?** allora, dove sei stato?

---

soak /səʊk/ vt mettere a bagno ● vi stare a bagno; **~ into** (liquid:) penetrare. □ **~ up** vt assorbire

soaking /ˈsəʊkɪŋ/ n ammollo m ● adj & adv **~ [wet]** 🔢 inzuppato

so-and-so /ˈsəʊənsəʊ/ n Tal dei Tali mf; (*euphemism*) specie f di imbecille

soap /səʊp/ n sapone m. **~ opera** n telenovela f, soap opera f inv. **~ powder** n detersivo m in polvere

soapy /ˈsəʊpɪ/ adj (-ier, -iest) insaponato

soar /sɔː(r)/ vi elevarsi; (prices): salire alle stelle

sob /sɒb/ n singhiozzo m • vi (pt/pp **sobbed**) singhiozzare

sober /'səʊbə(r)/ adj sobrio; (serious) serio • **sober up** vi ritornare sobrio

'so-called adj cosiddetto

soccer /'sɒkə(r)/ n calcio m

sociable /'səʊʃəbl/ adj socievole

social /'səʊʃl/ adj sociale; (sociable) socievole

socialism /'səʊʃəlɪzm/ n socialismo m. **~t** adj socialista • n socialista mf

socialize /'səʊʃəlaɪz/ vi socializzare

social: **~ se'curity** n previdenza f sociale. **~ worker** n assistente mf sociale

society /sə'saɪətɪ/ n società f inv

sociologist /səʊsɪ'ɒlədʒɪst/ n sociologo, -a mf. **~y** n sociologia f

sock[1] /sɒk/ n calzino m; (kneelength) calza f

sock[2] /sɒk/ n [T] pugno m • vt [T] dare un pugno a

socket /'sɒkɪt/ n (wall plug) presa f [di corrente]; (for bulb) portalampada m inv

soda /'səʊdə/ n soda f; Am gazzosa f. **~ water** n seltz m inv

sodium /'səʊdɪəm/ n sodio m

sofa /'səʊfə/ n divano m. **~ bed** n divano m letto

soft /sɒft/ adj morbido, soffice; (voice) sommesso; (light, colour) tenue; (not strict) indulgente; ([T]: silly) stupido; **have a ~ spot for sb** avere un debole per qcno. **~ drink** n bibita f analcolica

soften /'sɒfn/ vt ammorbidire; fig attenuare • vi ammorbidirsi

softly /'sɒftlɪ/ adv (say) sottovoce; (treat) con indulgenza; (play music) in sottofondo

software /n software m

soggy /'sɒgɪ/ adj (-ier, -iest) zuppo

soil[1] /sɔɪl/ n suolo m

soil[2] vt sporcare

solar /'səʊlə(r)/ adj solare

sold /səʊld/ ▷SELL

solder /'səʊldə(r)/ n lega f da saldatura • vt saldare

soldier /'səʊldʒə(r)/ n soldato m • **soldier on** vi perseverare

sole[1] /səʊl/ n (of foot) pianta f; (of shoe) suola f

sole[2] n (fish) sogliola f

sole[3] adj unico, solo. **~ly** adv unicamente

solemn /'sɒləm/ adj solenne. **~ity** n solennità f inv

solicitor /sə'lɪsɪtə(r)/ n avvocato m

solid /'sɒlɪd/ adj solido; (oak, gold) massiccio • n (figure) solido m; **~s** (food) cibi mpl solidi

solidarity /sɒlɪ'dærətɪ/ n solidarietà f inv

solidify /sə'lɪdɪfaɪ/ vi (pt/pp -ied) solidificarsi

solitary /'sɒlɪtərɪ/ adj solitario; (sole) solo. **~ con'finement** n cella f di isolamento

solitude /'sɒlɪtjuːd/ n solitudine f

solo /'səʊləʊ/ n (Mus) assolo m • adj (flight) in solitario • adv in solitario. **~ist** n solista m

solstice /'sɒlstɪs/ n solstizio m

soluble /'sɒljʊbl/ adj solubile

solution /sə'luːʃn/ n soluzione f

solve /sɒlv/ vt risolvere

solvent /'sɒlvənt/ adj solvente • n solvente m

sombre /'sɒmbə(r)/ adj tetro; (clothes) scuro

some /sʌm/ adj (a certain amount of) del; (a certain number of) qualche, alcuni; **~ day** un giorno o l'altro; **I need ~ money/books** ho bisogno di soldi/libri; **do ~ shopping** fare qualche acquisto • pron (a certain amount) un po'; (a certain number) alcuni; **I want ~** ne voglio

some: ~**body** /-bɒdɪ/ pron & n qualcuno m. ~**how** adv in qualche modo; ~**how or other** in un modo o nell'altro. ~**one** pron & n = **somebody**

somersault /'sʌməsɔːlt/ n capriola f; **turn a** ~ fare una capriola

something pron qualche cosa, qualcosa; ~ **different** qualcosa di diverso; ~ **like** un po' come; (approximately) qualcosa come; **see** ~ **of sb** vedere qcno un po'

some: ~**time** adv un giorno o l'altro; ~**times** adv qualche volta. ~**what** adv piuttosto. ~**where** adv da qualche parte • pron ~ **where to eat** un posto in cui mangiare

son /sʌn/ n figlio m

sonata /səˈnɑːtə/ n sonata f

song /sɒŋ/ n canzone f

sonic /'sɒnɪk/ adj sonico. ~ '**boom** n bang m inv sonico

'son-in-law n (pl ~**s-in-law**) genero m

sonnet /'sɒnɪt/ n sonetto m

soon /suːn/ adv presto; (in a short time) tra poco; **as** ~ **as** [non] appena; **as** ~ **as possible** il più presto possibile; ~**er or later** prima o poi; **the** ~**er the better** prima è, meglio è; **no** ~**er had I arrived than...** ero appena arrivato quando...; **I would** ~**er go** preferirei andare; ~ **after** subito dopo

soot /sʊt/ n fuliggine f

soothe /suːð/ vt calmare

sooty /'sʊtɪ/ adj fuligginoso

sophisticated /səˈfɪstɪkeɪtɪd/ adj sofisticato

sopping /'sɒpɪŋ/ adj & adv **be** ~ [**wet**] essere bagnato fradicio

soppy /'sɒpɪ/ adj (-**ier**, -**iest**) [T] svenevole

soprano /səˈprɑːnəʊ/ n soprano m

sordid /'sɔːdɪd/ adj sordido

sore /sɔː(r)/ adj dolorante; (Am:

vexed) arrabbiato; **It's** ~ fa male; **have a** ~ **throat** avere mal di gola • n piaga f. ~**ly** adv (tempted) seriamente

sorrow /'sɒrəʊ/ n tristezza f. ~**ful** adj triste

sorry /'sɒrɪ/ adj (-**ier**, -**iest**) (sad) spiacente; (wretched) pietoso; **you'll be** ~! te ne pentirai; **I am** ~ mi dispiace; **be** or **feel** ~ **for** provare compassione per; ~! scusa!; (more polite) scusi!

sort /sɔːt/ n specie f; ([T]: person) tipo m; **it's a** ~ **of fish** è un tipo di pesce; **be out of** ~**s** ([T]: unwell) store bene e fig classificare • **a** ~ **out** vt selezionare (papers); fig risolvere (problem); occuparsi di (person)

'so-so adj & adv così così

sought /sɔːt/ ▷ **SEEK**

soul /səʊl/ n anima f

sound[1] /saʊnd/ adj sano; (sensible) saggio; (secure) solido; (thrashing) clamoroso • adv ~ **asleep** profondamente addormentato

sound[2] n suono m; (noise) rumore m; **I don't like the** ~ **of it** [T] non mi suona bene • vi suonare; (seem) aver l'aria • vt (pronounce) pronunciare; (Med) auscultare (chest). ~ **barrier** n muro m del suono. ~ **card** n (Comput) scheda f sonora. ~**less** adj silenzioso. □ ~ **out** vt fig sondare

soundly /'saʊndlɪ/ adv (sleep) profondamente; (defeat) clamorosamente

'sound: ~**proof** adj impenetrabile al suono. ~**-track** n colonna f sonora

soup /suːp/ n minestra f. ~**ed-up** adj [T] (engine) truccato

sour /'saʊə(r)/ adj agro; (not fresh & fig) acido

source /sɔːs/ n fonte f

south /saʊθ/ n sud m; **to the** ~ **of** a sud di • adj del sud, meridionale

● adv verso il sud

south: S~ 'Africa n Sudafrica m. S~ A'merica n America f del Sud. S~ American adj & n sudamericano, -a mf. ~'east n sudest m

southerly /'sʌðəlɪ/ adj del sud

southern /'sʌðən/ adj del sud, meridionale; ~ **Italy** il Mezzogiorno m. ~er n meridionale mf

'southward[s] /-wəd[z]/ adv verso sud

souvenir /suːvə'nɪə(r)/ n ricordo m, souvenir m inv

sovereign /'sɒvrɪn/ adj sovrano ● n sovrano, -a mf. ~ty n sovranità f inv

Soviet /'səʊvɪət/ adj sovietico; ~ **Union** Unione f Sovietica

sow¹ /saʊ/ n scrofa f

sow² /səʊ/ vt (pt sowed, pp sown or sowed) seminare

soya /'sɔɪə/ n ~ **bean** soia f

spa /spɑː/ n stazione f termale

space /speɪs/ n spazio m ● adj (research etc) spaziale ● vt ~ [out] distanziare

space: ~**ship** n astronave f. ~ **shuttle** n navetta f spaziale

spade /speɪd/ n vanga f; (for child) paletta f; ~**s** pl (in cards) picche fpl. ~**work** n lavoro m preparatorio

Spain /speɪn/ n Spagna f

spam /spæm/ n spam m

span¹ /spæn/ n spanna f; (of arch) luce f; (of time) arco m; (of wings) apertura f ● vt (pt/pp spanned) estendersi su

span² ▷ **SPICK**

Span|iard /'spænjəd/ n spagnolo, -a mf. ~**ish** adj spagnolo ● n (language) spagnolo m; the ~ish pl gli spagnoli

spank /spæŋk/ vt sculacciare. ~**ing** n sculacciata f

spanner /'spænə(r)/ n chiave f inglese

spare /speə(r)/ adj (surplus) in più;

(additional) di riserva ● n (part) ricambio m ● vt risparmiare; (do without) fare a meno di; **can you** ~ **five minutes?** avresti cinque minuti?; **to** ~ (surplus) in eccedenza. ~ **part** n pezzo m di ricambio. ~ **time** n tempo m libero. ~ **'wheel** n ruota f di scorta

spark /spɑːk/ n scintilla f. ~**ing-plug** n (Auto) candela f

sparkl|e /'spɑːkl/ n scintillio m ● vi scintillare. ~**ing** adj frizzante; (wine) spumante

sparrow /'spærəʊ/ n passero m

sparse /spɑːs/ adj rado. ~**ly** adv scarsamente; ~**ly populated** a bassa densità di popolazione

spasm /'spæzm/ n spasmo m. ~**odic** adj spasmodico

spat /spæt/ ▷ **SPIT¹**

spate /speɪt/ n (series) successione f; **be in full** ~ essere in piena

spatial /'speɪʃl/ adj spaziale

spatter /'spætə(r)/ vt schizzare

spawn /spɔːn/ n uova fpl (di pesci, rane, ecc.) ● vi deporre le uova ● vt fig generare

speak /spiːk/ v (pt spoke, pp spoken) ● vi parlare (to a); ~**ing!** (Teleph) sono io! ● vt dire; ~ **one's mind** dire quello che si pensa. □ ~ **for** vi parlare a nome di. □ ~ **up** vi parlare più forte; ~ **up for oneself** parlare a favore di

speaker /'spiːkə(r)/ n parlante mf; (in public) oratore, -trice mf; (of stereo) cassa f

spear /spɪə(r)/ n lancia f

special /'speʃl/ adj speciale. ~**ist** n specialista mf. ~**ity** n specialità f inv

special|ize /'speʃəlaɪz/ vi specializzarsi. ~**ly** adv specialmente; (particularly) particolarmente

species /'spiːʃiːz/ n specie f inv

specific /spə'sɪfɪk/ adj specifico. ~**ally** adv in modo specifico

specify /'spesɪfaɪ/ vt (pt/pp -ied)

specificare

specimen /'spesɪmən/ n campione m

speck /spek/ n macchiolina f; (particle) granello m

specs /speks/ npl 🛈 occhiali mpl

spectacle /'spektəkl/ n (show) spettacolo m. **~s** npl occhiali mpl

spectacular /spek'tækjʊlə(r)/ adj spettacolare

spectator /spek'teɪtə(r)/ n spettatore, -trice mf

spectre /'spektə(r)/ n spettro m

spectrum /'spektrəm/ n (pl **-tra**) spettro m; fig gamma f

speculat|e /'spekjʊleɪt/ vi speculare. **~ion** n speculazione f. **~ive** adj speculativo. **~or** n speculatore, -trice mf

sped /sped/ ▷ SPEED

speech /spiːtʃ/ n linguaggio m; (address) discorso m. **~less** adj senza parole

speed /spiːd/ n velocità f; (gear) marcia f; **at ~** a tutta velocità ● vi (pt/pp **sped**) andare veloce; (pt/pp **speeded**) (go too fast) andare a velocità eccessiva. □ **~ up** (pt/pp **speeded up**) vi/i accelerare

speed: ~boat n motoscafo m. **~ camera** n Autovelox® m inv. **~ dating** n speed dating m. **~ limit** n limite m di velocità

speedometer /spiː'dɒmɪtə(r)/ n tachimetro m

speed|y /'spiːdɪ/ adj (**-ier, -iest**) rapido. **~ily** adv rapidamente

spell¹ /spel/ n (turn) turno m; (of weather) periodo m

spell² v (pt/pp **spelled, spelt**) ● vt how do you **~...?** come si scrive...?; **could you ~** that for me? me lo può compitare?; **~ disaster** essere disastroso ● vi he can't **~** ha molti errori d'ortografia

spell³ n (magic) incantesimo m. **~bound** adj affascinato

spelling /'spelɪŋ/ n ortografia f

spelt /spelt/ ▷ SPELL²

spend /spend/ vt/i (pt/pp **spent**) spendere; passare (time)

sperm /spɜːm/ n spermatozoo m; (semen) sperma m

spew /spjuː/ vt/i vomitare

sphere /sfɪə(r)/ n sfera f. **~ical** adj sferico

spice /spaɪs/ n spezia f; fig pepe m

spick /spɪk/ adj **~ and span** lindo

spicy /'spaɪsɪ/ adj piccante

spider /'spaɪdə(r)/ n ragno m

spike /spaɪk/ n punta f; (Bot, Zool) spina f; (on shoe) chiodo m. **~y** adj (plant) pungente

spill /spɪl/ v (pt/pp **spilt** or **spilled**) ● vt versare (blood) ● vi rovesciarsi

spin /spɪn/ v (pt/pp **spun**, pres p **spinning**) ● vt far girare; filare (wool); centrifugare (washing) ● vi girare; (washing machine:) centrifugare ● n rotazione f; (short drive) giretto m. □ **~ out** vt far durare

spinach /'spɪnɪdʒ/ n spinaci mpl

spin-'drier n centrifuga f

spine /spaɪn/ n spina f dorsale; (of book) dorso m; (Bot, Zool) spina f. **~less** adj fig smidollato

'spin-off n ricaduta f

spiral /'spaɪrəl/ adj a spirale ● n spirale f ● vi (pt/pp **spiralled**) formare una spirale. **~ 'staircase** n scala f a chiocciola

spire /spaɪə(r)/ n guglia f

spirit /'spɪrɪt/ n spirito m; (courage) ardore m. **~s** npl (alcohol) liquori mpl; **in good ~s** di buon umore; **in low ~s** abbattuto

spirited /'spɪrɪtɪd/ adj vivace; (courageous) pieno d'ardore

spiritual /'spɪrɪtjʊəl/ adj spirituale ● n spiritual m. **~ism** n spiritismo m. **~ist** n spiritista mf

spit¹ /spɪt/ n (for roasting) spiedo m

spit² n sputo m ● vt/i (pt/pp **spat**, pres

p **spitting**) sputare; (cat:) soffiare; (fat:) sfrigolare; **it's ~ing [with rain]** pioviggina; **the ~ting image of** il ritratto spiccicato di

spite /spaɪt/ *n* dispetto *m*; **in ~ of** malgrado ● *vt* far dispetto a. **~ful** *adj* indispettito

spittle /ˈspɪtl/ *n* saliva *f*

splash /splæʃ/ *n* schizzo *m*; (*of colour*) macchia *f*; (🔲: *drop*) goccio *m* ● *vt* schizzare; **~ sb with** schizzare qcno di qcsa ● *vi* schizzare. **~ about** *vi* schizzarsi. □ **~ down** *vi* (*spacecraft:*) ammarare

splendid /ˈsplendɪd/ *adj* splendido

splendour /ˈsplendə(r)/ *n* splendore *m*

splint /splɪnt/ *n* (*Med*) stecca *f*

splinter /ˈsplɪntə(r)/ *n* scheggia *f* ● *vi* scheggiarsi

split /splɪt/ *n* fessura *f*; (*quarrel*) rottura *f*; (*division*) scissione *f*; (*tear*) strappo *m* ● *v* (*pt/pp* **split**, *pres p* **splitting**) *vt* spaccare; (*share, divide*) dividere; (*tear*) strappare ● *vi* spaccarsi; (*tear*) strapparsi; (*divide*) dividersi; **~ on sb** 🔲 denunciare qcno ● *adj* a **~** second una frazione *f* di secondo. □ **~ up** *vt* dividersi ● *vi* (*couple:*) separarsi

splutter /ˈsplʌtə(r)/ *vi* farfugliare

spoil /spɔɪl/ *n* **~s** *pl* bottino *msg* ● *v* (*pt/pp* **spoilt** *or* **spoiled**) *vt* rovinare; viziare (*person*) ● *vi* andare a male. **~sport** *n* guastafeste *mf inv*

spoke¹ /spəʊk/ *n* raggio *m*

spoke², **spoken** /ˈspəʊkn/ ▷**SPEAK**

'spokesman *n* portavoce *m inv*

sponge /spʌndʒ/ *n* spugna *f* ● *vt* pulire (con la spugna) ● *vi* **~ on** scroccare da. **~-cake** *n* pan *m* di Spagna

sponsor /ˈspɒnsə(r)/ *n* garante *m*; (*Radio, TV*) sponsor *m inv*; (*god-parent*) padrino *m*, madrina *f*; (*for membership*) socio, -a *mf* garante ● *vt* sponsorizzare. **~ship** *n* sponsorizzazione *f*

spontaneous /spɒnˈteɪnɪəs/ *adj* spontaneo

spoof /spuːf/ *n* 🔲 parodia *f*

spooky /ˈspuːkɪ/ *adj* (**-ier, -iest**) 🔲 sinistro

spool /spuːl/ *n* bobina *f*

spoon /spuːn/ *n* cucchiaio *m* ● *vt* mettere col cucchiaio. **~-feed** *vt* (*pt/pp* **-fed**) *fig* imboccare. **~ful** *n* cucchiaiata *f*

sporadic /spəˈrædɪk/ *adj* sporadico

sport /spɔːt/ *n* sport *m inv* ● *vt* sfoggiare. **~ing** *adj* sportivo; **~ing chance** possibilità *f* reale

sports: ~car *n* automobile *f* sportiva. **~man** *n* sportivo *m*. **~woman** *n* sportiva *f*

spot /spɒt/ *n* macchia *f*; (*pimple*) brufolo *m*; (*place*) posto *m*; (*in pattern*) pois *m inv*; (*of rain*) goccia *f*; (*of water*) goccio *m*; **~s** *pl* (*rash*) sfogo *msg*; **a ~ of** 🔲 un po' di; **a ~ of bother** qualche problema; **on the ~** sul luogo; (*immediately*) immediatamente; **in a [tight] ~** 🔲 in difficoltà ● *vt* (*pt/pp* **spotted**) macchiare; (🔲: *notice*) individuare

spot: ~ 'check *n* (*without warning*) controllo *m* a sorpresa; **do a ~ check on sth** fare una controllata a qcsa. **~less** *adj* immacolato. **~light** *n* riflettore *m*

spotted /ˈspɒtɪd/ *adj* (*material*) a pois

spotty /ˈspɒtɪ/ *adj* (**-ier, -iest**) (*pimply*) brufoloso

spouse /spaʊz/ *n* consorte *mf*

spout /spaʊt/ *n* becco *m* ● *vi* zampillare (**from** da)

sprain /spreɪn/ *n* slogatura *f* ● *vt* slogare

sprang /spræŋ/ ▷**SPRING²**

spray /spreɪ/ *n* spruzzo *m*; (*preparation*) spray *m inv*; (*container*) spruzzatore *m inv* ● *vt* spruzzare. **~-gun** *n* pistola *f* a spruzzo

spread /spred/ *n* estensione *f*; (*of*

disease) diffusione *f*; (*paste*) crema *f*; (**!**: *feast*) banchetto *m* ● *v* /pt/pp

spread ● *vt* spargere; spalmare (butter, jam); stendere (cloth, arms); diffondere (news, disease); dilazionare (payments); ~ **sth with** spalmare qcsa di ● *vi* spargersi; (butter): spalmarsi; (disease): diffondersi. **~sheet** *n* (Comput) foglio *m* elettronico. ■ ~ **out** *vt* sparpagliare ● *vi* sparpagliarsi

spree /spri:/ *n* **!** **go on a** ~ far baldoria; **go on a shopping** ~ fare spese folli

sprightly /'spraitli/ *adj* (**-ier, -iest**) vivace

spring[1] /sprɪŋ/ *n* primavera *f* ● *attrib* primaverile

spring[2] *n* (*jump*) balzo *m*; (*water*) sorgente *f*; (*device*) molla *f*; (*elasticity*) elasticità *f inv* ● *vi* (pt **sprang**, pp **sprung**) ● *vi* balzare; (*arise*) provenire (from da) ● *vt* **he just sprang it on me** me l'ha detto a cose fatte compiuto. ■ ~ **up** balzare; *fig* spuntare

spring: ~**board** *n* trampolino *m*. ~**time** *n* primavera *f*

sprinkle /'sprɪŋkl/ *vt* (*scatter*) spruzzare (liquid); spargere (flour, cocoa); ~ **sth with** spruzzare qcsa di (liquid); cospargere qcsa di (flour, cocoa). ~**er** *n* spinkler *m inv*; (*for lawn*) irrigatore *m*. ~**ing** *n* (*of pepper, salt*) pizzico *m*; (*of flour, sugar*) spolveratina *f*; (*of knowledge*) infarinatura *f*; (*of people*) pugno *m*

sprint /sprɪnt/ *n* sprint *m inv* ● *vi* fare uno sprint; (Sport) sprintare. ~**er** *n* sprinter *mf inv*

sprout /spraʊt/ *n* germoglio *m*; [**Brussels**] ~**s** *pl* cavolini *mpl* di Bruxelles ● *vi* germogliare

sprung /sprʌŋ/ ▷**SPRING**[2] ● *adj* molleggiato

spud /spʌd/ *n* **!** patata *f*

spun /spʌn/ ▷**SPIN**

spur /spɜː(r)/ *n* sperone *m*; (*stimulus*)

stimolo *m*; (*road*) svincolo *m*; **on the** ~ **of the moment** su due piedi ● *vt* (pt/pp **spurred**) ~ **[on]** *fig* spronare [a]

spurn /spɜːn/ *vt* sdegnare

spurt /spɜːt/ *n* getto *m*; (Sport) scatto *m*; **put on a** ~ fare uno scatto ● *vi* sprizzare; (*increase speed*) scattare

spy /spaɪ/ *n* spia *f* ● *v* (pt/pp **spied**) ● *vi* spiare ● *vt* (**!**: *see*) spiare. □ ~ **on** *vi* spiare

squabble /'skwɒbl/ *n* bisticcio *m* ● *vi* bisticciare

squad /skwɒd/ *n* squadra *f*; (Sport) squadra

squadron /'skwɒdrən/ *n* (Mil) squadrone *m*; (Aeron), (Naut) squadriglia *f*

squalid /'skwɒlɪd/ *adj* squallido

squalor /'skwɒlə(r)/ *n* squallore *m*

squander /'skwɒndə(r)/ *vt* sprecare

square /skweə(r)/ *adj* quadrato; (*meal*) sostanzioso; (**!**: *old-fashioned*) vecchio stampo; **all** ~ **!** pari ● *n* quadrato *m*; (*in city*) piazza *f*; (*on chessboard*) riquadro *m* ● *vt* (*settle*) far quadrare, (*Math*) elevare al quadrato ● *vi* (*agree*) armonizzare

squash /skwɒʃ/ *n* (*drink*) spremuta *f*; (*sport*) squash *m*; (*vegetable*) zucca *f* ● *vt* schiacciare; soffocare (rebellion)

squat /skwɒt/ *adj* tarchiato ● *n* **!** edificio *m* occupato abusivamente ● *vi* (pt/pp **squatted**) accovacciarsi; ~ **in** occupare abusivamente. ~**ter** *n* occupante *mf* abusivo, -a

squawk /skwɔːk/ *n* gracchio *m* ● *vi* gracchiare

squeak /skwiːk/ *n* squittio *m*; (*of hinge, brakes*) scricchiolio *m* ● *vi* squittire; (hinge, brakes): scricchiolare

squeal /skwiːl/ *n* strillo *m*; (*of brakes*) cigolio *m* ● *vi* strillare; **x** spifferare

squeamish /'skwiːmɪʃ/ *adj* dallo stomaco delicato

squeeze /skwiːz/ *n* stretta *f*; (*crush*)

pigia pigia m inv ● vt premere; (to get juice) spremere; stringere (hand); (force) spingere a forza; (⚡: extort) estorcere (out of da). □ ~ in/out vi sgusciare dentro/fuori. □ ~ up vi stringersi

squid /skwɪd/ n calamaro m

squiggle /ˈskwɪgl/ n scarabocchio m

squint /skwɪnt/ n strabismo m ● vi essere strabico

squirm /skwɜːm/ vi contorcersi; (feel embarrassed) sentirsi imbarazzato

squirrel /ˈskwɪrəl/ n scoiattolo m

squirt /skwɜːt/ n spruzzo m; (⚡: person) presuntuoso m ● vt/i spruzzare

St abbr (Saint) S; abbr Street

stab /stæb/ n pugnalata f, coltellata f; (sensation) fitta f; (⚡: attempt) tentativo m ● vt (pt/pp stabbed) pugnalare, accoltellare

stability /stəˈbɪlətɪ/ n stabilità f inv

stabilize /ˈsteɪbɪlaɪz/ vt stabilizzare ● vi stabilizzarsi

stable¹ /ˈsteɪbl/ adj stabile

stable² n stalla f; (establishment) scuderia f

stack /stæk/ n catasta f; (of chimney) comignolo m; (chimney) ciminiera f; (⚡: large quantity) montagna f ● vt accatastare

stadium /ˈsteɪdɪəm/ n stadio m

staff /stɑːf/ n (stick) bastone m; (employees) personale m; (teachers) corpo m insegnante; (Mil) Stato m Maggiore ● vt fornire di personale. ~-room n (Sch) sala f insegnanti

stag /stæg/ n cervo m

stage /steɪdʒ/ n palcoscenico m; (profession) teatro m; (in journey) tappa f; (in process) stadio m; **go on the** ~ darsi al teatro; **by** or **in** ~s a tappe ● vt mettere in scena; (arrange) organizzare

stagger /ˈstægə(r)/ vi barcollare ● vt sbalordire; scaglionare (holidays etc); **I was** ~ed sono rimasto sbalordito

● n vacillamento m. ~ing adj sbalorditivo

stagnant /ˈstægnənt/ adj stagnante

stagnat|e /stægˈneɪt/ vi fig [ri]stagnare. ~ion n fig inattività f

'stag party n addio m al celibato

staid /steɪd/ adj posato

stain /steɪn/ n macchia f; (for wood) mordente m ● vt macchiare; (wood) dare il mordente a; ~ed glass vetro m colorato; ~ed-glass window vetrata f colorata. ~less adj senza macchia; (steel) inossidabile. ~ remover n smacchiatore m

stair /steə(r)/ n gradino m; ~s pl scale fpl. ~case n scale fpl

stake /steɪk/ n palo m; (wager) posta f; (Comm) partecipazione f; **at** ~ in gioco ● vt puntellare; (wager) scommettere

stale /steɪl/ adj stantio; (air) viziato; (uninteresting) trito [e ritrito]. ~mate n (in chess) stallo m; (deadlock) situazione f di stallo

stalk¹ /stɔːk/ n gambo m

stalk² vt inseguire ● vi camminare impettito

stall /stɔːl/ n box m inv; (in market) bancarella f; ~s pl (Theat) platea f ● vi (engine:) spegnersi; fig temporeggiare ● vt far spegnere (engine); tenere a bada (person)

stallion /ˈstæljən/ n stallone m

stalwart /ˈstɔːlwət/ adj fedele

stamina /ˈstæmɪnə/ n [capacità f inv di] resistenza f

stammer /ˈstæmə(r)/ n balbettio m ● vt/i balbettare

stamp /stæmp/ n (postage ~) francobollo m; (instrument) timbro m; fig impronta f ● vt affrancare (letter); timbrare (bill); battere (feet). □ ~ out vt spegnere; fig soffocare

stampede /stæmˈpiːd/ n fuga f precipitosa; (⚡: fuggi-fuggi m ● vi fuggire precipitosamente

stance /stɑːns/ n posizione f

stand /stænd/ n (for bikes) rastrelliera f; (at exhibition) stand m inv; (in market) bancarella f; (in stadium) gradinata f pr ~ll posizione f ● v (pt/pp stood) ● vi stare in piedi; (rise) alzarsi [in piedi]; (be) trovarsi; (be candidate) essere candidato (for a); (stay valid) rimanere valido; ~ **still** non muoversi; **I don't know where I ~** non so qual'è la mia posizione; ~ **firm** fig tener duro; ~ **together** essere solidali; ~ **to lose/gain** rischiare di perdere/vincere; ~ **to reason** essere logico ● vt (withstand) resistere a; (endure) sopportare; (place) mettere; ~ **a chance** avere una possibilità; ~ **one's ground** tener duro; ~ **the test of time** superare la prova del tempo; ~ **sb a beer** offrire una birra a qcno. □ ~ **by** vi stare a guardare; (be ready) essere pronto ● vt (support) appoggiare. □ ~ **down** vi (retire) ritirarsi. □ ~ **for** vt (mean) significare; (tolerate) tollerare. □ ~ **in for** vt sostituire. □ ~ **out** vi spiccare. □ ~ **up** vi alzarsi [in piedi]. □ ~ **up for** vt prendere le difese di; ~ **up for oneself** farsi valere. □ ~ **up to** vt affrontare

standard /ˈstændəd/ adj standard; **he ~ practice** essere pratica corrente ● n standard m inv; (Techn) norma f; (level) livello m; (quality) qualità f inv; (flag) stendardo m; ~**s** pl (morals) valori mpl; ~ **of living** tenore m di vita. ~**ize** vt standardizzare

'standard lamp n lampada f a stelo

'stand-by n riserva f; **on** ~ (at airport) in lista d'attesa

'stand-in n controfigura f

standing /ˈstændɪŋ/ adj (erect) in piedi; (permanent) permanente ● n posizione f; (duration) durata f. ~ **'order** n addebitamento m diretto. ~**-room** n posti mpl in piedi

stand: ~**point** n punto m di vista. ~**still** n come to a ~**still** fermarsi; **at a ~still** in un periodo di stasi

stank /stæŋk/ ▷STINK

staple[1] /ˈsteɪpl/ n (product) prodotto m principale

staple[2] n graffa f ● vt pinzare. ~**r** n pinzatrice f, cucitrice f

star /stɑː(r)/ n stella f; (asterisk) asterisco m; (Cinema, Sport, Theat) divo, -a mf, stella f ● vi (pt/pp starred) essere l'interprete principale

starboard /ˈstɑːbəd/ n tribordo m

starch /stɑːtʃ/ n amido m ● vt inamidare. ~**y** adj ricco di amido; fig compito

stare /steə(r)/ n sguardo m fisso ● vi **it's rude to** ~ è da maleducati fissare la gente; ~ **at** fissare; ~ **into space** guardare nel vuoto

'starfish n stella f di mare

stark /stɑːk/ adj austero; (contrast) forte ● adv completamente; ~ **naked** completamente nudo

starling /ˈstɑːlɪŋ/ n storno m

starry /ˈstɑːrɪ/ adj stellato

start /stɑːt/ n inizio m; (departure) partenza f; (jump) sobbalzo m; **from the** ~ [fin] dall'inizio; **for a** ~ tanto per cominciare; **give sb a** ~ (Sport) dare un vantaggio a qcno ● vi [in]cominciare; (set out) avviarsi; (engine, car:) partire; (jump) trasalire; **to** ~ **with,...** tanto per cominciare,... ● vt [in]cominciare; (cause) dare inizio a; (found) mettere su; mettere in moto (car); mettere in giro (rumour). ~**er** n (Culin) primo m (piatto m); (in race: giving signal) starter m inv; (participant) concorrente mf; (Auto) motorino m d'avviamento. ~**ing-point** n punto m di partenza

startle /ˈstɑːtl/ vt far trasalire; (news:) sconvolgere

starvation /stɑːˈveɪʃn/ n fame f

starve /stɑːv/ vi morire di fame ● vt far morire di fame

state /steɪt/ n stato m; (grand style) pompa f; ~ **of play** punteggio m; **be in a** ~ (person:) essere agitato;

lie in ~ essere esposto ● *attrib* di Stato; (Sch) pubblico; (with ceremony) di gala ● *vt* dichiarare; (specify) precisare. **~less** *adj* apolide

stately /'steɪtlɪ/ *adj* (-ier, -iest) maestoso. **~ 'home** *n* dimora *f* signorile

statement /'steɪtmənt/ *n* dichiarazione *f*; (Jur) deposizione *f*; (in banking) estratto *m* conto; (account) rapporto *m*

'statesman *n* statista *mf*

static /'stætɪk/ *adj* statico

station /'steɪʃn/ *n* stazione *f*; (police) commissariato *m* ● *vt* appostare (guard); **be ~ed in Germany** essere di stanza in Germania. **~ary** *adj* immobile

'station-wagon *n Am* familiare *f*

statistic|al /stə'tɪstɪkl/ *adj* statistico. **~s** *n & pl* statistica *f*

statue /'stætjuː/ *n* statua *f*

stature /'stætʃə(r)/ *n* statura *f*

status /'steɪtəs/ *n* condizione *f*; (high rank) alto rango *m*. **~ symbol** *n* status symbol *m inv*

statut|e /'stætjuːt/ *n* statuto *m*. **~ory** *adj* statutario

staunch /stɔːntʃ/ *adj* fedele. **~ly** *adv* fedelmente

stave /steɪv/ *vt* **~ off** tenere lontano

stay /steɪ/ *n* soggiorno *m* ● *vi* restare, rimanere; (reside) alloggiare; **~ the night** passare la notte; **~ put** non muoversi ● *vt* resistere. **~ the course** resistere fino alla fine. **□ ~ away** *vi* stare lontano. **□ ~ behind** *vi* non andare con gli altri. **□ ~ in** *vi* (at home) stare in casa; (Sch) restare a scuola dopo le

lezioni. **□ ~ up** *vi* stare su; (person:) stare alzato

stead /sted/ *n* **in his ~** in sua vece; **stand sb in good ~** tornare utile a qcno. **~fast** *adj* fedele; (refusal) fermo

steadily /'stedɪlɪ/ *adv* (continually) continuamente

steady /'stedɪ/ *adj* (-ier, -iest) saldo, fermo; (breathing) regolare; (job, boyfriend) fisso; (dependable) serio

steak /steɪk/ *n* (for stew) spezzatino *m*; (for grilling, frying) bistecca *f*

steal /stiːl/ *v* (pt **stole**, pp **stolen**) ● *vt* rubare (from da). **□ ~ in/out** *vi* entrare/uscire furtivamente

stealth /stelθ/ *n* **by ~** di nascosto. **~y** *adj* furtivo

steam /stiːm/ *n* vapore *m*; **under one's own ~** 🔲 da solo ● *vt* (Culin) cucinare a vapore ● *vi* fumare. **□ ~ up** *vi* appannarsi

'steam-engine *n* locomotiva *f*

'steamer *n* piroscafo *m*; (saucepan) pentola *f* a vapore

'steamroller *n* rullo *m* compressore

steamy /'stiːmɪ/ *adj* appannato

steel /stiːl/ *n* acciaio *m* ● *vt* **~ one-self** temprarsi

steep¹ /stiːp/ *vt* (soak) lasciare a bagno

steep² *adj* ripido; (🔲: price) esorbitante. **~ly** *adv* ripidamente

steeple /'stiːpl/ *n* campanile *m*. **~chase** *n* corsa *f* ippica a ostacoli

steer /stɪə(r)/ *vt/i* guidare; **~ clear of** stare alla larga da. **~ing** *n* (Auto) sterzo *m*. **~ing-wheel** *n* volante *m*

stem¹ /stem/ *n* stelo *m*; (of glass) gambo *m*; (of word) radice *f* ● *vi* (pt/pp **stemmed**) **~ from** derivare da

stem² *vt* (pt/pp **stemmed**) contenere

stench /stentʃ/ *n* fetore *m*

step /step/ *n* passo *m*; (stair) gradino *m*; **~s** *pl* (ladder) scala *f* portatile; **in**

~ al passo; **be out of** ~ non stare al passo; ~ **by** ~ un passo alla volta ● vi (pt/pp stepped) ~ **into** entrare in; ~ **out** of uscire da; ~ **out of line** sgarrare. □ ~ **down** vi fig dimettersi □ ~ **forward** vi farsi avanti. □ ~ **in** vi fig intervenire. □ ~ **up** vt (increase) aumentare

step: ~**brother** n fratellastro m. ~**daughter** n figliastra f. ~**father** n patrigno m. ~**ladder** n scala f portatile. ~**mother** n matrigna f

'stepping-stone n pietra f per guadare; fig trampolino m

step: ~**sister** n sorellastra f. ~**son** n figliastro m

stereo /'steriǝʊ/ n stereo m; **in** ~ in stereofonia. ~**phonic** adj stereofonico

stereotype /'oterɪǝtaɪp/ n stereotipo m. ~**d** adj stereotipato

steril|e /'sterail/ adj sterile. ~**ity** n sterilità f inv

sterling /'stɜːlɪŋ/ adj sterling; appreziabile; ~ **silver** argento m pregiato ● n sterlina f

stern¹ /stɜːn/ adj severo

stern² n (of boat) poppa f

stethoscope /'steθǝskǝʊp/ n stetoscopio m

stew /stjuː/ n stufato m; **in a** ~ 🔲 agitato ● vt/i cuocere in umido; ~**ed fruit** frutta f cotta

steward /'stjuːǝd/ n (at meeting) organizzatore, -trice mf; (on ship, aircraft) steward m inv. ~**ess** n hostess f inv

stick¹ /stɪk/ n bastone m; (of celery, rhubarb) gambo m; (Sport) mazza f

stick² v (pt/pp stuck) ● vt (stab) [con]ficcare; (glue) attaccare; (🔲: put) mettere; (🔲: endure) sopportare ● vi (adhere) attaccarsi (**to** a); (jam) bloccarsi; ~ **to** attenersi a (facts); mantenere (story); perseverare (in task); ~ **at it** 🔲 tener duro; ~ **at nothing** 🔲 non fermarsi di fronte a niente; **be stuck** (vehicle, person:)

essere bloccato; (drawer:) essere incastrato; **be stuck with sth** 🔲 farsi incastrare con qcsa. □ ~ **out** vi (project) sporgere; (🔲: catch the eye) risaltare ● vt 🔲 fare (tongue). □ ~ **up for** vt 🔲 difendere

sticker /'stɪkǝ(r)/ n autoadesivo m

'sticking plaster n cerotto m

stickler /'stɪklǝ(r)/ n **be a** ~ **for** tenere molto a

sticky /'stɪkɪ/ adj (-ier, -iest) appiccicoso; (adhesive) adesivo, (fig: difficult) difficile

stiff /stɪf/ adj rigido; (brush, task) duro; (person) controllato; (drink) forte; (penalty) severo; (price) alto; **bored** ~ 🔲 annoiato a morte; ~ **neck** torcicollo m. ~**en** vt irrigidire ● vi irrigidirsi. ~**ness** n rigidità f inv

stifl|e /'staɪfl/ vt soffocare. ~**ing** adj soffocante

still¹ /stɪl/ n distilleria f

still² adj fermo; (drink) non gasato; **keep/stand** ~ stare fermo ● n quiete f; (photo) posa f ● adv ancora; (nevertheless) nondimeno, comunque; **I'm** ~ **not sure** non sono ancora sicuro

'stillborn adj nato morto

still 'life n natura f morta

stilted /'stɪltɪd/ adj artificioso

stilts /stɪlts/ npl trampoli mpl

stimulant /'stɪmjʊlǝnt/ n eccitante m

stimulat|e /'stɪmjʊleɪt/ vt stimolare. ~**ion** n stimolo m

stimulus /'stɪmjʊlǝs/ n (pl -**li** /-laɪ/) stimolo m

sting /stɪŋ/ n puntura f; (from nettle, jellyfish) sostanza f irritante; (organ) pungiglione m ● v (pt/pp stung) ● vt pungere; (jellyfish:) pizzicare ● vi (insect:) pungere. ~**ing nettle** n ortica f

stingy /'stɪndʒɪ/ adj (-ier, -iest) tirchio

stink /stɪŋk/ n puzza f ● vi (pt stank,

pp **stunk**) puzzare

stipulat|e /'strpjʊleɪt/ *vt* porre come°condizione. **~ion** *n* condizione *f*

stir /stɜː(r)/ *n* mescolata *f*; (*commotion*) trambusto *m* ● *v* (*pt/pp* **stirred**) ● *vt* muovere; (*mix*) mescolare ● *vi* muoversi

stirrup /'strrəp/ *n* staffa *f*

stitch /strtʃ/ *n* punto *m*; (*in knitting*) maglia *f*; (*pain*) fitta *f*; **have sb in ~es** far ridere qcno a crepapelle ● *vt* cucire

stock /stɒk/ *n* (*for use or selling*) scorta *f*, stock *m inv*; (*livestock*) bestiame *m*; (*lineage*) stirpe *f*; (*Fin*) titoli *mpl*; (*Culin*) brodo *m*; **in ~** disponibile; **out of ~** esaurito; **take ~** *fig* fare il punto ● *adj* solito ● *vt* (*shop*) vendere; approvvigionare (*shelves*). □ **~ up** *vi* far scorta (**with** di)

stock: **~broker** *n* agente *m* di cambio. **S~ Exchange** *n* Borsa *f* Valori

stocking /'stɒkɪŋ/ *n* calza *f*

stock: **~pile** *vt* fare scorta di ● *n* riserva *f*. **~'still** *adj* immobile. **~-taking** *n* (*Comm*) inventario *m*

stocky /'stɒkɪ/ *adj* (**-ier, -iest**) tarchiato

stodgy /'stɒdʒɪ/ *adj* indigesto

stoke /stəʊk/ *vt* alimentare

stole[1] /stəʊl/ *n* stola *f*

stole[2], **stolen** /'stəʊln/ ▷**STEAL**

stomach /'stʌmək/ *n* pancia *f*; (*Anat*) stomaco *m* ● *vt* 🔲 reggere. **~-ache** *n* mal *m* di pancia

stone /stəʊn/ *n* pietra *f*; (*in fruit*) nocciolo *m*; (*Med*) calcolo *m*; (*weight*) 6,348 *kg* ● *adj* di pietra; (*wall, Age*) della pietra ● *vt* snocciolare (*fruit*). **~-cold** *adj* gelido. **~'deaf** *adj* 🔲 sordo come una campana

stony /'stəʊnɪ/ *adj* pietroso; (*glare*) glaciale

stood /stʊd/ ▷**STAND**

stool /stuːl/ *n* sgabello *m*

stoop /stuːp/ *n* curvatura *f* ● *vi* stare curvo; (*bend down*) chinarsi; *fig* abbassarsi

stop /stɒp/ *n* (*break*) sosta *f*; (*for bus, train*) fermata *f*; (*Gram*) punto *m*; **come to a ~** fermarsi; **put a ~ to sth** mettere fine a qcsa ● *v* (*pt/pp* **stopped**) ● *vt* fermare; arrestare (*machine*); (*prevent*) impedire; **~ sb doing sth** impedire a qcno di fare qcsa; **~ doing sth** smettere di fare qcsa; **~ that!** smettila! ● *vi* fermarsi; (*rain:*) smettere ● *int* fermo!. □ **~ off** *vi* fare una sosta. □ **~ up** *vt* otturare (*sink*); tappare (*hole*). □ **~ with** *vi* 🔲 stay with) fermarsi da

stop: **~gap** *n* palliativo *m*; (*person*) tappabuchi *m inv*. **~-over** *n* sosta *f*; (*Aeron*) scalo *m*

stoppage /'stɒpɪdʒ/ *n* ostruzione *f*; (*strike*) interruzione *f*; (*deduction*) trattenute *fpl*

stopper /'stɒpə(r)/ *n* tappo *m*

stop-watch *n* cronometro *m*

storage /'stɔːrɪdʒ/ *n* deposito *m*; (*in warehouse*) immagazzinaggio *m*; (*Comput*) memoria *f*

store /stɔː(r)/ *n* (*stock*) riserva *f*; (*shop*) grande magazzino *m*; (*depot*) deposito *m*; **in ~** in deposito; **what the future has in ~ for me** cosa mi riserva il futuro; **set great ~ by** tenere in gran conto ● *vt* tenere; (*in warehouse, Comput*) immagazzinare. **~-room** *n* magazzino *m*

storey /'stɔːrɪ/ *n* piano *m*

stork /stɔːk/ *n* cicogna *f*

storm /stɔːm/ *n* temporale *m*; (*with thunder*) tempesta *f* ● *vt* prendere d'assalto. **~y** *adj* tempestoso

story /'stɔːrɪ/ *n* storia *f*; (*in newspaper*) articolo *m*

stout /staʊt/ *adj* (*shoes*) resistente; (*fat*) robusto; (*defence*) strenuo

stove /stəʊv/ *n* stufa *f*; (*for cooking*) cucina *f* [economica]

stow /stəʊ/ *vt* metter via. **~away** *n*

passeggero, -a *mf* clandestino, -a

straggle /'strægl/ *vi* crescere disordinatamente; (*dawdle*) rimanere indietro. **~er** *n* persona *f* che rimane indietro. **~y** *adj* in disordine

straight /streɪt/ *adj* diritto, dritto; (*answer, question, person*) diretto; (*tidy*) in ordine; (*drink, hair*) liscio ● *adv* diritto, dritto; (*directly*) direttamente; **~ away** immediatamente; **~ on** *or* **ahead** diritto; **~ out** *fig* apertamente; **go ~** ◻ rigare diritto; **put sth ~** mettere qcsa in ordine; **sit/stand up ~** stare diritto

straighten /'streɪtn/ *vt* raddrizzare ● *vi* raddrizzarsi; **~ [up]** (*person:*) mettersi diritto. □ **~ out** *vt fig* chiarire (*situation*)

straight'forward *adj* franco; (*simple*) semplice

strain[1] /streɪn/ *n* (*streak*) vena *f*; (*Bot*) varietà *f inv*; (*of virus*) forma *f*

strain[2] *n* tensione *f*; (*injury*) stiramento *m* ● *s pl* (*of music*) note *fpl* ● *vt* tirare; sforzare (*eyes, voice*); stirarsi (*muscle*); (*Culin*) scolare ● *vi* sforzarsi. **~ed** *adj* (*relations*) teso. **~er** *n* colino *m*

strait /streɪt/ *n* stretto *m*; **in dire ~s** in serie difficoltà. **~jacket** *n* camicia *f* di forza. **~-laced** *adj* puritano

strand[1] /strænd/ *n* (*of thread*) gugliata *f*; (*of beads*) filo *m*; (*of hair*) capello *m*

strand[2] *vt* be **~ed** rimanere bloccato

strange /streɪndʒ/ *adj* strano; (*not known*) sconosciuto; (*unaccustomed*) estraneo. **~ly** *adv* stranamente; **~ly enough** curiosamente. **~r** *n* estraneo, -a *m*

strangle /'stræŋgl/ *vt* strangolare; *fig* reprimere

strap /stræp/ *n* cinghia *f* (*to grasp in vehicle*) maniglia *f*; (*of watch*) cinturino *m*; (*shoulder ~*) bretella *f*, spallina *f* ● *vt*

(*pt/pp* **strapped**) legare; **~ in** *or* **down** assicurare

strategic /strə'tiːdʒɪk/ *adj* strategico

strategy /'strætədʒɪ/ *n* strategia *f*

straw /strɔː/ *n* paglia *f*; (*single piece*) fuscello *m*; (*for drinking*) cannuccia *f*; **the last ~** l'ultima goccia

strawberry /'strɔːbərɪ/ *n* fragola *f*

stray /streɪ/ *adj* (*animal*) randagio ● *n* randagio *m* ● *vi* andarsene per conto proprio; (*deviate*) deviare (**from** da)

streak /striːk/ *n* striatura *f*; (*fig: trait*) vena *f* ● *vi* sfrecciare. **~y** *adj* striato; (*bacon*) grasso

stream /striːm/ *n* ruscello *m*; (*current*) corrente *f*; (*of blood, people*) flusso *m*; (*Sch*) classe *f* ● *vi* scorrere. □ **~ in/out** *vi* entrare/uscire a fiotti

streamer /'striːmə(r)/ *n* (*paper*) stella *f* filante; (*flag*) pennone *m*

streamline *vt* rendere aerodinamico; (*simplify*) snellire. **~d** *adj* aerodinamico

street /striːt/ *n* strada *f*. **~car** *n Am* tram *m inv*. **~lamp** *n* lampione *m*

strength /streŋθ/ *n* forza *f*; (*of wall, bridge etc*) solidità *f inv*; **~s** punti *mpl* forti; **on the ~ of** grazie a. **~en** *vt* rinforzare

strenuous /'strenjʊəs/ *adj* faticoso; (*attempt, denial*) energico

stress /stres/ *n* (*emphasis*) insistenza *f*; (*Gram*) accento *m* tonico; (*mental*) stress *m inv*; (*Mech*) spinta *f* ● *vt* (*emphasize*) insistere su; (*Gram*) mettere l'accento [tonico] su. **~ed** *adj* (*mentally*) stressato. **~ful** *adj* stressante

stretch /stretʃ/ *n* stiramento *m*; (*period*) periodo *m* di tempo; (*of road*) estensione *f*; (*elasticity*) elasticità *f inv*; **at a ~** di fila; **have a ~** stirarsi ● *vt* tirare; allargare (*shoes, arms etc*); (*person:*) allungare ● *vi* (*become wider*) allargarsi; (*extend*) estendersi; (*person:*) stirarsi. **~er** *n* barella *f*

strict /strɪkt/ *adj* severo; (*precise*)

s

preciso. **~ly** adv severamente; **~ly speaking** in senso stretto

stride /straɪd/ n [lungo] passo m; **take sth in one's ~** accettare qcsa con facilità ● vi (pt **strode**, pp **stridden**) andare a gran passi

strident /'straɪdənt/ adj stridente; (colour) vistoso

strife /straɪf/ n conflitto m

strike /straɪk/ n sciopero m; (Mil) attacco m; **on ~** in sciopero ● v (pt/pp **struck**) ● vt colpire; accendere (match); trovare (oil, gold); (delete) depennare; (occur to) venire in mente a; (Mil) attaccare ● vi (lightning:) cadere; (clock:) suonare; (Mil) attaccare; (workers:) scioperare; **~ lucky** azzeccarla. **□ ~ off, strike out** vt eliminare. **□ ~ up** vt fare (friendship); attaccare (conversation). **~-breaker** n persona f che non aderisce a uno sciopero

striker /'straɪkə(r)/ n scioperante mf

striking /'straɪkɪŋ/ adj impressionante; (attractive) affascinante

string /strɪŋ/ n spago m; (of musical instrument, racket) corda f; (of pearls) filo m; (of lies) serie f; **the ~s** (Mus) gli archi; **pull ~s** 🔢 usare le proprie conoscenze ● vt (pt/pp **strung**) (thread) infilare (beads). **~ed** adj (instrument) a corda

stringent /'strɪndʒənt/ adj rigido

strip /strɪp/ n striscia f ● v (pt/pp **stripped**) ● vt spogliare; togliere le lenzuola a (bed); scrostare (wood, furniture); smontare (machine); (deprive) privare (**of** di) ● vi (undress) spogliarsi. **~ cartoon** n striscia f. **~ club** n locale m di strip-tease

stripe /straɪp/ n striscia f; (Mil) gallone m. **~d** adj a strisce

strip-'tease n spogliarello m, striptease m inv

strive /straɪv/ vi (pt **strove**, pp **striven**) sforzarsi (**to** di); **~ for** sforzarsi di ottenere

strode /strəʊd/ ▷ **STRIDE**

stroke¹ /strəʊk/ n colpo m; (of pen) tratto m; (in swimming) bracciata f; (Med) ictus m inv; **~ of luck** colpo m di fortuna; **put sb off his ~** far perdere il filo a qcno

stroke² vt accarezzare

stroll /strəʊl/ n passeggiata f ● vi passeggiare. **~er** n (Am: push-chair) passeggino m

strong /strɒŋ/ adj (-**er** /-gə(r)/, -**est** /-gɪst/) forte; (argument) valido

strong: **~hold** n roccaforte f. **~ly** adv fortemente. **~-room** n camera f blindata

stroppy /'strɒpɪ/ adj scorbutico

strove /strəʊv/ ▷ **STRIVE**

struck /strʌk/ ▷ **STRIKE**

structural /'strʌktʃərəl/ adj strutturale. **~ly** adv strutturalmente

structure /'strʌktʃə(r)/ n struttura f

struggle /'strʌgl/ n lotta f; **with a ~** lottare con ● vi lottare; **~ for breath** respirare con fatica; **~ to do sth** fare fatica a fare qcsa; **~ to one's feet** alzarsi con fatica

strum /strʌm/ vt/i (pt/pp **strummed**) strimpellare

strung /strʌŋ/ ▷ **STRING**

strut¹ /strʌt/ n (component) puntello m

strut² vi (pt/pp **strutted**) camminare impettito

stub /stʌb/ n mozzicone m; (counterfoil) matrice f ● vt (pt/pp **stubbed**) **~ one's toe** sbattere il dito del piede (**on** contro). **□ ~ out** vt spegnere (cigarette)

stubble /'stʌbl/ n barba f ispida. **~ly** adj ispido

stubborn /'stʌbən/ adj testardo; (refusal) ostinato

stuck /stʌk/ ▷ **STICK²**. **~-'up** adj 🔢 snob

stud¹ /stʌd/ n (on boot) tacchetto m;

(on jacket) borchia f; (for ear) orecchino m [a bottone]

stud² n (of horses) scuderia f

student /ˈstjuːdənt/ n studente m, studentessa f; (school child) scolaro, -a mf. ~ **nurse** n studente, studentessa m infermiere, -a

studio /ˈstjuːdɪəʊ/ n studio m

studious /ˈstjuːdɪəs/ adj studioso; (attention) studiato

study /ˈstʌdɪ/ n studio m ● vt/i (pt/pp studied) studiare

stuff /stʌf/ n materiale m; (🇮🇹: things) roba f ● vt riempire; (with padding) imbottire; (Culin) farcire; ~ **sth into a drawer/one's pocket** ficcare qcsa alla rinfusa in un cassetto/in tasca. ~**ing** n (padding) imbottitura f; (Culin) ripieno m

stuffy /ˈstʌfɪ/ adj (-ier, -iest) che sa di chiuso; (old-fashioned) antiquato

stumbl|e /ˈstʌmbl/ vi inciampare; ~**e across** or **on** imbattersi in. ~**ing-block** n ostacolo m

stump /stʌmp/ n ceppo m; (of limb) moncone m. ~**ed** adj 🇮🇹 perplesso ● **stump up** vt/i 🇮🇹 sganciare

stun /stʌn/ vt (pt/pp stunned) stordire; (astonish) shalordire

stung /stʌŋ/ ▷ STING

stunk /stʌŋk/ ▷ STINK

stunning /ˈstʌnɪŋ/ adj favoloso; (blow, victory) sbalorditivo

stunt¹ /stʌnt/ n 🇮🇹 trovata f pubblicitaria

stunt² vt arrestare lo sviluppo di. ~**ed** adj stentato

stupendous /stjuːˈpendəs/ adj stupendo. ~**ly** adv stupendamente

stupid /ˈstjuːpɪd/ adj stupido. ~**ity** n stupidità f. ~**ly** adv stupidamente

stupor /ˈstjuːpə(r)/ n torpore m

sturdy /ˈstɜːdɪ/ adj (-ier, -iest) robusto; (furniture) solido

stutter /ˈstʌtə(r)/ n balbuzie f ● vt/i balbettare

sty, stye /staɪ/ n (pl **styes**) (Med) orzaiolo m

style /staɪl/ n stile m; (fashion) moda f; (sort) tipo m; (hair~) pettinatura f; **in ~** in grande stile

stylish /ˈstaɪlɪʃ/ adj elegante. ~**ly** adv con eleganza

stylist /ˈstaɪlɪst/ n stilista mf; (hair~) parrucchiere, -a mf. ~**ic** adj stilistico

stylus /ˈstaɪləs/ n (on record player) puntina f

suave /swɑːv/ adj dai modi garbati

sub'conscious /sʌb-/ adj subcosciente ● n subcosciente m. ~**ly** adv in modo inconscio

subdivi|de vt suddividere. ~**sion** n suddivisione f

subject¹ /ˈsʌbdʒɪkt/ adj ~ **to** soggetto a; (depending on) subordinato a; ~ **to availability** nei limiti della disponibilità ● n soggetto m; (of ruler) suddito, -a mf; (Sch) materia f

subject² /səbˈdʒekt/ vt (to attack, abuse) sottoporre; assoggettare (country)

subjective /səbˈdʒektɪv/ adj soggettivo. ~**ly** adv soggettivamente

subjunctive /səbˈdʒʌŋktɪv/ adj & n congiuntivo m

sublime /səˈblaɪm/ adj sublime. ~**ly** adv sublimemente

subma'rine n sommergibile m

submerge /səbˈmɜːdʒ/ vt immergere; **be ~d** essere sommerso ● vi immergersi

submiss|ion /səbˈmɪʃn/ n sottomissione f. ~**ive** adj sottomesso

submit /səbˈmɪt/ v (pt/pp -mitted, pres p -mitting) ● vt sottoporre ● vi sottomettersi

subordinate /səˈbɔːdɪnət/ adj subordinare (to a)

subscribe /səbˈskraɪb/ vi contribuire; ~ **to** abbonarsi a (newspaper); sottoscrivere (fund); fig aderire a. ~**r** n abbonato, -a mf

subscription /səb'skrɪpʃn/ n (to club) sottoscrizione f; (to newspaper) abbonamento m

subsequent /'sʌbsɪkwənt/ adj susseguente. ~ly adv in seguito

subside /səb'saɪd/ vi sprofondare; (ground:) avvallarsi; (storm:) placarsi

subsidiary /səb'sɪdɪərɪ/ adj secondario ● n ~ [company] filiale f

subsid|ize /'sʌbsɪdaɪz/ vt sovvenzionare. ~y n sovvenzione f

substance /'sʌbstəns/ n sostanza f

sub'standard adj di qualità inferiore

substantial /səb'stænʃl/ adj solido; (meal) sostanzioso; (considerable) notevole. ~ly adv notevolmente; (essentially) sostanzialmente

substitut|e /'sʌbstɪtjuːt/ n sostituto m ● vt ~e A for B sostituire B con A ● vi ~e for sb sostituire qcno. ~ion n sostituzione f

subterranean /sʌbtə'reɪnɪən/ adj sotterraneo

'subtitle n sottotitolo m

sub|tle /'sʌtl/ adj sottile; (taste, perfume) delicato. ~tlety n sottigliezza f. ~tly adv sottilmente

subtract /səb'trækt/ vt sottrarre. ~ion n sottrazione f

suburb /'sʌbɜːb/ n sobborgo m; in the ~s in periferia. ~an adj suburbano. ~ia n i sobborghi mpl

subversive /səb'vɜːsɪv/ adj sovversivo

'subway n sottopassaggio m; (Am: railway) metropolitana f

succeed /sək'siːd/ vi riuscire; (follow) succedere a ● vt ~ in doing riuscire a fare ● vt succedere a (king). ~ing adj successivo

success /sək'ses/ n successo m; be a ~ (in life) aver successo. ~ful adj riuscito; (businessman, artist etc) di successo. ~fully adv con successo

succession /sək'seʃn/ n successione f; in ~ di seguito

successive /sək'sesɪv/ adj successivo. ~ly adv successivamente

successor /sək'sesə(r)/ n successore m

succulent /'sʌkjʊlənt/ adj succulento

succumb /sə'kʌm/ vi soccombere (to a)

such /sʌtʃ/ adj tale; ~ a book un libro di questo genere; ~ a thing una cosa di questo genere; ~ a long time ago talmente tanto tempo fa; there is no ~ thing non esiste una cosa così; there is no ~ person non esiste una persona così ● pron as ~ come tale; ~ as chi; and ~ e simili; ~ as it is così com'è. ~like pron Ⓣ di tal genere

suck /sʌk/ vt succhiare. □ ~ up vt assorbire. □ ~ up to vt Ⓣ fare il lecchino con

sucker /'sʌkə(r)/ n (Bot) pollone m; (Ⓣ: person) credulone, -a mf

suction /'sʌkʃn/ n aspirazione f

sudden /'sʌdn/ adj improvviso ● n all of a ~ all'improvviso. ~ly adv improvvisamente

sue /suː/ vt (pres p suing) citare a (for per) ● vi fare causa

suede /sweɪd/ n pelle f scamosciata

suet /'suːɪt/ n grasso m di rognone

suffer /'sʌfə(r)/ vi soffrire (from per) ● vt soffrire (loss etc); (tolerate) subire. ~ing n sofferenza f

suffice /sə'faɪs/ vi bastare

sufficient /sə'fɪʃnt/ adj sufficiente. ~ly adv sufficientemente

suffix /'sʌfɪks/ n suffisso m

suffocat|e /'sʌfəkeɪt/ vt/i soffocare. ~ion n soffocamento m

sugar /'ʃʊɡə(r)/ n zucchero m ● vt zuccherare. ~ basin, ~-bowl n zuccheriera f. ~y adj zuccheroso; fig sdolcinato

suggest /sə'dʒest/ vt suggerire; (indicate, insinuate) fare pensare a. ~ion n suggerimento m; (trace) traccia f.

~**ive** *adj* allusivo. ~**ively** *adv* in modo allusivo

suicidal /suː'saɪdl/ *adj* suicida

suicide /'suːɪsaɪd/ *n* suicidio *m*; (*person*) suicida *mf*; **commit** ~ suicidarsi

suit /suːt/ *n* vestito *m*; (*woman's*) tailleur *m inv*; (*in cards*) seme *m*; (*Jur*) causa *f*; **follow** ~ *fig* fare lo stesso ● *vt* andar bene a; (*adapt*) adattare (**to** a); (*be convenient for*) andare bene per; **be** ~**ed to** or **for** essere adatto a; ~ **yourself!** fa' come vuoi!

suitable /'suːtəbl/ *adj* adatto. ~**y** *adv* convenientemente

'**suitcase** *n* valigia *f*

suite /swiːt/ *n* suite *f inv*; (*of furniture*) divano *m* e poltrone *fpl* assortiti

suik /sʌlk/ *vi* fare il broncio. ~**y** *adj* imbronciato

sullen /'sʌlən/ *adj* svogliato

sulphur /'sʌlfə(r)/ *n* zolfo *m*. ~**ic acid** *n* acido *m* solforico

sultana /sʌl'tɑːnə/ *n* uva *f* sultanina

sultry /'sʌltrɪ/ *adj* (**-ier, -iest**) (*weather*) afoso, *fig* sensuale

sum /sʌm/ *n* somma *f*; (*Sch*) addizione *f*. ~ **up** (*pt/pp* **summed**) *vi* riassumere ● *vt* valutare

summar|ize /'sʌmaraɪz/ *vt* riassumere. ~**y** *n* sommario *m* ● *adj* sommario; (*dismissal*) sbrigativo

summer /'sʌmə(r)/ *n* estate *f*. ~**-house** *n* padiglione *m*. ~**time** *n* (*season*) estate *f*

Summer camp Negli Stati Uniti indica il campeggio estivo cui moltissimi ragazzi si recano per socializzare e praticare attività ricreative e sportive all'aria aperta; tra queste il nuoto, il canottaggio, l'arrampicata e i corsi di sopravvivenza.

---

summery /'sʌmərɪ/ *adj* estivo

summit /'sʌmɪt/ *n* cima *f*. ~ **conference** *n* vertice *m*

summon /'sʌmən/ *vt* convocare; (*Jur*) citare. ~ **up** *vt* raccogliere (strength); rievocare (memory)

summons /'sʌmənz/ *n* (*Jur*) citazione *f* ● *vt* citare in giudizio

sumptuous /'sʌmptjʊəs/ *adj* sontuoso. ~**ly** *adv* sontuosamente

sun /sʌn/ *n* sole *m* ● *vt* (*pt/pp* **sunned**) ~ **oneself** prendere il sole

sun: ~**bathe** *vi* prendere il sole. ~**burn** *n* scottatura *f* (solare). ~**burnt** *adj* scottato (dal sole)

Sunday /'sʌndeɪ/ *n* domenica *f*

'**sunflower** *n* girasole *m*

sung /sʌŋ/ ▷**SING**

'**sun-glasses** *npl* occhiali *mpl* da sole

sunk /sʌŋk/ ▷**SINK**

sunken /'sʌŋkn/ *adj* incavato

'**sunlight** *n* [luce *f* del] sole *m*

sunny /'sʌnɪ/ *adj* (**-ier, -iest**) assolato

sun: ~**rise** *n* alba *f*. ~**-roof** *n* (*Auto*) tettuccio *m* apribile. ~**set** *n* tramonto *m*. ~**shine** *n* [luce *f* del] sole *m*. ~**stroke** *n* insolazione *f*. ~**-tan** *n* abbronzatura *f*. ~**-tan oil** *n* olio *m* solare

super /'suːpə(r)/ *adj* 🄸 fantastico

superb /suː'pɜːb/ *adj* splendido

supercilious /suːpə'sɪlɪəs/ *adj* altezzoso

superficial /suːpə'fɪʃl/ *adj* superficiale. ~**ly** *adv* superficialmente

superfluous /suː'pɜːflʊəs/ *adj* superfluo

super'human *adj* sovrumano

superintendent /suːpərɪn'tendənt/ *n* (*of police*) commissario *m* di polizia

superior /suː'pɪərɪə(r)/ *adj* superiore ● *n* superiore, -a *mf*. ~**ity** *n* superiorità *f*

superlative /suː'pɜːlətɪv/ *adj* eccellente ● *n* superlativo *m*

'**supermarket** *n* supermercato *m*

super'natural adj soprannaturale

'superpower n superpotenza f

supersede /su:pə'si:d/ vt rimpiazzare

super'sonic adj supersonico

superstiti|on /su:pə'stɪʃn/ n superstizione f. **~ous** adj superstizioso

supervis|e /'su:pəvaɪz/ vt supervisionare. **~ion** n supervisione f. **~or** n supervisore m

supper /'sʌpə(r)/ n cena f

supple /'sʌpl/ adj slogato

supplement /'sʌplɪmənt/ n supplemento m ● vt integrare. **~ary** adj supplementare

supplier /sə'plaɪə(r)/ n fornitore, -trice mf

supply /sə'plaɪ/ n fornitura f; (in economics) offerta f; **supplies** pl (Mil) approvvigionamenti mpl ● vt (pt/pp -ied) fornire; **~ sb with sth** fornire qcsa a qcno

support /sə'pɔ:t/ n sostegno m; (base) supporto m; (keep) sostentamento m ● vt sostenere; mantenere (family); (give money to) mantenere finanziariamente; (Sport) fare il tifo per. **~er** n sostenitore, -trice mf; (Sport) tifoso, -a mf. **~ive** adj incoraggiante

suppose /sə'pəʊz/ vt (presume) supporre; (imagine) pensare; **be ~d to do** dover fare; **not be ~d to** 🅣 non avere il permesso di; **I ~ so** suppongo di sì. **~dly** adv presumibilmente

suppress /sə'pres/ vt sopprimere. **~ion** n soppressione f

supremacy /su:'preməsɪ/ n supremazia f

supreme /su:'pri:m/ adj supremo

sure /ʃʊə(r)/ adj sicuro, certo; **make ~** accertarsi; **be ~ to do it** mi raccomando di farlo ● adv Am 🅣 certamente; **~ enough** infatti. **~ly** adv certamente; (Am: gladly) volentieri

surety /'ʃʊərətɪ/ n garanzia f; **stand**

~ for garantire

surf /sɜːf/ n schiuma f ● vt (Comput) **~ the Net** surfare in Internet

surface /'sɜːfɪs/ n superficie f; **on the ~** fig in apparenza ● vi (emerge) emergere. **~ mail** n **by ~ mail** per posta ordinaria

'surfboard n tavola f da surf

surfing /'sɜːfɪŋ/ n surf m inv

surge /sɜːdʒ/ n (of sea) ondata f; (of interest) aumento m; (in demand) impennata f; (of anger, pity) impeto m ● vi riversarsi; **~ forward** buttarsi in avanti

surgeon /'sɜːdʒən/ n chirurgo m

surgery /'sɜːdʒərɪ/ n chirurgia f; (place, consulting room) ambulatorio m; (hours) ore fpl di visita; **have ~** subire un'intervento [chirurgico]

surgical /'sɜːdʒɪkl/ adj chirurgico

surly /'sɜːlɪ/ adj (-ier, -iest) scontroso

surmise /sə'maɪz/ vt supporre

surmount /sə'maʊnt/ vt sormontare

surname /'sɜːneɪm/ n cognome m

surpass /sə'pɑːs/ vt superare

surplus /'sɜːpləs/ adj d'avanzo ● n sovrappiù m

surpris|e /sə'praɪz/ n sorpresa f ● vt sorprendere; **be ~ed** essere sorpreso (at da). **~ing** adj sorprendente. **~ingly** adv sorprendentemente

surrender /sə'rendə(r)/ n resa f ● vi arrendersi ● vt cedere

surreptitious /sʌrəp'tɪʃəs/ adj & adv di nascosto

surround /sə'raʊnd/ vt circondare. **~ing** adj circostante. **~ings** npl dintorni mpl

surveillance /sə'veɪləns/ n sorveglianza f

survey¹ /'sɜːveɪ/ n sguardo m; (poll) sondaggio m; (investigation) indagine f; (of land) rilevamento m; (of house) perizia f

survey[2] /sə'veɪ/ vt esaminare; fare un rilevamento di (land); fare una perizia di (building). **~or** n perito m, (of land) topografo, -a mf

survival /sə'vaɪvl/ n sopravvivenza f; (relic) resto m

surviv|e /sə'vaɪv/ vt sopravvivere a ● vi sopravvivere. **~or** n superstite mf; **be a ~or** 🆃 riuscire sempre a cavarsela

susceptible /sə'septəbl/ adj influenzabile; **~ to** sensibile a

suspect[1] /sə'spekt/ vt sospettare; (assume) supporre

suspect[2] /'sʌspekt/ adj & n sospetto, -a mf

suspend /sə'spend/ vt appendere; (stop, from duty) sospendere. **~er belt** n reggicalza m inv. **~ders** npl giarrettiere fpl; (Am: braces) bretelle fpl

suspense /sə'spens/ n tensione f; (in book etc) suspense f

suspension /sə'spenʃn/ n (Auto) sospensione f. **~ bridge** n ponte m sospeso

suspici|on /sə'spɪʃn/ n sospetto m; (trace) pizzico m; **under ~on** sospettato, **~ous** adj sospettoso (arousing suspicion) sospetto. **~ously** adv sospettosamente; (arousing suspicion) in modo sospetto

sustain /sə'steɪn/ vt sostenere; mantenere (life); subire (injury)

swab /swɒb/ n (Med) tampone m

swagger /'swægə(r)/ vi pavoneggiarsi

swallow[1] /'swɒləʊ/ vt/i inghiottire. □ **~ up** n divorare; (earth, crowd:) inghiottire

swallow[2] n (bird) rondine f

swam /swæm/ ▷**SWIM**

swamp /swɒmp/ n palude f ● vt fig sommergere. **~y** adj paludoso

swan /swɒn/ n cigno m

swap /swɒp/ n 🆃 scambio m ● v

(pt/pp swapped) 🆃 scambiare (for con) ● vi fare cambio

swarm /swɔːm/ n sciame m ● vi sciamare; **be ~ing with** brulicare di

swarthy /'swɔːðɪ/ adj (-ier, -iest) di carnagione scura

swat /swɒt/ vt (pt/pp swatted) schiacciare

sway /sweɪ/ n fig influenza f e vi oscillare; (person:) ondeggiare ● vt (influence) influenzare

swear /sweə(r)/ v (pt swore, pp sworn) ● vt giurare ● vi giurare; (curse) dire parolacce; **~ at sb** imprecare contro qcno; **~ by** 🆃 credere ciecamente in. **~word** n parolaccia f

sweat /swet/ n sudore m ● vi sudare

sweater /'swetə(r)/ n golf m inv

swede /swiːd/ n rapa f svedese

Swed|e n svedese mf. **~en** n Svezia f. **~ish** adj svedese

sweep /swiːp/ n scopata f, spazzata f; (curve) curva f; (movement) movimento m ampio; **make a clean ~** fig fare piazza pulita ● v (pt/pp swept) ● vt scopare, spazzare; (wind:) spazzare ● vi (go swiftly) andare rapidamente; (wind:) soffiare. □ **~ away** n fig spazzare via. □ **~ up** vt spazzare

sweeping /'swiːpɪŋ/ adj (gesture) ampio; (statement) generico, (changes) radicale

sweet /swiːt/ adj dolce; **have a ~ tooth** essere goloso ● n caramella f; (dessert) dolce m. **~ corn** n mais m

sweeten /'swiːtn/ vt addolcire. **~er** n dolcificante m

sweetheart n innamorato, -a mf; **hi, ~** ciao, tesoro

swell /swel/ ● v (pt swelled, pp swollen or swelled) ● vi gonfiarsi; (increase) aumentare ● vt gonfiare, (increase) far salire. **~ing** n gonfiore m

swept /swept/ ▷**SWEEP**

swerve /swɜːv/ vi deviare bruscamente

swift /swɪft/ adj rapido. **~ly** adv rapidamente

swig /swɪg/ n 🔲 sorso m • vt (pt/pp swigged) 🔲 scolarsi

swim /swɪm/ n have a ~ fare una nuotata • v (pt swam, pp swum) • vi nuotare; (room:) girare; **my head is ~ming** mi gira la testa • vt percorrere a nuoto. **~mer** n nuotatore, -trice mf

swimming /ˈswɪmɪŋ/ n nuoto m. **~-baths** npl piscina fsg. **~ costume** n costume m da bagno. **~-pool** n piscina f. **~ trunks** npl calzoncini mpl da bagno

'swim-suit n costume m da bagno

swindle /ˈswɪndl/ n truffa f • vt truffare. **~r** n truffatore, -trice mf

swine /swaɪn/ n 🔲 porco m

swing /swɪŋ/ n oscillazione f; (shift) cambiamento m; (seat) altalena f; (Mus) swing m; **in full ~in** piena attività • v (pt/pp swung) • vi oscillare; (on swing, sway) dondolare; (dangle) penzolare; (turn) girare • vt oscillare; far deviare (vote). **~-'door** n porta f a vento

swipe /swaɪp/ n 🔲 botta f • vt 🔲 colpire; (steal) rubare; far passare nella macchinetta (credit card); **~ card** n pass m inv magnetico

Swiss /swɪs/ adj & n svizzero, -a mf; **the ~** pl gli svizzeri. **~ roll** n rotolo m di pan di Spagna ripieno di marmellata

switch /swɪtʃ/ n interruttore m; (change) mutamento m; (exchange) scambiare • vt cambiare; **~ to** passare a. □ **~ off** vt spegnere. □ **~ on** vt accendere

switchboard n centralino m

Switzerland /ˈswɪtsələnd/ n Svizzera f

swivel /ˈswɪvl/ v (pt/pp swivelled) • vt girare • vi girarsi

swollen /ˈswəʊlən/ ▷SWELL • adj gonfio. **~-headed** adj presuntuoso

swoop /swuːp/ n (by police) incur-

sione f • vi **~ [down]** (bird:) piombare; fig fare un'incursione

sword /sɔːd/ n spada f

swore /swɔː(r)/ ▷SWEAR

sworn /swɔːn/ ▷SWEAR

swot /swɒt/ n 🔲 sgobbone, -a mf • vt (pt/pp swotted) 🔲 sgobbare

swum /swʌm/ ▷SWIM

swung /swʌŋ/ ▷SWING

syllable /ˈsɪləbl/ n sillaba f

syllabus /ˈsɪləbəs/ n programma m [dei corsi]

symbol /ˈsɪmbl/ n simbolo m (of di). **~ic** adj simbolico. **~ism** n simbolismo m. **~ize** vt simboleggiare

symmetr|ical /sɪˈmetrɪkl/ adj simmetrico. **~y** n simmetria f

sympathetic /sɪmpəˈθetɪk/ adj (understanding) comprensivo; (showing pity) compassionevole. **~ally** adv con comprensione/compassione

sympathize /ˈsɪmpəθaɪz/ vi capire; (in grief) solidarizzare; **~ with sb** capire qcno/solidarizzare con qcno. **~r** n (Pol) simpatizzante m

sympathy /ˈsɪmpəθɪ/ n comprensione f; (pity) compassione f; (condolences) condoglianze fpl; **in ~ with** (strike) per solidarietà con

symphony /ˈsɪmfənɪ/ n sinfonia f

symptom /ˈsɪmptəm/ n sintomo m. **~atic** adj sintomatico (of di)

synagogue /ˈsɪnəgɒg/ n sinagoga f

synchronize /ˈsɪŋkrənaɪz/ vt sincronizzare

syndicate /ˈsɪndɪkət/ n gruppo m

synonym /ˈsɪnənɪm/ n sinonimo m. **~ous** adj sinonimo

syntax /ˈsɪntæks/ n sintassi f inv

synthesize /ˈsɪnθəsaɪz/ vt sintetizzare. **~r** n (Mus) sintetizzatore m

synthetic /sɪnˈθetɪk/ adj sintetico • n fibra f sintetica

syringe /sɪˈrɪndʒ/ n siringa f

syrup /ˈsɪrəp/ n sciroppo m; treacle tipo m di melassa

system /'sɪstəm/ n sistema m. **~atic** adj sistematico

Tt

tab /tæb/ n linguetta f; (with name) etichetta f; **keep ~s on** 🄫 sorvegliare; **pick up the ~** 🄫 pagare il conto

table /'teɪbl/ n tavolo m; (list) tavola f; **at [the]** ~ a tavola; ~ **of contents** tavola f delle materie ● vt proporre. ~**cloth** n tovaglia f. ~**spoon** n cucchiaio m da tavola. ~**spoon[ful]** n cucchiaiata f

tablet /'tæblɪt/ n pastiglia f; (slab) lastra f; ~ **of soap** saponetta f

table tennis n tennis m da tavolo; (everyday level) ping pong m

tabloid /'tæblɔɪd/ n [giornale m formato] tabloid m inv; pej giornale m scandalistico

taboo /tə'buː/ adj tabù inv ● n tabù m inv

tacit /'tæsɪt/ adj tacito

taciturn /'tæsɪtɜːn/ adj taciturno

tack /tæk/ n (nail) chiodino m; (stitch) imbastitura f; (Naut) virata f; fig linea f di condotta ● vt inchiodare; (sew) imbastire ● vi (Naut) virare

tackle /'tækl/ n (equipment) attrezzatura f; (football etc) contrasto m, tackle m inv ● vt affrontare

tacky /'tækɪ/ adj (paint) non ancora asciutto; (glue) appiccicoso; fig pacchiano

tact /tækt/ n tatto m. ~**ful** adj pieno di tatto; (remark) delicato. ~**fully** adv con tatto

tactic|al /'tæktɪkl/ adj tattico. ~**s** npl tattica fsg

tactless /'tæktlɪs/ adj privo di tatto.

~**ly** adv senza tatto. ~**ness** n mancanza f di tatto; (of remark) indelicatezza f

tadpole /'tædpəʊl/ n girino m

tag[1] /tæg/ n (label) etichetta f ● vt (pt/pp **tagged**) attaccare l'etichetta a. ◻ ~ **along** vi seguire passo passo

tag[2] n (game) acchiapparello m

tail /teɪl/ n coda f; ~**s** pl (tailcoat) frac m inv ● vt (🄫: follow) pedinare. ◻ ~ **off** vi diminuire

tail light n fanalino m di coda

tailor /'teɪlə(r)/ n sarto m. ~**-made** adj fatto su misura

taint /teɪnt/ vt contaminare

take /teɪk/ n (Cinema) ripresa f ● v (pt **took**, pp **taken**) ● vt prendere; (to a place) portare (person, object); (contain) contenere (passengers etc); (endure) sopportare; (require) occorrere; (teach) insegnare; (study) studiare (subject); fare (exam holiday, photograph, walk, bath); sentire (pulse); misurare (sb's temperature); ~ **sb prisoner** fare prigioniero qcno; **be ~n ill** ammalarsi; ~ **sth calmly** prendere con calma qcsa ● vi (plant:) attecchire. ◻ ~ **after** vt assomigliare a. ◻ ~ **away** vt (with one) portare via; (remove) togliere; (subtract) sottrarre; **'to ~ away'** 'da asporto'. ◻ ~ **back** vt riprendere; ritirare (statement); (return) riportare [indietro]. ◻ ~ **down** vt portare giù (remove) tirare giù; (write down) prendere nota di. ◻ ~ **in** vt (bring indoors) portare dentro; (to one's home) ospitare; (understand) capire; (deceive) ingannare; riprendere (garment); (include) includere. ◻ ~ **off** vt togliersi (clothes); (deduct) togliere; (mimic) imitare; ~ **time off** prendere delle vacanze; ~ **oneself off** andarsene ● vi (Aeron) decollare. ◻ ~ **on** vt farsi carico di; assumere (employee); (as opponent) prendersela con. ◻ ~ **out** vt portare fuori; togliere (word, stain); (withdraw) ritirare (money, books); ~

out a subscription to sth abbonarsi a qcsa; ● **it out on sb** ⚏ prendersela con qcno. □ ~ **over** vt assumere il controllo di (firm) ● vi ~ **over from sb** sostituire qcno; (permanently) succedere a qcno. □ ~ **to** vt (as a habit) darsi a; **I took to her** (liked) mi è piaciuta. □ ~ **up** vt portare su; accettare (offer); intraprendere (profession); dedicarsi a (hobby); prendere (time); occupare (space); tirare su (floor-boards); accorciare (dress); ~ **sth up with sb** discutere qcsa con qcno ● vi ~ **up with sb** legarsi a qcno

take /~**off** n (Aeron) decollo m. ~**-over** n rilevamento m

takings /ˈteɪkɪŋz/ npl incassi mpl

tale /teɪl/ n storia f; pej fandonia f

talent /ˈtælənt/ n talento m. ~**ed** adj [ricco] di talento

talk /tɔːk/ n conversazione f; (lecture) conferenza f; (gossip) chiacchiere fpl; **make small** ~ parlare del più e del meno ● vi parlare ● vt parlare di (politics etc); ~ **sb into** sth convincere qcno di qcsa. □ ~ **over** vt discutere

talkative /ˈtɔːkətɪv/ adj loquace

tall /tɔːl/ adj alto. ~**boy** n cassettone m. ~ **order** n impresa f difficile. ~ **'story** n frottola f

tally /ˈtælɪ/ n conteggio m; **keep a** ~ **of** tenere il conto di ● vi coincidere

tambourine /tæmbəˈriːn/ n tamburello m

tame /teɪm/ adj (animal) domestico; (dull) insulso ● vt domare. ~**ly** adv docilmente. ~**r** n domatore, -trice mf

tamper /ˈtæmpə(r)/ vi ~ **with** manomettere

tampon /ˈtæmpɒn/ n tampone m.

tan /tæn/ adj marrone rossiccio ● n marrone m rossiccio; (from sun) abbronzatura f ● v (pt/pp **tanned**) ● vt conciare (hide) ● vi abbronzarsi

tang /tæŋ/ n sapore m forte; (smell)

odore m penetrante

tangent /ˈtændʒənt/ n tangente f

tangible /ˈtændʒɪbl/ adj tangibile

tangle /ˈtæŋgl/ n groviglio m; (in hair) nodo m ● vt ~**[up]** aggrovigliare ● vi aggrovigliarsi

tango /ˈtæŋgəʊ/ n tango m inv

tank /tæŋk/ n contenitore m; (for petrol) serbatoio m; (fish ~) acquario m; (Mil) carro m armato

tanker /ˈtæŋkə(r)/ n nave f cisterna; (lorry) autobotte f

tantrum /ˈtæntrəm/ n scoppio m d'ira

tap /tæp/ n rubinetto m; (knock) colpo m; **on** ~ a disposizione ● (pt/pp **tapped**) ● vt dare un colpetto a; sfruttare (resources); mettere sotto controllo (telephone) ● vi picchiettare. ~**-dance** n tip tap m ● vi ballare il tip tap

tape /teɪp/ n nastro m; (recording) cassetta f ● vt legare con nastro; (record) registrare

tape-measure n metro m [a nastro]

taper /ˈteɪpə(r)/ n candela f sottile ● **taper off** vi assottigliarsi

tape recorder n registratore m

tapestry /ˈtæpɪstrɪ/ n arazzo m

tar /tɑː(r)/ n catrame m ● vt (pt/pp **tarred**) incatramare

target /ˈtɑːgɪt/ n bersaglio m; fig obiettivo m

tarnish /ˈtɑːnɪʃ/ vi ossidarsi ● vt ossidare; fig macchiare

tart[1] n crostata f; (individual) crostatina f; (🔞: prostitute) donnaccia f ● **tart up** ⚏ ~ **oneself up** agghindarsi

tart[2] adj aspro; fig acido

tartan /ˈtɑːtn/ n tessuto m scozzese, tartan m inv ● attrib di tessuto scozzese

task /tɑːsk/ n compito m; **take sb to** ~ riprendere qcno. ~ **force** n (Pol)

tassel /'tæsl/ n nappa f

taste /teɪst/ n gusto m; (sample) assaggio m; **get a ~ of** sth fig assaporare il gusto di qcsa ● vt sentire il sapore (of di); **it's ~ly lovely it** è ottimo. **~ful** adj di [buon] gusto. **~fully** adv con gusto. **~less** adj senza gusto. **~lessly** adv con cattivo gusto

tasty /'teɪstɪ/ adj (-ier, -iest) saporito

tat /tæt/ ▷ **TAT²**

tatter|ed /'tætəd/ adj cencioso; (pages) strappato. **~s** npl **in ~s a** brandelli

tattoo¹ /tæ'tuː/ n tatuaggio m ● vt tatuare

tattoo² n (Mil) parata f militare

tatty /'tætɪ/ adj (-ier, -iest) (clothes, person) trasandato; (book) malandato

taught /tɔːt/ ▷ **TEACH**

taunt /tɔːnt/ n scherno m ● vt schernire

Taurus /'tɔːrəs/ n Toro m

taut /tɔːt/ adj teso

tax /tæks/ n tassa f; (on income) imposte fpl; **before ~** (price) tasse escluse; (salary) lordo ● vt tassare; fig mettere alla prova; **~ with** accusare di. **~able** adj tassabile. **~ation** n tasse fpl. **~ evasion** n evasione f fiscale. **~-free** adj esentasse. **~ haven** n paradiso m fiscale

taxi /'tæksɪ/ n taxi m inv ● vi (pt/pp taxied, pres p taxiing) (aircraft:) rullare. **~ driver** n tassista mf. **~ rank** n posteggio m per taxi

'taxpayer n contribuente mf

tea /tiː/ n tè m inv. **~-bag** n bustina f di tè. **~-break** n intervallo m per il tè

teach /tiːtʃ/ vt/i (pt/pp taught) insegnare; **~ sb sth** insegnare qcsa a qcno. **~er** n insegnante mf; (primary)

maestro, -a mf. **~ing** n insegnamento m

teacup n tazza f da tè

team /tiːm/ n squadra f; fig équipe f inv ● **team up** vi unirsi

'team-work n lavoro m di squadra; fig lavoro m d'équipe

teapot n teiera f

tear¹ /teə(r)/ n strappo m ● v (pt tore, pp torn) ● vt strappare ● vi strapparsi; (material:) strapparsi; (run:) precipitarsi. □ **~ apart** vt (fig: criticize) fare a pezzi; (separate) dividere. □ **~ away** vt **~ oneself away** andare via; **~ oneself away from** staccarsi da (television). □ **~ open** vt aprire strappando. □ **~ up** vt strappare; rompere (agreement)

tear² /tɪə(r)/ n lacrima f. **~ful** adj (person) in lacrime; (farewell) lacrimevole. **~fully** adv in lacrime. **~gas** n gas m lacrimogeno

tease /tiːz/ vt prendere in giro (person); tormentare (animal)

tea: **~-set** n servizio m da tè. **~-spoon** n cucchiaino m [da tè]

teat /tiːt/ n capezzolo m; (on bottle) tettarella f

'tea-towel n strofinaccio m [per i piatti]

technical /'teknɪkl/ adj tecnico. **~ity** n tecnicismo m; (Jur) cavillo m giuridico. **~ly** adv tecnicamente; (strictly) strettamente

technician /tek'nɪʃn/ n tecnico, -a mf

technique /tek'niːk/ n tecnica f

technological /teknə'lɒdʒɪkl/ adj tecnologico

technology /tek'nɒlədʒɪ/ n tecnologia f

tedious /'tiːdɪəs/ adj noioso

tedium /'tiːdɪəm/ n tedio m

teem /tiːm/ n (rain) piovere a dirotto; **be ~ing with** (full of) pullulare di

teenage /'ti:neɪdʒ/ adj per ragazzi; ~ **boy/girl** adolescente mf. ~**r** n adolescente mf

teens /ti:nz/ npl **the** ~ l'adolescenza fsg; **be in one's** ~ essere adolescente

teeny /'ti:nɪ/ adj (-**ier**, -**iest**) piccolissimo

teeter /'ti:tə(r)/ vi barcollare

teeth /ti:θ/ ▷**TOOTH**

teeth|e /ti:ð/ vi mettere i [primi] denti. ~**ing troubles** npl fig difficoltà fpl iniziali

telecommunications /telɪkəmju:nɪ'keɪʃnz/ npl telecomunicazioni fpl

telegram /'telɪgræm/ n telegramma m

telepathy /tɪ'lepəθɪ/ n telepatia f

telephone /'telɪfəʊn/ n telefono m; **be on the** ~ avere il telefono; (be telephoning) essere al telefono ● vt telefonare a ● vi telefonare

telephone: ~ **booth** n, ~ **box** n cabina f telefonica. ~ **directory** n elenco m telefonico

telephonist /tɪ'lefənɪst/ n telefonista mf

telescop|e /'telɪskəʊp/ n telescopio m. ~**ic** adj telescopico

televise /'telɪvaɪz/ vt trasmettere per televisione

television /'telɪvɪʒn/ n televisione f; **watch** ~ guardare la televisione. ~ **set** n televisore m

teleworking /'telɪwɜ:kɪŋ/ n telelavoro m

telex /'teleks/ n telex m inv

tell /tel/ vt (pt/pp told) dire; raccontare (story); (distinguish) distinguere (from da); ~ **sb sth** dire qcsa a qcno; ~ **the time** dire l'ora; **I couldn't** ~ **why...** non sapevo perché... ● vi (produce an effect) avere effetto; **time will** ~ il tempo ce lo dirà; **his age is beginning to** ~ l'età comincia a farsi sentire [per

lui]; **you mustn't** ~ non devi dire niente. □ ~ **off** vt sgridare

teller /'telə(r)/ n (in bank) cassiere, -a mf

telling /'telɪŋ/ adj significativo; (argument) efficace

telly /'telɪ/ n 🔲 tv f inv

temp /temp/ n 🔲 impiegato, -a mf temporaneo, -a

temper /'tempə(r)/ n (disposition) carattere m; (mood) umore m; (anger) collera f; **lose one's** ~ arrabbiarsi; **be in a** ~ essere arrabbiato; **keep one's** ~ mantenere la calma

temperament /'tempramant/ n temperamento m. ~**al** adj (moody) capriccioso

temperate /'tempərət/ adj (climate) temperato

temperature /'temprətʃə(r)/ n temperatura f; **have a** ~ avere la febbre

temple[1] /'templ/ n tempio m

temple[2] n (Anat) tempia f

tempo /'tempəʊ/ n ritmo m; (Mus) tempo m

temporar|y /'tempərərɪ/ adj temporaneo; (measure, building) provvisorio. ~**ily** adv temporaneamente; (introduced, erected) provvisoriamente

tempt /tempt/ vt tentare; sfidare (fate); ~ **sb to** indurre qcno a; **be** ~**ed** essere tentato (to di); **I am** ~**ed by the offer** l'offerta mi tenta. ~**ation** n tentazione f. ~**ing** adj allettante; (food, drink) invitante

ten /ten/ adj dieci

tenaci|ous /tɪ'neɪʃəs/ adj tenace. ~**ty** n tenacia f

tenant /'tenənt/ n inquilino, -a mf; (Comm) locatario, -a mf

tend vi ~ **to do sth** tendere a far qcsa

tendency /'tendənsɪ/ n tendenza f

tender[1] /'tendə(r)/ n (Comm) offerta

f: **be legal ~** avere corso legale ● vt offrire; presentare (resignation)

tender² adj tenero; (painful) dolorante. **~ly** adv teneramente. **~ness** n tenerezza f; (painfulness) dolore m

tendon /'tendən/ n tendine m

tennis /'tenɪs/ n tennis m. **~ court** n campo m da tennis. **~ player** n tennista mf

tenor /'tenə(r)/ n tenore m

tense¹ /tens/ n (Gram) tempo m

tense² adj teso ● vt tendere (muscle). □ **~ up** vi tendersi

tension /'tenʃn/ n tensione f

tent /tent/ n tenda f

tentacle /'tentəkl/ n tentacolo m

tentative /'tentətɪv/ adj provvisorio; (smile, gesture) esitante. **~ly** adv timidamente; (accept) provvisoriamente

tenterhooks /'tentəhʊks/ npl **be on ~** essere sulle spine

tenth /tenθ/ adj decimo ● n decimo, -a m/f

tenuous /'tenjʊəs/ adj fig debole

tepid /'tepɪd/ adj tiepido

term /tɜːm/ n periodo m; (Sch) (Univ) trimestre m; (expression) termine m; **~s** pl (conditions) condizioni fpl; **~ of office** carica f; **in the short/long ~** a breve/lungo termine; **be on good/bad ~s** essere in buoni/cattivi rapporti; **come to ~s** with accettare (past, fact); **easy ~s** facilità f di pagamento

terminal /'tɜːmɪn(ə)l/ adj finale; (Med) terminale ● n (Aeron) terminal m inv; (Rail) stazione f di testa; (of bus) capolinea m; (on battery) morsetto m; (Comput) terminale m. **~ly** adv **be ~ly ill** essere in fase terminale

terminat|e /'tɜːmɪneɪt/ vt terminare; rescindere (contract); interrompere (pregnancy) ● vi terminare; **~e in** finire in. **~ion** n termine m; (Med) interruzione f di gravidanza

terminology /tɜːmɪ'nɒlədʒɪ/ n

terminologia f

terrace /'terəs/ n terrazza f; (houses) fila f di case a schiera; **the ~s** (Sport) le gradinate. **~d house** n casa f a schiera

terrain /to'reɪn/ n terreno m

terrible /'terəbl/ adj terribile

terrific /tə'rɪfɪk/ adj **①** (excellent) fantastico; (huge) enorme. **~ally** adv **①** terribilmente

terri|fy /'terɪfaɪ/ vt (pt/pp -ied) atterrire; **be ~fied** essere terrorizzato. **~fying** adj terrificante

territorial /terɪ'tɔːrɪəl/ adj territoriale

territory /'terɪtərɪ/ n territorio m

terror /'terə(r)/ n terrore m. **~ism** n terrorismo m. **~ist** n terrorista mf. **~ize** vt terrorizzare

terse /tɜːs/ adj conciso

test /test/ n esame m; (in laboratory) esperimento m; (of friendship, machine) prova f; (of intelligence, aptitude) test m inv; **put to the ~** mettere alla prova ● vt esaminare; provare (machine)

testament /'testəmənt/ n testamento m; **Old/New T~** Antico/Nuovo Testamento m

testicle /'testɪkl/ n testicolo m

testify /'testɪfaɪ/ vt/i (pt/pp -ied) testimoniare

testimonial /testɪ'məʊnɪəl/ n lettera f di referenze

testimony /'testɪmənɪ/ n testimonianza f

'test: ~ match n partita f internazionale. **~-tube** n provetta f

tether /'teðə(r)/ n **be at the end of one's ~** non poterne più

text /tekst/ n testo m. **~book** n manuale m

textile /'tekstaɪl/ adj tessile ● n stoffa f

text message n sms m inv, breve messaggio m di testo

texture /'tekstʃə(r)/ n (of skin)

t

grana *f*; (*of food*) consistenza *f*; **of a smooth** ∼ (*to the touch*) soffice al tatto

Thames /temz/ *n* Tamigi *m*

than /ðən/, *accentato* /ðæn/ *conj* che; (*with numbers, names*) di; **older** ∼ **me** più vecchio di me

thank /θæŋk/ *vt* ringraziare; ∼ **you** [**very much**] grazie [mille]. ∼**ful** *adj* grato. ∼**fully** *adv* con gratitudine; (*happily*) fortunatamente. ∼**less** *adj* ingrato

thanks /θæŋks/ *npl* ringraziamenti *mpl*; ∼! **1** grazie!; ∼ **to** grazie a

that /ðæt/
● *adj & pron* (*pl* **those**) quel, quei *pl*; (*before s + consonant, gn, ps and z*) quello, quegli *pl*; (*before vowel*) quell' *mf*, quegli *mpl*, quelle *fpl*; ∼ **one** quello; **I don't like those** quelli non mi piacciono; ∼ **is** cioè; **is** ∼ **you?** sei tu?; **who is** ∼? chi è?; **what did you do after** ∼? cosa hai fatto dopo?; **like** ∼ in questo modo, così; **a man like** ∼ un uomo così; ∼ **is why** ecco perché; ∼'s **it!** (*you've understood*) ecco!; (*I've had enough*) basta così!; (*there's nothing more*) tutto qui!; ∼'s ∼! (*with job*) ecco fatto!; (*with relationship*) è tutto finito!; **and** ∼'s ∼! punto e basta! **all** ∼ **I know** tutto quello che so
● *adv* così; **it wasn't** ∼ **good** non era poi così buono
● *rel pron* che; **the man** ∼ **I spoke to** l'uomo con cui ho parlato; **the day** ∼ **I saw him** il giorno in cui l'ho visto; **all** ∼ **I know** tutto quello che so
● *conj* che; **I think** ∼...

thaw /θɔː/ *n* disgelo *m* ● *vt* fare scongelare (food) ● *vi* (food): scon-

gelarsi; **it's** ∼**ing** sta sgelando

the /ðə/, *di fronte a una vocale* /ðiː/
● *def art* il, la *f*; i *mpl*, le *fpl*; (*before s + consonant, gn, ps and z*) lo, gli *mpl*; (*before vowel*) l' *mf*, gli *mpl*, le *fpl*; **at** ∼ **cinema/station** al cinema/alla stazione; **from** ∼ **cinema/station** dal cinema/ dalla stazione
● *adv* ∼ **more** ∼ **better** più ce n'è meglio è; (*with reference to pl*) più ce ne sono, meglio è; **all** ∼ **better** tanto meglio

theatre /ˈθɪətə(r)/ *n* teatro *m*; (*Med*) sala *f* operatoria

theatrical /θɪˈætrɪkl/ *adj* teatrale; (*showy*) melodrammatico

theft /θeft/ *n* furto *m*

their /ðeə(r)/ *adj* il loro *m*, la loro *f*, i loro *mpl*, le loro *fpl*; ∼ **mother/ father** la loro madre/il loro padre

theirs /ðeəz/ *poss pron* il loro *m*, la loro *f*, i loro *mpl*, le loro *fpl*; **a friend of** ∼ un loro amico; **friends of** ∼ dei loro amici; **those are** ∼ quelli sono loro; (*as opposed to ours*) quelli sono i loro

them /ðem/ *pron* (*direct object*) li *m*, le *f*; (*indirect object*) gli, loro *fml*; (*after prep: with people*) loro; (*after preposition: with things*) essi; **we haven't seen** ∼ non li/le abbiamo visti/viste; **give** ∼ **the money** dai loro o dagli i soldi; **give it to** ∼ dagli/elo; **I've spoken to** ∼ ho parlato con loro; **it's** ∼ sono loro

theme /θiːm/ *n* tema *m*. ∼ **park** *n* parco *m* a tema. ∼ **song** *n* motivo *m* conduttore

them'selves *pron* (*reflexive*) si; (*emphatic*) se stessi; **they poured** ∼ **a drink** si sono versati da bere; **they said so** ∼ lo hanno detto loro stessi; **they kept it for** ∼ se lo sono tenuti per sé; **by** ∼ da soli

then /ðen/ *adv* allora; (*next*) poi; **by**

~ (in the past) ormai; (in the future) per allora; **since** ~ sin da allora; **before** ~ prima di allora; **from** ~ **on** da allora in poi; **now and** ~ ogni tanto; **there and** ~ all'istante ● adj di allora

theoretical /θɪə'retɪkl/ adj teorico

theory /'θɪərɪ/ n teoria f; **in** ~ **in** teoria

therapeutic /θerə'pju:tɪk/ adj terapeutico

therap|ist /'θerəpɪst/ n terapista mf. ~**y** n terapia f

there /ðeə(r)/ adv là, lì; **down/up** ~ laggiù/lassù; ~ **is/are** c'è/ci sono; ~ **he/she is** eccolo/eccola ● int ~, ~! dai, su!

there! ~**abouts** adv [or] ~ **abouts** (roughly) all'incirca. ~**fore** /-fɔ:(r)/ adv perciò

thermometer /θə'mɒmɪtə(r)/ n termometro m

thermostat /'θɜ:məstæt/ n termostato m

thesaurus /θɪ'sɔ:rəs/ n dizionario m dei sinonimi

these /ði:z/ ▷ **THIS**

thesis /'θi:sɪs/ n (pl -**ses** /-si:z/) tesi f inv

they /ðeɪ/ pron loro; ~ **are tired** sono stanchi; **we're going, but** ~ **are not** noi andiamo, ma loro no; ~ **say** (generalizing) si dice; ~ **are building a new road** stanno costruendo una nuova strada

thick /θɪk/ adj spesso; (forest) fitto; (liquid) denso; (hair) folto; (囗: stupid) ottuso; (囗: close) molto unito; **be 5 mm** ~ essere 5 mm di spessore ● adv densamente ● n **in the** ~ **of** nel mezzo di. ~**en** v/i ispessire; (sauce) ~ v/i ispessirsi; (fog:) infittirsi. ~**ly** adv densamente; (cut) a fette spesse. ~**ness** n spessore m

thief /θi:f/ n (pl **thieves**) ladro, -a mf

thigh /θaɪ/ n coscia f

thimble /'θɪmbl/ n ditale m

thin /θɪn/ adj (**thinner**, **thinnest**) sottile; (shoes, sweater) leggero; (liquid) liquido; (person) magro; (fig: excuse, plot) inconsistente ● adv ~ **thinly** ● v (pt/pp **thinned**) ● vt diluire (liquid) ● vi diradarsi. □ ~ **out** vi (of radars). ~**ly** adv (populated) scarsamente; (disguised) leggermente; (cut) a fette sottili

thing /θɪŋ/ n cosa f; ~**s** pl (belongings) roba fsg; **for one** ~ in primo luogo; **the right** ~ la cosa giusta; **just the** ~! proprio quel che ci vuole!; **how are** ~**s?** come vanno le cose?; **the latest** ~ ill l'ultima cosa; **the best** ~ **would be** la cosa migliore sarebbe; **poor** ~! poveretto!

think /θɪŋk/ v/t/i (pt/pp **thought**) pensare; (believe) credere; **I** ~ **so** credo di sì; **what do you** ~? (what is your opinion?) cosa ne pensi?; ~ **of/about** pensare a; **what do you** ~ **of it?** cosa ne pensi di questo?. □ ~ **over** vt riflettere su. □ ~ **up** vt escogitare

third /θɜ:d/ adj & n terzo, -a mf. ~**ly** adv terzo. ~**rate** adj scadente

thirst /θɜ:st/ n sete f. ~**ily** adv con sete. ~**y** adj assetato; **be** ~**y** aver sete

thirteen /θɜ:'ti:n/ adj tredici. ~**th** adj tredicesimo

thirtieth /'θɜ:tɪɪθ/ adj trentesimo

thirty /'θɜ:tɪ/ adj trenta

this /ðɪs/ adj (pl **these**) questo; ~ **man/woman** quest'uomo/questa donna; **these men/women** questi uomini/queste donne; ~ **one** questo; ~ **morning/evening** stamattina/stasera ● pron (pl **these**) questo; **we talked about** ~ **and that** abbiamo parlato del più e del meno; **like** ~ così; ~ **is Peter** (Teleph) sono Peter; **who is** ~? (Teleph) chi parla? ● adv così; ~ **big** così grande

thistle /'θɪsl/ n cardo m

thorn /θɔ:n/ n spina f. ~**y** adj

spinoso

thorough /ˈθʌrə/ adj completo; (knowledge) profondo; (clean, search, training) a fondo; (person) scrupoloso

thorough ~**bred** n purosangue m inv. ~**fare** n via f principale; '**no** ~**fare**' 'strada non transitabile'

thorough|**ly** adv (clean, search, know sth) a fondo; (extremely) estremamente. ~**ness** n completezza f

those /ðəʊz/ ▷ THAT

though /ðəʊ/ conj sebbene; **as** ~ come se ● adv **ⅰ** tuttavia

thought /θɔːt/ ▷ THINK ● n pensiero m; (idea) idea f. ~**ful** adj pensieroso; (considerate) premuroso. ~**fully** adv pensierosamente; (considerately) premurosamente. ~**less** adj (inconsiderate) sconsiderato. ~**lessly** adv con noncuranza

thousand /ˈθaʊznd/ adj one/a ~ mille m inv ● n mille m inv; ~**s of** migliaia fpl di. ~**th** adj millesimo ● n millesimo, -a mf

thrash /θræʃ/ vt picchiare; (defeat) sconfiggere. □ ~ **out** vt mettere a punto

thread /θred/ n filo m; (of screw) filetto m ● vt infilare (beads); ~ **one's way through** farsi strada fra. ~**bare** adj logoro

threat /θret/ n minaccia f

threaten /ˈθretn/ vt minacciare (**to do** di fare) ● vi fig incalzare. ~**ing** adj minaccioso; (sky, atmosphere) sinistro

three /θriː/ adj tre. ~**fold** adj & adv triplo. ~**some** n trio m

threshold /ˈθreʃəʊld/ n soglia f

threw /θruː/ ▷ THROW

thrift /θrɪft/ n economia f. ~**y** adj parsimonioso

thrill /θrɪl/ n emozione f; (of fear) brivido m ● vt entusiasmare; **be ~ed with** essere entusiasta di. ~**er** n

(book) [romanzo m] giallo m; (film) [film m] giallo m. ~**ing** adj eccitante

thrive /θraɪv/ vi (pt thrived or throve, pp thrived or thriven / ˈθrɪvn/) (business:) prosperare; (child, plant:) crescere bene; I ~ **on pressure** mi piace essere sotto tensione

throat /θrəʊt/ n gola f; **sore** ~ mal m di gola

throb /θrɒb/ n pulsazione f; (of heart) battito m ● vi (pt/pp throbbed) (vibrate) pulsare; (heart:) battere

throes /θrəʊz/ npl **in the** ~ **of** fig alle prese con

throne /θrəʊn/ n trono m

throng /θrɒŋ/ n calca f

throttle /ˈθrɒtl/ n (on motorbike) manopola f di accelerazione ● vt strozzare

through /θruː/ prep attraverso; (during) durante; (by means of) tramite; (thanks to) grazie a; **Saturday** ~ **Tuesday** Am da sabato a martedì incluso ● adv attraverso; ~ **and** ~ **and** fino in fondo; **wet** ~ completamente bagnato; **read sth** ~ dare una lettura a qcsa; **let** ~ lasciar passare (sb) ● adj (train) diretto; **be** ~ (finished) aver finito; (Teleph) avere la comunicazione

throughout /θruːˈaʊt/ prep per tutto ● adv completamente; (time) per tutto il tempo

throw /θrəʊ/ n tiro m ● vt (pt threw, pp thrown) lanciare; (throw away) gettare; azionare (switch); disarcionare (rider); (**ⅰ**: disconcert) disorientare; **ⅰ** dare (party). □ ~ **away** vt gettare via. □ ~ **out** vt gettare via; rigettare (plan); buttare fuori (person). □ ~ **up** vt alzare ● vi (vomit) vomitare

thrush /θrʌʃ/ n tordo m

thrust /θrʌst/ n spinta f ● vt (pt/pp thrust) (push) spingere; (insert) conficcare; ~ **[up]on** imporre a

thud /θʌd/ n tonfo m

thug /θʌg/ n delinquente m

thumb /θʌm/ n pollice m; **as a rule of ~** come regola generale; **under sb's ~** succube di qcno • vt **~ a lift** fare l'autostop. **~-index** n indice m a rubrica. **~-tack** n Am puntina f da disegno

thump /θʌmp/ n colpo m; (noise) tonfo m • vt battere su (table, door); battere (fist); colpire (person) • vi battere (on su); (heart:) battere forte. □ **~ about** vi camminare pesantemente

thunder /'θʌndə(r)/ n tuono m; (loud noise) rimbombo m • vi tuonare; (make loud noise) rimbombare. **~clap** n rombo m di tuono. **~storm** n temporale m. **~y** adj temporalesco

Thursday /'θɜːzdeɪ/ n giovedì m inv

thus /ðʌs/ adv così

thwart /θwɔːt/ vt ostacolare

Tiber /'taɪbə(r)/ n Tevere m

tick /tɪk/ n (sound) ticchettio m; (mark) segno m; (fam: instant) attimo m • vi ticchettare. □ **~ off** vt spuntare; (fam) sgridare. □ **~ over** vi (engine:) andare al minimo

ticket /'tɪkɪt/ n biglietto m; (for item deposited, library) tagliando m; (label) cartellino m; (fine) multa f. **~-collector** n controllore m. **~-office** n biglietteria f

tick|le /'tɪkl/ n solletico m • vt fare il solletico a; (amuse) divertire • vi fare prurito. **~lish** adj che soffre il solletico

tide /taɪd/ n marea f; (of events) corso m; **the ~ is in/out** c'è alta/ bassa marea • **tide over** vt **~ sb over** aiutare qcno a andare avanti

tidily /'taɪdɪlɪ/ adv in modo ordinato

tidiness /'taɪdɪnɪs/ n ordine m

tidy /'taɪdɪ/ adj (-ier, -iest) ordinato; (fam: amount) bello • vt (pt/pp -ied) **~ [up]** ordinare; **~ oneself up** mettersi in ordine

tie /taɪ/ n cravatta f; (cord) legaccio m; (fig: bond) legame m; (restriction) impedimento m; (Sport) pareggio m • v (pres p tying) • vt legare; fare (knot); **be ~d** (in competition) essere in parità • vi pareggiare. □ **~ in with** vi corrispondere a. □ **~ up** vt legare; vincolare (capital); **be ~d up** (busy) essere occupato

tier /tɪə(r)/ n fila f; (of cake) piano m; (in stadium) gradinata f

tiger /'taɪɡə(r)/ n tigre f

tight /taɪt/ adj stretto; (taut) teso; (fam: drunk) sbronzo; (fam: mean) spilorcio; **~ corner** (fam) brutta situazione f • adv strettamente; (hold) forte; (closed) bene

tighten /'taɪtn/ vt stringere; avvitare (screw); intensificare (control) • vi stringersi

tight: **~-fisted** adj tirchio. **~ly** adv strettamente; (hold) forte; (closed) bene. **~rope** n fune f (da funamboli)

tights /taɪts/ npl collant m inv

tile /taɪl/ n mattonella f; (on roof) tegola f • vt rivestire di mattonelle (wall)

till[1] /tɪl/ prep & conj = until

till[2] n cassa f

tilt /tɪlt/ n inclinazione f; **at full ~** a tutta velocità • vt inclinare • vi inclinarsi

timber /'tɪmbə(r)/ n legname m

time /taɪm/ n tempo m; (occasion) volta f; (by clock) ora f; **two ~s four** due volte quattro; **at any ~** in qualsiasi momento; **this ~** questa volta; **at ~s, from ~ to ~** ogni tanto; **~ and again** cento volte; **two at a ~** due alla volta; **on ~** in orario; **in ~** in tempo; (eventually) col tempo; **in no ~ at all** velocemente; **in a year's ~** fra un anno; **behind ~** in ritardo; **behind the ~s** antiquato; **for the ~ being** per ora; **what is the ~?** che ora è?; **by the ~ we arrive** quando arriviamo; **did you have a nice ~?** ti sei divertito?; **have a good ~!** divertiti! • vt scegliere il momento per; cronometrare (race); **be well ~d** essere ben calcolato

time: ~ **bomb** n bomba f a orologeria. **~ly** adj opportuno. **~-table** n orario m

timid /'tɪmɪd/ adj (shy) timido; (fearful) timoroso

tin /tɪn/ n stagno m; (container) barattolo m • vt (pt/pp **tinned**) inscatolare. ~ **foil** n [carta f] stagnola f

tinge /tɪndʒ/ n sfumatura f • vt **~d with** fig misto a

tingle /'tɪŋgl/ vi pizzicare

tinker /'tɪŋkə(r)/ vi armeggiare

tinkle /'tɪŋkl/ n tintinnio m; (🔊: phone call) colpo m di telefono • vi tintinnare

tinned /tɪnd/ adj in scatola

'**tin opener** n apriscatole m inv

tint /tɪnt/ n tinta f • vt tingersi (hair)

tiny /'taɪnɪ/ adj (-ier, -iest) minuscolo

tip¹ /tɪp/ n punta f

tip² n (money) mancia f; (advice) consiglio m; (for rubbish) discarica f • v (pt/pp **tipped**) • vt (tilt) inclinare; (overturn) capovolgere; (pour) versare; (reward) dare una mancia a • vi inclinarsi; (overturn) capovolgersi. □ **~ off** vt ~ **sb off** (inform) fare una soffiata a qcno. □ **~ out** vt rovesciare. □ **~ over** vt capovolgere • vi capovolgersi

tipped /tɪpt/ adj (cigarette) col filtro

tipsy /'tɪpsɪ/ adj 🔊 brillo

tiptoe /'tɪptəʊ/ n **on ~** in punta di piedi

tiptop /tɪp'tɒp/ adj 🔊 in condizioni perfette

tire /'taɪə(r)/ vt stancare • vi stancarsi. **~d** adj stanco; **~d of** stanco di; **~d out** stanco morto. **~less** adj instancabile. **~some** adj fastidioso

tiring /'taɪərɪŋ/ adj stancante

tissue /'tɪʃu:/ n tessuto m; (handkerchief) fazzolettino m di carta.

~-paper n carta f velina

tit¹ /tɪt/ n (bird) cincia f

tit² n **~ for tat** pan per focaccia

title /'taɪtl/ n titolo m. **~-deed** n atto m di proprietà. **~-role** n ruolo m principale

---

to /tu:/, atono /tə/

● prep a; (to countries) in; (towards) verso; (up to, until) fino a; **I'm going to John's/the butcher's** vado da John/dal macellaio; **come/go to sb** venire/andare da qcno; **to Italy/Switzerland** in Italia/Svizzera; **I've never been to Rome** non sono mai stato a Roma; **go to the market** andare al mercato; **to the toilet/my room** in bagno/camera mia; **to an exhibition** a una mostra; **to university** all'università; **twenty/quarter to eight** le otto meno venti/un quarto; **5 to 6 kilos** da 5 a 6 chili; **to the end** alla fine; **to this day** fino a oggi; **to the best of my recollection** per quanto mi possa ricordare; **give/say sth to sb** dare/dire qcsa a qcno; **give it to me** dammelo; **there's nothing to it** è una cosa da niente

● verbal constructions **to go** andare; **learn to swim** imparare a nuotare; **I want to/have to go** voglio/devo andare; **it's easy to forget** è facile da dimenticare; **too ill/tired to go** troppo malato/stanco per andare; **you have to** devi; **I don't want to** non voglio; **I'll be 90** vivere fino a 90 anni; **he was the last to arrive** è stato l'ultimo ad arrivare; **to be honest,...** per essere sincero,...

● adv **pull to** chiudere; **to and fro** avanti e indietro

toad /təʊd/ n rospo m. **~stool** n fungo m velenoso

toast /təʊst/ n pane m tostato; (drink) brindisi m ● vt tostare (bread); (drink a ~ to) brindare a. **~er** n tostapane m inv

tobacco /tə'bækəʊ/ n tabacco m. **~nist's [shop]** n tabaccheria f

toboggan /tə'bɒgən/ n toboga m ● vi andare in toboga

today /tə'deɪ/ adj & adv oggi m; a week ~ una settimana a oggi; **~'s paper** il giornale di oggi

toddler /'tɒdlə(r)/ n bambino, -a m/f ai primi passi

toe /təʊ/ n dito m del piede; (of footwear) punta f; **big ~** alluce m ● vt the line rigar diritto. **~nail** n unghia f del piede

toffee /'tɒfi/ n caramella f al mou

together /tə'geðə(r)/ adv insieme; (at the same time) allo stesso tempo; ~ with insieme a

toilet /'tɔɪlɪt/ n (lavatory) gabinetto m. ~ paper n carta f igienica

toiletries /'tɔɪlɪtrɪz/ npl articoli mpl da toilette

toilet roll n rotolo m di carta igienica

token /'təʊkən/ n segno m; (counter) gettone m; (voucher) buono m ● attrib simbolico

told /təʊld/ ▷ TELL ● adj all ~ in tutto

tolerab|le /'tɒl(ə)rəbl/ adj tollerabile; (not bad) discreto. **~y** adv discretamente

toleran|ce /'tɒl(ə)r(ə)ns/ n tolleranza f. **~t** adj tollerante. **~tly** adv con tolleranza

tolerate /'tɒləreɪt/ vt tollerare

toll[1] /təʊl/ n pedaggio m; **death ~** numero m di morti

toll[2] vi suonare a morto

tomato /tə'mɑːtəʊ/ n (pl -es) pomodoro m. ~ **ketchup** n ketchup m.

~ **purée** n concentrato m di pomodoro

tomb /tuːm/ n tomba f

'tombstone n pietra f tombale

tomorrow /tə'mɒrəʊ/ adj & adv domani m; ~ **morning** domani mattina; **the day after ~** dopodomani; **see you ~!** a domani!

ton /tʌn/ n tonnellata f (= 1,016 kg.); **~s of** [I] un sacco di

tone /təʊn/ n tono m; (colour) tonalità f inv ● **tone down** vt attenuare. □ ~ **up** vt tonificare (muscles)

tongs /tɒŋz/ npl pinze fpl

tongue /tʌŋ/ n lingua f; ~ **in cheek** (say) ironicamente. **~-twister** n scioglilingua m inv

tonic /'tɒnɪk/ n tonico m; (for hair) lozione f per i capelli, fig toccasana m inv; ~ [**water**] acqua f tonica

tonight /tə'naɪt/ adj adv stanotte; (evening) stasera ● n questa notte f; (evening) questa sera f

tonne /tʌn/ n tonnellata f metrica

tonsil /'tɒnsl/ n (Anat) tonsilla f. **~litis** n tonsillite f

too /tuː/ adv troppo; (also) anche; ~ **many** troppi; ~ **much** troppo, ~ **little** troppo poco

took /tʊk/ ▷ TAKE

tool /tuːl/ n attrezzo m

tooth /tuːθ/ n (pl teeth) dente m

tooth|ache n mal m di denti. **~brush** n spazzolino m da denti. **~paste** n dentifricio m. **~pick** n stuzzicadenti m inv

top[1] /tɒp/ n (toy) trottola f

top[2] n cima f; (Sch) primo, -a m/f; (upper part or half) parte f superiore; (of page, list, road) inizio m; (upper surface) superficie f; (lid) coperchio m; (of bottle) tappo m; (garment) maglia f; (blouse) camicia f; (Auto) marcia f in alta; **at the ~** fig al vertice; **at the ~ of one's voice** a squarciagola; **on ~/on ~ of** sopra; **on ~ of that** (besides) per di più; **from ~ to bottom**

da cima a fondo ● *adj* in alto; (official, floor) superiore; (pupil, musician etc) migliore; (speed) massimo ● *vt* (*pt/pp* **topped**) essere in testa a (list); (exceed) sorpassare; **~ped with ice-cream** ricoperto di gelato. □~ **up** *vt* riempire

top: ~ **floor** *n* ultimo piano *m*. ~ **hat** *n* cilindro *m*. **~-heavy** *adj* con la parte superiore sovraccarica

topic /ˈtɒpɪk/ *n* soggetto *m*; (*of conversation*) argomento *m*. **~al** *adj* d'attualità

topless *adj* & *adv* topless

topple /ˈtɒpl/ *vt* rovesciare ● *vi* rovesciarsi. □~ **off** *vi* cadere

top-'secret *adj* segretissimo, top secret *inv*

torch /tɔːtʃ/ *n* torcia *f* [elettrica]; (*flaming*) fiaccola *f*

tore /tɔː(r)/ ▶ TEAR¹

torment¹ /ˈtɔːment/ *n* tormento *m*

torment² /tɔːˈment/ *vt* tormentare

torn /tɔːn/ ▶ TEAR¹ ● *adj* bucato

tornado /tɔːˈneɪdəʊ/ *n* (*pl* -**es**) tornado *m inv*

torpedo /tɔːˈpiːdəʊ/ *n* (*pl* -**es**) siluro *m* ● *vt* silurare

torrent /ˈtɒrənt/ *n* torrente *m*. **~ial** *adj* (rain) torrenziale

tortoise /ˈtɔːtəs/ *n* tartaruga *f*

torture /ˈtɔːtʃə(r)/ *n* tortura *f* ● *vt* torturare

Tory /ˈtɔːrɪ/ *adj* & *n* 🄱 conservatore, -trice *mf*

toss /tɒs/ *vt* gettare; (into the air) lanciare in aria; (shake) scrollare; (horse:) disarcionare; mescolare (salad); rivoltare facendo saltare in aria (pancake); ~ **a coin** fare testa o croce ● *vi* ~ **and turn** (in bed) rigirarsi; **let's** ~ **for it** facciamo testa o croce

tot¹ /tɒt/ *n* bimbetto, -a *mf*; (🄱: of liquor) goccio *m*

tot² *vt* (*pt/pp* totted) ~ **up** 🄱 fare la somma di

total /ˈtəʊtl/ *adj* totale ● *n* totale *m* ● *vt* (*pt/pp* **totalled**) ammontare a; (add up) sommare

totalitarian /təʊtælɪˈteərɪən/ *adj* totalitario

totally /ˈtəʊtəlɪ/ *adv* totalmente

totter /ˈtɒtə(r)/ *vi* barcollare; (government:) vacillare

touch /tʌtʃ/ *n* tocco *m*; (sense) tatto *m*; (contact) contatto *m*; (trace) traccia *f*; (of irony, humour) tocco *m*; **get/be in** ~ mettersi/essere in contatto ● *vt* toccare; (lightly) sfiorare; (equal) eguagliare; (fig: move) commuovere ● *vi* toccarsi. □~ **down** *vi* (Aeron) atterrare. □~ **on** *vt fig* accennare a.

touch up *vt* ritoccare (painting). **~ing** *adj* commovente. **~screen** *n* touch screen *m inv*. **~-tone** *adj* a tastiera. **~y** *adj* permaloso; (subject) delicato

tough /tʌf/ *adj* duro; (severe, harsh) severo; (durable) resistente; (resilient) forte

toughen /ˈtʌfn/ *vt* rinforzare. □~ **up** *vt* rendere più forte (person)

tour /tʊə(r)/ *n* giro *m*; (of building, town) visita *f*; (Theat), (Sport) tournée *f inv*; (of duty) servizio *m* ● *vt* visitare ● *vi* fare un giro turistico; (Theat) essere in tournée

touris|m /ˈtʊərɪzm/ *n* turismo *m*. **~t** *n* turista *mf* ● *attrib* turistico. **~t office** *n* ufficio *m* turistico

tournament /ˈtʊənəmənt/ *n* torneo *m*

tousle /ˈtaʊzl/ *vt* spettinare

tout /taʊt/ *n* (ticket ~) bagarino *m*; (horse-racing) informatore *m* ● *vi* ~ **for** sollecitare

tow /təʊ/ *n* rimorchio *m*; **'on** ~' 'a rimorchio'; **in** ~ 🄱 al seguito di *fam* rimorchiare. □~ **away** *vt* portare via col carro attrezzi

toward[s] /təˈwɔːd(z)/ *prep* verso (with respect to) nei riguardi di

towel /ˈtaʊəl/ *n* asciugamano *m*.

~**ling** n spugna f

tower /'taʊə(r)/ n torre f ● vi ~ **above** dominare. ~ **block** n palazzone m. ~**ing** adj torreggiante, (rage) violento

town /taʊn/ n città f inv. ~ **'hall** n municipio m

toxic /'tɒksɪk/ adj tossico

toy /tɔɪ/ n giocattolo m. ~**shop** n negozio m di giocattoli. □ ~ **with** vt giocherellare con

trace /treɪs/ n traccia f ● vt seguire le tracce di; (find) rintracciare; (draw) tracciare; (with tracing-paper) ricalcare

track /træk/ n traccia f; (path, (Sport)) pista f; (Rail) binario m; **keep ~ of** tenere d'occhio ● vt seguire le tracce di. □ ~ **down** vt scovare

tracksuit n tuta f da ginnastica

tractor /'træktə(r)/ n trattore m

trade /treɪd/ n commercio m; (line of business) settore m; (craft) mestiere m; **by ~** di mestiere ● vt commerciare; ~ **sth for sth** scambiare qcsa per qcsa ● vi commerciare. □ ~ **in** vt (give in part exchange) dare in pagamento parziale

'trade mark n marchio m di fabbrica

trader /'treɪdə(r)/ n commerciante mf

trades 'union n sindacato m

tradition /trə'dɪʃn/ n tradizione f. ~**al** adj tradizionale. ~**ally** adv tradizionalmente

traffic /'træfɪk/ n traffico m ● vi (pt/ pp **trafficked**) trafficare

traffic: ~ **circle** n Am isola f rotatoria. ~ **jam** n ingorgo m. ~ **lights** npl semaforo msg. ~ **warden** n vigile m [urbano]; (woman) vigilessa f

tragedy /'trædʒɪdɪ/ n tragedia f

tragic /'trædʒɪk/ adj tragico. ~**ally** adv tragicamente

trail /treɪl/ n traccia f; (path) sentiero m ● vi strisciare; (plant:) arrampicarsi; ~ [**behind**] rimanere indietro; (in

competition) essere in svantaggio ● vt trascinare

trailer /'treɪlə(r)/ n (Auto) rimorchio m; (Am: caravan) roulotte f inv, (film) presentazione f (di un film)

train /treɪn/ n treno m; ~ **of thought** filo m dei pensieri ● vt formare professionalmente; (Sport) allenare; (aim) puntare; educare (child); addestrare (animal, soldier) ● vi fare il tirocinio; (Sport) allenarsi. ~**ed** adj (animal) addestrato (**to do** a fare)

trainee /treɪ'niː/ n apprendista mf

train|er /'treɪnə(r)/ n (Sport) allenatore, -trice mf; (in circus) domatore, -trice mf; (of dog, race-horse) addestratore, -trice mf; ~**ers** pl scarpe fpl da ginnastica. ~**ing** n tirocinio m; (Sport) allenamento m; (of animal, soldier) addestramento m

trait /treɪt/ n caratteristica f

traitor /'treɪtə(r)/ n traditore, -trice mf

tram /træm/ n tram m inv. ~ **lines** npl rotaie fpl del tram

tramp /træmp/ n (hike) camminata f; (vagrant) barbone, -a mf; (of feet) calpestio m ● vi camminare con passo pesante; (hike) percorrere a piedi

trample /'træmpl/ vt/i ~ [**on**] calpestare

trampoline /'træmpəliːn/ n trampolino m

trance /trɑːns/ n trance f inv

tranquil /'træŋkwɪl/ adj tranquillo. ~**lity** n tranquillità f

tranquillizer /'træŋkwɪlaɪzə(r)/ n tranquillante m

transatlantic /trænzət'læntɪk/ adj transatlantico

transcend /træn'send/ vt trascendere

transfer¹ /'trænsfɜː(r)/ n trasferimento m; (Sport) cessione f; (design) decalcomania f

transfer² /træns'fɜː(r)/ v (pt/pp

transferred ●*vt* trasferire; (*Sport*) cedere ● *vi* trasferirsi; (*when travelling*) cambiare. ~**able** *adj* trasferibile

transform /træns'fɔːm/ *vt* trasformare. ~**ation** *n* trasformazione *f*. ~**er** *n* trasformatore *m*

transfusion /træns'fjuːʒn/ *n* trasfusione *f*

transient /'trænzɪənt/ *adj* passeggero

transistor /træn'zɪstə(r)/ *n* transistor *m inv*; (*radio*) radiolina *f* a transistor

transit /'trænzɪt/ *n* transito *m*; **in** ~ (*goods*) in transito

transition /træn'zɪʃn/ *n* transizione *f*. ~**al** *adj* di transizione

transitive /'trænzɪtɪv/ *adj* transitivo

translat|e /trænz'leɪt/ *vt* tradurre. ~**ion** *n* traduzione *f*. ~**or** *n* traduttore, -trice *mf*

transmission /trænz'mɪʃn/ *n* trasmissione *f*

transmit /trænz'mɪt/ *vt* (*pt/pp* **transmitted**) trasmettere. ~**ter** *n* trasmettitore *m*

transparen|cy /træn'spærənsɪ/ *n* (*Phot*) diapositiva *f*. ~**t** *adj* trasparente

transplant[1] /'trænsplɑːnt/ *n* trapianto *m*

transplant[2] /træns'plɑːnt/ *vt* trapiantare

transport[1] /'trænspɔːt/ *n* trasporto *m*

transport[2] /træns'pɔːt/ *vt* trasportare. ~**ation** *n* trasporto *m*

trap /træp/ *n* trappola *f*; (🔒: *mouth*) boccaccia *f* ● *vt* (*pt/pp* **trapped**) intrappolare; schiacciare (*finger in door*). ~**door** *n* botola *f*

trapeze /trə'piːz/ *n* trapezio *m*

trash /træʃ/ *n* robaccia *f*; (*rubbish*) spazzatura *f*; (*nonsense*) schiocchezze *fpl*. ~**can** *n* Am secchio *m* della spazzatura. ~**y** *adj* scadente

travel /'trævl/ *n* viaggi *mpl* ● *v* (*pt/pp* **travelled**) ● *vi* viaggiare; (*to work*) andare ● *vt* percorrere (*distance*). ~ **agency** *n* agenzia *f* di viaggi. ~ **agent** *n* agente *mf* di viaggio

traveller /'trævələ(r)/ *n* viaggiatore, -trice *mf*; (*Comm*) commesso *m* viaggiatore; ~**s** *pl* (*gypsies*) zingari *mpl*. ~**'s cheque** *n* traveller's cheque *m inv*

trawler /'trɔːlə(r)/ *n* peschereccio *m*

tray /treɪ/ *n* vassoio *m*; (*for baking*) teglia *f*; (*for documents*) vaschetta *f* sparticarta; (*of printer, photocopier*) vassoio *m*

treacher|ous /'tretʃərəs/ *adj* traditore; (*weather, currents*) pericoloso. ~**y** *n* tradimento *m*

treacle /'triːkl/ *n* melassa *f*

tread /tred/ *n* andatura *f*; (*step*) gradino *m*; (*of tyre*) battistrada *m inv* ● *v* (*pt* **trod**, *pp* **trodden**) ● *vi* (*walk*) camminare. □ ~ **on** *vt* calpestare (*grass*); pestare (*foot*)

treason /'triːzn/ *n* tradimento *m*

treasure /'treʒə(r)/ *n* tesoro *m* ● *vt* tenere in gran conto. ~**r** *n* tesoriere, -a *mf*

treasury /'treʒərɪ/ *n* the T~ il Ministero del Tesoro

treat /triːt/ *n* piacere *m*; (*present*) regalo *m*; **give sb a** ~ fare una sorpresa a qcno ● *vt* trattare; (*Med*) curare; ~ **sb to sth** offrire qcsa a qcno

treatise /'triːtɪz/ *n* trattato *m*

treatment /'triːtmənt/ *n* trattamento *m*; (*Med*) cura *f*

treaty /'triːtɪ/ *n* trattato *m*

treble /'trebl/ *adj* triplo ● *n* (*Mus: voice*) voce *f* bianca ● *vt* triplicare ● *vi* triplicarsi. ~ **clef** *n* chiave *f* di violino

tree /triː/ *n* albero *m*

trek /trek/ *n* scarpinata *f*; (*as holiday*) trekking *m inv* ● *vi* (*pt/pp* **trekked**) farsi una scarpinata; (*on holiday*) fare trekking

tremble /'trembl/ vi tremare

tremendous /trɪ'mendəs/ adj (huge) enorme; (🔲: excellent) formidabile. **~ly** adv (very) straordinariamente; (adj Inf) enormemente

tremor /'tremə(r)/ n tremito m [earth] **~** scossa f [sismica]

trench /trentʃ/ n fosso m; (Mil) trincea f. **~ coat** n trench m inv

trend /trend/ n tendenza f; (fashion) moda f. **~y** adj (-ier, -iest) 🔲 di o alla moda

trepidation /trepɪ'deɪʃn/ n trepidazione f

trespass /'trespəs/ vi **~ on** introdursi abusivamente in; fig abusare di. **~er** n intruso, -a mf

trial /'traɪəl/ n (Jur) processo m; (test, ordeal) prova f; on **~** in prova; (Jur) in giudizio; **by ~ and error** per tentativi

triangle /'traɪæŋgl/ n triangolo m. **~ular** adj triangolare

tribe /traɪb/ n tribù f inv

tribulation /trɪbjʊ'leɪʃn/ n tribolazione f

tribunal /traɪ'bjuːnl/ n tribunale m

tributary /'trɪbjʊtərɪ/ n affluente m

tribute /'trɪbjuːt/ n tributo m; **pay ~** rendere omaggio

trick /trɪk/ n trucco m; (joke) scherzo m; (in cards) presa f; **do the ~** 🔲 funzionare; **play a ~ on** fare uno scherzo a ● vt imbrogliare

trickle /'trɪkl/ vi colare

trick|ster /'trɪkstə(r)/ n imbroglione, -a mf. **~y** adj (-ier, -iest) adj (operation) complesso; (situation) delicato

tricycle /'traɪsɪkl/ n triciclo m

tried /traɪd/ ▷TRY

trifl|e /'traɪfl/ n inezia f; (Culin) zuppa f inglese. **~ing** adj insignificante

trigger /'trɪgə(r)/ n grilletto m ● vt **~ [off]** scatenare

trim /trɪm/ adj (**trimmer, trimmest**) curato; (figure) snello ● n (of hair, hedge) spuntata f; (decoration) rifinitura f; **in good ~** in buono stato; (per son) in forma ● vt (pt/pp **trimmed**) spuntare (hair, hedge); (decorate) ornare; (Naut) orientare. **~ming** n bordo m; **~mings** pl (decorations) guarnizioni fpl; **with all the ~mings** (Culin) guarnito

trinket /'trɪŋkɪt/ n ninnolo m

trio /'triːəʊ/ n trio m

trip /trɪp/ n (excursion) gita f; (journey) viaggio m; (stumble) passo m falso ● v (pt/pp **tripped**) ● vt far inciampare ● vi inciampare (**on/over** in). **n ~ up** vt far inciampare

tripe /traɪp/ n trippa f; (🔲: nonsense) fesserie fpl

triple /'trɪpl/ adj triplo ● vt triplicare ● vi triplicarsi

triplets /'trɪplɪts/ npl tre gemelli mpl

triplicate /'trɪplɪkət/ n **in ~** in triplice copia

tripod /'traɪpɒd/ n treppiede m inv

trite /traɪt/ adj banale

triumph /'traɪʌmf/ n trionfo m ● vi trionfare (**over** su). **~ant** adj trionfante. **~antly** adv (exclaim) con tono trionfante

trivial /'trɪvɪəl/ adj insignificante. **~ity** n banalità f inv

trolley /'trɒlɪ/ n carrello m; (Am: tram) tram m inv. **~ bus** n filobus m inv

trombone /trɒm'bəʊn/ n trombone m

troop /truːp/ n gruppo m; **~s** pl truppe fpl ● vi **~ in/out** entrare/ uscire in gruppo

trophy /'trəʊfɪ/ n trofeo m

tropic /'trɒpɪk/ n tropico m; **~s** pl tropici mpl. **~al** adj tropicale

trot /trɒt/ n trotto m ● vi (pt/pp **trot ted**) trottare

trouble /'trʌbl/ n guaio m; (difficulties) problemi mpl; (inconvenience, Med) disturbo m; (conflict) conflitto *m*; **be in** ~ essere nei guai; (swimmer, climber:) essere in difficoltà; **get into** ~ finire nei guai; **get sb into** ~ mettere a qcno nei guai; **take the** ~ **to do sth** darsi la pena di far qcsa ● *vt* (worry) preoccupare; (inconvenience) disturbare; (conscience, cold wound:) tormentare ● *vi* **don't** ~**!** non ti disturbare!. ~**maker** *n* be a ~-maker seminare zizzania. ~**some** *adj* fastidioso

trough /trɒf/ *n* trogolo *m*; (atmospheric) depressione *f*

troupe /tru:p/ *n* troupe *f inv*

trousers /'trauzəz/ *npl* pantaloni *mpl*

trout /traut/ *n inv* trota *f*

trowel /'trauəl/ *n* (for gardening) paletta *f*; (for builder) cazzuola *f*

truant /'tru:ənt/ *n* **play** ~ marinare la scuola

truce /tru:s/ *n* tregua *f*

truck /trʌk/ *n* (lorry) camion *m inv*

trudge /trʌdʒ/ *n* camminata *f* faticosa ● *vi* arrancare

true /tru:/ *adj* vero; **come** ~ avverarsi

truffle /'trʌfl/ *n* tartufo *m*

truly /'tru:lɪ/ *adv* veramente; **Yours** ~ distinti saluti

trump /trʌmp/ *n* (in cards) atout *m inv*

trumpet /'trʌmpɪt/ *n* tromba *f*. ~**er** *n* trombettista *m inv*

truncheon /'trʌntʃn/ *n* manganello *m*

trunk /trʌŋk/ *n* (of tree, body) tronco *m*; (of elephant) proboscide *f*; (for travelling, storage) baule *m*; (Am: of car) bagagliaio *m*; ~**s** *pl* calzoncini *mpl* da bagno

truss /trʌs/ *n* (Med) cinto *m* erniario

trust /trʌst/ *n* fiducia *f*; (group of companies) trust *m inv*; (organization) associazione *f*; **on** ~ sulla parola ● *vt* fidarsi di; (hope) augurarsi ● *vi* ~ **in** credere in; ~ **to** affidarsi a. ~**ed** *adj* fidato

trustee /trʌs'ti:/ *n* amministratore, -trice *mf* fiduciario, -a

'trust|ful /'trʌstfl/ *adj* fiducioso. ~**ing** *adj* fiducioso. ~**worthy** *adj* fidato

truth /tru:θ/ *n* (*pl* -s /tru:ðz/) verità *f inv*. ~**ful** *adj* veritiero. ~**fully** *adv* sinceramente

try /traɪ/ *n* tentativo *m*, prova *f*; (in rugby) meta *f* ● *v* (*pt/pp* **tried**) ● *vt* provare; (be a strain on) mettere a dura prova; (Jur) processare (person); discutere (case); ~ **to do sth** provare a fare qcsa ● *vi* provare. □ ~ **on** *vt* provarsi (garment). □ ~ **out** *vt* provare

trying /'traɪɪŋ/ *adj* duro; (person) irritante

T-shirt /'ti:-/ *n* maglietta *f*

tub /tʌb/ *n* tinozza *f*; (carton) vaschetta *f*; (bath) vasca *f* da bagno

tuba /'tju:bə/ *n* (Mus) tuba *f*

tubby /'tʌbɪ/ *adj* (**-ier**, **-iest**) tozzo

tube /tju:b/ *n* tubo *m*; (of toothpaste) tubetto *m*; (Rail) metro *f*

tuberculosis /tju:bɜ:kju'ləʊsɪs/ *n* tubercolosi *f*

tubular /'tju:bjʊlə(r)/ *adj* tubolare

tuck /tʌk/ *n* piega *f* ● *vt* (put) infilare. □ ~ **in** *vt* rimboccare; ~ **sb in** rimboccare le coperte a qcno ● *vi* (□: eat) mangiare con appetito. □ ~ **up** *vt* rimboccarsi (sleeves); (in bed) rimboccare le coperte a

Tuesday /'tju:zdeɪ/ *n* martedì *m inv*

tuft /tʌft/ *n* ciuffo *m*

tug /tʌg/ *n* strattone *m*; (Naut) rimorchiatore *m* ● *v* (*pt/pp* **tugged**) ● *vt* tirare ● *vi* dare uno strattone. ~ **of war** *n* tiro *m* alla fune

tuition /tju:'ɪʃn/ *n* lezioni *fpl*

tulip /'tju:lɪp/ *n* tulipano *m*

tumble /'tʌmbl/ *n* ruzzolone *m* ● *vi* ruzzolare. ~**down** *adj* cadente. ~**drier** *n* asciugabiancheria *f*

tumbler /'tʌmblə(r)/ *n* bicchiere *m*

(conza etelo)

tummy /'tʌmɪ/ n 🔟 pancia f

tumour /'tju:mə(r)/ n tumore m

tumult /'tju:mʌlt/ n tumulto m. **~uous** adj tumultuoso

tuna /'tju:nə/ n tonno m

tune /tju:n/ n motivo m; **out of/in ~** (instrument) scordato/accordato; (person) stonato/intonato; **to the ~ of** 🔟 per la modesta somma di ● vt accordare (instrument); sintonizzare (radio, TV); mettere a punto (engine). □ **~ in** vt sintonizzare ● vi sintonizzarsi (**to** su). □ **~ up** vi (orchestra): accordare gli strumenti

tuneful /'tju:nfl/ adj melodioso

tuner /'tju:nə(r)/ n accordatore m, -trice mf; (Radio, TV) sintonizzatore m

tunic /'tju:nɪk/ n tunica f; (Mil) giacca f; (Sch) ≈ grembiule m

tunnel /'tʌnl/ n tunnel m inv ● vi (pt/pp **tunnelled**) scavare un tunnel

turban /'tɜːbən/ n turbante m

turbine /'tɜːbaɪn/ n turbina f

turbulen|ce /'tɜːbjʊləns/ n turbolenza f. **~t** adj turbolento

turf /tɜːf/ n erba f; (segment) zolla f erbosa ● **turf out** vt 🔟 buttar fuori

Turin /tjʊ'rɪn/ n Torino f

Turk /tɜːk/ n turco, -a mf

turkey /'tɜːkɪ/ n tacchino m

Turk|ey /'tɜːkɪ/ n Turchia f. **~ish** adj turco

turmoil /'tɜːmɔɪl/ n tumulto m.

turn /tɜːn/ n (rotation, short walk) giro m; (in road) svolta f, curva f; (development) svolta f; (Theat) numero m; (🔟 attack) crisi f inv; **a ~ for the better/worse** un miglioramento/peggioramento; **do sb a good ~** rendere un servizio a qcno; **take ~s** fare a turno; **in ~** a turno; **out of ~** (speak) a sproposito; **it's your ~** tocca a te ● vt girare; voltare (back, eyes); dirigere (gun, attention) ● vi girare; (person): girarsi; (leaves): ingiallire; (become) diventare; **~ right/**

left girare a destra/sinistra; **~ sour** inacidirsi; **~ to sb** girarsi verso qcno; fig rivolgersi a qcno. □ **~ against** vi diventare ostile a ● vt mettere contro. □ **~ away** vt mandare via (people); girare dall'altra parte (head) ● vi girarsi dall'altra parte. □ **~ down** vt piegare (collar); abbassare (heat, gas, sound); respingere (person, proposal). □ **~ in** vt ripiegare in dentro (edges); consegnare (lost object) ● vi (🔟: go to bed) andare a letto; **~ into the drive** entrare nel viale. □ **~ off** vt spegnere; chiudere (tap, water) ● vi (car:) girare. □ **~ on** vt accendere; aprire (tap, water); (🔟: attract) eccitare ● vi (allus) attaccare. □ **~ out** vt (expel) mandar via; spegnere (light, gas); (produce) produrre; (empty) svuotare (room, cupboard) ● vi (transpire) risultare; **~ out well/badly** (cake, dress): riuscire bene/male; (situation:) andare bene/male. □ **~ over** vt girare ● vi girarsi; **please ~ over** vedi retro. □ **~ round** vi girarsi; (car:) girare. □ **~ up** vt tirare su (collar); alzare (heat, gas, sound, radio) ● vi farsi vedere

turning /'tɜːnɪŋ/ n svolta f. **~-point** n svolta f decisiva

turnip /'tɜːnɪp/ n rapa f

turn: ~over n (Comm) giro m d'affari; (of staff) ricambio m. **~pike** n Am autostrada f. **~stile** n cancelletto m girevole. **~table** n piattaforma f girevole; (on record-player) piatto m (di giradischi). **~-up** n (of trousers) risvolto m

turquoise /'tɜːkwɔɪz/ adj (colour) turchese ● n turchese m

turret /'tʌrɪt/ n torretta f

turtle /'tɜːtl/ n tartaruga f acquatica

tusk /tʌsk/ n zanna f

tussle /'tʌsl/ n zuffa f ● vi azzuffarsi

tutor /'tju:tə(r)/ n insegnante mf privato, -a; (Univ) insegnante mf universitario, -a che segue individualmente un ristretto *numero di studenti.* **~ial** *n* discussione *f* col tutor

tuxedo /tʌkˈsiːdəʊ/ *n Am* smoking *m inv*

TV *n abbr* (television) tv *f inv*, tivù *f inv*

twang /twæŋ/ *n* (*in voice*) suono *m* nasale ● *vt* far vibrare

tweezers /ˈtwiːzəz/ *npl* pinzette *fpl*

twelfth /twelfθ/ *adj* dodicesimo

twelve /twelv/ *adj* dodici

twentieth /ˈtwentɪθ/ *adj* ventesimo

twenty /ˈtwentɪ/ *adj* venti

twice /twaɪs/ *adv* due volte

twiddle /ˈtwɪdl/ *vt* giocherellare con; **~** one's thumbs *fig* girarsi i pollici

twig[1] /twɪg/ *n* ramoscello *m*

twig[2] *vt/i* (*pt/pp* **twigged**) Ⓣ intuire

twilight /ˈtwaɪ-/ *n* crepuscolo *m*

twin /twɪn/ *n* gemello, -a *mf* ● *attrib* gemello. **~ beds** *npl* letti *mpl* gemelli

twine /twaɪn/ *n* spago *m* ● *vi* intrecciarsi; (*plant:*) attorcigliarsi ● *vt* intrecciare

twinge /twɪndʒ/ *n* fitta *f;* **~ of conscience** rimorso *m* di coscienza

twinkle /ˈtwɪŋkl/ *n* scintillio *m* ● *vi* scintillare

twirl /twɜːl/ *vt* far roteare ● *vi* volteggiare ● *n* piroetta *f*

twist /twɪst/ *n* torsione *f;* (*curve*) curva *f;* (*in rope*) attorcigliata *f;* (*in book, plot*) colpo *m* di scena ● *vt* attorcigliare (*rope*); torcere (*metal*); girare (*knob, cap*); (*distort*) distorcere; **~** one's ankle storcersi la caviglia ● *vi* attorcigliarsi; (*road:*) essere pieno di curve

twit /twɪt/ *n* Ⓣ cretino, -a *mf*

twitch /twɪtʃ/ *n* tic *m inv;* (*jerk*) strattone *m* ● *vi* contrarsi

twitter /ˈtwɪtə(r)/ *n* cinguettio *m* ● *vi* cinguettare; (*person:*) cianciare

two /tuː/ *adj* due

two: **~-faced** *adj* falso. **~-piece** *adj*

(*swimsuit*) due pezzi *m inv;* (*suit*) completo *m.* **~-way** *adj* (*traffic*) a doppio senso di marcia

tycoon /taɪˈkuːn/ *n* magnate *m*

tying /ˈtaɪɪŋ/ ▷**TIE**

type /taɪp/ *n* tipo *m;* (*printing*) carattere *m* [tipografico] ● *vt* scrivere a macchina ● *vi* scrivere a macchina. **~writer** *n* macchina *f* da scrivere. **~written** *adj* dattiloscritto

typical /ˈtɪpɪkl/ *adj* tipico. **~ly** *adv* tipicamente; (*as usual*) come al solito

typify /ˈtɪpɪfaɪ/ *vt* (*pt/pp* **-ied**) essere tipico di

typing /ˈtaɪpɪŋ/ *n* dattilografia *f*

typist /ˈtaɪpɪst/ *n* dattilografo, -a *mf*

tyrannical /tɪˈrænɪkl/ *adj* tirannico

tyranny /ˈtɪrənɪ/ *n* tirannia *f*

tyrant /ˈtaɪrənt/ *n* tiranno, -a *mf*

tyre /ˈtaɪə(r)/ *n* gomma *f,* pneumatico *m*

Uu

udder /ˈʌdə(r)/ *n* mammella *f* (*di vacca, capra etc*)

UK *n abbr* United Kingdom

ulcer /ˈʌlsə(r)/ *n* ulcera *f*

ultimate /ˈʌltɪmət/ *adj* definitivo; (*final*) finale; (*fundamental*) fondamentale. **~ly** *adv* alla fine

ultimatum /ʌltɪˈmeɪtəm/ *n* ultimatum *m inv*

ultra·violet *adj* ultravioletto

umbrella /ʌmˈbrelə/ *n* ombrello *m*

umpire /ˈʌmpaɪə(r)/ *n* arbitro *m* ● *vt/i* arbitrare

umpteen /ʌmpˈtiːn/ *adj* Ⓣ innumerevole. **~th** *adj* Ⓣ ennesimo; **for the ~th time** per l'ennesima volta

UN *n abbr* (United Nations) ONU *f*

un'able /ʌn-/ adj be ~ **to do sth** non potere fare qcsa; (not know how) non sapere fare qcsa

unac'companied adj non accompagnato; (luggage) incustodito

unac'customed adj insolito; be ~ **to** non essere abituato a

un'aided adj senza aiuto

unanimous /juːˈnænɪməs/ adj unanime. ~ly adv all'unanimità

un'armed adj disarmato; ~ **combat** n lotta f senza armi

unat'tended adj incustodito

una'voidable adj inevitabile

una'ware adj be ~ **of** sth non rendersi conto di qcsa. ~s adv **catch sb** ~s prendere qcno alla sprovvista

un'bearable adj insopportabile. ~y adv insopportabilmente

unbeat'able /ʌnˈbiːtəbl/ adj imbattibile. ~en adj imbattuto

unbe'lievable adj incredibile

un'biased adj obiettivo

un'block vt sbloccare

un'bolt vt togliere il chiavistello di

un'breakable adj infrangibile

un'button vt sbottonare

uncalled-for /ʌnˈkɔːldfɔː(r)/ adj fuori luogo

un'canny adj sorprendente; (silence, feeling) inquietante

un'certain adj incerto; (weather) instabile; **in no ~ terms** senza mezzi termini. ~ty n incertezza f

un'charitable adj duro

uncle /ˈʌŋkl/ n zio m

Uncle Sam Personaggio immaginario che rappresenta gli Stati Uniti, il suo governo e i suoi cittadini. Nell'iconografia è tradizionalmente rappresentato con la barba bianca, vestito dei colori nazionali bianco, rosso e azzurro, con un gran cappello a cilindro con le stelle della bandiera americana. Spesso utilizzato quando si fa appello al patriottismo americano.

---

un'comfortable adj scomodo; imbarazzante (silence, situation); **feel ~e** fig sentirsi a disagio. ~y adv (sit) scomodamente; (causing alarm etc) spaventosamente

un'common adj insolito

un'compromising adj intransigente

uncon'ditional adj incondizionato. ~ly adv incondizionatamente

un'conscious adj privo di sensi; (unaware) inconsapevole; be ~ **of** sth non rendersi conto di qcsa. ~ly adv inconsapevolmente

uncon'ventional adj poco convenzionale

un'cork vt sturare

un'couth /ʌnˈkuːθ/ adj zotico

un'cover vt scoprire; portare alla luce (buried object)

unde'cided adj indeciso; (not settled) incerto

undeni'able /ʌndɪˈnaɪəbl/ adj innegabile. ~y adv innegabilmente

under /ˈʌndə(r)/ prep sotto; (less than) al di sotto di; ~ **there** lì sotto; ~ **repair/construction** in riparazione/costruzione; ~ **way** fig in corso ● adv (~ water) sott'acqua; (unconscious) sotto anestesia

'undercarriage n (Aeron) carrello m

'underclothes npl biancheria fsg intima

under'cover adj clandestino

'undercurrent n corrente f sottomarina; fig sottofondo m

'underdog n perdente m

under'done adj (meat) al sangue

under'estimate vt sottovalutare

under'fed adj denutrito

under'foot adv sotto i piedi; **trample ~** calpestare

under'go vt (pt -went, pp -gone) subire (operation, treatment); **~ repair** essere in riparazione

under'graduate n studente, -tessa mf universitario, -a

under'ground[1] adv sottoterra

'underground[2] adj sotterraneo; (secret) clandestino ● n (railway) metropolitana f. **~ car park** n parcheggio m sotterraneo

'undergrowth n sottobosco m

'underhand adj subdolo

under'lie vt (pt -lay, pp -lain, pres p -lying) fig essere alla base di

under'line vt sottolineare

under'lying adj fig fondamentale

under'mine vt fig minare

underneath /ʌndə'ni:θ/ prep sotto; **~ it** sotto ● adv sotto

under'paid adj mal pagato

'underpants npl mutande fpl

'underpass n sottopassaggio m

under'privileged adj non abbiente

under'rate vt sottovalutare

'undershirt n Am maglia f della pelle

under'stand vt (pt/pp -stood) capire; **I ~ that...** (have heard) mi risulta che... ● vi capire. **~able** adj comprensibile. **~ably** adv comprensibilmente

under'standing adj comprensivo ● n comprensione f; (agreement) accordo m; **on the ~ that** a condizione che

'understatement n understatement m inv

under'take vt (pt -took, pp -taken) intraprendere; **~ to do sth** impegnarsi a fare qcsa

'undertaker n impresario m di pompe funebri; **[firm of] ~s** n impresa f di pompe funebri

under'taking n impresa f; (promise) promessa f

'undertone n fig sottofondo m; **in an ~** sottovoce

under'value vt sottovalutare

'underwater[1] adj subacqueo

under'water[2] adv sott'acqua

'underwear n biancheria f intima

under'weight adj sotto peso

'underworld n (criminals) malavita f

unde'sirable adj indesiderato; (person) poco raccomandabile

un'dignified adj non dignitoso

un'do vt (pt -did, pp -done) disfare; slacciare (dress, shoes); sbottonare (shirt); fig, (Comput) annullare

un'doubted adj indubbio. **~ly** adv senza dubbio

un'dress vt spogliare; **get ~ed** spogliarsi ● vi spogliarsi

un'due adj eccessivo

un'duly adv eccessivamente

un'earth vt dissotterrare; fig scovare; scoprire (secret). **~ly** adj soprannaturale; **at an ~ly hour** ⚠ a un'ora impossibile

uneco'nomic adj poco remunerativo

unem'ployed adj disoccupato ● npl **the ~** i disoccupati

unem'ployment n disoccupazione f. **~ benefit** n sussidio m di disoccupazione

un'ending adj senza fine

un'equal adj disuguale; (struggle) impari; **be ~ to a task** non essere all'altezza di un compito

unequivocal /ʌnɪ'kwɪvəkl/ adj inequivocabile; (person) esplicito

un'ethical adj immorale

un'even adj irregolare; (distribution) ineguale; (number) dispari

unex'pected adj inaspettato. **~ly** adv inaspettatamente

un'fair adj ingiusto. **~ly** adv ingiustamente. **~ness** n ingiustizia f

un'faithful adj infedele

unfa'miliar adj sconosciuto; **be ~ with** non conoscere

un'fasten vt slacciare; (detach) staccare

un'favourable adj sfavorevole; (impression) negativo

un'feeling adj insensibile

un'fit adj inadatto; (morally) indegno; (Sport) fuori forma; **~ for work** non in grado di lavorare

un'fold vt spiegare; (spread out) aprire; fig rivelare ● vi (view:) spiegarsi

unfore'seen adj imprevisto

unfor'gettable /ʌnfəˈgetəbl/ adj indimenticabile

unfor'givable /ʌnfəˈgɪvəbl/ adj imperdonabile

unfor'tunate adj sfortunato; (regrettable) spiacevole; (remark, choice) infelice. **~ly** adv purtroppo

un'founded adj infondato

unfurl /ʌnˈfɜːl/ vt spiegare

un'gainly /ʌnˈgeɪnlɪ/ adj sgraziato

un'grateful adj ingrato. **~ly** adv senza riconoscenza

un'happy adj infelice; (not content) insoddisfatto (with di)

un'harmed adj incolume

un'healthy adj poco sano; (insanitary) malsano

un'hurt adj illeso

unification /juːnɪfɪˈkeɪʃn/ n unificazione f

uniform /ˈjuːnɪfɔːm/ adj uniforme ● n uniforme f. **~ly** adv uniformemente

unify /ˈjuːnɪfaɪ/ vt (pt/pp -ied) unificare

uni'lateral /juːnɪ-/ adj unilaterale

uni'maginable adj inimmaginabile

unim'portant adj irrilevante

unin'habited adj disabitato

unin'tentional adj involontario. **~ly** adv involontariamente

union /ˈjuːnɪən/ n unione f; (trade ~) sindacato m. **U~ Jack** n bandiera f del Regno Unito

unique /juːˈniːk/ adj unico. **~ly** adv unicamente

unison /ˈjuːnɪsn/ n **in ~** all'unisono

unit /ˈjuːnɪt/ n unità f inv; (department) reparto m; (of furniture) elemento m

unite /juːˈnaɪt/ vt unire ● vi unirsi

unity /ˈjuːnətɪ/ n unità f; (agreement) accordo m

univer'sal /juːnɪˈvɜːsl/ adj universale. **~ly** adv universalmente

universe /ˈjuːnɪvɜːs/ n universo m

university /juːnɪˈvɜːsətɪ/ n università f ● attrib universitario

un'just adj ingiusto

un'kind adj scortese. **~ly** adv in modo scortese. **~ness** n mancanza f di gentilezza

un'known adj sconosciuto

un'lawful adj illecito, illegale

unleaded /ʌnˈledɪd/ adj senza piombo

un'leash vt fig scatenare

unless /ənˈles/ conj a meno che, **~ I am mistaken** se non mi sbaglio

un'like adj (not the same) diversi ● prep diverso da; **that's ~ him** non è da lui; **~ me, he...** diversamente da me, lui...

un'likely adj improbabile

un'limited adj illimitato

un'load vt scaricare

un'lock vt aprire (con chiave)

un'lucky adj sfortunato; **it's ~ to...** porta sfortuna...

un'married adj non sposato. **~ mother** n ragazza f madre

un'mask vt fig smascherare

unmistakable /ʌnmɪˈsteɪkəbl/ adj inconfondibile. **~y** adv chiaramente

u

un'natural adj innaturale; pej anormale. **~ly** adv in modo innaturale; pej in modo anormale

un'necessar|y adj inutile. **~ily** adv inutilmente

un'noticed adj inosservato

unob'tainable adj (product) introvabile; (phone number) non ottenibile

unob'trusive adj discreto. **~ly** adv in modo discreto

unof'ficial adj non ufficiale. **~ly** adv ufficiosamente

un'pack vi disfare le valigie ● vt svuotare (parcel); spacchettare (books); **~ one's case** disfare la valigia

un'paid adj da pagare; (work) non retribuito

un'pleasant adj sgradevole; (person) maleducato. **~ly** adv sgradevolmente; (behave) maleducatamente. **~ness** n (bad feeling) tensioni fpl

un'plug vt (pt/pp **-plugged**) staccare

un'popular adj impopolare

un'precedented adj senza precedenti

unpre'dictable adj imprevedibile

unpre'pared adj impreparato

unpro'fessional adj non professionale; **it's ~** è una mancanza di professionalità

un'profitable adj non redditizio

un'qualified adj non qualificato; (fig: absolute) assoluto

un'questionable adj incontestabile

unravel /ʌn'rævl/ vt (pt/pp **-ravelled**) districare; (in knitting) disfare

un'real adj irreale; 🔲 inverosimile

un'reasonable adj irragionevole

unre'lated adj (fact) senza rapporto (**to** con); (person) non imparentato (**to** con)

unre'liable adj inattendibile; (person) inaffidabile, che non dà affidamento

un'rest n fermenti mpl

un'rivalled adj ineguagliato

un'roll vt srotolare ● vi srotolarsi

unruly /ʌn'ruːlɪ/ adj indisciplinato

un'safe adj pericoloso

unsatis'factory adj poco soddisfacente

un'savoury adj equivoco

unscathed /ʌn'skeɪðd/ adj illeso

un'screw vt svitare

un'scrupulous adj senza scrupoli

un'seemly adj indecoroso

un'selfish adj disinteressato

un'settled adj in agitazione; (weather) variabile; (bill) non saldato

unshakeable /ʌn'ʃeɪkəbl/ adj categorico

unshaven /ʌn'ʃeɪvn/ adj non rasato

unsightly /ʌn'saɪtlɪ/ adj brutto

un'skilled adj non specializzato. **~ worker** n manovale m

un'sociable adj scontroso

unso'phisticated adj semplice

un'sound adj (building, reasoning) poco solido; (advice) poco sensato; **of ~ mind** malato di mente

un'stable adj instabile; (mentally) squilibrato

un'steady adj malsicuro

un'stuck adj **come ~** staccarsi; (🔲: project) andare a monte

unsuc'cessful adj fallimentare; **be ~** (in attempt) non aver successo. **~ly** adv senza successo

un'suitable adj (inappropriate) inadatto; (inconvenient) inopportuno

unthinkable /ʌn'θɪŋkəbl/ adj impensabile

un'tidiness n disordine m

un'tidy adj disordinato

un'tie vt slegare

until /ən'tɪl/ *prep* fino a; **not** ~ non prima di; ~ **the evening** fino alla sera; ~ **his arrival** fino al suo arrivo ● *conj* finché, fino a quando; **not** ~ **you've seen it** non prima che tu l'abbia visto

un'told *adj* (wealth) incalcolabile; (suffering) indescrivibile; (story) inedito

un'true *adj* falso; **that's** ~ non è vero

unused[1] /ʌn'juːzd/ *adj* non [ancora] usato

unused[2] /ʌn'juːst/ *adj* **be** ~ **to** non essere abituato a

un'usual *adj* insolito. ~**ly** *adv* insolitamente

un'veil *vt* scoprire

un'wanted *adj* indesiderato

un'welcome *adj* sgradito

un'well *adj* indisposto

unwieldy /ʌn'wiːldɪ/ *adj* ingombrante

un'willing *adj* riluttante. ~**ly** *adv* malvolentieri

un'wind *v* (*pt/pp* **unwound**) ● *vt* svolgere, srotolare ● *vi* svolgersi, srotolarsi; (🔁 *relax*) rilassarsi

un'wise *adj* imprudente

un'worthy *adj* non degno

un'wrap *vt* (*pt/pp* **-wrapped**) scartare (present, parcel)

un'written *adj* tacito

up /ʌp/ *adv* su; (*not in bed*) alzato; (road) smantellato; (theatre curtain, blinds) alzato; (shelves, tent) montato; (notice) affisso; (building) costruito; **prices are up** i prezzi sono in vendita; **be up for sale** essere in vendita; **time's up** tempo scaduto; **what's up?** 🔁 cos'è successo?; **up to** (as far as) fino a; **be up to** essere all'altezza di (task); **what's he up to?** 🔁 cosa sta facendo?; (*plotting*) cosa sta combinando?; **I'm up to page 100** sono arrivato a pagina 100; **feel up to it** sentirsela; **be one up on sb** 🔁 essere in vantaggio su qcno; **go up** salire; **lift up** alzare; **up against** *fig* alle prese con ● *prep* su; **the cat ran up the tree** il gatto è salito di corsa/è salito sull'albero; **further up this road** più avanti su questa strada; **row up the river** risalire il fiume; **go up the stairs** salire su per le scale; **be up the pub** 🔁 essere al pub; **be up on** *or* **in sth** essere bene informato su qcsa ● *n* **ups and downs** *npl* alti *mpl* e bassi

'upbringing *n* educazione *f*

up'date[1] *vt* aggiornare

'update[2] *n* aggiornamento *m*

up'grade *vt* promuovere (person); modernizzare (equipment)

upheaval /ʌp'hiːv(ə)l/ *n* scompiglio *m*

up'hill *adj* in salita; *fig* arduo ● *adv* in salita

up'hold *vt* (*pt/pp* **upheld**) sostenere (principle); confermare (verdict)

upholster /ʌp'həʊlstə(r)/ *vt* tappezzare. ~**er** *n* tappezziere, -a *mf*. ~**y** *n* tappezzeria *f*

'upkeep *n* mantenimento *m*

up-'market *adj* di qualità

upon /ə'pɒn/ *prep* su; ~ **arriving home** una volta arrivato a casa

upper /'ʌpə(r)/ *adj* superiore ● *n* (of shoe) tomaia *f*

upper class *n* alta borghesia *f*

'upright *adj* dritto; (piano) verticale; (honest) retto ● *n* montante *m*

'uprising *n* rivolta *f*

'uproar *n* tumulto *m*; **be in an** ~ essere in trambusto

up'set[1] *vt* (*pt/pp* **upset**, *pres p* **upsetting**) rovesciare; sconvolgere (plan); (*distress*) turbare; **upset sth** rovesciarsi qcsa; **he very** ~ essere sconvolto; **have an** ~ **stomach** avere l'intestino disturbato

'upset[2] *n* scombussolamento *m*

'upshot *n* risultato *m*

upside 'down adv sottosopra; turn ~ ~ capovolgere

up'stairs[1] adv [al piano] di sopra

'upstairs[2] adj del piano superiore

'upstart n arrivato, -a mf

up'stream adv controcorrente

'uptake n be slow on the ~ essere lento nel capire; **be quick on the** ~ capire le cose al volo

up-to-'date adj moderno; (news) ultimo; (records) aggiornato

'upturn n ripresa f

upward /'ʌpwəd/ adj verso l'alto, in su; ~ **slope** salita f ● adv ~[s] verso l'alto; ~s of oltre

uranium /juˈreɪnɪəm/ n uranio m

urban /'ɜːbən/ adj urbano

urge /ɜːdʒ/ n forte desiderio m ● vt esortare (to a). □ ~ **on** vt spronare

urgen|cy /'ɜːdʒənsɪ/ n urgenza f. **~t** adj urgente

urinate /'jʊərɪneɪt/ vi urinare

urine /'jʊərɪn/ n urina f

us /ʌs/ pron ci; (after prep) noi; **they know us** ci conoscono; **give us the money** dateci i soldi; **give it to us** datecelo; **they showed it to us** ce l'hanno fatto vedere; **they meant us, not you** intendevano noi, non voi; **it's us** siamo noi; **she hates us** ci odia

US[A] n[pl] abbr (**United States [of America]**) U.S.A. mpl

usage /'juːsɪdʒ/ n uso m

use[1] /juːs/ n uso m; **be of** ~ essere utile; **be of no** ~ essere inutile; **make** ~ **of** usare; (exploit) sfruttare; **it is no** ~ è inutile; **what's the** ~? a che scopo?

use[2] /juːz/ vt usare. □ ~ **up** vt consumare

used[1] /juːzd/ adj usato

used[2] /juːst/ pt be ~ **to sth** essere abituato a qcsa; **get** ~ **to** abituarsi a; **he** ~ **to live here** viveva qui

useful /'juːsfl/ adj utile. **~ness** n

utilità f

useless /'juːslɪs/ adj inutile; (☐: person) incapace

user /'juːzə(r)/ n utente mf. **~-friendly** adj facile da usare

usher /'ʌʃə(r)/ n (Theat) maschera f; (Jur) usciere m; (at wedding) persona f che accompagna gli invitati a un matrimonio ai loro posti in chiesa ● **usher in** vt fare entrare

usherette /ʌʃə'ret/ n maschera f

usual /'juːʒʊəl/ adj usuale; **as** ~ come al solito. **~ly** adv di solito

utensil /juːˈtensl/ n utensile m

utilize /'juːtɪlaɪz/ vt utilizzare

utmost /'ʌtməʊst/ adj estremo ● n one's ~ tutto il possibile

utter[1] /'ʌtə(r)/ adj totale. **~ly** adv completamente

utter[2] vt emettere (sigh, sound); proferire (word). **~ance** n dichiarazione f

U-turn /'juː-/ n (Auto) inversione f a U; fig marcia f in dietro

Vv

vacan|cy /'veɪk(ə)nsɪ/ n (job) posto m vacante; (room) stanza f disponibile. **~t** adj libero; (position) vacante; (look) assente

vacate /vəˈkeɪt/ vt lasciare libero

vacation /vəˈkeɪʃn/ n vacanza f

vaccinat|e /'væksɪneɪt/ vt vaccinare. **~ion** n vaccinazione f

vaccine /'væksiːn/ n vaccino m

vacuum /'vækjʊəm/ n vuoto m ● vt passare l'aspirapolvere in/su. **~ cleaner** n aspirapolvere m inv. **~ flask** n thermos® m inv. **~-packed** adj confezionato sottovuoto

vagina /vəˈdʒəɪnə/ n (Anat) vagina f

vague /veɪg/ adj vago; (outline) impreciso; (absent-minded) distratto; **I'm still ~ about it** non ho ancora le idee chiare in proposito. **~ly** adv vagamente

vain /veɪn/ adj vanitoso; (hope, attempt) vano; **in ~** invano. **~ly** adv vanamente

valentine /ˈvæləntaɪn/ n (card) biglietto m di San Valentino

valiant /ˈvæliənt/ adj valoroso

valid /ˈvælɪd/ adj valido. **~ate** vt (confirm) convalidare. **~ity** n validità f

valley /ˈvælɪ/ n valle f

valour /ˈvælə(r)/ n valore m

valuable /ˈvæljʊəbl/ adj di valore; fig prezioso. **~s** npl oggetti mpl di valore

valuation /væljʊˈeɪʃn/ n valutazione f

value /ˈvæljuː/ n valore m; (usefulness) utilità f ● vt valutare; (cherish) apprezzare. **~ added tax** n imposta f sul valore aggiunto

valve /vælv/ n valvola f

vampire /ˈvæmpaɪə(r)/ n vampiro m

van /væn/ n furgone m

vandal /ˈvændl/ n vandalo, -a mf. **~ism** n vandalismo m. **~ize** vt vandalizzare

vanilla /vəˈnɪlə/ n vaniglia f

vanish /ˈvænɪʃ/ vi svanire

vanity /ˈvænətɪ/ n vanità f. **~ bag** or **case** n beauty-case m inv

vapour /ˈveɪpə(r)/ n vapore m

variable /ˈveərɪəbl/ adj variabile; (adjustable) regolabile

variance /ˈveərɪəns/ n **be at ~** essere in disaccordo

variant /ˈveərɪənt/ n variante f

variation /veərɪˈeɪʃn/ n variazione f

varied /ˈveərɪd/ adj vario; (diet) diversificato; (life) movimentato

variety /vəˈraɪətɪ/ n varietà f inv

various /ˈveərɪəs/ adj vario

varnish /ˈvɑːnɪʃ/ n vernice f; (for nails) smalto m ● vt verniciare; **~ one's nails** mettersi lo smalto

vary /ˈveərɪ/ vt/i (pt/pp -ied) variare. **~ing** adj variabile; (different) diverso

vase /vɑːz/ n vaso m

vast /vɑːst/ adj vasto; (difference, amusement) enorme. **~ly** adv (superior) di gran lunga; (different, amused) enormemente

vat /væt/ n tino m

VAT /viːeɪˈtiː, væt/ n abbr (value added tax) I.V.A. f

vault[1] /vɔːlt/ n (roof) volta f; (in bank) caveau m inv; (tomb) cripta f

vault[2] n salto m ● vt/i ~ **[over]** saltare

VDU n abbr (visual display unit) VDU m

veal /viːl/ n carne f di vitello ● attrib di vitello

veer /vɪə(r)/ vi cambiare direzione; (Auto, Naut) virare

vegetable /ˈvedʒtəbl/ n (food) verdura f; (when growing) ortaggio m ● attrib (oil, fat) vegetale

vegetarian /vedʒɪˈteərɪən/ adj & n vegetariano, -a f

vehicle /ˈviːɪkl/ n veicolo m; (fig: medium) mezzo m

veil /veɪl/ n velo m ● vt velare

vein /veɪn/ n vena f; (mood) umore m; (manner) tenore m. **~ed** adj venato

velocity /vɪˈlɒsətɪ/ n velocità f

velvet /ˈvelvɪt/ n velluto m. **~y** adj vellutato

vendetta /venˈdetə/ n vendetta f

vending-machine /ˈvendɪŋ-/ n distributore m automatico

veneer /vəˈnɪə(r)/ n impiallacciatura f; fig vernice f. **~ed** adj impiallacciato

venereal /vɪˈnɪərɪəl/ adj ~ **disease** malattia f venerea

Venetian /vɪˈniːʃn/ adj & n veneziano, -a mf. **v~ blind** n persiana f alla veneziana

vengeance /'vendʒəns/ n vendetta f; **with a ~** 🄵 a più non posso

venison /'venɪsn/ n (Culin) carne f di cervo

venom /'venəm/ n veleno m. **~ous** adj velenoso

vent[1] /vent/ n presa f d'aria; **give ~ to** fig dar libero sfogo a ● vt fig sfogare (anger)

vent[2] n (in jacket) spacco m

ventilat|e /'ventɪleɪt/ vt ventilare. **~ion** n ventilazione f; (installation) sistema m di ventilazione. **~or** n ventilatore m

ventriloquist /ven'trɪləkwɪst/ n ventriloquo, -a f

venture /'ventʃə(r)/ n impresa f ● vt azzardare ● vi avventurarsi

venue /'venjuː/ n luogo m (di convegno, concerto, ecc.)

veranda /vəˈrændə/ n veranda f

verb /vɜːb/ n verbo m. **~al** adj verbale

verdict /'vɜːdɪkt/ n verdetto m; (opinion) parere m

verge /vɜːdʒ/ n orlo m; **be on the ~ of doing sth** essere sul punto di fare qcsa ● **verge on** vt fig rasentare

verify /'verɪfaɪ/ vt (pt/pp -ied) verificare; (confirm) confermare

vermin /'vɜːmɪn/ n animali mpl nocivi

versatil|e /'vɜːsətaɪl/ adj versatile. **~ity** n versatilità f

verse /vɜːs/ n verso m; (of Bible) versetto m; (poetry) versi mpl

versed /vɜːst/ adj **~ in** versato in

versus /'vɜːsəs/ prep contro

vertebra /'vɜːtɪbrə/ n (pl -brae /-briː/) (Anat) vertebra f

vertical /'vɜːtɪkl/ adj & n verticale m

vertigo /'vɜːtɪgəʊ/ n (Med) vertigine f

verve /vɜːv/ n verve f

very /'verɪ/ adv molto; **~ much**

molto; **~ little** pochissimo; **~ many** moltissimi; **~ few** pochissimi; **~ probably** molto probabilmente; **~ well** benissimo; **at the ~ most** tutt'al più; **at the ~ latest** al più tardi ● adj **the ~ first** il primissimo; **the ~ thing** proprio ciò che ci vuole; **at the ~ end/beginning** proprio alla fine/all'inizio; **that ~ day** proprio quel giorno; **the ~ thought** la sola idea; **only a ~ little** solo un pochino

vessel /'vesl/ n nave f

vest /vest/ n maglia f della pelle; (Am: waistcoat) gilè m inv. **~ed interest** n interesse m personale

vestige /'vestɪdʒ/ n (of past) vestigio m

vet /vet/ n veterinario, -a mf ● vt (pt/pp vetted) controllare minuziosamente

veteran /'vetərən/ n veterano, -a mf

veterinary /'vetərɪnərɪ/ adj veterinario. **~ surgeon** n medico m veterinario

veto /'viːtəʊ/ n (pl -es) veto m ● vt proibire

vex /veks/ vt irritare. **~ation** n irritazione f. **~ed** adj irritato; **~ed question** questione f controversa

via /'vaɪə/ prep via; (by means of) attraverso

viable /'vaɪəbl/ adj (life form, relationship, company) in grado di sopravvivere; (proposition) attuabile

viaduct /'vaɪədʌkt/ n viadotto m

vibrat|e /vaɪ'breɪt/ vi vibrare. **~ion** n vibrazione f

vicar /'vɪkə(r)/ n parroco m (protestante). **~age** n casa f parrocchiale

vice[1] /vaɪs/ n vizio m

vice[2] n (Techn) morsa f

vice versa /vaɪsɪ'vɜːsə/ adv viceversa

vicinity /vɪ'sɪnətɪ/ n vicinanza f; **in the ~ of** nelle vicinanze di

vicious /'vɪʃəs/ adj cattivo; (attack) brutale; (animal) pericoloso. ~ **'circle** n circolo m vizioso. ~**ly** adv (attack) brutalmente

victim /'vɪktɪm/ n vittima f. ~**ize** vt fare delle rappresaglie contro

victor /'vɪktə(r)/ n vincitore m

victor|ious /vɪk'tɔːrɪəs/ adj vittorioso. ~**y** /'vɪktərɪ/ n vittoria f

video /'vɪdɪəʊ/ n video m; (cassette) videocassetta f; (recorder) videoregistratore m ● attrib video ● vt videoregistrare

video: ~ **recorder** n videoregistratore m. ~**tape** n videocassetta f

vie /vaɪ/ vi (pres p **vying**) rivaleggiare

view /vjuː/ n vista f; (photographed, painted) veduta f; (opinion) visione f; **look at the** ~ guardare il panorama; **in my** ~ secondo me; **in** ~ **of** in considerazione di; **on** ~ esposto; **with a** ~ **to** con l'intenzione di ● vt visitare (house); (consider) considerare ● vi (TV) guardare. ~**er** n (TV) telespettatore m inv mf; (Phot) visore m

view: ~**finder** n (Phot) mirino m. ~**point** n punto m di vista

vigilan|ce /'vɪdʒɪləns/ n vigilanza f. ~**t** adj vigile

vigorous /'vɪgərəs/ adj vigoroso

vigour /'vɪgə(r)/ n vigore m

vile /vaɪl/ adj disgustoso; (weather) orribile; (temper, mood) pessimo

village /'vɪlɪdʒ/ n paese m. ~**r** n paesano, -a mf

villain /'vɪlən/ n furfante m; (in story) cattivo m

vindicate /'vɪndɪkeɪt/ vt (from guilt) discolpare; **you are ~d** ti sei dimostrato nel giusto

vindictive /vɪn'dɪktɪv/ adj vendicativo

vine /vaɪn/ n vite f

vinegar /'vɪnɪgə(r)/ n aceto m

vineyard /'vɪnjɑːd/ n vigneto m

vintage /'vɪntɪdʒ/ adj (wine) d'annata ● n (year) annata f

viola /vɪ'əʊlə/ n (Mus) viola f

violate /'vaɪəleɪt/ vt violare. ~**ion** n violazione f

violen|ce /'vaɪələns/ n violenza f. ~**t** adj violento

violet /'vaɪələt/ adj violetto ● n (flower) violetta f; (colour) violetto m

violin /vaɪə'lɪn/ n violino m. ~**ist** n violinista m

VIP n abbr (very important person) vip mf

virgin /'vɜːdʒɪn/ adj vergine ● n vergine f. ~**ity** n verginità f

Virgo /'vɜːgəʊ/ n Vergine f

viril|e /'vɪraɪl/ adj virile. ~**ity** n virilità f

virtual /'vɜːtjʊəl/ adj effettivo. ~ **reality** n realtà f virtuale. ~**ly** adv praticamente

virtue /'vɜːtjuː/ n virtù f inv; (advantage) vantaggio m; **by or in** ~ **of** a causa di

virtuous /'vɜːtjʊəs/ adj virtuoso

virulent /'vɪrʊlənt/ adj virulento

virus /'vaɪərəs/ n virus m inv

visa /'viːzə/ n visto m

visibility /vɪzə'bɪlɪtɪ/ n visibilità f

visible /'vɪzəbl/ adj visibile. ~**y** adv visibilmente

vision /'vɪʒn/ n visione f; (sight) vista f

visit /'vɪzɪt/ n visita f ● vt andare a trovare (person); andare da (doctor etc); visitare (town, building). ~**ing hours** npl orario m delle visite. ~**or** n ospite mf; (of town, museum) visitatore, -trice mf; (in hotel) cliente mf

visor /'vaɪzə(r)/ n visiera f; (Auto) parasole m

visual /'vɪzjʊəl/ adj visivo. ~ **aids** npl supporto m visivo. ~ **dis'play unit** n visualizzatore m. ~**ly** adv visualmente. ~**ly handicapped** non vedente

visualize /'vɪzjʊəlaɪz/ vt visualizzare

vital /'vaɪtl/ adj vitale. ~**ity** n vitalità f. ~**ly** adv estremamente

vitamin /'vɪtəmɪn/ n vitamina f

vivaci|ous /vɪ'veɪʃəs/ adj vivace. ~**ty** n vivacità f

vivid /'vɪvɪd/ adj vivido. ~**ly** adv in modo vivido

vocabulary /və'kæbjʊlərɪ/ n vocabolario m; (list) glossario m

vocal /'vəʊkl/ adj vocale; (vociferous) eloquente. ~ **cords** npl corde fpl vocali

vocalist /'vəʊkəlɪst/ n vocalista mf

vocation /və'keɪʃn/ n vocazione f. ~**al** adj di orientamento professionale

vociferous /və'sɪfərəs/ adj vociante

vogue /vəʊg/ n moda f; in ~ in voga

voice /vɔɪs/ n voce f ● vt esprimere. ~**mail** n posta f elettronica vocale

void /vɔɪd/ adj (not valid) nullo; ~ of privo di ● n vuoto m

volatile /'vɒlətaɪl/ adj volatile; (person) volubile

volcanic /vɒl'kænɪk/ adj vulcanico

volcano /vɒl'keɪnəʊ/ n vulcano m

volley /'vɒlɪ/ n (of gunfire) raffica f; (Tennis) volée f inv

volt /vəʊlt/ n volt m inv. ~**age** n (Electr) voltaggio m

volume /'vɒljuːm/ n volume m; (of work, traffic) quantità f inv. ~ **control** n volume m

voluntar|y /'vɒləntərɪ/ adj volontario. ~**y work** n volontariato m. ~**ily** adv volontariamente

volunteer /vɒlən'tɪə(r)/ n volontario, -a mf ● vt offrire volontariamente (information) ● vi offrirsi volontario; (Mil) arruolarsi come volontario

vomit /'vɒmɪt/ n vomito m ● vt/i vomitare

voracious /və'reɪʃəs/ adj vorace

vot|e /vəʊt/ n voto m; (ballot) votazione f; (right) diritto m di voto; **take**

a ~**e on** votare su ● vi votare ● vt ~**e sb president** eleggere qcno presidente. ~**er** n elettore, -trice mf. ~**ing** n votazione f

vouch /vaʊtʃ/ vi ~ **for** garantire per. ~**er** n buono m

vow /vaʊ/ n voto m ● vt giurare

vowel /'vaʊəl/ n vocale f

voyage /'vɔɪɪdʒ/ n viaggio m [marittimo]; (in space) viaggio m [nello spazio]

vulgar /'vʌlgə(r)/ adj volgare. ~**ity** n volgarità f inv

vulnerable /'vʌlnərəbl/ adj vulnerabile

vulture /'vʌltʃə(r)/ n avvoltoio m

vying /'vaɪɪŋ/ ▷**VIE**

Ww

wad /wɒd/ n batuffolo m; (bundle) rotolo m. ~**ding** n ovatta f

waddle /'wɒdl/ vi camminare ondeggiando

wade /weɪd/ vi guadare; ~ **through** 🔟 procedere faticosamente in (book)

wafer /'weɪfə(r)/ n cialda f, wafer m inv; (Relig) ostia f

waffle[1] /'wɒfl/ vi 🔟 blaterare

waffle[2] n (Culin) cialda f

waft /wɒft/ vt trasportare ● vi diffondersi

wag /wæg/ v (pt/pp **wagged**) ● vt agitare ● vi agitarsi

wage[1] /weɪdʒ/ vt dichiarare (war); lanciare (campaign)

wage[2] n, & ~**s** pl salario msg. ~ **packet** n busta f paga

waggle /'wægl/ vt dimenare ● vi dimenarsi

wagon /ˈwægən/ n carro m; (Rail) vagone m merci

wail /weɪl/ vi piagnucolare; (of wind) lamento m; (of baby) vagito m ● vi piagnucolare; (wind:) lamentarsi; (baby:) vagire

waist /weɪst/ n vita f. **~coat** n gilè m inv; (of man's suit) panciotto m. **~line** n vita f

wait /weɪt/ n attesa f; **lie in ~ for** appostarsi per sorprendere ● vi aspettare; **~ for** aspettare ● v i one's turn aspettare il proprio turno. **□ ~ on** vt servire

waiter /ˈweɪtə(r)/ n cameriere m

waiting: **~-list** n lista f d'attesa. **~-room** n sala f d'aspetto

waitress /ˈweɪtrɪs/ n cameriera f

waive /weɪv/ vt rinunciare a (claim), non tener conto di (rule)

wake¹ /weɪk/ n veglia f funebre ● vt (pt woke, pp woken) **[up]** ● vt svegliare ● vi svegliarsi

wake² n (Naut) scia f; **in the ~ of** fig nella scia di

Wales /weɪlz/ n Galles m

walk /wɔːk/ n passeggiata f; (gait) andatura f; (path) sentiero m; **go for a ~** andare a fare una passeggiata ● vi camminare; (as opposed to drive etc) andare a piedi; (ramble) passeggiare ● vt portare a spasso (dog); percorrere (streets). **□ ~ out** vi (husband, employee:) andarsene; (workers:) scioperare. **~ out on** vt lasciare

walker /ˈwɔːkə(r)/ n camminatore, trice mf; (rambler) escursionista mf

walk-out n sciopero m

wall /wɔːl/ n muro m; **go to the ~** far diventare matto qcno ● **wall up** vt murare

wallet /ˈwɒlɪt/ n portafoglio m

wallop /ˈwɒləp/ n colpo m ● vt (pt/pp walloped) colpire

wallow /ˈwɒləʊ/ vi sguazzare; (in self-pity, grief) crogiolarsi

wallpaper n tappezzeria f ● vt tappezzare

Wall Street Via di Manhattan, a New York, dove hanno sede la Borsa e altri istituti finanziari. Quando si parla di Wall Street ci si riferisce appunto a tali istituti.

walnut /ˈwɔːlnʌt/ n noce f

waltz /wɔːlts/ n valzer m inv ● vi ballare il valzer

wand /wɒnd/ n (magic ~) bacchetta f [magica]

wander /ˈwɒndə(r)/ vi girovagare; (fig: digress) divagare. **□ ~ about** vi andare a spasso

wane /weɪn/ n **be on the ~** essere in fase calante ● vi calare

wangle /ˈwæŋgl/ vt **[**rimediare (invitation, holiday)

want /wɒnt/ n (hardship) bisogno m; (lack) mancanza f ● vt volere; (need) aver bisogno di; **~ to have** voler fare qcsa; **~ to do** voler fare qcsa; **we ~ to stay** vogliamo rimanere; **I ~ you to go** voglio che tu vada; **it ~s painting** ha bisogno d'essere dipinto; **you ~ to learn to swim** bisogna che impari a nuotare ● vi **~ for** mancare di. **~ed** adj ricercato. **~ing** adj **be ~ing** mancare; **be ~ing in** mancare di

WAP /wæp/ n abbr (wireless application protocol) WAP m inv

war /wɔː(r)/ n guerra f; fig lotta f (on contro); **at ~** in guerra

ward /wɔːd/ n (in hospital) reparto m; (child) minore m sotto tutela ● **ward off** vt evitare; parare (blow)

warden /ˈwɔːdn/ n guardiano, -a mf

warder /ˈwɔːdə(r)/ n guardia f carceraria

wardrobe /ˈwɔːdrəʊb/ n guardaroba m

warehouse /ˈweəhaʊs/ n

magazzino m

war: ~**fare** n guerra f. ~**head** n testata f

warm /wɔːm/ adj caldo; (welcome) caloroso; **be** ~ (person:) aver caldo; **it is** ~ (weather) fa caldo ● vt scaldare. □ ~ **up** vt scaldare ● vi scaldarsi; fig animarsi. ~**hearted** adj espansivo. ~**ly** adv (greet) calorosamente; (dress) in modo pesante. ~**th** n calore m

warn /wɔːn/ vt avvertire. ~**ing** n avvertimento m; (advance notice) preavviso m

warp /wɔːp/ vt deformare; fig distorcere ● vi deformarsi

warped /wɔːpt/ adj fig contorto; (sexuality) deviato; (view) distorto

warrant /ˈwɒrənt/ n (for arrest, search) mandato m ● vt (justify) giustificare; (guarantee) garantire. ~**y** n garanzia f

warrior /ˈwɒrɪə(r)/ n guerriero, -a mf

'warship n nave f da guerra

wart /wɔːt/ n porro m

'wartime n tempo m di guerra

war|y /ˈweərɪ/ adj (**-ier**, **-iest**) (careful) cauto; (suspicious) diffidente

was /wɒz/ ▷**BE**

wash /wɒʃ/ n lavata f; (clothes) bucato m; (in washing machine) lavaggio m; **have a** ~ darsi una lavata ● vt lavare; (sea:) bagnare; ~ **one's hands** lavarsi le mani ● vi lavarsi. □ ~ **out** vt sciacquare (soap); sciacquarsi (mouth). □ ~ **up** vt lavare ● vi lavare i piatti; Am lavarsi

washable /ˈwɒʃəbl/ adj lavabile

wash-basin n lavandino m

washer /ˈwɒʃə(r)/ n (Techn) guarnizione f; (machine) lavatrice f

washing /ˈwɒʃɪŋ/ n bucato m. ~**-machine** n lavatrice f. ~**-powder** n detersivo m. ~**'up** n do the ~**-up** lavare i piatti. ~**'up liquid** n detersivo m per i piatti

wash: ~**-out** n disastro m. ~**-room** n bagno m

wasp /wɒsp/ n vespa f

waste /weɪst/ n spreco m; (rubbish) rifiuto m; ~ **of time** perdita f di tempo ● adj (product) di scarto; (land) desolato; **lay** ~ devastare ● vt sprecare. □ ~ **away** vi deperire

waste: ~**di'sposal unit** n eliminatore m di rifiuti. ~**ful** adj dispendioso. ~**'paper basket** n cestino m per la carta [straccia]

watch /wɒtʃ/ n guardia f; (period of duty) turno m di guardia; (timepiece) orologio m; **be on the** ~ stare all'erta ● vt guardare (film, match, television); (be careful of, look after) stare attento a ● vi guardare. □ ~ **out** vi (be careful) stare attento (**for** a). □ ~ **out for** vi (look for) fare attenzione all'arrivo di (person)

watch: ~**-dog** n cane m da guardia. ~**man** n guardiano m

water /ˈwɔːtə(r)/ n acqua f ● vt annaffiare (garden, plant); (dilute) annacquare ● vi (eyes:) lacrimare; **my mouth was** ~**ing** avevo l'acquolina in bocca. □ ~ **down** vt diluire; fig attenuare

water: ~**colour** n acquerello m. ~**cress** n crescione m. ~**fall** n cascata f

'watering-can n annaffiatoio m

water: ~**lily** n ninfea f. ~ **logged** adj inzuppato. ~**proof** adj impermeabile. ~**skiing** n sci m nautico. ~**tight** adj stagno; fig irrefutabile. ~**way** n canale m navigabile

watery /ˈwɔːtərɪ/ adj acquoso; (eyes) lacrimoso

watt /wɒt/ n watt m inv

wave /weɪv/ n onda f; (gesture) cenno m; fig ondata f ● vt agitare; **one's hand** agitare la mano ● vi far segno; (flag:) sventolare. ~**length** n lunghezza f d'onda

waver /ˈweɪvə(r)/ vi vacillare.

(hesitate) esitare

wavy /'weɪvɪ/ adj ondulato

wax¹ /wæks/ vi (moon:) crescere; (fig: become) diventare

wax² n cera f; (in ear) cerume m ● vt dare la cera a. **~works** n museo m delle cere

way /weɪ/ n percorso m; (direction) direzione f; (manner, method) modo m; **~s** pl (customs) abitudini fpl; **be in the ~** essere in mezzo; **on the ~ to Rome** andando a Roma; **I'll do it on the ~** lo faccio mentre vado; **it's on my ~** è sul mio percorso; **a long ~ off** lontano; **this ~** da questa parte; (like this) così; **by the ~** a proposito; **by ~ of** come; (via) via; **either ~** (whatever we do) in un modo o nell'altro; **in some ~s** sotto certi aspetti; **in a ~** in un certo senso; **in a bad ~** (person) molto grave; **out of the ~** fuori mano; **under ~** in corso; **lead the ~** far strada; **male ~** far posto (for a); **give ~** (Auto) dare la precedenza; **go out of one's ~** fig scomodarsi (to per); **get one's [own] ~** averla vinta ● adv **~ behind** molto indietro. **~ in** n entrata f

way'lay vt (pt/pp -laid) aspettare al varco (person)

way 'out n uscita f; fig via f d'uscita

way-'out adj [T] eccentrico

we /wiː/ pron noi; **we're the last** siamo gli ultimi; **they're going, but we're not** loro vanno, ma noi no

weak /wiːk/ adj debole; (liquid) leggero. **~en** vt indebolire ● vi indebolirsi. **~ling** n smidollato, -a mf. **~ness** n debolezza f; (liking) debole m

wealth /welθ/ n ricchezza f; fig gran quantità f. **~y** adj (-ier, -iest) ricco

weapon /'wepən/ n arma f; **~s of mass destruction** npl armi mpl di distruzione di massa

wear /weə(r)/ n (clothing) abbiglia-

mento m; **for everyday ~** da portare tutti i giorni; **~ [and tear]** usura f ● v (pt **wore**, pp **worn**) ● vt portare; (damage) consumare; **~ a hole in sth** logorare qcsa fino a fare un buco; **what shall I ~?** cosa mi metto? ● vi consumarsi; (last) durare. **□ ~ off** vi scomparire; (effect:) finire. **□ ~ out** vt consumare [fino in fondo]; (exhaust) estenuare ● vi estenuarsi

wear|y /'wɪərɪ/ adj (-ier, -iest) sfinito ● v (pt/pp wearied) ● vt sfinire ● vi **~y** vi stancarsi di. **~ily** adv stancamente

weather /'weðə(r)/ n tempo m; **in this ~** con questo tempo; **under the ~** [T] giù di corda ● vt superare (a storm)

weather: **~-beaten** adj (face) segnato dalle intemperie. **~ forecast** n previsioni fpl del tempo

weave¹ vi (pt/pp **weaved**) (move) zigzagare

weave² n tessuto m ● vt (pt **wove**, pp **woven**) tessere; intrecciare (flowers etc); intrecciare le fila di (story etc). **~r** n tessitore, -trice mf

web /web/ n rete f; (spider's) ragnatela f. **W~** (Comput) Web m inv, Rete f. **~bed feet** npl piedi mpl palmati. **~cam** n webcam f inv. **~ master** n webmaster m inv. **~ page** n pagina f web. **~ site** n sito m web

wed /wed/ vt (pt/pp **wedded**) sposare ● vi sposarsi. **~ding** n matrimonio m

wedding: **~ cake** n torta f nuziale. **~ring** n fede f

wedge /wedʒ/ n zeppa f; (for splitting wood) cuneo m; (of cheese) fetta f ● vt (fix) fissare

Wednesday /'wenzdeɪ/ n mercoledì m inv

wee¹ /wiː/ adj [T] piccolo

wee² vi [T] fare la pipì

weed /wiːd/ n erbaccia f; ([T]: person)

mollusco *m* ● *vt* estirpare le erbacce da. □ ~ **out** *vt fig* eliminare

'weed-killer *n* erbicida *m*

weedy /'wi:dɪ/ *adj* 🔢 mingherlino

week /wi:k/ *n* settimana *f*. ~**day** *n* giorno *m* feriale. ~**end** *n* fine settimana *m*

weekly /'wi:klɪ/ *adj* settimanale ● *n* settimanale ● *adv* settimanalmente

weep /wi:p/ *vi* (*pt/pp* **wept**) piangere

weigh /weɪ/ *vt/i* pesare; ~ **anchor** levare l'ancora. □ ~ **down** *vt fig* piegare. □ ~ **up** *vt fig* soppesare; valutare (*person*)

weight /weɪt/ *n* peso *m*; **put on/lose** ~ ingrassare/dimagrire. ~**ing** *n* (*allowance*) indennità *f inv*

weight-lifting *n* sollevamento *m* pesi

weir /wɪə(r)/ *n* chiusa *f*

weird /wɪəd/ *adj* misterioso; (*bizarre*) bizzarro

welcome /'welkəm/ *adj* benvenuto; **you're** ~! prego!; **you're** ~ **to have it/to come** prendilo/vieni pure ● *n* accoglienza *f* ● *vt* accogliere; (*appreciate*) gradire

weld /weld/ *vt* saldare. ~**er** *n* saldatore *m*

welfare /'welfeə(r)/ *n* benessere *m*; (*aid*) assistenza *f*. **W**~ **State** *n* Stato *m* assistenziale

well[1] /wel/ *n* pozzo *m*; (*of staircase*) tromba *f*

well[2] *adv* (**better, best**) bene; **as** ~ anche; **as** ~ **as** (*in addition*) oltre a; ~ **done!** bravo!; **very** ~ benissimo ● *adj* **he is not** ~ non sta bene; **get** ~ **soon!** guarisci presto!; ● *int* beh!; ~ **I never!** ma va!

well-behaved *adj* educato

well: ~**-known** *adj* famoso. ~**-off** *adj* benestante. ~**-to-do** *adj* ricco

Welsh /welʃ/ *adj & n* gallese; **the** ~ *pl* i gallesi. ~**man** *n* gallese *m*. ~ **rabbit** *n* toast *m inv* al formaggio

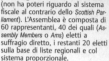

Welsh Assembly Istituita nel 1999 con sede a Cardiff, la *Welsh Assembly* ha poteri legislativi secondari limitati (non ha poteri riguardo al sistema fiscale al contrario dello *Scottish Parliament*). L'Assemblea è composta di 60 rappresentanti, 40 dei quali (*Assembly Members* o *Ams*) eletti a suffragio diretto, i restanti 20 eletti sulla base di liste regionali e col sistema proporzionale.

went /went/ ▷**GO**

wept /wept/ ▷**WEEP**

were /wɜ:(r)/ ▷**BE**

west /west/ *n* ovest *m*; **to the** ~ **of** a ovest di; **the W**~ l'Occidente *m* ● *adj* occidentale ● *adv* verso occidente; **go** ~ 🔢 andare in malora. ~**erly** *adj* verso ovest; occidentale (*wind*). ~**ern** *adj* occidentale ● *n* western *m inv*

West: ~ **'Indian** *adj & n* antillese *mf*. ~ **'Indies** /'ɪndɪz/ *npl* Antille *fpl*

'westward[s] /-wəd[z]/ *adv* verso ovest

wet /wet/ *adj* (**wetter, wettest**) bagnato; fresco (*paint*); (*rainy*) piovoso; (🔢: *person*) smidollato; **get** ~ bagnarsi ● *vt* (*pt/pp* **wet, wetted**) bagnare. ~**'blanket** *n* guastafeste *mf inv*

whack /wæk/ *n* 🔢 colpo *m* ● *vt* 🔢 dare un colpo a. ~**ed** *adj* 🔢 stanco morto. ~**ing** *adj* (🔢: *huge*) enorme

whale /weɪl/ *n* balena *f*; **have a** ~ **of a time** 🔢 divertirsi un sacco

wham /wæm/ *int* bum

wharf /wɔ:f/ *n* banchina *f*

what /wɒt/ *pron* che, [che] cosa; ~ **for?** perché?; ~ **is that for?** a che cosa serve?; ~ **is it?** (*what do you want*) cosa c'è?; ~ **is it like?** com'è?; ~ **is your name?** come ti chiami?; ~ **is the weather like?** com'è il tempo?; ~ **is the film about?** di

w

599 | whatever | whisker

cosa parla il film?; ~ is he talking about? di cosa sta parlando?; he asked me ~ she had said mi ha chiesto cosa ha detto; ~ about going to the cinema? e se andassimo al cinema?; ~ about the children? (what will they do) e i bambini?; ~ if it rains? e se piove? ● adj quale, che; take ~ books you want prendi tutti i libri che vuoi; ~ kind of a che tipo di; at ~ time? a che ora? ● adv che; ~ a lovely day! che bella giornata! ● int ~1 [che] cosa!; ~? [che] cosa?

whatever adj qualunque ● pron qualsiasi cosa; ~ is it? cos'è?; ~ he does qualsiasi cosa faccia; ~ happens qualunque cosa succeda; nothing ~ proprio niente

whatsoever adj & pron whatever

wheat /wiːt/ n grano m, frumento m

wheel /wiːl/ n ruota f; (steering ~) volante m; at the ~ al volante ● vt (push) spingere ● vi (circle) ruotare; ~ [round] ruotare

wheel: ~barrow n carriola f. ~chair n sedia f a rotelle. ~clamp n ceppo m bloccaruote

wheeze /wiːz/ vi ansimare

when /wen/ adv & conj quando; the day ~ il giorno in cui; ~ swimming/reading nuotando/leggendo

whenever adv & conj in qualsiasi momento; (every time that) ogni volta che; ~ did it happen? quando è successo?

where /weə(r)/ adv & conj dove; the street ~ I live la via in cui abito; ~ do you come from? da dove vieni?

whereabouts¹ /weərə'baʊts/ adv dove

whereabouts² n nobody knows his ~ nessuno sa dove si trova

whereas conj dal momento che; (in contrast) mentre

wherever adv & conj dovunque; ~

is he? dov'è mai?; ~ possible dovunque sia possibile

whet /wet/ vt (pt/pp whetted) aguzzare (appetite)

whether /'weðə(r)/ conj se; ~ you like it or not che ti piaccia o no

which /wɪtʃ/ adj & pron quale; ~ one? quale?; ~ one of you? chi di voi?; ~ way? (direction) in che direzione? ● rel pron (object) che; ~ he does frequently cosa che fa spesso; after ~ dopo di che; on/in ~ su/in cui

whichever adj & pron qualunque; ~ it is qualunque sia, ~ one of you chiunque tra voi

while /waɪl/ n a long ~ un bel po'; a little ~ un po' ago mentre; (as long as) finché; (although) sebbene ● while away vt passare (time)

whilst /waɪlst/ conj see while

whim /wɪm/ n capriccio m

whimper /'wɪmpə(r)/ vi piagnucolare, (dog:) mugolare

whine /waɪn/ n lamento m; (of dog) guaito m ● vi lamentarsi; (dog:) guaire

whip /wɪp/ n frusta f; (Pol: person) parlamentare mf incaricato di assicurarsi della presenza dei membri del suo partito alle votazioni ● vt (pt/pp whipped) frustare; (Culin) sbattere; (snatch) afferrare; (☐: steal) fregare. ~ up vt (incite) stimolare; (☐) improvvisare (meal). ~ped 'cream n panna f montata

whirl /wɜːl/ n (movement) rotazione f; my mind's in a ~ ho le idee confuse ● vi girare rapidamente ● vt far girare rapidamente. ~pool n vortice m. ~wind n turbine m

whirr /wɜː(r)/ vi ronzare

whisk /wɪsk/ n (Culin) frullino m ● vt (Culin) frullare. □ ~ away vt portare via

whisker /'wɪskə(r)/ n ~s (of cat) baffi mpl; (on man's cheek) basette fpl;

by a ∼ per un pelo

whisky /'wɪskɪ/ n whisky m inv

whisper /'wɪspə(r)/ n sussurro m; (rumour) diceria f ● vt/i sussurrare

whistle /'wɪsl/ n fischio m; (instrument) fischietto m ● vt fischiettare ● vi fischiettare; (referee) fischiare

white /waɪt/ adj bianco; **go ∼** (pale) sbiancare ● n bianco m; (of egg) albume m; (person) bianco, -a mf

white: **∼ 'coffee** n caffè m inv macchiato. **∼-'collar worker** n colletto m bianco

white 'lie n bugia f pietosa

whiten /'waɪtn/ vt imbiancare ● vi sbiancare

'whitewash n intonaco m; fig copertura f ● vt dare una mano d'intonaco a; fig coprire

Whitsun /'wɪtsn/ n Pentecoste f

who /hu:/ inter pron chi ● rel pron che; **the children, ∼ were all tired,...** i bambini, che erano tutti stanchi,...

who'ever pron chiunque; **∼ he is** chiunque sia; **∼ can that be?** chi può mai essere?

whole /həʊl/ adj tutto; (not broken) intatto; **the ∼ truth** tutta la verità; **the ∼ world** il mondo intero; **the ∼ lot** (everything) tutto; (pl) tutti; **the ∼ lot of you** tutti voi ● n tutto m; **as a ∼** nell'insieme; **on the ∼** tutto considerato; **the ∼ of Italy** tutta l'Italia

whole: **∼-'hearted** adj di tutto cuore. **∼meal** adj integrale

'wholesale adj & adv all'ingrosso; fig in massa. **∼r** n grossista mf

wholesome /'həʊlsəm/ adj sano

wholly /'həʊlɪ/ adv completamente

whom /hu:m/ rel pron che; **the man ∼ I saw** l'uomo che ho visto; **to/with ∼** a/con cui ● inter pron chi; **to ∼ did you speak?** con chi hai parlato?

whooping cough /'hu:pɪŋ/ n pertosse f

whore /hɔ:(r)/ n 🗓 puttana f

whose /hu:z/ rel pron il cui; **people ∼ name begins with D** le persone i cui nomi cominciano con la D ● inter pron di chi; **∼ is that?** di chi è quello? ● adj **∼ car did you use?** di chi è la macchina che hai usato?

why /waɪ/ adv (inter) perché; **the reason ∼** la ragione per cui; **that's ∼** per questo ● int diamine

wick /wɪk/ n stoppino m

wicked /'wɪkɪd/ adj cattivo; (mischievous) malizioso

wicker /'wɪkə(r)/ n vimini mpl ● attrib di vimini

wide /waɪd/ adj largo; (experience, knowledge) vasto; (difference) profondo; (far from target) lontano; **10 cm ∼** largo 10 cm; **how ∼ is it?** quanto è largo? ● adv (off target) lontano dal bersaglio; **∼ awake** del tutto sveglio; **∼ open** spalancato; **far and ∼** in lungo e in largo. **∼ly** adv largamente; (known, accepted) generalmente; (different) profondamente

widen /'waɪdn/ vt allargare ● vi allargarsi

'widespread adj diffuso

widow /'wɪdəʊ/ n vedova f. **∼ed** adj vedovo. **∼er** n vedovo m

width /wɪdθ/ n larghezza f; (of material) altezza f

wield /wi:ld/ vt maneggiare; esercitare (power)

wife /waɪf/ n (pl **wives**) moglie f

wig /wɪg/ n parrucca f

wiggle /'wɪgl/ vi dimenarsi ● vt dimenare

wild /waɪld/ adj selvaggio; (animal, flower) selvatico; (furious) furibondo; (applause) fragoroso; (idea) folle; (with joy) pazzo; (guess) azzardato; **be ∼ about** (keen on) andare pazzo per ● adv **run ∼** crescere senza controllo ● n **in the ∼** allo stato naturale; **the ∼s** pl le zone fpl sperdute

wilderness /'wɪldənɪs/ n deserto m; (fig: garden) giungla f

'wildfire n spread like ~ allargarsi a macchia d'olio

wildlife n animali mpl selvatici

will¹ /wɪl/ v aux he ~ arrive tomorrow arriverà domani; **I won't tell him** non glielo dirò; **you ~ be back soon, won't you?** tornerai presto, no?; **he ~ be there, won't he?** sarà là, no?; **she ~ be there by now** sarà lì ormai; ~ **you go?** (do you intend to go) pensi di andare?; **~ you go to the baker's and buy...?** puoi andare dal panettiere a comprare ~ ?; ~ **you be quiet!** vuol stare calmo!; ~ **you have some wine?** vuoi del vino?; **the engine won't start** la macchina non parte

will² n volontà f inv; (document) testamento m

willing /'wɪlɪŋ/ adj disposto; (eager) volonteroso; **~ly** adv volentieri; **~ness** n buona volontà f

willow /'wɪləʊ/ n salice m

'will-power n forza f di volontà

wilt /wɪlt/ vi appassire

win /wɪn/ n vittoria f; **have a ~** riportare una vittoria ● v (pt/pp **won**; pres p **winning**) ● vt vincere; conquistare (fame) ● vi vincere. **~ over** vt convincere

wince /wɪns/ vi contrarre il viso

winch /wɪntʃ/ n argano m

wind¹ /wɪnd/ n vento m; (breath) fiato m; (ℤ: flatulence) aria f; **get/ have the ~ up** ℤ aver fiato; **get ~ of** aver sentore di; **in the ~** nell'aria ● vt ~ **sb** lasciare qcno senza fiato

wind² /waɪnd/ v (pt/pp **wound**) ● vt (wrap) avvolgere; (move by turning) far girare; (clock) caricare ● vi (road:)

serpeggiare. □ ~ **up** vt caricare (clock); concludere (proceedings); ℤ prendere in giro (sb)

windfall /'wɪndfɔːl/ n fig fortuna f inaspettata

'wind farm n centrale f eolica

winding /'waɪndɪŋ/ adj tortuoso

wind: ~ **instrument** n strumento m a fiato. **~mill** n mulino m a vento

window /'wɪndəʊ/ n finestra f; (of car) finestrino m; (of shop) vetrina f

window: **~-box** n cassetta f per i fiori. **~-sill** n davanzale m

wine /waɪn/ n vino m

wine: **~glass** n bicchiere m da vino. **~-list** n carta f dei vini

'wine-tasting n degustazione f di vini

wing /wɪŋ/ n ala f; (Auto) parafango m; **~s** pl (Theat) quinte fpl. **~er** n (Sport) ala f

wink /wɪŋk/ n strizzata f d'occhio; **not sleep a ~** non chiudere occhio ● vi strizzare l'occhio; (light:) lampeggiare

winner /'wɪnə(r)/ n vincitore, -trice mf

wint|er /'wɪntə(r)/ n inverno m. **~ry** adj invernale

wipe /waɪp/ n passata f; (to dry) asciugata f ● vt strofinare; (dry) asciugare. □ ~ **off** vt asciugare; (erase) cancellare. □ ~ **out** vt annientare; eliminare (village); estinguere (debt). □ ~ **up** vt asciugare (dishes)

wire /waɪə(r)/ n fil m di ferro; (electrical) filo m elettrico

wiring /'waɪərɪŋ/ n impianto m elettrico

wisdom /'wɪzdəm/ n saggezza f; (of action) sensatezza f. ~ **tooth** n dente

w

m del giudizio

wise /waɪz/ *adj* saggio; (*prudent*) sensato. ~**ly** *adv* saggiamente; (act) sensatamente

wish /wɪʃ/ *n* desiderio *m*; **make a** ~ esprimere un desiderio; **with best** ~**es** con i migliori auguri ● *vt* desiderare; ~ **sb well** fare tanti auguri a qcno; **I** ~ **you every success** ti auguro buona fortuna; **I** ~ **you could stay** vorrei che tu potessi rimanere ● *vi* ~ **for sth** desiderare qcsa. ~**ful** *adj* ~**ful thinking** illusione *f*

wistful /ˈwɪstfl/ *adj* malinconico

wit /wɪt/ *n* spirito *m*; (*person*) persona *f* di spirito; **be at one's** ~**s' end** non saper che pesci pigliare

witch /wɪtʃ/ *n* strega *f*. ~**craft** *n* magia *f*. ~**-hunt** *n* caccia *f* alle streghe

with /wɪð/ *prep* con; (*fear, cold, jealousy etc*) di; **I'm not** ~ **you** 🄸 non ti seguo; **can I leave it** ~ **you?** (task) puoi occupartene tu?; ~ **no regrets/money** senza rimpianti/soldi; **be** ~ **it** 🄸 essere al passo coi tempi; (*alert*) essere concentrato

with'draw *v* (*pt* **-drew**, *pp* **-drawn**) ● *vt* ritirare; prelevare (money) ● *vi* ritirarsi. ~**al** *n* ritiro *m*; (*of money*) prelevamento *m*; (*from drugs*) crisi *f inv* di astinenza; (*Psych*) chiusura *f* in se stessi. ~**al symptoms** *npl* sintomi *mpl* della crisi di astinenza

with'drawn ▷**WITHDRAW** ● *adj* (person) chiuso in se stesso

wither /ˈwɪðə(r)/ *vi* (flower:) appassire

with'hold *vt* (*pt/pp* **-held**) rifiutare (consent) (**from** a); nascondere (information) (**from** a); trattenere (smile)

with'in *prep* in; (*before the end of*) entro; ~ **the law** legale ● *adv* all'interno

with'out *prep* senza; ~ **stopping** senza fermarsi

with'stand *vt* (*pt/pp* **-stood**) resistere a

witness /ˈwɪtnɪs/ *n* testimone *mf* ● *vt* autenticare (signature); essere testimone di (accident). ~**-box** *n*, *Am* ~**-stand** *n* banco *m* dei testimoni

witticism /ˈwɪtɪsɪzm/ *n* spiritosaggine *f*

witty /ˈwɪtɪ/ *adj* (**-ier, -iest**) spiritoso

wives /waɪvz/ ▷**WIFE**

wizard /ˈwɪzəd/ *n* mago *m*. ~**ry** *n* stregoneria *f*

wobb|le /ˈwɒbl/ *vi* traballare. ~**ly** *adj* traballante

woe /wəʊ/ *n* afflizione *f*

woke, woken /wəʊk, /ˈwəʊkn/ ▷**WAKE**

wolf /wʊlf/ *n* (*pl* **wolves** /wʊlvz/) lupo *m*; (🄸: *womanizer*) donnaiolo *m* ● *vt* ~ [**down**] divorare. ~ **whistle** *n* fischio *m* ● *vi* ~**-whistle at sb** fischiare dietro a qcno

woman /ˈwʊmən/ *n* (*pl* **women**) donna *f*. ~**izer** *n* donnaiolo *m*. ~**ly** *adj* femmineo

womb /wuːm/ *n* utero *m*

women /ˈwɪmɪn/ ▷**WOMAN**. **W**~**'s Libber** *n* femminista *f*. **W**~**'s Liberation** *n* movimento *m* femminista

won /wʌn/ ▷**WIN**

wonder /ˈwʌndə(r)/ *n* meraviglia *f*; (*surprise*) stupore *m*; **no** ~**!** non c'è da stupirsi; **it's a** ~ **that...** è incredibile che... ● *vi* restare in ammirazione; (*be surprised*) essere sorpreso; **I** ~ **is** quello che mi chiedo; **I** ~ **whether she is ill** mi chiedo se è malata?. ~**ful** *adj* meraviglioso. ~**fully** *adv* meravigliosamente

wood /wʊd/ *n* legno *m*; (*for burning*) legna *f*; (*forest*) bosco *m*; **out of the** ~ *fig* fuori pericolo; **touch** ~**!** tocca ferro!

wood: ~**ed** /-ɪd/ *adj* boscoso. ~**en** *adj* di legno; *fig* legnoso. ~ **wind** *n* strumenti *mpl* a fiato. ~**work** *n* (*wooden parts*) parti *fpl* in legno; (craft) falegnameria f. **~worm** n tarlo m. **~y** /wʊlɪ/ adj legnoso; (hill) boscoso

wool /wʊl/ n lana f ● attrib di lana. **~len** adj di lana. **~lens** npl capi mpl di lana

woolly /ˈwʊlɪ/ adj (-ier, -iest) (sweater) di lana; fig confuso

word /wɜːd/ n parola f; (news) notizia f; **by ~ of mouth** a viva voce; **have a ~ with** dire due parole a; **have ~s** bisticciare; **in other ~s** in altre parole. **~ing** n parole fpl. **~ processor** n programma m di videoscrittura, word processor m inv

wore /wɔː(r)/ ▷ WEAR

work /wɜːk/ n lavoro m; (of art) opera f; **~s** pl (factory) fabbrica fsg; (mechanism) meccanismo msg; **at ~** al lavoro; **out of ~** disoccupato ● vi lavorare; (machine, ruse) funzionare; (study) studiare ● vt far funzionare (machine); far lavorare (employee); far studiare (student). **~ off** vt sfogare (anger); lavorare per estinguere (debt); fare sport per smaltire (weight). **~ out** vt elaborare (plan); risolvere (problem); calcolare (bill); **I ~ed out how he did it** ho capito come l'ha fatto ● vi evolvere. **~ up** vi **I ~ed up an appetite** mi è venuto appetito; **don't get ~ed up** (anxious) non farti prendere dal panico; (angry) non arrabbiarti

workable /ˈwɜːkəbl/ adj (feasible) fattibile

worker /ˈwɜːkə(r)/ n lavoratore, -trice mf; (manual) operaio, -a mf

working /ˈwɜːkɪŋ/ adj (clothes etc) da lavoro; (day) feriale; **in ~** order funzionante. **~ class** n classe f operaia. **~-class** adj operaio

work: **~man** n operaio m. **~manship** n lavorazione f. **~shop** n officina f; (discussion) dibattito m

world /wɜːld/ n mondo m; **a ~ of difference** una differenza abissale; **out of this ~** favoloso; **think the ~ of sb** andare matto per qcno. **~ly**

adj materiale; (person) materialista. **~-'wide** adj mondiale ● adv mondialmente

worm /wɜːm/ n verme m ● vi **~ one's way into sb's confidence** conquistarsi la fiducia di qcno in modo subdolo. **~-eaten** adj tarlato

worn /wɔːn/ ▷ WEAR ● adj sciupato. **~-out** adj consumato; (person) sfinito

worried /ˈwʌrɪd/ adj preoccupato

worry /ˈwʌrɪ/ n preoccupazione f ● v (pt/pp worried) ● vt preoccupare; (bother) disturbare ● vi preoccuparsi. **~ing** adj preoccupante

worse /wɜːs/ adj peggiore ● adv peggio ● n peggio m

worsen /ˈwɜːsn/ vt/i peggiorare

worship /ˈwɜːʃɪp/ n culto m; (service) funzione f; **Your/His W~** (to judge) signor giudice/il giudice ● v (pt/pp -shipped) ● vt venerare ● vi andare a messa

worst /wɜːst/ adj peggiore ● adv peggio [di tutti] ● n **the ~** il peggio; **get the ~ of it** avere la peggio; **if the ~ comes to the ~** nella peggiore delle ipotesi

worth /wɜːθ/ n valore m; **£10 ~ of petrol** 10 sterline di benzina ● adj **be ~** valere; **be ~ it** fig valerne la pena; **it's ~ trying** vale la pena di provare; **it's ~ my while** mi conviene. **~less** adj senza valore. **~while** adj che vale la pena; (cause) lodevole

worthy /ˈwɜːðɪ/ adj degno; (cause, motive) lodevole

would /wʊd/ v aux **I ~ do it** lo farei; **~ you go?** andresti?; **~ you mind if I opened the window?** ti dispiace se apro la finestra?; **I ~ come if he could** verrebbe se potesse; **he said he ~n't** ha detto di no; **~ you like a drink?** vuoi

w

qualcosa da bere?; **what ~ you like to drink?** cosa prendi da bere?; **you ~n't, ~ you?** non lo faresti, vero?

wound[1] /wuːnd/ n ferita f ● vt ferire

wound[2] /waʊnd/ ▷ **WIND**[2]

wrangle /ˈræŋgl/ n litigio m ● vi litigare

wrap /ræp/ n (shawl) scialle m ● vt (pt/pp wrapped) ~ [up] avvolgere; (present) incartare; **be ~ped up in** fig essere completamente preso da ● vi ~ **up warmly** coprirsi bene. **~per** n (for sweet) carta f [di caramella]. **~ping** n materiale m da imballaggio. **~ping paper** n carta f da pacchi; (for gift) carta f da regalo

wrath /rɒθ/ n ira f

wreak /riːk/ vt ~ **havoc with sth** scombussolare qcsa

wreath /riːθ/ n (pl ~s /-ðz/) corona f

wreck /rek/ n (of ship) relitto m; (of car) carcassa f; (person) rottame m ● vt far naufragare; demolire (car). **~age** n rottami mpl; fig brandelli mpl

wrench /rentʃ/ n (injury) slogatura f; (tool) chiave f inglese; (pull) strattone m ● vt (pull) strappare; slogarsi (wrist, ankle etc)

wrestl|e /ˈresl/ vi lottare corpo a corpo; fig lottare. **~er** n lottatore, -trice mf. **~ing** n lotta f libera; (all-in) catch m

wretch /retʃ/ n disgraziato, -a mf. **~ed** adj odioso; (weather) orribile; **feel ~ed** (unhappy) essere triste; (ill) sentirsi malissimo

wriggle /ˈrɪgl/ n contorsione f ● vi contorcersi; (move forward) strisciare; ~ **out of sth** 🔲 sottrarsi a qcsa

wring /rɪŋ/ vt (pt/pp wrung) torcere (sb's neck); strizzare (clothes); ~ **one's hands** torcersi le mani; **~ing wet** inzuppato

wrinkle /ˈrɪŋkl/ n grinza f; (on skin) ruga f ● vt/i raggrinzire. **~d** adj (skin,

face) rugoso; (clothes) raggrinzito

wrist /rɪst/ n polso m. **~-watch** n orologio m da polso

writ /rɪt/ n (Jur) mandato m

write /raɪt/ vt/i (pt wrote, pp written, pres p writing) scrivere. □ ~ **down** vt annotare. □ ~ **off** vt cancellare (debt); distruggere (car)

'write-off n (car) rottame m

writer /ˈraɪtə(r)/ n autore, -trice mf; **she's a ~** è una scrittrice

writhe /raɪð/ vi contorcersi

writing /ˈraɪtɪŋ/ n (occupation) scrivere m; (words) scritte fpl; (handwriting) scrittura f; **in ~** per iscritto. **~-paper** n carta f da lettera

written /ˈrɪtn/ ▷ **WRITE**

wrong /rɒŋ/ adj sbagliato; **be ~** (person:) sbagliare; **what's ~?** cosa c'è che non va? ● adv (spelt) in modo sbagliato; **go ~** (person:) sbagliare; (machine:) funzionare male; (plan:) andar male ● n ingiustizia f; **in the ~** dalla parte del torto; **know right from ~** distinguere il bene dal male ● vt fare torto a. **~ful** adj ingiusto. **~ly** adv in modo sbagliato; (accuse, imagine) a torto; (informed) male

wrote /rəʊt/ ▷ **WRITE**

wrought'iron /rɔːt-/ n ferro m battuto ● attrib di ferro battuto

wrung /rʌŋ/ ▷ **WRING**

wry /raɪ/ adj (-er, -est) (humour, smile) beffardo

Xx

Xmas /ˈkrɪsməs/ n 🔲 Natale m

'X-ray n (picture) radiografia f; **have an ~** farsi fare una radiografia ● vt passare ai raggi X

Yy

yacht /jɒt/ n yacht m inv; (for racing) barca f a vela. **~ing** n vela f

yank /jæŋk/ vt 🄴 tirare

Yank n 🄵 americano, -a mf

yap /jæp/ vi (pt/pp yapped) (dog:) guaire

yard¹ /jɑːd/ n cortile m; (for storage) deposito m

yard² n iarda f (= 91,44 cm). **~stick** n fig pietra f di paragone

yarn /jɑːn/ n filo m; (🄵: tale) storia f

yawn /jɔːn/ vi sbadigliare. **~ing** adj **~ing gap** sbadiglio m

yeah /jeə/ adv sì

year /jɪə(r)/ n anno m; (of wine) annata f; for **~s** 🄴 da secoli. **~book** n annuario m. **~ly** adj annuale ● adv annualmente

yearn /jɜːn/ vi struggersi. **~ing** n desiderio m struggente

yeast /jiːst/ n lievito m

yell /jel/ n urlo m ● vi urlare

yellow /ˈjeləʊ/ adj & n giallo m

yelp /jelp/ n (of dog) guaito m ● vi (dog:) guaire

yes /jes/ adv sì ● n sì m inv

yesterday /ˈjestədeɪ/ adj & adv ieri m inv; **~'s paper** il giornale di ieri; **the day before ~** l'altroieri

yet /jet/ adv ancora; **as ~** fino ad ora; **not ~** non ancora; **the best ~** il migliore finora ● conj eppure

yield /jiːld/ n produzione f, (profit) reddito m ● vt produrre; fruttare (profit) ● vi cedere; Am (Auto) dare la precedenza

yoga /ˈjəʊgə/ n yoga m

yoghurt /ˈjɒgət/ n yogurt m inv

yoke /jəʊk/ n giogo m; (of garment) carré m inv

yokel /ˈjəʊkl/ n zotico, -a mf

yolk /jəʊk/ n tuorlo m

you /juː/ pron (subject) tu, voi pl; (formal) lei, voi pl; (direct/indirect object) ti, vi pl; (formal: direct object) la; (formal: indirect object) le; (after prep) te, voi pl; (formal: after prep) lei;

> **tu** is used when speaking to friends, children and animals. **lei** is used to speak to someone you do not know. **voi** is used to speak to more than one person. Note that you is often not translated when it is the subject of the sentence

~ are very kind (sg) sei molto gentile, (formal) è molto gentile (pl & formal pl) siete molto gentili; **~ can stay, but he has to go** (sg) tu puoi rimanere, ma lui deve andarsene; (pl) voi potete rimanere, ma lui deve andarsene; **all of ~** tutti voi; **I'll give ~ the money** (sg) ti darò i soldi; (pl) vi darò i soldi; **I'll give it to ~** (sg) te/(pl) ve lo darò; **it was ~** (sg) eri tu/(pl) eravate voi; **~ have to be careful** (one) si deve fare attenzione

young /jʌŋ/ adj giovane ● npl (animals) piccoli mpl; **the ~** (people) i giovani mpl. **~ lady** n signorina f. **~ man** n giovanotto. **~ster** n ragazzo, -a mf; (child) bambino, -a mf

your /jɔː(r)/ adj il tuo m, la tua f, i tuoi mpl, le tue fpl; (formal) il suo m, la sua f, i suoi mpl, le sue fpl; (pl & formal pl) il vostro m, la vostra f, i vostri mpl, le vostre fpl; **~ mother/father** tua madre/tuo padre, (formal) sua madre/suo padre; (pl & formal pl) vostra madre/vostro padre

y

yours /jɔːz/ poss pron il tuo m, la tua f, i tuoi mpl, le tue fpl; (formal) il suo m, la sua f, i suoi mpl, le sue fpl; (pl & formal pl) il vostro m, la vostra f, i vostri mpl, le vostre fpl; **a friend of ~** un tuo/suo/vostro amico; **friends of ~** dei tuoi/vostri/suoi amici; **that is ~** quello è tuo/vostro/suo; (as opposed to mine) quello è il tuo/il vostro/il suo

your'self pron (reflexive) ti; (formal) si; (emphatic) te stesso; (formal) sé, se stesso; **do pour ~ a drink** versati da bere; (formal) si versi da bere; **you said so ~** lo hai detto tu stesso; (formal) lo ha detto lei stesso; **you can be proud of ~** puoi essere fiero di te/di sé; **by ~** da solo

your'selves pron (reflexive) vi; (emphatic) voi stessi; **do pour ~ a drink** versatevi da bere; **you said so ~** lo avete detto voi stessi; **you can be proud of ~** potete essere fieri di voi; **by ~** da soli

youth /juːθ/ n (pl **youths** /-ðːz/) gioventù f inv; (boy) giovanetto m; **the ~** (young people) i giovani mpl. **~ful** adj giovanile. **~ hostel** n ostello m [della gioventù]

Yugoslav /ˈjuːɡəslɑːv/ adj & n jugoslavo, -a mf

Yugoslavia /-ˈslɑːvɪə/ n Jugoslavia f

Zz

zeal /ziːl/ n zelo m
zealous /ˈzeləs/ adj zelante. **~ly** adv con zelo
zebra /ˈzebrə/ n zebra f. **~ 'crossing** n passaggio m pedonale, zebre fpl
zero /ˈzɪərəʊ/ n zero m
zest /zest/ n gusto m
zigzag /ˈzɪɡzæɡ/ n zigzag m inv ● vi (pt/pp **-zagged**) zigzagare
zilch /zɪltʃ/ n [1] zero m assoluto
zinc /zɪŋk/ n zinco m
zip /zɪp/ n ~ **[fastener]** cerniera f [lampo] ● vt (pt/pp **zipped**) ~ **[up]** chiudere con la cerniera [lampo]
'Zip code n Am codice m postale
zipper /ˈzɪpə(r)/ n Am cerniera f [lampo]
zodiac /ˈzəʊdɪæk/ n zodiaco m
zombie /ˈzɒmbɪ/ n [1] zombi mf inv
zone /zəʊn/ n zona f
zoo /zuː/ n zoo m inv
zoolog|ist /zəʊˈɒlədʒɪst/ n zoologo, -a mf. **~y** zoologia f
zoom /zuːm/ vi sfrecciare. **~ lens** n zoom m inv

Verbi inglese irregolari

Infinito	Passato	Participio passato	Infinito	Passato	Participio passato
be	was	been	**drive**	drove	driven
bear	bore	borne	**eat**	ate	eaten
beat	beat	beaten	**fall**	fell	fallen
become	became	become	**feed**	fed	fed
begin	began	begun	**feel**	felt	felt
bend	bent	bent	**fight**	fought	fought
bet	bet,	bet,	**find**	found	found
	betted	betted	**flee**	fled	fled
bid	bade, bid	bidden, bid	**fly**	flew	flown
bind	bound	bound	**freeze**	froze	frozen
bite	bit	bitten	**get**	got	got, gotten US
bleed	bled	bled	**give**	gave	given
blow	blew	blown	**go**	went	gone
break	broke	broken	**grow**	grew	grown
breed	bred	bred	**hang**	hung,	hung,
bring	brought	brought		hanged	hanged
build	built	built	**have**	had	had
burn	burnt,	burnt,	**hear**	heard	heard
	burned	burned	**hide**	hid	hidden
burst	burst	burst	**hit**	hit	hit
buy	bought	bought	**hold**	held	held
catch	caught	caught	**hurt**	hurt	hurt
choose	chose	chosen	**keep**	kept	kept
cling	clung	clung	**kneel**	knelt	knelt
come	came	come	**know**	knew	known
cost	cost,	cost,	**lay**	laid	laid
	costed (vt)	costed	**lead**	led	led
cut	cut	cut	**lean**	leaned,	leaned,
deal	dealt	dealt		leant	leant
dig	dug	dug	**learn**	learnt,	learnt,
do	did	done		learned	learned
draw	drew	drawn	**leave**	left	left
dream	dreamt,	dreamt,	**lend**	lent	lent
	dreamed	dreamed	**let**	let	let
drink	drank	drunk	**lie**	lay	lain

Verbi inglese irregolari

Infinito	Passato	Participio passato	Infinito	Passato	Participio passato
lose	lost	lost	spend	spent	spent
make	made	made	spit	spat	spat
mean	meant	meant	spoil	spoilt, spoiled	spoilt, spoiled
meet	met	met			
pay	paid	paid	spread	spread	spread
put	put	put	spring	sprang	sprung
read	read	read	stand	stood	stood
ride	rode	ridden	steal	stole	stolen
ring	rang	rung	stick	stuck	stuck
rise	rose	risen	sting	stung	stung
run	ran	run	stride	strode	stridden
say	said	said	strike	struck	struck
see	saw	seen	swear	swore	sworn
seek	sought	sought	sweep	swept	swept
sell	sold	sold	swell	swelled	swollen, swelled
send	sent	sent			
set	set	set	swim	swam	swum
sew	sewed	sewn, sewed	swing	swung	swung
shake	shook	shaken	take	took	taken
shine	shone	shone	teach	taught	taught
shoe	shod	shod	tear	tore	torn
shoot	shot	shot	tell	told	told
show	showed	shown	think	thought	thought
shut	shut	shut	throw	threw	thrown
sing	sang	sung	thrust	thrust	thrust
sink	sank	sunk	tread	trod	trodden
sit	sat	sat	under- stand	under- stood	understood
sleep	slept	slept			
sling	slung	slung	wake	woke	woken
smell	smelt, smelled	smelt, smelled	wear	wore	worn
			win	won	won
speak	spoke	spoken	write	wrote	written
spell	spelled, spelt	spelled, spelt			

Italian verb tables

1. in -are (*eg* compr|are)

Present ~o, ~i, ~a, ~iamo, ~ate, ~ano

Imperfect ~avo, ~avi, ~ava, ~avamo, ~avate, ~avano

Past historic ~ai, ~asti, ~ò, ~ammo, ~aste, ~arono

Future ~erò, ~erai, ~erà, ~eremo, ~erete, ~eranno

Present subjunctive ~i, ~i, ~i, ~iamo, ~iate, ~ino

Past subjunctive ~assi, ~assi, ~asse, ~assimo, ~aste, ~assero

Present participle ~ando

Past participle ~ato

Imperative ~a (*fml* ~i), ~iamo, ~ate

Conditional ~erei, ~eresti, ~erebbe, ~eremmo, ~ereste, ~erebbero

2. in -ere (*eg* vend|ere)

Pres ~o, ~i, ~e, ~iamo, ~ete, ~ono

Impf ~evo, ~evi, ~eva, ~evamo, ~evate, ~evano

Past hist ~ei or ~etti, ~esti, ~è or ~ette, ~emmo, ~este, ~erono or ~ettero

Fut ~erò, ~erai, ~erà, ~eremo, ~erete, ~eranno

Pres sub ~a, ~a, ~a, ~iamo, ~iate, ~ano

Past sub ~essi, ~essi, ~esse, ~essimo, ~este, ~essero

Pres part ~endo

Past part ~uto

Imp ~i (*fml* ~a), ~iamo, ~ete

Cond ~erei, ~eresti, ~erebbe, ~eremmo, ~ereste, ~erebbero

3. in -ire (*eg* dorm|ire)

Pres ~o, ~i, ~e, ~iamo, ~ite, ~ono

Impf ~ivo, ~ivi, ~iva, ~ivamo, ~ivate, ~ivano

Past hist ~ii, ~isti, ~ì, ~immo, ~iste, ~irono

Fut ~irò, ~irai, ~irà, ~iremo, ~irete, ~iranno

Pres sub ~a, ~a, ~a, ~iamo, ~iate, ~ano

Past sub ~issi, ~issi, ~isse, ~issimo, ~iste, ~issero

Pres part ~endo

Past part ~ito

Imp ~i (*fml* ~a), ~iamo, ~ite

Cond ~irei, ~iresti, ~irebbe, ~iremmo, ~ireste, ~irebbero

Notes

• Many verbs in the third conjugation take **isc** between the stem and the ending in the first, second, and third person singular and in the third person plural of the present, the present subjunctive, and the imperative:

fin|ire *Pres* ~isco, ~isci, ~isce, ~iscono, *Pres sub* ~isca, ~iscano *Imp* ~isci.

• The three forms of the imperative are the same as the corresponding forms of the present for the second and third conjugation. In the first conjugation the forms are also the same except for the second person singular: present compri, imperative compra. The negative form of the second person singular is formed by putting *non* before the infinitive for all conjugations: *non comprare*. In polite forms the third person of the present subjunctive is used instead for all conjugations: *compri*.

Irregular verbs:

Certain forms of all irregular verbs are regular (except for *essere*). These are: the second person plural of the present, the past subjunctive, and the present participle. All forms not listed below are regular and can be derived from the parts given. Only those irregular verbs considered to be the most useful are shown in the tables.

accadere *as* cadere

accendere
Past hist accesi, accendesti
Past part acceso

affliggere
Past hist afflissi, affliggesti
Past part afflitto

ammettere *as* mettere

andare
Pres vado, vai, va, andiamo, andate, vanno
Fut andrò *etc*
Pres sub vada, vadano
Imp va', vada, vadano

apparire
Pres appaio *or* apparisco, appari *or* apparisci, appare *or* apparisce, appaiono *or* appariscono
Past hist apparvi *or* apparsi, apparisti, apparve *or* appari *or* apparse,

apparvero *or* apparirono *or* apparsero
Pres sub appaia *or* apparisca

aprire
Pres apro
Past hist aprii, apristi
Pres sub apra
Past part aperto

avere
Pres ho, hai, ha, abbiamo, hanno
Past hist ebbi, avesti, ebbe, avemmo, aveste, ebbero
Fut avrò *etc*
Pres sub abbia *etc*
Imp abbi, abbia, abbiate, abbiano

bere
Pres bevo *etc*
Impf bevevo *etc*
Past hist bevvi *or* bevetti, bevesti
Fut berrò *etc*
Pres sub beva *etc*
Past sub bevessi *etc*
Pres part bevendo
Cond berrei *etc*

cadere
Past hist caddi, cadesti
Fut cadrò *etc*

chiedere
Past hist chiesi, chiedesti
Pres sub chieda *etc*
Past part chiesto *etc*

chiudere
Past hist chiusi, chiudesti
Past part chiuso

cogliere
Pres colgo, colgono
Past hist colsi, cogliesti

Pres sub colga
Past part colto

correre
Past hist corsi, corresti
Past part corso

crascere
Past hist crebbi
Past part cresciuto

cuocere
Pres cuocio, cuociamo, cuociono
Past hist cossi, cocesti
Past part cotto

dare
Pres do, dai, dà, diamo, danno
Past hist diedi *or* detti, desti
Fut darò *etc*
Pres sub dia *etc*
Past sub dessi *etc*
Imp da' (*fml* dia)

dire
Pres dico, dici, dice, diciamo, dicono
Impf dicevo *etc*
Past hist dissi, dicesti
Fut dirò *etc*
Pres sub dica, diciamo, diciate, dicano
Past sub dicessi *etc*
Pres part dicendo
Past part detto
Imp di' (*fml* dica)

dovere
Pres devo *or* debbo, devi, deve,
  dobbiamo, devono *or* debbono
Fut dovrò *etc*
Pres sub deva *or* debba, dobbiamo,
  dobbiate, devano *or* debbano
Cond dovrei *etc*

essere
Pres sono, sei, è, siamo, siete, sono

Impf ero, eri, era, eravamo, eravate,
  erano
Past hist fui, fosti, fu, fummo, foste,
  furono
Fut sarò *etc*
Pres sub sia *etc*
Past sub fossi, fossi, fosse, fossimo,
  foste, fossero
Past part stato
Imp sii (*fml* sia), siate
Cond sarei *etc*

fare
Pres faccio, fai, fa, facciamo, fanno
Impf facevo *etc*
Past hist feci, facesti
Fut farò *etc*
Pres sub faccia *etc*
Past sub facessi *etc*
Pres part facendo
Past part fatto
Imp fa' (*fml* faccia)
Cond farei *etc*

fingere
Past hist finsi, fingesti, finsero
Past part finto

giungere
Past hist giunsi, giungesti, giunsero
Past part giunto

leggere
Past hist lessi, leggesti
Past part letto

mettere
Past hist misi, mettesti
Past part messo

morire
Pres muoio, muori, muore, muoiono
Fut morirò *or* morrò *etc*

Pres sub muoia
Past part morto

muovere

Past hist mossi, movesti
Past part mosso

nascere

Past hist nacqui, nascesti
Past part nato

offrire

Past hist offersi *or* offrii, offristi
Pres sub offra
Past part offerto

parere

Pres paio, pari, pare, pariamo, paiono
Past hist parvi *or* parsi, paresti
Fut parrò *etc*
Pres sub paia, paiamo *or* pariamo,
    pariate, paiano
Past part parso

placere

Pres piaccio, piaci, piace, piacciamo,
    piacciono
Past hist piacqui, piacesti, piacque,
    piacemmo, piaceste, piacquero
Pres sub piaccia *etc*
Past part piaciuto

porre

Pres pongo, poni, pone, poniamo,
    ponete, pongono
Impf ponevo *etc*
Past hist posi, ponesti
Fut porrò *etc*
Pres sub ponga, poniamo, poniate,
    pongano
Past sub ponessi *etc*

potere

Pres posso, puoi, può, possiamo,

possono
Fut potrò *etc*
Pres sub possa, possiamo, possiate,
    possano
Cond potrei *etc*

prendere

Past hist presi, prendesti
Past part preso

ridere

Past hist risi, ridesti
Past part riso

rimanere

Pres rimango, rimani, rimane,
    rimaniamo, rimangono
Past hist rimasi, rimanesti
Fut rimarrò *etc*
Pres sub rimanga
Past part rimasto
Cond rimarrei *etc*

salire

Pres salgo, sali, sale, saliamo, salgono
Pres sub salga, saliate, salgano

sapere

Pres so, sai, sa, sappiamo, sanno
Past hist seppi, sapesti
Fut saprò *etc*
Pres sub sappia *etc*
Imp sappi (*fml* sappia), sappiate
Cond saprei *etc*

scegliere

Pres scelgo, scegli, sceglie, scegliamo,
    scelgono
Past hist scelsi, scegliesti *etc*
Past part scelto

scrivere

Past hist scrissi, scrivesti *etc*
Past part scritto

Italian verb tables

sedere

Pres siedo *or* seggo, siedi, siede, siedono
Pres sub sieda *or* segga

spegnere

Pres spengo, spengono
Past hist spensi, spegnesti
Past part spento

stare

Pres sto, stai, sta, stiamo, stanno
Past hist stetti, stesti
Fut starò *etc*
Pres sub stia *etc*
Past sub stessi *etc*
Past part stato
Imp sta' (*fml* stia)

tacere

Pres taccio, tacciono
Past hist tacqui, tacque, tacquero
Pres sub taccia

tendere

Past hist tesi
Past part teso

tenere

Pres tengo, tieni, tiene, tengono
Past hist tenni, tenesti
Fut terrò *etc*
Pres sub tenga

togliere

Pres tolgo, tolgono
Past hist tolsi, tolse, tolsero
Pres sub tolga, tolgano
Past part tolto
Imp fml tolga

rarre

Pres traggo, trai, trae, traiamo, traete, traggono

Past hist trassi, traesti
Fut trarrò *etc*
Pres sub tragga
Past sub traessi *etc*
Past part tratto

uscire

Pres esco, esci, esce, escono
Pres sub esca
Imp esci (*fml* esca)

valere

Pres valgo, valgono
Past hist valsi, valesti
Fut varrò *etc*
Pres sub valga, valgano
Past part valso
Cond varrei *etc*

vedere

Past hist vidi, vedesti
Fut vedrò *etc*
Past part visto *or* veduto
Cond vedrei *etc*

venire

Pres vengo, vieni, viene, vengono
Past hist venni, venisti
Fut verrò *etc*

vivere

Past hist vissi, vivesti
Fut vivrò *etc*
Past part vissuto
Cond vivrei *etc*

volere

Pres voglio, vuoi, vuole, vogliamo, volete, vogliono
Past hist volli, volesti
Fut verrò *etc*
Pres sub voglia *etc*
Imp vogliate
Cond vorrei *etc*

Numbers/Numeri

Cardinal numbers/ Numeri cardinali

0	zero **zero**
1	one **uno**
2	two **due**
3	three **tre**
4	four **quattro**
5	five **cinque**
6	six **sei**
7	seven **sette**
8	eight **otto**
9	nine **nove**
10	ten **dieci**
11	eleven **undici**
12	twelve **dodici**
13	thirteen **tredici**
14	fourteen **quattordici**
15	fifteen **quindici**
16	sixteen **sedici**
17	seventeen **diciassette**
18	eighteen **diciotto**
19	nineteen **diciannove**
20	twenty **venti**
21	twenty-one **ventuno**
22	twenty-two **ventidue**
30	thirty **trenta**
40	forty **quaranta**
50	fifty **cinquanta**
60	sixty **sessanta**
70	seventy **settanta**
80	eighty **ottanta**
90	ninety **novanta**

100	a hundred **cento**
101	a hundred and one **centouno**
110	a hundred and ten **centodieci**
200	two hundred **duecento**
1,000	a thousand **mille**
10,000	ten thousand **diecimila**
100,000	a hundred thousand **centomila**
1,000,000	a million **un milione**

Ordinal numbers/ Numeri ordinali

1st	first **primo**
2nd	second **secondo**
3rd	third **terzo**
4th	fourth **quarto**
5th	fifth **quinto**
6th	sixth **sesto**
7th	seventh **settimo**
8th	eighth **ottavo**
9th	ninth **nono**
10th	tenth **decimo**
11th	eleventh **undicesimo**
20th	twentieth **ventesimo**
21st	twenty-first **ventunesimo**
30th	thirtieth **trentesimo**
40th	fortieth **quarantesimo**
50th	fiftieth **cinquantesimo**
100th	hundredth **centesimo**
1,000th	thousandth **millesimo**

Abbreviations/Abbreviazioni

adjective	*adj*	aggettivo
abbreviation	*abbr*	abbreviazione
administration	*Admin*	amministrazione
adverb	*adv*	avverbio
aeronautics	*Aeron*	aeronautica
American	*Am*	americano
anatomy	*Anat*	anatomia
archaeology	*Archeol*	archeologia
architecture	*Archit*	architettura
astrology	*Astr*	astrologia
attributive	*attrib*	attributo
automobiles	*Auto*	automobile
auxiliary	*aux*	ausiliario
biology	*Biol*	biologia
botany	*Bot*	botanica
British English	*Br*	inglese britannico
chemistry	*Chem*	chimica
commerce	*Comm*	commercio
computers	*Comput*	informatica
conjunction	*conj*	congiunzione
cooking	*Culin*	cucina
definite article	*def art*	articolo determinativo
et cetera	*ecc*	eccetera
electricity	*Electr*	elettricità
et cetera	*etc*	eccetera
feminine	*f*	femminile
figurative	*fig*	figurato
formal	*fml*	formale
geography	*Geog*	geografia
geology	*Geol*	geologia
grammar	*Gram*	grammatica
humorous	*hum*	umoristico
indefinite article	*indef art*	articolo indeterminativo
interjection	*int*	interiezione
interrogative	*inter*	interrogativo
invariable	*inv*	invariabile
law	*Jur*	legge/giuridico
literary	*liter*	letterario
masculine	*m*	maschile
mathematics	*Math*	matematica
mechanics	*Mech*	meccanica
medicine	*Med*	medicina